A COMPANION
TO
ARCHAIC GREECE

BLACKWELL COMPANIONS TO THE ANCIENT WORLD

This series provides sophisticated and authoritative overviews of periods of ancient history, genres of classical literature, and the most important themes in ancient culture. Each volume comprises approximately twenty-five and forty concise essays written by individual scholars within their area of specialization. The essays are written in a clear, provocative, and lively manner, designed for an international audience of scholars, students, and general readers.

ANCIENT HISTORY

Published

A Companion to the Roman Army
Edited by Paul Erdkamp

A Companion to the Roman Republic
Edited by Nathan Rosenstein and Robert Morstein-Marx

A Companion to the Roman Empire
Edited by David S. Potter

A Companion to the Classical Greek World
Edited by Konrad H. Kinzl

A Companion to the Ancient Near East
Edited by Daniel C. Snell

A Companion to the Hellenistic World
Edited by Andrew Erskine

A Companion to Late Antiquity
Edited by Philip Rousseau

A Companion to Ancient History
Edited by Andrew Erskine

A Companion to Archaic Greece
Edited by Kurt A. Raaflaub and Hans van Wees

A Companion to Julius Caesar
Edited by Miriam Griffin

A Companion to Byzantium
Edited by Liz James

A Companion to Ancient Egypt
Edited by Alan B. Lloyd

A Companion to Ancient Macedonia
Edited by Joseph Roisman and Ian Worthington

A Companion to the Punic Wars
Edited by Dexter Hoyos

A Companion to Augustine
Edited by Mark Vessey

A Companion to Marcus Aurelius
Edited by Marcel van Ackeren

A Companion to Ancient Greek Government
Edited by Hans Beck

LITERATURE AND CULTURE

Published

A Companion to Classical Receptions
Edited by Lorna Hardwick and Christopher Stray

A Companion to Greek and Roman Historiography
Edited by John Marincola

A Companion to Catullus
Edited by Marilyn B. Skinner

A Companion to Roman Religion
Edited by Jörg Rüpke

A Companion to Greek Religion
Edited by Daniel Ogden

A Companion to the Classical Tradition
Edited by Craig W. Kallendorf

A Companion to Roman Rhetoric
Edited by William Dominik and Jon Hall

A Companion to Greek Rhetoric
Edited by Ian Worthington

A Companion to Ancient Epic
Edited by John Miles Foley

A Companion to Greek Tragedy
Edited by Justina Gregory

A Companion to Latin Literature
Edited by Stephen Harrison

A Companion to Greek and Roman Political Thought
Edited by Ryan K. Balot

A Companion to Ovid
Edited by Peter E. Knox

A Companion to the Ancient Greek Language
Edited by Egbert Bakker

A Companion to Hellenistic Literature
Edited by Martine Cuypers and James J. Clauss

A Companion to Vergil's *Aeneid* and its Tradition
Edited by Joseph Farrell and Michael C. J. Putnam

A Companion to Horace
Edited by Gregson Davis

A Companion to Families in the Greek and Roman Worlds
Edited by Beryl Rawson

A Companion to Greek Mythology
Edited by Ken Dowden and Niall Livingstone

A Companion to the Latin Language
Edited by James Clackson

A Companion to Tacitus
Edited by Victoria Emma Pagán

A Companion to Women in the Ancient World
Edited by Sharon L. James and Sheila Dillon

A Companion to Sophocles
Edited by Kirk Ormand

A Companion to the Archaeology of the Ancient Near East
Edited by Daniel Potts

A Companion to Roman Love Elegy
Edited by Barbara K. Gold

A Companion to Greek Art
Edited by Tyler Jo Smith and Dimitris Plantzos

A Companion to Persius and Juvenal
Edited by Susanna Braund and Josiah Osgood

A Companion
to
Archaic Greece

Edited by

Kurt A. Raaflaub and Hans van Wees

A John Wiley & Sons, Ltd., Publication

This paperback edition first published 2013
© 2013 Blackwell Publishing Ltd

Edition history: (hardback, 2009)

Blackwell Publishing was acquired by John Wiley & Sons in February 2007. Blackwell's publishing program has been merged with Wiley's global Scientific, Technical, and Medical business to form Wiley-Blackwell.

Registered Office
John Wiley & Sons Ltd, The Atrium, Southern Gate, Chichester, West Sussex, PO19 8SQ, UK

Editorial Offices
350 Main Street, Malden, MA 02148-5020, USA
9600 Garsington Road, Oxford, OX4 2DQ, UK
The Atrium, Southern Gate, Chichester, West Sussex, PO19 8SQ, UK

For details of our global editorial offices, for customer services, and for information about how to apply for permission to reuse the copyright material in this book please see our website at www.wiley.com/wiley-blackwell.

The right of Kurt A. Raaflaub and Hans van Wees to be identified as the authors of the editorial material in this work has been asserted in accordance with the UK Copyright, Designs and Patents Act 1988.

Library of Congress Cataloging-in-Publication Data

A companion to Archaic Greece / edited by Kurt A. Raaflaub and Hans van Wees.
     p. cm. – (Blackwell companions to the ancient world)
   Includes bibliographical references and index.
   ISBN 978-0-631-23045-8 (hardcover : alk. paper) ISBN 978-1-118-45138-0 (pbk :   )
1. Greece–Civilization–To 146 B.C.   I. Raaflaub, Kurt A.   II. Wees, Hans van.
   DF77.C6955 2009
   938–dc22

                                                                        2008046992

A catalogue record for this book is available from the British Library.

Cover image: Head of a warrior from the Temple of Aphaia in Aegina, Greece, 490 BC. Staatliche Glyptothek, Munich. Photo © The Art Archive / Corbis / Alfredo Dagli Orti.
Cover design by Workhaus

Set in 10/12.5 pt Galliard by Graphicraft Limited, Hong Kong

1   2013

Contents

Illustrations

Maps

Figures

Tables

Contributors

Carla M. Antonaccio is Professor of Archaeology and Chair of Classical Studies at Duke University. Her main interests concern the archaeology of Greek colonization and of Greek ethnicity and identity, Greek burial practices, and tomb and hero cults. Pertinent publications include *An Archaeology of Ancestors: Tomb Cult and Hero Cult in Early Greece* (1995); "Elite Mobility in the West," in Simon Hornblower and Catherine Morgan (eds.), *Pindar's Poetry, Patrons and Festivals: From Archaic Greece to the Roman Empire* (2006): 265–85; "Colonization: Greece on the Move," in H. A. Shapiro (ed.), *The Cambridge Companion to Archaic Greece* (2007): 201–24; "Ethnicity Reconsidered," forthcoming in T. Hodos and S. Hales (eds.), *Material Culture and Social Identities in the Ancient World* (2009).

Zosia Halina Archibald is Lecturer in Classical Archaeology at the University of Liverpool. She has been researching topics that combine archaeological and historical perspectives, notably Greek and Roman economies; the cultural and economic connections between the Mediterranean and Iron Age Europe; the emergence of urban centers; ancient metallurgy and technologies; ancient geography and historiography; and the functions of writing. She is the British team coordinator of an international project at Vetren, Bulgaria (identified with ancient Pistiros). Recent publications include: "A River Port and Emporion in Central Bulgaria: An Interim Report on the British Project at Vetren,," *ABSA* 97 (2002): 309–51; and four co-edited volumes: *Hellenistic Economies* (2000); *Making, Moving, and Managing: The New World of Ancient Economies, 323–31 BCE* (2005); *Pistiros: Excavations and Studies* 2 (2002); 3 (2007).

Jan Paul Crielaard teaches Greek archaeology at the Free University Amsterdam. His research has focused on the Early Iron Age and archaic period of Greece, including long-distance exchanges and colonization, elites and elite behavior, Homeric archaeology, and ethnicity. He is currently director of excavations at L'Amastuola, an archaic indigenous-Greek settlement in the periphery of Taras (Taranto). Recent publications pertinent to the current volume include an edited volume, *Homeric Questions: Essays in Philology, Ancient History, and Archaeology* (1995); "*Basileis* at Sea: Elites and External Contacts in the Euboian Gulf Region from the End of the Bronze Age to the Beginning of the Iron Age," in: S. Deger-Jalkotzy and I. S. Lemos (eds.), *Ancient Greece: From the Mycenaean Palaces to the Age of Homer* (2006): 271–97; "The Ionians in the Archaic Period: Shifting Identities in a Changing World," in A. M. J. Derks and N. G. A. M. Roymans (eds.), *Ethnic Constructs in Antiquity: The Role of Power and Tradition* (2009).

John K. Davies was Rathbone Professor of Ancient History and Classical Archaeology at the University of Liverpool 1977–2003, was elected FBA in 1985, FSA in 1986, and Corresponding Member of the German Archaeological Institute in 2000, and was Leverhulme Research Professor 1995–2000. He is the author of *Athenian Propertied Families 600–300 BC* (1971, revd. edn. in progress), *Democracy and Classical Greece* (2nd edn. 1992), and *Wealth and the Power of Wealth in Classical Athens* (1981), besides much activity on jointly edited volumes and as editor of *JHS* 1973–77 and of *Archaeological Reports* 1972–4. His many scholarly interests include the economies of the Hellenistic world, Delphi, Gortyn, the administrative and cultic history of the Greek states, the problems of post-Mycenaean state-formation, and the modern historiography of ancient Greece.

Nick Fisher is Professor of Ancient History in the Cardiff School of History and Archaeology at Cardiff University. He has published widely on the political, social, and cultural history of archaic and classical Greece. His books include *Hybris: A Study in the Values of Honour and Shame in Ancient Greece* (1992); *Slavery in Classical Greece* (1993); a translation with introduction and commentary of Aeschines, *Against Timarchos* (2001), and a co-edited volume, *Archaic Greece: New Approaches and New Evidence* (1998).

Lin Foxhall is Professor of Greek Archaeology and History at the University of Leicester. Her field projects include an archaeological survey in Methana, Greece, and currently a survey and excavation in Bova Marina in southern Calabria, Italy. She co-edited *Greek Law in Its Political Setting: Justifications Not Justice* (1996), and *Money, Labour and Land: Approaches to the Economies of Ancient Greece* (2002), is author of *Olive Cultivation in Ancient Greece: Seeking the Ancient Economy* (2007), and has written extensively on gender, agriculture, and land use in classical antiquity.

Hans-Joachim Gehrke is President of the German Archaeological Institute in Berlin. In the period 1987–2008 he was Professor of Ancient History at the University of Freiburg. His research and publications range widely, from archaic, classical, and hellenistic Greece to the Roman republic and empire, from social and political history to the history of political concepts and theories. His main publications include *Stasis: Untersuchungen zu den inneren Kriegen in den griechischen Staaten des 5. und 4. Jahrhunderts v. Chr.* (1985); *Geschichte des Hellenismus* (3rd edn., 2003); *Alexander der Grosse* (4th edn., 2005, translated into many languages), and *Geschichte der Antike: Ein Studienbuch* (2nd edn., 2006).

Jonathan M. Hall is the Phyllis Fay Horton Professor in the Humanities, Professor and Chair of Classics, and Professor in the Department of History and the College at the University of Chicago. His interests include the construction and maintenance of social, cultural, and ethnic identity in antiquity and the relationship between literary texts and material culture. He is the author of *Ethnic Identity in Greek Antiquity* (1997), which won the American Philological Association's Charles J. Goodwin Award for Merit in 1999; *Hellenicity: Between Ethnicity and Culture* (2002), which won the University of Chicago Press' Gordon J. Laing Prize in 2004; and *A History of the Archaic Greek World* (2007).

Sanne Houby-Nielsen is Director of the Museum of Mediterranean and Near Eastern Antiquities and of the Museum of Far Eastern Antiquities, both in Stockholm. She was keeper of the Royal Cast Collection (National Museum of Fine Arts, Copenhagen), 1995–7 and on-site leader of the Greek–Danish Excavations at Chalkis in Aetolia, Greece, 1995–2005. She has published several articles on burial customs in ancient Athens in *Proceedings of the Danish Institute at Athens* and is editor-in-chief of the journal *Medelhavsmuseet: Focus on the Mediterranean*. A volume on *Chalkis Aitolias, II: The Archaic Period* is forthcoming.

Nigel Kennell is currently a senior associate member of the American School of Classical Studies and instructor at the International Center for Hellenic and Mediterranean Studies in Athens. His research interests include Spartan history, Greek epigraphy, and Greek civic institutions. He is the author of *The Gymnasium of Virtue: Education and Culture in Ancient Sparta* (1995), which was a *Choice* Outstanding Academic Book for 1996; *Ephebeia: A Register of Greek Cities with Citizen Training Systems in the Hellenistic and Roman Periods* (2006), and *Spartans: A New History* (in press).

Iphigeneia Leventi is Assistant Professor in Classical Archaeology in the University of Thessaly. She has taken part in several excavations in the Peloponnese, Naxos, and Athens. Since 2004 she has been assistant director of her university's excavation at Soros in Magnesia. Her main research and teaching interests are sculpture, iconography, and cult. Recent publications include *Hygieia in Classical Greek Art* (2003); "The Mondragone Relief Revisited: Eleusinian Cult Iconography in Campania," *Hesperia* 76 (2007): 107–141; "Der Fries des Poseidon-Tempels in Sounion" (forthcoming).

Nino Luraghi is Professor of Classics at Princeton University. His main areas of interest include Greek historiography, the history and culture of the Greeks of Sicily and southern Italy, archaic Greek tyranny, and ethnicity and ethnic memory in the ancient Peloponnese. He is the author of *The Ancient Messenians: Constructions of Ethnicity and Memory* (2008) and co-editor of *Helots and Their Masters in Laconia and Messenia* (2003) as well as *The Politics of Ethnicity and the Crisis of the Peloponnesian League* (2009).

Irad Malkin is Professor of Greek History at Tel Aviv University, Incumbent of Cummings Chair for Mediterranean History and Cultures, and co-founder and co-editor of the *Mediterranean Historical Review*. His interests focus on Greek religion, colonization, ethnicity, networks, and, more generally, Mediterranean history.

His publications include *Religion and Colonization in Ancient Greece* (1987); *Myth and Territory in the Spartan Mediterranean* (1994); *The Returns of Odysseus: Colonization and Ethnicity* (1998), and *Networks in the Archaic Mediterranean* (forthcoming).

Alexander Mazarakis Ainian is Professor of Classical Archaeology at the University of Thessaly (Volos). He is the scientific director of several European Union research programs and director of excavations at the Early Iron Age settlement at Oropos in Attica, the archaic–hellenistic sanctuary of Kythnos, the ancient harbor of Kythnos, and the sanctuary of Apollo at Soros in Thessaly. His main field of specialization is the archaeology and architecture of Early Iron Age and archaic Greece. His publications include *From Rulers' Dwellings to Temples: Architecture, Religion and Society in Early Iron Age Greece, 1100–700 BC* (1997); *Homer and Archaeology* (2000, in Greek) as well as co-edited volumes on *Kea-Kythnos: History and Archaeology* (1998), and *Oropos and Euboea in the Early Iron Age* (2007).

Catherine Morgan is Director of the British School at Athens and Professor of Classical Archaeology at King's College London. Her interests focus on the art and archaeology of Early Iron Age and archaic Greece, with particular reference to the Peloponnese and western Greece. She currently directs the Stavros Valley Project on Ithaca for the British School, and co-directs the School's excavations in the ancient theatre at Sparta. Her recent publications include *Pindar's Poetry, Patrons and Festivals* (co-edited, 2006); *Early Greek States Beyond the Polis* (2004), *Isthmia* VIII (1999), and *Athletes and Oracles: The Transformation of Olympia and Delphi in the Eighth Century BC* (1990).

Ian Morris is Jean and Rebecca Willard Professor of Classics and Professor of History at Stanford University. His interests cover economic and social history, long-term comparative history, and archaeology. From 2000 to 2006 he was director of Stanford University's excavations on the acropolis of Monte Polizzo, Sicily. His recent publications include *The Cambridge Economic History of the Greco-Roman World* (co-authored, 2007); *The Greeks: History, Culture, and Society* (co-authored, 2nd edn., 2009); *Why the West Rules? For Now* (2009). He is also co-editor of *The Dynamics of Ancient Empires* (2009).

Oswyn Murray is a Fellow of the Society of Antiquaries, the Royal Danish Academy, and the Scuola Normale di Pisa. He was a Classics Fellow at Balliol College, Oxford (1968–2004). His books include *Early Greece* (2nd edn., 1993, translated into six languages) and (co-)edited volumes: *The Oxford History of the Classical World* (1986); *The Greek City from Homer to Alexander* (1990), *Sympotica: A Symposium on the Symposion* (1994), and *A Commentary on Herodotus I–IV* (2007).

Massimo Nafissi is Associate Professor in Greek History at the University of Perugia. His research focuses on Spartan history, Olympia and Elis, colonization and South Italy, Greek religion, and epigraphical work in Iasos (Caria). His publications include: *La nascita del kosmos. Ricerche sulla storia e la società di Sparta* (1991); "From Sparta to Taras: Nomima, Ktiseis and Relationships between Colony and Mother City," in S. Hodkinson and A. Powell (eds.), *Sparta: New Perspectives* (1999): 245–72; "The Great Rhetra (Plut. *Lyc.* 6): A Retrospective and Intentional Construct?" In

L. Foxhall, H. J. Gehrke, and N. Luraghi (eds.), *Intentionale Geschichte: Spinning Time* (forthcoming).

Thomas Heine Nielsen is Lecturer (Associate Professor) in Ancient Greek in the Section for Greek and Latin in the Saxo Institute at the University of Copenhagen. In 2003 he was awarded the prize for young scholars for research in the Humanities by the Royal Danish Academy of Sciences and Letters. His publications include *Arkadia and Its Poleis in the Archaic and Classical Periods* (2002); *Olympia and the Classical Hellenic City-state Culture* (2007), and a co-edited volume, *An Inventory of Archaic and Classical Poleis* (2004).

François de Polignac is Directeur d'Etudes at the Ecole Pratique des Hautes Etudes, Paris. His main interests bear on religion, society, and institutions in ancient Greece, on the archaeological history and anthropology of archaic Greece, the history of archaeology in Rome, and the legend of Alexander the Great in Arabic medieval literature. He currently serves as the Director of the Centre Louis Gernet de recherches comparées sur les sociétés anciennes, Paris, and coordinator of the research program CIRCE (cultual interpretations, representations, and constructions of space in ancient societies). His publications include *La naissance de la cité grecque: cultes, espace et société VIIIe–VIIe siècles av. J.-C.* (1984, Engl. translation 1995) and recently *Athènes et le politique. Dans le sillage de Claude Mossé* (2007), as well as a coedited collection, *L'individu et la communauté. Regards sur les identités en Grèce ancienne*, Revue des Études Anciennes 108 (2006): 5–153.

Kurt A. Raaflaub is David Herlihy University Professor and Professor of Classics and History as well as Director of the Program in Ancient Studies at Brown University. His research has been devoted mainly to the social, political, and intellectual history of archaic and classical Greece and the Roman republic as well as the comparative history of the ancient world. Among his recent publications are *The Discovery of Freedom in Ancient Greece* (2004, winner of the James Henry Breasted Prize of the American Historical Association); *Origins of Democracy in Ancient Greece* (co-authored, 2007), and *War and Peace in the Ancient World* (ed., 2007). A co-edited volume on *Epic and History* is forthcoming (2009).

Peter W. Rose is Professor of Classics at Miami University of Ohio. His main academic interests are Greek literature, history, literary theory, and film. He is the author of *Sons of the Gods, Children of Earth: Ideology and Literary Form in Ancient Greece* (1992). More recently he has published "Teaching Classical Myth and Confronting Contemporary Myths," in Martin Winkler (ed.), *Classical Myth and Culture in the Cinema* (2001): 291–318, and "Divorcing Ideology from Marxism and Marxism from Ideology: Some Problems," *Arethusa* 39.1 (2006) 101–36.

James Roy is Honorary Research Fellow in the School of Humanities at the University of Nottingham, where he taught for many years before his retirement. His research interests are Greek social and institutional history, the Greek countryside, and the local history and archaeology of Arkadia and Elis. Recent publications include "The Achaian League," in K. Buraselis and K. Zoumboulakis (eds.), *The Idea of European Community in History*, II (2003): 81–95; "Elis," in M. H. Hansen and

T. H. Nielsen (eds.), *An Inventory of Archaic and Classical Poleis* (2004): 489–504; "The Ambitions of a Mercenary," in R. L. Fox (ed.), *The Long March* (2004): 264–88.

Henk Singor teaches Ancient History at the University of Leiden. His main interests are Greek military history and Sparta as well as the history of Early Christianity. His publications include "*Eni prōtoisi machesthai:* Some Remarks on the Iliadic Image of the Battlefield," in J. P. Crielaard (ed.), *Homeric Questions* (1995): 183–99; "The Military Side of the Peisistratean Tyranny," in H. Sancisi-Weerdenburg (ed.), *Peisistratos and the Tyranny* (2000): 107–29; "The Spartan Army at Mantinea and Its Organization in the Fifth Century BC," in W. Jongman and M. Kleijwegt (eds.), *After the Past: Essays in Ancient History in Honour of H. W. Pleket* (2002): 235–84.

Michael Stahl is Professor of Ancient History at the Technical University of Darmstadt. His interests focus on archaic and classical Greece, politics and culture in the Roman empire, Romans in Germany as well as Greece and Rome in the eighteenth to twentieth century. Some of his publications: *Aristokraten und Tyrannen im archaischen Athen* (1987); two volumes on *Gesellschaft und Staat bei den Griechen* (2003, archaic and classical periods, respectively); *Botschaften des Schönen. Kulturgeschichte der Antike* (2008).

Elke Stein-Hölkeskamp teaches at the University of Münster, Germany. She is a corresponding member of the German Archaeological Institute. Her main interests concern the cultural history of archaic and classical Greece and Imperial Rome. Her publications include *Adelskultur und Polisgesellschaft. Studien zum griechischen Adel in archaischer und klassischer Zeit* (1989, 2nd edn., forthcoming); "Perikles, Kleon und Alkibiades als Redner: Eine zentrale Rolle der athenischen Demokratie im Wandel," in C. Neumeister and W. Raeck (eds.), *Rede und Redner: Bewertung und Darstellung in den antiken Kulturen* (2000): 79–93; *Das römische Gastmahl. Eine Kulturgeschichte* (2005).

Carol G. Thomas is Professor of History, Chair of European Studies, and Chair of Hellenic Studies at the University of Washington, Seattle. Her interests have focused on pre-classical Greece through the archaic age, Linear B, ancient historiography, and, most recently, ancient Macedonia with special interest in its historical geography. Her co-authored book, *Citadel to City State: The Transformation of Greece 1200–700 BCE* (1999, paperback 2003) achieved History Book Club status. Recent publications include *The Trojan War* (co-authored, 2005); *Finding People in Early Greece* (2005); *Alexander the Great in His World* (2006).

Gocha R. Tsetskhladze teaches classical archaeology at the Centre for Classics and Archaeology at the University of Melbourne. His main interests are the archaeology of the archaic and classical Mediterranean, Black Sea archaeology, and Greek colonization. His most recent publications include *The Eastern Edge of the Ancient Known World: A Brief Introduction to Black Sea Archaeology and History* (2007); *Greek Colonisation: An Account of Greek Colonies and other Settlements Overseas*, 2 vols. (ed., 2006, 2008). He is founder and editor-in-chief of the journal *Ancient West & East* and of its monograph supplement *Colloquia Antiqua*.

Christoph Ulf is Professor of Ancient History at the University of Innsbruck, Austria. His main research interests focus on the history of archaic Greek societies, the interaction between archaic Greece and the cultures of the near east, sports, and ancient society, and the impact of political beliefs on historiography. His many publications include *Die homerische Gesellschaft. Materialien zur analytischen Beschreibung und historischen Lokalisierung* (1990); *Wege zur Genese griechischer Identität. Die Bedeutung der früharchaischen Zeit* (ed., 1996); *Griechische Archaik zwischen Ost und West: Interne Entwicklungen – externe Impulse* (co-ed., 2004).

Robert W. Wallace is Professor of Classics at Northwestern University. He has worked widely in Greek history, law, music theory, and numismatics. Among many publications, he is the author of *The Areopagos Council, to 307 BC* (1989); "The Sophists in Athens," in D. Boedeker and K. A. Raaflaub (eds.), *Democracy, Empire, and the Arts in Fifth-century Athens* (1998): 203–22; *Reconstructing Damon: Music, Wisdom Teaching, and Politics in Democratic Athens* (forthcoming), and co-author of *Origins of Democracy in Ancient Greece* (2007).

Uwe Walter is Professor of Ancient History at the University of Bielefeld. His research interests are devoted to archaic and classical Greece, the political culture of the Roman republic, Greek and Roman historiography, and *Wissenschaftsgeschichte* in the field of ancient history. He is co-editor of *Historische Zeitschrift* and one of the leaders of the collaborative research center "The Political as Communicative Space in History" at his university. His main publications: *An der Polis teilhaben. Bürgerstaat und Zugehörigkeit im Archaischen Griechenland* (1993); "Das Wesen im Anfang suchen: Die archaische Zeit Griechenlands in neuer Perspektive," *Gymnasium* 105 (1998) 537–52; "The Classical Age as a Historical Epoch," in Konrad Kinzl (ed.), *A Companion to the Classical Greek World* (2006): 1–25.

Hans van Wees is Professor of Ancient History at University College London. He has published widely on the social and economic history of archaic Greece, as well as on archaic and classical Greek warfare. He is the author of *Status Warriors: War, Violence and Society in Homer and History* (1992); *Greek Warfare: Myths and Realities* (2004), and *The World of Achilles* (forthcoming); he has edited or co-edited several volumes, including *Archaic Greece: New Approaches and New Evidence* (1998).

James Whitley is Professor of Mediterranean Archaeology at Cardiff University. His main interests have focused on the archaeology of Early Iron Age and archaic Greece, particularly Crete, as well as mortuary archaeology, ethnicity, hero cults, social agency, and literacy. He has directed surveys and excavations around the city of Praisos in eastern Crete and was Director of the British School at Athens (2002–7). His recent publications include *The Archaeology of Ancient Greece, 1000–300 BC* (2001, winner of the Runciman prize in 2002); "Praisos: Political Evolution and Ethnic Identity in Eastern Crete, c.1400–300 BC," in S. Deger-Jalkotzy and I. Lemos (eds.), *Ancient Greece from the Mycenaean Palaces to the Age of Homer* (2006): 597–617; *Building Communities: House, Settlement and Society in the Aegean and Beyond* (co-ed., 2007).

Josef Wiesehöfer is Professor of Ancient History at the University of Kiel and Director of its Department of Classics. He is a member of the Centre for Asian and African Studies at his university, corresponding member of the German Archaeological Institute and the Academy of Sciences at Göttingen, and (co-)editor of various series: *Oriens et Occidens* (Stuttgart), *Asien und Afrika* (Hamburg), *Achaemenid History* (Leiden), and *Oikumene* (Frankfurt). His main interests are in the history of the ancient near east and its relations with the Mediterranean world, in social history, the history of early modern travelogues, and the history of scholarship. His main publications include *Das antike Persien von 550 v. Chr. bis 651 n. Chr.* (4th edn., 2005; English translation 3rd edn., 2001); *Das Reich der Achaimeniden. Eine Bibliographie* (co-authored, 1996); *Das frühe Persien* (3rd edn., 2006); *Iraniens, Grecs et Romains* (2005).

John-Paul Wilson is currently Research Development and Training Officer at the Graduate Research School of the University of Worcester, UK. His research interests have focused on early Greek literacy, the alphabet, colonization, trade and exchange, and research student training and development. His recent publications include "The 'Illiterate Trader'?" *Bulletin of the Institute of Classical Studies* 44 (1997–8): 29–53; *Greek and Roman Colonization: Origins, Ideologies and Interactions* (co-ed., 2006), and "Ideologies of Greek Colonization," in the same volume, 25–58.

Preface

Nothing seems certain any longer in the study of archaic Greece. In recent years, staples of older textbooks such as "tyranny," "colonization" and "the rise of the hoplite phalanx" have been thoroughly reconceptualized or even consigned to the dustbin of history – at least by a few scholars. Most historical dates, beginning with the year 776 BC as marking the foundation of the Olympic Games and the start of the archaic age, are now widely considered unreliable. Iconic events such as the Lelantine and Messenian Wars may never have taken place. Perhaps some of the scepticism driving such reassessments has gone too far, but it is certainly an important positive development that recent scholarship has been characterized by a more critical approach to the literary evidence. Meanwhile, other kinds of evidence – archaeological and iconographic – as well as numerous topics in the field of social, economic, and cultural history have been demanding increasing attention. As a combined effect of these developments, archaic Greek history has virtually been transformed beyond recognition. Recent surveys by, for example, Robin Osborne (1996) or Jonathan Hall (2007), make an admirable effort to highlight new perspectives and assessments. Still, the task has perhaps become almost too complex for one scholar, and it is high time for an even more comprehensive approach. As is typical of the genre, this *Companion to Archaic Greece* pursues two complementary goals: to offer, from the perspective of many specialists in various fields, a multi-authored survey of the current state of the evidence and the latest insights on the period, and to give new impulses or suggest new directions for future research.

The Introduction establishes the context of this volume in two ways. It provides the intellectual background by tracing changes in historiography since the nineteenth century that have brought us to the present state of scholarship (ch. 1), and it lays out the physical context of geography and communications in the wider Mediterranean world, which did so much to shape Greek history (ch. 2).

A narrative history of the archaic age has always been difficult to write, even for those with great confidence in the accuracy of our later sources for the period. By now it seems virtually impossible. The written record mentions very few events or individuals, scattered across the cities and centuries. More importantly, much that has survived is not contemporary but represents archaic Greece as selectively remembered by later generations with their own interests, agendas and presuppositions. Nevertheless, enough contemporary texts and material remains survive to allow us to reconstruct the history of the period in broad outline, as shown in Part II, Histories. We begin with the long-term historical background to developments of the archaic period in what is rightly no longer called "the Dark Age" (ch. 3) and proceed with an analysis of the changes of the eighth century BC and the beginnings of urbanization which shape the fundamental structures of the archaic age (ch. 4). Alongside the archaeological evidence on which these two chapters are based, the society and culture of the early archaic period are potentially illuminated by the controversial evidence of Homer and Hesiod, which is analysed next (ch. 5). The political, military and social history of the following centuries is outlined in three chapters which concentrate on the widespread phenomenon of tyranny (ch. 6) and on the only two states about which we are sufficiently well informed to attempt a continuous and coherent interpretation of developments, Athens (ch. 7) and Sparta (ch. 8), the latter a subject of particularly lively debate in the last decade or so. Part II closes with a study of relations between Greece and Persia, stripped as far as possible of its usual Greek bias, culminating in the great war which conventionally marks the transition to the classical period (ch. 9).

The ever bigger, better and better-published body of evidence from archaeological excavation and survey is the main focus of Part III, Regions. As several of the contributors note, the areas covered by each of the chapters are not always unified and often have notable similarities to and links with other regions with which they might profitably have been combined in a single study. In order to ensure comprehensive and even coverage, however, we have divided up the Greek world into eight broad regions each of which has at least some significant distinguishing characteristics. In view of their special status in Greek history, the territories of Athens (ch. 10) and Sparta (ch. 12) deserve separate treatment, while the rest of the Greek homeland is covered in four wide-ranging chapters on the cities of the Aegean (ch. 11), the Peloponnese (ch. 13), Crete (ch. 14) and northern Greece (ch. 15). We have unfortunately been unable to include the very different world of the Greeks in Cyprus, but the "colonial" Greek settlements receive their due in two chapters dedicated to the western Mediterranean (ch. 16) and the Black Sea area (ch. 17).

The fourth, final and longest part, Themes, offers fourteen new perspectives on key themes in archaic Greek society and history. The rise of a world of poleis is studied from several angles, taking in urbanization as well as the developments of the concepts of "city" and "countryside" (ch. 18), the nature of the "foundation' of cities and the creation of Mediterranean-wide networks linking them (ch. 19), the establishment of complex republican institutions and popular sovereignty (ch. 20), the continuing role of charismatic political leadership in its various guises (ch. 21), and the crucial role of sanctuaries and festivals in binding communities together at every level (ch. 22). Basic features of archaic society are surveyed in studies of economy (ch. 23) and class (ch. 24) as forces for historical change, and on concepts of gender as expressed in literature and material culture (ch. 25). The symposium (ch. 26) and sporting and other competitions (ch. 27) not only dominated social life but also inspired a great deal of the literature and art of the period – among the most remarkable achievements of Greek culture, along with the adoption of the alphabet and the spread of literacy (ch. 28), and, perhaps most important of all, the spirit of critical enquiry which produced scientific, philosophical and political thought (ch. 29). The volume closes with a look at the Greek world as an international system, analysing both the changing shapes of war and diplomacy (ch. 30) and the formulation of ethnic identities in a world where many cultures met and influenced one another across the Mediterranean and Near East (ch. 31).

Many more themes might have been added. Readers may be surprised to find no chapter devoted to, for example, art and architecture, or lyric poetry. These and other topics are not ignored, but discussed – albeit relatively briefly – under different headings, as an aspect of, say, economic development or of sympotic culture, as well as in the regional surveys. We believe that in such cases the loss of detail in the treatment is off-set by the insights gained from looking at these subjects from a broader historical perspective.

Not the least important feature of this *Companion* is that the contributing authors represent an exceptionally wide range of scholarship and scholarly traditions: thirty-five authors of a dozen different nationalities working in thirteen different countries, all leading experts with innovative approaches to their subjects, including some whose important work is rarely published in English. Both the range and the sheer size of this volume – which could have been much larger still if we had not brutally cut large amounts of excellent material from numerous chapters – are, we think, eloquent testimony to the renewed vitality and enduring fascination of archaic Greek history and culture.

The first drafts of many of the papers in this volume were written several years ago, and comprehensive updating has not always been possible, but authors and editors have made every effort to include the most recent bibliography. US spelling and punctuation have been adopted as standard; all ancient Greek has been transliterated, and contributors have been allowed their own preference in rendering long vowels (marked by circumflex, macron, or acute accent, or not marked at all). The editors wish to acknowledge the important contributions made to this volume by David Yates who, together with Jennifer Yates, translated a chapter and compiled the indices, by Amy Flynn and especially by Mark Thatcher, who did most of the work towards compiling the consolidated bibliography of more than 2,500 entries, by Al Bertrand, who commissioned the project, and staff at Blackwell for their assistance at various stages of the long road towards completing this *Companion*. We are also grateful to Errietta Bissa for further assistance with the bibliography and to Nino Luraghi for help with the maps, which are based on relief maps provided by C. Scott Walker of the Harvard University Maps Collection.

Thanks for financial assistance in funding the work of graduate students are owed to the Humanities Research Fund and the Royce Family Fund for Teaching Excellence at Brown University.

Kurt A. Raaflaub
Hans van Wees

Abbreviations

Chronology

EIA	Early Iron Age	ca. 1100–700 BC
LBA	Late Bronze Age	ca. 1600–1100 BC
LG	Late Geometric	ca. 750–700 BC
LHIIIC	Late Helladic IIIC	ca. 1200–1100 BC
LMIIIC	Late Minoan IIIC	ca. 1200–1100 BC
MG	Middle Geometric	ca. 850–750 BC
PG	Protogeometric	ca. 1050–900 BC
SPG	SubProtogeometric	ca. 900–750 (in Euboea)
Archaic		ca. 750–480 BC

Standard Works

DK	Diels and Kranz 1951–2
DNP	*Der Neue Pauly*
Icr	*Inscriptiones Creticae*: Guarducci 1935–50
IG	*Inscriptiones Graecae*
Inventory	Hansen and Nielsen 2004
ML	Meiggs and Lewis 1969 (1988)
Nomima	van Effenterre and Ruzé 1994–5
OCD	*Oxford Classical Dictionary*
RE	*Realencyclopaedie der classischen Altertumswissenschaft*
SIG	*Sylloge Inscriptionum Graecarum*

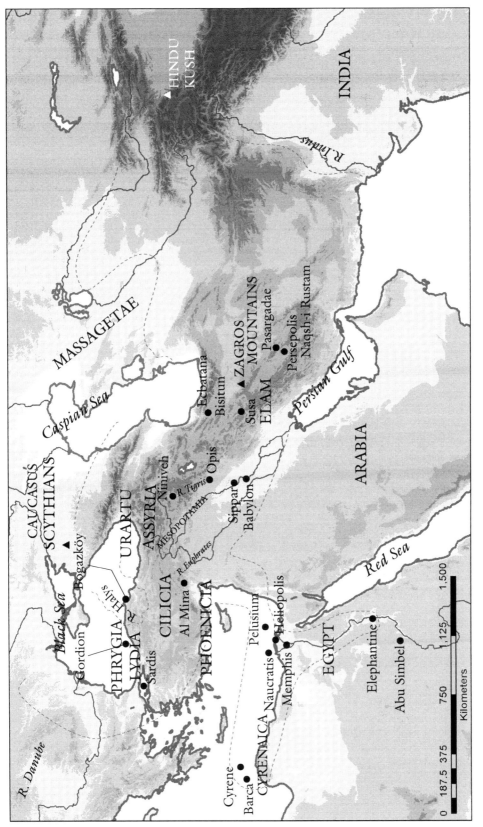

Map 1 The eastern Mediterranean and the Persian empire

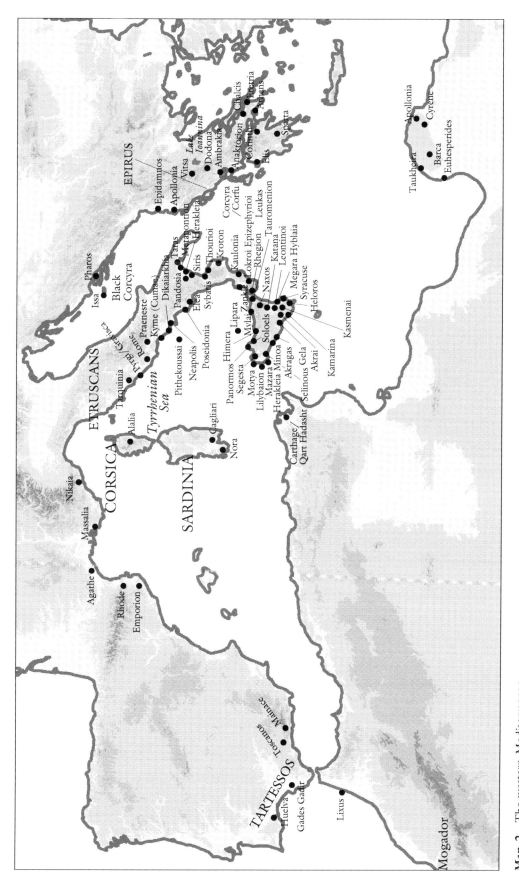

Map 2 The western Mediterranean

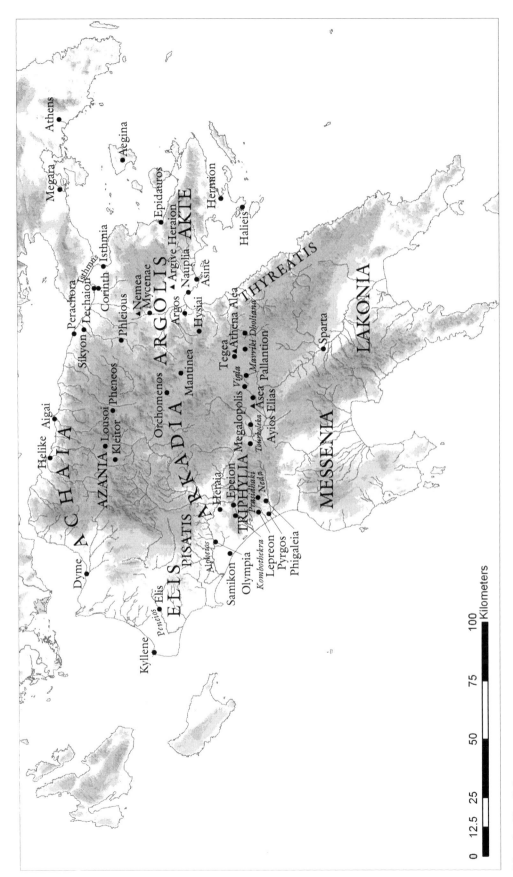

Map 3 The Peloponnese

Argos

Hysiae

THYREATIS

Tegea

MOUNT
PARNON

Sellasia
Tsakona
Sparta
Menelaion
Amyclae

R. Eurotas

Geronthrae

MOUNT
TAYGETOS

Helos
Plain

Aigiai

Gytheum

Molaoi

Epidauros
Limera

Asopos

CAPE
TAENARUM

CAPE
MALEA

CYTHERA

0 4.5 9   18   27   36

Kilometers

Map 4 Laconia

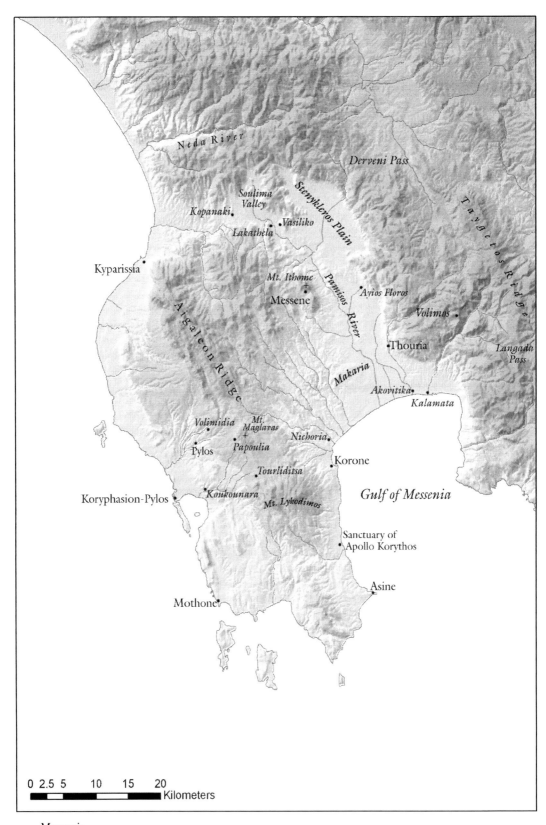

Neda River

Derveni Pass

Soulima Valley

Stenykleros Plain

Kopanaki

Vasiliko

Lakathela

Taygetos Ridge

Kyparissia

Mt. Ithome

Pamisos River

Ayios Floros

Messene

Volimos

Algaleon Ridge

Thouria

Langada Pass

Makaria

Akovitika

Kalamata

Volimidia

Mt. Maglavas

Nichoria

Pylos

Papoulia

Korone

Tourliditsa

Gulf of Messenia

Koryphasion-Pylos

Koukounara

Mt. Lykodimos

Sanctuary of Apollo Korythos

Asine

Mothone

0 2.5 5   10   15   20
Kilometers

Map 5 Messenia

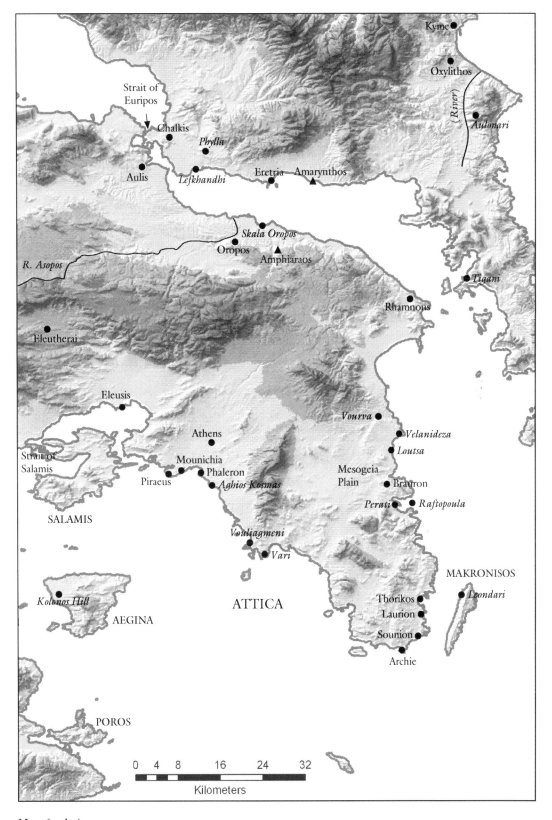

Map 6 Attica

Map 7 The central Aegean

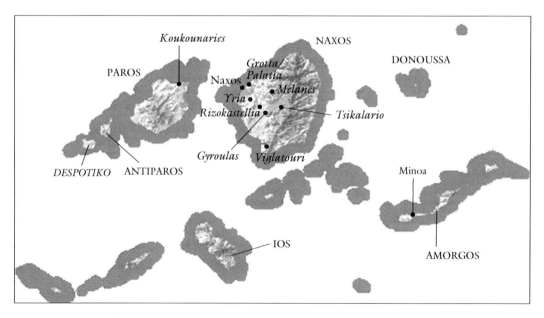

Map 8 Naxos and Paros

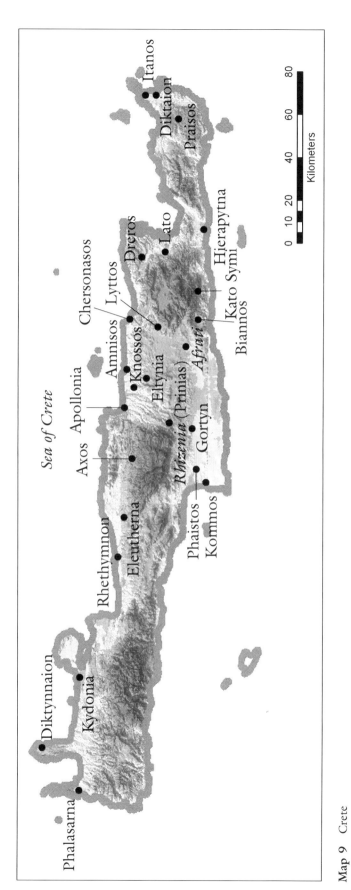

Map 9   Crete

Map 10 Greek Asia Minor

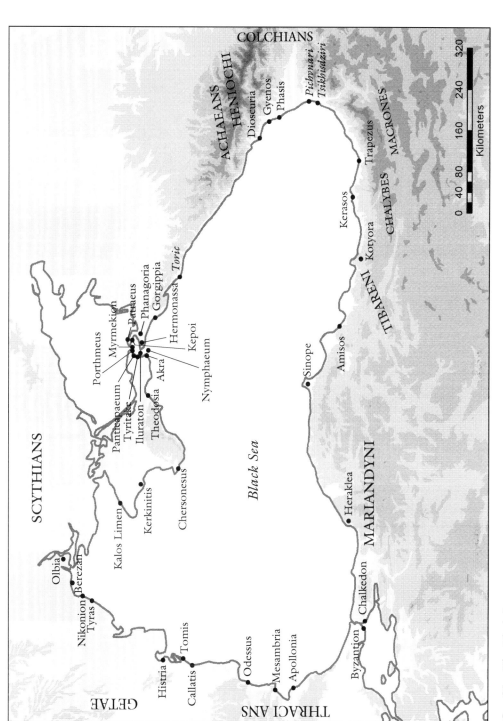

Map 11 The Black Sea

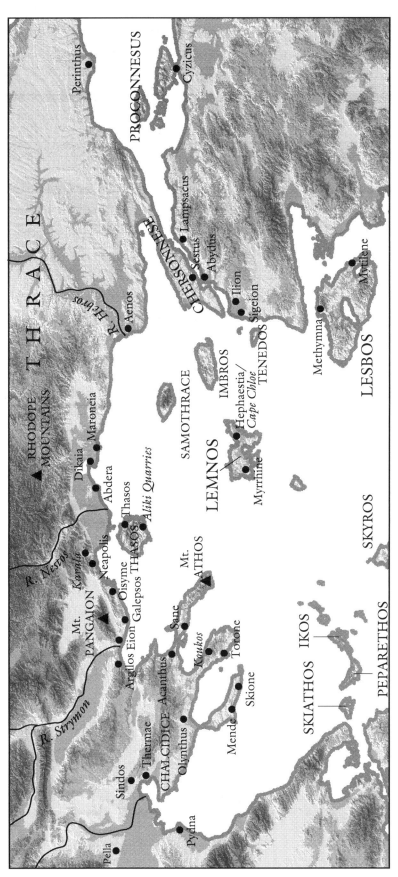

Map 12 The northern Aegean

PROCONNESUS

Perinthus

Cyzicus

Lampsacus

Sestus
Abydus

Ilion
Sigeion

Myrtilene

Methymna

LESBOS

CHERSONNESE

Aenos

R. Hebros

T H R A C E

RHODOPE
MOUNTAINS

SAMOTHRACE

IMBROS

Hephaestia/
Cape Chloe

TENEDOS

Maroneia

Dikaia

Abdera

Thasos
Aliki Quarries

THASOS

LEMNOS

Myrrhine

R. Nestos

Kavala

Neapolis

Oisyme

Galepsos

Mt.
ATHOS

SKYROS

Mt.
PANGAION

Argilos Eion

Acanthus

Sane

Koukos

IKOS

Torone

Skione

R. Strymon

Thermae

CHALCIDICE

Olynthus

Mende

PEPARETHOS

SKIATHOS

Sindos

Pydna

Pella

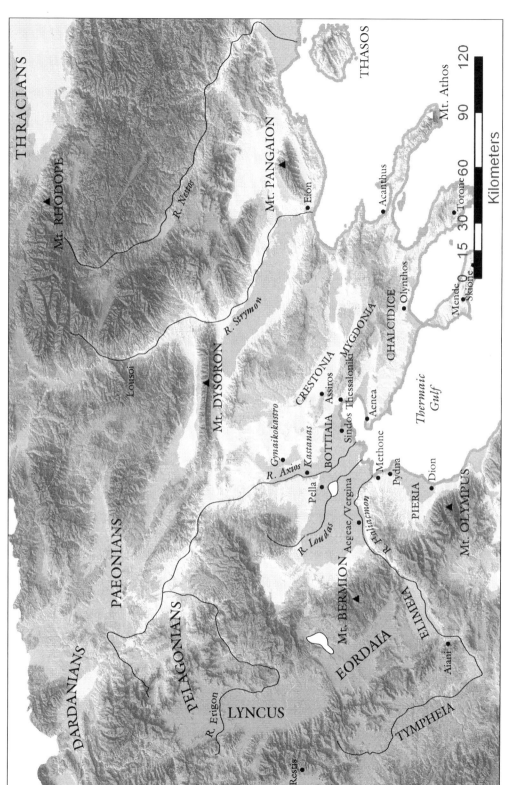

Map 13 Macedonia

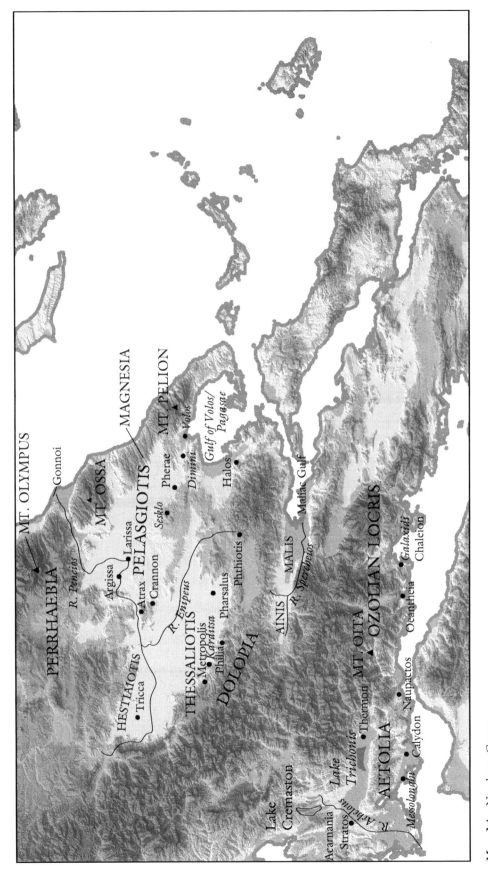

MT. OLYMPUS

PERRHAEBIA

R. Peneios

Gonnoi

MT. OSSA

MAGNESIA

MT. PELION

HESTIAIOTIS

Tricca

Larissa

Argissa

Atrax

Crannon

PELASGIOTIS

Sesklo

Pherae

Dimini

Volos

Gulf of Volos/
Pagasae

R. Empeus

THESSALIOTIS

Metropolis

Karatsa

Philia

Pharsalus

Phthiotis

Halos

DOLOPIA

AINIS

R. Spercheios

MALIS

Maliac Gulf

Lake
Cremaston

MT. OITA

OZOLIAN LOCRIS

Galaxidi

Chaleion

Lake
Trichonis

Thermon

Oeantheia

R. Achelous

Acarnania

Stratos

AETOLIA

Calydon

Naupactos

Mesolongi

Map 14 Northern Greece

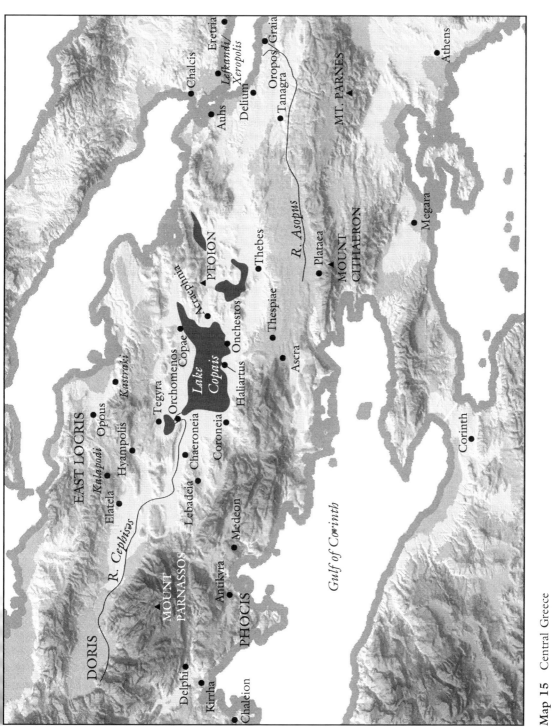

Map 15 Central Greece

Athens

Eretria

Lefkandi/
Xeropolis

Oropos/Graia

Chalcis

Auhs

Delium

Tanagra

MT. PARNES

R. Asopus

Megara

PTOION

Thebes

Plataea

MOUNT
CITHAERON

Acraephnia

Onchestos

Thespiae

Orchomenos

Copae

Ascra

Tegyra

Lake
Copais

Kastraki

Haliartus

Corinth

EAST LOCRIS

Opous

Coroneia

Kalapodi

Hyampolis

Chaeroneia

Elatela

Lebadeia

Gulf of Corinth

R. Cephisos

Medeon

DORIS

Antikyra

MOUNT
PARNASSOS

PHOCIS

Delphi

Kirrha

Chaleion

PART I

Introduction

CHAPTER ONE

The Historiography of Archaic Greece

John K. Davies

The Trap of Terminology

"Modern convention sets the start of the Archaic period in 776 BC, the year when the Games were said to have been officially founded at Olympia in Elis."[1] So it does: but the convention hides a contradiction. Normal practice, as encapsulated by the *Oxford English Dictionary*, uses "archaic" for whatever is "marked by the characteristics of an earlier period; old-fashioned, primitive, antiquated" – but what the reader will find in this book is the story of an exceptional, energetic, effervescent culture which developed and expanded with extraordinary speed and innovative assurance, in ways which it would be absurd to describe as "old-fashioned" or "antiquated." Nor is "archaic" the only metaphor in play, for "primitive Greece," "early Greece" and "medieval Greece" have all been in use among historians at various times to denote the period covered by this book, while "Dark Age Greece" has come to be the conventional label for the period between the collapse of the Mycenaean kingdoms and the Greeks' re-adoption of literacy by the mid-eighth century.

Such labels have three characteristics in common. First, they gaze backwards, whether from our own modern vantage-point or from that of the higher culture or greater sophistication which we attribute to "Classical Greece" (itself a dangerous label). Thereby they seriously hinder our attempts to re-create the experiences of the men and women who lived through these centuries: such people did not – could not – think of themselves as "primitive," "early," or "archaic." Second, they all imply comparison, whether with medieval Europe or with post-Roman "Dark Age" Britain or with other chronologically distant civilizations. The comparison with medieval Europe has been especially influential, the Greek city-states being seen as politically and economically very similar to the Hansa states, the Swiss cantons, and the Italian communes:[2] but all such comparisons are shortcuts, which mislead more than they help. Third, they reflect decisions about periodization. Of course, all historians have to decide where to start and stop, but it is all too easy to inherit a decision without identifying and testing the criteria which underlie it. Specifically with this volume: just as 776 is a dangerously fragile peg on which to hang the recognition of a new period, so too the Graeco-Persian Wars of 499–479 might not nowadays be taken as marking the break between "Archaic" and "Classical" if Herodotus' text had not survived.[3]

The traps set by terminology do not end there. "Archaic" itself may have started off in art history, since the *OED*'s first citation, of 1846, comes from a book on the Elgin Marbles.[4] "Archaeology" in the sense of "ancient history" is much older, the first citation being of 1607, but the semantic shift towards its present-day meaning was also an early nineteenth-century affair (the two relevant pages of the *OED* are most instructive for intellectual history). But in fact Greece, like all Mediterranean countries, has a long and intricate human "pre-history," which stretches back at least to ca. 40,000 BC and includes major sites of the Neolithic period as well as the Mycenaean age (1600–1100) with its wealth, its palaces, and its Linear B writing in Greek. As is clear from myths and allusions in historical sources, the Greek peoples of the "Archaic" period knew perfectly well that they lived in a landscape long moulded by previous inhabitants, with whose legacy they came to terms in various ways. Nor, as contact by sea with the rest of the Eastern Mediterranean gathered pace again after ca. 900, could they avoid awareness that out there, "beyond the noble Ocean" (Hesiod, *Theog.* 215), lay cultures and societies which could look, and in many ways were, vastly richer and older than their own: Egypt especially made a great impression. That is not to deny that there had been significant disruption throughout the Eastern Mediterranean between ca. 1200 and ca. 1000, or that late Mycenaean Greece in particular had experienced some sort of systems failure, generating depopulation, political and cultural discontinuity, and the felt need to create a new order of society. The currently lively debate about the nature, degree, and duration of that discontinuity is not the direct concern of this book,[5] but the reader should bear continually in mind the tension between the new starts which post-Mycenaean societies had perforce been making and the antiquity of the human landscapes which formed their backdrop. Indeed, a neglected short book (Ure 1921) and a now classic volume of papers (Hägg 1983b), surveying what it calls "The Greek Renaissance of the eighth century BC," use a much more fitting metaphor than "Archaic," though it too evokes perilous comparisons. Though they are not inserted hereafter, "archaic" should always be read with mental quotation marks.

The modern historiography of Archaic Greece[6] is the product of three distinct styles. They emerged at different dates, and remained separate for the best part of a century, but since around 1980 have experienced a complex and very uncomfortable process of convergence. They are, first, the long-established approach of the ancient historians, based primarily on the historical, geographical, and antiquarian traditions of the later Greeks themselves with some admixture from "literary" texts such as the epic and lyric poets; second, the style adopted by cultural historians, who came to be concerned above all with how institutions, habits, cult and mythology could be "read," both as reflections of a social order and as representations of the ways in which contemporaries interpreted their world and thereby made sense of it; and third, the approach taken by archaeologists, who until the 1970s were concerned mainly

with establishing relative and absolute chronologies for the various genres of artifacts which came within their purview, but also, and derivatively, with establishing
the history of the occupation of specific sites such as the major sanctuaries (Delos,
Delphi, Olympia, etc.), since these had been the object of the earliest professional
attention. Each style has had a very different trajectory. Once their development has
been traced in outline, the processes of convergence since 1980 can be traced in
slightly more detail.

The Large-scale Narratives

The first "current" to formalize itself was that adopted by the text-based ancient
historians, for whom the multi-volume single-authored narrative survey was adopted
right from the start as the preferred format.[7] Within that format, and once the
writing of what we now term "ancient history" became established as an art-form
in the eighteenth century, the Greek archaic period naturally required inclusion. That
task at once presented the problems of separating myth from reality and of weaving
tiny fragmentary narratives into a coherent whole. Both problems were, and remain,
ferociously intractable. Adequately to tackle the former required either formulating
usable criteria for isolating possible historical cores in the material of epic, myth,
legend, and folktale, or developing techniques to detect symbolic "meaning." Some
progress has been made in "reading" myths symbolically, much less in re-historicizing
them, not least because awareness that stories are preserved because they have a purpose (so the purpose is what matters, not the content) has combined with a far more
detailed understanding of how the verbal transmission of narratives can transform
(or distort) the material.[8] True, the temptation to take the Trojan War as history is
perennial, but the only respectable course has proved to be the drastic one taken
by George Grote in 1846, in excluding mythic material from the historical domain
altogether. That decision drove him to begin his historical treatment in 776 and
thereby to set the convention with which this chapter began.

However, the second problem remained, viz. that of combining fragmentary narratives. Whereas, say, the history of Roman Italy or of each of the post-medieval
European powers can be presented as a narrative with a single thread (albeit at the
serious cost of marginalizing the histories of subordinated areas), not even Classical
(i.e. post-480) Greece allows its history to be presented thus, for at a minimum Sparta,
Athens, Thebes, Syracuse, Asia Minor, and Macedonia each need focused attention.
Pre-Classical Greece is even more polycentric: each island, each micro-state, each
sanctuary presents a certain number of pieces of information – but they turn out to
be pieces from a huge number of different jigsaws. Either, then, the historian presents a set of simultaneous micro-narratives, at the cost of obscuring links and similarities, or s/he groups them in various ways, at the cost of occluding differences,
or s/he identifies recurrent themes and patterns of behavior, at the cost of losing
the thread of processes which unfold and intersect through time.

Three multi-volume classics each provide an illustrative example of one of these
expedients, while their chronological order of publication also reveals how academic
preoccupations and styles of presentation changed over the decades between the 1840s

and the First World War. As is conventional, I begin with George Grote (1794–1871), for though his History, appearing in twelve volumes in 1846–56,[9] was very far from being the first full-dress *History of Greece*, both its quality, as a careful account soberly based on the critical evaluation of sources, and its tone, reflecting both moral earnestness and a sympathy for democracy and the Athenian Empire, were recognized as setting a wholly new standard of scholarship in the subject, thereby giving it widespread authority and influence for the next fifty years.[10] In organizing his material, his sense that "the history of Greece, prior to 560 BC, [is] little better than a series of parallel but isolated threads, each attached to a separate city"[11] led him to begin his Part II with three ethno-geographical chapters, and then to devote one or more chapters to each of the main Greek-speaking polities or regions. He breaks off only for two chapters on the Panhellenic festivals and lyric poetry before narrating sixth-century Athenian affairs in detail, the growth of the Persian empire as far as the Battle of Marathon, the Ionian Enlightenment and the impact of Pythagoras on the Greeks of south Italy, the Persian wars, the Sicilian tyrannies, the growth of Athens' Aegean empire, and so on – noticeably marking no sharp break between "archaic" and "classical" in the way which has become customary. Grote's *History* can still be read with pleasure, for his style is eminently readable, weaving summaries of the primary evidence into an exposition which always flows attractively while offering the reader a measured interpretative reading. Of course, especially for the archaic period it reflected the clustering of the information available in the literary sources, for Grote was writing just before the discoveries of inscriptions and papyri – first a trickle, then a flood – began to make any serious impact and before the challenge of incorporating archaeological evidence became inescapable. Yet it also reflected how choices could still be made, e.g. by concentrating on peoples rather than on personalities, by giving attention to Greece's eastern Mediterranean neighbors, by offering regional surveys, and most notably by offering a far more sympathetic reading of radical or populist politics and politicians than his predecessors had done.

By the 1880s and 1890s, however, a younger generation of historians in Germany was developing very different readings of pre-480 Greece. They were influenced in part by their experiences of nation-formation and authoritarian leadership, in part by new evidence from inscriptions and excavations, and in part by the emergence of newer academic agendas in world history and economic history.[12] Of the innumerable scholarly creations of this golden generation two in particular need attention here. The first, the *Griechische Geschichte* of Georg Busolt (1850–1920), first appearing in two volumes in 1885 and 1888 but best used through the four published volumes of the second edition (1893–1904), was seen at once as *the* authoritative treatment of the period,[13] offering a very different balance. The archaeological work of Schliemann and others allowed him to start with a 120-page section on the Mycenaean period, followed by an even longer section on the emergence and expansion of the historical world of the Greek states (I 127–509). Especially interesting is the third section of volume I, with chapters on Lykourgos and the Spartan constitution, the Messenian Wars and Pheidon of Argos, tyranny in the Isthmos states, and the Delphian Amphiktyony and the Peloponnesian League, for behind the preoccupation with state-formation and the crystallization of power-groups in this section it is hard not to detect a reflection of the Bismarckian power-politics which Busolt admired. Geographically, the focus has narrowed, to concentrate above all on the better-documented polities of Peloponnese and the Saronic Gulf with their colonial offshoots, at the expense of Northern Greece or the eastern Aegean. Stylistically, too, the contrast with Grote is marked, for, to put it kindly, narrative was not Busolt's forte. Instead, the focus above all is on constitutional antiquities, documented in close-packed footnotes which usually cover at least half the page. The result is a meticulously systematic and all-embracing but sadly static and stodgy presentation, which traces the growth and expansion of Greek presence and culture with all the grace of a sledge-hammer, while its unfinished state and the total absence of an index make it a penance to consult. These are matters of much regret, for Busolt did not just encapsulate the scholarship of his time but advanced it with critical shrewdness, encyclopaedic knowledge of the sources, and a real if hidden interpretative agenda which even now would deserve a measured assessment.

What it received, instead, was a fierce rejoinder from his slightly younger rival K. J. Beloch (1854–1929).[14] As with Busolt, his *Griechische Geschichte* is best viewed not via its first edition of 1893–1904 but via its second, of 1912–27, for that allows the work as a whole, and especially the volume dealing with archaic Greece (I², in two parts, 1912 and 1913), to serve as the apogee of the comprehensive monograph. Plan, style, and tone are all a world away from Busolt. Putting essays on specific problems and details into a separate volume (I² 2) allowed Beloch to minimize footnotes and to paint a vivid picture of flow and development. His chapter headings alone give the gist clearly: Personality in history, Transmitted information, The Aegean coastlands, The beginnings of the Greek people, The Minoan–Mycenaean period, Expansion across the Aegean, Myth and religion, Heroic poetry, The age of cavalry, Sea-power, The transformation of economic life, The transformation of cultural life, The growth of larger polities, Tyranny, The foundation of the Persian Empire and of Greek hegemonies, Society and art in the age of the tyrants, and Religious reform and the foundation of scholarship. Here at last was a real interpretative essay, giving the period shape, life, and a proper sense of its intensive and rapid development.

Yet it had serious defects, which re-echo even now. One was an "Aryan" racism which generated some stupefying paragraphs[15] and led him to down-date or to minimize (in marked contrast to Busolt) Phoenician presence and influence in the Aegean and the Mediterranean.[16] A second, more forgivable, defect was an attitude of deep skepticism towards the veracity of the information transmitted in the antiquarian tradition. It led him *inter alia* to down-date much of the traditional chronology of the archaic period, a view which found some adherents[17] but crumbled once the chronology of Greek ceramic artifacts had been established and calibrated against firm dates from eastern Mediterranean sites. A third, in itself commendable and far-sighted, was to proclaim the importance of economic history,[18] but that led him to embrace wholeheartedly the comparison between the growth of the mini-states of central Greece and the growth, institutions, and social dynamics of the Hansa towns, in ways which few could now accept.

All the same, Beloch's work offered a framework and a model. The trouble was, as became ever clearer in the 1920s and 1930s, that the increasing flow of new primary documentation, especially of inscriptions and site reports, rendered exhaustive and knowledgeable coverage of the whole of Greek history by one scholar virtually impracticable. As a result, after Beloch the mainstream narrative genre broke apart. One sub-form, the single-author summary narrative of Greek history as a whole, generated authoritative textbooks, some of astonishing longevity,[19] which however inevitably summarized existing knowledge without breaking much new ground. A second sub-form, mostly initiated by publishers for a student market, comprised a series of monographs, each treating a major "period" of two to three hundred years and each written by a specialist. It is this format which has provided the main narrative surveys of archaic Greece since the 1920s.[20] As their chapter headings show, they all share a strong family resemblance. True, there has been evolution, as scholars ceased to attempt to cover the Bronze Age or the Dark Age, or introduced explicit sections on sources, or gave cultural history a higher profile, but all have clearly found their formats being determined more by geography than by theme. Nor was anything very different offered by the third sub-form, the multi-volume, multi-author production shaped and guided by a team of editors. First applied to archaic Greece in vols III (1925) and IV (1926) of *The Cambridge Ancient History*, and perpetuated in a far more elaborate and extended form in the volumes of the second edition, the material was again, though with a few exceptions,[21] mostly distributed among a series of narrative chapters, each embracing a geographical region. It is striking how little this genre has changed since Grote.

The other main narrative format has addressed the history of regions and single polities. This genre took a long time to emerge from being histories above all of antiquarian traditions and constitutional development, a preoccupation which the publication of the Aristotelian *Constitution of Athens* in 1890 merely served to perpetuate. What was needed was to marry that approach with a sensibility for landscape and settlement and for archaeological and epigraphic evidence. Perhaps not surprisingly, the first enterprises in that direction[22] reviewed areas where the paucity of evidence from literary sources both encouraged such a marriage and required a long chronological overview: until recently, books on the Western Greeks and on Delos were unusual in surveying the Archaic period only.[23] However, since the 1970s a convergence of historically minded archaeologists and archaeologically minded historians has extended the genre both to well-documented regions[24] and more recently back to regions and epochs where the discourse still has to start from landscape, installations, and artifacts:[25] activity in northern Greece is particularly lively at present, fuelled by surface survey, by the proliferation of local archaeological journals, and by dedicated monograph series.[26]

Other forms of narrative have been marginal. Of course, the Graeco-Persian Wars of 499–479 have been exhaustively treated, but what little is known of other wars has rightly either been accommodated within large-scale narratives or, as with conflicts arising from settlement overseas, been treated as elements of ongoing processes. Likewise, given the fragility of the source material, narratives of individual lives have been near-impossible (Plutarch's *Lykourgos* is as imaginary as his *Theseus*). Only for Solon, for Peisistratos on his own or with the other pre-480 tyrants of the mainland as a group, and for one or two major Athenian figures of the Graeco-Persian Wars has it been worth making the effort,[27] but even here it has been more a matter of dis-entangling the processes by which biographical information (or pseudo-information) emerged and was transformed in later sources than of presenting a documented life within its political context and cultural milieu, in the way that is possible for Perikles (just about), Alkibiades, King Agesilaos, or Demosthenes.

Cultural History

Narrative history, even if envisaged within the generation-long blocks of time which are often the smallest practicable units of description for archaic Greek history, is essentially linear. As such it is liable to bypass the constants of life and to under-estimate the extent to which habits, values, and expectations differed from our own. One may, for example, take "expectation" literally, for recent studies of ancient demo-graphic patterns suggest that average life expectancy at birth (e_0) was less than 30, with all that that implies for pressures on child-bearing and for the instability of households – experiences that are unfamiliar in societies which have passed through the great demographic transition. Indeed, it is not just that a multitude of such stabilities and differences has to be identified, described, and knitted together before "the narrative" can be adequately framed, but that in many ways, and for many people, the frame is more interesting and important than the (often tentative or trivial) nar-rative which unfolded within it.

   Not surprisingly, therefore, for over two centuries scholars have been attempting to construct that frame. That activity began by assembling the evidence for "anti-quities" – constitutional, legal, military, social, and familial – but gradually transformed itself from the 1860s onwards into an attempt to reconstruct the experience of the individual person of Greek antiquity within a network of relationships that embraced family members, neighbors and rivals, friends and enemies, formal and informal com-munities, and gods and heroes with their powers and rituals. Of course, this scholarly endeavor addressed ancient Greece as a whole, not just the archaic period, and since its main source-material comprised the literary texts of all periods, including later antiquarian writers and essayists such as Pausanias and Plutarch, archaic Greece was only part of the picture. Nonetheless, both because that period offered texts of primordial importance for cultural history (Homer, Hesiod, the lyric and elegiac poets, the earlier Presocratic philosophers, and much of Herodotus' material), and because scholars rightly saw it as the paramount period during which what was distinctively Greek (institutions, customs, mythic representations) was created and developed, the archaic period has got its due, perhaps even more than its due. It is not chance that *Griechische Kulturgeschichte*,[28] the prime work of the main creator of cultural his-tory, Jacob Burckhardt, shows precisely such a chronological bias. It used two closely linked bodies of evidence, Greek religion with its cults and myths, and Greek art and literature, in order to paint a portrait of Greek sensibility and experience, and though there was a lengthy quasi-diachronic sketch of "The polis in its historical development," Burckhardt's prime aim was to reject the "tyranny of the historical fact" in favor of identifying mentalities, patterns, and beliefs.

His approach combined with other existing genres of scholarship to generate a hugely influential inheritance, as central to the twentieth-century study of archaic Greece as it is impossible to map coherently. Part of that incoherence derives from the ways in which scholarly interests and agendas have expanded, so that it has become more and more difficult to identify themes and processes round which a unified picture could be drawn. Partly, also, it stems from the existence of ongoing debates within specific subject areas. Some of these have been triggered by seemingly contradictory primary evidence (as when scholars attempt to locate women within an archaic Greek world which presents itself as unthinkingly and overbearingly male),[29] while others, such as the emergence of legal enactments and the partial systematizations of custom, derive from the difficulty of identifying actors and processes through the fog of later tradition and political myth. Partly, again, it derives from radical differences of approach. They are nowhere more divergent than in respect of cult and religion, which may serve as a "worked example." One strand of scholarship, with the Swedish scholar Martin Nilsson as its doyen, has explored and presented Greek cults and religious practices as a more or less autonomous area of life. A second view, influenced by Durkheim, has seen Greek religion as deeply embedded in society, manipulated by its politicians and serving communal interests first and foremost. A third view, owing much first to Freud and then to Lévi-Strauss, has sought rather to understand how rituals and myths evolve, or are constructed, so as to reflect human desires and assuage their fears, via symbolisms which are largely timeless. A fourth view, taking practicality to extremes, has interpreted cult and ritual above all in terms of redistributing surplus produce, providing a locus for meetings on safe neutral ground, and offering a sanctified mode of maximizing personal or communal prestige via display. In sharp contrast, a fifth view takes Greek spirituality seriously and sees its two main manifestations as being, first, the central role which oracles came to play in Greek public and private life in the archaic period, and, second, the evidently strong appeal which mystery cults and ceremonies of initiation had for Greeks of all classes and both genders. A sixth, complementary view sees the gods of the Greek polytheistic system above all as encapsulations of the powers – psychological as well as external – which affected human life and which therefore had to be neutralized or harnessed as effectively as possible. In truth, all these views have some validity, the proper balance among them being still a deeply elusive grail.[30]

While religion and gender subsequently became standard topics in cultural history, another, more recent *Kulturgeschichte* (Müller 1976) offered a very different picture of archaic Greece, focused above all on modes of production. With or without its Marxist coloring, by the 1960s that theme had already redirected attention towards foodstuffs, raw materials, agricultural techniques, and dietary needs, thereby bringing the countryside and its inhabitants into the picture in ways which after the Second World War came also to be influenced by the findings of anthropological fieldwork. Likewise, the inter-war years brought awareness that substantial quantities of archaic-period pottery made in Greece were being distributed in all directions across the Mediterranean and that, perhaps in return, Greece was benefiting from imports both visible (e.g. high-value bronzework) and inferred (especially iron from Etruria). Debate about how far such movements constituted "trade," and therefore about whether "traders" should be seen as economically (and perhaps even politically) significant, began in the 1950s in belated reaction to Hasebroek's classic statement of minimalism[31] and has continued energetically but inconclusively ever since, generating in its turn what was until recently the principal theoretical construct for interpreting the ancient economy.[32] Its terms were further transformed when numismatists brought the adoption of coined money by Greek states down to after ca. 550 BC,[33] which renewed the debate about the reasons for its adoption,[34] forced scholars to devise coinage-free models of economic growth, and fostered a heightened awareness of the symbolic weight which coinage carried in contemporary texts.[35] Equally a growing interest in consumption, the third component of elementary economic description, has generated study of its social contexts, especially of banqueting, symposia, and feasting within sanctuaries,[36] and consequently also of the human relationships which such occasions created or formalized.

Here four aspects of such relationships have attracted especial attention. Kingship is one, in proportion as the importance of its post-Homeric survival or re-invention has been belatedly recognized.[37] The second is "aristocracy," a term which appears to reflect contemporary terminology from Homer onwards but has proved hard to define save as a loosely connected set of behaviors affordable only by a rentier leisure class.[38] Apart from intermarriage and expedients aimed at retaining and maximizing political power, the most striking among them has been seen as the emergence of a culture of competing in various physical and paramilitary contests, a perception which has yielded much work on the "athletic ideal" and the growth of the Panhellenic Games.[39] A third preoccupation, mainly fuelled by the antiquarian tradition about pre-Solonian Athens, attempted to create a credible picture of archaic Greek "pre-state" polities as composed of tribes, clans, brotherhoods, etc. Though carried out with much elaboration and scholarship,[40] the task ended in disorder when two studies of the 1970s exposed its illogicalities and showed that such entities, so far from being deep-rooted, were constructs created as part of the processes of systematization and segmentation which yielded the well-organized micro-states of the late archaic and classical periods.[41]

Instead, a fourth quest, initiated in 1937 and still in active progress, has sought to trace and explain "the rise of the *polis*." It has constructively superseded older preoccupations with "constitutional antiquities" and has generated, in the shape of the Copenhagen Polis Project, one of the most important and useful international research projects in Greek studies to crystallize since the Second World War.[42] It has also focused attention on "citizenship" as an integral component of the *polis* as an institution. Belated recognition that the idea is not self-explanatory and may have no straightforward congeners elsewhere in the archaic Mediterranean has taken scholars back to the terminology of the Greek texts, with their repeated use of the phrase "to have a share in the polity," and thereby towards comparing archaic (and later) Greek states to companies or clubs composed of shareholders who share, equally or unequally, in the benefits and the responsibilities of membership.[43]

On the whole, since the 1960s cultural history has been more inquisitive about archaic Greece, and more innovative in its techniques, than narrative history. It has addressed at least part of the agenda of social theory by attempting to show how archaic Greek societies worked as systems. Furthermore, its impact has affected both scholarship as an activity and its modes of publication. Whereas in the 1960s the book and the journal article (both single-authored) predominated, supplemented on occasion by a senior scholar's collected articles in book format, multi-authored and jointly edited volumes of thematically linked papers (with or without a preceding conference) are now the norm:[44] the Copenhagen Polis Project's volumes illustrate the transformation. Even more striking have been the planning and publication of two major Italian-edited collective works, Ranuccio Bianchi Bandinelli's *Storia e civiltà dei Greci* and Salvatore Settis' *I Greci*. The material contained in the two relevant volumes of the former begins with a brief section on the post-Mycenaean transition and then offers a sequence of century-long periodizations, each interweaving literary, artistic, and social-economic aspects. *I Greci*, more recent, much larger and more complex, has a first volume, *Noi e i Greci* (1996), which uses a long series of sections in order to map the complex relationships between Greece and Greeks as a real community in past time and Greece and Greeks as they are seen or imagined or used. Its plan thus vividly reflects the preoccupation with the "reception" of a culture by subsequent generations which has deeply affected classical scholarship since the 1980s. Similarly, a second volume, *Formazione* (1996), focusing more precisely on the "archaic period," explicitly reviews the main components of archaic Greek culture, virtually ignoring narrative as such. After a century in which Burckhardt's unifying vision was clouded by layers of antiquarian specialization and divergent readings, these and other volumes are performing a valuable service of reunification.

The Physical Evidence

The last, but in many ways the most important and innovative, current of scholarship for the understanding of Archaic Greece comprises the study of the physical record of sites and artifacts. Here, the rhythm and trajectory of work followed a wholly different pattern, for whereas historians have had their texts ready to hand, published and emended by philologists and papyrologists, students of the physical record had first to find, study, classify, and publish the primary material themselves. While the assumptions accepted, the processes involved, and the categories used have themselves become a matter of debate and analysis,[45] the two main traditional focuses of study – objects and sites – are clear enough and are best sketched separately.

Very broadly, objects came first, driven by the tastes of eighteenth-century collectors and connoisseurs but needing over a century's worth of assemblage and discussion thereafter before dates and origins could be assigned, while remaining close (perhaps too close) to art-historical agendas. From the late nineteenth century onwards the influx of material from graves and the "big digs" (see below) helped to round out catalogues and to allow robust classifications to be established. Because of its profusion and indestructibility, pottery was a prime focus, and the inter-war and immediate post-war years saw the creation and publication of authoritative guides to the main pottery styles of the archaic period.[46] Such activity, which naturally continues,[47] used the changes in style through time of regional pottery industries in order to create relative chronologies for the major fabrics, while the appearance of pottery of a given stage in such sequences at sites which were destroyed or founded at known dates[48] has (after much debate) allowed the establishment of absolute chronologies which are nowadays accepted for the major fabrics as accurate to within 10–15 years. Not only can phases of occupation at excavated sites thereby be dated, but also the scatter of pottery sherds which is visible on the ground from the field-walking technique known as intensive surface survey can often give a clear – and sometimes surprising – profile of when a given area was intensely or sparsely inhabited.[49] As with pottery, so also for other objects the first task had to be cataloguing and classifying by genre of object. Much work inevitably ranged widely in time, but the archaic period especially was given system by classic older works such as those on Cretan bronze reliefs, decorations on bronze vessels, *kouroi* statues, or dress pins,[50] followed more recently by comparable general works, e.g. on gems and finger rings, on armor and weaponry, *korai* statues and archaic sculpture as a whole, architectural terracottas, and faience,[51] and throughout by a steady stream of catalogues raisonnées of material from excavations on specific sites.

Here the second traditional line of study enters. Once the initial phase of identifying on the ground place-names known from literary texts had run its course, what had largely been desultory or treasure-hunting activity was transformed after the 1870s into the systematic exploration and excavation of accessible major sites under the auspices of Greek and Italian authorities or of schools of archaeology sponsored in various ways from abroad. Apart from the "holy rock" of the Athenian acropolis, where Greek investigations go back to the 1830s, the earliest "big digs" were on sanctuary sites – initially Olympia, Delos, and Delphi, later Isthmia, Samothrake, Nemea, Perachora, Artemis Orthia at Sparta, Lindos, and Bassai. Cemetery sites such as Athens' Kerameikos or Perati followed, as too did investigations of major settlements (in whole or part) such as Priene, Pergamon, Gortyn, Akragas, Selinous, Korinth, the Athenian Agora, Argos, and above all Olynthos.[52] Nearly all of these, of course, were multi-period sites, but especially for the high-status sites the hope of recovering some of the major pieces of archaic or classical-period statuary mentioned by Pausanias or Pliny was a significant factor. Partly as a result, but also because of the need to catalogue and classify the finds, the art-historical agenda has been influential in shaping definitive site-publications, which typically devote a separate volume to each genre of find or each site feature.[53] As a result, while there have been numerous presentations of the (mostly figurative) creations of archaic Greek art,[54] interpretative studies, which reviewed the evidence synoptically and placed sites and artifacts within the framework of human needs and social values, were till recently sadly sparse.

The Story Evolves

In consequence, until about the late 1970s each of the three currents of activity described above regarded the others with polite incomprehension, not so much because the primary evidence was diverse as because interpretative skills, intellectual agendas, and cultural assumptions had come to diverge substantially. For "Classical" Greece, that is still largely true, alas, but the study of "Archaic" Greece is undergoing a revolution. It has become ever clearer that none of these currents can flow much further on its own: they have to be made to converge. It is not a comfortable process, for convergence always creates turbulence. Moreover, since it is still in train, its history cannot yet be tidily written. All that can be offered here is a sketch of its main components, coupled with a warning to the reader that a later sketch in fifteen years' time may present a very different aspect again.

First, the literary texts. As classical scholars have absorbed, and contributed to, the general transformation of the repertoire of literary criticism by applying ideas of critical theory – "gaze," "genre," intertextuality, narratology, "voice," and so forth – to Greek texts, those texts have come to assume aspects ever more complex, more remote, and less usable by the historian: few could now trustingly construct a portrait of archaic Greece round the post-Homeric poets as Burn did in 1960, not to mention the endless debate about "a historical Homeric society." [55] Herodotus, too, is increasingly seen primarily as a literary artist whose main concern, to construct an edifice as complex and as grandiose as Homer's, has rendered it very difficult to assess the truth-value of its component narrative-units (*logoi*) independently of the roles which they are accorded in his narrative. Since, moreover, the degree of difficulty increases directly with the distance of the dramatic date of this or that episode from his own time, while many of his *logoi* palpably emanate from earlier processes within Greek communities of re-ordering or recreating their own pasts, at least for the period before ca. 550 historians increasingly sense that they are building on sand.[56] Since later historical texts, such as those deriving from the fourth-century historian Ephoros or the local historians of Athens, are even less reliable, a narrative text-based history of archaic Greece such as Jeffery's is ceasing to be viable.

One constructive response, which cuts across individual authorial voices and therefore offers the cultural historian greater reliability, has been to study the uses of complex words, both those, such as *timê, hybris, kalokagathia, aidôs, aretê,* or *agôn*, which are taken to reflect the behaviors and the "values" of the leisure class[57] and those such as *dikê, nomos, euthyna, eggyê,* or *telos*, which reflect the ways in which legal and other relationships were conceptualized and managed.[58] However, such studies have also raised the questions whether those "values" were consistent or stable, and whether a different set of non-aristocratic values, appropriate for a yeoman or peasant society, can be identified.[59] A second response, similarly standing back from the individual "author" or creator and assimilating the analysis of texts to that of other artifacts, has been to view images (statuary, bas-reliefs, vase-paintings, etc) not just as illustrations and portrayals, whether of funerals or episodes from myth or of individual gods or mortals, still less as stages of development in accurate anatomical rendering, but as conscious or unconscious representations of what individuals or groups felt were appropriate projections of their identity.[60] This development has broadened the ways in which the relationship between "craftsman" and "patron" or "purchaser" can be seen.[61]

A third response, pioneered in the 1970s and similarly viewing artifacts not as items to be catalogued but as components of a complex interwoven culture, redefined the term "orientalizing" to denote not so much an artistic style, as earlier scholarship had done, but rather a set of choices and behaviors.[62] That in turn helped to start a process of replacing Beloch's model of largely autonomous cultural development by one which acknowledged the extent to which archaic Greece borrowed, accepted, adapted, and transformed a huge range of cultural goods and techniques from her eastern (and other) neighbors. Though of course the most visible borrowing, that of the alphabet, has always been acknowledged, and though the scholarly process has had its excesses, it is serving to locate archaic Greece within the economic and cultural networks of the Mediterranean and the Balkans so as to offer a radically different "narrative"[63] and to ask how far Greek political institutions were influenced by Levantine models.[64]

In turn, that relocation is now offering a very different analysis of the polis from that described above. Partly, it challenges the conventional view of the city-state as a Greek creation *sui generis* rather than as a version of a general development within the Iron Age Mediterranean, partly it insists on the need to distinguish between state-formation and the growth of towns, partly it wishes to rebut the portrayal of the ancient city as "consumer" rather than "producer" which Moses Finley influentially took over from Max Weber, partly it warns against being over-influenced by later political theory and, therefore, undervaluing the importance of monarchic and cantonal polities such as Macedon or Aitolia.[65] As the information from survey and rescue archaeology and epigraphy increases for patterns of settlement and state-formation in those regions of "Greek" culture which barely feature in the textual sources,[66] this alternative analysis is likely to gather force.

In these ways our understanding is gradually emancipating itself from the interpretative frameworks, amounting all too often to stereotypes, which are offered consciously or unconsciously by the extant source material. Fittingly (though such preoccupations are perhaps still too influenced by Herodotus's anachronistically polarized picture of sixth-century Greek politics), Athens and Sparta have been the main focuses. Sparta has benefited most, for a simplistic reading of her society once based above all upon Plutarch and Aristotle, obsessed with Lykourgos and the "Great Rhetra," and in some pre-Second World War quarters identifying politically with a conservative militaristic society, has been able to shake off the "Spartan mirage," focus on Lakonia as a coherent economic region, and see Sparta's society and government as lying much nearer to the Greek mainstream.[67] Instead, the focus of ideological preoccupations has moved elsewhere, for while the tendency to view the history of archaic Athens as a series of intricate and insoluble crossword-puzzles has weakened, her later emergence as the flag-carrier of "democracy" has recently generated a torrent of publication, the themes of which flow back at least to the pre-480 generation, if not to Solon. Traditional work of a descriptive and largely antiquarian kind[68] has been supplemented by monographs and collective volumes which highlight the Kleisthenic reforms and steer the reader to compare and contrast Athenian with modern democracy.[69] Their purpose is two-fold: both to test the appropriateness of "democracy" as a descriptive term, whether for ancient polities in general or for Athens in particular, and (especially from within American scholarship) to hold up a mirror for contemporary society to use and ponder. As with work on archaic colonization (see below), the danger of collapsing the past into the present has not always been avoided,[70] but the debate has had the merit of bringing what are often unstated but powerful assumptions and attitudes out into the open.

Not that revisionism ends there, for other radically different (meta-)narratives have also emerged. Six deserve special attention. The first, Snodgrass's *Archaic Greece* of 1980, was perhaps the most important, for it took further the convergence of textual evidence with physical evidence by marrying data from various excavated sites or surveyed areas in order to identify various "interacting processes" (p. 55) of change, especially those visible in the fast-moving eighth century: a rise in population, changes in military technology, the growth of sanctuaries, the explosive rise in dedications within them and the corresponding decline in interring valuable objects with the deceased, the recovery of literacy, the growth of monumental temples, major changes in settlement patterns, and so forth. Though some aspects of this portrayal have been challenged, overall, by showing that a unified interpretation using all genres of evidence is both possible and essential, it provided the foundation for a far more satisfying reading. Of especial value was his emphasis on the growth of sanctuaries, which are now being read in terms of usage (cult acts, contests, assemblies, conflict-resolution, statements of status, feasting), user-groups, and changing user-needs, not just in terms of installations and finds.[71]

The impact of literacy has stimulated a second meta-narrative. Prompted by the problem of how and when Homeric poetry came to be written down after a protracted period of oral composition and revision, by the work of Goody and others on the uses made of literacy in different societies, and by the better chronology of extant inscriptions which distinguished epigraphists have given us,[72] a coherent debate about the extent to which being literate changed Greek society has become possible.[73] In turn, this has led to further study of the changing processes and content of formal education, as well as to renewed awareness that effects differed significantly by region. Spartan minimalism, for example, came to contrast strikingly with the abundant flow of dedications set up on the Athenian acropolis before 480,[74] but Crete's many legal texts may reflect social control and oppression rather than democratization fuelled by literacy.[75]

Warfare, long taken for granted in spite of its prominence in the literary texts and the ubiquity of weaponry in early graves and in sanctuaries, has prompted a third narrative, not focused so much on specific wars (the "Lelantine War" of an earlier generation has largely faded from sight)[76] as on assessing the political impact of its evolving technologies. Though there has been argument about when the trireme emerged,[77] the recognition that serious sea-power wielded by states controlling pub-licly funded navies barely pre-dated the 540s and 530s[78] and that the predominance accorded to the "naval mob" in the 420s ([Xen.] *Ath. Pol.* i.2) was a fifth-century growth channeled attention on land warfare and especially on the emergence of heavy-armed infantry ("hoplites") as the predominant fighting force. Here scholarly opinion has shown an interesting evolution. Attention focused first on matters of brigading (in what became phalanx formation) and tactics, the mid-seventh century being seen as a major turning-point: this nurtured the hypothesis of a causal link with the emer-gence of tyrant regimes in Korinth and elsewhere. However, increased awareness that "hoplite" armor and weaponry were well established by the late eighth century, together with subsequent insistence on the importance of infantry in the narrative of the *Iliad*, made the hypothesis of "political hoplites" increasingly implausible, and fostered an alternative interpretation, couched in social terms, which detected changes in masculinity and social status instead and linked the erosion of the habit of carrying weapons with the growth of leisure class customs such as symposia and ritualized "contesting" at Olympia and other sanctuaries. A simple, perhaps simplistic, explanation has thus given way to one which locates visible behavior within a matrix of symbolisms and (self)-representations.[79]

The enlargement of geographical horizons, together with the emergence of a reasonably reliable chronology for the Dark Age, is beginning to provide a fourth narrative. Not only is Iron Age and Archaic Crete at last emerging from long neglect,[80] but also increasingly detailed archaeological work is bringing the northern mainland, the islands, and the less fashionable parts of Peloponnese back to life.[81] Their polities, settlement patterns, and cults are all benefiting from such attention, in a way which complements (but also challenges) the intense preoccupation with the polis which has characterized recent scholarship. It is also allowing the archaic polis as an at least proto-urban settlement to be viewed as the product of a process of concentration of populations,[82] a process which must have some connection, not as yet fully understood, with the pressures which created the ethnic identities of the late Archaic and classical periods at the expense of older labels such as Leleges or Lapithai. Indeed, an obsession with "ethnicity" has replaced the earlier discourse about tribes.[83]

A fifth meta-narrative, not yet fully articulated or appreciated, highlights the recovery and enlargement of craftsman and technological skills, whether in building, in stone statuary, in metalwork in precious or base metals, in ceramics, in mining, in shipping, or in infrastructure projects.[84] No economic historian of the archaic period can now fail to acknowledge such progress, not just because it nullifies portrayals of this period of the ancient economy as primitive or static[85] but also because it carried two major consequences. First, it stimulated the development of managerial skills, whether in organizing major building projects such as temples or wall circuits or in running workshops and workforces profitably. Second, it drove a major extension of the system of chattel slavery beyond the domestic context which is visible in Homer, for only a bought labor force could be moved forcibly to the locations, whether mines or workshops or households, where extra labor was needed.[86] Taken together with recent work on serf societies, both in Lakonia and elsewhere,[87] and with the substantial body of known depictions of workplaces, a much fuller view of the roles of labor in production is beginning to emerge.

Archaeological work is also generating a sixth, and the most radical, meta-narrative. Whereas the traditional historian's instinct is to look backwards from the vantage-point given by written sources, the instinct of archaeologists and of some economic and social historians, influenced by approaches developed within archaeology or adapted from the social sciences, is to look forwards, to construct models which explain development and change, to test them against extant evidence, and to compare the trajectory of one society against that of another. Coupled with an ever more intense interest in the post-Mycenaean "Dark Age," in "continuity," and in the construction of ethnicities, it is dissolving the (never very clear) boundary between "Dark Age" and "Archaic" in favor of portrayals of post-Mycenaean Greece which challenge much conventional wisdom.[88] Two final examples must suffice. The first concerns Greek expansion and settlement overseas, traditionally known by the shorthand term "colonization" and recognized on all sides as a core component of the crystallization of the Greek world before Alexander. Led in part by Herodotus' detailed narrative of the foundation of Kyrene, historians have seen it as a public process steered by "Korinthians," "Chalkidians," and others. However, an alternative view seeks to dismantle it as a guided process, arguing both that historians' terminology and attitudes have been unduly influenced by nineteenth-century activities and ideologies, that models of "cultural interactions" should replace models of invasion, occupation, or domination, and that antiquarian traditions of datable foundations, of named founders of colonies, and of collective acts by "Korinthians" or "Chalkidians" reflect a later style of foundation and were applied anachronistically to actions which were in fact far more individual and unorganized.[89] A second example cuts even more deeply, by arguing that as applied to any period before the Persian wars, perhaps even before Herodotus' generation, the term "the Greeks" is an anachronism, asserting a common ethnic identity vis-à-vis the rest of the world which owes more to nineteenth-century nationalisms than to the realities of peoples' lives and sensibilities.[90] It remains to be seen whether such constructive subversion can also be extended to what still dominates, a reluctance to locate "archaic" "Greece" fully in a comparative perspective.

NOTES

1   Jeffery 1976: 24; but fifth-century authors saw things differently (Bichler 2004a).
2   The comparison, amounting to an interpretative analysis worked out in detail, was made in different ways a century ago by Meyer and Beloch, and was explicit in Ure 1922. Cf. also Burn 1965: 35 ff.
3   Heuss 1946; 1981; I. Morris 1997c.
4   Further detail in Most 1989.
5   See instead Snodgrass 1971 (²2000), Desborough 1972, Musti et al. 1991, and Mazarakis Ainian 1997.
6   Earlier surveys include von Pöhlmann 1902; Lenschau 1905; Bengtson 1950: 1–16; Christ 1972; Starr 1987: 1–17; Gehrke 1995b (on ancient history in general); Ampolo 1996; Ampolo 1997; Raaflaub 1997a; Davies 2000a; Davies 2002.
7   Further detail in Ampolo 1997: 150–2 and Davies 2000a.
8   Cf. Henige 1974; R. Thomas 1992.
9   Details of new editions up to 1861 in Clarke 1962: 189–90.
10   Basic are Momigliano 1952; Clarke 1962: ch. 5; Turner 1981: 212–44; Morris 1994: 29–31.
11   Grote 1846–56: ch. 29 (1872 III: 321).
12   Cf. Lenschau's excellent summary (1905: 155–68), with Christ 1972: 286–333, Calder and Demandt 1990, and Ampolo 1997: 90–3 for the universal historians von Ranke and Eduard Meyer.
13   Lenschau 1905: 186–7; Bleicken 1989: 122–7; Chambers 1990; briefly Ampolo 1997: 95.
14   Cf. Christ 1972: 248–85.

15 Beloch 1924: 66–7 with 67 n.1; 94. Not that Beloch was alone: Dinsmoor's early account of the origins of Greek monumental architecture (1927: chs. 1–2) is equally "Aryan," as noted by Wright 2003: 39.

16 Beloch 1926: 65–76 and 245–53.

17 Will 1955: 363–440; Burn 1960: 403–8, with explicit acknowledgement to Beloch. Contrast Morris 1996a.

18 "Darum sollte, wer den historischen Werdeprozeß verstehen will, mit dem Studium der Wirtschaftsgeschichte beginnen" (Beloch 1924: 2).

19 Notably (von) Pöhlmann 1889 ([5]1914), eventually replaced in the *Handbuch* by Bengtson 1950 ([5]1977; itself soon to be replaced by a multi-volume work by Niemeier, Gschnitzer and Gehrke); Wilcken 1924 ([9]1962) eventually replaced by Schuller 1980, and above all Bury 1900 ([4]1975 revised and corrected reprint 1978).

20 Thus Glotz-Cohen 1925 for P.U.F. (Pierre Lévêque's replacement did not to my knowledge appear); Burn 1960; Jeffery 1976 for Benn; Murray 1980/1993 for Fontana/dtv; Osborne 1996a for Methuen; Baurain 1997 for Nouvelle Clio.

21 E.g. in III[2]: 3, chs. 45a "Economic and Social Conditions in the Greek World" (C. G. Starr) and 45b "The Material Culture of Archaic Greece" (J. Boardman), and in IV[2] a five-section survey (ch. 7) of "Archaic Greek Society."

22 E.g. Stählin 1924 (Thessaly); Kophiniotis 1892 deserves honorable mention for its initial pages on the topography, flora, and fauna of the Argolid.

23 Dunbabin 1948; Gallet de Santerre 1958.

24 Tomlinson 1972 (Argos); Buck 1979 (Boiotia); Cartledge 1979 (Sparta and Lakonia); Griffin 1982 (Sikyon); Salmon 1984 (Korinth).

25 E.g. Morgan 1990 (Phokis); Archibald 1998 (Thrace).

26 Especially *Meletemata* and *Studien zur Geschichte Nordwest-Griechenlands*.

27 E.g. Andrewes 1956 (tyrants); Masaracchia 1958 (Solon; cf. Blok and Lardinois 2006); Sancisi-Weerdenburg 2000 or Lavelle 2005 (Peisistratos); Podlecki 1975 (Themistokles); Berve 1937 (Miltiades). Lévêque and Vidal-Naquet 1964 is not really a biography of Kleisthenes.

28 Burckhardt 1898–1902, with Burckhardt 1958 for the abridged version translated into English as Burckhardt 1963, but Burckhardt 1998 is a fuller and much more satisfactory abridged translation, with Murray's helpful biographical introduction and Christ 1972: 119–58. Baumgarten et al. 1908 follow Burckhardt's lead more succinctly.

29 E.g. W. Schuller 1985: 24–33, Osborne 1996a: 226–32, or Lardinois and McClure 2001: 19–92 for the archaic period, besides the many books of the 1980s and 1990s on women in antiquity in general.

30 See ch. 22 for discussion of aspects of religion.

31 Hasebroek 1928/1933; Boardman 1957; Coldstream 1977: 17–21 for overtly mercantilist language.

32 Finley 1973a (1985), with Osborne 1996b, Tandy 1997, von Reden 2002, and Reed 2003 among many more recent contributions. See ch. 23.

33 Review of evidence and arguments in Kim 2001.

34 Kraay 1964; Howgego 1995: 12–18; Martin 1996b.

35 Seaford 1994; Kurke 1999; Seaford 2004.

36 Cf. Murray 1990b, especially Schmitt-Pantel 1990 and Bookidis 1990; Schmitt-Pantel 1992; Bookidis 1993. See ch. 26.

37 Drews 1983; Carlier 1984; Ogden 1997.

38 Toepffer 1889; Arnheim 1977; Herman 1987; Morris 1996b; Duplouy 2006.

39 See ch. 27.

40   E.g. de Sanctis 1912: 40–76; Halliday 1923: 69–139; Hignett 1952: 47–85.
41   Bourriot 1976; Roussel 1976; Donlan 1985; Smith 1985; Welwei 1988; Donlan 1989;
     T. Schneider 1991; Davies 1996.
42   Ehrenberg 1937; Snodgrass 1980a: 15–48; Sakellariou 1989; Mitchell and Rhodes 1997;
     Greco 1999; Hansen and Nielsen 2004, with a list of associated titles at xii–xiii.
43   Walter 1993a; E. W. Robinson 1997: 127–130; Davies 2004.
44   Improved travel opportunities, the quest for individual or institutional prestige, and the
     need for student textbooks have also contributed.
45   Cf. especially Cook 1997: 275–311; Snodgrass 1987; Morris 1994: 15–26; Shanks 1996;
     Shanks 1999; Rouet 2001: 1–40; Whitley 2001: 1–59.
46   Most notably Friis Johansen 1923 and Payne 1931 for Protocorinthian and Corinthian,
     Desborough 1952 for Protogeometric, Beazley 1956 and Boardman 1974 for Attic
     Black-figure, Boardman 1952 and 1957 for Euboian, Friis Johansen 1957 for Rhodian
     Geometric, Beazley 1963 and Boardman 1979 for Attic Red-figure, and Coldstream 1968
     (2008) for Geometric.
47   E.g. Lemos 1991 for Chios: much further detail in Cook 1997: 331–56.
48   Hannestad 1996; Morris 1996a; Whitley 2001: 60–74 for evidence and references.
49   Whitley 2001: 47–50.
50   Respectively Kunze 1931; Jacobsthal and Langsdorff 1929 and Jantzen 1955; Richter
     1942; Jacobsthal 1956.
51   Respectively Boardman 1968 and 1970; Snodgrass 1964; Richter 1968 and Ridgway 1977;
     Winter 1993; Webb 1978.
52   For publication details, see *OCD*[3] or *Der Neue Pauly*.
53   Thus also genre-specific monographs or collaborative volumes such as Berve and Gruben
     1961 (temples); des Courtils and Moretti 1993 (general); Coulton 1976 (stoas); Lavas 1974,
     Tomlinson 1976, Marinatos and Hägg 1993, and Alcock and Osborne 1994 (sanctuaries).
54   E.g. Homann-Wedeking 1968; Charbonneaux et al. 1968; Schweitzer 1969; Robertson
     1975; Pedley 1993.
55   Cf. Griffiths 1995 and R. Thomas 1995; Finley 1954; Snodgrass 1974; van Wees 1992;
     2002c; Osborne 1996a: 137–160; Morris and Powell 1997; Raaflaub 1998; Donlan 1999.
56   Luraghi 2001c; Bakker et al. 2002; Derow and Parker 2003; Marincola 2006.
57   E.g. Dodds 1951; Miller 1991; Fisher 1992; Cairns 1993. Burckhardt had already sketched
     the basics (1898–1902: I 159–165).
58   More detail in Davies 2003: 333–4.
59   E.g. Adkins 1960; Walcot 1970; Arnheim 1977; Millett 1984; Dougherty and Kurke
     1993; Morris 1996b; Kistler 2004.
60   Cf. Bérard et al. 1989; Niels 1992; Kurke 1999.
61   One may contrast Webster 1972 with Snodgrass 1980a: 178–87 and Morgan 1990:
     194–205.
62   Bianchi Bandinelli 1978b: 462–509 (F. Canciani); Murray 1980/1993: ch. 6.
63   Dunbabin 1957; Bernal 1987; Burkert 1992; Gras 1995/1997; West 1997; Harris 2005.
64   Raaflaub 1993a; Davies 1997: 33–4; E. W. Robinson 1997: 16–25; papers in Rollinger
     and Ulf 2004b, especially Raaflaub 2004c.
65   Cf. Gawantka 1985; Gehrke 1986; Brock and Hodkinson 2000; Vlassopoulos 2005;
     Osborne and Cunliffe 2005.
66   E.g. Rizakis 1991; Archibald 1998; McInerney 1999; C. Morgan 2003.
67   Forrest 1968, with bibliography of earlier work; Cartledge 1979; Powell 1989; Powell
     and Hodkinson 1994; Hodkinson and Powell 1999; Hodkinson 2000; Powell and
     Hodkinson 2002.

68 E.g. Hignett 1952; Forrest 1966; Ostwald 1969; Bicknell 1972; Hansen 1991; Lambert 1993; Bleicken 1985; Hansen 1991; Ste. Croix 2004.

69 E.g. Finley 1973b; Dunn 1992; Rahe 1992; Euben et al. 1994; Raaflaub 1995; Ober 1996; Ober and Hedrick 1996; Morris and Raaflaub 1998.

70 For critiques, Anderson 2003; Davies 2003; Rhodes 2003.

71 E.g. Morgan 1990; Alcock and Osborne 1994; Morgan 1997; Ulf 1997; Naso 2006; Davies 2007.

72 Guarducci 1967–78; Jeffery 1961a/1990.

73 Harris 1989; B. B. Powell 1991; R. Thomas 1992; Svenbro 1993; Robb 1994; Yunis 2003.

74 Cartledge 1978.

75 Whitley 1997 (shorter version Whitley 1998); Davies 2005.

76 Contrast Forrest 1957 with Osborne 1996a: 146–7; but cf. V. Parker 1993.

77 The controversy can be followed from Morrison and Williams 1968 via Lloyd 1980 to Wallinga 1992.

78 De Souza 1998.

79 Snodgrass 1965; Cartledge 1977; Salmon 1977; Latacz 1977; van Wees 1994; 1998b; 2004; Raaflaub 2005b.

80 Prent 2005; a far cry from Willetts 1955 or Willetts 1962.

81 See n. 66 above.

82 Snodgrass 1980a: 154–8; Kolb 1984: 58–95; de Polignac 2005b.

83 Hall 1997; Hall et al. 1998; Hall 2002.

84 E.g. Burford 1972; Coulton 1977; Healy 1978; Conophagos 1980; Rihll and Tucker 1995; Wikander 2000.

85 Sherratt and Sherratt 1993.

86 E.g. Lauffer 1979; Burford 1993; Osborne 1995.

87 Lotze 1959; 2000; Hodkinson 2000; Ducat 1990b; 1994; Luraghi and Alcock 2003.

88 See e.g. Deger-Jalkotzy and Lemos 2006.

89 Contrast Forrest 1957, Blumenthal 1963, Boardman 1964 (1980/1999), or Graham 1964a with Osborne 1996a: 119–129 and 232–242; J.-P. Wilson 1997b; Lepore 2000; Braund 2005; Owen 2005; Snodgrass 2005.

90 Morgan 2001a; Hurst and Owen 2005.

CHAPTER TWO

The Mediterranean World in the Early Iron Age

Carol G. Thomas

Long before the Greeks began to actively explore the sea in the eighth century, the Mediterranean had been a link between the peoples who inhabited its shores. In fact, during the Bronze Age the Mycenaeans and Minoans were familiar seafarers in both the eastern and central Mediterranean waters and may well have penetrated the western half of the great sea as well as found their way through the Bosporus straits into the Black Sea. During the difficult centuries of the early Iron Age, however, Greeks like most people of the Mediterranean sphere traveled far less by either land or water. Consequently, routes, winds, and currents had to be relearned. Peoples along those routes would also be unfamiliar. To set the scene for this new knowledge, this chapter will explore, first, the nature of the Mediterranean sea and the land that rings it; next, the inhabitants of its shores; and, finally, Greek ability to navigate the water of the Great Sea.

The Mediterranean Sea

Although it was identifiable as a body of water 150 million years ago, the final shaping of the Mediterranean occurred some fifteen million years ago. In size, the sea is 2,965,500 square kilometers. It extends 3,733 kilometers from west to east and its width varies considerably due to the configuration of the surrounding land: the southern coast is generally smooth while the northern coast is defined by jutting peninsulas and deep bays that are seas in their own right. The configuration draws continents together at several points, but separates them in other regions. In the west, the Iberian peninsula is separated from northern Africa by the Strait of Gibraltar which, at its narrowest point, is a little more than 24 kilometers. Moving eastward, the islands of Corsica and Sardinia are separated from the mainland by the Ligurian Sea in the north and the Tyrrhenian Sea in the east that extends to the 1,046 kilometer long peninsula of Italy. The toe of Italy is narrowly separated from the Island of Sicily which, in turn, is roughly 160 kilometers from the north coast of Africa. The Adriatic Sea divides the Italian from the Greek peninsula while the Aegean stands between the Greek peninsula and Anatolia. A voyage of more than 885 kilometers, as the crow flies, must be undertaken to reach the coast of Africa from the Northern Aegean. Even in the more expansive eastern waters, a sailor is rarely out of sight of land, either a portion of the coastal ring of land encompassing the sea or one of the numerous islands that dot the waters of the sea (Carrington 1971: ch. 1 on physical characteristics).

The Mediterranean is connected with other bodies of water by straits in both the west and the east: the Strait of Gibraltar leads to the Atlantic Ocean and the Dardanelles provide an entrance to the Propontis and ultimately to the Black Sea. Inflow of water from these two points provides much of the replenishment of an otherwise essentially static body of water. This contained nature of the water produces a high salinity due to a greater rate of evaporation than precipitation of new water. The seafloor is deep, in most parts of the Mediterranean the water's depth is at least 10,620 feet; in the Ionian Sea soundings have indicated a depth of twice that amount. Water temperature remains quite constant at 13 degrees centigrade throughout the year.

Since it is so tightly enclosed, the water is virtually tideless. Currents, which cause its movement, are dependent upon the inflow of water, particularly that coming through the Strait of Gibraltar which is stronger than the current from the Black Sea. The current from the Atlantic continues along the north African coast, up the coast of the Levant, and west along the southern shore of Anatolia. Moving westward, the current flows west along the Greek coast and into the Adriatic. At Sicily, the current turns north along the Italian coast, then it flows along the coasts of southern France and Spain. Smaller, local currents exist in several areas such as the eastern and western coasts of Crete and off southern France.

Prevailing winds blow from both north and south into the Mediterranean. Strongest are the two paths of Mistral which join over southern France; second in force is the Bora which reaches the Adriatic in the north-east. The Meltemi push down the Dardanelles into the Aegean in the summer months and the Scirocco winds head northward into the Mediterranean along much of the African coast. The areas experiencing the strongest force of winds are the Aegean, the northern Adriatic, and the coastal area of southern France near Marseilles. Knowing and using the winds is essential to navigation in the Mediterranean. Thus, if the Mistral was blowing, it would provide power for eastward travel and if it was strong "then it and the east-bound north African current between them would carry the ship two-thirds of the way there, almost automatically, leaving the captain with no problem in seamanship more profound than managing to dodge Sardinia and Sicily" (Hodge 1998: 27). In sailing westward, on the other hand, the task was to avoid the Mistral which, coming head-on, would impede rather than aid the journey.

The lands enclosing the great sea and the large number of islands in its midst share many features. Low-lying coast is generally limestone or earth impregnated with lime and, thus, the soil is often thin. Certain river mouths, such as the Nile, Po, and Rhone, are especially fertile. The coastal land does not extend deeply into the hinterland which is regularly separated by mountains. Toward the interior, larger expanses of land take the opposite forms of arable plains and deserts depending on the prevailing climate of the region; the Saharan climate of Africa produces more of the latter while the more temperate climate of the European region results in more arable land. In the north, extensive mountain ranges and their spurs divide the plains from one another.

Broad regional differences exist between both the east and west basins of the Mediterranean and the north and south coasts. The two basins divide at the Sicilian channel between that island and the peninsula of Cap Bon in modern Tunisia. In addition to their different configurations, the western basin is smaller in size and more temperate in climate than the eastern. Mountains extend almost to the coast-line leaving a narrow strip of land by the sea in the west while they do not reach so near the shore in the east. Mountains are greater in extent and size in the northern Mediterranean lands than in the southern, a mixed blessing since in return for the valuable resources they provide they exact a regular toll in volcanoes and earthquakes. The southern Mediterranean lands, by contrast, are characterized by deserts: the Sahara desert seems endless with its 14,811,562 squares kilometers relieved only by occasional oases. This contrast identifies another difference, namely in the rainfall which is greater in the north and west than in the south and east.

Climatic and environmental conditions of lands bordering or situated in the Mediterranean are capable of sustaining life of plants, animals, and humans. Much of the land is maquis and garigue, that is, rough land that can support a combination of shrubs such as laurel, myrtle, and wild olive; undershrubs including broom, daphne, and gorse; and herbaceous plants including clovers, grasses, and asphodel. True forests exist in northern and eastern regions, from the cedars of the Levant through the mountain forests of Macedonia and the Apennines to the significant forests of southern Spain. Most dominant are varieties of oak and pine (Meiggs 1982). In addition to their fruit and timber, the forests were homes for a number of wild animals: deer, bears, wolves, lynxes, panthers, leopards, lions, and boars as well as smaller animals. Regions without great forests also had a large complement of wild animals: lions, deer and smaller animals in the north and the more exotic elephants, monkeys, hippopotami, and camels of North Africa (Rackham 2003 on the physical setting).

Some of the once-wild animals had been domesticated: elephants and camels lessened the loads collected by humans in the southern Mediterranean but far more widespread were sheep, goats, cattle, donkeys, and horses. Transhumance of flocks of sheep and goats between summer and winter pastures was a common way of life for people living in the northern and eastern lands of the sea. However, the land also supported a sedentary existence even in upland areas; Fernand Braudel, who knew and understood the Mediterranean world as well as anyone can, painted a vivid picture with his description that "every mountain [in the Mediterranean region] has some arable land, in the valleys or on the terraces cut out of the hillside" (1972: 42). Basic grain crops were wheat, barley, oats and green millet; a range of legumes; orchard fruits and nuts; grapes; and olives. In fact, the Mediterranean region can be defined as the land in which the olive grows for, as Lawrence Durrell described this hearty tree, "it seems to live without water although it responds readily to moisture and to fertilizer when available . . . it will stand heat to an astonishing degree and keeps the beauty of its grey-silver leaf; . . . the wood . . . can be worked and has a beautiful grain when carved and oiled. Of the fruit it is useless to speak unless it be to extol its properties" (197: 65–6).

The sea also contributed to the livelihood of humans even though its high salinity and exhaustion through its great longevity made it difficult for some species of fish to survive in its waters. Even so, a variety of marine life was present. The tunny is perhaps the most important fish; swordfish, octopus, and squid are present along with several varieties of shell fish.

The northern Mediterranean lands possessed much of the mineral wealth of the region. Copper was available in Cyprus, the Balkans, northern Italy, Sardinia, Anatolia, and southern Spain but, in the southern Mediterranean, only in the Sinai peninsula where there were also gold resources. The Northern Aegean, Attica in Greece, and the Cyclades had silver resources; there are gold resources in the northern Aegean, the eastern Black Sea, Cyprus and Spain; iron was plentiful in northern Italy and Spain; tin was rarer, although it was present in Spain, the northern Aegean, perhaps the Levant and northern Italy. Base metals occur in much of the north as well as along the western African coast and flint and obsidian, the black volcanic stone, are found in Anatolia, and the islands of Melos in the Aegean, the Lipari islands north of Sicily, and Sardinia (Lombard 1974).

Stretching between three continents where so many of the earliest developments in human history occurred, the Mediterranean experienced and supported a human presence even in the Paleolithic Age. As people learned to use its water for travel, ideas as well as humans and objects moved between the northern and southern coast and from its eastern to western extremes (Stampolidis and Karageorghis 2003). The ecological and geological diversity of the region produced a variety of cultures; however, groups of people were not greatly distanced from one another (Horden and Purcell 2000; Rackham 2003). Life for Greeks was changed in every fundamental respect by the renewed skill to course through Poseidon's realm as the Dark Age gave way to the archaic age of revolution.

Regions and Peoples of the Mediterranean in the Iron Age

Well into the 1960s, the prevailing assessment of the early Iron Age in the Aegean sphere was that it was a time of collapse, both of population and way of life characterized by misery with little progress out of that miserable state. The words of the poet Hesiod, who lived toward the end of the eighth century and the early part of the seventh, neatly described the life of everyone from 1150 to 750: "now indeed is the race of iron. By day there is no end to labor and misery, nor escape from perishing by night" (*Works and Days* 176–8; author's tr.). For his part, Hesiod wished that he had died earlier or been born after this age of woes (175). Such a dark picture has been lightened considerably by recent study. The Bronze Age kingdoms with their citadel strongholds, centralized administration necessitating written records, and participation in Mediterranean affairs did collapse. And there was a precipitous decline in population. However, some of that reduced population continued to live at the centers of the former kingdoms – at Athens and Thebes and Tiryns – and archaeological evidence demonstrates sufficient continuity of culture to establish the roots of many major features of archaic and classical culture in the Bronze Age past (Thomas and Conant 1999).

Nor did all contact with the sea disappear although it was diminished (Stampolidis 2002; Stampolidis and Karageorghis 2003). As early as the eleventh century, inhabitants of the Greek mainland sailed across the wine-dark waters of the Aegean to found settlements on the coast of Asia Minor. To the west, ceramic evidence reveals mainland pottery in Italy in the darkest, early centuries following the major destructions. The enigmatic site of Lefkandi on the island of Euboea has produced imports from Cyprus or Crete and the Levant in the eleventh and tenth centuries. Finds in the northern Aegean attest to Euboean activity during the same period. It must be acknowledged that such activity was not typical of the whole of Greece nor was it sustained even by the first adventurers. Greece remained largely secluded, by comparison with other Mediterranean peoples, from the eleventh century into the eighth. Then, by contrast, the outward thrust of the Greeks expanded from the Aegean sphere southward into the Eastern Mediterranean, then westward across the Adriatic and eventually into the waters of the western Mediterranean (see figure 2.1). This itinerary is a useful tool to employ in identifying the "others" – both peoples and lands – whom Greeks would come to know during the Archaic Age.

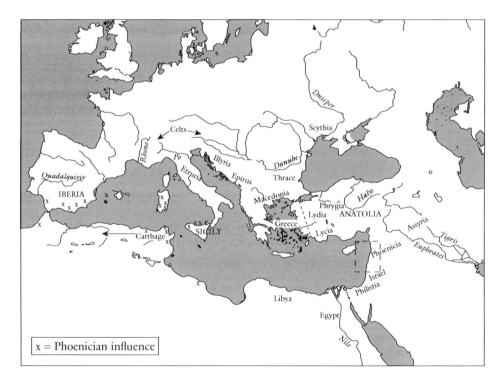

Figure 2.1 Peoples of the Mediterranean

Anatolia

The coast of the eastern Aegean was familiar to Greeks in the Bronze Age; a settlement in the middle of that long strip of land had been a Mycenaean outpost in the second half of the second millennium. It was known to the Hittites as Millawanda and, following the difficulties of the late thirteenth and early twelfth centuries, was resettled in the Iron Age as Miletus (as appreciated by Desborough 1972: 353ff). That the immigrations came from a number of parts of the mainland is shown by linguistic and cultural differences among the settlements. In the north, the Iron Age migrants spoke Aeolic, the dialect of Greek present in north-eastern Greece; in the middle region, the dialect was Ionic, that of Attica and Euboea; and in the south, it was Doric, that of the Peloponnese. Their settlements were located on a jagged rocky coastline often on peninsulas that were easily defensible; sometimes at ports located in the mouths of river valleys running down from the interior plateau of Anatolia; and on offshore islands. The land was suitable for farming and herding; the hill slopes supported trees and shrubs; clay was good for ceramic production. Lacking were metals and sufficient fertile land for large quantities of grain.

Consequently, in addition to arriving by sea, the immigrants were encouraged to continue their seafaring. Sailors from Kyme in the north, for example, propelled boats for the kings of landlocked Phrygia while inhabitants of that same Greek town participated in some of the earliest colonization in the central Mediterranean (Strabo 6.2.2). These adventurers enjoyed winds and currents that facilitated a southerly route through the Cyclades. Those settlements that were further south were also helped by Etesian winds that blew from the northwest while, further north, winds came in from due north.

The Aegean was not a "Greek Lake" before the archaic age but the western and eastern arcs of that circle had been established well before the end of the "Dark" Age as a result of the migrations to western Anatolia. Knowledge of the Anatolian interior, however, was minimal. Mountains that ring the upland plateau hamper communications with the sea along the western, northern, and southern coasts while the Taurus mountains on the eastern land mass are a formidable barrier. Nor would Greeks settled on the coast be tempted to penetrate the hinterland in search of arable land for the interior was generally less well watered than the coastal plains. A search for other resources would have been more enticing: silver, gold, copper, and iron had drawn others, especially the Assyrians from the northern Tigris, to establish trade centers in southern Anatolia as early as 2000 BCE. Timber in the north was another asset.

Another deterrent was other peoples well established in the early Iron Age. Phrygians had created a good-sized kingdom in the center of the interior after migrating into Anatolia following the collapse of the Hittite kingdom in the late thirteenth century (Muscarella 2003). South-eastern Europe seems to have been the homeland of the newcomers; their language and material culture is related to that of inhabitants of Thrace and Illyria identifying them as Indo-Europeans. The wealth of Phrygia is remembered in the tale of its most famous king, Midas, who was touted as having the power to turn everything he touched into gold. Archaeological excavation of the capital at

Gordion substantiates the material wealth of the kingdom (Voigt and Henrickson 2000). We have seen that at least some Greeks of the coast knew the Phrygians, who relied on the ships of Kyme for trade. A tradition tells of the marriage of Midas to the daughter of one Agamemnon of Kyme (Julius Pollux, *Onomasticon* 9.83). However, the inland kingdom would not endure to become part of the archaic Greek horizons: new dating of the destruction of the capital suggests a date in the ninth century rather than the eighth century.

Succeeding the Phrygians as the Greeks' most powerful neighbors were the Lydians, who were much closer than the Phrygians had been to the band of settlements along the coast: the capital at Sardis was little more than fifty miles inland on the Hermus River. Indo-European Lydians inhabited west central Anatolia during the Bronze Age; in fact the settlements were probably on or near the Aegean coast. Arrival of Greeks at the end of the second millennium pushed them into the hinterland. Under Phrygian sway until the demise of that kingdom, Lydia became an independent, organized state by the seventh century although it required outside assistance to ward off an attack of invaders from the Black Sea region early in that century. Eventually the Lydian kingdom would be extensive and sufficiently powerful to contend against major players in a bid for authority in the eastern Mediterranean. But at the start of the archaic age, Lydia was a congeries of agricultural villages, with a single larger center at Sardis. Part of the foundation for future expansion was based on production of admired products, woolen textiles for example. More important was use of metals – both native, such as gold and silver, and imported – to produce objects for trade and to spur the invention of coinage. Greeks served the Lydians as intermediaries, just as they had aided the Phrygians, and relations were cordial in the early decades of the relationship. In the sixth century, King Croesus made magnificent offerings to Delphian Apollo including a gold sculpture of a lion weighing nearly 272 kilograms (Hdt 1.50–2). Shortly thereafter, relations deteriorated as Lydia determined to return to the coast (Hanfmann 1983).

Further south were the Lycians, whose Bronze Age presence is attested archaeologically and by references in Hittite records and in documents naming groups associated with the "Land and Sea" peoples who brought destruction to many eastern Mediterranean lands in the late thirteenth and twelfth centuries. One named group is the Lukka. Herodotus wrote that they originally came from Crete when its population was entirely non-Greek (1.172). Linguistic theory may substantiate Herodotus in placing roots of the Lycians in an early period when proto-Indo-European was diverging from proto-Indo-Hittite (Bryce 1998). Their settlements were located on the mountainous land jutting into the Mediterranean on the south-western coast of Anatolia. Much of the eastern shore is inaccessible; indeed Lycia was relatively removed from contact with surrounding regions. Even Croesus, according to Herodotus, was unable to subdue the Lycians (1.28).

South-eastern Europe

Intrepid seafarers determined to explore the northern Aegean would encounter descendants of Trojan allies remembered in the *Iliad* such as:

> Rhesos their king, the son of Eïoneus.
> And his are the finest horses I ever saw, and the biggest;
> They are whiter than snow, and their speed of foot is the winds' speed;
> His chariot is fairly ornate with gold and with silver,
> And the armor is golden and gigantic, a wonder to look on.
>> (10.435–9; tr. Lattimore)

Not only stalwart warriors, the Thracians were remembered as suppliers of the wine "that Achaean ships carry day by day from Thrace" (9.71–2) and as providers of homes for youthful Trojans such as

> Iphidamus, Antenor's son, the huge and stalwart,
> Who had been reared in generous Thrace, the mother of sheepflocks.
>> (11.221–2; tr. Lattimore)

The home of the Thracians essentially coincides with modern Bulgaria. Two theories of their origin are best combined into one explanation: there was continuous development of an indigenous population as well as ongoing migration into the region which drew immigrants through its fertile agricultural land and a range of metals – copper, tin, lead, and gold (Hoddinott 1981). Pasturage was excellent for horse-raising. Thrace could support a sizeable population: in his contest against Philip II of Macedon, an Odrysian ruler raised an army of 150,000. It was not, however, a unified state; rather, shifting relationships between various tribes led by chieftains and kings determined its politics. The presence of Thracian names in the Mycenaean Linear B tablets indicates a Bronze Age acquaintance with these horse-riders, an acquaintance that faded in the early Iron Age.

By contrast, Greeks probably had little knowledge of the Thracians' eastern neighbors before the archaic age. At the bay of the western shore of the Black Sea where the Ister/Danube joins the sea, Scythia begins (Hdt 4.99). The Scythians are akin to their Thracian neighbors in grouping together in several diverse tribes. The three main groups include the "royal" Scythians who dwell closest to the Black Sea; the "nomadic" Scythians who reside north and east of the "royal" tribes; and the "sedentary" Scythians who are located to the north and west. Herodotus's statement that Scythians who do business on Black Sea ports use seven different languages and require seven different interpreters reveals their diversity (4.24).

The region possesses rich, well-watered land with excellent pasture, rivers almost as numerous as canals in Egypt in Herodotus' opinion (4.48), forest steppe becoming deciduous woodland in the north, and, in the south, mountains that provide a variety of metals. Herodotus does not believe the tradition that the Scythians received a gift from heaven of a golden plough, yoke, battle-axe, and cup although one senses that he had to fight against that belief (4.5).

Hesiod is the earliest written source for the Scythians whom he knows as milk-feeders who have wagons for houses (*Catalogues of Women and Eoiae* fr. 39). Greek colonization in the northern Black Sea in the sixth century would bring direct knowledge – often dreaded – of these warriors whose custom was to drink the blood of the first man each has killed.

Just as unfamiliar during the early Iron Age were the peoples of what would become the kingdom of Macedonia: the future subjects of Philip II and Alexander III seem to have arrived about 700. The region bounded on the east by the Thermaic Gulf was a crossroad between east and west, north and south and, consequently, witnessed regular migrations and invasions. One group that decided to remain rather than move on settled at the end of the eighth century into a strip of land along the coast that extended some 97 kilometers north to south between the Haliacmon and Vardar rivers. The name of this tribal group was Makednons and they were led by a clan known as the Argeads. Similarities of language and material culture with other peoples indicates that they were Indo-European. Related tribal groups inhabiting the hinterland were independent of one another; mountains were something of a barrier with the northern territory of the Greek mainland.

The natural resources of the region were incentives to establish a village way of life: there were fertile plains both in lower, coastal Macedonia and in upper regions where the land was irrigated by more rainfall that the lower peninsula received as well as by the water of perennial rivers. Herodotus reported that these rivers provided such an abundance of fish that horses were fed on fish. The higher inland reaches had excellent timber resources and could boast a plentitude of wild animals. Minerals and metals were abundant. The combination of low-lying and more elevated land encouraged herding that utilized summer and winter pasturage of sheep and goats and the raising of horses.

This way of life fostered villages and upland settlements that were not tightly cohesive even into the fifth century. The inhabitants, and even their kings, were regarded as backward by Greeks to the south as late as the fourth century even though they valued Macedonian resources (Thomas 2007).

Eastern Mediterranean

Somewhat surprising, at least initially, is the greater and earlier knowledge of peoples of the eastern Mediterranean on the part of the Greeks. In large part, the precocious level of culture in the Levant and Egypt led entrepreneurs from those regions into the Aegean and, in turn, drew bold Aegean seafarers southward (Boardman 1991; Van de Mieroop 2004).

Particularly enterprising were the Phoenician survivors from the Bronze Age who inhabited a coastal strip some 320 kilometers long by roughly 48 kilometers deep. Their several city-states had played an important role in trade in the second millennium and valuable resources had drawn other major states into the region, for both peaceful and covetous reasons. Both of these roles continued into the first millennium.

The population of the independent city-states shared a common Semitic culture and language but geography characterized by mountain spurs, river valleys, and separation from the interior by mountains fostered individual communities governed by kings and councils composed of heads of leading families. The Lebanese mountains provided timber, metals, and wild animals while the coast offered good harbors on easily defended headlands or islands. Fish and purple dye from sea snails were valuable products together with timber, especially cedar; olives, wine, and honey; and manu-factured items of glass, metal, and ivory. Such products and their location made the Phoenicians the main seafarers of the early Iron Age. Eumaios, the faithful swineherd of Odysseus was the son of a king of an island that, unfortunately for him, was visited by "renowned seafaring men, the Phoenicians" who came ashore to trade. Part of their gain was the kidnapped son of the king who was eventually sold to Odysseus' father (*Odyssey* 15.403–84). Archaeological evidence is mounting to demonstrate the reach of the Phoenicians into the central and western Mediterranean in the ninth century and perhaps even earlier. Carthage was a Phoenician "new town" (Qart-hadasht) founded according to literary sources in 814 although archaeological evidence has not yet confirmed this dating. Much of the west African and southern Spanish coasts would become part of an extensive trading empire quite early in the Greek archaic age. Study of the interaction between Phoenicians and Greeks has achieved a new sophistication as scholars examine evidence for their largely contemporaneous seafar-ing activities. Perhaps there was collaboration between them and growing acquaint-ance with one another was likely to result in cultural borrowings (Aubet 1993; Niemeyer 1990b).

Greeks knew people to the south of the Phoenician city-states and, in fact, may well have been part of the formative mix of people who are known as the Philistines. Southern Levant was as much a crossroads as the Phoenician coast in antiquity as it is now. After the movements of various groups known collectively as the "Land and Sea" peoples in the thirteenth and twelfth centuries, the coastal area and region some-what inland in the southern Levant became the land of the Philistines. In the Old Testament, they are identified by their formidable military skills and in earlier Egyptian records they may be recognized as the "Peleset." Following the attempted invasions of the Egyptian delta and the destructions along the Levantine coast, a mixed culture marks the presence of earlier and new inhabitants. Mycenaean pottery is a strong element in this culture along with earlier Canaanite elements and Egyptian motifs. It seems increasingly likely that Bronze Age Greeks joined with others in both the destructions and the eventual settlement. However, continuing contact with the Aegean is uncertain. When the mainland Greeks returned to the eastern Mediterranean, the Philistines had been defeated by the Israelites in their consolidation of a united kingdom (Dothan 1992).

Those Israelites inhabited an area of approximately 15,000 square kilometers of rocky hill country west of the Jordan river, land good for pasturage but not well suited for agriculture except along the coastal plain. Nor was that plain blessed with good harbors. While the region was settled much earlier, archaeological evidence demonstrated new unwalled villages in the central hill country of the eventual state in the early twelfth century that were abandoned in the late eleventh/early tenth centuries with the emergence of the Israelite state. Such evidence may describe tribal groupings under local leaders who consolidated for purposes of war – against the Philistines and others. Unification under King David is dated to the start of the first millennium; consolidation of a larger territory and a significant role in events of the region persisted to the last two decades of the tenth century when the kingdom was divided, easier prey for a more forceful power (Dever 1992).

The Assyrians were that power. A Semitic people living in the northern reaches of the Tigris, they had been active in Near Eastern affairs in the Bronze age, first as traders in Anatolia in quest of metal resources and then as aggressive expansionists: a grandson of the Assyrian king became king of Babylon in 1360. Assyria is recognized as an important kingdom in the Hittite records of the second half of the second millennium. Repercussions of the late Bronze Age disruptions were felt as far inland as Assyria but the ninth century witnessed a renewal of their expansion in the Levant and southern Mesopotamia. An Assyrian empire included Egypt by 745; the northern half of Israel was subjected to Assyria in 743; Phoenicia was invaded in 727. Greeks were defeated in battle by the Phoenicians off southern Anatolia, now part of the Assyrian Empire, in 696. Another interface was Al Mina in the northern Levant, where Greeks may have been active – or even among the founders – in the ninth century (Boardman 1991; Van de Mieroop 2004).

The Assyrians did not conquer the land west of Egypt, where the nearest western neighbors of Egypt were a people known from antiquity as Libyans. Written evidence from late Bronze Age Egypt identifies them as Tehenyu and Libu. The first indications of Bronze Age Libyans in their homeland dates to the fourteenth century site on Bates Island, in the lagoon of Marsa Matruk, although the larger region had human occupants as early as one and three-quarters or one and a half million years ago. Anthropological evidence coupled with archaeological finds indicates that the late Paleolithic population was a hybrid of indigenous Africans and peoples from the Levant.

For most of prehistory, the basic economy of the Libyans was pastoral nomadism, a way of life conditioned by a region in which 95 percent of the land is flat desert elevated in three regions by mountains that reach to 1,448 meters. For the most part, soil is arid due to rare and irregular rainfall. Large reserves of water, existing beneath the sands, produce interior oases and support some extensive plains closer to the Mediterranean coast. It was in these coastal regions that a sedentary life developed during the late Bronze Age and Iron Age. That these towns would be centers in larger Mediterranean context is shown in ceramic finds from the Bates Island site that indicate connections with both the Levant and Cyprus (Gueneron 1976).

Society was ordered by chieftains and their retinues who enjoyed the reputation of experienced charioteers. In this capacity, Libyans were all too familiar to the Egyptians. Armies of Pharaoh Merenptah contended with an invasion of people of Libya and their allies in 1230 and Rameses III fought again against Libyans and cohorts of other peoples in the first quarter of the twelfth century. Some Libyan prisoners were conscripted and settled in forts in the eastern Nile delta. By the end of the twentieth dynasty (1087), a Libyan population was well established in the delta and dynasties 22 and 23 are identified as the Libyan period in Egypt (Leahy 1990).

Seafarers from Aegean waters were drawn to the eastern Mediterranean for a variety of reasons; particular reasons would determine the region to be favored. If land for settlement were the objective, the northern coast of Libya was the most likely choice while if trade were the incentive, the Levantine coast was preferable. For any Greeks inclined to offer services as warriors, native Egyptian pharaohs were plausible employers of any who might aid them in freeing Egypt from foreign control. Only incipient trade seems to have been undertaken in Egypt earlier than the seventh century.

Eastern Adriatic

Travel to the central Mediterranean had been attractive to Greeks in the Bronze Age and attractions would become apparent again in the later Dark Age. The route north of Corcyra via the Strait of Otranto to the eastern coast of Italy could be accomplished in less than a day and, on arrival, the Greeks would be spared foes akin to the Assyrians. Euboeans may have been among the first to undertake the long and distant voyage across the Adriatic. Of mainland Greeks, the Corinthians were particularly active in western waters. Corinthian influence begins in the Corinthian Gulf and in the Ionian Islands, especially at Ithaca where dedications indicate 780 as a date for a Corinthian presence there. Later in the eighth century, Corinth established new settlements in Ambrakia, Epidamnos, Apollonia, and on the islands of Leukas and Corcyra (Morgan 1988). At the three mainland sites they would encounter western counterparts of the inhabitants of what would later be the kingdom of Macedonia under Philip II, namely the Illyrians and the peoples of Epirus.

Illyrians occupied what is modern Albania but, when combined under the rule of an energetic king, they regularly spilled in all directions. The core is west of the Balkan watershed. Rivers that flow into the Adriatic stretch along the upland plains into the coastal plain. A large scale movement of tribes from the late eleventh century into the ninth brought newcomers to this region. Divided as it was by rivers and mountains, the location fostered continuity of the earlier way of life as semi-nomadic pastoralists. Similarities of culture indicate that the Illyrians were related to peoples who moved into northern Italy at the same time. Both eastern and western groups were Indo-Europeans (Wilkes 1992).

Further south was the land of Epirus, a region west of the Pindus range characterized by valleys tightly folded into limestone ranges. Comparison of the physical culture of new people migrating into the area toward the end of the third millennium indicates a likeness with the Indo-European culture of the northern Balkans. Initially a pastoral life continued but toward the end of the second millennium an increasing number of sedentary sites is attested. Movement into Epirus was frequent, bringing Molossi, Thesprotes, and Chaones by the end of the Dark Age. Interaction between Greeks and the Epirotes began early: one of the earliest major Greek sanctuaries – that of Zeus at Dodona – was in Epirus and is mentioned in both the *Iliad* (16.233–5) and *Odyssey* (14.327; 19.296). The sustained contact was beneficial to both parties: the Greeks, primarily the Corinthians, had access to resources that were scarce in Corinth and the Epirotes developed a sedentary way of life that allowed for consolidation into a unified kingdom in the fourth century.

Central Mediterranean

Even earlier than the time when the Corinthians were establishing settlements on the Adriatic coast, other Greeks – notably those from the island of Euboea – were investigating waters of the Tyrrhenian Sea. Earlier still, the peninsula of Italy had been familiar to Aegean seafarers of the Bronze Age and some contact persisted even in the first centuries of the Dark Age. As we have seen, the voyage was not difficult;

even the Straits of Messina were navigable into the Tyrrhenian Sea. It is not surprising that the first Greek associations with Italy were in the south of the peninsula. Nor did Greeks penetrate deeply into the interior, which is approximately 201 kilometers wide at its greatest point (Malkin 1998).

Nature made the interior less attractive. The Apennine mountains run through Italy's length and shoot out spurs that divide the land into pockets much of which is of low quality for agriculture. A shortage of navigable rivers would also have been a deterrent. What is more, those areas with fertile plains and the rich resources of timber, tin, iron, stone, and salt pans were already spoken for by others.

The occupants were a patchwork of peoples. A relatively homogeneous Neolithic culture had been replaced by increasing cultural differences among regions. Along the Apennines and eventually spreading into Campania were the Sabellian peoples, Oscans in the south and Umbrians in the north. The east was occupied by Venetians and Messapians, Indo-Europeans allied to the Illyrians; both groups migrated into the Adriatic from the eleventh century branching in opposite directions at the head of the sea. Picentines holding the east central coast were a mixture of Indo-European and non-Indo-European peoples while Ligurians and Raetians – also Indo-Europeans combined with an earlier substratum – shared the north of the peninsula with the Etruscans. In the south were Sicels, whose language resembles Latin and Messapian. They, like the Philistines, may be among the late Bronze Age "Land and Sea" peoples identified in Egyptian records as the Sheklesh (Ridgway and Ridgway 1979).

The most powerful people of Italy in the early Iron Age may also have migrated from the eastern Mediterranean: they are the Etruscans who held Etruria, modern Tuscany from the Arno to the Tiber river, from the Apennines to the Tyrrhenian Sea. The east was characterized by hills and narrow plains; low-lying plains sometimes rocky or marshy typified the west. The region was inhabited during the Bronze Age but witnessed major changes from the twelfth century to the tenth as people moved from upland sites to hill summits that often were on sites of the future Etruscan cities. While communal and social organization remained loose, dwellings became larger and the dead received grander burials and more impressive objects. In addition to agriculture and herding, metallurgical production increased (Torelli 2000).

Debate over the cause of these changes has been lengthy and the issue has not been resolved. Even in antiquity there were quite different explanations for the origin of the Etruscans: Herodotus described them as immigrants from the east (1.94), an explanation that may be supported by the presence of "Tursha" among the pesky "Land and Sea" peoples as well as through evidence from the island of Lemnos in the northern Aegean in an inscription showing similarities with Etruscan. Dionysius of Halicarnassus, on the other hand, believed that the Etruscan civilization was an indigenous development (1.28). Somewhat ambiguous is Hesiod's attribution of rule over the glorious Tyrsenians to the sons of Odysseus and Circe (*Theogony* 1011–15). Until the language of the Etruscans is determined, it is impossible to associate them with any broad group of peoples.

Internal development was certainly notable in Etruria in the ninth century. Population grew, villages coalesced and increased in size, and the Etruscan sphere expanded south to the Campania for agricultural and commercial purposes as well as north to the Po valley which would quickly become a major producer of bronzes. Imported goods are apparent among the indigenous products. Social stratification became sharper with leadership of villages in the hands of aristocratic families in whose honor great monumental tombs with diameters up to 265 meters were erected. In the eighth century larger settlements took the form of cities and Etruscan influence soon extended to the small, strategically located village of Rome. Outside contacts expanded to include interaction with Phoenicians and Greeks, especially those from Euboea, the Cycladic islands, and Crete. What appears to be the earliest Greek settlement in the central Mediterranean was founded ca. 780 on the island of Pithekoussai, offshore from the bay of Naples. Since the coast of Italy was in Etruscan hands, newly arrived Greeks discovered an offshore location for settlement but one that would facilitate contact with the Etruscans. Archaeological evidence does indeed reveal a mix of cultures at Pithekoussai that served as a trade center for Greeks, Etruscans, and Phoenicians (d'Agostino 1999b; Gialanella 2003).

Etruscan power would abide into the fifth century causing a reputation like that rendered by Cato: "almost all of Italy was under the control of the Etruscans" (*Tuscorum iure paene omnis Italia fuerat*, in Servius *ad Aeneidem* 11.567). Greeks recognized the value of Etruscan resources and manufactured objects. They may also have feared the lords of Etruria for it was believed that Greeks did not trade in Sicily for ten generations after Trojan War due to Etruscan piracy. In return, Etruscans imported Greek goods and customs to such a degree that present knowledge of archaic Greek pottery depends heavily on Etruscan finds.

Sicily and Sardinia

The island of Sicily divides the eastern and western basins of the Mediterranean and comes close to providing a link between its northern and southern halves. Consequently, whenever seafaring is widespread in the Mediterranean, Sicily will be involved. In the Bronze Age, Mycenaean Greeks and Minoan Cretans were familiar with the route to Sicily. In fact, tradition remembered that it was this island to which the inventive Daidalos fled from King Minos of Knossos. Bronze and early Iron Age inhabitants of Sicily were known collectively as Sicels who seemed to have arrived from southern Italy in the eleventh century. In addition two other named groups shared the island: Sicans who may have been earlier inhabitants, perhaps immigrants from Iberia, and Elymi who are identified as people fleeing from Troy (Thuc. 6.2). Archaeologically there are no major differences between them in the early Iron Age (Brea 1957).

The fertility of Sicilian land was another attraction; it was later regarded as the bread-basket of the Mediterranean. Gentle hills and rolling uplands in the center and plains in the east and northwest provide arable land for cultivation of wheat, grapes, olives, and fruit while the mountains – a continuation of the Apennines – supply forests of oak, chestnut, pine, and fir. Metal resources are scarce but harbors permit travel in all directions from the triangular, strategic location.

The island of Sardinia also attracted eastern visitors in the Bronze Age as Mycenaean pottery discoveries and metalwork showing Cypriot/Levantine influences reveal. A

Phoenician settlement in the south dates to the Iron Age and pottery finds indicate a Greek presence on the island (Tronchetti 2003).

Western Mediterranean

When Greeks ventured into the western Mediterranean, they would encounter both familiar and new peoples. The largest single group of unfamiliar people were the Celts whom Greeks would meet first in the south of France and, later, in the south of Iberia. Originating in Bohemia and Austria, tribal groups formed a confederation in the early Iron Age, a development that fostered movement in several directions and an acceleration of trade activity. Approximately in the mid-eighth century, Celts arrived in what is modern France. At a site on the sea entrance of the Étang de Berre evidence from the eighth century has been discovered and the primitive huts of the inhabitants have been preserved. Ligurian is the name given to these inhabitants of southern France who lived in *oppida* (Latin for towns) which were usually fortified settlements on defensible hilltops directed by local chiefs. Later evidence indicates that these *oppida* were numerous and varied, extending from 7 to 25 hectares. Products of the land were diverse: grain, olives, grapes, salt, herbs, fish, animals (especially rabbits) metals and stone, some of which were precious (Cunliffe 1994b).

When Greeks visited the Mediterranean coast of southern Iberia before the third century, they would not have encountered the Celts but, rather, a mixed population whose culture was akin to groups in northern and western Europe. During the early centuries of the first millennium, the main cultural traditions suggest an ancestry in what is known as the Hallstatt culture of trans-Alpine Europe. From approximately 750, a series of immigrations brought yet another tradition into the north-east region which is also traceable to central Europe. Advanced bronze technology characterized much of Iberia, including the lower Guadalquivir valley where more than three hundred settlements dating to the ninth and eighth centuries have been identified. Artifacts and language indicate a mixture of Indo-European and non-Indo-European elements (Castro 1995).

Readiest access to valuable minerals (including iron, zinc, lead, and copper) of the hinterland came through the settlements along the Guadalquivir river. The interior is a large plateau (about 40 percent of the land of modern Spain) surrounded by rugged hills. Some 30 percent percent of the land is arable, another 21 percent supplies good pasture, and more than 30 percent is forested. The valleys of the south have especially rich soil.

Well before the Greeks began to explore southern Iberia, the Phoenicians had traveled there. They were drawn by metals, especially silver, to the southern region of the peninsula know as Tartessos. At Gadir on the Atlantic coast north of the Straits of Gilbratar, the first Phoenician imports date to ca. 770–760. A second site beyond Gibraltar was on the southern coast at Likos. Much of the African coast was now Phoenician. Sites in Libya were Leptis, Oia, Sabrata; in Tunisia, Carthage, Utica, Neapolis; in Morocco, Tingis. In the north, Phoenicians were situated at Solus, Panormus, and Nora in Italy and were, as mentioned above, involved at Pithekoussai. Melita on Malta was Phoenician as were Malaka and Karteia in Spain (Aubet 1993).

Like Odysseus, Greeks venturing beyond their Aegean communities would "see the towns of many men and learn their way of thinking" and, also like the heroic wanderer, they might "suffer many woes upon the sea" (*Odyssey* 1.3–4).

Greek Seamanship in the Early Iron Age

The Mediterranean and its appendages were relatively easy to navigate, once seafarers had learned the nature of its currents, winds, and obstacles. They learned some of the sea's secrets very early since islands were inhabited from ca. 9000 BCE (Cherry 1990). Beyond acquisition of land, sailors ventured by sea in search of other resources for although similarities exist in the lands that center round the Mediterranean, there are sufficient absences of vital resources in much of the region to stimulate travel in search for those requisites. And, as we have reviewed, there were people established round the Mediterranean sphere who possessed raw materials and manufactured goods that they were willing to trade for objects desirable or insufficient in their own corners of the Great Sea (see figure 2.2). If they were unwilling to barter, they might be forced to share their native wealth. We have seen that Greeks did venture into the Aegean and, later, into the larger Mediterranean so it is necessary to inquire after reasons that prompted them to do so and means that enabled the seafaring.

How well did the Greeks know the realm of Poseidon? Knowledge of that realm began far earlier than the Iron Age. Not only is the use of seacraft being pushed earlier and earlier but certain regions are seen as "potential nurseries for the development of maritime technology and navigation" (Rainbird 1999: 231), and the Aegean is one of those regions. Even before the Bronze Age, travel by sea is clearly attested. Ships brought the first settlers to the island of Crete about 6000 BCE and those settlers continued to rely on the sea for purposes of trade. Ships also carried the first settlers to the islands of the Aegean known as the Cyclades about 4300 BCE. It is increasingly clear that lively interaction existed within the Aegean as early as the late

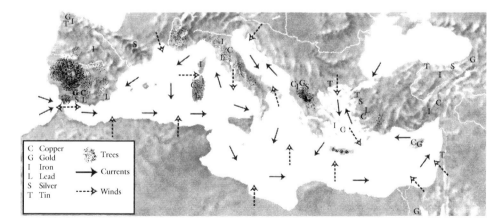

Figure 2.2 Resources in the Mediterranean world

fourth and early third millennia. Initially, settlers in the Cyclades employed their long-ships, developed around 3000 BCE, among the islands and then beyond to gain goods unavailable on their rocky homes in trade for their own craft products, like elegant marble vessels and sculptures, and produce such as olive oil and wine. These seafarers moved among the islands and beyond them to other parts of the Aegean. Excavations in the summer of 2001 have uncovered remains of a flourishing, fortified settlement on the south-western coast of Andros dating to ca. 4500–3300. The excavator, Christina Televantou, discovered incised pictures of ten ships between 20 and 30 centimeters in length on the outer face of the defensive wall as well as two ships on the wall's rock foundations (Televantou 2001). And they appear to have reached the eastern Mediterranean. The Carmel mountain ridge in the Levant has a number of incised pictures of boats of various forms and sizes. One boat, dated to the Neolithic period, is an Aegean type of vessel (Artzy 2000: 444–5).

Inhabitants of Crete soon expanded this incipient trade in the Aegean attested by great quantities of imported Minoan vases at a number of sites (Wiener 1987). Locations in Anatolia, too, show that same presence through objects and, in several cases, through actual settlements (Mee 1998). Well beyond the Aegean, Minoan goods and influence were felt in Egypt, the Levant, and the central Mediterranean (Davies and Schofield 1995). Inhabitants of mainland Greece involved themselves in this intensive network of trade during the second half of the second millennium. Increasing presence of mainland goods, and surely mainlanders, extends eastward from the Aegean islands, to the Anatolian coast and neighboring islands, southward to Crete, and on to Egypt and the Levant. Even before these eastern interests, Mycenaeans had been active in the central Mediterranean as finds from southern Italy and Sicily demonstrate.

Moreover, a new explanation of the history of the penteconter (a 50-oared ship) dates its origin to the thirteenth century, that is the Mycenaean age rather than the archaic age. Michael Wedde makes a compelling case in his study of the nature of Bronze Age ships based on representations of ships. Evidence exists from the late Bronze Age for partial decking to create hulls capable of carrying the greater weight of a second level of rowers. One advantage of the decking is the greater speed produced by the additional rowers; another is that the greater weight produced by adding a second level provided greater rigidity making the hull more resistant to impact. In addition to decking, developments in sails and their rigging occurred at approximately the same time. A loose-footed sail that appears to be an Aegean invention brought greater scope for trimming the sail to suit wind conditions (Wedde 2000). Built according to Bronze Age techniques of construction, a 16.46-meter-long craft – named the *Argo* – equipped with twenty oars and carrying a large rectangular sail on its seven and a third meter mast completed a 1,500 nautical mile voyage from northern Greece to the eastern coast of the Black Sea in 1984. The feat demonstrated that it was possible to survive the clashing rocks of the Dardanelles and reach the goal of the original *Argo* associated with Jason's search for the Golden Fleece (Severin 1985).

It is possible, of course, that these skills of construction and navigation were lost in the period following the collapse of the Bronze Age kingdoms of the Aegean and elsewhere in the Mediterranean. As we know, however, Greeks from the mainland had the ability to transport themselves to the coast of Anatolia in the eleventh century. Nor did contact with the central Mediterranean cease; inhabitants of the Cyclades and the Aegean island of Euboea, "famed for its ships" (*Homeric Hymn to Apollo* 219), were moving about by sea in the tenth and ninth centuries (d'Agostino 1999b; Kearsley 1999).

Ships obviously figure prominently in the Homeric epics. They are of two sizes. The smaller are twenty-oared, such as the vessel that Telemachus employs to seek news of his father (*Odyssey* 1.280). Larger vessels are penteconters – they have fifty oars, like the ships of the contingents of Achilles and Philoktetes (*Iliad* 16.169–70; 2.719–20). Common adjectives describe both sizes: they are narrow, long, low, lightweight, and have a single sail mounted on a mast (Casson 1971; Morrison and Williams 1968).

Archaeological evidence adds more detail especially through painted representations painted on vases. Of the forty-four representations of ships from the Geometric Age – ca. 900–700 – forty-three date to ca. 760–710 (Morrison and Williams 1968). A deck became common in the eighth century when a mortise and tenon system for joining the planks replaced the technique of sewing the planks together with cords. The newer technique is far more durable over time or in storm conditions (Dougherty 2001: 27–9). Deck area, translated into quantity of cargo that could be carried, indicates capacities ranging from nine tons of grain or 375 amphoras for the smaller vessels and fifty tons or 1,000 amphorae for the larger (Scott 2000: 112–13). In size, then, vessels capable of transporting people and goods were available in the eighth century.

Hesiod also knows that men take to the sea and even offers instructions about the proper times to sail and the cargo to carry. These instructions begin at line 618 of his *Works and Days* when he speculates on the chance that "desire for rough seafaring seizes you." The poet describes the two seasons when seafaring is possible: the fifty days following the summer solstice and in spring when leaves at the very top of the fig tree are as large as a crow's footprint. One should never venture out to sea when the Pleiades are hiding themselves. At that time, tend to your ship and its equipment. When you do fill your ship with cargo, remember that the greater cargo brings the greater profits. But, the advice continues, do not trust all of your livelihood to a hollow ship but leave the larger part on shore, gambling on the smaller portion. "You will escape grief only with great difficulty." What is more, he recounts that his own father took to the sea leaving his home in Asia Minor to settle in central Greece:

> Then he came to this place, crossing the wide sea,
> having left Aeolian Kyme, in a black ship (634–5) . . .
> He settled close to Helikon in this wretched hamlet,
> Askra, bad in winter, difficult in summer, never good.
> (639–40; author's tr.)

Evidence, then, suggests that sea travel was undertaken during the early Iron Age. In fact, in recent studies of colonization, many scholars insert a "pre-colonization" phase of exploration prior to the establishment of permanent settlements (Graham

1990; Popham 1994). Moreover, the physical nature of Greece indicates incentives to experience what Hesiod knew as stormy and rough business. Greece can support life but it is not an easy life: as Herodotus said "poverty is always a companion in Greece" (7.102). Mountains comprise 75 percent of the land; the islands are, in fact, peaks of submerged mountains; consequently, plains suitable for farming are extremely limited. The mountains also divide Greece into small pockets of territory which have only difficult communication with one another. Nor are there perennial, navigable rivers in the southern Greek mainland that help to link the regions. Rainfall is restricted and uncertain, usually most plentiful in the winter when vegetation is hibernating but ceasing during the growing season. Climate is variable to the degree of creating micro-regions within the pockets of land encouraging farming families to cultivate several crops in a variety of locations in hopes of being self-sufficient. However, this strategy requires resources – especially metals and timber – that are scarce or even absent in many parts of Greece. Hesiod's advice was that one must "work and then work more" (*Works and Days* 382). But he also knew that men take to the sea and, by this time, would-be sailors had goods in their cargo that were likely to be welcome in other regions of the Mediterranean, among them wine and olive oil in various forms along with their containers.

Consequently, there was great incentive to resort to the sea. Conditions in Greece both necessitated and facilitated seafaring. Ancestors of the Iron Age inhabitants had learned the rules of the Mediterranean as well as the Aegean and Adriatic Seas and that knowledge had not been lost during the darkest period of the early first millennium. Although the Mycenaean centers had been seriously weakened if not obliterated in the late Bronze Age, Mycenaeans lived on both in mainland Greece and in other areas of the Aegean, and perhaps as distant as Italy and the Levant. Strength by sea marks the periods when Greece has flourished throughout its long history. The archaic age is one of those periods when Greeks and non-Greeks met face to face in remote parts of the Mediterranean, with momentous consequences to the cultures of all the participants.

PART II

Histories

CHAPTER THREE

The Early Iron Age

Catherine Morgan

From the collapse of the Mycenaean palaces (ca. 1200), the Early Iron Age runs to the point, around 700, where we can begin to recognize the social and political world attested by archaic literary sources. It was no Dark Age, even though the hindsight which encourages us to look for signs of "progress" towards an ideal of the archaic and classical polis may simplify approaches to it. This chapter explores the multiple histories of traders and raiders, princes and priests, city-builders and craftsmen. Not all prove to be the kind of supra-regional or long-term stories which demand their place in textbooks. But 500 years is a long time, and "Greek" lands (strikingly defined by phenomena such as the swift spread of the Greek alphabet and pantheon) extensive and varied. What with hindsight may seem to be transient or distinctive to certain periods and places is just as important in understanding this period as are the roots of longer-term historical phenomena.

After the Palaces

Almost all of our stories start in the twelfth century, in a post-palatial (Late Helladic IIIC) phase of what Klaus Kilian aptly termed "Late Mycenaean city life" (Kilian 1988: 135). Here he had in mind the Greek mainland, and especially the Argolid, where almost all of the major palatial centers – Tiryns, Mycenae, and Midea included – had substantial settlement on and/or around the earlier citadels, with earlier fortifications repaired and maintained.[1] At Tiryns and Midea, the partial reconstruction of the megaron of the previous palace was presumably intended to house the community ruler. These new buildings incorporated the previous altar and throne (Maran 2001; Walberg 1988), thus alluding to the authority of the Mycenaean ruler or *wanax*, and similar claims can be found in other areas of elite behavior. Alongside the major changes in burial ritual discussed below, twelfth-century cemeteries at a number of sites have produced a small proportion of exceptionally rich graves, a significant number of which contained arms and armor (Papadimitriou 2006). Indeed, even below this super-rich elite, symbolizing male warrior status in burial is widespread during this period – in, for example, the extensive cemeteries of western Achaia.[2] Whether or not the dead really were leading warriors (Whitley 2002), they were treated as such in burial, and it is tempting to suggest that the practice reflects an adaptation from the military ideology of Mycenaean kingship (Davies and Bennett 1999).

In this post-palatial world, previous symbols of authority were reused and adapted within a wide variety of (generally geographically more extensive) political recon-figurations. Yet the transition from Mycenaean kingdoms ruled by a *wanax*, with the *qa-si-re-u* as a second order magistrate, to a proliferation of local *basileis* during Early Iron Age, is one of the least understood aspects of our period. We do not know exactly how the authority of a *basileus* was conceived (let alone how it may have dif-fered according to place and time), and since every modern translation of the term, apart, perhaps, from the anodyne "ruler," carries its own connotations, care is needed.[3] In most regions, there is some archaeological evidence for social hierarchy (in house size and location as at Nichoria, Klazomenai or Thermon, for example, or in cult roles or funerary expenditure), albeit less marked than in the Late Bronze Age. Where we have a large enough sample of graves to make statistical analysis viable (chiefly, but not exclusively in Athens), attention has been devoted to considering what we can learn about communal frameworks for the expression of status and power over time from patterns of mortuary behavior.[4] Kinship was the likely basis for (and primary means of expression of) the "leader plus followers" structure which we commonly infer for Early Iron Age societies across Greece. But since kinship is a social rather than a biological phenomenon, this observation is rarely informative. Usually, we cannot tell whether status was inherited or won by economic, military or other means in a "big man" system.[5]

Burial and Society

This uncertainty largely derives from problems of interpretation which follow changes in burial customs. The widespread (although far from universal) fashion for single burial from Late Helladic IIIC onwards, ending multiple interments in chamber tombs or, for the elite, *tholoi*, and sometimes involving the complete abandonment of earlier cemeteries, was in many areas accompanied, or rapidly followed by, a wholesale shift from inhumation to cremation (Lemos 2002: ch. 5). Cremation had been practiced at various stages of the Bronze Age, but was now favored on an unprecedented scale (Stampolidis 2001). As has commonly been observed, the relative frequency with which favored rites changed through the Early Iron Age precludes a primarily religious explanation: surely more significant was the social capital to be gained from the spectacle and investment involved in a key rite of passage (Morris 1987: chs. 3, 8). Cremation dealt in spectacular fashion with the perishable body, and facilitated con-spicuous consumption of other offerings. It thus gave scope to prolong celebrations at the grave, and to draw greater attention to the deceased and his family, which was fully exploited in the succeeding centuries as tumuli and/or grave markers became ever larger and more elaborate. The richness of the warrior cremation in the central shaft of the Toumba building at Lefkandi (ca. 950) is a case in point (see below). Usually, the major loss resulting from a switch to single burial is that of the physical association of individuals in shared family or kin-group tombs. In some regions, multiple burials survived or were revived for varying reasons. For example, the cemetery at Elateia in Phocis may have reached a peak of wealth in the immediate post-palatial period, but new if smaller chamber tombs continued to be built into Protogeometric and beyond, and remained in use even longer (Dakoronia 1993a). At Argos, the appearance of ever-larger cist tombs with multiple burials in the eighth century probably indicates renewed emphasis on lineage among the elite (Hägg 1983a; Foley 1988: 35–40). And perhaps most strikingly, at Knossos the long-term use of chamber tombs and shaft graves in the North Cemetery allows us to reconstruct patterns of inherited rights and custom, such as the right to be buried with weaponry (Cavanagh 1996; Snodgrass 1996). In regions such as Macedonia, Epirus and Thessaly, the continuing popularity of tumuli through the Early Iron Age and beyond is usually taken to represent long-lived kin associations. This may be so, although usually only small parts of very extensive cemeteries have been excavated, and recent discoveries in Thessaly in particular have shown differences in age/sex representation, offerings, and spatial arrangements of graves within individual tumuli which imply that they could contain different forms of group. A good, archaic, example of this is an apparent military association at Ag. Giorgios near Larisa (Tziaphalias 1994).

Nonetheless, in most parts of the southern mainland in particular, addressing questions of inherited versus acquired power demands that we identify and interpret spatial associations between single burials and where possible, correlate their pattern of offerings. The existence of family burial plots has been claimed at a number of sites, and certain examples predate the eighth century (Lemos 2002: 187–8). A small early/mid-ninth century grave group on the north slope of the Areiopagus in Athens, for example, has been tentatively identified as the family plot of the Medontid genos.[6] This includes the grave of the "Rich Lady" (ca. 850) whose 81 offerings included a variety of orientalia, and a ceramic chest with five granary models on the lid which likely symbolizes one source of family wealth (another being the eastern trade discussed below). Most groups, however, date from the eighth century onwards, when new burial plots appear, pressure on space made the preferential use of certain parts of existing cemeteries (such as the Athenian Kerameikos) an important issue, or when the laying out of whole new cemetery areas (as at Eretria) allows us to trace contemporary perceptions of who belonged where. Such groupings vary in strength, and their interpretation as direct representations of family or *genos* is controversial. Certainly, it is a further step to see them as simple precursors of archaic and classical groups which present their own difficulties in interpretation (Houby-Nielsen 1995). In the Athenian Kerameikos, for example, there is clear variation in the ties between the burial groups represented in the great Archaic tumuli, and, for example, the largely male dead in Grave-mound G and the South Mound who shared the symposiastic aspects of the luxurious, Lydianizing lifestyle of *tryphe* (Houby-Nielsen 1995: 152–63). The ties symbolized here span the range of elite male activities, from kinship to warfare and drinking and dining associations – the public virtues which played such an important part in constructing the reputation of the good aristocrat. For the Early Iron Age, however, we still lack the large multi-period sample from any region necessary to put such expression into context.

Settlement Histories

It was long thought that the Early Iron Age saw a major decline in population, with small, scattered settlements coalescing into larger polis centers only from the eighth century onwards. There was certainly a great increase in the number and size of archaeologically-visible settlements across the Greek world during the eighth century, although since the EIA is more or less invisible in the majority of surface surveys, the contrast may be exaggerated. Overall, it is now clear that earlier depopulation is largely an artifact of archaeological research. Over the past decades, excavation and publication of material from regions as diverse as East Locris (Dakoronia 1993b) and the Cyclades (Gounaris 1999) has confirmed the continued importance of regional central places with associated socio-political identities focused upon them. The location of these sites, and the way in which they operated within hierarchies, in relation to peer sites, or as centers of territories, varied greatly, however, and in many areas is still barely understood (C. Morgan 2003: chs. 2, 4). Across the mainland and in many parts of Crete, there was long-term continuity in settlement at, or close by, many Late Bronze Age big sites. This does not imply an unchanged regional role, although the loss of the information provided by Linear B leaves us dependent on archaeological evidence to reconstruct this. In some cases, there seems to have been a more or less immediate decline in size and/or complexity in relation to previous second-order sites or new foundations. Early Iron Age Pylos (Griebel and Nelson 1998) seems to have been a notably smaller settlement than Nichoria, at least until the abandonment of the latter sometime before the mid-eighth century, even though Bronze Age Nichoria had previously been a substantial village incorporated into the Further Province of Pylos as one of seven local economic centers.[7] Elsewhere, however, the growth in regional importance of sites such as Athens or Knossos, and the relegation of others such as Mycenae or Tiryns, occurred only centuries later as part of the larger (and sometimes violent) processes which surrounded the formation of polis hierarchies.

An important phenomenon of the first centuries of the Early Iron Age is the expansion of activity around the fringes of certain previous palatial centers, although since these usually continued to be occupied, this should be seen not in terms of "refugee" movement but rather of liberation of dependencies, with consequent freedom to exploit their position in key locations solely for their own advantage (Foxhall 1995: 246–7). A notable example, following the demise of the palace at Thebes, is the expansion of settlement on Euboea,[8] at the port of Pyrgos-Kynos on the Locrian coast opposite (previously the seat of a *qa-si-re-u*), and along the road inland which connects with the north-south route towards Delphi and the Corinthian Gulf (Crielaard 2006). The *koine* characterized by close material connections between Euboea, Thessaly, Macedonia, Attica and the neighboring islands, usually termed "Euboean" although without implying that Euboea necessarily initiated it, lasted from ca. 1100 into the ninth century (Lemos 1998). Moving inland, the cemetery at Elateia is one of a group along this road which saw a striking wealth of investment in the immediate post-palatial period (Dakoronia 1993a). In the midst of these cemeteries is the sanctuary at Kalapodi, founded in Late Helladic IIIB2 as home to a large-scale festival involving the sacrifice and consumption of meat (including many wild species invoking hunting activity favored by the male elite and appropriate to the patron deity, Artemis) and cultivated and wild plants. The dedication of spinning and weaving equipment reflects a further aspect of Artemis' persona of particular relevance to women, and small metal offerings are closely similar to their more plentiful counterparts from the Elateia graves.[9]

The wealth of the Lefkandi elite reached a peak around 950, when two outstandingly rich burials, a male cremation and a female inhumation, were placed under the floor of a vast building (some 50 m long) at the site now named Toumba after the mound subsequently erected over the structure. This was probably a funerary building rather than the ruler's own house, though the latter possibility cannot be completely discounted (Coulton and Catling 1993; Lemos 2002: 140–6). These burials were accompanied by rich textiles, jewelery, weapons and orientalia (including heirlooms), by four horses in a separate pit, and by a vase as a grave marker (Lemos 2002: 166–8; Popham 1994). Heroizing, Homeric, overtones have been widely noted (e.g. Antonaccio 1995b), and the cemetery which rapidly formed around the structure contained the cremations and inhumations of elite men, women and children who seemingly claimed association with the power of the dead rulers. Was this a perhaps a *basileus* and his clan? Burials continued for over a century (until ca. 825), and from ca. 950 onwards were mirrored by rich graves and settlements on the opposite, Locrian coast (including pyres at Tragana with oriental imports: Onasoglou 1981), and by a marked expansion at Kalapodi, when the *temenos* was extended and metal dedications increased in size and number.[10] Outside Crete, Lefkandi offers perhaps the closest Greek parallel for the princely burials which were such a feature of surrounding lands to east and west in the eighth and seventh centuries – at Salamis on Cyprus, for example (Karageorghis 2003), and in Campania and the Bay of Naples (D'Agostino 1999a). The major differences are the date of the Lefkandi burials and the concept of heroization which they embody (Morris 1999b). Spectacular as these archaeological remains are, this Early Iron Age story had limited longer term implications.

The same is true of a second distinctive phenomenon of the earliest centuries of our period, the so-called "refuge" settlement which is most spectacularly shown in the mountains of eastern and central Crete. Settlement of this kind was not new, but from the end of LMIIIB (ca. 1190) it occurred on a larger scale than ever before. It is therefore tempting to interpret it in terms of flight in the face of post-palatial incursions. Yet the topography of Crete, the largest Aegean island, is characterized by a sharp transition between its mountainous spine and a coastal plain, the latter generally more extensive and hospitable in the north. This juxtaposition of ecologies, combined with the island's location on the major east-west trade routes of the southern Aegean (Jones 2000: esp. ch. 4), sustained a complex pattern of responses to various outsider contacts. Around 120 defensible Early Iron Age sites are so far known (Nowicki 2000). A few are true refuges in the sense of being extremely difficult of access and only occasionally inhabited. But these tend to be closely linked to the more common defensible upland sites, in more accessible locations, which enjoyed vantage points over inland plains and the coast alike, and access to routes to the shore for desirable purposes such as trade (albeit involving difficult climbs which offered their own protection). Communities such as those at Karphi, Vrokastro, and Kavousi had access to a wide variety of imported goods, maintained relations with lowland settlements, were able to exploit well-watered arable uplands and to sustain often large populations, yet were reached only via steep and often difficult paths. They formed part of upland settlement networks, the nature and scale of which varied over time. Kavousi Vronda, for example, was founded in Late Minoan IIIC (ca. 1190–1070) as one of ten interdependent nucleated hamlets and villages in distinct niches around a complex of upland valleys (Haggis 1996; 2001). Together, these sites indicate dense settlement of the area (Haggis estimates 600–1,200 inhabitants), but since they each maintained their own shrines and cemeteries, some form of (perhaps clan-based) divisions must have precluded their amalgamation. By Protogeometric times, common concerns are indicated by the foundation of a shrine at Makellos, roughly equidistant between settlement clusters, which continued in use into the archaic period. But a combination of resource constraints and the pull of the sea resulted in a reduction in site numbers from LMIIIC into Protogeometric, yet expansion both at those which survived and in many parts of the lowlands (including former palaces such as Knossos, where the North Cemetery was founded in the mid-eleventh century). The very variable history of mountain settlement across Crete reflects differences in this balance as well as the extent of local resources. In the Lasithi area, Karphi is typical in expanding swiftly from a village to a large town with a territory and satellite villages (Nowicki 1999; 2000: 157–64, 238), but then being abandoned at the end of LMIIIC in favor of lower sites such as Lato, which seemed to offer a better balance of resources, protection, and access to the coast. Elsewhere, mountain sites closer to the coast, such as Kavousi Kastro and Vrokastro, expanded through the Protogeometric and Geometric periods. By ca. 750, Kavousi was a densely packed site at its peak of population; it declined markedly after 700 but was not completely abandoned until classical times (Coulson et al. 1997). Clearly, Cretan mountain sites were far from just the refuges of panicking coast-dwellers fleeing incursions from the sea. They were a complex response to the opportunities and dangers involved in accessing upland, coastal and maritime resources, and their long-term fate depended on the perceived advantages to be gained from the various contacts involved.

Mobility, Migration, and Trade

Until relatively recently, two common views of the Early Iron Age emphasized migration and depopulation. These rested on an unfortunate alliance of literal readings of archaic and later epichoric myth-histories, in which the origins of particular communities were located in the supposed tribal migrations of the deep past (notoriously, the Dorian invasion), and interpretations of the archaeological record which attempted to define material "cultures" in terms of peoples, and accepted as meaningful what we now understand as mere gaps in research. This is not to imply that there were no significant changes in population level in some areas, merely that they were fewer, less dramatic, and less peculiar to this period than previously supposed. Demographic mobility is certainly evident throughout our period, but in widely paralleled circumstances which owe nothing to great tribal migrations. Long-term cycles of settlement movement within a relatively confined area can be seen in the pattern of creation and abandonment of sites around the Pagasitic Gulf in Thessaly. The abrupt abandonment of the major Mycenaean site at Iolkos (modern Dimini) coincides with a marked expansion at modern Volos-Palia, which probably then assumed the name of Iolkos (Adrymi-Sismani 2006). Sudden as this shift may seem, the longer-term perspective of the succeeding 500–600 years reveals similar expansion and contraction and the appearance of other new or re-foundations around the Gulf, including Demetrias and Pagasai, which show how the relationship between Dimini and Volos-Palia fits within larger processes (C. Morgan 2003: 95–102).

Shorter-term demographic instability is evident in the Early Iron Age settlement history of the Cyclades and neighboring islands, long thought to have been largely uninhabited before a general increase in archaeologically visible settlement in the eighth century. Recent research has shown the record to be much fuller and more complex, however, with near continuous activity at many principal settlements at least from Protogeometric onwards,[11] yet considerable variety in overall settlement strategies at island level. This variety depended on such factors as mineral and agricultural resources (the latter comparatively scarce on such small and rugged islands, and particularly vulnerable to the effects of bad years), and the proximity of neighboring islands, the mainland, and trade routes. The use of stone as a readily available building material, combined with often confined settlement locations which made tight planning essential, has left an unusually rich record of well preserved abandoned sites, such as Koukounaries on Paros, Zagora on Andros, or Emborio on Chios (Coldstream 1977 (2003): ch. 12). Much can be learned, therefore, about planning in relation to community and household size and structure, but it is hard to generalize on the basis of the knowledge so gained (C. Morgan 2003: 49–54). Prominent as these sites may seem when studying Early Iron Age architecture and town planning, even within their island context they need to be understood as part of the complex settlement dynamics that were a particular feature of island history. It is therefore not surprising to find Cycladic communities prominently involved in often quite short-distance resettlements (internal "colonizations") in the archaic period if not earlier.[12] Equally, given the potential for conflict in such situations, it is surely no coincidence that the earliest polyandrion so far discovered is a construction of the end of the eighth century near Paroikia on Paros (Zapheiropoulou 2000a). When communities did crystallize into poleis – a phenomenon which may have occurred relatively late, after the Late Geometric period (as Gounaris 1999 suggests) – they did so in ways which echoed localized patterns of cross-island and trade-route connections, producing sometimes quite high numbers of poleis in small areas (Kea, for example, had four), not all of which survived in the longer term (Reger 1997).

More individual forms of mobility included the travels of craftsmen, traders, and small groups of foreign settlers within established communities. The Homeric picture of the traveling *demiourgos*, touting his skills from household to household, is an appealing one, as is the rural smithy in Hesiod's *Works and Days* (493–4). Neither, however, is easy to find in the archaeological record, where attention rather focuses on more visible fixed installations, such as the kilns in the Potters' Quarters at Athens and at Torone,[13] or the metalworking facilities at Geometric Argos and eighth-century Oropos.[14] Installations for crafts such as pottery or metalworking, which used readily transportable raw materials, were certainly connected with settlement centers through-out the Early Iron Age, and the link grew stronger as settlement expansion from the eighth century onwards increased the local market for these products (Hasaki 2002: 285–95; C. Morgan 2003: 71–3). But this is only part of the story: sanctuaries too were important centers of (mostly seasonal) manufacture, mainly of metalwork but not only of votives.[15] They were major economic centers, with the ability to com-mand resources and craftsmen on a large scale, and were so deeply embedded in most regional economies that often no meaningful distinction can be drawn between the sacred and the secular (C. Morgan 2003: 119–20, 149–55).

Tracing the movements of individual craftsmen tends to rely on the usually highly problematic identification of individual objects as the work of immigrant or itinerant craftsmen, on the basis of style or the skills required to work certain imported mater-ials (ivory, for example). Debate has long surrounded the origins of the craftsmen who produced works such as the spectacular bronze votive shields from the Idaean Cave on Crete[16] or the five ivory female figurines from the mid-eighth-century Odos Peiraios grave 13 in Athens (Lapatin 2001: 44–5). Was it possible to learn to work new materials, or familiar materials in new ways, without the physical presence of experienced craftsmen?[17] Known workshop areas, such as an eighth-century gold-smith's shop at Eretria (Themelis 1981), reveal nothing of the ethnic origins of the craftsmen who used them. Not until the sixth century can we trace such origins via craftsmen's names. Attempts to identify graves as those of craftsmen, let alone as those of craftsmen of a certain origin, have proved even more controversial, as the case of the Tekke *tholos* at Knossos shows (Hoffman 1997: ch. 4). It seems certain that itinerant craftsmen, and specifically, itinerant specialists in handling rarer mater-ials or producing certain artifact types, operated in many parts of Greece through-out the Early Iron Age. But tracing individual cases in the archaeological record can be highly problematic.

Equally, while foreigners visited and/or lived in Greek communities, their visibil-ity largely depends on the extent to which they chose to represent their ethnicity in an archaeologically retrievable way (e.g. Hoffman 1997: ch. 3). Prominent cases include the late ninth- to early/mid-seventh-century Phoenician tripillar shrine in Temple B at Kommos, which served as a facility for travelers along the trade route which passed along the southern coast of Crete (Shaw 1998), and the distinctive Phoenician grave-stones found at Knossos and Eleutherna.[18] In other instances, hybridization, or just simple changes in the execution of customs which probably developed over time, may raise doubts about their origins and significance. The curious seventh-century urn burials at Arkades are a case in point,: while anomalous on Crete, they also show differences from their supposed North Syrian prototypes (Hoffman 1997: 165–72). The most secure reconstructions rest on the kind of combination of clues used to trace the presence of Levantine residents at Pithekoussai – graffiti, distinctive forms of ritual behavior (burials in this case), and the use in both domestic contexts and graves of particular types of artifact. Plates, for example, were rare in the Greek home, but at Pithekoussai, after their initial import in Phoenician red slip ware, they were rapidly copied.[19] Visible cases were likely the tip of the iceberg, and the decision to mark a distinctive identity itself raises questions. Many migrants may have chosen to assimilate to a host community or to express their identity in ways which left no material trace.

Patently, trade during the first centuries of the Early Iron Age trade differed in scale and perhaps also nature from that of the Late Bronze Age. Yet Greece was hardly isolated, and by the ninth century at the latest, there is plentiful evidence for rich and complex connections (especially with the east) to rival those of the Bronze Age (Jones 2000: 50–82; Crielaard 1998; Stampolidis and Karageorghis 2003). The notion of elite gift exchange has been used to explain the movement of certain (usually costly and/or antique) items treated by their recipients as luxuries (Crielaard 1998). More generally, however, identifying the origins of traders raises problems similar to those noted above – and this is all the more frustrating since traders were uniquely placed not only to recognize and supply local needs, but to make markets by identifying what might interest whom. Who but such a middleman would have known that an Athenian potter's malformed *hydria* could be transformed into a tall *krater* for the Cretan market (Papadopoulos 1998), or could persuade Euboean potters that there were customers in Tyre for plates, as well as *skyphoi*, with pendent semi-circle decoration?[20] In the later eighth and seventh century, the range of local scripts in which graffiti were written on local pots at Kommos allows us to identify what Csapo has termed "an international community of traders" (Csapo 1991; 1993). But usually our only evidence is the origin of the goods carried, and while this can provide clues as to possible carriers, it is never conclusive, as is clear from the debates surrounding the nature and extent of "Greek" trade with the Near East (to which we will return), or Euboean involvement in long distance trade to the north, east and west.[21]

Discussion of Early Iron Age trade has tended to focus on the movement of raw material (such as metals, to which we will return), or finished goods like fine decorated pottery which can be readily provenanced via style. But a particularly significant phenomenon is the use of distinctive transport amphorae, with their implications for commodity transport, organization of shipping and marketing. The earliest post-Bronze Age group so far identified comprises two very closely related types with semicircle decoration, which were probably produced somewhere in southern Macedonia, and remained in circulation for some three hundred years across a broad arc around the northern Aegean, from Lefkandi to Troy and Lesbos (Catling 1998). The coarseware transport amphorae so familiar in later centuries made their first appearance in the late eighth century, on Lesbos and in Corinth and Athens.[22] The most likely explanation for this development is a desire on the part of shippers for a standard, readily stackable shape to facilitate the loading of the maximum quantity of liquid. This in turn implies the co-existence of a much larger movement of agricultural produce (including oil and wine) in conventional containers, highlighting the importance of long-distance trade in such commodities. It is therefore interesting to note the routes along which these amphorae first appeared. In the case of Corinth, a form of proto-Corinthian A amphora developed from earlier storage jars was first found at Syracuse and especially Otranto. In the latter case it was accompanied by Corinthian fine drinking and pouring vessels which formed part of the imported drinking sets of the local elite, marking an escalation of contacts which date far back into the ninth century. In turn, it fed a taste for symposium equipment transmitted by the elite of Otranto to their Messapian peers (D'Andria 1995). The absence of these amphorae at sites *en route* to the Salento suggests direct trade with Corinth, but whether this was solely in the hands of Corinthians, let alone whether Corinthians were permanently or seasonally resident at Otranto, is less clear (Yntema 2000: 23–32).

Subsistence

When we consider the nature of Early Iron Age subsistence economies, it is now clear that the world of the small farmer, so graphically described in Hesiod's *Works and Days*, probably depicted reality in most parts of Greece throughout the Early Iron Age. Suggestions that depopulation and the collapse of palace economies fueled a resurgence of pastoralism (Snodgrass 1987: 192–209) in part reflects over-emphasis on apparent contrasts with the Linear B record, even though this reports only that small portion of the Mycenaean economy in which the palaces were directly involved (Halstead 2001; Shelmerdine 2006). Instead, the ending of upward mobilization of subsistence commodities in the command economies of the palaces had the effect of liberating local communities to focus on their own interests (Foxhall 1995: 244–5). This, rather than a complete change of strategy, may explain phenomena such as the different kill patterns evident in the herds of Early Iron Age Nichoria.[23] The eleventh to ninth centuries saw neither extensive depopulation nor a wholesale shift to specialist pastoralism (for which evidence is generally very scarce) but, in John Cherry's words, "a reversion to more localized, intensive, mixed, non-specialized farming systems in which animals served much the same functions as they had before the rise of stratified states in the Aegean" (Cherry 1988: 28). At settlements such as Volos Palaia (Iolkos) or Assiros (G. Jones 1982; 1987), there is ample evidence for the cultivation and storage of a wide range of cereals, pulses and garden crops, something echoed in the record of foodstuffs consumed during religious celebrations at Kalapodi (Kroll 1993). Storage and exchange were necessary buffers against bad years, as Hesiod describes. But it is also worth emphasizing the central importance of animal sacrifice and the shared consumption of a wide range of foodstuffs at Early Iron Age sanctuaries across the Greek world. There are Mycenaean precedents for the practice of burnt animal sacrifice at Pylos (Isaakidou et al. 2002), and ritual banqueting was, as noted, a major feature of palace life.[24] Yet the scale and central role of consumption at Early Iron Age shrines is striking, and the change in setting, from the confined context of a palace or shrine to the open air, must also have changed perceptions of the events (Hamilakis and Konsolaki 2004). At Kalapodi, the Amyklaion, Olympia and Isthmia, shared sacrifice and dining cemented social ties and enabled individuals to display their personal command of resources (Morgan 2002b). From its very beginning in Late Helladic IIIC, the festival at Kalapodi featured mass consumption of a range of foodstuffs, including wild animals and plants, and a variety of grains that led the excavator to characterize the festival as a *panspermion*, symbolizing both hunting and cultivation (Felsch 1999). In most regions of Greece, figurine dedications now focused on animals and other symbols of human activity rather than the highly abbreviated personifications of deity/worshipper current during the Late Bronze Age (French 1981) although the image of the goddess with upraised arms lingered somewhat longer on Crete (Nicholls 1970). As has already been noted, throughout the Early Iron Age, sacred and secular aspects of economic activity were inextricably intertwined, a situation which become ever more complex (and arguably more skewed) with the expansion of cult systems from the eighth century onwards.

Sanctuaries

Prior to 750, the major cult centers of the southern and central Greek mainland were open air sites without specifically religious buildings. This is not to imply that rituals were temporally or spatially unstructured. The sacrifice and dining practiced at open-air sanctuaries implied a recognized location and occasion (Morgan 1999a: ch. III.2). The ever-increasing volume of dedications (the mass of tripods at tenth- and ninth-century Olympia, for example) must have made spectacular monuments in their own right, and required some management of display and probably recycling (C. Morgan 2003: 153–4). The range of gender, age and status interests symbolized in votive offerings gradually widened through the tenth and ninth centuries and expanded markedly during the eighth, with ever greater investment differentiating rich from poor. This is particularly evident at shrines such as the Samian Heraion, where waterlogged conditions have preserved materials lost elsewhere, allowing us to see the full spectrum of dedications from the gold and ivory of the wealthy to the simplest gifts of the poor (Kyrieleis 1988; Brize 1997). At most mainland shrines the first major building activities were landscaping operations designed to manage space for assemblies and the display of votives – the mid-tenth-century terrace at Kalapodi is a case in point.[25] From Submycenaean onwards, large-scale images of deities are strikingly absent on the mainland.[26] They lingered longer on Crete, but even here, there is a gap until the three late eighth- or early seventh-century *sphyrelaton* figures from the altar of the Dreros temple (Prent 2005: 174–200; Romano 2000). Large-scale anthropomorphic imagery reappears with the spectacular eighth-century amber and ivory figures which "peopled" the *temenos* at Ephesos, although since the earliest temple here held a base for a cult statue, these probably represent worshipers or cult personnel rather than the deity (Muss 1999; 2007). In general, the rich imagery of Early Iron Age votives tends to reveal more about the interests and social personae of worshipers than deities.

Alongside these open air sanctuaries, a number of settlements have produced evidence for ritual within prominent domestic structures ("rulers' houses"), Nichoria is a much-cited case,[27] but one might also consider Aetos on Ithaka which continued long past the eighth century (Symeonoglou 2002: 51–3). These two models of cult organization were not simple alternatives, but in many regions operated in parallel. Thus it seems likely that the Nichoria elite who reinforced their status by control of the ritual activities in Units IV–1 and IV–5 also made offerings at Olympia, staking their claims to recognition in a wider forum (Morgan 1990: 65–85). In the southern and central mainland, purpose-built temples were a phenomenon of the late eighth and seventh centuries, but they are attested much earlier elsewhere. The Protogeometric Building Στ at Mende Poseidi in Macedonia is the earliest mainland candidate yet discovered (Moschonissioti 1998: 265–7), but evidence from Crete is much more plentiful (Prent 2005). Cretan settlements more commonly contained cult rooms or complexes, as those at Karphi[28] or Kephala Vasilikis (Eliopoulos 1998), and where settlements focused on old palace sites, such as Knossos or Phaistos, cult facilities sometimes exploited these ruined structures to create deliberate links to past authority (Prent 2005: 508–54). Open-air sanctuaries are known (Kato Symi for example: Lebessi 1981), but in general, cult activity seems more settlement-based than in much of the mainland.

Metallurgy, Cult, and Warfare

The development which gave its name to our period and left a particularly prominent mark is the acquisition of iron working technology in the Aegean. Following the demise of the Hittite empire, which had guarded its secrets carefully, this technology was transmitted during the eleventh century via Cyprus, where it dates back to the twelfth century, and in time allowed Greeks to transform what had previously been a sporadic and luxury import into a central element of local economies.[29] Emphasis upon sanctuaries as centers of conspicuous consumption also extends to the use of metals, since, together with military requirements, the manufacture of votives was one of the principal uses of metals in the early Greek world. Admittedly, the record is biased towards graves and sanctuaries, where recyclable metal was permanently removed from circulation (votives could be melted down, but the metal remained the property of the deity). But it seems unlikely that the picture is wholly inaccurate. There is evidence of metalworking installations attached to settlements, but care was taken to recycle where possible, and so metal finds in settlements are relatively rare. We are dependent on Homer, and especially Hesiod, for an impression of how metals could be used, and an understanding of the very large range of (often perishable) alternatives. Indeed, the extent to which metal use really penetrated into the everyday lives of all but the elite remains a matter of speculation. Unlike bronze, which demands the import of tin from many hundreds of miles beyond Greek lands, iron was readily available across Greece. And while 10% tin is required to create a bronze which rivals iron in hardness, most bronze alloys during the Late Bronze and Early Iron Ages contained a much higher proportion of copper, and were thus softer although perfectly good for jewelry or votives such as tripods (Snodgrass 1989: 29). Yet iron is far more complicated and time-consuming to work. There is a degree of exoticism and mystery in Homer's use of the verb *pharmasso* (to drug or bewitch) to describe ironworking in the context of a simile in which he likens the sound of iron quenched in cold water to the hissing of the stake as it entered the Cyclops' eye (*Odyssey* 9.391–4). The suggestion that iron use had a democratizing effect on activities from agriculture to warfare (Childe 1942: 183) therefore seems unlikely. It was hardly cheap, it had the potential to liberate bronze for ever more luxurious uses, and in so far as we can reconstruct its use in ritual contexts (despite problems of preservation), it was treated as of significant value in its own right (Haarer 2000).

The decision to divert so much metal to military purposes rested on two interconnected factors – the importance of warrior status to aristocratic masculinity, and the relationship between equipment and favored military tactics (Snodgrass 1999: ch. 2, 134–6). The former can be traced throughout our period, but since expensive equipment could be bequeathed down the generations, it is not surprising to find offensive arms more commonly offered in graves than defensive armor. Panoply graves are always exceptional whenever and wherever they occur, be it Submycenaean Tiryns, eighth-century Argos or fifth-century Corinth (Morgan 2001b: 22–4). If Alcaeus' later description is any guide (Z 34 Lobel Page), armor and weapons may rather have been displayed in the halls of the elite (a custom attested also in Persia: Herodotos 1.34.3), although inevitably, this is hard to trace archaeologically – a rare exception is the so-called "sanctuary" or *andreion* at Afrati on Crete.[30] For much of our period (at least from ca. 1100 onwards), it is clear that the mode of fighting demanded little or no armor (presumably perishable materials like leather would have sufficed), and just a light shield, a sword and either a pair of throwing spears or a bow and arrows. From the last quarter of the eighth century, however, the various elements of the hoplite panoply – the corselet, greaves, helmet, and shield (Snodgrass 1999: 48–60, 136–8) – begin slowly to appear and to be refined. Nowadays, few would subscribe to the old notion of a hoplite reform which linked equipment and tactics in a model of far-reaching social and political change (ultimately leading to the rise of tyranny: for a review, see Morgan 2001b: 20–2). More plausibly, a gradual tightening of the open warfare of earlier centuries, with a more complex mix of battlefield tactics, created a need for greater personal protection, and the resulting improvements in equipment themselves speeded a process which in time produced the classical phalanx (van Wees 2000a; 2004). Tactics aside, such evidence as we have for the causes of early warfare and military leadership emphasizes the role of local rulers in mobilizing their followers (sometimes supplemented by "loans" from friendly peers) in causes of immediate concern. Thucydides' review of the nature of early warfare (1.15), while designed to demonstrate the unusual importance of his real subject, the Peloponnesian War, emphasizes this local aspect. His sole exception, the Lelantine War (of which we otherwise know little), was singled out because it drew in wider alliances rather than for the fundamental nature of the cause or the forces involved. Localized conflicts were not necessarily trivial; there are rare instances of wholesale destruction and/or conquest, in the Argive sack of Asine, for example, or the first Messenian war.[31] But the fundamental role of aristocrats leading their dependants or followers can be traced well down into the archaic period (Morgan 2001b: 27–38). Not only was the motif of vengeance long-lived (Lendon 2000), but aristocratic self-interest was frequently wrapped up in personal defense of what could be claimed to be wider "state" interests, as the seventh- and early sixth-century history of Attica shows (Frost 1984).

Eighth-century Expansion

In any account of the Early Iron Age, the eighth century stands out as a period of transformation. At this point, we can recognize many traits familiar in the archaic world of city-states – an extensive network of sanctuaries and temples, growing towns, alphabetic writing, and overseas settlements. It is often seen as a "Greek Renaissance," although as we have come to understand the rapidly expanding archaeological record of previous centuries, the analogy with the European Renaissance becomes less precise. Instead, we find a more complex and regionally variable mixture of tradition, transformation, and innovation. Certain continuities and transformations have already been mentioned. Perhaps the most obvious changes in the archaeological record follow from the expansion of settlement both in the countryside and at population centers. Although the level of pre-eighth-century settlement in most parts of Greece has been greatly underestimated, there was undoubtedly a significant increase in evidence for rural settlement (chiefly burials), as well as expansion at principal sites, from the eighth century onwards. This was initially attributed simply to population increase (Snodgrass 1980a: 20–4), although this is unlikely to be the sole explanation and no straightforward correlation can be made between the volume of material evidence and population size. In the case of graves, it is essential to consider when and where particular categories of people were granted the rite of formal burial, as well as the nature and visibility of mortuary practices (Morris 1987). Nonetheless, in the great majority of cases, expansion at principal settlements, like Athens or Thebes, was accompanied by increased activity across ever-larger areas of countryside (Bintliff and Snodgrass 1988; Mersch 1997). Physical synoikism cannot be the main reason, despite later tradition (C. Morgan 2003: 171–6), and a number of other factors may have been in operation – residential groups may split to create temporary or permanent bases close to distant land, or to allow established principles of residential organization to be maintained. Expansion at major settlements probably demanded the ranking of available resources by distance and accessibility, and even when new settlements were created, more land would be needed (eventually drawing in marginal land) if the same strategies of exploitation were to be maintained without intensification.[32]

Population pressure and pressure on land are relative concepts. In both cases, the desire to maintain the status quo in terms of settlement density, the residential rights of individuals or families in particular areas, access to certain agricultural or pasture land, or cultivation of the same crops using the same practices, could lead to extensification before, or alongside, intensification. The movement to colonize, which in the west began with Euboean settlement at Naxos immediately followed by Corinthian at Syracuse (according to Thucydides 6.3), must therefore be understood within the wider context of movement across and beyond Greek speaking lands, be it over relatively short distances, within what was to become the territory of the state concerned (Dyme in the case of Achaia, for example: Morgan and Hall 1996: 186–9) or further, into areas such as the northern Aegean and the islands (Snodgrass 1994b). To some extent, the distinction between internal and external colonization rests on the anachronism of modern national borders. Yet there were real differences in the nature of the host populations, not only in terms of social and political organization and attitudes to material wealth, but in their identification (however poorly understood) with broader notions of Hellenism, noting especially the geographical extent of the spread of the Greek alphabet in the late eighth and seventh centuries (Johnston 1999). Neither internal expansion nor migration commonly led to the settlement of virgin territory. The responses of established settlers varied greatly. For example, the custom of making offerings at conspicuously old (usually Bronze Age) tombs is found in many parts of Greece during the eighth and seventh centuries, chiefly in Messenia, the Argolid, and Attica, but also widely elsewhere.[33] Anonymous tomb cult has been variously interpreted as asserting rights to the land of one's ancestors in the face of incomers, or establishing "ancestral" or "founder" claims in new territory.[34] Whatever the case, the desire to anchor a personal or collective past in the landscape is clear, and there is a long-recognized conceptual link between offerings to the nameless dead of the deep past, and other forms of ritual connected with community ancestors – feasting in cemeteries, for example, as at Mycenae, Asine or Naxos, or more rarely cults of named heroes like Helen and/or Menelaos in Sparta (Antonaccio 1995a: ch. 3, 199–207).

Greeks Overseas

Of all the developments considered in this chapter, permanent settlement overseas, which escalated dramatically with the beginnings of western colonization in the last decades of the eighth century, was perhaps of the greatest long-term significance. The full story of its motivation, development, and consequences belongs in later chapters. It is now clear that most of the earliest colonies attested by Thucydides were founded within native settlements which were either destroyed (in the case of Syracuse) or gradually displaced. They were also small-scale; the laying out of a *chora* and systematic town planning on any scale lay some way ahead.[35] A rather different picture emerges from the long and complex history of overseas connections to east and west through the Early Iron Age which formed the background to permanent settlement. To the west, the twelfth century was a period of intensive contact with Italy, and Apulia in particular (Jones 2000: 44–6; Fisher 1988: ch. 5). The intensity and wealth of settlement around the periphery of the former kingdom of Pylos – notably in the Patras area and the Ionian islands – created a new focus of interaction across the Ionian and southern Adriatic seas, indicated both by the movement of pottery and by Italian emulation of Aegean ceramics. The principal Apulian findspots, Roca Vecchia on the coast near Lecce, and Punto Melisso by Cape Leuca (within sight of Corfu), confirm the importance of this network (Benzi 2001; Guglielmino 1996). Thereafter, there is a hiatus in material evidence until the beginning of systematic imports (initially Corinthian) into Otranto from the ninth century onwards. Whether or not Corinthians lived at Otranto even temporarily, the Messapian identity of the settlement, as of the entire region, is clear. When Corinth did establish a colony along this route, it was rather on Corfu. As Douwe Yntema (2000) has emphasized, the problems of interpretation surrounding imported artifacts at Otranto recur in even more complex form elsewhere along the Ionian coast, and attempts to characterize "native" as opposed to "Greek" phases of particular settlements are fraught with difficulty. In the case of Incoronata, for example, it is debatable whether the quantity of Greek imports which distinguished the coastal site of Incoronata Greca from its inland neighbor, Incoronata Indigena, should be seen as reflecting the distinctive identity of its inhabitants, rather than native interest in imports which encouraged a second settlement by the coast (Yntema 2000: 11–13).

Some Greek settlements were founded anew in areas where Greek goods, and probably also travelers, had circulated for some time. Pithekoussai on the island of Ischia in the Bay of Naples is such a case. The settlement was clearly Euboean, both in archaeologically visible customs and ancient tradition, although other ethnic groups traded and probably settled there too (Ridgway 1992: 31–42, 107–20). Following Strabo (5.4.9) and Livy (8.22.5–6), Eretrians and Chalcidians were involved in the foundation, and the identity of the oikists of the related mainland colony of Cumae (Megacles of Chalcis and Hippocles of Cyme) draws in Euboea's third major settlement, Cyme, now known to be an extensive eighth-century town (Sapouna-Sakellaraki 1998). The foundation of Pithekoussai consolidated Euboean engagement with well-established networks of Phoenician, Sardinian and various Italian groups which extended out to Sardinia and up to Etruria and beyond, perhaps attracted by trade in metals and metalwork.[36] This multi-ethnic milieu, where Greeks and Phoenicians traded and probably lived in close proximity, is exactly the kind of situation in which, during the eighth century, Greeks must have learned to write their own language using an adapted Phoenician alphabet. The role of the Phoenicians as teachers was emphasized in antiquity (Herodotos 5.58.1–2), and its importance is clear from the fact that the simple presence of inscribed Phoenician objects in much earlier Greek contexts[37] had no impact. The Bay of Naples is not the only candidate for the place of transfer – Al Mina, Crete, Rhodes, or a mainland city such as Athens or the cities of Euboea have also been proposed (Coldstream 1990). But the case is greatly strengthened if a graffito on a local flask in grave 482 of the Osteria dell'Osa cemetery in Latium is accepted as Greek, as the grave can date no later than 775 (Ridgway 1996). The reading remains controversial, however, and the wider issue unresolved (see further ch. 28, below). A second long-term consequence of Euboean settlement in this area stems from its proximity to the increasingly hierarchical native societies of Campania and southern Latium (e.g. Pontecagnano: Cuozzo 2003). Following the establishment of Greek settlement on the neighboring mainland at Cumae, there are indeed similarities between the rich early seventh-century warrior and "princely" cremation burials on the acropolis and burials of the super-elite in the Euboean homeland, such as the West Gate at Eretria (Crielaard 2000, 500–3). Even stronger, however, are links with the burials of the "princely" elite of Campania and Latium noted above: the aristocracy of Cumae positioned themselves between their Euboean roots and the values of the native elites with whom they most closely interacted.

Connections with the east were even richer and more complex, with a palimpsest of shifting regional Greek, Cypriot, and Levantine interests moving and utilizing a variety of products from dining pottery to gold jewelry. In the eastern Aegean, strong connections between Crete, Cyprus, and the Levant continued through the twelfth and eleventh centuries, when contacts with the mainland Greek world were in temporary decline (Stampolidis 2003b: 48–55). By the tenth century, oriental imports were plentiful in elite burials at Lefkandi too (Stampolidis 2003b: 51; Popham 1994), and they increased in number in the following centuries. From this time, pottery of probable Euboean origin is also found in Cyprus and in very small quantities in the Levant, notably at Tyre and Ras al Bassit/Posideion (Lemos 2001). Yet when one examines find-contexts, the nature and purpose of import seems somewhat different. On Cyprus, Greek pottery (mostly Euboean and some Attic drinking vessels and other tableware) circulated as exotica in local elite-controlled exchange systems from the later tenth century until ca. 700. Together with a range of other non-Greek imports, these vessels formed part of the banqueting sets found mostly in funerary contexts and certain sanctuaries, and seem, therefore, to have answered a specific desire among the Cypriot elite to command imports from far and wide (Crielaard 1999a). In the Levant, by contrast, tenth-century imports at Tyre and Ras al Bassit were initially closed container vessels, implying the movement of commodities (perhaps fine-quality olive oil), with a full table-setting appearing somewhat later.[38] As noted, the identity of the carriers involved in this trade remains a matter of debate, especially as the late tenth century also saw the beginning of Phoenician expansion westwards which proceeded rapidly thereafter (Markoe 2000: ch. 7). The establishment of the tripillar shrine at Kommos dates to the early ninth century, the first Phoenician presence at Kition on Cyprus to the mid-ninth, and in Iberia, a phase of "precolonial" contact was followed by settlement by the end of the century (Almagro-Gorbea 2001). There is no shortage of possible carriers, and every likelihood that most routes were frequented by almost all nationalities at some point in this long period.

As in the west, the eighth century saw an increase in the volume, variety, and geographical spread of Greek imports, raising the possibility of temporary or permanent Greek settlement. Here too, the full story falls outside our period, and we can only touch upon its beginnings. Perhaps the most debated case is that of Al Mina on the river Orontes, the probable port of the neo-Hittite state of Unqi which had its capital at Tell Tainat on the Amuq plain. Prior to the foundation of Al Mina, at the very beginning of the eighth century, Greek imports (exclusively pottery) were relatively few in number and found in high-status contexts (Crielaard 1999a: 280–4). Thereafter, they increased greatly in quantity, shape, range, and origin, including, by the second half of the century, Cypriot imitations of mainland vessels too. Who controlled this flow? Did the coincidence of the foundation of the settlement and the expansion of imports represent a local re-orientation of trade, or a Greek initiative? The question of whether (and at what point) Al Mina had a permanent or seasonal Greek population remains open, and the partial publication of the site makes arguments based upon find statistics somewhat risky. It is, however, worth noting that the architecture of the early site fits local standards, and the pottery assemblage does not look much like usual Greek kitchen kit. While it seems an unlikely Greek foundation, the idea of some seasonal residence remains attractive (Luke 2003: esp. ch. 3).

City Life

In the old Greek world the foundation of new settlements and marked expansion at almost all established centers during the latter part of the eighth century in particular, raises new questions about the wider role of "cities." What social and political needs can be seen in their physical organization and the form of public building and landscaping projects undertaken? A certain amount can be learnt from town planning, even though the long-term success of major settlements (notably Athens: Parlama and Stampolidis 2000) leaves us dependent upon the vagaries of rescue excavation. It is certainly true that settlements constructed in physically constrained locations – island sites, many of which were chosen for their defensive potential[39] – tend to be more compact, with more effort expended to adapt existing buildings to changing social needs than would have been necessary had there been freedom to expand. Where land was available, as for example, at Corinth, Eretria, or Pherai, small residential groupings replicated themselves over larger areas (C. Morgan 2003: ch. 2), indicating a desire to maintain the kind of kin and/or resource-focused ties that had underpinned previous settlement before accepting any shift in scale or intensity. Where house structures are well preserved, they reveal similar provision across a wide geographical area.[40] And where access and water supply permitted, acropoleis formed a focus and often a religious center, as at Athens.[41] But whether settlement expansion involved a scalar shift in intensity or simply extension across a wider area, the result was an unprecedented need to deal with the demands of proximal residence. Thus "elite" quarters could be privileged over others,[42] water supplies were guarded carefully, and we find the beginnings of the mechanisms for community regulation which came to complement customary, oral law. Oracles were an important means of gaining divine approval for new or contentious strategies: early consultations of Delphi dealt with matters such as religious practice, military alliances and the adoption of laws, as well as western colonial ventures (Morgan 1990, 186–90), and the rather later record of Dodona shows a rich compendium of issues from inheritance to overseas travel (Parke 1967: ch. 6). From the second half of the seventh century onwards, legal inscriptions, such as those on the temple of Apollo Delphinios at Dreros on Crete (ML no. 2), used the authority of writing and divine sanction to reinforce specific provisions within what probably remained a primarily oral context (Thomas 1996; C. Morgan 2003: 76–80). Prominent among the earliest uses of writing were those, such as the marking of property and sanctuary dedications, which exploited the longevity and exoticism of the written word to publicize and prolong the significance of what had hitherto been orally-expressed understandings (Thomas 1992: 56–61).

   Public architecture and planning – especially the earliest agoras, with their implication of political debate – have long been seen as evidence for the emergence of the form of poleis familiar in subsequent centuries (Morgan and Coulton 1997: 107–9). In the old Greek world, it is clear that the formalization of, for example, agora areas was a phenomenon of the sixth century onwards, and this has drawn unfavorable comparison with "advanced" residential and public planning in certain colonies (e.g. Megara Hyblaea) which are seen as embodying political ideals in advance of their motherlands.[43] Yet this is a false comparison. Topographical constraints aside, the use of space in mainland cities – be they independent poleis, such as Corinth, or poleis within *ethne*, such as Aigion in Achaea – was not "unplanned," but was, rather, articulated by a long history of social and economic relationships (C. Morgan 2003: 48–71). It is, therefore, highly unlikely that changes in the use of space (in the areas devoted to certain activities and in the exclusivity of that association) would occur in the same way and at the same time as in new colonial foundations. More striking is the creation of new sanctuaries in both the old world and the colonies, in poleis and *ethne* alike. As the case of Corinth well illustrates, shrines such as those at Perachora, Isthmia, Solygeia and the various cult places of the city itself, could be related within physical and ritual networks which connected major centers to key points in community territory (villages, border locations, roads and passes), and which could be augmented over time as settlements grew or declined in importance and social priorities changed (Morgan 1999b: ch. III.3; Bookidis 2003). They thus provide a communal framework for thinking about territory and the place of individual settlements, social identities and interest groups within it (De Polignac 1995a). This extended to the symbolism of wealth and social persona in dedication, as noted above, especially where particular forms of offering appear in greater quantities at certain shrines within a region. In the Corinthia, for example, arms and armor tend to be offered at Isthmia, and iron spits and orientalia at Perachora (Morgan 1999b: 411). But perhaps the most obvious change, at least in the southern and central mainland, is the appearance of purpose-built temples from the late eighth century onwards, again in both independent poleis (such as Eretria) and poleis which were to form part of *ethne* (Tegea, for example, or Ano Mazaraki in the territory of Aigion: Østby 1997; Petropoulos 2002). Across the Greek world, the very varied appearance, decoration, interior arrangement, and contents of these buildings point to a complex range of motivations for their construction. Early seventh-century Isthmia seems to have served as an elaborate store for offerings and supplies for the rapidly expanding festival (Morgan 1999b: 203, 144–8), whereas thanks to its internal organization and sculptural scheme, "Temple A" at Prinias on Crete has been interpreted as an *andreion*, or meeting house, akin to a Near Eastern *marzeah* house (Carter 1997: 86–96). All were, of course, votives in their own right, even if we can only guess at the mechanisms by which materials were assembled and labor commanded for their construction.

Elites in the Eighth Century

Such changes form the context within which an escalation in other aspects of elite status expression occurred through the eighth century. In most parts of Greece, aristocratic wealth and power did not compare with that of the princes of eighth-century Campania and Cyprus, or seventh-century Etruria and Latium (Morris 1999b). Exceptions tend to occur on the margins, where rulers were in regular contact with their non-Greek neighbors. Cumae is such a case, as noted, and at Eleutherna on Crete, the beheading of a captive at the grave of an elite warrior reveals the ability to command life and death (Stampolidis 1996). This is not to imply that celebrations of individual and/or family status in the Greek world were in themselves modest. In most areas of Greece, funerary expenditure increased markedly from ca. 750 onwards, where necessary privileging external display over offerings placed in the grave, although such selectivity was often unnecessary, as the rich gold jewelery of the Dipylon graves in Athens well illustrates (Coldstream 2003: 119–37). Grave markers of many kinds became larger and more prominent. In Athens, the huge vases placed on elite graves in the city center from ca. 760 and in rural cemeteries from the 730s, bore scenes of lavish, idealized funerals, often with other forms of elite-aspirational activity such as chariot processions. For the first and almost the last time, the works of the Dipylon and Hirschfeld Painters and their successors made vase painting a public, monumental art. Much eighth-century funerary imagery has close Late Bronze Age parallels (see e.g. Skoinas 1999; Immerwahr 1990: 154–8), and while the aniconic nature of earlier Early Iron Age vase painting has often been noted, the votive record featured human and animal figurines, the placing, association, and juxtaposition of which we can only guess. What is innovative is the specific association between image, object, and context, tying known aristocrats to idealized, even heroizing, images of specific activities, on vessels used in contexts such as cemeteries (and in some regions also for symposia) where their status was publicly commemorated (Snodgrass 1980a: 65–77; 1987: ch. 5). Symbolism and iconographical conventions may have varied from region to region (Boardman 1983), but the start of a process which in time produced the complex narrative art of, for example, archaic symposium settings, was not confined to Athens. In seeking physical evidence for the place of elite families within the expanding communities of the eighth and early seventh centuries, it is important to stress the rarity of monuments of communal significance, like the early seventh-century heroon at the West Gate of Eretria (Bérard 1970), or of major architectural differentiation between private residences. The archaic poets may speak of aristocratic halls, but physical evidence for anything exceptionally lavish is extremely rare. It is in the religious sphere that real power was displayed, not only in the ability to command resources for sacrifice, dedication and construction, but in the exercise of the religious roles via which social status was expressed and legitimized anew.

Archaic poleis may, in Lin Foxhall's words, have been "little more than a stand-off between the members of the elite who ran them" (Foxhall 1997: 119). But even this implies the existence of an entity worth competing for – the form of polis which was just beginning to be visible by the end of the eighth century.

NOTES

1   Maran 2000; Papadimitriou 1998; Iakovidis and French 2003: 10, 26, *passim*.
2   Papadopoulos and Kontorli-Papadopoulou 2001; Eder 2006; Deger-Jalkotzy 2006.
3   See most recently Carlier 2006.
4   E.g. I. Morris 1987; 1992: chs. 1, 7; Whitley 1991a.
5   As proposed by Whitley 1991b; see also Whitley 1991a: chs. 6, 7.
6   Coldstream 1995, with previous bibliography.

7 McDonald et al. 1992; McDonald and Coulson 1983.
8 Especially at Lefkandi: Lemos 2006; Lemos 2002: 160–8.
9 Felsch 1999; Felsch 2001; C. Morgan 2003: 114–18.
10 Felsch et al. 1980: 47–63; Felsch et al. 1987: 5–13.
11 Gounaris 1999: 111, 112; Lemos 2002: 147, 178–80, 207–8.
12 Andros' engagement in Chalkidice is a case in point: Reger 1997: 471–3; Rhomiopoulou 1999.
13 Papadopoulos 2003: ch. 2; 1989; Hasaki 2002: 220–5.
14 Argos: Courbin 1963: 98–100; Oropos: Mazarakis Ainian 1998c: 202–3.
15 As weapons manufacture at Philia and Kalapodi shows: Risberg 1992; Kilian 1983.
16 For a review, see Hoffman 1997: 160–5.
17 For a flavor of the negative arguments, see Papadopoulos 1997a.
18 Kourou and Karetsou 1998; Stampolidis 2003a.
19 Ridgway 1992: 111–18; 1994; Coldstream 1998.
20 Coldstream and Bikai 1988: 38–40; Coldstream 1998: 304–5.
21 Ridgway 2000a provides a flavor of the arguments.
22 Whitbread 1995: 3–7, 20–2, 154–5; D'Andria 1995: 476–7, fig. 13.
23 *Contra* Snodgrass 1987: 202, citing Sloan and Duncan 1978.
24 As is well demonstrated by the various contributions to Wright 2004.
25 Felsch, Keinast, and Schuler 1980: 47–63; Felsch et al. 1987: 5–13.
26 The latest being an Late Helladic IIIC near life-size terracotta female from the Amyklaion: Demakopoulou 1982: pls. 25, 6.
27 Mazarakis Ainian 1997: 74–80, and see more generally 381–92.
28 Mazarakis Ainian 1997: 218 with bibliography.
29 Snodgrass 1980b; 1989; Sherratt 1994; Stampolidis 2003b: 41–2.
30 Hoffmann 1972: ch. 5; Viviers 1994: 244–9; cf. van Wees 1998b.
31 Frödin and Persson 1938: 15–20, 149–51, 437; Morgan 1990: 99–103.
32 C. Morgan 2003: 54–5 with bibliography.
33 The most recent discovery being at Metropolis in Thessaly: Antonaccio 1995a: ch. 2; Morgan 2003: 192.
34 For a review, see Antonaccio 1995a: 257–68.
35 DiVita 1996: 270–4, 279–80; Fischer-Hansen 1996; on Naxos, see Lentini 2001.
36 Bailo Modesti and Gastaldi 1999; Ridgway 2000a; Markoe 2000: 174–80.
37 Such as the bronze bowl in Tekke Tomb J at Knossos, ca. 900: Coldstream 1990: 146–8.
38 Coldstream and Bikai 1988; Courbin 1993.
39 E.g. Xobourgo on Tinos (Kourou 2001b), Ag. Andreas on Siphnos (Televantou 2001), the sites on Crete mentioned earlier, or mainland sites like Delphi (Coldstream 1977 (2003): ch. 12).
40 As, for example, at Delphi: Luce 2002, with comparanda.
41 Papadopoulos 2003: ch. 5; Gauss and Ruppenstein 1998.
42 As at Eretria or Kastanas in Macedonia: C. Morgan 2003: 50–2; Mazarakis Ainian 1997: 124–5.
43 Martin 1987: 155–85; Fischer-Hansen 1996; for a critical review, see Danner 1997; Varela 2003: 219–34.

CHAPTER FOUR

The Eighth-century Revolution

Ian Morris

Introduction

In the eighth century BC the communities of central Aegean Greece (see table 4.1; figure 4.1) and their colonies overseas laid the foundations of the economic, social, and cultural framework that constrained and enabled Greek achievements for the next five hundred years. Rapid population growth promoted warfare, trade, and political centralization all around the Mediterranean. In most regions, the outcome was a concentration of power in the hands of kings, but Aegean Greeks created a new form of identity, the equal male citizen, living freely within a small *polis*. This vision of the good society was intensely contested throughout the late eighth century, but by the end of the archaic period it had defeated all rival models in the central Aegean, and was spreading through other Greek communities. Only a minority of Greeks were free male citizens, but the struggles around this social category made Greek society distinctive.

Ever since a post-Mycenaean Dark Age was defined in the 1890s, archaeologists have seen the eighth century as the beginning of a revival from it. In the first archaeological synthesis of early Greek history, Starr suggested that "the age of revolution, 750–650, was the most dramatic development in all Greek history" (1961: 99), and Snodgrass's interpretation of the period as a "structural revolution" (1980a: 15–84) has shaped all subsequent scholarship. Snodgrass argued that population growth stimulated state formation, and that Greeks made sense of the changes going on around them through artistic, poetic, and religious innovations.

In the 1990s some scholars suggested that this model exaggerated the scale of collapse after 1200 BC, the depth of the Early Iron Age depression, and importance of the eighth-century revival (e.g., de Polignac 1995b; Foxhall 1995; Langdon 1997a; S. Morris 1992). They were right that the explosion of fieldwork since the 1960s had complicated the picture, syntheses (Lemos 2002) still reveal tenth-century Greece as impoverished, simple, and isolated compared to the Late Bronze or archaic ages. The critics also pointed out that Greek society continued to change throughout archaic

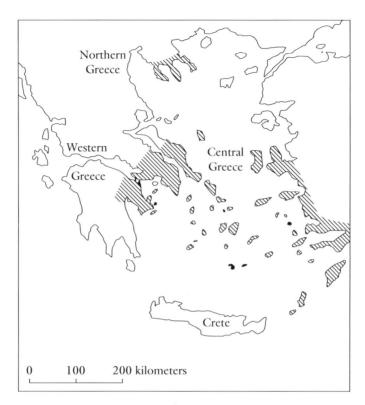

Figure 4.1 Four material culture regions in Aegean Greece

and classical times; post-eighth-century Greece inherited much from the Early Iron and even the Bronze Age; there were variations within the Greek world; and post-eighth-century Greece had much in common with other Mediterranean societies. All these assertions were true: classical Greece did not leap fully formed and unique from Zeus' head in the eighth century in an absolute break with the past. But these criticisms of the structural revolution thesis, nevertheless, missed the core point: there are few episodes in world history before the industrial revolution when a society experienced such profound change in the course of a hundred years. A quarter-century of research has modified Snodgrass's model in many ways, but its core features (demography, state formation, social conflict) must remain at the heart of any balanced discussion. The 1990s revisionists systematically avoided such economic and sociological issues. The title the editors chose for this chapter – "the eighth-century revolution" – is appropriate.

Background: The Dark Age

The destruction of the Aegean palaces around 1200 BC was part of an east-Mediterranean-wide pattern. From Egypt and the Levant to Sicily and Sardinia the

following centuries saw recession, albeit at varying scales and paces; but Greece –
and particularly the central Aegean – experienced the most severe collapse. Population, craft techniques, and social hierarchy declined in the twelfth and eleventh
century. Standards of living fell sharply; adult heights and ages at death were lower
than in Late Bronze or classical times, houses were smaller and less well built, household goods poorer, and civic amenities almost entirely absent (Morris 2007). In the
1990s many historians rejected the label "Dark Age" for the period ca. 1100–750 BC,
but life in Greece in this era was more wretched than at any other time in antiquity
(see ch. 3 above).

Economics

Demography

The population of Greece, defined as the Aegean basin and its overseas colonies,
probably doubled in the eighth century. This is, of course, a guess, and an average;
population grew more rapidly in some places, such as Euboea and Corinthia, than
in others, such as the western mainland. Snodgrass (1977a; 1980a: 18–24) once suggested from grave counts that growth reached 3–4 percent per annum in Athens
and Argos, meaning that population doubled every twenty years. I have argued that
ritual changes inflate the number of known eighth-century graves relative to those
of the Dark Age, making graves no guide to demography (Morris 1987; 1998b; cf.
Scheidel 2004a). However, settlement excavations and surface surveys do show that
population grew (Scheidel 2003; Morris in prep.). Around 1000 the largest communities (e.g., Athens, Knossos) had perhaps 1,500 people; by 700 they numbered
at least 5,000 (Morris 2006b).

Greek population growth was part of a broader Mediterranean revival. Despite the
difficulties of comparing survey data (Alcock and Cherry 2004), preliminary study
suggests that population grew everywhere from Iran to Iberia in the eighth century
(Morris in prep.). Again, the precise timing varied, and local factors such as Assyrian
deportations could have devastating consequences, but the general pattern is clear.

The reasons are less clear, although the geographical scale of the phenomenon
probably rules out cultural factors (e.g., changes in marriage patterns or birth spacing)
as the prime mover. Demographers generally argue that mortality rates drive sustained
growth and decline, and that the exogenous disease pool and climate matter more
than endogenous factors.[1] Roman evidence suggests that ancient Mediterranean populations conformed to "natural fertility regimes," in which women began bearing
children soon after menarche, and continued as rapidly as possible until death (or,
for those women who lived long enough, menopause; Scheidel 2002; 2007). In
natural fertility regimes, women's average age at death largely determines population size.

There is some evidence that climatic changes might have increased ages at death
across the Mediterranean. Between 850 and 750 there was a broad shift from a hot,
dry sub-Boreal climate regime to a cool, wet sub-Atlantic system. According to one

paleoclimatologist, "If such a disruption of the climate system were to occur today, the social, economic, and political consequences would be nothing short of catastrophic" (Bradley 1999: 15). Palynology reveals countless local variations, but the general outcome was disastrous for temperate Europe, where the main factor in mortality would have been pneumonic infections in winter and the main limitation on agriculture was cold weather and unworkably heavy bottomlands, but good for the Mediterranean, where the main killers were intestinal complaints in summer (Shaw 1996; Scheidel 2001) and the main agricultural problem was interannual variability in rainfall (Garnsey 1988). The cooler, wetter sub-Atlantic regime exacerbated problems in Europe and eased them in the Mediterranean.[2]

But whatever the cause, the consequence was more mouths to feed. Doubling population usually means more than doubling society's problems. If 90 out of every 100 people had access to a socially acceptable level of resources in 800 and the population doubled in the absence of other changes, then only 90 out of every 200 would have done so in 700. Unless my estimate that the population doubled is very wide off the mark, we must conclude that either (1) the numbers of the poor and hungry multiplied dramatically, (2) resources were redistributed, (3) new resources were brought into use, (4) output per capita increased sharply, or (5) massive social dislocations ensued – or some combination of the above.

Responses

Three broad categories of response were available: intensification, extensification, and reorganization. Intensification of agricultural production became possible because population growth made more labor available. Inputs per hectare probably increased, although the ratio of producers to consumers may have worsened. Greeks may also have applied more capital per hectare. There are no signs of major technological advances, although iron tools perhaps came into wider use; the earliest examples from a domestic context date around 700 (Mazarakis Ainian 1998a), though their scarcity may reflect excavators' priorities more than technological trends. Manuring may have increased; the "haloes" of sherds around sites in some Greek regions now seem certain to be refuse included in manure. But 75–80 percent of the sherds in Boeotian haloes are classical (Bintliff 2002: 30), and intensive manuring may have been a fifth- and fourth-century phenomenon.

Hanson suggests that irrigation and arboriculture increased in the eighth century (1995/1999b: 60–3, 77–81). Seeds from Miletus (Stika 1997) and Samos (Kucan 2000) reveal a wide range of fruits grown in the seventh century, and olive pollen increases sharply in Messenia after the Dark Age (Zangger et al. 1997: 589–94). But direct evidence for irrigation remains elusive. Similarly, despite advances in work on agricultural terracing, little is clear about the eighth century. Study of Iron Age seeds and animal bones is in its infancy, but what data there are reveal stronger geographical than diachronic variations.[3]

The second response was *extensification*, whether internal, external or long-distance. In many parts of Greece, population apparently fell so low in the Dark Age that good arable land was unoccupied in the eighth century. Surveys suggest that much population growth in the eighth and seventh centuries consisted of "internal colonization." In Attica, Dark Age settlement had focused on the coasts, and new sites appeared in inland areas in the eighth century. The "external" approach was to take land from neighbors. The classic example is, of course, Sparta. Despite revisionist criticisms (Luraghi and Alcock 2003), most historians believe that Sparta conquered Laconia in the ninth century and reduced much of the population to helotage, then tried to reduce social tensions by repeating this in Messenia, probably in the 720s. Stories of other late-eighth-century wars may mean that other groups also tried expansion, but none was so successful.

"Long-distance" extensification first occurred before 750 at Pithekoussai and in 734 in Sicily, when some Greeks relocated to fertile lands far away. Many settlements no doubt failed, and even the successful ones started out small. De Angelis (2003: 44) estimates that Megara Hyblaea increased from about 225 people in the years 725–700 to 2,275 by 525–500. Pithekoussai grew even faster, reaching 4,000 by 700 (Morris 1996a: 57). The large number of Corinthian, Euboean, and Milesian colonies must have reduced local problems, but we should not exaggerate colonization's impact on Aegean population. Scheidel (2003) estimates the total number of Aegean emigrants between 750 and 650 at around 30,000, probably just 1–2% of Aegean Greeks who lived in those years.

But colonization was not just a way to export people. The west – especially Sicily – had more arable land than the Aegean, and more reliable rainfall (De Angelis 2000). By 500 colonization more than doubled the amount of arable land owned, and vastly increased food production. Unusually large grain silos suggest that settlers at Megara Hyblaea were already producing beyond subsistence before 700. While we cannot prove that they exported grain to the Aegean, this seems very likely (De Angelis 2002).

The third possible response to demographic pressures was *reorganization*. Efficient property rights and low transaction costs can be decisive in economic growth (North 1981). We hear several stories about attempts to promote family properties in this period. There are hints of equal-sized, family-run plots in early western colonies, and Aristotle comments that Pheidon of Corinth and Philolaos at Thebes passed laws to preserve family plots, probably in the late eighth century (*Politics* 1265b13–16, 1274a31–b6). But other regimes persisted: in seventh-century Attica aristocratic *Eupatridai* apparently held most land, with the poor working it as sharecroppers, lacking secure property rights (Aristotle, *Constitution of Athens* 2.2). The most famous (and problematic) story has Lycurgus divide Laconia and Messenia equally among Spartiates, with helots working it as sharecroppers (Hodkinson 1992; 2000).

Some communities probably responded to population growth by redistributing land more equally, improving land : labor ratios and raising productivity,[4] and by improving property rights, as ideas of citizenship became stronger. This produced varied landscapes of free, property-owning farmers, generally occupying about as much land as a nuclear family could effectively work by itself (Foxhall 2003). However, the evidence is anecdotal, and we cannot construct a systematic picture. Similarly, while there is clear evidence for trade and the expansion of Greek settlement, there is as yet no way to quantify the gains from exploiting comparative advantages.

Living standards

Despite their obscurity, Greek responses to population growth were apparently effective. The evidence is coarse-grained, but as population rose, perhaps ten-fold between 900 and 300, standards of living rose even faster (Morris 2004b). Skeletal measures of age at death and stature show some decline after 1200, then steady improvement across archaic and classical times. The data remain too unrefined to distinguish eighth-century trends from later archaic ones, but output apparently kept pace with population growth. The evidence for morbidity, nutritional stress, and physical injuries is more complicated, with inter-site variations overshadowing diachronic change (Morris 2007).

Data on housing are more abundant. The size and quality of houses declined after 1100 BC, from median Mycenaean sizes around 70 m² to about 50 m² in the tenth and ninth centuries. Mean house size changed little across the eighth and seventh centuries, hovering around 45–50 m², but variation around the mean increased (table 4.1). Rich houses got richer, and poor houses poorer in the late eighth century. The only two large buildings from the Dark Age, the Lefkandi "heroon" (ca. 600 m²) and Thermon Megaron B (157 m²), seem to be special-purpose structures rather than conventional houses, but around 700 the "Great House" (H19/22/23/28/29) at Zagora on Andros probably covered 256 m², and may have had a second floor. Only one very small house, the Smyrna trench H oval house (14 m²), is known from the Dark Age, but houses under 20 m² proliferated around 700. Interestingly, most come from Naxos, Syracuse, and Megara Hyblaea in Sicily, where eighth-century houses were typically just 4 × 4 m, suggesting that life was harder for the first colonists than for Greeks who stayed in the Aegean, but there are also small houses at Smyrna and in Zagora area J (Morris 2004a). Exceptionally big or small houses became rare by the late seventh century. Sixth- and fifth-century houses clustered tightly around the mean, which rose to about 125 m² after 525 (see table 4.1).

Construction – stone foundations with mudbrick walls in most areas, but all-stone construction in the Cyclades and Crete; thatched or flat, clay roofs – changed little across Dark Age and archaic times, but the quality of workmanship declined after 1100, then revived in the late eighth century. By 700, some houses had drains, and bathtubs appeared in the seventh century for the first time since the Bronze Age. Clay roof tiles were used occasionally in the Bronze Age, and were common on temples after 675, but only became normal on houses after 525.[5]

Table 4.1 25th percentile, mean, and 75th percentile of Greek house sizes (m²), 1000–600 BC

Period	Percentile		
	25	50	75
ca. 1000–800 BC	40	50	55
ca. 800–600 BC	33	48	69

Overall economic trends

Eighth-century Greeks intensified, extensified, and reorganized production. The details are unclear, but trends in living standards show that their responses worked. In fact, the eighth century began one of the most sustained and rapid improvements in aggregate and per capita consumption known from the pre-modern world.[6]

We could conceptualize these responses in terms of a system finding a new equilibrium as exogenous climate changes shifted its demographic parameters. Technological, institutional, and legal subsystems all reacted, feeding back on each other to maintain balance, and triggering further responses in political and symbolic subsystems (cf. Renfrew 1972). Since the 1980s theories of this kind have lost favor in archaeology,[7] but a systems model does make sense of Greek history, which moved from a low-level Dark Age equilibrium with a small population, poor living standards, limited hierarchy, and limited crafts to a high-level classical equilibrium (by premodern standards).[8]

But understanding what happened in the eighth century also requires less abstract frameworks. We need to trace how individuals and groups contested the available responses, how competition limited their choices, why certain responses emerged within the Greek world, and why Greeks reacted to shared population growth differently from other Mediterranean peoples.

Social Structures

All the responses sketched above will have strained pre-existing social relationships. For example, extensification (whether internal, external, or long-distance) might create sturdy independent farmers, or support the rise of wealthy landlords, depending on who is involved and how capital is distributed; but it is unlikely simply to reproduce, on a larger scale, the relations of production that previously applied. Similarly, intensification might widen gaps between peasants with capital and those without, or might encourage kin- or village-based cooperation, again depending on how it is organized. As eighth-century Greeks scrambled to make a living, their decisions generated resistance and conflict.

State formation

A major outcome was the creation of somewhat more organized and centralized communities. I say "somewhat," because compared to most ancient states, eighth-century Greek organizations were very weak (cf. Trigger 2003: 71–275). Some historians (e.g., Berent 2000; Hansen 2002) even debate whether we should call classical *poleis* "stateless societies."

Territorially extensive political organizations probably existed before the eighth century, with local chiefs (perhaps called *basileis*) having some influence within particular villages or groups of villages, and coming together in larger confederations for defense, religion, and perhaps trade (cf. Donlan 1985). These confederations probably recognized one chief as paramount ruler. Coldstream (1983) noted that Dark Age pottery styles often coincide roughly with the borders of later *poleis*, suggesting that these organizations grew out of earlier spheres of cultural and perhaps political interaction. Archaeology cannot provide direct evidence for political institutions, but the most plausible theory is that the eighth century's challenges provided incentives for chiefs to work together more closely, forming something like primitive states; and that those chiefs who worked together successfully had advantages over neighbors who did not, forcing the neighbors either to copy them or be replaced by more organized rivals. As this process went on, offices and powers were increasingly formalized, and rudimentary states took shape.

For the purposes of this chapter I take "state" to mean "coercion-wielding organizations that are distinct from household and kinship groups and exercise clear priority in some respects over all other organizations within substantial territories. The term therefore includes city-states, empires, theocracies, and many other forms of government, but excludes tribes, lineages, forms, and churches" (Tilly 1992: 1–2). "The state" was normally one of many organizations within a given area, defined by its superiority over other organizations in wielding force. Its officials might claim to monopolize legitimate violence within a given area, but rarely actually did so. Rather, "a state is an organization with a comparative advantage in violence, extending over a geographic area whose boundaries are determined by its power to tax constituents" (North 1981: 21). It makes little sense to try to set a threshold, saying that coercion-wielding organizations of a certain size and power count as states and those that are smaller and weaker do not; rather, we should imagine a continuum of organizations and the eighth century as a time when, in most parts of Greece, political organizations got more powerful. As population grew, the tempo of state formation accelerated, but Greek states remained weak by east Mediterranean standards (Morris 1991; 1997a; 2001a).

I suggest that eighth-century chiefs found that Dark Age institutions (whatever they were) no longer worked well. Population growth seriously affected access to land, grazing, water, housing, rituals, and decision-making. Families that had flourished under the old order now struggled; others that had struggled now flourished. Chiefs who did not deal with the conflicts this created would not last long, but those who did resolve them, successfully managing larger groups of people, became much more powerful than Dark Age *basileis*. The challenges and opportunities were probably greatest in larger towns, like Knossos, Athens, and Argos, and in settlements like Corinth and Eretria, which grew from almost nothing to several thousand people in the eighth century.

It seems reasonable to imagine increasing tensions between villages as well as within them, with regional chiefs facing similar problems as village-level leaders did. No doubt many solutions were tried, but across archaic times limited political centralization was the most effective. Local chiefs/*basileis* agreed to work together, surrendering some powers they had previously exercised within their villages in return for a share in broader powers in a larger territory. It must have taken time for the boundaries of these larger territories to crystallize, as leaders addressed various urgent questions. Should Eleusis join Athens, even though Eleusinian chiefs might be junior partners, or try to go it alone? Could Argos tolerate Asine as an independent organization? De Polignac (1995a) plausibly suggests that the placement of religious sanctuaries helped formalize frontiers in the late eighth century.

As well as working out the geographical scale of their political organizations, members of chiefly councils had to negotiate what powers they wanted central institutions to have, and what they wanted to preserve at the local level. Again, conflict was inevitable. Some chiefs may have been champions of small government, wanting the central council to be an institution of the last resort, perhaps organizing major wars, ruling on disputes that could not be resolved locally, and keeping peace between the *basileis*, but doing little else. Others may have wanted officials like the *archon* or *kosmos* to be able to replace local customs with centralized rules, extract resources, and run religion. Personalities and accidents must have played a huge role in local outcomes, yet there was a slow, overall trend toward centralization.

Most likely war was the immediate catalyst. Councils of *basileis* who could not fight off more effective neighbors would be replaced by ones who could. Councils had to mobilize and train warriors, and above all, make sure that chiefs pulled together, bringing their men to fight external enemies. We might read the *Iliad* and *Odyssey* as being cautionary tales about the costs of intra-elite conflict.[9] When Agamemnon and Achilles feuded over *timê*, only the Trojans profited; when the suitors refused to act decently, Ithaca became a failed state, only saved from *stasis* by divine intervention. It is therefore not surprising that the earliest lawcodes emphasize procedure over substance (Gagarin 1986: 6–17; see also ch. 20, below). The code from Dreros (ca. 625) has the top officials – the *kosmos*, the *dêmioi*, and the Twenty of the City – swear not to cooperate with anyone who tries to be *kosmos* more than once in ten years (ML no. 2; Fornara no. 11). Refusal to surrender offices remained a problem into the sixth century (e.g., Aristotle, *Constitution of Athens* 13.2).

The precise forms of eighth-century political organizations varied. There was a general trend toward making the old regional *basileis* figureheads or annual officials elected from an aristocratic college. Sparta, as so often, was an exception, keeping two kings with very real powers, perhaps as a compromise when villages pooled their power in the ninth or eighth century. Sometimes, as in seventh-century Athens, narrow aristocracies used state institutions to protect their own interests; elsewhere, the men who controlled state offices negotiated with the mass of citizens.

But state institutions were always weak. Confiscated property, fines, voluntary contributions, and indirect taxes on markets and harbors were their main sources of revenue in archaic times: direct taxation was always considered incompatible with freedom. States were therefore poor. They organized warfare, but individuals bore the main costs (armor, training, food). Fleets barely existed before 550. Fortifications were simple. States also paid for some religious activities, and temple-building may have been their main outlay. But sales of plunder after military victories probably covered many of the costs. These generalizations applied *a fortiori* in the eighth century. Put simply, states did not do much except keep the peace, call up the army for war, and spend windfall profits on temples. Even organizing colonial ventures may have been largely in private hands.

Egalitarianism

In addition to resistance from aristocrats eager to preserve their own powers, state officials also faced resistance from below. The strength of male egalitarianism and communal solidarity in the face of would-be rulers were, in comparative terms, the most unusual and most important features of archaic society. By 500, in some *poleis* they produced *dêmokratia*, opening decision-making to mass male participation.

The immediate cause of the shift in political power toward the poor in the late sixth century (Robinson 1997) was new ideas about egalitarianism, but late-archaic developments built on the eighth-century revolution, which redefined ideas of community and equality that had grown up since the eleventh century. Explaining this – the heart of the eighth-century revolution – requires a long-term approach, encompassing the whole Greek world, and combining archaeological and textual data.

After a chaotic period in the twelfth and eleventh centuries, a new ritual system formed in the central Aegean by 1000. It drew a line within the community. The funerals of people of property, well-off peasants as well as chiefs, produced distinctive burials with high archaeological visibility (Morris 1987), and the worship of the gods largely, though not entirely, went on inside chiefs' houses, physically limiting the number of people who could take part (Mazarakis Ainian 1997). Poorer Greeks, excluded from both these arenas, were rendered archaeologically almost invisible.

But having divided the community into two groups, Dark Age rituals denied strong distinctions within the upper group. Burials, cult, and housing were all simple and homogeneous. The broad Dark Age elite effaced conflict, division, and difference within its own ranks. Its rituals also made sense of the post-Mycenaean world of poverty, isolation, and decline, drawing sharp lines between present and past, and the local context and the broader world (Morris 2000: 208–38).

The expansion of Mediterranean trade around 900 challenged this ritual system, and it broke down completely after 750, as population growth and connectivity soared. New rituals – more open, competitive, and varied – flourished. We see them at Corinth as early as 775, then at Athens, Argos, and Eretria by 750. The evidence is poorer elsewhere in central Greece, but elements of the new ritual package are nonetheless widely apparent by 700. Large cemeteries open to the whole community appeared, at first with great variations in burial forms, grave goods, and monuments. Simultaneously, open-air sanctuaries proliferated, with millions of dedications, ranging from household pottery to precious metals. As noted above, people built the first really big houses, and larger numbers of really small ones. The new rituals recognized a broader community than before, and made room for difference and competition.[10]

This redefinition of community was the core of the eighth-century revolution. The old elite/non-elite boundary started dissolving in the central Aegean. We cannot prove that population growth caused this massive ritual upheaval, but given the responses to demographic pressure and the forces of state formation described above, the connection seems likely. The earliest literature implies conflicts between mass and elite and within the elites. There is no way to link texts directly to artifacts, but I would like to describe one possible set of connections, which, I believe, accounts for all the available evidence.

Population growth caused redistributions of power all around the Mediterranean in the eighth century (generally, see Ruby 1999). In Italy, burials suggest that the first strong chiefs emerged, and in Sardinia the Early Iron Age lords reached the peak of their wealth and power. In Sicily, southern France and eastern Spain, developments were slower, but there is also good evidence for increasingly centralized wealth and political power between 800 and 500.[11] In the eastern Mediterranean, where texts provide a fuller picture, Egypt and Assyria saw local institutions flourish at the expense of central courts in the mid-eighth century. In Assyria this phase, known as "the Interval" (783–744), ended with Tiglath-Pileser III's coup and transformation of royal power, and in Egypt the Nubian 25th Dynasty also built stronger central institutions. In Anatolia, the Phrygian and Lydian kingdoms became major forces in the eighth century.[12]

Only in the Aegean, it seems, did the eighth century *not* produce more powerful kings. There, local chiefs pooled their resources to form oligarchic colleges, rotating through limited-term offices. By 650, any man who would be king was marginalized as a *tyrannos*, an illegitimate usurper. The most important questions to ask about the eighth century are how and why the central Aegean moved toward male citizenship rather than kingship. I see four relevant variables: history, economics, war, and religion.

History

By 750, there was a quarter-millennium-old tradition of homogeneous Dark Age elites, denying internal differences and competition in their rituals. Dark Age regional *basileis* claiming the right to command lesser local rulers must have been *primi inter pares*, with limited powers. By the eighth century this legacy of elite homogeneity, as old to eighth-century Greeks as the Enlightenment legacy is to us, may have been a serious ideological barrier for men trying to centralize power in their own hands.

Economics

In archaic Greece, there were no very rich men. Herodotus was impressed that the Athenian Cleinias (Alcibiades' father) paid for a trireme from his own pocket in 480 BC, but also says that in the same year a Lydian named Pythios offered Xerxes 2,000 talents of silver and 3,993,000 gold darics (8.17; 7.28). The richest eighth-century Greeks may simply have lacked the wherewithal to set themselves above rivals who wanted to keep them in check. Possibly there were extremely rich men in the ninth and eighth centuries whose estates were broken up in the seventh and sixth centuries; Homer has Eumaeus say that "not even twenty men put together have such great wealth" as Odysseus (*Od.* 14.98–9). But the wealth he describes – 59 flocks of cows, sheep, goats, and pigs, plus a treasure room guarded by an old lady (*Od.* 2.337–47; 14.96–104) – would not have impressed Lydians or Phrygians, let alone Assyrians or Egyptians. If some Dark Age aristocrats really did stand out for their wealth, we would need to explain why none of them (except, perhaps, the one buried under the Lefkandi apsidal building) left any signs of it.

War

If a handful of warriors dominated the battlefield, they might be able to centralize power. Great heroes certainly swept all before them in the *Iliad*, though Achilles' skills weakened, not concentrated, political power. Further, it seems as if Homer told stories about how he thought great heroes *ought* to act, set against a contemporary reality of mass infantry armies (van Wees 1997; 2004). Certainly in the seventh and sixth centuries there was no scope for super-warriors to slice their way through citizen armies, and this had probably been true for several centuries previously.

Religion

One of the strongest contrasts between archaic Greece and the Near East was the importance of divine kingship and priestly castes in the latter and their almost total absence in the Aegean. West Asian kings regularly claimed special access to the gods, supported by powerful temple institutions, and Egyptian kings claimed to *be* gods. Religion may have been an important source of social power in the Bronze Age Aegean, but not in archaic times. Mazarakis Ainian (1997) argues that Dark Age chiefs conducted religious ceremonies in their homes and appealed to divine authority. The earliest texts claim that good *basileis* receive wisdom and protection from the gods (Hesiod, *Theogony* 79–93; cf. *Odyssey* 8.166–77), and Martin (1984) shows that these ideas probably go back to an older hexameter advice-poetry tradition. We should probably assume that Dark Age *basileis* claimed privileged access to the gods, and that many Greeks accepted this. The separation of secular and divine power that Mazarakis Ainian traces between 750 and 700 was one of the most important sociological developments in Greek history.

We cannot assign primacy to history, economics, war, or religion: all four factors turned together in a tight circle, multiplying each other. They raised barriers to would-be great men who tried to exploit the new possibilities of the eighth century for their own ends. A few men succeeded, becoming the archaic tyrants so reviled in the literary tradition, but it seems important that as early as Solon and Theognis, *topoi* about tyrants insisted that they appealed to the mass of citizens for support against a corrupt aristocracy (McGlew 1993).

I suggest that as the Dark Age aristocracy fragmented in the eighth century, producing the fluidity and competition we see in the archaeological record, appeals to the poor (exemplified by the assembly debate in *Odyssey* 2) became increasingly important. Champions of old visions of an undifferentiated elite reached out across the barriers between elite and non-elite, to preserve the principle that no one aristocrat should dominate the others. The fact that kingship did not take hold suggests that, by and large, they succeeded. But the price they paid to defeat would-be kings was the collapse of the old elite/non-elite boundary. Increasingly, the old elite conceded that the whole male community now belonged to a relatively undifferentiated group. The old elite homogeneity was generalized to the entire resident male population, creating a new category of identity, the citizen (*politês*), and a new definition of community (*polis*).

The late-eighth-century struggles transformed older notions about class, gender, ethnicity, the past, the east, and the gods into two broadly opposed ideologies that I have called "middling" and "elitist" (Morris 2000: 155–91). Ancient authors do not self-identify in this way; the middling/elitist opposition is a model that simplifies a more complex and unstable reality. But this is the point of models (Morris 2000: 159–61). The simple middling/elitist contrast makes sense of a range of phenomena, from the poems themselves to coinage (Kurke 1999), burials, house design, and cult practices (Morris 1998a).

The core of the middling ideology was the idea that all local men were more or less the same, and that all others – foreigners, women, slaves – were utterly different. The only legitimate authority came from within the local male community. Appeals to ties with gods, eastern monarchs, and ancient heroes were worthless. Elitists claimed precisely the opposite: their divine, oriental, and heroic connections set them above the rabble, and they alone should rule.

The middling poets were rich men, singing for other rich men. They were not proto-democrats. Throughout their poetry, they insisted that they should rule, but should do so as particularly wise representatives of the moderate citizen community. The first verbal expression of the middling philosophy comes in Hesiod's *Works and Days*, at the beginning of Greek literary production, around 700, and the archaeological evidence for the redefinition of community makes it seem likely that these attitudes took shape over the previous generation or two, in the late eighth century. The elitist vision, I suggest, formed in opposition to middling ideologies in the same period, and the variability of the late-eighth-century archaeological record reflects the use of material culture to express competing visions of the good society.[13]

The issues had to be worked out separately in each of the formative *poleis*, and no two followed exactly the same path. On the whole, central Aegean communities embraced the middling ideology by 700. A stable symbolic system developed in the seventh century, featuring poor, homogeneous graves in large cemeteries. Warrior burials disappeared. Sanctuaries became the main context for spending, chiefly on elaborate communal temples. People dedicated very large numbers of poor offerings. Rich metal offerings continued until about 650, but then declined. Elaborate orientalizing motifs were tamed. Houses slowly grew larger, and their diversity declined, until by 600 nearly all were multi-room rectilinear structures around central courtyards (Morris 1998a: 13–31).

But this, like the middling ideology itself, is a model simplifying a more complex reality. At Athens, trends were reversed around 700, and distinctly old-fashioned rituals once again divided the community in the seventh century. In Ionia, some of the Cyclades, and Boeotia, the full archaic ritual package only appeared around 550, by which time Athens had returned to the general central Aegean pattern.[14] In the western colonies there were planned settlements at Naxos, Syracuse, and Megara Hyblaea before 700, but few communities had the resources to build major temples for another hundred years. The large eighth-century cemetery at Pithekoussai (Buchner and Ridgway 1993) is quite like contemporary central Aegean graveyards, but few eighth-century burials are known from other sites; and in archaic and classical times, Sicilian cemeteries were more varied than Aegean ones (Jackman 2005).

Greeks outside the central Aegean and its colonies shared in some, but not all, of these developments. Cretans and western mainlanders built temples like Aegean Greeks, and westerners may have pioneered the new religious practices (but see ch. 14, below). Western mainland settlements and cemeteries remained small until the sixth century, and are poorly known; Sparta, which responded to the eighth century so distinctively, has produced almost no archaic remains other than its temples, although the recent Laconia survey (Cavanagh et al. 1996; 2002) may change that. Cretans also opened up their cemeteries like Aegean Greeks in the late eighth century, but mortuary variability increased on Crete throughout the seventh century, with warrior burials remaining popular. Warrior burials and mounds were also popular in northern and western Greece. Only at the end of the sixth century, when the elitist ideology collapsed, did regional patterns converge (Morris 1998a: 36–68; Whitley 2001: 231–55). In the fifth century, broadly similar rhythms operated in material culture all over the Greek world except for Crete, which we are only now beginning to understand (Erickson forthcoming).

Culture

There are hints in the texts that the conflicts of the eighth century were sometimes settled by violence, but the main arena of debate was probably cultural. The period saw an explosion of cultural innovation. Everything from mythology to house design was turned upside down. Archaeological sites give an impression of feverish energy. Eighth-century settlements have much thicker deposits than Dark Age ones, reflecting a frenzied level of building, demolition, and rebuilding; and they simply have *more* material culture.

Art historians regularly speak of the late eighth century as the start of an orientalizing period, when the Greeks, drawn into a wider Mediterranean world as population and trade grew, saw and adopted Near Eastern designs. This is reasonable, but the most significant development was the Aegean Greeks' redeployment of Near Eastern techniques to respond to the unique social issues of the conflicts between middling and elitist ideologies.

The most obvious example is the Greek alphabet. Greeks had known of Near Eastern scripts since at least 900, but only developed their own writing, based on west Semitic consonantal scripts, around 750. The adapter improved the script's ability to represent vowels, but the remarkable thing about the earliest Greek inscriptions is how many of them are poetic (Powell 1991: 119–86). This usually means one or two lines (mostly hexameters) scratched on pots, but since Albert Lord's pioneering work (Lord 1953), most Homerists have believed that around 700 BC someone took down by dictation the 28,000 lines of the *Iliad* and *Odyssey*, the 2,000 lines of the *Theogony* and *Works and Days*, plus countless lines of now-lost poems (Janko 1998). There are competing theories, imagining a drawn-out process of fixation without texts (e.g., Nagy 1996a: 65–112), which raise interesting questions but seem less plausible.

There is little evidence for commercial writing before the sixth century and none at all for scribal bureaucracies of Near Eastern types[15] to compare with the poetic inscriptions and the likelihood of major dictated poems. Powell (1991; 2002) has argued that the main impetus for the creation of the alphabet was to fix in writing accounts of the past, at a time when the relationship between present and past became acutely important (cf. Morris 2000: 261–7; 2001b: 81–2). The earliest poetry over-whelmingly concerns the heroic age and theogonies.

The same concern with thinking through relationships between the present and the heroic past may lie behind the explosion of figured art in the late eighth century. Greek vase painters had occasionally shown humans and animals across the Dark Age, but around 800 Corinthians and Argives adopted animal friezes, probably inspired by Eastern examples, and around 750 Athenians pioneered the use of human figures (Hurwit 1985: 71–124; Snodgrass 1987: 132–69). Everything about these scenes remains controversial, but Snodgrass has made a good case that the scenes were generically "heroizing" (Snodgrass 1980a: 65–77; 1998). Just as an adapter developed Near Eastern scripts so that particular poetic visions of the heroic past could be preserved, painters did the same with Near Eastern artistic techniques, constantly using the heroic past to think about the present. Powell suggests that Near Eastern art also stimulated the development of Greek mythology, as an attempt to make sense of the unfamiliar images now entering the Aegean (2002: 146–87).

Much in Greek myth can be traced back to Near Eastern prototypes (S. Morris 1992; West 1997), but it is hard to know whether the shared elements developed in tandem in the Bronze Age, or were Iron Age imports to the Aegean, like writing and representational art. Herodotus' stories (1.46–58; 2.54–57) that Croesus of Lydia consulted Greek oracles and that Egyptians claimed that some Greek oracles had Egyptian founders, via Phoenician intermediaries, suggest that East Mediterranean peoples inserted Greece into their own theogonies, just as Greeks inserted Italians and Sicilians into their own mythical genealogies.[16] Herodotus accepted Near Eastern and Egyptian origins for several Greek divinities, just as Elymians and Romans some-times accepted Greek stories about their origins.[17]

Greeks also started copying Near Eastern monumental sculpture in the late eighth century and Egyptian in the late seventh, but did not have the sort of palaces and grand mansions where such statues were commonly displayed in the East. Late-eighth-century Cretans displayed statues in cemeteries, but after 700 this practice declined, except in Attica, where tomb monuments seem to have been an important part of attempts to preserve unusual social distinctions (D'Onofrio 1982; 1988). Funerary sculpture seems to have been thought inconsistent with middling attitudes; sanctu-aries were the only places where such displays were acceptable.

The way eighth- and seventh-century Greek patrons and artists took Near Eastern forms and used them in different contexts may have a lot to do with the innovation and energy of archaic Greek art. Operating outside the often-rigid institutional frame-works of Near Eastern and Egyptian palaces, Greek artists were free to experiment, and indeed had to experiment, to make these adopted media speak to their concerns. Greek craftsmen then took their hybridized styles to the west Mediterranean. In the eighth century, only small amounts of Greek material reached westerners. In Sicily, southern Italy and Sardinia natives always used these artifacts within traditional rituals,[18] just as Greeks had adapted Near Eastern media to their own needs, and only in the sixth century did Greek material culture have a serious impact on local ways of life.

Eighth-century Greece in Comparative Perspective

Since the 1990s there has been a major shift toward Mediterranean-scale history, expressed most forcefully in Horden and Purcell's *The Corrupting Sea* (2000). When Snodgrass developed his structural revolution model, it seemed reasonable to treat Greece largely on its own terms, but that is no longer the case (see ch. 2, above). This broadening of perspectives was one of the major accomplishments of 1990s scholarship. In this chapter, I have argued that the motors of change in eighth-century Greece – demography, perhaps climate, competition, centralization – affected the whole Mediterranean, but the Greeks' responses to them – particularly the creation of egalitarian male citizenship and the set of cultural conflicts around it – were unique to the Aegean and its colonies.

But although 1970s discussions of eighth-century Greece now seem to lack a Mediterranean context, Snodgrass (1977a) had in fact looked toward a much wider context, linking eighth-century Greece to archaeological debates on state formation in other parts of the world. Non-classical archaeologists only rarely take Iron Age Greece into consideration, but two aspects of the Greek case seem important for current arguments. The first is archaic Greece's peculiarity. Generalizing models trade off explanatory power against specificity, so we should not expect them to describe any particular case exactly; but archaic Greece's basic social structures seem incompatible with most models of state formation (I. Morris 1997a; Trigger 2003: 142–3). Since the 1990s comparative archaeologists have developed alternatives to neo-evolutionary models, particularly the "dual-processual" model, recognizing the possibility of relatively unhierarchical, "corporate" social structures like Greece (Blanton et al. 1996: esp. 2, 7) as well as more individualistic "network" systems. The rapid improvement in living standards and growth of markets in archaic and classical Greece also challenges much conventional thought in archaeology (see Smith 2004).

Secondly, eighth-century Greece is not just a problematic example of a worldwide phenomenon of state formation; it is also one of the best-documented cases of the more specific process of the regeneration of complex society after collapse. Building on 1980s interest in the collapse of complex societies, regeneration is now emerging as a major research topic.[19] "Collapse" and "regeneration" are varied phenomena, making systematic comparisons difficult. But if we take Childe's (1950) famous ten criteria of civilization (urban centers, craft production, taxation, monuments, non-productive elites, writing and numeracy, practical sciences, art, long-distance trade, craft specialization) as our starting point, eighth-century Greece is one of the clearest cases of regeneration after collapse (Morris 2006a).

Conclusion

The eighth century was a turning point in Mediterranean history. The Greeks were caught up in larger processes of climate change, population growth, expanding trade, and political centralization. In another essay I have called this "Mediterraneanization," a speeding-up of connectivity that increased competition, creating new winners and losers (Morris 2003).

One of the main advances in classical scholarship in the past twenty years has been the movement toward seeing Greece in its Mediterranean context, but a comparative approach in fact highlights the peculiarities of the Greeks as well as the ways they belonged to a larger system. Demography and Mediterraneanization drove state formation, but central Aegean Greeks uniquely tempered this process with increasing male egalitarianism. The middling ideology obstructed the development of state powers and derailed kingship as a viable institution. In the conflicts between middling and elitist ways of seeing the world Greeks developed unusual ideas about the gods, the past, class, gender, and ethnicity. These established the parameters of archaic and classical Greek culture, providing the whole reason why we continue to study the Greeks today.

NOTES

1 E.g., Galloway 1986; 1988; Reher and Osona 2000.
2 Bouzek (1997) and Kristiansen (1998: 28–31, 408–10) both stress the inverse relationship between demographic patterns in Iron Age Europe and the Mediterranean, and link it to climate change.
3 E.g., Klippel and Snyder 1993; Legouilloux 2000; Snyder and Klippel 2000.
4 See Link 1991 for seventh- and sixth-century examples; cf. van Wees 1999a; 1999b.
5 Darcque and Treuil 1990; Lang 1996; Mazarakis Ainian 1997; Morris 2004a; 2007.
6 Goldstone 2002; Morris 2004b; Scheidel 2004a.
7 Hodder 1986: 18–33; Shanks and Tilley 1987: 31–60.
8 Saller (2002) suggests that per capita consumption peaked around 1.4 times subsistence in the western Roman Empire; I have suggested similar figures for classical Greece (Morris 2004b).
9 Among many other things; for my own views, see Morris 2001b; cf. Raaflaub 1998.
10 De Polignac 1995a; D'Onofrio 1993; 1995; Houby Nielsen 1992; 1995; 1996; Mazarakis Ainian 1997; C. Morgan 1990; 2003; Osborne 1996a: 70–136; Snodgrass 1980a; Whitley 1991a; 1996; 2001: 77–265.
11 Italy: Bietti Sestieri 1997. Sardinia: Webster 1996. Sicily: Albanese Procelli 2003. France: Dietler 1997; Py 1993. Spain: Ruiz and Molinos 1997.
12 For a good overview, see Kuhrt 1995: 473–646.
13 Morris 1998a: 4–13; 2000: 190–1; cf. Kistler 2004.
14 Morris 1987; 1998a: 31–6; 2000: 287–305.
15 Cf. Postgate 2001 on the variety of such bureaucracies.
16 E.g., Herodotus 1.94, 166–67 (Etruscans), 7.169–71 (Iapygians); Thucydides 6.2 (Elymians).
17 Hdt. 1.131; 2.43–64; Harrison 2000: 208–22.
18 Sicily: Albanese Procelli 2003: 131–6. Southern Italy: Burgers 1998: 183–6. Sardinia: van Dommelen 1998: 104–12.
19 Schwartz and Nichols 2006; cf. Tainter 1988; Yoffee and Cowgill 1988.

CHAPTER FIVE

The World of Homer and Hesiod

Christoph Ulf

Preliminary Remarks

Any attempt to describe the world of Homer and Hesiod must start with their texts.[1] Homer's *Iliad* and *Odyssey* and Hesiod's *Theogony* and *Works and Days* are classified as epics and generally dated to 750–650 in histories of Greek literature.[2] The epic is conventionally regarded as a genre which conveys to its audience already existing traditions without much intervention by the poet. It is commonly held that these texts therefore reflect the societies of the periods in which the traditions brought together in the epics originated, i.e., that epics are a more or less consciously created "amalgam" of different periods, down to the time they were written down. However, the ever-continuing discussion of the nature of these texts and the historical realities they contain indicates that things cannot be so simple.[3] The debate, which has become almost impossible to survey, cannot be covered in detail here, but we will briefly set out our views on the main points.

Central to every historical analysis is the answer to the question of how Homer's and Hesiod's texts were created. For a long time, the dominant view was that they are part of a long tradition of "oral poetry," which survived because it was recorded in writing. Although oral poetry changed constantly, it, nevertheless, preserved core elements which reached back to Mycenaean times at least. Texts were produced, it was thought, through "composition in performance," in which bards reproduced existing texts, which however they would modify – to an extent unwittingly – with every recital. Homer and Hesiod were to be seen as such oral poets, with the qualification that their texts differed from older, unpreserved versions in scale and quality. Proponents of this view continue to argue about when the extant written versions were produced – according to the most extreme idea it did not happen until the classical age.[4]

This kind of reduction of the bard to an anonymous figure was opposed by advocates of so-called "neoanalysis" who emphasized the independent creative contribution of the poet to the epic text (Kullmann 1984). The poet would have made use of fixed oral or oral-derived texts consciously to create a new work of his own. Where neoanalysis already markedly reduces the significance of orality, "narratology" is only marginally interested in the possible oral pre-history of the texts. Narratologists analyze the written epic texts by means of literary methods, and shift to the "oralists" the burden of proof that the epics' oral origins make this inappropriate (De Jong 1995; Blaise 1996).

These three views on the origin and thus the character of the epics are by no means based merely upon linguistic or philological arguments. They are also linked to underlying assumptions about the nature of the historical reality in which the texts originated. For example, those who take "oral poetry" as their starting point also postulate that the epic emerged in a "heroic age" characterized by a heroic-aristocratic competitive ethos. In their oral performances, the poets conveyed values central to this "heroic age" for the aristocracy's pleasure and instruction. Why the traditions of this world should have endured throughout turbulent historical epochs into the Archaic Age is rarely explicitly explained. Implictly, however, it is assumed that a "Greek" people existed from at least the second millennium BCE, and that the existence of a people entails the existence of (national) oral traditions which preserve their core despite all historical change.

Neoanalysis and narratology, by contrast, in their different ways allow the poet to comment upon well-known, distinct oral or written texts which are not subject to continuous change. This liberates the poets from both the almost compulsory association with a "heroic age" and from dependence upon a supposed national tradition. This makes it possible for them to adopt a non-aristocratic perspective as well, and even to criticize existing conditions by means of commenting on existing texts. Since they postulate that fixed motifs and texts formed the basis for the creation of new works, neoanalysis and narratology tend to assume that the poets' world knew and used writing, and also to allow for the possibility of external influences.

When it comes to deciding in favor of one of these positions with a view to historical evaluation of Homer's and Hesiod's works, one is in danger of falling into circular argument. In the absence of other evidence, one is forced to deduce from the epics themselves the historical conditions under which they were created. An important step in breaking out of this circle is to examine the central modern concepts usually used in describing the "historical" worlds of the texts, because these concepts are not mere translations of key terms preserved in the texts, but they place the world of the texts into overarching historical frames of reference. This step can here be illustrated, by way of example, only with the concept of "a people" or "nation" (*Volk*), as used especially in German-language scholarship. Without "a people," of course, an oral "national" tradition (*Volkstradition*) could not have existed. The simple question is: what is a people, and where does it come from?

Contrary to what is often assumed, even today, "peoples" are not early but very late forms of human community. The belief that the "nation" is a primordial entity arose from Romantic thought as it developed in the late eighteenth century. Against this, more recent scholarship has been able to show – particularly by means of an analysis of the peoples of the so-called European migrations – that "nations" emerge only under certain demographic conditions and with the aid of fictive stories of origin so that, as a distinct political unit, they may advance their claims to power more successfully. But even when they had come into existence in this manner, nations were not – and still are not – fixed entities defined by straightforward (ethnic and/or cultural) criteria. To describe the complex processes which lead to the emergence of a nation, the term "ethnogenesis" has been coined (Pohl and Reimitz 1998; Gillett 2002). The notion of a highly characteristic "national tradition" which reaches far back into the past thus no longer has any foundation, nor is there any reason left to think that the different forms of human society are not comparable to one another.

As with the term "people," which plays such a crucial role in some traditional interpretations, we must examine carefully whether other key terms such as "state," "king," "aristocracy," "office" and "justice" are applicable to the period in which Homer's and Hesiod's texts were created.[5] Archaeological research has shown that the inhabitants of the Balkans and the coast of Anatolia lived in small settlements, distinct but with an essentially simple structure. Before the start of the seventh century, demographic developments in many places produce small towns.[6] We can infer that the works of Homer and Hesiod were composed in a world where "states" were only just beginning to form. Accordingly, a historical and literary evaluation of these texts should not merely apply concepts derived from the world of the state but take into account the entire spectrum of concepts and models developed by anthroplogy (cf. Sahlins 1972; Johnson and Earle 1987), philology and historical theory. A convincing interpretation will choose from this array with the aid of a model which accommodates as many as possible – ideally all – of the elements which make up the world of the epics. Since this chapter analyzes texts, it can only discover literary worlds.[7] These, however, can then be compared with the worlds "reconstructed" by archaeology and its models, and with information derived from Near Eastern sources (Morris 2000; chs. 3, 4, above). It is only this comparison which enables us to draw conclusions about the historicity of the societies portrayed in the epics.

Homer's World

The two epics attributed to Homer, the *Iliad* and the *Odyssey*, recount completely different events. They, nevertheless, share important basic characteristics which are of fundamental significance for the reconstruction of Homer's world and its place in history. In the following brief summaries of the poems, we shall focus upon these aspects alone.

The Iliad: *societies at war*

The *Iliad* is one of many stories about the Trojan War, but only deals with a period of 51 days in the tenth year of the siege of Troy, not including the conquest of Troy itself. Sections of the long text are linked to one another by means of flashbacks and flash-forwards. The story incorporates other tales familiar to its audience, such as the story of Meleager or old Nestor's reminiscences of his youth. These comment on the main story line and clearly signal the intentions of the text.

Both combatants are comprised of many different groups with distinct names, listed in the "Catalogue of Ships" and the "Catalogue of Trojans." The besiegers are collectively called "Achaeans" or "Danaeans," and submit – voluntarily – to the supreme command of Agamemnon. The defenders of Troy, called "Trojans" or "Dardanians," consist of the inhabitants of the city of Troy and allies, won over by Priam by means of gifts. Since he himself is too old, Hector, his eldest son, must lead the army. The events of war, covering only four days, are depicted at length, but they are not the central theme of the story.

The central theme is: how should a leader behave in order to ensure the well-being of the community as a whole (*demos*)? This theme shapes the events on both the Achaeans' and the Trojans' side. Amongst the Achaeans, the focus is on the conflict between Agamemnon and Achilles, usually seen as a mere private problem, and Achilles' resulting wrath (*menis*). A parallel treatment of the theme is found at the level of the gods. According to a belief which pervades the Homeric epics, the gods largely but not exclusively determine the fate of man, and they take sides not only with Trojans or Achaeans but also with individuals. This may embroil them in quarrels with one another, and if this does not lead to open fighting among them it is only thanks to Zeus, who is represented in both *Iliad* and *Odyssey* as the authority to whom the other gods must ultimately bow down.

The quarrel between Agamemnon and Achilles arises over a plague sent by Apollo to afflict the Achaean army because Agamemnon has seized the daughter of his priest. Agamemnon initially refused to recognize the problem, and then tried to solve it by returning the woman, Chryseis, to her father, but by way of compensation taking a slave woman, Briseis, whom the Achaeans had given to Achilles after the same campaign. Achilles accuses Agamemnon of being cowardly and greedy. He withdraws from battle, and no one is able to stop him

> You dog-eyed, fawn-hearted drunk! You have never had the courage to arm yourself for battle alongside the men (*laoi*) or to join the best of the Achaeans in an ambush. To you, that seems like certain death. Of course it is much easier to rob men of their gifts across the great Achaean army, whenever someone speaks out against you, you *basileus* who devours his people, because you rule over nobodies!
>
> (1.224–31; tr. van Wees)

Agamemnon cannot refute Achilles' accusations in the following battles. The result is twofold danger for the Achaeans: they are threatened by an internal conflict which destroys the community (*polemos epidemios*) and by annihilation at the hands of the Trojans. In this situation, Agamemnon is forced to admit to his weaknesses and to try to compensate for his behavior towards Achilles by material and ideal means. He must also acknowledge the partial superiority of other leaders, who signal that they no longer accept Agamemnon as paramount leader. Agamemnon gives way in every respect, and in parallel the Achaeans gain the upper hand. The funeral games (*athla*) for Patroclus, organized by Achilles for all the Achaeans, are symbolic of the internal unity recovered under the new conditions (Ulf 2004).

The Trojan counterpart of this internal conflict arises as a result of the opportunity created, at the very start of the action, to end the war by means of a treaty and single

combat between the main adversaries, Menelaos and Paris (3.82–115). Paris however flees combat with the help of Aphrodite, and the Trojans proceed to break the
armistice agreement. This not only makes continuation of battle between Achaeans
and Trojans inevitable, but also gives rise to debate amongst the Trojans concerning the correct behavior of a leader (*basileus*). Paris is forced to listen to Hector's
and Helen's vehement accusations of cowardice:

HECTOR: "Wretched Paris, you are the best man only in appearance, you woman-
          crazy seducer! If only you had never been born and died unmarried.
          I would really prefer that, and it would really be much better than for
          you to be such a disgrace and an object of contempt to everyone."

                                                                    (3.39–42)

HELEN: "Have you returned from battle? If only you had fallen on the spot,
          brought low by a strong man who was once my husband. You used
          to boast that your strength and fists and spear were superior to those
          of warlike Menelaus."

                                                        (3.428–31; tr. van Wees)

In doing so, he has endangered Troy. Later, Hector himself is also criticized for
having lost sight of the actual goal, to protect the people and the city. He overestimates his own abilities, which ultimately leads him to his death in combat against
Achilles, who thereupon defiles his corpse. It is at this point that the two strands of
internal events amongst the Achaeans and the Trojans converge. Achilles is forced
once more to contain his inhuman wrath, this time towards the defeated foe. With
the approval of Zeus, old Priam turns to Achilles with the plea that he return Hector's
corpse for burial. In a touching dialogue, Achilles accepts Priam's gifts and grants
his request. Priam returns to Troy and Hector can be buried. Thus, the *Iliad* not
merely keeps well away from the end of the tale of Troy as the audience knew it
from other accounts, ending with the conquest and destruction of the city, but virtually contradicts this implacable conclusion.

   With this ending, the reign of Zeus over the Olympian gods, which the epics
deliberately reinforce and systematize by means of genealogical connections, also
proves meaningful. For not only has Zeus been able to get the other gods to agree
to this conclusion, but even earlier, when all the gods intervened in battle between
Trojans and Achaeans (the "Battle of the Gods") he had been able to prevent an
open confrontation among them.

The Odyssey: *a society in danger*

The Odyssey offers no mere chronological description of Odysseus' return to Ithaca
but artfully elaborately interweaves two main story lines: the different stages of Odysseus'
dangerous homeward voyage, and the events and situation in Ithaca. In the last stage
of his journey, among the Phaeacians, Odysseus himself describes how close to home
after only a few adventures, he and his comrades ruined their chances of an immediate

homecoming. Odysseus' men (*hetairoi*) believed that he did not want to give them a share of the valuable gifts of the wind god Aeolus. So they opened the bag into which Aeolos had bound the winds that could endanger their journey. The winds escaped and drove the ships completely off course (10.34–50). Thus, in the *Odyssey* as in the *Iliad*, a smooth solution of problems is prevented by erroneous behavior – on the part of both Odysseus and his companions. Odysseus alone can escape the dangers of the mythical world into which they stray as a result.

He is shipwrecked and then rescued by the Phaeacians. The island society of the Phaeacians, located between the mythical and real worlds, represents a sort of counter-image to the situation in Ithaca. Ithaca, the story's destination, has not had a paramount *basileus* since Odysseus' departure for Troy. A new one can only be designated by Penelope, Odysseus' widow, marrying one of her young suitors. But the way in which these suitors court the widow violates almost all accepted norms. Not only do they destroy the economic basis of Odysseus' household with their daily feasts at his house, but they even attempt to murder Telemachus, Odysseus' son and potential heir. When Odysseus returns to this world, he recovers his position by force, fighting first against the suitors and then against their relatives. As in the *Iliad*, the story is resolved with the help of the gods: Athena is instructed by Zeus to prevent a civil war and force the Ithacans to recognize Odysseus as their paramount *basileus*.

In view of the plot lines of the *Iliad* and the *Odyssey* described above, these two epics can be read as complementary texts which deal with a common theme from different perspectives and with an eye on different societies, and which are guided by a common message: a conflict (*neikos*) which cannot be resolved "privately"[8] must not carry on by means of violence. Internal cohesion and a leader's duty to keep the public good in mind must not be endangered by egoism and *hubris*. These clear, complementary prescriptions are hardly conceivable without the existence of fierce conflict and a discussion of the qualities required of leaders in the reality of the poet's times. But before we can pursue this thought any further, we must first examine the chief elements of which the societies described in the poems are constructed.

Subsistence economy and trade

A simple agricultural economy prevails in Homer, despite the presence of a few luxury goods, and in contrast to the economy of the Mycenaean age or of Near Eastern empires. Agriculture is the almost exclusive source of subsistence. Farmland was owned by households (*oikoi*). In the *Iliad* and the *Odyssey* only the households of the elite are described. They are located near or within settlements and have the best land at their disposal. The plots of land are large enough to be divisible amongst heirs (*Il* 14.208–10), or for pieces to be given away to slaves. Besides the owner's family, the *oikos* includes male and female slaves, servants, and hired laborers (*thetes*), who either own no land at all or too little to subsist on; and in addition free men who have come as refugees and are dependent upon support (*therapontes*). The men energetically cultivate the land, above all to produce grain; they also work in vineyards and orchards. The women are responsible for all tasks related to housekeeping. Livestock breeding plays a special role in that cattle serve as a status symbol and – presumably for this very reason – as a measure of value. Members of the elite pride themselves on personally being able to perform all tasks particulary well.

Apart from land owned by *oikoi*, not only common land but also uncultivated and unallocated land of lesser quality seems to have been available. This might explain the conspicuous absence of any hint of conflict over land between rich and poor.

Besides the people living in the *oikos*, we find in the epic world professional traveling specialists, such as the seer, healer, carpenter or singer, who are important enough to be called *demiourgoi*, "workers for the *demos*," i.e. the whole community (*Od.* 17.382–6). There is no direct mention of permanent local markets or trade, but both may have existed. Long-distance trade is dominated by foreigners, notably the Phoenicians, but the elite also takes part in, and derives special advantage from, it. Because it is directed toward profit (*kerdos*) and may be connected with piracy, foreign trade is regarded with ambivalence.[9]

> Strangers, who are you? Why are you sailing the wet lanes of the sea? Is it on some business? Or are you traveling at random across the sea, as raiders do – men who wander and put their lives at risk as they bring harm upon foreigners?
>
> (3.71–4; tr. van Wees)

The principle of reciprocity

Reciprocity is a principle which is essential to the functioning of Homeric societies as a whole, not only of their elites. According to this principle, the exchange of goods and services simultaneously creates social and economic obligations between individuals or groups, which are to be discharged immediately or at some later point. The services of a leader can be recompensed by the community as a whole (*demos*) with a plot of land (*temenos*) or a special gift (*geras*). Leaders (*gerontes*) convened in council drink wine (*gerousios oinos*) placed at their disposal by the *demos* in exchange for their advice, and some of them receive a special piece of meat by the paramount leader in return for special services. Reciprocity is also involved in the relationships between guest-friends in their exchange of gifts, as well as the relationship that is forged between Priam and Achilles by means of the goods which redeem Hector's corpse.[10]

The typology of reciprocity established by Marshall Sahlins can help clarify what the effects of reciprocity may be (Sahlins 1972; van Wees 1998c). With regard to the relationship between giver and receiver, we can distinguish "generalized," "balanced," and "negative" reciprocity. "Balanced reciprocity" is normally to be found in gifts between guest-friends. "Generalized reciprocity" presupposes the generosity of the giver, but puts the receiver into a position of dependency for as long as he is not in a position to return similar gifts. This is Agamemnon's intention when he offers Achilles goods and services in exceptional quantity and quality to win him back as ally. This is also what happens when the Phaeacians fill Odysseus' ship with countless gifts for his return to Ithaca. "Negative reciprocity" means that goods and services are demanded and received, but the expected compensation does not follow, or is not adequate.

If one wishes to avoid the obligations created by reciprocity, one can only refuse to accept the goods and services offered. This is why Achilles does not accept the gifts offered by Agamemnon. Yet the individual is not free to accept or refuse at will the gifts offered. If one is in a weak social position, one cannot turn down such an offer. Thus, for example, Agamemnon must accept the prize which he receives from Achilles at Patroclus' funeral games, but in doing so falls, as he himself recognizes, into dependence on Achilles. Because this game of acceptance and refusal is closely connected to raising and lowering social status, it also entails intense competition within the Homeric elite, as in all societies of this kind.[11]

In this competition it is an advantage always to have goods (*keimelia, ktemata*) at one's disposal. For this reason, as many valuable commodities as possible are hoarded at home. Such goods are textiles produced by the women in the *oikos*, animals raised on the farm, and metal artwork or raw metals (gold, iron) obtained through foreign trade. *Basileis* who present gifts can demand compensation from the *demos*, but probably only when they do so as representatives of the community, rather than as individuals. On the whole, however, we must remember that the number of such luxury goods is small, despite the efforts to depict a rich and splendid world; generally only between one and three luxury items are exchanged or given away at a time.

Social status

Homeric societies are patriarchal in the sense that the power of decision-making (*kratos*) lies with the men.[12] This is not to say that the female sex or its sphere of action was devalued. For on the one hand this male power does not imply the use of force, and on the other hand the (elite) woman has the same authority in her domain as the man has in his. Men are explicitly assigned the areas of (public) speech and warfare, women domestic work and the supervision of free and unfree maid-servants (*Il.* 6.488–93; *Od.* 1.346–59; 21.344–53). In exceptional circumstances, the boundary between the gender spheres is crossed. In the face of the threat to Troy, Andromache advises her husband Hector on how best to defend the city. Penelope must – and can – manage the whole *oikos* as long as her husband is away and her son is not yet an adult. Similar situations are found in the mythical fantasy world where Calypso and Circe live. But the influence of women in the "real" world can also exceed their normal sphere. The mothers of Nestor and Andomache are both explicitly designated as leaders (*basileia*), and Arete, wife to the paramount leader of the Phaeacians, sets out the parameters for decision-making by the men.

The position of an individual within Homeric societies depends upon two factors: his socio-economic and socio-political esteem. Economic success is considered essential proof of a person's quality. This makes it necessary to display one's prosperity and to consume it in the company of others. However, Achilles' accusation that Agamemnon is greedy, for instance, or the negative view of the long-distance trader, suggest that it matters *how* one achieves economic success. One's own work as well as the successful organization of work are valued positively, while success achieved at the cost of others is valued negatively. Only free men and women are included in this spectrum of evaluations. The foreigner, who often arrives as a refugee to become a "resident alien" (*metanastes*), like the free hired laborer (*thes*) and the occasional begger (*ptochos*) or slave (*dmos*), cannot attain the same status as full members of society. And yet, there are differences in the treatment of these lower-ranking persons. The *thetes* are subject to their master's moods and can even be cheated out of their rightful pay, like the gods Poseidon and Apollo, when they built the walls of Troy in the guise of hired laborers (*Il.* 21.441–52; *Od.* 11.489–91). By comparison, the small number of female and male slaves, who are all part of an *oikos*, are definitely better off (Raaflaub 1997b: 638–9).

The degree of prestige a person has within society is what lies behind the term *time*. As a sociopolitical term, it covers the link between standing and prestige. The extremes of the range of *time* are marked as "the best" (*aristos*) or "good" (*agathos*), and "bad" (*kakos*). A person's ranking within this range is not fixed once and for all, but can vary according to context. *Basilees* may count fundamentally as *agathos* or *aristos*, and also enjoy a special relationship to Zeus, but they are differentiated according to their prestige. For example, at the beginning of the *Iliad*, Agamemnon has more of the quality of a leader (*basileuteros*) than Achilles. On the other hand, Achilles is *aristos* in combat which Agamemnon is not. Agamemnon – and he is not alone – can even lose his position as *basileus* if he does not take the well-being of the *demos* into consideration, for the *demos*, or the *laos*, is the point of reference of every evaluation. If he would no longer fulfill his role as "shepherd of the people," his *time* in public opinion (*pheme*) would be much reduced (Ulf 1990b: 41–8).

Gradations of *time* can be in evidence in all areas of human endeavor, and are encountered in the organization in age groups, from child to old man, which pervades all of society (Ulf 1990b: 51–83). The child is foolish (*nepios*), youths and young adults (*kouros, koure*) have not yet developed their full intellectual abilities. From the age of about 30, male adults are designated *gerontes* and have more prestige due to the greater qualities ascribed to them. But each age group is further differentiated according to individual ability, which can result in a younger person receiving more *time* than an older one. Concretely, Diomedes, for instance, who in age is still a *kouros*, is nevertheless reckoned among the *gerontes*, as wise Nestor insists:

> Son of Tydeus, you are exceedingly strong in war, and in council you are the best of all your contemporaries. Not a single Greek will scoff at your speech or contradict you, yet you have not brought the debate to an end. You are after all a young man, and might be my youngest son . . . But come, I, who can claim to be older than you, shall have the final word and run through everything; no one will disrespect my speech, not even lord Agamemnon.
>
> (*Il.* 9.53–62; tr. van Wees)

Descent from a "good" elite family does endow a child with the important advantages of this milieu, but the complaint about the bad offspring of good parents indicates that they are not exempt from the competition for *time* (*Od.* 2.276–7; Ulf 1990b: 194–7). A person has to prove himself above all in warfare, in council, and in the mediation of conflicts. A "strong warrior" who is able "to think simultaneously ahead and back" (*Il.* 1.343), has the best chance of improving his personal prestige and thereby his social status.

Socio-political units

The establishment of a person's status by means of socio-economic and socio-political criteria takes place within what we may call a political framework, delimited by the concept of *time*. Only a full member of the community (*polites*) can have *time*. This does not include either the refugee (*phygas*) who as resident alien (*metanastes*) enjoys no *time*, nor the slave, because Zeus has deprived him of half of the qualities of a free person (*arete*).[13]

Just as the epics depict diverse societies, their political units do not look uniform. In the *Iliad*'s Catalogue of Ships and Catalogue of Trojans, the contingents engaged in the war are portrayed as *ethne*; they appear in the *Odyssey* as e.g. Ithacans, Thesprotians or Phoenicians. At the same time, numerous cities, such as Troy or the town of the Phaeacians, but also the Achaean camp, exhibit the characteristics of a *polis* (city-state).[14] An *ethnos* can encompass an entire region with several, differently structured settlements. The specific characteristic of the *polis* is its openly visible communal institutions: it has a public square, streets, temples and a city wall; and political arrangements are more easily set in motion within it. But both of these forms of political community have *basileis* and a council of *gerontes*. These, and the public assembly (*agora*), operate according to fixed rules, such as the summoning by heralds, or a particular order of speakers.[15]

What the political unit is expected to achieve can be deduced from the goal pursued by all deliberations. It is not a matter of imposing one's own view, but rather of presenting a persuasive argument which promotes the common good; in other words, which above all avoids internal conflict. How important a point this is can be inferred from the plots of the *Iliad* and the *Odyssey* outlined earlier, and from the safeguarding of this duty by divine supervision: Zeus and Themis ("the norm") watch over good order in the political community. Decisions in the *agora* are not made exclusively by the elite, but on the principle described earlier by which individual abilities and economic success (must) coincide, the elite are not only granted political leadership but also dominate the formation of public opinion.[16]

The unambiguous obligation to make political decisions collectively is formulated in the face of latent tensions within the political units. These tensions arise out of the parallel existence of an overarching political framework and of smaller units, which each create identity and demand loyalty. For instance, the age groups of the *gerontes* and the *kouroi*, i.e. of older and younger adults, can have virtually opposite views on important issues. This is the case e.g. in the *agora* in which the Achaeans publicly discuss the correct method of warfare against the Trojans (*Il.* 9.50–68). Here it becomes evident that a youthful leader such as Diomedes can represent a danger for the internal peace of a community when he is supported by his peers. We also hear of kinship groups, rarely and vaguely, but not only at weddings or when a murdered man is to be avenged. Some Arcadians, for instance, are characterized as group by their residence near the tomb of Aipytos, perhaps a collective ancestor (*Il.* 2.603–4), and Hector gathers the Trojan leaders in a council at the tomb of Ilos, eponymous founder of Ilion, in the plain outside the city (*Il.* 10.414–15; cf. 11.166–7).

This recalls Nestor's advice that the Achaean army be subdivided by *phratries* (brotherhoods) and *phylai* (sections) (*Il.* 2.362–3). The impression that kinship groups are meant here is confirmed by the fact that Hector originally planned to fend off the Achaeans without Trojan soldiers (*laoi*) or allies (*epikouroi*), but "with his brothers-in-law and own brothers" (*Il.* 5.472–4). In Ithaca, another group which may be based on kinship makes an appearance in connection with Eupeithes, father of the suitor Antinoos. This group took part in a raid against Thesprotians in the face of protests from the Ithacans and is therefore attacked by the *demos* (*Od.* 16.424–29). The relationship between these kinship groups and the *oikoi* cannot be clearly determined. In any case, the *oikoi* represent a third kind of group which as a focus of identity and loyalty can come into conflict with the interests of the *demos*.

The tensions within societies also result from the near-impossibility of classifying the actions of any individual as unambiguously private. This is because the community as a whole (*demos*) not only dominates as the point of reference for the allocation of *time*, but also takes action in its own right. It awards gifts of honor from booty, or else land. It contributes to processes of arbitration (*Il.* 18.497–508), can proclaim a penalty (*thoe*) when the collective interest is harmed, and in its gatherings (*agora*) creates the space for political decision-making, in which it also participates (*Il.* 3.205–24; 7.345–78). Whoever harms the common interest for selfish reasons, even if only by influencing a speaker in assembly by means of a gifts, loses *time* (*Il.* 9,123–4; *Od.* 2,184–6).[17]

The tensions thus inherent in the political units seem to be reproduced in the classification of the individual as one of four distinct types of relationship between *hetairoi* (companions), which are characterized by different forms of reciprocity (cf. Ulf 1990b: 127–38). Parallel membership in different groups could produce conflicts of loyalty, all the more so since groups of *hetairoi* were not confined to the elite.[18]

The relationship between political communities

Homer's political communities are not self-contained, completely autonomous entities, any more than his *oikoi* are. We can tell this not only from the common practice of (long-distance) trade, but also from the fact that e.g. Troy or the Phaeacians' *polis* are newly-founded cities (*Il.* 20.215–18; *Od.* 6.3–10). The ambivalent experience[19] of trade contact and foundation of settlements abroad finds expression in, on the one hand, the ethnographical interest shown by the epics and Zeus' role as protector of the stranger, and, on the other hand, the image of the violent foreign *basileus* who has people's noses and ears cut off and genitals ripped out.[20]

The relationship between political units is often not peaceful, and the reasons for this are not uniform. In his "lying tales," Odysseus tells of how hunger and poverty drive people into foreign parts (*Od.* 14.214–15; Ulf 1990b: 180–2), but other stories reveal a more complex picture. It seems that single members of the community, especially young men, hope to improve their social status as well as profit economically. This seems to be the case for the series of plundering expeditions between the Pylians and the Eleans (*Il.* 11.668–762), Achilles' raids around Troy (*Il.* 6.414–28; 20.188–94), and Odysseus' alleged adventures in Egypt (*Od.* 14.222–34), but also for Paris' behavior in Sparta which leads to the Trojan War. All this is not far removed from piracy, represented by e.g. the Taphians, regarded as kidnappers (*Od.* 15.427–49).

The different kinds of aggression – from small-scale raid to organized warfare between political communities – may well have also been linked to different forms of warfare. The great Trojan War is no more than a conflict between political units, blown up to panhellenic proportions. These exaggerated dimensions presumably also explain why forms of warfare corresponding to different occasions for military conflict were all projected into the Trojan War. The very variable equipment of the Achaean contingents might suggest this.[21]

The political unit as a whole is also put at risk even when only one section wages war. Although the danger of retribution becomes smaller as the victims are more remote, but if claims for compensation are made, they are addressed to the political unit as a whole. Hence political units try to find solutions beyond guest-friendship, which links only individuals. The Trojan War gives an exemplary demonstration of possible procedures. Menelaos and Odysseus were sent to Troy as envoys authorized to clarify how the conflict could be resolved. Although no solution was reached in this way, the attempt was made to prevent a war by concluding an actual treaty. The alliances of different political units which constitute the Trojans and Achaeans are also based upon such formal agreements.[22] Such alliances were apparently not confined to military situations (*Od.* 16.424 – 9), but details are unclear.

Hesiod's World

In our description of Hesiod's epics, we will limit ourselves to emphasizing those aspects that are relevant to a reconstruction of Hesiod's world, and those that have bearing upon the comparison of Homer's and Hesiod's worlds.

Theogony: *the order of Zeus*

The *Theogony* justifies the reign of Zeus and the Olympian gods. Hesiod does not, however, represent "the" Greek religion, but rather one – and the only surviving – attempt of many to systematize the multitude of religious ideas amongst the Greeks. The particular world of Hesiod's *Theogony* also contains important Near Eastern elements, which cannot be given their due here.[23]

In the beginning, the Void (*chaos*), Earth, and Eros emerged. Gaia, the Earth, brought forth the sky and the sea. She then gave birth to a generation of gods named Titans, fathered by Uranus. Uranus hates his children because they are a threat to his power. So he "would not suffer them to come up into the light" (157). Only the youngest child, Cronus, dares to resist. With his mother Gaia's help, he cuts off his father's genitals and himself takes power amongst the gods. But he knew "from Gaia and starry Uranus that, for all his strength, he was doomed, by the plan of great Zeus, to be subjected by his own son" (459–65). With this reference to Zeus, who has not even been born at this time, Hesiod shows that Zeus is the endpoint of his entire genealogy of the gods. Cronus then devours all the children he begot with his sister Rhea, but Rhea outwits him by giving him a stone wrapped in swaddling-bands instead of Zeus. Thus Zeus can grow up and rescue his siblings. With the youngest of the Olympian gods, Zeus, a new era begins. He forgoes the violence upon which Uranus and Cronus had relied. He liberates the Cyclopes and in return they give him the necessary instruments of power: thunder and lightning. Supported by the Hundred-Handers, gods whom he has also set free, Zeus is able to defeat the Titans, who rebel against the new regime, in a ten-year battle that shatters heaven and earth. At the request of the gods, Zeus establishes his new order, in which he assigns all deities a status (*time*) corresponding to their qualities. Furthermore, he binds the most important goddesses to himself by marriage, and in this way begets further deities – such as, by Themis, Eunomia (good order), Dike (justice) und Eirene (peace), to whom fall important tasks in the new divine order (901–3). A wealth of further deities and stories are tied to this chronological and substantive framework, to fulfill the aim of systematization but also to reinforce the basic idea.

The order of Zeus is not completely new but composed of elements which had been positively valued in connection with the earlier generations of gods, including the gift given in the appropriate measure and manner; the recognition of achievements which are to the benefit of all; the farsighted thinking which can see even through tricks; quick and good decisions based on such thinking; the consideration of good advice; the exercise of one's power to the advantage of all, which means that it should not be used in excess. Zeus completely embodies all of these characteristics, while other deities do so partially (e.g. Gaia, Nereus and the Nereids, Oceanus and the Oceanids, Hecate, the Horae, the Moirae, the Charites and the Muses). The contrasting negative characteristics and behaviors have already been mentioned: violent use of power to one's own advantage; resort to trickery to damage others; hate. It is significant that the evaluation of the *basileus* Zeus is not unquestionably established from the outset, since he too has means of power which could be used in negative ways. Only when it becomes clear that he puts these to wise use, does the latent positive evaluation prevail.

Works and Days: *daily life stripped of heroism*

At the center of this work is an inheritance conflict (30–9, 395–9) to which the individual sections relate. Only those who assume an oral composition and tradition of the text doubt this autobiographical element, and the historicity of the poet Hesiod with it (Nagy 1996b). Hesiod accuses his brother Perses of pursuing a wrong form of ambition (*eris*). Because he wrongly disagreed with the division of their joint inheritance, Perses had turned to the *basilees*. Against this background, an image is created which transfers into daily life the kind of dispute settlement portrayed in the ideal world of the description of the shield of Achilles in the *Iliad* (18.497–508). Although Perses gave the *basileis* not only his entire inheritance, but also property stolen from Hesiod, they had not judged in his favor. "For we had already divided our estate, and you had seized and carried off much else besides, paying great honor to the *basileis* who eat gifts (*dorophagoi*) who were keen to settle this dispute" (37–9).

The reason for Perses' failure was that he had pretended to be wealthy. And now he came to him to ask for support. "Do your work, foolish Perses, as ordained for mankind by the gods" (397–8).

To give his admonitions a foundation, Hesiod ties this conflict and his advice to the rules of a more comprehensive divine and human order. To this end he describes parts of the divine world insofar as necessary for his argument. Two aspects of the human order are represented. Against the power of the *basilees*, wrongly understood and selfishly used in his own world, he places the behavior and rules which can overcome the problems of life to the advantage of all. In this way, Hesiod lends events and situations in the little town of Askra in Boeotia the character of a generally valid paradigm. He speaks to Perses and the audience of a just human order safeguarded by Zeus, of the *basilees'* tasks, of the significance of material wealth to social recognition (*time*) and of the importance of working for it.

Unlike the Homeric epics, in Hesiod's works it is not the world of the wealthy elite which dominates, but rather the perspective of the owner of an *oikos* of middling size who works on his land himself, together with a few servants, slaves, and animals (but cf. ch. 23). Such an *oikos*, ideally dependent on no one, can only be successful when the principle of maximum thrift is added to one's own intensive work, to prudent planning and to the observance of all economic and social rules (423–36, 538–46). Kinsmen are less important in this than neighbors, whose support may be needed in daily work. Hesiod's thoughts are not concerned with survival, but are to be understood as instructions for attaining prosperity.[24] For prosperity is a prerequisite for social recognition. The path taken by Perses in seeking a legal decision by the *basilees* in the *agora* without this prerequisite is therefore foolish, since "capability and renown attend upon wealth" (312).

Hesiod presents these rules of conduct not merely to assert himself in his own world, but also intends with their aid to lead foolish people (*nepioi*) like Perses and the *basilees* back onto the straight and narrow. By means of four narrative strands, Hesiod aims to make them see the error of their ways and at the same time to present rules to guide the community. The sketch of how Hesiod is robbed by his brother, and how Perses in turn is robbed by the *basilees*, is immediately followed by the story of Prometheus, who tried to dupe Zeus. Zeus proved his superiority by giving Pandora to Prometheus' brother Epimetheus ("after-thinker"). The famous story which ensues about the succession of human types (*genos*) ends with the Iron Age, in which Hesiod's contemporaries must live lives of toil and suffering. For them, Hesiod prophesies the mutual destruction of cities because they respect violent man who has given in to *hybris* (188–92). This general diagnosis is followed by the fable of the hawk and the nightingale which warns the *basilees* that only a fool fights stronger opponents (201–11). What this means is explained by the depiction of the "unjust" and the "just" *polis*.

> For those who indulge in bad aggression (*hybris*) and evil deeds Zeus, far-seeing son of Cronus, ordains punishment, and often an entire city shares the fate of one bad man who commits crimes and performs reckless deeds.
>
> (237–40)

But, Hesiod warns, "a fool suffers first and understands later" (218). To avoid this, one should organize one's community in accordance with the rules of *dike*, justice. Then, the city will flourish and be protected by Zeus, his chosen guardians, and Dike herself (225–37).

This diagnosis leads Hesiod to exhort Perses to change his behavior. He should be guided by justice and turn away from violence (*bie*). Wealth obtained by violence and deception rather than persuasion will be short-lived (320–5). Hesiod offers detailed instructions for the practical application of this exhortation in the main part of the epic, in more than 500 verses, often derived from rustic proverbs.[25] Work precedes prosperity. Only property acquired by a year's labor with one's own hands will last. Farmwork dominates but Hesiod briefly also mentions seafaring and trade, albeit primarily their risks (617–93).

Just like the *Iliad* and *Odyssey*, the *Theogony* and *Works and Days* can be seen as complementary texts whose structure derives from a clear poetic intention.[26] The proems of both works leave no doubt that Zeus is the sole point of reference for the order represented by Dike and presented by Hesiod as the right one. To show this order in the right light, Hesiod makes complex use of the antithesis "positive-negative." At the beginning of *Works and Days*, we find two types of conflict (*eris*) defined in these terms. In *Theogony*, only one type of *eris* is mentioned, but, unlike the older gods, Zeus has chosen the right kind. We encounter the same contrast in the two paths humans can choose to take. Perses should choose the more demanding path and desist from deceit and violence. Zeus does the same in the *Theogony*. In contrast to the older gods, he refrains from violence so long as he is not forced to use it. This opposition is continued in the juxtaposition of the "just" and the "unjust" *polis*. The good *basilees* in the just *polis* behave like Zeus in *Theogony* and the ideal *basileus* in the *Odyssey* (*Od.* 19.109–14). The bad *polis* ends in ruin because *dike* is not respected and the *basilees* rely on *hybris*, deception, and violence instead.

With the story of Prometheus and Pandora, told in both texts, Hesiod creates a link between his two works, and here too the opposition "good-bad" is fundamental. Because of Prometheus' deception of Zeus, which should have brought advantages, mankind suffers misery in the form of Pandora ("all gifts"). This woman, called "a beautiful evil" (*Th.* 585. *kalon kakon*) has only one jar (*pithos*) – not two, like Zeus in the *Iliad* (24.527–30) – which contains only the negative gifts. It is part of Zeus' deception that her name suggests that she will bring all. But Pandora seems to be only half. For there are some indications that this woman, created as a punishment by Zeus, does not represent womankind *per se*, as is generally assumed, but only embodies the "more feminine" kind of woman (*genos gynaikon thelyteraon*, *Th.* 590–1), of which Hesiod says in *Works and Days* (372–4) that they confuse a man's mind – just as Hera, here negatively characterized, does to Zeus in the *Iliad* (14.214–21). Hesiod contrasts this type with the hard-working, sensible woman (*WD* 694–704), represented in the divine world of the *Theogony* by female figures such as Gaia or Hecate.[27]

Thus *Theogony* and *Works and Days* have the same goal: the establishment of an order based upon justice (*dike*). Hesiod reinforces his exhortation to uphold its rules to the benefit of all by pointing to divine sanctions. Those who drag Dike away not only make the *demos* grumble (*WD* 219: *rhothos*), but they are also threatened by

Zeus' punishment. This message is proclaimed by both Hesiod and Homer with a claim to truth that is guaranteed by their having been made singers by the Muses and Apollo.

The World beyond Homer's and Hesiod's Texts

The differences between Homer and Hesiod are unmistakable. In Hesiod's world, the elite is not the center of attention. Hesiod, Perses and the *basilees* are part of a highly concrete political unit. A problem affecting this group of people is the point of departure for an analysis of the shortcomings and fundamental problems of everyday life. However, Hesiod does not see any way of fundamentally changing the conditions of life. He puts his faith much more heavily than Homer in the power of Dike rather than in participation in public life in the *agora*.[28] Perhaps this distance from the community is related to the fact that Hesiod, being the son of an immigrant, was not wholly integrated into Ascran society. This in turn could explain why he regards kinship as less important than neighborly assistance, with which the Homeric epics are also familiar (*Il.* 5.488–90; *Od.* 9.48–50).

The Homeric epics examine in a more fundamental way a wider world of societies which are not the same but similar, from the point of view of two exceptional situations, which makes them seem more "political" than Hesiod's works. Only at first glance, however, do the Homeric epics appear to focus upon the elite, because the elite is always related to the community.[29] The *Iliad* and the *Odyssey* seem to want to draw attention above all to the means by which internal social hierarchies should be organized. The *basilees* must do justice to their privileged position in thought and action to maintain their standing. This conception is not entirely alien to Hesiod either. It finds drastic expression in a passage where people who pursue their self-interest with brute force are compared to animals (*WD* 275–9). This is also how Achilles is characterized when he defiles Hector's corpse in breach of all norms (*Il.* 23.344–54; 24.39–54).

Neither the problematic concept of the "nation" briefly noted at the outset nor the kind of differences sketched above entitle us to attribute the differences between Homer and Hesiod to an evolutionary development of "the Greeks." The basic economic, social and political structures of the societies portrayed by the two authors largely coincide: agriculture prevails; trade only occurs on a relatively small scale; the elite sets itself apart from the community through wealth and behavior; *basilees, agora,* and the problem of conflict settlement feature in both. Nor can the differences between Homer and Hesiod be explained by their different social backgrounds, as this would presuppose the assumption erroneously deduced from Homeric epics that the historical world of Homer and Hesiod was characterized by an elite which lived in its own (heroic) world that was clearly separate from the *demos.*

How, then, can the differences and similarities be explained? First of all, one should simply remember that a text cannot represent everything but must make a selection. As there nonetheless are such striking correspondences between the societies described, it seems reasonable to suppose that the works do indeed refer to a common historical

world. If the texts date between 750 and 650 – without our being able to date individual epics more exactly within this period – they were composed in a historical
world that was not ethnically, culturally or politically uniform and was also going
through a process of transformation. Neither archeological finds nor written sources
from the Near East leave any doubt about this. The historical situation is made even
more complex by the fact that neither the demographic nor the social, economic
and cultural changes took place at the same pace everywhere.[30] One consequence of
these changes was an increase in mobility, which from ca. 750 brought individuals
or even whole groups of people into intensive contact with foreign worlds, and probably also brought Hesiod's father from Cyme in Asia Minor to Boeotia. This explains
the interest in ethnography and the adoption of Near Eastern and Egyptian knowledge and culture in the Greek world.

The engagement with this inwardly and outwardly changing world was by no means
restricted to epic texts like those of Homer and Hesiod, but is also found in archaic
lyric poetry (Dalby 1998; Patzek 2004). The differences one can see between Homer
and Hesiod might be due to their looking at historical processes from two different
geographical viewpoints, Hesiod from Boeotia and Homer from Ionia.[31] At all events,
both poets were attentive observers and keen analysts of their times, so that they
came to very similar conclusions about the questions and problems of their age. An
experience they evidently shared was the effect of an unprecedented increase in social
differentiation, which led to "power," based on wealth and prestige, gaining an autonomous status which was felt to be unjust. The use of violence and fraud, especially
attractive to youthful leaders, is a related phenomenon. Apart from deployment of the
gods as ideological tools, only the personal qualities of individuals and the pressure of
public opinion can counter this trend. These are the only means to control the prestige and thereby the power of the new elite. From Homer and Hesiod to Solon and
Theognis, this theme features ever more strongly in archaic Greek literature.[32]

Hesiod and Homer alike attempt to give their arguments special weight by means
of two literary techniques. Both avow that they proclaim the truth, and, like many after
them, appeal to the Muses on this point. And both make use of the past to make their
conclusions appear irrefutable. Homer projects everything into a past heroic age. He
consciously creates a heroic world furnished with archaic elements and wondrous
things, about which he pretends to be well-informed. However, his plots are not taken
from any concrete knowledge of the past, but from traditional stories, which he combined with completely new elements to create his own. The result is, on the one
hand, what has been called "epic distance" (J. M. Redfield), and on the other hand,
an "organic amalgam" (Raaflaub 1998: 188) which reflects the poet's intention. By
contrast, Hesiod constructs a much more systematic world of the gods and a divinely
ordained human order, in which his own world represents the final phase of a progressive decline of types of man. This construct is designed to lend persuasive power
to his conclusions and instructions for righteous conduct.

Homer's and Hesiod's texts thus are neither a mere passing on of old stories, nor
are they a depiction of conditions in their time: they are "intentional history."[33] They
aim to offer solutions to the problems of their own historical societies in an age of
transition. Hence one should not dismiss out of hand the idea, only recently formulated,

that Homer's, and Hesiod's, epics do not simply represent the end of a long oral tradition but are literary experiments which successfully exploited this tradition to draw attention to their "political" concerns. The stories are not mere tales of heroes (*Heldenlieder*), but offer wholly new arguments. The old tales are given new accents and inserted in the narrative arc of the new story. Furthermore, this new form of epic not only draws on Near Eastern models, but, like these, also shapes its own story as a kind of compendium of contemporary knowledge (Ulf 2003; Patzek 2004). It can hardly be denied that the complexity and length of these works were only possible in the new medium of writing. In this way, the epics of Homer and Hesiod were not only especially large but also particularly successful forms of expression among the various literary genres of their age.

Finally, we must ask once more to whom the poets addressed their "intentional" texts. The argument of the texts, more in Hesiod than in Homer, aims at open criticism of, not the existence of an elite, but its conduct. Thus the conclusion, suggested by the texts themselves, has been drawn that they were not exclusively meant for the elite, but addressed the *demos* at large (Dalby 1995). Only if this is true can we properly understand the panhellenic orientation of Homer's and Hesiod's texts,[34] since it fits well with the ambition of the "genre experiment" (Wolf 1995) to have maximum impact on the new political and cultural situation. This however does not mean that a panhellenic forum already existed in historical reality. Quite the contrary, it was only the changes of the Greek archaic age, including the development of new literary forms, which led to larger entities, such as those of the Dorians and Ionians, taking shape, and with them also the sense of a "Greek" unity. Not until this point in time, in the sixth century, did Homer and Hesiod gain a wide appeal.[35]

NOTES

1   Cf. the overview in Cairns 2001c.
2   Dating: West 1995; Dalby 1997; van Wees 2002c. 650–600 BC: Dickie 1995.
3   Snodgrass 1974; in contrast: Morris 2001b.
4   Nagy 1996b; Lamberton 1988; Rosen 1997.
5   This also goes for the notion of a heroic age: Haubold 2000; Dickie 1995; Dalby 1995, Morris 2000: 84–94; van Wees 2002c: 115–17.
6   Whitley 2001; see below n. 30.
7   Cairns 2001c: 1–56; Blümer 2001. On the modern theoretical debate, see Rosen 1997.
8   Nagy 1979: 312–13; Ulf 1990a; Tandy and Neal 1996: 46–7; Cairns 2001a.
9   Cf. e.g. *Od.* 3.70–4; *Il.* 7.467–75; von Reden 1995, 61–68; Donlan 1997a; Foxhall 1998; Wagner-Hasel 2000: 246–60.
10 Donlan 1981; Scheid-Tissinier 1994; friendship: Herman 1987; Ulf 1990b: 191–212.
11 Emphasized by Stein-Hölkeskamp 1989. Method of comparison: van Wees 2002a.
12 Wagner-Hasel 1997; Wickert-Micknat 1982; van Wees 1998a.
13 *Il.* 9.648; 24.534–5; *Od.* 17.322. Walter 1993a: 76–88; Raaflaub 1997a: 629–33.
14 *Ethnos* and *polis*: Funke 1993; C. Morgan 2003; and Raaflaub 1993b: 46–59; 1997c; Donlan 1989; Ulf 1990b: 215–23.
15 See e.g. *Od.* 2.25–9; Raaflaub 1997c: 8–20; van Wees 1992: 31–8.

16 Hölkeskamp 1997; Raaflaub 2000: 27–34; Hammer 2002; Patzek 1992: 131–5; Ulf 1990b: 106–17.
17 Ulf 1990b: 41–5, 99–105, 154–7, 160–2 (*thoe*), 206–7; Raaflaub 1997b: 632–6, 644–5; 1997c, 6, 19–23; Wagner-Hasel 2000: 167–8.
18 Raaflaub 1997b refers to this. *Od.* 21.214–16; 14.62–6.
19 Osborne 1998b; Papadopoulos 1997b; Haider 1996.
20 Echetos: *Od.* 24.474–7; Laomedon: *Il.* 21.441–57; 7.452–3. Cf. Bichler 1996; Dougherty 2001.
21 Fiction: Ulf 1990b: 118–25; Raaflaub 1997c: 6. War: Raaflaub 1997d; Ulf 1990b: 138–57; van Wees 2000a; van Wees 2004: 153–65, 203–6, 249–52.
22 Friendship: Herman 1987. Messengers and contracts: Raaflaub 1997c: Rollinger 2004. Alliances: Donlan 2002.
23 Burkert 1992; Bernabé 2004; Walcot 1966; West 1966; 1978; 1997.
24 Millett 1984; Donlan 1997a: 649–51; Schmitz 2004b.
25 Association with ancient Near Eastern "wisdom literature": West 1978; 1997; skeptical: Schmitz 2004a.
26 Blaise 1996; Rosen 1997; Blümer 2001; differently: West 1978: 46–7.
27 Similar: Clay 2003: 100–28. For the meaning of *genos* cf. Bourriot 1976: 266–9.
28 Rosen 1997: 484–8; Hesiod: Raaflaub 1993b: 60–4; 2000: 34–7; Homer: Ulf 1990b: 100–1.
29 Differently: van Wees 1992: 78–83, 87–9.
30 C. Morgan 2003; chs. 3 and 4, above. Demography: Scheidel 2003. Near east: Lanfranchi 2000, Rollinger 2001.
31 Dickie 1995; Latacz 1996: 24–30; West 1966: 40–8.
32 Ulf 2001; Raaflaub 1993b; 2000; differently: Stein-Hölkeskamp 1989.
33 Gehrke 2001; similarly: Raaflaub 1998: 183–4; Patzek 1992.
34 According to Nagy 1999; cf. Patzek 1992: 98–101.
35 Ulf 1996a; Hall 1997; ch. 31, below; Malkin 2001; Siapkas 2003; Burkert 2001; West 1966: 48–50; 1978: 60–1.

CHAPTER SIX

The Tyrants

Elke Stein-Hölkeskamp

Introduction

In Aristophanes' *Birds*, produced in 414, a herald promises the enormous reward of a talent to the citizens of "Cloudcuckooland," if they eliminate one of the "long dead tyrants."[1] The poet here pokes fun at the Athenians' fear of tyranny, which was by that time as unfounded as it was anachronistic: there had been no tyrannies in mainland Greece, the Aegean islands, or the *poleis* of Asia Minor for generations. Yet this did not reduce the great interest and the peculiar mixture of fear and fascination that tyranny aroused in the Greeks – and particularly in the citizens of democratic Athens. This interest found expression repeatedly and variously in the literature of the fifth and fourth centuries, from Herodotus and Thucydides to the tragedians and Plato, Aristotle and their schools. All these authors, each in his own way, investigated the causes and emergence of tyranny in the archaic period. They developed processual models for the tyrants' rise to power, distinguished and classified various types of autocratic rule, and described in terms of "ideal types" the character, conduct and self-presentation of tyrants and the instruments of oppression peculiar to their regime. Moreover, when *Birds* was performed, tyranny had already been converted into an evocative metaphor for the Athenians' own form of government: indeed, the rule of the Athenian *demos* over *polis* and empire – a rule that was not and could not be limited – was suggestively reflected in contemporaneous conceptions of the violent rule of erstwhile tyrants. By reinventing archaic tyranny in historiography, drama, and philosophy, the Athenians thus reflected in a variety of ways on their own identity.[2]

One expression of such intensive and variously motivated discussion of tyranny is found in Thucydides' suggestion that it originated as a consequence of economic growth in the archaic period: "As Greece became more powerful and acquired more wealth than it had previously, tyrannies were established in nearly every city"

(1.13.1). In *Politics*, Aristotle attempts to categorize systematically the causes of the rise of tyrannies, identifying four basic types: they stemmed from the emergence of a demagogue, from the abuse of the powers of a regular office by an ambitious and power-hungry incumbent, from the deterioration of traditional kingship and neglect of time-honored customs, or from the delegation to an individual of central authority previously wielded by an oligarchy. Yet all tyrants, Aristotle concludes, essentially began as leaders of the people in their struggle against oppression by an elite.[3]

Socrates, as portrayed by Xenophon in *Memorabilia* (4.6.12), thought of tyranny as rule against the wishes of the people, exercised by the will of the ruler without consideration for the law. Plato and Aristotle characterize tyranny as a type of rule that exclusively serves the personal interests of its holder. The aim of each tyrant is to enjoy the pleasures of life. Consequently, a life of luxury and decadent extravagance, including voluptuous meals and drinking, splendid clothing, prostitutes, catamites, and indeed sexual excesses of every kind are regarded as typical of the tyrant's lifestyle which by necessity corresponds to immense personal greed and an extraordinary and unprecedented accumulation of wealth at the tyrant's court.[4]

The proverbial wealth, the analysis continues, which the tyrant amasses through confiscations, taxes, and fees – that is, at the expense of the community – serves not only to satisfy his own desires but also to protect his rule from opposition and conspiracy. Typically, therefore, according to Aristotle, the tyrant relies on mercenaries and a bodyguard. Several tyrants deprived the citizens of power (and even arms) so as to eliminate any threat on their part (*Pol.* 1311a8ff). Moreover, tradition generally considers it characteristic of a tyrant constantly to monitor and spy on the citizens. To paraphrase Plato (*Symp.* 182b–c), Aristotle (*Pol.* 1313a40ff and b10ff), and Isocrates (*Or.* 3.54), tyrants regarded ties of friendship as a threat to their rule and accordingly outlawed *hetaireiai* (associations of friends) and alliances.

The detail and variety of the discussion of tyranny in the classical sources starkly contrast both quantitatively and even qualitatively not only with the few explicit assessments by contemporaries that survive in the fragments of archaic lyric poetry, but also with the scanty information about circumstances and events related to individual tyrannies which we are able to extract from those same fragments and from Herodotus' stories. Modern scholarship tends to disregard as much as possible the abstract and systematizing reflections of later authors because they seem to obstruct rather than advance our understanding of archaic tyranny, and to focus instead on contemporary evidence and a cautious interpretation of the relevant passages in Herodotus. Of course, even the latter cannot at all be taken at face value. For example, when Herodotus worked on his *Histories*, considerably more than three generations had passed since Cypselus' rise to power in Corinth; these events therefore lay far beyond the three-generation period accessible to more-or-less reliable oral memory. In the case studies on specific archaic tyrannies offered below it is therefore crucially important to be methodologically thorough and explicit, to identify the gaps and to make clear what we can and cannot say in any given case.[5]

Case Studies

Corinth

The epoch of archaic tyranny began with the rule of Cypselus over Corinth.[6] In 660 he overthrew the ruling Bacchiads and assumed sole power. The Bacchiads formed a hereditary, closed aristocracy who sought to preserve their monopoly of power through endogamy. They owned the best land in the territory of Corinth. According to Strabo, they controlled foreign trade and imposed fees both on the exchange of goods and the export of agricultural products. The Bacchiads had ruled collectively by monopolizing all political privileges and rotating the highest political office annually among members of their group. Obviously, there were other families as well who in a broad sense belonged to an elite upper class. Many of them apparently were of pre-Dorian origin. Their estates lay on the periphery of Corinthian territory.[7]

The archaic, pre-political structure of Bacchiad rule seems to have retarded the political and institutional development of Corinth. In other spheres, however, Bacchiad Corinth made rapid progress and emerged as a comparatively wealthy *polis*. A gradual rise in population beginning in ca. 800 resulted in the active role that the *polis* played in early colonization. The founders of Syracuse and Corcyra, Archias and Chersikrates, were Corinthians and members of the Bacchiads. Once these colonies in the west and north-west had been established, Corinth because of its favorable geographical location became the most important trading center for commerce between them and mainland Greece (Thuc. 6.3.2; Strabo 6.2.4).

Nevertheless, even before Cypselus' time Bacchiad rule seems to have suffered from a crisis that had various causes. A major factor undoubtedly was the Bacchiads' inability over an extended period to legitimate their power through foreign policy and military successes. Indeed, a few years before the coup of Cypselus, Corinth lost control over its colony on the island of Corcyra and failed to regain it despite considerable efforts. Moreover, the Bacchiads were unable to prevent either the expansion of Argive influence or the rise of neighboring Megara (Thuc. 1.13). In addition to these failures and defeats, they faced challenges in adapting to the broad structural changes that began to take effect throughout Greece in the early seventh century. In this period, Megara may have adopted the new hoplite tactics. If they wished to hold their own in conflicts with their neighbor, the Bacchiads were thus forced to base Corinth's army on a broader class of citizens.[8] In the short term, the need to equip themselves with the panoply must have been an economic burden for the affected farmers. In the middle or long term, however, this development brought about a revaluation of that class and consequently an increase in its self-confidence, expectations, and demands. Against this backdrop, the concentration of the best land in the hands of the Bacchiads perhaps caused increasing dissatisfaction. At the same time, other well-to-do elite families, who so far had been excluded from the decision-making processes and now claimed a share in political power, probably helped increase pressure on the Bacchiads' legitimacy and power and eventually proved an essential factor in the overthrow of the Bacchiad regime and the rise of Cypselus.

The ancient sources offer two different accounts of Cypselus' rise to power. Herodotus, who gives most space to the fairy-tale elements of the story, relates that

Labda, daughter of one of the Bacchiads, but unable to find a husband among them because she was lame, married an outsider. Because the Delphic oracle predicted great power for the male offspring of this union, the Bacchiads decided to kill Labda's firstborn. Yet she saved him by hiding him in a chest (*kypsele*). When Cypselus grew up, another oracle from Delphi encouraged him to overthrow the unjust rule of the Bacchiads and to usurp their power for himself and his children. The topos, pervasive in mythology, of a disabled person who brings destruction upon those who rejected her, is here used as a leitmotif for the entire episode (Hdt. 5.92b).

The other version of the story of Cypselus' coup goes back to the fourth-century historian Ephorus, and survives in the fragments of the universal history of Nicolaus of Damascus (time of Augustus; *FGrHist* 90 F57.1–7). Although aware of Cypselus' miraculous rescue from the Bacchiad henchmen, Nicolaus is more interested in the concrete actions by which Cypselus prepared his takeover. He stresses that Cypselus enjoyed great authority because of his military prowess and was finally elected to the office of *polemarchos*. In stark contrast to his Bacchiad predecessors, he supposedly exercised the civil and judicial duties entailed by this office with leniency and fairness, refraining from placing defendants in fetters and from exacting the customary severe punishments from insolvent debtors. His "valiant and public-spirited" style of administration won him extraordinary popularity. Yet Cypselus did not, according to Nicolaus, overthrow the Bacchiad regime as leader of an uprising of the dissatisfied *demos*, but with the help of a conspiracy among the nobility (*hetairikon*). Thus the would-be tyrant sought and found support primarily among those members of the elite who, because of the Bacchiad's monopoly of power, had not been able to realize the claims to prestige and influence characteristic of men of their status. After his coup, Cypselus had many Bacchiads killed; others he sent into exile, confiscating their land. Some scholars have assumed, on the basis of Nicolaus' terminology, that the *demos* no less than Cypselus' aristocratic followers profited from such redistribution of land, but this seems questionable at least.[9] Cypselus certainly did not enact a program of sweeping redistribution of land or of comprehensive economic and social reform. The organization of further colonies rather suggests that demographic pressure and, correspondingly, demand for land continued to be a problem during his reign. Leucas, Ambracia, and Anactorium, among others, were founded under the leadership of his sons. A steady rise in the export of Corinthian pottery confirms that manufacturing and trade flourished under the tyrant.[10]

Construction of a treasury in Delphi – according to the dedicatory inscription a personal donation of Cypselus – as well as a number of dedications in Delphi and Olympia, as splendid as they were unusual, including a large bronze palm tree and a golden statue of Zeus, indicate the tyrant's desire to demonstrate his status in the central arenas of the panhellenic aristocracy. Simultaneously they make it clear that it was a matter of great importance to the tyrant to present himself, through behavior that befitted his status, as an accepted member of a community of cult that transcended individual *poleis*.[11]

Cypselus died after a thirty-year reign, succeeded by his son Periander. In the ancient tradition Periander is the prototype of the evil and cruel tyrant, to whom every possible excess and perversion, even incest and necrophilia, were attributed. Aristotle describes him as the inventor of all those measures that served as violent means of maintaining tyranny: bribery, corruption, spying, and terror (*Pol.* 1313a36ff). Yet there were also essentially positive judgments of Periander, and he was occasionally counted among the "Seven Sages" (D.L. 1.13). Given the difficult source situation, very little can be said with any certainty about his political and legislative activities.[12] He seems to have scored some military and political successes, continuing colonization and regaining control over Corcyra. He was well integrated into the inter-*polis* elite and participated regularly in the panhellenic festivals in Olympia and elsewhere. The authority he enjoyed in these circles is confirmed by the fact that he was chosen as an arbitrator in a conflict between Athens and Mytilene (Hdt. 5.95; Ephorus *FGrH* 70 F178). In Corinth he appears consistently to have taken action against the competing claims of other aristocratic families; at least he is supposed to have enacted a series of sumptuary laws that decisively restricted the self-presentation of the elite. He is said to have prohibited unauthorized meetings and tried to limit access to the city center; unless these measures are *topoi* of fourth-century typologies of tyranny that were falsely ascribed to Periander, they must reflect his efforts to safeguard his rule from increasing opposition (Ephorus *FGrH* 70 F179; Nicolaus of Damascus *FGrH* 90 F58.1). Even in antiquity, Periander was considered a great builder, responsible for a temple, a spring house, a harbor, and the *diolkos*, a paved road over which boats laden with cargo could be dragged on carts across the Isthmus.[13] Although these works were primarily motivated by the tyrant's desire for personal glory, they nevertheless greatly advanced the process of urbanization at Corinth.

After Periander's death his nephew Psammetichus assumed power.[14] He was eliminated by an aristocratic plot after only three years. Tyranny was replaced by the "polycratic" rule of a wealthy aristocratic elite (Nicolaus of Damascus *FGrH* 90 F59.4, 60.1–2).

Sicyon

Orthagoras established a tyranny at Sicyon in c. 650.[15] Our source for his rise to power and rule is an anonymous "History of Tyranny" that probably goes back to Ephorus. According to this source, Orthagoras, whose father Andreas allegedly was a simple cook, first distinguished himself as a border sentry and was then promoted to watch commander and later to *polemarchos* (*FGrH* 105 F2; Diod. 8.24). The fragmentary and only partially credible tradition includes no specific information on Orthagoras' assumption of power or on his and his immediate successors' reigns. Aristotle's opinion is vague and positive. He emphasizes that the tyrants of Sicyon were moderate toward their subjects, for the most part observed the laws, and won the masses' approval by caring for their well-being. Other sources, however, mention strife within the ruling family and violent, indeed bloody, fights about the succession.[16]

Cleisthenes, who ruled over Sicyon in the first third of the sixth century, is the first tyrant whom we know in some detail. According to Aristotle, he was a distinguished general. His military fame was primarily due to his participation in the Sacred War which the Delphic Amphictyony and its allies waged in 590 against the Phocian *polis* of Crisa (Arist. *Pol.* 1315b16ff; Paus. 10.37.5f). Moreover, under Cleisthenes the Sicyonians are said to have conquered the neighboring *polis* Pellene and carried on a military conflict with Argos (with unknown results). Since its founding, Sicyon had maintained close ties with Argos. Cleisthenes apparently attempted to sever those ties and free Sicyon from Argive influence. For this purpose, tradition reports, he enacted a series of highly unusual measures: for example, he prohibited the recitation of the Homeric epics in Sicyon because they glorified the deeds of Argive heroes; he abolished tragic choruses in honor of Adrastus, the Argive hero, who according to legend had once been the king of Sicyon, and even expelled him from his shrine in the agora, in spite of vehement resistance from Delphi. The cult and sacrifices for Adrastus were transferred to the Theban hero Melanippus who supposedly was an arch-enemy of Adrastus. Cleisthenes even had Melanippus' bones transferred from Thebes to Sicyon and buried in a shrine near the council building. This act represented a remarkable interference with the Sicyonians' collective memory and a substantial alteration to the town's sacral and monumental topography (Hdt. 5.67.1ff).

A much-debated issue among scholars is the interpretation of Cleisthenes' tribal reform. Herodotus mentions it in connection with the tyrant's other anti-Argive activities. He states that Cleisthenes ridiculed the Sicyonians by renaming the three Dorian tribes (Hylleis, Pamphyli, and Dymanatae), giving them derogatory names of animals instead. He dubbed them the "swine-men," the "donkey-men," and the "pig-men," whereas he called the fourth tribe, to which he and his family belonged, the *Archelaoi* or "leaders of the people" (Hdt. 5.68.1). This measure has frequently been taken as evidence for a division of the Sicyonians into a Dorian upper class and pre-Dorian lower class, which was considered the real cause of all social and political conflicts in that *polis*. According to this theory, the Orthagorid tyrants drew their support from the pre-Dorian group to which they themselves belonged. The tribal reform consequently was interpreted as a measure designed to weaken the Dorian upper class and simultaneously to improve the position of the previously disadvantaged pre-Dorian population who formed the fourth tribe.[17]

This interpretation has recently been called into question by K.-W. Welwei, who attempts to fit the tribal system and its reorganization, both in Sicyon and in other communities, into the general process of early *polis* formation. He stresses that comparison with the tribal systems of other *poleis* makes it unlikely that Sicyonian tribes in the sixth century reflected a division by ethnic, social, or regional criteria. He, therefore, argues against the existence, at that time, of three traditional tribes exclusively made up of Dorians. More likely, Dorian immigrants and remains of the pre-Dorian population had to some extent become intermixed, and this must have had an effect on the composition of the tribes as well. In Sparta, for example, even before 750 BC the pre-Dorian inhabitants of Amyclae were incorporated into the tribes (but cf. ch. 7, below). The very idea of limiting membership in the three old tribes to the Dorian nobility by means of relegating the pre-Dorian lower class to a fourth tribe is hardly convincing, since the Orthagorids themselves were members of the latter. Welwei suggests that the fourth tribe originated in the course of territorial expansion from an effort to integrate the population of border areas. Regional differences gradually disappeared because the population fluctuated within the *polis* territory but changes in domicile did not affect tribal affiliation. Hence Welwei considers the aim of the tribal reform – in analogy to that instituted by the Athenian

Cleisthenes – to have been an even distribution of men fit for military service throughout the tribes with a view to quick and effective mobilization of the army for the
tyrant's many military undertakings.[18]

Even this interpretation of Cleisthenes' reform has to rely to some extent on speculation. It does, however, accord better with what little we know of the character
and function of the subdivisions of early Greek communities. Obviously it deprives
Cleisthenes of the aura, frequently attributed to him, of the tyrant as defender
of an underprivileged ethnic minority. Instead it illuminates Cleisthenes' efforts, by
restructuring the subdivisions, to overcome rifts within the community and in this
way to limit the potential for conflict. The interpretation of his reform as a measure
intended to stabilize both his rule and his community is completely consistent with
the fact that the Orthagorid dynasty continued to rule over Sicyon for some decades
after the death of Cleisthenes and that his tribal reform was cancelled only after its
overthrow.[19]

There is no reliable evidence on other domestic measures enacted by Cleisthenes.
He allegedly sought to keep small farmers from visiting the city center by compelling
them to wear even there their rustic garb, a sheepskin coat. The historicity of this
measure is highly controversial. Herodotus mentions an *agora* and *prytaneion* in the
center of Sicyon; this admits the possibility that assembly and council continued to
meet under the tyranny. Yet nothing is known of their functions and powers.[20]

Like Periander, Cleisthenes regularly participated in the great panhellenic festivals,
which offered archaic Greek aristocrats a chance to meet with their peers from other
poleis, to show off their wealth and personal excellence, and also to seek public recognition in a larger forum. He competed in the games with considerable success and
won the four-horse chariot race in the Pythian games of 582 and at Olympia in 576.
In connection with the latter victory an event occurred that would do more to secure
Cleisthenes' lasting fame than any of his political and military activities. Indeed, its
description by Herodotus is still considered a key to reconstructing the world of the
archaic aristocracy.[21]

Herodotus states that Cleisthenes announced to the aristocrats, assembled in Olympia
from around the entire Greek world, that he intended to give his daughter, Agariste,
in marriage to the best possible candidate; all who considered themselves worthy
were invited to present themselves in Sicyon within sixty days. Thirteen suitors from
various parts of Greece and even southern Italy accepted this invitation. Cleisthenes
first inquired about their descent and then subjected them to extensive and manifold
tests, including courage, education, and manners. They had to prove their individual
talents in athletics and especially at *symposia*, that is, at those occasions that were
considered the defining activities of the aristocratic way of life. Cleisthenes chose
Megacles, a scion of the Alcmaeonid family of Athens, to be his son-in-law – a
success that supposedly made that family famous far beyond its home town, indeed
throughout the Greek world (Hdt. 6.126–30).

This story exemplifies the extent to which tyrants were an integral part of the
aristocratic society of the archaic period. In their values, lifestyles, and methods of
self-presentation, men like Cleisthenes distinguished themselves only slightly from
other aristocrats. Even when they acted against other aristocrats in their own *poleis*,

they did so primarily in order to restrict the latter's capacity of proving, presenting, and advancing themselves and, as a consequence, to stand unrivaled in power and honor. Typically, aristocrats holding a tyranny in their home town were not excluded from the established forms of interaction with the aristocracies of other *poleis.* Apparently the tyrants' position or role was perceived as neither strange nor shocking nor generally "anti-aristocratic." Rather, other aristocrats admired and envied them and attached great importance to forming familial ties with them.

Cleisthenes died some time after 570. Another Orthagorid, Aeschines, then took control of Sicyon. Some decades later, the tyranny was overthrown either by intervention or at least with the support of Sparta (Hdt. 5.68; *FGrHist* 105 F1).

Megara

The tyranny of Theagenes in Megara was contemporaneous with those in Corinth and Sicyon.[22] Nothing is known about his rise to power. That he was able to marry his daughter to the Athenian Cylon, a member of the aristocracy of the Eupatridae (Thuc. 1.126) suggests that he belonged to the aristocratic elite of Megara. Aristotle reckons Theagenes among those tyrants who took advantage of a political and military office in the aristocratic community to seize control of the *polis.* He characterizes him, in fifth- and fourth-century terminology, as a *prostates* (leader), who used the people's hatred of the wealthy to gain the trust of the masses. As far as we can tell, Megara already had an assembly and council at that time. Exploiting his influence with the *demos,* Theagenes was able to obtain permission from the assembly to maintain a personal bodyguard with whose support he later seized power (Arist. *Pol.* 1305a7ff; *Rhet.* 1357b31ff).

After he had gained control of Megara, Theagenes is said to have mounted a spectacular action to seize the flocks of the wealthy. He had the animals that were grazing by the river captured and slaughtered (Arist. *Pol.* 1305a24ff). Both the exact details of this report and the more general question of what economical, social, and political issues lay behind these events are much debated. The conventional interpretation assumes that by this time the Megarian aristocracy was already extensively involved in the production and exportation of wool and woolen garments. As a corollary, the importation of grain from Megarian colonies in the Black Sea area had steadily increased. Consequently, the wealthy elite rapidly and recklessly expanded pastoralism which was a prerequisite for the production of wool. In doing so, they occupied large portions of the scarce Megarian lands that were suitable for farming and had till then been used by small farmers. As a result, the economic situation of the lower classes deteriorated seriously. Their irritation and discontent could easily be exploited by a skillful demagogue like Theagenes.[23]

Thomas Figueira has recently called this interpretation into question.[24] He points out that the river (*potamos*) mentioned by Aristotle does not exist in the territory of Megara. A further problem that needs to be explained lies in the fact that the animals were slaughtered and not expropriated. Figueira interprets the term *potamos* as referring here to an old cult center where sacrifices and communal cult meals were held regularly. The cattle that were grazing nearby, intended for these sacrifices, were illegally seized by the wealthy herd owners. By seizing and killing them, Theagenes merely returned them to their original purpose. Because there is no evidence other than Aristotle's brief report, any interpretation of this event must necessarily entail some degree of speculation. Everything we know about the structural problems of archaic *polis* economies and the mentality of the elites suggests that here too an individual aristocrat used the temporary support of the dissatisfied *demos* to enhance his own power at the expense of his peers, when they pursued their own interests all too recklessly and thereby destabilized the internal order of their community.

Once again, nothing is known about the concrete details and strategies of Theagenes' rule. Pausanias states that he commissioned an aqueduct that was several kilometers long, and a fountainhouse that was famous for its multitude of columns and unusual beauty (1.40.1, 41.2).[25] These measures helped advance the process of urbanization and doubtlessly improved living conditions in the town. Yet in Theagenes' case, too, one may doubt that this was indeed the crucial motivation for his building program, since so far as we know he initiated no further measures to better the situation of the *demos*. The expectations which he may have raised before his coup were probably not satisfied, as is also suggested by the fact that in local popular traditions of later generations he plays no role.

In 630 Theagenes supported his son-in-law in an attempt to establish a tyranny in Athens (ch. 8, below). The complete failure of this undertaking seems to have weakened Theagenes' position in Megara as well. At any rate, he was overthrown soon thereafter (Thuc. 1.126). According to Plutarch, a constitution based on *sophrosyne* (self-restraint and moderation) followed his regime, that is, a system that would later be characterized as a "moderate oligarchy" (*Mor.* 295c–d).

Samos

In 538 Polycrates established a tyranny in Samos that, however, lasted only till 522.[26] In his *Histories*, Herodotus provides detailed information about his rule over the great Aegean island. Polycrates came from a distinguished family of the Samian upper class. His father Aiakes was probably a member of the landholding nobility, the so-called *Geomoroi*, who in sixth-century Samos not only shared out the land among themselves, but also collectively exerted political control. Along with his brothers Pantagnostus and Syloson, Polycrates then toppled the rule of the *Geomoroi*. They allegedly staged their violent coup during the annual festival honoring the goddess Hera. In a solemn procession, in which all Samians participated, the colossal cult statue of the goddess was carried from its temple to the sea where it was washed and clothed in new robes. When this ceremony was completed, the citizens laid aside their weapons and performed the customary sacrifices. At exactly this moment Polycrates and his brothers began their uprising and brutally massacred many of the celebrants. Then they seized the *acropolis* which, according to ancient notions, put them in control of the entire *polis*. The brothers shared power for some time, but then Polycrates eliminated the other two and became the autocratic ruler of Samos.[27]

Herodotus states explicitly that the usurpers staged their coup with the help of only fifteen armed men, all fellow aristocrats, whom Polycrates supposedly won over to his cause with lavish gifts (Hdt. 3.39, 120, 125). The small number of those actively involved suggests that the Samians themselves put up no notable resistance. It is even conceivable that they welcomed the fall of the *Geomoroi* because they considered tyranny as the lesser of two evils. It is in any case notable that Polycrates subsequently did not experience any threat to the stability and continuity of his rule from the general population. He directed repressive measures to safeguard his position only against the aristocratic former masters of Samos and their families. Accordingly, Polycrates is said to have ordered the demolition of the *palaistrai* (wrestling grounds), that is, those sporting facilities where young aristocrats gathered for the athletic exercise and competition which were typical of their lifestyle. Presumably, from Polycrates' point of view wrestling grounds were hives of conspiratorial activity by the young men of those families which suffered most under his tyranny. After all, Polycrates had monopolized all the opportunities to win glory, gain wealth, and exercise power that had previously been open to all *Geomoroi*.[28]

It is well attested that Polycrates made extensive use of such opportunities in the early years of his regime. In a short time, he reportedly conquered several neighboring islands and numerous towns on the Anatolian mainland. These expeditions were successful not least because the Persians, after Cyrus' campaigns of conquest had brought many Greek cities under their control (ch. 9, below), had retreated far to the east and left a kind of power vacuum in the eastern Aegean. Polycrates' fleet consisted of a modified type of 50-oared vessel, the so-called *Samaina*, which was fast and maneuverable and had an exceptionally large capacity to carry men and goods. With these ships, a large number of mercenaries, and a thousand archers Polycrates soon controlled the sea lanes of the eastern Mediterranean. In all these activities war, trade, and piracy converged; indeed, in people's perceptions at the time they were generally not differentiated clearly from each other. To contemporaries, Polycrates' dominion over the sea, his *thalassokratia*, must have appeared to be so extensive and enormous that it was comparable only to that of the mythical king Minos.[29]

All this not only enhanced Polycrates' personal glory but also brought considerable financial resources to an already prosperous *polis*, as is suggested by the lively building program which developed here throughout the sixth century and especially during the tyrant's reign. Herodotus considers the Samian buildings the greatest in all of Greece. His admiration focused particularly on the great harbor mole, the aqueduct, and the temple of Hera, all of which have been thoroughly explored by archaeologists. The harbor mole consisted of a 300 meter long dam which was built around the harbor basin and functioned as a breakwater on the stormy south-eastern side. An even more magnificent feat of early Greek engineering was the underground aqueduct, the design of which was attributed to the architect Eupalinus of Megara. This aqueduct brought water from a reservoir outside the city walls into the center, through a tunnel more than 1,000 meters long which ran under the acropolis. The third structure identified by Herodotus – the temple of Hera – was in the fifth century still considered the greatest temple the Greeks had ever built. A monumental temple had already been erected around 570 in the precinct of Hera to the south-west of the city. Yet only a generation later it was razed, possibly because it had been seriously damaged by an earthquake. In the 530s the sanctuary was rebuilt; at 55×112 meters it was larger than its predecessor. No fewer than 123 columns surrounded the cella in a double ring. Later the so-called *Laura*, a kind of oriental bazaar, in which all manner of luxury goods were produced and sold, was also ascribed to Polycrates.

These projects were not, of course, intended to create jobs for the poor – to impute such objectives to Polycrates, as occasionally happened in earlier scholarship, would be anachronistic.[30] True, these building projects were in part designed to win the citizens' loyalty, which was essential to the security of the tyrant's reign. Such loyalty, however, was cultivated not by providing employment but by turning Samos into a better place to live. Polycrates gave it a certain luster that elevated it above other *poleis*, filled the citizens with pride, and made it easier for them to identify with this city and its tyrant.

In all likelihood, Polycrates also built a splendid residence for himself. Herodotus mentions costly furnishings, which were located in the men's hall (*andron*) of this palace. Here Polycrates hosted his friends and confidants as well as famous artists such as the poets Anacreon and Ibycus. At these *symposia*, which were typical of the lifestyle of Greek aristocrats, it was customary for poets to entertain their host and patron with songs that celebrated his glory, beauty, and generosity.[31] All this conferred a luster to the tyrant with which none of the other Samian aristocrats could ever hope to compete. In this type of court life and in the building program the difference is particularly visible between the autocratic rule of a tyrant and the collective, partly cooperative, partly competitive, rule of an aristocracy. Yet it is also clear that the difference in these spheres was mostly quantitive, not qualitative, in nature. In cultural practice and self-presentation the tyrant basically operated within the traditional frame of aristocratic society.[32]

The partial restriction of their customary range of activities and the overwhelming competitive power of the tyrant induced some Samian aristocrats to leave their homeland. Among them was, for example, the philosopher Pythagoras (Strabo 14.638; Diog. Laert. 8.3). A substantial group of these exiles went to Italy and founded a colony on the gulf of Naples. They called it *Dikaiarchia* and thereby emphasized that they intended to distinguish themselves from their homeland primarily through their "just exercise of power." In trying to remove another group of disgruntled citizens from Samos, Polycrates used a trick. In 525, as Cambyses prepared for an invasion of Egypt, the tyrant considered it opportune to side with the Persian King. He offered him forty triremes to aid him in his attack on Egypt, manned these ships with his opponents, and, to make things doubly sure, sent a message to Cambyses, indicating that he did not wish them to return. Yet the crews saw through the tyrant's plan. They turned around before they arrived in Egypt and made their way back to Samos. Shortly before they reached home, they met a Samian fleet and, after a successful naval battle, made a landing on the island. They were, however, defeated in a subsequent land battle and were again compelled to leave their homeland. The dissidents then made their way to Sparta and there requested military aid. After some hesitation, the Spartans offered them assistance and crossed the Aegean, for the first time in their history (Cartledge 1982). The Corinthians also joined the expedition, seeing a very real threat to their own unrestricted ability to navigate the seas and trade in Polycrates' notorious involvement in piracy. Together they besieged Samos for forty days but were then forced to withdraw without having achieved anything. Apparently, they found no support among the Samian population, primarily because opposition to the tyrant was still limited to a few aristocratic families. Moreover, the city was all too well prepared for such a siege: monumental fortifications protected its center and the harbor, and the besieged population was provided with water by means of Eupalinus' tunnel. The tyrant once again remained victorious (Hdt. 3.44, 54ff).

Even so, this episode suggests that Polycrates' scope for action was gradually becoming narrower. His unbridled rule over the Aegean, which had expanded his own sphere of influence well beyond his own homeland while at the same time curtailing that of other *poleis*, was increasingly arousing opposition. It was clear that his enemies would use every opportunity to take action against the man who, according to Herodotus, was the first Greek to "have had a good chance to become master of Ionia and the islands" (3.122). Yet in the actual overthrow of Polycrates these factors played at best an indirect role. Rather, a most tempting offer proved the beginning of Polycrates' end. Oroites, the Persian satrap of Sardes, sent a messenger to request refuge in Samos, because he allegedly felt threatened by King Cambyses. As compensation, Oroites offered half of all his treasure and wealth – a fortune, so the messenger supposedly stressed, that was sufficient to make Polycrates master over all of Greece. Polycrates' interest had been aroused: the skillful appeal to his greed and ambition obviously caused him to throw caution to the winds. He first sent out his confidant Maiandrios to confirm the existence of this treasure. The satrap showed him eight chests filled with stones with a layer of gold on top. Maiandrios was fooled and brought back a positive report. Thereupon Polycrates traveled with a great retinue to Magnesia on the Maeander, where Oroites resided. He was immediately seized by the satrap's henchmen and executed in so brutal a way that Herodotus refused to reveal the details to his readers. The corpse was then crucified on Cape Mycale, directly opposite Samos. Herodotus was no longer able to say exactly what prompted Oroites' attack on Polycrates. Yet there are some indications that the tyrant's huge ambition and unprecedented power in the region made him dangerous to the Persian satrap no less than to the Greeks (Hdt. 3.120ff).

In the rise and fall of Polycrates the ethos and ideal of the Greek aristocracies at the end of the archaic period manifest themselves in a unique way. Polycrates was immensely wealthy, he cultivated a particularly splendid lifestyle, and he proved himself both in numerous military campaigns and other adventurous undertakings. His influence reached far, and his connections supposedly extended all the way to Egypt. In all this he surpassed his peers by far, whose competitive ethos, typical of their class, forced them constantly to measure themselves against one another in these very areas. That he also succeeded for a short time in monopolizing political power caused later generations to see him as a tyrant and strongman. To his contemporaries and even many later Greeks, however, this final intensification of aristocratic ambition made him an icon of good fortune and success. It was only when Polycrates began to reach far beyond his homeland and sought to acquire more power than any of the tyrants before him had ever held, that "the great fortune of Polycrates," as Herodotus puts it, ended. The immense power of his protopolitical regime proved no longer acceptable in the face of growing consolidation of political structures in many Greek cities on the mainland and in the Persian empire.

Common Features and General Patterns

The phenomenon of archaic tyranny provides the best illustration of the profound polarity between the aristocratic individual and the *polis* community – a polarity that must be considered one of the basic structural patterns of the cultural and political life of the archaic Greek city-states. Contemporary texts therefore characterize the tyrant in a thoroughly negative way. Their judgments combine the perspectives of those who sought to advance remedies for internal strife and to bring peace to their communities and those who saw in the person of the tyrant an envied (because victorious) rival for the highest goal of the individual aristocrat's ambition. Thus Alcaeus and Solon condemn tyrants as unscrupulous despots, who seize power for themselves against law and custom and destroy the established order. In the collection of elegies that survive under the name of Theognis of Megara, the tyrant appears as an opportunistic manipulator who exploits strife and even civil war in his home *polis* to achieve autocratic rule. Remarkably enough, all of these authors recognize serious misconduct on the part of the leading class and therefore the failure of their own peers as the primary cause of the crisis which the tyrant exploits for his own purposes. The *hybris* and excess of the "leaders of the people" (*demou hegemones*) are indispensable conditions for the would-be tyrant among their own ranks to successfully realize his ambitions.[33]

Yet all four case studies discussed here demonstrate that the fragmentary state of the tradition does not permit a detailed reconstruction of the political and social conditions that existed before the rise of the tyrants. The scarce information we have about the situation in Corinth, Samos, and Megara, however, all points in the same direction: usurpers had a chance only when the ruling aristocracies – the Bacchiads, the *Geomoroi*, and the Megarian elite – somehow or other overstepped their bounds and thereby jeopardized the legitimacy of their predominance. Whether such social and economic factors as are mentioned in Hesiod's *Works and Days* (35ff, 202ff, 349ff, 392ff) and in the poems of Solon (esp. fr. 3 GP) also played a significant role is no longer verifiable in each individual case. Phenomena that are clearly visible in Hesiod's Ascra and Solon's Athens (increasing burdens of debt and widespread impoverishment among farmers as well as corresponding pressure exerted on the farmers by the elite; see chs. 8, 22, 23, below) cannot be confirmed in any of the cases considered here. This does not, of course, preclude the possibility that all or some of the general crisis factors that affected the archaic period – population growth, fragmentation of landownership through division by inheritance, and a general shortage of agricultural resources – were also operative in Corinth, Samos, and Megara and that they contributed to destabilizing conditions there as they did elsewhere. Indeed, there is no doubt about the active participation of at least Corinth and Megara in colonization, which can be seen as a symptom of crises of this kind.[34]

We are on firmer ground when assessing another crisis factor that was widespread in the archaic period and was inseparably tied to the economic and legal problems of the farmers – namely the distinctive ethic of aristocratic competition and, resulting from it, an unbridled rivalry for power, status, and influence that in many cases intensified the aristocracy's pressure on the *demos*.[35] Well-known examples such as Athens and Mytilene on Lesbos show that perennial conflict within the aristocracy jeopardized the community's internal and external peace and paralyzed the working of institutions that were still in the process of being consolidated.[36] In at least two of the cases considered here, Corinth and Samos, there is explicit evidence that the would-be tyrants relied on a group of aristocratic conspirators to topple the ruling aristocratic faction. In the case of Polycrates, there is mention of an economic aspect cementing this connection: the later tyrant's generosity toward his supporters. By contrast, in none of these cases did the *demos* play an active part in the establishment of tyranny. Ultimately, it must have made very little difference for the vast majority of the population whether a single aristocrat or a group of aristocrats ruled the *polis*. We might even think it likely that the *demos* kept quiet when tyrants seized power because they expected from them an improvement of their condition, just because they cracked down on aristocratic rivals. Accordingly, in all our examples the tyrant's efforts to maintain his power were directed not against the *demos* who did not pose any danger, but against the tyrant's aristocratic peers.

It is certainly the case that none of these tyrants put forward a progressive reform program that in any way improved the *demos'* situation. They did not undertake a radical redistribution of land. They never questioned in principle the predominance and privileges of the aristocracy – even if hostile aristocrats were regularly dispossessed, banished, or even murdered. Nowhere were traditional social hierarchies overturned or social distinctions leveled. The archaic tyrants were clearly no social reformers, and they did not assume the role of lawgivers, draft new constitutions, or design forward-looking plans for the comprehensive reorganization of the *polis*.[37] As we saw, the tribal reforms in Sicyon did not even survive the fall of the Orthagorid tyranny. Measures that eventually guaranteed the stable and reliable operation of communal institutions and provided greater legal security for the citizens were developed rather in opposition to tyranny – one might almost say, as a sort of program to prevent one-man rule. Only in this indirect way, and by forcing the aristocracy out of power and thus weakening its structures of social and political control, did tyranny contribute to the further development of those ideals and concepts which, as is best attested in the case of Athens, were eventually connected with terms like good order (*eunomia*), equality (*isonomia, isegoria*), and finally even democracy (*demokratia*). Consequently and from hindsight, tyranny became the perfect opposite of good order, but it did not directly or immediately help establish such an order.[38]

To summarize and conclude, the actual measures of the tyrants primarily served to maintain and stabilize their own positions of power. This is true not only for oppressive actions that, as noted above, were mostly directed against their aristocratic peers as potential rivals. All of their other political, economic, and cultural activities served the same purpose: to secure recognition in their own *poleis* and, in addition, the active

support or at least the passive acceptance of their regimes among the broadest possible citizen circles. This explains their support for farmers, participation in colonization
and similar ventures abroad, patronage of poets, promotion of religion, cults, and
festivals, and not least their extensive building activities in their own *poleis* and in
the panhellenic centers and sanctuaries. Moreover, all these efforts demonstrate that
the tyrants remained tied into the traditional value system and behavior patterns of the
Greek aristocracy. All the tyrants dealt with here made use of the traditional forms
and semantics of elite self-presentation. Sparing no expense or effort, they displayed
their power, wealth, and capacity for consumption commensurate to their status. Indeed,
they greatly increased, without changing it in principle, the dimensions and opulence
of such "conspicuous consumption."

Consequently, tyranny cannot be interpreted as an alternative to traditional
aristocracy; rather, it represents the ultimate culmination of aristocratic rule that was
possible within the framework of political, social, and economic structures existing
in the archaic *polis*.[39] When these structures finally changed for good and became
more resilient, and when the central institutions – assembly and council – were firmly
enough established for their weight and the force of the citizen body represented in
them to be able effectively to discipline and integrate even ambitious and energetic
individuals, tyranny became obsolete as a viable form of governance. At the same
time, the aristocracy's leading role was placed on an entirely new basis which in turn
required new forms of legitimation and self-presentation. But that brings us back to
where our discussion began, in democratic Athens.

NOTES

1   1074ff; cf. *Wasps* 463ff, 473ff, 489ff.
2   On all these aspects, see esp. the chapters by Dewald, Raaflaub, Seaford, and Henderson
    in K. Morgan 2003. Cf. now Anderson 2005: 174f, who calls for a new conceptual frame-
    work for the interpretation of archaic tyranny. On *demos tyrannos*, see Kallet, in the same
    vol. On *polis tyrannos*, see Raaflaub 2004b: 132–4, 141–3.
3   *Pol.* 1305a6ff, 1308a19ff, 1310b12ff.
4   Pl. *Rep.* 344a–b, 572e; Arist. *Pol.* 1311a8ff and a30ff, 1314b1ff and 28ff.
5   On the methodological problems posed by the interpretation of Herodotus, see Gray
    1996; Dewald 2003. For complementary discussions of tyranny, see also chs. 8, 21, and
    23, below. On oral tradition and memory, see Vansina 1985; Ungern-Sternberg and Reinau
    1988.
6   Will 1955: 441–571; Andrewes (1956) 1974: 43; Berve 1967: 14–27, 521–31; Oost 1972:
    10–30; Drews 1972: 129–44; Welwei (1983) 1998: 78–81; Salmon 1984: 186–230;
    McGlew 1993: 61–74, 174–82; De Libero 1996: 135–78; Osborne 1996a: 194–6; Gray
    1996; Stein-Hölkeskamp 1996: 658–62. Cf. Anderson 2005: 190ff on Cypselid dedi-
    catory activities in Delphi.
7   Hdt. 5.92b; Diod. 7.9.1ff; Strabo 8.378; Paus. 2.4.5, 5.18.7.
8   But the date and impact of the development of the hoplite phalanx is much debated:
    see ch. 30, below, and e.g. van Wees 2000a; 2004; Raaflaub 1997d; Hanson 1995.
9   Thus, for example, Will 1955: 477–81. *Contra:* De Libero 1996: 143–4.

10 Hdt. 8.45; Thuc. 1.30; Strabo 8.352, 10.452.

11 Hdt. 1.14; Plut. *Mor.* 164a, 399f, 400d–e; Paus. 10.13.5.

12 Hölkeskamp 1999: 157–8; and ch. 21, below.

13 Salmon 1984: 201–2 offers a survey of archaeological evidence. It seems anachronistic to interpret such construction as an effort to provide labor and as part of broader measures to prevent laziness. On the *diolkos*, see Raepsaet 1993.

14 The name illuminates the father's far-reaching international connections.

15 Andrewes (1956) 1974: 57–61; Berve 1967: 27–33, 531–5; Rudolph 1971: 75–83; Griffin 1982: 40–59; Welwei (1983) 1998: 82–4; Stein-Hölkeskamp 1996: 662–7. De Libero 1996: 179–205 considers reports about Orthagoras' lowly origin completely unhistorical. Specifically on dating, see Parker V. 1992.

16 Arist. *Pol.* 1315b12ff; for a genealogy of the Orthagorids, see Hdt. 6.120; Nicolaus of Damascus *FGrH* 90 F61.

17 Thus, for example, Skalet 1928: 52, 59–60; Andrewes 1956: 58–61; Berve 1967: 29–32; Griffin 1982: 51.

18 Welwei (1983) 1998: 82–4. Kinzl 1979: 302–8 was the first to emphasize that on linguistic principles the new tribal names cannot have been derived from the names of animals. He thinks they must be connected, as was usual, with the names of heroes. See further Parker 1994. On the military aspects of the Athenian tribal reform, see Siewert 1982. On "tribes" and other subdivisions in Greek *poleis*, see N. F. Jones 1987.

19 For a different recent interpretation of these tribal reforms, see van Wees 2003.

20 Theopompus *FGrHist* 115 F176, 311; Menaechmus of Sicyon *FGrHist* 131 F1; Hdt. 5.67.1ff.

21 Murray 1980: 202–3; Stahl 1987: 50–1; Stein-Hölkeskamp 1989: 117–19. On the integration of tyrants into the panhellenic network of marriage alliances cf. now Anderson 2005: 190ff.

22 Berve 1967: 33–4, 536; Oost 1973: 186–96; Legon 1981: 86ff; Welwei (1983) 1998: 84; De Libero 1996: 224–30; Stein-Hölkeskamp 1996: 667–9.

23 Berve 1967: 33–4; Oost 1973: 190–1; Legon 1981: 86ff.

24 Figueira 1985: 112–58; cf. now Anderson 2005: 194ff.

25 On the archaeological evidence that mostly dates to the first quarter of the fifth century, see Glaser 1983.

26 Berve 1967: 107–14, 581–7; Labarbe 1974: 21–41; Welwei (1983) 1998: 85; Shipley 1987: 68–99, who considers it possible that Aiakes, Polycrates' father, was tyrant before him. For detailed discussion of the difficult source problems, see De Libero 1996: 249–59. See also, more recently, Stein-Hölkeskamp 1999: 105–12.

27 Hdt. 3.39; Polyaenus 1.23; Diog. Laert. 2.5.

28 Hieronymus of Rhodes fr. 34 Wehrli; more generally on this pattern, Arist. *Pol.* 1313a39–b21. Recent scholarship doubts the historicity of this specific report; see, e.g., De Libero 1996: 273. On the archaeological evidence, Tölle-Kastenbein 1969.

29 Hdt. 3.39, 122; Thuc. 1.13.6; 3.104.2; Plut. *Per.* 26.

30 Berve 1967: 110 still argues this way; Shipley 1987: 83, 92–93 is much more cautious.

31 Stein-Hölkeskamp 1989: 104–22.

32 Hdt. 3.60ff, 121, 123; Arist. *Pol.* 1313b22ff; Paus. 1.2.3.

33 Solon, frr. 3.12–20; 8; 10; 23 GP; Alcaeus, frr. 24a, 27 GP; Theognis 39–52, 823–4, 855–6, 1081ff. On Alcaeus, see Rösler 1980; on Theognis, Stein-Hölkeskamp 1997; on Solon, chs. 8, 21, 23, below.

34 On the crisis of the period, see in general Starr 1986; Osborne 1996a.

35 On the connection between agrarian crisis and aristocratic competition, see Stein-
    Hölkeskamp 1989: 64–85.
36 For references, see n. 33.
37 On Pittakos of Mytilene as "elected tyrant," "arbitrator" (*aisymnetes*) and "lawgiver" (Arist.
    Pol. 1274b18ff, 1285a30ff and 35ff), see Hölkeskamp 1999: 12–13, 219–26.
38 On this, see Hölkeskamp 1992b; Hölkeskamp 1999: 262–85 and *passim.*
39 See now Anderson 2005: 173 and passim, who considers the regime of early tyrants as
    a kind of mainstream oligarchic leadership in its most amplified form.

CHAPTER SEVEN

Sparta[1]

Massimo Nafissi

Any introduction to the archaic history of Sparta must begin with some discussion of the prudent use of evidence. Non-Spartan observers have produced an idealized version of Sparta, the distorting effects of which (the "*mirage spartiate*") have long been recognized;[2] even Sparta's own local traditions are now considered of doubtful reliability. Historians of Sparta must also be aware of the invention of tradition. During the Classical and Hellenistic periods, contemporary dispositions were frequently attributed to Lycurgus (Flower 2002), and earlier evidence poses similar problems. Dates and details contained in such unreliable later narratives (Starr 1965) still creep into modern reconstructions of Spartan history, but rigorous source criticism casts doubt on even the few "facts" previously regarded as sound. Accordingly, there is little common ground in current historical research on archaic Sparta, and the only conclusions that command any general agreement tend to be vague and suggestive. To construct an intelligible account of early Spartan history while remaining faithful to rigorous methodological standards is a major challenge.

The Foundation of Heraclid Laconia: Identities and Forms of Dependence

Research into the origin and nature of the Spartan *polis* has benefited from a greater understanding of the transmission of memory in oral culture, the relationship between memory and collective identity, and the nature of ethnicity as a cultural construct, not a natural and biological fact. The Dorian issue is a case in point: attention now focuses on the question of the ethnogenesis of the Dorians rather than on their role in the collapse of Mycenaean culture. The social and settlement instability that characterized post-Mycenaean Greece was particularly pronounced in Laconia. Between the end of the Bronze Age and the Protogeometric Period (eleventh to tenth century) the region was drastically depopulated. Despite a certain mobility of human groups, many today consider it improbable that the Dorians arrived in the Peloponnese as an already defined entity, even in small groups:[3] Dorian ethnogenesis is essentially a phenomenon of the early Iron Age (Hall 1997; 2002: 82–9).

According to ancient tradition, the arrival of the Dorians in Laconia coincided with the return (*kathodos*) of the Heraclid kings (Prinz 1979: 206–313; Malkin 1994b: 15–45). The canonical form of the myth recounts the simultaneous creation of three kingdoms: Argos, Messenia, and Laconia. This view is probably of archaic origin (but see Luraghi 2001a; 2008: 46–67), and is in any case, like all ancient accounts of the Dorian and Spartan conquest of Laconia, an "intentional" history: that is, an account which reflects the needs of the society which produced it.[4] Ancient traditions concerning the origins of Sparta probably tell us nothing about the late Bronze Age or the arrival of the Dorians but can perhaps advance our understanding of Sparta and the Lacedaemonians between the tenth and seventh centuries.

Spartan tradition begins with the myth of Heracles and Hippocoon. The latter took the kingdom of Lacedaemon from its legitimate owner, Tyndareos. In a quarrel with the sons of Hippocoon, Heracles returned the kingdom (*basileia*) to Tyndareos. It should have passed back to Heracles or his descendants but went to Atreus' son Menelaus, husband of Tyndareos' daughter Helen, and then to Orestes, who united the dominions of his father Agamemnon and uncle Menelaus. The Heraclids returned with the Dorians, a people who had lived in central Greece, to retake possession when Orestes' son Tisamenus was king. These traditions establish Dorian identity, the right of kings of the line of Heracles to inherit Tyndareos' rule over the community of Lacedaemonians, and the very existence of this community, made up of people dwelling in many Laconian places under the kings of Sparta.

Tradition thus spotlights the Heraclid kings at the centre of Dorian ethnogenesis in Laconia. They resided in Sparta, a group of villages which probably arose in the tenth century on a site of apparently scant importance in the late Bronze Age (Welwei 2004: 15–16). The myth of a Dorian ancestral homeland possibly retained the memory of a provenance beyond the Peloponnese, but a Dorian identity first crystallized in the Spartan community in Laconia and was then assumed by other groups as well.[5] Between the tenth and eighth centuries, this process accompanied the development of a homogeneous regional material culture and culminated in the formation of a Lacedaemonian identity.[6]

As Jonathan Hall (2000) points out, the Spartans used the concept of "Lacedaemon" as a unified region to justify their dominance over all other inhabitants of this area, whom they called *perioikoi* ("dwellers round about"). Linear B tablets found in Thebes show that the toponym "Lacedaemon" already existed in the Mycenaean period,[7] but this does not necessarily mean that a continuous Lacedaemonian identity existed from the Bronze to the Iron Age. The word Lacedaemon may simply have been transmitted in epic tradition as the name of the seat and land of powerful heroic kings. When Sparta was later identified as the former seat of these heroes, the city and its territory began to be called Lacedaemon. The foundation of the cult of Menelaus and Helena, ca. 700, on a hill opposite Sparta (Antonaccio 1995a: 155–66), presupposes and sanctions this identification, and it is also recognized by the *Odyssey* (Hall 2000: 85), which makes Menelaus king of Sparta and thereby bestows panhellenic legitimacy upon the claims of the Heraclid kings.[8] "Lacedaemonians" thus became a term that referred to Spartans and *perioikoi* together: members of a community became Lacedaemonians as soon as they paid the correct honors (*timai*) to the kings of Sparta. As new communities accepted these obligations, Lacedaemon and the *Lakonike* grew progressively. By the end of the eighth century, Sparta had already forced obedience upon parts of Laconia and Messenia.[9]

The extension of the Dorian identity and the development of traditions concerning the Heraclid origins of the Spartan kings (*basileis*) and their right to the kingdom of Tyndareos probably both reflected and consolidated their successes. These were not limited to the small Laconia of Heraclid tradition but comprised what was to become *Lakonike*, extending westwards beyond the Taygetus mountain range. This brings us to the three best documented conflicts, those with Amyclae, Helos, and Messenia, and thus to the history of Spartan expansion.

In the early Iron and archaic ages, Amyclae was the second centre in Laconia, as is demonstrated in particular by the sanctuary of Apollo and Hyacinthus.[10] Earlier tradition placed the conquest of Amyclae at the time of the return of the Heraclids, or before Lycurgus.[11] Pausanias (3.2.6, cf. 19.6) says, however, that the native inhabitants of Amyclae, Pharis, and Geronthrae were not driven out until the reign of Teleclus (whom modern scholars place around the mid-eighth century). Moreover, Pausanias dates the war against Helos in the reign of Teleclus' successor, Alcamenes (3.2.7, 20.6). This chronology, allowing the conquest of Laconia to be separated from the "return of the Dorians," has seemed more plausible to modern historians. Scholars in the 1960s accepted it entirely (Huxley 1962: 22; Kiechle 1963: 55–67). Recent attempts to defend Pausanias' information (Parker V. 1993: 45–8; Kõiv 2003: 77–100, 133–40) seem too optimistic, although his chronology is used tacitly even in sober reconstructions of the early history of Laconia that sometimes turn a war of conquest into an incorporation of Amyclae into the Spartan community.[12]

Yet these traditions are not genuine memories of a real opposition between Dorians and native "Achaeans" or between Sparta and Amyclae. They represent, rather, a Spartan attempt to transfer to Laconia, and specifically to Amyclae, the seat of Agamemnon and thus the kingdom of Orestes and Tisamenus that united the kingdoms of Menelaus and Agamemnon.[13] As the sanctuary of Agamemnon and Cassandra at Amyclae confirms, this claim (possibly reflected also in *Od.* 4.514ff) originated as early as the seventh century, in connection with rivalry between Sparta and Argos (Salapata 2002). On this premise, the return of the Heraclids had to culminate in the conquest of Amyclae. Pausanias preserves a variation of this tradition in which the traditional link between Lycurgus and the growth of Spartan power (Hdt. 1.65–6; Ephorus *FGrH* 70 F118) is presented in an extreme form: Sparta was able to overcome native "Achaean" resistance only because Lycurgus had established "good order" (*eunomia*). This variation may actually reflect developments in Sparta in the second century BC: its problematic relationship with the perioikic cities after they had been freed in 195 and entrusted to the protection of the Achaean League, and its long craving for the restoration of the ancient Lycurgan laws after they had been abolished by Philopoemen in 188.[14] From a sober historical perspective it seems probable that Amyclae was from the very beginning part of a pre-political community which also included the villages in the area of Sparta (Welwei 2004: 24–34); it thus never needed to be conquered by the Spartans.

The notion of a Spartan conquest of the southern Eurotas Valley, distinct from taking control of the middle valley (Welwei 2004: 37ff), is founded on an ancient folk or learned – but in any case groundless – etymology. The name Helots (*heilotes*) was said to derive from the town of Helos in the lower Eurotas valley: when Sparta conquered it, its inhabitants became the first Helots.[15] The connection of Helos with Helots was entirely arbitrary, and the agreement of ancient sources proves only the authority of tradition, not its historical worth.[16] Some scholars (Cartledge 2002: 83) prefer a debated etymology from *heilon* ("I took") and *haliskomai* ("I am taken"), which would suggest an origin of helotage in conquest without tying it to a specific area.

The authority of the Heraclid *basileis* could certainly not have been imposed peacefully everywhere, but reliable information on the conquest of Laconia is lacking. Evidence concerning the Messenian wars is sound but scanty. Some fragments of Tyrtaeus record the victory obtained by king Theopompus and "the fathers of our fathers" during a twenty-year conflict against the Messenians, who were finally forced to abandon Mount Ithome and their rich lands.[17] Other narratives of these wars echo opinions and debates raised by the Messenian revolt of ca. 464–455, sparked by an earthquake, and subsequent events down to the refoundation of Messene in 369, and even by the later experiences of the new *polis* (Luraghi 2003; 2008: 68–106). In particular, the romantic account of the Messenian Wars in Pausanias' fourth book presents a fresco as rich as it is unreliable. Its main sources are two Hellenistic authors, Myron of Priene and Rhianos of Bene. Other material Pausanias uses originated at best in sources of the late fourth century.[18] Modern attempts to save these traditions emphasize the oppressed Messenians' desire to preserve the memory of their own history, and archaeological evidence does hint at "contexts for remembrance" for the Helots and *perioikoi* of Messenia, but their memories were inevitably subject to change, not least because archaic and classical Messenia was an integral part of the Laconian world.[19]

That we are not certain how many Messenian Wars were fought show just how little we know, but a few facts about these wars can be ascertained. Fifth-century historians know only of one Spartan war of conquest and one revolt, after the earthquake.[20] The rebirth of Messene in 369 led to the rediscovery of Tyrtaeus' war, also known as the Second Messenian War. Supporters of the alliance between Athens and Sparta claimed an Athenian origin for Tyrtaeus (Fisher 1994: 362–4) and a Messenian revolt that hindered the eager Spartans from fighting with the Athenians against the Persians at Marathon (Plato *Laws* 3.692d, 698d–e; Dusanic 1997). So from the fourth century, three (Diod. Sic. 15.66.2–5) or, when Plato's revolt was added, four (Strabo 8.4.10) Messenian wars appeared in the sources. Doubts about the historicity of Plato's war are not sufficient to discredit the war of Tyrtaeus too, but his elegies contain few and unclear traces of a conflict against the Messenians in his time (fr. 23.6 W). Certainly the ancients, having made the poet a protagonist of the Second Messenian War, read more into his poems than was legitimate.

Ancient views of the chronology of the Messenian wars differed. The first was generally placed well in the eighth century. Pausanias gives precise dates: 743–724 and, for Tyrtaeus's war, 685–668, whereas, according to Rhianus (*FGrH* 265 F43 *ap.* Paus.

4.15.2), the latter was fought during the reign of Latychidas I. (roughly third quarter of the seventh century). In fact, all these chronologies were developed with the list of Spartan kings at hand (which was put together in the late fifth century), starting from Tyrtaeus' references to Theopompus and "the fathers of our fathers" (Jacoby 1943: 114; Schneider 1985). The same information was used to construct dates for the poet's life (centered in 640–637 or 636–633), because Tyrtaeus did not name the kings under whom "his" war had been fought (Paus. 4.15.2; Mosshammer 1979: 205, 208–9). None of these or other learned chronological constructs possess documentary value. Nor do the products of intentional history transmitted by Pausanias (4.23.6–9; 24.2–3) or other authors,[21] even though they seem plausible in themselves and some scholars still accept them (Parker 1991; M. Meier 1998: 94–6). Any attempt to date the Messenian wars depends therefore on the genealogy of King Theopompus.[22] A count of generations suggests an approximate date for Theopompus' reign – lower than that proposed by the ancients who assumed excessively long generations – in the early seventh century at the latest.

It is worth noting that Sparta's victory in the First Messenian War resulted in the conquest of only one town with its territory. There is no reason to believe that Messene, the urban settlement at the foot of Mount Ithome, controlled the entire region, as stories of the return of the Heraclids imply (Luraghi 2003: 111–12; 2008: 71, 132). The destruction of Nichoria on the south-eastern border of the Pamisus Valley in the mid-seventh century may, therefore, be due to Spartan expansion in that area (Luraghi 2008: 132). The poems of Homer seem to know the Spartans' dominion over Messene and reflect their efforts to legitimize their expansion beyond the Taygetus (Luraghi 2003: 112–13; 2008: 72–3). A date around 700 BC thus seems most probable for the war of Theopompus. As for Tyrtaeus, ancient historians and chronologists understood the expression "the fathers of our fathers" as meaning "grandfathers" and therefore counted two generations between Theopompus and the poet: this could be correct but in some scholars' opinion Tyrtaeus' words refer to distant forefathers.[23]

We have already mentioned recent discussion of the position of the Helots which now needs to be inserted into the more general debate on Spartan land tenure. In both respects, Sparta appears more similar to other *poleis* than was long believed; on this point, as the works of M. I. Finley, Paul Cartledge, and Stephen Hodkinson indicate, current scholarship has reached fairly general agreement.

Some problems still require further study but the idea of substantial public control over Spartan landholdings, current in various forms until very recently, should be discarded.[24] Rightly, the opinion now prevails that "land was transmitted hereditarily within the lineage from one generation to the next by means of the normal Greek system of partible inheritance, that is by dividing it among one's heirs."[25] Similarly, concerning the Helots, broad agreement now emphasizes the essentially private nature of property relationships.[26] Anthropological and comparative perspectives, and the rigorous re-examination of ancient traditions, have prompted stimulating research and exciting new results.[27] Archaeological surveys in Laconia and Messenia and excavations (for example, of the great edifice of Kopanaki in the Solima Valley, Messenia) furnish important, albeit controversial, information.[28]

The Helots and their condition are now seen by many scholars as a phenomenon that evolved in interaction with Spartan society, and not as the decisive factor which at an early stage turned Sparta into a closed and military community. Even if some scholars still disagree, it now seems reasonable to accept that an obsession with the threat posed by the Helots developed only after the earthquake revolt.[29] This is all the more probable if, as seems plausible, one of the engines of Helotic revolt, a Messenian identity, emerged only then: to support their own territorial claims, the rebels asserted descent from the ancient inhabitants whose achievements were recounted in the tradition of the Heraclids' return.[30] By contrast, traditional opinion maintains that Helotism was born, in a distant past, by mass enslavement of an ethnically homogeneous conquered population that remained on its own land. This contradicts Greek custom, and in the general history of slavery no parallels can be found for a successful undertaking of this kind (*contra* van Wees 2003). Rather, it seems, Helotism was given its classical form, by regulating and homogenizing different forms of dependent labor, only in the sixth century, in the context of reforms that also produced the status of *homoioi* (Luraghi 2002b: esp. 233–38).

True, with only one exception, the interpretation of which is controversial (Antiochus *FGrH* 555 F 13; Luraghi 2003: 115–17), ancient tradition generally agrees that the Helots of Laconia and Messenia were reduced to servitude after being conquered in war. But, as already stated, the traditions on the origin of helotage in Laconia are inconsistent and the meaning "prisoner" for the term *heilotes* debated. True, too, every year the newly elected ephors declared war on the Helots (Arist. fr. 538 Rose = 543 Gigon) but this does not necessarily throw light on their origins: as M. Whitby observes (1994: 106), this "might have been a practice introduced as late as the 460s . . . to assume new significance after the liberation of Messenia."

Debate about the outcome of the first Messenian war turns on these lines of Tyrtaeus:

> Like asses worn out by heavy burdens,
> bringing to their masters out of grievous necessity
> half of all the produce that the land brings forth . . .
> Wailing for their masters, they and their wives alike
> whenever the baneful lot of death came upon any.
>   (fr. 6–7 W *ap.* Paus. 4.14.4–5, transl. Gerber)

The prevalent opinion is that the Messenians were turned into Helots and the land was distributed among individual Spartans, but some believe, like Pausanias and his sources, that Tyrtaeus refers to some form of dependence of the Messenian community.[31] Anyway it is not clear that the ancients (cf. Ael. *VH* 6.1) were right in recognizing Messenians in the men reduced to these conditions, or that these lines describe classical helotage.[32] I would not exclude the possibility that Tyrtaeus speaks derisively of a perioikic community that had rebelled against Sparta, likening its members to slaves and exaggerating its economic plight.

Discussion of the origins of helotage has been intensified by the revisionist proposals of Luraghi, although the traditional view continues to be defended.[33] It seems probable that in Laconia in the eighth to seventh centuries different types of agricultural dependents co-existed: free, semi-free, and eventually also debt-bondsmen and chattel-slaves. In Sparta, as elsewhere, the *polis* elite exerted heavy economic pressure on other members of the community. This is probably all that can be extracted from Aristotle's reference to *staseis* in the time of Tyrtaeus: "unrest occurred during the [second] Messenian war, as is clear from the poem of Tyrtaeus called *Eunomia*; for some people afflicted by the war were demanding land redistribution" (*Pol.* 1306b36–07a2 = fr. 1 W; that the crisis was caused by the war was an inference drawn by the ancient interpreters of Tyrtaeus, not necessarily a fact stated by him). Following events akin to those known from Solonian Athens (see ch. 8, below), free people may have been reduced to conditions resembling slavery. In some cases, the Spartans may have enslaved defeated local populations, but their individual owners are likely to have forced them to move away from their own homes and families to work elsewhere within *Lakonike*.

The *perioikoi* have been objects of much recent study, stimulated by Anglo-Dutch surveys in Laconia and initiatives of the Copenhagen Polis Centre.[34] In classical times, the *Lakonike* covered 8,500 sq km, more than three times the territory of Athens (2,500 sq km) which was already extraordinary by Greek *polis* standards. What accounts for this anomaly is the existence of the perioikic communities. They were often small and their economic base was primarily agricultural, although some also disposed of other resources (Shipley 1992; Catling 2002: 243–8). It is debated whether they should be considered dependent poleis or rather civic subdivisions (Hansen 2004; Mertens 2002). In fact, we know very little about their institutions before their liberation by the Roman proconsul Flamininus in 195.[35]

The concept of Lacedaemonians embraced both the Spartans and *perioikoi*. In the Classical age the experience of the battlefield fed the collective solidarity of all Lacedaemonians. Such unity must also have possessed a religious component. Not only was the religion of the *perioikoi* strongly influenced by that of Sparta (Parker 1989: 145) but, as the catalogue of Damonon's victories in the late fifth and early fourth centuries (*IG* V 1.213) shows, a cycle of festivals was celebrated in all of Laconia. Furthermore, information on the Hekatonbaia, a festival connected with the notion of "the hundred cities of Laconia,"[36] suggests the existence of common, "pan-Lacedaemonian" cults (Strabo 8.4.11 with Hesychius s.v. *Hekatonbeus*). Unlike other ethnic communities of ancient Greece, however, the community of Lacedaemonians in the broad sense of Spartans and *perioikoi* never adopted a federal type of organization: it was not a political community. Only the Lacedaemonians from Sparta, citizens with full rights of the polis Sparta-Lacedaemon, constituted a political community, and their decisions were binding on all Lacedaemonians. This reflected the pre-political origins of the regional Lacedaemonian community and the centrality of Sparta-Lacedaemon, seat of the kings. The currently prevailing view of the *perioikoi* as Lacedaemonian citizens of inferior status is, however, well grounded in classical perceptions of the *polis* Sparta-Lacedaemon (Hall 2000: 79–81; cf. Mertens 2002: 288).

On the origins of the dependence of the *perioikoi* on Sparta recent research shows healthy caution (Shipley 1997: 203–5; Hall 2000: 82–7). Certainly the perioikic status, like that of the Helots, was not simply the result of Doric invasion and/or repopulation of Laconia, and not all *perioikoi* acquired their status in the same way (Cartledge 2002: 84). Some communities must already have been formed between the tenth and the eighth centuries before recognizing the authority of the Heraclid kings. Others, though, emerged later on land that was already Lacedaemonian: for instance, Sellasia appears not to have existed before the sixth century (Catling 2002: 238–40). We hear also of colonization promoted by Sparta,[37] and of communities like Asine and Nauplia which were encouraged by a generous Sparta to take refuge in Messenia from oppression by Argos. Even if such traditions – with the probable exception of Asine – do not necessarily have a historical foundation,[38] they point to an awareness of diverse origins, and it is reasonable to imagine that some *poleis* began as outlets for demographic growth among the *perioikoi* themselves or as settlements for those who were excluded from Spartan citizenship when the latter was legally defined.

The problem of the exclusion of the *perioikoi* from political rights (*timai*) interested fourth-century authors (Ephorus *FGrH* 70 F117; Isocr. 12.177–181) and certainly also the perioikic elites (Xen. *Hell.* 5.3.9; Shipley 1997: 202) who must have shared the Spartan passion for honor. With the tightening of the legal criteria that deter-mined membership in the Spartan community they probably lost the occasional chance for integration among the privileged. This may have led them to introduce a local system of honors, and eventually political offices (*timai, archai*) inspired by the Spartan model. The perioikic *poleis* thus possibly arose as a response to the local elites' need for self-representation. If this was primarily an endogenous phenomenon it would provide an additional reason to consider these communities dependent *poleis* rather than subdivisions of the civic body.

The Development of Political Institutions

The recent suggestion that Spartan structures reached their full development as late as the mid-fifth century (Thommen 1996) is a warning against any image of a "fossilized" Sparta: the *polis*' institutions continued to develop during the Classical age. Still, there remain good reasons to accept Moses Finley's classic opinion, that the Spartan system was the result of a long historical process but fundamental changes can be ascribed to a "sixth-century revolution."[39] This process can be divided schematically into four phases: (1) development of the pre-political community, of which we have already traced the main characteristics; (2) reinforcement of the kingship (*basileia*); (3) first definition of political institutions (citizenship, assembly and *gerousia*); (4) maturation of these institutions (rise of the ephorate) and "classical" definition of the legal status of citizenship with effects on the dependent classes and communities (Helots and *perioikoi*) in a "sixth-century reform."

The return of the Heraclids provided the mythical foundation for the preroga-tive of the two families which had exclusive rights to the kingship, the Agiads and Eurypontids (Huttner 1997: 48–58). Although in classical times the power of the kings was formally restricted, they could surpass its limits by means of their poten-tially enormous authority.[40] Aristotle undervalues their *basileia* when he describes it as "a hereditary and perpetual generalship with full powers" (*Pol.* 1285a7–8); their military command gave the kings the opportunity to develop considerable economic and symbolic capital. Herodotus records scrupulously the honors reserved for the kings (6.56–9). The grandiose royal funerals were sensational; the unbridled manifestations of mourning by all members of Lacedaemonian society stood in stark contrast to Greek and even Spartan custom. (Whether the *basileis* after death were the object of hero-cult is debatable; see Lipka 2002b: 248–51.) Even in life the kings were honored on every public occasion so as always to be acknowledged as the first men – with a sole exception: "All rise from their seats out of respect for the king, save the ephors from their official thrones" (Xen. *Lac. Pol.* 15.6). Thus even the ephors rose, save when they were seated on the symbol of their office: for their honors derived from their official position, whereas the honors of the kings derived from their own persons – a clear indication of the difference between political and pre-political authority. Yet even the *basileis* were now dramatically subordinated to the *polis*: all citizens every month witnessed the kings swearing an oath to obey the law on pain of losing their honors (Xen. *Lac. Pol.* 15.7), as happened to many kings who fell into disgrace.

The saga of the return of the Heraclids not only elevated the *basileis* among the Spartans but defined their status among all Lacedaemonians. Even the *perioikoi* honored them both in death (at their funerals: Hdt. 6.58.2) and in life: in some poleis they held royal estates (*temene*: Xen. *Lac. Pol.* 15.3), the others probably paid the royal tribute (Pl. *Alc. maj.* 123). The *basileis* headed the Lacedaemonians army, comprising both Spartans and *perioikoi*, they made sacrifices when the army left Laconian soil, and they held the priesthood of Zeus Lakedaimonios and Zeus Ouranios (Hdt. 6.56). Although it has been suggested that perioikic status was based upon unequal alliances obliging the *perioikoi* "to follow withersoever the Spartans might lead and to have the same friends and enemies as they" (Cartledge 2002: 153), the bonds uniting the *perioikoi* with Sparta appear to have been of a different kind: quite simply, the *perioikoi* were obliged to follow the kings of the Lacedaemonians.[41]

On the origins of the double kingship, the dyarchy,[42] we observe only that the non-monarchical nature of *basileia* in Homer, where many leading men within a community have the title *basileus*, is compatible with the coexistence of two kings. Homeric kingships were based on authority and social prestige but highly unstable, particularly in the transition to the next generation. Traditions claiming descent from Zeus and Heracles secured for the *basileis* of Sparta extraordinary charisma that probably explains an early fixation of their honors (*gerea*) and certainty of transmission of the *basileia* within the regal families. As stated earlier, the elaboration of traditions concerning the Heraclids and Sparta and their rights over the kingdom of Tyndareos was the consequence of important military successes. The foundation of the cult of Menelaus (end of eighth century) reflects the later stages of this development. The consolidation of Spartan kingship must be more ancient. It had a long-lasting impact on the institutions of the polis: the Spartans were aware that the charismatic leadership of the Heraclids presented a powerful threat to order, but for religious and political reasons they did not want to abolish it: the prestige of the Heraclid kings was an important factor even for Spartan hegemony in the Peloponnese and Greece. Two anomalies in Sparta are closely tied together: the continuation of kingship, indeed dyarchy, well beyond the time when "the hereditary *basileiai* of clearly assigned privileges" (Thuc. 1.13.1) disappeared elsewhere, and the extraordinary territorial development of the Lacedaemonian community.

In the study of the dawn of political institutions, Spartan scholars appear privileged in having access to an ancient document that might constitute a foundation charter: the great *rhetra*. The text of the *rhetra* is preserved by Plutarch (*Lyc.* 6), who declares it to be a Delphic oracle received by Lycurgus. He derived text and comment from the lost Aristotelian *Constitution of the Lacedaemonians*:

> 1. Having founded a cult of Zeus Syllanios and Athena Syllania, having divided the people [or: "kept the divisions"] in tribes (*phylas phylaxanta*)[43] and having divided it in *obai* (*obas obaxanta*), having appointed a council (*gerousia*) of thirty members, including the founders (*archagetai*), regularly celebrate the Apellai between Babyka and Knakion.
> 3. Bring forward (*eispherein*) and reject (*aphisthasthai*)[44] (proposals) as follows (*houtos*):
> 4. to the people must go . . . and final decision, 5. but if the people speaks crookedly [or: "asks for something crooked"[45]] the elders and the founders are to be rejecters (*apostateras*).

> (author's tr.; numeration added)

Plutarch declares that clause 5 was surreptitiously added to the *rhetra* by kings Theopompus and Polydorus (thus it is usually called the "rider"), but this is clearly a fabrication of fourth-century scholars.[46] They declared clause 5 a later addition because, by separating the "rider" from the *rhetra*, they sought to reconcile the tradition of Lycurgus' oracle with the evidence of Tyrtaeus (fr. 4 W), who referred to an oracle given to Theopompus and Polydorus.[47] By linking the "rider" with Theopompus, they also connected it to the creation of the ephorate which a fourth-century theory attributed to this same king (Plut. *Lyc.* 6–7.3; see below). The upshot of all this was to claim that the Spartan constitution had preserved the balance dear to its admirers: while the "rider" limited the powers of the people, the people's representatives, the ephors, received the right of proposal and the presidency of the assembly. In fact, however, clauses 3–5 are strictly bound together. *Houtos* refers to what follows, and both the indirect and direct understood objects of *eispherein* (the people, and proposals) are dealt with in the last two clauses: 4 is seriously corrupt but the reference is certainly to the people, *damos*,[48] while 5 explains how to reject the proposals, and in the term *apostateras* clearly recalls the verb *aphisthasthai* of clause 3.

A clue to the nature of the *rhetra* lies in the use of the term *archagetai* for the kings (Plutarch *Lyc.* 6.3). This is elswhere an honorary title for founders, leaders of colonial undertakings (Malkin 1987: 241–50), and we should follow the few scholars who have accorded the term its natural meaning.[49] The *rhetra* must be referring to the first Heraclid kings, Eurysthenes and Procles, and to the foundation of Sparta, the preservation or institutionalization of the tribes of the Dorian settlers, the first *gerousia*, the creation of a place of assembly, and the distribution of the people into *obai*. If *obai* means villages, as it did in Roman times and as Hesychius seems to confirm,[50] this alludes not only to the people's distribution into civic subdivisions but to their settlement in villages. It is usually supposed that royalty, *gerousia* and the assembly already existed before the promulgation of the great *rhetra*, but this is no more than an assumption based on the belief that the text represents an authentic archaic enactment. In fact, the *rhetra* is not a law but a supposed founding prescription for the establishment of the state, which projected back to the beginning the institutions which existed in archaic Sparta. This explains the absolute uniqueness in form and content of the *rhetra* among archaic legislative documents (Hölkeskamp 1999: esp. 272). Although the last sentence in its conditional form ("but if") resembles a written law (Gagarin 1986: 54 n. 9) and shows familiarity with archaic legislative practice, archaic laws never have such general and generic content; rather, as Hölkeskamp (1992b: 91) observes, they are "single enactments, independent, complete and self-contained statutes."[51]

The *rhetra*, however, is not simply a fake:[52] it is a retrospective reconstruction inserted into an intentional elaboration of a past that was largely accepted by Spartan society. It reflects the tendency of the traditions on legislators (Hölkeskamp 1999: 44–59) and of oral culture to concentrate on origins, at the expense of later events which are left obscure in a so-called "floating gap."[53] Even if it does not attest to a historical act of organization, the *rhetra* offers unique insight into a community that has reached a certain level of political institutionalization. Citizenship is connected with hereditary membership in the *phylai* and *obai*; the *basileis* firmly enjoy hereditary status as descendants of the founders; the *gerontes* are now a well established council with a fixed number, and the kings are integrated into the *gerousia;* relations between council and assembly, their respective powers, and the frequency of their meetings are clearly established.

The chronology of the *rhetra* is usually believed to be fixed by six lines of an elegy by Tyrtaeus that was later entitled *Eunomia (Good Order)*. These lines are cited by Plutarch (*Lyc.* 6.10, Tyrtaeus fr. 4 W) who declared they seemed (*pou*) to recall the "rider."[54] The lines contain part of a Delphic oracle on correct deliberation. Kings, *gerontes*, and *damos* take part. Tyrtaeus probably mentioned Theopompus and Polydorus in lines lost to us; hence the attribution of the rider to these two kings.[55] It used to be assumed that Tyrtaeus was aquainted with the *rhetra:* but Hans van Wees has demonstrated how difficult it is to prove this (I suspect it is impossible).[56] In that light, and since the *rhetra* is not a law, the crucial question of its relationship to Tyrtaeus must be expressed in the following terms: were Spartan institutions in Tyrtaeus' time organized as the *rhetra* ordains? Perhaps yes. Tyrtaeus seems to place greater value on the authority of the *basileis* and this has been labelled more Homeric (van Wees 1999b: 24; 2002b: 93–5), but the difference has also been explained by referring to the different historical context and the different nature of the *Eunomia* elegy in comparison to the *rhetra* (Whitby 2002: n. 34; Link 2003: 149). Tyrtaeus knew the tradition on the Heraclids (hence *archagetai*), *gerousia* and the Doric *phylai* (see n. 8), and both he and the *rhetra* date back to a moment when Spartan civic institutions and decision making could be spoken of without mentioning the ephors.[57] They bear witness to the third stage of the political development of the *polis* as outlined at the beginning of this section, perhaps in the second half of the seventh or early sixth century.[58]

The *rhetra* must also find a place in the *traditions* on Spartan institutions. Some have claimed that originally the *rhetra* was not considered an oracle, for *rhetra* means "law" (Nafissi 1991: 71; van Wees 1999b: 22–3), but maybe it was always considered a legislative text based upon an oracle, or an oracle which confirmed a bill (Walter 1993a: 159 n. 66; Meier 2002: 86 with biblio.). Its use of participles in the accusative singular suggests that the *rhetra* was attributed to a single individual, presumably Lycurgus. Possibly, the text was originally formulated in the dual, with the kings carrying out its provisions, but later re-elaborated (Bringmann 1975: 356–62). If so, it could have influenced Hellanicus of Lesbos, who in the late fifth century attributed the creation of Spartan institutions to Eurysthenes and Procles, the founders. If, on the other hand, the *rhetra* referred to Lycurgus as is more likely, it would explain why Xenophon places the legislator in the age of the Heraclids (Xen. *Lak. Pol.* 10.8).[59] In that case the *rhetra* would be later than Tyrtaeus, who fails to name Lycurgus.

In seventh-century Sparta, as elsewhere in Greece, there certainly existed a class whose superiority depended on hereditary wealth, bravery in war and an elevated lifestyle. Members of this elite were proud both of their riches and of their athletic prowess (Tyrtaeus, fr. 12 W). They held ostentatious banquets which, lacking the restraint of the Classical *syssitia* (Alcman, fr. 17 Davies), resembled the usual gatherings of aristocrats (*symposia*).[60] Probably the *gerousia* was their preserve but we do not know if access was formally restricted by family or census.[61] Other members of the community, small landholders or peasants, who fought in Tyrtaeus' battles only with light arms (*gymnetes*, fr. 11.35 W; cf. *gymnomachoi*, fr. 23a.14 W), were to a greater or lesser extent in socio-economic difficulties. Serious tensions arose, which Tyrtaeus mentions, as we have seen (fr. 1 W *ap.* Arist. *Pol.* 5.1306b36–1307a2).

The Messenian land distribution of Tyrtaeus' war may have somewhat relaxed these tensions. At any rate, some, including Tyrtaeus, recognized that personal ambition was a good thing only when it was placed in the service of the *polis*. To live up to the glorious Spartan past required the exercise of political and military virtue (frr. 2, 5 W). The former found expression in wise choices and obedience to leaders, especially the kings (fr. 4 W, above n. 54), the latter in willingness to offer the supreme sacrifice: all the illustrious and noble values of old had value only if demonstrated on the battlefield (fr. 12 W). Whoever fought bravely in the front line would be rewarded with the highest civic honors. The exaltation of the community recurs in Alcman too, who prefers simple food over luxurious repasts because they are typical of the community (*ta koina*), of the *damos* (fr. 17 Davies). These are clear heralds of classical Spartan custom.

To many, Sparta is the most resounding example of the impact of the "hoplite revolution or reform" (Snodgrass 1965a; 1993): the transformation in military tactics that was to stimulate the evolution of democracy in Greek society as it required the integration of the peasant class into military and political structures.[62] This transformation, it is claimed, was connected with the great *rhetra* and/or the age of Tyrtaeus, whose songs described a hoplite formation. Land distributions following the Second Messenian War founded or enlarged this class. Yet doubts have been raised about whether Tyrtaeus really describes fully developed hoplite fighting: combat still seems fluid, the formation rather open, and much use is made of missiles hurled by lightly armed warriors.[63] In fact, the problem is more radical. While already in "epic society" mass fighting is decisive,[64] the rigorously homogeneous nature of the hoplitic phalanx is an illusion. Apparently towards the end of the eighth century, when hand-to-hand fighting increased in importance, the essential elements of the panoply were introduced for the elites who wanted to exhibit their wealth as well as their courage (van Wees 2004: 49–50, 52–4, 166). For a long time, not all hoplites wore the expensive bronze panoply that distinguished the wealthiest warriors and those readiest to engage the enemy in hand-to-hand conflict. Hoplite tactics are compatible with a hierarchical society. On these premises the hoplite lead figurines dedicated in the Spartan shrines from the mid-seventh century onwards[65] prove not the immediate transformation of the entire community into hoplites, uniformly armed and aware of their social position,[66] but only the existence of warriors vaunting prestigious armor (ch. 30, below). Besides, some Spartan hoplites of the seventh century probably showed off their status by reaching the battlefield on horseback.[67] As Kurt Raaflaub concludes, the hoplite revolution is a phantom that we should expel from our textbooks (1997d: 53; cf. 1999: 132–41).

What turned Sparta into a hoplite community and a *polis* of Homeric character was neither "hoplite tactics" nor the integration of non-citizens into the army and community during or after the Second Messenian War (Nafissi 1991; Förtsch 2001: 15–6). Nor was it the permanent threat exerted by the Helots (Raaflaub 1999: 134–8), but, rather, a civic, aristocratic and hoplitic ideal and, I would add, the prestige and the extraordinary self-admiration of the Spartans.

The (new?) allotment to Spartiate citizens of Messenian territory was not planned to create a great hoplite phalanx. Roughly between the mid-seventh (the age of Tyrtaeus) and the mid-sixth century a rational and coherent system was established, based on one simple and traditional principle:[68] the Spartans rightly considered themselves the best among the Greeks. We learn from Herodotus (1.68.6) that in the middle of the sixth century the Peloponnese was under their control and their courage on the battlefield was matched by a long series of triumphs in panhellenic competitions (Hodkinson 1999; Mann 2001). They decided that the first *polis* in Greece ought to consist only of the best and to be governed by a rigorously selected elite. They therefore established strict conditions for citizenship: monthly contributions in the form of food for the common tables (the *syssitia*, Arist. *Pol.* 1271a26–37). The elevated census which they imposed on themselves (Hodkinson 2000: 190–9) suggests that the citizens had to procure the panoply privately. Despite these limitations, the success of the polis in previous centuries – not only during the Second Messenian War – made citizenship accessible to several thousand men. They set up an educational system that eventually became mandatory, governed and administered by the civic authorities. This system, partly founded on pre-existing rites and certainly developed further over time, was intended to create full-time warriors, dedicated to the good of the polis and respect for communal norms (*nomos*). Constant competition in socially approved virtues resulted in the emergence of a highly competent elite whose performance was subject to continuous scrutiny (Ducat 1999; 2006).

We do not know if all those who in the period of Tyrtaeus had asked for land redistribution were now satisfied. Certainly, some Spartans now rose to the ranks of the aristocracy. The Helots produced harvests on their farms, and all citizens, freed from manual labor, used their time for political and religious activities, hunting, athletics, and banquets. A strict opposition was now created, between free (full citizens) and unfree (Helots). The various conditions of dependent peasants, no matter their original status and how and when they became dependent, were homogenized. Perhaps Helot status itself was legally (re)defined. The distinction between *perioikoi* and citizens became sharper. The Spartan and Athenian response to social and economic tensions was to define what each person deserved. Solonian Athens defended the weaker members of the community and openly acknowledged the role of wealth. Sparta condemned those falling below a minimum census to life in worse conditions and loss of status, excluding them from full citizenship, while at the same time declaring equality of all citizens.

In fact, the Spartans were called *homoioi*, peers, equal in value and therefore in dignity (Cartledge 2001: 68–75). The term, used in the late fifth century (Shimron 1979), signifies the overcoming of former social differences, while implicitly distinguishing the peers from everyone below their own level in Lacedaemonian society and perhaps beyond. Probably the emphasis on parity was a direct result of sixth-century changes.[69] Parity was reflected in lifestyle too. Thucydides writes that the Spartans adopted a modest, strongly egalitarian lifestyle (1.6.4), and in the Classical age restrictions on the display of private wealth, for instance regarding feminine decorum, are well documented (Hodkinson 2000: 214–30). Immoderate greed for wealth was considered a threat to civic harmony; luxury and relaxation were condemned as dangerously effeminate fascinations for people who were expected to endure every hardship and demonstrate their manliness in brutal fighting. The Spartans' resulting determination to preserve a severe and traditional way of life was supported by the menacing power of the ephors. Individual status (*time*) was bestowed by the polis and reflected individual dedication to the community and its ethical, political, and religious values. The city chose and rewarded the best. Economic differences and shows of prestige were not allowed to interfere with this decision. Wealth, in general, was not valued socially. Economic differences were not eliminated but reduced to secondary rank and only occasionally allowed to be displayed, in accordance with civic values. Similarly, citizens were free to pursue economic interests, and possession of precious metals was not banned. Generosity among citizens, however, was highly praised, and the most valuable exchanges took mostly place in kind (gifts, dowries, testaments) and usually involved reciprocity.[70]

In my opinion it is beyond doubt that the famous sixth-century ephor, Chilon, was among the promoters of this politico-cultural effort aiming to produce such an exceptional citizen body, but details are lost and the evidence, even from Classical times, cannot be pressed too far. A heroic relief with the inscription [*Ch*]*ilon* has been attributed to him (Förtsch 2001: 218 n. 1842, no. 3, figs. 210–11). However that may be, the inclusion of Chilon in the variable canon of the "Seven Sages" reflects his importance in the archaic history of Sparta.[71]

The ephorate played an important role in this transformation, but reliable information on its origin and history are lacking.[72] The most ancient sources attribute its creation to the ever-present Lycurgus (Hdt. 1.65). Only later and, in my opinion, prompted by the need to counter King Pausanias' attempt to discredit the office, arose a tradition that assigned its institution to King Theopompus.[73] Later information concerning Elatus, the first ephor, depending as it does on the latter tradition (Plut. *Lyc.* 7.1; 754–753 BC: Jacoby 1902: 138–42), or the partisan account by Cleomenes III on Asteropus (Plut. *Cleom.* 10), are even less credible. Claims that Chilon was the first ephor are no less doubtful (Diog. Laert. 1.68: cf. above n. 71). That the ephorate should be placed in this recent phase of Sparta's development seems assured by its highly political function (above) and the *rhetra's* silence. In this case, the argument from silence seems sound, especially if, as explained above, the *rhetra* is not a legislative document but a text describing Spartan institutions and their supposed origin.

The essential task of the ephors, as suggested by their original title ("overseers") was to guard respect for laws and customs. Probably, then, the office was instituted in the context of the sixth-century reform. Its creation reflects the community's political maturation. Those appointed as ephors were expected to be men of excellent virtues and rewarded with outstanding *timai*, including the right to preside over assemblies and the most revered ephoral seat (Xen. *Lac. Pol.* 15.6). Annual election stimulated open competition among adults, similar to that among elders at the election of *gerontes*, and the ephors in turn indirectly controlled the selection of the most excellent youths (above n. 67). Competition in virtue, the essential characteristic of Spartan civic culture, therefore passed from generation to generation.

Aristotle affirms that, whereas the *gerousia* was the prerogative of an elite, defined primarily in ethical terms (*kaloi kagathoi*), the ephorate was open to the entire *damos* (*Pol.* 1270b23ff; 1294b29ff). Combined with traditional theories concerning the role of hoplites, this has prompted attempts to interpret the rise of the ephorate and the transformation of Sparta as the outcome of a struggle between nobles and *damos* (Oliva 1971: 128–31; Nafissi 1991; Sommer 2001). The value of Aristotle's evidence is dubious, however. His theory of the mixed constitution encouraged the assignation of a social basis to each of the elements of government (monarchy, oligarchy, democracy) and the idea that virtue was confined to the "best" of the community led ancient theorists to conceive of candidates for the *gerousia* as a distinct group within the *damos*. The sixth-century reform certainly was not achieved without tensions but it is misleading to assume a rigid opposition between nobles and *damos*.

What, then, was the ephors' relationship with the kings? Attempts have been made to reconstruct either a slow growth in power from an earlier "little ephorate" which collaborated with the kings or a delayed rise of the ephorate in the late sixth and early fifth century, due in part to abuses of royal power by ambitious kings like Cleomenes I.[74] The available evidence permits neither confirmation nor refutation of such hypotheses.[75] Even Herodotus' information on political life in Sparta in the sixth and fifth centuries is episodic and anecdotal; it attests specifically to only one innovation (5.75: the law of 507/6 prohibiting the simultaneous presence of both *basileis* in one campaign) and does not suggest essential changes in the relationship between ephorate and *basileia* (Luther 2004: 94–137). It is not unlikely that the functions of the ephors broadened gradually as the community faced new challenges and needs. A fifth-century origin of the monthly oath (Xen. *Lac. Pol.* 15.7) cannot be excluded *a priori*, but the principle that even the kings were subjected to the *nomos* must have been much older. The spread of tyrannies in Greece probably prompted new sensitivity towards the kings' power which, however, could only be harnessed, not eliminated.

Figure 7.1 A Laconian cup by the
Naucratis painter, ca. 560 BC, probably
showing Zeus enthroned, with an eagle
Source: Louvre E688. Photo by Bibi Saint-Pol.

Archaeological evidence has often
been consulted for information concerning the date and nature of Sparta's
socio-cultural transformation.[76] Recent
detailed analysis has illuminated the
process that can loosely be called the
decline of Laconian art (Förtsch 2001).
Yet analysis and historical interpretation continue to be quite difficult. Not
all phenomena can be reduced to internal causes. For example, the disappearance of Laconian black-figured pottery
is largely attributable to the success
of its Attic counterpart (Hodkinson
1998: 97–102). By contrast, in the
area of internal consumption, quantitative analysis of bronze votive offerings
approximates much more closely what
is found in the rest of Greece, but the available sample is severely limited
(Hodkinson 2000: 271–301; cf. Förtsch 2001: 37 n. 336). Broadly, however, we
note a gradual extinction of artisan traditions and a preference, considered conscious
by some, for cruder artistic forms. The process seems to have reached a critical stage
in the mid-sixth century (Förtsch 1998; 2001; cf. Boss 2000 for lead figurines).

The number of lead figurines dedicated to Artemis Orthia grew dramatically during
the sixth century, from around 200 a year between 650 and 580 to 860 a year between
580 and 500,[77] and the latter period also saw a great increase in the number of hoplite
figurines.[78] Black-figure Laconian vases in the middle decades of the sixth century
(see figure 7.1) reflect persistence of a luxurious symposiastic tradition that contrasts
with the habits of the Classical *syssition*.[79] The slow appearance of battle scenes, encountered only from the beginning of the sixth century, and, in the second half of the
same century, representations of hoplites and athletes seem to indicate the growing
importance of the celebration of *arete* (Förtsch 2001: 99–104, 106–9, 115–29, 222–4).
By the second half of the sixth century, the stamp of communitarian ideals had been
imposed on Laconian art, causing political and military values to prevail over the
individual self-representation of a leisured class.

The results of the "Laconia Survey" now offer further proof of the importance
of the middle decades of the sixth century for the development of classical Sparta.
In the middle of the century, or a little earlier (the nature of the evidence allows
only approximate dates), the lands around Sparta, until then without settlements,
were dotted with many tiny farms. Elsewhere in Greece too the countryside tends
to become more densely occupied in the late archaic and classical ages, but in Laconia
the process was particularly sudden, and apparently spontaneous (followed by a rapid
decline that was certainly connected to the concentration of properties and the shortage of citizens which hit Sparta in the fifth century, at the latest). No evidence of
land distribution on the part of the polis can be detected.[80] Obviously the greater

part of these lands was owned by Spartans, though earlier they had failed to farm them intensively. It is reasonable to postulate a connection with the decision to fix a monthly contribution to the common tables as a condition of citizenship.[81] Stephen Hodkinson has shown that the classical Spartan system of agriculture presupposes a certain degree of intensive cultivation, stemming, among other causes, from the range of compulsory mess contributions and the subsistence pressure on the helot tenants (Hodkinson 2000: 133–5). Soon the need to produce sufficient food to qualify as *homoioi* must have induced forms of land exploitation which required a more stable and continuous presence of laborers.

The reforms which decreed the status of the *homoioi* profoundly influenced also the life of dependent agricultural classes: the displacement of the unfree population to permanent dwellings in the countryside was probably both an expression of contempt and the result of economic considerations. Perioikic status – probably also defined in legal terms from this time on – possibly offered an outlet for those excluded from citizenship. This is suggested, at that very time, by the rise of Sellasia (Catling 2002: 238–40), a perioikic community in which, as far as possible, the Spartan way of life was emulated.

Conclusion:
An Outline of Archaic Spartan History

Military success was the key-note of Spartan history from the tenth to the sixth century. The earliest victories, with the partial exception of Theopompus' war against Messene, are historically shadowy. However, in their wake traditions were created which shaped the complex communal identity of Sparta and the Heraclid ancestry of its *basileis*. The strength of Sparta and the prestige of its kings impelled many communities in the southern Peloponnese to follow the Lacedaemonians and their *basileis*. Thanks to the heroic lineage ascribed to the latter, Sparta soon enjoyed some of the stable power which its ancient admirers credited to the genius of Lycurgus. In the seventh century the *polis* faced social unrest, but the elite was able to retain control, partly through appeals to their highly praised kings and warlike traditions. By then, Sparta valued its own political system so highly that it produced a charter of its origins, the *great rhetra*. Common scholarly opinion probably overestimates the importance of the Helots and uniform hoplite culture in the construction of Classical Sparta. The latter was more an effect than a cause of the historical process which led, in the first half of the sixth century, to a deep political reform. Fuelled chiefly by the Spartans' self-esteem, its main features were the high census required to qualify as citizen and the equality between those who qualified – much to the disadvantage of the Helots, whose status and conditions probably now began to take their classical form. By this time the civic institutions formed a complex system of honors, the wrestling-ground, so to speak, where the proud Spartans competed in the contest of virtue. The ephors, probably a new institution, loudly demanded compliance to the *nomos*. Their voice seems to threaten the majesty of the *basileis*: it is, however, not clear if fear of tyranny was a real danger, or a phantom to conjure with. Spartan ambition to be recognized as first among the Peloponnesians (if not all Greeks) is evident in the early attempt to locate Agamemnon in Amyclai. The origin of the Peloponnesian league, which we have not been able to sketch above, has its origins in the sixth century and Thucydides (1.18.1) was probably not too wide of the mark when he connected it to Spartan intervention against tyrants.[82] In any case, in the glorious day of the Persian war, Spartan hegemony rested not only on preexisting treaties and the renown of the city's army, but also – as the terms of the negotiatons between Sparta and Argos and Syracuse show (Hdt. 7.148, 159) – on the mythical and genealogical discourse surrounding its *basileis*. The Spartan mirage had very deep roots.

NOTES

1   I thank Dr. Rosemary Alabaster for translating this chapter into English. Further thanks to the editors, Kurt Raaflaub and Hans van Wees, for their careful reading and helpful suggestions.
2   Ollier 1933–43; cf. Tigerstedt 1965–78; Powell and Hodkinson 1994.
3   But see Cartledge 1992; Malkin 1994b: 15–45; Eder 1998.
4   On "intentional history," see Gehrke 2001.
5   The concept of "Traditionskern," adopted by Wenskus 1961: 54–82, esp. 75–7, in medieval history, has usefully been applied to Greece, e.g., by Luraghi 2001b: 294–9; Gehrke 2003b: 13.
6   Protogeometric or Dark Age pottery: 950–750 BC. Cartledge 2002: 71–80, 85–6, 92; Coulson 1985; Eder 1998: 99–113.
7   Aravantinos et al. 2001: 214–5 and commentary on Fq 229.4; see Hall 2000: 85–6.
8   The traditions which justify these claims are documented very early: Tyrtaeus frr. 2.12–5, 19.8 W; Alcman fr. 3.1–12 Calame (1983) = 1.1–12 Davies (1991).
9   Successes of Sparta in this period are probably also reflected in the first construction of a temple in the sanctuary of Artemis Orthia at the end of the eighth century (Boardman 1963; Cartledge 2002: 308–12).
10   Cult continuity from the Bronze Age is debated (Eder 1998: 97–107, 127–30).
11   Pind. *Pyth.* 1.65; *Isthm.* 7.12ff; Ephorus *FGrH* 70 F117, cf. 118; on Arist. fr. 532 Rose; cf. Nafissi 1991: 324 n. 214.
12   Cartledge 2002: 90–3; 1992: 54–5; Lévy 2003: 16–7; Welwei 2004: 28. Amyclae would then have been the fifth village (*oba*) of Sparta, but it cannot be excluded that it was a perioikic centre during the Classical period (Kennell 1995: 162–9). Pausanias' failure to mention the Amyclaeans among the communities that originally honored Artemis Orthia, proves nothing (3.16.9); it reflects the Amyclaeans' late incorporation into Roman Sparta.
13   Laconia: Stesich. fr. 216 Davies; Simon. fr. 549 Page; Hdt. 1.67–8. Amyclae: Pind. *Pyth.* 9.32; *Nem.* 11.34.
14   Kennell 1995: 8–11; Cartledge and Spawforth 1989: 78–90; Kennell 1999: 191–2; Luraghi 2003: 131.
15   Hellanicus *FGrH* 4 F188; Ephorus *FGrH* 70 F117; Theopompus *FGrH* 115 F13; Paus. 3.20.6.
16   Luraghi 2003: 119–20, 133–5; Ducat 1990b: 11; *contra* van Wees 2003: 52–3.
17   frr. 5.1–2 W *ap.* Paus. 4.6.5; 5.4–8 W *ap.* Strabo 6.3.3; cf. fr. 8 W *ap.* Strabo 8.4.10.
18   Jacoby 1923–54: vol. 3a: 109–95; Pearson 1962; Musti and Torelli 1991: esp. xii–xxviii.

19 Alcock 1999; Luraghi 2002a; Luraghi 2008: 107–46.

20 Antiochus of Syracuse *FGrH* 555 F13 *ap.* Strabo 6.3.2; Thuc. 1.101.2; cf. Hdt. 3.47.1.

21 Plut. *Mor.* 194b; Ael. *VH* 13.42; see Den Boer 1954: 81–2. Fragments of the lists of Olympic victors record Messenian successes between 768 and 736 BC and one in the long distance race some time after 716 BC; the historical value of this information and its significance for Messenian history is debated (Parker 1991: 27–8; M. Meier 1998: 92–3; Christesen 2007).

22 The proposal to place the war in the sixth century (Shaw 1999: 275–82; 2003: 100–45), ignores this one solid date.

23 Schwartz 1899: 429; Musti and Torelli 1991: 225. The traditional interpretation is defended by Jacoby 1902: 136; 1943: 154; M. Meier 1998: 97–8.

24 For a rapid overview, see Hodkinson 2000: 66–8; Lupi 2003; Figueira 2003; 2004a.

25 See the "monumental" argument for this view by Hodkinson 2000, esp 65–6 n. 2 (quote: 81).

26 Ducat 1990b: 19–29; Hodkinson 2000: 113–16; Luraghi 2002b: 228–33. Cartledge 2003: 17–9 defends the collective nature of Helotic serfdom, but see Patterson 2003: 298–9.

27 Ducat 1974; 1990b; Cartledge 1985b; Luraghi 2002b; van Wees 2003: 66–71; Hodkinson 2003. Generally Luraghi and Alcock 2003.

28 Alcock 2002b; Hodkinson 2003: 259–60, 266, 270–4; cf. Luraghi 2002b: 231–2; 2008: 107–46.

29 Roobaert 1977; Talbert 1989; Ducat 1990b: 145–53; Whitby 1994; cf. Cartledge 1991; 2003: 20–3; Link 2000.

30 Figueira 1999; Luraghi 2001b; 2002a; 2003; 2008; Hall 2003b.

31 For the *communis opinio*, see the bibliography quoted by M. Meier 1998: 267 n. 112. Hodkinson 2000: 127–8; 2003: 262–3; Link 2004. Collective dependence: Kiechle 1959: 56ff; Figueira 2003: 221–2; Welwei 2004: 55–7.

32 So Hodkinson 2000: 126–31, but see Ducat 1990b: 59–61; Luraghi 2002b: 235–6.

33 van Wees 2003; Hodkinson 2003: 262–3; Link 2004; but see Raaflaub 2003a: 171–2.

34 Shipley 1992; 1997; 2000; 2004a; 2004b; Hall 2000; Eremin 2002; Mertens 2002; Hansen 2004.

35 Kennell 1999. It is possible, though far from certain, that the ephors mentioned in the inscriptions of the Tainaron sanctuary (mostly fourth century BC) were not Spartan ephors but those of the local perioikic city (Ducat 1990a).

36 Cf. also Steph. Byz. *s.v Aithaia, Amyklai, Anthana, Aulon, Aphrodisia, Dyrrachion, Epidauros, Krokeai, Tenos* and perhaps *Augeia*. For lists of perioikic settlements and *poleis* in Laconia and Messenia, see Shipley 2004a; 2004b.

37 Beginning with Thucydides (7.57.6; cf. 4.53.2), but, as Shipley 1997: 204 notes, the reference is to Cythera, an island. Cf. Paus. 3.22.6; Strabo 8.4.4; Nep. *Conon* 1.1.

38 The destruction of Asine is attested archeologically: Hall 1995: 581–3, but for Mothone see Luraghi 2008: 142.

39 Finley 1968; cf. Hodkinson 2000: 3–4; I will speak of this transformation as a "reform."

40 De Ste. Croix 1972: 125; Cartledge 2001: 61. Generally on Spartan kings Carlier 1984 is fundamental; see also briefly Cartledge 2001: 55–66.

41 On links between kings and *perioikoi*, see Kahrstedt 1922: 78–9; Bringmann 1975: 382 n. 89; van Wees 2003: 56. In the classical age they were subject also to other Spartan authorities (Isoc. 12.181; cf. Mertens 2002: 293–5; Hodkinson 2000: 188–90).

42 Oliva 1971: 23–8; Cartledge 2002: 89–92; Welwei 2004: 24–6.

43 *Phylaxanta* probably alludes to two verbs: *phylasso* (to preserve) and *phylazo* (to divide into *phylai*): Nafissi 1991: 80–1; Walter 1993a: 160–1.

44   Cf. Thuc. 4.118.9.
45   Wade-Gery 1943–1944: I. 70; van Wees 1999b: 34 n. 62.
46   On the role of fourth-century scholarship: Meyer 1892; David 1979; Nafissi 1991: 51–71; van Wees 1999b: 14–22; Sordi 2004; Bertelli 2004. For the rider as integral part of the *rhetra*: Wade-Gery 1943–4: I. 65, III. 115; Jeffery 1961b: 147 n. 28; Forrest 1963: 157–66; West 1974: 185; Cartledge 1980: 99–100; Musti 1996; Thommen 1996: 34; Liberman 1997; M. Meier 1998: 187; van Wees 1999b: 19–21; Welwei 2004: 60–1; *contra* the authors cited by van Wees 1999b: 36 n. 70 under (3), and e.g., Ruzé 1997: 161–72; Richer 1998: 93–109; Luther 2004: 25–59. Ogden 1994 suggests that the rider antedates the *rhetra*, which is difficult to accept; see further Nafissi, forthcoming.
47   Forrest 1963: 159–60, 165–6; Jones 1967: 31; West 1970: 151; Liberman 1997.
48   Plut. *Lyc.* 6.6: "the *damos* had the power to give a decisive verdict"; for a list of the numerous amendments which have been suggested, see Luther 2004: 39 n. 124.
49   Jeffery 1961b: 144–7; Roussel 1976: 243 n. 13; Lévy 1977: 94–5; *contra*: Carlier 1984: 312 n. 445; Richer 1998: 94 and n. 10.
50   Roussel 1976: 237 thinks of groupings analogous to the phratries; cf. Lévy 1977: 91–4; Welwei 2004: 64–5.
51   The *rhetra* goes well beyond the determination of the responsibility of officials (cf. Osborne 1997); *pace* Luther 2004: 33–5, 42–3, 59, the *rhetra* is not a simple description of measures enacted by Lycurgus, but a prescription: the participles indicate actions to be carried out once only, while the infinitives concern actions that must be repeated in the future.
52   As suggested in different ways by Meyer 1892: 261–9 (cf. Sealey 1976: 74–8); Jeffery 1961b; Lévy 1977: 44–5 (cf. 2003: 27–36, 204–5). My own opinion is closer to Roussel's (1976: 235), whose precise chronology and conclusion, however, are over-optimistic.
53   Vansina 1985; cf. Ungern-Sternberg and Reinau 1988.
54   For a survey of opinions, see van Wees 1999b: 35–6 n. 70.
55   Plut. *Lyc.* 6.9; Hammond 1950: 49; Kiechle 1963: 167–8; Forrest 1963: 158–62; Murray 1980: 161; but see van Wees 1999b: 12–13; 2002: 98–9.
56   Van Wees 1999b; 2002b; cf. Luther 2004: 90–2; *contra* Meier 2002; Link 2003; Raaflaub 2006. Lines 3–6 appear with slight variations in Diod. Sic. 7.12.6 (= fr. 4 W), where they are cited as part of an oracle received by Lycurgus. This oracle was published at the beginning of the fourth century by king Pausanias in a pamphlet written "against the Laws of Lycurgus" (Strabo 8.5.5 cf. Ducat 2006: 42–4) and evidently used at least some material from Tyrtaeus. But it does not necessarily follow that lines 1–2 and 7–9 of the oracle in Diodorus also derived from Tyrtaeus, who did not recollect constitutional norms, but exhorted obedience to the kings and communal decisions (Nafissi 1991: 77; van Wees 1999b; 2002: 92–8).
57   *Pace* Nippel 1980: 132; Richer 1998: 98–106; Link 2000: 19–30; Luther 2004: 44–59.
58   Many consider it possible that, despite a "Lycurgan" prohibition of written laws (Plut. *Lyc.* 13.1–4), the *rhetra* was quickly put into writing (Jeffery 1961b: 145–6; Thommen 1996: 42–3 n. 96; Millender 2001: 127–9; Lipka 2002a; 2002b: 24–7).
59   Lévy 1977: 95. For a different explanation: van Wees 1999b: 13.
60   Generally on the evolution of banquets from Alcman to the classical *syssition*: Nafissi 1991: 206–26; Hodkinson 1997: 90–2; on the classical *syssition*: Fisher 1989.
61   As suggested, for example, by Welwei 1979: 431–3.
62   Andrewes 1954; Andrewes 1956: 75, "the first hoplite constitution of Greek history"; Cartledge 1980; Murray 1980; Bringmann 1980; Förtsch 2001.

63 Wheeler 1991: 129–31; van Wees 2000a: 149–52; 2004: 172–4; see also Latacz 1977: 232–7; ch. 30, below.

64 Latacz 1977; Pritchett 1985a: 1–33; van Wees 1994; Raaflaub 2005b.

65 Dawkins, Droop et al. 1929: 262; see Boardman 1963 for the date: 650–620 BC; cf. Boß 2000: 154–62.

66 Snodgrass 1965: 116; Cartledge 1977: 26–7; Murray 1980: 159; Osborne 1996a: 183.

67 From extant sources we know only of the *hippeis* of the Classical Age (Xen. *Lac. Pol.* 4.3; Hodkinson 1983: 247–9), to whom horses were made available (cf. Hdt. 8.124; Ephorus *FgrH* 70 F149.18). It is likely that these were created in a sixth-century reform (Nafissi 1991: 153–62; *pace* Thommen 1996: 61; see also ch. 30, below).

68 On Sparta as a system, see Finley 1968; on rationality and the possibility of recognizing a general pattern in the development of archaic Sparta, see Hodkinson 1997: 86–89.

69 Ehrenberg 1933 [1965]: 218–19; Link 2000: 113–17; differently Shimron 1979; Thommen 1996: 51, 136–7.

70 Hodkinson 2000: 151–86, 199–201; on iron money see also Christien 2002; Figueira 2002, the latter suggesting that it buttressed a barter economy.

71 Ancient testimonies place Chilon variously in the early or mid-sixth century (Fehling 1985); the date of his ephorate (556/5: Diog. Laert. 1.68) probably has no documentary foundation. Modern opinion ranges from being excessively skeptical (Thommen 1996: 76–78; Luther 2002) to being unduly uncritical (Ehrenberg 1925; Stibbe 1985; Nafissi 1991: 124ff, 138, 347–8; Richer 1998: 117–34, 230–2).

72 Recent monographs on the ephorate: Richer 1998; Sommer 2001; Luther 2004.

73 Arist. *Pol.* 5.1313a25–33, but see already Pl. *Leg.* 3.692a; Nafissi 1991: 63–5.

74 See Welwei 2004: 86–93, 126–9; Thommen 1996: 92–8, 105–12, respectively; cf. Meier 2000. Note the law against both kings going on campaign together (Hdt. 5.75) and the trials against individuals of royal blood from the 490s to 460s.

75 Herodotus' account of Anaxandridas, coerced into taking a second wife by the ephors (5.39ff), assumes that ephors were already in full possession of their powers around the mid-sixth century (Link 2000: 2–11), but this may be anachronistic.

76 Hodkinson 1998: 94–7; Förtsch 1998; Förtsch 2001: 34–7.

77 Hodkinson 1998: 107; the chronology of Boß 2000: 147–75 implies an even more pronounced growth.

78 Kennell 1995: 136; Hodkinson 2000: 290. The remodelling of the sanctuary (according to Boardman 1963 in 575–560 BC) may have been connected with a reorganization of the cult which reflected its greater role in the boys' upbringing as hoplites (Kennell 1995: 136–7; cf. Hodkinson 2000: 290–1).

79 Nafissi 1991: 206–26; Powell 1998; Förtsch 2001: 139–56.

80 Catling 2002: esp. 157–74, 235–8, 250; cf. Hodkinson 2003: 259–60.

81 Contra Catling 2002: 234, who links it to the failed attempt to conquer Tegea (Hdt. 1.66).

82 On the league see especially Ste. Croix 1972: 101–24, 333–46; Lendon 1994; also Bolmarcich 2005; Kimmerle 2005; Yates 2005.

CHAPTER EIGHT

Athens

Michael Stahl and Uwe Walter

Where to begin?

When Jacob Burckhardt warned against beginning the study of history at the beginning, he might with good reason have cited Athens. For here any attempt to determine origins runs into problems. What archaeologists tell us about the first settlements on the slopes of the Acropolis, the Mycenaean fortress there, possible population movements into and within Attica, and economic and social conditions as revealed especially by grave-goods – all this is important and informative, but it is neither a story nor history.[1]

In historical times the Athenians prided themselves on being autochthonous, that is, having always lived in Attica (Loraux 1993: 37–71). Nevertheless, their mythical memory included a marked act of foundation, connected with the figure of Theseus. They saw him as a liberator, because he had terminated the humiliating obligation, imposed by king Minos of Crete, of sending every ninth year fourteen young men and women as a sacrifice to the Minotaur. Having become king himself, Theseus was believed to have established Athens as a proper state through an act of unification (*synoikismos*). In a nice piece of "conjectural history" on Athens' earliest period (2.14.2–16.2), Thucydides writes:

> Under Cecrops and the first kings, down to the reign of Theseus, Attica had always consisted of a number of independent townships, each with its own town hall and magistrates. Except in times of danger the king at Athens was not consulted; in ordinary seasons they carried on their government and settled their affairs without his interference; sometimes even they waged war against him, as in the case of the Eleusinians with Eumolpus against Erechtheus. In Theseus, however, they had a king of equal intelligence and power; and one of the chief features in his organization of the country was to abolish the council-chambers and magistrates of the petty cities, and to merge them in the single council-chamber and town hall of the present capital. Individuals might still enjoy their private property just as before, but they were henceforth compelled to

have only one political centre, viz., Athens; which thus counted all the inhabitants of Attica among her citizens, so that when Theseus died he left a great state behind him.

(2.15.1–2; tr. Crawley)

Such mythical stories tell us much about Athenian self-consciousness in the classical period and the construction of their identity from the late sixth century (Walker 1995; Anderson 2003: 136–43). But for the question of the beginning of a political organization or state in Attica they have no value. Myths do not turn into history simply by being purged of all implausibilities and subjugated to laws of reason – critical thinkers knew this already in antiquity. But the public needed its founding heroes (e.g., Plut. *Thes.* 1.3; cf. Welwei 1990/2000). Later, Theseus, whose rule supposedly predated the Trojan War, was even identified as the creator of Athenian democracy.[2] He was for the Athenians an idealized portrait of themselves: brave, just, helpful, and clever.

Yet the mythical construct of Theseus' synoikism is intuitively based on the right question: what made it possible to unify the large territory of Attica (ca. 2,650 km^2) with its old and proud towns and sanctuaries? Even if Athens was the most prominent settlement already in the Bronze Age, what enabled it to become the center of a process of state formation? And, from a broader perspective, what prompted Athens' rise to predominance in Greece in the fifth century?

Even to a critical modern historian the extant sources suggest an account of the history of Athenian state formation which follows a chain of powerful individuals. We shall reconstruct this history here as a continual process with several stages: beginnings (Draco), brilliant design (Solon), latency (Peisistratus), revolution (508), and institutional consolidation (Cleisthenes). To be sure, different and more discontinuous narratives are possible. For example, Anderson (2003) suggests that the course of Athenian history was dramatically altered between 510 and 490. But the model presented here, of a logical evolution of the Athenian citizen-state, has a significant advantage: it attributes less importance to the oft-posed question of when democracy, in a specific sense, began in Athens. Of course, the intense and permanent mobilization in politics of large sections of the citizenry would hardly have been possible without Athens' victory in the Persian Wars and the rise of the city to great imperial power in their aftermath; hence undoubtedly contingent factors did play a role. But the psychological and institutional preconditions that were established in the archaic period were decisive.[3]

Violence, Law, and Procedure: Cylon and Draco

The series of eminent Athenians extolled by tradition begins in the last third of the seventh century with Cylon and Draco. Both illustrate an elementary fact: the development of structures and procedures that resulted in the typical Greek "citizen-state" (Hansen 1993b) was neither natural nor automatic (ch. 20, below; Stahl 2003a: 94–116). Rather, this development was a response to actual conflicts and potential uses of force which threatened to destroy the internal peace of a community with still weak institutions – and thereby destroy the whole community. In Athens one particular event was carved deeply into collective memory: the "Cylonian Conspiracy" (Welwei 1992: 133–7). At an undetermined date before the tyranny of Peisistratus, Cylon reportedly tried to seize absolute power (*tyrannis*). With a group of men of his own age he occupied the Acropolis but was unable to hold it. To save themselves, the conspirators sought refuge at a cult statue of Athena. A group of officials in charge – Herodotus mentions the "heads of the Naucraries," Thucydides the nine archons – persuaded them to surrender under guarantee of their lives. Cylon and his brother escaped, but his followers were murdered. The noble family of the Alcmeonids was held responsible for this bloody deed. Since members of this family were prominent in Athenian politics for generations thereafter, the memory of the "Cylonian curse" remained alive.[4]

This escalating bloodshed was probably the culmination of a power struggle (*stasis*) between rival elite leaders and their followers (Seaford 1994: 92–8). Unlike in other *poleis*, the issue apparently was not permanent control of the highest office. Even earlier, the Athenians had entrusted communal duties like the command of the citizen militia or the supervision of cult to yearly magistrates. Yet the large number of these offices – three archons and six thesmothetes – made them unsuitable as a base for predominance in the *polis*. Instead, Cylon had gained prominence as an Olympic victor and through his marriage to a daughter of the tyrant of Megara, Theagenes. He had surrounded himself with a group of noble young men, a *hetaireia* (Hdt. 5.71.1), and felt strong enough to pursue a lasting position of leadership, allegedly supported by a troop of soldiers supplied by his father-in-law. (Such armed assistance by outside allies is well attested for other revolutionary coups in archaic history too). Cylon's coup failed because he was unable to win the consent of the citizen population. Already at this early date, around 630, therefore, "politics" in Athens was evidently not the preserve of the nobles (Manville 1990: 78), even if after the end of the acute crisis the Athenians left its resolution to the officials (Thuc. 1.126.8). The affair confirms both the communal spirit of the Athenian *polis* and the functioning of the institutions on which it relied, but the violent outcome shows that procedures and institutions were threatened by the elite's tendency in their intense competition (*stasis*) to humiliate and permanently weaken their defeated opponents.

Violent excesses of this kind posed an enormous problem to the *polis*-community, since in competitions for honor, reputation, and glory the strict rule was reciprocity in doing good and in doing harm (Herman, *OCD*³ 1295; Gill et al. 1998). Whoever failed to return favors for assistance and good deeds, and to avenge bad deeds and insults, lost his honor. Gift-exchange and reciprocal obligations were central in Greek social relations. Violence among nobles threatened the existence of the entire community because the dynamic of revenge and counter-revenge might cause ever wider ripples and undermine security in an entire region (McHardy 2008; Stahl 2003a: 77–80). General insecurity was enhanced further because probably in this early phase of developing state organization not all areas of Attica's large territory were equally pacified. During any *stasis*, nobles and their followers may have controlled their own districts. Likely zones of potential violence were remote pastures and roads. Cylon, however, had violated customary rules by trying to seize by force the Acropolis, that is, the *polis*'s center which belonged to everyone and where, therefore, peace needed to be preserved. His opponents' retaliation made the matter worse, since now even the shrine of Athena, the community's patron goddess, no longer offered a "neutral zone." In a worst case scenario, force of arms was now to be expected everywhere, in the most sacred heart of the *polis* no less than on a mountain pasture. Communal space had virtually lost its structure; no safe haven remained where one could seek refuge in order to take the impetus out of a violent conflict and gain time to sort out the offenses, and to seek solutions as calmly as possible.

Regulations intended to facilitate precisely such quests for solutions are found in Draco's statutes (*thesmoi*) on homicide. According to conventional (although by no means certain) dating, they were enacted in 621/0 and publicly displayed on rotating wooden blocks (*axones*). It is very unlikely that Draco was the author of a comprehensive codification of existing law. Rather, his regulations seem to have covered only kinds of homicide in which conventional forms of arbitration no longer functioned and immediate self-help in the form of retaliation threatened to cause an escalating cycle of vengeance. That they were made effective retroactively confirms their urgency. Draco's homicide law was recorded anew on stone in 409/8 in the context of a revision of all Athenian laws; an extant section concerns murder without premeditation and, despite possible modifications, certainly preserves the authentic core of Draco's statute.[5]

First, specific relatives or members of the victim's phratry had to bring public accusation against the murderer. The claim to blood revenge hereby announced was limited by the subsequent intervention of *polis* institutions. If an exchange of oaths between accuser and plaintiff brought no result, a committee of 51 *ephetes* had to decide whether the deed had been committed with or without premeditation. If it was ruled intentional, blood-revenge was explicitly permitted; if unintentional, the killer, who would have fled the country as a precaution, could obtain reconciliation and pardon (*aidesis*) from the victim's immediate relatives.

It was decisive for the process of state-formation that specific communal institutions were involved in dealing with such offenses. Those seeking revenge were no longer entitled to strike immediately but compelled to submit to a fixed procedure. By leaving Attica, a person guilty of unpremeditated murder created time and opportunity for this procedure which, importantly, took place in public in the Agora. The *busileis* – presumably the tribe-leaders (*phylobasileis*) and an archon (*archon basileus*) – were joined by a new committee, the *ephetes*. Their large number (51) and their selection by social prestige (*aristinden*) guaranteed authority and acceptability of their decisions. Even those who disagreed would have to yield to the pressures of social consensus. Short of taking over the entire process of prosecution and punishment (which at the time was inconceivable), the only practical way to assert the *polis*'s authority consisted of sanctioning and limiting the self-help of injured parties through communal institutions. In addition, the committee of 51 embodied another fundamental principle of the citizen-state: all important decisions were passed not by individuals but by collective bodies ideally representing the entire *polis* (even if in this case representation was limited to elite large landowners).

Even so, great obstacles impeded the killer's return. Not only the victim's immediate relatives (father, brother, or son) had to approve *aidesis* (mostly in exchange for material compensation) but also distant relatives and in some cases the phratry-members, which shows how far the duty of vengeance extended – potentially involving large parts of the community and making it far more than a "private affair" – and how seriously it was taken. The law says twice, "the one opposing it shall prevail," that is, one opposing voice could prevent the deal. Undoubtedly, therefore, its purpose was not merely purification (which was in any case primarily achieved by religious means) but lasting communal peace (Osborne 1996a: 188).

As long as the murderer remained in exile, he was protected by the law; duty of vengeance did not justify his killing. Clearly, this passage responded to a central problem of the Cylonian affair: the exile was explicitly prohibited from staying in places that were visited by many people. This may suggest an attempt to prevent killers from abusing places of asylum where violent revenge caused especially big problems, and to protect from desecration places and events (such as festivals) that were sacred for the entire *polis* and thus especially attractive for those who sought sanctuary (Schmitz 2001).

Lack of sources makes it impossible to tell how successful Draco's regulations were. Yet there is an argument from silence: there is no tradition of escalation of deadly violence in later *stasis*-struggles; we hear of another political assassination only in 462/1, when Ephialtes was killed.

Solon "Invents" the Athenian *Polis*

To us, Solon is the most eminent personality of archaic Greece. A substantial body of evidence, above all remains of his own poetry, although not easy to assess, presents for the first time in Athenian history the clear outline of a historical figure.[6] With hindsight, Solon's individual measures and regulations together form a "grand design" for a comprehensive new communal order. Conversely, the often isolated and fragmentary notices about his regulations and statements on "social politics," jurisdiction and the legal system, citizenship, and political education must always be interpreted from the perspective of this grand design. Overall, the years around 600 form an epochal turning point in the history of Athens; a straight line leads from here to the classical citizen-state of the fifth and fourth centuries. It is Solon's personal merit to have shown the Athenians the way into this future.[7]

Date and social background

The only secure clue to Solon's lifetime is his archonship in 594/3 (Diog. Laert. 1.62). This office required no minimum age, entailed no special power even at this early date, played a primarily supporting role (see above), and could be held even by young men. Solon therefore may well have been born between 630 and 620 and it could be correct that, in old age, he witnessed the beginning of Peisistratus' tyranny around 560 (Plut. *Sol.* 29.2–5). Even his meeting with Croesus, king of Lydia from ca. 560, famously recounted by Herodotus (1.29–32), should not simply be discarded as fictitious, as it usually is.

Solon certainly descended from an aristocratic family. Although he sharply criticizes the offensive behavior of his aristocratic peers (below), he was familiar with many aspects of aristocratic life (guest-friendship, *symposia*, pederasty, horse-breeding and hunting: frs. 19, 23, 25, 26)[8] and offers no hint that he belonged among a new and rising social class. His own statements suggest that he traveled widely around the eastern Mediterranean – nothing exceptional among aristocrats at the time – probably visiting Egypt, Cyprus (frs. 28, 19), and the centers of Greek Asia Minor. The eastern world's social and political structures, exotic to Greek eyes, as well as the exchange of ideas and the intellectual climate elsewhere, must have raised his awareness of the qualities of his native society and impressed upon him that Athens needed to strengthen the traditional foundations of its communal life and develop further the political forms based on them.

To Solon, tradition was first and foremost rooted in Homer – not surprisingly, given Homer's immense significance for Greek thought and action (Havelock 1963). In diction and style, Solon's poems reflect Homer's epics, and he often self-consciously identifies with Homer's most "modern" hero, Odysseus, who trusts his versatility, intelligence, and persuasive speech rather than his sword (Vox 1984). Solon modeled himself on this "prototype of European man" (Andreae 1982); he paradigmatically embodied his combination of intellectual authority and vigorous political action and we may regard him as the first "Western statesman."

Solon and the Athenian crisis

Solon achieved political prominence when he was appointed – by the majority of both his aristocratic peers and the people – to resolve a crisis that threatened to paralyze Athens. His accomplishments thus lack revolutionary flavor, even if they eventually placed the commonwealth on an entirely new foundation. Solon was a *diallaktes* (reconciler); that the *Ath. Pol.* (5.2) also calls him *archon* is due to its misconception of the early archonship which, as said above, offered no base for wide-reaching reforms. Their implementation must have required several years anyway. Rather, Solon's reforms should be separated from his archonship and perhaps dated later, ca. 580–570.[9] Clearly, though, he must have been known as an Athenian patriot, who cared about his community's well-being. Part of this background is probably reflected in his celebrated "Salamis elegy" (frs. 1–3) which calls his countrymen to renew their efforts to recover the island of Salamis from Megara:

> I have come as a herald from lovely Salamis,
> And have composed a song, an ornament of words, instead of speech . . .
> May I be then a man of Pholegandros or Sikinos
> Instead of an Athenian . . .
> For this would shortly be men's common talk:
> "This man is an Athenian, one of the family that let Salamis go." . . .
> Let us go to Salamis, to fight for an island
> That is lovely, and repel grievous shame.[10]

The deep social crisis that troubled Athens certainly had several causes; the sources give no direct information but permit some conclusions. A massive population increase in Attica in the eighth and seventh centuries was earlier taken for granted but is now debated (Scheidel 2003: 126–31). Athenians seem to have participated only minimally in the foundation of colonies; possibly they first concentrated on cultivating unused farmland in Attica.[11] Here as elsewhere the division of land by inheritance appears to have posed problems for many a small farmer. Like Hesiod in Boeotia, Solon advised men to marry late, around age 35 (fr. 27.9), but the consequences of such patterns of behavior, such as the spread of pederasty and prostitution – into which many daughters were sold – created serious new problems (see Solon's law, F31a). Besides demographic changes, scholars also suspect the overuse and subsequent exhaustion and erosion of soil as an extraneous factor, which is however not attested in the sources. The introduction of coinage or the monetization of economic life played no role: these processes began later and took a long time to achieve far-reaching effects.

Other contexts offer better clues. Hesiod's *Works and Days* (*WD*), composed roughly a century before Solon, is our only source for conditions in an archaic rural *oikos* and its relations to other *oikoi* (Tandy and Neale 1996). Hard work, we hear, is necessary to maintain the mostly self-sufficient life of the landowner, or preferably to enhance his prosperity (*WD* 299–300, 311ff). Neighbors covet their property, and whoever fails to take care of it will soon lose it (340). Land is scarce but cultivated diligently and used optimally. Stored harvest prevents hunger, poverty, and the risk of needing to beg for help and being rejected (364–7). Only those who achieve enough profit to be able to give can expect help themselves (549–51). Everybody occasionally needs to borrow seed, animals, fodder, wood, tools, and food. Loans are short-term, offered without interest, guided by the principle of reciprocity, and expected to balance out in the long term, since lender and borrower come from the same familiar, if socially heterogeneous, community of neighbors (353–4). The principle of self-sufficiency, typical of agrarian societies, is therefore only viable in combination with reciprocity.[12]

Apparently, in the second half of the seventh century the rules of reciprocity were increasingly disregarded. Small unreturned gifts or loans accumulated and quickly grew into enormous debts (*WD* 359–62). If this happened only to a few individuals, it did not disturb the community, and those affected could try with hard work to pay off the debt. If they failed the creditors were entitled by customary rules of self-help to seize the borrowers and/or their property, since in common perception failure to repay a loan was equivalent to a loss or theft of property. If, however, changing social dynamics made it impossible for entire groups of the rural population to observe the rules of reciprocity and if, in addition, the lenders systematically exploited customary rules to weaken traditional social structures in order to advance their own interests, then society was in danger of falling apart in a tangle of greed for wealth and power, theft, and moral failings (Balot 2001). Even worse, if ever fewer independent *oikoi* survived, the foundations of the emerging citizen-state with its collective institutions would be destroyed. The "strong principle of equality" (Morris 1996b), an essential condition for their development, would be lost if large numbers of *oikoi* became permanently dependent on a few aristocratic families that disposed of additional means of income and probably needed additional workers.

This background helps understand the crisis mentioned in Solon's poems. Indebted farmers lost their land and became dependent laborers. Some were even sold into slavery; others, to avoid this fate, fled from Attica, hoping, often in vain, to start a new life abroad (fr. 36.10–12). A most serious innovation concerned the *hektemoroi* (sixth-parters), who annually paid a fixed portion of their income to secure their release from the creditor's right of seizing their bodies. These payments, therefore, did not reduce the debt but were, so to speak, lifelong interest payments that could affect even farmers who were not entirely impoverished. The result were statuses of permanent social dependence and the subversion of traditional social relations. In effect, the activities of the elite produced an entirely different type of society. Many aristocrats had profited from the foundation of colonies, trade, piracy, or even the appropri-ation of communal property (*demosia*: fr. 4.12) and thus acquired immense wealth. They too were under pressure. If they wanted to maintain or improve their status they had to engage in "conspicuous consumption" and form large and stable groups of followers and dependents; both were indispensable for success in the rivalries and *stasis*-conflicts that marked aristocratic politics from the seventh century.

The core of the crisis, therefore, was not economic, but social and political. High and low statuses had always existed. Now, however, permanent chains would hold the weak down and keep the strong on top (Stahl 2003a: 190). Whether one identifies causes, as we do here, mainly in the economic and social sphere, or prefers, as Harris (1997) suggests, to interpret the farmers' payments to aristocrats as protection money and fees, the result was the same. The agrarian society of Attica was in danger of becoming dependent and feudal through the establishment of structures of clientele.[13] The *Athenian Politeia* anachronistically sees the reason in an oligarchic constitution but grasps the core of the problem correctly: "The harshest and bitterest aspect of the constitution for the masses was the fact of their enslavement (*douleuein*), though they were discontented on other grounds too: it could be said that there was noth-ing in which they had a share" (2.3; tr. Rhodes 1984).

This break with traditional forms of communal life – a veritable social and polit-ical "revolution from above" – caused widespread anger and threatened even those who so far had preserved their independence. Many aristocrats too must have been disconcerted, fearing as a result of escalating *stasis* either the self-destruction of the community or a tyranny. The community, no longer securely rooted in pre-state tradi-tions and not yet sufficiently protected by new political institutions, was unable to cope. At last a coalition was formed that entrusted Solon with the task of resolving the crisis and saving the community. He appeared trustworthy: although commanding his own followers, he expressly refused to seize tyranny (see below).

Short-term reform, long-term vision

Solon's first measure, called *seisachtheia* (shaking-off of burdens), is usually taken as a cancellation of all debts, but probably refers more specifically to the liberation of the *hektemoroi* (mentioned above). Their obligations abolished, they became owners

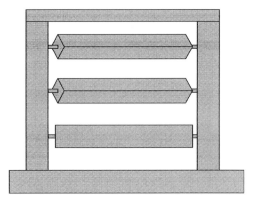

Figure 8.1 A reconstruction of Solon's *axones*

of their land; men who had been enslaved for debt were freed, and enslavement for debt was abolished once and for all. But a "good order" (*eunomia*; Ehrenberg 1946: 70–93) could only be restored permanently by strengthening public institutions (Stahl 2003a: 232). The traditional norms of communal life remained valid but Solon developed them further and gave them precision in many details and, by recording them for the first time publicly as written laws,[14] he made the Athenians fully conscious of them (see figure 8.1). These laws, surviving only in fragments quoted by later authors (collected in Ruschenbusch 1966), represent neither a constitution nor a systematic legal code. Rather, they contain a great variety of regulations, from (in modern terms) private and criminal law to issues of economics and religion. Old customs that had proved useful were fixed and stood next to new norms that took into account recent changes in communal life. Since it was not possible to reform the community from a (nonexistent) position of central power, the laws themselves represented such power. Later, the fifth-century poet Pindar found a catchphrase for this: "the law is king" (*nomos basileus*: fr. 169 in Snell and Maehler 1975). In a culture that was still overwhelmingly oral, the new, enacted laws (*thesmoi*; Solon, fr. 36.18) held a special position. They were publicly displayed on the Acropolis, the religious center, and thus reinforced the community's focal point. Yet they could only be effective if they – and the lawgiver – combined authority and justice.

> And these things by the power
> of law, by a combination of force and justice,
> I accomplished, and completed them as I promised.
> Ordinances for high and low alike,
> setting up straight justice for each man,
> I wrote.
>
> (fr. 36.15–20)

Justice is here created through reconciliation that considered individual circumstances; the legal order manifested itself as a space for the civic community that encompassed society as a whole. Whoever belonged in this space was henceforth a member of the citizen community, with all the rights and obligations arising from it (Manville 1990: 132–3; Walter 1993a: 198–200). The citizen enjoyed personal freedom (Raaflaub 2004b: 45–57) and participated in communal life. While inequalities between rich and poor, nobles and commoners continued, permanent social dependence of a citizen was excluded. The citizens' main responsibility was armed defense of the community. Their military capacity was determined by their economic capacity, measured in annual grain yield. Hence the citizens were divided into four property classes: *pentakosiomedimnoi* (500-bushel men), *hippeis* (horsemen), *zeugitai* (farmers with a team of oxen), and *thetes* with little or no landed property. The members of the first three classes fought as hoplites in the phalanx, even if they could afford a horse. As citizens, all were politically equal in the assembly, except that only members of the first class could hold the office of archon. Thus the circle of the political elite was reduced, since economically the aristocratic *hippeis* (300 bushels) were closer to the *zeugitai* (200 bushels) than to the *pentakosiomedimnoi*.[15]

Ultimately, power was located in the citizens' collective institutions, especially the assembly; only these institutions held political responsibility and were entitled to make decisions. The experience and social prestige of the aristocracy was assembled in the Areopagus, the council of former archons. Additional committees functioned as law courts; to these Solon added the *heliaia* (Hansen 1981–2). The people's power was strengthened further by the introduction of a form of "public prosecution" – by which any citizen was entitled to prosecute an offense on behalf of the victim (*Ath. Pol.* 9.1). Collective bodies could only function, however, if individual citizens geared their behavior wholly towards the community. Without such an attitude, if citizens lived exclusively by the mottos of individual ambition and gain, which of course made sense for an individual *oikos*, communal crisis was inevitable (Balot 2001: 59). Solon formulates and explains this connection programmatically in the famous *Eunomia* elegy (fr. 4), which one might call an ancient "We the People" manifesto.

> Our city will never perish in accordance with the decree of Zeus
> and the will of the blessed immortal gods;
> for such a great-hearted guardian, daughter of a mighty father,
> Pallas Athena holds her hands over us;
> but to destroy a great city by their thoughtlessness
> is the wish of the citizens, won over by riches,
> and unrighteous is the mind of the people's leaders, who are about
> to suffer many pains from their great presumption [*hybris*].
>
> (fr. 4.1–8)

The citizens alone are held responsible for the condition of their community, no longer – as Hesiod had assumed (*WD* 213ff) – the ultimately inscrutable intervention of the gods. Solon postulates an entirely mundane connection between human behavior and communal well-being. This realization marks the beginning of political thought in Europe (Raaflaub 2000) and permits both a sober analysis of connections between social-political causes and effects, and the formulation of a concept for crisis resolution (Stahl 1992 with biblio.; Mülke 2002: 88–159).

> Thus the public evil comes to each at home,
> and house doors can no longer keep it out,
> it has leapt over high fences, found people in all ways,
> even one who runs and hides in his chamber's recess.
>
> (4.26–9)

Since all citizens are equally affected by the consequences of disorder (*dysnomia*), no one can remove himself from the political community. The effects of the citizens' offenses will appear "surely with time" (16). For the *polis* that is founded on the citizens' actions, it is therefore indispensable that every individual give highest priority to the common good. This applies particularly to the aristocrats, "for they know not how to restrain excess" (9). To them, civic responsibility must mean *sophrosyne*, i.e. moderation, self-control, and reason. The climax of his poem is the line "This my spirit (*thymos*) bids me tell the Athenians" (30), which shows how Solon understood his own political actions: as motivated not only by rational insight but also by the deepest internal drive of human existence (*thymos*).

The demand for a political ethic embodied in every citizen was the focal point of Solon's concept of the citizen-state. It was to be realized in two ways. One consisted of connecting political ethics and traditional *polis* religion. The citizens were to think of the city's patron goddess, Athena, as the mother of all Athenians. An important line of continuity in Athenian history lies in the ongoing development of the Athena cult, beginning with Solon and culminating in the building program on the Acropolis in Pericles' time (Kasper-Butz 1990). A second path was suggested to Solon by his personal talents, on which he had already relied in the "Salamis" elegy (mentioned above). Through the means of poetry and in the public space of the *agora* he extolled the power of *peitho*, the peaceful and peace-making force of persuasion that uniquely fitted the role of the arbitrator and reconciler. In the tradition of epic, poetry was a crucial medium of communication in the oral culture of the archaic period.[16] Like other archaic poets, Solon struggled to build a moral foundation for the citizen-state, fighting those traditional social values that stressed the individual's striving for pre-eminence (to be the best, *aristos*) rather than civic ideals. Realizing that the elite's *aristeia*-ideal tended to result in tyranny, Solon explicitly distanced himself from it. In his poetry, he lets an aristocrat represent the conventional ideals of behavior and then refutes them:

> Solon was not a deep thinker or a wise man;
> for when the god gave him good fortune, he did not accept it.
> After encompassing his prey, out of amazement he did not pull in the great
> net, failing in spirit and deprived of wits.
> I would have chosen to have power, to have taken limitless wealth
> and been tyrant of Athens only for a single day,
> and then to have been flayed for a wineskin and had my posterity wiped out.
>
> (fr. 33)

> If I have spared
> my country, and of tyranny and cruel violence
> not laid hold, defiling and disgracing my good name,
> I am not ashamed; for thus I think I shall be more superior
> to all mankind.
>
> (fr. 32)

Solon personally represents the new model; his "sound mind" (*noos artios:* fr. 6.4) transforms the *aristeia*-ideal with its destructive consequences of egotism and lust for power, thus creating an ethics of politics and meeting an elementary need of the emerging *polis*. In Solon's view, the masses with their "empty mind" *(noos chaunos:* fr 11.6) could only grow into a citizenry if they all internalized such ethics. The "soundness of the political order . . . depends on the soundness of the invidual moral consciousness of citizens" (Balot 2001: 94). Solon sought to imprint on this consciousness a strong patriotic component. When he spoke of the common "Attic tongue" (fr. 36.11), the "black Earth" (36.5), and the "native land" (32), and called Athens "Ionia's oldest land" (4a.2), he aimed at integrating a citizenry that still had strong regional loyalties.

Solon's bold and pioneering model of a communal order thus was based entirely on the citizens' common will and action: in its core it was already democratic.[17] Since it presupposed a new political mentality, it could not be realized overnight; the Athenians needed to learn it in a long process, but later "it did provide a moralistic, oppositional language to Athenian greed that would remain important throughout the archaic and classical periods" (Balot 2001: 79). Moreover, the rules and institutions of the citizen-state first needed to prove successful. The half-century after Solon represents, therefore, a transitional period, in which the planted seeds sprouted under the protection of Peisistratid tyranny – paradoxically, since the latter seemed to move in the opposite direction.

The Latent Citizen-state:
The Tyranny of Peisistratus and His Sons

The *stasis*-conflicts that broke out with renewed vigor after Solon's retirement from politics included efforts by the aristocrat Peisistratus to achieve a position of absolute predominance. It took him more than one attempt to establish a tyranny which, in its final phase, lasted from 546 to his death in 527. He was succeeded by his sons Hippias who ruled from 527 to 510, and Hipparchus, who was assassinated in 514 (see figure 8.2).[18] Although these rulers relied not least on superior external resources, their long control of power was only possible because they did not ignore the needs of the Athenian citizenry and their communal life (cf. *Ath. Pol.* 16.2, 7, McGlew 1993). While the memory of other tyrants entails violence and threats (ch. 6 above), the tradition about Peisistratus emphasizes rather his eloquence and cunning (Hdt. 1.59.4–5, 60). Other Athenian aristocrats were able to share in the prestige of the highest offices[19] if they were willing to cooperate; otherwise they suffered exile. In view of his sacred and secular building projects and his efforts to strengthen a sense of community, it seems justified to speak of Peisistratus' "Solonian tyranny."

Naturally, in everything they did, Peisistratus and his sons sought to enhance their own prestige and the acceptance of their rule. But in doing so, they also strengthened and advanced the evolving forms of communal order, including both Solon's legislation and judicial system, which remained intact, and the archonship and its responsibilities. Certainly, the Peisistratids did not allow outspoken opponents to hold the archonship, and they carefully supervised those who did (Thuc. 6.54.6); but the offices were now filled regularly and, together with the Areopagus council, met their

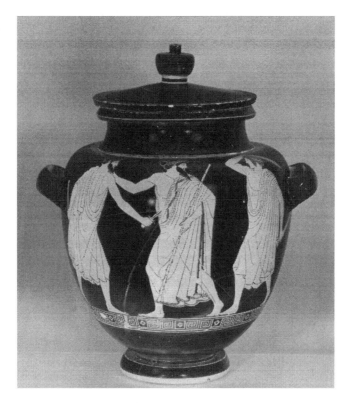

Figure 8.2   Vase painting of Harmodius and Aristogeiton killing Hipparchos

obligations efficiently and without disruption, because the tyrants' mere presence and power eliminated the vicissitudes of *stasis*-conflicts. All this demonstrated to the citizens that the institutions of government could operate effectively and in particular were able to bring greater legal security (Stahl 2003a: 255–9).

Among the tyrants' innovations were the "deme judges" ([Arist.] *Ath. Pol.* 16.5), charged with settling in Attica those disputes which did not reach the ordinary court of the assembly (*heliaia*). Again, political stability ensured the authority of these single judges, whose success contributed to integrating the large Attic territory by emphasizing throughout the principle of conflict resolution by mandatory judicial procedures. The nature of this institution, however, was incompatible with the general norm that offices be based on collegiality and collective control; it seemed too closely connected with the tyrants' personal power, and the Athenians soon abolished it (only to revive it in 453/2). Other laws of the tyrants, too, were subject to later revision, such as a tax on income from landed property and procedures used for naturalization. Still, even these measures ultimately strengthened the idea of the state. The former raised the citizens' awareness that the community requires permanent sources of finance for state-purposes – a need met in the classical period by the system of liturgies (Hansen 1991: 110–12). And the enfranchisement of new citizens came to be one of the most carefully supervised public actions under the democracy (Manville 1990: 215).

In the sphere of foreign relations too the tyrants picked up earlier threads and joined them to a web of connections that became an increasingly important part of state action. Carefully safeguarding their own power and the interests of other aristocrats, they shaped for the first time dynamic policies that also took into consideration the needs of the community as a whole. The goals were diverse: to gain, in a long-standing conflict with neighboring Megara, control over the island of Salamis; to establish on the coast of the Troad an Athenian colony, Sigeum, which, like Salamis, had high symbolic value; to establish an Athenian sphere of influence in the Hellespont, on the Thracian coast, and on various islands of the north and central Aegean. In all these cases the tyrants' actions laid the foundations for Athens' foreign policy that was continued with great vigor after 510 (Stahl 1987: 201–28) and, in hindsight, already outlined the power politics initiated later by democracy. Moreover, such external activities, subject to different norms, taught the citizens to appreciate the special quality of the community's inner space – which again strengthened awareness of the citizen-state's order. This applies even to the central issue of Solon's concept, political ethics. In order to be accepted by the citizens, the tyrants had to seek representative forms of expression for their rule. Here they had no choice but to latch onto prevailing cultural traditions. For instance, in the sphere of cult and religion, they enhanced and reorganized the main festivals of Dionysus and Athena; through the performance of drama, dance, and song at the Dionysia, and games and processions at the Panathenaea, these festivals later attained a central function in the democratic community's self-understanding. Cultivation of the Homeric tradition and support for contemporary poets played an equally large role. Sculpture and vase-painting flourished. Moreover, the Peisistratids undertook extraordinary efforts to build up Athens as a city, especially by enhancing the large sanctuary of Athena on the Acropolis with numerous temples and shrines (Hurwitt 1999), by establishing, for the first time, a political center in the Agora (Camp 1986) (see figure 8.3), or by creating an urban infrastructure, markedly visible in an eight km-long aqueduct into the heart of the city (Tölle-Kastenbein 1994). We cannot discuss in detail here the cultural rise of Athens in the time of the tyrants (Stahl 1987: 233–55; Shapiro 1989), which was naturally supported by an economic prosperity made possible by political peace. The crucial point is, however, that the tyrants' cultural activities were at the same time reflections of Athens' *polis*-culture and thus fostered civic consciousness.

Events after the expulsion of Hippias in 510 show how much the political ethics inaugurated by Solon had grown during half a century. The tyranny represented neither a slow-down nor a detour, but acted as a catalyst for the final breakthrough of the Athenian citizen-state. In the end, it outlived its usefulness as Hippias' rule became increasingly hard to bear. State power and political activity, which had for some time and with beneficial consequences lain in the hands of the tyrants, returned to the place where Solon, very sensibly in view of the social conditions of communal life, had located them: *es meson* (cf. Hdt. 3.142.3), in the middle of the citizen body.

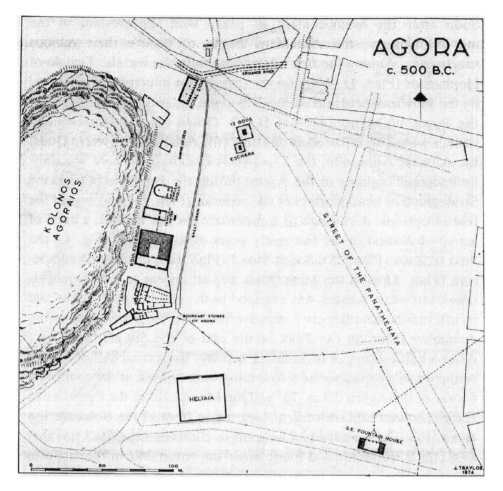

Figure 8.3 A plan of the Agora ca. 500 BC
Source: After Camp (1990: 23).

Revolution and Reform: The People of Athens and Cleisthenes

A revolutionary moment

In 510 the Spartan king Cleomenes intervened with a detachment of troops and expelled Hippias. Previously, leading Athenian aristocrats, above all the Alcmeonids, had tried to orchestrate the tyrants' overthrow from exile. Since their own forces proved insufficient, they focused on attracting outside assistance – a typical device in aristocratic *stasis* – and prompting Spartan action. At the same time, the Spartans pursued their own interests, hoping to tie Athens closely to themselves and perhaps to expand their alliance system even beyond the Peloponnese. Under the rules of reciprocity, their assistance in liberating Athens imposed an obligation on the new Athenian regime.

But what *was* this new regime? According to Herodotus (5.66), "the chief authority was lodged with two persons, Cleisthenes, of the family of the Alcmeonids . . . and Isagoras, the son of Tisander . . . These two men strove together for the mastery; and Cleisthenes, finding himself the weaker, embarked on the process of becoming the *demos'* trusted comrade" (*ton demon proshetairizetai,* tr. Rawlinson, modified). Further statements shed light on the preferences of the majority of Athenians, explaining why they eventually helped Cleisthenes achieve victory.

First, they did not want a new tyranny. By the end, Hippias' regime had turned oppressive (*Ath. Pol.* 19.1) but been unable to prevent the armed uprising of competing nobles or the intervention of Sparta; he succumbed to both relatively quickly, and the people apparently did not interfere. Now, however, the reintroduction of *stasis* seemed to lead directly to renewed autocracy, especially since the Spartans intervened again in support of one party.

Second, expectations focused not on noble *hetaireiai,* but on the collective *polis* institutions. During the tyranny, their functioning and traditional aristocratic politics of competition had come to be perceived as diametrical opposites; Athens as the focus of civic self-awareness had gained in importance.

Third, Isagoras' victory in the current *stasis* would have renewed civic strife, since he apparently intended to settle accounts with the tyrants' supporters and to disenfranchise, in a "review of the citizen body," numerous families that had recently moved to Attica (*Ath. Pol.* 13.5; Walter 1993a: 203–5). How such a split among citizens could be avoided had already been demonstrated, for example, in Cyrene: the distribution of the free population among newly created civic subdivisions offered a good means to clear the heavy atmosphere of insecurity and vengefulness (Arist. *Pol.* 1275b36–9; 1319b19–26). This was one of Cleisthenes' motives for creating ten new tribes (Hdt. 5.66.2) – and one of the primary reasons for his success.[20]

The sources do not permit us to clarify exactly either the chronology of Cleisthenes' reforms (most recently, Badian 2000) or the capacity in which Cleisthenes (who had been archon in 525/4) acted. A late source calls him *rhetor,* a politician who speaks in the assembly and proposes motions (Philod. *De rhet.* 3). The majority of Athenians obviously approved of his words and proposals, which must have been decided upon in the assembly. In any case, the *demos'* actions in the dramatic days of 508 show remarkable consistency and determination:

> Cleisthenes was, now that the common people took his part, very much more powerful than his adversaries. Isagoras in his turn lost ground; and therefore, to counter-plot his enemy, he called in Cleomenes the Lacedaemonian, who had already, at the time when he was besieging the Pisistratids, made a contract of friendship with him . . . At this time the first thing that he did was to send a herald and require that Cleisthenes, and a large number of Athenians besides, whom he called "the Accursed," should leave Athens.

> This message he sent at the suggestion of Isagoras: for in the affair referred to [the Cylonian affair], the blood-guiltiness lay on the Alcmaeonids and their partisans, while he and his friends were quite clear of it . . . When the message of Cleomenes arrived, requiring Cleisthenes and "the Accursed" to quit the city, Cleisthenes departed of his own accord. Cleomenes, however, notwithstanding his departure, came to Athens, with a small band of followers, and on his arrival sent into banishment seven hundred Athenian families, which were pointed out to him by Isagoras. Succeeding here, he next endeavored to dissolve the council, and to put the government into the hands of three hundred of the partisans of that leader. But the council resisted, and refused to obey his orders; whereupon Cleomenes, Isagoras, and their followers took possession of the citadel. Here they were attacked by the rest of the Athenians, who unanimously took the side of the council, and were besieged for the space of two days; on the third day they accepted terms, being allowed – at least such of them as were Lacedaemonians – to quit the country.
>
> (Hdt. 5.69.2–70; 72–3; tr. Rawlinson, modified)

Isagoras is not mentioned again; many of his followers were executed. The entire event was truly an unprecedented, revolutionary affair. The Athenians must have been fully aware of the dangers of inaction, which inevitably would result in increasing weakness: in Cleomenes' guest-friend Isagoras (archon in 508/7) and his supporters the Spartans had a "fifth column" in Athens. Armed foreigners entered the city at will, laid down the law and further weakened the citizen body by purges. Then came a bold attack on their ability, only recently regained, to govern themselves through the council (*boule*). Scholars debate whether this refers to the old Solonian council of 400 or to the new council of 500 established by Cleisthenes (if only in a preliminary form). Since we know nothing about Solon's council and broad support for Cleisthenes could manifest itself rather in and through the "mixed" new council, most likely it was this new council that was to be dissolved and replaced by a partisan regime of Isagoras' followers (Petzold 1990: 156–7). At least it is suggestive that the people apparently identified unanimously with the council (*ta auta phronesantes*) when it refused to be dissolved. And the citizens became active. Already Cylon's coup had united the Athenians from the countryside in an effort to defeat the plot but they had left the conclusion of the matter to the officials. In 508 they could rely neither on officials nor other leaders, since Isagoras was archon and Cleisthenes was in exile. There is no record that hoplites were mobilized. Nevertheless, the citizens consistently brought to a conclusion what they had started.

It is reasonable to argue that constitutions that are based on the actual and active exercise of power by the entire citizenry and therefore called "democracies" in the ancient sense of the word, require certain institutions, agencies, procedures, and rules in order to function. Democracies furthermore require regular practice by which the citizens learn and internalize politics through routine consultation and decision-making. In addition, the citizen body needs an experience in which it realizes its own power and potential, acts spontaneously and without long preparation or expert guidance, and defends its own collective interests against foreign or external determination. If there was in Athenian history a revolutionary moment in the modern sense of the word, then it happened in those three days in 508.[21] This event must be fitted into the evolution of the Athenian citizen state: with the victory over Isagoras and his supporters the Athenians successfully warded off all aristocratic attempts at restoration and emphatically announced their demand for a larger political share. What had been prepared by Solon's reforms and – although inadvertently – matured under Peisistratid tyranny now bore fruit. The civic self-awareness of broad sections of the populace had asserted itself for the first time politically and was to become the decisive factor in the further evolution of the Athenian political order in the classical period.

When Cleisthenes returned from exile, he completed what he had previously proposed to the *demos*, securing such wide support. But he did this not as a lawgiver, not, as it were, like Solon, as a father of the *polis*. Cleisthenes is never called *nomothetes*; by contrast, once he appears as "leader and champion of the people" ([Arist.] *Ath. Pol.* 20.4). His position was, in fact, more complicated: "though Cleisthenes is indeed a very important player in Athens' revolutionary drama, the key role was played by the *demos*. And thus, *demokratia* was not a gift from a benevolent elite to a passive *demos*, but was the product of collective decision, action, and self-definiton on the part of the *demos* himself" (Ober 1996: 35). Cleisthenes' genius did not lie in his ability to formulate a democratic vision or, conversely, to disguise behind a fair facade selfish interests that would serve his own power and family,[22] but rather in his ability to "read" acurately the new Athenian discourse that had emerged in a moment of revolution and to recognize that the collective action of the three days in 508 had created new political realities (Ober 1996: 52). Now the challenge consisted of converting these realities into a stable and effective form of government; put differently, the significance of the event needed to be captured in institutions in order to gain permanence.

Grassroots democracy, mobilization, and integration

Cleisthenes' reforms following the events of 508/7 had to tackle precisely those aspects that had revealed potential and weaknesses. The potential lay in the citizens' readiness to stand up for their collective interests; their weakness had proved to be fragmentation during *stasis*: follower groups vs. unattached citizens, old vs. new citizens, an urban population capable of spontaneous action vs. rural populations that were harder to mobilize. Such divisions were enhanced by the great size of Attica and by continuing local isolation that expressed itself not in secessionism but rather in an outlook that was limited to one's own rural community. Another basic weakness was military in nature. Twice the Athenians had been reduced to watching powerlessly the intervention of a small group of Spartans; the citizen militia was obviously no longer intact, a rusty sword at best.

Cleisthenes' reform therefore began with a political reorganization of the citizen body in Athens and Attica, with the communities (or townships) called demes as building blocks. Most of them had previously existed as such, especially in the country, but not everywhere in this form. Therefore Cleisthenes' reform amounted, first of all, to a general re-structuring of communities, based on existing settlement conditions and neighborhood relations. Vastly different deme sizes indicate that the division into demes was, at least in the country, not artificial; for instance, the largest deme had some twenty times the inhabitants of the smallest. Small village settlements with a few dozen inhabitants stood next to urban districts with more than a thousand. In the city of Athens, where some demes were newly created, deme sizes probably were more even. The entire territory was now divided into individual communities, both in the city of Athens and outside it. Every Athenian was entered into a deme register, which was at the same time a list of citizens, in the deme where he lived. Henceforth every Athenian identified himself by the *demotikon*, the name of his deme; only the addition of the patronymic revealed his family affiliation (thus, for example, "Pericles, son of Xanthippos, from [the deme] Cholargos"). Serving as the "building blocks of Cleisthenes' three-tier civic structure' (Whitehead 1996: 447), the demes received their own political institutions: a deme assembly and an annual magistrate, the *demarchos*. Yet the demes were not administrative districts but, rather, associations of persons with shared cults and festivals (e.g., *IG* I³ 244, tr. in Dillon and Garland 2000: 146) within which citizens could practice on a manageable level – and always together with other citizens – their self-determined role in taking a share of responsibility for the entire *polis*. Scholarship has made much progress in localizing individual demes. Because nearly all sources are much later and it is not clear how many changes were made over time, it is debated whether the demes numbered 139 already in Cleisthenes' time.²³ Yet there is absolutely no doubt that the demes were the living foundation of Athenian "grassroots democracy."

Of course, the problem of the integration of Attica was not yet solved by establishing the demes. The next step was to form from these demes ten new tribes (*phylai*) of approximately equal size (in terms of citizen population: see table 8.1). Each of the new tribes took a third of its members from the city of Athens and its environs (*astu*), a third from the coastal region (*paralia*), and a third from inland Attica (*mesogeion*). The demes of each region that were to form a tribe were combined into so-called *trittyes* (thirds). In each region, therefore, there were ten *trittyes*, hence 30 altogether. Three *trittyes*, one from each region – city, coast, inland – formed one tribe, resulting in 10 tribes. Like the demes, the tribes too were associations of persons with their own administration, consisting of three officials (phylarchs) and a treasurer, a tribal assembly and common cults. These included the cult of an eponymous hero (an Athenian mythical figure) who helped crystallize a common identity and had the same function as Theseus for the entire *polis* (Kearns 1989; Anderson 2003: ch. 5). The *Athenaion Politeia* (21.2) is quite correct in interpreting the intention and effect of Cleisthenes' tribal organization as a "mixing" of the Athenians, in order to bring together through communal activity the 25,000–30,000 citizens in the large

Table 8.1 List of the ten Attic tribes (*phylai*)

1 Erechtheis	2 Aigeis
3 Pandionis	4 Leontis
5 Akamantis	6 Oineis
7 Kekropis	8 Hippothontis
9 Aiantis	10 Antiochis

region of Attica. The distance from the extreme south of Attica, around Sunion, to Athens is about 50 km, to the northern border of Attica (Oropos in the north-east or the Kithairon range in the north-west) about 100 km. The "mixture" achieved by Cleisthenes' deme-*trittys*-tribe structure literally made the Athenians familiar to one another and strengthened the identity of the *polis*.

The tribes were of enormous importance to the communal life of the citizens; they performed many functions in the military, political, religious, and financial spheres. For example, they functioned as recruiting units for the newly constituted citizen army. The fighting strength of each tribal regiment consisted of around 1,000 hoplites, and each tribe contributed in addition a small contingent of horsemen. In these regiments, therefore, citizens from different regions in Attica came to fight side by side for their *polis* Athens. Undoubtedly, the reorganization of the citizen army, which had been neglected under the tyrants, represented one of the most urgent tasks for Cleisthenes. At least in terms of citizen population, Athens was the largest *polis* in Greece, and humiliations such as those suffered by the double intervention of Cleomenes were hard to tolerate. It has even been suggested that it was the very need for rapid and effective mobilization of the army that determined at least partially the details of the geographical arrangement and combination of *trittyes* and tribes.[24] This cannot be excluded but overall it fails to explain the "grand design" of the whole reform. Nevertheless, it is incontestable that within a short time after 508–7 Athens became more powerful and determined (on the "new order at war," see Anderson 2003: ch. 6). Herodotus reports that a renewed Spartan military intervention, combined with the attack of no less than two neighbors (Thebes in Boeotia and Chalcis on Euboea), were successfully repulsed.[25] The Athenians even confiscated some territory of Chalcis and settled there several thousand Athenians as a military colony (called cleruchy). Herodotus' explanation of this success is informative:

> Thus did the Athenians increase in strength. And it is plain enough, not from this instance only, but from many everywhere, that equal right to political involvement (*isegoria*) is an excellent thing since even the Athenians, who, while they continued under rule of tyrants, were not a whit more valiant than any of their neighbors, no sooner shook off the yoke than they became decidedly the first of all. These things show that, while undergoing oppression, they let themselves be beaten, since then they worked for a master; but so soon as they got their freedom, each man was eager to do the best he could for himself.
>
> (5.78; tr. Rawlinson, modified)

In the period of Cleisthenes, for the first time Athenian cleruchies were established not only on Euboea but also on the islands of Lemnos and Imbros (Figueira 1991: ch. 5). Miltiades (Lazenby 1996: 981–2) had conquered these islands when he was tyrant in the Thracian Chersonese, and left Athenians there as settlers. The impression of an increasingly active political involvement of Athens is confirmed by indications that in those very years the status of the cleruchs already settled on the island of Salamis was adjusted and that they were integrated more firmly into the Athenian citizen body.[26]

The new council of 500 (*Boule*) is directly connected with the reorganization of the tribes: it was the political centerpiece of the Cleisthenic reforms. The council, chosen annually for one year, is the one representative element in what is otherwise a system of direct democracy. Each tribe sent a tenth of the council-members, i.e. 50 men, who were selected by the individual demes in proportion to their number of citizens. The largest deme, Acharnae, alone had 22 council members; other demes were so small that they had to share one council member. Most demes were represented by between two and eight *bouleutai*; these were probably at first elected but by the second half of the fifth century at the latest chosen by lot. The minimum age was 30. In this way, political life in the demes was closely connected to the political life at the center of Athens (Meier 1990a: ch. 4). Initially, this council, in purely quantitative terms, was probably not too busy. But over the next decades – especially during and after the Great Persian War – its military and political agenda increased enormously, and for the council as the collective body that handled continuous business and prepared the assembly's agenda, large responsibilities accrued. Accordingly, all Athenians could be involved in the intensification of politics. The specific method of recruiting the council provided a representative distribution of public functions and secured cooperation and compromise among different groups of the population, because citizens from all parts of Attica were now obliged to deliberate and decide together in a new and institutionally intensive way in the political bodies that met in the center of Athens. The exchange of information between the center and the local units intensified in both directions; the council members kept their fellow citizens in demes and tribes up to date and urged them to participate in the assembly when important issues arose. They did not, however, represent purely local or particularist interests, as is the case in some modern parliamentary systems. Such interests were to a large extent mutually balanced and neutralized through regional distribution in the tribes, the council, and the army.

Thus the conditions were created that in the long run enabled the regular and natural participation of larger segments of the citizen body even in everyday politics and routine affairs. Of course, it was primarily the nobles who continued to speak in the assembly and proposed motions, but they were no longer able either there or in the council to rely on groups of personal followers and special interests. Moreover, the council as a permanent representation of the citizens made it possible to react quickly against offenses and in emergencies. Generally, the citizens were now in a position to monitor closely the aristocrats' politics and behavior in office; they could regularly be brought into play. The non-elite citizens' weakness in the preceding period had been that they had no leaders of their own, came together rarely, and, when they did, were for the most part limited to approving passively what was going to happen anyway. Those days were now over.

The Cleisthenic reorganization can thus be seen as a successful attempt to overcome two political impediments: the regional particuliarization of affiliations and interests, and the isolation of individual citizens and small regional groups. Both tended to encourage passivity. "Only in 508/7, with the passage of Cleisthenes' political reforms, did a united Attica become a functional reality" (Anderson 2003: 5).

The presence of the citizens, organized in demes and tribes, their involvement in politics, and their prospects for exercising control over events and decisions in the center had clearly increased and had the potential to increase further. As a political body enhancing the participation of the citizens (*politai*) in communal life, administration, and government, every single tribe channeled rights and duties toward the community; we need only think of military service and extraordinary financial contributions (called liturgies). Festivals too promoted tribal integration. Each tribe had its own cults and festivals; moreover, tribal teams took part in many of the athletic and musical competitions that were held at the large *polis* festivals; they also ate together at the sacrificial banquets. Through their pronounced connection with the *polis*, the tribes enhanced centralization and the institutionalization of the state.

Despite many uncertainties in dating specific measures, and despite the general scarcity of sources, there is one remarkable fact: no notice survives about a refusal to accept the new order, or of resistance against it. One reason may be that most of the old political powers resigned themselves to the new conditions, learned to live and deal with them, and soon gained experience in working with the new council and the assembly. Furthermore, the authority, expertise, and eloquence of the elite continued to count for much, so that, as long as the newly created political rules were obeyed, the Athenian citizenry at large trusted their leadership. Members of the old noble houses, therefore, for the most part still guided Athens' political fortunes in the time after Cleisthenes, but they did so no longer on the basis of their own power but rather in collaboration and with the approval of the majority of citizens. Still, it would hardly have been possible to consolidate the new political arrangements in such an astonishingly peaceful way if those profound changes had not been accompanied by major successes in foreign policy. Already in the twenty years before the Battle of Marathon one finds the almost dialectical relationship between developments in foreign and domestic affairs which would become characteristic of the fifth century. The transformed *polis* readily assumed, so to speak, the role of a "super-aristocrat." This is visible not least in Athens' willingness to take over aristocratic enterprises like those of Miltiades in the northern Aegean, continuing them in the form of early colonies or cleruchies (Ehrenberg 1946: 116–43; Figueira 1991: 131–60).

Cleisthenes and the development of the Athenian citizen-state

Warfare, joint and communal activities as well as the practice of politics on the local and *polis* levels guaranteed that the institutions created by Cleisthenes were full of life. Old-style aristocratic party politics and parochialism concerned only with local matters were no longer viable. To overcome factionalism and particularism was to Solon a matter of political thought and to Cleisthenes a matter of political organization. Both Solon and Cleisthenes, therefore, belong among the founders of republican discourse (Rahe 1992). The fathers of the American constitution saw the cure for factionalism and particularism in a representative system that rests on smaller units. Representation in the center of power and participation "at home," however, could only function when they were nourished by a corresponding political ethic, a civic virtue. The Cleisthenic *polis* was very close to this model. His system ensured that political participation was spread broadly enough regionally and socially and that it was important enough to the citizens – or at least many citizens – that the assembly was not controlled by special interests. Such broadening and steadiness of participation was institutionally anchored in the council of 500, which was decisive in making the entire *demos* the subject of politics. Hence the assembly itself did not need to be reformed.

No texts by Cleisthenes survive as they do from Solon. Still, the order he devised, and the energy with which the Athenians immediately took things into their own hands – in the war against their neighbors, but also, for instance, in putting up new public buildings, so that "during the years 510–490, the Acropolis was . . . stamped with the mark of a new political culture" (Anderson 2003: 109) – show that Cleisthenes is to be considered, on equal terms with Solon, the second founding father of the Athenian citizen state. Cleisthenes succeeded in binding the revolutionary impulse of the year 508/7 into something permanent and institutional. Only in the political spaces (or "infrastructure") created by Cleisthenes could that special kind of thinking prosper that according to Rousseau is indispensable for successful government: the interests of the community have to stand above particular interests (Osborne 1996a: 311). As the reference to Rousseau indicates, we are not of course speaking here of a model of liberal democracy.

And Cleisthenes himself? He is mentioned only in connection with his reforms. Hence it is usually assumed that he died soon afterwards. That may well be true (Anderson 2007), but perhaps his unsung, noiseless, disappearance contains a deep historical truth. Cleisthenes had played midwife to a political revolution that was not inevitable – such radical ruptures never are – but was part of the logical evolution of Athens as a citizen-state, continuing what Draco and Solon had set in motion. Once the people had been established in the saddle, the maker of the bridle could silently step down.

NOTES

1 See ch. 10, below; Thomas and Conant 1999: 60–84 (tenth century); Scheidel 2004b (demography).
2 Eur. *Supp.* 352–3, 406–8; Paus. 1.3.3; Ruschenbusch 1958.
3 For the debate, see, e.g., Bleicken 1995/1998; Hansen 1994; Raaflaub et al. 2007. Against efforts to identify the so-called reforms of Ephialtes in 462/1 as the beginning of democracy in Athens, see Stahl 2003b: 64–86.
4 Stanton 1990: 17–26 for sources; cf. Lang 1967; Rhodes 1993: 79–84.
5 *IG* I³ 104; ML 86 = Fornara 1983a: no. 15; Stanton 1990: 27; see Stroud 1968; Gagarin 1981; Humphreys 1991; Carawan 1998 (but cf. R. W. Wallace, *BMCR* 2000.05.02); Stahl 2003a: 213–26.
6 See Stanton 1990: 34–85; Dillon and Garland 2000: 66–90 for the sources; Almeida 2003: ch. 1; Mülke 2002 for discussion of evidence and scholarship.
7 For in-depth discussions, see Stahl 2003a: 176–200, 228–51; also Rhodes 1993: 118–79; Welwei 1992: 150–206; Raaflaub 1996b. For fundamental criticism of some features of Blok and Lardinois (2006), see U. Walter, *Historische Zeitschrift* 286 (2008) 685–7.
8 Laws are cited after Ruschenbusch 1966, translations of Solon's fragments are from Dillon and Garland 2000 (sometimes modified).
9 Sealey 1979; this is contested, see, e.g., Wallace 1983. Wallace (2007b: 75) believes that Solon was still alive and active when Peisistratus seized tyranny for the first time, ca. 560.

10 The first two verses show that this poem was conceived of as the equivalent of a political speech (*ant' agores*) and therefore performed in public context rather than the usual setting of the private symposium; see further below at n. 16. The places named are small Aegean islands.

11 Stanley 1999: 142–6, but see K.-W. Welwei, *Gymnasium* 110 (2003) 600–2.

12 Millett 1984; Stahl 2003a: 182–5; Schmitz 2004b.

13 In a classic study, Fustel de Coulanges (1830–1889) recognized this long ago (1873, orig. 1864: bk. 4, ch. 6.2; see Murray 1980: 183–4). For a different interpretation of the problems of Solonian Athens, see van Wees 1999a.

14 See, in general, Hölkeskamp 1992a, 1992b, 1999; also, this vol. ch. 28.

15 *Ath. Pol.* 7.3–4; Hansen 1991: 43–6; all this is debated, however; see De Ste. Croix 2004; van Wees and Raaflaub in Blok and Lardinois 2006; Raaflaub et al. 2006.

16 Gentili 1988. Simonides' recently published elegy on the Greek victory at Platea in 479 now offers a splendid example of an elegy intended for public performance: Aloni 2001 and other chapters in Boedeker and Sider 2001.

17 Stahl 1992; Wallace 1998 and in Raaflaub et al. 2006: ch. 3; for debate, see also chs. 4–5.

18 Sources: Stanton 1990: 87–137; Dillon and Garland 2000: 91–122. See, in general, Andrewes 1982b; Stahl 1987; Lewis 1988; Smith 1989; Welwei 1992: 229–65; Rhodes 1981 (1993): 189–240; Sancisi-Weerdenburg 2000; Lavelle 2005.

19 *IG* I³ 1031 = Fornara 1983a: no. 23C; Stanton 1990: 111–12.

20 For sources on Cleisthenes' reforms, see Stanton 1990: 138–90; Dillon and Garland 2000: 123–46; for interpretation, see Ostwald 1988; Meier 1990a: 53–81; 1998: ch. 4; Rhodes 1993: 240–83; Osborne 1996a: 292–311; Ober 1998; Stahl 2003b: 20–63; Welwei 1999: 1–27. Develin and Kilmer 1997 offer a reductionist reading of the sources. Anderson's purpose (2003) is "to show how the many changes implemented during the age of Cleisthenes would profoundly alter the course of Athenian history."

21 Ober 1996; 2007; Funke 2001b: 1–7.

22 Stanton 1984 is profoundly misleading on this aspect; see, rightly, Osborne 1996a: 299–304.

23 See, generally, Osborne 1985; Whitehead 1986; Traill 1986.

24 Siewert 1982 with an important revd. by D. M. Lewis, *Gnomon* 55 (1983) 432–6.

25 *IG* I³ 501 = Fornara 1983a: no. 42; see Anderson 2003: 112, 155–6.

26 *IG* I³ 1 = Fornara 1983a: no. 44; see Figueira 1991: 142–8; Taylor 1997.

CHAPTER NINE

Greeks and Persians

Josef Wiesehöfer

Introduction

In the second half of the sixth century BCE the political map of the ancient Near East changed profoundly. The rival powers of Elam, Media, Babylonia, Lydia and Egypt were supplanted by the Persian empire, the first world empire in history, which, in the course of time, incorporated its predecessors and pushed its borders towards Thrace in the north-west, Sogdia in the north-east, the Indus valley in the south-east and Libya and Egypt in the south-west. The Persian conquest of western Asia Minor under Cyrus, the revolt of the Ionian cities under Darius, and the failure of the Persian invasions of Greece under Datis and Artaphernes at Marathon (490) and under Xerxes at Salamis and Plataea (480–479) feature prominently in our "European" tradition. Less familiar are the problems posed by the source material for this period and the questions of how, why, and with what consequences Persian rule in western Asia Minor affected existing political, economic, social, and cultural structures. The causes and goals of the Ionian revolt and Persian wars, rarely discussed in textbooks or popular accounts, remain a matter of debate, as does the nature of early Greek literary and iconographic representation of the Persians and Persian views of the Greeks. These are the issues to be addressed in this chapter.

Understanding Graeco-Persian Contacts

Among all the civilizations which the ancient Greeks encountered, the Iranians have a special place in the European imagination as the Greeks' enemies and opposites. Nineteenth- and early twentieth-century Europeans, whatever their nationality, took it for granted that ancient Greek civilization was indigenous and exemplary, while its Iranian counterpart was strange and alien, Greek culture creative and active, Eastern culture passive and derivative (Hauser 2001a: 93–4). European historical thought, following ancient Greek models, perceived Iran (like the other cultures of the Ancient Near East) as hardly more than a "culture on the fringes of the Mediterranean," as a kind of outer or even counter-world. This antinomy did not change fundamentally even when the kinship between the Iranian (Aryan) and European languages was recognized, and when theories about "national consciousness" gave rise to a belief in a close affinity between all Indo-European peoples and their shared cultural superiority. True, this resulted in a more positive assessment of the ancient Persians, but it did not change the distinct preference for the art, culture, and government which evolved in Greece (mainly Athens) and was often seen as continuing in a direct line to the present day (Hauser 2001a: 85–90). In Germany, this ideology was replaced, but in part also reinforced, by the National Socialists' view that the "Aryan" Persians had been adversely affected by the racial and biological influences of the "Semitic" Orient. A negative assessment of "Semites" and "Semitic" cultures was not, of course, an exclusively German phenomenon. After the war – again not only in Germany – the idea of an unbridgeable gap between Persian despotism and Greek love of freedom became predominant (Wiesehöfer 1988; 1990; 2002). Only since the 1980s have interdisciplinary scholarship[1] and the more inclusive discourse of such research topics as cultural diversity, ethnicity, Orientalism, the "strangeness" of Greek culture (Hölscher 1989) promised a paradigmatic change which would treat non-Greek cultures more fairly. At the moment, however, we are again seeing a rejection of such a broader perspective and a revival of Eurocentric constructs of cultural continuity, a trend set off by controversies over the relevance of Classics in Higher Education and by the search for pan-European and/or occidental identities (Hauser 1999). In the process, the real and most lasting legacy of Greek culture, political theory and practice (Flaig 2001), is often pushed into the background.

This chapter reviews the political and cultural relationship between Greeks and Persians in pre-classical times in two ways. First, it is concerned with the history of scholarly and popular perceptions of those relations in both Europe and Iran. It seeks to expose the weaknesses inherent in many of those views in light of new ideas about, for example, the invention of tradition, ethnicity, collective identities, and cultural complexity. Secondly, drawing on recent research on the sources (especially Herodotus) and the history of events, it stresses the variety of political and cultural relations between Hellas and Iran and of the Greeks' perceptions of their mighty neighbor in the East.

In this chapter, the term "culture" will be used to mean not only "high" culture, but the whole range of acquired perception, knowledge, ethics, and aesthetics. This is important since the transfer of practical knowledge and techniques, as well as of utilitarian and luxury goods, was a distinguishing mark of Graeco-Persian cultural contacts. Ancient civilizations were shaped by cultural differences, and hardly at all by ethnic characteristics (despite our sources' occasional claims to that effect). This chapter adopts the concept of "transculturality," which sees the relationship between cultures as a process of exchange and appropriation, within which what is one's own and what is foreign is constantly being negotiated. Through loss, selection, innovation, and borrowing something completely new may emerge on both sides (Welsch 1999: 194–213). Finally, cultures must be understood in their historical context.

As far as material culture is concerned, where Classical and Near Eastern archaeology overlap the tendency is still to emphasize the Greek side of cultural contact: "good taste" in art is sometimes attributed only to Greeks, and Iranian interest in or understanding of Greek culture is denied. The Orient may be presented as a "debtor of Greece, and relevant only insofar as it participated in 'our Hellenic-European evolution'" (Hauser 1999: 334). On the other hand, in our effort to escape the traps of "Orientalism" and "Eurocentrism" (Kurz 2000; cf. Hauser 2001b) and to give the Iranian contribution to cultural contacts and creative processes its due, we may run the risk of underestimating Greek involvement and the appeal to Iranian and indigenous elites of what the Greeks had to offer. Only a careful analysis of the nature, social and cultural contexts, and audiences of literary and artistic genres will enable us to balance imperial Achaemenid influence against regional traditions and fusions of the two. The fact that Near Eastern specialists are now being asked to review the validity of their own, post-colonial, world view (Østergård 1991) is a welcome development.

Historical myths, aimed at securing the identity of groups and peoples, are found in Asian as well as European and Western societies (Conermann 1999). In Iran, for example, a – futile – authoritarian attempt was made to impose the myth of the 2,500th anniversary of Iranian imperial kingship (Wiesehöfer 1999). "National" Iranian interpretations of Graeco-Persian or Irano-Arabic relations, which – like their western (Greek) counterparts – equate ethnic, cultural and "national" identities, and other ideas propagating an allegedly immutable kind of "Iranianism," are still quite popular in Iran and the Iranian diaspora.

The preceding remarks point to further weaknesses of earlier (and the most recent?) historical research. First, terms like "Iran/Persia" or "Greece," and "Iranian/Persian" or "Greek culture," tend to obscure the variety of political and cultural "styles" found within the Ancient Near East and Greece. Thus, in Greece, a stock of common cultural and political ideals and institutions[2] coexisted with a wide range of traditions peculiar to particular regions and periods, many of them adopted from abroad and adapted as appropriate. The history of Greece was determined to a large extent by the tension between particularism and the pursuit of hegemony or even empire. Nor was ancient Iran, with a territory far larger than the modern state, ever a culturally homogeneous entity. An example of cultural variety and exchange in the east is the Persian ethnogenesis in an Elamite environment before the foundation of a "Persian" empire by Cyrus (Rollinger 1999). Furthermore, in the military encounters of the Persian wars Greeks faced not only Iranians, but also other Greeks, Macedonians and all the main peoples subject to the Great Kings (Wiesehöfer 2002).

Secondly, for generations before the Persian wars a variety of ethnic, cultural, and religious communities had been living side by side in Iran and Mesopotamia, and processes of transculturation, of a different kind and intensity, had long been on-going. We know the peoples of antiquity by names which define them primarily as linguistic or cultural communities; ethnic affiliations and origins are harder to determine. But the modern insistence on assigning a particular "nationality" would surely have baffled people in the Ancient Near East, and besides: what do collective names and origins really tell us about cultures and attitudes? Only a closer look at the direction, significance and paths of cultural exchange in antiquity will allow us to understand different social milieus and aspects of culture, and to account for "syncretistic" or "hybrid" phenomena such as Achaemenid imperial art where in the course of time something completely new developed.

Thirdly, many modern observers – depending on their views on such matters in their own society – consider ethnic variety and social and cultural heterogeneity in imperial societies either an abnormality and handicap or a positive advantage and virtue. In the National Socialist era, for example, German "scholars" regarded the abandonment of the so-called "völkisches Prinzip" ("national principle"), alongside "Rassenmischung" ("racial mixing"), as the root of all evil, a sign of decadence and decline. More generally, European scholarship long after the Second World War continues to compare ancient empires with modern national states (Wiesehöfer 2004a: *passim*). Instead of passing such judgements, historians ought to describe and analyze the complex processes of creating identities in ancient multi-cultural societies, both at the level of ethnic and religious groups and at the level of the individual.

Fourthly, many of the problems raised and deplored so far have their origin not only in the biases of Classicism, Eurocentrism, and "Orientalism," but also in inadequate use of sources. This applies in particular to material culture and archaeological remains, but to a lesser degree also to the written sources, which contain a great deal more information on relations and interaction between Greeks and Persians than we might expect. It is vital to read the literary and epigraphic texts closely with due consideration of their genre, date of origin, and the world view of their authors – and indeed to read them "against the grain."

The Sources

Lydians, Medes, Persians, and Greeks

Lydia and the Greeks of Asia Minor under Lydian and Persian rule became part of the literary version of history only with Herodotus' *Histories*, written in the 430s and 420s. This work has often been misinterpreted as a "history of the Persian wars," but offers much more than that: a picture "of the whole inhabited world in its diversity . . . of the spaces in which different peoples dwelt, of their different customs and cultural achievements, of their deeds and their fate, in order to take them as models for an understanding of one's own history – that is, the history of the Greeks – and to make this the focus of universal history" (Bichler and Rollinger 2000: 11). Since Lydian literature and archives have been lost, it is this much later work of art that remains our most important testimony for the Persian conquest of Western Asia Minor. Before Herodotus, the Lydian kings and their capital Sardis had only been mentioned casually by Near Eastern sources (Assyrian royal inscriptions) and Greek poets. While the former emphasized the tributary dependence of Gyges and his son, the first kings of the Mermnad dynasty, on Assyria (Aro-Valjus 1999), the latter described Lydia as a rich superpower with a special relation to Hellas but also cited it to illustrate the transitory nature of power and luxury. Later Greek authors saw these dangers confirmed by the fall of Sardis (Bichler 1996; Ehrhardt 2005). Likewise, Herodotus does not present a genuine "Lydian history," but fits the rise and fall of Lydia into an account of the fortunes of empires and peoples which centers on questions of guilt and fate, force of circumstance, and personal responsibility. For him, the Lydian king Croesus is the first of a group of rulers who increasingly threaten the freedom of the Greeks (1.5.3–6.3) but who, blinded by their unlimited power, wealth, luck, and success, ultimately fail because they do not recognize the limits imposed by the gods (1.26–92). Herodotus makes Sparta, the hegemonial power in Greece, part of this central idea of his *Histories* by linking it through an (alleged) alliance to Croesus, the oppressor of Greek freedom in Asia (Asheri 1988: 312; Bichler 1985: 65–8); this treaty therefore corresponds to Athens' later (historical) arrangement with Darius I (507–506), which – temporarily – made the Athenians, too, allies of an Asian super-power which threatened freedom. The history of Lydia between Gyges and Croesus was obviously almost unknown to Herodotus and is only covered in retrospective (1.7–25); his account of Lydia ends with comments on local customs (1.93–4).

Our view of the rise of the Persian empire is also decisively determined by Herodotus' account.[3] He presents Assyria and Lydia as former rulers over Asia and builds up the Medes as another Asian superpower which alongside the Lydians and the Babylonians succeeds the Assyrians. Herodotus' "Median story" (*medikos logos*), with its impressive account of the rise to power of Deioces is a tale "in the spirit of Greek [i.e. sophistic] political philosophy."[4] Not until Cyrus overthrows the Median king Astyages, defeats Croesus, and puts an end to Babylonian rule, do the Persians make a name for them-selves. The legendary story of Cyrus' exposure, his childhood, and the revelation of his true identity supports the impression of a rapid rise to power, and also makes Cyrus Astyages' grandson – most probably a Herodotean invention. Cyrus is convinced that *tyche*, who guides him (1.126) will help him conquer almost the whole continent facing Europe (1.153). By crossing the river Araxes, representing the border of Asia, in his war against the Massagetae, the Herodotean Cyrus also crosses the limits set for him by the gods – comparable to Croesus' earlier crossing of the Halys and Xerxes' later crossing of the Hellespont. Thus, the history of the admirable founder of the Persian empire ends in a terrible tragedy (not least because of fatal advice by Croesus). In studying events where Lydian, Persian and Greek history overlap, one must be aware of this particular view of Herodotus' and of the nature of his *Histories* (Bichler 2000).

Archaeological research at Sardis and elsewhere and Lydian-Achaemenid coinage also throw light on the transition from the Lydian to the Persian period in Western Asia Minor, but both types of evidence have their limitations: only parts of Sardis have been explored or excavated so far, and the problem of who minted the famous gold Croeseïd coins has only recently been settled in favour of Croesus.[5]

Ionian revolt and Persian wars

One of the most important results of the paradigmatic shift in current research[6] has been to make us see that we cannot recover a Persian perspective on the Greeks or the "Greek Wars." The views attributed to Persians in Greek historiography cannot be treated as such: as Sancisi-Weerdenburg provocatively put it, "Persians on Greeks are really Greeks on Persians and therefore Greeks on Greeks" (2001: 340). Attempts to uncover royal plans for Greece or reflections of the military encounters between Greeks and Persians in the pictorial or epigraphic announcements of the Great Kings have remained unsuccessful. Royal inscriptions and lists and reliefs of subject peoples show that the only thing about the Asiatic Greeks which really mattered ideologically to the Achaemenid rulers was that these "Yauna" ranked among their subjects (Kuhrt 2002). In other words, for the Ionian revolt and the Persian wars Herodotus remains our only informant. Evidence closer to the events, whether poetic (Pindar, Simonides), dramatic (Aeschylus), or pictorial (a painting in the Stoa Poikile, and vase paintings, among other things), does not contribute to a history of events, although it is important for the history of ideas. Later historiographical work (Ctesias, Ephorus, Trogus) or biographies (Nepos, Plutarch), insofar as it does not rely on Herodotus, makes only minor contributions to our knowledge, as do epigraphic and archaeological material.

Many scholars have used Herodotus' *Histories* as a kind of military log to be quarried for the reconstruction of the motives, plans, and actions not only of the *poleis* of the Hellenic League, but also of the Persians. The assumption has been that Herodotus derived his knowledge of Persian foreign policy and war aims from close contacts with Persians (Bäbler 1998: 102) or Greek members of the Persian administration (Lewis 1985) who had intimate knowledge of Persian institutions and customs. Recent scholarship has been able to show, however, that Herodotus' representation of Persian institutions and traditions, beyond the basics of personal names and terminology, is overwhelmingly shaped by a Greek or personal perspective. If Herodotus did have information from good Persian sources, we would have to conclude that he did not understand it or deliberately obscured its meaning. It makes much more sense to suppose that Herodotus instead drew on a range of contemporary Greek views and debates concerning foreign civilizations and traditions – debates initiated by direct contacts across the borders, as well as by the reports of diplomats, mercenaries or artists.[7] Herodotus actively engaged in such discussions,[8] absorbing and transforming them in his work with such skill that even today some historians are persuaded that his description of the Persians is an only slightly revised documentary report (e.g. Hammond 1988), and the continuous narrative of events in modern textbooks largely just reproduces Herodotus' account.

> We thus become familiar with Herodotus' version of events before we realize that it is his, and it is difficult to view his narrative with properly critical detachment.
> (West 2002: 15–16)

Yet a critical appreciation of Herodotus' literary intentions, based on an understanding of the concept of the *Histories* as a whole, is vital when we are dealing with the principles of Persian foreign policy and goals in the wars with the Greeks. The contents of major pronouncements by the Great Kings, or crucial debates between rulers and their advisors – often quoted in direct speech by Herodotus – cannot have been known to many and probably not to anyone whom the historian was able to contact. It is now also generally accepted that the characterization of the Kings and stories of "tragic warners" and misleading dreams are equally Herodotus' own creations (Bichler 2000).

His authorship is betrayed not least by inconsistencies in the text that make literary and philosophical but hardly historical sense.

Nevertheless, so far few have drawn the inescapable conclusion that the announcements and decisions of the Persian kings in Herodotus' work need to be subjected to a systematic, not just selective, critical analysis. For example, modern works often follow Herodotus in accepting that the Athenians gave earth and water to Darius in 507–506 and then instantly broke the relationship thus created (5.73), but rarely mention that Herodotus has Spartan envoys in 479 blame the Persian wars on the Athenians (8.142), surely referring to this earlier broken agreement.[9] Similarly, no one accepts as historical Herodotus' portrayal of Darius as initially ignorant of Athenian affairs and later obsessed with Athens ("O Zeus, grant me my revenge against the Athenians" and/or "O master, remember the Athenians": 5.105), but even recent studies take it for granted that nothing had higher priority for the Great King than revenge on Athens and Eretria. Hardly anyone believes Herodotus' claim that the Persian planned the subjection of Hellas even before the Ionian rebellion (3.134ff; cf. 4.143; 5.31–2) and that the expedition of Datis and Artaphernes already aimed at all of Hellas (6.94), but many rigidly adhere to his assertion that after the Ionian rebellion even uninvolved Greek cities were ordered by Darius to submit.[10] The gigantic numbers of the Persian forces in Xerxes' Greek campaign, matching the king's alleged plans for world domination, have rightly been reduced to more plausible levels (Cuyler Young 1980; Barkworth 1993), and the scenario of a simultaneous threat to the Greeks in both Hellas and Sicily has rightly been deemed unhistorical (Bichler 1985), but scholars still accept Herodotus' statement that Xerxes not only took over the war goals of his father Darius, but ultimately strove for world domination, for an empire "bordering the sky of Zeus" (7.8a–c; e.g. Harrison 2002: 577). A closer examination of the conception of Herodotus' work and of the eastern sources proves such an interpretation of the principles of Achaemenid foreign policy to be a phantom.

Western Asia Minor and the Persian Empire to the End of the Ionian Revolt

According to Herodotus' *Histories*, Croesus tried to take advantage of the Persian conquest of Media by the former Median "vassal" Cyrus by extending his realm east of the Halys River – previously the frontier between the Lydian and the Median empires (1.6.1; 1.28, 72). However, new studies of the Median "empire" cast doubt on the imperial character of Median rule, a continuing Median presence in Eastern Anatolia, and the historicity of the Halys border.[11] They prefer to speak of a Median confederation of "tribes" that united and formed an alliance with the Babylonians in order to fight against their deadly foes, the Assyrians, but did not set up a lasting empire and did not force the Persians into vassalage. (The Persian model of empire was rather Elamite.)[12] Certainly, much speaks for military conflict[13] and other contacts between Lydians and Medes, which explain the Greek use of the term *Medoi* for "Persians" and *medismos* for "collaboration with the Persians,[14] but the Babylonian presence in Northern Mesopotamia, Syria, and Cilicia makes Median rule over Eastern Anatolia unlikely. Finally, the Halys borderline separating the Lydians and Persians is a construct based on information about frontiers of Persian provinces in Anatolia in the fifth century, created by Herodotus because of his preference for conspicuous borderlines that demarcate territories assigned by divine will to specific peoples or empires (Rollinger 2003b: 310–13).

When Croesus opened hostilities against Cyrus, a member of the Persian Teispid clan,[15] is uncertain. The Nabonidus Chronicle (II 15–18; Grayson 1975: no. 7, 107–8) has been cited in support of dating the conquest of Lydia and Croesus' death to the year 547, but this is no longer tenable.[16] The Persian sack of Sardis is, however, archaeologically attested, and it is highly probable, *pace* Herodotus, that the last Mermnad king died during this event.[17]

Ionian and Aeolian troops probably supported Croesus in his war against the Persians (Hdt. 1.141) as Lydian "vassals." According to Herodotus, only Miletus was able to reach an agreement with Cyrus that continued the terms previously granted by the Lydians.[18] The historian's account of Ionian and Aeolian efforts to secure Spartan support and of mutual threats between Spartans and Persians (1.152–3) does not make historical sense, but fits well into the overall concept of the *Histories*: Aristagoras' later quest for military support in Hellas and Athens' support for the Ionians thus have earlier counterparts. Once again, Herodotus succeeds in integrating the two Greek hegemonial powers which will eventually defeat the Persians into the earlier history of wars between Greeks and Asian superpowers. Moreover, for the first time, he hints at the Persian kings' overestimation of their own abilities and their fatal underestimation of the particular qualities of the Greeks.

Herodotus has the Persian army withdrawing very quickly (1.153) and leaving the Lydian Pactyes in charge. This might be explained by urgent preparations for campaigns in Eastern Iran or against Babylon, but is hardly conceivable if Lydia had not yet been pacified and Ionia left humiliated by unilaterally imposed peace terms. Therefore, the imposition of such unfavorable terms, and an Ionian request for help from Sparta, if historical at all, make sense only after the failure of Pactyes' rebellion and the reconquest of the coastal regions by Cyrus' generals, Mazares and Harpagus. Herodotus' statement that (only) the gold from Sardis enticed the inhabitants of the coastal cities to join Pactyes' revolt (1.154), seems to support such a sequence of events.

Sardis, with its strategically favorable location, fortifications, proven political and administrative infrastructure, and public spaces, was the obvious place to set up a satrapal residence and the administrative center of Western Asia Minor (see figure 9.1). From the Persian army's quick departure to the east, Herodotus' account and the later parallel in Babylon we can deduce that the Persian king not only kept in post – under the supervision of the Persian Tabalus – numerous locals (like Pactyes) whom he considered loyal, but also took over most existing administrative and fiscal institutions, among them those which regulated the dependent status of the Greek cities. The rebellion of Pactyes which, according to Herodotus, infected wide sections of the population of the region, surprised the Persians and forced Cyrus, despite his other commitments, to act immediately.[19] If we trust Herodotus, the rebellion could

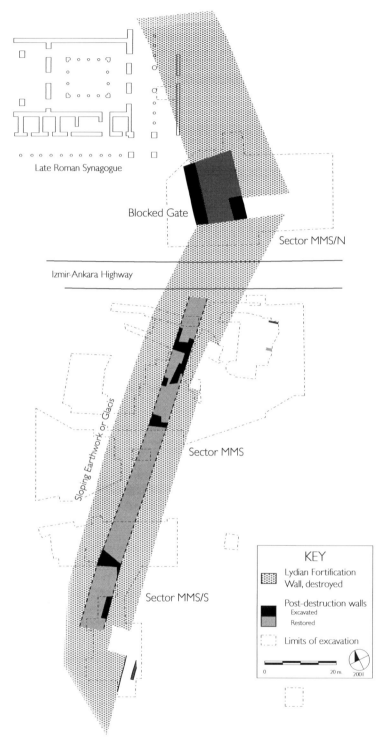

Figure 9.1 Schematic plan of Achaemenid fortifications at Sardis
Source: Archaeological exploration of Sardis, Harvard University, MMS-143.02.08.02.

only be quashed after several years, but was not supported by those cities and sanctuaries which had negotiated favorable terms with the Persians, or indeed – like Didyma, Aulae[20] and probably Clarus – had been given privileges by Cyrus, following Croesus' example.[21] Herodotus gives little information on Persian sanctions against the conquered cities, but reports that Harpagus made them promise to take part in his military campaigns against the Carians and Lycians, against Halicarnassus and Cnidus (1.171).[22] Whether the participation of Lydian and Ionian sculptors and artists in the building of the Persian royal residences at Pasargadae, and later at Susa and Persepolis (see below),[23] was a consequence of Pactyes' revolt, we do not know.

The Persian Oroetes succeeded Tabalus as "governor of the Sardians," i.e. satrap of Lydia and Ionia (Hdt. 3.120, 127); his residential centers were Sardis and Magnesia-on-the-Maeander (Hdt. 3.121, 126).[24] One of his main duties was probably to defend Cyrus' possessions in western Asia Minor against the aspirations of Polycrates of Samos, who – according to Herodotus – reckoned that he would have good prospects "to rule over Ionia and the islands" because of his fleet (3.39; Thuc. 1.13; Strab. 14.1.16). Oroetes remained in office under Cyrus' son Cambyses; he then eliminated Polycrates (Hdt. 3.120–7), who had helped Cambyses against Egypt but pursued a policy which competed with that of the satrap of Sardis (cf. Diod. 10.16.4).[25] Oroetes tried to exploit the disputed succession to the throne after Cambyses' death by pushing his border east and having the satrap of Hellespontine Phrygia and his son executed (Hdt. 3.126), but later paid dearly for his opposition against the usurper Darius I (Hdt. 3.126–8). The satrap of Sardis is not mentioned among the defeated "liar kings" in Darius' *res gestae*, probably since he had not striven for independent rule. We do not know who succeeded Oroetes.[26] It has been supposed that Darius gave decisive influence over the affairs of Western Asia Minor to the satraps of Cappadocia (Debord 1999: 89–91).

Perhaps in the 510s, Darius appointed his brother Artaphernes satrap of Lydia; it was this man who in 507–506 received earth and water from the Athenian envoys and who defended the acropolis of Sardis against the rebellious Ionians and their allies. The Elamite Fortification Tablets from Persepolis testify to the importance of the satrapal residence Sardis for the years between 509 and 494, as well as to the close links between Lydia and the Imperial centers and the employment of craftsmen from Western Asia Minor in Achaemenid Persis.[27] That Sardis became Xerxes' military basis and winter quarters in 480 and 479 (Hdt. 8.116; 9.108–9) shows its function as administrative, military, and economic center at the same time.

In the coastal Greek cities, unlike in other conquered territories, the Persians came across extremely unstable political conditions, due not least to the existence of "isolated aristocrats, tyrants striving for survival, and powerless priests." The tyrants – not all of them appointed by the Persians – became their contacts and allies: only these autocrats guaranteed a consistent loyal policy, not least because of a personal pledge of loyalty to the Great King,[28] and they more than anyone benefited from Persian backing, since this support secured their position: the overthrow of a tyrant would normally provoke Persian reprisals.[29]

No problem in Achaemenid studies has been discussed as intensively and polemically as the so-called administrative and tributary reforms of Darius I. The main reason for the harsh fundamentalism of this debate lies in the ancient evidence: the very nature and historical value of the two main testimonies – the lists of peoples/countries in Persian royal inscriptions and chapters 3.89–94 of Herodotus' *Histories* – are highly disputed. Scholars who try to use the lists for dating purposes are opposed by

Figure 9.2 Croeseïd coin
Source: www.achemenet.com.

others who deny these lists any historiographical value; scholars who more or less trust Herodotus' account of an administrative and fiscal re-organization of the empire argue with those who are highly skeptical about that account. Among the latter, some dismiss the whole reform, while others believe in a reform but regard Herodotus' list of twenty satrapies as a Greek construct.[30] In my own view, when Croesus' "treasures" had been taken to the Iranian treasuries (probably after Pactyes' revolt), his former subjects were required to pay tribute and to join the army: every conqueror relied on such obligations, and they are presupposed by the grants of privileges and exemptions mentioned above. Therefore – even if Herodotus' list of satrapies, which follows existing "catalogue" traditions (Bichler 2000: 286–7), is mostly meant to illustrate the territorial extent and economic power of Darius' empire and thus useless for a reconstruction of a satrapal reform, and even if one has to accept greater continuity between the rule of Darius and his two predecessors than is usually done (Briant 2002a: 69–70) – there is no reason to deny the authenticity of Darius' reforms or to dismiss all later evidence for it as derived from Herodotus.[31] The new tributary system, as Herodotus and others emphasize, was designed to regularize assessment standards and the amount and frequency of tax-payments – concerns very familiar to a fifth-century Greek. It did not exclude incorporation of existing regional or local systems. Last but not least, it makes historical sense, if it is true that the building of a Persian fleet had led to overtaxation and to a moratorium on tax (Wallinga 1984; 1987). The survey of the territories of the Greek cities of Western Asia Minor organized by Artaphernes after the Ionian revolt to alleviate conflicts within and between the *poleis* (Briant 2002a: 494–6), and the reassessment of their taxes (on almost the same level as before; Hdt. 6.42), probably followed the model of Darius' reform and subsequently served as the model for the assessments of the contributions of the members of the Delian League (Wallinga 1989).

There are no signs of a change in the economic structures of western Asia Minor; even the mint at Sardis was taken over by the Persians. From the beginning of their rule over the region the Persian kings showed much interest in minting, but it has long been a matter of controversy whether Cyrus merely continued to strike, or himself introduced, the gold-and-silver coinage attributed to Croesus (the so-called *kroiseioi statêres*: see figure 9.2).[32] Scholars do agree that a new phase in the history of bi-metallic coinage in Western Anatolia began when the Persian *dareikoi* and *sigloi* were first struck around 520, on the standard of the *kroiseioi*. The darics, primarily designed to finance military campaigns and to serve as "gifts," ultimately became the most important gold coinage in Greece before the *Philippeioi* of Philip II of Macedon.

Scholars have sometimes assumed that economic changes were among the causes of the Ionian revolt: it has been supposed that the integration of Phoenicia and Egypt into the Persian trade system brought these two regions into competition with the Ionian cities (Miletus in particular), to the Ionians' disadvantage (Lenschau 1913), or that Darius placed overseas trade in the hands of state-approved entrepreneurs rather than Greeks (Högemann 1992: 290–1). Neither Herodotus' *Histories* nor the archaeological evidence speak in favor of an economic crisis in Ionia or Miletus, restrictions on Milesian trade or a preference for non-Greek entrepreneurs. What is more, the abolition of internal borders in the Persian empire ought to have benefited the Ionians and given them an advantage over their rivals in the *poleis* of Greece. As for Miletus, Herodotus stresses that the city reached its cultural and economic acme under Persian rule (5.28).[33] In pre-Persian times, the city appears to have suffered a series of extraordinarily brutal civil wars over more than two generations, which had only been brought to an end through the mediation of Parians.[34]

Against the background of latent tensions within the Ionian cities, documented by Herodotus and other authors, and testified to by the prevalence of Persian-backed tyrannies, a political interpretation of the Ionian revolt is to be preferred. In this interpretation, the decisive role is played by the endeavors of the tyrant of Miletus, Aristagoras, to secure his power and status in a situation of internal *stasis*. The tyrant had tried to improve his standing in the city and in the empire by mounting a campaign of conquest against Naxos, but had failed and had annoyed his overlord by underestimating the strategic and economic risk of the operation. To anticipate Persian reprisals and to secure his political position, Aristagoras saw no other choice than to persuade the Ionians to revolt against the Persians and to request external help. An Ionian revolt could only be successful if the Persian-backed tyrants were expelled and the social basis of the rebellion was broadened with the help of political concessions, and this is exactly what Herodotus says happened. "And first [Aristagoras] made a pretence (*logôi*) of giving up his despotism and gave Miletus equality of government (*isonomiê*), so that the Milesians might readily join in his revolt; then he did likewise in the rest of Ionia" (5.37). In other words, Aristagoras sought to divert the political and social tensions within the city – perhaps intensified as a result of socially unbalanced taxation, and the example of successful "isonomic revolutions" in Athens and Naxos – into collective action against the Persian overlord (cf. Briant 2002a: 151–2). Despite their final victory, the Persians learned their lesson: the regulation of territorial conflicts between the Ionian cities, the reassessment of tribute, and Persian non-interference in the political reorganization of the cities in 493–492 "benefited" the Ionians and helped to secure internal and external peace (Hdt. 6.42–3; Briant 2002a: 493–7).

The influence of Persian rule on the culture of Lydia has long been difficult to assess, but a new book on Persian Sardis (Dusinberre 2003) has remedied this problem by demonstrating a quick consolidation of Lydian affairs. This was accomplished by a combination of imperial influence on both ideology and way of life, and a return to, or preservation of, "Lydian" tradition. Such processes of acculturation or transculturation not only permanently shaped the identity and the self-representation of the local and regional polyethnic elites, but were later also partially internalized by the rest of the population and thus became part of local tradition well beyond the downfall of the Achaemenid empire.

As we have seen, Miletus "had been at the height of her fortunes" before the Ionian revolt, "and was indeed the chief ornament of Ionia" (Hdt. 5.28; Gorman 2001). Undoubtedly, Herodotus referred not only to the economic status of Miletus, but also to its role as a cultural center. Scholars used to find it hard to reconcile Miletus' political attachment to Persia with its intellectually highly stimulating atmosphere (the "Ionian Enlightenment"; see ch. 29, below), but it has long since become clear that the Ionian beginnings of a philosophy of nature, science, and analytical geometry, as well as important progress in the disciplines of geography and ethnography, occurred "in the shadow of the rise of the Persian empire" (Burkert 2003). Ephesus, whose sanctuary of Artemis had probably welcomed the Persians' arrival and whose "temple of Croesus" (Bammer and Muss 1996) reached its completion under Persian domination (Burkert 2003: 113–15), also took part in this development (see figure 9.3). It was not initiated by the Persians, but was favored by the absence of internal and external wars and the unification of the oriental world under one ruler. Aside from the possible forced use of specialists after Pactyes' rebellion and the Ionian revolt, Persian supremacy also opened up lucrative new opportunities for Ionian artists, craftsmen, doctors, and members of other professions in the empire, and even at the Great King's court (Walser 1984: 20–6).

Figure 9.3 Temple of Artemis at Ephesos

The Ionian revolt was a turning point in the history of Ionian-Persian relations, but one which did not affect all cities in the same way as Miletus, which was destroyed and had part of its population deported. Ephesus apparently refused to support the revolt and introduced a political system according to the principles of isonomy in 492 (Heracl. fr. 121 D). And even in Miletus "the element of continuity [prevailed], since the rest of its population was able to preserve its home, traditions and therefore its identity far beyond the years of Persian rule" (Ehrhardt 2003: 18). After the Persian defeats at Salamis, Plataea, and Mycale (480–479), the local enemies of tyranny in many Greek cities of the islands and Asia Minor used the supremacy of the Hellenic fleet to expel their city lords, shake off Persian rule and join the Delian League. Other cities were then or later unwillingly forced into the alliance.

The borderline between the territories of the Delian League and the possessions of the Great King never became an "iron curtain." Papyrological and archaeological evidence testifies to the fact that western Asia Minor remained a zone of intensive cultural contacts and diplomatic networks for the purpose of the maintenance of local peace.[35]

The Persian Wars and Persian Plans for Greece

The central topic of Herodotus' *Histories* is how and why the great figures of this world succumb to the temptations and dangers of rule, why their urge to expand their realm makes them forget the responsibilities of power, and why and against which opponents they ultimately fail.[36] In this conception, divinely set limits play an important role, and the conqueror who exceeds these suffers fatal consequences. Against the background of the Athenian glorification of their surprising victory over the Persians as a triumph of free citizens over servile royal subjects (Wiesehöfer 2002b), Herodotus assigns the full range of qualities of men of power to his Persian characters: the patriarchal founding hero Cyrus, the mad despot Cambyses, the magnanimous and capricious Darius, always seeking his own advantage, the ambitious but overstretched Xerxes, and the vain Mardonius. In the end, they all fail because of their excessive ambition for conquest.[37]

It is usually claimed that the notion of three successive world empires of Assyria, Media, and Persia, found in the works of Herodotus (cf. 1.95.130) and Ctesias (*FGrH* 688 F 1.5) and in an expanded form in the book of Daniel and in Roman literature (Wiesehöfer 2003b), derives from the official Achaemenid view of history, intended to underline the legitimacy of Persia as the heir to the empires of the Near East.[38] However, doubts about the historicity of a "Median empire" and new insights into Achaemenid royal ideology force us to reconsider this thesis. First, the "three-kingdom" sequence cannot be found in Achaemenid royal inscriptions or other official statements of the Persian kings, and the views of history which the Achaemenids did try to impose on their subject peoples could not have inspired the Herodotean model. The Great Kings regarded themselves as truly "Persian" rulers and not as successors to the Medes. Secondly, the model is neatly compatible with Herodotus' own view of world history. He makes all the territories of the earlier kingdoms merge into the

Persian empire, which alone is capable of ruling "the whole of Asia," and not merely "upper Asia" or "on this side of the river Halys." Moreover, he focuses, as we have seen, on the origin, consolidation, erosion, and – in the cases of Assyria and Media – collapse of the Asian empires, which he causally relates to guilt and fate, to the responsibility and compulsion of the rulers in question.[39] Thirdly, later accounts may well be Hellenistic reworkings of Herodotus rather than reflections of an Achaemenid conception; the figure of "Darius the Mede" in the Book of Daniel, at any rate, is modeled after the Herodotean Darius (Wiesehöfer 2005). However, the author of the book of Daniel did diverge from Herodotus insofar as he turned the three Asian empires into real world empires.

Although the Great Kings in their inscriptions underline their religious and moral right to world domination, ordained by Auramazda, they do not demand possession of the whole inhabited world, the *oikumene*.[40] They address only the peoples of the empire, whose well-being and loyalty matter to the Great Kings; the *poleis* of Hellas, not to mention the rest of Europe, remain outside the world which is asked to internalize the instructions of the kings and to recognize the rulers' efforts for its well-being:

> A great god (is) Auramazda, who created this earth, who created yonder heaven, who created man, who created blissful happiness for man, who made Darius king, the one king of many, the one master of many. I (am) Darius, the great king, king of kings, king of the countries containing all races, king on this great earth even far off . . . Proclaims Darius, the king: By the favor of Auramazda these (are) the countries which I seized outside Persia; I ruled them; to me they brought tribute. What has been said to them by me, that they did.
>
> (DNa 1–21; tr. R. Schmitt)

At least politically, the Great Kings seem to have been quite satisfied with their rule over Asia and Egypt alone, an idea which Herodotus' courageous queen Artemisia seems to convey when she tells Xerxes after Salamis that he has achieved the goal of his expedition by burning Athens, and that any further conquests would be no more than an added bonus (8.102).

Darius had no "European" plans beyond subjecting the coastal regions of Thrace, making Macedonia a vassal, and, later, punishing Eretria and Athens. And that Darius' son Xerxes had no intention of conquering the western Mediterranean (despite Herodotus 7.8 and Ephorus ap. Diod. 11.1.4–5) is made perfectly clear by Thucydides: "Ten years afterwards the barbarian returned with the armada for the subjugation of Hellas" (1.18.2). But what about Xerxes' plans for Greece before and after a victory over the Hellenic League?

Herodotus tells us that Mardonius wanted to become "governor of Greece" (*tês Hellados hyparchos*: 7.6.1), but we may wonder how our author could have known such private information, and should be aware that this motivation is part of a literary portrayal of Mardonius as an overambitious and self-interested advisor of Xerxes. Herodotus' claim that the Persians aimed at the subjugation and permanent control of Greece as a whole does not make much historical sense.[41] How are we to explain that neither the unbeaten Persian army after Salamis, nor Mardonius after his second occupation of Athens in 479, campaigned against the Peloponnese, where they would probably have been supported by the enemies of Sparta? The Macedonian delegation to Athens (8.136,140–3) suggests that both Xerxes and Mardonius were primarily concerned with the political and military conduct of Athens, and hoped that, if it changed sides, the remaining members of the Hellenic League and neutral states such as Argos would reach a settlement with the Great King. Lengthy operations far away from the centers of the empire would surely have been doomed to fail, since these would have surpassed the Persians' military and logistic capacities. Finally, it is hard to see how the Persians could have made Greece into a satrapy, separated from the satrapy of Thrace by the vassal kingdom of Macedonia: reducing previously autonomous persophile Greek *poleis* and *ethnê* to dependent subjects would have alienated support, and it would have been difficult to exercise royal supervision over a distant area of such geographical and political divergence. What the Persians demanded from their neighbors and subject states was a readiness to accept royal rule in the "land of the king" and to recognize the primacy of Persian interests in areas just beyond the empire's borders, and this could have been ensured simply by placing Greek supporters in leading positions in the most important *poleis*. The Greek exiles accompanying Xerxes on his campaign are likely to have featured prominently in his plans. The best-known of these characters is the former Spartan king Demaratus, who was undoubtedly meant to become the Persian stakeholder in Sparta. The exact political organization of submissive states was of minor importance to the Persians, as is proven by Mardonius' measures after the Ionian rebellion (Hdt. 6.43).

Such indications in Herodotus' work fit perfectly with current research on the dynamics of empire which concludes that empires always favor indirect rule (Goldstone and Haldon 2008). A later source, rarely considered in this connection, appears to refer to Persian plans for indirect rule: Demosthenes tells us that the Athenians before Plataea declined a Persian offer, delivered by Alexander of Macedon, "to rule over the rest of the Greeks" (*tôn loipôn archein Hellênôn*), in return for bowing to the will of the Great King (*hypakouein basilei*; 6.11). Of course, this alleged Persian offer serves the orator to emphasize the Athenians' will-power in resistance. Herodotus is unfamiliar with it (but reports an offer of additional territory: 8.140a; 9.7a), and it would certainly have encountered violent opposition from the persophile Thebans and Demaratus of Sparta. On the other hand, the Persians might indeed have been eager to control Hellas with the help of a politically and militarily balanced system of Greek hegemonial powers. By contrast, it seems unlikely that Demaratus or the other friends of Persia would ever have obeyed, and have persuaded their compatriots to obey, a Persian satrap of Greece, who would have been in need of a very large occupation force.

Persian Views of Greeks and Greek Views of Persians

Mainland Greece remained outside Persian visions of imperial space. The Greek subjects of the Great Kings – called *Yauna* and divided into three groups, the

"Ionians of the land," "(Ionians) who are on the sea and the peoples beyond the sea," "*pelte*-carrying Ionians" – appear in inscriptions among "tribal" peoples such as Thracians and Scythians; on the accompanying reliefs, they are barely distinguished from the Carians and Lydians. In Darius' vision of the empire,[42] "the Ionians . . . are not (even) deemed distinctive enough to serve as a significant boundary marker" (Kuhrt 2002: 22). Although this Persian view of the Greeks should not be used to minimalize the importance of the "Greek Wars" for the Persians, it might nevertheless help us to avoid "hellenocentric" traps.

As we have seen, Greece's perception of the Persians was influenced by its impression of Median influence on Near Eastern affairs. Hence the early expansion of the Persian empire was seen as the empire-building of "the Mede" (Xenophanes F 18 D), the Persian wars as *ta Mêdika*, and Greek collaboration with the Persian enemy as *mêdismos*. In 472, Aeschylus still presented the Persian monarchs as descendants of an eponymous Medos (*Pers.* 765). However, many Greeks' first experience of the Persians was the sight of the Persian army and booty at Marathon, Salamis and Plataea. Contemporary Greek poets who commented on these military encounters stressed the extraordinary threat of the Persian campaigns and the heroism of the Greek soldiers (Hutzfeldt 1999: 16–23). A few years later, Athens' part in the victories of Marathon and Salamis acquired mythical proportions in Aeschylus' tragedy *Persai*. Although the dramatist already philosophized about the contrast between Greek (Athenian) and Persian norms and behavior, the Persian empire's association with despotism and luxury was a product of later Athenian propaganda.[43]

In Greek art, the conceptual change in which the "foreigner" becomes the "enemy," and an asymmetric opposition develops between Greeks and Persians, occurred notably later than the time of the Persian wars, at a time when Athens developed a highly ideological perspective on its victories. Previously, Attic representations of Graeco-Persian combat had not shown unique forms of victory but followed the normal contemporary iconography of Greek combat scenes, which were far more numerous than Graeco-Persian battles.[44]

Greeks in the Early Persian Empire

Persia was the new home of many Greek refugees who became "servants" of the Great Kings after 479, and we also know of pre-war commuters across the border. Those seeking the protection of the king after suffering political reverses at home, included not only the Spartan king, Demaratus, but the Athenian tyrant, Hippias, the soothsayer, Onomacritus (Hdt. 7.6.3), the Athenian, Dicaeus (Hdt. 8.65), and the Sicilian, Scythes of Zancle (Hdt. 6.23–4, 7.164; Athen. 415–416). Demaratus is said to have been given "land and cities" by Darius (Hdt. 6.70.2), like Pytharchus of Cyzicus by Cyrus (Agathocles Babyl. *FGrH* 472 F 6.42) and Theomestor and Phylacus of Samos (Hdt. 8.85.2–3), Xenagoras of Halicarnassus (Hdt. 9.107) and the prisoner-of-war Metiochus, son of Miltiades (Hdt. 6.41.4), by Xerxes. And "the few surviving names of Greeks who moved between worlds must (only) be a small fraction of the numbers of Greeks actually involved" (Miller 1997: 100; cf. 97–108).

Apart from the doctor Democedes of Croton in Herodotus' fairytale-like story (3.129–37; Griffith 1987), Greeks mentioned in the service of Persian kings include sculptors, secretaries, soldiers, and textile workers, mostly of East Greek origin. Most famous are the architect Mandrocles (Hdt. 4.87) and the craftsmen Pytharchus and Nicon who left their graffiti in the quarry near the terrace at Persepolis (Boardman 2000, 131–2). Most of the working gangs mentioned in the Persepolis Tablets were, like the deportees from Miletus (494) and Eretria (490), probably never allowed to return to their homeland.

Greeks and Persians, 559–479: A Short History of Events[45]

Center of the Persian empire was a region in south-western Iran which bore the Persians' name (Old Persian *Parsa*, Greek *Persis*) and with which they felt a particular affinity. The Persians were not the original inhabitants of Persis, and their ethnogenesis is still a highly disputed matter. Only for the seventh and sixth centuries are we able to lift the veil and see the processes of acculturation between Elamite and Iranian political and cultural entities, acknowledged by Cyrus II when he called himself and his forebears "Kings of Anshan." Cyrus fundamentally changed the political landscape of the ancient Near East. After winning the territories of the Elamite kingdom, Cyrus defeated Astyages, the leader of the Median confederacy, which, sixty years before, had conquered the Assyrian royal cities. Cyrus successfully expanded his new territory to the north-west and thwarted Lydian plans to profit from the turmoil in the east. Although he failed to induce Lydia's Greek subjects to desert their king Croesus, Cyrus was able to conquer Lydia. The Lydian king probably died during the siege of Sardis, to survive only in parts of Greek tradition, which mythologically (Bacchylides) or rationally (Herodotus) glossed over the catastrophe and at the same time established the tradition of the "generous victor" Cyrus. That this tradition has nothing to do with reality is proven by the Persian king's reaction to the rebellion of the Lydian treasurer Pactyes, supported by most of the Greek cities. Cyrus' generals not only punished the rebel, but also took revenge on his allies: Mazares conquered Priene, enslaved its political elite, and pillaged Magnesia, while Harpagus forcibly took possession of Smyrna, Phocaea, and other cities, securing the whole coastal region up to Lycia. Only Miletus, autonomous in Lydian times, which had supported Cyrus against Croesus and had not been involved in Pactyes' revolt, was allowed to keep its favored political status.

Babylonia, under its king Nabonidus, must have been alarmed at Cyrus' successes in Elam, Media and Anatolia. What finally caused the fatal confrontation of the two powers, we do not know. After a massacre of Babylonian troops at Opis and the capture of Sippar, Cyrus sent his general Ugbaru ahead to Babylon, which opened its gates to him. Cyrus had probably presented himself beforehand to the priests of Marduk and the city's elite as the instrument of the god and as a promising political alternative to Nabonidus. His own entry into the city in October 539 took a Babylonian ceremonial form (which the last Pahlavi Shah tried to recall in 1971), as did his

Figure 9.4 Tomb of Cyrus at Pasargadae
Source: Author's photo.

Figure 9.5 Palace at Pasargadae
Source: Author's photo.

Figure 9.6 The Zendan at Pasargadae
Source: Author's photo.

first measures in the city and in the region. Cyrus' cylinder inscription, drafted by Babylonian experts, introduces the new king as legitimate ruler of Babylon, fostered by Marduk, a king who fulfils his duties to the god and the people. This prudent behavior made collaboration of the Babylonian elite with the foreign ruler much easier. It is unclear to what extent Cyrus' integration of former territories of the Babylonian empire into his own realm followed a Babylonian model or innovated. Despite the Jewish tradition which presents him as Yahweh's Messiah and as the man who repatriated the exiles and rebuilt the Temple, decisive measures in Jewish affairs were taken only under his successors. However, the fact that our sources report no rebellions in Babylonia or Transeuphratene speaks in favor of a successful policy in the newly conquered territories. This success is confirmed by Cyrus' conquest of Eastern Iran, probably in the 530s; about which we have no further details. Greek authors tell us that Cyrus died during his wars against the peoples of the steppe and that his corpse was brought to Persis and buried in his newly built residence Pasargadae. The remains of this "garden residence" still bear witness to Cyrus' use of Near Eastern and Greek artistic models and to the special skill of the king's artists and craftsmen, including Ionian sculptors (see figures 9.4–9.6). Even if the traditional view of Cyrus, not least thanks to his own endeavors, is much too positive and hides the dark side of the conqueror's personality and policy, it is clear that the founder of the first world empire in history must have been a man with extraordinary abilities. It is no wonder that in Iran and other parts of the ancient Near East numerous stories, modeled after older traditions, bestowed praise on this exceptional ruler.

From Cyrus' time, the Persians had a common border with Egypt, the only other remaining superpower. Its king Amasis tried to meet the Persian threat with an impressive fleet, the support of Polycrates of Samos, then a rival to the Persian satrap at Sardis, and the occupation of Cyprus as a naval base. Cyrus' son Cambyses responded to these measures by the time- and money-consuming building of a Persian navy, manned by experienced subjects and commanded by Persian officers. He then conquered Cyprus and, crossing the Sinai with the help of Arab tribes, won a victory at Pelusium (525), took Memphis, and captured king Psammetichus III. His success was made complete by the voluntary submission of Libyan territories, the diplomatic securing of Egypt's southern frontier, and probably also by winning control of the big western oases. Like his father in Babylonia, Cambyses tried to adapt his policy and royal representation to Egyptian traditions and to win the loyalty and support of the Egyptian elite. The career of the Egyptian commander and doctor Udjahorresnet shows how successful he was in that plan.[46] However, reductions in the revenues of some temples, and probably also the later experience of the unsuccessful Egyptian rebellions of 486–485 and 460–454, were responsible for a distorted picture of the foreign conqueror Cambyses in Egypt, as handed down to us by Herodotus: here, the Persian king appears as a brutal, almost mad, despot who shows no mercy and no appreciation of Egyptian customs and traditions.

A serious crisis afflicted the empire during Cambyses' stay in Egypt, as a result of the high economic and military demands he made on his subjects, and probably also as a result of tensions between the king and both the mighty Persian aristocracy and his brother Bardiya. Although both Herodotus and Darius' *res gestae* inscribed on the rock of Bisutun (DB) refer to it, the course of this crisis is still disputed. Most probably, Gaumata, a Median *magus*, left behind as high functionary in Persis by Cambyses, took advantage of the Persian nobility's unhappiness with the king and his murder of Bardiya to present himself as the king's brother: he took the throne and gained support by a series of highly popular measures, not least a moratorium on taxes and military service. Other scholars suppose that Bardiya himself revolted against his brother. Whether or not Darius I, to whom we owe the Gaumata-version, and who after Cambyses' death killed Gaumata/Bardiya with the help of six conspirators, was a regicide, he surely was a usurper without right to the throne. This is underlined by the fact that he tried to legitimize his rule by linking his descent with Cyrus' Teispid line, and by the numerous rebellions which he was able to quash only with great difficulty and great brutality (522/1). He would not have been successful without the support of parts of the Persian higher nobility, which had been dissatisfied with both Cambyses and Gaumata/Bardiya: the financial, political and military effort of expansion and empire building had probably led to dissent between monarch, population and aristocracy over the future of the empire and the roles of ruler, nobility, and subjects. That Darius succeeded in securing the cohesion of the empire and in making the aristocracy dependent on his royal family, points to his political and diplomatic skills, his military genius and his unscrupulousness at the same time.

Darius' reign was probably the most important phase of the history of the Achaemenid empire. It was the time of the greatest extent of the realm, decisive fiscal and administrative reforms and the development of a specific Persian ideology of kingship and rule. Unfortunately, our information about events after Darius' succession to the throne is scanty and highly biased. The Bisutun inscription mentions Darius' campaigns against Elam and the Scythians of Central Asia (in the second and third years of his reign), but after that the Persian sources fall silent. Only two late-Achaemenid Babylonian chronicles and a few historical details from "Astronomical Diaries" hint at later events in the east. Almost all other relevant historical information is provided by foreign records, hostile or at any rate highly ideologically colored, which almost exclusively deal with Graeco-Persian relations and Greek views of their neighbors in the East.

Darius not only expanded the empire, but also guaranteed its military and economic stability. In the west, he incorporated the Cyrenaica (513), Thrace, the strategically important straits, and Samos (519) into the empire, and made Macedon (510 [?] and after 494) and Athens (507/6) acknowledge the Great King's supreme power in foreign affairs. In the east, he conquered "Indian" territories, and in the north probably regarded the Danube as his frontier, after an unsuccessful campaign against the "European" Scythians (513) beyond that natural border. His later policy of consolidation suffered a bitter setback when in 498 the Ionian cities revolted against their Persian overlord. The rebels won over Caria and the greater part of Cyprus, and, assisted by the Eretrians and Athenians, took Sardis (except the acropolis), setting fire to the city. Only a supreme effort, and disunity amongst the Ionians, enabled Darius to suppress the revolt. Over the next few years steps were taken to safeguard the Ionians' loyalty for the future, and Darius prepared to punish Eretria and Athens for their role in the revolt (and, in the case of Athens, also for the city's violation of the treaty of 507/6). The Persian defeat at Marathon (490) was the ignominious end of an otherwise successful expedition in the Aegean, surely not the failed start of a Persian attempt to conquer Greece or even Europe. Historically more important than the Persian setback was the repercussion of the Athenian victory on the internal affairs of the city – the expulsion of the (alleged) friends of the Peisistratids and Persians – and the subsequent emergence of a special Athenian identity.

Darius was also drawn into the affairs of Egypt, where the short reign of Cambyses had not provided political stability. The most notable of his many measures were the withdrawal of his predecessor's fiscal orders, the confirmation of former privileges of sanctuaries and priesthoods, the completion of Necho's canal, and the sending of naval expeditions to and from Egypt which served to demonstrate the special qualities of Persian rule by emulating past pharaonic feats. Royal images and inscriptions from Egypt – in particular, the texts on the monumental statue of Darius excavated at Susa, but originally put up at Heliopolis – show the king as both a pious, successful Egyptian Pharaoh and a universal ruler. Darius also started the building of the two most impressive Achaemenid residences – first Susa, then Persepolis. The tablets from Persepolis and the *Burgbau*-inscription from Susa (DSf) reveal the empire-wide importance of those projects: the king was seen as mobilizing the labor forces and resources of the whole empire in order to create the residences which he deserved and which gave architectural, pictorial and textual expression to his vision of Achaemenid kingship and Persian rule. Darius' rock-cut tomb at Naqsh-i Rustam with its new cross-shaped form and its inscriptions (DNa, DNb) and reliefs also stresses the king's role as the gods' human representative on earth.

It was a difficult task for Xerxes (486–465) to protect and preserve Persian rule. Recent scholarship has rightly emphasized that Xerxes' reign was much more successful than Greek authors want us to believe, acquitting him not only from the charge of having destroyed Babylonian temples and taken away the statue of Marduk, but also from the accusation that he was a man lacking in ideas, a coward, brutal despot and strategic failure all at the same time. Xerxes' reign did not trigger an irreversible process of decadence and decline in Persian power, as Greek authors of the fourth century claimed. Quick to learn his father's lessons, Xerxes was highly successful in consolidating the empire through a carrot-and-stick policy, granting local autonomy on the one hand and exercising strict supervision on the other. Culturally, one might even call Xerxes' rule the highlight of Persian civilization.

The king failed, however, to force mainland Greeks to accept Persian power of decision in foreign affairs. Some important Greek *poleis* and *ethnê* (Thebes, Thessaly) did join him on his campaign against Greece, while others proceeded tactically (Delphi) or remained neutral (Argos), but thirty or so Greek states formed a Hellenic League against him and, after initial defeats, were ultimately victorious over the Persian fleet (Salamis, 480) and army (Plataea, 479). Even if Athenians and Lacedaemonians, Plataeans and Corinthians, Eretrians and Aeginetans neither fought for Europe against Asia, nor for democracy and humanity against barbarism and despotism, but simply for their independence from foreign rule, the results of their victories were significant. The Persian empire was confined to its territories in Asia Minor (now without the coastal region), the Levant and Egypt; Athens, with the help of its Delian League, became a hegemonial power and a rival to Sparta; and finally the Athenians, and to some extent all Greeks, developed an "anti-barbarian" identity, creating a vision of a "barbarian" counter-world of despotic monarchs and slavish subjects which continues to be influential to this very day.

NOTES

1 For example, in the *Achaemenid History Workshops*, beautifully organized by the late H. Sancisi-Weerdenburg, or in the Melammu conferences, initiated by S. Parpola and others (most recently in Innsbruck in 2002: Rollinger and Ulf 2004a).

2 It has, however, been rightly stressed that the Persian wars were crucial for the development of this kind of panhellenism (Hall 2002: 205–20; and ch. 31, below).

3 Herodotus on Persians: Rollinger 2003a; Persian foreign policy: Wiesehöfer 2004c.

4 Bichler 2000: 235; Panaino 2003 for an Iranianist's view of this *logos*; on Deioces, see Wiesehöfer 2004b; also Dewald 2003.

5 Excavations: Mierse 1983; Greenewalt 1995a; 1995b; Dusinberre 2003. Coinage; Cahil and Kroll 2005.

6 See n. 1, above, and the groundbreaking work of Pierre Briant (2002a; originally 1996).

7   Rollinger 2004; Miller 1997; Hutzfeldt 1999; Hölscher 2000; Thomas 2000: 75–100.
8   See Raaflaub 1987; 2002a; 2002b.
9   See Welwei 1999: 23, 345 n. 87. On giving earth and water, see Kuhrt 1988.
10   Hdt. 6.48; see the bibliography in Zahrnt 1992: 276ff; Welwei 1999: 350 n. 133.
11   Such doubts are raised in most chapters of Lanfranchi et al. 2003b.
12   For criticism of Persian "vassalage," see Rollinger 1999; Henkelman 2003; for the Elamite heritage: Vallat 1996; Liverani 2003: 10–11 and in particular Henkelman 2003.
13   Cf. the "night battle" in Hdt. 1.74; not to be linked with the solar eclipse of May 28, 585: Rollinger 2003b: 309–10.
14   Rollinger 2003b: 318 n. 141 rightly stresses the fact that the "Median" terminology is normally used to underline the special character of the dangers coming from the east.
15   For Cyrus' origins, see TUAT I 409.21 (confirmed by an inscription from Ur). Later inscriptions which make him an Achaemenid (CMa-c; cf. DB I 27–29) were attempts to legitimize the rule of Darius I. The story in Herodotus (1.107–8; cf. Xen. *Cyr.* 1.2.1) which makes Cyrus the son of the Median princess Mandane is meant to offer ideological support for Persian claims to Media and Lydia (for Egypt, see Hdt. 3.2.1–2). The story of Cyrus' birth and childhood (Hdt. 1.107–21; cf. Justin 1.4.10; Nic. Dam. *FGrH* 90 F66; Ctes. *FGrH* 688 F9) has Mesopotamian parallels (Sargon of Akkade) and is Iranian in character.
16   See Rollinger 2008 and 1993: 188–97; Oelsner 1999/2000, esp. 378–9; Schaudig 2001: 25 n. 108. The Chronicle here probably refers to a campaign against Urartu instead.
17   See Greenewalt 1992; Burkert 1985a; Bichler 2000: 251–4; West 2003: 418–20.
18   See Hdt. 1.22. Walser 1984: 14–15 dates Miletus' agreement with Persia to the time after Pactyes' rebellion and interprets it as the result of Miletus' refusal to support Pactyes.
19   Hdt. 1.154–69; Plut. Mor. 859 A-B; Justin 1.7.11. For the fate of the Lydians, see Herodotus 1.155.2, with Bichler 2000: 255.
20   The authenticity of the so-called "Gadatas Letter" (ML12), which mentions the agreement with Aulae, is disputed (cf. Schmitt 1996a with Briant 2003; Gauger 2000: 205–12).
21   For the history of Pactyes' rebellion, cf. Briant 2002a, 37–8, 882–3 (with the older literature).
22   Cilicia continued to be governed by a dynast who had the title *syennesis* (Hdt. 1.74; called "king of the Cilicians" by Herodotus 5.118) In Lycia, local dynasts probably had the greatest political say; nominally, however, they had to accept Persian lordship.
23   Nylander 1970; 1974; Roaf 1983; Boardman 2000. Cf. the praise of the Lydian and Ionian sculptors in Darius I's *Burgbau*-inscription from Susa: DSf 47–9, 51–2.
24   Achaemenid lists give the name *Sparda* for Lydia, which seems to represent the Lydian ethnic term *Śfarda*, "Sardians" (Schmitt 2003a, 293–4). An attempt to distinguish between (early and changeable) "great," "major," and "minor" satrapies (Jacobs 1994) is unconvincing.
25   For Polycrates: de Libero 1996: 253–97; Briant 2002a: 52–3, 886; ch 6, above.
26   Balcer 1984: 185, speculates that it was Bagaeus, Darius' tool in the murder of Oroetes.
27   Cf. the overview in Schmitt 2003a, 293–4.
28   Walter 1993b: 275; cf. 273–5. It is not enough to interpret the Persian appointment of tyrants only as a "rewarding of loyal supporters" (as does de Libero 1996: 415).
29   Hdt. 6.9–10, 13 notes that the tyrants flee to Persia after their expulsion; the Ionians interpreted the political system of their cities as joint rule of Persians and tyrants (Hdt. 6.22).
30   For an overview of the debate (and a firm personal opinion), see Jacobs 2003.
31   See Plat. *Leg.* 695c; Plut. *Mor.* 172f; Polyaen. 7.11.3; Chron.Pasch. 145 C Dindorf; with Jacobs 2003: 308. Plato's version is particularly revealing, since unlike Herodotus it uses the older (and original) Greek term for "tribute," *dasmos*, rather than the later *phoros*.

32 Hdt. 1.54, 94; *IG* I³ 458.29. A sixth-century gold refinery has been excavated at Sardis: Ramage and Craddock 2000. For the Croeseïds, cf. note 5.

33 Hdt. 5.28. Although Herodotus presents Miletus' prosperity as the starting-point of Aristagoras' excessive quest for power, as well as the root of all evil for the city (Walter 1993b, 268), the prosperity itself should not be doubted.

34 Hdt. 5.28–9; Heracl.Pont. fr. 50 Wehrli; Plut. *Mor.* 298 C-D; cf. Hesych. s.v. *aeinautai.*

35 Balcer 1985; Miller 1997: 97–108; Whitby 1998b; Wiesehöfer 2004d.

36 Bichler 2000: 213ff gives an excellent summary of this topic with many valuable observations in detail.

37 Raaflaub 2002a argues that Athens' Sicilian expedition (415–413) may have shaped Herodotus' views of imperialism and expansionism vs. desire for freedom and political unity.

38 The following points are discussed in detail in Wiesehöfer 2003a.

39 Ctesias' slightly different view is best explained as the author's deliberate play on the version of his famous predecessor: Bichler 2004a; 2004b.

40 Walser 1987.

41 Cf. the counterfactual history ("The Persians Win at Salamis, 480 BC") in Hanson 1999a; contrast: Zahrnt 1992; Wiesehöfer 2002.

42 DPh 3–8: "This (is) the kingdom which I hold, from the Scythians who (are) beyond Sogdiana, from there as far as Nubia, from the Indus province, from there as far as Lydia."

43 Wiesehöfer 2002. Gehrke (2003a) has rightly pointed out that, after the crisis of the Peloponnesian War, the battle of Marathon as an exclusively Athenian victory became much more important for the cultural memory of Athens and for that of antiquity in general.

44 Schneider, personal communication.

45 Cf. Briant 2002a; Wiesehöfer 2006.

46 Bareş 1999: 38–43; Weinberg 1999.

PART III

Regions

CHAPTER TEN

Attica: A View from the Sea

Sanne Houby-Nielsen

Introduction

The scholarly view of archaic Attica has changed greatly within the last hundred years or so.[1] In the late nineteenth and early twentieth century, French and German handbooks on Greek art liked to indulge in vivid descriptions of oriental influences on archaic Greece and Attic art. Max Collignon stated that Homeric culture was half oriental, and that the prototype for the buildings described in the *Odyssey* could be found in Assyria rather than Greece. He visualized the seventh century BC as a melting pot of "Asiatic" influences and "Hellenism" resulting in new pottery styles and works of art (1881: 29–33). Similarly, Ernst Buschor painted a positive and colorful picture of early archaic Greece in which oriental influences reached and changed Greece via two main routes, "via the Greek East (Rhodes, Samos, Miletus) and above all via Crete" (1913: 43).

During the following decades research increasingly toned down external influences as explanations of cultural change. Cultural relations were seen as far more complex and the "recipient" as a far more autonomous agent, actively selecting among foreign values. This line of thinking also influenced approaches to Attica. Explanations for profound changes in social structure – such as those leading to the formation of the Athenian city state – or for the characteristic development of Athenian religion were sought exclusively within Attica[2] without looking at the contemporary Mediterranean cultural context. Typically, maps show the Attic peninsula in complete isolation from surrounding islands and regions, never mind the Aegean and Mediterranean.[3] Some important recent studies do stress Oriental influences on Greece, but Attica is not their main object of investigation (S. Morris 1992).

The intention of this chapter is not to evaluate the degree of orientalism in early Attica,[4] but to remind readers that stressing cultural autonomy runs counter to recent studies in ethnicity which emphasize hybridization and multiculturalism. The older open-mindedness towards "orientalism," which saw that Attica was almost like an island in the Mediterranean, exposed to foreign cultures from all sides, was in this respect more in tune with the latest research.

For several thousand years, Attica was inhabited by people who lived mainly on its very fringes, in the coastal zones, and interacted so closely with neighbors on the shores of Euboea, the Cyclades, the islands and other coasts of the Saronic Gulf that in the early archaic period the cultural and political "border" of Attica was still a grey zone, difficult to outline. Interaction with neighboring regions also drew Attica into the larger traffic between the eastern and western Mediterranean. In general, this chapter will show the difficulty of defining the region of Attica and ask whether it is meaningful to study the cultural history of the Attic peninsula in isolation. Many major features of archaic Attica – apart from imports and influences in pottery and art – are best understood when Attica is viewed from the sea.

The Definition of Attica as a Region

The territory of Athens was known in antiquity as *Attike ge*, the land of the Athenians. According to the earliest sources this land was controlled by aristocratic families and may have been divided into "kingdoms" ruled by "*basileis*" (Stanton 1990: 6). However, we know little about how developed the notion of Attica as a region was in the early archaic period.

The reforms of Cleisthenes in 508 BC give us the earliest detailed idea of the political organization of Attica: they divided the Athenian people afresh into 139 or 140 *demes*, village-like units in the countryside or sectors within the city of Athens. Rhamnous and Eleusis formed the extremes of this "Cleisthenic map."[5] However, Athenian interests went far beyond the extension of the Cleisthenic *demes* and consequently the political borders of Attica changed throughout the later archaic (and classical) period.[6] Athens continuously struggled to control the waters leading to the strait of Euripos and the Corinthian Isthmus, and the mountain passes connecting Boeotia and Attica. The late archaic fort at Phylla (between Chalcis and Eretria) is likely to have been built in connection with Athens' victory over the Boeotians in 507–506 BC, followed by the occupation of the territory of Chalcis by one of Athens' first cleruchies. The continuous strife between Athens, Boeotia, and Euboea over the community of Oropos and the nearby sanctuary of Amphiaraos, situated immediately to the south of the Asopos river, may also be partly due to a wish to control the Euripos. Between 490 and the first century BC, Oropos is known to have changed hands twelve times, which raises questions about the scholarly habit of treating the Asopos river as the border between Boeotia and Attica (Camp 2001: 322). To the west, Athens waged continual wars with Megara for control of the sea routes towards the crucial isthmus of Corinth. The subjection of Eleusis in the seventh century and Salamis around 600 was part of these wars.[7] The transference to Athens of the Dionysos cult at Eleutherai – situated at an important pass into western Boeotia – should probably be seen in the same context (Paus. 1.20.3).

Attic *social* contacts with neighboring regions and beyond were intense from the early Iron Age onwards.[8] Euboean-type pendent-semicircle *skyphoi* and plates, traded as far as Asia Minor and Chalcidice, were also found in Attica. Conversely, Attic Geometric pottery was imitated in Euboea, and Attic pottery was conspicuous among the imports from the Toumba excavations in Lefkandhi.[9] The so-called SOS amphorae, widely distributed in the Mediterranean, were made both in Athens and in Chalcis and Eretria, and were imitated in the western Greek colony of Pithecusae (Johnston and Jones 1978). Studies of archaic Athenian art long ago noted Oriental and eastern Greek influences. Well-known cases are late eighth-century Attic ceramic imitations of Phoenician silver bowls and ivory imitations of Oriental Astarte figurines (Coldstream 1977: figs. 35b–c, 42 b–d). Ritual vases produced in the seventh century – so-called middle Protoattic pottery – and early Attic Black Figure vases from the early sixth century were the result of a mixture of Attic, Corinthian and East Greek pottery traditions.[10] Several *kouroi* and some *korai* – marble sculptures of respectively naked young men and richly dressed young women, mainly from the sixth and early fifth centuries – from the Ptoon sanctuary in Boeotia clearly stand in an Attic artistic tradition. Conversely, a Boeotian made a dedication on the acropolis in Athens (Karakasi 2001: 144–5).

With regard to more distant regions, social interaction between Asia Minor – or Ionia – and Attica appears especially strong. While the *production* of *kouroi* and *korai* stands in a Cycladic tradition,[11] the ritual practice of *erecting korai* was an Eastern Mediterranean feature, most popular in Ionia and especially in Athens (Karakasi 2001, distribution map). A huge, freestanding column with an Ionic capital contemporary with the famous Naxian column in Delphi stood on the acropolis in imitation of Ionian sanctuaries. Funerary customs and social habits of the ruling classes, "court" life, and temple buildings under the rule of the tyrant Peisistratos and his sons appear to have imitated Eastern Greek practices.[12] Also, one of the best early Black Figure painters in Athens, whose works were among the first to be exported, the Nettos painter, may have come from Asia Minor (Boegehold 1962).[13]

Scholarly perceptions of Attica as a region vary. Some use the "Cleisthenic map" as a guide to borders even though this is much later than the periods under investigation (Morris 1987: fig. 60; Whitley 1991b: 199–201). Others include Oropos, using the Asopos river as a border (Parker 1996: map II; Camp 2001: fig. 7). Archaeological guides tend to follow the modern *nomos* of Attica which includes the Megarid, the islands in the Saronic Gulf (such as Salamis, Aegina, Poros) and even part of the eastern coast of the Argolid, thereby including, for instance, the sanctuary of Perachora, but also the harbor of Aulis, located immediately to the south of the Euripos strait and in antiquity normally counted as Boeotian (Goette 1993; Tomkinson 2002: 5). The studies of the archaic remains in Attica summarized below are generally confined to the Attic peninsula and thus at least indirectly use the "Cleisthenic map."

The Archaic Remains: A Brief Summary

Several recent studies have provided excellent overviews of the archaeology of Athens and Attica in all periods,[14] while more specialized studies of the development of the Athenian city state have focused on burials and settlement traces from the late Iron Age.[15] The study of archaic painted vases from Attica has almost developed into an academic discipline of its own.[16] Later archaic sanctuaries and art have been closely analyzed, often in relation to Peisistratos and his sons (Shapiro 1989). The evidence for Iron Age and archaic Athenian religion has been summarized and invest-igated (Parker 1996: 10–101) and the outstanding funerary and votive marble sculp-ture of the sixth century – especially the statues of *kouroi* and *korai* – has long been an object of interest to art historians and archaeologists.[17] Historical and epigraphic evidence has been compiled by Jeffery (1976: 83–108; 1990).

As is clear from these studies, burials form by far the most abundant source for the early archaic period. Evidence from settlements and sanctuaries is scarce. The only major exception is a series of peak sanctuaries, perhaps dedicated to Zeus, the earliest of which go back to the tenth century (on Mt. Hymettos and Mt. Parnes) while the others are mostly characterized by seventh century material. All of these sanctuaries were extremely rustic, with no elaborate architecture or any imported dedications, in strong contrast to contemporary sanctuaries from the coastal regions, to which we shall return. Similarly, the late Iron Age votive deposit found at Menidhi is the only inland example of a hero-cult. The other known hero-cult in Attica was located near Thorikos, in a coastal region (Parker 1996: 29–42, for references). It is, therefore, also clear from these studies that the evidence is concentrated in the coastal zones, in Athens and its immediate vicinity, and in the Mesogeia plain, the latter areas visible from, and within easy reach of, the coast. Evidence from surveys in the Attic countryside (unfor-tunately rare) point in the same direction: before the sixth century, nothing much goes on inland.[18]

The rest of this chapter will survey settlement patterns, burial customs and belief systems in the Attic peninsula and its border areas in relation to the wider Mediterranean. It will try to show that even though Athens was never a colonizing power much of social life in Attica responded to the colonial world, no doubt due to Attica's central geographical position in the Mediterranean. For convenience, I use the standard terms Boeotia, Euboea, and Attica for the regions although, as just argued, their borders were not static and tended to overlap.

Coastal Settlement in the Bronze and Iron Ages: Offshore Islands and Promontories

From the late Neolithic until the sixth century BC, for more than 2,500 years, people in Attica, including Salamis, and Euboea mainly lived in the coastal zones, settling in bays, on promontories, small peninsulas and tiny offshore islands.[19] These coastal settlements were often established at locations opposite one another on either side of the Euboean Gulf, or on either side of the waters between Cythnos, Kea, Andros, Aegina, Salamis, and the west coast of Attica. No doubt the reason for settling in "pairs" was the ease of communication with neighbors across the sea, compared to the difficulty of crossing mountainous inland regions. Accordingly, in Euboea the majority of prehistoric settlements were situated on the west coast, facing Attica and Central Greece (Sampson 1981: distribution map).

Some early and middle Bronze Age settlements were located on tiny islands or peninsulas situated opposite particularly fertile coastal regions of Attica and Euboea. This preference is of particular interest since such sites came to play a special role for archaic Attica, demonstrating continuities in settlement experience over long periods of time. The communities on the tiny offshore island of Raftopoula (cf. Camp 2001: 280; *ArchRep* 2002/3, 11) and on the Amarynthos promontory in Euboea, the isthmus of which is so narrow that it almost counts as an island, no doubt profited from their location at the mouth of large river valleys which transected Attica and Euboea respectively and created rare opportunities for communication routes inland. The major exception to the rule of coastal settlement are traces of settlements found along these two river valleys and at the eastern mouth of the Euboean river, the Erasimos.[20] The Raftopoula settlement must have flourished, because the extensive and rich late Bronze Age cemetery on the Perati peninsula indicates that the community at one time moved to, or expanded on to, the mainland of Attica and developed into a prosperous Mycenaean community (Iakovidis 1981). Other offshore island settlements were established on Makronisos at Leondari, facing the southeast coast of Attica (Schallin 1993: 16, no. 20), on Archie opposite Sounion (Goette 2000: 18), and on a tiny island opposite Vouliagmeni. In the bay of Phaleron, the settlement of Aghios Kosmas was situated on a small promontory, which – just like Amarynthos – is connected to the mainland only by a very narrow strip of land (Mylonas 1959).

These coastal and offshore settlements were not an isolated Attic-Euboean phenomenon, but followed the pattern of sixty or so prehistoric Cycladic settlements likewise located on promontories, coastal hills and offshore islands (Schallin 1993: 37–9). These again reflected a widespread Mediterranean way of living, of which the Neolithic settlement on the small rocky island of Petra tou Limniti, no more than 80 m from the north coast of Cyprus (SCE I, 1–2) is a prominent early example. In the late Bronze Age, Mycenaeans settled on the island of Thapsos off the coast of Sicily (Voza 1999a: opposite fig. 61), as did the Phoenicians in their "home" settlements, Tyre and Sidon, situated on coastal islands in the Levant, and in numerous other places, such as Cerro del Villar on a tiny island in the alluvial plain of the Río Guadalhorce in Spain or on the tiny island of Motya east of Sicily (Niemeier 1995: 74).

The experience of living on small offshore islands was not lost in the Dark Age. On the contrary, Attic and Euboean promontories, peninsulas and coastal islands were once again settled in the early Iron Age, as were the coasts of Aegina (Kolonas hill) and Andros (Zagora).[21] Just as in the Bronze Age, these settlements were often situated "in pairs" on either side of the water, forming socio-cultural subregions which makes a separation of South Boeotian, Attic and Euboean culture both arbitrary and difficult. For instance, Chalcis and Eretria on the Euboean side faced Aulis and the important settlement at Skala Oropos on the South Boeotian coast. All four communities no doubt stimulated each other, as they developed at an even pace and all experienced a floruit in the eighth and seventh centuries, as shown by the abundant layers of late Geometric–early archaic material and by complex cultic activity and metal industry at Eretria and Skala Oropos.[22]

Similarly, the promontory settlements of Carystus and Zagora – on the south coast of Euboea and the island of Andros respectively – faced the settlements of Thorikos and Laurion, as well as the rich settlements of the Mesogeia plain[23] and the sanctuaries at Loutsa and Brauron on the Attic coast. Judging from their location, all sites must have formed a subregion interacting across the Euboean Sea in much the same way as for instance the three colonies of Megara – Byzantium, Chrysopolis and Chalcedon – communicated across the Bosporos or Aetolian and Achaean communities communicated across the Corinthian Gulf. In fact, the Corinthian Gulf was still conceived of as so coherent a region in later antiquity that both coasts shared the same name, and Augustus moved the cult of Artemis Laphria from Calydon on the Aetolian side to Patras on the Achaean side to consolidate his synoecism of the region (Houby-Nielsen 2001). These subregions, with roots in the Bronze Age, must be taken into consideration when evaluating Euboean and Attic interaction in the Iron Age and early archaic period.

Interestingly, these new early Iron Age settlements on promontories and offshore islands were founded at the same time as settlements of a Greek appearance were founded in similar locations in Asia Minor (Akurgal 1983: 13). Ancient tradition claimed that Athens and Attica played a leading role in the so-called "Ionian Migration." The foremost of the new Eastern Greek cities, Ephesus and Miletus, were said to have been founded by sons of Kodros, a legendary king of Athens.[24] Attica and Euboea have also been associated with the earliest known Greek colony in the West due to, among other things, the presence of Euboean and Attic pottery in the earliest strata at Pithecusae (Ridgway 1992), which, again, was founded on a large offshore island, Ischia, in the bay of Naples.

Even if the alleged Ionian migrations and the foundation myths of the Ionian cities were mere attempts to construct a historical anchorage in the mainland (Hall 1997: 51–6) and the presence of Euboean and Attic pottery in Pithecusae was nothing more than the result of Phoenician trade (Papadopoulos 1997b), the coincidence in time of the foundation of coastal settlements in the Attic–Euboean region, Asia Minor, and the west is worth considering. So too is the striking similarity in topographical setting between Pithecusae, Lefkandhi, and Amarynthos, and Ay. Kosmas and Mounichia in the Old Phaleron bay of Athens: all located on small promontories with a narrow isthmus and resembling Phoenician settlements such as Nora in Sardinia (Bonetto and Oggiano 2004: fig. 1). This indicates the integration of the Iron Age settlement pattern in the Attic region with early colonial Greek settlement patterns, and their dependence on Phoenician experiences.

Survivals of Bronze Age settlement experiences could also take a different shape, however. It was hardly a coincidence that the Artemis sanctuary at Brauron, and probably also the Apollo sanctuary at Prasiai (Pausanias 1.31.2), were founded near the harbor of Perati – opposite the island of Raftopoula – in the river valley leading across the fertile plain of central Attica to Athens, while on the Euboean coast the Artemis sanctuary at Amarynthos was founded at the entrance to the Erasinos river valley.[25] The location of these sanctuaries again formed part of a wider phenomenon: the oldest large peristyle building known, probably an Artemis sanctuary, dating to the late eighth century, was recently discovered in Achaea in the valley of the Selinous river, which had functioned since prehistoric times as an important route of communication between the interior of the Peloponnese and the coast as well as between Bouprasion and Aigaleos in the north-west.[26]

Offshore Islands and Promontories in the Archaic Period

By the later archaic period, many offshore and promontory settlements had developed into flourishing communities after having first expanded further into the mainland. The prosperity of the communities in the Mesogeia plain is indicated by the fact that the majority of the archaic funerary *kouroi* found in Attica stem from this region, as we shall see. Also, the only parallels so far known to the exceptionally large grave tumuli in the Kerameikos in Athens, lay in the Mesogeia (at Velanideza and Vourva). Similarly, once they had expanded on to the mainland, the settlements of Makronisos, Archie and the Vouliagmeni islet grew into flourishing communities in the early archaic period, just as they had done in the late Bronze Age. Excavations near Laurion and Thorikos point to successful extraction of silver ores – perhaps stimulated by the silver mining in nearby Naxos – and extensive Geometric and early archaic cemeteries have been excavated at Sounion, Vouliagmeni and the bay of Phaleron. In Vouliagmeni, two sanctuaries have been excavated on the Lathoureza hill, and the rich archaic cemeteries at Vari belonged to this community. It profited from easy access to several harbors, and can perhaps be identified with the important deme of Anagyrous. And Sounion soon developed into an important deme, rich enough to built the impressive Poseidon and Athena sanctuaries, the former surrounded by a fortification in later times.[27] In Phaleron, several sanctuaries mentioned in later sources may well go back to the early archaic period. In fact, the Ay. Kosmas promontory mentioned above may be the cape mentioned by Herodotus in connection with the battle of Salamis (Hdt. 8.96), in which case it was crowned by the temple of Kolias Aphrodite (Paus. 1.1.5), and was close to the sanctuary of Demeter and Kore in which Athenian women celebrated the Thesmophoria (Mylonas 1959: 9).

Some small islands near Attica were still inhabited in the late Iron Age, such as the islet of Vryokastri, off the island of Kythnos, the ties of which to Southern Attica were especially strong. Its settlement expanded on to Kythnos itself during the late Iron Age and archaic period (Mazarakis Ainian 1998b). The Athena sanctuary in Karthaia also appears to have started on a tiny island (Ostby 1980: 189–223). It is tempting to add the Chalcis peninsula of Euboea, which socio-geographically acted as a large coastal island off the South Boeotian shore, the width of the strait at this point being no more than 72.5 m. The settlement gradually extended over most of the peninsula, and in the classical period the city had expanded over to the mainland, providing the city with two acropoleis (Bakhuizen 1985: 48–9, 94–6).

This general development which Attica and her near neighbors underwent, the movement from offshore island or promontory to the mainland or the expansion on to the mainland, again recalls the larger Greek colonial situation in the early archaic period. A few examples will suffice. In the north-western Aegean, Mytilene in Lesbos may originally have started on the island just off the main shore (Spencer 2000: fig. 4.5). In Magna Graecia, Pithecusae expanded on to the mainland to found Cumae. The late Bronze Age settlement on Thapsos off Sicily, mentioned above, was followed centuries later by a Greek colony founded on the island of Ortygia not far from Thapsos and soon expanding on to the mainland to become Syracuse, one of the largest and richest Greek cities in the Mediterranean (Voza 1999a).

This significance of the offshore island in early Greek colonial settlement is beautifully recalled in the much later, famous foundation myth of Alexandria on the small island of Pharos (turned into a promontory through silting) off the coast of Egypt. According to this, Alexander the Great had a dream that a man looking just like Homer appeared and recommended the founding of a city on "an island in the much-dashing sea, *in front of* Egypt; Pharos is what men call it" (Plutarch, *Alexander* 26.3–4; emphasis added).

The "Invention" of the Strait and the Harbor Spring

Increasing seaborne communication from ca. 750 onwards not only gave a new importance to coastal settlements but also shaped a new perception of geography. The "strait" as a social and cultural-geographical concept now developed and became the scene of a certain lifestyle centered on trade and more generally on the control of sea traffic. The borders of the Attic sphere of interest can be defined by two major and two minor straits. The major straits were those of Euripos and the Corinthian Isthmus which functioned as a strait. The minor ones were the strait created by the Rhamnous and Tigani promontories on the Attic and Euboean coasts respectively, and the strait in between Eleusis and Salamis.

The growing importance of the Euripos is apparent from the development of the Chalcis peninsula (Bakhuizen 1985: esp. 39–49). Survey results and the distribution of tombs on the western slopes of the Vathrovouna show that, by the late Iron Age, settlement was concentrated in the much larger harbor of Ay. Stephanos on the south side of the peninsula, which had a copious spring. This must have attained a special significance by the late Iron Age, as it appears to be mentioned in the *Odyssey* under the name of Arethusa (13.408).

Eleusis, in the western border zone of Attica, was, as mentioned, situated on a strait formed by the island of Salamis and the coast of Attica. Ships heading for the Corinthian Isthmus or the cities on the east coast of the Peloponnese had to pass through this narrow strait, which of course gave the harbor city of Eleusis a crucial location. Here too lay an important spring (made into a well). The so-called *Homeric Hymn to Demeter*, now dated to the end of the seventh century, attributes to this well, called Kallichoron, a major part in the foundation myth of the early archaic Demeter sanctuary at Eleusis (Binder 1998).

Chalcis and Eleusis became good examples of a new "model" town with a location close to a strait, large harbor(s) and copious spring(s). Homer's reference to the spring at the harbor in Aulis opposite Chalcis (*Il.* 2.308–30) may reflect this model. Again this archetype is easy to identify in the colonial world, at places such as Syracuse or Halicarnassus. By the Hellenistic period, the actual settlement at a spring on a promontory in the harbor of Halicarnassus was recalled in an inscription found in situ in 1995: "Having settled the lovely promontory sung of as dear to the immortals by the sweet stream of Salmakis, she [Halicarnassus] controls the beautiful dwelling of the nymph" (Isager 1998: with translation).

The notion that the ideal (that is maximum) extension of Attic territory should be confined by two major straits agreed well with a current colonial Greek world view. Firstly, the majority of Greek colonies in the Black Sea, along the shores of North Africa, the Iberian peninsula and Asia Minor, were founded near small, narrow straits formed by opposing promontories or islands off main shores. Communication between the Sea of Azov and the Black Sea was controlled by settlements on the promontories forming the narrow Straits of Kertch, and Athens' own colonies, Elaious and Sigeion, were founded on the straits of the Dardanelles around 600.[28] Secondly, the whole colonial "world" of the Mediterranean Sea was clearly conceived, from an early date, as being bounded by the Straits of Gibraltar and the straits of the Hellespont. In his geographical tour round the Mediterranean in the late sixth century, Hecataeus of Miletus significantly started his description at the Hellespont and moved to Gibraltar and back again. The westernmost site he mentioned was Metagonium, a name in later times applied to a promontory near Thinga, modern Tangiers (Bunbury 1883: 138–45).

Attic awareness of this world view in the early archaic period is indirectly apparent in the story of Heracles and Geryones and Heracles and Nereus and Triton, already mentioned by Hesiod (*Theog.* 287–92). These adventures took place near the straits of Gibraltar and the Gardens of Hesperides, associated with Cyrene in Libya. Interestingly, a Protocorinthian *pyxis* carrying the earliest known depiction of Heracles fighting Geryones was found in Attica, in a grave near the harbor of Phaleron, indicating that its owner had good access to sailors' yarns. After about 575, the Heracles-Geryones theme became extremely popular in Attic art: we meet it twice in the sculptural decoration of the earliest monumental temple on the acropolis (Brize 1980). All in all there is little doubt that the people of Attica were familiar with the geographical extremities, defined by straits, of the then known world, and this will have influenced their perception of their own region.

This increasing importance for Attica of settlements at straits in the late eighth and early seventh century must be related to a general formalization of strait settlements in the Greek world and the Mediterranean, such as Corinth, Actium (Preveza), Leucas, Chalcis (Negroponte), Rhegion-Zancle, Messina, and the Byzantium–Chrysopolis–Chalkedon triangle, which maintained their importance until medieval and modern times.

New Interest in the Saronic Gulf

In the late Iron Age and early archaic period, the bay of Phaleron appears to have suddenly gained a new importance as harbor, to judge from the extensive cemeteries lying around it (Morris 1987: 226 no. 35). One of the few large buildings known from Attica at this time has recently been found in Phaleron (*ArchRep* 2002/3, 10, no. 49). The Artemis sanctuary on the Mounichia promontory now flourished, as seen by the plentiful early archaic votives the character of which indicate a purely local, Athenian, function (Paliokrassa 1991). During the seventh century, Athens appears to have become increasingly tied to the bay of Phaleron but also to the bay of Eleusis and to some extent to the Piraeus. Athens thereby followed a general tendency to focus on large harbors, as did for instance her neighbors Chalcis in Euboea and Zagora in Andros, but also responded to increasing trade in the Saronic Gulf.

One of the main actors was the city of Corinth, which was establishing a series of colonies in Sicily and in the Corinthian Gulf, Corfu, and the Ambracian Gulf, often followed up by the foundation of Apollo sanctuaries (Tzouvara-Souli 2001). In addition, Corinth traded extensively in the whole of the Greek colonial world and in the Aegean, to judge by the distribution of seventh-century Corinthian pottery. Another important actor much closer to Athens was the island of Aegina. The sanctuary on Kolonna Hill and to some extent the Aphaia sanctuary attracted large quantities of pottery and exotic votives from the Eastern Greek region, Naucratis in Egypt, Cyprus, but also from Argos, and of course Corinth.[29] Already Hesiod (fr. 205 Merkelbach-West) alluded to the Aeginetans as skilled seafarers.

Athens may have started its own trade on a modest scale, or traded via Aegina. Exotic "oriental" votives and eastern Greek pottery now reached Athens and Eleusis. Conversely, the characteristic Attic "SOS" *amphorae*, some of which date as early as the seventh century BC have been found in Northern Africa, Spain, France, Italy, the Levant and the Black Sea.[30]

Another result of the lively commerce and traffic in the Saronic Gulf was the increasing importance of the cemeteries to the north-west of the acropolis (in the Kerameikos), which extended along the roads leading to the harbor of Eleusis, and to Piraeus. Since the late Geometric period, the funerary vases placed on top of tumuli and tombs had become increasingly frontally accentuated. They now carried elaborate figural scenes on the "front" while the "rear" side was black-glazed or carried ornamental decoration. In other words, the marker vases no longer belonged to the urnfield culture of the Iron Age, but represented the beginning of the long tradition funerary art designed to be seen from the road (Houby-Nielsen 1996: 44 n.s. 11–13). By far the most numerous and elaborate marker vases and clusters of tumuli have been found along roads in the Kerameikos. This shows that in the seventh century, the face of the young city-state of Athens, in the shape of roads lined with the most prestigious graves, was now concentrated in the area where roads to Eleusis started. The status of these cemeteries continued to rise during the archaic and later periods as the "sacred road" to Eleusis and the harbor of Piraeus grew in importance. The "sacred road" came to be lined with state burials; the most prestigious town gate, the Dipylon Gate, was erected here (Houby-Nielsen 1995; 2000); and monumental sixth-century grave sculptures have so far only appeared in the Agora-Kerameikos district in Athens. A spectacular new *kouros* and other monumental grave sculptures have recently been excavated here (Niemeier 2003).

Increased contact with the Saronic Gulf also resulted in a more cosmopolitan ideology of death and burial, which was partly shared with aristocratic families living in

Eleusis, Phaleron, Piraeus, and Aegina. A good indication of this is the appearance of an "eclectic" pottery style, produced either in Athens or in Aegina (probably the latter: Morris 1984): so-called middle Protoattic (the "Black and White style"). This very different pottery was eclectic in the sense that it combined several distinct, attractive styles traded in the Saronic Gulf. The oriental or exotic and mythological motifs were taken over from Protocorinthian, while the silhouette technique was east Greek, and the monumentality and variety of shapes stood in a strictly late Geometric Attic tradition (Morris 1984: 31–50). The new pottery was clearly designed for ceremonial purposes and confined to the Athens–Piraeus–Aegina–Eleusis region. It was used solely in elaborate funerary rituals, in rites connected with the worship of ancestors, or to be dedicated at prominent sanctuaries (Whitley 1994). It was most numerous in Aegina, where it was found in the Kolonna hill sanctuary and in rock-cut tombs. In Athens, the vessels served as grave markers on tumuli and were burned in a dramatic holocaust together with the deceased (see below). Some vases have also been found in the archaic cemetery near the Areopagus. The number of vases from sanctuaries is smaller in Athens than in Aegina (Morris 1984: 84–9). A small number of sherds come from the acropolis, and the Nymph sanctuary on the slopes of the acropolis. Sherds from the Olympieion region stem from either graves or sanctuaries. Fragments of the so-called Kerameikos painter and the Chimaera-Nessos painter have been found in the Artemis Mounichia sanctuary. In Eleusis and Piraeus, spectacular vases derive from burials. This distribution shows that the same type of ceremonial pottery was consumed by leading families in Aegina, Eleusis, Athens, and Piraeus. The only difference was that the Athenians were more inclined to use the pottery in funerary rituals, for which reason deep bowls and conical stands with protomes and funerary motifs were more usual in Athens. The Aeginetans, on the other hand, used it for dedications in sanctuaries, which is why ovoid kraters and *dinoi* with stand and neck-handled amphorae with mythological motifs were more numerous (Morris 1984: 84–9).

It is clear that the much-debated Protoattic pottery was never made for export: its quality could not compete with that of contemporary Corinthian pottery, and certainly not with the sophisticated Chiot pottery produced in Naukratis which all aristocracies in the Mediterranean appear to have wanted, including Athens–Aegina. Rather, the pottery was a cheap imitation, meant purely for display in local funerary and sacred rituals where it served to demonstrate that Athenian–Aeginetan–Eleusinian leading families shared the sophisticated life of eastern Greek region and the Corinthian world.

Another indication of the new cosmopolitan climate in Athens in the early archaic period is the appearance of ostentatious new "performance rituals" at death and burial. The rituals were performed in the area of the Kerameikos close to the "sacred road" and thus clearly visible to passers-by. Among other things, they consisted of the display of an elaborate banquet service of Protoattic pottery intermixed with fowl and vines. The service and food were displayed on wooden benches up to 12 m long. Each bench was placed on a pyre in a low trench dug parallel to the accompanying grave while the grave was still open. The deceased lay on a bier on top of a funerary pyre inside the grave. The service was then deliberately broken and burned simultaneously with the cremation of the deceased in the open grave beside it, creating an elaborate holocaust ritual. Afterwards, offering trench and tomb were covered by a common tumulus. This ritual may have been an almost theatrical enactment of male values, such as the power of the deceased to hold banquets, a right restricted to leaders of households, and a theme running through the *Odyssey* (Houby-Nielsen 1996). The banquet service also recalled the ritual oriental reclining banquet, the *marzeah* (Kistler 1998), a custom spreading especially among the upper classes in central Italy. The ritual performed in the Kerameikos would therefore have been understood by anyone familiar with Homeric values and the oriental reclining banquet, as most aristocratic families in the Greek east and west were.

Athens: The Formalization of a Riverbank Settlement

Some settlements on offshore islands and promontories which extended down towards nearby rivers began to shift their focus towards these rivers and deltas during the late Iron Age and early archaic period. The most prominent are Athens, Eleusis, and Skala Oropos in Attica, and Eretria in Euboea. The fact that these four important settlements are situated on riverbanks is rarely underlined in handbooks. In Athens, the dominant rock of the acropolis is normally highlighted, due of course to the later importance of its sanctuaries, but it should be remembered that Athens, and in particular early archaic Athens, was also – and especially – a riverbank settlement. Three rivers determined its immediate environment. First and foremost the huge Kephissos river which sprang from the foothills of Mt. Parnes and emptied into the bay of Phaleron. Secondly, the Ilissos river which sprang from Mt. Hymettos, and thirdly the Eridanos river which sprang from the hills of Lykabettos and joined the Kephissos. Our image of the modern city of Athens makes it difficult to grasp the impact which these rivers had on the landscape. Plato's description of the Ilissos river bank as an idyllic wooded area (*Phaedrus* 227c) and photographs from nineteenth-century Athens are helpful in recalling the vigor and greatness of the rivers and the fertility of nearby land (figure 10.1).

In the early Iron Age, large cemeteries extended on either side of the two rivers and all the way around the acropolis, indicating that settled areas lay to the north, east and south-west of the acropolis and probably also to the north of the Eridanos (Papadopoulos 2004, fig. 5:15). The acropolis itself was probably inhabited. In the late Iron Age and early archaic period, Athens developed urban characteristics. An extremely large amount of late Geometric pottery and a wealth of bronzes from the acropolis indicate that a highly important sanctuary had now been established on the rock (Hurwit 1999: 85–98). Below it, along the banks of the Eridanos in the area of the classical Agora and Kerameikos, pottery and dye workshops mingled with a hero shrine and old and new cemeteries.[31] New investigations of wells and other deposits in this area proved them to be either refuse wells or rubbish pits, while some yielded large quantities of potter's refuse, such as test-pieces and draw-pieces. These wells, and the frequent mention of burials in older excavation reports, show that the area of the classical agora was not inhabited in the late Iron Age – as hitherto thought

Figure 10.1 The river Illissos in Athens in 1906
Source: Photo from the collection of Haris Yiakoumis, photographer unknown; after H. Yiakoumis, *Apo tin Olympia stin Athina* (Toubis 2004), fig. 113.

Figure 10.2 View from the Acropolis over the "heart" of early archaic Athens, between Artemis Agrotera, above the Illissos river and the possible site of the early archaic Agora
Source: Photo by Sanne Houby-Nielsen.

– but used both as a burial ground and for the pottery industry (Papadopoulos 2003: 271–5).

Furthermore, new studies in the topography of the old agora, mentioned by Apollodoros (*FGrH* 244 F113), place this to the east of the acropolis under present-day Pl. Ay. Aikaterini, on the grounds of new inscriptions and architectural finds (Papadopoulos 2003: 282, with references). This agora accordingly formed an extension of the actual "heart" of early archaic Athens, namely an old sanctuary complex situated in the marshes along the River Ilissos, to which we shall return below (see figure 10.2). This complex comprised sacred springs, one of which, the Enneakrounos-Kallirhoe fountain (Thuc. 2.15.4–5), later became the most venerated of all Athenian public monuments. Also, it was in this area that a truly monumental temple, perhaps the earliest in Athens, was erected: a massive M-shaped foundation 2.5 m thick beneath the enormous late archaic temple for the Olympian Zeus probably stems from an earlier huge temple-related structure (Parker 1996: 68). Similarly, the earliest sanctuary in the late archaic and classical Agora situated to the north of the acropolis – the altar of the Twelve Gods – was located on the banks of the Eridanos river (Camp 2001: 32–4). To the north-west of Athens, the Poseidon Hippios cult on the Kolonos Hippios overlooked the Kephissos river in much the same manner as the Poseidon cult in Helice in Achaea or the Artemis Laphria cult in Calydon in Aetolia overlooked the deltas of huge border rivers.

It is of importance for the development of Athens that much the same city plan is found in Eretria and to some extent right opposite Eretria on the Attic coast, at Skala Oropos. Iron Age Eretria was situated in the very delta of a river. In fact, in the early part of the Iron Age, the settlement was encircled by water as it was situated in between a branch of the river, the river itself and the coast of the Euripos Sea (Auberson and Schefold 1972). The poor burials, pottery and other finds clearly show that the early Iron Age settlement was small and insignificant, and hardly extended beyond the river and its branch. In the late Iron Age, however, there is a clear boom in material. Rich late Geometric layers were found in all trenches of the excavations, indicating that the settlement now extended from the seashore all the way up to the acropolis, situated about 1.5 km inland, amounting to a habitation area of about 45 ha. As in Athens, the sacred, "public" and industrial heart of the settlement was situated on the riverbank, and the industrial quarters lay near or among rich cemeteries and a hero shrine.

Right opposite Eretria, a very similar settlement has been excavated in recent years at Skala Oropos. Early Iron Age remains are few, while the site clearly blossomed in the late Iron Age and early archaic period. The settlement lies in flat, marshy territory at the outlet of a large river. Again a cluster of apsidal buildings for cultic and industrial purposes extended along the river, among which metal industry was prominent. A spring near the river was perhaps the object of veneration, as in Athens: the large *peribolos* structure enclosing finds of cultic character may have been devoted to the nymph Alia, later named Leukothea, to judge by an inscription of the Hellenistic period found in the vicinity (*ArchRep* 1997/8, 17–18).

This sudden focus on rivers, producing hero shrines, industries and complex sanctuaries on the actual riverbanks, probably also emerged elsewhere in Greece. Many classical sanctuaries situated on rivers were originally – that is, in the late Iron Age and early archaic period – "sacred hearts" of urban communities which became "suburban" or "extra-urban" after the community had moved to a larger center as a result of a synoecism process and thus "left them behind." This was the case, for example, with the Artemis Triklaria and Larisaean Athena sanctuaries in Achaea, on the banks of the Meilichos and Larisa rivers, respectively (Paus. 7.20.7–9; 17.5), and probably the Artemis Limnatis and Artemis Nemydia sanctuaries in the same region.[32] The late Geometric-early archaic sanctuaries in the plains of the Acheloos river – the largest river in Greece – revealed by surveys in the region of Stratos in Acarnania could be yet other examples.[33] Other cities at large rivers such as Trikala, Arta, Orchomenos and Larisa are likely to have a similar prehistory, and striking parallels in the Mediterranean make the Attic-Euboean and Greek riverbank communities stand out as a "settlement type." Apart from Phoenician or Phoenician-influenced forerunners in Cyprus such as Ledra (Nicosia) which was divided by the Pedieos river and Salamis at the outlet of this river, one thinks of Greek parallels such as Ephesus and Miletus on the Maeander, Naucratis in the Nile delta, or the Greek ports at Agde and Narbo on the Iberian coast in the delta of the Herault and the Atax rivers respectively. Greek-influenced centers such as Lydian Sardis and Etruscan Rome provide other parallels. In the latter, a strongly Greek-influenced archaic sanctuary complex has been excavated at St. Omobono on the banks of the Tiber, with architectural decoration which partly recalls the Artemis temple in Corfu (Bartoloni 1982: 115–21).

All in all, the riverbank settlement became formalized in Attica and neighboring regions at a time when contacts between the East and the West of the Mediterranean were intensifying and Greek colonial enterprises had started in earnest; Eretria and Skala Oropos, supported by Athens, appear to have been greatly involved. Studies of archaic Athens which overlook the location of Athens on rivers, therefore, omit one of the most important and characteristic aspects of archaic Attic social life.[34]

The Appearance of Water-related Sanctuaries

The way in which settlements turned their attention to nearby rivers is especially visible from a series of important sanctuaries founded on riverbanks and in deltas at the same time as other sanctuaries were founded close to the seashore and at springs. New categories of sanctuaries, all focused on water, came into existence, and those in Athens were particularly impressive.

In the late eighth and the seventh century, no fewer than eleven sanctuaries were founded in marshy deltas or directly on the seashores of South Boeotia, Attica, and Euboea. At Aulis, the Artemis sanctuary was founded on a spring close to the seashore. Opposite Aulis, in Eretria, the earliest sanctuary was situated not far from the seashore, in marshy fields on the western riverbank of a branch of a large river.[35] Approximately 5 km to the south lay the famous Artemis sanctuary at Amarynthos on the southern bank of the Erasinos, about 1.5 km inland. Opposite these, at Skala Oropos, ellipsoidal buildings which appear from their finds to have served cultic purposes were founded in the marshes of a river delta. Further to the south, an important sanctuary was founded at Brauron in the alluvial marshland of a river in between two rocky hills; we ought to locate the Apollo temple at Prasiai here as well (Pausanias 1.31.2). Only a few kilometres to the south, at Loutsa, another Artemis sanctuary was founded no more than 50 m from the sea. In classical times this became the so-called Artemis Tauropolos sanctuary at Halai Araphenides, so important in Greek drama. Rounding the tip of Attica, we find the Apollo, Artemis, and Leto sanctuary situated on the very shore of the bay of the Vouliagmeni promontory. In Eleusis, the late Geometric–early archaic sanctuary stretched from near the seashore along the slopes of the Eleusinian promontory and thus faced the western bank of another large river called Kephissos which empties into the bay.

Finally, as already indicated above, the oldest, largest, and most complex group of sanctuaries in Athens and Attica lay on the banks of the Ilissos. From early times this river was connected with the cults of Artemis Agrotera, Pan, the river god Acheloos and the Nymphs, as well as Apollo Pythios and Delphinios, Ge, Dionysos *en limnais* (in the marshes) – the seat of one of the oldest festivals in Athens, the Anthesteria – Zeus Olympios, Aphrodite, and Demeter.[36] The archaeological evidence from the early period is sparse, as the area has not been systematically excavated. On the northern bank, old excavations mention a two-roomed building and an apsidal compartment dated to the eighth century and probably located near the eastern side of the classical Apollo Delphinios temple (Mazarakis-Ainian 1997: 245).

An image of Pan is carved in the rock and the remains of a fine Ionic *in antis* temple similar to the Nike temple on the acropolis still stand high above the river. This may be identified with the Artemis Agrotera sanctuary and is likely to have had a much earlier predecessor. The most powerful reminder of the importance of the area is the enormous late archaic temple for Zeus Olympios, begun by Hippias and Hipparchos and finished by Hadrian, which, as mentioned earlier, may have had a pre-Peisistratid monumental forerunner. Although Doric in style, it was designed to compete in size and splendor with the Ionian temples in Samos, Miletus, and other places. The topographical setting of this new category of sanctuaries close to a river or the seashore must have determined their activities in many ways.

The Eridanos and Ilissos rivers were tributaries of the great River Kephissos, which caught up all the water from the mountains surrounding the Attic plain and nourished the Attic fields through countless canals and wells. However, in spite of the idyllic atmosphere along the Ilissos described by Plato, the rivers were also feared in antiquity for their vast inundations. In 1896 the Kephissos and Ilissos rivers still caused an inundation which drowned 35 people.[37] Likewise, the Eleusinian Kephissos river was feared in antiquity due to its strong torrents and frequent inundations. During the time of Hadrian the whole sanctuary of Eleusis was flooded and dams were built. The impressive size and strength of the Hadrianic bridge (50 m long, 5.30 m wide, four arches, the central one of which has a span of 6.90 m) built at the spot where the Sacred Road crossed the Kephissos, about one kilometre to the east of the sanctuary, suffice as testimony to the power of the river (Travlos 1950). Excavations at Skala Oropos, Eretria, and Brauron have also proved that the rivers here often flooded the sanctuaries, and that inundations finally caused the destruction of those at Brauron and Skala Oropos. The sanctuaries at the Ilissos probably suffered too. Similarly, the

Artemis Tauropolos and the Apollo, Artemis and Leto sanctuaries lay so close to the waterfront that inundations must have constituted a severe threat.

It is a curious fact that it was close to these coastlines and the outlets of these rivers – the annual rhythm of which people knew from thousands of years of living in the coastal zones of Attica – that people in the early archaic period placed their most prestigious sanctuaries. Elsewhere in Greece and the Mediterranean regular inundations sometimes formed an integrated part of the rituals in river and seashore sanctuaries. Certain cases are the Artemis Orthia in Sparta, probably also the fertility sanctuary on the banks of the Acheloos river separating Aetolia and Acarnania, and certainly the rural fertility cult near the village of Ay. Irini in Cyprus, where hundreds of votive statuettes each year were literally and intentionally "drowned." [38] The Apollo sanctuary in Halieis in the Peloponnese drowned in the sea, and near Syracuse an archaic sanctuary has been excavated in sand dunes no more than 60 m from the sea (Jameson 1974). On the small promontory of Aliki (probably originally an island) in Thasos, an archaic Artemis sanctuary has been excavated on the beach.

Perhaps one of the major reasons for the sudden appearance of water-related sanctuaries in Attica and neighboring regions – and also in the wider Mediterranean – should be sought in Ionia. The most prominent river-delta sanctuary in the Greek world was the Artemis sanctuary in Delos, situated on the bank of the Inopos and dating back to at least the eighth century. According to the so-called *Hymn for Apollo*, the god was born under a palm tree at the side of a lake created by the delta of the River Inopos. A sanctuary enclosing the tree lay here and for centuries was the focus of a procession. In archaic times, it was first controlled by Naxos, then by the Peisistratids of Athens and then the tyrant Polycrates of Samos, showing its extreme importance. The Athenians appear to have built a sanctuary situated further up the hill – for Hera – in Delos as early as 650.

A related sanctuary was the Artemision in Ephesus, founded in the eighth century and situated both on the spot of a freshwater spring and on the bank of the river Selinus. Like Eretria, Skala Oropos and the Ilissos river sanctuary, early Ephesus consisted of a sanctuary complex, not just a single temple (Bammer 1998). The Apollo sanctuary in Didyma was also centered on a spring and lay right on the seashore, and in Miletus, Artemis possessed a *temenos* of her own already from the seventh century, complete with spring, rock basin, and altar. The Artemis Tauropolos in Ikaria lay right at the outlet of the Chalares river into the Aegean Sea, and hot springs are found nearby, strongly reminiscent of the archaic sanctuary on the shore of Vouliagmeni in Attica. This connection between water and Artemis is interesting, as several of the Attic-Euboean water cults may be connected with Artemis or Apollo in the late archaic period. Apart from Eretria, Amarynthos, Brauron, it should be remembered that Apollo and Artemis were also very strong in early Athens. In fact, the earliest monumental depiction of gods in Attic art is of Artemis and Apollo shown as a Delian pair on the so-called Orestheia krater from about 650 BC. Artemis also appears as *Potnia Theron*, "mistress of the animals," on vases by the Sophilos painter from the early sixth century.

All in all, the reputations and religious ideas of the great Delian and Ephesian sanctuaries may well have spread like ripples across a pond throughout the Greek

world, promoting the appearance of water-related sanctuaries in Attica and neighboring regions. If so, the character of the early cults in Attica constitute additional
evidence for intimate social interaction between Attica and Asia Minor noted at the
start of this chapter.

The Sixth-century Transformation:
The Filling-in of the Attic Countryside

Since the coasts of Attica were part of major cultural developments characterizing
the early archaic Mediterranean, they must have been inhabited by a multicultural
and cosmopolitan population. However, the material and written sources for this
period are few and one-sided, and evidence for inland settlement is especially poor.
In these respects, sixth-century Attica stands out as totally transformed (Parker 1996:
67–101). All of a sudden, monumental remains of not only sacred but also civic
buildings and extensive cemeteries with elaborate grave markers appear, and these
remains, especially the grave markers, are not restricted to the coastal zones but appear
in plenty in the inland. Written sources – though admittedly mostly of a later date
– and epigraphic testimony in combination with archaeology may even provide us
with glimpses of individual personalities and political struggles, and give us a good
idea of social values, reform programmes, laws and sacred calendars. The sources
combine to indicate that by the middle of the century, Athens dominated all of the
Attic peninsula, from Eleusis in the south-west, including Salamis, to Eleutherai in
the north-west, and all the way up to Oropos in the north-east. Many nearby islands
were also under Athenian domination. Whereas formerly coastal subregions communicated as much with neighbors across the waters as with each other, now one
center exerted its influence on all subregions and struggled to extend her domination
to neighboring regions. This unification was known to the ancients as *synoecism* and
attributed to the mythological figure of Theseus.

Evidence that Athens has become a true civic and religious center for all of the
Attic peninsula appears at the beginning of the sixth century and is regarded by many
scholars as the earliest sign of a true Athenian city-state. As mentioned, a huge M-
shaped foundation beneath the Olympieion may be connected with a monumental
stone temple which is likely to predate the Peisistratid temple by at least some decades
(Parker 1996, 68, n. 4). Nearby, an Ionic peristyle complex has been excavated on
the lower eastern slopes of the acropolis (under the present-day Pl. Aiaikaterini) and
identified with an early archaic city hall (*prytaneion*) alluded to in ancient sources
(Papadopoulos 2003). If this identification is correct, the agora in Attica was first
formalized at this stage, and placed in such a way as to form an extension of the
sacred Ilissos river area. Perhaps these early buildings are connected with Solon, and
perhaps Athens also acquired its first city wall in this period; at any rate, passages in
Thucydides may be interpreted in this way (Thuc. 1.89.3, 93.2; 6.57.1–3).

Another piece of evidence is the sudden explosion in pottery industry and export,
in particular to Asia Minor. The Black Figure technique becomes highly developed
and the pottery is so similar in style, and non-regional, that a coherent group of

craftsmen must lie behind it. In Asia Minor, Attic Black Figure pottery begins to appear 600–575, and in most places the number of imports increases dramatically in 575–550 or 550–525 (Tuna-Nörling 1995: 103–47). Most of this industry is likely to be associated with the archaeological remains of pottery workshops to the north of the acropolis, in the area of the classical agora.

Major new developments around 550 provide further evidence of the pre-eminence of Athens. On the acropolis, already a site of cult activity in earlier periods, the first certain signs of an important cult of Athena appeared. The *Iliad* and *Odyssey* allude to a house or temple shared by Erechtheus and Athena on the acropolis (*Il.* 2.554; *Od.* 7.81) and the earliest – possible – depiction of Athena in Attic art, on an *amphora* by the Polyphemos painter (ca. 650), was found in a grave in Eleusis. In 575–550, however, there are many signs that Athena was being promoted as the protectress of Athens. The acropolis suddenly became the object of a major building programme: the first *korai* appeared, soon followed by the erection of a monumental stone temple. Fragments of brightly painted pedimental sculpture of limestone and a large number of column fragments point to a large Doric temple dating to ca. 550. At approximately the same time, a polygonal retaining wall for a monumental ramp leading up to the acropolis was built (Camp 2001: 31, fig. 27). Furthermore, a bronze statuette of Athena as Palladion found on the acropolis must be dated to this period (Hurwitt 1999, 22, fig. 20). In subsequent decades, the production of *korai* accelerated. All in all, no less than 297 *korai* have been found on the acropolis, making Athens the busiest producer of *korai* in the eastern Mediterranean. The majority date to 510–480, and were most likely set up by families of girls elected as *arrephoroi*, that is, given the privilege of carrying the *peplos* for the cult statue of Athena.

Perhaps contemporary with the building programme on the acropolis, another major change appears to have taken place. Pottery industry and burial activity were cleared from the area to the north of the acropolis and a new agora was laid out, turning the focus of the city from the areas to the east to those to the north of the acropolis (Papadopoulos 2003: 276–9). These major changes on the acropolis and in the Agora have been connected with the establishment of the Greater Panathenaea, a festival of panhellenic appeal, which began with a procession crossing the new agora and culminating on the acropolis. They have also been attributed to the tyrant Peisistratos, who was also said to have promoted ancient cults in the Ilissos river area and to have established there the oldest and most venerated of all Athenian public monuments, the Enneakrounos-Kallirhoe fountain (Thuc. 2.15.4–5).

Many other measures were taken to make Athens the center of Attica. By the end of the sixth century, local cults – often celebrated in the border zones of Attica – had been copied or moved to Athens. A well-known case is the Demeter cult at Eleusis which had attained Panhellenic status and was copied in Athens through the so-called city Eleusinion and Metroon in Agrai. The important cult of Dionysos at Ikaria to the north of Mt. Pentelicon was established in Athens on the south slope of the acropolis and a city festival for Dionysos was founded to match a rural Dionysia festival. The Artemis Brauronia cult appears to have been copied on the acropolis and the cult statue of Dionysos at Eleutherai, mentioned earlier, was probably transferred to Athens in this period (Shapiro 1989: 67–101; Parker 1996: 92). Burial customs changed abruptly around 560 BC. In the Kerameikos cemeteries, the ritual of placing a ritual banquet service in a separate offering trench disappeared. Instead, adults were equipped with oil flasks (*lekythoi*), a custom which was to last for more than a century and spread to Asia Minor (Houby-Nielsen 1992: table 8; 1995: 137).

In the decades 510–480, yet another important change occurred. The acropolis appears to have been given a whole new monumental aspect through the erection of a new temple for Athena (on the so-called Dörpfeld foundation). A few years later, a splendid new temple, all in marble, and a new entrance building were begun, predecessors to the Parthenon and the Propylaia (Hurwit 1999: 110–15). The Agora became monumentalized through the building of the Royal Stoa in the north-west corner. Burial customs indicate the arrival of new social values. For the first time in the history of Athens and Attica, a concept of "infancy" and "early childhood" up to the age of around 3 or 4, perhaps 5 or 6, was clearly expressed in burial customs and the number of infant and small-child burials increased dramatically. They continued to be numerous throughout most of the fifth century and may be related to a new concern by the burying families and the Athenian city-state to underline the importance of legitimate children, that is, future citizens (Houby-Nielsen 1995: 147–50; 2000).

Turning to the Attic countryside, we find towards the middle of the sixth century the first undeniable sign in millennia of new and much more intense settlement activity: the erection of very large grave mounds, up to 40 m in diameter, elaborate grave stelae with images of the deceased in relief or painted, and the erection of funerary *kouroi*, and occasionally *korai* (Houby-Nielsen 1995: 153–6) (figure 10.3). These rich funerary monuments which mostly commemorate men with a certain public status may be related not only to growing wealth among country people but also to a new road network across the Attic countryside which facilitated communication with Athens. The grave stelae and funerary *kouroi* were erected *beside* the grave mound (not on top), close to the road (D'Onofrio 1982). Their bases carried inscriptions which sometimes directly addressed passers-by and commemorated public virtues of the deceased, shared by upper classes in Attica and Athens (Houby-Nielsen 1995: 132).

The new importance of the countryside is indicated also by the formalization of the road network by the setting up of *herms*, marble shafts with a set of male genitalia and crowned by a portrait of the god Hermes. Plato refers to roads in the country marked with posts and carrying moral maxims of Hipparchus, son of Peisistratos (*Hipparchos* 228–9). Actual herms have recently been found in Rhamnous, Sounion, and Koropi (Parker 1996: 80–3). Apparently a very fine one said "the Memorial of Hipparchos: deceive not a friend" and stood on the Steireian road, which followed the old route connecting the harbor of Perati and the sanctuary at Brauron with Athens (Camp 2001: 37–8). It is also now that Pan, the god of *eschatiai*, the marginal lands or the edges, suddenly becomes popular. Besides at Athens and Eleusis, his caves have been found on Mt. Parnassos, Mt. Pentelicon, Mt. Hymettos, and Mt. Aigaleos (Borgeaud 1988; Camp 2001, 50). Certain peak sanctuaries also acquired a somewhat more monumental aspect in the sixth century (Lauter 1985; Langdon 1976).

Many of the developments described above have traditionally been attributed scholars to the lawgiver Solon, the popular tyrant Peisistratos and his sons, and the reformer

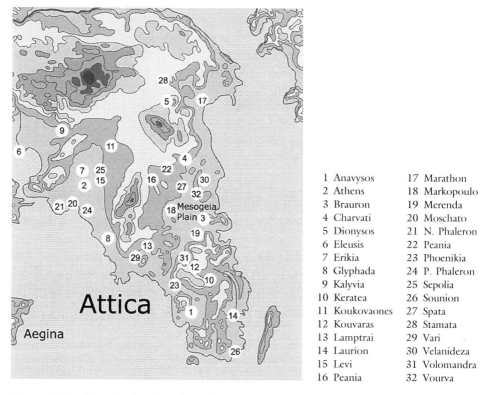

1 Anavysos	17 Marathon
2 Athens	18 Markopoulo
3 Brauron	19 Merenda
4 Charvati	20 Moschato
5 Dionysos	21 N. Phaleron
6 Eleusis	22 Peania
7 Erikia	23 Phoenikia
8 Glyphada	24 P. Phaleron
9 Kalyvia	25 Sepolia
10 Keratea	26 Sounion
11 Koukovaones	27 Spata
12 Kouvaras	28 Stamata
13 Lamptrai	29 Vari
14 Laurion	30 Velanideza
15 Levi	31 Volomandra
16 Peania	32 Vourva

Figure 10.3 The distribution of archaic grave monuments in Attica
Source: Map drawn by Lars Östling, based on data by Richter (1961; 1968; 1970) and Curtius and Kaupert (1881–1903).

Cleisthenes. However, none of these men acted in a vacuum. Rather, their actions and cultural-historical developments in the sixth century responded to developments elsewhere. The festival of the Greater Panathenaea was established in competition with the old Panhellenic festivals in Nemea, Isthmia, Delphi, and Olympia. The monumentalization of sanctuaries in the Ilissos river area and on the acropolis responded to contemporary, ambitious large-scale temple building at e.g. Didyma and Miletos (Niemeier 1999: 373–413) and the monumentalization of the Demeter Malophoros sanctuary on the banks of the Sele river in Sicily, just as the choice of the Doric order for the Olympieion probably owes much to the huge contemporary temples at Acragas in Sicily. Similarly, the transfer to or "copying" of sanctuaries in Athens reminds one of the cults of the communities of Aroe, Mesoa, and Antheia which were moved to Patras as part of a synoecism (Houby-Nielsen 2001: 267). Unusually huge grave mounds and the character of the associated grave gifts and burial customs recall Lydian "luxury," *tryphe*, which spread to Asia Minor (Houby-Nielsen 1995: 166–7). The monumentalization of some Attic peak sanctuaries is matched, for instance, by the monumentalization of the Zeus sanctuary on Mt. Oros in Aegina (Goette 1993: 272–5), or the rich finds from two archaic sanctuaries in the mountains behind Carystos in Euboea (Keller 1985, 188–9, sites 33, 56).

The sudden leap in the cultural and social development of Athens in the sixth century, therefore, cannot be attributed to three outstanding men, but needs to be seen in the light of the intensified trading and other contacts which made Athens' position on the main route between east and west very central and tightened her contacts with Asia Minor. In fact, the whole process of filling-in of the countryside reminds one of the Greek colonies where an initial and tentative settlement on a promontory or offshore island is often followed by a gradual filling-in of the hinterland and founding of scattered rural sanctuaries (as at Metapontum: Carter 1994). The Cleisthenic reforms provided a much-needed administrative system to cope with a new interest in the countryside in Attica, as elsewhere in the Greek world. Archaic Athens and Attica may rightly be characterized as prosperous and flowering. The recipe, however, for this success was openness to ideas, influences and persons from outside Attica. The Persian wars have come to stand as a turning point in western history and mark the end of a formative period – the archaic age – in Greek history. In a way, however, they were the extreme expression of intimate ties between Attica and the east across millennia and constitute the ultimate proof that Attica is best understood from the sea.

NOTES

1 In this chapter, the term "early Iron Age" refers to the Protogeometric and middle Geometric period (1000–750), while "late Iron Age" refers to the late Geometric and early archaic period (750–600), and "later archaic period" to the sixth century BC.
2 Morris 1987; Whitley 1991b; Parker 1996.
3 Similarly the neighboring island of Euboea is often shown in complete isolation, disregarding its closeness to Attica and Boeotia, even in recent studies (Walker 2004: maps 1 and 2, pp. 1 and 2).
4 Whitley concluded that Attica as a region "seems reluctant to 'Orientalize'" (2001: 117).
5 Traill 1986; map reproduced in Camp 2001, opposite 39.
6 For similar line of thought, see Osborne 1993a: 148–50.
7 Phylla: Sapouna-Sakellaraki et al. 2002: 6. Amphiareion: Camp 2001: 322. Western expansion: Jeffery 1976: 83–4; Binder 1998; an alliance with Megara is attested at the time of the failed coup of Cylon: sources in Stanton 1990: 17–26.
8 Compare Morris 1992: 139.
9 Catling and Lemos 1990: 1; Popham 1994: 27.
10 Dunbabin 1950; Jackson 1976; Morris 1984: 31–50.
11 Ridgway 1977: 52–3, 71–2; Shear et al. 1978.
12 Column: Korres 1997. Imitation of Greek East: Houby-Nielsen 1995: 159–63; Shapiro 1989.
13 In late Hellenistic and Roman Athens, Milesians were still the most significant group of foreigners (Vestergaard 2000).
14 Hurwit 1999; Goette 2000; Camp 2001; Travlos 1971 and 1988 are still indispensable.
15 Morris 1987; Whitley 1991b; Houby-Nielsen 1995; 1996; D'Onofrio 1997.
16 Boardman 1974, 1979; Bérard et al. 1989, with references.
17 Richter 1961; 1968; 1970; D'Onofrio 1982; 1988; Karakasi 2001.
18 Lohmann 1993; Cherry and Davis 1998.

19 Mylonas 1959; Sampson 1980; Wickens 1986: 143–7; Lolos 2001.

20 Sampson 1981: Oxylithos, Kyme, Aulonari.

21 Whitley 1991b: 55–8; Sapouna-Sakellaraki 1997; Keller 1985; Cherry and Davis 1998.

22 Auberson and Schefold 1972: 16; Mazarakis-Ainian 1987; *ArchRep* 1997/8: 17–18 and 1998/9: 17–18 and 2000/1: 16; *ArchRep* 2002/3, no. 49, 11; Walker 2004.

23 Compare especially the cemeteries at Velanideza and Vourva: Morris 1987 nos. 69, 71.

24 Hdt. 1.146, 9.97, 9.106; Hellanikos *FGrH* 4 F125; Pherekydes *FGrH* 3 F155; Strabo 14.1.6; Paus. 7.2.1–3.

25 Knoepfler 1988; cf. Shapiro 1989: 65, for their later status.

26 Houby-Nielsen 2001: 260; Petropoulos 2001.

27 Vouliagmeni: Lauter 1985; Goette 2000a: 149–54 with references. Sounion: *ArchRep* 2002/3: 11, no. 49; Goette 2000b.

28 Hdt. 4.38; 6.34–7, 140; Pottier 1915.

29 Morris 1984: 91–115 with references; Lemos 1991: 199 and figs. 103–4.

30 Lemos 1991: 199 for Chiot pottery in Athens; Coldstream 1977: 80, 375 for the Isis tomb. SOS amphorae: Johnston and Jones 1978; Domingues and Sanchez 2001: 86–90; *ArchRep* 30, 1984, 79.

31 Burr 1933; Papadopoulos 2003: 271, 279.

32 Athen. 460d; Strabo 8.3.11; Houby-Nielsen 2001: 267 and fig. 4.

33 Funke 2001a: 194, 197; Lang 2001.

34 Cf. Morgan 2000: fig. 11.4, map meant to show "archaic Athens" but excluding Ilissos area.

35 Walker 2004: map 4: 17–17 p. 97, the Ptekhai and the east–west road which follows the original east-flowing river.

36 Thuc. 2.15.4; Dem. 59.76; Paus. 1.18.7, 19.1.

37 *RE* 11, 1922, Kephisos (3), 244–7.

38 *SCE* II, 666–74; Houby-Nielsen, forthcoming.

CHAPTER ELEVEN

The Aegean

Alexander Mazarakis Ainian and
Iphigeneia Leventi

The Cyclades and Euboea

It is quite common to study the history and archaeology of the islands of the Cyclades and Euboea in relation to the surrounding continents with which they interacted at all periods.[1] Each island developed its own cultural characteristics, especially at the beginning of the Early Iron Age, although especially in the classical period these gradually became less evident as powerful city states, notably Athens, tried to impose their rule in the Aegean. From an early date, however, the chain of islands of the Cyclades and Euboea communicated closely with one another and formed a bridge between east and west. A Cycladic *koine* is discernible, as is an even more widespread Euboean *koine* (Lemos 1998) extending to the coasts of northern Greece, Thessaly, Phthiotis and East Locris. Both Euboea and the Cyclades maintained particularly strong ties with Attica in this early formative period. Several cultural features are common to all these islands, as well as to the Sporades, Skyros in particular (Sapouna-Sakellaraki 2002). Moreover, Euboean influence is clearly manifested in the material culture of some Cycladic islands, such as Naxos and Andros, especially during the Geometric period. According to Strabo (10.1.10), Eretria was in control of several islands, including Andros, Tenos and Kea; at what date this may have happened is, however, a matter of conjecture.

The Protogeometric and Geometric periods

At the end of the thirteenth and throughout the twelfth century BC the Aegean region is characterized by a series of violent destructions. Some of them may be safely assigned to human action, as for instance at Koukounaries on Paros (Schilardi 1984), others to earthquakes (Phylakopi on Melos, Grotta on Naxos). In some places settlements were abandoned, while in others occupation continued,[2] usually after a period of desertion, and often at a slightly different location, as at Grotta, where the area of the previous settlement now served as a burial ground and the community apparently resided on the low acropolis (Lambrinoudakis 1988). A number of new settlements were founded some way inland, presumably for the sake of safety from threats coming from the sea. This phenomenon is most characteristic of Crete (Nowicky 2000), but may be observed on a smaller scale in the Cyclades as well. Xobourgo, on Tenos, is a good example of a naturally defensible site of the Dark Ages, though the lower settlement was provided with a "Cyclopean" circuit wall which was extended during the archaic period (Kourou 2001a; 2001b; 2002). Other such protected sites inhabited during the Dark Ages were Koukounaries on Paros, Froudi tou Kalamitsiou on Siphnos, Rizokastelia on Naxos (Kourou 2001b: 171). Ay. Andreas on Siphnos and Ay. Spyridon on Melos have also been said to fit the pattern, but this seems less probable today.[3] Natural defensibility combined with proximity to protected harbors seems to have conditioned the choice of most major island settlements of the EIA. The danger of sea raids was presumably great and this may be why Cycladic settlements were fortified earlier than those of the mainland. Xobourgo, Vathy Limenari at Donousa, Zagora and Ypsili on Andros, Minoa on Amorgos were already fortified by the end of the Geometric period, sometimes reusing pre-existing fortifications of the LBA (Koukounaries, Ay. Andreas on Siphnos).[4] Most Cycladic *poleis* appear to have acquired substantial fortification walls by the time of the Persian wars, though lack of excavation means that their dating cannot yet be accurately fixed.[5] The Euboean settlements, on the other hand, appear to have been fortified rather late, perhaps due to their naval supremacy which minimized threats from the sea. Eretria was apparently fortified only in the archaic period. Indeed, it seems probable that the so-called "fortification wall" of ca. 700 served primarily to preserve the inhabited area from inundation by the torrent which passed through the settlement, rather than for purposes of defence.[6]

The breakdown of the LBA centers of power and the population movements in the mainland, through the islands, and to the shores of Asia Minor gradually led to the formation of the geopolitical map of the historical era. In the Cyclades at least 120 EIA sites have so far been recorded, 27 of which have produced evidence for occupation during the PG period (Gounaris 1999: 111), while in Euboea 44 EIA sites have been catalogued, half of which bear evidence for occupation during the PG period (Gounaris 2002: 705). These figures should be considered with caution, since they represent the progress of archaeological research of the last century or so, which has been rather selective.[7] According to the available data, however, Euboea seems to have been more densely settled than the Cyclades in the PG period. The most flourishing settlement of the period must have been Lefkandi, judging by the wealth of the funerary offerings of the known cemeteries and the monumental apsidal building with the "heroic" burials on the summit of the Toumba hill.

Around the end of the eleventh century we seem to witness a process of reorganization of social and political communities in the wider Aegean area and a new ruling class appears to take over, as suggested also by the changes in burial customs which brought "order" after "chaos" (Morris 2000: 195–256). As a rule in each island a new main settlement had been founded during the Dark Ages and only occasionally did future *poleis* develop upon the ruins of a substantial LBA settlement, as at Naxos. This process, as the material evidence suggests, was well on its way during the later Geometric period. It is interesting to note that in some islands (for instance Kea, Mykonos, Syros, Amorgos) there was more than one city-state from the archaic period onwards. No single explanation will suffice for this phenomenon; each case must be examined separately. For instance, it has been argued that the division of Kea into four territories reflects either different periods of settling, or Athenian intervention designed to break the power of a single *polis* which was a poten-tial danger to the Athenian state.[8] It is noteworthy that the largest Cycladic islands, such as Naxos, Andros, Paros, Melos, had only one single *polis*. By contrast, Euboea, due to its great size, was divided into large territories controlled by independent city-states.

In the uncertain conditions which characterized the Dark Ages, communications with other regions of the Mediterranean and the Aegean were curtailed, though the sea routes were not totally forgotten and contacts did not altogether cease. Lefkandi in particular seems to have renewed contacts with Cyprus and the Levant already in the mid-tenth century (Popham 1994). They were intensified from the ninth century onwards, presumably thanks to improving standards of living, and motivated not least by the need for metals. Several scholars believe that the Greeks derived their knowledge of metal technology from Cyprus, and that the Euboeans traded iron in return of copper (Kourou 1990/1: 273–4; 1994). Such an explanation accords well with the moulds found at Xeropolis, dated ca. 900, which were used for casting bronze tripods in the Cypriot style.[9] Archaeological finds in the Aegean testify to the movement of artisans, especially metalworkers, from the Levant, and to the intensification of the islanders' contacts with Asia Minor and the Eastern Mediterranean.[10] This mingling of artists, artisans, merchants, and perhaps mercenaries from both areas allowed a series of developments which would thereafter charac-terize the culture of the islands. The widespread use of iron had a dramatic impact on societies not only in the Greek world but throughout the entire Mediterranean basin. Certain islands, especially the Western Cyclades and Euboea, thanks to their rich metal ores (Siphnos: Herodotus 3.57.4–6, Pausanias 10.11.2), seem to have played a leading role not only in the trade and exchange of metals but also in the transmission of the new technology, which appears to have spread from the East to the West. Moreover, one of the reasons for the Greek expansion towards the North Aegean (especially Chalcidice) and initially the west (Pithekoussai and Kyme), in which Chalcis and Eretria were pioneers, was doubtless the trade for metals. Some Cycladic islands such as Naxos, Paros, Andros and Thera,[11] also founded *emporia* or colonies, many of which were at or near areas rich in metals. In view of this, one could argue that those who managed the metal "industry" and the trade in metals must have attained great power (Mazarakis Ainian 2006).

Euboea and, to a lesser degree, the Cyclades played a leading role in the adoption and spread of the alphabet. Greek inscriptions of the late eighth and early seventh century have been found at Xeropolis-Lefkandi, Eretria, Oropos, Zagora, Grotta, Thera, Amorgos, Anaphe and Syros, as well as in remote areas where Euboean presence was strong, in Syria (Al Mina) and South Italy.[12] Interaction and common interests with the Phoenicians in the Aegean and elsewhere led to the adoption of their alphabet (see Herodotus 5.58.1–2). Tangible evidence of such inter-action is a Semitic graffito of the late ninth or early eighth century, scratched on a local MG I cup, recently identified among the numerous graffiti from the sanctuary of Apollo at Eretria,[13] alongside significant numbers of Orientalia encountered in both sacred and funerary contexts all over the Aegean during the Geometric period. Among the places where Greeks, especially Euboeans, met Phoenicians and adopted their alphabet, Al Mina (Jeffery and Johnston 1961a: 11–12) and Pithekoussai (Coldstream 1993; Jeffery and Johnston 1990: 7) have been cited, as well as the Dorian islands where interaction with Phoenicians is either documented archaeologically (Crete[14]) or through later sources (Thera,[15] Rhodes[16]), but current archaeological evidence points, rather, to a location in the South Euboean channel, in the region of Chalcis-Eretria and Oropos.[17] The Eretrian graffito suggests that it is likely that when Pithekoussai was first settled around 775, the Euboean colonists were already acquainted with writing. It is in any case beyond question that the Euboeans played a crucial role in the adoption and dissemination of the alphabet.

The islands flourished during the Geometric and archaic periods but subsequently declined. Until the Persian wars, as a rule, each island city-state retained its polit-ical autonomy, despite the fact that Athenian interests in the area were manifested already during the sixth century. Thus most islands had, for example, struck silver coins already by the end of the century.[18] During this period of "autonomy" we hear of several interstate wars. Rivalry for control of sea routes led to clashes between the more important powers of the era, such as Naxos and Paros. Chalcis and Eretria were involved in the protracted conflict known as the Lelantine War, in which other powers of the Aegean also participated (for instance Paros and Naxos probably supported Eretria and Chalcis, respectively). The reasons for this conflict must have been complex and were certainly not restricted to control of the fertile Lelantine plain. The date of the war is still a matter of debate, but is best placed around 700, when Hesiod won a tripod in the musical contest at the funeral games of king Amphidamas of Chalcis (*Works and Days* 654–9). The abandonment shortly before 700 of Xeropolis-Lefkandi (sometimes identified with "Old Eretria": Strabo 9.403; 10.448), the "prince" buried by the future West Gate at Eretria (Bérard 1970), a skyphos containing ca. 500 gr. of gold hidden beneath the floor of an oval house at Eretria around the same period (Themelis 1983; Le Rider and Verdan 2002) may be linked with the same war, as may the praise of Archilochos of Paros for the Euboeans' heroic style of fighting. Strabo (448) mentions an inscription in the sanctuary of Artemis Amarynthia in Eretria which stipulated the rules of warfare.[19] The *polyan-drion* on Paros, which contained the funerary urns of ca. 150 warriors who presumably fell in battle (Zapheiropoulou 1999), is a further indication of clashes between rising states in this period.

The prevailing architectural forms in EIA Euboea, including Oropos which appears to have originated as an Eretrian outpost, were the apsidal and oval. The former was perhaps best suited for the dwellings of the elite (Lefkandi/Toumba; the so-called "Daphnephoreion" at Eretria; Oropos Θ2), though two-roomed oval buildings, otherwise rarely encountered in the EIA, could serve similar functions (Viglatouri; Oropos Building Θ1). Normal dwellings were usually oval single-roomed buildings but by the end of the eighth century they started being replaced by rectangular structures. Round buildings mainly served for storage, and occasionally as shrines. Interior furnishings consist of pit hearths and less often of stone-built benches. The superstructure was of mud bricks, resting on a stone socle, and roofs were thatched. Orientation towards the South prevails, in order to avoid the northern winds. Clusters of buildings seem to have formed family units (*oikoi*; Mazarakis Ainian 2002a; 2003), often surrounded by an enclosure wall (Viglatouri; Xeropolis-Lefkandi; Oropos). Within these "compounds" there were various household and artisans' installations, including pottery kilns and wells. At Oropos and Eretria intensive metalworking activities were carried out near certain important units (Mazarakis Ainian 1998c; 2002a; 2002b; Verdan 2007; Doonan and Mazarakis Ainian 2007). In both places, infants and children were buried near these compounds during the LG and early archaic periods, but this practice ceased before the mid seventh century (Vlachou 2007; Blandin 2005). A similar situation occurs at the site of the future Athenian Agora, which contained workshops in the EIA, as argued recently (Papadopoulos 2003), which probably served as dwellings at the same time. Archaeological evidence suggests that during the EIA craft specialization had not yet advanced beyond household level.[20]

In the Cyclades the situation is quite different. Houses and cult buildings were as a rule constructed entirely of stone, while marble architectural members (bases for wooden columns, thresholds, etc.) were already being used in the eighth century in public architecture (Melanes, Yria). Settlements in the Geometric and archaic periods consist of rectangular agglutinative units usually adapted to the sloping landscape and making use of the natural bedrock. Curvilinear plans are uncommon but not unknown, especially in the PG period (Koukounaries). Corners of houses were often rounded in order to facilitate traffic. Roofs were presumably flat, though pitched roofs will characterize temple architecture and public buildings from the sixth century onwards. It seems that the idea of replacing the flat ceiling with a sloping roof was invented by the Naxians, ca. 550 (see esp. the "Telesterion" at Gyroulas, near Sangri). Interior furnishings comprise central hearths lined with vertical slabs, benches along the walls for sitting and storage, and various cists and bins for storage.[21]

In the Cyclades, unlike Euboea, agglutinative units were the norm. A good example are the houses at Zagora. These originally consisted of one main room and a porch, serving a variety of functions, and later developed into multi-roomed courtyard houses with differentiated functions. All houses were turned inward and were accessible via a narrow door which opened onto the public space.[22]

In a number of EIA settlements certain buildings which stand out for their architectural layout, location, furnishings and movable finds may be identified as rulers' dwellings (Mazarakis Ainian 1997). It has been possible to trace such buildings in larger settlements which have been excavated to a significant degree.[23] In smaller settlements which have revealed most of their layout it has not been possible to identify such structures (Donousa, Ay. Andreas); this may be explained either by the character of these sites[24] or the nature of the preserved data (i.e. they could be archaeologically "invisible" to us).

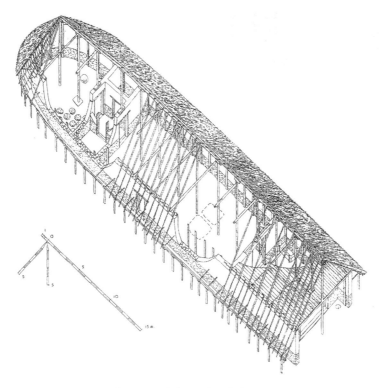

Figure 11.1   Reconstruction drawing of the Lefkandi heroon

The case of the so-called "Heroon" at Lefkandi-Toumba (figure 11.1) remains ambiguous, since scholars continue to disagree whether this unique mid-tenth-century monumental apsidal building, surrounded by a wooden stoa, represents the dwelling of the couple buried inside (a warrior cremation, a rich female inhumation, and the skeletons of four horses),[25] or a funerary monument imitating such an outstanding dwelling (Coulton 1993: 49; Lemos 2002: 145)[26] The fact that this outstanding edifice lies at some distance from the settlement of Xeropolis, which we know was inhabited during the period that the so-called "heroon" was in use (Lemos 2002: 140; 2007) strengthens the latter theory. Recent discoveries at Mitrou (Van de Moortel and Zahou 2003/4; 2005; 2006) and Halos (Malakasioti and Mousioni 2004), however, seem to support the former hypothesis. Others maintain that the apsidal building was originally a house, subsequently transformed into a heroon (Crielaard and Driessen 1994). The hypothesis that the prevailing pattern in Euboea until the end of the ninth century was one of widely dispersed independent *oikoi* situated on the summits of hills, cannot be proven.[27]

In the architectural organization of settlements, the layout of cemeteries, the funerary rituals and offerings, one observes a social stratification into classes. At Zagora, for instance, the central habitation nucleus comprises more spacious dwellings than those of the periphery. At Eretria the area around the future sanctuary of Apollo

(a)   (b)

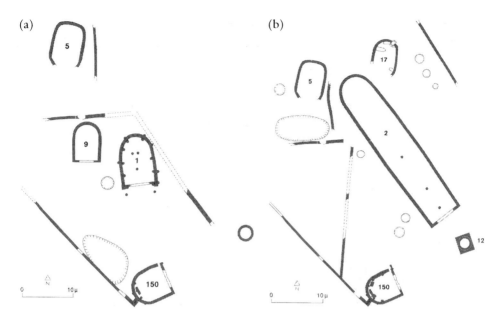

Figure 11.2 Plans of temple of Apollo at Eretria: (a) Middle Geometric phase; (b) Late Geometric phase

Daphnephoros (figure 11.2) seems to have been inhabited by members of the elite, while the area by the harbor, judging by the architectural layout, appears to have been more densely populated by less prosperous families (Mazarakis 1987), though this idea has been question on account of a scatter of rather wealthy burials by the sea (Blandin 2005; Crielaard 2006). It has been argued that the conspicuous differences in pottery and burial customs between Naxos city and Tsikalario on Naxos reflect two major social groups, residents of the city laying claim to "ancestral nobility" and the inland population displaying "wealth and vitality" (Lambrinoudakis 2001: 15; 2004).

Just to the south of the presumed ruler's dwelling in Zagora, an open area in the center of the settlement, which includes an open air sanctuary and an altar, may have functioned as a primitive agora. The lower settlement at Koukounaries, dating to the early seventh century, is also suggestive: the houses are multi-roomed and within the "urban" tissue we find a temple, a building identified as a "Prytaneion," and an open space. Such open spaces may not have been agoras in the strict sense of the term, since it would be odd for communities which failed to develop into *poleis* and were abandoned to have developed *polis* institutions. One could argue, however, that it was precisely the development of such institutions which led these communities to decide to re-settle in places which allowed more expansion and growth.

In several places, as in Crete and certain mainland sanctuaries, we witness continuity of cult from the LBA (Ay. Irini Kea, Yria Naxos) or a tendency to establish a link with the past (Artemision on Delos). At Ay. Irini, the head of a LHII terracotta statue was reused as a cult idol in the Geometric period (Caskey 1986; 1998). The tendency to create a link with the past is also reflected in the cases of veneration of ancestors which in some places developed into hero cults, as in Euboea (Lefkandi;[28] Eretria; Oropos) and in the Cyclades.[29]

The first urban temples, as elsewhere in the Greek world, were built during the eighth century (Eretria, Ypsile, Koukounaries, Minoa) or later, though cult buildings were in place much earlier in extra-urban sanctuaries (Ay. Irini on Kea, Yria on Naxos).[30] Indeed, from very early times sub- or extra-urban sanctuaries were founded, several of which were of a "rural" character and would have served the surrounding communities (Gyroulas). In some cases cult was performed in the open air, in the vicinity of the dwellings of the members of the elite (Eretria, Zagora). Inside the earliest cult buildings there is evidence that meals were held in the interior (Yria II and III, Oikos of the Naxians, Ypsile and perhaps Koukounaries). In the absence of an urban temple, such meals would have been held inside the ruler's dwelling, as one can assume for Zagora and Eretria. Koukounaries stands as an exception to the model according to which settlements failed to develop into *poleis* when they did not acquire a temple dedicated to a poliad divinity (see Snodgrass 1977a; Gounaris 2005a).

The process of synoecism is well documented in the Cyclades. On Andros, Paleopolis apparently received an influx of population from Zagora and Ypsile, while Paroikia on Paros must have been partly populated by the inhabitants of Koukounaries. The construction of monumental temples (Eretria, Zarakes, Yria, Delos), fortification walls (Louyot 2005) and drainage works (Eretria, Oropos) point towards a communal organization which was well established by 700. This will become much more obvious during the seventh and especially sixth centuries, when monumental temples, aqueducts (for instance the 11-km-long aqueduct which brought water from Melanes to the city of Naxos) and circuit walls became the rule.

The archaic period

From the seventh century onwards contacts with the east intensified. The spread of the Homeric epics and the need of the new communities to define their identity led to a series of innovations such as narrative art, establishment of hero cults, and "Homeric" burials. This was also a period of social restructuring thanks to the wealth acquired by agriculture and trade.

Many islands expressed an individual cultural identity through their specific style in art. The Naxians, Parians and, to a lesser degree, Tenians exploited fine marble quarries and dared to produce colossal sculptures, thus contributing to the development of monumental sculpture. The antagonism of Naxos and Paros in the seventh and sixth centuries is evident in the sculptured dedications in the Panionion sanctuary on Delos, as well as other panhellenic sanctuaries.[31] Throughout the seventh and early sixth centuries, the Naxians seem to have excelled in producing such sculpture, but in the second half of the sixth century Parian workshops took over (figure 11.3).[32] This was partly due to the high quality of Parian marble, praised by Strabo (10.5.7) and Pindar (*Nemean* 4.81).[33] In ceramics, the local workshops followed different, mostly conservative, trajectories which continued the Geometric

Figure 11.3   Statue of Gorgo from Paros

tradition but gradually incorporated models and ideas from the East.[34] Of great interest are the huge *pithoi* which bear relief decoration, often with strikingly original
narrative or mythological scenes (esp. the Tenian workshop; Simantoni-Bournia 2004).

   The rising *poleis*, which as we have seen had already emerged by 700, used not
only monumental sculpture but also monumental temple architecture to express their
wealth and power in rivalry with one another. Several of the most prosperous Cycladic
islands, as well as Euboea, appear to have played a major role in the process which
led to the shaping of the canonical form of the monumental classical Greek temple.
Two major temples were built shortly after 700 on Delos (Oikos of the Naxians,
Artemision E). Both reflect a similar development on the island of Naxos.[35] Here,
the second temple at Yria (ca. 730) replaced a smaller one of ca. 800, and now had
four naves, a hearth, and a bench for meals which could accommodate ca. 80 seated
participants (figure 11.4). Monumentality is expressed here in temple architecture
for the first time. The early seventh-century temple became more canonical, with
three naves (though the central nave was narrower than those of the sides), and acquired
a monumental wooden prostasis which was unusual for the period but later came
to characterize many Ionic temples. The greatest leap forward came with the construction of the fourth temple (580–570), with its marble threshold and adyton,
Ionian columns, monumental door jambs, and even a pitched marble roof (note that
Byzes of Naxos was said to have invented marble tiles: Pausanias 5.10.3). Some of

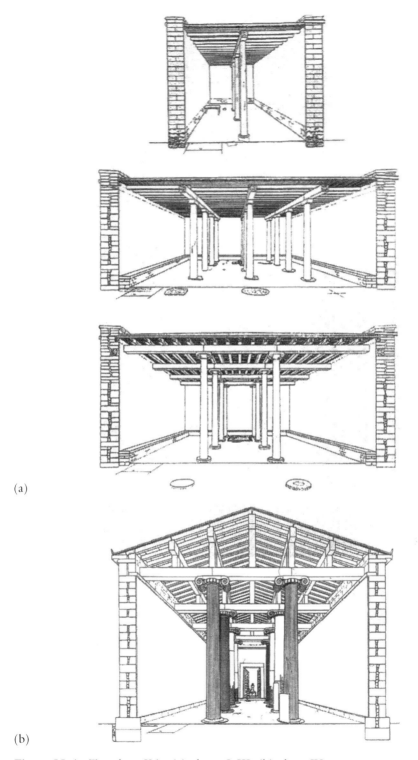

(a)

(b)

Figure 11.4 Temple at Yria: (a) phases I–III; (b) phase IV

these innovations – the use of marble for bases and threshold, and the monumentalization of the facade – can already be seen in the otherwise modest early seventh-century *oikos* at Melanes, built next to an earlier *oikos* of the eighth century. The temple of Gyroulas, dated ca. 530, during the rule of Lygdamis, is the first in the Naxian series to have been built entirely of marble. It presents features that we will see ca. 100 years later in the Athenian Parthenon, such as the application of curved lines to the entire building and the marble roof. The Ionic temple of Apollo Delios in the city of Naxos was even more monumental and its planning included a peristyle which, however, was never completed. Naxos undoubtedly played a leading role in the shaping and development of the Ionic order (Yria, Palatia, Gyroulas, Oikos of Naxians). At Paros, the amphiprostyle temple of Athena, built around 525 (Ohnesorg 2005, for bibliography), and the small but elegant marble temple of Artemis at the Delion (M. Schuller 1991), rivaled those of nearby Naxos.

The display of wealth so prominent in these architectural achievements can be compared with the variety and richness of the offerings in various sanctuaries, such as the Delion on Paros (Rubensohn 1962), the Apollo sanctuary on the small island of Despotiko near Antiparos (Kourayos 2004a; 2004b; 2005) and especially one of the sanctuaries of the ancient town of Kythnos which may have been dedicated to Artemis and Apollo (Mazarakis Ainian 2005) (figures 11.5–11.7). Other finds pointing in the same direction come from sanctuaries of Artemis (?) at Kastro on Siphnos, Dionysos at Yria, an unidentified divinity at Kaminaki on Naxos, and Aphrodite at Thera.[36] In many of these sanctuaries, although only a small portion of the offerings

Figure 11.5   Aerial view of sanctuary on Kythnos
Source: Author's photo.

Figure 11.6 *Adyton* of the sanctuary on Kythnos
Source: Author's photo.

has been preserved, it is clear that that the divinities both in major and peripheral cult places received valuable gifts. At Despotiko in particular, fine marble sculptures add to this picture of available wealth. The case of the otherwise unpretentious archaic temple in Kythnos, built entirely of schist stones and a Doric entablature of local mussel stone, is unique since the offerings contained inside the *adyton* were found in situ and intact. Hundreds of similar votives were also found in an extensive votive deposit nearby. The finds from the *adyton* consist mostly of luxurious items, especially precious jewellery from the early seventh to the early fifth centuries, though certain objects date back to the Early Iron and Late Bronze Ages.

Figure 11.7 Gold rosace found in the *adyton* of the sanctuary on Kythnos
Source: Author's photo.

Among the offerings there were several "orientalia," as well as imports from South Italy and Sicily. There were also significant numbers of terracotta seated female figurines and numerous intact orientalizing, Corinthian and black figure vases, some of which may be linked to master painters. This picture of a sanctuary belonging to a rather unimportant island *polis* provides a new insight of the display of wealth that one should take into account when assessing the evidence from other more important sanctuaries of the same period.

Display of wealth in sanctuaries is also observed in Euboea, especially in Eretria. The diversity of the "orientalia" in the sanctuary known as the "Aire Sacrificelle Nord" next to that of Apollo Daphnephoros, perhaps dedicated to the cult of Artemis, is indicative of a wider network of communications with the eastern Mediterranean from which Eretria still benefited during the early archaic period (Huber 2003). Monumental *hekatompedon* temples were built at Eretria and Zarakes already by the end of the eighth century. The first temple at Eretria preserved the apsidal plan deeply anchored in the local building tradition. This temple was rebuilt twice during the archaic period, now following the new trend of rectangular construction. The second archaic temple, destroyed by the Persians, was provided with sculptured decoration (Touloupa 2002). At Zarakes the temple was apparently provided with a *peristasis* already by the end of the eighth centuries (Chatzidimitriou 1997; 2003; 2003/4). The *peristasis* which had been occasionally attached to apsidal and oval domestic buildings throughout the EIA (the earliest example is the "Heroon" at Lefkandi) became typical of temple architecture during the succeeding centuries. The peristyle was, however, rarely applied in the Cyclades, where emphasis lay on the monumentalization of the temple's facade.

The architectural layout of archaic *poleis* in the Cyclades and Euboea remains elusive. Koukounaries and Hypsile, when published, will certainly contribute towards understanding better the process of urbanization;[37] a recently published study of Eretria moves in the same direction (Charalampidou 2003), though the fragmentary character of the data leaves room for much speculation. Noteworthy are the extensive and expensive marble fortification walls of the late sixth century on the acropolis of Kastro Siphnos and the 11 km long aqueduct of Naxos (Papadopoulou 2002). Such works reflect the tendency of *poleis* to demonstrate their wealth, often under the rule of tyrants, such as Lygdamis on Naxos. The Siphnians' contemporaries regarded this extreme display of wealth as an expression of arrogance which led to their punishment by the gods (Herodotus 3.57–8).[38] Judging by recent excavations, however, even smaller and less prosperous islands, such as Kythnos, seem to have been rather wealthier and participated in wider networks of communication than previously thought.

"The Greeks Overseas" in the East Aegean and Asia Minor

In the long formative phase of Greek Iron Age civilization from the end of the eleventh to the eight century, Greek populations launched to settle down in the islands of the east Aegean and the west coast of Asia Minor. Colonization of the shores and the islands of the east Aegean created city-states which took a leading part in subsequent political developments in the Greek world, and in the further colonization of the western Mediterranean, the Black Sea and even Naucratis in Egypt. Some of these Greek colonies were preceded by Mycenaean Greek and Minoan settlements. In Ephesus, pottery finds show that the area of the sanctuary of Artemis was occupied continuously from the fourteenth to the eighth century, and the situation was similar in Miletus and the Dodecanese.

Greek tradition spoke of the colonization of the coast of northern Asia Minor by Aeolians from Lesbos and coast opposite, south of the river Maeander. These regions are characterized by Grey Ware in the Early Iron Age, not found south of Miletus (Cultraro 2004: 215, fig. 1). Soon afterwards, the Ionians followed and took over the territory up to the river Hermos. Greek settlers occupied peninsulas and promontories on bays, often at the mouth of rivers – now silted up – as at Miletus on the Maeander, Ephesus on the Cayster, and Smyrna on the Hermos, which offered safe anchorage or a well-sheltered harbor and a cultivable hinterland, situated on trade routes to the Aegean and mainland Greece by sea and to central Anatolia along navigable rivers. The pattern of coastal settlement in the Greek colonization of western Asia Minor followed an east Mediterranean tradition with Bronze Age roots, known from both Phoenician and Greek colonies as well as the Greek mainland. The new settlers had to face successive attacks by Cimmerians, Lydians and finally Persians, who in 545 occupied Sardis. Although many sites in Ionia, Aeolis and Troas have archaic fortifications (Teos, Kyme, Larisa-Kale, Kalabaktepe in Miletus, Neandreia) colonists' relations with local inhabitants was for the most part peaceful, as attested not only by the wave of Orientalizing art encouraged by their co-existence, but also by the development of common cults, hellenized versions of the local cults which the Greeks encountered. Witness to mutual influence are the sixth-century limestone statue of the Phrygian mother goddess Cybele and her attendants from Bogazköy, in the Ankara Museum, and the reflection of Phrygian rock-cut throne-shaped shrines of Cybele in the early sixth-century rock-cut model of the goddess's shrine on Chios (Boardman 1980: 93–4, figs. 106, 109).

Peaceful coexistence between native Anatolian populations, such as Phrygians and Lydians, and Greek colonists is mentioned in literary sources. An interesting example is the case of Ephesus, governed by kings who according to a later fabrication were descended from the Athenian Neleid founder Androclos[39] and connected by marriage to the Lydian aristocracy. The Lydians later engineered the resettlement of Ephesus around the sanctuary of Artemis, whose cult they patronized, in order to gain greater control over the powerful aristocratic Greek families traditionally associated with sanctuaries in Greek Asia Minor.[40]

Settlement patterns and early urbanization

The best investigated early Greek city in Asia Minor is Old Smyrna (Bayrakli). From the mid-eleventh century to ca. 700 the settlement's pottery is predominantly Aeolian. An impressive defensive wall was constructed already in the mid-ninth century and rebuilt in the eighth and sixth centuries. Circular granaries, partly subterranean, are

Figure 11.8 Temple at Old Smyrna

attested ca. 900. In the eighth century, when urbanization began at the site, most houses were rectangular. Ionians eventually captured the city and erected a temple to Athena on a platform near the defensive wall in ca. 700.[41] The later Athena temple (630–610) displayed Proto-Ionic features in its architecture with Aeolic column capitals on its *peristasis* (figure 11.8). The offerings in the Athenaion in Old Smyrna were set on terraces laid out to the east and west of the temple. A characteristic offering to the goddess, whose cult was widespread both among Aeolians and Ionians, were small votive shields (cf. the sanctuary of Athena at Emporion on Chios). Old Smyrna was laid out with streets following the natural terrain in north–south and east–west directions, thought to be an early form of a grid plan which could be characterized as "proto-hippodamian." Akurgal (1987) estimated that the population of Old Smyrna was ca. 3,000 inhabitants from the late seventh to the mid-sixth century.

An even earlier temple of Athena may have existed in Erythrae (Ildir), where Ionians from Chios settled in the eighth century, as is evident from pottery, megaron-type houses, and the walls of a temple platform.[42] The sixth-century temple was also built on a platform. Another temple dedicated to Athena or Apollo, at Neandreia in Aeolis in the early sixth century, featured a colonnade along the length of its cella, as well as Aeolic column capitals.

Cyme in Aeolis has been identified with the settlement in S. Tepe, which yielded eleventh-century Protogeometric pottery along with imported Corinthian and Attic wares and large amounts of locally produced grey monochrome pottery (Mitchell

1985: 80–1). Clazomenae was inhabited between the seventh and early fifth century BC, when the city was abandoned as a result of the Ionian Revolt (494). A sixth-century road and domestic buildings on the acropolis, as well as a defensive wall, have been detected (Mitchell 1985: 82–3).

A prosperous and populous city was Miletus, which enjoyed considerable stability and founded a great number of colonies along the Aegean and Thracian coast. The plan of the important settlement on the acropolis (Kalabaktepe), first built in the Geometric period, was aligned with the fortification wall; there are no traces of a hippodamian orthogonal grid plan in the lower city either. The cult of Artemis K(h)ithone thrived here.[43] Outside the city walls at Zeyintepe was a sanctuary of Aphrodite Oikous where hundreds of archaic terracotta statuettes have come to light; this site also yielded the most important finds of imported Egyptian material in the Mediterranean in the seventh century.

On the fortified acropolis of Emporio on Chios the so-called Megaron Hall was constructed in the late eighth century, possibly as the chieftain's dwelling or as a building for community gatherings (figure 11.9). There was possibly an altar of the same date at the site and the finds attest outdoor cult activity. The altar was later incorporated in a temple of Athena, built in the mid-sixth century when the settlement had been abandoned. Clay votive shields were an important find among the sanctuary's offerings (Boardman 1967a: 5–31). There was also a high percentage of Cypriot ivories among the votives, as was also the case in the Heraion on Samos, in Old Smyrna, and in the temple of Athena at Lindos on Rhodes (Boardman 1967a: 31–4).

The defensive wall of the ancient city of Chios in the second half of the seventh century may have been located in the area of modern Palaiokastro, north of the medieval Genoese castle, as is suggested by burials and the sporadic finds of pottery workshops. In the cemetery at Rizari in the modern town of Chios, social stratification in the seventh century can be deduced from the different types and sizes of sarcophagi

Figure 11.9 Megaron Hall at Emborio, Chios

as well as the difference between pithoi-amphorae with linear decoration and coarse undecorated vessels of this type (Lemos 1997).

The archaic cemeteries at Ialysos and Camirus on Rhodes are of prime importance. Camirus featured rock-cut chamber tombs. The difference in burial customs and grave goods between these immense archaic cemeteries corresponds to the contrasting social, economic, and artistic development of the two cities: Ialysos strengthened its ties with Athenian trade in the third quarter of the sixth century, whereas Camirus retained stronger contacts with East Greece (Samos, Chios) and Corinth (Gates 1983).

Another seventh-century settlement, at Vroulia in southern Rhodes, already displays orderly town planning with houses arranged in two parallel rows, suggesting affinities with Gordion in Phrygia. The first row of houses is built against a wall with a tower near the entrance, the defensive character of which has recently been disputed.[44]

On the island of Cos, the main city extant from the seventh to the fourth century was Cos-Meropis on the hill Serraglio. On top of the Mycenean settlement was situated the Geometric cemetery with cist graves, child burials in pots, and plain terracotta sarcophagi, mainly of the Clazomenian type furnished with a hole in the lid for funerary libations.

Geometric to archaic curvilinear buildings are known from Mytilene, Pyrrha, and Antissa on Lesbos. Some are apsidal, though this type is rare on east Greek islands and the west coast of Asia Minor; they may be dwellings, or in some instances, when the finds can be securely recognized as votive offerings or cult objects, cult buildings (Mazarakis 1997: 84–5, 89–93). In the archaic period detached houses prevail over conglomerate settlements. In the seventh century public buildings with different functions appear in sacred and secular contexts (*stoa, telesterion, hestiatorion*). Temples assume distinct architectural styles (Ionic, Doric) as well as tile roofs and demand specialized labor for their construction. In the same period the city is clearly differentiated from its *chora*. All these aspects and especially the construction of fortification walls and public buildings reflect the consolidation of the *polis* and its central organization in Greek territories (Lang 1996).

Sacred landscapes and a taste for monumentality

Artemis of Ephesus was a Bronze Age Anatolian vegetation goddess, whom the Ionian settlers fused with Artemis, recasting the image of the Greek goddess in Western Anatolian iconography, the most conspicuous element of which were the breast-shaped bulbs on the lower chest of statues of the goddess, symbols of fecundity (Morris 2001). The temple erected in the late eighth century is the first in Greek Asia Minor with a *peristasis* made up by wooden columns. This important element of Greek temples was developed at the same time in mainland Greece (Thermos in Aetolia, Mazaraki in Achaea) and on Samos (Hekatompedon I and II of the Heraion), possibly after a remote predecessor, the Heroon at Lefkandi, which was, however, covered by a tumulus. In the Artemis temple the wooden *peristasis* was combined with an open-air *oikos* having in its interior an orthogonal base for both the cult statue of the goddess and the altar, roofed by a baldachin. Thus the older Anatolian tradition of open-air sanctuaries was combined with traditional Mycenaean palatial features (the megaron hearth) and innovative Greek architectures (the *peristasis*).[45]

Since the Lydians could not manage to seize Miletus and the extra-urban sanctuary of Didyma, their king Croesus chose to erect a huge new marble Ionic dipteral temple at Ephesus.[46] This Anatolian patronage is reminiscent of the donations for architectural projects made by the Hecatomnid rulers of Caria to free mainland Greek sanctuaries (Delphi, Tegea) in the fourth century BC (Waywell 1993). It was almost contemporary with the dipteral Ionic temple of Apollo at Didyma, and was a rival also to the slightly earlier temple by the architect Rhoikos on Samos, from which its dipteral design was drawn. The Ephesian temple, however, was superior to the Rhoikos temple in its use of marble and figural architectural reliefs. Relief decoration may have adorned the upper drum and the orthogonal base of each column on the west and east sides, depicting a sacrificial procession. A sculpted frieze with chariots and symposium scenes as well as mythological subjects carried on an early Anatolian tradition. This East Ionian decorative mode established by the Ephesian Artemision was followed in the Doric temple of Athena at Assos (Behramkale), ca. 550–525, which had relief metopes but also a relief frieze adorning the architrave with mythological, heroic, and decorative subjects (Finster-Hotz 1984). The temple of Apollo at Didyma also shared this uncanonical position of relief decoration found in archaic East Greek temples.

The Rhoikos temple in the Heraion on Samos is the first monumental Ionic temple (570–560). Its architectural decoration, although non-figural, was of high quality and showed a strong sense of plasticity. This temple marked the inception of monumental art on Samos and in Ionian Asia Minor in general. Along with it, a monumental altar was erected in the Heraion, and the first dedications of monumental marble *kouroi* and *korai* appear. In the second quarter of the sixth-century monumental limestone sarcophagi and palmette-stelae in the archaic west cemetery of the city of Samos (Pythagoreion) have been connected with the family tumuli of local aristocrats (Tsakos 2001), who developed a taste for monumentality.

The dipteral temple of Hera erected by Polycrates acquired a third row of columns on its short sides. Monumentality was a hallmark of the art of the tyrants both on Samos and in Athens where a first Doric peripteral temple was erected before the mid-sixth century, in the first period of the tyranny of Peisistratos, for Zeus Olympios' sanctuary on the river Ilissos. The much larger Peisistratid Doric temple which replaced it was obviously influenced by the Samian Heraion of Polycrates in adopting a third row of columns at both ends (Gruben 2001, 246–7). The Athenian examples attest to a lively rivalry between Ionian tyrants on both sides of the Aegean. Moreover, Peisistratos instigated significant building projects for the water supply of Athens, just as Polycrates ordered the creation of the famous aqueduct by the architect Eupalinos for the city of Samos (Kienast 1995), and intensified maritime trade by building a harbor mole and ship-sheds.

The Rhoikos and Polycrates temples in the Samian Heraion influenced the sanctuary of Apollo at Phanai on Chios, while the late archaic Ionic temple at Phanai betrays the influence of the Ephesian Artemision *dipteros* in its more elaborate architectural ornaments.[47]

In the Apollo sanctuary at Branchidae–Didyma, the first temple was erected ca. 700, the second in the sixth century. The latter was a monumental dipteral Ionic temple around an open-air cella in the form of an internal court known as *adyton*. The *prodomos* comprised two compartments, the outer of which possessed twelve columns in three rows, thus obscuring the view into the lower-level interior court where cult practice took place in front of a *naiskos*. In line with Carian cult tradition the *naiskos* housed not the cult statue of the god, but a sacred spring, associated with an oracle which became very famous. Miletus was connected with Didyma by a sacred processional road, just as Samos was connected with the Heraion, Ephesus with the sanctuary of Artemis, Argos with the Heraion at Prosymna and Athens with the sanctuary of Eleusis. A processional Sacred Way between city and extramural sanctuary may be seen as a means of securing the deity's protection for the city (Tuchelt 1992: 38). On another level, the close association between polis and extra-urban sanctuary helps the city to mark the extent of its *chora* and consolidate its territory (de Polignac 1995a: 33–4).

A special characteristic of the Sacred Way between Miletus and Didyma was that it was lined with precincts where the sacred procession stopped to perform cult actions, as at the sanctuary of the Nymph and at a family cult precinct of the Milesian aristocracy. The latter's main feature, unusual for the archaic period, was a semi-circular *exedra* with ten statues of enthroned men and women in the Milesian Archaic style, in front of a terrace where sacred performances were held. Another oddity of this precinct was that in the late sixth century six Sphinx statues were erected on the *peribolos* wall exactly opposite the *exedra*. This is the first occurrence of the figure of the sphinx in the archaic sculpture of Asia Minor. This line of statues of a fabulous creature recalls the archaic lions lining the way to the sanctuary of Leto on Delos (Tuchelt 1992: 56) and the "Branchidai" statues lining the Sacred Way from the Apollo temple at Didyma to Panormos. No sacrificial altar was detected in the *temenos* but the great number of amphorae and *phialae* discovered attest to meals without cooking. The deliberate destruction of the sculptural decoration in the early fifth century indicates a possible punishment by the Persians or the Athenians of an aristocratic Milesian family demonstrating its power through gatherings in this sacred precinct (Tuchelt 1992: 50).

The sanctuaries of Delphinion in Miletus, Didyma-Branchidae, Ephesus, Poseidon's sanctuary at cape Monodendri (Tekağaç), and the Poseidon Helikonios sanctuary at Mycale (the seat of the Ionian League since the ninth century), all belong to the type of a precinct with a *peribolos*-cella or open-air sanctuary which is considered characteristic of early Ionia. In the sanctuary of Apollo at Branchidae-Didyma, a strong Carian influence in forms of cult is combined with Greek architectural elements (Voigtländer 2004: 286–94).

Dedications and artistic influences

In the extramural sanctuary of Hera on Samos numerous votives attest to relations of Samians with the Mediterranean, Asia Minor, Persia, and Mesopotamia. Nowhere else in Greece have so many and such varied oriental imports been unearthed. The earliest Greek *stoa* was erected in this sanctuary (640–630) to provide shelter for worshipers. Samian metalwork was legendary, and Samos also had an innovative school of sculptors who produced mainly *kouroi* and *korai* which combine full-volumed bodies with subtle modelling and engraving on the surface (Freyer-Schauenburg 1974). The colossal bronze cauldron dedicated as a tithe from seafaring enterprises by the Samian captain Kolaios (Hdt. 4.152) and the dedication of ship models in the Heraion from the late seventh century onwards point to a social group which derived its wealth and status from overseas trade and/or raiding, and may have been in rivalry with the aristocratic landowners who dedicated colossal marble statues in the same period.

The family statuary group signed by the sculptor Geneleos (figure 11.10) comprised the dedicator, shown as a reclining symposiast; his wife, seated; a son, draped and playing the double pipe; and three daughters, of an identical *kore*-type, possibly alluding to their choral performance in honor of the sacred marriage of Hera at her annual festival, the *Tonaia* (Karakasi 2003: 29). The Geneleos group may also represent a glimpse of the symposium, a hallmark of archaic Greek *polis*-culture.[48] At the local festival, cult meals took place in the open air, where worshippers reclined on the ground, on lygos branches, the so-called *stoibades*. These cult meals may be reflected in scenes on Laconian painted pottery and on Samian painted amphorae as well. Moreover a special kind of pottery for everyday use was used in these ritual meals and was afterwards inscribed to the goddess and dedicated at her sanctuary (Kron 1988). Family-group dedications to Hera attest to the self-assertion of prominent Samian families. In east Ionia, *korai* were almost always dedicated in

Figure 11.10 Geneleos statue group from Samos

sanctuaries, as were the majority of *kouroi*; funerary *kouroi* may have been extant only on Samos. The phenomenon may be associated with attempts by the elite to circumvent restrictions imposed by local tyrants, by displaying their wealth through the erection of impressive sculptural dedications outside the *polis* sanctuaries.

On Rhodes, as on neighboring Cos, monumental architecture in stone did not develop before late classical times,[49] but the archaic Rhodian sanctuaries of Athena at Ialysos and Camirus have important votive deposits. At Ialysos, occupation dates back to Mycenean times, but votive deposits begin in the tenth century (Martelli 1988; 1996). These contain numerous Cypriot statuettes of female votaries from the late seventh and the first half of the sixth century; fibulae of island types and Anatolian, Phrygian or Italiotic origin; ivory pendants portraying nude figures of mixed Syrian and Greek Daidalic character; and Egyptian material.

The Wild Goat Style of the seventh century and the Fikellura Style of the second half of the sixth century in Greek vasepainting are now recognized as originating in Miletus. Miletus was also an important center for bronzeworking, as attested by the mainly orientalizing bronzes from the temple of Athena which betray Urartian and Near Eastern influence. A thriving school of sculpture developed in archaic Miletus. Most famous are the enthroned statues lining the Sacred Way from Panormos to Didyma, the so-called Branchidai, representing local rulers and their wives (Voigtländer 2004: 287). In the decade 540–530, the corners of the architrave of the Ionic *dipteros* temple of Apollo Philesios at Didyma were adorned with running Gorgons flanked by antithetical lying lions, sculptural types that owe much to Egyptian and Phoenician artistic traditions.

Chios founded one colony, Maroneia in Thrace, and took part in the establishment of Naucratis in Egypt in the last quarter of the seventh century. Maroneia gave its metropolis access to the silver mines of the Thracians, and Chian silver coins traveled to Egypt in the sixth century. A Chiot school of Ionic architectural decoration was recognized from the late sixth century onwards, characterized by rich and original variations of the egg-and-dart moulding and the lion's-paw form of anta bases (Boardman 1959: 170–97). The extensive trading relations of archaic Chios are better reflected in the distribution of Chian pottery. The main style of painted Chian pottery in the seventh and first half of the sixth centuries was a local refinement of the so-called Wild Goat Style, and the distinct shape was the Chian chalice with painted decoration on a white slip (Lemos 1986; 1991).

A remarkable combination of Greek mythological subjects in the East Greek artistic tradition with scenes of Anatolian and Persian inspiration like the funerary feast is found in the early fifth-century painted interiors of tombs at Lycia (Elmali) (Boardman 1980: 107 figs. 122–3).

Sea Routes in the North Aegean

On the island of Lemnos a sixth- to fifth-century settlement has been excavated at Hephaisteia, but better known is the archaic cemetery from the second half of the eighth down to the fifth century. The excavator discerned a significant change in burial customs in the beginning of the fifth century which he connected with the arrival of Athenian settlers, who according to Herodotus (6.140) expelled the "Tyrrhenian" population from the island.[50] On the acropolis stood a sanctuary of the Great Goddess, dated to the second half of the seventh century: the temple, which resembled a *telesterion*, had internal benches and a hearth. In the Cabirion sanctuary on Chloe promontory a mystery cult was practiced from the late eighth century to the late Hellenistic period.[51] The Great Goddess of Lemnos was in the sixth century assimilated to the Thracian Bendis and the Greek Artemis. The late seventh century produced terracotta figurines of the Great Goddess with raised arms, a tube-shaped body with painted decoration on the front only, and a very expressive face. Pottery production bears witness to Lemnos' relations with nearby areas, especially the Troas, Lesbos and Thasos (Beschi 2004). The "Tyrrhenians" who inhabited eighth-century Lemnos and Imbros were in linguistic terms akin to the Etruscans but their material culture and religious life were totally different and associated instead with the north-east Aegean region (Beschi 1998).

The city of Thasos was founded on the north side of the island of the same name by colonists from Paros (traditional date: 680), and in turn founded a series of colonies on the Thracian mainland opposite. From the sixth century date sanctuaries of Artemis and Heracles. The gates of the defensive wall were decorated in the late sixth to early fifth centuries with monumental reliefs depicting a variety of deities, protectors of the city (e.g. Dionysos, Herakles, Zeus and Hera, Hermes and the Charites). Also in the sixth century, the important marble quarries at Aliki began to be exploited.

The rich valleys of the lower courses of the rivers Strymon and Nestos with their marshy plains, wooded mountains and rich mineral resources, notably the gold and silver mines of Mt. Pangaion, attracted Greek ventures and settlements from an early date. Thasos founded Galepsos, Neapolis, and Oisyme here in the seventh century. Galepsos is known from its sixth- to fourth-century cemetery and from a cult of Demeter which is epigraphically attested. In Neapolis a monumental Ionic temple of Athena Parthenos replaced an earlier wooden structure in the sixth century. A temple on the acropolis of Oisyme had decorated terracotta antefixes from the seventh to the fifth century and was assigned to Athena on the evidence of votive figurines and bronze shields dedications (cf. the Athena temples at Emporion on Chios and at Old Smyrna). Another sixth-century fortified Thasian settlement on the mainland was Pistyros, described as an *emporion* in ancient sources. The fact that another *emporion* with the name Pistyros existed in the upper Hebros valley attests to the successful penetration of the Thasians in the Thracian hinterland (Loukopoulou 2004: 866–7). Thasos retained under Persian occupation financial control of her mainland possesions (*peraia*) and especially her rights in exploiting the rich mines of Mt. Pangaion.

On the island of Samothrace, Ionic and Aeolian Greeks settled in the Iron Age, succeeding the earlier Thracian inhabitants. The importance of the Samothracian *polis* in the archaic period led to the colonization of the Thracian coast between the Hebros river and Mt. Ismaros with a series of fortified towns which initially had an agrarian character but in the late archaic and classical periods became important trading posts. Samothrace is best known for the Sanctuary of the Great Gods or Cabiri, whose mystery cult was according to Herodotus founded by the "Pelasgians." Mystery cult activity is attested already in the seventh century by Greek pottery finds, especially a hearth and lamps, under the building with the dancers.[52] Important are pottery fragments from the sanctuary bearing votive inscriptions in Greek letters but in a non-Greek *lingua sacra* from the sixth century, and in the Greek language from the mid-fifth century. These inscriptions have parallels in Zone, where they are connected with the cult of Apollo, and on Samothrace itself outside the sanctuary of the Great Gods and in the southern part of the island, at Mantal' Panagia, where they are associated with an unfortified Thracian settlement and a sanctuary of Artemis. These texts suggest the peaceful coexistence of Thracians and waves of Greek colonists (first Aeolians, later Samians), and the continuation of local cults by Greek settlers.[53] Prehellenic cults of the Cabiri are also attested on Tenedos and Lemnos, where "Tyrrhenian" graffiti and dipinti on votive pottery again attest to an initially non-Greek cult, taken over, after a hiatus, by Greek settlers in the mid-fifth century.

Megalithic tombs on Samothrace, also known from the Thracian inland, indicate relations with the Balkan region. The Early Iron Age fortification on Blychos belongs to a type of inland settlement on a naturally defended site with complementary fortifications which is found all over the Aegean in the Late Bronze and Early Iron Ages.

In the region of Thrace between the Nestos and Hebros, the wealthy cities of Abdera, Maroneia, Dikaia, and Ainos had a pivotal position as intermediaries between the Thracian hinterland and the Greek Aegean. Abdera was the largest city on the North Aegean coast with a population of between 40,000 and 100,000. It was situated on the eastern bank of the Nestos and had one of the very few natural harbors in the region. A defensive wall dating from the third quarter of the seventh century was discovered north of the classical city, and may have marked the settlement of the first colonists from Clazomenae in Asia Minor. In the mid-sixth century new colonists arrived from Teos, fleeing from Persians. Relations between the two groups were peaceful as shown by finds of the period 575–550 and the literary tradition regarding the common cult of the Clazomenian founder of the city, Timesios. In the late sixth century Teians built a new defensive wall, outside which stood an open-air sanctuary with altars, perhaps dedicated to the Nymphs or Demeter and Kore. Abdera developed into a major financial power in the late sixth century when it issued silver coins with a wide circulation in the East, possibly as a result of gaining access to the silver mines of Mt. Symbolon.

An archaic to fifth-century city on the mainland opposite Samothrace, renamed Zone or Orthogareia in the fourth century, is a rare Greek settlement on the coast of Thrace – most other seventh-century Greek colonies in the region were situated inland on the top of hills with natural defences or man-made fortifications. Its archaic temple, which remained in use in the fifth century, is the only temple of Apollo in Thracian territory.

The Chalcidic peninsula

The Chalcidic peninsula was colonized by the Corinthians, Andrians, and Eretrians in the eighth and seventh centuries. The traditional scholarly view which stresses the role of early Euboean maritime or colonial expansion in cities like Mende, Koukos, Torone, and Dikaia has recently been challenged on the basis of accumulating evidence from excavation. In pottery, architectural features, and linguistic remains, a strong east Greek influence (from Ionia and Aeolis) has been detected. Some traits which appeared to establish connections with Euboean sites are now regarded as more widespread in the Aegean world. For example, the peculiar eighth-century circular stone platforms of Mende – according to the literary evidence a colony from Eretria – occur not only in the Xeropolis settlement at Lefkandi (Euboea) but also at other sites in mainland Greece and West Asia Minor, such as the Argolid, Troad and Miletus. It has even been suggested that the name of the Chalkidic peninsula does not derive from the city of Chalcis in Euboea, but from the rich metal deposits of the region already exploited in the Middle Bronze Age. The archaeological record shows that metal may have been extracted at Koukos and distributed from Torone (Papadopoulos 1996a: 166–74). Large and thriving cities (Akanthus, Olynthus, Mende, Torone, Poseidaia, Argilos) alongside smaller settlements developed in oppostion to the Thracians who lived in the hinterland. In the eastern Chalcidice, archaic and classical architectural features depend largely on Thasian and Cycladic models.[54] At Sane the temple of Apollo was decorated with terracotta architectural sculptures portraying man-sized Nikai, ca. 530/520. At Poseidion in the territory of Mende a sanctuary of Poseidon was thriving already in the Protogeometric period, though building activity on the site dates between the sixth and the fourth century. Habitation in Mende, a colony of Eretria according to Thucydides (4.123.1), is now dated back to the ninth century, based on a Geometric wall on the acropolis, and houses as well as a Geometric cemetery on the coast. At Koukos an Early Iron Age fortified settlement with a long building used as a metal workshop has come to light (Lemos 2002). In Torone the recent excavation on the Lekythos (Promontory 1) has yielded scanty Late Geometric and archaic pottery and more abundant finds from the Early Iron Age, along with architectural remains of storage facilities (Cambitoglou and Papadopoulos 1988).

Greek settlements all over the Aegean coast and islands were primarily orientated towards Mediterranean and Black Sea trade routes and developed a high level of civilization which included the earliest stages of Greek philosophy and scientific thought, especially at Miletus and Ephesus. The eastern Greeks, moreover, engaged in lively interaction with the peoples of Anatolia and Thrace, thus creating the cultural foundation for the further evolution of art, city-planning, architecture and philosophical thought in the Greek world at large.

NOTES

1 For a general overview of the archaeology of the islands of the Aegean see Ekschmitt 1986; Vlachopoulos 2005.
2 As on Xeropolis-Lefkandi: Lemos in Whitley 2004/5; 2007.
3 The site of Ay. Andreas is considered to have been abandoned during the first half of the eleventh century and resettled during the Geometric period. An Attic krater of the

late tenth-early ninth century is regarded as an "antique." For Ay. Spyridon (Renfrew and Wagstaff 1982: 306, n. 94) see Catling 2005: 71, n. 14 who suggests that the LBA site was resettled in the early archaic period.

4   Mazarakis Ainian 1997: 376, 384–5 with references. On Ay. Andreas, see now also Televantou 2005, with earlier bibliography.

5   These include Xobourgo, Kythnos, Kastro on Siphnos, Thera, Paros, Melos, Karthaia and Koresia on Kea, Ios, Ermoupolis and presumably Naxos: Louyot 2005: 95–170.

6   Mazarakis Ainian 1987: 14–16, with references. A similar wall was uncovered in 2006 to the East of the EIA settlement of Oropos, bordering the left bank of the dangerous river or torrent which flowed to the East of the site (see *Ergon* 2006).

7   For instance, systematic surveys have been conducted in Euboea (Sackett et al. 1966), Melos (Renfrew, Wagstaff 1982), Kea and Kythnos (Cherry, Davis, Mantzourani 1991; Mendoni, Mazarakis Ainian 1998c; Mazarakis Ainian 1993; 1995; Louyot, Mazarakis Ainian 2005) and Amorgos (Marangou 2002; Dalongeville and Rougemont 1993).

8   Cherry, Davis, Mantzourani 1991: 5, 8; see also Gounaris 1999: 101, 104.

9   Catling suggested the presence of an itinerant bronzesmith trained in the east (Popham, Sackett, Themelis, 1980: 93–7) and Popham was of the opinion that this smith may have even resided at Lefkandi (Popham 1994: 22).

10 For the notion of itinerant oriental craftsmen in the Aegean in the later Dark Ages, see Boardman 1980; Burkert 1992.

11 Naxos: Lentini 2004; Paros: Zapheiropoulou and Matthaiou 2000; Andros: Balkas 1988; Thera: Boardman 1980: 153–9.

12 At Osteria dell'Osa/Gabii in Latium, ca. 800–775; Bologna, 800–750; and especially Pithekoussai, including the famous inscription on "Nestor's cup," a Rhodian vessel of ca. 720. For references see Powell 1991: 119–80; Mazarakis Ainian and Matthaiou 1999; Mazarakis Ainian 2000: 119–32.

13 Kenzelmann Pfyffer, Theurillat and Verdan 2005; Theurillat 2007.

14 Guarducci 1987: 17–19.

15 Herodotus (4.147–8) mentions eight generations of Phoenicians on the island, but their presence has not been proven by archaeological finds.

16 Diodorus 5.58 concerning the Phoenician presence on the island.

17 See already Pugliese-Carratteli 1976; not unrelated is the opinion that the Homeric epics took their final shape in the same area: West 1988b: 166 (notable is the absence of the Cyclades from the Catalogue of Ships in the Iliad: Gounaris 2005b).

18 Liampi 1988; for Kythnos, see now Kyrou and Artemis 1998.

19 In general concerning the Lelantine War, see Parker 1997 with earlier bibliography.

20 Mazarakis Ainian 2002b: 166–8, 174. On the other hand, at Xeropolis-Lefkandi, intramural burials are not encountered. Child burials are included in the known cemeteries of the PG and SPG periods, while two LG child burials were recently uncovered outside the settlement, suggesting that there was a reserved burial ground for children during this period (Lemos 2007).

21 On Naxos, see Lambrinoudakis and Gruben 1985/7; 1987; Lambrinoudakis 1991; 2001; 2004; 2005. In general, see Mazarakis Ainian 1997.

22 Cambitoglou 1971; 1988; Morris 1998a: 28–9; Nevett 1999: 158–60; Coucouzeli 2004.

23 So at Lefkandi-Toumba (Coulton 1993; Mazarakis Ainian 1997: 48–58), Viglatouri (Sapouna-Sakellaraki 1998), Eretria (area of sanctuary of Apollo: Mazarakis Ainian 1987: 20–1; 1997: 60–1), Oropos (Building Θ: Mazarakis Ainian 1998c; 2002a; 2002b;

2004b), Zagora (Unit H19, etc.: Cambitoglou 1971: 18–19, 30–1; 1988: 79–106; Mazarakis Ainian 1997: 171–6) and Koukounaries (Buildings A, B, C: Schilardi 1983; Mazarakis Ainian 1997: 82–3, 183–4).

24 Fagerström 1988, 72 has suggested that Vathy Limenari at Donousa may have been a pirates' nest. On the contrary, Ay. Andreas is sometimes identified with Minoa mentioned in the sources (Televantou 2005).

25 According to a recent opinion, not unanimously accepted, the edifice is considered as "an unfinished longhouse, a type of dwelling characteristic of stateless, small-scale, kinship-based societies" (Coucouzeli 2004).

26 For other theories, see Calligas 1988; Crielaard and Driessen 1994; Mazarakis Ainian 1997: 48–57; Coucouzeli 1999; Morris 2000: 195–256.

27 Lefkandi: Calligas 1984/5. Chalcis: Calligas 1988/9: 94.

28 According to Morris, the Greek concept of the hero would have taken shape at Lefkandi, since he is of the opinion that the deceased warrior was honored like a hero, even if traces of subsequent worship are invisible to us. The new elites of the tenth century defined themselves through such cults (Morris 2000: 237).

29 At Grotta (Lambrinoudakis 1988), Paros (Zapheiropoulou 1999), Minoa (Marangou 2002: 207–24). In general on EIA hero cults, see Mazarakis Ainian 2004b, with bibliography.

30 Mazarakis Ainian 1997; for a complete list of cult places an temples in the Cyclades, see Gounaris 2005a.

31 For example, the treasury of the Siphnians dedicated at Delphi, ca. 525 (Pausanias 10.11.2), and the sphinx of the Naxians at Delphi.

32 See more recently the impressive Gorgon found in Paros (Zapheiropoulou 2000b), presumably, according to Ohnesorg (2005, 143) representing a corner acroterion of an unidentified temple.

33 On archaic Paros, see Berranger 1992. Naxos: Costa 1997.

34 On the so-called "Melian" workshop, see Zapheiropoulou 1985; 2003.

35 At Melanes, Yria, Palatia, Sangri: Lambrinoudakis 1991; 1992; 2001; 2004; 2005; Lambrinoudakis and Gruben 1985/7; 1987.

36 Siphnos: Brock and Mackworth Young 1949; Yria: Simantoni-Bournia 2001/2; Naxos: Kontoleon and Karouzos 1937; Kontoleon 1939; Thera: Sigalas 2000.

37 Concerning the unusual temple-*hestiatorion* of the sixth century there see Televantou 1993; 1996; 1998; 1999; 2004.

38 Herodotus (3.57) mentions also an Agora and Prytaneion of marble on Siphnos.

39 See the literary sources in ch. 10, n. 24.

40 Boardman 1980: 23–34; Hueber 1997: 28–33.

41 Mazarakis 1997: 205. See also Cook and Nicholls 1998.

42 Akurgal 1983; Mazarakis 1997: 248.

43 Compare similar rites known from the sanctuary of Artemis Brauronia in Attica where the sacred hunt also played a major role: Reeder 1995: 321–7. Karakasi 2003: 50.

44 See Sørensen 2002, contra Kinch 1914; Melander 1988.

45 Bammer and Muss 1996: 33–8; Gruben 2001: 380–90.

46 The temple was sponsored by Croesus according to the dedicatory inscription on the torus of its columns, and Herodotus 1.92.

47 Note also, at Klopedi on Lesbos, two archaic temples dedicated to Apollo Napaios: Spencer 1995: 24 n. 111; Aeolic column capitals from the region are stored in Lesbos Archaeological Museum at Mytilene.

48   Walter-Karydi 1985; Karakasi 2003: 28–30. pl. 29. For the Cheramyes *korai*, see Karakasi
     2003, pls. 4–9. On the Greek banquet, see recently Schmitt-Pantel and Lissarague et al.
     2005: esp. 243 n. 166 (Geneleos group).
49   Rocco 1996; Livadiotti and Rocco 1999.
50   Mustilli 1932/3; Graham 2002: 255; Cultraro 2004.
51   Beschi 1998; Mazarakis 1997: 197.
52   Lehmann and Spittle 1982: 267–9, fig. 22; Graham 2002.
53   Graham 2002; Matsas 2004.
54   Note the agora at Stageira, houses at Argilos, and the temple in Sane: Winter 1999.

CHAPTER TWELVE

Laconia and Messenia

Nigel Kennell and Nino Luraghi

The Archaeology of Laconia

South of the Argive and Tegean territories lies Laconia, which comprises all of the south-east Peloponnese. The Spartans dwelt in the relatively central Eurotas valley between the breathtaking Taygetus range to the west and the less dramatic but still formidable ramparts of Parnon in the east. They lived in a cluster of hilltop communities ringing the end of a low, broken spur of Taygetus thrusting down into the valley from the north, situated in an area enclosed eastwards by the Eurotas, one of the few Greek rivers not to dry up in the summer, on the south and south-west by the course of a tributary known today as the Magoulitsa, and on the north by the modern Mousga.

Sparta and Laconia are a problem. However legitimate the traditional picture of Sparta's history and customs that has been handed down by writers such as Xenophon, Plato, and Plutarch, there is no other Greek state where the coordination of literary and archaeological evidence is so fraught with difficulties, controversies, and down-right contradictions. Ever since excavations of the sanctuary of Artemis Orthia in the early years of the last century brought to light signs of a lavish lifestyle among the archaic elite that simply did not jibe with the austere, boot-camp society of the literary sources, historians and archaeologists have been struggling to readjust their ideas to accommodate the artifactual reality (Förtsch 2001). This ongoing reassessment is hampered by two peculiarly Laconian obstacles – the almost total absence of native informants in the guise of Spartan, or even Laconian, writers from any period of the city's ancient history and the surprisingly thin record of excavation in the region.

For Sparta itself, the reason is obvious. The modern city, founded soon after the end of the Greek War of Independence, is built right on top of the ancient city, whose massive redevelopment in the Roman period had evidently obliterated most of the classical and earlier structures. But outside the urban area, major sanctuary sites such as the shrine of Apollo Hyperteleates near the town of Molaoi, the admittedly rather remote temple of Poseidon Taenarius, and even the Amyklaion, sacred to Apollo and located only a few kilometers south of Sparta near a main road, remain largely unexcavated, while town sites in Laconia have hardly been explored at all. The shelves of Sparta's archaeological storerooms groan under masses of understudied pottery and other artifacts from rescue excavations (despite efforts by the local archaeologists to interest specialists in examining them systematically) that could add significantly to our understanding of the processes at play in Sparta and Laconia during the archaic and classical periods. The recent Anglo-Dutch survey[1] of a swath of land north-east of Sparta has, as we shall see, provided information about long-term processes of settlement, exploitation, and recurring abandonment of land that will have to be incorporated into any future history of Sparta, but the archaeological story of Laconia still remains largely untold.

Given the scarcity of material evidence that can uncontroversially be held to illuminate any aspect of the traditional view of Spartan society – *syssitia*, "*agoge*," *homoioi*, etc. – in what follows we avoid attempting to coordinate the archaeological with the literary evidence on that subject. A recent paper shows the pitfalls of using Roman-era texts to elucidate archaic and classical material evidence (Stibbe 2002). By focusing on the archaeology of Laconia, we can expect an internally consistent picture to emerge, which will prompt further investigation in the field as well as renewed interpretation of the artifacts already recovered.

Questions of urban development do not really apply to archaic and classical Sparta, as what we would recognize as urbanization in a tangible sense did not take place until the hellenistic period, when the area of the city's four constituent communities – Limnae, Cynosoures, Pitane, and Mesoa – finally received a wall. It has even been doubted that "acropolis" is an appropriate term before then for the hill upon which the temple of Athena Chalkioikos stood. Until the later third century, Sparta's settlements were distinct from one another, separated by extensive unbuilt areas. Like people all over Greece, the inhabitants of each community (*oba*) buried their dead on the outskirts of their villages in order to keep the worlds of the living and the dead separate. After the enclosure of the city, Spartans continued for a while to bury their dead in the same places, giving rise to the misconception that, in exception to the Greek norm, they had always buried their dead within the city's walls (Kourinou 2000: 90, 217).

The first area to be occupied was that of the *oba* Limnae, between the Eurotas and Toumpano, the easternmost hill of the acropolis heights, where the greatest concentrations of Protogeometric and Geometric artifacts have been found. Here, dug into virgin soil and beneath rich Protogeometric layers, were very simple Early Iron Age graves so early in date that they were originally thought to be from the Bronze Age (Raphtopoulou 1996/7: 272–3). Excavations in this area have continued to uncover similar burials from the first centuries of settlement at Sparta. Grave goods are not on the whole plentiful, though small objects of bronze or iron are sometimes found (Themos, Zavvou et al. 1997: 162–3).

Relative to the rest of Sparta, Limnae has long been particularly fruitful archaeologically. The sanctuary of Artemis Orthia, the best-known site in the city, has produced a wealth of material (Dawkins 1929). Several deposits and terracotta plaques of a kind peculiar to Laconia were also discovered in the area, along with a building taken to be a heroon.[2] Perhaps the best-known single artifact from this part of the city is a partially preserved stone "hero" relief from the late sixth century bearing a fragmentary inscription that can be restored to produce the name of Chilon, the famous Spartan sage and ephor (Wace 1937).

Another potential hero shrine has recently been found a little to the north of the graves just mentioned. A votive pit was excavated in 1996 containing many artifacts, among hundreds of terracotta dedicatory relief plaques and large numbers of miniature lead votives. In a nearby room, underneath a layer of classical and hellenistic pottery, were very many votives and a mound of stones with an almost circular opening in the top. Under this opening a stone slab covered remains of a person wearing a bronze ring on the right hand, while between the slab and the mound's opening was found a large quantity of Geometric pottery. The complex underwent at least two building phases; on its east, it faced a road running north-south.[3] Full publication of the material from this important site, including an inscribed relief mentioned in the preliminary report, should shed valuable new light on Spartan burial practices and veneration for their honored dead, especially as the mound of stones here resembles the "tumulus" upon which the well-known Chrysapha relief was found over a century ago.

The most important Laconian shrine of Artemis was located on the west bank of the Eurotas river on the eastern edge of Limnae. Probably founded in the ninth century, by the end of the eighth the site boasted an altar and temple inside a paved, enclosed cult area. Between 570 and 560 a massive flood may have devastated the sanctuary, causing a new altar and stone temple to be built on top of a layer of river sand spread over the site.[4] The sanctuary is characterized by finds of terracotta masks representing a variety of types, from handsome youths to wrinkled old women and grotesque monsters, and by a staggering quantity of small lead votives (figures 12.1 and 12.2). These lead votives are typical of shrines elsewhere in Laconia; they have been found in significant numbers not only here, but also at several other sites including the Menelaion and the perioecic shrine at Aigies (Bonias 1998: 103). A few came to light during the excavations at the sanctuary of Zeus Messapeus, north-east of the city (Catling 2002: 75), and several hundred appeared on the acropolis near the temple of Athena Chalkioikos. However, these numbers pale into insignificance compared with the 100,773 lead votives dedicated to Artemis Orthia.[5] Ranging in date from the seventh to the end of the sixth century, with the bulk from after the renovation of the sanctuary, the moldmade votives depict divinities, *daimones* of various sorts, winged female figures, dancers, musicians, warriors, and objects such as wool-carding implements and wreaths, of which there is an especially large number. Particularly important are images of stags, an attribute of Artemis, that replace earlier images of horses after 570–560 (Boss 2000: 153). All these votives were found, here and elsewhere, mixed in with bone-and-ash debris from sacrifices but showed no signs of contact with heat, indicating that they were placed on the altars or tossed onto the ground nearby when sacrifices were not occurring. According to one calculation, an average of 650 lead votives was deposited annually at the Orthia sanctuary alone, so we should imagine a steady stream of devotees visiting the altar throughout

Figure 12.1   Masks from Artemis Orthia sanctuary
Source: Dawkins (1929: pl. 47).

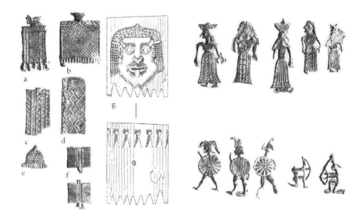

Figure 12.2   Votives from Artemis Orthia sanctuary. Left: lead models of textiles (a–d), a hat (e), and weaving combs (f); a bone weaving comb (g). Right: lead figurines of ornately dressed women (top) and warriors and archers (bottom)
Source: Dawkins (1929: pls. 181, 183).

the year. The votives, it used to be thought, were merely cheap substitutes for more expensive dedications, but a better explanation rests on the special properties of lead, which was used in antiquity as the medium for magical incantations such as curses. They probably functioned much like the metal votives (*tamata*) found in Greek Orthodox churches today (Boss 2000: 195–8). The source of lead has been identified as Laurion in Attica, a proposal which invites interesting speculations about trade in luxury goods between Athens and Sparta in the late archaic period (Vickers and Gill 2002). But the methodology used to assign metal artifacts to specific ore sources has lately been questioned (Budd, Pollard et al. 1995: 74), so the Attic origin of the material for these characteristic Laconian dedications must remain only a possibility.

The masks, on the other hand, remain quite mysterious, although they evidently played a significant role in sixth-century cultic activity at the site. Depicting perhaps various characters in a sort of sacred play, the surviving clay examples cannot have actually been worn by participants, because several are smaller than life-size and many lack holes for the attachment of string or strips of leather to fasten the mask onto a participant's head. Perhaps the working masks were of wood, like the elaborate ceremonial masks of the Haida and Kwakiutl peoples of British Columbia.

On a hill near the settlement of Amyclae, approximately two hours walk south of Sparta, stood the pre-eminent Apolline sanctuary in Laconia. In the later sixth century, the god received at the Amyklaion one of his more unusual offerings, a massive statue seated on or standing in the midst of a gigantic throne, the work of the Ionian artist Bathycles. The towering bronze statue of an armed Apollo must have been visible from nearly everywhere in the Eurotas valley, and so much figured decoration covered the god's elaborate throne that the Roman-era periegete Pausanias devoted several paragraphs to a detailed description (3.18.9–19.5). All now, of course, is lost. Sporadic excavations on the hill in the first half of the last century revealed a few archaic architectural members and a retaining wall from the same period, but nothing came to light of the Throne of Apollo or of the grave of the pre-Greek divinity Hyacinthus located underneath (Faustoferri 1996).

Despite the lack of spectacular finds, the Amyklaion is a site of prime importance for the history of Laconia and of Greece as a whole after the end of the Bronze Age, since it was a locus for cult for both Mycenaean and Iron-Age Laconians. Pottery found by a retaining wall seems to show a break in its sequence between the very end of the Bronze Age in the twelfth century and the beginning of the local style of Iron Age pottery usually dated no earlier than 950. Accounting for this break or bridging it has implications for the historicity of Greek stories about the return of the sons of Heracles to the Peloponnesus to claim their patrimony sometime after the Trojan War, which many modern researchers identified as invasions by speakers of the Dorian dialect who violently brought an end to Mycenaean civilization. As usual for a site in Laconia the situation is complicated, this time by the nature of the depositional record. Instead of a clear stratigraphy resulting from levels of occupation debris such as are found in settlements, no proper layers of pottery exist at the Amyklaion for the crucial period.

The surviving fragments were found in a layer of clay, one meter deep, with Geometric pottery at the top, Mycenaean ware at the bottom, and Protogeometric sherds in between, among which were a very few pieces of Mycenaean artifacts as well as later bronzes (Cartledge 1979: 81–2). Due to the deposit's nature, we cannot simply assume that the Mycenaean and Protogeometric sherds come from objects that were on display in the sanctuary at the same time. Adding to the problem is the gap of well over a century between the two styles. Their decoration is strikingly different, with the fluid lines of the Mycenaean replaced by cross-hatched full- and half-diamond shapes on pots mostly glazed black, often with incised grooves and an unmistakable metallic sheen. On the other hand, several of the shapes Laconian potters threw in the early Iron Age were closely related to those used by their Bronze Age predecessors,[6] perhaps implying some continuity. Finds from elsewhere in Laconia, notably a vessel found on the Malea peninsula which undoubtedly continues a shape known from the middle of the Mycenaean period (Coulson 1988: 21, 23), and further afield in the Peloponnese, a Laconian Protogeometric sherd discovered at Asine on the Argolid in the earliest Iron Age occupation layer dating to the eleventh century (Wells 1983: 42), while intriguing, are by themselves insufficient evidence for a continuous ceramic tradition at Amyclae from the Bronze Age to the tenth century (Coulson 1988: 23, n. 13). We are left then with evidence that can support two opposing viewpoints: that the discontinuity is best explained as resulting from an influx of newcomers from the north-west – the Dorians;[7] or that the hints of a stylistic connection between the Mycenaean and Iron Ages, when placed in a wider context, are enough to consign those same Dorians to the scrapheap of history (Hall 1997: 114–28). However, now that excavations may start again, we can hope that new evidence will soon help unravel this particularly knotty problem (Eder 1998: 97–9).

Beyond the Spartan plain, excavations on the acropolis of Geronthrae (mod. Geraki), 26 km to the south-east, are at present the only systematic archaeological investigation to be undertaken at a perioecic town site. The picture that is emerging conforms to what has been reconstructed for the rest of Laconia. The site shows no signs of habitation for many years from the Middle Helladic period to the Early Iron Age, with a few Protogeometric and Geometric sherds washed down from the top of the hill indicating a resumption of human activity in the area. A tentatively identified late archaic or classical wall built on top of leveled remains from the Early Bronze Age further attests to the dramatic discontinuity characterizing the Laconian archaeological record.[8] Architectural fragments and a votive deposit suggest the existence of the expected sanctuary in the archaic period, but unfortunately large-scale redevelopment in the later classical and hellenistic periods caused the removal of many earlier remains (Crouwel, Prent et al. 1997: 71–2). Apart from a temple to Apollo with an ivory cult statue that burned down before Pausanias visited in the second century CE (3.22.7), there may also have been a cult building dedicated to the major Laconian deities, the Dioscuri.[9] Despite the wholesale destruction of earlier remains, an anvil uncovered during 2003 in a classical context associated with some tentatively identified pieces of iron slag, either from smelting or reworking metal, may for the first time provide some evidence for industrial activity among the *perioikoi* (M. Prent, personal comment).

One other full-scale excavation of a perioecic site has been undertaken recently, at a rural sanctuary near the ancient city of Aegiae, a short distance north-west of Sparta's port, Gytheum. The earlier cult building on the site, from the middle of the seventh century, is the only such apsidal structure found in Laconia so far. The presence of votive pits (*bothroi*) and lack of evidence for burnt sacrifice suggest that the object of devotion at this stage was a hero. The first quarter of the sixth century saw this building converted into a temple-like construction, possibly in the Doric order, with terracotta architectural adornment. Within the temple were found fragments of a booted *kouros* statue from 540–520 and pieces of an early classical seated female figure of such size and quality that the excavator identified it as the cult statue of a female deity, probably Artemis.[10] The dedications, ranging mostly from the mid-seventh century to the early fifth, tend to bear out this interpretation: they include an early Mistress of Animals figurine and statuette groups of a female flanked by smaller figures recalling the so-called Eileithyia statuette found at the sanctuary of Artemis Orthia (Bonias 1998: 83). In addition to the ubiquitous miniature lead votives, there are seated children of the "temple boy" type, female busts, the earliest of which is a late daedalic example from ca. 620, women mounted sidesaddle using *astrabai* (a type known from many Peloponnesian sites), as well as some articulated "doll" torsos (possibly children's toys), a few articles of jewelry – dedications pointing to a predominantly female-oriented cult. Somewhat different from these sorts of votive offerings were a strigil and a jumping weight (*halter*) dedicated by Tachistolaos ("Swiftest of the people") to Timagenes, the hero who shared worship at the site with the deity.[11] It has been suggested that Tachistolaos had won his victory in the Olympic games but he is just as likely to have been successful in local games similar to those catalogued in the famous Damonon inscription (*IG* V.1 213).

North-east of Sparta, the state sanctuary of Zeus Messapeus at Tsakona was in use continuously from the late eighth or early seventh century to the second century, followed by a revival of activity approximately three centuries later in the Roman period. In contrast to the Aegiae shrine, masculine sexuality seems to have been the cult's main concern, since eighty percent of the hundreds of handmade terracotta figurines found on the site represent crouching males grasping their erect phalluses. A much smaller number of female figurines, some displaying their genitalia, others pregnant or giving birth, may attest to a certain level of female involvement. Fragments of a stone *halter* and a bronze spearhead, perhaps from the javelin competition of the pentathlon, also indicate a connection with athletic victory (Catling 2002: 73–80, 90). The most intriguing artifacts, though, are six small rectangular rods, each bent at one end and hammered flat at the other to form a sort of blade. The excavator identifies these instruments as scalpels and, associating them with some small, spherical *aryballoi* that may have served as receptacles for a bodily fluid such as blood, proposes that ritual circumcision may have been performed here, a suggestion he rightly expects "to find little favour."[12] Whatever the ritual activity here, Zeus Messapeus was evidently connected with male maturation rituals, as was Artemis Orthia, at whose shrine were found similar figurines but in quite different proportions (Catling 2002: 90).

Regarding the history of settlement in Laconia as a whole, the results of the Anglo-Dutch Laconia Survey for the first time afford researchers some firm data with which to work. This survey, which covered an area of approximately seventy square kilometers, ranging from the eastern bank of the Eurotas river near Sparta at its southern end to the village of Palaiogoulas (probably ancient Sellasia) at its northeastern, has produced a surprising picture of settlement in the archaic period (figure 12.3). The Iron Age saw Laconians confined to the Eurotas valley itself, clustered together in a very few, highly nucleated, discrete settlements, each situated some distance from its neighbors – a pattern found in most of Greece at the time. However, when other Greek settlements began to spread out over the empty spaces between settlements after the middle of the eighth century due probably to a population increase (Morris 1998a: 16), Laconian villages remained static within the bounds established in the

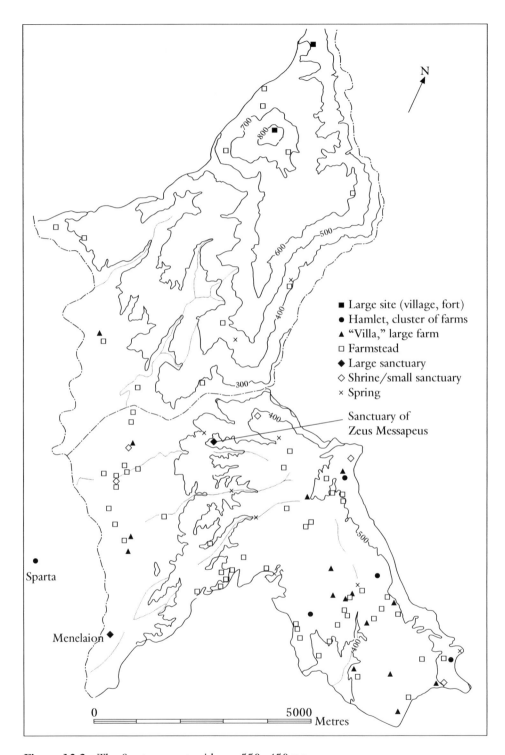

Figure 12.3   The Spartan countryside, ca 550–450 BC

previous centuries. Not even from the next century, when Sparta is supposed to have embarked on the grueling, but ultimately successful conquest of the rich lands of Messenia, were there signs of an expansion to make full use of the agricultural potential of the Eurotas and the lands to the north-east.

Compared to the rest of Greece, then, archaic Sparta and Laconia were unique. They were not completely isolated from other panhellenic trends, however, since the foundations of extra-urban cult sites such as the Menelaion and the northern sanctuary of Zeus Messapeus can be traced back to the end of the eighth century, while the wealth and cosmopolitan taste of Spartan aristocrats at this time is evident in the sophisticated Laconian pottery they used and the orientalizing ivory dedications they made at Artemis Orthia and elsewhere. Nonetheless, outside the few areas of habitation, seventh-century Laconia was essentially an empty land, with later perioecic towns such as Gytheum, Asopus, and Epidaurus Limera not yet in existence. The dam finally burst in the sixth century, when, within the astonishingly short space of only about fifty years, this wilderness was transformed into a landscape of farms, villages, and small towns. Interestingly, the survey evidence tends to indicate that the one perioecic town within its area, Sellasia, may have been founded at this time, as there is no evidence for prior habitation. One factor in the rapid development of north-east Laconia, apart from simple land hunger, may have been Sparta's wresting control of the disputed northern borderlands from Argos at about this time (Cartledge 1979: 140–2). Whether or not a large slice of eastern Laconia from the Thyreatis to Cape Malea in the south remained under Argive control until the Battle of the Champions ca. 545 (Herodotus 1.82.1), the archaeological evidence, such as it is, from various sites in the Parnon range and on the eastern seaboard is remarkably consistent with that of the survey area: the earliest securely datable artifacts cluster around the second half of the sixth century (Cavanagh, Crouwel et al. 1996: 269, 277–312). Something dramatic definitely happened then, perhaps linked with the great increase in conspicuous consumption by the Spartan elite already noted around that time.

What the surveyors did not find also raises some challenging questions. In the entire region investigated, only one settlement, Sellasia, located north of Sparta, was just large enough to support specialist artisans, such as metalworkers and potters, to manufacture the commodities needed by farmers, let alone the high-grade weapons used by Spartiate warriors. Where, then, were these products made? In Sparta itself is one suggestion.[13] Although this flies in the face of the traditional view that production and commerce were the province solely of the *perioikoi*, who are supposed to have lived outside the Spartan territory proper, some archaeological clues point to the existence of industry within the city.[14] That larger perioecic communities did possess some forms of industrial production is now established by the classical anvil found at Geronthrae, but it is still far from clear how such activities were distributed through the Laconian landscape.

Even more surprising is the lack of reliable early evidence for small settlements in the plain around the city (Cavanagh, Crouwel et al. 2002: 232–4). Although hamlets, farmsteads, and villas were scattered throughout the area in the fifth century, the lands outside Sparta and Amyclae were devoid of human habitation before the great wave of Spartan expansion in the sixth century. The situation is mysterious, to say the least, because these fields in the Spartan heartland are supposed to have been worked by helots, whose labor allowed the Spartiates to devote themselves to training up for war. Conventionally thought of in antiquity as the oppressed descendants of the conquered original inhabitants of Laconia, helots as a social class are held today to have existed since the early years of the Spartan state.[15] In the fifth century, the helots probably lived in small settlements, some close to Sparta, as they quickly massed to attempt a raid on the city after the violent earthquake of ca. 465 (Plut. *Cim.* 16.6–7). But the situation earlier must have been quite different, since no dwelling places of any kind existed outside the centers of Sparta and Amyclae. This raises the intriguing question of where the helots lived during the seventh and early sixth centuries. One answer might be that the lands were farmed from Sparta itself (Cavanagh, Crouwel et al. 2002: 232), but that would have entailed substantial numbers of helots barracked among Spartiates in the city. Another might be that the lack of evidence for habitation in the survey area is simply a matter of chance, a proposition which would no doubt be rejected by the surveyors themselves, who emphasize that, within the limits of our knowledge, nothing suggests that the results from the survey area are unrepresentative of the region as a whole (2002: 156).

The success of the Sparta Survey can be gauged by the unexpected questions it provokes, many of which can be answered only by the spade. Since Sparta itself seems unlikely to yield any more sites of the importance of Artemis Orthia to students of archaic and classical Greece, then archaeologists' attention should shift to the settlements and sanctuaries liberally scattered over the Laconian landscape. With time and patience, our ignorance of the lifestyles of *perioikoi* and helots might not be quite so absolute, and our understanding of their evolving relationships with the Spartiates somewhat less dependent on tendentious foreign sources.

The Archaeology of Messenia

The south-western part of the Peloponnese was known at least since the hellenistic age as Messenia. To the east, the Taygetos chain, whose southernmost part forms the Mani peninsula, separates it from Laconia. To the north, the deep valley of the River Neda marks its border towards Triphylia and Arkadia. The only easy access to the region is from southern Arkadia, over the Derveni Pass, crossed by the modern road from Megalopolis to Kalamata. Messenia is divided in two main areas, the valley of the River Pamisos, the most rich and fertile portion, and the western coastal region, separated from each other by a line of mountains culminating in Mount Aigaleos to the north and Mount Maglavas and Mount Lykodimos to the south, and ending in the Akritas Peninsula. The upper Pamisos Valley, called Stenyklaros in antiquity, is separated from the lower valley, the ancient Makaria, by a row of hills immediately to the east of Mount Ithome. To the north, a narrow plain connects the north-western harbor town of Kyparissia and its coastal plain to Stenyklaros, opening up along the way in the Soulima Valley, the third most important plain of Messenia.

The modern traveler going from Sparta to Kalamata cannot but be impressed by their surprising proximity: with modern means of transportation, Kalamata is in fact closer to Sparta than Gytheion – or put the other way around, in Laconia, Sparta is the closest point to Messenia. Of course, in antiquity crossing the steep passes over the Taygetos was much more troublesome than it is today, but an archaic or classical road that connected Sparta to Kalamata by the shortest way, the Langada pass, has recently been identified (Pikoulas 1991). Adding that the Pamisos valley is probably the richest agricultural area of the Peloponnese, it is fair to say that geographical conditions explain much of the history of Messenia during the archaic age.

Judging by the number of sites, Bronze Age Messenia must have been one of the most prosperous and densely populated parts of the Greek world. Its main center lay in the western coastal region, where the palace of Pylos controlled a network of minor settlements that in due course probably came to embrace almost the whole of later Messenia. The second most important settlement of the region seems to have been located not far from the Gulf of Messenia, on a hill to the east of the river Pamisos, the site of the later town of Thuria. During the Mycenaean Age, this place may have been called Leuktron and functioned as capital of the eastern province of the kingdom of Pylos (Davis 1998). In general terms, the western part of the region seems to have been more densely populated than the Pamisos Valley, especially than the Stenyklaros plain, where there are hardly any Bronze Age sites.

All this prosperity disappeared at the end of the Bronze Age, and Iron Age Messenia offers the usual desolated landscape (Eder 1998). The small settlement on the hill of Nichoria, overlooking the western corner of the Gulf of Messenia, has been the focus of sustained archaeological investigation and is one of the best-known Dark Age settlements anywhere in the Greek world (McDonald, Coulson et al. 1983). Originally a thriving Bronze Age village, with streets and stone-built drains, after being deserted for about a century Nichoria was settled by a small group of people around the second quarter of the eleventh century. At its peak, between the tenth and ninth centuries, Iron Age Nichoria was home to perhaps forty families or some 200 people, whose apsidal houses clustered around a similar but larger building, over ten meters long, clearly the home of some sort of chief or leader, that seems to have functioned as a focus for the religious life of the community, too (Thomas and Conant 1999). But the eighth century was a period of decline, both in terms of size of the settlement and of contacts with other regions, culminating in the destruction and abandonment of the site around the middle of the century. The site was not reoccupied in antiquity.

If the archaeological record of Messenia in the Late Geometric and Early Archaic period is untypical in any way, it is probably in its failure to emerge in a sustained way from this situation of stagnation. While elsewhere in Greece larger settlements or sanctuaries start to appear, eighth-century Messenia has nothing really noteworthy to offer. This may be to some extent a misleading impression, resulting from the convergence of two factors that influence in a negative way our understanding of the history and archaeology of archaic Messenia. The first is the predominance of the Bronze Age which has by and large set the agenda for research in the region, resulting for instance in most attention being devoted to the area around Pylos, which was clearly not very important in the later history of Messenia. The second negative factor is lack of information from written sources that might guide the search for important sites of early archaic date. However, it is probably correct to say that the current state of the evidence for the archaic age in Messenia cannot be purely a consequence of the combined effect of these two factors. The meager archaeological record of archaic Messenia is perhaps the most visible consequence of its history, that is, of the fact that throughout the period the real political center of the region was in fact across the Taygetos. In all likelihood, Spartan domination also accounts for an important long-term transformation in the distribution of settlements in Messenia. While in the Dark Age the concentration of settlements remained highest in the western part of the region, especially on the Navarino plateau, with the archaic age human presence in Messenia becomes stronger in the Pamisos Valley and around the Gulf of Messenia, assuming the shape that it will preserve for the rest of antiquity (Eder 1998: 178).

Apart from this, it is fair to say that, while the Spartan conquest must have been the main event in the archaic history of Messenia, it has left no unequivocal traces on the ground. Nichoria was apparently destroyed by fire and abandoned around the mid-eighth century, which most scholars would say is too early for a connection with the Spartan conquest to be suggested. Probably the Spartan conquest of Messenia should not be envisioned as the result of one war, as the ancient sources depict it, but rather as a longer and more complex process, that included, beside outright military conquest of some parts of the region, other sorts of episodes, such as some smaller, village-like communities being absorbed into the orbit of Sparta very much like *perioikoi* of Laconia also may have been, or the foundation of new settlements by Spartan initiative, perhaps by relocating population from other parts of the Peloponnese, including Laconia. The perioikic town of Asine, on the western coast of the Gulf of Messenia, allegedly populated by exiles who had left Asine in the Argolis at the time of the Argive conquest, may be a case in point.

Archaeological evidence for archaic Messenia comes mostly from a handful of sanctuaries, often through stray finds or rescue excavations (Luraghi 2008: 117–32). At least three locations have produced finds dating to the first half of the eighth century and continuing through the archaic period. One of them was located in a place called Lakathela, on the hills south of the corridor that links the Pamisos Valley with the Gulf of Kyparissia, not far from the medieval castle of Mila and the Bronze Age acropolis of Malthi (Karagiorga 1972). Small bronze and clay figurines of animals seem to go back to the second quarter of the eighth century. The sanctuary acquired monumental appearance later in the archaic age, when a 28-m-long *stoa* was built, together with a rather puzzling circular building. The complex was destroyed and abandoned in the early decades of the fifth century, possibly in connection with the revolt in Messenia in the 460s. The finds speak strongly in favor of a sanctuary, but there is no way to tell which deity was worshipped in it.

Late Geometric materials have been found also in a place that was destined to have a great symbolic meaning in the history of Messenia. The site is known in scholarship as Volimos or Volimnos, and is marked today by a small chapel dedicated to the Panayia Volimiotissa, high up in the mountains north-east of Kalamata, probably on or close to the ancient itinerary across the Langada Pass (Luraghi 2008: 123–4). In antiquity, the sanctuary of Artemis Limnatis stood here, the alleged theatre of the episode that ignited the First Messenian War and a bone of contention between Messenians and Spartans ever since the Messenian independence in 369. Although the site has been visited by scholars many times from the nineteenth century onwards, no excavation has ever taken place, and all the information we have derives from inscriptions of the imperial age built into the walls of the chapel and stray finds. One of the latter, a bronze mirror dedicated to Limnatis and tentatively dated to the second quarter of the fifth century,[16] confirms that this goddess was worshipped here already before the liberation of Messenia. The name "Limnatis" probably means "the goddess of Limnai," that is, Artemis Orthia. The earliest votives date back to the mid-eighth century (Luraghi 2008: 114), but they have no specific link with Artemis, so it is not possible to say with certainty how old the cult really was.

Sherds and bronze votives suggest an early eighth-century date for the sanctuary of Poseidon at Akovitika, not far from the coast and the mouth of the river Pamisos (Luraghi 2008: 121–3). Most likely, the sanctuary belonged to Thuria and was the place where the festival of Poseidon mentioned in the Damonon inscription (*IG* V.1, 213.18–23) was held. A rescue excavation conducted at the site brought to light a peristyle dating to the sixth century, partially built with spoils from an earlier building. There is no doubt that more buildings remain to be uncovered.

The only two archaic sanctuaries that have been object of regular, if short, excavation campaigns are the sanctuary of Apollo Korythos at Ayios Andreas, on the western side of the Gulf of Messenia, between Asine and Corone, not far from the coast, and the sanctuary of the river god Pamisos at Ayios Floros, north of Thuria. The architectural history of the sanctuary of Apollo Korythos is rather unclear.[17] Votives seem to go back to the seventh century and are, for archaic Messenia, unusually rich, including three archaic or early classical inscriptions. The bronze statuette of a hoplite with a very elaborate armor and plates covering his arms and thighs is a frequently met icon in books on ancient Sparta (Cartledge 2002: pl. 11). The relative abundance of weapons among the offerings suggests that Apollo was worshipped here especially in his warlike aspect. The most striking find from the site is a large marble Doric capital, certainly votive and datable to the mid sixth century, with a very elaborate decoration under the echinus (Barletta 1990: 51). Very close parallels for this exquisite piece are to be found among the architectural remains of the throne of Amyklai and in a capital of unknown provenance reused in a church near Sparta.

In the sanctuary of Pamisos votives go back to the first half of the seventh century and include pottery, mostly miniaturistic, bronze figurines of animals and a few statuettes (Valmin 1938). In all likelihood, the archaic statuette of a warrior hurling a spear, carrying a dedication by Pythodoros to the god Pamisos, now in the Princeton University Art Museum, came from this site, but it surfaced on the antiquities market without a provenance record.[18]

Finally, much to scholars' surprise, abundant votives referring to at least two sanctuaries that date back to the mid seventh century have been found during excavations on the site of Messene, the city founded by Epaminondas in 369. Soundings in the courtyard of the hellenistic temple of Asclepios and the excavation of a small sanctuary west of the square stoa that surrounds the temple have brought to light a respectable amount of remains of archaic date (Luraghi 2008: 124–7). Apart from pottery about which very little is known, the votives consist of terracotta plaques similar to those found in sanctuaries at Sparta and in Laconia, including a group of three figures sitting on a bench, two of which, dressed, flank and support a third one, female and naked, who raises her hands to her head in a gesture of mourning. Very close parallels come from Amyklai, from Aigies, and from the votive deposit of the Dimiova cave, near Kalamata.[19] The same iconography is displayed also by a group worked in the round (Papaephthimiou 2001/2). A few fragments of large terracotta relief plaques, of remarkable quality and characteristically Laconian style, go back to the sixth century. The architectural history of the area during the archaic age is unclear, but a fragment of a Laconian terracotta acroterion testifies to the presence of at least one sacred building (Themelis 1994: 150). Which deities were worshipped here is not easy to tell. A kourotrophic goddess such as Artemis or Eileithyia is a very likely candidate.

The economic and social level displayed by these assemblages, and comparison with sanctuaries from Laconia, suggest to see in the sites just listed the sanctuaries of the *perioikoi* of Messenia. Except for the obviously local river-god Pamisus, they show a remarkable homogeneity with cults of *perioikoi* in Laconia (Parker 1989: 145). The same homogeneity is revealed by the style of the objects found in these sanctuaries, which regularly find close parallels in Laconia and often nowhere else. There is no real trace of a distinct material culture of archaic Messenia – a conclusion confirmed by all other finds from the region. If we compare this situation with the Dark Age, it seems appropriate to speak of a thorough cultural Laconization of Messenia. Signs of continuity in sanctuaries and settlements however are a warning against assuming widespread immigration from Laconia. What we see is Messenia growing to be a part of the Lacedaemonian state. The presence of a probable settlement of *perioikoi* on the site of later Messene has come as a surprise to scholars: it does not perhaps call into question the notion that the Stenyklaros plain was occupied by land lots belonging to the Spartiates, but it certainly opens up a number of questions relating to the identity of Messenian *perioikoi*.

Vidal-Naquet famously observed that, so far, archaeology has not uncovered many Helots (1986: 175). However, the situation may be just beginning to change. The results of the Laconia survey, discussed above, must refer in large part to land that belonged to the Spartiates, and was therefore tilled by Helots. In Messenia, the pattern observed in the area of the Pylos Regional Archaeological Project (PRAP), characterized by the presence of very few quite large settlements and almost no evidence for isolated farmsteads, has been taken tentatively as representative of Helot settlement (Alcock 2002b). The notion that Helots in Messenia lived in large villages rather than scattered through the countryside could have interesting consequences for how we imagine their social organization and everyday life (Hodkinson 2003: 269–75). However, while it is possible that the area investigated by PRAP, south-west of Mycenaean Pylos, might have been inhabited by Helots, it must be admitted that, mildly put, this area it is not a prime candidate for the location of the Spartiates' estates. Evidence from the Stenyklaros and Soulima Valleys would carry much more weight. As it happens, two large square buildings of late archaic date, quite similar in shape and size, have been excavated in the general area of the Soulima Valley, at Kopanaki and Vasiliko. Both are multi-room complexes organized around a central courtyard, and were certainly provided with an upper floor (Luraghi 2008: 130–1). They are much larger than normal farmsteads – so much so that one of them was originally interpreted as a small fort – and may suggest a pattern of settlement and exploitation of land and workforce quite different from the one that has been reconstructed based on the results of PRAP.

Finally, a typically Messenian class of evidence remains to be addressed, offerings at Bronze Age tombs.[20] Two dozen Late Geometric vases of rather high quality, including imports from Corinth and Laconia, were found inside two chamber tombs in the Volimidia necropolis, not far from Pylos (Coulson 1988). More Late Geometric materials may come from other tombs, including ones at Kopanaki and Nichoria, but nothing coming even close, in terms of quantity and quality, to the deposition at Volimidia. During the archaic age, a thin but continuous stream of evidence includes an Orientalizing *pyxis* from one of the *tholoi* at Koukounara, the fragments of eight drinking cups, mostly Laconian and dated to the late seventh-early sixth century from Papoulia, on the plateau to the west of Mount Maglavas, fragments of an archaic amphora from Tourliditsa, sherds of a Proto-Corinthian vase from Vasiliko, a couple of small black glazed pots from Volimidia. This material has often been interpreted as evidence of a sort of cultural resistance by the Helotized Messenians against their Spartan oppressors (Alcock 2002a: 146–52).

While this interpretation suffers from the tendency to see archaic Messenia in terms of a simplified dialectic Helots-Spartiates, offerings at Bronze Age tombs may have been a way for inhabitants of Messenia, both Helots and *perioikoi*, to articulate a separate identity, which in due course evolved into the Messenian irredentism that emerged in the first half of the fifth century.

NOTES

1   Cavanagh, Crouwel et al. 2002; 1996.
2   Salapata 1992: 164; Kourinou 2000: 45–6.
3   Themos, Zavvou et al. 1996: 123–5.
4   Cartledge 1979: 357–61; Boardman 1963.
5   Wace in Dawkins 1929: 249–84.
6   Coulson 1985: 45, 52, 57, 64.
7   Cartledge 1979: 81–8; 1992.
8   Sherds: Crouwel, Prent et al. 1997: 71–2. Wall: Crouwel, Prent et al. 2002: 43.
9   Crouwel, Prent ct al. 2000: 48; 2001: 7.
10 Bonias 1998: 27–30 (hero), 30–2 (temple), 38–51 (statues).
11 Bonias 1998: 60–99, and 107–8 (Tachistolaos).
12 Catling 2002: 82, 87–9; cf Hdt. 2.104.2, 4.
13 Cavanagh, Crouwel et al. 2002: 196, 226.
14 Salapata 1992: 188; Boss 2002: 197.
15 Cartledge 1979: 97; van Wees 2003: 48–53.

16   Parlama 1973/4; *SEG* 29.395.

17   Versakis 1916; Dengate 1988.

18   Mitten and Doeringer 1967: 62–3.

19   Amyklai: Stibbe 1996: 248; Aigies: Bonias 1998: 199–200; Dimiova: Themelis 1965: 207.

20   van der Kamp 1996; Boehringer 2001.

CHAPTER THIRTEEN

The Peloponnese

Thomas Heine Nielsen and James Roy

Introduction

The Peloponnese is primarily a geographical concept, the southernmost part of the Balkan peninsula lying beyond the Isthmus of Corinth. Its topography is fragmented, and any regional solidarity seems to have emerged only under Spartan hegemony, i.e. from the late archaic period onwards (Purcell in *OCD*³ 1133). This chapter is about the Peloponnese other than Lakonia and Messenia, in other words about a geographical area which for most of the archaic period had no political or ideological unity at all. Within the area different communities varied in their evolution, as will be seen. However, the area included such obviously important archaic centres as Corinth and Argos, and lay close to other influential communities in central Greece. Contemporary trends in development penetrated the Peloponnese, and in fact reached not only Corinth and Argos but also much smaller and more obscure settlements.

Comparing how different areas of the archaic Peloponnese evolved is made more difficult by the very uneven evidence, whether literary, epigraphic, or archaeological. The progress of archaeological research has brought much new information, but some areas remain virtually unknown. One such case is the area between the rivers Alpheios and Neda (which later – around 400 – became Triphylia). It barely appears in the literary evidence. The sanctuary of Artemis at Kombothekra (Sinn 1978; 1981), already important in the archaic period, has been excavated, but we still do not know who controlled it. Some archaic material has also been found at Prasidaki near Lepreon, where the late classical temple had an archaic predecessor,[1] and at the probable sites of such classical communities as Epeion and Pyrgos.[2] Nonetheless the archaic history of the area generally is barely known, and it hardly appears in this chapter.

The uneven coverage offered by the available evidence creates obvious difficulties, for instance for anyone trying to explain how Achaea came to launch several important colonies in Magna Graecia. Nonetheless, despite the inevitable gaps, it is possible to see how different communities in the various regions of the archaic Peloponnese participated in major developments of the period, and in some cases led the way.

Regionalism and Identity

The Peloponnese is traditionally seen as made up of a number of regions – Achaea, Sicyon, Corinth, the Argolid, Laconia, Messenia, Elis (or Eleia), and Arcadia in the centre – and many Peloponnesians adopted an identity associated with their region (Nielsen 2002a: 45–88). While the origins of such regionalization were no doubt earlier, still in the archaic period the regions were not sharply defined, but there was a transition towards the more stable classical network of identities (although even then significant shifts of identity were still possible).[3]

By the eighth century both Corinth and Sicyon had unified their territories as single political entities, and they then remained remarkably stable as territorial states, whatever internal changes they underwent (Legon in *Inventory* 462); but most regions were a patchwork of numerous separate communities. In several cases, however, it was uncertain how many communities were covered by a particular regional identity (e.g. in Eleia, where regional identity developed and spread as the influence of Elis grew: Roy 1999), and border areas in particular were often not clearly defined. Even among such uncertainties Achaea is a particularly difficult problem since the concept of Achaean identity probably developed before the archaic period, but the region is not a natural geographical unity and how political communities evolved within Achaea in the archaic period is still obscure.[4]

In several parts of the Peloponnese, particularly in border areas, communities had a choice of identity (Roy 2000a). How such communities exercised their choice must have been affected by the tendency of more powerful communities to extend their influence. Elis, for instance, was originally a community of the Peneios valley in northern Eleia, but by the sixth century it controlled Olympia and quite possibly also territory south of the Alpheios: as Elis expanded its control, some territory, such as Pisatis around Olympia, was incorporated directly into the Elean state, while other communities were made perioikic, and by 500 at least Elis had created a network of subordinate perioikic allies (Roy in *Inventory* 489–91). Communities south of the Alpheios not yet controlled by Elis in 500 would have to decide how to align themselves in view of the obvious likelihood (which became reality in the fifth century: e.g. Hdt. 4.148.4) that Elis would seek to extend its control over them too.

Argos destroyed Asine in the eighth century and conquered Nauplia in the seventh, thus achieving domination of the entire valley in which it lay, and it continued to expand its influence over its neighbors: another aspect of Argive ambition was the long-lasting struggle with Sparta for control of Thyreatis. While there was a tendency in antiquity to distinguish the territory of Argos itself from "the cities of the Acte" (the peninsula adjacent to the Saronic Gulf), the term "cities of the Acte" was a loose one, and Argive strength does not seem to have provoked the coalescence of an anti-Argive identity, though it was presumably among the factors which led these cities to join the Spartan-led Peloponnesian League.[5]

In northern Arcadia Kleitor campaigned in the later sixth century against "many *poleis*," presumably neighbors, and commemorated its success in a dedication at Olympia (see below): Kleitor may have established some hegemonial organization in the area (Nielsen 1996: 86–7). In the same area the Azanian identity, which had united several northern Arcadian communities and possibly extended into Achaea, collapsed for unknown reasons and simply disappeared except as a memory: evidently the formerly Azanian communities preferred to rely on their own local identities within the wider Arcadian regional grouping.[6] The power of Mantinea and Tegea in eastern Arcadia probably also faced their smaller Arcadian neighbors with choices of alignment, though Mantinean and Tegean expansion into adjacent areas is not actually attested until the fifth century (Nielsen in *Inventory* 517–20, 530–3).

As the power and influence of Sparta grew in the archaic period beyond the limits of Laconia and Messenia that development too reshaped the identities of communities on Sparta's borders. In some cases smaller and weaker communities had no real choice: Elis, Argos, Sparta, and probably also Kleitor achieved some of their expansion by force of arms, but in other cases a less powerful community probably exercised a genuine choice: Heraea, situated in the boundary area between Arcadia and Elis, for instance, may have preferred to assert an Arcadian identity rather than allow itself to be linked to Elis.[7] There are also problems with the way shifts of identity are presented in later sources: for instance, control of border areas between Laconia and southern Arcadian communities was still being disputed in the hellenistic period, and accounts circulating in the hellenistic and Roman periods of the areas' earlier history were obviously slanted to support later territorial claims (Shipley 2000: 369–76). While early Spartan expansion on this border is presented as military conquest, Spartan strength may have offered an attractive security to small communities that found themselves between, say, Sparta and Tegea.

Inter-state relations were not all, however, colored by tension and anxiety, nor were they all shaped by adherence to a region. The development, probably in the seventh to sixth centuries, of a network of wagon-roads in the Peloponnese (see below) shows both a willingness on the part of states to cooperate in creating and maintaining such roads, and a readiness to facilitate traffic extending beyond the region.

Sanctuaries in the archaic Peloponnese also blended local and wider interests. Many sanctuaries were of course of purely local significance, but others had a regional role. The sanctuary of Poseidon at Samikon, for example, was evidently ancient, and important in the region south of the Alpheios that later became Triphylia (Ruggeri 2004: 96–102). Whatever its precise relationship to Argos and other nearby communities, the Argive Heraion was clearly another such sanctuary of major regional importance (Hall 1995; Piérart 2003: 61). But the attraction of a sanctuary could draw worshippers across regional boundaries, and the prime Peloponnesian example of such a shrine is of course Olympia, used from the eighth century not only by inhabitants of Eleia but also by worshippers, and dedicants, from elsewhere in the Peloponnese, notably Arcadia, Argos, Messenia and Lakonia – and by Greeks from outside the Peloponnese, on whom see below (Morgan 1990: 57–105).

Such evidence shows that the archaic history of the Peloponnese must be seen not only as marked by increasing regional definition and differentiation, but also as a time of considerable interaction and cooperation between communities and regions. It is nonetheless true that the period saw the evolution of increasingly structured, though still elastic,[8] regional identities, leading to the well-known regional pattern of the classical Peloponnese recorded, for instance, in the *periplous* of Pseudo-Skylax (40–4).

Cities and Their Infrastructure

In the archaic period major urban centres developed in the Peloponnese. The evidence is patchy, but enough to show that towns grew in different patterns. At Halieis part of the town was laid out in planned form already in the sixth century if, as seems likely, the sixth-century street plan matched that followed in the fourth-century reconstruction (figure 13.1),[9] but less structured development was more common. At Tegea the town evidently grew up in the archaic period alongside the sanctuary of Athena Alea, which had been important since the Early Iron Age, though the settlement pattern within the town is still more or less unknown.[10] On the site of the town of Elis settlement had existed from the eleventh/tenth centuries, and developed in the archaic period, probably as a cluster of small settlements with their various cemeteries around a central public space. Public building is attested at Elis from the beginning of the sixth century (Eder and Mitsopoulos 1999). The case of Elis is instructive because

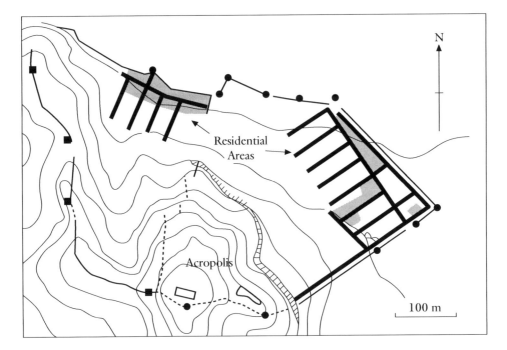

Figure 13.1 Halieis may have been a planned city already in the sixth century: the fourth-century roads of this plan probably reflect the sixth-century layout
Source: Owens (1991: fig. 19).

the archaeological record clearly does not support the view derived from literary accounts that the town was created by a *synoikismos* in 471 (Roy 2002b).

Two major centres, Corinth and Argos, have both been the object of considerable archaeological investigation, but present rather different images as archaic urban centres. At Corinth considerable public building is known from the eighth century onwards (Legon in *Inventory* 467–8). The settlement area however appears to have been loosely structured, and to have been interspersed with unbuilt areas.[11] At Argos from the late eighth or early seventh century settlement, which had previously stretched out into the plain, was concentrated around Pron (a southward projection from the acropolis hill Larisa), and workshops clustered around the agora. Though isolated burials continued to occur within the city walls throughout antiquity, areas of habitation were differentiated from space for burials and two main cemeteries developed (the south-western necropolis and the northern necropolis). Centres of public and religious life, on the other hand, are still not well known. Several small sanctuaries have been found, but only one of Aphrodite has been identified: it was probably in use from the late seventh century, but a temple was built for it only in the second half of the sixth century. There is a marked contrast between the limited archaic remains of monumental building known in the city and the major works carried out at the nearby Heraion from the late eighth or early seventh century (Piérart 2003); after all, although Argos probably gained control of the sanctuary only in the early classical period, from their city the people of Argos could see it across the plain (cf. Hall 1995). Nonetheless, despite the limitations and variations of our evidence, and the diversity of patterns of development, there was clearly a general trend, naturally most marked in major centres, towards urban centres equipped with buildings to serve public purposes.

An essential part of an ancient Greek city (Hansen in *Inventory* 135–7) and probably the most expensive of its public buildings[12] was its circuit wall. Most preserved Greek circuits are post-archaic in date and the traditional assumption is that such walls were not usually built before the early fifth century (Frederiksen 2003: 1–2). However, recent research by Frederiksen (2003) suggests that the extent to which circuits were built even in the earlier archaic period has been seriously underestimated and that the building of circuits gained momentum already in the sixth century. Perhaps not surprisingly most early fortifications are found in colonial areas, but a few cities of the north-eastern Peloponnese were in fact protected by walls in the archaic period: Argos, Corinth, and Halieis in the southernmost Argolid.[13] At Halieis – by no means a major community – there are remains of a presumably seventh-century wall protecting at least the acropolis if not the lower town as well (Frederiksen 2003: cat. A 118). Situated on the coast, the city may have feared seaborne piratical raids, but the object of fear may also have been aggressive Argives (Osborne 1996a: 288). At Argos itself, the two dominating hills of Larisa and Aspis seem to have been fortified, the Larisa as early as the seventh century and the Aspis by the sixth century.[14] At the so-called Potters' Quarter in Corinth is preserved a stretch of a double faced fortification wall, ca. 70 m long, 2.40 m wide and dating to the later seventh century (Frederiksen 2003: cat. A 112). Though it has been disputed, the probability is that this stretch was part of a continuous circuit enclosing the entire site of Corinth, perhaps as much as 300 ha.[15] Wealthy but vulnerable, Corinth was presumably prompted by its exposed topographical position – open to attack from all sides – to construct this massive fortification.

Temples form another important and far more widespread group of monumental public buildings of the archaic Peloponnese. Their obvious function was to cater to the religious needs of the communities which erected them, but this was not their only and perhaps even not their most important function. Apart from temples erected at Panhellenic sanctuaries (such as the Heraion at Olympia, traditionally dated ca. 580; Lawrence 1996: 78–9) temples were built in a wide range of places: major communities such as Corinth and Tegea, of course, built several temples,[16] but just as importantly, temples were also constructed by minor communities such as Dyme and possibly Helike in Achaea,[17] Halieis and Hermione in the Argolid,[18] and Asea and Pallantion in Arcadia.[19]

In Arcadia, in particular, an impressive number of temples was constructed in the archaic period (Voyatzis 1999) and they conveniently illustrate the extra-religious importance of such buildings (Nielsen 2002a: 176–84) (figure 13.2). The evidence

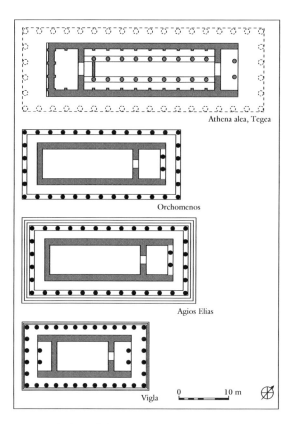

Athena alea, Tegea

Orchomenos

Agios Elias

Vigla

0 — 10 m

Figure 13.2 Reconstructed plan of the temple at Ayios Elias and of some closely related Arkadian temples
Source: Nielsen and Roy (1999: 173, fig. c).

at present available suggests that temple building in Arcadia gained momentum only in the late seventh century when numerous other communities around the Greek world had already put up temples; however, once started, the Arcadians constructed temples in surprising numbers, perhaps as many as 38 from the late seventh to the early fifth century (Nielsen 2002a: 176). Some of these temples were, it should be emphasized, quite substantial: the temple at Ayios Elias near Asea of ca. 500–490 which replaced a sixth-century predecessor (Forsén, Forsén and Østby 1999: 177–8), is a Doric *peripteros* (6 × 14 m) with a stylobate measuring 12.0 × 29.51 m and with an elevation above the stylobate entirely of Dholiana marble that had to be brought in from the quarry some 10 km south-east of Tegea, perhaps traveling altogether some 27 km to the site and rising some 500 m above the Asea valley to an altitude of ca. 1,100 m above sea-level! There are no fragments of metopal or pedimental sculpture at Ayios Elias, but pedimental sculptures are known to have embellished the Doric peripteros of ca. 540–530 at Vigla, also near Asea, and since pedimental sculpture at this period is rare outside Athens and Korkyra, the figures again emphasize that these Arcadian temples are by no means unsophisticated buildings (Morgan 1999a: 401). But they also illustrate the fact that Peloponnesian communities looked outside the region for architectural and artistic inspiration. The

Figure 13.3
Monumental sculpture is comparatively rare in the archaic Peloponnese, though there is the odd piece here and there. The figure illustrates a fragmentary *kouros* from Tourkoleka near the later Megalopolis, dated ca. 540–530 BC
Source: Palagia and Coulson (1993: 15, fig. 3).

peninsula itself, of course, produced sculptors such as the Argive artists who produced the early sixth-century twins at Delphi.[20] However, when compared to areas such as Attica, comparatively little monumental archaic sculpture has been found in the Peloponnese itself (Stewart 1990: 127; Boardman 1991: 76, 89) though there is the odd piece here and there such as a mid-sixth-century *kouros* from Arcadian Phigaleia, now in the Olympia Museum (Papachatzis 1980: fig. 370), the fragment of a *kouros* of ca. 540–530 from Tourkoleka near the later Megalopolis (Kokkorou-Aleura 1993) (figure 13.3), or the reliefs from the acropolis of Mycenae.[21] Moreover, Peloponnesian communities did not hesitate to bring in sculptors from other parts of Greece: thus, the Tegeans brought in Endoios of Athens to create the cult statue of Athena Alea (Nielsen 2002a: 180).

To return to temples: the erection of a temple, or rather the *decision* to erect one, presupposes more than community cult: decision-making bodies, financial capability, and the wish to assert the *identity* of the community undertaking the construction.[22] In some cases how the communities constructing temples conceived of themselves is evident: when the Tegeans built their temple of Athena Alea with the slightly older Argive Heraion as the architectural model, it seems probable that they were asserting for their sanctuary a significance not just local but regional (Voyatzis 1999: 143–4; Nielsen 2002a: 180). Likewise the Ayios Elias temple at Asea – the ambitiousness

Figure 13.4 Wheel-road near Pheneos in Arcadia

Source: Nielsen and Roy (1999: 267, pl. 4).

of which was emphasized above – took nothing less than the new temple of Apollo at Delphi as the model for its capitals.[23] Such examples speak clearly of the self-assertiveness of Tegea and Asea.

In this way temples attest that the local communities of archaic Arcadia were very much aware of general Greek developments. But they probably also watched each other carefully and when for instance Mantinea and Orchomenos construct temples almost simultaneously around 530 we may see in this an instance of inter-community rivalry and efforts to assert their separate local identities in each other's face, which must have contributed significantly to the consolidation of these communities (Voyatzis 1999: 147–8; Nielsen 2002a: 181).

Traditionally, temples have been thought of as presupposing the existence of *poleis* or at least as one of the factors contributing to their emergence,[24] and we may close this section with a particularly clear example supporting this view. An essential feature of the *polis* in the classical period was its control of a territory (Hansen in *Inventory* 70–1). For the earliest archaic period "territory" may perhaps be an anachronistic concept, but it is quite certain that at least some Peloponnesian communities possessed well-defined terrieries by the end of the archaic period: thus, Herodotus (8.124.3) reports that after the Battle of Salamis the Spartans paid Themistocles of Athens – the brains behind the victory – the unprecedented honor of an escort by select Spartiates from Sparta itself "as far as the borders of Tegea," which, then, must have been defined in some way. Moreover, some temples were situated in the centre of a *polis* such as all four constructed by Pallantion (above, n. 19), but others were situated at considerable distance from the cities constructing them, and in this we may reasonably see a claim to ownership of the land from the city up to the site of the temples, if not beyond.[25] Thus, the Tegean temple at Mavriki near the Dholiana marble quarry is probably to be interpreted among other things as a claim by Tegea to ownership of the quarry. Asea constructed some five temples in its hinterland and some of them in conspicuous locations which invite the conclusion that they were intended to serve as markers of both territorial claims and boundaries. In this way, they presuppose the existence of an Asean territory and/or will themselves have served to consolidate such a territory (Nielsen 2002a: 181–3).

Finally, mention should be made of a major means by which traffic between Peloponnesian cities took place: roads (figure 13.4). In recent years, largely thanks to the pioneering work of Pikoulas (esp. 1995; 1999), our knowledge of ancient Greek roads in the Peloponnese (and elsewhere) has improved enormously. For these roads to cross rocky terrain two parallel ruts at a standard distance of 1.4 m apart were chiseled in the rock so that wagon-wheels could run smoothly. Such roads have now been recorded in many parts of the Peloponnese, if the local stone is hard enough to preserve traces of the ruts. It is obviously difficult to date ruts cut in natural rock (though not impossible, e.g. by referring to associated buildings or to destinations of known date), and also difficult to identify the nature of the goods or people carried by the wagons that used them. Pikoulas has suggested that many of the Peloponnesian roads were constructed in the seventh to sixth centuries primarily for military purposes, and, while Forsén has questioned these views and suggested that many of the roads will have been constructed originally to facilitate moving building materials, Forsén himself also sees the seventh to sixth centuries as the likely period for the growth of the Peloponnesian road network (2003: 63–75). These roads typically connected two separate communities, and their upkeep will have needed regular attention, just as their use would require an agreed system to prevent carts traveling in opposite directions from blocking each other, so that the roads show not only growing traffic among Peloponnesian settlements in the later archaic period but also a willingness among individual city-states to cooperate with neighbors in developing and maintaining such roads.

Political Developments

In so far as the political form taken by archaic Peloponnesian communities is known at all, it was the *polis*. In the Greek world as such, the *polis* had developed into recognizable form at the latest by 650 though some of the colonial foundations presumably developed into *poleis* shortly after their foundation, i.e. as early as the late eighth or early seventh century (Hansen in *Inventory* 17–19). In the Peloponnese, the *polis* spread gradually throughout the archaic period so that by the end of the period it was the basic form of political organization in the peninsula. Some major communities such as e.g. Sicyon and Argos had presumably developed into *poleis* before the sixth century,[26] whereas others seem to have so developed *during* the century: thus, though e.g. Arcadia has traditionally been conceived of as a backwater in terms of *polis* organization (Nielsen 2002a: 11 n. 2), it seems reasonably certain that *poleis* had developed there at least by the sixth century, when Heraea, Mantinea and Tegea – to name only a few – appear in our record as highly indivualized communities waging wars, building temples, striking coins and concluding alliances.[27] In Achaea, *poleis* are recognizable as early as the early fifth century when Aegae strikes its own coinage of silver triobols on the Aeginetan standard (Head 1911: 412).[28] The situation in Elis is a little more obscure. Elis itself was surely a *polis* by the sixth century, but there may well have been a number of other, minor, *poleis* within the wider region of Elis. The evidence is tricky and these minor *poleis* are hard to identify, but a community such as Kyllene is a good candidate.[29]

These *poleis* in various ways interacted freely with near neighbors as well as more distant communities. The important institution of *proxenia*[30] developed in the sixth century and it was a development in which at least one Peloponnesian *polis* participated: the earliest grant of proxeny by the city of Elis belongs to the period 550–500 (Roy in *Inventory* 496) and it has been suggested that Elis, the organizer of the Olympic Games, was in fact the pioneer in the use of *proxenia* in the late archaic period.[31] Two other archaic grants by Elis, both to Spartans, are also known from inscriptions at Olympia (*SEG* 11.1180a; 26.476).

The road network described above is a fine example of what must have been extensive collaboration between cities. Another example of interaction is provided by the processes (described above) by which some of the major *poleis* such as Elis and Argos expanded their influence and power. But in contrast to the fourth century when, for instance, Achaea and – though only briefly – Arcadia, by then firmly established as regions, were organized as federal states comprising all or most of their *poleis*,[32] there seems to have been no similar political unity on a regional level in either region in the archaic period;[33] in Arcadia, what evidence there is for archaic *polis* interaction in fact concerns mainly wars (Nielsen 2002a: 228). The picture, then, is one of a large number of more or less independent cities collaborating with or fighting each other as occasion demanded.

As for the constitutional set-up of the *poleis* the evidence is exiguous and for an area such as Achaea wholly post-archaic. Though still patchy, the evidence relating to Arcadian communities is a little better. Robinson argues that Mantinea may have been a democracy by the mid-sixth century, though, as he admits, the evidence is far from conclusive.[34] It is worth noting, however, that in the mid-sixth century Cyrene in Libya called in Demonax of Mantinea to act as arbitrator in a civic crisis and that he carried through a constitutional reform which must count as sophisticated for its time (Nielsen 2002a: 218–19; and below); the implication is that refined political thinking was found in archaic Mantinea. In addition, an official by the title of *damiorgos* and with limited tenure is attested in a northern community, either Kleitor, Lousoi, or Pheneos (Nielsen 2002a: 219). And so the sparse evidence at least allows the inference that the internal political structure of at least some Arcadian communities was being formalized in the sixth century.

But most of the surviving evidence on constitutional matters relates to the major *poleis* and in particular to the rise of tyrants. Tyrants are attested in Corinth, Epidauros, Phleious and Sicyon. The sixth-century tyrant of Phleious, Leon, is a shadowy figure. A little more is known of Procles of Epidauros: he rose to power in the second half of the seventh century and established dynastic relations with the Cypselids of Corinth by marrying his daughter to Periander. This dynastic alliance, however, ended in failure for Prokles when a Corinthian army descended upon Epidauros and took the city (Jeffery 1976: 151).

At Sicyon, the tyrannical dynasty of the Orthagorids ruled the city for a century from the mid-seventh century (Osborne 1996a: 281). Its most well-known figure is Cleisthenes (ca. 600–570) who around 575 established a marriage connection with the Alcmaeonidae of Athens by selecting Megacles as husband for his daughter Agariste from among a number of invited suitors from many parts of the Greek world (Jeffery 1976: 165). He is reported to have participated, as the only Peloponnesian power, in the First Sacred War for control of Delphi in the early sixth century[35] and to have waged war with Argos (Hdt. 5.67), as a consequence of which different aspects of cultic life at Sicyon were reformed with an anti-Argive propagandistic twist. He was thus clearly pursuing a very active foreign policy, but he is also known to have introduced a reform of the tribal structure of Sicyon itself which outlasted him by sixty years (Osborne 1996a: 282–3).

The other great tyrannical dynasty of the Peloponnese was the Cypselids of Corinth who ruled the city from the mid-seventh to the early sixth century and expelled many, perhaps most Bacchiads, the narrow aristocracy previously ruling the city (Salmon

1997: 63). It is likely that during Cypselus' reign the Corinthian tribal structure was reformed for military and political purposes,[36] as at Sicyon; and in both cases modern scholars have pointed out that such reforms will have contributed to sharpening the self-awareness and citizen identity of the populace.[37] Other political innovations have been attributed to the Cypselids (see Salmon 1997: 66 for the *probouloi*) but their most remarkable undertakings are probably their public constructions: the fortification of the city, the building of temples, the creation of an artificial harbor at Lechaeon and of the *diolkos* for transporting vessels across the Isthmus (Salmon 1997: 66). In terms of foreign policy, the Cypselids were busy founding colonies which were kept under unusually tight control (see below); and as noted, marriage alliances were established with the tyrant of Epidauros and with a prominent Athenian family (Hdt. 6.128).

The overall picture, then, is one of rulers taking an interest in political reforms, pursuing active foreign policies, establishing relations with prominent families in other cities, and, particularly in the case of the Cypselids of Corinth, providing their cities with monumental public amenities. In all cases, however, the tyrannies eventually fell and were replaced, not by democracies but by remarkably stable oligarchies which survived long into the Classical period.

The Peloponnese in the Greek World

Of the areas of the Peloponnese considered here only Corinth and Achaea sent out colonies that can be securely dated to the archaic period. Other foundations, some from other areas, might also belong to the same period – e.g. the four Elean colonies in Epirus (Funke et al. in *Inventory* nos. 88, 90, 94, 104) – but cannot be dated accurately enough. Corinth founded Syracuse (733), Corcyra (706), Ambracia and Anactorion in Acarnania (650–625), Leucas (650–625) and Apollonia (600) in the Adriatic, and Potidaea in Chalcidice (600). Corinthians were also involved in the foundation by Corcyra of Epidamnus/Dyrrachium in the Adriatic ca. 625. The Achaean foundations were all in southern Italy: Croton (709/8), Sybaris (co-founded with Troizen in the late eighth century), Metapontium (630), and Pandosia (sixth century).[38] It is clear that, with the notable exception of Potidaea, both Corinth and Achaea colonized in the west. In other respects, however, the patterns of their colonization are very different.

From the eighth century Corinth was well organized and already engaged on a significant export trade. The most obvious evidence of Corinth's export is the Corinthian pottery found at many sites, particularly among western Greeks and neighboring areas (Salmon 1984: 101–16). Corinthian colonization created settlements in the Adriatic, southern Italy, and Sicily, but Corinth, initially at least, kept some control of these new communities, appointing reliable men in charge, and evidently expected the colonies to foster Corinthian interests in the area.[39] The situation in Achaea was quite different: the *polis* seems to have emerged in the region relatively late, and it is unclear what links there were among the various archaic communities of Achaea. It is consequently unclear who the "Achaeans" were who sent out the colonies. It does however seem clear that the Achaean colonies developed faster and became more prosperous than the settlements of Achaea itself.[40]

Colonization shows the strength of the archaic Peloponnese's connections to the west (also seen e.g. in the treasuries set up by western Greeks at Olympia, see below), but it also shows how Peloponnesian regions varied: several did not colonize at all, and Corinth and Achaea, which did, produced different patterns of colonization.[41]

The Peloponnese was home to no fewer than three of the so-called Panhellenic sanctuaries: Olympia, Isthmia, and Nemea, where athletic games took place and came to attract competitors from all over the Greek world. The most prestigious games were of course the Olympics (supposedly founded 776: Lee 1988), but the games at the two other sites were sufficiently important to be incorporated, with the Olympics and the Pythian Games, into the *periodos* in the early sixth century: this was a formal arrangement whereby these four festivals were made to follow each other in fixed order.[42] The promotion of these four above the innumerable local athletic festivals throughout the Greek world[43] shows clearly that they were of outstanding importance and that in this respect the Peloponnese was at the heart of Greek interaction. Due to their enormous prestige (Golden 1998: 33–7, 80–1), the history of the Olympics is far better known than that of the Nemean or Isthmian Games. The archaic catchment area of the Olympics is illuminating: cities of the Peloponnese itself, of course, were blessed by victories of their citizens,[44] but a large number of victors came from outside the Peloponnese, from Sicily, Magna Graecia, the Adriatic, Phocis, Boeotia, Aegina, Athens, Euboea, East Locris, Thessaly, Ionia; in short, from most parts of the Greek world.[45]

But Olympia was not only a meeting place for athletes: it was an important centre of interaction and display for the city-states of archaic Greece. So city-states would post important acts of state there in the form of inscriptions, thus adding Zeus' sanction to the act. But that was presumably not all: for instance, display of interstate treaties served to announce new loyalties and to show strength on the part of the senior parties to such treaties (Lewis 1996: 140–2). The patron of the Olympic sanctuary, Elis itself, as explained above, was a *polis* which expanded its power to the detriment of lesser communities, and Elis naturally used Olympia to publish its treaties: a treaty of ca. 500 between Elis and an otherwise unknown community, the Ewaoioi, with Elis as the leading power, was published at Olympia, obviously as a show of strength to the international gathering flocking there (ML 17; Roy and Schofield 1999). So was the mid-sixth-century treaty by which the powerful *polis* of Sybaris – a western colony founded from Achaea – announced the entry into its hegemonic league of a new ally, the obscure Serdaioi (ML 10; Fischer-Hansen et al. in *Inventory* 296).

By publishing such treaties, then, communities displayed their stature and affirmed their place in the Greek world. Naturally, however, similar statements could be made by dedications. For example, "an unparalleled collection of arms and armour" (Snodgrass 1999: 12) has been found in the German excavations; they certainly originally belonged to dedications whereby a victorious belligerent offered part of the spoils taken from the defeated enemy to Zeus Olympios. Such dedications were probably not prompted only by piety: as pointed out by Snodgrass, they were intended to communicate with other communities and will "have impressed the citizens of other *poleis* with the prowess of one's own."[46] Victory dedications could also take the form of sculpture financed by spoils, as when Arcadian Kleitor in 550–500 dedicated a figure of Zeus from booty taken "from many *poleis*."[47] But dedications took an even more monumental form: on the northern edge of the Altis, the Olympian *temenos*, below the Kronion hill, is the so-called Terrace of Treasuries. A treasury (*thesauros*) was a small temple-like building erected by an individual *polis* as a gift to Zeus, the god of the sanctuary. On the terrace are remains of twelve such treasuries; a few may be early fifth century, but the bulk is archaic. The Megarian treasury preserves remains of magnificent pedimental sculpture (Bol 1974) and all in all these are splendid dedications. What is particularly notable is that most of these were erected by western colonies: Syracuse, Epidamnus, Sybaris, Selinous, Metapontium and Gela. As pointed out above, Peloponnesian colonization was primarily directed towards these areas and the treasuries are traditionally, and obviously correctly, interpreted as monumental expressions of the colonies' efforts to maintain contacts with the old homeland and, importantly, to define themselves as Greeks. The Olympic sanctuary, then, developed into one of the nodal points of Panhellenic interaction and so, no doubt, did the sanctuaries at Nemea and Isthmia.

Conclusion

In many respects, the archaic Peloponnese was fully in the mainstream of general Greek developments. Silver coinage provides a nice example: introduced into the Greek world in the mid-sixth century, it spread rapidly and was produced by more than a hundred cities before the end of the archaic period (Osborne 1996a: 253–5). Among them were a few Peloponnesian communities: Corinth possessed a very prolific mint striking on a local standard which spread to other areas (Legon in *Inventory* 468), but other Peloponnesian communities simply adopted the Aeginetan weight standard, e.g. Aegae in Achaea (ca. 500), Elis (late sixth century), Heraea in Arcadia (ca. 510), or Sicyon (late sixth century).[48] Another example may be found in the development towards major urban centres, where the Peloponnese also follows the general Greek trend of the archaic period. The evidence for archaic Peloponnesian urbanism is uneven and patchy, but enough to show that major urban sites certainly developed there, e.g. at Corinth, but also, it seems highly likely, at such sites as Tegea and Elis. One Peloponnesian city, Halieis, even seems to have been grid-planned in the archaic period, a unique example in Greece itself in the period, when most grid-planned cities were situated in the western colonial area.[49] The most well-known type of monumental public building of the Peloponnese is the temple, but a few cities, such as Corinth, also constructed defensive circuit walls, a huge undertaking. Here again, the Peloponnese follows Greek trends: the building of circuit walls gained momentum in the sixth century (Frederiksen 2003) and the sixth century was "the great age of temple building" (Murray 1980 (1993): 242; cf. Osborne 1996a: 262). Again, Peloponnesian communities are seen to follow general Greek developments.

Such physical city centres as arose in the archaic Peloponnese were connected by a network of roads, which will have needed collaboration between city-states for maintenance, and which presupposes extensive traffic and communication between cities and which will itself have greatly facilitated such interaction. At present, a system of roads is best known from the Peloponnese: the most intensive research has focused on the Peloponnese but similar roads are known from other parts of Greece and their emergence may very well turn out to be a general characteristic of the archaic Greek world.

In the political sphere as well, the Peloponnese followed the general trend: the *polis* was the basic form of political organization by the end of the archaic period, except perhaps in Achaea where the *polis* may have developed only in the very latest archaic period. In other parts of Greece, such as Boeotia, Thessaly, Phocis, and possibly East Locris,[50] the late sixth century saw the emergence of political organizations which united local communities on a regional level. However, despite the regionalization of the archaic Peloponnese, no such organizations are visible there on present evidence and the formation of local powerbases presumably took other forms, such as colonization in the case of Corinth and expansion by single cities in the cases of Elis and Argos.

But even so the communities of the central and northern Peloponnese played their part in various major processes that marked the archaic Greek world. Corinth and Achaea, at least, participated in the process of founding new Greek settlements generally labeled colonization: some colonies sent out by other Peloponnesian regions might also be archaic, but cannot be securely dated to the period. With the notable exception of Potidaea, the Corinthian and Achaean colonies lay to the west, in areas in which Corinthian products were traded in quantity. Corinth was the major trading community of the Peloponnese, and led the way in the export of fine pottery until the sixth century. Since pottery can readily be detected and identified archaeologically while other goods that Corinth might have traded cannot, it is difficult to know how far finds of exported Corinthian pottery mark the range and intensity of all Corinthian trade, but Corinthian products traveled across the Greek world, probably with a bias towards the west.[51] Peloponnesian communities could also take advantage at home of trends in the Greek world, such as the development of techniques of temple-building. While it is not surprising that Corinth, with its far-flung contacts, followed the archaic Greek pattern of temple-building with several major constructions, it is striking that even small communities in Arcadia, situated in the central Peloponnese where it might be supposed that new ideas would be slow to penetrate, could draw inspiration from the most advanced work of the day. Examples are the mid-sixth century temple at Vigla near Asea with its pedimental sculpture, and the late archaic Ayios Elias temple at Kandreva, also near Asea, with capitals modeled on those of the new temple at Delphi.

There was also interaction in more narrowly inter-state matters between archaic Peloponnese and the rest of the Greek world. As noted (n. 39), a late archaic arbitration by Corinth and Corcyra between Gela and Syracuse is reported by Herodotos, and he also reports arbitration by Periander, the Cypselid tyrant of Corinth, between Mytilene and Athens (5.95.2; cf. Salmon 1984: 224). But more important is the sending of Demonax by Mantinea to Cyrene as arbitrator in the mid-sixth century, since it was the Delphic oracle that recommended that the Cyreneans seek help from Mantinea (Parker 2000: 92) which obviously implies that Mantinea was known at Delphi and thus that even lesser Peloponnesian communities had some international repute.

There are, then, a number of respects in which the Peloponnese was fully in the mainstream of general Greek developments. In other respects, however, communities of the Peloponnese actually led the development. Corinth, in particular, is a case in point: Corinthian potters developed the black-figure style and their products dominated the Greek market well into the sixth century, and while the city may not have erected the earliest temples in the Peloponnese, in the mid-seventh century Corinth built ostentatiously magnificent stone temples of Apollo on Temple Hill and of Poseidon at Isthmia, thus embellishing both the city itself and the international sanctuary over which it presided. These constructions "must have given Corinth the lead in architectural development for some years" if not for generations.[52] Arcadia, moreover, was clearly among the leaders as far as numbers of temples are concerned, and so in this important respect the Peloponnese stands out in the archaic Greek world.

Likewise, there are important archaic political developments which are headed by Peloponnesian communities or at least particularly visible in the Peloponnese. Murray has pointed out that one of the most important political developments of the archaic period was the creation or reformation of civic subdivisions such as "tribes" (*phylai*) and that this "was a well-recognized way of resolving various types of political conflict" (1990a: 13; 1997; cf. Nielsen 2002a: 219). As noted above, reforms of civic subdivisions ("tribes") are known from archaic Corinth and Sicyon and a Peloponnesian, Demonax of Mantinea, carried out such a reform in Cyrene in Libya. Another political development, this time in inter-state relations, in which a Peloponnesian community may have been in the frontline, is the development of *proxenia*, in which Elis seems to have been among the pioneers.

There is also a sense in which the Peloponnese is the centre of the Greek world, i.e. by being the home of the three great Panhellenic sanctuaries of Isthmia, Nemea, and, most importantly, Olympia which developed into one of the prime centres of Greek interaction: athletes came to compete there from all over the Greek world, and city-states communicated with each other there by means of dedications and posting of important inscriptions. Among the treasuries set up in Olympia in the archaic period in honor of its god, Zeus Olympios, are several built by western colonies such as Sybaris and Epidamnus, but the city of Byzantium on the Hellespont erected one as well.

By the late sixth century much of the non-Spartan Peloponnese was linked to Sparta through the network of alliances known as the Peloponnesian League: the significant exceptions were Argos, which never joined the League, and the Achaean communities, which joined only from 430 onwards.[53] Even once the League was established Sparta did not totally dominate it, and Corinth, especially, sometimes proved a difficult ally (Salmon 1984: 240–52). Nonetheless from the late sixth century until the fourth Sparta, through the Peloponnesian League, was the greatest single influence in the Peloponnese. There are also reports of Spartan involvement with communities north of Laconia and Messenia well before the creation of the Peloponnesian League: according to Pausanias (2.24.7), Argos defeated Sparta at Hysiae in 669/8, presumably in an early phase of the long struggle for control of the eastern coast of the Peloponnese between the Argolid and Laconia, and Herodotos (1.66–8) believed that there was considerable warfare between Sparta and Tegea before Tegea allied with Sparta in the mid-sixth century. Despite such earlier involvement, however, Spartan dominance in the Peloponnese came only at the end of the archaic period, and for most of the period developments in the other Peloponnesian communities were not shaped by Sparta nor heavily influenced by resistance to Sparta. Instead, the several regions in varying degrees – Corinth, for instance, much more than Achaea – matched the patterns of development in the Greek world as a whole and, in some respects, led the way.

NOTES

1   See Yalouris 1971; 1973: 155; Arapogianni 1999.
2   Epeion: Papakonstantinou 1982. Pyrgos: Yalouris 1956: 187, 191; 1958: 194, 198.
3   See e.g. Nielsen 2002a: 229–69 on Triphylia. Origins: e.g. Gehrke 2000a: 168.
4   Morgan and Hall in *Inventory* 472–77; cf. Walbank 2000.
5   Piérart in *Inventory* 599–600. For the early history of the Peloponnesian League, see Wickert 1961: 7–33; see also Cawkwell 1993.
6   Nielsen and Roy 1998; cf. Pikoulas 1981–2; Tausend 1993.
7   Cf. Nielsen 2002a: 95. ML 17 is a treaty of Elis with the *Ewaoioi*, not with Heraea: see below.
8   The regional identity of Triphylia did not emerge until ca. 400: see Nielsen 2002a: 229–69.
9   Piérart in *Inventory* 609 (Halieis no. 349), cf. Owens 1991: 67.
10 Morgan and Coulton 1997: 111; Nielsen in *Inventory* 531 (no. 297). The results of the Norwegian Survey in Arcadia may well throw light on such settlement.
11 Morgan and Coulton 1997: 92, 94, 106–7. The comments of Salmon 1984: 79–80 concern the degree of sophistication of public building rather than the pattern of habitation.
12 Camp 2000: 46–7, esp. 47: "fortifications represent by far the greatest physical expression of public, communal participation, whether we think in terms of money, labor, or organisation."
13 Oresthasion in southern Arcadia may just possibly have had a pre-classical acropolis wall: Frederiksen 2003: cat. C 341.
14 Frederiksen 2003: cat. A 110 (Aspis), cat. C 303 (Larisa).
15 Salmon 1984: 220; Frederiksen 2003: 171–4; cat. A 112.
16 Corinth: (1) seventh-century temple of Apollo on Temple Hill, rebuilt in the mid-sixth century; (2) temple of Poseidon at Isthmia ca. 650; (3) temples of Hera at Perachora, several phases from ca. 800 onwards; cf. Legon in *Inventory* 468. Tegea: (1) temples of Athena Alea, first monumental structure from the late seventh century; (2) sixth-century (560–550) prostyle Doric temple (14 × 6 m) at Mavriki constructed in marble from the nearby Dholiana quarry; Nielsen in *Inventory* 531–2.
17 Cf. Morgan and Hall in *Inventory*. Dyme: small archaic temple at Santameri (482); Helike: small archaic temple at Nea Keryneia which may be associated with the acropolis of ancient Helike (482).

18 Cf. Piérart in *Inventory*. Halieis: early seventh-century temple of Apollo (609); Hermione: late sixth-century temple of Poseidon (610).

19 Cf. entries by Nielsen in *Inventory*. Asea: e.g. two important extra-urban temples: (1) a sixth-century one at Vigla, to Athena and Poseidon, and (2) a large temple at Ayios Elias of ca. 500 (510); Pallantion: on top of the acropolis and on its southern slope are four modest temples constructed ca. 600–550 (cf. Østby 1990/1). Cf. above for an archaic temple in what was probably the territory of Lepreon.

20 See Stewart 1990: 112, figs. 56–7; Boardman 1991: 24, fig. 70; Hall 1995: 594–6.

21 The best preserved of these, "The Lady at the Window," is depicted in most handbooks of Greek art: e.g. Stewart 1990: fig. 77; also Palagia and Coulson 1993: fig. 1. For a *kouros* of ca. 550 from Tenea near Corinth, see Boardman 1991: 76, fig. 121; for a head of a *kore* of ca. 530 from Sicyon, see 1991: 89, fig. 183.

22 Burkert 1988, 43 ("a temple is the most prestigious and lasting monument into which the available surplus of society is transformed – a monument of common identity"), 44 ("a Greek temple is the sumptuous and beautiful *anathema* by which a *polis*, yielding to the divine, demonstrates to herself and to others her existence and her claims"); 1996; Nielsen 2002a: 176.

23 Forsén, Forsén and Østby 1999: 176; Nielsen 2002a: 180.

24 Snodgrass 1980a: 58–62; 1991: 17–18; Burkert 1995: 205–7.

25 See Osborne 1996a: 102, and the classic study by de Polignac 1995a.

26 For Sicyon, see Legon in *Inventory* no. 228; for Argos, see Piérart no. 347.

27 On the status of local communities of archaic Arcadia, see Nielsen 2002a: 159–228. On Heraea, Mantinea, and Tegea, see Nielsen in *Inventory* nos. 274, 281, 297.

28 Morgan and Hall 1996: 174: "in our opinion, the decision to issue in the early fifth century a series of coins carrying an emblem (the goat protome) which evidently serves as an aetiological commentary on the self-appointed city-ethnic *AIG[AION]* implies a strong political consciousness"; 193. On Aegae, see Morgan and Hall in *Inventory* no. 229.

29 Roy in *Inventory* nos. 251 (Elis), 254 (Kyllene); 489–504 (minor poleis; cf. Roy 1997; 2002a, b).

30 On the institution of *proxenia*, see ch. 29, below, and Hansen in *Inventory* 98–103.

31 See Perlman 2000: 20, referring to Wallace 1970.

32 Federated Achaea: Beck 1997: 55–66; federated Arcadia: Beck 1997: 67–83 (cf. Dusanic 1970; Roy 2000b; Nielsen 2002a: 474–99). A fifth-century Arcadian Confederacy has traditionally been assumed (e.g. Wallace 1954 and Williams 1965) on the basis of coins inscribed *ARKADIKON* (or abbreviations thereof) but did not exist (Nielsen 2002a: 121–41).

33 Achaea: Morgan and Hall 1996: 193–7; Arcadia: Nielsen 2002a: 228.

34 Robinson 1997: 113–14; also discussing the possibility of democracies at Argos (82–4, sixth century; 84–8, early fifth century), Elis (108–11, ca. 500), and Megara (114–17, sixth century).

35 Jeffery 1976: 163–4. The historicity of this Sacred War is debated: see Davies 1994.

36 Salmon 1997: 64; Legon in *Inventory* no. 227.

37 Salmon 1997: 65 (Corinth), 66 (Sicyon); Osborne 1996a: 283 (Sicyon).

38 For details, see *Inventory* 1390–6, and the individual entries for the various *poleis*.

39 Jeffery 1976: 50–9; Salmon 1984: 62–7, 209–19. Syracuse seems not to have been under Corinthian control, but Corinth retained an interest in the city (Hdt. 7.154.2.3: late archaic arbitration by Corinth and Corcyra between Syracuse and Gela).

40 Morgan and Hall 1996. There is considerable relevant material in Greco 2002.

41 The uncertainties of evidence on when colonies were founded would make little differ-
    ence to the argument: e.g. even if Elis' four Adriatic colonies were founded in the archaic
    period, they were minor settlements.
42 Morgan 1990: 212ff; 1993: 35–6; Golden 1998: 10–11.
43 See Morgan 1990: 212: "Pindar, writing in the mid fifth century named some 30 other
    contests and implied that many more existed."
44 See *Inventory*: Megara (no. 225); Corinth (227); Sicyon (228); Aegeira (230); Dyme
    (234); Pellene (240); Dyspontion (250); Elis (251); Lenos (257); Heraea (274); Lousoi
    (279); Phigaleia (292); Sparta (345); Argos (347); Epidaurus (348); and Cleonae (351).
    For the pride taken by cities in the victories of its citizens, see Nielsen 2002a: 208–9.
45 See *Inventory*: Acragas (no. 9); Gela (17); Himera (24); Camarina (28); Naxos (41); Croton
    (56); Locri (59); Rhegion (68); Sybaris (70); Taras (71); Apollonia (77); Epidamnus
    (79); Delphi (177); Orchomenos (213); Thebes (221); Aegina (358); Athens (361); Chalcis
    (365); Eretria (370); Carystos (373); Opous (386); Crannon (400); Pelinna (409); Pharsalus
    (413); Astypalaea (476); Peparethos (511); Thasos (526); Chios (840); Miletus (854);
    Samos (864); Smyrna (867).
46 Snodgrass 1986b: 55. For a list of mostly archaic dedications of spoils, among them one
    made by Psophis in the border area between Elis and Arcadia, see Pritchett 1979: 290–1.
47 Paus. 5.23.7. Dedication and epigram: Richter 1931: 200; Maddoli 1992; historical impli-
    cations: see Roy 1972; Nielsen 2002a: 181, 187, 193, 198, 201, 212, 534–6, 562.
48 See the entries in *Inventory* nos. 229, 251, 274, 228.
49 See in particular Fischer-Hansen 1996; also the entries in *Inventory* for cities with archaic
    grid plans: Massalia (no. 3); Acragas (9); Acrae (10); Himera (24); Camarina (28); Casmenae
    (29); Leontini (33); Megara (36); Naxos (41); Selinous (44); Syracuse (47); Zankle (51);
    Hyele (54); Croton (56); Locri (59); Metapontium (61); Poseidonia (66); Taras (71);
    Ambracia (113).
50 Boeotia: Hansen in *Inventory* 431; Thessaly: Decourt et al. in *Inventory* 680; Phocis:
    McInerney 1999: 178–80; East Locris: Nielsen in *Inventory* 666.
51 Salmon 1984: 101–58, esp. 139–47; Salmon 2000.
52 C. Morgan 1990: 162; also 2003: 150: these temples "imply conscious innovation rather
    than simple peer pressure"; Snodgrass 1980a: 60–1 ("generations"); Osborne 1996a:
    211–14.
53 On the difficult question of how the Peloponnesian League developed see e.g. Osborne
    1996a: 287–91. Pellene was the first Achaean polis to join the league, in 430: Morgan
    and Hall in *Inventory* 484 (no. 240).

CHAPTER FOURTEEN

Crete

James Whitley

Introduction: Sources and Problems

No region of archaic Greece is typical, but some are less typical than others. Crete and Macedonia are, in their opposite ways, perhaps the least typical of all. The material record of Macedonia in the sixth century is rich – but it is not rich in votives or the elaborate temples we find further to the south. Its wealth was deposited in its graves, which are especially rich in finds in the late sixth and early fifth centuries. The "warrior graves" of Sindos and Archontiko Giannitson are full of armor, weapons, gold masks, and imported Corinthian and Attic painted cups and kraters, which clearly reference the symposium. Female graves are no less richly furnished. This sixth-century efflorescence is all the more surprising since it appears to come out of nowhere – seventh-century and Early Iron Age graves, while extensive, are not particularly "rich," and the houses of the *toumbes* and *trapezes* of archaic Macedonia are not particularly commodious. The Cretan picture is the very opposite of this. Crete's material efflorescence is most marked in the eighth and seventh centuries, when it had wide contacts with many other parts of the Eastern Mediterranean. There are many archaic Cretan "firsts": the first Orientalizing style (Protogeometric B), the first examples of elaborately figurative art which could be called "narrative," the first temples, and the first law codes inscribed in stone. But this head start was not followed up. The sixth century saw a marked trough in the material record – burials from Knossos disappear, votives are few and poor, imports (particularly imported "symposium" shapes) are rare, and what pottery we have is certainly the plainest in all the Aegean. But, like the statues of Easter Island, Cretan cities and their written laws remain.

This material peculiarity may also be reflected in the written record. Crete had a reputation both for wisdom and for oddity in ancient times. It was an island where ancient religious mysteries and ancient forms of political justice had been maintained – hence the stories about Minos, Rhadamanthys (see Plato *Laws* and Ps-Plato *Minos*) and Epimenides (DK 27–37 = *FGrH* 457) – and a region where odd local customs, peoples and languages had been preserved. This reputation however is discussed, almost entirely, by authors who are not Cretans – Ionians, Athenians, and later the anti-quarian writers and historians of Hellenistic and early Roman Greece. What archaic Cretans thought and wrote about themselves generally does not survive: the only archaic Cretan poem we have is the song of Hybrias, a drinking song preserved in Athenaeus (15.695f–696b; skolion 909 Page) and thought to date to the late sixth century (Bowra 1961: 398–403). The source problems we have for Crete are very similar to those for archaic Sparta. Just as there is a Spartan mirage, an optical illu-sion of Spartan austerity diffracted through Athenian idealization, antiquarianism, and disdain, so a fog of ancient misconception hangs over archaic Crete. This is not merely a "source problem": it affects the kind of history we can write.

One kind of history we cannot write is a standard political history. For regions such as Sparta, Athens, and Samos from about 550 onwards, Herodotus provides a basic narrative framework of personalities and events. This framework can be supplemented by later authors and filled out through the inscriptions preserved from the Athenian acropolis, Olympia, and other major sanctuary sites. But there is no such framework for Crete, no thread that links the bits and pieces that Herodotus chooses to tell us about the island. Crete first appears in his narrative in the account of the coloniza-tion of Cyrenaica from Thera (4.150–7). Herodotus provides two different stories, involving two different Cretan cities: one emphasizes the role of Korobios, a murex fisherman from Itanos, the other that of Etearchos, the *basileus* (king?) of Oaxos (Axos). Then Cydonia appears as a bit-player in a story of the rivalry of Samos and Aegina (3.44–59); and finally "the Cretans" deliberate whether or not they will be joining the coalition against the Persians (they choose not to: 7.169–71). And that, apart from the odd antiquarian titbit, is all Herodotus tells us. Yet he is the best source we have. He is the nearest to a contemporary observer, and (when we can check) his observa-tions are usually accurate. What Homer, the Homeric hymns and Hesiod can tell us of Crete is set in a legendary past; references in Pindar and other poets are usually obscure; Thucydides and Xenophon write later, and have less interest in the island than "the father of history"; Plato and Aristotle are writing not history, but philo-sophy, and so are prone to making generalizations about the "Cretans" unsupported by particular examples; later writers such as Dosiadas, Ephorus, Pythion, and Strabo provide much useful information, but information colored by a romantic antiquarian-ism and detached from any chronological scheme.

But if political history is out, institutional history is more promising. Archaic and early classical Crete is rich in public inscriptions, chiefly "law codes," which mention many of the institutions that ancient authors refer to. The *kosmos*, Aristotle's prin-cipal Cretan magistrate, is mentioned as early as ca. 650 on an inscription from Dreros, and confirms that oligarchic republicanism had established itself in Crete from a very early date.[1] The *andreion* ("men's club") is both fully described by Strabo (10.4.16; 4.18, 20, 21, quoting Ephorus) and referred to in many Cretan inscriptions.[2] One such is an inscribed *mitra* (ca. 500) which came to light in 1970 (figure 14.5), but this find also reveals the limits of our literary sources, since it concerns a Cretan official, the *poinikastas* or scribe, unattested by any ancient writer (Jeffery and Morpurgo-Davies 1970). So the inscriptions do allow us both to qualify and to supplement the picture from the literary sources. But that does not mean that these public inscriptions enable us to write a history. Their occurrence is so sporadic and their dating so imprecise that it is very difficult accurately to trace how institutions develop.

This leaves a number of options. One could discuss the source problems and call the result a history – many scholars do. Or one could base one's history on evidence whose chronological development we can trace with some degree of accuracy: material evidence, principally archaeological. This approach is not without its pitfalls, since material evidence rarely sheds light in a straightforward manner. Archaeology throws up some very strange cases, and none is stranger than archaic Crete. Crete's peculiarity can be illustrated in many ways: in ancient Cretan cult and sanctuaries, in burials, settlements, and houses, in patterns of production and consumption of pottery and metalwork, in art, visual culture and iconography, in relations with the rest of the Aegean and the Mediterranean, and in epigraphic habits and literacy. All of which in turn are relevant to the question of Cretan institutions. But before these deep questions are discussed, some basic facts of geography, topography, and the material record need to be set out.

Geography and Regionalism

Crete is the largest and most mountainous island in the Aegean; it is only on the map that its unity is apparent. The massifs of the White Mountains, Ida (Psiloritis), Dikte, and Thriphte make overland communication difficult, and effectively divide the island into regions (map 9): the far west, the center and the far east, with some grey areas in between. Regionalism is apparent both in material culture and in "ethnicity" – the *Odyssey* (19.172–7) mentions five "peoples" (Achaeans, Eteocretans, Cydonians, Dorians, and Pelasgians), and Herodotus (7.170–1) marks out the inhabitants of both Polichna (in the west) and Praisos (in the east) as being different from other Cretans.

The far west comprises a number of settlements (later "cities") in the southwest corner of the island, whose archaic phases are little known, and the cities of Phalarssana, Polyrrhenia and Polichna, whose archaic phases remain underexplored. Ancient Cydonia (modern Khania) is the most important city of this region. This is the area of the Cydonians and Polichnitai (if they are not the same), and its pottery was distinct from the center from Protogeometric times onwards. To the east, the region of Sphakia (around Anopolis), the Ayios Vassilios valley, the cities of Aptera, Lappa, and "Onythe behind Rethymnon," and the Amari valley (comprising ancient Sybrita) are something of a gray area. What little we know indicates closer affinities with the center than the far west.

The center, from Eleutherna in the west to Dreros in the east, is the largest region, and the one that figures most prominently in the literary and epigraphic record. It comprises the cities north of Mt. Ida, Eleutherna and Axos (Oaxos), and then Knossos, Eltynia, Lyttos and Dreros. To the south, it encompasses the cities of Phaistos, Gortyn (Gortys), Prinias (Rhizenia), Priansos, Afrati and Biennos (modernViannos).[3] Though there are some slight differences between north and south, in material terms it is fairly homogeneous. To the east is another "grey area," comprising the cities of Olous, Lato, Malla and Hierapytna and the complex of settlements around modern Kavousi. None of these cities seem to have been prominent in archaic times. Over the Thriphte range is the Siteia peninsula, the far east of Crete, at whose center is ancient Praisos, city of the Eteocretans. This is R. C. Bosanquet's "Cretan Wales" (1940: 64), in whose "Pembrokeshire," in the north-east corner, is the Greek city of Itanos.[4]

This regional diversity makes any "Cretan" generalization hazardous, and should raise suspicions about the tendency in ancient authors to refer to the "Cretans" rather than to the inhabitants of Lyttos, Knossos, and so forth. Similar caveats apply to the material record.

Material Sequence and Terminology

The type site for Geometric and archaic Crete remains Knossos. Rescue excavation in Khania and systematic excavations of Geometric and Archaic deposits from Eleutherna, Kommos, Afrati, Kato Symi, and the Kavousi area may change this picture eventually, but for the time being the Knossian sequence provides the essential chronological yardstick for the whole of Crete, since it is only from Knossos that we can closely relate burial, sanctuary, and domestic deposits (chiefly from wells).[5]

A word of caution is needed about absolute chronology. Just as there is no narrative of Cretan political history, so there is no Cretan event (such as the Persian destruction of the Athenian acropolis) that directly connects the historical and archaeological sequences. Our only link with the broader Greek sequence (on which see generally Whitley 2001: 60–74) is through imports. There are therefore no true absolute dates for archaic Crete; dating is often purely "stylistic," and the best we can do is to divide the sequence into slots of 25 years or so.

At Knossos around 800 there was no one "style." There are at least two styles of painted pottery, the "Protogeometric B," a mix of Protogeometric and essentially Orientalizing styles, and the atticizing "Early Geometric." Contemporary metalwork is by contrast overwhelmingly "Oriental" in technique, style, and iconography. This mix of style persists during the later eighth century, the "Middle Geometric," and even, towards its end, in Knossian Late Geometric. Euboean and Attic imports allow us to link these phases to the broader Greek ceramic sequence.

The Geometric is followed in the seventh century by the so-called Orientalizing phase, divided into "Early" and "Late." This too can be tied in with the broader Greek sequence through Corinthian and east Greek imports. But the burial record of Knossos ceases abruptly around 630, and no domestic deposits can be dated to between 600 and 525. Nor can any central Cretan metalwork be securely assigned to this period. After 525, the Knossian sequence can again be linked to the broader Greek through a number of Attic and Laconian imports.

This break in the Knossian sequence has been called the "archaic gap" (Coldstream and Huxley 1999). But the gap is more artistic than archaeological, and more Knossian than Cretan. Some time ago, archaic pottery with a south Cretan chemical "signature" and stylistic similarities to Knossian Late Orientalizing had been identified in sixth-century levels at Tocra (Taucheira) in Libya.[6] More recently, a sequence of sixth-century pottery has been identified through close examination of stratified deposits from Eleutherna and Afrati.[7] This fineware pottery is very plain, which perhaps explains why hitherto it has been overlooked.

Gods, sanctuaries, and cult[8]

At first sight, the shrine of Kato Symi Viannou seems a Cretan Delphi. It is set high in the mountains, amongst pine trees, below a cleft in a south-facing limestone cliff. As at Delphi, the light seems to shine from the rock itself, and to the east a cold spring (Krya Vryssi) bubbles from the ground. But if the aesthetics seem identical, the experience of a worshiper coming to this shrine in ancient times would be markedly different. For here was neither temple nor oracle, neither treasuries nor games. The agonistic spirit, between man and man and state and state, which Delphi exemplifies, is here conspicuous by its absence. A visitor/worshiper arriving at this shrine in, say, 650, is likely to have been a very young man from the polis of Biennos (Viannos), coming perhaps not as an individual but as part of a group during his initiation into his *agele*, or "herd." He would offer, either as a thank-offering or as a prayer for future success, a bronze inscribed plaque or animal figurine to the male deity of the place, later identified as Hermes. But he would, most probably, leave no trace, no inscription of his name nor that of the deity on his offering.[9]

Kato Symi illustrates the difference between Cretan and mainland cult. For neither the pantheon nor the iconography, neither the architecture nor the topography of Cretan sanctuaries conform to any mainland or Aegean "Greek" pattern. To be sure, by classical times the Olympian gods Aphrodite, Apollo, Athena, Demeter, Hermes, and Zeus can be identified, and other mainland deities (Eileithyia, Rhea) are also known. Cretan cults to Apollo (Apollo Pythios at Gortyn, Apollo Delphinios at Dreros) had clear links to Delphi (but not Delos) – Cretan seafarers indeed are held responsible for the foundation of Apollo's cult in the Homeric *Hymn to Pythian Apollo* (3.391–6). But we also know of important Cretan deities with no mainland equivalent, such as Dictynna and Britomartis. The Dictynnaion in western Crete, a sanctuary linked particularly to Cydonia, was, according to Strabo, one of the most important shrines in Crete.[10] Moreover, even if Cretan Zeus shares the name of the deity worshiped at Olympia, he shares few of the attributes. This is not merely a matter of epithets. Cretan Zeus seems to be more of a youth-cum-fertility god, the "greatest youth," born in a cave and attended by other youths (the Kouretes), than the sky-god and father figure of Homer.[11]

The same oddities can be seen in the iconography. The great series of votive shields (or tympana) from the sanctuaries of Zeus at the Idaean cave and Palaikastro (e.g., figure 14.1) have scenes which cannot be linked to any mainland cycle, or assimilated into any mainland myth.[12] More peculiar still is the iconography of female deities, in particular the "Goddess with Upraised Arms" (Alexiou 1958). This image goes back at least to the late Bronze Age, and survives into the Geometric and Archaic. Figure 14.2 shows two sides of a "Protogeometric B" (PGB) straight-sided *pithos* from the North Cemetery at Knossos (around 800).[13] On one side, the goddess

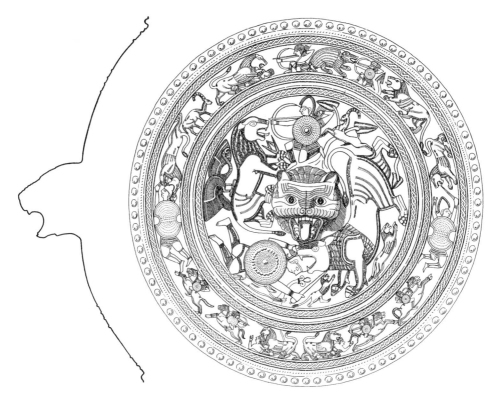

Figure 14.1   The Hunt Shield, a bronze votive tympanum from the Idaean cave
Source: After Kunze (1931: fig. 1).

(apparently in summer/spring) is being wheeled out on a cart; she holds her arms upraised and a bird in each hand; on the other (in winter) she has her arms lowered, and she drops the birds. So she seems to be some kind of fertility deity, and, if one were determined to identify her with one of the Olympians, either Persephone or Demeter suggests herself. Persephone is unknown in Crete. Demeter however was certainly worshiped at Knossos, her cult being identified by an inscription dating to around 450 (Coldstream 1973a: 131–3 no. 14). But, even if the name was the same, as with "Cretan Zeus" the iconographic and cultic attributes are different. She is not a mainland Demeter.

   All this suggests that we are dealing, not with a standard regional variation of the Olympian pantheon, but with a distinct Cretan pantheon that is being gradually assimilated into the Olympian. Other considerations support this hypothesis. First, the Bronze Age pedigree of Cretan cult is much clearer than it is on the mainland. The shrine at Kato Symi, for example, begins in the Old Palace period and cult continues unbroken into Roman times. Second, the epigraphic attestation for the "Olympian" names for these deities is late – that of Demeter at Knossos being one of the earliest. Third, a particular Cretan pantheon would help to account for Cretan peculiarities of sacred architecture and sacred topography.

Figure 14.2 Protogeometric B straight-sided pithos from Knossos, north cemetery
Source: KMF 107.14.

The characteristic Cretan temple is the hearth temple, a rectangular structure with stone benches around the inside and a central hearth (see figure 14.3). Such temples seem to be derived from the bench temple of LMIIIB to Protogeometric times. The earliest such structure is temple A at Kommos dated to around 1020. By 650, hearth temples are found at Kommos (temple B), Prinias (Rhizenia) and Dreros in central Crete.[14] Such architecture presupposes a very different set of cult practices from the mainland. For one thing, hearth temples would have been far less suitable for the sacrifice of large animals than the huge open-air altars of Olympia or the Samian Heraion. Analysis of the animal bones from Kommos reveals that sheep/goat, cattle, pig, birds and fish were consumed, probably after sacrifice, and that such consumption probably took place within the hearth temple itself (Reese 2000). Large open-air altars are rare in Crete. This is not to say that there were no altars – small altar(s) existed at the shrine of Kato Symi near Viannos and (less certainly) at several sanctuaries close to Praisos in the east. And architectural types other than the hearth temple existed – the late archaic temple of Apollo Pythios (Riccardi 1987) and the structure at the acropolis shrine (to "Athena"),[15] both at Gortyn, are cases in point.

Two major factors seem to determine the location of mainland sanctuaries: the identity of the deity worshiped, and the "politics" of cult, that is the relationship of

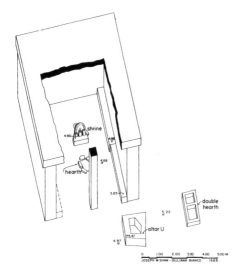

Figure 14.3 Isometric reconstruction of Kommos, temple B
Source: After Shaw and Shaw (2000: pl. 1.31).

the sanctuary to the city it served.[16] From what evidence we have, however, the mainland seems a poor template for Crete. A Cretan "Athena" seems to have been worshiped within the acropolis at Gortyn, but the two certain sanctuaries of Apollo (at Gortyn and Dreros) are located at the heart of the city, and not set in some remote or mountainous location, like the great sanctuaries of Delphi or Delos. And Cretan Zeus fits no mainland model.

Cretan Zeus was not a god of mountain tops – there are few (if any) "peak sanctuaries" in Iron Age and archaic Crete. His richest shrines are the cave sanctuaries of Psychro (the so-called Dictaean cave) and Ida,[17] and his two principal other shrines are coastal: Zeus Thenatas at Amnisos in the territory of Knossos and Dictaean Zeus at modern Palaikastro in the territory of Praisos.[18] It is these two sanctuaries that seem best to fit de Polignac's model for the location of "extra-urban" sanctuaries, since both lie at the very extremity of each city's territory. The shrine at Palaikastro lies just south of the river bed that probably formed the boundary with the neighboring city of Itanos, to which the sanctuary is far more accessible than from Praisos. Elsewhere, however, the politics of cult are harder to discern. The cave sanctuaries at Psychro and Ida do not seem to have been controlled by any single city; we cannot tell which state controlled Kommos – it ought to be Phaistos, but the relationship is far from certain. Cydonia's Dictynnaion is set at the end of a barren peninsula, territory hardly worth contesting.[19] No prominent sanctuaries have been found interposed between the warring states of Knossos, Eltynia and Lyktos, or between Prinias (Rhizenia) and Gortyn. Politics therefore was not the principal factor in the location of cult sites.

But if not politics, then what? And if the identification of cult is so uncertain, what approach should we adopt? Two are possible. One is to examine, in some detail, the types of locations chosen for cult sites – the phenomenological approach. The other is to look in detail at the types of votives. Both approaches require comparisons with the mainland. In the topography of cult, the Cretans' preference for cave sanctuaries (mainly to Zeus, but sometimes to Hermes) is unusual from a mainland perspective. Cave shrines, principally to Pan and the Nymphs, do not become prominent in Attica at least until after the battle of Marathon. Here too there are regional variations (Whitley 2001: 147). In the Siteia peninsula in east Crete, caves are used for burials, not for cult (Tsipopoulou 1987; 1990). In this region two other types of location are prominent. First are the apparently open-air "spring shrines" at Mesamvrysis, Vavelloi and Roussa Ekklesia with rich deposits of terracotta plaques and lamps (Forster 1902; Papadakis 1989). Second are the "ruin cults," sanctuaries built over Bronze Age ruins, such as Tou Koukou tou Kephali near Zakros and, most prominent of all, Dictaean Zeus at Palaikastro, erected over the remains of the Bronze Age town.[20] Such preferences are, however, not quite so obvious in central Crete. In many places (Knossos, Phaistos, Ayia Triada) Bronze Age ruins could hardly be avoided, and there are few major deposits of terracottas associated with springs.

Cretan votive assemblages have not been much studied, still less quantified. It is only from Kato Symi that we can begin to make a systematic comparison with mainland practices. Here the bronze animal figurines and incised bronze plaques seem to peak in the years just before 600 (table 14.1). Metal votives in the sixth century number in the tens,[21] rather than the hundreds or even thousands from the Argive Heraion, Olympia, or Artemis Orthia near Sparta (Whitley 2001: 146, 311). This picture is consistent with other sanctuaries. The bronze tympana and tripods that are such a characteristic feature of shrines to Zeus on Mt.Ida and at Palaikastro date to around 700, and fall off thereafter (table 14.2; Kunze 1931; Maass 1977). The finds from the acropolis sanctuary of Gortyn[22] and the Demeter sanctuary at Knossos do not suggest that what Cretans lacked in metal deposition they made up in terracottas. Nor is Cretan parsimony in votive deposition compensated by an ambitious programme of temple building. Seventh-century hearth temples are small, and only

Table 14.1 Bronzes from the Sanctuary of Kato Symi, Viannou

Period (BC)	Votive type (total)	Bronze plaques	Anthropomorphic figurines	Animal figurines
tenth cent. (PG)	0	2	30	32
ninth cent.	0	2	135	137
eighth cent.	1	8	281	290
seventh cent.	51	13	86	150
sixth cent.	13	3	0	16
fifth cent.	2	0	0	2
Total	67	28	532	627

Source: Lebessi (1985; 2002); Schürmann (1996).

Table 14.2 Late Geometric (eighth-century) bronzes at Cretan sanctuaries

Sanctuary	Idaean cave	Dictaean Zeus (Palaikastro)	Praisos (Altar Hill)
Type of votive			
Shield (tympana)	83	4	0
Tripod	35	8	2
Total	118	12	2

Source: Kunze (1931); Maass (1977); Langdon (1993: 165–7, no. 62).

two Cretan temple structures can be dated to the sixth century: Apollo Pythios at Gortys, and Dictaean Zeus at Palaikastro. In this, as in so many other areas, Crete runs counter to mainland trends.

Settlements, Houses, and Burials

By 800, Cretans had, by and large, abandoned the upland "refuge settlements" that had been occupied from around 1300–1200 onwards. Not all Cretans had fled to the hills of course – the lowland site of Knossos had been occupied continuously from the end of the Bronze Age. But by 800 coastal sites are rarer than they had been in the Late Bronze Age. Defensible hilltops, situated some way inland but much closer to good arable terrain than the refuge settlements (on which see Nowicki 2000), are now the preferred locations. Not all such locations became the nuclei of later poleis: Ligourtino is one of several low hills above the Mesara plain occupied around 800, but for not much longer thereafter. Yet most were, and by the eighth century the acropoleis of Eleutherna, Phaistos, Gortyn, Prinias, Lyktos, Afrati, Dreros, and Praisos were well established.[23] It is hard accurately to measure their size; indications from Praisos suggest a range between 10 and 16 hectares.

Until recently, we knew very little about the internal structure of these settlements. From Knossos we have mainly well deposits; from Phaistos there are some Geometric houses with streets preserved; the phases at Prinias are hard to define; and the only complete plans of archaic houses come from Onythe Goulediana (Platon 1954; 1955; 1956). These, though relatively large, are still simple two-room structures, with a series of single rooms opening straight onto an open area (not necessarily a court). There are no signs of any internal courtyard houses: one- and two-room structures remain the norm in classical and hellenistic Crete.[24] Excavations at Azoria in the Kavousi area have changed this picture. Several archaic structures have been found. Such structures seem to have been built out of a "spine wall," and otherwise arranged to follow the contours of the hill.[25] One particularly large structure, with a destruction horizon dating to ca. 500, has been interpreted as an *andreion* (on which more below).

Major settlements were surrounded by their cemeteries. The cemeteries of the acropolis sites of Eleutherna, Prinias, and Afrati have been thoroughly investigated, but the clearest picture comes from Knossos. Here were extensive cemeteries of chamber tombs; the North Cemetery being the largest, with the smaller Fortetsa cemetery to the west. Scattered groups of tombs were also found to the south (Gypsades) and east (Coldstream 1984a; Coldstream and Huxley 1999). For adults, interment was, by 800, mainly a case of cremation in an urn, which was then placed in the chamber or dromos of the rock-cut chamber tomb.[26] Urns, such as the straight-sided *pithos* in figure 14.2, could be elaborately painted, but many were much more simply decorated. In the ninth and eighth centuries the simpler urns are "coarse" in fabric. By the seventh, the elaborate polychrome "Orientalizing" necked *pithoi* are balanced by those painted in a linear style. Such plain urns do not seem to have been poorer in grave goods than the more elaborately painted examples. In any case, few goods were actually placed inside the urn. This is not to say that the tombs were poorly furnished – often they are full of elaborate bronze and iron work, such that tombs can be "ranked" in a general hierarchy.[27] But such offerings are not clearly associated with any individual – they seem to belong to the "group."

What were these groups? The natural inference is that they are families, and there is indeed some (slight) support in the human osteology for this hypothesis (Musgrave 1996). If so, there appear to have been major changes to the kinship structure of Knossos between 850 and 630. Many tombs seem to have been established just before 800 and stayed in use until at least 700, a period of four or five generations. The number of interments in urns peaks in the Late Geometric period, and declines thereafter. In the seventh century, fewer tombs are in use, but some tombs have many more urns. Tomb P from Fortetsa, for example, has 27 Early Orientalizing and 36 Late Orientalizing interments, compared to an average of 4 for a "Proto-Geometric B/Early Geometric" tomb and 5 for a Late Geometric one (table 14.3).[28] This picture suggests a move from a position where the basic kinship unit of Knossos was the "nuclear family," to the establishment of "segmentary lineages" by 700 and larger clans by the end of the Orientalizing period. Of course, such a "plain reading" is full of pitfalls, but it is hard to avoid the inference that Knossian kinship structure changed considerably in this period.

After 630, the burial record of Knossos stops abruptly. Though some burials at Afrati can be dated after this, the same seems to be true of most of central Crete.

Table 14.3 No. of interments (cremations in urns) in EIA tombs from the Fortetsa and Lower Gypsades cemeteries at Knossos

Tomb	Period (interments/ period)	PGB/EG	MG	LG	EO	LO	Totals average
L	7	—	—	—	—	7	7
OD	4	—	—	—	—	4	4
X (chi)	6	6	6	—	—	18	6
VIII	—	2	2	1	—	5	−1.66
TFT	4	4	4	1	—	13	4.33
F	4	2	3	5	—	14	4.66
VII	2	3	3	3	3	14	2.8
P2 (rho2)	—	1	6	8	2	17	4.25
II	—	—	4	8	10	22	7.33
P (rho)	2	1	7	27	36	73	14.6
Lower Gypsades	3	6	12	9	4	34	6.8
Totals	32	25	47	62	55	221	
Average no of interments per tomb, per period	4	3.125	5.22	7.62	11		

Source: Brock (1957); Coldstream et al. (1981).

Though there are some late archaic (post-525) finds in one or two tombs, the burial record of Knossos does not really pick up again until the hellenistic period. It seems highly unlikely that Knossians simply stopped burying their dead. There are many ways of disposing of dead bodies that the archaeologist is unlikely to pick up, cremations in pits or plain *pithoi* being two possibilities.

Production and Consumption:
Pottery and Metalwork

Archaic Crete produced only as much fine painted pottery as it could consume locally. Very little Cretan pottery was exported. Finds from the Orientalizing kiln at Knossos suggest local production for local demand (Coldstream and MacDonald 1997: 197–9), and very few Knossian pots found their way to other parts of Crete. Patterns of production and consumption of large coarseware storage jars (*pithoi*) may have been different – modern parallels suggest more specialized production in fewer centers and a wider pattern of distribution. But such coarsewares have yet to receive the attention they deserve from ceramic petrologists. Moreover the marked difference between shapes found in tomb and domestic (well) assemblages from Knossos suggest that production was geared to particular, specialized demands. The painted polychrome *pithoi* from Fortetsa and the North Cemetery can have served no purpose other than as ash urns – the bright paint is poorly bonded to the fabric of the pot, and would quickly disappear in domestic use. It is the same with coroplasty. Though there are significant iconographic similarities between the terracotta plaques from Gortyn and the Praisos area,[29] it is clear that moulds did not travel. The deposits represent two local schools of terracotta production deposited in local sanctuaries.

Metalwork is a slightly different story. Cretan bronze and iron production had, of course, continued throughout the Early Iron Age. Most simple jewellery (pins, fibulae) and cosmetic equipment (razors, tweezers) were of bronze. By 700 ironworkers had extended their range beyond the usual weapons and small tools, and were making the elaborate firedogs we find in the North Cemetery of Knossos. Such facts could easily be fitted into the general model of "localism," were it not for a spectacular change that took place at around 850. Suddenly elaborate bronzes (such as quivers) and gold jewellery are being produced and consumed in Knossos. The sophisticated techniques required to produce such bronzes have no local antecedents, and the style and iconography of the objects is reminiscent of North Syria. Boardman long ago suggested that these were made by an immigrant group of North Syrian craftsmen, adapting their skills to local demand.[30] The tympana or shields found in the Idaean cave and at Palaikastro seem to be the later products of this workshop (e.g., figure 14.1). But here the line ends. The Cretan bronzes being produced around 600, in particular the cuirasses, helms, and *mitrai* from Rethymnon, Onythe, Axos, Afrati and Dreros, owe nothing to this workshop (Hoffmann 1972).

The demand for armor is normally created by warfare, and our (very late) sources suggest that inter-city wars in Crete were as endemic as they were in any other part of Greece. This warfare may not have been of the standard hoplite type. Crete had a reputation for archery, and Cretan equipment lacks one crucial element – the shield. To be sure, votive miniature shields have been found at Gortyn and Praisos, and there are representations of hoplites with shields on the terracotta frieze from Palaikastro. But it is odd that no shield turned up in the Afrati deposit, and no bronze shield has been traced to Crete. A more "open" style of warfare than the hoplite phalanx, perhaps requiring a clearer vision than the Corinthian helmet allows, might also explain the absence of a nose-piece on the Cretan helmet.[31]

Oddities in Cretan pottery production may also be linked to the peculiarities of Cretan demand. In the Early Iron Age, Crete, like any other part of Greece, was producing kraters and drinking vessels. This assemblage has, rightly, been seen as related to drinking practices ancestral to the symposium. In most parts of Greece, this assemblage becomes more elaborate through time – the kraters and even the cups are covered with figure scenes, and a full range of pouring and storing vessels appears. Archaic Crete bucks this trend. Cretan kraters, and particularly Cretan kraters with figured scenes are more common in the years before 800 than they were thereafter. The drinking assemblage becomes plainer and simpler, the monochrome one-handled cup ousting other drinking shapes (in particular the bell *skyphos*) by about 700 (tables 14.4 and 14.5). This is one of many indications that symposium culture

Table 14.4 Pottery from temples at Kommos

	Kraters	%	Drinking vessels	%	Total
Temple A deposits (1020–800 BC)	23	(15)	76	(49.7)	153
Temple B deposits (800–600 BC)	8	(3.8)	102	(48.6)	210
Totals (averages)	31	(8.5)	178	(49)	363

Source: From Callaghan and Johnston (2000).

Table 14.5 Pottery from domestic deposits at Knossos

	Kraters	%	Drinking vessels	%	Total vessels
10th/9th cent. deposits	57	(20.4)	87	(31.1)	280
8th cent. deposits	30	(20.4)	46	(31.3)	147
7th cent. deposits	47	(12)	71	(18.2)	391
Late archaic deposits (535–480 BC)	19	(7.5)	73	(28.95)	253
Early classical deposits (480–400 BC)	3	(10.7)	10	(35.7)	28
Totals (averages)	156	(14.2)	193	(17.6)	1099

Source: From Coldstream (1972; 1973; 1992; 1999); Coldstream and Sackett (1978); Coldstream and Macdonald (1997); Callaghan (1992: 90–4).

did not take root in Crete. This, and the peculiarities of its visual culture, set Crete apart, not only from archaic Greece, but from much of the archaic Mediterranean in the sixth century.

Visual Culture: Art and Iconography

Archaic Greek visual culture takes two principal forms: sculpture and painted pottery. The setting for sculpture was the tomb or the sanctuary, and the context for much painted pottery the symposium. By 700, Cretan bronzeworkers had managed to produce small freestanding sculptures in the round using the *sphyrelata* technique; but no examples of large cast bronzes using the lost wax method have been traced to Crete. Similarly, there are many seventh-century examples of limestone sculpture, from the frieze at temple A at Prinias to the daedalic *kouros* from Astritsi. But Crete has only one small fragment of archaic marble sculpture; sixth-century Cretan sculpture is represented principally by some large terracottas from Axos and the Praisos area.[32]

On the mainland and through much of the Aegean, it is painted pottery that earliest becomes the vehicle for visual narrative. Most of the shapes of the painted pottery from Corinth, Attica, the east Aegean, and Laconia are symposium shapes – kraters, cups, amphoras, and pouring vessels (hydrias, *oinochoai*). Cups in particular have a tendency to become larger and more elaborately decorated, and it is on cups, amphoras, and kraters that most complex narrative scenes are to be found. There is nothing like this in archaic Crete. The Orientalizing polychrome funerary *pithoi* from Knossos are decorated with lotus palmettes and bird panels; but the figured scenes are in many ways less complex (if more accomplished) than earlier Protogeometric B examples. Imported symposium shapes are rare. Two East Greek *dinoi* are found with symposium assemblages from the Knossian North Cemetery.[33] But in the sixth century, imports are fewer – there are two imported Attic kraters, one from Knossos (post-525; Coldstream 1973b) and an earlier "Sophilan" dinos from Gortyn (Johannowsky 1956). The most popular import is the Laconian stirrup krater, which is imitated, but the attraction of this shape seems to have lain in its almost total lack of visual interest – all examples have a shiny black glaze, the only decoration being around the rim. This preference is in keeping with the austere Cretan drinking vessel – the monochrome necked cup. It seems that, just after the symposium crystallized in Corinth and Athens around 630, Crete turned its back on this institution. This seems to have inhibited the development of narrative art.

Now of course there was figured art in late seventh and sixth century Crete, the outstanding examples being bronze armor. But most of these are decorated with antithetical figures (human or animal) that are more heraldic than narrative. There are more complex scenes – the Rethymnon mitra (figure 14.4) is the outstanding example, and there has been no lack of ingenious attempts to identify such scenes with episodes from the corpus of Greek myth.[34] No such identification has ever commanded wide assent, because the scenes lack the standard iconographic or epigraphic clues that would make identification secure. They may not allude to known "Greek" myths at all. The most plausible interpretation of the Rethymnon mitra is that it represents some kind of Cretan initiation rite.

Figure 14.4 The Rethymnon mitra
Source: After Poulson (1906: fig. XXIII).

This move away from visual narrative is all the more surprising if we consider what came before. For between 850 and 700 Crete had the richest visual culture of the whole Aegean world; figured scenes are common on Protogeometric B pottery, and some (like figure 14.2) can plausibly be called narrative. The scenes on bronze shields from the Idaean cave, particularly the "Hunt Shield" (figure 14.1), are complex and can hardly not be classed as narrative art. Crete had clearly failed to live up to its early promise. Here the standard explanations of classical art history – "influence," "individual genius," "craft tradition," and so forth – fail us. The explanation, whether cultural or social, must lie deeper and should be sought by looking at other aspects of Crete's material expression and its relation with the wider world.

External Relations

Crete, as Arthur Evans saw clearly, is at the crossroads of the eastern Mediterranean. Geography dictates that of all the Aegean islands it is most liable to influence. A consideration of Crete's position in the late ninth and early eighth centuries bears this out, for there are many signs of contact both with the Levant and other parts of the Aegean. The earliest phase of the shrine at Kommos appears to be a "tripartite shrine" of a known Canaanite (Phoenician) type;[35] a school of north Syrian metal-workers was active in north central Crete; pot painters at Knossos were incorporating motifs derived from both Levantine metalwork and Attic painted pottery in the Protogeometric B, and Early, Middle and Late Geometric styles. Protogeometric B is indeed the first "Orientalizing" style of the Iron Age Aegean. The find of both an inscribed Phoenician bronze bowl (Snycer 1979) and a Sardinian *askos* from late ninth-century contexts from Knossos (Vagnetti 1989) testify to the role that Crete played in east–west trade in the wider Mediterranean. Though Corinthian and East Greek imports oust the earlier Attic and Euboean wares in seventh-century Knossos, it is clear that wider Aegean networks are being maintained. In the later seventh century, Cretans played a role in the colonization of both Sicily (Gela: Thuc. 6.4.3) and North Africa (Taucheira in Libya). Then comes the "archaic gap."

A commonsense interpretation of the gap is that it is the result of some external force – a drought or plague. Recent scholarship has however emphasized that the gap is not so much archaeological as artistic – it is a gap in visual culture. Public inscriptions continue throughout the sixth century in central Crete (see below), and there is no gap in the ceramic sequence. It is just that the pottery is very plain. Imports too testify to a wide range of external contacts. Proponents of the drought or civil strife theories might argue that the plainness of the pottery is a sign of impoverishment. But the gradual simplification of Cretan figured scenes had been going on throughout the seventh century, and so the sixth-century Cretan preference for the plain over the ornate can more plausibly be seen as the culmination of a more gradual process of turning away from visual culture.

One thing is clear – Crete may have been "impoverished," but was not isolated. Both the practice of inscribing law codes, and the peculiar Cretan name for scribe (*poinikastas*) show Crete's continuing debt to the Near East. More striking, however, is the number of Cretans who went abroad. The mercenaries who inscribed their names on the Memnonion at Abydos in Egypt,[36] Hybrias with his drinking song (mentioned above), Ergoteles from Knossos but "racing for Himera" in the foot race at Olympia (Pindar *Ol.* 12), and Dipoinis and Skyllis, the Cretan sculptors who worked at Kleonai and Sicyon (Pliny *NH* 36.9–10) were full participants in the East Mediterranean cultural mix. What were these Cretans getting away from?

Law, Literacy, and the Cretan *Polis*

Cretan literacy is unique in the Aegean world. From Thera to Athens, and from Euboea to Pithekoussai the Greek alphabet seems to have encouraged personal and poetic expression in the years around 700. Crete's strong and early links with the Near East, and in particular the presence of literate Phoenicians before 800, led an earlier generation of scholars to suggest that the island might be one of the points from which the alphabet was first adapted and then transmitted to the rest of the Aegean. But the earliest Cretan inscription, from Phaistos,[37] is clearly later than the earliest Euboean and Attic examples. The Greek alphabet was developed elsewhere, and for purposes for which Cretans had little use (see, generally, Powell 1991). When Cretans came to employ it, alphabetic literacy took a very strange turn.

Archaic Cretans had a remarkable propensity for inscribing laws in large letters on stone. Legal fragments dating to between 650 and 450 have been found in almost all the major cities of central Crete – Eleutherna, Axos, Phaistos, Gortyn, Prinias (Rhizenia), Afrati, Knossos, Eltynia, Lyktos (Lyttos), and Dreros. Unlike other examples of early Greek law, few laws are procedural (see below). Most have a very specific application, governing everything from terms of office to pasturage rights. Many prescribe equally specific penalties for breaking the law. Cretan laws leave very little room for interpretation, that is, for the discretion of a magistrate or a judge. While public inscriptions are common, personal inscriptions and names are rare.[38] Such graffiti, votive inscriptions, and inscribed tombstones as do exist tend either to be early (as at Kommos) or to be found on coastal sites principally in the eastern or western extremities of the island (tombstones at Cydonia, graffiti on rocks in the Itanos area). Many such informal inscriptions are not in Cretan, but in Boeotian or Aeginetan scripts.[39] Either fewer individuals were literate than elsewhere in the Aegean, or personal expression through writing was in some way discouraged. In any case, the bulk of archaic Cretan writing seems to be monumental writing in the service of the *polis*. And public writing was a skill with relatively high status, as the Spensithios inscription makes clear (figure 14.5).[40] This seems to be a contract between Spensithios and the "Dataleis." Spensithios and his descendants are to be the *mnamon kai poinikastas* ("remembrancer and scribe") of this community, having a monopoly of public writing, "both human and divine." In Crete a scribe seems not merely to be a kind of secretary: Spensithios was admitted to the community's *andreion*, or men's club. This put him very close to the oligarchic elite.

With one exception, all our sources agree that Cretan (and especially central Cretan) cities were oligarchies, run by *kosmoi* or "regulators," who were elected annually.

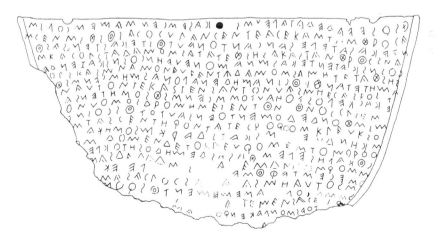

Figure 14.5 The Spensithios inscription and mitra
Source: BM 1969.4.2.1, side A.

Strict rules governed the frequency with which any individual could hold office (Dreros). Clear and specific penalties were defined for individuals who broke the rules. Cretan laws also governed other institutions; the conduct of youths in the *agelai* (Eltynia); the dues owed to one's *andreion*.[41] The institutions described by Strabo and other late hellenistic/Augustan writers (Dosiadas) were therefore well developed by late archaic times.[42] Indeed, they seem not to have changed very much, if at all, in the course of three hundred years.

Here we again run into the fundamental source problem of archaic Crete. It is later writers who provide the most detailed picture of Cretan institutions, but it is these very writers who present these institutions as representing an unchanging essence of "Cretanness." Cretan institutions may have changed little, but they can hardly not have changed at all. Can archaeology – in particular "archaeological history" – help?

Let us take the example of the *andreion*. Our sources agree that this was a kind of Cretan mess hall, a club for male citizens who would dine and (presumably) drink together. These late sources liken the Cretan *andreion* to the Spartan *syssition*, a "dining together." The *andreion* is an institution that ought to leave some material trace – a building, or signs of communal dining and drinking. Our late sources suggest that, while there may have been more than one *andreion* per city, an *andreion* would have had to accommodate at least fifty, if not a hundred, diners at one sitting. Can we identify such a building? None of the candidates so far suggested seem quite to fit the bill. Meat was certainly consumed in and around the hearth temples, which may indeed have been "multi-functional," but, as said earlier, they are all too small; the same applies to the "armories" at Dreros and Afrati – these have all the right masculine associations, but the buildings are no more than 5 m wide and 10 m long (Xanthoudides 1918; Lebessi 1969; 1970). Larger late-archaic structures with a central *eschara* have been found at Itanos and Ayia Pelagia (Apollonia); these could just about have accommodated fifty or so people (Alexiou 1972: 235–9; 1984; Greco et al. 2000: 551–5). Preliminary reports of a large building at Azoria near Kavousi, with finds of drinking vessels and "krater stands," are certainly suggestive.[43] What is more suggestive, however, is the clear, archaeological evidence for the direction in which Cretan drinking practices were going. The Cretan plain black necked cup and plain black krater can hardly have suited the small, intimate, "aristocratic" groups of the symposium, groups which elsewhere encouraged a close link between visual and alphabetic literacy. They must instead be associated with a more austere, but also less intimate form of communal drinking – exactly the picture that Dosiadas and others present.

In traditional histories, it is the rise both of the *polis* and of the individual that represent archaic Greece's distinctive achievement. But these processes to a degree pulled in different directions. The polis was a male "citizen state," a form of collective male power that placed a greater value on one's duty to participate in, decide for, and defend one's home community than on one's duty to oneself or one's kin (Runciman 1990: esp. 348–9). The "aristocratic" individual operated on a wider canvas, his arena was international. "Aristocratic" individualism finds expression as much in the inscribed marble *kouroi* and *korai* that grace the sanctuaries of the Heraion at Samos and the Athenian acropolis as in the iambi of Archilochus or the odes of Bacchylides.

This "aristocracy" was not one that depended primarily on birth or wealth – it was, rather, an aristocracy of performance (Duplouy 2006; ch. 27, below). This performance could be relatively intimate – as in the symposium – or more public, as in the games and dedications at the major panhellenic sanctuaries of Delphi and Olympia. But, as much as individualism was agonistic, it was, in equal measure, unstable. Status had to be achieved – it could not be inherited or ascribed. This instability, together with the inherent contradiction between the "communal" *polis* and the international "aristocratic" ideal, may help to explain much that is remarkable about archaic Greece as a whole. But it does not seem to apply to Crete. By 500, the Cretan *polis* had arisen, but the Cretan individual had not. The community seems to have prevailed over the individual. It would be facile to interpret Cretan *poleis* as, in some way, proto-totalitarian, suppressing free movement and free expression, and regulating every detail of a person's (particularly a man's) course through life, however much this picture may explain Plato's attraction to Crete and accord with modern readings of that philosopher. Cretan states were oligarchies, and there had to be something in them for the oligarchs. The answer is not "power," but stability. One of the outstanding features of the Gortyn law code is its obsessive concern with rules of inheritance within the kin group, and so with assuring the essential continuity of families and family property from one generation to the next (Willetts 1967: 18–27). In Crete, birth and wealth, not performance and display, were the marks of the aristocracy. And, if stability is our major criterion, Cretan poleis were very successful, surviving as effective independent entities until the Roman conquest of 67.

Conclusion

All history is contemporary history – even, or perhaps especially, ancient Greek history. One of the driving forces behind modern scholarship on the archaic period is an interest in the origins of republican polities, and especially democracy. Recent scholarship has also emphasized that "democracy" cannot be explained by recourse to a simple narrative of political events in central Greece between 550 and 479. Democracy is more than what Cleisthenes did and suffered – it has deeper origins in the cultural practices (literacy and the symposium) of archaic Athens. What ancient historians and archaeologists both have to explain is as much the culture that made democracy possible as the political (that is, constitutional) arrangements that formally define it. Crete has two roles to play in this debate. First, epigraphy and archaeology suggest that the institutions of the Cretan *polis* had crystallized in the years around 500. In Crete, the rule of law and oligarchic republicanism emerged early in the archaic period, but democracy never developed. Crete therefore raises, in rather acute form, the question "why didn't democracy emerge more often?"[44] Second, Crete provides an important counterfactual to narratives that lay great stress on purely political arrangements. The absence of a rich visual culture, the steep fall in the number of votive offerings, the restricted use of literacy and the apparent indifference towards the symposium are features that characterize the Cretan material record in the sixth century, and it is these very features that provide important (albeit negative) clues towards any explanation of the origins of "democratic culture." The final irony, of course, is that the intellectual and cultural legacy of archaic Crete lies principally in the political discussions of the philosophers Plato and Aristotle. Crete may not have produced its own philosopher after the shadowy Epimenides, but it remains, as an anthropologist might say, "good to think with."

NOTES

1 Demargne and van Effenterre 1937: 333–48 = ML 2; Jeffery 1961 (1990): 315 no. 1a. Perlman 1992 offers the most intelligent discussion of Aristotle's "Cretan constitution," which is based mainly on that of Lyctos.
2 Guarducci, *ICr* I.10.2 (Eltynia), II.4.1 (Axos); IV.4 (Gortyn).
3 For the topography and identification of Cretan cities, see generally Faure 1960. The ancient name of Afrati remains disputed. Guarducci (*ICr* I.5 [pp. 6–7]) proposed Arkades, but Viviers 1994 suggests it was in fact "Dattalla," to which the Spensithios inscription (Jeffery and Morpurgo Davies 1970) obliquely refers.
4 On the archaeology of the "Eteocretans," see more recently Whitley 1998b.
5 For the Knossos sequence, see Brock 1957: 142–5, 213–19, qualified by Coldstream 1968: 233–55 and 327–31. For the Orientalizing, see Moignard 1996; 1998.
6 Boardman and Hayes 1966: 78–80; 1973: 36–8; Boardman and Schweizer 1977: 280.
7 Erickson 2000; 2002, building on the work of Callaghan 1978.
8 For this topic, see now the large-scale synthesis by Prent (2005).
9 Lebessi 1985: 188–98, basing her interpretation on Ephorus *FGrH* 70, 149 = Strabo 10.4.16–22; on the very few inscribed dedications found at this sanctuary, see Lebessi 1973: 191.
10 Strabo 10.4.12–13; cf. Hdt. 3.59; for the material remains, see Welter and Jantzen 1951.
11 Here I part company with the most comprehensive treatment of this subject by Verbruggen (1981), who emphasizes the similarity between the Cretan and Olympian Zeus. Verbruggen's arguments are however mainly directed against those who would deny the "Hellenic" character of Cretan Zeus.
12 Kunze 1931: 204–35; this generalization applies with particular force to the Hunt Shield (1931: 8–12, no. 60).
13 KMF 107.114; Coldstream and Catling 1996: 155; see Coldstream 1984b.
14 Kommos: Shaw and Shaw 2000: 8–24. Prinias: Pernier 1914; Watrous 1998. Dreros: Marinatos 1936. For the architecture of Dreros and Prinias A, see Beyer 1976.
15 Rizza and Scrinari 1968; Johannowsky 2002.
16 Scully 1979; de Polignac 1984; 1995a; ch. 22 below.
17 Dictaean Cave: Hogarth 1900; Boardman 1961: 1–75; Watrous 1996: 43–5, 53–5, 100–5. Ida: Halbherr 1888; Sakellarakis 1988; Kunze 1931.
18 Amnisos: Schäfer 1992: 159–78, 226–39. Palaikastro: Bosanquet 1905.
19 The epigraphic evidence (*ICr* I.12) indicates that both Axos and Gortyn were involved in cult at the Idaean Cave, and the setting for dialogue in Plato's *Laws* (625b) is the path from Knossos to the Cave. The Dictynnaion does seem to have changed hands: Herodotus 3.59 reports that it was founded by the Cydonians, but by Strabo's day (10.4.13) it lay within the territory of Polyrrhenia.
20 See D'Agata 1998 for Ayia Triada; generally, Prent 2003.
21 Lebessi 1985: 21–57; 2002: 56–142; Schürmann 1996.

22 Rizza and Scrinari 1968; Johannowsky 2002.

23 For settlement change, see Sjögren 2003; Wallace 2003.

24 For comparison with developments in the rest of the Aegean, see Morris 1998a; ch. 4 above.

25 *AR* 49 (2002–3) 83–4; 50 (2003–4) 86–7.

26 For the relevant evidence, see Brock 1957; Coldstream and Catling 1996. For discussion of the burial customs, see Cavanagh 1996. It is not entirely clear what the general rule for child burial was, though it seems that the only persons not cremated in = eighth and seventh century Knossos were infants. For plain and decorated urns, see Whitley 2004. For a hierarchy of tombs based on bronze and iron finds, see separately Catling 1996 and Snodgrass 1996, respectively.

27 Musgrave 1996, esp the bones from KMF tomb 285 (p. 681).

28 For tomb P, see Brock 1957: 102–38. The averages are arrived at by counting the urns of PGB to LO date from tombs L, OD, X, VIII, TFT, F, VII, P2, II and P in the Fortetsa cemetery together with those from the Lower Gypsades tomb (Coldstream et al. 1981).

29 Cassimatis 1982 (Gortyn); Halbherr 1901; Forster 1905; Dohan 1931 (Praisos).

30 For bronze and iron working generally, see Catling 1996; Snodgrass 1996. For the Fortetsa girdle (no. 1568) and quiver (no. 1569), both from tomb P, see Brock 1957: 134–6, 197–9. For the hypothesis of the North Syrian metalworkers guild, see Boardman 1961: 129–59; 1967b. This hypothesis has recently been criticized: see Hoffman 1997.

31 Cretan archers, from Lyttos (and elsewhere) are said to have intervened on the Spartan side in the second Messenian war (Pausanias 4.19.4); see Snodgrass 1977b.

32 For *sphyreleta* sculpture, see Boardman 1961: 137–8; for limestone sculpture, Davaras 1972; Adams 1978: 4–107; for the single marble *kouros* (no. 177) from Gortyn, Richter 1970: 128, 143. Praisos sculpture: Bosanquet 1940: pls. 18–19; Forster 1902: 272–8; pls. 13–14.

33 Whitley 2004; Coldstream and Catling 1996: 82–5, 94–8; figs. 79–82, 87–90.

34 On the Rethymnon mitra, see Poulsen 1906: 373–91; Hoffmann 1972: 25–26, 31–32. For an early attempt at "mythological" interpretation, see Payne 1928: 240, 286; also Moignard 1998. For the whole question, see Blome 1982: 65–104, esp. 98–104: "Bilder griechischer Sagen sind auf Kreta selten."

35 Shaw and Shaw 2000: 8–14; Shaw 1989.

36 Pedrizet and Lefebvre 1919; Masson 1976.

37 Levi 1969 = Jeffery and Johnston 1990: 468 no. 8a.

38 See, generally, Whitley 1997 with references to earlier work; criticisms: Perlman 2002.

39 The 73 seventh-century inscriptions from Kommos are mainly in Boeotian script (Csapo et al. 2000). The tombstones from Cydonia and the Ayia Pelagia inscriptions are in Aeginetan script.

40 Jeffery and Morpugo Davies 1970: 124–5, 148–52.

41 For the *kosmoi* in the Dreros inscription, see Demargne and van Effenterre 1937. For the *agelai* in the Eltynia inscription, see *ICr* I.10.2 (pp. 90–2); for mention of the *andreion* in archaic inscriptions, see ibid. line 6 (Eltynia); *ICr* II.4.1 (Axos); IV.4 (Gortyn); and the Spensithios inscription side B lines 10–12 (Jeffery and Morpugo Davies 1970: 143–4).

42 For discussion in the late sources of *syssitia* and *andreia* in particular, see Ephorus, *FGrH* 70 F149 (= Strabo, *Geography* 10.4.16); Dosiadas, *FGrH* 458 F2 (= Athenaeus *Deipnosophistae* 4.143a–f); Pyrgion, *FGrH* 467.

43 *AR* 49 [2002–3] 83–4; *AR* 50 [2003–4] 86–7; Haggis et al. 2004.

44 A question posed by Whitley 1997; 2001: 231–65; Morris 1998a; 2000.

CHAPTER FIFTEEN

Northern Greece

Zosia Halina Archibald

Introduction

Since Greece was far from being a unified area in pre-Classical times, a survey of the mainland can be divided up in a number of different ways. In this chapter all regions north of Attica will be treated together.[1] Such an approach has the merit of avoiding unduly arbitrary cultural distinctions. It also makes possible broad comparisons between regions that are rarely considered alongside one another in most narrative histories.

The lands and sites explored here include some, like Delphi in Phocis, or Thebes in Boeotia, which are virtually household names, as well as whole regions that still remain largely unknown (Aetolia, Acarnania, western Phocis, parts of Thessaly, and Macedonia), and are certainly under-explored, by historians and archaeologists alike. The geography and ecology of northern Greece are very diverse, although a few general characteristics do prevail across the whole region. The west is wetter, more mountainous and inaccessible, but enjoys a more marked Mediterranean climate, while the eastern side has colder winters, drier, hotter summers, and more low-lying terrain. The high peaks of the Pindus mountains, which are the Greek peninsula's spine from north to south (extending, in geological terms, into the Aegean as the Cycladic islands), are folded in a westerly direction, and trap much of the average rainfall on their western slopes. In antiquity, the eastern half of the peninsula was not as dry as it is today. Clay, silt, and gravel has filled what were once much deeper bays and inlets, notably the Thermaic and Malian gulfs. River water was higher, with far more water meadow, lakes, and streams, although, less attractively, coastal marshlands were periodically infested with malarial mosquitoes.[2]

Since Neolithic times, the optimal conditions of altitude, soils, and groundwater encouraged longer-term settlement in the river valleys of the eastern half, which were far more intensively settled than those in the west. The high summits of Pindus are composed of rugged, impenetrable limestone, interleaved with impermeable sandstones and shales, particularly in the north and center, as well as in the central Aetolian mountains of the south-west. The waterless limestone massifs of the region have discouraged settlement even in recent times. Instead, villages have naturally arisen at spring lines in the foothills, where limestone met impermeable rock, clays and shales. The deeper soils of the major river valleys of the east, notably the Axius, Loudias, and Haliacmon in Macedonia; in Thessaly the Peneius, its northern tributary the Titaresius, and southern Enipeus; in Boeotia the Cephissus feeding into Lake Copais, and the Asopus, could support larger population units which exploited local resources intensively over many centuries. The larger lowland sites, which generally became the earliest to acquire urban features, were not isolated pockets, but nuclei of wider activity. Extensive use of mountain resources held an important place in the lives of many communities. Pastoralism is certainly one, involving temporary shepherds' shelters during the summer months.

In terms of landscape and settlement analysis, the scale of research, archaeological as well as historical, has been uneven across northern Greece. A series of research projects focused on Boeotia and Thessaly has provided more specific data relating to longer-term research questions, such as "How was the landscape populated?,"[3] and "How did big sites in the north differ from their counterparts in the rest of Greece?" (Hansen 1995; C. Morgan 2003: 85–105). Perhaps the most striking progress has taken place in the far north. Beyond Thessaly, the expansion of research-directed fieldwork in Macedonia has provided new, and, to some extent, unexpected data, which for the first time offers historians the chance to make legitimate comparisons between this region and others in archaic Greece, even when written sources are lacking.

The modern history of the Balkan peninsula has crystallized into a number of nation states, whose territorial relationship to ancient polities is far from straightforward. We are prone to thinking of communities in terms of coherent and well-defined relationships between lands and peoples. Our assumptions are based on a lengthy process of historical development, during which various pragmatic and institutional mechanisms have been applied to deal with matters concerning inter-personal and inter-community disputes (especially over differential access to resources). This was the period when certain patterns of regional settlement and cult activity became established that would shape social organization in northern Greece for centuries to come.

Until quite recently, northern Greece was perceived as being different from the south and the islands of the Aegean. Many of the cultural features that have been identified as distinctive of this period – the emergence of *polis*-type communities, monumental temple architecture, collective burial in cemeteries composed of individual graves, figurative art, as well as more ephemeral phenomena (sports festivals, symposium culture) – have been regarded as characteristic primarily of central and southern Greece. The north was thought of as dominated by *ethne*, understood as tribal communities (Gschnitzer used the term *Stammstaaten*: 1955; 1960), living in dispersed, isolated villages, with underdeveloped political and social institutions. They were thus predominantly pastoral peoples, and urban centers developed comparatively late, under southern influence. This surprisingly polarized view of the Greek peninsula was apparently supported by near-contemporary writers, like Thucydides, who wrote that the Aetolians may have been numerous and warlike, but lived in scattered villages.

He added, rather more graphically, that the largest Aetolian grouping, the Eurytanians, spoke a barely comprehensible dialect and ate raw flesh (3.94.4–5). By taking such statements at face value, it was not difficult to accept the more deliberate rhetorical slur of "barbarians," heaped upon Macedonian kings and commoners alike by fourth century writers and orators, as a reflection of seemingly profound cultural differences (Hall 2001).

But recent research has demonstrated that the supposed polarity owes more to lack of investigation than to objective differences. Temples, or structures that resemble temples, have been discovered at a growing number of sites in the north (Schmidt–Dounas 2004). At Thermon, west of the most inaccessible highlands of Aetolia, above Lake Trichonis, lie the remains of one of the oldest temples in Greece. Many northern settlements were large, in some cases quite complex sites. Political organ-ization is another aspect of northern societies where modern perceptions have undergone revision. *Polis* structures can no longer be considered a late imitation of southern practices. Cities often had lengthy histories in the north. Although our under-standing of their institutional development is still rather sketchy for the archaic period, clear analogies can be drawn with other parts of the Greek world, though we can also form some idea of the distinctiveness of northern communities.[4]

Regions

Boeotia

The development of separate regional communities in central Greece (between the valley of the River Spercheus and the gulf of Corinth) was partly a consequence of natural geographical factors, and partly the result of historical dynamics. A chain of mountains extends the Pindus range as far as the Corinthian gulf, creating a natural barrier between the western and eastern coastal plains. In the south-east, a narrow mountain chain, Cithaeron in the west, Pateras and Parnes in the middle, and Mavrovouni in the east, constitutes the border land between Boeotia and Attica. The principal modern roads follow the preferred access routes of historical times from Thebes, in Boeotia, south-east of Lake Copais, branching at Lebadea and Orchomenus west of the Lake. One route leads due westwards, via Delphi, skirting the coast-line as far as Missolonghi, where it turns north, following the broad lowland plain east of the River Achelous, in the direction of the Ambracian gulf (gulf of Arta). A second follows the Upper Cephissus valley in northern Phocis, joining the main north–south route from Itea on the coast as far as the Pass south of Thermopylae. A third route skirts the eastern side of the Copais Basin, and thence along the coast-line, northwards to east Locris, south to Aulis, Delium, and Oropus. These modern roads trace the pattern of ancient overland and marine routes. They chart human traffic rather than physical roads, whose detailed pattern can sometimes be sketched close to settlements, but rarely demonstrated at any distance.[5] Most known sites are located in, or close to, lowland areas (figures 15.1 and 15.2). The exceptions tend to be communal meeting places, which had collective symbolic significance.

Figure 15.1 View of the Theban plain and Lake Helice from Mt. Ptoion, looking north
Source: © Christel Muller.

Figure 15.2 View of the Theban plain from Mt. Ptoion, looking towards the modern town of Kastri
Source: © Christel Muller.

Settlements

In Boeotia, intensive survey carried out between 1979 and 1984 of selected blocks of land belonging to the ancient communities of Thespiae and Haliartos, including a previously unknown concentration that has been identified as Ascra, the home of the poet Hesiod, has brought to light a dramatic change in settlement density and size that took place between the eighth and sixth centuries,[6] though its effects are visible mainly towards the end of this timescale (Schachter 1989). The increase of population reflected in the survey applies as much to smaller, rural sites, as it does to larger, proto-urban ones. Similar population changes can be documented in other parts of central Greece, notably in Attica and Euboea (Morris 1998a: 15–16). Recent investigations at a complex of structures at ancient Oropus suggest that there is still a great deal more to be learned about the earlier part of the archaic period in the region. The excavator has identified this site with Homeric Graia, subsequently renamed Oropus, and activities ranging from the eighth to the sixth centuries have been studied. In the western part of the excavated area, a variety of apsidal structures are associated with an unusually large rectangular enclosure, which may have served as a temporary fort. Important new evidence has emerged about iron technology and the organization of smithing, while in the main quarter an apsidal-ended building has been plausibly interpreted, on the basis of votive offerings, as a *heroon* – a shrine to a hero (Mazarakis Ainian 2002a).

The sixth century seems to represent a period of rapid development in Boeotia. This is most clearly reflected in the expansion of sites around the shores of Lake Copais, which was once the largest lake in the Greek mainland, extending some 10 km north–south and rather more east–west (Strabo gives it a circuit of 380 *stadia*). Seasonal flows of water from the rivers that fed the lake fluctuated dramatically, so the principal settlements were concentrated just above the flood plain surrounding the lake: Orchomenus and Copae in the north, Acraephia in the east, Coronea and Haliartus on its southern reaches. Other large sites were located on the fertile plains west (Chaeronea, Lebadea) or south of the lake (Thespiae, Thebes). Systematic attempts to control the outflow of water from the lake were in operation from the Middle Bronze Age onwards, and were renewed at various periods in antiquity.[7]

Sanctuaries

Excavations have focused on the most visible and accessible remains, often those of sanctuaries or cemeteries, rather than habitation sites. The oracular shrine of Apollo on the summit of Mount Ptoon (near Perdikovryrsi, on the western slopes of Mt. Pelagia), was situated on three terraces. Spring water from above the highest terrace fed a cistern, and thence a fountain, on the lowest terrace. The fountain was the earliest formal structure in the sanctuary, succeeded by a temple on the top terrace, in the sixth century. Dedications, consisting of bronze statuettes and tripod fragments, pottery, and relief-decorated bronze plaques, began to accumulate in the eighth century. The most spectacular individual votives were marble statues of youths and girls, principally in the second third of the sixth century (Ducat 1971). From the final third of the century, the people of Acraephia preferred to leave their personal dedications to the Hero Ptoios, at Kastraki, in the direction of Acraephia (Guillon 1943; Schachter 1989: 75). At the shrine of the Cabiri, west of Thebes, at that of Poseidon of Onchestos, and in the cities of Thebes and Orchomenus, the earliest evidence of monumental religious buildings, in the form of stone constructions and sculptural decoration, also belongs to the late sixth century.

A string of oracular shrines skirted Lake Copais, each with its own festivals and some structural elaboration: Apollo at Tegyra, near Orchomenus; Apollo Thourius near Chaeronea; Telphousa near Haliartus and Coronea; Trophonius at Lebadea; Apollo Ptoios on Mount Ptoion, and Amphiaraos, either at Thebes or at Oropos, where his cult is subsequently attested. Most of these cults were already thriving by the middle of the sixth century, while some, like Athena Itonia at Coronea, had a more precocious architectural history, with a shrine and statue established some time before the early sixth century.[8]

These developments represent the late flowering of cult traditions that had far older roots. Outside the citadel of Thebes was the sanctuary of Apollo Ismenios, where the remains of a mudbrick and wood superstructure on a stone socle have been identified with a temple of the late eighth century. Cult paraphernalia from Early to Late Geometric in style has also been used to identify additional extra-urban shrines at Thebes, as well as religious sites at Haliartus (Athena), Mount Mavrovouni (Artemis Agrotera), Coronea (?Athena Itonia), Aulis (Artemis), and Oropus (Mazarakis Ainian 1997: 242, 312–13).

Locris and Phocis

Sites

Between Boeotia and the coast opposite Euboea was the country of the east Locrians, also known as the Opuntian Locrians, after the principal population center of Opus (alternatively, "Hypocnemidian" or "Locrians under Mount Cnemis"). The people of Boeotia spoke a dialect more akin to the Thessalian. Both dialects are classified by philologists as belonging to the "Aeolic" group, whereas the Locrians used a variant of "North-west Greek." The east Locrians had become separated from their west Locrian neighbors (who were confined to the uplands between Aetolia and Phocis, with harbors at Naupactus and Oeanthea), by the expansion of the Phocians, who occupied most of the central upland region (figure 15.3), as well as the upper Cephissus valley and the southern coastal plain. The restricted scope of cultivable arable land in central Greece north and west of Boeotia resulted

Figure 15.3 View of Mt. Parnassos in Phocis
Source: © C. B. Mee.

in serious tensions between neighboring communities, when population numbers, or social pressures, made the acquisition of additional arable resources a collective priority.[9]

Sanctuaries

At the beginning of the first millennium, the sanctuary at Kalapodi in northern Phocis was also the principal shrine of central Greece. In Classical times the sanctuary was dedicated to Artemis Elaphebolus and Apollo, and at that time was controlled by the city of Hyampolis. There was a cult center at Kalapodi from the Late Bronze Age (LHIIIC: eleventh century) until the early Christian era. Around 950, the center lost much of its earlier regional importance and was reorganized. It had long been, and continued to be, the focus of communal dining for many communities living in Phocis (C. Morgan 2003: 113–20). Beneath two rectangular early archaic mud-brick temples (ca. 700–ca. 600/580), whose design has been preserved, were traces of earlier constructions (open to the air), partly obscured by these and later successors. The early archaic temples had internal ash deposits, which are thought to have been low hearth altars, or *escharai*. Temple A, slightly north of the previous focus of cult behavior, contained an axial wooden colonnade, while temple B, close to an extensive area of ash, animal bone and other votive deposits, had vertical columns on poros bases supporting the long walls and a tetrastyle columned porch.[10] Votives from the eighth century onwards have stylistic connections with Thessaly, Euboea and central Greece, though some may have been manufactured at the sanctuary, since bronzeworking debris has been discovered (Felsch 1983). Both shrines were rebuilt as peripteral stone temples, which were destroyed during the Persian invasion of 480.

Judging by the kinds of objects found at early first millennium Delphi (figure 15.4), in graves belonging to an

Figure 15.4 View of the sanctuary of Apollo at Delphi, looking eastwards
Source: © C. B. Mee.

extensive site at Medeon, on the Bay of Antikyra, and in the Corycaean Cave on a south-western slope of Mount Parnassus, the communities of southern Phocis were orientated, like many of their neighbors further west, towards the Corinthian gulf (C. Morgan 1990: 116–17, 122–6; 2003: 120–4, 213–18). Delphi was a prosperous settlement that had developed since the Late Bronze Age (LHIIIB-C: fourteenth–eleventh centuries), and continued to thrive after dedications to Apollo, in the form of bronze tripods, jewelery, and zoomorphic figurines, began to accumulate from ca. 800. There is no evidence that Pythian Apollo was worshipped here before that time and no specific indications of a cult building before the second quarter of the sixth century (Mazarakis Ainian 1997: 312; C. Morgan 2003: 122–3).

The origin of dedications, and the identity of those making them, should tell us a good deal about how the sanctuary evolved, but cannot easily be deduced. Among eighth-century finds, Peloponnesian, particularly Corinthian (or Corinthianizing) artifacts are more prominent than central Greek ones. In the seventh century Athenian votives joined this repertoire. The two most noticeable categories that distinguish votives at Delphi from those at Kalapodi are bronze tripods (with Peloponnesians and perhaps Boeotians as donors: *LSAG* 91 nos. 2a–c, 9) and Oriental-looking objects, which include faience scarabs, Cypro-Cretan and Cypro-Levantine bronze stands and other sheet bronze articles (Rolley 1969; 1977; Amandry 1987). Similar exotic imports are found among seventh century dedications to Hera at Perachora, the extra-urban sanctuary of Corinth on the Isthmus, facing west across the Corinthian gulf. At Delphi there are some Italian-made artifacts too (Kilian 1977).

The exceptional character of many of the dedications at Delphi, by interregional, not just regional standards, reflects a developing momentum at the site, at a time when virtually nothing has been revealed that defines a sanctuary as such. This is a salutary reminder of the difficulties of reconstructing the early phases of a site with a history of intensive monumentalization from the end of the first quarter of the sixth century for the next several hundred years (Jacquemin 1999). Many of these later constructions have been conserved in place for modern visitors. But this means that investigation of what came earlier is limited to "keyhole" activities between, and occasionally below, later buildings. The presence of conspicuous dedications presupposes a designated area within which they would have been displayed, whether sheltered by a roofed building of some kind, or in the open air.

It is not yet clear when the first temple was built. The seventh-century roof tiles that have sometimes been connected with a temple may belong to a *stoa* (a covered hall), or some other type of communal building. Delphi continued, until at least ca. 575, when the first *peribolos* wall was built to define the limits of the sanctuary of Apollo, to be a settlement. Houses may have gone on being built until the fire of 548, which destroyed large parts of the interior, including the first temple. This primary shrine was decorated, or redecorated, with a marble gutter in the period ca. 580–50 (Jacquemin 1993: 217–23). The first temple of Athena, in the sanctuary of "Marmaria," south-east of the shrine of Apollo, probably dates from the same period as the first temple of Apollo. Pits between the rocks in this lower sanctuary contained pottery, animal bones and ashes, belonging to dedications made in the eighth and seventh centuries (including a reburial of Late Bronze Age ceramic figurines).

The territorial and civic dimensions of Delphi have only relatively recently been examined in detail (Rousset 2002). The relationship between the settlement of Delphi, and a contemporary site at Ayia Varvara, 1km south–west of the modern village of Chryso, has yet to be clarified. Ayia Varvara has been identified with Cirrha or Crisa, the historical community that dominated the plain extending from the mountains above Delphi to the port of Cirrha on the Corinthian gulf (Skorda 1992; C. Morgan 2003: 124–5), allegedly until the "First Sacred War." Archaeological evidence from the vicinity of Delphi has yet to provide coherent, let alone conclusive, information that might help us to understand the circumstances behind the conflict that historians have dubbed "The First Sacred War" (ca. 595–586).[11] The later histories of major religious centers of the Greek mainland, including Delphi and Olympia, show that there is nothing inherently implausible about an armed conflict whose ultimate rationale was political and economic control of the sanctuary. But written accounts of the origins and early history of the cult of Pythian Apollo[12] post-date the alleged events by a considerable margin and are framed in terms that justify the outcome of the supposed conflict. No clear exposition is given of the issues, except for vague suggestions of sacrilege.

Among the pretexts for armed intervention on the part of a Thessalian force (under the command of one Eurylochus and a Hippias), Athenians (under Alcmaeon), and Sicyonians (under the tyrant Cleisthenes), was the levying of tolls by the Crisaeans on pilgrims visiting the sanctuary and the tilling of sacred land. It is impossible, on the basis of such sources alone, to separate earlier from later accretions, and to distinguish partisan elements from local legend. But that is not all the evidence we have to rely on. The "Homeric" *Hymn to Pythian Apollo*, written no later, and perhaps no earlier, than the beginning of the sixth century (Davies 1994: 203), seeks to assert the establishment of outsiders (Cretans) as priests of Delphi. The tenor of the poem, particularly the final four lines, reinforce the separation of sanctuary interests from purely local ones. Such a conscious omission of the local, Phocian, dimension that we might logically expect, presupposes a deliberate attempt to justify a different authority.

Events that followed the alleged dispute nevertheless suggest that tensions escalated, not only because of wilful brinkmanship on the part of (some) local Phocians, but as a result of the growing disjunction between the needs and interests of sanctuary users and those of local inhabitants (McInerney 1999: 168–72). One of the most prominent outcomes of the conflict was the sequestration of the Crisaean Plain, to be used in future exclusively as sacred land (Isocrates 14 [*Plataicus*] 33). Rousset has argued convincingly that the almost total absence of any archaeological traces dating from the Archaic and Classical periods in the lands between Mount Kirphis and the Corinthian gulf, and more particularly the Desphina peninsula to the south, strongly suggests that this area corresponds to the sacred land where accommodation, industries, and agriculture were prohibited (Rousset 2002: 57–9, 183–92). Another was the reorganization of terraces within the *temenos*, or precinct of Apollo, and the rapid expansion of monumental dedications and treasury buildings to house some of them (Laroche and Nenna 1993; Jacquemin 1999: 245–62). There was a practical reason why the sanctuary needed to acquire and own landed property. The "sacred economy" of Delphi involved the maintenance of substantial herds, which, on the one hand,

provided the sacrificial victims for clients (McInerney 1999: 91–108), but also constituted an important source of revenue as live animals (Rousset 2002: 283–4;
Chandezon 2003: 292).

The physical definition and reorganization of space within the precinct was dictated
by perceived needs of display. The material value of the early dedications suggests
that, from the eighth century onwards, Delphi provided a forum for the prominent
display of public piety from a broad, and consistently expanding, geographical area.
The focus of attention were the oracular responses of Apollo's sacred laurel tree
(*Homeric Hymn to Apollo*, 393–6), which came to be pronounced by a local woman,
acting as the god's mouthpiece, and called Pythia. It was the oracle that made such
a remote and topographically awkward location into the most prestigious shrine in
mainland Greece after Olympia. Its reputation as a reliable source of advice gave
the sanctuary special prestige (Parke and Wormell 1956; Fontenrose 1978). But the
potential political ramifications of oracular pronouncements may not have been
appreciated until the late sixth century, when we first hear of attempts by members
of the Athenian Alcmaeonid family to ingratiate themselves with the Amphictions,
or guardians of Delphi (Hdt. 5.62–3). It has recently been suggested that the timing of oracular pronouncements, on "Apollo's birthday," on the seventh day of the
Delphic month Bysios, was determined by the first sighting of the heliacal rising of
the constellation Delphinios (Salt and Boutsikas 2005). Since this sighting would have
occurred a month earlier than in most lowland parts of Greece, because of the high
horizon on Mount Parnassus, the festival of Apollo became a reliable calendrical marker,
and thus an event of wide significance, independent of the oracular pronouncements
that also took place.

Today's historians face an intractable problem in attempting to make sense of the
symbolic references and social significance of the "First Sacred War" (if "war" is the
appropriate term for what happened). One key to understanding what happened in
the early years of the sixth century lies in the mechanisms that were developed to
manage the sanctuary's affairs. Unfortunately, it is still difficult to map the mosaic
of disparate data into historical time. Like other major Greek sanctuaries, the Pythian
was under the control of a particular community, in this case the Delphians. At some
point between the early seventh and early sixth centuries, administration of the
sanctuary became the responsibility of a joint body, or Amphictiony (those "dwelling
around"; Hdt. 2.180: referring to the fire of 548), though we do not know exactly
when this body came into being. The Delphic Amphictiony is usually thought to
have been an extension or expansion of a similar body of representatives, which met
at the sanctuary of Demeter at Anthela, on the coast of Malis (Lefèvre 1998: 13–16).
The "Pylaean" Amphictiony (as in the later Delphic Amphictiony, delegates were called
"Pylagorai," or "delegates at the Gates," after Thermopylae, the "Hot gates," a reference to the mineral springs nearby) consisted of a number of peoples (*ethne*). The
sources list between ten and twelve members: those geographically nearest to the
shrine of Demeter, and their neighbors.[13] Those nearest were Malis, together with
Ainis and Doris (all nestling around Mount Oeta and flanking the River Spercheus),
as well as their immediate neighbors, the east Locrians, south-east of the estuary;
Achaea Phthiotis, to the north of it; and the obscure Dolopians (from the southern

Pindus mountains). The more distant members were Ionians (from Euboea?), Phocians, Boeotians, Thessalians of the plains, and the "perioecic" communities of Perrhaebia, in the hill country west of Mount Olympus, and Magnesia, the heavily wooded ridge of mountains extending from Mount Ossa through Mount Pelion into the peninsula that protects the gulf of Volos.

Fourth-century historians who wrote about these early community associations attempted to make sense of incomplete traditions. There seemed to be a clear local logic among many of the adherents, but no easy way of demonstrating how the Athenians (and later the Spartans), had become members of an enlarged body, this time acting as a kind of steering group for Apollo's sanctuary, which also included Boeotians and (some) Phocians. Androtion and Theopompus gave the list a distinctly evolutionary slant by framing them as the *ethne* ruled by Deucalion (the Greek Noah) and his son Amphictyon. Thus "Ionians" (hence, eventually, Athenians), Boeotians, and Phocians found their rightful places in a kind of topographical genealogy of the east mainland (Hall 2002: 134–54). But such attempts to smooth out the inconsistencies of the past have made it difficult to distinguish nuggets of genuine tradition about Amphictionic origins, maintained in one way or another by contemporary practice, from retrospective rationalization.

Thessaly

Sites

Occupying an area larger than all of central Greece (Acarnania, Aetolia, Phocis, Locris, and Boeotia), Thessaly contained some of the most prominent and active mainland communities of the archaic period. Recent research has underscored the importance and longevity of a string of Late Bronze Age settlements inland of the Volos gulf. Evidence of Early Iron Age activity, frequently in the vicinity of earlier sites, is widespread and plentiful. Thessaly is a prominent region of the mainland in the Homeric poems – Phthia is the home of Achilles – and most of the sites referred to in the "Catalogue of Ships" (*Iliad* 2.681–759, 928–33), insofar as they can be located, have produced ceramics of Proto-Geometric or Geometric type. The *Iliad* does, therefore, provide some reflection of genuine Iron Age activity. But the choice of locations offered by the poet is neither systematic (various known sites are ignored), nor does his galaxy of sites cohere with the pattern of settlement that can be traced from the seventh, or even from the eighth century onwards.[14] A comparison of the site names that occur in Homer and those documented from the eighth century onwards shows that few of the "Homeric" sites continued to be important in later times. Halos and Pherae are the exceptions. However, although our principal focus is on sites of growing importance, we should not ignore major settlements of the Proto-Geometric and Early Geometric phases (tenth to ninth centuries) that were subsequently eclipsed, notably Dimini, Volos "Palia" and Sesklo.[15]

The lowlands of Thessaly occupy two plains separated by a low ridge. They correspond to two out of the four historical divisions or "tetrads" of the plains, alongside Phthiotis, already referred to: Thessaliotis in the west and Pelasgiotis in the east, separated by the River Peneus from the fourth division, Hestiaiotis, to the north. These land divisions were topographical labels, although later a more technical function was applied to this land division for military purposes. Two sites in Pelasgiotis illustrate how cities in inland Thessaly evolved. The acropolis of Larissa (Phrourio hill) was one of a group of sites within the territory of the modern city occupied in Late Bronze Age (Mycenaean) times. The stronghold continued to be inhabited in the early first millennium, and settlement spread outwards onto the slopes and surrounding lowlands, particularly in the sixth century, when a regular pattern of streets and house units first emerged. The appearance of imported artifacts, including Attic black and red figure tableware, confirms that the city was flourishing. In the vicinity were other settlements, some of which, including Atrax, Argissa, and Crannon, grew to be independent political units in their own right. A plethora of distinctive archaeological remains, including settlement debris and burials, can be associated with the ancient community of Crannon and its immediate neighbors. In the fifth and fourth centuries Crannon was associated with the Scopadae, one of Thessaly's dynastic clans, like the Aleuadae at Larissa, and the Echecratidae of Pharsalus.

The other civic center in Pelasgiotis that has been extensively investigated is Pherae (modern Velestino), inland of the gulf of Volos. As at Larissa, occupation here seems to have continued without apparent interruption from the Late Bronze Age onwards, albeit in a reduced area. Although modern structures, and intensive reconstruction in antiquity, including substantial changes in the sixth century, have hindered attempts to map early civic activity, the pattern that is emerging on the ground looks very similar to that of Corinth or Argos in the archaic period. The distribution of finds, both settlement remains and cemeteries, dating from the eighth to sixth centuries, would indicate dispersed nuclei, perhaps consisting of kin groups, or simply different residential foci, which later coalesced to form the city of Pherai.

Sanctuaries

One of the most important Thessalian pre-Classical shrines lay just beyond the northern periphery of Pherae. This was the temenos of Enodia and Zeus Thaulius. The cult of Enodia, a divinity connected with the underworld and with roadways, was centerd at Pherae, but spread to many parts of Thessaly and beyond. The shrine was probably open to the air until a temple was built in the sixth century. More than 3,700 votive objects, consisting mainly of dress pins, or animal or bird figurines, and made of bronze or iron, were deposited at the sanctuary. The majority date from the eighth and seventh centuries, and represent an overwhelmingly local clientele. Only 2 percent of the finds came from outside Thessaly, principally from further north in the Balkans, plus a few exotic items derived from Italy or Egypt (C. Morgan 2003: 135–9).

The sanctuary of Athena Itonia at Philia in Thessaliotis was also an open-air shrine (until the third century), with a similar range of Thessalian votive objects: bronze fibulae, bird and vase pendants, double axes, occasional bone and ivory goods. Among the more unusual items were iron spits, among the earliest dedications of this type anywhere in the Aegean, together with spearheads and swords. Some of these were manufactured at the sanctuary, judging by metallurgical debris.

Elsewhere in Thessaly temple-like structures were beginning to appear. The construction of large public monuments, particularly when accompanied, as in a growing number of Thessalian cases, with carved or painted ornaments, is symptomatic of the overall level of wealth achieved by at least half a dozen sites in each region. This is particularly visible in the sixth century. At Gonnoi, Pelasgiotis, an apsidal hall was built on the summit of the acropolis during the second half of the seventh century (Mazarakis Ainian 1997: 86, 310). Among the most spectacular and surprising discoveries in the region during the 1990s was the sixth century temple 2 km outside the ancient city of Metropolis, west of Karditsa, and below Mount Agrapha in the Pindus range (Intzesiloglou 2002). The architectural remains have yet to be studied in detail, but the Doric column capitals are carved with alternating lotus buds and palmettes in an Ionian manner. The bronze cult statue of Apollo shows him as an armed hoplite with a raised spear. The finds at Metropolis put into context other discoveries of architectural elements that most likely adorned temples at sites in all regions of Thessaly (C. Morgan 2003: 87–8, 140–2). Reassessments of such evidence suggest analogies not only with central and southern Greece, but more northerly areas too. Close connections between central Greece and Thessaly on the one hand, Macedonia, Epirus, and other parts of the Balkans on the other, have long been detected in some votive offerings, particularly bronze ornaments (Bouzek 1997: 183–6, 210–14, 218–23, 224–36). But common spatial and architectural characteristics are something new.

Macedonia

In ecological and geological terms, the mountains and lowlands of Macedonia are northerly extensions of the features in Thessaly (figure 15.5). Two parallel mountain ridges, running from north-west to south-east, in the same direction as Pindus, separate the principal areas of settlement. Lake Lychnitis, and its two neighboring waters, Great Prespa and Little Prespa, formed a border region between Illyrian groups further west, upland communities north of the River Erigon (Pelagonians, Paeonians, Dardanians), and Macedonian lowlanders of the upper and middle reaches of the Haliacmon: Orestis and Tymphaea below the foothills of Pindus; Lyncus, Eordaea and Elimia west of Mount Vermion; and the alluvial plain inland from the Thermaic gulf to the east, called Bottia, and its southern extension, Pieria. The innermost part of the gulf has silted up over the centuries. In early antiquity the gulf extended more than 20 km inland in some areas. Gradual silting at the sea end created a large lake in the lower estuary of the River Loudias. As a result, settlements in the area of the lower estuary were either coastal at that time, or much closer to the coast.

Sites

Recent research in all regions of Macedonia has begun to fill out its settlement history between two phases that are rather better known archaeologically, namely the mound sites of the Bronze Age and the expansion of urban planning from the late fourth century onwards. The most intensive investigations have been conducted around

Figure 15.5 The Haliacmon river in Macedonia, looking towards the southern bank and the site of ancient Aegea (modern Vergina)
Source: © Z. H. Archibald.

the rapidly expanding modern city of Thessaloniki. At sites like Assiros and Kastanas, to the north-east (Lang 1996: 260–74), and now at a range of sites in and around the city itself (notably Toumba "Kalamarias" and Souroti), local communities went on building and rebuilding homes in the same localities as their Bronze Age ancestors had done (Archibald 2000: 223–8). Although Assiros and Kastanas did not survive into the archaic period, many sites closer to the Thermaic gulf flourished. There is now a wealth of evidence, in the form of settlement data and cemeteries, dating from the eighth to sixth centuries, which can be mapped and identified with known historical communities.[16]

From a regional point of view, the preponderance of research in the area around the Thermaic gulf, which also includes the magnificent Classical remains at Pella, means that we know far more about the development of those regions that were progressively annexed to the kingdom of Macedonia after the Persian Wars (territories east of the Loudias), than we do about the evolution of the "old kingdom" in Pieria, Elimia, and Bottia (Hatzopoulos 1996: 1, 105–23, 463–86). During the first half of the first millennium BCE, Crestonia, Mygdonia, the Chalcidic peninsula, the lowland regions either side of the Strymon and Nestos estuaries, together with the island of Thasos, were fertile areas with rich mineral resources that attracted numerous settlers, as well as nurturing indigenous populations.[17]

The range of new discoveries in the Thermaic gulf provides useful comparative data for sites in "Old Macedonia." Manolis Andronikos' excavations in the cemetery at

Vergina can now be viewed in the light of cremation burials at Gynaikokastro, and other sites along the lower Axios valley, as well as Early Iron Age burials north and west of Dion (Andronikos 1969; Vokotopoulou 1985). Although the sites where these populations lived have not been exposed, the longevity of local burying communities demonstrates continuity of settlement. Systematic excavations at Aeane, nestling in the Elymian foothills, and further north-west, in the Voion district, have shown that urban life was indeed developing in the sixth century.[18] Elsewhere in "Old Macedonia" eighth to sixth century activities are confirmed at many later urban sites by loose finds and the presence of cemeteries nearby.

Acarnania and Aetolia

Acarnania and Aetolia were identified, by fifth-century writers, as separate political entities. The south-western corner of the north Greek peninsula is a region isolated by the mountains of eastern Aetolia, which prevent easy communication with western Phocis. Travelers wanting to go to Aetolia westwards from Phocis, or eastwards from Aetolia to Phocis, either had to go by sea along the Corinthian gulf, braving local currents in the channel, or northwards up the Achelous valley, as far as Lake Cremastum, and thence follow the gorge cut by the River Spercheius. Aetolia has attracted new scholarly interest since the re-evaluation of long-term activities at the principal Aetolian cult center of Thermum above Lake Trichonis (Mazarakis Ainian 1997: 44–5, 125–32, 310). Here a Middle Helladic (Middle Bronze Age) secular structure (a ruler's house?) with an apsidal end, "Megaron A," was succeeded around the beginning of the first millennium by a rectangular hall, "Megaron B," used for communal dining. By the eighth century, this structure had become recognizably associated with the cult of Apollo, and was replaced in the seventh by one of the earliest known Doric temples.

At Kallipolis, in north-east Aetolia, a rectangular building ("B"), immediately below the Hellenistic temple, represents an eighth century cult building associated with sacrifices and dining. It was succeeded by a stone-built altar surrounded by votive offerings of the late sixth to fourth centuries. At Kalydon, Geometric-style bronze figurines were found in the later sanctuary of Artemis Laphria, outside Kalydon, where the earliest temple dates from the seventh century. A survey of Aetolia has yielded more information about its settlement history.[19] The traditional boundary with Acarnania was the River Achelous. Early archaic Aetolian settlements are concentrated in the lower river valley, with just a few upland centers, which were centers of cult. In the seventh and sixth centuries, habitation spread further south, in the area of Kalydon, and eastwards along the coastal plain, as well as into the more fertile areas around the southern side of the lake.

Little is known about Acarnania before the fifth century. The main city in the region at that time was Stratos (Thuc. 2.80.8), situated at the point where the outlying foothills of the southern Pindus meet the alluvial clays of the middle Achelous valley, on its broader left bank (Gehrke and Wirbelauer 2004 with refs). Recent survey work in the vicinity of the city has revealed traces of a sixth-century temple with carved and painted revetments some 4 km to the west, at Spathari, and, underlying it, an older construction still. A second sanctuary has also been located between Spathari and the ancient city (*AA* 1995: 783–6; 1996: 557–8).

Immigrants and Natives

Much scholarly attention has in the past been devoted to tracing colonizing initiatives, mainly in the seventh and sixth centuries. The influx of Parians to Thasos and the mainland opposite from the second quarter of the seventh century, of Corinthians to Potidaea, of various Euboeans to Chalcidice, and of Klazomenians and Teans successively to Abdera, does play an important part in the story, although it is still difficult to distinguish informal early activity from later historiographical simplifications. But there are other elements equally deserving of attention. Excavation and scientific analysis indicates that the role of Ionian commercial and cultural activity in the north Aegean has been under-appreciated (Papadopoulos 1996a). Even more striking has been the omission of an indigenous perspective. Discoveries around the Thermaic gulf and Chalcidice show that the organization of indigenous settlements, burial practices, and many material expressions have much in common with other parts of northern and central Greece. Perceptions of the indigenous–colonial discourse need to change in the light of discoveries such as the extra-urban shrine at Mende–Poseidi, where a long, apsidal structure was built in the tenth century around an ash altar, whose origin is Late Bronze Age or Sub-Mycenaean (Moschonissioti 1998) (figure 15.6). The chronological and structural resemblances between this building and the Proto-Geometric apsidal structure at Toumba, Lefkandi (Popham et al., 1993), suggest that cultural connections between the far north of the Aegean and other coastal areas were much closer than scholars have been in the habit of imagining.

One of the most important sources of information about the people of archaic Greece is burial evidence. Skeletal material can provide a wide range of information about the health history and physical background of individuals. Systematic investigation of mortuary data has only been completed in a limited number of case studies (e.g. Agelarakis 1999), which are relevant to specific locations. Future work is likely to provide more nuanced interpretations of biological histories, as well as a range of comparative evidence. Most of the accumulated published data from burials has focused on mortuary customs, particularly on typologies of tombs and the range of grave goods. Changes in burial practice have sometimes been interpreted as indications of population change. In cases where it is now possible to compare larger numbers of burials, particularly in Thessaly, different practices can now be seen as methods of affirming the status of the deceased, rather than the introduction of foreign customs (Georganas 2002). Such studies will prompt a reconsideration of other mortuary evidence from northern Greece that has been interpreted in terms of cultural intrusion. We may nevertheless expect cemeteries to contain evidence about the many immigrants and migrants known to have traveled in the north. Among the most celebrated examples is the cenotaph on Corcyra (ca. 550) in memory of Menecrates, son of Tlesias, of Oiantheia in western Locris, who was *proxenos*, or advocate of the Corcyreans, and immortalized by them through this inscribed monument

Figure 15.6 View of the excavated sanctuary of Poseidon at the modern town of Poseidi in the westernmost promontory of the Chalcidic peninsula
Source: © Z. H. Archibald.

after his death at sea (*Nomima* I: 34). The influence of Corinth, founder city of Corcyra, was profound and wide ranging, and includes the distribution of Corinthian products (already referred to above with regard to votives in Phocis and beyond). But traces of local dialect forms reflect the imprint of inland cultural interconnections.

The recognition and investigation of long-term agricultural settlements of the early first millennium, whether we call them large villages or small towns, displaying spatial and structural characteristics that provide good analogies with central and southern Greece, is matched by a growing number of documents that indicate sociopolitical and institutional mechanisms familiar from further south. As outlined earlier, it is no longer feasible to distinguish northern societies as having a wholly different way of life, which was gradually modified as a result of contacts with cities further south. The differences between north and south can be attributed in part to differing responses towards local ecologies, and in part to the development of local institutional devices. The two organizing principles that can be seen at work in the formation of Early Iron Age communities in Greece, namely the granting of citizenship status on the one hand to one's neighbors, or, on the other, according to some preconceived pattern of kinship or hierarchy, disregard simple geographical rules (Davies

1996). The former solution, which is especially characteristic of strongly nucleated communities, was also the pattern adopted in Attica, for instance, while the latter puts much of Thessaly alongside Lakonia and most Cretan settlements.

Access to land and resources constituted a potential source of anxiety, and thus a major driver in the development of fixed principles. One of the most revealing documents in our area is the law outlining the terms on which east Locrian and local Chaleian settlers at Naupactus could take up land plots and become Naupactians, and how inheritance questions, or failed settlers, should be dealt with (*Nomima* I: 43; see Ch. 20, below). Elsewhere in the region the intense preoccupation with equal status and treatment, apparent in this document, is less evident, although we have, as yet, far too few examples of collective decision-making. In Phocis, Boeotia, and Thessaly, there were people who went out of their way to make their membership of certain inner social groups popularly known.[20] On the other hand, although there is evidence, archaeological as well as historical, of a social élite in Thessaly, a growing body of civic statutes concerning various public issues shows that the inhabitants applied the same kinds of rights and constraints on each other as did their peers further south.[21]

Inland and External Networks and Communication: Trade and Economies

From the early centuries of the first millennium there is evidence of regular, though not necessarily widespread, contact between the regions west and east of the Pindus mountains. A distinctive type of matt-painted pottery is found across the Balkan peninsula from southern Illyria (the area of Elbasan, south of Albanian Tirana) as far east as the Chalcidic peninsula in the north, Acarnania and the gulf of Volos to the south (Kilian 1985: 237–47). There are general cultural resemblances in burial forms, personal ornaments, and tools within this region, extending westwards to the gulf of Otranto in southern Italy. The distribution of specific mobile items suggests that extensive social networks were maintained within and outside the Pindus range, at a time of considerable dislocation elsewhere in the Greek mainland.

From the eighth century onwards, Corinthian and Corinthianizing products chart these networks, between the Korçë area (eastern Albania) and Pelagonia, via Lake Ohrid; between Thesprotia in southern Epirus (figure 15.7), supplied from Corinthian and local merchants at Corcyra, and Ambracia; from Dodona and the plain above Lake Ioannina through the principal passes of Pindus – northwards, along the valley of the River Sarandaporos into the Grevena region of western Macedonia, and eastwards through the Metsovo pass and Meteora into north – west Thessaly.[22] In the *Iliad*'s "Catalogue of Ships," the Perrhaebians are said to set up homes around "wintry Dodona," but they also till fields on the banks of the River Titaresius (2.750); while the Phthiotid Achilles invokes Zeus of Dodona and his interpreters, called Selli (16.234). Modern political borders have worked to conceal rather than reveal connections that surpassed local ones. The visible symptoms of exchange tend to survive in very small numbers, so individual artifacts carry much more significance than they possess intrinsically.

The maintenance of these social and cultural networks has often been attributed to pastoral strategies. Shepherds did cross local boundaries in order to move herds from their host villages to suitable pasture. The best evidence for the seasonal migration of herds comes from Epirus, particularly the settlement of Vitsa, in the Zagoria region north of Ioannina (Vokotopoulou 1986). This upland site was inhabited from at least the ninth to the fourth centuries. The house forms are rather more substantial than simple chalets – many had stone foundations and were quite robust structures. Recent

Figure 15.7 View of the lower estuary of the River Acheron in Thesprotia, north-west Greece
Source: © C. B. Mee.

research on long-term pastoral management in the Balkans shows that similar strategies have been adopted in different periods of the past, but the scale and scope of herd movements has been determined by the labor force available and by the marketability of by-products (Nixon and Price 2001).

Travel was by horse or donkey, if not on foot. Most of the inter-community conflicts reported in our sources as taking place in Thessaly and further north were resolved in cavalry battles. Horses and cattle constituted valuable as well as vital resources, which were far more easily accumulated in northern Greece than further south, enabling the rapid growth of wealth by those who were able to put such resources into circulation. Formal and symbolic expressions of wealth are often displayed in rich grave goods, including gold jewelery, gold foil ornaments and imported bronze and clay tableware.[23] The metal items are the ultimate products of mining activities east and north-east of lake Ohrid (Damastium), at Dysoron, in Paeonia (Hdt. 5.17.2), in Mount Pangaion, east of the Strymon estuary, probably in Chalcidice, and at a variety of sites in Rhodope and central Thrace. These mines produced precious and base metals in considerable quantities. The precious metals were evidently converted to ingot form, stored as plate, or coined. Some of the earliest gold and silver coin issues from the Aegean were produced by authorities operating along the north Aegean coast (Carradice and Price 1988: 38–41). The desire to convert metal into stamped gold and silver coinage reflects a lively pattern of exchange, linked to Persian as well as wider Aegean markets (Archibald 1998: 89–90, 126–34; Kim 2001). The range and distribution of metal artifacts seems to indicate that the desire for suitable ores and for finished items was among the principal drivers that brought the coastal communities of the north Aegean into contact with upland peoples, not only in Macedonia and Illyria, but also in inland Thrace.

The emergence of coined money in the north is clearly linked to the expansion of mining and metal production, but our perception of how these processes were linked is still rather sketchy. The minting of money was by no means a systematic process. Coinage was struck irregularly, and is distributed equally irregularly. The earliest accounts of major civic projects reveal that coin was but one form of early money, while ingots and a variety of other, inorganic as well as organic goods, circulated as alternative methods of payment within these economies. Public or state projects provide the clearest evidence of how fiscal mechanisms may have developed. The fourth-century reconstruction of the temple of Apollo at Delphi provides a useful comparative model of how the same process could have been conducted following the fire of 548 (Davies 2001a; cf. 2001b, for accounting procedures). We know that a contract for tender was put out by sanctuary officials, which implies a costing procedure of some kind (Hdt. 2.180). The Athenian Alcmaeonidae chose to enhance the finished structure with Parian marble (Hdt. 5.62.2–3). In the fourth century most of the suppliers and craftsmen were Peloponnesians, and it seems likely that there was a similar relationship less than two hundred years earlier. Notwithstanding the active role played by Thessalians and other central Greeks at the sanctuary (Lefèvre 1998: 24–9), local experts and suppliers were conspicuous by their absence. Timber was supplied from Arcadia, while Corinthians shipped the heavy freight and perhaps provided a range of on-site services.[24] In his description of the monuments erected in the aftermath of the Greek victories over the Persians, Herodotus illuminates a further, symbolic as well as economic, dimension of the emerging leaders from the north. Alexander I of Macedon commissioned a portrait statue of himself, which, according to the historian, was made of beaten gold (Hdt. 8.121). Technically speaking, it would not be feasible to construct an all gold figure of such size. But whether it was made of gilded bronze or gold foil over another medium, this was an extraordinary, pioneering creation, remarkable as much for the subject as for the unusual technology.

NOTES

1 Cf. e.g. Lang 1996: 152ff, esp. 260–98; Morris 1998a: 10–12; C. Morgan 2003: 16–31, 79–105, 113–43, 168–76, 206–25.
2 Sallares 1991: 271–81; Grove and Rackham 2001: 141, 157–61, 343.
3 Bintliff 1999; Bintliff and Snodgrass 1988; 1989; Bintliff, Howard, and Snodgrass 1999; Bintliff et al. 2007.
4 Karamitrou-Mentesidi 1993; 1996; Davies 1997; 2000b; Archibald 2000; C. Morgan 2000; 2003; Hatzopoulos and Paschidis 2004; Stamatopoulou 2007.
5 Rousset 2002: 54–7 on Delphi region; Pikoulas 1999 for roads in another mountainous region, Arcadia.
6 See references to works by Bintliff and Snodgrass in n. 3.
7 The lake was canalized and drained from the late 1880s onwards: Horden and Purcell 2000: 244–7, 586–7.
8 Shachter 1981: 117–18; 1986; 1989: 78.
9 *Nomima* I: 43, ca. 560–550, a law outlining terms of settlement for Locrians and Chaleians at Naupactus, see further below; cf. I: 44, ca. 525–500, law governing property in Locris or Aetolia.
10 Felsch et al. 1987; Felsch 1991; Mazarakis Ainian 1997: 137–40.
11 C. Morgan 1990: 135–6; 2003: 124–5; Davies 1994; 2007; McInerney 1999: 165–72, 310–12; Rousset 2002: 44–59, 283–6; rejecting the historicity of the conflict: Robertson 1978.

12 Notably Aeschines 3.107–13; Callisthenes *FGrH* 124 F 1; Paus. 10.37.4–8; Plut. *Solon* 11; Davies 1994: 206–10 with translations.

13 Androtion *FGrH* 324 F 58; Theop. *FGrH* 115 F 63; Aesch. 3.115–16; cf. Paus. 10.8.2; Lefèvre 1998: 16.

14 Helly 1995: 76–9; some would even date the emergence of the civic network between the ninth and seventh centuries: Auda et al. 1990: 103–4.

15 Archibald 2000: 226–7; C. Morgan 2003: 95–102.

16 Hatzopoulos 1996: 1, 106–7; Chrysostomou 2000; Chrysostomou and Chrysostomou 2002; Tiverios and Gimatzidis 2002; Tiverios, Manakidou, and Tziafaki 2002; Soueref 2000; Soueref and Havela 2002.

17 Archibald 1998: 71–8; Morris 1998a: 36–52; Sgourou 2002; Koukouli-Chrysanthaki 2002.

18 Karamitrou-Mentessidi 1993; 1996; 1999; Ginouvès 1994: 29–32.

19 Bommeljé et al. 1987; Lang 1996: 17 fig. 2; Freitag, Funke, and Moustakis 2004, with further refs.

20 Labyadae at Delphi: *Nomima* I: 71; cf. 72; "friends" at Acraephia: I: 69; "chosen ones" at Tanagra, I: 70.

21 Jeffery 1990: 97–8 no. 1; 99 nos. 2 and 6; *Nomima* I: 102.

22 Hammond 1994: 422–36; Andrea 1993; Vasić 1993; Herman 1987 on the social mechanism of "guest friendship."

23 Hammond 1994: 425–6 (Trebenishte); Archibald 1998: 71–90; Ginouvès 1994: 29–39.

24 cf. *Nomima* I: 33, the people of Thetonion in Thessaly granted privileges to a Corinthian, Sotairos.

CHAPTER SIXTEEN

The Western Mediterranean

Carla M. Antonaccio

Preliminaries

Unlike many of the other regions covered in this volume, the western Mediterranean is neither an ancient political territory nor topographically distinct and self-contained. Nor does it constitute a region, like that of the Black Sea, which is defined by the complete shoreline of a bounded body of water and the interior behind that shore, or like the Aegean, a conventionally accepted sub-region of the Mediterranean and conceptualized as such in antiquity (Margomenou et al. 2005). Instead, "the western Mediterranean" is a term used in a way similar to "the west" in the modern world. Indeed, a shorthand reference that echoes a contemporary usage of "the west" has been extended into antiquity, where "the west" sometimes refers to the Greek colonial world, and also to the far reaches of the western Mediterranean basin frequented and settled by Greeks. This notion of the ancient west is paralleled by "the East," "the Near (or Middle) East," and further refined by "the far west" (like the modern "Far East") to indicate an even greater degree of remove, unfamiliarity, and exoticism. Yet it can be argued that already in Greek antiquity there was a concept of "the west" or the western Mediterranean, and even notions of a near and far west.[1] The far western Mediterranean – west of Sardinia and Corsica, including modern Spain and coastal France – was certainly not as thickly settled by Greeks as the middle west, i.e. Italy and Sicily.

The western Mediterranean is, from the point of view of Greek history, simply the sea and landscapes west of the conventional Greek homeland of the Balkan peninsula, and for the Greeks it was a prime space of travel, trade, and colonization – not the only such space, but the scene of some of the earliest voyages, exchanges, and permanent settlements. One could make a case that parts of the central Mediterranean, or "midwest" (including part of coastal north Africa), should not be considered anything other than part of what we conventionally call "Greece" in the archaic period.[2] The Greek communities of Sicily and southern Italy, for example, were established at the same time as the *polis* coalesced in "Greece" – indeed, the colonies may have led the way toward the integration and urbanization of the metropolitan communities (e.g. Morris 2006b). It is an old habit to see the Mediterranean midwest as fundamentally different from, say, Crete or Rhodes, a reflex grounded in modern national boundaries and old notions of cultural territories, as well as the sense that the territory once home to the Mycenaeans in particular is the original homeland of the Greeks. The notion of the mobility of early Greeks, a theme of this chapter, is predicated on this idea of a homeland; the traditional founders of western colonies, who for the early colonies were all held to come from the old country, followed in the mythic footsteps of heroic predecessors. But neither the Balkan peninsula nor the Aegean alone comprise "Greece" in the first millennium.

Looked at from the Phoenician (or Carthaginian) point of view, the central Mediterranean, and the Tyrrhenian littoral in particular, including the north and west coasts of Sicily as well as the islands of Corsica and Sardinia, forms the eastern "shore" of the western Mediterranean. From this point of view even Gibraltar – the traditional boundary of the Mediterranean, and of the known world – formed no real obstacle to trade or settlement. The western Mediterranean may be a bounded inland sea, but the silver riches of Iberian Tartessos and the markets and resources of the Atlantic were an incentive to found Gades (Cádiz), Huelva, Lixus and Mogador, all on the Lusitanian and African coasts (see below). Even the Greeks knew of Tartessos. The regionality of this part of the Mediterranean is, therefore, not entirely fixed nor strictly bounded.[3]

This chapter will survey developments in a part of the Mediterranean that today comprises Italy, Sicily, Sardinia, Spain, and France but focus on relatively few sites, given the space constraints here. While the subject is the region's particular "Greek" history, informed by the distance of this space and its shores and islands from the Greek homelands, it will not simply recapitulate the story of Greek colonization. Indeed, to tell the story of colonization in the western Mediterranean would be to give an account not only of the Greek, but also of the Phoenician and Carthaginian settlements in the west, which were many and began earlier than the Greeks'. Rather, the theme will be the conceptualization of the western Mediterranean as a "region" in which interconnected diversity reigns. The variety found in the west is predicated not only on the different origins and fortunes of the Greeks who frequented these waters, but also the presence of Levantines in the same seas: Phoenicians and perhaps North Syrians early; later the Carthaginians – in north Africa to the west of the main area of Greek colonization in Libya (i.e. Cyrene and its territory)[4] – and the Etruscans. The archaic period in this region, as will be seen, is complex and heterogeneous, the groups sometimes in cooperation, at other times in conflict, in cohabitation, and in permanent settlements under the political authority of one group or another.

Connectivity, Networks, and the Middle Ground

The archaic period per se is grounded in connections, networks, and movements that, in fact, stretch back to the Bronze Age and often originate, or at least implicate, the eastern Mediterranean and its hinterlands as well as the west.[5] Rather than to see it simply as a vague geographical location, or some nebulous space into which the Greeks ventured and settled rather less than elsewhere, the western Mediterranean's regionality can be predicated on its status as a field of interactivity – what Malkin, borrowing a phrase used of space and modes of interactions of Europeans and native Americans in the upper midwest of North America, has termed a "Middle Ground."[6] As Michel Gras remarks, the context for the archaic history of the Greeks of the west, the Greeks of the homeland, and of the Carthaginians, is founded in a Mediterranean that is "characterized by great demographic dynamism and, partly in consequence, great geographic mobility of people and goods."[7] This quality does not map solely onto this part of this body of water, of course – indeed, the eastern Mediterranean saw many and similar interactions unfold, some between the same actors. (The western Mediterranean is conceived as including the coast of north-west Africa, whereas the eastern Mediterranean includes Egypt.) Yet, there is a different quality to the eastern and western Mediterraneans; the early and numerous cities of the eastern Aegean littoral anchor the Greek presence in the east to a degree that is not the case in the far west. The Levantine eastern Mediterranean is not a region of settlement for the Greeks either (never mind the somewhat ambiguous status of Cyprus).[8] The Greeks' eastern limits, pushed much farther by Alexander, in the archaic period were on the coast of Asia Minor and the Black Sea. The movement in the west noted by Gras has its particular causes and conditions. These conditions, which implicated the Greeks in webs of relations that included other groups, inform the region and its history as a whole, while they also make comprehensible the Greeks' particularity.

What was referred to above as interactivity, has also been termed connectivity, or sometimes described as the operation of networks. So too the study of particular cultures or groups in and around the Mediterranean has recently emphasized their connections, mutual intelligibility and temporal continuities.[9] Within Mediterranean connectivity there was (and is) distinctiveness, predicated on ever deeper pasts in which connectivity was, at times, not very pronounced and, without arguing for any original, indigenous purity of particular groups, what we can call "identities" were formed (Hall 2002). In these various places different languages were spoken, distinctive forms of material culture used, and particular ritual practices employed, by inhabitants that constitute what are often called ethnic groups or cultures – Phoenicians, Greeks, and so on, living in settlements of various types and purposes with their own histories. All this diversity might be considered variations on a theme in a broad sense. There are obvious commonalities across the Mediterranean with reference to ritual, elite practices, and so on. Indeed, the emphasis on mutual intelligibility rather than difference has led to the introduction of another metaphor: that of a decentered rhizome, an "endless, interconnected root system (a network with no center) giving rise to leafy plants above the surface."[10]

This metaphor may indeed describe some aspects of the high archaic period from a Mediterranean-wide perspective. Even a rhizome, however, spreads by runners from established points that give rise to the abundant and varied life "above ground" (to carry through with the metaphor). The chief factor in difference may be social stratification and the degree of urbanization in a given community, more than ethnic or cultural difference; indeed, the latter may also articulate the former. To comprehend the Greek experience in the west – to understand how the Greeks caught a wave, so to speak – is to start in the east in the late Bronze Age and the early Iron Age. The end of the Bronze Age around 1200 BC seems to have been a turning point for the entire central and eastern Mediterranean basin. In the case of the Phoenicians, a combination of environmental degradation (desertification) and population growth created conditions that both restricted their territory and encouraged their expansion westwards. This is of some interest because famine and overpopulation have been conventional reasons for Greek colonization, but trade has always been the standard explanation for Phoenician settlements abroad (Aubet 2001: 70ff). Tyre became the dominant city of Phoenicia, and its craft industries supplied luxury goods especially to Assyria, but from the ninth century in a trade that also ultimately encompassed Anatolia and the Aegean. Assyrian conquests in the eighth century cut the Phoenicians off from their markets in Asia, but by then the Phoenicians had already gone west, to North Africa and Iberia, and established permanent presences – settlements. They had access to the supply of silver, the dominant standard of value in the early first millennium, in the area of Huelva (Tartessos) beginning in the late eighth century.[11] Large amounts of silver were coming into the Assyrian sphere from the late eighth century. The western expansion also brought access to supplies of foodstuffs, but especially to raw materials (including gold, tin, and copper in addition to silver; Aubet 2001: 70–96; cf. Aubet Semmler 2002).

Phoenicians were out in front in the far west (Sardinia, Iberia and beyond). Among the Greeks it is the Euboeans who seem to be pre-eminent participants in mobility from at least the middle of the Iron Age (i.e. the tenth century), creating outposts in the North Aegean (e.g. Mende and Torone). They operated in tandem with Phoenicians and with inhabitants of north Syria (speakers of Aramaic) at Pithekoussai on the island of Ischia, and were prominent in the establishment of the first colonies of Sicily. The Euboeans were also well ahead of the curve in the east, as the cemeteries of Lefkandi have shown, with clear ties to Cyprus, Syria, and the Levantine coast, Egypt, and even Mesopotamia. Euboeans were also clearly involved in the activities at the site of Al Mina on the Orontes River in Syria, long recognized as an early example of long distance overseas trade and exchange though they may not have been the prime movers in this region. Indeed, Gras has gone so far as to suggest it is as a consequence of the long Euboean experience in the *east* that they arrive in the west, "in conditions which remain far from clear but appear to be closely linked to Phoenician sea travel."[12]

The Phoenicians struck out into the far west and to North Africa at nearly the same time, creating a large zone of influence along the Atlantic coast of Iberia and the western African coast (including settlements at the sites of Lixus and Mogador). There was also a series of Phoenician settlements on the Mediterranean coast of Iberia.[13] On the Mediterranean coast, the most important site was arguably Toscanos, founded in the middle of the eighth century. The presence of a large market building has led to the site's characterization as a "commercial enclave" (Aubet 2001: 317) with connections to Pithekoussai, Cyprus, and the eastern Mediterranean, and the cemeteries include rich graves with Phoenician imports that testify to the high status of local individuals (see also Niemeyer 2002). A transition from this early Phoenician phase to a Punic, or "Carthaginian" phase when the balance of power shifted to the north African colony, came in the middle of the sixth century. The silver mines of Tartessos were no longer as profitable then, and Tyre had fallen to the Assyrians in the first quarter of the sixth century. Although Tyre recovered by the mid-sixth century, the Phoenician west saw profound changes as a result of these developments, and Carthage ascended at the expense of the Phoenician homeland.

This history, though not centrally Greek, had several effects of interest to Greek history per se: after an initial, cooperative period a more confrontational mode of operation resulted in conflicts between Carthage and western Greek communities, as well as with an ascendant Rome; the abandonment of Phoenician settlements on the Mediterranean coast of Iberia; and the cessation of Phoenician activity in the area of Gadir – a hiatus which may coincide with the Phocaean expansion described below.

Nostoi

Parallel to this archaeologically derived narrative is that of the proto-historical Greek tradition, epic poetry, the poetry of Homer. To some ways of thinking, Homer marks the beginning of a specifically Greek colonialist consciousness at least of horizons beyond the Aegean, and many of these seem to lie to the west. Colonization, too, that permanent settling down that both the Phoenicians and the early Greeks engaged in, has been a kind of summary term for a turn, or a return, a turning again, perhaps: to voyaging, trade, and settlement that slowed dramatically, but did not end, with the end of the Bronze Age as just discussed, and to contacts with overseas regions and their inhabitants who practiced different cultures. Non-Greeks appear as early as Homeric poetry itself, as do far-off lands. But their representation in Greek and Roman sources is just that, and representation has its own purposes.

It is the *Odyssey* that contains the references most usually associated with knowledge of the west and an awareness of colonization. In recounting the stories of the *nostoi*, the returns of the Greek heroes from Troy (of which Odysseus is only one), the poem describes several locations that Odysseus encounters which lie in the western Mediterranean, the most obvious being the Straits of Messina (the location of Scylla and Charybdis; *Od.* 12.253ff), the island of Aeolus (10.1ff), the island Thrinacria (Sicily, 12.285ff), and of course Scheria (Corfu), which is on the westward path towards Sicily and the Tyrrhenian Sea. But more interesting is the reflection of a colonizing consciousness detected especially in two episodes. In Book 6 the story is told of how the king of the Phaeacians, Nausithoos, resettled his people from Hyperia to Scheria, as a colonial founder might; and similarly, how he divided up the land, built a city wall and houses, and precincts for the gods (6.4–10). Equally intriguing, in 9.130–42, Odysseus describes an island neighboring the Cyclopes' territory, uninhabited except for goats, in terms that identify it as a likely place for human habitation – for colonization, since the soil would yield grain and grapes, staples that would sustain a permanent settlement. Just as striking, though, the poet has Odysseus describe the beach, which provides a perfect place to draw up ships on the sand without need for anchorage. And most telling of all, it is said at the start of the passage that the Cyclopes lack ships and shipwrights to make vessels, so that they do not go out to sea to trade with other men. The episode is permeated with an awareness of mobility as much as colonization.

Of course, the Phaeacians are fantastic sailors; the other major epic poet we have, Hesiod, tells of sea voyages and trade, and describes how his father because of the difficulty of life in seventh-century Asia Minor, sought a better life abroad in Boeotia (*W&D* 630–40). Thus, farming and seafaring are not mutually exclusive, so that voyaging for trade and permanent settlement need not be either. At the same time, Homer neither uses the word *apoikia* nor names or describes an actual colony, or an *emporion*. Whether this knowledge is suppressed for the purposes of the epic tradition is impossible to say for certain.[14] Relations with strangers in Homer are governed by the norms of *xenia* – as on Scheria – unless the hosts are monstrous barbarians – like the Cyclopes or Laestrygonians. In these cases the exceptions prove the rule. The edges of the known world hold hideous dangers, magical places and creatures, and supernatural terrors. The Phoenicians appear in both Homeric epics, and Hesiod provides a most intriguing reference to the Etruscans (*Theogony* 1011–18), but the status of both mentions is highly contested.[15]

This is the early poetic backdrop again which we investigate the early first millennium from a specifically Greek point of view. These investigations necessarily entail reconstructing the movements of goods and persons. Of course, the relationship of material culture, traces of some of the goods and the persons who set them in motion, indeed of all cultural *indicia*, to cultural identity or ethnicity is highly contested (see ch. 31, below). It is therefore very uncertain whether archaeological cultures correspond to literary accounts of ethnic groups, and dangerously circular to argue from one side or the other of this question. Nevertheless, archaeology is what we have to write the history of the late Iron Age and early archaic west in particular (from roughly 1000 BC). The movements of individuals into and out of different regions are traceable above all by changing artifactual assemblages and their contexts. (Whether these index the physical presence of individuals who also made the objects is open to question.) Archaeology is the only way to investigate directly settlement patterns, ritual landscapes and practices, and interactions with indigenes. Excavation and survey provide not only data on sites and regions not well documented in written sources, but also challenge written texts with discourses of things and histories other than those written about in antiquity (and/or preserved to us). Finally, archaeology documents pre- and proto-historical experience, which sometimes meshes with the written accounts available to us, and sometimes does not.

An archaic example of a written account is the story of the Corinthian Demaratus, who conducted trade with the Etruscans and settled at Tarquinia, eventually becoming the ancestor of the Tarquinii, or Roman kings. We also have the story of the Samian Kolaios's voyage to Tartessus, beyond the Straits of Gibraltar (see below), and the trading ventures of the Aeginetan Sostratos have a tantalizing reflection, perhaps, in the dedication of an anchor to Aeginetan Apollo by a person of the same name at Gravisca.[16] Such encounters, however, occurred probably much earlier than the sixth century. Both Phoenicians and Greeks used the conventions of gift exchange to pave the way for trade with indigenous groups – witness the presence of ostentatious prestige objects such as the Praeneste silver in Italy, on the Phoenician side, and the Vix krater in France, on the Greek side, in the seventh and sixth century respectively. It seems safe to say that while some of those encountered by Greeks came to be represented as *barbaroi*, in the earliest period they were perhaps more like *xenoi*, strangers (and, under some conditions, guest-friends). In any case, and in contradiction to older views, mutual intelligibility seems to have played a large role in the Greek experience in the west, even if hostility, warfare, and cultural assimilation were also present. There is ample evidence for interaction in the form of transfers of artistic styles, mythological narratives (Heracles and Odysseus have already been mentioned), elite ideologies (like sympotic practices and burial customs), to say nothing of commodities and finished goods in trade and exchange. While some of these interactions had been occurring for centuries before the eighth and indeed might be either continuations or revivals of Bronze Age contacts, they intensified with the establishment of permanent settlements.[17]

Thus, the oft-stressed importance of the colonization movement of the eighth century, frequently supported by reference to Homeric geography and the apparent reflection of colonial features in the *Odyssey* as sketched above, should not obscure pre-existing geographical, historical, and cultural connections, nor substitute for archaeological evidence of movement and exchange.[18]

The Western Greeks

The space of return: enoikismos *and colonization*

In the shared space of the western Mediterranean – a "Middle Ground" – in which actors of various origins interacted, competed, struggled, settled, and continually created new forms of identities, cultures, and symbolic and political systems, the Greeks produced several of each. The western Mediterranean was not *mare incognitum* for the Greeks of the eighth century who were the first to establish *apoikiai* (see ch. 19). Nor was it empty: the western Mediterranean was already populated by indigenes whose presence stretches far into prehistory, and provided encounters not with strange flora and fauna, such as have characterized other colonial episodes in human history, but with human strangers. It was also shared space, both with the Phoenicians, who seem to have been first off the mark in the west as we have seen, and with the Etruscans, vying for territory and markets on the islands and coasts of the west Mediterranean in particular. The presence of other groups not indigenous to the western Mediterranean, who also left their homelands to travel, trade, and settle abroad, means that the Greeks were not alone in their expansion. The movements of people from one place to a permanent settling down elsewhere, bringing with them distinctive forms of material culture, social structures, languages, political organization, and so on, is one way to define colonization, however inapt this term is to describe, much less explain, anything in this period of antiquity. Often such communities, like their *metropoleis*, had an admixture of non-citizens from the same cultural and geographical origin, and from other cultures.

It is important to note that the "colony," or *apoikia*, is only one of the possible forms settling took; in addition to the *emporion*, or trading station, we may note the model of *enoikismos*, "cohabitation," proposed by H. G. Niemeyer (1990a), according to which Greeks and others lived, intermarried, traded, manufactured, and farmed together without the settlement being either a colony or a trading post.[19] Pithekoussai is the single best-known example, but others might be found in the far west. Ancient sources speak of famine, civil disturbances and exile, or personal tragedy as reasons for groups of Greeks to leave home to settle permanently elsewhere. Famine came to be generalized as "land-hunger" in modern scholarship, and colonization came to be viewed as a kind of safety valve for societies under social or economic pressure. Alternatively, colonization was viewed as a state-sponsored enterprise aimed at securing lucrative resources (grain, metals, timber, fish) or trade with native populations (as seen especially in ceramic exports, which include transport amphorae and so indicate the trade of commodities and possibly cultural practices that come with these). Colonization, however, is a concept that must be qualified when speaking of the Greeks. It is more a process than an event, and less a manifestation or effect of imperialism than a settling down of a group of individuals, not always from the same original community, who might otherwise only trade or raid. They form a new, independent, permanent community in new territory (Jeffery 1976: 54; Osborne 1998b).

It was long the perception that "trade before the flag" was somehow transformed into settlement, colonization *per se*, and the reasons for this were endlessly debated. The very concept of "pre-colonial," however, is no longer favored in archaeological discourse (see Ridgway 2000b). It seems certain that voyaging for exchange and trade, and the contacts and human relationships, as well as the knowledge of winds, currents, places that it is based on, never wholly died out after the end of the Bronze Age, and these factors contributed to the conditions that led to permanent settlements that constitute colonization. Yet, despite the presence of *bona fide* Greek colonies in this midwest, the colonization model adumbrated above is not entirely sufficient or appropriate. Certainly *emporia*, or ports of trade, were more than just trading posts that received goods from elsewhere and facilitated their distribution. Their scope of activity included the fabrication of finished goods from local raw materials – and might involve cooperation and/or cohabitation of different groups of individuals from different cultures and origins.

The Mediterranean midwest

Sicily and Italy were the middle west, or "the intermediate stages,"[20] to the far western Mediterranean. The Phoenicians are clearly present in this region at a very early stage. This is documented not only by artifacts, but epigraphically. One of the most important written documents is the Nora Stele from near Cagliari in Sardinia. Discovered in 1773, published in 1835, this inscription probably dates to the late ninth century, early in the period under discussion here. It commemorates the founding of a temple to the god Pumay or Pumai (*Pmy*) by an arriving contingent of Phoenicians. This coincides with the Phoenicians' dispersal to Libya and Cyprus and, at the end of the eighth century, with the foundation of Carthage – as well as the early Greek colonies on Sicily. The late ninth century also saw the expansion of the Iberian demand for metal, both raw and finished products, as already noted. From Iberia, it was a short hop to Sardinia – and to Sicily. But despite these early activities, a firmly established Phoenician presence in permanent settlements in the west seems to belong mostly to the eighth century and later, as does the Greek.[21]

In this midwest, Pithekoussai is among the most celebrated early sites for Greek history – and for Phoenician history, as it turns out. Though incompletely excavated and only partially published, it is also one of the best documented. Parts of the acropolis, necropolis, and town including an area used for the smelting of iron, have been explored. Most scholars agree that the community, established in the ninth century, was of mixed origins, including Greeks from more than a single community, but certainly Euboeans among them. This fact makes the site important to understanding the phenomenon of Greek and Phoenician settlement, for Phoenicians were also present – if artifact types and origins, and the evidence of inscriptions in Greek and Phoenician, are anything to go on at all. Indeed, it appears that the community may have been a very diverse mix of individuals: "families whose original individual members came from Campania, Etruria, Latium vetus, North Africa, Sardinia, and doubtless more besides as well as from Euboea, Corinth, North Syria, and Phoenicia."[22] Pithekoussai is therefore not only early, but a hinge in the history of the western Mediterranean, where three of the main protagonists of the archaic period (and others) actually came face to face and cooperated in the same place. Indeed, Pithekoussai, Carthage, and Phoenician settlement in Sardinia are all contemporary; Phoenician settlements in western Sicily (Motya in particular) are somewhat later but more or less contemporary with Greek settlements in eastern Sicily (see below). Moreover, late Geometric style pottery from Carthage seems Pithecussan in origin.

There is general agreement that Pithekoussai was not a colony, Greek or otherwise. For one thing, there is not enough arable land to support the population extrapolated from the cemeteries at some thousands of inhabitants (men, women, children). It is also interesting to note that the cemetery, so far as it is known, seems to have had a mixture of grave goods from the beginning, with some female burials featuring indigenous Italian types of metalwork. This may indicate that the community was socially and ritually integrated, with possible intermarriage and a basic agreement on burial customs. Inhumations were sometimes placed in Levantine amphorae recycled to this purpose; the grave goods included ornaments with "oriental" origins (seals of the "Lyre-Player Group" from North Syria, scarabs, and other "orientalia.") Indeed, *enoikismos,* "cohabitation," better describes the situation at Pithekoussai than does *emporion.* The co-existence of Greeks and the heavily hellenizing Etruscans here and at Cumae would have had a strong influence on the Phoenicians of the west from the beginning (i.e. the eighth century).

The Greek midwest

After the establishment of this cooperative, productive, influential outpost in the Tyrrhenian Sea a major movement unfolds. Indeed, Pithekoussai for all its importance was not the wave of the future beyond the eighth century.

As already noted, the perspective imposed by modern political maps conditions how we frame the boundaries of Greece, sometimes taking into account the "Ionian Islands" and, less often, the Adriatic coasts as far as the limits of archaic Greek colonization (present-day Albania and Croatia). Yet it is a short coasting voyage from Corcyra to Otranto in the far south of peninsular Italy, shorter than many routes between neighboring islands in the Aegean, and shorter, in fact, than that from Ithaca to Corcyra.[23] The sea path along the south coast of Italy to Sicily is easy to trace, and indeed there is good evidence for contact between the Mycenaeans and southern Italy, and early (if not continuous) contacts from the earliest Iron Age as well (Holloway 1981; d'Andria 1995; see ch. 31, below). It should be noted that some Greek colonies, in actuality, were founded in what we might regard as home territory, because of the locations in the Aegean or Adriatic Seas: Corcyra, Leucas, Ambracia, Naupactos in the north-west; Thasos, the Chalcidice, and Thrace in the north Aegean, Thera in the central Aegean. In some ways, then, colonization can be considered an infilling of space, which occurred even within the territory (*chora*) of *poleis* like Athens in the course of the eighth and especially the seventh centuries, and proceeding with secondary colonizations in the sixth and fifth. A distinguishing feature of the western "colonial" movement is its concentration in time, the richness and success of many of the foundations, their impact on developments in the homeland, and their prominence and importance in ensuing Greek history – at least, as long as they lasted, which in some cases was not very long.[24]

The earliest *apoikiai* in the Mediterranean midwest were founded in the space of about a generation throughout the Mediterranean, and beyond. Italy and Sicily, situated in the middle west or central Mediterranean, saw some of the first. The very first were in Sicily, and founded by Euboeans: Naxos and Leontinoi, only a few years apart, reportedly by the same oecist (founder), Thucles of Chalcis. A Corinthian named Archias, meanwhile, founded Syracuse within a year of Naxos; an intended co-founder, Chersicrates, stopped instead at Corcyra. Catane was founded by another Chalcidian, Evarchus. Within the decade, Megarians had settled at Megara Hyblaea, after a number of failures, including a joint venture with the Euboeans at Leontini. By the end of the eighth century, Zancle and the dependent Mylai were founded at the straits of Messina, probably by Chalcidians and other Euboeans, with an admixture of individuals, reputedly pirates, from Cumae – itself established in the wake of the Pithecussan period (according to Thucydides 6.4 a foundation of Chalchis).

Thus, once again, the Euboeans were out in front, continuing into south Italy by founding Rhegium (together with Messenians). But in southern Italy it was the Achaeans who were pre-eminent; they established Sybaris (possibly with colonists from Troizene), and Croton. The Achaean initiative in south Italy presents a different path to establishing homes away from home – it was not driven by trade and exchange, and it happened somewhat after the Sicilian foundations, despite the knowledge of this coast which early contact suggests. Meanwhile, Taras was reputedly settled by Spartans under the authority of Phalanthus. Sparta colonized very little, though; aside from Thera in the south central Aegean, its only colony was Taras. Among pre-eminent homeland communities, Athens is an anomaly, completely uninvolved in early colonial activity, although Athenian transport amphorae are found throughout

Carla M. Antonaccio

the west Mediterranean, and Athens was in contact with the east from at least the ninth century.

All of these new communities were in existence before the end of the eighth century. These permanent settlements in the midwest, at least in south Italy, would seem to follow earlier trading contacts; the purpose of settlement in the eighth century, however, is primarily to create a new, independent, and largely self-sustaining community, which meant having access to arable land and other resources. Indeed, the proverbial wealth of many of the western Greek colonies was predicated on their territory and its productivity. The early foundations were located on the east cost of Sicily, accompanied at nearly the same moment by colonies in coastal southern Italy. If viewed from a western perspective, they seem to be a natural part of the central Mediterranean that includes the west coast of Greece and the Ionian islands, and face the Greek homeland. Indeed, the sanctuary at Olympia, in the western Peloponnese, is in many respects a western Greek sanctuary as much as a Panhellenic one, with early material from Italy and Sicily and a number of later treasuries dedicated by communities (and not only Greek ones) in the west (Antonaccio 2007, with references to earlier work).

The following century saw new colonies in both Sicily and south Italy, still with the participation of Achaeans at Metapontum, probably early in the century. The eastern Greeks joined in during this second phase: Siris was founded, reputedly by Ionians from Colophon, ca. 700, and Locri founded Locri Epizephyri in the early seventh century. Similarly, Rhodians from Lindus and Cretans founded Gela on Sicily's southern coast during the first quarter of the century. Thus, not only were the original colonies of Sicily and south Italy joined by others sent from homeland *metropoleis*, the original colonies themselves became *metropoleis*, establishing secondary colonies that extended Greek settlement well into the south and west of Sicily and the south and west Italian coasts. This phenomenon was led by Syracuse, which founded Helorus and Acrae early in the seventh century, and Camarina around 600. Megara Hyblaea founded Selinus in the second quarter of the seventh century, and Selinus turned around and founded Heraclea Minoa about a century later. Gela founded Acragas early in the sixth century in the face of Megara's extension of settlement; Zancle founded Himera in the last quarter of the seventh century.[25] Colonists could come from different Greek communities and different regions; and it is not unlikely that once established, local women and perhaps men may have resided among the Greeks and intermarried with them. (That indigenous individuals also lived in Greek communities as slaves or in some other subordinated status is also likely.) Certainly, Greeks from the homelands moved to the colonies, and vice versa (see further below on sanctuaries and festivals).

And east met west again, several hundred years after the earlier movements discussed above. In this context, the Phoenicians were founding their great second city, Qart Hadasht, "new city" or Carthage, in Tunisia, by the end of the ninth century according to literary tradition but not until the late eighth century judging by the archaeological evidence (Hodos 2006: 3, 159), and trade with Iberia was developing as well. In Sicily the Phoenicians founded cities at Panormus (modern Palermo), Motya off the west coast, and Soloeis (Solunto), as well as Mazara. The latter was relinquished when Selinus was founded. The foundations of Himera, on the north coast facing Phoenician colonies just mentioned, and Selinus, in the sphere of Motya, set the stage for confrontation. This came in the early sixth century, with the foundation of Acragas. Meanwhile, a group of east Greeks from Cnidus and Rhodes under the leadership of Pentathlus, attempted to found a colony at Lilybaeum. Siding with the Selinuntines in a conflict with Segesta, Pentathlus was killed. In this episode, according to Thucydides, the Elymian (indigenous western Sicilian) inhabitants of Segesta and the Phoenicians were allied. The foundation of Lilybaeum, had it succeeded, would have put a community of Greeks in a good strategic position to participate in the trade with Iberia, but geographical placement is not the only factor in the pursuit of trade or settlement – witness the Euboeans.[26]

The far west

Despite earlier contacts,[27] it was only at the end of the seventh century that trade was a regular activity between the Greeks of the eastern Mediterranean and the far west. As the Euboeans dominated early midwestern colonization and pre-colonial trade, it was the Phocaeans, Greeks of Ionia, the eastern Aegean, who founded colonies in modern France and Spain (Lombardo 2002) – another east-west encounter. This westward movement was prefigured by earlier settlements and trading ventures: having founded Lampsacus at the end of the seventh century, they headed west, founding Alalia on Corsica in the process, in ca. 565 – just the moment of the Phoenician "crisis" in the mid-sixth century. The Phoenicians had come under increasing pressure in the eighth and seventh century from the Assyrians. By the middle of the seventh century, Tyre's coastal territory was in Assyrian hands and cities in the north were destroyed. It was the neo-Babylonian empire, however, in the third quarter of the sixth century that dealt the decisive blow. After taking Nineveh and Jerusalem, as well as Damascus, Nebuchadnezzar's long siege effectively ended the Tyrian kingship. Sidon, in southern Phoenicia, benefited from the eclipse of Tyre, but Phoenician cedar trade was now in the hands of the Babylonians, and access to southern and eastern trade routes was hampered (Markoe 2000: 47–8; Aubet 2001: 59–60).

The most important of the Phocaean western colonies included Massalia (modern Marseilles, founded ca. 600), and Phocaea the metropolis together with Massalia her colony reportedly founded Emporion (modern Ampurias). Yet, the Phocaeans seem to have been more concerned with trade than with permanent settlement until the Ionian Revolt: the cities lay along the trade routes.[28]

The status of many archaic sites in the far west, including Rhode (modern Rosas) and the most western, Mainace, are disputed: whether they were *apoikiai* or *emporia*, whether Greek, Punic, or mixed, and the dates of their establishment and the role of the preexisting local populations in any of these endeavors. Imports to the far west, however, indicate much earlier contacts than these with indigenous groups, and perhaps not by Ionian Greeks (i.e. Phocaeans): at Huelva on the Atlantic coast beyond Gibraltar (belonging to the Iberian kingdom of Tartessus, ruled by the famous Arganthonius: Herodotus 1.163), the first known imported Greek object is an Attic Middle Geometric II pyxis krater – which may not have been carried by Athenians, of course, since the Athenians were not part of the early westward movements.[29] Indeed, recent work has suggested that the Phoenicians carried early Greek imports, including Attic SOS transport amphorae and Corinthian Subgeometric and Proto-corinthian *kotylai*.[30] Phoenician pottery (Red Slip and Polychrome wares, late seventh/early sixth century) was actually more widely distributed than Greek wares, and occurs further west though not so early. In the early seventh century, Greek material drops off. In the late seventh century, however, imports increase in variety and number, including much from east Greece and Etruscan bucchero, and following this material from Athens, Corinth, Sparta, and Ionia, including metalwork and terracottas, and faience. The story of the voyage of Kolaios of Samos beyond the Straits of Gibraltar, to Tartessus (Herodotus 4.152), is to be placed in this period.

The notion of Phocaean presence and influence is so prevalent and well attested in written sources that every Greek or hellenizing object in the far west can be (and has been) attributed to them. Our impression of the importance of Phocaean activities is due in part to Herodotus, who says they were the first Greeks to undertake lengthy voyages and to establish extremely friendly relations with king Arganthonios of Tartessus (1.163). In recent years, however, with more excavation and publication it has become clear that the majority of the pottery imports in Iberia are Attic, and a very wide variety characterizes the rest. There is no particular link to Ionia in this material. The celebrated "Tartessian" stone sculptures, which have been seen as proof of Phocaean influence because of their East Greek style, have been redefined as products of Iberian workshops influenced probably not by major sculpture or Greek sculptors but by terracottas in wide circulation throughout the Mediterranean (Rouillard 2001).

Nevertheless, the establishment of Massalia by ca. 600 seems to have changed the balance of trade, so to speak, in this region, shifting it from imports of Etruscan pottery and comestibles (wine and oil) in the late seventh century to Greek goods by mid-sixth century, including much Massaliot Greek pottery. The west then offered a refuge for those in the Phocaean metropolis who fled the Persians in 546, settling in the previously founded Alalia on the east coast of Corsica facing Etruria (and who, according to Herodotus, sailed in pentekonters, engaging in piracy). This presented a challenge to both the Etruscans and the Carthaginians, who joined forces to face it at the Battle of Alalia, fought between 540 and 535. Though the Phocaeans drove off this allied navy, they still retreated from Corsica, scattering to Rhegium and ultimately to Elea (Velia) north of Poseidonia (Paestum) on the Italian mainland.[31]

This row is emblematic of the complex reconfiguration of relations: fluid, but more confrontational in the mid-archaic period than they were earlier. The story of the Spartan Dorieus exemplifies it further. In the late sixth century, Dorieus, the younger brother of King Cleomenes, left Sparta to found a colony, making attempts first on the north coast of Africa (at a site between the related city of Cyrene, and Carthage itself, and possibly aided by Therans) but was forced to leave. His next destination was western Sicily, already staked by the Phoenicians and various Greeks, but mythically traversed by the Dorian Heracles. The region of Eryx was already in the orbit of native Elymians, Phoenicians who had arrived two centuries earlier, and Carthaginians – who therefore combined forces to kill Dorieus. Ostensiby to avenge Dorieus, Gelon (of Gela and later of Syracuse) fought a war to free what are referred to as the *emporia* in either north Africa or perhaps in western Sicily.[32]

Thus, an early cooperation and mutual intelligibility, articulated by interactivity and permeability, was transformed to confrontation and hostility later in the archaic period. The transition to permanent settlement and the second or third generation colonies, and the accompanying need for territory, created conflicts with both the local populations and among the colonizing Greeks, Etruscans, and Phoenicians/ Carthaginians. The battles of Himera (480, Greeks under Gelon of Syracuse defeating the Carthaginians) and Cumae (Cumaeans again with Syracusan help in 474, defeating the Etruscans) mark the end of the archaic period – events providing not only convenient, conventional dates for the end of an historical era. They also exemplify a conflictive, territorial mode, leading to mutual exclusion, and mutual hostility. Conflict, the destruction of Greek cities by other Greeks, and the removal and resettlement of populations also marked the sixth and fifth centuries in the mid and far west Mediterranean. The astonishingly brief *floruits* of rich cities such as Sybaris (founded in the late eighth century, destroyed in a war with Croton ca. 510) are an indication of the fluidity, or instability, of the networks with which we began. Yet, despite the "decolonization" of the west Mediterranean, the archaic Greek expansion was an important element of the mixing that characterizes the Mediterranean throughout history.[33]

As David Abulafia suggests (in Harris 2005: 68), both Braudel, who argued for the unity of the Mediterranean, and Horden and Purcell, who insist on its regional variation (as well as its connectivity), are right: "the Mediterranean had possessed such a high measure of unity . . . ever since long-distance trade linked the shores of Lebanon to the *Qart Hadasht* or 'New City' known now as Carthage, and then moved further west to reach the Mediterranean shores of Spain and even Cádiz beyond the Straits of Gibraltar." These unifying activities began even before the eighth century, as we have seen, and perhaps extended far back into prehistory. In this frame of reference, the archaic western Mediterranean is one of several Mediterraneans, and one with particular importance for the history of the Greeks.

NOTES

1 Horden and Purcell 2000: 11; cf. Abulafia 2005.
2 See Bowersock 2005. Acknowledging the imprecision of the term, Fernand Braudel suggests that "pre-em" encompasses "central Europe, from the Alps to the Baltic and the North Sea, the Italian peninsula (rather than the surrounding islands), the territory that would become Gaul, the Iberian peninsula, and North Africa . . . from the Gulf of Gabès to the Atlantic" (2001: 165). It is interesting to note that in this context he identifies the Greeks together with Phoenicians and Etruscans as "peoples from the east" (177). He is not alone; cf. Malkin 2004, Rouillard in Settis 2001.
3 For another perspective on the western Mediterranean and the Atlantic, see Cunliffe 2001.
4 See Aubet 2001: ch. 1 on the terminological confusion between Canaanites, Phoenicians, Carthaginians, and the term "Punic." Adapting the approach of Aubet (2001: 13), in what follows the term "Phoenicians" will be used of the inhabitants of the coastal plain

of Lebanon up until the sixth century, "Carthaginians" will apply to inhabitants of Carthage, founded in the eighth century, and "western Phoenicians" will be preferred for those voyaging and settling in the west.

5   Aubet 2001: 52: "Thus the ultimate causes of the [Phoenician] expansion westwards must be sought fundamentally in the internal dynamics of Phoenician society in the east."

6   Malkin 1998; 2002a; 2004; cf. Gosden 2005: 82–114.

7   "Caractérisé par un grand dynamisme démographique et, en partie par voie de conséquence, par une grande mobilité géographique des personnes et des biens": Gras 2002: 183; see also Ridgway 2000b.

8   On Cyprus in the archaic period, see for example Reyes 1994.

9   Horden and Purcell 2000: 123–72; Malkin 1998. See also LaBianca and Scham 2006.

10 Malkin 2004: 359, drawing on the work of Deleuze and Guattari; cf. Knappett 2005: 76.

11 As Aubet comments, "Classical historiography is unanimous in recognizing the silver trade as the objective of Phoenician expansion into the far west . . . the procurement and production of silver on a large scale means Gadir [Cadiz] and its immediate hinterland, Tartessos. For once the archaeological record provides an abundance of elements corroborating this historical fact" (2001: 257). On the settlements in the area, see Ruiz Mata 2002a; 2002b; cf. Aubet Semmler 2002; Jurado 2002.

12 Gras 2002: 189 ("dans des conditions qui demeurent encore peu claires mais qui apparaissent comme très liées aux navigations phéniciennes"); see also Fletcher 2006. As will be noted further below, the presence of a particular style of pottery or other artifact is no necessary index of the presence of a particular group, and Euboean pottery at Al Mina does not prove Euboeans were in charge. See ch. 19, below, on the debate over "phantom Euboeans," and J. Papadopoulos's skepticism in particular. This extreme skepticism is not very widely shared, however, and what seems clear is that Euboeans were part of the picture as much as Phoenicians were.

13 The cult of Melqart, whom the Greeks called Heracles, figured in founding Gadir, and a major temple to this divinity was located there. Melqart may have been a mediating figure in the same way that Odysseus was for the Greeks and Etruscans. See Aubet 2001: 194–211, 260–2, 273–9; Malkin 2004. For the Atlantic settlements, see Bierling 2002: part II.

14 See Dougherty 2001 and Malkin 1998 on the figure of Odysseus in the context of early voyaging, trade, and colonization.

15 See Aubet 2001: 127–32 on the Homeric treatment of Phoenicians, and Malkin 1998: 180–91 on the Hesiodic passage.

16 On Demaratus, see Cornell 1995: 124–5; for Kolaios and Sostratos, Möller 2000 (and on Sosatratos' dedication at Gravisca, Cornell 1995: 109–11).

17 See Ridgway 2000b summarizing much other work.

18 On "pre-colonial," see Ridgway 2000b and the scathing comments of Purcell 1997.

19 His model seems preferable to earlier views (summarized in Hodos 2006: 19–24) because, unlike a colony, an *enoikismos* does not imply political control by one group or another, and unlike a trading post, it is both durable and exploits the territory for its subsistence.

20 "Le tappe intermedie": Pugliese Caratelli 1990, speaking of Sicily and Sardinia.

21 Aubet 2001 is the best account so far of the Phoenician expansion into the western Mediterranean; on the Nora stele, 206–9. See also Markoe 2000 (Nora inscription, 176–8).

22 Ridgway 2000b: 30; cf. Boardman in Lévêque 1999: 46; Docter and Niemeyer 1994.

23 Horden and Purcell 2000: 127, map 9, shows what parts of the Mediterranean were out of sight to sailors at sea; cf. fig. 35 in Aubet 2001: 169.

24 The scholarly literature on colonization is very extensive; see ch. 19, below.

25 Keeping in mind Braudel's definition of the west, we should remember that this fissioning occurred elsewhere in the Greek ambit; Thera, an early colony of Sparta, founded Cyrene in Libya, which in turn spread other foundations throughout the Cyrenaica.

26 The unsuccessful Knidians went on to found a colony at Lipari and to fight the Etruscans who were active in these waters, and who may have been trading partners with the Greek cities on the Tyrrhenian coast (e.g. Laos). Cf. Thuc. 6.2.6.

27 Chapman 2003 on the prehistory of the western Mediterranean; Ruiz and Molinos 1998.

28 Niemeyer 1990a: 47. Indeed, it is for the case of Emporion that Niemeyer has suggested the model of *enoikismos* rather than *apoikia* for the Greek presence in the far west.

29 Niemeyer 1990a: 39; cf. Ruiz and Molinos 1998: 51; Dominguez and Sánchez 2001: 10 and fig. 4 no. 1, with additional references. As Aubet points out, Arganthonius' name is rooted in the Greek word for silver, directly reflecting the commodity that was the object of the Phoenician and also Greek interest in the area.

30 Aubet 2001: 287. On pottery imports, see Dominguez in Dominguez and Sánchez 2001.

31 Hdt. 1.166–7. See Hodge 1998 on France with an emphasis on Marseilles.

32 Hdt. 5.42ff; 7.158; see Dunbabin 1948: ch. XI, 410–14; Malkin 1994b.

33 On the notion of decolonization in the ancient Greek case, see Asheri 1996 (on the rise of indigenous Italian groups such as the Lucanians, Bruttians, Oenotrians, etc. and the decline of the Greek communities in their areas).

CHAPTER SEVENTEEN

The Black Sea

Gocha R. Tsetskhladze

This sea was not navigable, and was called Axine [Inhospitable] because of its wintry storms and the ferocity of the tribes that lived around it, and particularly the Scythians, in that they sacrificed strangers, ate their flesh, and used their skulls as drinking-cups; but later it was called "Euxine" [Hospitable] when the Ionians founded cities on the seaboard.

(Strabo 7.3.6; tr. Loeb)

The Black Sea, known in ancient times as the Euxine Pontus (Hdt. 1.72), before it was colonized by Greeks, primarily Ionians, was wrapped in myth, a distant area of legend, famed for its riches. In Greek mythology, the Scythian snake-footed goddess held Heracles captive for a while, and he left his footprint, as well as his descendants, near the River Tyras. Euripides told the story of Iphigeneia, carried off to the Temple of Artemis among the Taurians. Achilles led his post-mortal life on the island of Leuce, north-east of the Danube delta. The Hyperboreans sent gifts to the temple of Apollo on Delos and Hyperborean Apollo rode on a winged griffin from lands to the north of Scythia. The Sarmatians were supposedly begotten on the shores of Lake Maeotis (the Sea of Azov) when migrating Amazons met a group of young Scythians. Orpheus, the greatest of singers, was a native of Thrace. Prometheus was punished for giving man fire by being chained to Mount Elbrus in the Great Caucasus, where his liver was eaten each day by birds of prey. Io journeyed to the Caucasus, land of the one-eyed, gold-hoarding Arimaspeans and of the part-lion, part-eagle, treasure-guarding griffins, and then on to Scythia. Best known is the myth of Jason and the Argonauts, who voyaged to Colchis, for the Greeks the eastern edge of the known world, to steal the Golden Fleece with the help of the sorceress Medea. Both Aeschylus and Sophocles wrote several plays based on aspects of the Argonautic adventures, but Euripides' *Medea* was the most influential work on this topic. No ancient historian or geographer could write about the Black Sea without mention of the Argonauts and the peoples and places they visited.

For Greeks of the archaic period, many of these peoples and places remained distant, largely legendary. Only later, from the fifth century onward, was an attempt made to identify them, such as Aia, in Jason's story, with Colchis (Hdt. 7.193). Initially, the Greeks found the waters of the Black Sea dangerous: there were no islands and the peoples dwelling along the shore practiced piracy (Tsetskhladze 2000/1). It was not until the time of Herodotus that the Greeks estimated the extent of a sea whose beauty had impressed the Great King Darius:

> Darius, when in his march from Susa he came to that place in the territory of Calchedon where the Bosporus was bridged, took ship and sailed to the Dark Rocks (as they are called) which the Greeks say did formerly move upon the waters; there he sat on a headland and viewed the Pontus, a marvelous sight. For it is of all seas the most wonderful. Its length is eleven thousand one hundred furlongs [about 2,000 km], and its breadth, at the place where it is widest, three thousand three hundred [about 600 km]. The channel at the entrance of this sea is four furlongs broad; and in length, the narrow neck of the channel called Bosporus, across which the bridge was thown, is as much as a hundred and twenty furlongs. The Bosporus reaches as far as to the Propontis.
>
> (Hdt. 4.85; tr. Loeb)

In reality, the sea measures 1,174 km in length and is 260 km across (from the Crimea to Inebolu on the Turkish coast): overall, an area of about 423,000 km² (King 2004: 15).

Local Societies

Before the Greeks founded their cities and settlements, the Black Sea was home to many tribes and peoples (see map 11), with whom Greek colonists established contacts from the first. Sometimes the land for settlement and agriculture was given to the Greeks by local tribal rulers, either by special agreement or in return for payment of a moderate tribute (Strabo 7.4.6). In most areas, groups of the local population formed part of Greek settlements from the outset, whilst some Greeks went to live in local settlements (see below); the gradual blossoming of these relations gave rise to the creation of a completely new and unique phenomenon, Graeco-barbarian art (Boardman 1994: 182–223). Of course, in some other parts of the Black Sea the Greeks were confronted by hostile locals.

In the western Black Sea the Greeks encountered Thracian tribes (Archibald 1998), who occupied lands from the Aegean to Transdanubia, as well as straddling the Propontis into the Troad and Bithynia. Homer mentions them in the *Iliad* and the *Odyssey*.[1] The western frontiers with the Illyrians and Macedonians were vaguer. Thrace was well stocked with fish and game and possessed some very large, fertile plains (especially the Danubian); other parts were rich in precious metals and iron and copper (and the Thracians quite advanced at metalworking): some rivers yielded gold-bearing sand, whilst gold and silver were mined in Aegean Thrace. The Greeks valued timber from Thrace's many forests for shipbuilding.

What the Thracians called themselves is unknown, if indeed they had a common name; the terms Thrace and Thracians were labels applied by the Greeks. The Thracian tribes (Triballi, Rhodopians, Dardani, Haemians, etc.) were numerous, a warlike, non-urbanized people ruled by various local dynasties, and in the Early Iron Age they practiced ritualized human sacrifice (Tonkova 2005). Those south-east of Dacia, the Getae, formed a large group consisting of several tribes occupying large territories on both banks of the Danube. In Dobruja, with the assimilation of the Getae and the Thracians by the Dacians (from the second half of the sixth century), a Getic–Dacian culture was formed.

After Greek colonization of western Pontus, Thracians became customers for some fine Greek imports. Between ca. 513 and 479 Thrace was held by the Persians. The results of exposure to both Greek and Persian influence are apparent to differing degrees. The cultural influence of the Scythian Animal Style was also quite strong (see below).

Scythian tribes occupied the Black Sea coastal regions and hinterland in an arc of territory from north of the Danube across to the northern Caucasus, including the Crimea.[2] They settled in the rich valleys and plains of the Danube, Dniester, Bug, Dnieper, and Don, and most of the southern Ukraine as far north as Kiev, following migration from northern Siberia at the beginning of the seventh century into the North Pontic steppes previously controlled by the Cimmerians, whom they pursued through both the Caucasus and Thrace to Asia Minor and Anatolia.

Ancient authors mention many groups as living in Scythia, of whom the Scythians were just one. The term Scythian embraces different ethnically related but often opposed groups (Alazones, Callippidae, Geloni, Budini, etc.), not all of them nomads. The most valiant and numerous of the Scythian tribes (Hdt. 4.20), and those enjoying the closest relation with the Greeks of the northern Pontus, were the "Royal Scythians," who regarded all other Scythians as their slaves. In the mid-seventh century the Scythians migrated to western Asia, passing through the Caucasus, as had the Cimmerians, and overthrowing the Medes, Assyria, Urartu, and others to become "masters of Asia" (Hdt. 1.104). Then, at the end of the seventh or beginning of the sixth century, the Scythians returned by a similar route to the North Pontic steppes. But it was not until the end of the sixth century that North Pontic Scythia was created – even then it was bicephalous, with territory on the lower Dnieper not far from the Greek *polis* of Olbia and in the Crimean steppe close to the Bosporan kingdom (Hind 1994) – and, in its wake, close Graeco-Scythian relations developed.

Scythian territory was not highly urbanized; its characteristic archaeological site is the burial tumulus – although there are a few fortified settlements such as Belsk and Kamenskoe. Scythian art, known as Animal Style, is that of a nomadic culture, expressed mainly in small objects – dress, weapons, and horse trappings – made from gold, bronze, bone, wood, and various textiles. Some examples of the last two have been preserved in excellent condition in the frozen sites of Siberia. In the Greek cities of the northern Black Sea, Scythian and Greek cultures met and combined to create the unique Scythian-Greek art, especially in the classical period (figures 17.1–17.3), with Greek craftsmen in the North Pontic colonies adapting their output to produce highly artistic gold and silver jewelry and vessels for the Scythian elite, crafted to Scythian taste and requirements.

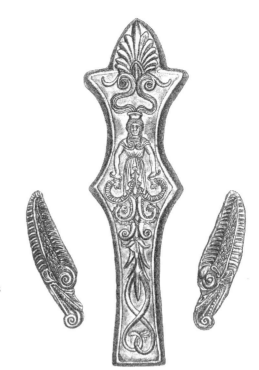

Figure 17.1 Gold bridle set: cheek-pieces
(left, right) in the form of dolphins,
L. 17.8 cm, 18.2 cm; chamfron (center)
with the image of a serpent-bodied female,
L. 41.4 cm, Bolshaya Tsimbalka tumulus
Source: After Jacobson (1995: figs. 141–3).

Figure 17.2 Spherical vessel: whole vessel and details of images of Scythian males, gold
or electrum, H. 13.0 cm, Kul Olba tumulus
Source: After Jacobson (1995: fig. 84).

Figure 17.3 Amphora with tendril ornament, frieze of men and horses, and scenes of griffins savaging deer, silver-gilt, H. 70.0 cm, D. 40.0 cm, Chertomlyk tumulus
Source: After Jacobson (1995: fig. 90).

Other local peoples were to be found around the northern Black Sea: Tauri in the Crimea (difficult to distinguish archaeologically); Maeotians in the eastern part of Lake Maeotis/Sea of Azov; and Sindians in the Taman Peninsula and the Kuban (Tsetskhladze 1998b: 44–50). Whereas the Tauri lived in the mountains, practiced piracy and had hostile relations with the Greek colonists, the two last were agricultural tribes in close and amicable relations with the Greeks and were influenced strongly by Greek culture, especially from the fourth century when they became part of the Greek Bosporan kingdom.

South of the Caucasus mountains, the eastern part of the Black Sea was called Colchis – another instance of a Greek appellation; the local name is unknown – after the leading element in a multi-ethnic region which had achieved political unification, and applied to the territory as a whole (Tsetskhladze 1998c: 165–89). A Colchian kingdom developed by the middle of the fifth century. Natural conditions along this coast were unwelcoming: swamps, marshes, and wetlands (Hippoc. *Airs, Waters, Places* 15). So too were the tribes of northern Colchis, the Heniochi and Zygi, notorious pirates who used to attack the Greek cities. But the other Colchians were agricultural peoples. Cimmerians and Scythians passed through Colchis en route to western Asia; the latter passed that way again, some settling there, on their journey back to the northern Pontus. Scythian-type weapons and objects in the Animal Style were widespread. Colchis formed a link between east and west and its culture, although endogenous, shows Greek and Persian influences, as well it might.

The pattern of the southern Black Sea is even more homogeneous: many local peoples were very hostile towards Greeks. The long expanse of coast between Byzantium and Heraclea Pontica contained neither Greek cities nor settlements although there were good harbors and fertile lands suited to their establishment. The main reason for their absence was the unfriendliness of the local people (Xen. *Anab.* 6.4.2–6). Dorian Heraclea Pontica (see below) was established on the lands of the Mariandynoi, a people gradually assimilated by the Thracians. According to Strabo, the colonists "forced the Mariandynoi, who held the place before them, to serve as Helots, so that they sold them, but not beyond the boundaries of their own country (for the two peoples came to an agreement on this)" (12.3.4).

The south-eastern Black Sea littoral was populated by the Tibareni, Chalybes, Drilae, Mossynoeci, Macrones, and Colchians. Most of these tribes were included in the Achaemenid empire. Archaeologically, little is known about them, and although we know more about the Colchians from the eastern Black Sea, we have no means of determining whether those around Trapezus shared the same material culture as Colchis proper. The Chalybes were few in number, most engaged in ironworking. The Colchians in the vicinity of Trapezus lived in numerous villages; they were hostile towards the Greeks. The Drilae lived in fortified settlements in the mountains behind Trapezus. Both their houses and fortifications were wooden. So too were those of the Mossynoeci, who dwelt in numerous villages in the mountains between Kotyora and Kerasos.[3] Their houses were towers of seven levels. According to Xenophon, the Mossynoeci were "the most uncivilized people whose country they [the Greeks] traversed, the furthest removed from Greek customs."[4]

The area between Sinope and Amisos probably was home to some Phrygian settlements; and to Cappadocians and/or Paphlagonians, called by the Greeks "Syrians" or "White Syrians" (Hdt. 1.7.2; Strabo 12.3.9). The area around Trapezus and the Diauehi country were under Urartian political influence. These territories were also known as Chaldia, and the Chaldians were thought to be descendants or remnants of the Urartians.[5]

Greek Colonies of the Pontus in the Archaic Period

Greek exploration and settlement of the Black Sea region began in the second half of the seventh century (Tsetskhladze 1994) (see map 11). The principal manifestation of this was the colonizing activity of Miletus, said to have possessed as many as 75 or even 90 colonies.[6] In the words of Strabo: "The city [Miletus] is known to many, and mainly thanks to the large number of its colonies, since the whole Pontus Euxinus, Propontis and many other places have been settled by Milesians" (14.1.6). Of course, other Ionian centers took part (see below): Miletus itself was just the organizer of the process and was unable to found and populate so many colonies on its own (Ehrhardt 1988; Gorman 2001: 47–86).

The reasons for Ionian colonization are highly complex (Tsetskhladze 1994: 123–6). It was long held that the search for metals in the southern and eastern Black Sea and for grain on its northern shore provided the main spur to this colonizing activity. More recent studies have shown the former regions to be less metal-rich than was thought (Tsetskhladze and Treister 1995), whilst the northern Black Sea could not have been a source of grain in the seventh to fifth centuries, as many scholars would like to believe: there is no evidence; indeed, archaeological and palaeo-botanical sources show that grain could not have been obtained from the Scythians until the late fifth or fourth century, when the lifestyle of the vast majority of Scythian tribes shifted from nomadic to pastoral (Gavrilyuk 1999: 28–85, 292–300). Most probably, if and when Athens needed grain in the seventh to fifth centuries, it resorted to fertile areas much nearer to hand, such as the Peloponnese (Keen 2000: 65; cf. Whitby 1998a: 102–5).

Every mother-city had particular reasons for sending forth colonists, and these must be examined. Only through analysis of these cities and their circumstances can we identify what reasons and motives obliged the Greeks to emigrate. Greek colonization was never exclusively agrarian, commercial or connected with the need for metals; nor was it simply a consequence of over-population. Study of the situation in seventh-century Asia Minor suggests that enforced emigration was paramount: first Lydia and then, in the mid-sixth century, the Persians, pursued a hostile policy towards Miletus and other Ionian cities. The Persians eventually annexed the region. The upshot was a reduction of the cities' *chorai* and a fierce political struggle within Miletus itself, fueled by internal tensions as much as reaction to the external threat.[7] In the circumstances, emigration provided a solution, albeit a very radical one (Tsetskhladze 1994: 123–6). As written sources make clear, thanks to the Achaemenid conquest, the Ionians were left with two stark choices: to leave their homeland or to stay and be enslaved or killed. At that time the one region not yet colonized by other Greek cities was the Black Sea, and that is principally where Miletus and other Ionian cities looked.[8]

There are problems with the foundation dates of the Black Sea colonies given by written sources, compounded by a trend towards dating by Olympiads and their four-year cycle instead of using other Greek or near eastern events, or even the reign of a king, to anchor them.[9] Christian writers of the late Roman imperial period stirred the era of Abraham into the pot. Eusebius and Jerome (*Chron.* 95b) provide spuriously exact dates, based on previous pagan traditions tabulated much later, and these have won wide acceptance as actual foundation dates for some of the Pontic colonies – Histria in 657, Olbia in 647, Sinope in 631. But these dates cannot be accepted as canonical. And a fourth date relating to Trapezus, found in the Armenian version of Eusebius (*Ann. Abr.* 1260) should be discounted as a mistake: it refers to Cyzicus.

Thus, archaeological evidence must have the last word in clearing away the obstacle of these discrepant written sources. The earliest Pontic colonies were founded at the same time as Byzantium and Chalcedon in the Propontis (Tsetskhladze 1994: 115–18). The first settlements in the northern Black Sea were those at Berezan in the third quarter of the seventh century (Solovyov 1998) and the so-called Taganrog settlement in the last third of the seventh century, which has now been completely destroyed by the sea (Larenok and Dally 2002). Berezan was identified with the Borysthenites (Avram et al. 2004: 937), and study of the archaic pottery shows that the majority came from Miletus, while Samos, Ephesus and possibly Smyrna also participated in its foundation. Among the earliest Milesian colonies in the western Black Sea are Histria (ca. 630) and Apollonia (ca. 610); and on the southern shore, Sinope and Amisos, both in the late seventh century (Avram et al. 2004: 954, 960–1).

The earliest *apoikiai*, situated on peninsulas, were all well protected by the natural environment and possessed convenient harbors. Apollo was worshipped: the Milesians and other Ionian cities sought advice in Didyma, the oracular sanctuary of Apollo founded by Miletus and shared by all the Pontic colonies, according to which their god and protector was Apollo Ietros, "the Healer" (Avram, Hind and Tsetskhladze 2004: *passim*).

From the beginning of the sixth century Milesian colonizing activity expanded (Tsetskhladze 1994: 119–20). In Berezan a new wave of settlers appeared. This new population ushered in the gradual penetration of the mainland by Greeks from the peninsula, and the opening up of *chorai* clustered on the left bank of the Berezan estuary and in the western part of the Dnieper-Bug estuary. A similar situation may be observed at Histria where the first city walls were built in 575 (Avram, Hind and Tsetskhladze 2004: 932–3). As existing colonies were extended, so too were new cities established: Tomis in the western Pontus and Olbia, not far from Berezan, in the north, between 590 and 580. Olbia soon extended its zone of influence and founded rural settlements on the lower reaches of the Bug. In the archaic period, Olbia's *chora* comprised 107 settlements. Between ca. 580 and 560, Miletus settled new territories: the Kerch and Taman peninsulas (the Cimmerian Bosporus). In the Kerch Peninsula (European Bosporus) the cities of Panticapaeum, Nymphaeum, Theodosia, Myrmekion, and Tyritake were founded; in the Taman Peninsula (Asiatic Bosporus) Kepoi, Patraeus, a city since destroyed by the sea to which the Tuzlian cemetery belonged, and Hermonassa, a joint colony of Miletus and Mytilene.[10]

The first stages of the Persian conquest of the Greek cities of Asia Minor sent a new wave of Ionian colonists to the shores of the Black Sea (ca. 560–530). One aspect of this period is the appearance of colonies founded by people other than Milesians – for example Heraclea, which was established to the south of the Pontus in 554 by Megarians and Boeotians – but their number is small. On the western shore, Odessos was founded by the Milesians, and the expansion of existing Greek cities in the western Pontus caused many small settlements to appear (Avram, Hind and Tsetskhladze 2004). In the north of the Black Sea, Olbia was already a *polis*, a large city possessed of an extensive *chora*, and issuing its own coinage. Berezan had become part of Olbia. In the mid-sixth century new cities such as Tyras and Nikonion appeared, together with the approximately 50 settlements which formed their *chorai*. Within the Cimmerian Bosporus, Gorgippia, Toricos, Akra, Porthmeus and Iluraton were founded, and on the Taman Peninsula in ca. 542 the Teians founded Phanagoria. Another Teian colony, Abdera, was established in Thrace at the same time (Avram, Hind and Tsetskhladze 2004). The Ionians began to settle new territories: the north-western Crimea and eastern Pontus (Colchis). In the territory where Chersonesus was to be founded in 422/1 by Heraclea Pontica, a small, probably Ionian, settlement appeared (Avram, Hind and Tsetskhladze 2004: 941–2). Colchis was colonized by the Milesians, who established three cities (Phasis, Gyenos, and Dioscurias) and two settlements (Pichvnari and Tsikhisdziri). These colonists' official cult was of Apollo Hegemon.[11]

The last wave of Ionian penetration of the Pontus dates from the end of the sixth century to the first quarter of the fifth century when the Ionians, defeated in their revolt against the Persians, were again obliged to flee their native cities (Tsetskhladze 1994: 120–3). During the same period existing cities were expanding and new settlements of Milesians and by other Greek centers were appearing. Mesambria was founded to the west of the Black Sea by Chalcedonians and Byzantines who, according to Herodotus (6.33), fled at the time of the Ionian Revolt. In the western Crimea, the Ionians established Kerkinitis and Kalos Limen, later to be absorbed by Chersonesus.

The sixth century, the second half particularly, was an important period in the history of the Pontus and its Greek cities. Colonization seems to have been more directly organized. The written sources give us the names of the *oikistes* of several Greek colonies: Hermonassa, where the *oikistes* even became ruler of the city, Phanagoria and Phasis.[12]

Social Structures and Culture

From the mid-sixth century the first Greek *apoikiai* matured into *poleis* with their own strong state and religious institutions, laws and social structure. These city-states began their own craft production. The *chorai* of Olbia, Bosporus, and Histria were now very extensive (Avram et al. 2004).

The earliest colonies had been small: Panticapaeum occupied some 7.5 ha in the sixth century, its population no more than 2,000–3,000 (Blavatskii 1964: 25), while in the first half of the century Olbia had had an area of about 6 ha, rising to 16.5 ha in the second half (Vinogradov and Kryzickij 1995: 28). Phanagoria was built on a hill; its area was 20–22.5 ha in the second half of the century. For this colony some regulation can be identified: buildings are next to each other along both sides of streets 1.5–3 m wide (Tsetskhladze 2002b). It is the only settlement of the period to show signs of proper planning and a regular layout of streets. In none of these towns is there any evidence of a distinct *agora* or a *temenos* until the last quarter of the sixth century. The architecture of sanctuaries was quite primitive and, for example in Olbia, indistinguishable from the domestic. The "sanctuary" of Demeter in Nymphaeum may in fact be a production complex (Tsetskhladze 2003: 136). A small temple of the late archaic period dedicated to Aphrodite has been discovered recently in Berezan (figure 17.4).[13]

It is true that there was no grand temple architecture in the archaic period but the evidence demonstrates the existence of quite advanced religious practices and ceremonies. Orphism is attested in Olbia (West 1983: 17–20). A bone plaque with a graffito was found in Berezan, dating to the end of the sixth or beginning of the fifth century (Onyshkevych 2002; figure 17.5). Its interpretation is still a matter of debate. There are seven texts written on the bone (Onyshkevych 2002: 163–4, with translations). Text A reads:

> Seven. A weak wolf.
> Seventy. A fierce lion.
> Seven hundred. A friendly archer – a gift
> to the power of the physician.
> Seven thousand. A wide dolphin.
> Peace to the Olbian polis. I bless her.
> I remember Leto.

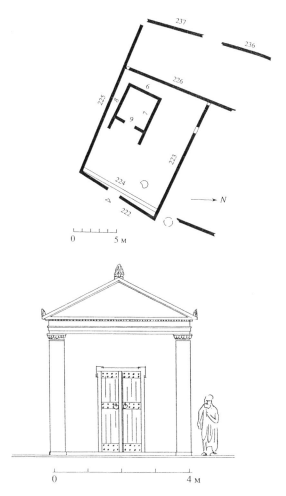

Figure 17.4 Temple dedicated to Aphrodite at Berezan: plan (1) and reconstruction of facade (2)
Source: After Kryzhitskij (2001: figs. 1, 5).

Texts B–E translate as:

> Seven.
> To Apollo,
> the Didymaian,
> the Milesian.
> Bringer of fortune of the mother (or motherland).
> Victor of the north (or northern wind).
> To the Didymaian/The Didymaian.

Text F is restored as "seventy oxen to Didymaian (Apollo)." Text G repeats a phrase from text D. Some interpret the plaque as bearing elements of resemblance

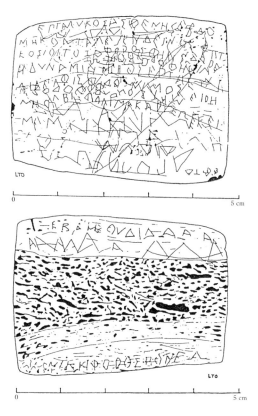

Figure 17.5 Drawing of bone plaque from Berezan: front (1) and reverse (2)
Source: After Onyshkevych (2002: figs. 6, 7).

to the three Olbian Orphic plaques and having Orphic connections itself. Although it is not possible to divine the exact meaning of the texts, many elements suggest strongly a link to a cult of Apollo Hebdoman in the Berezan-Olbia area, and a possible connection to the Orphic cult known later in Olbia. In part, the purpose of the plaque was probably votive; the texts may represent a hymn or prayer used in the cult.

Domestic architecture from the end of the seventh through the late sixth century possessed some distinctive features (Tsetskhladze 2004). Two main types of dwelling may be identified: one in Milesian colonies, the other in Teian (e.g. at Phanagoria). Milesian foundations around the whole Black Sea are characterized by the presence of dugouts and semi-dugouts. This kind of architecture survived into the last quarter of the sixth century or a little later. It is not surprising when new evidence from Miletus itself is taken into account. Milesian domestic architecture was very simple and some evidence there points to the existence of subterranean houses. In the Teian colony of Phanagoria we have one-room mudbrick houses and also wattle-and-daub architecture. In general, stone architecture and regular town-planning do not appear around the Black Sea until the late archaic period, especially from the middle of the fifth century. The most plausible explanation for this change is the arrival of Athenians (Tsetskhladze 2004).

The late archaic period marked the end of colonization of the Black Sea by the Greeks, but this does not mean that no further waves of Greeks came to the Black Sea. The Athenians showed great interest in the area, but most of their permanent settlements did not appear until the second half of the fifth century and were unconnected with the waves of colonization undertaken by the Greek world in the eighth–sixth centuries. Rather, it was a completely new phenomenon, a manifestation of Athenian imperialism. Admittedly, early Attic black-figure pottery, which dates from ca. 600–550, has been found in Berezan, Histria, and Apollonia, but this was precisely the time that Athenian political expansion reached the Propontis. The most important Athenian foundations were Sigeion and the settlements in Thracian Chersonesus. In the wake of the growing difficulties the Ionians experienced with the Persian empire and the suppression of the Ionian Revolt, the colonial and commercial activities of the Ionians decreased and Athens began to turn its attention to the Black Sea market. During the Graeco-Persian wars it was difficult to sail through the Straits. We do not find many imports of Attic pottery there at this time. After the consolidation of the Athenian maritime empire, the amount of fine Attic pottery increases. It was marketed in all parts of Pontus but the largest share seems to have gone to the Bosporan area, to Olbia and Apollonia Pontica (Tsetskhladze 1998c).

Crafts and Trade

Soon after its establishment, every Greek city became a center of craft production (Tsetskhladze 1998b: 42–3; 2003: 144–7). Many started to manufacture pottery imitating East Greek shapes, expanding step by step to produce terracottas, tiles, amphorae, etc. Nearly every Greek city has left traces of metalworking, based on the use of ingots specially produced for them – for example the cities of the northern Black Sea obtained these supplies from wooded-steppe Scythia (Tsetskhladze 1998b: 66–7). As we have seen, the Pontic cities were largely founded by Ionians. It is unsurprising that the bulk of their craftsmen came from Asia Minor as well (Treister 1998; 2001: 59 78), although there is evidence that some were from elsewhere in the Greek world, for example from Eleutherna in Crete and Helike in the Peloponnese (Treister and Shelov-Kovedyaev 1989).

Special metal workshops sprang up in the late archaic period, producing objects in styles familiar to the local Scythian and Thracian elites, the Hallstatt chiefs of central Europe, and others. In these shops craftsmen of Milesian, Ephesian, and Lydian origin worked alongside each other (Treister 1998; 2001: 59–78).

Fine pottery and amphorae are the principal evidence used to study trade relations.[14] Pottery from southern Ionia was widespread throughout the Pontic region in the seventh century and the early sixth; pottery from northern Ionia later displaced it. Transport amphorae from Chios, Lesbos, and Clazomenae are commonplace. Ionian merchants probably brought the small quantities of goods from Corinth and Naucratis that have been found, and, with Aeginetans, were responsible for the appearance of the first archaic Athenian pottery in the region.

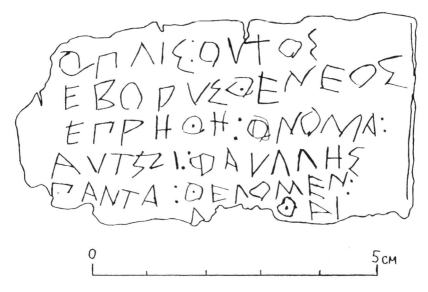

Figure 17.6 Drawing of lead plaque from Phanagoria
Source: After Vinogradov (1998: fig. 3).

Trade relations between the Greek Pontic colonies were also quite well developed. The best sources are lead letters (Vinogradov 1998). One such, found in Phanagoria on the Taman Peninsula, dating from the 530s to the 510s, reads: "This slave was exported for sale from Borysthenes, his name is Phaulles. We wish all (debts?) to be paid" (Vinogradov 1998: 160–3) (figure 17.6). It demonstrates the existence of a slave trade between Phanagoria and Borysthenes/Olbia. To date we have five letters on lead or *ostraka* indicating that a slave trade was also well developed at least along the northern Black Sea littoral (Vinogradov 1998).

Each large city possessed a fine harbor. According to Strabo, Theodosia "is situated in a fertile plain and has a harbor that can accommodate as many as a hundred ships; this harbor in earlier times was a boundary between the countries of the Bosporus and the Taurians" (7.4.4); Nymphaeum possessed a good harbor, while Panticapaeum controlled the entrance to the Sea of Azov and its harbor could hold up to 30 ships (Strabo 7.4.4). Along the north-west shore, deep harbors were few but the mouths of the major rivers were both sources of fish and easy routes into the hinterland. Herodotus writes:

> The Borysthenes . . . is . . . the most valuable and productive not only of the rivers in this part of the world, but anywhere else, with the sole exception of the Nile . . . It provides the finest and most abundant pasture, by far the richest supply of the best sorts of fish, and the most excellent water for drinking – clear and bright . . . no better crops grow anywhere than along its banks, and where grain is not sown the grass is the most luxuriant in the world.
>
> (Herodotus 4.53; tr. Loeb)

Discussion of trade relations between Pontic Greek cities and local peoples has been based on finds of Greek pottery in local settlements up to 500 km inland from the Black Sea. Examples are discovered at about one local site in ten of those known and excavated, but they are usually few in number (as is the case in both the Thracian and Colchian hinterlands). Trade is an important but complex matter, and its scale and *modus operandi* are so far unknown. It is no longer possible to hold to a simple explanation – that of a close trading relationship between Greeks and locals. To rely on pottery to prove these links when there are other explanations for the presence of pottery in local settlements is methodologically dubious. And such are the quantities that they give no encouragement to the view that the greater they are, the more intensive and closer the links. The Athenian painted pottery found in many tombs of the local elite could just as easily have been a gift from the Greeks as a traded commodity. We do not know what interpretation the locals placed on the scenes depicted; we do know that these tombs contained jewelry and metal vessels, and that the local elite was much keener on such objects (Tsetskhladze 1998b: 51–66).

Deep in the hinterland were several settlements, usually very large, which served as political and economic centers for the local ethnic groups and may well have been distribution centers for goods. Study has shown that they had Greek inhabitants as well (see below), and great quantities of Greek pottery have been found: the 10,000 pieces at Belsk in Scythia, not far from Poltava on the Ukrainian steppes, are just one example (see below).

It is not surprising that everyone investigating trade between the Black Sea and the Mediterranean focuses on the particular commodities exchanged, especially grain and metals sent from the Black Sea (Tsetskhladze 1998d). Usually, the information given in written sources describing later periods is unthinkingly transposed to the earlier period, and opinions formulated several decades ago have become the new orthodoxy despite a lack of hard evidence to underpin them (Davies 1998: 228–9). As mentioned, there is no evidence to suggest the export of grain from the Black Sea to the Mediterranean, particularly Athens, until the late fifth century or the beginning of the fourth, and even then it is not a regular occurrence.[15] While Herodotus (7.147) does say that Xerxes saw ships conveying corn from the Black Sea passing through the Hellespont en route to Aegina and the Peloponnese, one should agree with T. G. Figueira (1981: 43–6) that Aegina, mentioned directly in this passage, was the destination of the grain ships, not Athens as many would like it to be: Aegina frequently required grain in large amounts to feed its population (Hahn 1983: 34).

Indeed, Athens was usually able to feed its own population, and only needed to import grain in an emergency (Whitby 1998a). Like Athens, the Black Sea colonies kept a reserve fund to purchase grain in times of famine.[16] The Black Sea colonies acquired metals from the local peoples of the hinterland; they had no such resources of their own. Although local societies were keen on luxurious metal objects (the Scythians and Colchians on gold jewelry and decorations produced by Greek craftsmen but styled to the tastes of local elites), we still lack evidence to show where the metal originated. If one were to impose later realities on earlier uncertainties, one might follow Polybius, writing in the second century:

as regards necessities, it is an undisputed fact that the most plentiful supplies and best qualities of cattle and slaves reached us from the countries lying around the Pontus, while among luxuries, the same countries furnish us with an abundance of honey, wax and preserved fish; from the surplus of our countries they take olive-oil and every kind of wine. As for grain, there is give and take – with them sometimes supplying us when we require it and sometimes importing it from us.

(4.38.4–6; tr. Loeb)

Greeks among Local Communities

New excavation, and re-evaluation of material already known, allows us not only to re-examine Greek pottery found in local contexts and supposedly predating the foundation of the Pontic colonies but also to suggest that Greeks visited and lived in local settlements of the deep hinterland from early times.

A few dozen pieces of East Greek pottery discovered in Scythian settlements and tumuli situated some 500 km from the Black Sea coast have been known for a long time. They were interpreted as evidence of some form of pre-colonial contact because it was thought that they predated the establishment of the first Greek colonies. Applying the most up-to-date chronology of East Greek pottery, in conjunction with other evidence, allows us to challenge this orthodoxy (Tsetskhladze 1998b: 10–15). Might it be that Greeks did not just establish settlements on the coast but penetrated the hinterland inhabited by local peoples? From what we know at present, this interpretation seems more than possible (Tsetskhladze 2003: 149–59). Let us look at the northern Black Sea littoral.

In the Scythian Trekhtemirovskoe settlement, the earliest Ionian pottery was found on the altar in a dugout construction (Rusyaeva 1999: 94–5). It seems very difficult to understand why Scythians were offering Greek pottery to their deities. Could this not indicate instead that Greeks lived in this settlement? So far, we can say no more than that it is highly likely. Turning to another settlement, one near the village of Zhabotin in the Ukrainian hinterland (Rusyaeva 1999: 96), a "large quantity" of East Greek pottery was found on the altar of a shrine. Not much is said about the altar itself, but it seems to have been large and rectangular, with a baked clay floor containing the remains of a wooden pillar. The altar contained ornaments which, according to the publisher, have parallels in Ionian art. It is again probable that this shrine belonged to a seventh-century Greek inhabitant of this settlement. The possibility that Wild Goat Style pottery was produced in the Nemirovskoe settlement has already been proposed in the literature (Tsetskhladze 2003: 134).

As mentioned above, some 10,000 pieces of Greek pottery were discovered in the Belsk settlement, believed to be the city of Gelonus, inhabited by the Budini and the Geloni (Shramko 1987: 121–6, 174–9). What kind of settlement was Gelonus/Belsk? Let us turn to Herodotus, who tells us that:

The Budini are a great and numerous nation; the eyes of all of them are very bright, and they are ruddy. They have a city built of wood, called Gelonus. The wall of it is thirty furlongs in length on each side of the city; this wall is high and all of wood; and their houses are wooden, and their temples; for there are among them temples of Greek gods, furnished in Greek fashion with images and altars and shrines of wood; and they honor Dionysus every two years with festivals and revels. For the Geloni are by their origin Greeks, who left their trading ports to settle among the Budini; and they speak a language half Greek and half Scythian. But the Budini speak not the same language as the Geloni, nor is their manner of life the same.

(4.108; tr. Loeb)

The site's excavator believes that he has found a small sanctuary of the sixth-fourth centuries built with wooden columns. Inside it is an altar; not far away a pit containing cult offerings (Shramko 1987: 127–40). There is some discussion of whether Herodotus' Gelonus is Belsk, but if it is, it had Greek-type sanctuaries and a Greek population from the archaic period.

A further settlement worth mentioning is Vasil Levsky, not far from Vetren in the Thracian hinterland, where remains of monumental stone buildings and painted Corinthian-type roof tiles have been found (Kisov 2004: 48–68). This settlement, established in the late archaic period, did not survive beyond the early fourth century. Unfortunately, it has not been well studied archaeologically (Archibald 1998: 141; Bouzek 2000–1).

Thus, we can suppose that the first colonists did indeed visit the settlements of the local population, which were also political centers, and that some of them lived there. This is not surprising. The Greeks had arrived in an already populated region and were dependent on the goodwill of the existing inhabitants and their leaders. As we saw, Strabo states explicitly that land for colonies was, in many cases, given directly by local chieftains in return for a moderate tribute. Collaboration between Greeks and local rulers deepened in the classical period, when the Greeks were obliged not just to pay tribute to the locals but to manufacture luxurious metal objects for the local nobility among the Scythians, Colchians, and Thracians, and to design and construct their residences, even their tombs.

NOTES

1　*Il.* 6.130; 9.5; 14.227; 21.390; 10.434–5; 10.558–9; 11.222; etc.; *Od.* 8.361.
2　Sulimirski and Taylor 1991; Alekseev 2003.
3　Xen. *Anab.* 5.5.1 (Chalybes); 4.8.20 (Colchians); 5.2.2; 5.3.3 (Drilae); 5.4.26 (Mossynoeci).
4　Xen. *Anab.* 5.5.34. Houses: Diodorus 14.30.6.
5　Hdt. 2.104; 3.94; Xen. *Anab.* 4.8.9; Strabo 12.3.18, 28.
6　75: Seneca *Helv.* 7.2; 90: Pliny *HN* 5.112. Most of these settlements were either secondary colonies or later foundations. The initial colonies established in the archaic period numbered about 25.
7　Dandamaev 1989: 153–4; Briant 2002a: 35–8.
8　Arrian *Byth.* fr. 56 Roos; Tsetskhladze 1994; 2002a; 2003.
9　Hind 1999; Avram, Hind and Tsetskhladze 2004: 924–5.
10　Tolstikov 2002; Treister 2002; Kuznetsov 2002; Tsetskhladze 2002b; Avram, Hind and Tsetskhladze 2004.

11 Tsetskhladze 1998c: 7–37; Avram, Hind and Tsetskhladze 2004: 952–3.
12 Hermonassa: Eustathius *GGM* II 324; Phanagoria: Arrian *Byth.* fr. 71 Roos; Phasis: Pompon. 1.108.
13 Nazarov 2001; Kryzhitskii 2001.
14 Tsetskhladze 1998b: 51–4; Cook and Dupont 1998: 142–91.
15 Tsetskhladze 1998d; Burstein 1999.
16 Stroud 1998: 109–20; Anghel 1999/2000: 107–12.

PART IV

Themes

CHAPTER EIGHTEEN

Cities[1]

Jan Paul Crielaard

Introduction: The Importance of Context

The rise of cities and city-states provides the key to our understanding of what was going on in the archaic period. The development of the phalanx, the creation of temples and sanctuaries, the birth of philosophy and the flourishing of lyric poetry are all unthinkable outside the context of the *polis* and outside an urban setting. Not surprisingly, the rise of the city-state has long been central to the study of the period. More recently, however, it has been recognized that it is possible, and perhaps even necessary, to distinguish between the process of urbanization – which created "cities" – and the process of state formation, which created "states."[2] This chapter accordingly concentrates on cities and urbanization; the process of state formation is dealt with in ch. 20.

Over the last decades, archaeologists and ancient historians have also come to recognize that the rise of the city (and, indeed, of the state) was a long-drawn-out process: it took most of the archaic period and had not reached completion even by the end of the sixth century. The appearance of monumental architecture in the late eighth century marks an important step in the creation of an urban ambience in centralized settlement nuclei, but on the whole ancient Greek urbanism can only be understood by using a rather long timescale.[3]

The "city" is notoriously difficult to define. Historians, sociologists, economists, architectural historians, social psychologists, town planners and geographers all use very different concepts and definitions.[4] Their criteria variously stress the city's distinct legal status, size, occupation density, morphology, way of living, type of society, or mentality. There are numerous exceptions to the rule even at the level of single definitions. Size may seem to be an unproblematic criterion, but it is not. For instance, a nucleation of 250 inhabitants would count as a village in the United States, but in Sweden would have the status of a town. Occupation density is not always a distinctive criterion: there are fewer people per square kilometre in the city of Los Angeles than in some rural areas in Asia. As far as ways of living and economic activities are concerned, towns in north-west Europe during the Middle Ages may be rightly characterized as centers of craft production and trade. However, this does not apply to modern cities in Sicily and Andalusia, which are large agro-towns. Finally, impersonal relationships may determine the type of society and mentality that prevails in cities of the modern, industrialized world, but such a qualification hardly matches what we know of medieval towns.

Yet another problem is that sometimes settlements gradually expand and their sociopolitical organization and social interactions become more complex. This raises the question at what point exactly such a settlement stops being a village and starts to meet the criteria that make it a city. It is, of course, impossible to fix this point in time.

Thus, cities are multifaceted, variable and dynamic phenomena to which universalizing criteria and simplifying definitions can do no justice. The city must be understood in its specific temporal and spatial context. This observation has implications for the study of archaic Greece. If the city is a culturally specific phenomenon, we should study the city on the basis of contemporary sources of information. We must ask our sources three important questions: What were archaic Greek cities like? How did the Greeks themselves see them? And how did these cities come into being and develop?

The limitations of the source material determine how one tackles these questions. Political treatises on the institutions of some major Greek cities, and philosophical essays about what the ideal city should look like, are available only from the classical period. There is only very fragmentary written documentation for the archaic era, but by piecing together scraps of evidence it is possible to reconstruct how archaic Greeks saw the city. One of the positive qualities of the main literary sources of this period – Homer, Hesiod and the lyric poets – is that they are part of a tradition of oral poetry: because such poetry was performed for a live audience, the ideas and values expressed are likely to have been shared by a large group of people, and are thus very valuable sources for a reconstruction of mentalities. It will become evident that the source material allows the reconstruction of a coherent picture of the ideational and ideological side of city and city life, and of life in the countryside.[5]

Visual imagery is another important source of information for the archaic period. However, the information provided by the iconographic evidence is patchy. The archaic Greeks seem not to have been interested in producing images of cities and landscapes, in contrast to their Minoan and Mycenaean forebears, their contemporaries in the Near East and later the Romans. Archaic Greek depictions of nature or of man's built environment often follow the principle of *pars pro toto*. An isolated column may indicate the presence of public architecture, just as a single olive tree may show that a scene takes place in the countryside.[6] Moreover, the images are especially concerned with the high life of the urban elite.[7] For a more comprehensive and more diversified picture of towns and countryside, one has to depend on reconstructions made on the basis of archaeological findings.

Terminology

In archaic Greek literature, the words most often used for town or city are *astu* and, especially, *polis* (or sometimes *ptolis*). These words have their roots in Mycenaean

Greek, although in Linear B documents only *wa-tu / wastu* occurs as *terminus tech-nicus* for "city" and "inhabitants of a city" (Deger-Jalkotzy 1995: esp. 367–9). In the poetry of Homer and Hesiod, "*polis*" evokes an image of the city as a whole, often in conjunction with its city wall; it refers to the city as seen from the exterior. It is mostly a topographical term, although it is also used in a political sense, referring to both city and countryside, or even to a "political entity" or "state" – no matter how weakly developed the "state" is in Homer and Hesiod. *Astu*, on the other hand, is the city viewed from within; the focus is on its inhabitants. In the epics, *politai* refers to all the free inhabitants of a *polis* (mostly in its narrow meaning of "city"), including women and children.[8] The term *astos* for "townsman" or "citizen" is also known from Homer onwards, but in later sources it can have a negative connota-tion in the sense of "commoner."[9]

The term *dêmos* designates a well-defined territory and all the free people who inhabit it. It is found in Linear B documents as *damos*, meaning "village." *Kômê* is used in Hesiod's *Works and Days* (639) and in the *Shield of Heracles* (18) to denote a village or hamlet. Remarkably enough, there is no specific term for "village" in the Homeric epics (Donlan 1970; 1985: 288–9), but this may be part of a more general disinterest in villages that is also attested in later sources (*Inventory* 75).

Images of City and Country

Figure 18.1 represents a bird's eye view of the city of Smyrna in about 600. The picture is based on one of the very few instances of a fairly completely excavated archaic town. The drawing is by R. V. Nicholls and was first published in the late 1950s (Cook 1958/9: 15, fig. 3). Since then it has been reproduced in many text-books on the archaic period, and has become part of the collective memory. The drawing shows an agglomeration of houses surrounded by mighty fortification walls with gates and towers. The town is small and compact: one can see the roofs of some 160 buildings (representing an even smaller number of domestic units[10]), tightly packed together but built along a regular laid-out street grid. Public buildings, situ-ated around a small, open area, are also visible. The town is set on a headland and surrounded on three sides by the sea. Ships are moored to moles or have been hauled up onto the beach. Habitation continues outside the circuit wall, but in a much more dispersed form.

This is probably the image most archaeologists and ancient historians have of an archaic Greek city. Archaic Greeks may not have had a very different image them-selves, since Nicholls included a number of elements in his reconstruction that seem to have been inspired by Homer's *Odyssey*,[11] which takes one to Scheria, home of the legendary Phaeacians.

> But when we come to the city, and around this is a towering
> wall, and a handsome harbour either side of the city,
> and a narrow causeway, and along the road there are oarswept
> ships drawn up, for they all have slips, one for each vessel;

Figure 18.1 Smyrna: imaginative reconstruction of the town in about 600 BC
Source: Cook (1958–9: 15, fig. 3).

> and there is the place of the assembly (*agorê*), put together with quarried
> stone, and built around a fine precinct of Poseidon,
> and there they tend to all that gear that goes with the black ships.
>
> (6.262–8)

The city wall, the precinct of Poseidon and the *agorê* are the most conspicuous elements of the city's public space. The *agorê* is the place where the community's leaders and men of counsel assemble (*Od.* 8.5ff), and where, later, all the Phaeacians gather to watch the dancing and athletic contests (109ff). In the poet's description of the shield that Hephaestus makes for Achilles, another imaginary city is portrayed and here, too, the *agorê* occupies a most prominent place. In this scene, people have assembled to attend a court session conducted by the elders of the community.[12] Although Scheria is a fictional town, it is not pure fantasy: there are many correspondences between the view of Scheria and the manner in which other Homeric towns are described.[13] Rather, Scheria represents an ideal world: it gives an impression of what the poet and his audience thought a city *should* look like.

Both Homer and Hesiod say that the city cannot prosper without the countryside, and that when the country suffers, the city suffers (*Od.* 19.111–14;

W&D 227–47). The reason for this is, of course, that a large majority of the town-dwellers earned their livelihood from agricultural activities. In the *Iliad* and *Odyssey*, people leave the town each morning to work their fields, which extend right up to the city walls, and at the end of the day they go back to town (e.g. *Il.* 18.541–7; *Od.* 6.259–60). Members of the urban elite make regular trips to the countryside to inspect their fields (*agroi*) and estates, which are worked by slaves. Still further away from the town are pens where herdsmen tend cattle, sheep, and pigs.[14]

Despite this symbiosis of town and country (*polin kai gaian*: *Od.* 6.177–8), the poet makes it clear that there is a spatial and conceptual distinction between city and countryside. *Agros/agroi* and *p(t)olis* very often occur as an antithetic pair.[15] This distinction also relates to the people associated with either locality. In one of the few passages showing that it is taken for granted that not all community members live in the city, Alcinous distinguishes between "people living in the *astu* and those living around it" (*hoi perinaietaousin*: *Od.* 8.551).

The City as Concept

The literary sources for our period feature three closely connected major themes in Greek perceptions of the city: the city as center of order and civilization, the city as a sacred place, and the city as a community of men. These themes will be discussed in the following sections.

The city as center of order and civilization

A good starting point to investigate ideas and concepts concerning the city are charter myths about the origins of cities. The foundation stories of Scheria and Troy, mythical or legendary cities, can be expected to reflect ideas and experiences common among the poet's audience.

Scheria is a newly founded city. Alcinous' father, Nausithous, led a migration of the Phaeacians to the new territory, "and drove a wall about the city, and built the houses, and made the temples of the gods, and divided the arable land" (*Od.* 6.9–10). Nausithous' tasks are very similar to those traditionally performed by the founders of new settlements in the archaic period. The emphasis in this passage is on the fact that the Phaeacians' new home was planned and executed according to certain ordering principles. These include provisions for protection, division between religious, civic and private space, organization of subsistence, and division of property, which most probably means a regular – or at least orderly – layout of town and country. This order and degree of organization is also one of the things that Odysseus seems to admire most when he enters the city (see above: 6.262–8). In this respect, Scheria is again a model town.

The degree of organization prevailing at Scheria becomes even more evident when the Phaeacians' habitat is compared to the land of the Cyclopes, their former neighbors:

> These people have no counselling or law-establishing assemblies,
> rather they make their habitation in caverns hollowed
> among the peaks of the high mountains, and each one is the law
> for his own wives and children, and cares nothing about the others.
>
> (*Od.* 9.112–15)

These cavemen "neither plough with their hands nor plant anything" (108), but live the life of hunter-gatherers and pastoralists. They have no ships or shipwrights to make them "strong-benched vessels" to visit "all the various cities of men," as other people do (126–9). The Cyclopes are "lawless" (106); they are indifferent to the will of the gods and disrespectful to strangers and suppliants protected by Zeus Xenios (268–78).

We find here a set of oppositions which relate especially to the living conditions of the Phaeacians and the Cyclopes: houses v. caves, coastal settlement v. mountain dwellings, community v. isolated families, agriculture v. pasturage and food gathering, and political institutions v. lawlessness. From this set of oppositions one can distil a package of positive qualities that may be designated as civilized values and civilizing activities. The most salient are community life, hospitable behavior and communications with other city communities. Civilization and civilized life are associated specifically with an urban community and urban infrastructure (*agorē*, nucleated settlement delineated by a circuit wall, harbor). Already for Homer and his audience, city life is the norm for civilized communities.[16]

A number of these elements are also found in the story of the founding of Troy. The inhabitants of the Troad (the region surrounding Troy) originally lived in the wilderness, scattered over the slopes of Mount Ida (*Il.* 20.218), just as the barbarous Cyclopes live in dispersed mountain dwellings. The Trojans-to-be became settled when they built a city on the plain (217). The founding of a city thus embodies the transition from wild nature to culture. This transition is materialized by the building of a community and the creation of an urban environment by means of a specific set of architectural elements. Foremost among these are city walls, which not only serve defensive purposes, they also have an important symbolic dimension: they separate the *polis* from nature's randomness, create order and identify space that is exclusively human. It is not without reason that the building of Troy's walls is said to have "citied" Troy (*polissamen*: *Il.* 7.453), and that "driving a wall about the city" is mentioned as the first of Nausithous' actions (Scully 1990: 24–5). Also, a defensive wall can spread fame (*kleos*, *Il*.7.451ff).

Many of the walls' symbolic properties extend to the city as a whole. This is especially clear from the set of epithets frequently used for cities, which qualify the *polis* as "well-built," "well-founded" or "well-walled" (*euktimenos, eudmētos, euteikheos*) or, indeed, *euruaguia* ("with wide streets"), *hupsipulos* ("with lofty gates") and *eu naiomenos* ("well-inhabited"; Scully 1990: 49, 78, 131–3). These epithets emphasize the city's technical or technological aspects as an important characteristic of the urban landscape. More importantly, they show that urban architecture was closely associated with a civilized mode of life and, more particularly, with good order (cf. Ehrenberg 1960: 27, 84–5, 140–1).

The sacred city

Homer, Hesiod, Alcaeus, Theognis and Pindar were all familiar with the idea that the city was sacred.[17] In the epics, cities are often called *hieros*, *ēgatheos*, *zatheos* or *dios*. In fact, of all city and place epithets in Homer, the most common are those referring to "sacredness," not only of cities but also of their constituent parts – walls, temples, sanctuaries and the *agora*.[18] It is not self-evident why the *polis* is sacred. Although it contains sanctuaries which are the abodes of gods and goddesses – as well as an *agora* which is sacred since it houses the collective force around which civic life is organized – it also has secular inhabitants: it is "a city of mortal men" (e.g. *Il.* 4.45; 20.217). Moreover, the city consists of an aggregate of *oikoi* which individually are never called sacred.

It may be that the city is holy because its inhabitants are pious people who make sacrifices to the gods, and in return receive divine protection and other favors.[19] However, the city is sacred primarily because its founding and construction are considered sacred acts inspired or guided by divine powers. Gods sometimes even literally take part in the founding of cities. Troy, for example, is said to have been established through the agency of Zeus, while its walls were built by Poseidon. Many historical cities also claimed divine support for their foundation,[20] and in many foundation stories of archaic colonies Apollo played a guiding and civilizing role (Dougherty 1993). The city is also holy because it encompasses order and civilization, as noted, and houses a human community, including "women and (innocent) children,"[21] and thus shelters human life itself. In sum, the city is thought to protect human life and to create and preserve order, tasks which belong to the domain of the gods.

What is important in this connection is that the city is walled. The city wall makes the *polis arrēktos*, "unbreakable" (e.g. *Il.* 21.446–7). In other words, the fortification walls give permanence to the order created and provide human culture with long-term protection. These functional and symbolic properties help to explain what is meant when a city like Troy is called "well-walled" (*euteicheos*) and the walls are "sacred" (*hieros*, *theios*, *theodmētos*). It is this aspect of stability and well-founded order that further enhances the city's sanctity.

Zeus creates and protects cities, but is also instrumental in their devastation.[22] This is why the Greek heroes before Troy pray especially to Zeus to grant them the destruction of that city. Achilles' prayer to Zeus – "May we undo Troy's holy veil" – suggests a desire to violate the city, to desecrate the walls which symbolize the hallowed bonds of civilization.[23] It is important to stress that to defeat or kill the enemy was one thing, but to seize or destroy a city was something of an entirely different magnitude (see e.g. Callinus F 5a, 4; cf. Archil. F 20 West; Hdt. 6.21.1). If the "sacred" and "unbreakable" city is thought to guarantee order, stability and continuity, it follows quite naturally that its destruction stands for something that goes against the natural order of things. Hesiod is very clear about this: for him the sacking of cities is associated with times of anarchy and reversal of the existing order (*W&D* 189).

The destruction of a city is thought not to happen without reason. A frequently given explanation is that a town was destroyed as a punishment for committing *hybris*

(*Il.* 16.384–92; 21.522–4). This applies not only to a mythical city like Troy but also to such historical towns as Magnesia, Smyrna, and Colophon, which were devastated during the archaic period. Troy had violated the laws regarding the sacrosanct institution of *xeinia* (*Il.* 6.55–60; 13.621–7; 24.27–30). The historical towns of Asia Minor were thought to have provoked their destruction by violent behavior, an excessively luxurious lifestyle or the persistence of *stasis*, which had disrupted the existing order.[24] The logic behind this way of thinking is that, when internal, "god-given" order is destroyed, the physical devastation of a city becomes virtually unavoidable. A city that loses its divinely inspired order also loses its right to exist.

Men, not stones, make a city

Homer and other authors of the archaic period may use the term *polis* to refer to the city, to the community of the city's inhabitants or to the city's territory – just as *dēmos* sometimes refers to territory and sometimes to the people occupying a territory (Sakellariou 1989: 155ff, 185ff, 205). These overlapping meanings indicate that city, territory and inhabitants are thought to constitute an inseparable unity. A closely related idea is that "men make a *polis*," a notion frequently expressed in our sources, especially by means of metaphors comparing people to fortifications. Thus Odysseus, after slaughtering his rivals, exclaims: "we have killed the city's *herma*" – the "stay," "support," or "defence" of the city – that is, its "finest young men" (*Od.* 23.121–2; cf. *Il.* 16.550), who no doubt constitute the elite of Ithaca.

The idea that men make a *polis* relates especially to those men who are able and willing to defend themselves and their community. A fragment of Alcaeus of Mytilene (ca. 600) says "for men are the warlike tower of a city" (*polios purgos areuios*: F 112.10 Voigt). Another version is given by the orator Aelius Aristides, who paraphrases "the words which the poet Alcaeus spoke long ago and which all surely have since borrowed from him, that cities are not stones or timbers or the craft of builders, but wherever there are men who know how to defend themselves *there* are walls and a city (*polis*)."[25]

Alcaeus was certainly not the first to use this metaphor. In Homer, Achaeans and Trojans are collectively and individually compared to a "tower" (*purgos*) or "bulwark" (*herkos*: Scully 1990: 58–9). Callinus of Ephesus (ca. 675–650) reminds his audience that people honor the stout-hearted man who dies defending "country, children, wedded wife": "alive, he equals the demigods, for in the people's eyes he is a tower of strength, his single efforts worth a company's" (F 1 West; cf. Tyrtaeus F 12 West). Theognis, finally, tells us that "a man of worth is the witless people's citadel and rampart."[26]

These passages provide a consistent picture of the city as a collective of inhabitants, and more specifically express the idea that, if the community forms the city, the elite constitutes the foundation of the *polis*, while those who fight on the front lines are its most prominent defensive works. The metaphorical language employed confirms once again that the city wall was considered one of the most notable features of the city. It also underscores how strongly the idea of the city and the community was interwoven with war and violence.

City and Self-image: Self-definition by Opposition

The archaic Greek city not only defined itself in opposition to fictional savage creatures like the Cyclopes, but also exploited oppositions with the countryside. Country-
people expressed antithetic feelings of a similar kind. This is something of a surprise
in view of the earlier conclusion that city and countryside were conceptually one.

View from the city

The local elites of archaic Greece were both based in and strongly oriented towards
the city. The lifestyle of city-based local elites, especially in towns on the east side
of the Aegean, is illuminated by lyric poetry, which places much emphasis on personal adornment, clothing, and the consumption of food and drink. This urban lifestyle was intended to accentuate contrasts not only with commoners but also with
country-people and country life.

The *agora* was in many respects the heart of the city. In the towns portrayed by
Homer, the people come to the *agora* to attend court sessions, games, and assemblies, but on other occasions it is the sole domain of the community's leaders and
men of counsel, as noted above. The special importance of the *agora* to members
of the elite is underlined by the poet-politician Alcaeus (F 130b.1–4 Voigt). From
his place of exile in an out-of-the-way corner of Lesbos, the poet or his persona
pities himself and complains that he longs "to hear assembly (*agora*) called and
council." By contrasting his present "rustic" living situation (*moiran agroïōtikan*) with
the town's quintessential activities, he makes it clear that the city is the political epi-
center – the natural habitat of aristocrats.

The *agora*, however, is not only a political arena but also a meeting place, where
people gather for everyday social intercourse. In Homeric Ithaca, the men congre-
gate every morning at the *agora* to talk and gossip, the most distinguished among
them carrying weapons and attended by dogs.[27] In the course of the archaic period
the *agora* appears to have become more and more the playground of the leisure class
in some cities, at least. Xenophanes of Colophon (ca 565–473) scolds his fellow-
citizens in the following terms:

> They would go to the *agorē* in full purple robes,
> a thousand of them at the very least,
> proud in the splendour of their finely coiffed hair
> and sleek with unguents of the choicest scent.
>
> (F 3.3–6 West)

The "thousand" to whom Xenophanes refers are probably members of a ruling
élite of fixed size, and are said to have learnt this "useless luxury from Lydia." The
Colophonian oligarchs were certainly not unique in this regard, as the tyrants of
Erythrae (possibly in the seventh century) and the nobles of Samos (perhaps in the
sixth century) are described as behaving in a similar way.[28] And then there was Alcman

(Sparta, ca. 600), drawn "along to the *agora*, where I'll be tossing my flaxen hair" (F 3.6–7). Elsewhere, dominant groups took rigorous measures to claim the *agora* for themselves: in Thessaly, craftsmen, farmers and other such persons were not permitted to enter the "free *agora*" (Arist., *Pol.* 1331a30).

Smaller groups of aristocrats met in private or public dining halls to feast together (see ch. 26, below). Anacreon (late sixth century) refers to "tables covered with good things of every sort" (F 435 Page). He aims to eat "for breakfast sweet sesame cake, and drink a whole flagon of wine, in luxury" (F 373 Page). This type of food is contrasted with the countryman's diet by his contemporary Hipponax: "I have to dig the rocky hillside, munching modestly on a few figs and barley cobs – slave's fodder – not champing hare and francolin, not I, not tarting up pancakes with sesame, or dripping waffles into honeycombs" (F 26–26a West). What Hipponax calls "slaves' fodder" must be the standard fare of the agricultural laborer. It corresponds to Hesiod's recommendation to give a plough-hand a day's ration comprising "a loaf of bread, of four quarters and eight slices, for dinner" (*W&D* 442).

Somewhere halfway between these two extremes of consumption were the *maza* (barley cakes made with goat's milk), veal and Bibline wine that Hesiod's farmer consumes during the dog-days of summer, when agricultural work comes to a temporary standstill.[29] As a place to celebrate this exceptional occasion, he – typically – prefers the rustic setting of a shady rock (589), far removed from the great dining halls where urbanites recline.

Clothing and other forms of personal adornment were also used to make explicit the distinction between city- and country-people. The "Lesbian maidens with trailing robes (*helkesipeploi*)" whom Alcaeus sees in his place of exile are surely city girls who have come to the countryside for an annual beauty contest (F 130b.18–9 Voigt). Trailing garments carry associations with the heroic past,[30] and also belong to the elegant attire of archaic city women, as is clear when Sappho asks: "who is this country colleen that enchants your mind . . . wearing a country garb . . . who hasn't learned to arrange her shift well down over her calves?" (F 57 Voigt). A country girl (*agroïōtis*) is distinguished not only by her country garb (*agroïōtin stolan*), but also by the fact that she is unable to wear her dress according to what is proper or fashionable – as determined by urbanites. Other poems make it clear that fashion is all about wearing the latest headbands, kerchiefs, aprons and slippers derived from such cities as Phocaea and, of course, Sardis – the city *par excellence*.[31]

A poem by Theognis of Megara (ca. 600) visualizes a reversal of the existing social order in terms of a change from country garb to city dress: "Cyrnus, the town's a town still, but it has new folk who knew no justice previously, no laws. They used to wear old goatskins on their flanks, and lived outside the town like deer" (53–6).[32] This situation is reminiscent of one encountered by Anacreon: "He used to wear a rough cloak, pinched in at the waist, and wooden baubles in his ears, and around his ribs a hairless cowhide, the unwashed covering of a cheap shield . . . And now he wears gold ear-rings, rides about in traps" (F 388). The wooden earrings that this upstart is wearing are "wooden knucklebones" (*astragaloi*). Rich tombs excavated in Smyrna and Lydia have yielded earrings in the shape of stylized knucklebones that fit Anacreon's description, except that they are made of gold plate.[33] *Astragaloi* made of wood must be regarded as down-market imitations, and they are in this poem surely meant to exemplify the sorry attempt of a rustic to follow city fashion.[34]

In lyric poetry the elite thus defined itself as decisively urban by creating oppositions with countrymen's dress and consumptive behavior. At the same time, the elite associated itself – at least in the East Greek cities – with Sardis, the city of cities. This scheme also operated on a wider geographical and social scale, to judge from Alcman: "He was no yokel, no fool even among experts; not of Thessalian stock, no shepherd from Erysiche, but from the center of Sardis" (F 16 West). Alcman puts the yokel (*anēr agreios*), the stupid man (*skaios*), the Thessalian and the shepherd into the same category, in order to draw a contrast with the man from the center of Sardis (*Sardiōn ap' akran*, literally: "of highest Sardis"). These lines reveal that the opposition between city and country operated even in a Panhellenic context. Thessaly and Acarnania (where Erysiche is located) are Greece's backwaters, the ultimate examples of "boorish" regions in which the *polis* is unknown. The other end of the spectrum is represented by Sardis, the finest of cities; its center is truly the center of civilization.

The antithesis between town and country is also – and even more strongly and explicitly – expressed in negative qualifications of country-people similar to those used in English ("boor," "rustic"), as when Sappho typifies the "country colleen" wearing "country garb" (*agroïōtis, agroïōtin stolan*) or Alcaeus uses the same term to describe his miserable, rustic state. Similar terminology and stereotypes can be found already in the *Odyssey*. When Eumaeus and Philoetius – two herdsmen loyal to Odysseus – start to weep at the sight of their lost master's bow, Antinous calls them "Stupid rustics [*agroiotai*], who can only think of today, wretched pair!" (21.85–6). These qualifications are more than expressions of a young nobleman's disdain of dull farmhands. Implicitly, urban sophistication is contrasted with the lack of restraint and the narrow-minded outlook thought of as countrified.[35]

Conversely, Eumaeus scolds Melantheus, Odysseus' unfaithful farm worker, for having acquired some affectations and mannerisms (*aglaia*) bred by life in the city and by his close association with the suitors (*Od.* 17.244–6). He expresses the rural point of view which equates the idle luxury of the suitors and their class with town life. This is contrasted with the hard work in the fields that is the norm for country-people, an attitude also encountered in Hesiod. The rustic is made into an outsider, since he is unaware of the social intricacies of a city code of behavior. What is more, both sides – noblemen/city-dwellers and base people/country folk – agree that it is better for rural folk to remain outside town, as they may suffer from the dangerous lack of customary restraint that accompanies town life.[36]

View from the countryside

For the archaic urban elite, and probably for city-dwellers in general, the city was what the countryside was not. Defining self in opposition to others is not a mechanism restricted to urbanites, however. "Othering" is something that country-people do, too. Hesiod's *Work and Days* is a rich source of information for reconstructing opposing views.

Hesiod's description of Ascra does not mention the *agora*, walls or armed forces at all, while ships, seafaring and external communications play only a marginal role in the life of Hesiod's farmer. A key passage is his advice to his brother Perses:

> O Perses, put these things in your spirit,
> and do not let the evil-rejoicing Strife hold your spirit back from work,
> while you closely watch and listen to the wrangles of the *agora*.
> Little concern has he with wranglings and agoras
> whose seasonal sustenance does not lie stored up
> in abundance indoors, what the earth bears, Demeter's grain.
>
> (*W&D* 27–32)

This passage illuminates one of the poem's central themes: a good farmer works his land and stores his provisions in the right order.[37] The point that is stressed here is that a farmer has things to do and cannot afford to waste his time in the city.[38]

The advice to stay away from the city and to stick to one's own kind also reverberates in Hesiod's recommendation to be respectful to one's neighbors, since they are the only people one can rely on (343–51), even though there is competition within the village for wealth (23). Neighbors are also recommended as appropriate marriage partners (700–1) and table companions (343) to create a social network. The focus on endogamy within the *kōmē* community is in marked contrast with, for instance, Sappho's girls, who are married off to Sardis (F 96 Voigt). As for the question whom to invite for dinner, an elitist like Theognis urges his audience to be much more selective when choosing table companions (31–7; 113–4), and Solon does not think of his next-door neighbors when he states that it is a guest-friend in foreign lands that gives the greatest pleasure (F 23 West).[39]

Thus, the oppositions that helped to shape the countryman's conception of self were village v. city; territory (*dēmos*, 261) v. center (represented by its rulers, the *basilēes*)[40]; hard-working farmers v. members of the leisure class; and neighborliness v. "wrangles of the *agorē*." In a more indirect way, there is also the opposition between marrying and mingling with village members v. establishing marriage and *xeinia* links with one's equals in other *poleis*. Finally, there is also a contrast in the pace of life. Whereas the rustic life of the Hesiodic farmer is determined by the endless cycle of the seasons, Sappho and her like live the fast life of urbanites, determined by the latest trends and fashions of cosmopolitan culture.

The common element in most of these oppositions is the contrast between the socially inferior villagers and the superior elite of *basilēes*.[41] It is relevant to this discussion of town–country relationships that the *basilēes* of Thespiae had jurisdiction over conflicts in Ascra brought before them. For the rest, *Works and Days* does not suggest that the *basilēes* exercised much economic or political control over the village.[42] The impression the poem gives is that *polis* and *kōmē* were very loosely integrated in almost every respect. Thespiae must have been larger, wealthier and more powerful than Ascra, while the latter was a less complex, less hierarchized and less centralized community. Its ideal was self-sufficiency and independence at the level of both the *oikos* and the *kōmē*. There was a sense of community, although it hardly transcended incidental cooperation between neighbors.

The world of the Hesiodic farmer was circumscribed by the boundary of his village. This also determined his view of the city and his perception of self: city and country are worlds apart, and Hesiod's explicit advice is to preserve the situation as it is. This is highly revealing of the state of urbanization in archaic Greece. By means of a range of oppositions, city-dwellers made country-people into outsiders, but remarkably enough this situation was reinforced by villagers who shaped their identity by distancing themselves from the city.

The Growth of Urban Centers

This final section deals mainly with archaeological data. I will distinguish some dominant trends in the process that led to the creation of an urban environment and a spatially defined urban culture, and briefly discuss changes occurring in the occupation of the countryside during the Early Iron Age and the archaic period.[43]

Settlement patterns, settlement size, and settlement layout

Regional surveys show that after the fall of the Mycenaean palaces most regions in Greece witnessed a sharp reduction in the number of occupied sites. Only in the Euboean Gulf area and in Crete was the decline in the level of occupation much less dramatic (Crielaard 2006, with further references). Early Iron Age settlements were generally small, although it has been suggested that major sites like Athens, Knossos and Argos occupied roughly 200, 100, and 50 hectares, respectively, and housed several hundreds or even thousands of people. It should be added, however, that these sites consisted of hamlets or small clusters of houses separated by open areas (Morris 1991: 29). This settlement pattern of individual habitation nuclei continued to exist into the archaic period and beyond (e.g. at Corinth, Argos, Megara, Eretria, Miletus, and Ephesus).[44] As Thucydides tells us, the Spartans of the late fifth century were still living in scattered villages (1.10.2).

From the eighth century onwards, both the number and the size of settlements increased markedly. It is estimated that during the later archaic period the free population of larger poleis such as Metapontum, Aegina, Samos, Miletus, and Athens numbered somewhere between 40,000 and 60,000; the majority of these people will have lived in the city.[45] The increase in size was interrelated with developments in house type. The change from single-room huts to multiple-room house complexes (see below) led not only to a growth in the size of individual houses, but also to an increase in the total settlement area. At the same time, the rectangular house plan that became more popular in the seventh century made more economical use of space and allowed a more densely organized settlement. At Smyrna, for instance, an earthquake in around 700 was taken as an opportunity to reconstruct the town according to a more tightly knit, rectilinear plan.[46] What is also interesting is that during the later eighth and early seventh centuries, granaries or olive and wine presses were still found within the settlement area (e.g. at Lefkandi, Mende, Smyrna: Mazarakis Ainian 1997: 119–22), but these agricultural installations seem to disappear thereafter. With a more densely organized settlement, the agrarian elements were expelled from the urban area, creating an even stronger differentiation between town and countryside.

Some settlements grew rapidly thanks to synoecism. Habitation nuclei were formally united by the construction of an *enceinte*, or the open spaces between them just gradually filled up. In other cases, settlements that were inhabited during the Early Iron Age were abandoned to create a new *polis* center (e.g. on Andros, Paros, and Chios during the seventh century).

Greek colonies in the west were among the first to implement a rationalized layout of the settlement space. Megara Hyblaea in Sicily in the seventh century contained an orthogonal street grid with rectangular residential plots and a division between cultic and civic space demarcated by an *agora* and plots on which shrines and stoai were built.[47] It is even possible that the regular town-plans of Megara and of its fellow Sicilian colonies Syracuse and Naxos were designed when these colonies were founded in the 730s and 720s.[48] In the Greek motherland, one of the first orthogonally planned settlements appears in the early sixth century (Boyd and Jameson 1981).

Until the late archaic period, craft and industry were carried out in domestic or cultic contexts.[49] Sometimes part of the settlement was dedicated to specialized craft activities, including the production of metals (e.g. Thorikos, Sardis) or pottery (Miletus, Corinth, Athens), and there is evidence of specialized sites for metalworking at Pithekoussai and Skala Oropou, and olive oil extraction at Clazomenae (figure 18.2; next door to a blacksmith's workshop).[50] Still, these hardly amount to specialized industrial quarters. Craft production remained small-scale, probably as a part-time household operation (Morris 1991: 38–9).

Houses

During the Early Iron Age, two main house types can be discerned. The most widespread were houses of rectilinear plan, consisting either of one room or – especially in Crete and the Cyclades – of multiple room units (figure 18.3). The other main house type consisted of freestanding, hut-like houses, oval or apsidal in shape, and generally comprising a single room. They were made of mud bricks or wattle-and-daub, and covered with a thatched roof. Elevated social status had an architectural element in the form of houses with larger dimensions and more complex internal divisions.

In the late eighth and early seventh centuries, there was a progressive replacement of curvilinear houses by buildings with a rectangular layout. These generally comprised two or more rooms and an integrated courtyard, sometimes with a porch built against one or more rooms – the hallmark of so-called *pastas* and *prostas* houses. The increase in size and complexity allowed for the segmentation and relative specialization of internal space for different functions, activities, individuals and genders (see figure 18.4a).[51] In the seventh century, houses became more uniform in size and design; links between architecture and differences in social status became less obvious. Terracotta roof tiles were introduced in ca. 700, but it is not certain when they were first used for covering domestic structures; one of the earliest known examples is a house at Sardis dating to the late seventh century.[52]

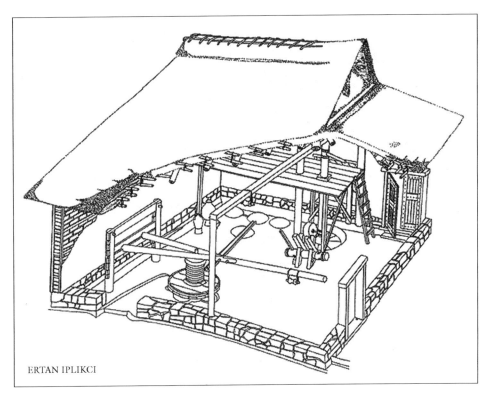

Figure 18.2 Clazomenae: olive oil extraction plant, 525–500 BC
Source: Koparal and Iplikçi (2004: fig. 13).

City walls

Around 1200, most Mycenaean citadels were destroyed. Many arts and crafts were lost, but not the art of fortification. Small fortified settlements of the LH IIIC period are attested in the Cyclades (Siphnos, Keos, Melos, Paros), Crete, western Anatolia (Bademgediği Tepesi) and the Peloponnese (e.g. Teichos Dymaion). As late as ca. 1100, Grotta on Naxos had a large urban center with defence works and harbor installations. Fortifications recently discovered on the islands of Salamis and Tenos were possibly in use from the LH IIIC to the Protogeometric or Geometric period.[53]

A new era of fortification started in the ninth and, especially, the eighth century. The first generation of defensive settlements were again found on the islands of the Aegean (Andros, Siphnos, Amorgos, Chios, Donousa, Crete) and in western Asia Minor (Smyrna, "Melie," Iasos). They were generally small sites, located in inhospitable places, and most were not long-lived. On the Greek mainland, fortified sites mostly date from the seventh century onwards. In central and northern Greece they begin only in the sixth century.[54]

Four types of fortified settlements can be distinguished in the archaic period: walled hilltops or acropoleis acting as places of refuge (e.g. Emporio on Chios, "Melie");

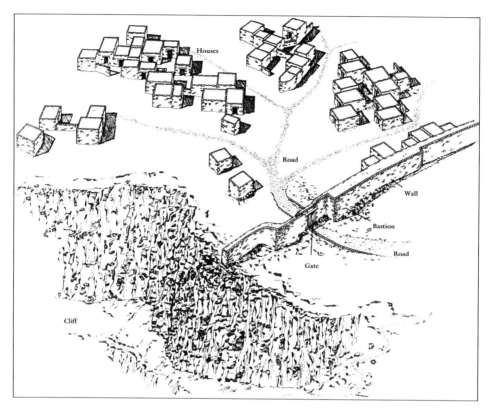

Figure 18.3 Zagora on Andros: hypothetical reconstruction of the settlement and its
fortification wall (later eighth century)
Source: Cambitoglou et al. (1991: 25, fig. 5).

settlements defended by a straight fortification wall across the neck of a promontory
or peninsula (e.g. Zagora on Andros [figure 18.3], Vroulia on Rhodes); separate
fortified enclaves within the settlement area (possibly at Miletus [figure 18.4a], Corinth
and Eretria); and the city *enceinte* enclosing most of the settled area (Smyrna,
Oikonomos on Paros, Pythagorion on Samos, Gortyn on Crete). The last-mentioned
type of fortification became increasingly dominant from the seventh century onwards.
It was also adopted by settlements that started out with a different defensive
system.

Fortification walls almost always consisted of a mudbrick superstructure built upon
a foundation of large stones. Sometimes rectangular towers or bastions were added
– often just one, usually flanking a gate (Zagora [figure 18.3], Oikonomos, Minoa
on Amorgos, "Melie"). For the rest, there is little standardization in design or construction techniques. Only in the course of the seventh century were important improvements made: large rectangular or polygonal stones were used to make tightly fitted
walls, while gates and towers became more strategically placed.

As we have seen, Smyrna is sometimes considered the archetypal archaic city. In many respects, however, Smyrna is exceptional – above all because of its defensive works. Its late ninth-century city wall is by far the earliest in the Greek world, and is also one of the first examples of an *enceinte* round a coastal site. Even more remarkable is that until its destruction in around 600 by the Lydian king Alyattes, this wall was rebuilt twice. In its final form of the later seventh century (see figure 18.1) it was no less than 10–18 m wide, which was without parallel in the Greek world and perhaps inspired by Lydian fortifications.[55] The rebuilding of walls on an ever-larger scale underlines that city walls offered not only protection but also prestige.

Another unusual aspect of Smyrna's fortifications is the location of a temple dedicated to Athena dating to the seventh century. The large platform on which it was built was situated close to the north-east gate and its tower, and was in fact part of the city *enceinte* (figure 18.1; Cook and Nicholls 1998: 128). Perhaps this was how Smyrna's inhabitants honored Athena as their patron goddess protecting their city and walls. At the same time, the association of temple and defensive wall brings to mind earlier observations about the sacred nature of the city and the city's walls.[56]

It is important to be aware that only a minority of settlements were walled. The slowness of the process is remarkable: it seems that many major cities, starting with Athens, did not possess a city *enceinte* by the end of the archaic period. Even in classical times, *poleis* like Elis and Sparta still did not have city walls, or indeed "costly temples" and other public edifices (Thuc. 1.10.2; *Inventory* 133–7). The lack of city walls may be connected with the preferred mode of warfare, which is the open hoplite battle (see ch. 30, below).

Temples, agorai, and public buildings

Archaeological evidence shows that during the Early Iron Age the house of the local ruler served certain cult purposes. Especially in the eighth century these chieftain's dwellings were replaced by or transformed into sacred buildings, presumably when the ruler lost control of the community's religious affairs. Particularly during the latter half of that century there was a tendency towards clearer separation and distinction of religious space. All over the Aegean shrines or temples were erected for patron deities protecting the *polis*; some of these represent the first examples of post-Late Bronze Age monumental architecture (e.g. the *hekatompeda* at Eretria and Samos; Mazarakis Ainian 1997).

In quite a number of Early Iron Age settlements, the house of the local ruler gave on to an open area that probably functioned as a "proto-*agora*," as an assembly place and perhaps also an open-air sanctuary for outdoor religious ceremonies (Mazarakis Ainian 1997: 378). The stepped area in the hollow between the two citadels of Dreros forms the earliest-known spatially defined *agora* in the Greek world (around 700). The first examples of a monumentalized *agora* occur during the later seventh century, for instance in the colony of Megara Hyblaea, where the *agora* was delineated by temples, public buildings and stoai (see above). At Metapontum, a monumental *agora* was created between ca. 600 and 530 with the construction of a series of temples, sanctuaries, altars and an amphitheater-like assembly building (capacity:

7,000–8,000 people), replacing an earlier wooden grandstand (*ikria*; Carter 2000). The *agora* at Athens, finally, is a little later in date, but more modest in design. In addition to temples, altars and a stoa, civic buildings and a fountain house were constructed (basically in the second half of the sixth century). Directly to the north of the *agora*, a series of shops was found. The *agora* was formally delimited by boundary (*horos*) stones.[57]

Occupation of the countryside

In comparison to the detailed archaeological information we have about the archaic city, the countryside is still largely *terra incognita*, although regional surface surveys do shed some light on it. Survey evidence suggests that by the seventh century a hierarchy of settlements had emerged. In addition to the dominant, first-order sites that exploited the land in the immediately adjacent settlement area, second-order sites existed at some distance into the countryside. These consisted of farming villages or hamlets rather than isolated farms.[58]

There were regional differences in the way that rural areas were inhabited during the archaic period.[59] In Boeotia and East Locris, alongside fortified first-order sites, there were smaller walled towns dispersed over the countryside (Snodgrass 1986a: 130). In the seventh century, the countryside around Miletus was exploited by means of "houses on the lands," possibly landed estates (Hdt. 1.17; cf. Lohmann 1997: 290–1). The *chora* of Teos, and presumably of other East Greek *poleis* as well, was during the late sixth and fifth centuries divided by *pyrgoi* and *teichē*. These were presumably towered manors and fortified villages that acted as centers of agricultural production and storage for the oligarchic families and their clients. It has been suggested that Teichioussa in the *chora* of Miletus is an example of this type of defensive estate (Balcer 1985: 25–7, 38). Whatever the case, Teichioussa (modern Akbük) gives us an idea of what a second-order site in the countryside looked like. It has yielded several complexes with rooms centered on a courtyard (figure 18.4b), as well as structures associated with a number of conspicuous tombs.[60] This kind of architecture has a decidedly urban feel to it. An interesting contrast is provided by a number of roughly built complexes comprising a large, walled area, bordered by oval or rectangular structures, which are found in the mountainous hinterland of the Milesian peninsula (figure 18.4c). Some of them may date to the archaic period. They can be identified as herding stations, and attributed to Carians (cf. Hdt. 6.20), who lived in similar compounds in the Halicarnassus peninsula.[61]

There is evidence that some *poleis* organized their *chora* in a rationalized manner, comparable to the layout of the town center. This happened, for instance, in Halieis in the early sixth century, and in Metapontum during the second half of that century. This process can best be followed in the Metapontine *chora*. Initially, the population lived dispersed in hamlets or the occasional isolated farmhouse, but after 550 farmsteads started to spread over the countryside; not much later the *chora* was divided into parallel strips by a system of country lanes. The orientation of these division lines is very similar to that of the town grid (figure 18.5), suggesting that *polis* and *chora* were restructured roughly at the same time.[62]

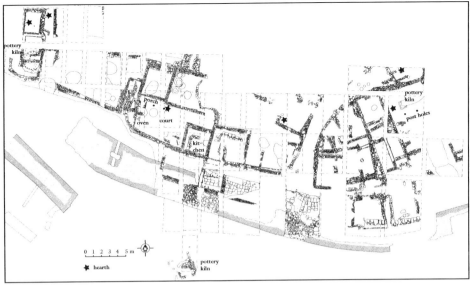

(a)

(b)

(c)

Figure 18.4 Miletus and Milesia, archaic structures: (a) Miletus-Kalabaktepe – fortification wall, overlap gate, and courtyard house (later sixth century) with pottery kilns of earlier phase (latter half of seventh century); (b) Teichioussa – courtyard house (sixth century); (c) Saplatansırt region – oval buildings around central courtyard, possibly shepherds compound (first half of sixth century)

Source: Senff (2000: 31, fig. 5), adapted by J. Fokkema. M. J. Mellink, *AJA* 93, 1989, 122, fig. 9. W. Voigtländer, *AA* (1988: 574, fig. 6).

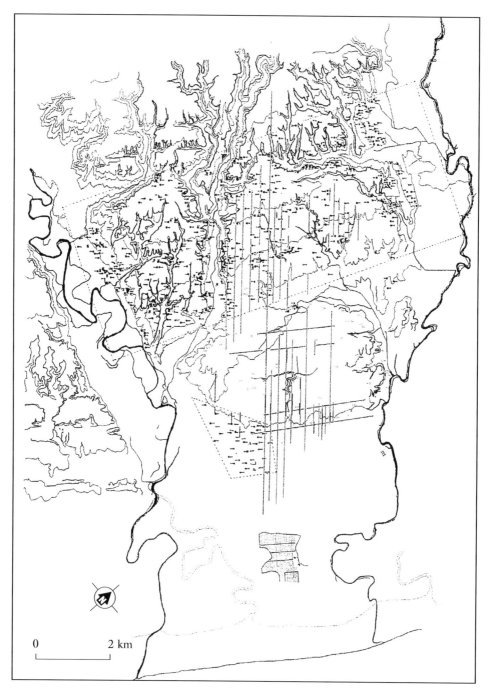

Figure 18.5 Metapontum and surroundings: plan of the *chora* between the Bradano and Basento rivers (later sixth century)
Source: Carter (2000: colour pl. II/1).

Concluding Remarks

Archaeological and literary sources provide complementary and often even fairly similar information about the archaic city. Temples, *agorai* and fortifications were the city's most distinctive features and contributed to its sacred nature. The city was seen as the center of civilization and order, symbolized by urban architecture and a specifically urban layout which itself helped to create and preserve good order. The land that was part of the town's catchment area belonged spatially and conceptually to the town. Far away in rural areas were hamlets which continued to exist in relative isolation until an advanced stage of the archaic period.

Archaeology suggests that urbanization was a long-drawn-out process. What is even more significant is that the pace of development differed markedly from place to place. The construction of city walls is a case in point. Local differences in settlement layout and in degree of urbanization were probably related to differences in socio-political organization, just as the organization of the countryside was probably related to prevailing agricultural systems. The only phenomena that occurred largely simultaneously throughout the Greek world were the building of temples and sanctuaries for patron deities and their rebuilding on an ever grander scale. The self-assertion and the incipient rivalry of the developing *poleis* ("peer polity interaction") was manifest especially in this aspect of urbanization (Snodgrass 1980a: 58–60).

However, there are also differences between the literary and the archaeological record. From Homer and Hesiod onwards a clearly defined conceptual distinction existed between city and countryside. Oppositions between town-dwellers and country folk found expression in different modes of life, behavior and world views. This is in marked contrast to the picture that archaeology provides of urbanization proceeding at a slow pace and with strong local variations. The conclusion must be that an urban mentality and, indeed, ideology existed long before the typical Greek city had been conceptualized in a spatial sense.

The antithesis between town-dwellers and countryfolk partly overlapped with the opposition between upper class and commoners. It is possible that this reflects the actual situation. Aristotle (F 558 Rose) tells us that in archaic Naxos the town was the domain of the wealthy, whereas the rest of the population lived in villages in the countryside. However, this was probably not a common pattern of residence in archaic Greece. In most towns, part of the population consisted of farmers. It is therefore more likely that the equation of town-dwellers with upper class and of rural folk with commoners was rhetorical. Members of the sophisticated urban elite saw themselves as the typical town-dwellers, and may have found it convenient to qualify the rest of the population as "peasants."

NOTES

1   I wish to thank Kurt Raaflaub, Reinhard Senff, Hans van Wees, and Douwe Yntema for reading the manuscript and for their useful remarks, and Jaap Fokkema for digitalizing

and editing the drawings. For quotations from ancient authors, I have used translations by R. Lattimore (*Iliad* and *Odyssey of Homer*, Chicago/New York, 1961, 1975), M. L. West (*Greek Lyric Poetry*, Oxford, 1993) and D. W. Tandy/W. C. Neale, *Hesiod's Works and Days*, Berkeley/Los Angeles, 1996), in some cases with minor adaptations.

2   See e.g. Sakellariou 1989: 154; Hansen and Nielsen 2004: 35.

3   See Morris 1991, with replies in Hansen 1997; Morgan and Coulton 1997.

4   Cf. Finley 1977; Kolb 1984: 11–7; Jameson et al. 1994: 249.

5   The Greeks' unusual awareness of the city and urbanization makes ancient Greece a special case for the study of ancient urbanism: see. C. Lloyd 1983: 12.

6   On landscape and architectural setting in Attic vase painting, see Hedreen 2001.

7   Osborne 1987: 16–21 rightly notes the tendency to ignore the countryside in archaic and classical Greek art and literature.

8   E.g. *Il.* 15.558, 22.429; *Od.* 7.131; with Scully 1990: 8–9, 56. But cf. *Il.* 2.806 (= combatant). *Inventory* 30–2, for terminology in lyric poetry.

9   *Il.* 11.242; *Od.* 13.192. Pind. *Pyth.* 3.71 opposes *hoi astoi* to *hoi agathoi*; cf. Hdt. 3.142–3.

10 Although Cook (1958/9: 22) estimates that Smyrna at this time housed some 1,000 households or 6,000 inhabitants.

11 Smyrna claimed to be Homer's birthplace, and the poet's portrait of Scheria may actually be a portrait of a Ionian city (so e.g. Cook 1958–9: 12). Similar to Scheria and in contrast to many archaic Greek *poleis*, the town of Smyrna did not possess an *acropolis*.

12 *Il.* 18.497–508; cf. *Il.*16.387; *Od.* 12.439–40; *Theog.* 80–93, 434; *W&D* 28–30.

13 van Wees 1992: 28–31, 41–2; Crielaard 1995a: 243–5; Mazarakis Ainian 1997: 363–7; Scully 1990: 6–15.

14 Country estates: *Il.* 12.313–4; *Od.* 4.517; 11.187–8; 15.504–5. Remote pigsties: *Od.* 14.1–12. See van Wees 1992: 42, 49–53; Edwards 1993; Schnapp 1996.

15 E.g. *Od.* 1.185, 189–90; 2.22; 11.188; 15.504–5; 17.18–9, 182; cf. 22.47: *agros* v. *megara*, "halls."

16 Vidal-Naquet 1986; cf. Anac. F 348 Page; Thuc. 1.1–8. *W&D* 276–8 contrasts men and lawless animals.

17 Hesiod: e.g. *Theog.* 292 (Tiryns). Alc. F 69.4 Voigt. Thgn. 603. Pindar uses *hieros* for Acragas (*Ol.* 2.9), Thera (*Pyth.* 4.6), Sicyon (*Nem.* 9.53), Athens (F 95.4), *theios* for Cyrene (*Pyth.* 4.26). Much of what follows is based on Scully's brilliant analysis (1990: esp. 16–53).

18 Fortifications: e.g. *Il.* 4.378; 16.100; 21.526. Temples: e.g. *Il.* 6.89. *Agora*: e.g. *Il.* 18.504.

19 Cult and divine protection: e.g. *Il.* 4.44–9; 5.445–8; 6.86–95, 269, 279, 297–310; 7.81–3; 24.64–70. Other examples of gods favoring cities: e.g. *Il.* 5.423; 6.305–10; 9.418–20 = 685–7; *Od.* 5.101–2; *Shield of Heracles* 104–5; Callinus F 2, 2a West.

20 Troy: *Il.* 20.215–8, 242–3; 21.446–7. Cf. Boeotian Thebes: *Od.* 11.260–5; *Shield of Heracles* 104–5. Megara: Thgn. 773–4. Further examples in Scully 1990: 52.

21 E.g. *Il.* 6.95; 8.57; 17.224; 24.730.

22 Zeus protecting cities: e.g. *Il.* 4.378; 9.418–20 = 685–7. Zeus' devastating powers: e.g. *Il.* 2.116–8; 4.51–3, 163–8; 9.23–5; 13.621–5; 20.192. It is also Zeus who – on an even larger scale – creates and destroys the generations of men: *W&D* 47–201.

23 Prayers: e.g. *Il.* 1.128–9; 2.111–14; 8.240–3, 287–8; "holy veil" (*hiera krēdemna*): *Il.* 16.100; cf. *Od.* 13.388.

24 See e.g. Mimn. F 9.4 West; Thgn. 603–4, 1103–4, with Fisher 1992, 213–16; also 188ff on *hybris* and Zeus' destruction of the generations of men in *Works and Days*.

25 Aelius Aristides, *Or.* 46.207 = Alc. F 426 Voigt. For later authors expressing this idea, see Sakellariou 1989: 109–10; Scully 1990: 58–9.

26 *Akropolis kai purgos*, 233–4. Pindar calls Theron, winner of the chariot races at Olympia in 476, "the bulwark of Acragas" (*ereism' Akragantos*: *Ol.* 2.7).

27 E.g. *Od.* 17.61–70. See further van Wees 1992: 30ff.

28 Hippias of Erythrae, *FGH* 421 F 1; Asius *ad* Douris of Samos, *FGH* 76 F 60 (= Athen. 12.525f.); also Eratosthenes, *FGH* 241 F 11.

29 *W&D* 585–92; cf. Archil. F 2 West. "Bibline wine" (589) was probably imported from Thrace: West 1978: 306 *ad loc.*

30 E.g. Troy: Hom. *Il.* 6.442 etc; Thebes: Hes. F 193.2 M-W; *Shield of Heracles* 83; Stesichorus F 222.6. Further *Il.* 13.685 and *Hom. Hymn Ap.* 146–7: dress of Ionians.

31 See e.g. Sappho FF 39.2, 98.11–2, 101 Voigt. On Sardis also F 132.

32 On Thgn. 53–8, see further van Wees 2000b, 61–3. Alc. F 379 Voigt could refer to a similar sort of outfit. Cf. *W&D* 535–46, for the winter-clothes that Hesiod's farmer' wears.

33 Smyrna: Akurgal 1998: 36, 46 pl. 14 (sarcophagus, ca. 600–575?). Lydia: Greifenhagen 1965: pl. 6:5 (female tomb, mid-sixth century); further Özgen/Öztürk 1996: 204–6.

34 For further comments on this fragment, see Kurke 1999: 197–8.

35 *Theog.* 26 offers an interesting parallel for abuse and stereotypes of shepherds.

36 See further the discussion of these passages in Lloyd 1983: 15–6.

37 Esp. 21–2, 30–2, 364–5, 405, 471–2, 601; cf. 502–3. For Hesiod, hard work is important (303–13); it is man's destiny (42ff, 289–90); see also ch. 23, below.

38 Hesiod's visit to the city of Chalkis is one of the few times he leaves his own environment, to enter a world of almost epic dimensions, where he mingles with the high life of the aristocracy; see *W&D* 650, with Crielaard 2002: 256–9.

39 Schmitz 2004b: 52–147 offers a detailed discussion of differences in social networks of aristocrats (relying on guest-friends and *hetairoi*) and farmers (relying on neighbors).

40 Tandy/Neale 1996: 78; Edwards 2004: 65–6.

41 Cf. 210–1: "only a fool tries to stand up to those who are better/stronger (*pros kreissonas*)," which probably reflects Hesiod's position towards the *basilees*. Cf. 215: *deilos* v. *esthlos*.

42 See Millett 1984: 90ff; Edwards 2004: esp. 37, 65–79, 121–7, 166.

43 General works on the archaeology of the archaic Greek city: Snodgrass 1980a: esp. ch. 1; Kolb 1984: ch. 3; Lang 1996; Pugliese Carratelli 1996: 233–96.

44 Lang 1996: 26. Ephesus: Hüber 1997: 32. Megara: Plut., *QG* 17 (*Mor.* 295b).

45 Osborne 1987: 46; Greaves 2002: 100–2; Hansen and Nielsen 2004: 135.

46 Coldstream 2003: 261–2, 303–4; Kolb 1984: 69, 98–9.

47 Fusaro 1982: 15ff; Kolb 1984: 100–7; De Angelis 2003.

48 Lang 1996: 12, with n. 16; Malkin 2002: 202–7, 216; De Angelis 2003: 20 (with nn. 57–8), 33. In early Megara Hyblaea and possibly Syracuse open areas existed between habitation nuclei and sanctuaries: de Polignac 1999; Voza 1999b.

49 Metal production in sanctuaries: Risberg 1997.

50 Pottery production: Crielaard et al. 1999: esp. 52ff, 84ff, 220ff, 291ff, with Senff 2000: 34–7 (Miletus). Sardis: Ramage and Craddock 2000. Clazomenae: Koparal and Iplikçi 2004. Thorikos, Pithekoussai, Skala Oropou: Mazarakis Ainian 1997: 147, 254; 1998c: 200–3.

51 This process can be followed e.g. at Smyrna and Miletos, see Senff 2000: 33–6.

52 Lang 1996: 78–117; 2005, 14–28; Mazarakis Ainian 2001; also Morris 1991: 31–3, 38–40. For tiles used in a later eighth-century kiln at Tiryns, see Blackman 2001: 30–1. For archaic house architecture in Magna Graecia and Sicily, see D'Andria and Mannino 1996.

53   See Karageorghis and Morris 2001; for Bademgediği Tepesi, see Meriç/Mountjoy 2002. Some Early Iron Age communities (e.g. at Tiryns and Mycenae) may have found protection in surviving Mycenaean citadel walls, see Mazarakis Ainian 1997: 159–61, 245–6.

54   Snodgrass 1986a; Lang 1996: 21–54; Cobet 1997. Note that Lohmann 2004 has raised doubts against the traditional view that the site of Güzelçamlı-Kaletepe can be identified with Melie.

55   According to Lang (1996: 28, 41, 241) the late ninth-century Wall 1 was a retaining rather than a defensive wall. Archaic fortifications at Sardis: Lang 1996: 28–9; Greenewalt and Rautman 2000: 656ff.

56   At Emporio, the "Megaron," which probably had a ceremonial or cultic function, was built directly against the late eighth-century fortification wall and opposite the entrance gate, as were the two slightly later buildings on the *Oberburg* of "Melie": Lang 1996: figs. 66, 70.

57   Hölscher 1991: 363–8; Lang 1996: 63–8; Camp 1998: 37–57; Kenzler 2000. The location of the old *agora* of Athens is debated: Robertson 1998; Kolb 1999 (with references to earlier literature). Note that in literary sources before Herodotus the *agora* never has an economic meaning ("market place"): see Möller 2000: 71–4; also Kurke 1999: 73–6.

58   See e.g. Jameson et al. 1994: 374–5; Lohmann 1999: 446, 463–5.

59   Generally on this topic: Doukellis and Mendoni. For the colonial Greek world: De Caro and Gialanella 1998; Greco 2001; Osanna 2001.

60   Brief reports in English: *AJA* 1987: 16–7 figs. 19–20, 22; 1988: 123; 1989: 122 fig. 9, 124.

61   Lohmann 1997: 291–3; 1999: 446–51, 464–5; Voigtländer 2004: 206–22.

62   Boyd and Jameson 1981; Carter 2000.

CHAPTER NINETEEN

Foundations

Irad Malkin

What Is Foundation?

If we search for archaic Greeks on a map we note their amazing spread along the coasts of the Mediterranean and the Black Sea, from Georgia to Spain. Except in what is today Greece's mainland, for the most part Greek settlements appear as dots on islands, promontories, and river mouths with relatively narrow coastal strips and hinterlands. In time such dots came to constitute a "Greek network" whose virtual center was the sea, a kind of a vast salt lake, connecting points along the major "banks" of the Black Sea and the Mediterranean. The various, multidirectional flows of goods, ideas, artistic and architectural conventions, immigrants, and religious contacts along the nodes of this Greek network came to constitute Greek "civilization." The creation of these dots, therefore, is a major aspect of Archaic history.

Reflecting on their past from the vantage point of the fifth century, Greeks could see these dotted settlements as the result of a series of foundations, in a process that lasted several centuries since the aftermath of the Trojan War. Modern scholars tend to characterize the early Dark Age "Ionian migration" as a mass exodus, in contrast with archaic colonization where the founding polis is not emptied of its citizens. Ancient sources sometimes make similar distinctions yet tend to speak of the Dark Age foundations in terms familiar from later periods: a founder-leader (an *oikistes*), who first consults at Apollo's oracle, then leads the migration and takes the land from some natives (or from other Greeks; Graham 1964a (1983): 25–8). This lack of distinction between "Ionian migration" and "archaic colonization" actually enlarges the body of evidence about Archaic attitudes and practices.

One salient aspect of Archaic foundations is their maritime position, and here our Classical sources are right to obliterate any distinction between Dark Age and Archaic foundations. A comparative typology of settlement sites reveals a perspective "from ship to shore." Greeks in both periods chose precisely the same kind of sites: offshore islands, promontories, river mouths, or a combination of an island and hinterland on the coasts opposite (*peraia*). Homer, for example, has Odysseus (*Odyssey* 9) pondering the settlement option of the empty offshore island facing the rich land of the Cyclopes, a non-maritime civilization. Both Dark Age and Archaic foundations were maritime in character, implying a growing variety of multi-directional connections. The multiplying Greek foundations came to form a Greek network.

With the exception of some poetic fragments most of our sources about Archaic colonization come from the Classical period.[1] Can we trust such traditions? One position sees tradition as fluid and changing with circumstances. Its value is perhaps, sadly, only as good as "the last person speaking to Herodotus" (Osborne 1996a: 5–7). Moreover, the validity of the very idea of "foundation" as a single event (Detienne 1990: Introduction) seems questionable to those who, in line with current trends in historical theory, prefer to think of foundation as a "process." Some go so far as to demand the elimination of chapters on Greek colonization from history books (Osborne 1998b with 1996a: 8–15).

Yet the fluctuating narratives of "tradition" may contain historical facts. A minimal list of elements of colonial traditions can often be trusted, conforming to what Greeks cared to remember: origins (mother-city), time of foundation, and the name of the founder (Malkin 2003a). For example, most of the founders' names that come down to us are totally obscure, without any apparent reason why they would have been invented. Note especially the persistence of the names of Euboian founders, even though Euboia sharply declined after ca. 700. When Kroton invented Herakles as founder in the fifth century, it still retained the memory of its human founder, a certain Myskellos.[2]

Names of founders probably had their independent vehicle of tradition in the form of the annual heroic cult accorded to founders in the *agora* of each city, where they were customarily buried. Thus it was ritualized collective memory, rather than the interest of any individual family, that kept the memory of the founders' name. It was the first cult that, by definition, could not have been imported from the mother-city and hence was the first to express the collective identity of the new foundation. The evidence for its existence is wide-ranging and includes the excavated *agora*-tomb of Battos in Cyrene (of ca. 600) and a simple cup from Sicilian Gela with the inscription "Mnasithales dedicated me [the cup] to Antiphamos (one of Gela's two founders)" (Malkin 1987: 189–266).

The entire system of the religious, social and political order in a Greek city was articulated by *nomima*, "customary institutions," which included the sacred calendars and festivals (see below). Such *nomima* were apparently decided upon rather quickly, within the first, founding generation, under the oikist's overall responsibility. They were also tied in with the physical aspects of foundation that included comprehensive territorial planning and demarcation of plots for individual use and as religious precincts. Such *nomima* solidified collective memory of the foundation.

Foundational rituals involved professional seers (*manteis*) and the transfer of sacred fire from the mother-city to light a new fire on the new common hearth (*koine hestia*). Common hearths (in later periods we find them in the Prytaneion), were the meeting (and dining) point for magistrates and ambassadors, and hence quickly came to presuppose each other (Gernet 1968; Malkin 1987: 92–134) in the inter-polis network that was emerging along the coasts of the Mediterranean and the Black Sea. The widespread existence of a *koine hestia* in Greek cities helped focus identity and preserve memories associated with foundations.

Foundation memories depended not only on the colony, but also on the home community (or "mother-city') for whom colonization was sometimes both a traumatic and formative experience (see below). Finally, collective memories of foundations depended on the panhellenic network associated with the Delphic oracle. Delphi was active in the foundations of Greek colonies since the second half of the eighth century and owed much of its panhellenic status to colonization, which kept expanding the oracle's network (Malkin 1987: 17–91).

The practice of consulting Delphi before foundation was therefore of interest not only to colonists but especially to Delphi, which had a vested interest in standardizing it. Herodotus, for example, criticizes Dorieus who, in the late sixth century, set out to colonize and "neither consulted at Delphi nor did any of the other customary things" (4.44.2). This points to the normative powers of the Delphic oracle as creating panhellenic expectations and practices of foundation.

So what is a "foundation?" The oikist cult indicates how Greeks understood it. Information about a "foundation date" such as "Naxos was founded in 734," is often treated with skepticism by modern scholars, yet Greek settlers apparently saw the foundation as beginning with a "moment" of arrival and ending with the death of the founder. The authentic Greek perspective indicates that foundation was both an "event" *and* a "process." It was punctuated by two temporal points of reference, opening and closing the notion of "foundation": initial arrival, e.g., "734" and foundational rituals such as setting up the altar to Apollo Archegetes at Sicilian Naxos (below), and the death of the founder, with its attendant, symbolic founder's cult that provided the foundation with a closure. In between, there were many "foundations" in a more concrete sense: setting up of altars and precincts, providing the settlement with a social and political order, or parceling and distributing lands.

The foundation of a colony, therefore, starts with arrival and ends with the death of the founder. It is sufficiently limited in time – a period in a mature man's life, between twenty and forty years – to still be considered an "event," and it is sufficiently processual not to be arbitrary. *Symbolically*, a first arrival "in 734" nicely punctuates and defines foundational time. *Historically* an entire generation is what constitutes a foundation, when the physical, social, religious, and political orders are implemented and consolidated to create a collective polity with its own identity.

Founding the Mother-city?

Our view of the world of Greek foundations has been distorted, I think, by the separation of "overseas" settlements from "Greece" (a modern national state born in 1821). Our mental maps of "homelands and overseas" perhaps still adhere to European conceptual frameworks current since the Crusaders' *outremer* through the colonization "overseas" of the New World. Moreover, these mental maps retain implied hierarchies of centers and peripheries, sometimes even of "backwaters" and colonial

"provincialism" that are inappropriate for the dotted Greek world of sovereign political communities of the Archaic period.

The eighth and seventh centuries saw all kinds of contemporaneous human mobility, migration and settlement which modern scholarship often artificially separates
into different categories.[3] Aside from overseas settlements, *apoikiai*, there were short-
distance colonies, often directly dependent on their mother-city. Sicilian Syracuse,
for instance, was independent of its mother-city Corinth, but its own short-distance
colonies in Sicily, Kasmenai, and Akrai were dependent on Syracuse. In "Old
Greece" Sparta provides a whole spectrum: after winning the First Messenian War,
it settled the fugitives of Asine as colonists in New Asine on the south-eastern Rhion
peninsula (ca. 700) to serve its own interests in relation to Messenia.[4] Mothone, in
the south-west of the same peninsula, was settled by Sparta with refugees from Nauplia
(ca. 600).[5] In 431 Sparta settled the Aiginetans who were driven out by Athens in
Thyreatis, at the frontier between Argos and Lakonia. These three cases (Asine,
Mothone, Thyreatis), spanning from the end of the eighth century to the fifth, indicate
a consistent internal "colonial" use of non-Lakedaimonian populations. In addition,
during the eighth century Sparta was busy with both short-distance colonization and
conquest in the Peloponnese, while also sending groups of settlers overseas, to Italian
Taras (706); perhaps earlier settlers left Lakedaimon for Thera and Melos.[6]

Another example of the connection between short-distance and overseas foundations may be seen at the island of Paros where some hinterland sites (notably
Koukounaries) were being abandoned in favor of coastal locations (Schilardi 1975;
1983; 1996). At the same time Parians founded (overseas) Thasos and fought Thracians
on the coasts opposite the island.[7] Perhaps some of the people involved came from
the same families; one can imagine a family from Koukounaries moving to a sea-front
location in the bay of Naussa while one of its sons, perhaps of Archilochos' age,
joined Archilochos' father Telesikles, the founder of Thasos. Instead of sharply distinguishing between "Thasos" as an overseas colony and the bay of Naussa settlements as "internal colonization" it is better to see "Paros" as being politically formed
through the variety of the contemporary settlements of its people.

Similarly, Athens hardly sent any colonies overseas, yet Attica was "internally settled"
and its countryside "filled" during the eighth and seventh centuries. Corinth, a major
mother-city ruled by an aristocratic family-oligarchy (the Bacchiads) which sent its
members to Corcyra (Chersikrates) and Syracuse (Archias), there to found a
"planned" city, was itself not "urbanized" before the seventh century.[8]

The horizon of opportunities for a Greek living in the eighth and seventh centuries
included all of the above foundational opportunities ("internal," short-distance, overseas), as well as individual migration, mercenary service abroad, and trade, including participation in a "trading station" (*emporion*), whether exclusively Greek, as at
Naukratis in Egypt,[9] or with a majority population of non-Greeks (as at Gravisca
and Pyrgi in Italy, Pistiros in Thrace, or Emporion in Spain).[10]

The complexities and varieties of eighth- and seventh-century foundations indicate how "colonial procedures" were not fully formed *a priori* but consisted in a
process of crystallization of norms and conventions; in fact, when we reach the fifth
century, we can already detect serious deviations from expected conventions (the

Athenian Hagnon, for example, did not bother to stay in Amphipolis, the colony he founded, and had his name inscribed on the Hagnoneia, its public buildings; Thuc. 5.11.1 with Malkin 1985).

Although colonization did not start off with standard procedures for relations between mother-city and colony, these developed and crystallized very quickly, both on the panhellenic level (with the active, self-interested encouragement of the Delphic oracle) and for each new settlement. It helped that colonization diluted the prominence of powerful individuals. Differentiation of material wealth appears in western colonies only after the first two or three generations (Shepherd 2000; 2005). The colonial situation was very dynamic, frontier oriented, and the authority of a prominent individual could be easily shaken off by an evolving community conscious of itself and its deserts precisely because of the novelty of the situation. Colonization was a "middle ground" of experimentation both in relation to the native world and politically, in the relation of individuals to their newly created, "colonial" society (Malkin 2002a).

Oikists apparently learnt their limits quickly. One of the earliest was Thoukles who led Chalkidians to Naxos in Sicily (734), then founded Leontinoi where he expelled the natives with the help of some Megarian colonists (whom he too expelled); he then founded a third colony, Katana, on the shore. The Katanaians had enough: they rebelled against his exceptional status (oikist of three cities!) and chose for themselves their own founder, a certain Euarchos (Thuc. 6.3.3). Thoukles should not be judged according to later criteria of how oikists were supposed to function, namely, a single oikist per city. He is, rather, comparable to his Spartan contemporary Teleklos, who was busy with a series of short-distance colonizations and conquests in the Peloponnese (Malkin 1994b: 82–9). The Spartan, working closer to home, extended the authority of his city where he could, but the open frontiers of the Sicilian situation may have made it possible to assert independence from Thoukles.

This is a good illustration of how colonial patterns were quickly being formed and asserted. It is no accident that after Thoukles, and throughout the entire Archaic period, we never hear of oikists (tyrants excepted) trying to found whole series of cities, nor of dynasties of oikists, with the exception of the royal house at Cyrene. We do not hear of this even in invented traditions. In time, what happened was that instead of a single oikist founding several cities, several oikists could found a single city, probably checking each other's authority (Graham 1983: 29–39).

Greek foundations following the second half of the eighth century seem to belong to the "world of the polis," but not in a one-sided, cause-and-effect relationship. The polis was not a pre-condition for colonization; no fully developed idea of a polis needed to be exported in order for colonization to succeed. In fact, it seems that the numerous foundations of "centrifugal" colonies with their abstraction of the social order and their foundational needs projected "back" to the older Greek world (cf. Lévêque and Vidal-Naquet 1996). The Achaian colonies in Italy, for example, were founded as *poleis*, but without a mother-polis behind them.[11] "Homeland" Achaia did not know *poleis* before the fifth century. It would seem, rather, that the phenomenon of colonization provided the overall rise of the polis with an enormous impetus, precisely because of the founding of new political communities. Younger men, less constricted by tradition, left home; mixed groups of colonists made mutual awareness of differences, as well as the need to resolve them, more acute. *Nomima* had to be deliberately regulated and decided upon by the founders. The comprehensive foundation of a new social order necessitated an *abstraction* of such an order; territorial and urban planning (first attested at eighth-century Megara Hyblaia in Sicily) translated abstract social and political concepts into a living reality.[12]

Colonization contributed towards social cohesiveness both "at home" and in the new foundation. What is remarkable about Greek colonization is this two-way foundational aspect. Social groups whose existence may have been perceived as an obstacle to political integration left so that the home community could homogenize more easily. At the same time, such groups became themselves more close-knit and with the experience of sailing away and creating a new society identified themselves more cohesively as, say, "Spartan," "Megarian," or "Chalkidian" colonists.

Other individuals or small groups probably joined them. In the mid-seventh century, Archilochos – himself a colonist – implies a mixed bag of settlers when he exclaims: "the misery of all the Greeks (*panhellénôn*) has rushed together (*sunedramen*) to Thasos!"[13] And yet there is no question, neither in our sources, nor even among modern scholars, that Thasos was a "Parian" colony. These "panhellenes" might have joined either as small groups, like the Megarians who hitched a colonial ride to Syracuse, or all those roaming individuals who quickly co-opted the new collective identities that were rapidly being formed in the new foundations. The term *panhellenes*, here used in one of its earliest attestations (Hall 2002: 131–4), also indicates a generalized view of "Greeks" expressed precisely in the context of mobility and colonization.

This co-optation is a familiar feature of modern immigration-societies such as Canada, Australia, USA, and Israel, where an overwhelming numerical majority of immigrants who come from very different backgrounds co-opt to the culture and language of the much smaller, yet cohesive nucleus that offers them a share in a new collective identity. Hence the homogenizing references in our sources to "Milesians" or "Chalkidians" that so confuse modern research should be understood in terms of co-optation. Historians justifiably doubt the existence of a large number of Milesians or Chalkidians who could furnish so many colonists for so many "Chalkidian" settlements. Miletus, for example, is reputed to have colonized close to ninety new settlements in the Black Sea.[14] It may be more fruitful to think about colonization in terms of cohesive nuclei of settlers, led by their *oikistes*, to which were added many other Greeks and possibly natives (especially women). These may have outnumbered the nucleus, yet quicky co-opted into its collective identity.

This approach goes a long way to explain the difference between consistent, homogenizing foundation-traditions that seem exaggerated and at odds with the variability in the material evidence. John Papadopoulos (1997b) rightly raises the question of Euboians as "phantoms" of archaeologists. However, the approach suggested here may provide the answer: many simply *became* "Euboian" because of colonization (Malkin 2002a).

According to this reconstruction, we see a three-way process of social and political formation: because of colonization the mother-city itself was being created (more below); the group led by the oikist acquired contours of collective identity, conceived in kinship terms as the "children" of the "parent" community, yet acted sovereignly and independently; the nuclei of settlers attracted numerous others and perhaps local women to form, especially by the formal means of cult and *nomima*, a collective identity of a "Chalkidian" or "Milesian" colony.

In general, the role of women, whether new arrivals or native, must have been important for such processes, but it mostly eludes us because of the lack of evidence. The general assumption that (some?) colonists were men who married native women is only a reasonable hypothesis with no proof, resting on debatable archaeological markers (such as fibulae), and some aetiological anecdotes. Religious needs must have necessitated the participation of some Greek women with special knowledge, and we have a few examples of those. In contrast, foundation-lore sometimes has a native "Pocahontas," usually a local princess, mediate relations with the new arrivals. One expects that women perhaps did not come in the initial military contingent such as the two warships sent by Thera to Cyrene, but probably joined the large numbers of new immigrants that directly followed (see Graham 1984; Coldstream 1993).

In Cyrene, for example, the number of non-Therans who joined was apparently significant. Some were even encouraged by a pan-hellenic Delphic oracle addressed to "all Greeks" who cared to join (Hdt. 4.162). Archaeologically we see that Cyrene's own colony at Taucheira was already a large settlement within the first generation of Cyrene's foundation (ca. 640–600). Eventually, when the monarchy was abolished, Cyrene's three tribes were reformed into "Therans and dispossessed Libyans," "Peloponnesians and Cretans," and "all the islanders." Clearly the original Theran nucleus did not form a majority, yet in terms of identity there was nothing "un-Theran" in Cyrene's *nomima*, down to the Roman period. Every Cyrenaian, for example, worshipped Apollo Karneios, the main divinity of Thera (Malkin 1994b: 174 n.13, 43–68).

The theorizing perspective of a Greek thinker of the fourth century BCE is relevant here. In case there are too many citizens in the state, says Plato, "there still remains that ancient device which we have often mentioned, namely, the sending forth, in a friendly manner from a friendly nation, of colonies consisting of such people as are deemed suitable" (*Laws* 740e). A colony, he says, is "like a swarm of bees (curiously, another early meaning of the Greek word *apoikia*), a single *genos* goes out from a single country and settles, like a friend coming from among friends, being either squeezed out by lack of room (*stenochoria*) or forced by some other such pressing need"; sometimes, "the violence of civil strife (*stasis*) might compel a whole section (*morion*) of a state to emigrate; and on one occasion an entire state went into exile because of external attacks" (*Laws* 708b). Plato, a keen observer and theorist who chooses the foundational framework of colonization for the utopian state in the *Laws* (e.g. 702c–d) here singles out some "push factors" while providing an insight into a major motive cause of colonization: the integrity of the (mother-)state.

The "narrow space" at home is here perceived more in a political sense rather than overpopulaton or lack of resources. This could apply also to powerful individuals. Finding his political space too narow because of Peisistratos's tyranny, Miltiades the Athenian took Athenians with him to the Thracian Chersonese to become ruler of the Dolonkoi (Hdt. 6.35.3–36.1), and Dorieus the Spartan, having failed in his bid to become king, led colonists to Sicily.[15] These are sixth-century examples, but they could easily have applied to the preceding two centuries, as some foundation folk-lore, mostly regarding motifs of *stasis*, seems to illustrate. Whatever other interests colonization may have served, one of its driving forces was the issue of political "space" within the mother-city.

In general, research has paid too little attention to what colonization did *to* the metropolis, especially its formation and consolidaton as a polis.[16] The issue may be illustrated through the "right of return" of colonists (whether as individuals or entire groups) which has direct bearing on issues of citizenship and ownership of *kleroi*, individual plots of land. Shortly after their settlement, the Eretrian colonists to Corcyra were expelled by Chersikrates and his Corinthian colonists. Trying to return home, they were "repulsed by slings" and were sent to colonize Methone in Chalkidike.[17] Plutarch, who gives the story, mentions Eretria together with Magnesia as examples of cities sending their sons as "First Fruits" (*aparchai*), comparable to the story of another Euboian group from Chalkis that was dedicated as a tithe to Delphi. Apollo then joined them to "other Chalkidians" who colonized Rhegion and Strabo adds that "Rhegion is a foundation of the Chalkidians who according to an oracle were consecrated as a tithe to Apollo beacuse of dearth; later, it is said, they set out to Rhegion as colonists from Delphi, taking with them also others from home" (Strabo 6.1.5–6; C257). The motif of the tithe (*dekate*) is explicitly mentioned only for Rhegion, but may reflect ritualized practices which give the separation a particular touch of finality: such colonists no longer have a mother-city to return to as Delphi has taken its place (Malkin 1987: 31–41).

The severe oath that binds the entire sending community (including its women) at Thera, accompanied by curses and the melting down of wax images, serves as a reminder of the socio-religious dimensions of the process of colonization insofar as these affected the home societies, of which we usually know nothing.[18] "Dearth" as signifying sterility, a punishment from the Gods, is a common motif in foundation lore.[19] The *dekate* group that settled Rhegion exemplifies an awareness of discrete groups who could not be integrated in the home society; it also confirms that various kinds of groups, aware of their differences, could collaborate in order to found a city: not only "other Chalkidians" but also a group from ('colonial') Zankle with their own oikist, and a group of Messenians fleeing the hardships of the First Messenian War joined in colonizing Rhegion, again through Delphi's mediation.[20]

We cannot be certain how far we can trust such stories, but as inventions they would be very curious and it is preferable to regard their "annalistic" aspects as genuine. There is no *a priori* reason to doubt, for example, a short-lived presence of Eretrians at Corcyra, and no argument from silence (the absence of Eretrian pot-tery) can have much force in view of the patchy excavations relevant to the period (Morgan 1998) and our ignorance of where the settlement might have been.

While some dispossessed Messenians went to Rhegion, some distinct social groups of Spartans who missed out on the spoils of Messenia colonized Taras in Italy (ca. 706). Variously called by terms that our sources do not seem to understand, *Parth-eniai* or *Epeunaktai*, such groups seem to have been dissatisfied with their share in the state and, especially, in the Messenian *kleroi* distributed among individual Spartans after the victory. We noted that Sparta was also busy forming short-distance settlements in the Peloponnese, while laying the basis for the society of its "Equals" through the distribution of *kleroi*. The Spartans, according to Ephoros, who calls the estranged groups "brothers" (*adelphoi*), resolved the *stasis* by sending them to Taras in southern Italy: "And if the place of which they took possession sufficed them, to stay there, but if not, to come on back and divide among themselves the fifth part of Messenia."[21]

They are comparable to the "new citizens" at Sparta, the *neodamodeis* of the fifth century, who were sent off to colonize Lepreon in order to guard the frontiers of Triphylia against Elis together with the "Brasideioi," the armed, enfranchised Helots (421; Thuc. 5.34.1). These *neodamodeis* are one of several groups, such as the *hypomeiones* (inferiors) or the *mothakes*, who were superior to Helots yet not fully integrated into the body of Equals, an in-between status which may have engendered the idea, in some versions of the story, that Taras was founded by "bastards" (Malkin 1994b: ch. 4).

The Spartans' refusal to share the *kleroi* of Messenia with a group large enough to occupy, in principle, "a fifth of Messenia," is another example of what Plato's *stenochoria* could mean: those excluded from the allocation of land were also excluded from full civic rights and from the consolidation of the political community of Sparta, newly emerging after a war of conquest. Instead of getting a state-allocated *kleros* at home, the colonists won an equivalent (or larger) allotment abroad in a new settlement: thus the two processes, consolidation at home and foundation abroad, were perceived as inextricably linked.

In the foundation decree of Cyrene, colonists retain a collective right of return after a minimum stay of five years, and Therans, as individuals, were guaranteed the right of future immigration to Cyrene. The decision is made by the entire Theran community and conscription, as in the Homeric army,[22] forces each household with more than one son to send another as a settler on the pain of death. Other Therans may join, now or later. However, if the "Therans are unable to help them and they suffer inescapable troubles up to five years, let them return from that land without fear to Thera, to their possessions and to be citizens."[23] The decision, ritualized by a communal oath, applies to "Therans," an apellation that applies both to those who stay and those who leave.

The Theran colonists are neither a faction in *stasis* nor any other distinct social group, but a comprehensive selection "from each household" in the community. Plato similarly speaks of fixing the "number of hearths," and thus of *kleros*-holders, in the new settlement, by ensuring that there will always be one, and only one, son as inheritor (*Laws* 740b–e). The strong sense of a comprehensively "counted community," that is, a *political community*, argues for centrally organized foundations.

At Thera the reason for the "forced" colonization is dearth, a *topos* of foundation stories; but the fact that it is a *topos* does not mean that it is necessarily false, since actual dearth is common, especially in the Aegean islands, which have known long periods of abandonment (Kolodny 1966; 1974; 1976). In short, both the cause and procedure of colonization are portrayed in terms of the well-being of the mother-city, with hardly a word about the colony as such. Colonization is again seen primarily from an internal perspective.

Sparta and Thera provide different motivations for colonization that both result in the re-formation of the home societies. Both could only consolidate themselves into the city-states which they became through the export of the disaffected, or the young landless. Moreover, these two very different states illustrate how conceptual frameworks of colonization and foundation were essential to collective identities. Sparta, we need to remember, was itself perceived as a "colony of the Dorians," as Pindar calls it.[24] Proud of the antiquity of their Heraklid royal houses and their ancient legitimating charter, the Spartans nevertheless saw themselves as colonists, keenly stressing their *new* arrival, as Dorians, to the ancient "Homeric" city of Lakedaimon (see ch. 7, above). In the Classical period such conceptions were explicitly translated into political and colonizing action: Sparta twice sent military aid to its mother-city Doris, and colonized Herakleia Trachinia.[25]

In sum, "colonization" and "foundation" should be considered as a two-way process, a formative force in the general rise of the city state. Eretria, a major Euboian mother-city, was itself being "founded" when Eretrians were founding colonies, and Corinth, as we have seen, was probably undergoing synoikistic processes when Chersikrates founded Corcyra and Archias Syracuse (Krause 1982; cf. Walker 2004). The general process during the eighth and seventh centuries was both simultaneous and reciprocal: by sending out colonies cities could close ranks and crystallize more sharply as *poleis*.

Sanctuaries and Foundation

To understand what Greeks may have meant by "foundation" the role of religion is of the utmost importance. Religion mediated both the vertical link with the gods and the horizontal networking of human society. What we know of Greek religion in general may provide us with a few general *a priori* assumptions about its role in foundation. Few would contest that (1) Greeks believed in their gods; (2) that they mediated this belief through ritual actions; and (3) that religion functioned socially, mediating membership in society, while helping to define the community as such.

Comparative anthropological studies indicate that religion articulates foundational acts in most human societies (Detienne 1990). Expressing a sense of beginning, societies need symbolic acts to mark them. When Cortez landed in a new territory he would plant a cross in the ground, read aloud some proclamation of taking possession, and go around slashing tree-trunks with his sword to "mark" his presence (Greenblatt 1991). Such actions seem no stranger than planting a flag on the moon.

Visiting foreign shores, Greeks would pour libations "to Earth, to the gods of the land (*epichorioi theoi*), and to the souls of its dead heroes," as Apollonius describes the Argonauts doing (*Argonautica* 2.1271ff). The scholiast adds: "For those who have arrived in a foreign land the custom was to sacrifice to the local gods and heroes." Gods and heroes were perceived as "holding the land" (*echein ten gen*) – whether or not humans knew their particular local attributes. This conforms with a general religious attitude that belongs to the common substratum of polytheism. Conversion of natives was never the agenda in Greek colonization, in contrast to the Christianizing imperative during the colonization of the New World. For a Greek such as Thales the "world was full of gods," and the gods of "others" were either unfamiliar ('new gods') or, simply the "same," but known by different names and attitudes. Religion was *langue*, the names of the gods and their particular cults were *parole*. When Herodotus tells us the Egyptian name of Zeus, he sees a "Zeus" in the Egyptian deity (*langue*) although his name, cult and even status may be peculiarly Egyptian (*parole*).[26]

This attitude goes a long way to explain the merging of cults of native populations with those of Greek colonists (syncretism), which may account, for example, for the exceptional prominence of the cult of Demeter and Persephone in Sicily (Zuntz 1971). However, in terms of foundation, it is the arrival of the Greek gods that seems to matter in the initial stages. The Argonauts, in passing, poured libations; disembarking, a Greek would sacrifice on the shore to Apollo *ekbasisios*, the god of disembarkation from ships, or to Apollo *delphinios*, the dolphin God who finds the paths across the sea. This attribute of "pathfinder" belongs to Apollo also on land, where Apollo Agyeus or Archegetes opens up routes for humanity to settle (Detienne 1998: 85–133).

"The first Greeks to sail over to Sicily," says Thucydides, "were some Chalkidians from Euboia who settled Naxos with Thoukles as founder, and set up an altar in honor of Apollo Archegetes. This is now outside the city, and on it sacred *theoroi*, whenever they sail from Sicily, first offer sacrifice" (6.3.1). Some seven centuries later Octavian, the future Roman Emperor Augustus, moored his ships and disembarked by the shrine of the Archegetes, containing a small (hence probably Archaic) cult statue of Apollo Archegetes that had been set up by the founders of Naxos (Appian *BC* 5.109). When Octavian landed, the city of Naxos had been in ruins since 402/3 but the sanctuary was probably both too sacred and too "Sicilian" to be moved.

It was a "Mayflower" altar, commemorating the first landfall of Greeks who came *to stay*. Powerful co-optative forces came into play in the colonial situation to create a *regional* Greek identity: the Greek inhabitants of Sicily were in the fifth century sometimes known as *Sikeliôtai*. Considering the great differences of cult-*nomima* between Dorians and Ionian colonies (e.g., Syracuse was Corinthian–Dorian, Naxos Chalkidian–Ionian), what Thucydides tells us is remarkable: that *all* religious ambassadors (he uses no limiting article to qualify *theoroi*), coming from all Greek cities in Sicily, would first stop at the altar before leaving for the panhellenic sanctuaries.

The foundational act of setting up the altar to Apollo Archegetes, pathfinder and colonizer, therefore, first, ritually articulates "first arrival"; secondly, signifies the "opening up" for settlement of new land that is implicitly "Greek"; and thirdly, articulates the idea of founding a new "land," as opposed to merely a new "city." Similarly, at Massalia (founded ca. 600) the Ionian Phokaian colonists established a cult to Apollo Delphinios intended to be common to all Ionian Greeks (Strabo 4.1.4; C179). Like Naxos or Cyrene, Massalia was the first Greek city in a new "land" where no other Greek had settled before.

Foundational, colonial acts afford a glimpse into the new mentality of the eighth and seventh centuries, when the new experience of (to use Ian Morris' term) "time-space compression," caused the world suddenly to get smaller with new traffic between far-flung settlements, and with Greek societies experiencing important changes both in their social order and mindset (Morris 2005). Such acts and accompanying symbolic rituals, involved applying comprehensive, ambitious notions to entire lands of the ancient Mediterranean. The oracular charters for the founding of Cyrene, for example, speak consistently of settling *all of Libya*, implying a charter for further foundations, such as Apollonia, Euhesperides, or Barke. Furthermore, all of Libya had come to be seen as the sacred precinct of one god, Zeus Ammon (Malkin 1994b: 169–74, with references).

How did the gods land in their new settlements? One of our *a priori* assumptions about colonization must be that permanent settlers needed "places in which to set up altars and consecrate precincts to the gods" (Hdt. 2.178.1), even if the settlement was an *emporion*, such as Naukratis (to which the quotation refers) or Gravisca, where the Greeks constituted only a small minority yet worshipped at their own sanctuary. *A fortiori* this was the case in major colonies, such as Syracuse or Olbia. During the first generation or two, sanctuaries usually took the form, not of free-standing temples, but of sacred precincts (*temene*) and altars (*bomoi*). Just as settlers divided *kleroi* among themselves, the oikists allocated sacred plots of lands to the gods, probably among the first acts of the overall land division, all forming part of the comprehensive physical foundation (Malkin 1987: 135–86).

Discussion of sanctuaries within the general framework of the rise of the *polis* has taken central place in current scholarship. Public sanctuaries, and especially free-standing temples built inside them, are taken to signify a collective, self-aware effort. The open-air sacred precinct allowed *all the community* to participate in the sacrifice. The emergence of the *temenos* with its clearly demarcated boundaries signified a change from a notion of "sacred place" (such as a sacred spring, or a chief's residence which holds some cult object, inherently limiting access) to "sacred space," a clearly defined *public* domain. It also reflected the new value attached to land-ownership as expressing participation in the *polis*: gods too had become sharers in the city, possessing plots of land (some very large, revenue-bearing estates). The sacred precinct marked the sovereign, unmediated relation of the community with the gods.

This communal, sacred space has been variously assessed, mostly in terms of "town planning." Roland Martin suggests a model of urbanization which distinguishes between the "centripetal" and the "centrifugal" city (Martin 1974). The former "pulls in" settlements towards the center, unifying them in a so-called *synoikismos*, as at Corinth, or at Athens where legend had Theseus putting out the fires in local Attic *prytaneia* leaving a single one burning in the common hearth, the *koine hestia* (Thuc. 2.15.2; Plut. *Theseus* 24). The "centrifugal" city, by contrast, is founded at a single spot and radiates outwards, as is typical of colonies.

In the urban plan the "synoikistic" city is characterized by new land-allocation and building activity converging towards the center, by stressing central cult sites and even reduplicating cults such as the twin Eleusinian cult on the Athenian acropolis and in Eleusis. By contrast, in colonies public spaces were more widely spread out and differentiated (Martin 1983; Brunet 1999). For example, by the beginning of the seventh century the sacred and public areas of Corinth were organized not on the acropolis but around the areas of the temple of Apollo and the agora, whereas in Corinth's colony Syracuse the Athenaion was established right from the start on the top of a hill (in the initial area of settlement, the islet Ortygia), and the Apollonion some distance below. The two formed, between them, the central axis of the city. The temples of Olympian Zeus and of Demeter were probably founded a little later towards the periphery of the city. The *temenos* of Apollo Temenites, which became famous during the Athenian siege of Syracuse in the fifth century, was distinctly peripheral (Bergquist 1992: 113; cf. Wilson 1981–2: 87–8).

When founding a new colony, how did Greeks know where to worship their gods?[27] We never hear of divine epiphanies, no equivalent of divine voices rising out of the Burning Bush announced to the founders that the earth they were treading upon was sacred. We must try to understand their choices in the context of the overall spatial and territorial organization of the settlement. We should avoid conjectures about epiphanies, inherent sacredness, natural ambience, memories of Mycenaean presence, or native cult sites for which there is no compelling evidence, and try to discern instead the criteria which governed all the elements of the "urban" lay-out. These criteria seem rational and functional. In any case, the very existence of a *temenos* and *bomos* at the time of settlement, especially as an element in an overall city-plan, indicates a comprehensive vision of both settlement and society. In other words, it implies an act of real "foundation."

Yet the assessment is not simple. Since a sacred area without a building appears simply as an empty lot, how do we know that it had been deliberately so designed by the settlers? The question is directly relevant to the influential thesis of François de Polignac which places the foundation of sanctuaries at the heart of the "birth of the city" (1995a). De Polignac sensitively discusses the spatial or territorial dimension of sanctuaries in relation to the polis. He is especially interested in the relationship between "urban" (central), sub-urban (peripheral), and extra-urban (several kilometers distant) sanctuaries, arguing that (1) the city was a "bi-polar" entity, its territory defined and united by urban sanctuaries at the center and extra-urban ones at the border; (2) the foundation of extra-urban sanctuaries, because of its implicit encompassing territorial vision, was tantamount to the foundation of the *polis*; (3) central and extra-urban sanctuaries were founded "at once," as it were; (d) the location of the extra-urban sanctuaries at the limits of territory signified both a claim to that territory, and a point of separation and mediation with the "Other" and the "Beyond" outside it. The thesis applies both to mainland Greece and beyond it, to the colonies.

The major problem of this approach is that outside of mainland Greece it involves the identification of "extra-urban" sacred lands, the sacred status of which can only be attested in periods much later than the initial settlement (Alcock and Osborne 1994; Malkin 1996). I prefer to study sacred foundations where a contemporary context is available, as at Megara Hyblaia in Sicily where the eighth-century spatial planning reserved an "agora" area (which included altars and, later, built temples) amidst the surrounding "blocks." That sacred areas were among the first to be allocated stands to reason and may also be attested in the fifth-century foundation decree of Brea, with the explicit injunction that the "reserved" sacred precincts should remain just as they are, implying that these had been chosen and separated first, even before the implementation of the plan to settle (ML 49.9–11). The public agora, as such, was also a sacred area (Martin 1951: ch. 2). Thus Megara's "town plan" leaves us with the impression of a high degree of sophistication, a firm grasp of the situation, and a bold and concentrated effort of "foundation."[28]

A more general conclusion also emerges: the archaeological evidence points to the foundational colonial situation as a new field of experimentation. Megara Hyblaia was not a copy of its home town, presupposing the *synoikismos* that was probably taking place at Megara Nisaia at this time. Nor, in its ambitious scale, did it follow the model of small clusters which we find in some earlier "regularized" sites such as Zagora on Andros.[29] This colonial experimentation was motivated not by any utopian ideology or plan but by the imperatives and conditions of the novel situation: new terrain, a new community, and the immediate need for *kleroi*, *temene* for the gods, a physical infrastructure (such as roads, necropoleis), and social, political, and religious organization. We thus find Greeks as early as the last third of the eighth century deliberately and consciously making decisions about location, reservation, and demarcation of sacred precincts as an integral part of re-defining their societies. In terms of the history of Greek religion this was a momentous step: the colonial circumstances made people experience an *objectification* of the Gods' worship and of their entire social order.

What is remarkable in all this is the temporally limited, yet absolute, authority that oikists seem to have had. In some sense they are comparable to the archaic Roman *dictator*, nominated for specific purposes, whose authority evaporated when his task was done. In the fifth-century Athenian foundation decree to Brea the oikist is explicitly entitled *autokrator*, although he is limited by many impositions by Athens and the personnel sent with him, a feature of Classical colonization when the mother-city had a much tighter control over the foundation process (Graham 1983: 29–39).

Oikists belong to a fascinating category known to archaic Greeks yet alien to our own political culture: the "Supreme Arbitrator."[30] As founders of a new social order, the oikist is very similar to the reformer, tyrant, or professional arbitrator who "sets things right" (*katartister*), such as Demonax of Mantineia (cf. ch. 21, below). Many such figures had special relationships with Delphi, are reputed to have set up cults and sanctuaries, and disappeared when their work was done. Pittakos of Lesbos abdicated, Solon of Athens is said to have gone into a self-imposed exile, and oikists did not create dynasties. Their cult elevated them above society but also provided closure to their exceptional authority. It was as supreme arbitrators that oikists settled Gods and colonists, together, on the terrain of the new foundation.

Nomima

Most traditions about foundations reach us through sources of the Classical period and are thus suspect *a priori* of accretion, manipulation, folkloristic elaboration, and invention. However, we can also glimpse the social and religious framework of foundation and its perception through the more reliable evidence of *nomima*, "customary institutions." With a few significant exceptions,[31] this category of evidence has been overlooked by research in this context. Perhaps this is because most of those who have dealt with the relevant corpus were epigraphers or historians of religion, who have often left its more general historical implication for others to study.

Nomima were the identifying features of a Greek polis among which were sacred calendars, the terms by which judicial, military, religious, and political magistracies and institutions were known, and the names and number of "tribes" and other subdivisions. Calendars provide particularly meaningful evidence because they were "sacred" in the sense that they were based on theophoric names, cults and festivals (Samuel 1972: 61). *Nomima* mediate the social order among settlers but also their arrangements with the gods, who also came to settle along with their sacred days, cults, festivals, and unpleasant threats of pollution.

Scholars who imagine settlement abroad as a process driven by the gradual arrival of disparate, multicultural groups miss the point that settlers needed to organize quickly as a community, if only for safety reasons. Safety, we need to remember, was something both military (many colonies were settled by force) and religious. Along with an adventurous spirit and hopes for a new future, migration must have involved traumatic experiences that were probably articulated and assuaged in terms of the divine. Delphi helped in providing general charters that allowed the oikist, once at the site, to make *ad hoc* religious decisions. *Manteis* (seers) could help the oikist implement such decisions and provide colonists with immediate interpretations and prophecies (Malkin 1987: 92–113). However, for a society to live as such (and we need to regard groups of settlers living together at a site and undergoing common experiences for significant periods of time as "societies') the bonds which had held their home societies together needed re-assertion and re-articulation. An oikist must have made active, deliberate choices, mediating a social and religious order for the new collective, an order without which people simply could not live together for very long without incurring the anger of the gods or losing even the semblance of social cohesion.

In the classical period Thucydides considered *nomima* a salient feature of a colony's identity and from what he reports it seems that colonists too were aware of this. He says that the *nomima* of Gela were "Dorian," a comprehensive term referring to the Rhodian and Cretan origins of the colonists. But later, when Gela founded Akragas, it "gave it the *nomima* of Gela.[32] Now Thucydides is specific: no longer the generalized "Dorian," but specifically the *nomima* of Gela, Akragas's mother-city.

An even more explicit example is the chain of Chalkis, Zankle and Himera. Zankle, on the tip of Sicily facing the Italian "boot," was initially settled by Greeks from Kyme in the Bay of Naples; thus it is unclear to what extent we may treat the initial settlement as "foundation." It then became a political community with the joint foundation of people from Kyme (itself a Chalkidian colony) and Chalkis in Euboia, with two respective oikists, one from Kyme (Perieres), the other from Chalkis (Krataimenes). Thucydides also comments that this was a *nomos* (1.24.2): to have an oikist come from the mother-city when a daughter itself founded a colony, thus illustrating an authentic Greek ritual and conception.

Himera, on the north-eastern shore of Sicily, was founded by Zankle, probably in 648 BC, and for this third link of the colonial chain three oikists are mentioned (Eukleides, Simos, Sakon). It was settled by many Chalkidians. Then it again became "mixed': exiled Myletidai, a distinct Dorian group from Syracuse joined the foundation. The language of Himera resulted in a mixture of "Doric and Chalkidic," says Thucydides, but the *nomima* that prevailed were just Chalkidian (Thuc. 6.5.1). These two kinds of social mediation, the linguistic and the institutional, are important: the colonial situation produced a linguistic mixture because language did not play the prominent role it has had in modern nation-building, but was neutral. By contrast, since having *nomima* was *a priori* necessity, no one could afford to wait for an evolutionist mixture to emerge; rather, deliberate selection and exclusion were probably necessary and the Dorian Myletidai needed to conform to the Chalkidian *nomima*. That too is part and parcel of the notion of "foundation": express decisions, arbitrating and mediating the social and religious order, had to be made and newcomers needed to conform to this formative middle ground, a pattern which finds many parallels in modern colonial societies.

Another example is that of Sparta, Thera, Cyrene, and Taras, all reputed to have been Spartan colonies. They variously had kings and ephors, and in three the cult of Apollo Karneios was particularly prominent.[33] These facts are independent of any suspect oral tradition. Rather, precisely because of their neutral value, these *nomima* appear to corroborate the colonial chains. Such *nomima* also explain the explicit chain of cult-transfers of Apollo Karneios from Sparta to Thera to Cyrene. For once, the pottery evidence, especially with regard to the Cyrenaica, may confirm a specific origin. Sparta is said to have sent the Olympic victor Chionis to Cyrene as co-founder with Battos,[34] and at Taucheira, a settlement of Cyrene, was found a large quantity of low-grade Lakonian pottery, not for export, which dated to the first generation of settlement and disappeared thereafter.[35]

Turning to the east, we may note Samos and her colonies Perinthos, Bisanthe, and Heraion on the north shore of the Propontis, and on the island Amorgos (Loukopoulou 1989: 96–7). Similarities of cults between Samos and her Propontid colonies have been noted; about a generation after the foundation of Perinthos we find two Perinthians, entitled *oikeioi* ('kinsmen'), coming to Samos and dedicating a *dekate* (tithe) to Hera in the form of a gold Gorgon and a silver Siren. The inscription recording this is variously interpreted either as a formal Perinthian dedication, or one by returning citizens, or simply a private dedication. In any case the two are called "kinsmen," revealing close colonial ties between the two cities. Another inscription, this time from Perinthos, indicates the prominence of Hera, probably at Heraion, a site 24 km west of Perinthos. The goddess, perhaps the most prominent in the Samian pantheon, also appears on Perinthian coins. Finally, at the political level, we find Perinthos at the beginning of the sixth century as the point of departure for the Samians against their oligarchs, the *geomoroi*.[36]

Another aspect of *nomima* is religious calendars, with the names of the months often following a prominent cult. If a colony adopted the same theophoric month-names it is also legitimate to assume that it adopted the associated cult, as the case of Paros (mother-city) and Thasos seems to illustrate (Graham 1978; 1982b; Salviat 1948: 212–19). We have the order of Samian months and can observe that Samos and Perinthos had at least 7 months in common. Sometimes colonial *nomima* reveal the situation at a mother-city before she underwent certain reforms, as seems to be the case with the calendar of Amorgos (Loukopoulou 1989: 113–17).

The initial copying of institutions, especially when the organizing nucleus was consistently, say, "Chalkidian," was perhaps ideological to the extent that it declared a focus of identity. But there was no dependence: the Amorgos calendar remained independent of developments in the mother-city. Colonies were usually sovereign states, not dominions of their mother-cities; that is probably why colonies did not think it an issue to make changes when *nomima* in the mother-city were changed. This is especially evident with the division of a society into tribes: Perinthos' tribes follow the traditional Ionian names. This probably reflects the situation at Samos when Perinthos was founded, before the reforms that replaced the Ionian kinship tribes at Samos with two, region-related, tribes, the "River area," Chesia, and the "Old City," the Astypalaia (Loukopoulou 1989: 129).

To date, the best-researched *nomima* of colonial cities are those of Megara (Hanell 1934 with Antonetti 1997). A list of Megarian colonies and sub-colonies include Megara Hyblaia in eastern Sicily (founded in 728) and her daughter colony Selinous (Selinunte) in western Sicily (628); Chalkedon and Astakos on the Asian side of the Bosporos and Byzantion and Selymbria on the European; Herakleia Pontike and its own colonies Mesembria, Apollonia, Kallatis and (the Tauric) Chersonesos in the Black Sea.

The pantheon of Sicilian Selinous (a colony of Megara Hyblaia) is similar to that of the "grandmother" city, Megara (Nisaia) in mainland Greece. At Byzantion we also find prominent Megarian cults, such as that of Pythian Apollo; Demeter Malophoros; Artemis Orthosia; the diviner Polyeidos; Ajax son of Telamon. Apollo Archegetes and Daphnephoros was also very prominent at Selymbria. We have no information about the calendar of Megara, in contrast to the full cycle of Byzantion. But there are distinct similarities between the calendars of Byzantion and Selymbria, and the sub-colonies of Herakleia Pontike, Kallatis and Tauric Chersonesos. All these point to a common, Megarian, source (Hanell 1934: 192; Loukopoulou 1989: 120–2).

Megara had the three customary, kinship-based, Dorian tribes. But a Megarian citizen was called by his name, a patronymic, and the name of his *hekatostys*. This term of social and probably military division related not to the fictional kinship tribes, but to a regional division, the five *komai* (*pente mere*), from which the main magistrates, the five archons and the five *strategoi* were drawn up. The unit (based on the figure of one hundred) served various reforms, allowing for the inclusion of new citizens, as it did also in Byzantion. The names of the magistracies too are indicative: an annual, eponymous, *basileus* at Megara and a board of five *aisymnatai*, chaired by the *proaisymnon*. These are found in all the colonies except Byzantion: Selymbria, Chalkedon, Herakleia Pontike, the Tauric Chersonesos, Kallatis, and Selinous in Sicily, thus probably implying also Megara Hyblaia (Loukopoulou 1989: 138–42).

Colonies did not blindly copy cults from the mother-city. Where it was important to assert independence colonists expressed it through the heroic cult of their oikist, through panhellenic dedications at Olympia, possibly through new mortuary practices, and sometimes through a special emphasis on a major cult that had little role in the mother-city. Thus in Thasos, the famous temple to "Thasian Herakles," as he is called in inscriptions (Bonnet 1988: 359), was clearly dedicated to the city's major god, yet in Paros, the mother-city, Herakles had no special standing. It looks as if the Thasian cult was taken over from the previous Phoenician cult to Melqart (identified by Greeks as Herakles; Malkin 2005a) and that the emphasis on the independence of the cult was not a "rebellion" but something that evolved gradually.

Research on calendars holds much promise for the future. A spiral inscription on a bottom of a vase of ca. 450 gives a full list of Olbian months that correspond precisely to those of Miletus.[37] François Salviat has noted similarities between the sacred calendars of Phokaia (mother-city) and Massalia and Lampsakos – two very distant cities (Salviat 2000). Others have noted the prominent position of a "mother goddess"-type at Phokaia that is linked with a particular sculptural representation (*naiskos*) of a seated goddess found in Phokaia and the Phokaian colonies Massalia and Velia (Özyigit and Erdogan 2000; Hermary 2000). Salviat observes especially close overlaps between Paros and Thasos, as does Catherine Hadzis who compares Corinthian and Corcyrian calendars (and tribal names; Salviat 1992; Hadzis 1995). Most remarkable in current research are the exhaustive and detailed epigraphical studies by Denis Knoepfler of the calendars of the "Chalkidians" in Thrace. In two complementary studies he has shown that most months in several cities in Chalkidike have characteristically Euboian (not just generally Ionian) names and orthography, and appear in the same order, with the same beginning of the year, as in Euboia. He sees in this confirmation of Euboian origins, implying a refutation of the charge that the Euboians, credited with so much colonization activity, are a mere "phantom" of archaeological interpretation (see above; Knoepfler 1989; 1990; Papadopoulos 1997b).

Calendars can thus serve as an independent confirmation of "origins" although, as noted above, it need not mean that the *majority* of settlers came from the mother-city, only that the oikist and the culturally dominant nucleus came from there. Therefore, in terms of both practice and self-perception it seems that the notion of the social and religious contract was taken from the home community and that it was applied by the oikist and the nucleus of settlers to the new colony as a deliberate, foundational act.

Conclusion

Distance gives the objectivity that time will eventually provide even to compatriots.
(Edmund White 2001)

Greek settlements and their territories, created between the end of the second millennium and the fourth century BC, are like fractals, dotted along the coasts of mainland Greece, the Aegean, Asia Minor, the Propontis and the Black Sea, Italy, Sicily, France, Spain, and North Africa. Each political community had its own micro-region, with varying relations among components such as towns, sanctuaries, Greek and non-Greek neighbors and overarching links with other Greek cities, metropoleis, and panhellenic sanctuaries. When Fernand Braudel pioneered his study of the Mediterranean he introduced the concept of *réseau*, network. A port city may be studied as such, but its very existence implies another port city somewhere else. A study of criss-crossing lines among settlements changes our perspective and focus. The "Greek Wide Web" that emerged as a result of the founding of hundreds of new city-states lends itself to such a network-approach. Braudel's *réseaux* form the basis of his *longue durée* view of Mediterranean history: such networks could persist for centuries, bypassing traditional periodization. To this must be added the sophisticated conceptual analysis by Peregrine Horden and Nicholas Purcell in their own Mediterranean study, *The Corrupting Sea*, where the emphasis is on Mediterranean micro-regions and the nature of their connectivity. In each such region many of the pan-Mediterranean, "Braudelian" patterns appear, much like fractals ("fractals" is not their expression). The Mediterranean can still be interpreted along Braudelian lines ("The Mediterranean is exchange"), but more as a network connecting the micro-regions (Braudel 1972; Horden and Purcell 2000).

The numerous types of networks, panhellenic (e.g. those created by Olympia, Delphi), regional (e.g. across Sicily), trade-related (e.g. centered on *emporia* or on the Hellenion, the "Greek" temple at Naukratis), colonial (the conceptual or real links between mother-city and new foundation), or other, grew diachronically to create a new "Greek convergence" in the ancient Mediterranean and Black Sea. Early Greek colonization extended Greek horizons to an unprecedented degree. Greeks settled in a remarkable variety of areas, and came from a variety of homes, some regional ("Achaia"), some *ethnos*-related ("Lokrians"), some *polis*-oriented ("Corinthian," "Milesians"). We need to remember that wherever they came from, they did not come from "Greece," as this national state is a modern creation. The sense of "a Greek place" was very different from that of the modern nation. It was one of diffusion, not centralization. Colonization disseminated no religious truths, nor did it create huge empires, filling the coffers of imperialistic metropoleis. Its fragmentary nature, its polytheistic and more open religious *mentalité*, allowed the network to spread more easily and opened the way to the reception of "Hellenization" but not in the mode of "cultural imperialism," a popular term in postcolonial studies (Malkin 2004).

The settlers of the new city-states met an enormous variety of populations. These included peoples as different from each other as Scythians in the Ukraine, Libyans in North Africa, Egyptians, Sikels in Sicily, and Etruscans in Italy. A Phokaian in Lampsakos met very different kinds of people from a Phokaian in Corsica, Massalia, or Velia (Elea), and is likely to have told someone about it. Images of these new places, and especially their marked differences from what now came to be understood as "familiar," as well as the commonalities of colonial experiences, must have been spoken of along sea-lanes and in ports, in the same way that overseas adventures were the stuff of epic poetry. Again Archilochos singing of both Italian Siris and near-Thracian Thasos, provides a nice illustration. What matters here is that the growing distance of these settlement-horizons probably had an impact on the way the people we call Greeks came to see themselves. When closely packed together people often pay attention to their differences. Widely distributed, commonalities come to the foreground. Such awareness may have begun already in Ionia, as Santo Mazzarino stressed in his *Fra Oriente e Occidente* (1947). In the west, following the eighth century, colonial investment in panhellenic sanctuaries and their panhellenic myths indicates an emphasis on overarching identities.

Overseas colonization informed and strengthened the nascent idea of Hellenism also because of the newly perceived differences from various "Others" and because of the common experiences of colonization shared across the network. Greek identity was not formed just because colonists met people different from themselves (cf. Hall 2002: 190–1; ch. 31 below; Shepherd 2005), but because such encounters combined with the colonizing experience which they shared as Greeks. The binary opposition of self/other, of "identity formed along boundary lines" is too simple. It ignores the development of identity over time and its spread along network lines, which the study of colonial commonalities allows us to see. Such commonalities include foundational religious practices (oracular consultation, *mantike* at the site, sacred fire) and the creation of similar *nomima* and religious institutions (sanctuaries, calendars); the role of the founder (*oikistes*) and leader of the settlement expedition; similar perceptions of the beginning and ending of "foundation" – starting with sanctuaries and ending with the founder's cult; similar tensions in the establishment of identity, between independence from and dependence on the sending community; the co-optation of settlers who joined nuclei of organized groups; a shared sense of becoming colonists (*apoikoi*); similar needs to organize the physical space of the new territories to serve very similar functions; the modalities of relations with native populations; and special investment in the great panhellenic sanctuaries.

Geographical distance fulfills a similar function to temporal distance, as Edmund White says: it makes us forget difference and awakens the urge to affirm "sameness." For ancient Greeks distance functioned as a mental filter along with the growing recognition that so many elements of "sameness" constitute an identity. Shared Hellenization kept closely at the heels of geographical expansion, down to the Hellenistic period and the emergence of a new common dialect, the first ever truly "Greek" language, the *koine*.

No wonder, then, that both fractal and network imagery seem appropriate: the same criteria for inclusion in cultic membership in a village operated also on a panhellenic scale. It seems that colonists took such ideas with them when settling on distant shores, re-worked, and abstracted them. Then they incorporated their various identities – civic ('Syracusan'), colonial (Corinth as mother-city), sub-ethnic ('Dorian'), regional ('Sikeliote') – into an overall "Greek" identity. What we call "colonization," therefore, was a significant, formative historical force, its currents running through the lines of the Greek Wide Web. The longer the lines of the network stretched and extended the stronger they became. The combination of distance and foundation helped create the virtual "center" which we call Greek civilization.

NOTES

1   For an overview see Graham 1982a; 1982c. Cf. Pugliese Carratelli 1996.
2   Myskellos: Strabo 8.7.5 (C387); Herakles on coins: Lacroix 1965: 76–8. More references: Malkin 1994b: 134.
3   Mobility: Purcell 1990; Giangiulio 1996; D'Ercole 2005. Mercenaries: Parke 1933; Trundle 2004.

4   Paus. 2.36.4; 3.7.4; 4.14.3, 34.9. Discussion: Malkin 1994b: 84–5.

5   Paus. 4.24.4, 35.2; cf. Theopomp. *FGrH* 115 F 383.

6   For Sparta in the Peloponnese, the Aegean, and Italy see Malkin 1994b: 67–142.

7   Graham 1978. See also the volumes *Études thasiennes*, published since 1944 by the École Française d'Athènes.

8   Williams 1995: 31–45; cf. Salmon 1984: ch. 4.

9   Naukratis: Möller 2000; Coulson 1996; Bowden 1996; Höckmann and Kreikenbom 2001; Sullivan 1996; Malkin 2003b; James 2003.

10   Gravisca: Torelli 1971; 1977; 1982; 1988; Frau 1982; Solin 1981. Pistiros: Demetriou 2005 with Bouzek, Domaradzki, and Archibald 1996; Bravo and Chankowski 1999; von Bredow 1997; Chankowski and Fouache 2000; Loukopoulou 1999. Emporion (Spain): Bosch Gimpera 1976; Cabrera Bonet 1996; Domínguez 1986; Peña 1992; Sanmartí 1990.

11   Snodgrass 1977a; Morgan and Hall 1996; contra: Walbank 2000. See also Greco 2002.

12   Megara Hyblaia: De Angelis 2003. The full original publication: Vallet, Villard, and Auberson 1976. The fifth volume has now come out, supporting the main conclusions of the site's original, organized layout: Gras, Tréziny, and Broise 2004. For the debate over its implications see also Svenbro 1982; Polignac 1999; Malkin 2002b.

13   Archilochos fr. 102 = Strabo 8.6.6. (C370). Translation Gerber 1999a (modified).

14   Snodgrass 1994: 2. Miletus: Gorman 2001; Greaves 2002.

15   Hdt. 5.42–7; Malkin 1994b: 192–218.

16   Malkin 1994a also for the examples discussed here.

17   Plut. *QG* 293a; cf. Strabo 6.2.3–4 (C269).

18   *SEG* ix.3; ML 5; translated in Graham 1983: 224–6.

19   Delcourt 1938; Gierth 1971; for foundation lore in general: Schmid 1947; Prinz 1979; for the position in relation to the home society (murder, *stasis*) Dougherty 1993; McGlew 1993.

20   Strabo 6.1.6 (C257) (Timaios? See Jacoby's commentary on Antiochos of Syracuse *FGrH* 555 F 9); Heraclides Lembos *FHG* 219. Malkin 1987: 31–41.

21   Ephorus *FGrH* 70 F 216 = Strabo 6.3.1–3 (C278–9).

22   Cf. van Wees 1992: 42; 1995, 168–70.

23   ML 5.34–37, trans. Graham 1983: 225. Cf. Graham 1960.

24   Pind. *Isthm.* 7.12–15. See Malkin 1994b: 15–45.

25   Hdt. 8.31; Thuc. 1.107.2; 3.92; Malkin 1994b: 219–35.

26   Herodotus in particular was sensitive to the distinction between the gods and their names: e.g. Hdt. 2.50, 53.

27   Malkin 1987: 135–86.

28   See now also Gras, Tréziny in Gras, Tréziny, and Broise 2004: 523–46 and the general conclusion of the volume, 585–9.

29   Cambitoglou et al. 1988 with Reger 1997: 469 and Snodgrass 1994a.

30   For discussion and references see Malkin 1989.

31   An exemplary study, regarding Megara and her colonies, is Hanell 1934 with Antonetti 1997. See Malkin 2005c: 67–71, some of which is reproduced here. For other studies that concern *nomima* see Bilabel 1920; Samuel 1972; Jones 1987; Loukopoulou 1989; Knoepfler 1989; Knoepfler 1990; Hadzis 1995; Reichert-Südbeck 2002. Also Effenterre and Ruzé 1994.

32   Thuc. 6.4.4. Cf. Pind. *Pyth.* 1.60–6 on "Dorian ways."

33   Chamoux 1953: 214–16; Malkin 1994b: 143–58.

34   Paus. 3.14.3 with Malkin 1994b: 82.

35   Schaus 1985; other references: Malkin 1994b: 174 n.13.

36   For discussion of these issues and the colonial significance of "kinsmen" see Graham 1964b;
     Loukopoulou 1989: 101–2.
37   The dedication is to "Apollon Delphinios, Iatros, Thargelios." See Dubois 1996 who
     confirms the order of the months suggested for Miletus by Samuel 1972: 61 who, at
     the time of writing, suggested that "the mother-city's calendar was adopted *in toto*."

CHAPTER TWENTY

States

Hans-Joachim Gehrke

Introduction: Greek States and the Rule of Law

In the seventh and especially in the sixth century, an elementary conflict pervaded Greek history, a struggle between tyranny and self-determination, between a monarchical and communal order, or, in still more pointed terms, between despotism and law, monarchy and republic. The latter was victorious – not least thanks to the Spartans' consistent hostility to tyranny – even if Sicily remained a notable exception. Thus at this very time the socio-political organization which we call the *polis* emerged, to some extent even in regions where communities had no urban center and the Greeks spoke of an *ethnos*. Where this had not happened yet by 500, developments caught up later.

The forms of organization discussed here generally encompassed a defined territory (that of the *polis*) and always claimed to apply to all members of the community, including the power over life and death. They made specific arrangements for the application of force through justice and law, so that the distinction between legitimate and illegitimate use of force was usually clear. Even by modern criteria, therefore, these organizations may be credited with the characteristics of a state, and rightly called "states."[1] The crucial connections were surely clear to contemporaries as well: the Athenian lawgiver Solon himself claims to have combined *bia* and *dike*, force and justice (fr. 36.16 W). We see here, as elsewhere, the impact of tyranny, a form of organization rejected as such, which was characterized precisely by the application of constraint and force.

If we wish to distinguish the Greek states historically – that is, from comparable forms of state – we have to define the specifics of this kind of statehood. They lie above all in the type and character of rules that determined social life. Previously, this had been the function of social norms that were handed down orally. In essentially agrarian communities, cooperative values were emphasized above all, and they were enforced by clear sanctions, so-called "shaming punishments" ("Schandstrafen";

Schmitz 2004b). We know about certain institutions and procedures, mostly in the mirror of Homeric epic (Finley 1978; Raaflaub 1997b; 1997c). There were leaders who had religious, military, and judicial responsibilities and therefore acted as priests, war leaders, and arbitrators. Distinguished persons formed councils, and on various occasions the people were convened. Yet all this did not happen regularly, membership and powers were not clearly demarcated, and the people were little more than an audience, a body which applauded rather than decided. Leaders could not simply expect that their orders would be obeyed. Hence there was no rule (*Herrschaft*) in Max Weber's sense (1972: 28), and we cannot yet speak of a state here.[2]

These loose structures contributed to the almost unchecked expression of the considerable potential for conflict inherent in these communities (Van Wees 1992). Bitter confrontations among the wealthy and notables which sometimes had catastrophic social and economic consequences and tended to result in tyranny, could not be controlled by traditional means. Conflicts that frequently prompted violence required the application of force which the community had to exercise itself, unless it was ready to submit to a tyrant with his cronies and mercenaries. In the "Solonian" crisis at Athens we grasp most clearly the mechanisms and connections at play, as well as the concepts and measures needed to resolve these problems (ch. 8, above). The phenomenon as such, however, and this way of dealing with it, were widespread.

The response of many communities to these critical developments was to have recourse to legal regulation through laws recorded in writing and sanctioned by religion. These new laws partially confirmed old social norms and partially transformed them (Schmitz 2004b). This trend toward "legalization," however, did not result in comprehensive regulation – especially when compared with the situation in the modern world – and many areas of life in any case continued to be governed by tradition and customary norms. But the areas which caused problems for the community were extensively regulated by means of the new methods and new media. The recording of law was neither systematic nor based on first principles, but everything which was or seemed problematic could be covered by legislation. Since its purpose was primarily to establish secure foundations for peaceful cohabitation – a crucial issue for the community – this order based on law became the specific characteristic of the *polis*. We may call it "nomocracy" (Ostwald 1986). From the end of the archaic period the Greeks had a clear sense that the law ruled and at the same time guaranteed their freedom.[3] Since, as mentioned above, the *polis* thus defined shows significant elements of statehood, I use the concepts of *polis* and state as synonyms insofar as the specific Greek form of state is embodied in the polis.[4] Likewise, I use "community" and similar terms in the same sense, so as to underscore the specific character of such very early statehood and to emphasize its difference from modern forms (to be discussed below).

Although sources for the Archaic period are problematic, we know the basic elements of these political organizations quite well, precisely because the phenomenon was widespread and because the recording and display of written laws was one of its characteristic features. Many of these laws are extant, even if most often fragmentary; they are easily accessible in recent collections (Koerner 1993; van Effenterre and Ruzé 1994–95). We are therefore not dependent on later, often anachronistic, literary reports; what follows is based upon documentary material. In his book on legislation, K.-J. Hölkeskamp (1999) analyzes relevant examples from fifty-three *poleis*, not including Athens and Sparta, which is enough to show how common the phenomenon was. Given the condition of the surviving evidence we may assume that a far larger number of comparable regulations once existed.

An inscription, probably from Chios, may serve as an example and starting point.[5] The text, certainly of sixth-century origin (dated to 575–550 by L. H. Jeffery [1956]), primarily regulates relations between various officials and boards – what we would call today constitutional bodies. Among them are two officials, the *demarchos* and the *basileus*, whose titles indicate their high rank. By analogy with the Athenian *archon basileus*, the *basileus* ("leader, king") was probably the chief religious dignitary. The *demarchos* ("leader of the people") was evidently the highest-ranking representative of the community. His tasks included arbitration and jurisdiction – which were subject to appeal.

For the officials were integrated into an established order in which other bodies and not least the people played an important role. We hear most about the People's Council (*bole demosie*). Its name justifies the assumption that it co-existed with another council with a more traditional, aristocratic, character, similar to the Athenian Areopagus. Members of the People's Council were appointed by election, each of the *phylai* (older subdivisions of the community) being represented by fifty councillors. The Council met regularly on fixed dates, at least once a month. Its powers were extensive. It was the instance of appeal in trials, in which it was either entitled to decide by itself or prepared the Assembly's decision. It had the right to impose fines and to deliberate on all issues that concerned the people. All this anticipates some of what we know about the Council of 500 in Athens, and the Solonian *Boule*, if historical, would have been the closest parallel.[6]

The text unequivocally indicates, however, that the central political and judicial power was the people (*demos*). They made decisions (*rhetrai*) – which certainly included court rulings – and did so in the popular Assembly. We do not know how many people belonged to the *demos* as an institution – that is, how far the circle of those entitled to participate extended. The term itself and the existence of a People's Council suggest, at any rate, that *demos* comprised not only the aristocratic elite but rather a broader stratum of society. On the basis of analogies in other poleis we might think of those qualified to fight in the army.

Especially characteristic is an effort to clarify procedural questions. A course of legal action is established. Arrangements are made to ensure that in certain situations decisions will be taken. It helped that the council had regular meeting dates and above all that officials were forced to observe their duties under threat of punishment. Here we have the precise elements which are characteristic of early Greek statehood: the community itself established the rules and had the final decision; procedures and dates were fixed and not left to the whims of the powerful. They too – they especially – were, in their capacity of polis-officials, subject to the coercive authority of the community. The rules were therefore supposed to be binding upon all and, if necessary, could be enforced by judicial means. Not without reason, W. G. Forrest describes this order as "an early step on the road to democracy" (1960: 180).

While we have an important and, in some repects, much better known analogy in Athens (ch. 8, above), Sparta's "Great Rhetra" offers an older parallel. The Rhetra's wording will always be debated, but Tyrtaeus' testimony (fr. 4 W) leaves no doubt about its historical authenticity, at least in its core.[7] Here we find comparable institutions (kings, council, and popular assembly) among which the people (*damos*) has the ultimate decision – no doubt subject to some sort of normative control exerted by the Council (*gerousia*). The people decides by majority vote and must be convened at regular intervals by the kings, as chief state-officials.

Comparable institutions can be found in other sources which, despite great variation between *poleis*, clearly reveal common structures and trends.[8] We will therefore present in synopsis the essential elements of these early states: first their institutions, then their procedures, and finally the content of various legislative efforts.

Institutions

Everywhere, high officials were the leaders of these states. They served in those functions which members of the elite exercised previously as well, in religious life, in the administration of justice, and in the military sphere (about which the extant sources reveal little). In contrast to their predecessors, these officials were subject to binding rules. One of the oldest surviving inscribed laws of this type – from Dreros on Crete and generally dated to ca. 600 – firmly prohibits the highest officials, the *kosmoi*, responsible for jurisdiction, from having another term of office within ten years.[9] Similar restrictions are attested in Gortyn (Koerner 121; *Nomina* I.82). This implies that the term of office was limited, presumably to one year, as parallels suggest. The principle of annuity was thus known.

Officials were above all formally required to perform their duties. An office was therefore not only an honor but also an obligation. Quite frequently, therefore, a – usually substantial – punishment was imposed for neglect of duty. Correspondingly, citizens were often entitled to sue officials. In some cases there apparently existed a special office to check on the officials, such as the *titas* (punisher) in Gortyn (Gehrke 1997: 60).

The titles of the officials varied but frequently have a clear meaning. In addition to the *demarchos* in Chios and elsewhere there is the *damiorgos* or *damiourgos*, the *archos* or *archon*, the *kosmos*, *prytanis*, etc. Although priestly offices were generally distinct, they were always integrated into the civic order. Offices could be filled by one or more persons, and thus officials could act as a board (particularly on political issues) or as individuals, especially in jurisdiction. Moreover, responsibilities could be divided among several officials, as was the case with the original three and later nine archons in Athens. Similarly, among the *kosmoi* of Gortyn there was a special "*kosmos* for foreigners" (comparable to the *praetor peregrinus* in Rome), responsible for noncitizens and for lawsuits between them and citizens,[10] and possibly a foreman or speaker of the *kosmoi*, the *protokosmos*.[11]

Moreover, we find functionaries who were responsible for the execution of punishments and financial affairs. Occasionally, the community hired and paid secretaries, persons well versed in the rules, who assisted the officials. They were called *mnamones* ("rememberers") or "scribes"; one of them is even termed an "expert in Phoenician letters" (*poinikastas: Nomima* I.22.B1). These employees of the *polis* need to be distinguished from the secretaries who as elected officials were responsible especially for recording, storing, and publishing the decisions of the various boards.

Various councils played an important role in the preparation of decisions. Little is known about their composition. Frequently, as in the case of the Spartan *gerousia* and the Athenian Areopagus, traditional councils will have continued to function, even if their composition and procedures were formalized. Hence we find several "councils of Elders." At least in Chios, as mentioned above, an additional "People's Council" is attested, something of a new type of council. All councils have in common that they were firmly integrated into the system of executive bodies, including the administration of justice. Some of them – for example, the "Elders" in Cretan Rhittenia (*Nomima* I.7) and probably the Athenian Areopagus – were to some extent in charge of supervising the officials and making sure that popular decisions corresponded to current law (thus probably the Spartan *gerousia* and perhaps the Areopagus, but this is debated).[12] Regardless of their precisely defined powers, some of these councils must have had great authority by virtue of the experience, reputation, and skill usually assembled in them; one might compare the Roman Senate.

Even if the real distribution of power between various institutions mostly eludes us, there is no doubt that the formal power of decision-making rested with the people, that is, the popular Assembly, which our sources usually call *damos/demos* or simply *polis*. "So decided the polis" (*ad' ewade poli*), begins the above-mentioned oldest surviving constitutional law from Dreros (ML 2). In this way the community itself arranged everything that mattered to it (*demion*, already attested in *Od.* 2.32, 44), even if the assembly was usually convened by the responsible officials, guided by proposals and motions prepared by these officials or by the relevant councils, and bound by existing norms. Among the powers of the people were the election of officials – even if the right to hold office was at least partially restricted, as at Athens – and in some cases (see Chios) also of councils. The assembly could also charge committees with specific tasks.

The people acted as a corporate body. It owned property and raised dues, decreed honors for specific individuals and groups and could even enter into a relation of "guest-friendship" (*proxenia*) with a citizen of another *polis*, who was in this way awarded a status of particular honor. Moreover, it concluded contracts with individuals and treaties with other states, and to this extent, as the people of a state, it was a subject in international law and foreign relations.

The question of membership in this state and people was clear to all involved and could certainly be decided by legal action in case of dispute. Those who belonged were citizens (*politai*) and designated by the name of their polis as Athenians, Gortynians, or Thebans – collective designations that regularly appear even in the opening formulae of public decrees. The men thus designated were citizens of the state, in the sense of the French *citoyen*; they exercised political rights and participated in the communal order (Walter 1993a).

The entire citizen body was divided into subunits of various types and purposes. Overall, we are still able to recognize that these referred to earlier social organizations determined by kinship, friendship, comradeship, or neighborhood, such as phratries, tribes, *hetaireiai*, dining- and drinking-clubs (*syssitia* and perhaps the puzzling *platiwoinoi* in Tiryns [Koerner 1993: 31; *Nomima* I. 78]), among others. But these organizations had clearly been transformed, and in some cases even created artificially, by the polis (Roussel 1976; Gehrke 2000a). In the shape in which we know them, they had been fully absorbed into the civic order – even if many other kinds of social contacts and groupings continued to exist, including some with political purposes. Significantly, those associations that were tied into the civic order adopted fixed regulations as well: the *hetaireiai* in Cretan Gortyn had judges, and contributions to the local *syssitia* were governed by certain rules and subject to control (Gehrke 1997: 55); the drinking club in Tiryns probably had communally-owned property and certainly a "chairman" (*platiwoinarchos*) who had disciplinary power and was obliged to exercise it, on pain of punishment, like a state official (Gehrke 1993: 55).

Most of the time we cannot determine with certainty how far the citizen body extended. The concept itself suggests that it comprised a rather broad group. In Sparta and Crete, we see that the subdivisions already mentioned (primarily dining-clubs) encompassed persons who owned a certain amount of property and thus could afford a modest standard of living but above all were active as soldiers for the *polis*. The connection between soldier and citizen status probably was important elsewhere too, but one cannot posit this as a hard and fast rule. Still, for the archaic period there are good reasons to identify the citizens with hoplites, although it remains controversial whether this was true in Solonian Athens as well.[13]

Procedures

We know relatively little about procedures of decision-making by the people, but the most important elements are clear. In whatever way an assembly was convened, agenda and proposals prepared, or debate conducted, at the end stood a majority decision. Typically, pebbles (*psephoi* or *psaphoi*) were used in voting, which provided one of the common words for "popular decision," *psephisma*. What was involved, therefore, was not simply the principle of majority decision but rather, unlike in Sparta or Rome, that of "one man one vote."[14] This clearly demonstrates that in these communities there was no question of a patient search for consensus, but contested decisions in disputed cases were acceptable or even desirable, as if in a situation of conflict which has winners and losers.[15] The concern with precise vote-counts probably led to the requirement of a certain number of votes or level of participation, i.e. a quorum, on particularly important matters.[16]

As has already been emphasized, the people could in principle decide about everything. Yet, in contrast to ordinary popular decrees, certain rules were distinguished as "statutes" or "laws." Although these could be produced in other ways as well (below), they most frequently originated in a popular decision. They are therefore often indistinguishable from "normal" decrees of the assembly, and there are no clear distinctions in content or subject matter either (Quass 1971). The difference probably lay in the higher esteem and importance accorded to laws – not surprisingly since, as already suggested, the specific characteristic of the early Greek form of statehood was the rule of law. Hence obedience to the law was a common definition of justice, and legislation was the most important procedure in Greek states.

Not infrequently communities chose a different method to enact laws, selecting for this purpose particular persons who were known for their intellectual abilities and expected to be capable of resolving current problems. They were given extraordinary power – Aristotle even speaks of an "elected tyranny" established for a fixed time or specified task (*Pol.* 1285a30ff). They bore titles like *diallaktes* ("Reconciler") or *aisymnetes* ("Pronouncer") and were later combined under the collective title *nomothetai* ("Lawgivers"). Many tyrants too were counted among them. The best-known of these lawgivers is Solon of Athens; among the others, Draco of Athens, Pittacus of Mytilene, Charondas of Catane, and Zaleukos of Locri were particularly famous. Although many of these figures (most prominently Lycurgus of Sparta) have become obscured by legend, the content and intention of their laws can be reconstructed fairly well.[17] We even have a piece of Draco's legislation as recorded later (*IG* I^3 104; Koerner 1993: 11) and this fits quite well with what we know from extant epigraphic texts.

It was decisive that these laws were fixed in an authoritative way and displayed publicly. In often turbulent times they were to represent firmness and stability. Accordingly, the new medium of writing, adapted from Phoenician models (Gehrke 2000b: 144 with n. 7; ch. 28, below), was used to record the new laws word-for-word on imperishable material for eternity. Moreover, in order to endow the laws with a religious aura, they were frequently recorded on temple walls or set up in temples, placed under the protection of divinities, and confirmed by oaths. It was probably not uncommon to consult an oracle before passing a law. The "Great Rhetra" in Sparta was even composed as an oracle. The particular nature of this form of regulation was also expressed in the common habit of referring to laws as "the writing" (*graphos*) or "that which is written" (*gramma*). Conversely, older terms such as *thesmos* and *tethmos* indicate that the laws also included or adapted older rules and social norms, previously passed down orally. This serves to remind us that much in civic society continued to be governed by wholly traditional norms and that the process of "legalization" discussed here concerned only certain areas of life.

It is a particular characteristic of early Greek statehood that such laws and other regulations, which formed the basis of the political and legal systems, focused above all on procedures (Gagarin 1986). Even the rules imposed on high officials, who were after all primarily active as judges, reveal an effort to ensure a decision wherever possible, as we have seen: where there was a plaintiff, there ought to be a judge. Conversely, the right to prosecute also extended widely, to all citizens of the *polis*. Highly characteristic was the feature of Solon's legislation in Athens that enabled every citizen (*ho boulomenos*) to act as a plaintiff on behalf of a third party (the so-called *Popularklage*), in cases where the polis itself was affected or the victim, being underage or dependent, was unable to do so. Comparable laws may have existed elsewhere. Furthermore, the institution of a *kosmos* for foreigners in Gortyn (see above) indicates that the legal system paid attention even to noncitizens (resident aliens or

visiting foreigners). It is not impossible, therefore, that they too had a right to prosecute, as is perhaps suggested by the *kseneia dika* in Crete (*ICret* IV. 80.8), which
must have been a "*droit des étrangers*" (*Nomima* I: p. 32).

It was therefore considered extremely important that the opportunity for a
lawsuit be available, that a legal procedure was provided for it, and that thanks
to publication of the relevant laws everybody knew, or at any rate could know,
how to conduct a lawsuit. The laws defined the content, meaning, and course of
lawsuits, including time-limits to be observed. Special care was devoted to defining
the roles of the plaintiff, defendant, judge, and witnesses, their duties, responsibilities, and legal competences. It was made clear what evidence and criteria for decisions were valid, particularly how the swearing of oaths was to be arranged. And of
course the scope for imposing penalties, above all the level of fines and compensa-
tions, was precisely regulated, as were the actions required to ensure payment of
these sums.

Even in its fragmentary state the extant evidence reveals in what minute detail the
conduct of lawsuits was fixed. There must have been good reasons for such almost
obsessive efforts: we can infer a strong commitment to neutralizing a high potential
for conflict within the community by making it possible to pursue disputes through
regulated channels. If the preservation of domestic peace is among the tasks of the
state (Herzog 1971: 110ff; Walter 1998: 22ff), we have here another clear feature
of statehood in the early Greek *polis*.

Nevertheless, in this area there remain marked differences from modern forms of
statehood. Most importantly, the judge handed down a ruling, but was not responsible for carrying it out. Modern states have specific agencies that deal with such tasks.
It is therefore possible to act immediately upon the judge's decision. In the early
Greek poleis, however, after the ruling was made it was once again the turn of the
contending parties. Whoever won the case had to carry the ruling out himself. He
had no more than a legal claim, but at least he was now entitled to realize it by
means of "permitted self-help" (Steinwenter 1925: 45). Other officials entered the
action only when the polis itself was affected. We can easily imagine that this arrangement encouraged the continuation of conflicts on another level – and prompted more
lawsuits. The further development of Greek law confirms this vividly.[18]

Scope of Legislation

Since nothing was in principle exempt from regulation, the subjects of legislation
were extraordinarily manifold. A glance at the table of contents of *Nomima*, the important publication of archaic laws by Henri van Effenterre and Françoise Ruzé
(1994–5), is enough to show this. Modern scholars (in particular legal historians)
tend to sort the various regulations by content and to correlate these with fields of
modern law. Yet in archaic Greece any kind of systematic arrangement of laws was
at best rudimentary. The common notion of "codification" is therefore in some respects
misleading. The laws of Solon or the so-called Codex of Gortyn (or the Twelve Tables
in Rome) are no more than collections of disparate laws, not systematically conceived

constitutions. Even so, we find clearly recognizable basic tendencies and constantly recurring content.

Two areas stand out among all the variety. In addition to procedural law in the broadest sense (discussed above), there were above all laws concerning sacred matters. Just as legislation itself was steeped in a religious aura – although everyone knew that it was man-made – so its subjects too were very often related to cult. Especially when dealing with the gods great care was needed lest the safety of community and citizens be jeopardized (Plato, *Euthyphr.* 14b). The gods were expected to show gratitude for generous sacrifices and to exact gruesome punishment for neglect and offenses.

Minutely detailed rules therefore abounded for all sorts of religious matters, including, above all, ritual purity. In spaces defined as "sacred," strict requirements for the maintenance of purity were applied. Pollution through blood or, concretely, through persons tainted by blood was a particular concern. Conversely, it was possible to appease the gods through rituals of atonement for which again rules were drawn up. Moreover, a multitude of regulations fixed even the smallest details of sacrifices, including what type of animal to offer to which god. Corresponding regulations were laid down for processions and festivals, for participants and for the sacred envoys who attended these events.

Characteristically, all these prescriptions were the responsibility of the community, the people (Sourvinou-Inwood 1990). Among the tasks of a scribe hired by Dattalla in Crete, we read that he is responsible for "public matters, divine as well as human" (*ta damosia ta te theia kai t'anthropina: Nomima* I. 22.4). In other words, the public domain, i.e. the domain of the state, encompassed both the religious and secular spheres. The political and religious communities were not distinguished; there was no separation of church and state, indeed the very word and concept of "church" is out of place here. The polis was also a religious association. Therefore the priests were among the most important public officials and the polis also made decisions in religious matters, albeit in particularly close consultation with oracles. Not even here was a fundamental difference perceived between sacred and secular matters. Thus religious business was always the first item on the assembly's agenda, in Athens (*Ath. Pol.* 43.6) and surely elsewhere as well.

Another important area of legislation was concerned with problems posed by the political system, the relation between institutions, their powers, and limitations, as mentioned above. Here again construction was not systematic, not based on a blueprint for a constitution, but it was nevertheless a considered effort, which started with problem areas that required regulation. Much continued to happen according to convention and tradition, but some things which were particularly important or urgent (such as jurisdiction and legal procedures) were given legal form and acquired the force of law.

Next, and closely related, were the state's relations to the outside world in the broadest sense, from honors and privileges bestowed on individuals to international treaties, as well as relations with foreigners living in the community, or with neighboring *poleis*. Issues of status played a significant role, including dealings with serfs, slaves, and freedmen. Regulations concerning offenses like manslaughter, bodily injury, rape, and slander, and the associated claims for compensation and punishment featured prominently. What was at issue here clearly was less the criminal act as such than the violation of prestige which it entailed. Accordingly, in a law about bodily injury from Eltynia on Crete a higher punishment was set for an offense committed in a public place or at a public function.[19] Similarly, laws concerning adultery or limiting the consumption of alcohol probably were prompted less by moral principles than by a desire to reduce the potential for conflicts in which affronts to honor could easily occur.

Other regulations, sometimes very precise, concerned matters of the *oikos*, that is, house, property, and especially family life. Here too the state interfered with its regulations where it seemed necessary and sensible, without allowing itself to be hampered by any concept of a private sphere (Gehrke 1993: 63ff; 1997: 51ff). Again it was above all areas rife with potential for conflict that attracted the lawgiver's attention: inheritance and dowry, property rights of children of various statuses, relations between natural and adopted children, distribution of property affecting divorcees or widows, and care for the elderly. The state also protected the weak, women, widows, and children, and even to some extent serfs, from excessive patriarchal power, certainly not out of social compassion but in order to promote peace under the law and to safeguard the next generation of citizens.

The laws included rules on economic issues such as sales, lending, and leasing with various types of contracts. Here particular attention was given to problems of mortgage and debt, especially when debt bondage was at issue. Given the economic developments especially at the end of the seventh and in the sixth century – as in Athens (chs. 8 and 23, this volume) – this was essential. It was precisely through debt that many were in danger of slipping into permanent dependence, while creditors on the other hand insisted on their rights. This was an area of considerable social stress.

Moreover, some of our texts attest to an interest in issues of settlement and land division. A law probably enacted in western Lokris confirmed, with strict sanctions, the validity of a previous division of land in a certain area, which amounted to a clear guarantee of ownership.[20] Only limited further settlement in the area was to be permitted, and only under special conditions. Any attempt even to propose a further distribution of land was to be treated like murder and punished most severely. It is hardly a coincidence that at a time when calls for the cancellation of debt and redistribution of land were widespread (Asheri 1966: 21ff, 61ff), special attention was given to regulations of debt and landownership.

Furthermore, we find laws that were designed to prevent an excessive display of wealth and luxury, particularly at funerals and private celebrations, such as weddings, in which the public also took an active part. Finally areas were considered that were likely to cause quarrels between neighbors: the construction of houses, access to water, rights of way, the exploitation of arable land, and viticulture.

The density of our discussion, and the accumulation of subjects which are often only attested once, may create an exaggerated impression of an extreme density of regulation which could easily stand comparison with the present day, and one ought therefore to be rather careful in calculating the volume and impact of such prescriptions. But the fact remains that the legal formalization sketched above was by no means a

marginal phenomenon. It constituted, in its details and its specificity, a characteristic feature of the Greek *polis* and Greek statehood.

The Nature of the Early Greek State

To summarize, three elements should be underscored as specific characteristics of
the early Greek state. First, a broadly comparable degree of institutionalization and
formalization appears everywhere. We find holders of established posts (in modern
parlance often but not quite fittingly called "magistrates"), small bodies (councils)
essentially engaged in deliberation and preparation, and finally actual general assemblies of the community, in which all citizens were entitled to participate and vote and
where usually each vote counted equally. Their decisions, which could have the force
of law, were final, not least in dealing with actions of the officials and proposals of
the council. Traditional forms of social organization as well as concerns of individuals and families (*oikoi*), were taken into account within this institutional frame
and thus integrated into the organization of the state. The community chose its own
officials, and in external relations with individuals and states acted as a corporate entity,
in the full legal sense.

Second, formalization in the socio-political sphere was characterized by the use of
laws, i.e. the publication and making permanent of rules through the medium of
writing, on durable material, and with religious sanction. It was precisely against annul-
ment and change that these laws were protected in a very special manner, by oaths
and threats of punishment, often again of a religious kind. Quite often, one who
acted against such provisions, by attempting to change a law for example, risked being
made an outlaw.

Third, extant laws throughout show massive state involvement in two areas. One
was an effort to regulate relations to the gods precisely and to protect the religious
sphere from any kind of desecration. The other, most importantly, concerned the
ever-present potential for conflict in the community and resulted in highly energetic
attempts to reduce such conflicts or at least to force them into regulated channels
where they were subject to legal procedures and state control. Here, then, was one
of the principal tasks of the officials, which they were obliged to carry out. In order
to prevent them from becoming too powerful as a result, their terms of office were
limited, usually to one year (annuity), and repeated office-holding (iteration) was
made more difficult, for example, by requiring a mandatory interval. In any case
the people exercised some control over the officials, expressed in the fact that the
citizens elected them and had the right to prosecute them.

We see or at least sense much that is familiar to us from modern constitutional
states: some kind of accountability on the part of officials, checks and balances between
various institutions, and not least the basic importance of the legal order itself and
of the citizens' active political participation. Even if we wish to detect in "So the
community decided" the same self-confidence as in the proud "We, the People,"
and even if we bear in mind that those modern political orders in many respects,
albeit by very tortuous routes, reach back to Greek forms of state and Greek

constitutional thought, we must nevertheless first and foremost be aware of the enormous differences. Early Greek statehood appears deeply alien to us in key respects, even if we disregard the existence of relations of extreme dependence, vast gender differences not least in law, and the absence of human rights. The foundations on which modern constitutional states are built simply did not exist.

Entirely lacking, first of all, was the marked separation of church and state that has been constitutive from the Enlightenment at least for so-called western state formation and especially prominent in the French tradition. The Greek state was no less responsible for sacred matters than for secular ones; the term "public" or "state" covered both. In contrast to the modern state, the *polis* was thus also a religious institution: this was and remained a central principle.

Moreover, the Greek state was far from embracing the concept of separation of powers. In particular, there was no independent judiciary branch functioning as a "third power." Again, the opposite was true. The state's sphere of action was, strictly speaking, not administrative and executive, but juridical. This was due to specific conditions that were decisive: there simply was no bureaucracy, paid officials or functionaries were rare, and, in contrast to Rome for example, the power base controlled by wealthy families was not great enough to permit development of such an apparatus. The regular changes of officials made that impossible in any case. At best, this would have been conceivable in a tyranny – but tyrannies were shortlived, entirely focused on one person or family, and thus severely limited in other ways (chs. 6 and 21, this volume). Above all, it was the peaceful, legal resolution of conflicts that was a central concern in developing the Greek state order. Jurisdiction was, so to speak, the executive or, put another way, the executive itself, as we have seen, remained rather weak.

Finally, the Greek states lacked the protection of the private sphere as it has developed in the modern world, especially in the Anglo-Saxon legal system. Self-confident as he was, a Greek noble would no doubt happily have said, "my home is my castle," and indeed might have been right to describe the actual building in this way, i.e. as a fortification – many farms with fortification towers are known, at least from later periods. But in a legal sense the polis did not respect the home at all. The laws of Solon and those from Gortyn demonstrate with all the clarity one could wish for that the state interfered in the affairs of families and homes whenever this seemed necessary or opportune. Indeed, the state paid particular attention to this sphere in view of its inherent conflict and its importance for the regular regeneration of the citizen body, not least in order to protect the weak. True, a distinction was made between the "public" or "official" (*damosion*) and the "individual" and "private" (*idion*); this distinction was a sign of statehood. Yet the borders were drawn and conceived differently from the modern contrasting pair, "public" and "private." Here, as in other areas, one must not be misled by the appearance of similarity into ignoring fundamental differences.

That such state forms were widespread in Archaic Greece, at least by the end of the sixth century, has been pointed out several times. We know this not only from the documentary evidence – the primary basis for the present discussion – but also from the literary tradition. The latter is rich especially for those states, which later played a conspicuous role and thus are privileged in our sources: Sparta and even more so Athens, but also other poleis such as Corinth and Thebes. All the more important poleis are included, as well as many smaller ones, among which some are scarcely known otherwise. Crete apparently had a particularly large output of laws. This cannot be due to the chance of archaeological discovery but must have its cause in the concentration of potential conflict and violence here (Gehrke 1997) and in processes of imitation and emulation (Gehrke 2000b: 150; see also ch. 14, above). In any case, we can almost speak of a ubiquitous phenomenon.

As far as we can see, some rather remote regions – particularly Aetolia and Acarnania in western Greece, but also Thessaly and areas bordering on it – were, at least initially, not affected by these processes. In these regions tribal structures remained dominant until well into the fifth century at least, such as the tribe and its subtribes among the Aetolians (Funke 1997). In such cases the Greeks spoke of an *ethnos* which they distinguished clearly from the *polis*.[21] On the other hand, a clear tendency toward the formation of *poleis* can be observed even in those areas where similar tribal associations were maintained for a long time, such as Phocis, Achaea, and Arcadia, even if we scarcely know the details of these organizations. This alone is enough to show how attractive the model of the state was.

Elis offers a graphic example (Gehrke 2005). It became a polis with a clearly demarcated center only in 471 through a political act of synoecism. Previously the people lived mostly scattered in the country. Yet this synoecism was to all appearances a matter of settlement practice, rather than of public law, even if it was linked to changes in the constitution (Gehrke 1985: 52–3). For the Eleian *ethnos* – as we should call this type of non-*polis* community according to the Greek terminology just cited – had a degree of political organization that we generally associate with the *polis*. It showed all the elements of statehood described above and its inscriptions offer many pertinent examples of important regulations. The *ethnos* had a place of assembly (an *agora*) with corresponding buildings (cult-places, law-courts) at the site of Elis itself, the future center of the polis (Siewert 1994; Eder and Mitsopoulos-Leon 1999). A fragmentary inscription recently published by Peter Siewert (1994) indicates that regulations fixed in writing, that is, laws and legal rules, were stored there. It is possible that the centrality of this site was not yet uncontested, for in the middle of the sixth century the place designated for the publication of the ever-increasing number of regulations was moved to the Temple of Zeus in Olympia (Siewert 1994: 27). Also already in the sixth century, this *ethnos*, organized as a state, was capable of expanding its sphere of influence and to attach to itself as allies (*symmachoi*) other groups along and beyond the Alpheios River (Ebert and Siewert 1997–9). It thereby created relations of dependence by means of the system of hegemonial alliance that the Spartans had developed shortly before.

All this suggests that distinctions between *ethnos* and polis were not strict at all. Even if the connections between Greek ethnicity, tribal structures, and *polis* formation continue to pose many puzzles, the process of state formation appealed to tribal conglomerations as well. In the end, the latter's various subunits evolved into *poleis*, while on a higher level of organization they preserved their unity and mutated into federal states. For the Acarnanians we can demonstrate this in the fifth century (Gehrke

1994–5), while among the Aetolians the process probably extended well into the fourth (Funke 1997). This goes beyond our chronological limits, but the look ahead helps to underscore once again the general significance of the process of Greek state formation.

The ubiquity of this process confirms at the same time that its decisive precondition was also widespread: the constant and alert willingness of the rich and influential to demonstrate their power and strength and to display and protect their honor, as well as their inability to yield and compromise. Again and again, this disposition led to conflicts which often escalated into violent confrontations, particularly in the seventh and sixth centuries. Nor was it only the feuds within the elite that proved dangerous, but still more their collective efforts to establish themselves as a ruling class, and the aspirations of single members to rise above the community by establishing a tyranny. Against all these efforts stood the law, "the friend of the weak" as Friedrich Schiller put it.

These connections, emphasized strongly in recent scholarship, were already recognized by Friedrich Nietzsche who characterized them with weighty words (1969: 151):

> Smelling out "beautiful souls" in the Greeks, "golden means" and other perfections, admiring in them, for instance, calm in grandeur, an ideal disposition, elevated simplicity – I was protected from this "elevated simplicity," which is in the end *niaiserie allemande* [German foolishness], by the psychologist in me. I saw their strongest instinct, the will to power; I saw them tremble before the boundless force of this drive – I saw all their institutions arise from security measures, in order to make themselves safe in the face of each other's inner explosives.
>
> (tr. in Nietzsche 1997: 88)

Did this work?, we finally have to ask. How successful were these intensive and intelligent attempts to use political order combined with coercive power exerted by the community and its laws – that is, to rely on state organization – to channel conflicts and thereby to achieve and secure internal peace? It is not possible to give an unequivocal answer to these questions. On the one hand, these institutions made it possible to contain or at least slow down the rise of tyranny, which at times seemed unstoppable. Despite all challenges, the citizen community of this type remained the only legitimate form of social and political organization among the Greeks, and, as the history of democracy shows, it even offered possibilities for further development.

On the other hand, this order was and remained precarious. Although legal recourse was available, in the absence of strong state agencies the execution of a court's judgement raised new problems if, for example, permitted self-help went too far. And what happened if the officials serving as judges, in spite of all controls and threats of punishment, did not fulfill their duties? Aristotle uses the example of contemporary Crete to paint an alarming picture of the possible consequences (*Pol.* 1272b3ff):

> The *kosmoi* are often expelled from office either by a conspiracy of their colleagues or of private persons. It is also possible for *kosmoi* to resign in the middle of their term. But it were better if all these things took place according to law (*kata nomon*) and not human wish, which is no safe standard. Basest of all, however, are the frequent abolitions

of *kosmoi* brought about by the powerful when they do not wish to submit to punishment, from which it is also clear that the Cretan order (*taxis*) has some elements of a constitution (*politeia*) but is not really a constitution but rather an arbitrary regime of a few powerful people (*dynasteia*). The habit of the powerful is to create rival followings among the people and their friends and to exploit the resulting condition of anarchy to engage in civil strife (*stasis*) and fight against each other. Yet what is the difference between such behavior and the *polis* periodically ceasing to exist and the constitutionally ordered community dissolving?

(tr. Simpson 1997, modified)

This passage, far too rarely noted, is a *locus classicus* for the specifically Greek form of violent political conflict within a polis (*stasis*). It demonstrates how – as Aristotle sees it – the state (*polis*) and the community of citizens (*politike koinonia*) were jeopardized by *stasis* and, conversely, that they were organized to prevent such internal strife. This passage also makes clear that in this organization the judicial competence of the highest officials played a central role, and why intensive efforts were made to compel these officials to perform their duties, most especially in the arbitration of quarrels. It was precisely when this function (held in this case by the *kosmoi*) was not served well or even consciously obstructed, that is, when *anarchia*, anarchy, reigned, that open civil war could break out. We would today speak of mafia-like structures (van Wees 2000b).

Aristotle sees here a deficiency of Cretan statehood. In line with the creators of the forms of state analyzed in this chapter, he pleads for "firm legal rules," for *nomos*, which in his view had not been pushed far enough in Crete.[22] Since even our limited knowledge shows that Cretan legal systems were meticulous, it is clear that the laws had a limited effect. All we know about civil war, amply attested in Greece in the seventh and sixth centuries and later (Lintott 1982; Gehrke 1985), shows that this certainly did not apply to Crete alone. In any case, efforts to develop state regulations that would direct conflicts into peaceful channels were faced with a highly competitive mentality and corresponding values, as well as a barely limited readiness to resort to violence. Their constant interaction meant that political and legal organization remained precarious: an unstable equilibrium of order and anarchy.

Here probably lies the most fundamental precondition for the perpetual warfare among Greek states, for their attempts to foster domestic peace by promoting enmity against those outside, to satisfy agonistic ambition in this way and to weld the *polis* together as a community of fighters. That is another story (ch. 30, below), but this aspect of Greek statehood had to be mentioned at least. Here too Nietzsche can serve as our crown witness, when he continues after the passage cited above:

The immense internal tension then discharged itself in frightening and ruthless external hostility: the city-states ripped each other to shreds so that the citizens might, each of them, attain peace with themselves. It was necessary to be strong; danger was nearby – it lay in ambush everywhere.

What would have been needed here was a Leviathan – which the Greeks feared even more. Hence they lived in states but ultimately these were far different from ours.

NOTES

1   Jellinek 1914: 394ff, on the so-called "three element theory"; see now Walter 1998: esp. 19ff; also Davies 1997.

2   On early developments, see esp. Donlan 1989 (in part going farther than I would) Ulf 1990b; van Wees 1992; Raaflaub 1998; further bibliography Raaflaub 1993b: 87 n. 2.

3   Orph. Hymn 64.1ff; Heracl. 22 B114 D-K; Pind. fr. 152B; Hdt. 7.102.

4   For a complementary perspective on the accelerated development of the polis in archaic Greece, see Raaflaub 1993b, which does not concentrate on the topic of statehood and primarily uses literary rather than documentary sources, but reaches very similar conclusions. Raaflaub also illuminates contemporary reflection on the developments analyzed here, that is, early forms of political thought (cf. Raaflaub 2000; 2001).

5   ML 8; Koerner 1993: 61; *Nomima* I.62. Origin: Meiggs and Lewis 1988: 17; interpretation: Gehrke 1993: 51ff.

6   On the question of authenticity, see Beloch 1912 (1924): 366; Hignett 1952: 92ff; Chambers 1990a: 178–9 (all *contra*); Busolt 1895–1904: 2. 279; Busolt and Swoboda 1926: 845; Rhodes 1972: 208–9; 1981: 153–4 (all *pro*).

7   My interpretation owes much to Ehrenberg 1933 (1965a); and Bringmann 1975; 1980; cf. Raaflaub 1993b: 64ff. For different views, Nafissi, 1991: 5ff, and ch. 8, above; van Wees 1999b.

8   See esp. Willets 1967; Gagarin 1986; Camassa 1988; Link 1991; Maffi 1992; Hölkeskamp 1992a, 1999; Thomas 1996, Schmitz 2004b. For my own position (and more references than I can include here), see Gehrke 1993, 1995a, 2000a, 2000b, and 1997 (on Crete).

9   ML 2; Koerner 1993: 90; *Nomima* I.81.

10 Koerner 1993: 153–154; *Nomima* I.16, 30; *Cod. Gortyn* XI.16.

11 The title is attested only later; this *protokosmos* has been identified with the *startagetas* (*strategos*, "general": *Nomima* I.7.4–5) attested in the early fifth century (Guarducci, comm. on *ICret* IV.80, p. 185), but this is far from certain.

12 Martin 1974: 29ff is skeptical, but see Rhodes 1972: 201ff on this debate; see also Bleicken 1985 (1988; 1991; 1994): 454–5 and, generally, Wallace 1989.

13 See generally the lucid observations of Raaflaub 1993b: 80; on the debate concerning Athens: Bleicken 1994: 442 and recently Raaflaub 2006; van Wees 2006; and the discussion between Ober, Raaflaub, and Wallace in Raaflaub et al. 2007.

14 On Sparta's vote by shouting or dividing, see, e.g., Thuc. 1.87; Flaig 1993. On the Roman group vote, Staveley 1972: esp. 133ff.

15 Ruzé 1984: 253; see, generally, Larsen 1949.

16 This is suggested by the formula *zamos plathyon* (perhaps: "the people in full numbers") in Elis (Koerner 1993: 38; *Nomima* I.108; Ruzé 1984: 257). A similar formula (*demos plethyon*) is attested in fifth-century Athens but probably goes back to the archaic period: Ostwald 1986: 32–6; Ryan 1994.

17 See Link 1992, 1994; Hölkeskamp 1992a; 1999: 44ff. Generally, see ch. 21, below.

18 As illustrated by [Demosthenes] 47.52–61; cf. Bravo 1980; and the Twelve Tables in Rome.

19 *ICret* I.X.2; Koerner 1993: 94; *Nomima* II.80; Gehrke 1997: 43–44.

20 *IG* IX² 1.3.609; ML 13; Koerner 1993: 47; *Nomima* I.44.

21 Hdt. 5.2; 7.8; 8.108; cf. Funke 1997: 145 and, generally, C. Morgan 2003.

22 On Aristotle's concept of law, see now Piepenbrink 2001: 15ff.

CHAPTER TWENTY-ONE

Charismatic Leaders

Robert W. Wallace

Tyrants and lawgivers play a critical but contested role in Archaic history. According to some ancient sources, many seventh-century communities, beset by dysfunctional aristocracies, empowered charismatic individuals to rule as tyrants – the word still lacked negative connotations – or else to legislate judicial or political reforms. Early tyrants curtailed abusive aristocrats and safeguarded the – possibly hoplite – masses who promoted and supported them, an important step on the road to democracy.[1] Ancient texts also assign lawgivers major roles in resolving social crises.

Many scholars have challenged these conceptions, as reflecting anachronistic fourth-century theory and an overestimation of the *demos'* role. Following different sources, they view tyrants as dominant aristocrats, often abusing the people. Others question the historical significance of lawgivers, viewing most early legislation as *ad hoc*.[2] Indisputably, both lawgivers and tyrants attracted much mythology, especially for biographical details.[3]

The current chapter focuses on three *poleis*, Mytilene, Megara, and Athens, for which Alcaeus, Theognis, and Solon supply contemporary testimonia. They and other early evidence will help to confirm the first, positive vision of seventh-century tyrants. At the same time, early evidence also indicates that by the end of that century, most tyrannies had become problematic – the root of alternative, now hostile interpretations of tyranny – and laws proved weak. A third type of charismatic now emerged on the scene: the sage or *sophos*. Seeking to mediate the strife that afflicted their communities, some *sophoi* became civic reformers, combining political authority with wisdom and restraint.

Elites in Crisis

Seventh- and sixth-century poets voice frequent complaints against aristocratic violence, arrogance, judicial abuse, and economic exploitation.[4] Within their *poleis*, elites

contended for status (*timê*), wealth, and power, sometimes with damaging consequences. Our earliest Greek (and panhellenic) text, the *Iliad*, takes as its theme Achilles'
and Agamemnon's private quarrel over honor and booty, bringing death and destruction to their warrior community despite elite ideals of fostering the demos (see, e.g.,
Agamemnon and Menelaos "fearing lest the Argives suffer some hurt," *Il.* 10.1–35).[5]
Achilles calls Agamemnon a *basileus* who "feeds on his people" (*demoboros:* 1.231),
the ranker Thersites lambasts Agamemnon for greed (2.225–34), Priam calls his
surviving sons "shameful, boasters and dancers, the best men of the dancefloor,
robbers of sheep and goats among their own people" (24.260–2, tr. van Wees).
Around the same time as Homer, Hesiod laments,

> There is angry murmuring when right is dragged off wherever gift-swallowers choose
> to take her as they give judgment with crooked verdicts . . . Often a whole community
> together suffers in consequence of a bad man who does wrong and contrives evil . . .
> Zeus either punishes those men's broad army or city wall, or punishes their ships at sea
> . . . Beware of this, lords, and keep your pronouncements straight, you gift-swallowers,
> and forget your crooked judgments altogether.
>
> (*Works and Days* 213–73, tr. West, adapted)

Similar difficulties afflicted seventh-century Mytilene, Athens, and Megara. At Mytilene,
after overthrowing the Penthilid dynasty perhaps ca. 640, aristocratic "clans" (*genê*)
began a murderous competition for power and prestige, fighting or else fleeing into
exile. Alcaeus fled at least twice; Sappho also fled. The names of three Mytilenean
genê, Kleanaktidai, Demoanaktidai, and Archeanaktidai (Alc. fr. 112.23, 24; 296b1
Liberman), reflect their ruling pretensions (the element "-anak-" derives from *anax*,
"master"). In fr. 305a Alcaeus expresses unhappiness at the "endless" fighting between
his *genos* and another. Penthilids continued to manoeuvre among rival *genê*, not shed-
ding their reputation for violence. Aristotle (*Pol.* 1311b) notes that one night a certain Penthilos dragged out from beside his wife and beat a certain Smerdis, who
killed him. Between elite and *demos*, issues included upper class excesses unregulated
by law, popular hatred for elite violence, elite scorn for community warfare and for
ordinary citizens whom they called *kakoi*, "base," "ugly," "worthless" (Alc. fr. 296a.7),
and ethnic discrimination against Mytileneans of Thracian or Anatolian origin.[6]

In seventh-century Attica an elite calling itself *eupatridai*, "sons of good fathers,"
dominated the land. Solon calls them "you who have pushed through to glut yourselves with many good things" (fr. 4c.2 West). "Out of arrogance many griefs must
be endured," for Athens' rulers "do not know how to restrain their greed or to order
their present festivities in the peacefulness of the banquet" (fr. 4.8–10). Eupatrid
extravagance weighed especially on dependent farmers (Murray 1993: 189–94), some
of whom were sold abroad into slavery (Solon fr. 4.23–5). Prospering non-
Eupatrids and the *demos* had difficulty gaining political status. Solon's defensive, even
self-contradictory, claim "to the people I gave as much privilege (*geras*)/ power (*kratos*)
as sufficed them, neither taking away *timê* nor holding out still more" (fr. 5 = *Ath.
Pol.* 12.1/ Plut. *Sol.* 18.5) shows that the revolutionary masses were demanding greater
political standing, which he failed to satisfy. His proclamation that he wrote laws

"equal for elite and *kakoi* alike, straight justice" (fr. 36.18–19) implies earlier complaints by the *kakoi* about crooked justice. Meanwhile, elites fought among themselves "for a long time" after the Alcmaeonid *genos* killed some "companions" (*hetairoi*) of Kylon, attempting to become tyrant in 632 (Plut. *Sol.* 12). The Alcmaeonids fled into exile four times between 600 and 508. Solon mentions "civil discord and war" (fr. 4.19).

At Megara also, early evidence points to economic exploitation, aristocratic disorder, and judicial abuse. Sometime before 550 (Lane Fox 2000: 40 dates him ca. 600–560) the elite poet Theognis mentions murderous civil strife (51) and aristocratic outrage: "Cyrnus, this polis is pregnant, and I fear that it will give birth to a man who will be a straightener of our base *hubris*" (39–40, tr. Nagy; cf. 41–52). He complains that the elite has yielded to the masses in administering justice: "Cyrnus, this *polis* is still a *polis*, but its people are different. Formerly they knew nothing of legal decisions or laws but wore goatskins around their flanks – wore them to shreds – and grazed like deer outside this *polis*. And now they are *agathoi* [elite], son of Polupaos, and those who were formerly *esthloi* [noble] are now *deiloi* [base cowards]" (53–60). As we shall see, Aristotle's comment that Megara's tyrant Theagenes won the people's trust "by slaughtering the cattle of the rich" (*Pol.* 1305a) points to earlier economic injustice. Van Wees remarks that in aristocratic Megara, as elsewhere, "violence and greed were structural phenomena, rather than aberrations which could be blamed on 'the bad men'" (2000b: 66).

Tyrants

Amid these crises, tyrants came to dominate many *poleis*. What were their functions and who supported them?[7] In an important passage Aristotle concluded that in larger *poleis*

> a tyrant is set up from among the people and the masses to oppose the notables, that the people may suffer no injustice from them. This is manifest from the historical record. For almost the greatest number of tyrants have risen, it may be said, from being demagogues, having won the people's confidence by slandering the notables.
>
> (*Pol.* 1310b)

Aristotle and his research group reconstructed detailed political and constitutional histories of 158 *poleis*, using and sometimes quoting archaic poetry now mostly lost. Although all but one of these histories are also lost, *Politics* preserves his general reflections on this material. Aristotle was not alone in thus interpreting the installation of tyrants. Plato wrote: "Is it not the way of a *demos* to put forward one man as its special champion and protector, and cherish and magnify him? . . . This is plain, that when a tyrant arises he sprouts from a protectorate root" – i.e., from protecting the *demos* (*Rep.* 565cd). In the fifth century, Herodotus' presentation of the Mede Deioces (1.96–100) reflects a similar conception – "the despotic template" (Dewald 2003: 27–8). The people of Deioces' village chose him to administer justice and his reputation spread, as "corrupt practices of law were causing much distress." The Medes later made him *basileus*/tyrant (Herodotus uses both words). "We cannot continue to live in this country under the present intolerable conditions. Let us appoint one of our number to rule us so that we can get on with our work under orderly government, and not lose our homes altogether in the recent chaos."

These statements all describe the appointment of tyrants to safeguard the *demos*: the positive vision of tyranny. However, these same writers present quite negative pictures of tyrants once in power. Immediately following his description of the installation of tyrants as popular leaders, Aristotle observes, "the tyrant does not look to the public interest at all, unless it happens to contribute to his personal benefit" (*Pol.* 1310b); "it is clear that tyranny has the evils of both democracy and oligarchy: it copies oligarchy in making wealth its object . . . and in putting no trust in the masses, which is why they resort to the measure of stripping the people of their weapons, and why ill treatment of the mob and its expulsion from the city and settlement in scattered places is common to both forms of government" (*Pol.* 1311a). Similarly, Plato (*Rep.* 571a–576c) and Herodotus' Otanes (3.80.2) state that absolute power leads to savage and unnatural violence against the community. These writers indicate that tyrants began as popular leaders promoted by the *demos* to curtail aristocratic abuse, but in time turned bad. How far will archaic evidence confirm these conceptions?

The first Greek tyrant, Pheidon of Argos, remains shadowy. Called both tyrant and *basileus* (here perhaps "ruler"), he may have led a mass hoplite army to defeat the Spartans at Hysiae in 669 (Andrewes 1956: 39–42; Murray 1980 (1993): 141–3). He also introduced a system of weights and measures (Hdt. 6.127), arguably analogous to the specification of legal norms (Salmon 1997: 64) and certainly benefiting his community.

In Corinth during the 650s Cypselus seized power from the Bacchiad *genos*. Herodotus' story that baby Cypselus was saved from the murderous Bacchiadae by smiling points to a positive view of his tyranny (5.92.b; cf. Murray 1993: 148). Contemporary evidence (Salmon 1984: 186–8) makes clear that social justice and adjudication were major issues. A contemporary Delphic oracle proclaimed that Cypselus would "bring justice" to Corinth (Hdt. 5.92b, also calling him *basileus*). Similarly, "Cypselus' Chest" at Olympia – inscribed (Pausanias notes) with archaic *boustrophedon* writing – depicted justice choking injustice (Paus. 5.18.2, 6). This dedication – "not a relic, but a symbol of Cypselus' . . . rise to power" (Drews 1972: 132 n. 14) – was also contemporary: as we shall see, no one after his son and successor Periander would have dedicated such a chest. Its central panel displayed military scenes, perhaps supporting the story (in Nicolaus *FGH* 90 F 57.5, from Ephorus?) that, like Pheidon, Cypselus had been a military commander. In 607/6, Athens and Mytilene chose Periander to mediate their struggle over Sigeion (D.L. 1.76). Many scholars have observed that he would never have been awarded that task had he been a wicked despot. In the late seventh century, as again we shall see, Periander was also considered *sophos*, a sage. According to Aristotle (*Pol.* 1315b), Cypselus did not need a bodyguard, the tyrant's standard protection against menacing aristocrats. If so,

Corinth's aristocracy may also have opposed the Bacchiad dynasty and not threatened Cypselus.

In the 650s or later, Orthagoras gained power in nearby Sicyon. One contemporary datum is illuminating: a successor born probably around the time of Orthagoras' accession was named Isodamos, "Equalpeople."[8] The Orthagorids ruled for a century, the longest tyranny known to Aristotle, and were only expelled by Spartan intervention: "they treated their subjects with moderation and generally obeyed the laws . . . By their diligence in many matters they gained the leadership of the *demos*" (Arist. *Pol.* 1315b12). They never attracted negative stories.

In Megara before 550, we have seen, Theognis mentions aristocratic abuse and warns Megara's elite against a "man who will be a straightener of our base *hubris*." Thus Theognis also viewed early tyranny as protecting against abusive elites. Theagenes became tyrant ca. 640, according to Aristotle gaining the *demos*'s trust "by slaughtering the livestock of the rich." The violence of that report suggests that it derives from archaic poetry hostile to Theagenes, defending the *demos* against a wealthy elite. According to later sources, ca. 620 Theagenes was replaced by an oligarchy, but the *demos* soon seized power, still outraged at economic exploitation.[9] Quite possibly drawing on Aristotle's *Constitution of the Megarians*, the conservative Plutarch writes (*Mor.* 295c–d):

> among their shocking acts of misconduct toward the wealthy, the poor would enter their homes and insist upon being entertained and banqueted sumptuously. But if they did not receive what they demanded, they would treat all the household with violence and *hubris*. Finally, they enacted a decree whereby they received back again the interest which they paid their creditors, calling the measure "return interest."

At Mytilene, the first tyrant we can clearly identify is Melanchros, dated only by his assassination by Pittacus and Alcaeus' brothers in the forty-second Olympiad, 612–19 (D.L. 1.74, *Suda* P1659). Alcaeus himself praises Melanchros as "worthy of respect toward the *polis*" (fr. 331), perhaps attesting discord within his *genos*. Citing "the so-called *stasiotika* [civil strife] poems of Alcaeus," Strabo (13.2.3) describes intense aristocratic in-fighting (*dichostasiai*, "apart-civil-struggles," a word Solon also uses [fr. 4.37]), periods of tyranny, and what he calls *dunasteiai* for some fifteen years after Melanchros' murder. Soon after his death, a new tyrant, Myrsilos, was brought in by ship, from exile or retreat. The scholiast on fr. 305a quotes Alcaeus' "if only there were no war between myself and you," and says, "this is addressed to someone called Mnemon who provided a boat for the return of Myrsilos. He says, then, that he does not blame him or quarrel with him for this." Again, elite discord is evident. As for popular support, like Smerdis (who killed Penthilos), Myrsilos' name is Anatolian: like Pittacus later, he seems to have represented Mytilene's non-Greek population. Alcaeus fr. 383 attests a Myrsileon, a heroic shrine to Myrsilos erected soon after his death, suggesting widespread popularity.

Alcaeus and his "companions," including Pittacus, tried to kill Myrsilos, and fled (schol. Alc. fr. 114). However, Pittacus, of noble but also Thracian stock, now shifts sides. Alcaeus prays:

Come . . . rescue us from these hardships and from grievous exile; and let their Avenger [i.e., of the conspirators] pursue the son of Hyrrhas [Pittacus], since once we swore, cutting [the throat of an animal for sacrifice?] never [to abandon?] any of our *hetairoi*, but either to die at the hands of men who at that time came against us . . . or else to kill them and rescue the *demos* from its griefs. But Pot-Belly [Pittacus] did not talk to their hearts; he recklessly trampled the oaths underfoot, and devours our *polis*.

(fr. 129)

Alcaeus' stated purpose, "to rescue the *demos* from its griefs," reflects elite ideologies of fostering the *demos* as we saw with Agamemnon and Menelaos. Pittacus joined Myrsilos, but probably not as joint tyrants, as Pittacus was not tyrant after Myrsilos' death. Their collaboration may have been what Strabo called a *dunasteia*, and we a popular junta.

Finally, in response to elite violence and exploitation at Athens, some revolutionaries in 594/3 wanted Solon to become tyrant (fr. 32 West; Plut. *Sol.* 13–14). For reasons we shall consider, he declined. In the 560s, however, after the mixed success of his reforms, Solon indicates that the *demos* wanted and were responsible for Peisistratus' tyranny. He warned them:

from great men a city is destroyed, and into the slavery
of a single ruler [*monarchos*] by ignorance the *demos* falls.
Once a man is raised too high, it is not easy to restrain him
thereafter. Now is the time to see all this coming.

(fr. 9.3–6 West)

Once Peisistratus gained power, Solon blamed the *demos*:

If you have suffered terrible things through your own baseness (*kakotês*),
do not put the blame for this on the gods.
For you yourselves increased these men, giving pledges,
and through these things you have evil slavery . . .
You look to the tongue and to the words of a flattering man,
but do not look to the deed that arises.

(fr. 11 W)

The *demos* voted Peisistratus a bodyguard of club-bearers, and when he seized the Acropolis they did not besiege him as they had besieged Cylon (Hdt. 1.59). These data support Aristotle's claim (*Pol.* 1305a) that the *demos* trusted Peisistratus, and the view of *Ath. Pol.* (14.1) that he was *dêmotikôtatos*, "most inclined to the *demos*" (see Lavelle 2005). As Salmon notes (1997: 70), the sources indicate no popular opposition to the Peisistrateans until their overthrow. By contrast, if some of Athens' aristocrats briefly cooperated – Peisistratus' marriage to the daughter of Megacles, head of the Alcmaeonid *genos*, quickly collapsed (Hdt. 1.60.2) – rival aristocrats mostly hated tyrants and tried to kill them. Megarian aristocrats killed Theagenes; Mytilene's aristocrats killed Myrsilos; Athenian aristocrats Harmodios and Aristogeiton killed Hipparchos and tried to kill Hippias, Peisistratus' successors. Bodyguards, including

Myrsilos' spear-bearers (Alc. fr. 60), Cleisthenes of Sicyon's club-bearers (Pollux 3.83; 7.68), and Peisistratus' club-bearers, aimed to protect tyrants against murderous aristocrats. By contrast, the unprejudiced use of the word "tyrant" in classical poetry and tragedy has preserved archaic usage, reflecting the early, positive period of tyranny (Andrewes 1956: 23).

If for these early *demoi* tyrants did not constitute a further abusive regime but relief from abuse, the power of the masses underscores the dynamics of tyrant rule. Already in our earliest evidence, the community – "the *demos*," "the *polis*" – played an important role in community affairs, sometimes installing what Aristotle called democracies (as in Megara) by the later seventh century.[10] Although scholars have not yet reached consensus on this point, no source indicates that these *demoi* were limited to the hoplite class. Spinning a tale of life on Crete, Homer's Odysseus remarks that, although he was unwilling to fight at Troy, "the harsh voice of the *demos* compelled me" (*Od.* 14.239). Our earliest inscription, from mid-seventh century Dreros in Crete, begins "This has been decided by the *polis*" (ML 2). Early regimes should not be called "aristocracies" without configuring the power of popular assemblies (e.g., *Od.* 16.370–82), free speech, resistance to elite abuse, and pervasive mentalities of personal independence among the Greek populace (Raaflaub and Wallace 2007). If early *demoi* were not necessarily ready to govern themselves, they did demand a voice in determining who would govern them. Mass support for popular tyrants helped unify the polis and showed the *demos* what communal action could accomplish.

Lawgivers

For many *poleis*, lawgivers were the alternative to tyrants – a momentous discovery that a few written lines had the strength to regularize justice and even replace governments. As with tyrants, narrative accounts of famous lawgivers are mostly fabricated. Aristotle himself reported of Locri (Gerace) in southern Italy:

> when the Locrians asked the oracle how they might find relief from the considerable turmoil they were experiencing, the oracle responded that they should have laws enacted for themselves, whereupon a certain shepherd named Zaleukos ventured to propose to the citizens many excellent laws. When they learned of these and asked him where he had found them, he replied that Athena had come to him in a dream. As a result of this he was freed and was appointed lawgiver.
>
> (fr. 548 Rose, tr. Gagarin)

History transformed into myth, Szegedy-Maszak (1978: 208) reconstructs the lawgiver's typology: "(1) Initial stage – crisis in the state; rise of one man, uniquely suited for the task of legislation because of his virtue, education and experience. (2) Medial stage – the crisis is suspended; the man is selected to be lawgiver, promulgates the code and triumphs over a challenge to it. (3) Final stage – the crisis is resolved; the code is firmly established, with some provision for its permanence, and the lawgiver departs."

At the same time, such typologies distilled essential realities. Early lawgivers promulgated many laws – although not law codes (Hölkeskamp 1992a: 58–60) – in an effort to diffuse social crises. Although many worked in cities whose histories attracted little attention by ancient scholars, some important evidence is preserved.

As Aristotle noted, early lawgivers were of two types, depending on whether their legislation also revised their cities' polities (*Pol.* 1273b). The first lawgivers he mentions also revised polities. Philolaus, a Bacchiad older than Diocles (Olympic victor in 728), is said to have left Corinth for Thebes and written laws for that city (*Pol.* 1274ab). Aristotle's account is shot through with legend. In particular, Philolaus may exemplify the outside savior: Oedipus, too, left Corinth and rescued Thebes. However, because Aristotle was interested in different ways of distributing landed property, he mentions "some" of Philolaus' measures on "the begetting of children, which the Thebans called 'laws of adoption.' They consist of an enactment, peculiar to Philolaus, designed to keep fixed the number of land lots." As Hölkeskamp says (1992b: 89), the early laws that Aristotle quotes appear to be genuine. This particular measure is constitutional although its purpose is uncertain, targeting either the subdivision or the abandonment of properties. Aristotle does not mention Philolaus' other laws, but he was important enough to attract biographical details. The Thebans still pointed out his tomb in Aristotle's day.

Philolaus' provision echoes another which Aristotle attributes to Pheidon of Corinth, "one of the earliest lawgivers," almost certainly from the Bacchiad period.[11] Pheidon legislated that "the number of houses and the number of citizens should be kept equal, even if to begin with they all had estates of varying magnitude" (*Pol.* 1265b). Both Oost (1972: 13–14) and Hölkeskamp (1999: 153–4) regard this measure as "stabilizing," "conservative." Hölkeskamp (1999: 155–7) suggests that it identified citizenship with land-owning – possibly the first definition of citizenship. All men with property, regardless of size, belonged, and none could be excluded, protecting the farmers but excluding the landless. Salmon (1984: 63–5) canvasses various possible interpretations of this measure, which he seeks to link with land displacements caused by colonization. In any case, this measure patently addressed important social and political problems, although much remains unclear.

Sparta's great reformer Lycurgus also stands at the dawn of history, probably after Sparta's defeat at Hysiae in 669. Few now question Lycurgus' existence, although our sources assign him certain later institutions (Hodkinson 1997). Lycurgus' measures did not regulate justice: Sparta had no such provisions. He is linked with the Great Rhetra ("pronouncement": Plut. *Lyc.* 6) reforming Sparta's constitution. The Rhetra established the dates and times of assembly meetings, fixed the size of the council of elders, and gave the assembled *demos* final authority. In most important seventh-century *poleis*, like Sparta's, articulated governments replaced unstructured aristocracies. Thus, Dreros had a college of Damioi, a council (?) called "the Twenty," and the *kosmos*, a chief official with adjudicatory functions. Basic polis structures were instituted either by lawgivers or by copying the work of lawgivers elsewhere.

Greece's most famous lawgivers were Zaleukos (Hölkeskamp 1999: 187–98) and Charondas of Sicilian Katane (ibid. 130–44). Traditionally, Zaleukos promulgated laws in 662 (Locri was founded in 679 or 673). Charondas may have worked somewhat later. Various laws are attributed to these men, including constitutional measures. Thus, Charondas is said to have regulated participation in the law courts, heavily fining the wealthy if they avoided service, while only lightly fining the poor. Probably their work was linked not with social crises (which moving overseas helped resolve) but with new settlements, often of mixed populations and lacking traditional rules.

Sometime between 682 and 621, the Athenians began appointing six annual *thesmothetai* (*Ath. Pol.* 3.4), literally "lawgivers," a significant misnomer reflecting legislation's new importance throughout Greece. In fact Athens' *thesmothetai* were probably specially designated judges. Their institution reflects the seventh-century panhellenic movement toward regularizing justice.

Rejecting Cylon as tyrant in 632, in 621 the Athenians appointed Draco to write laws (not a constitution: Arist. *Pol.* 1274b), displayed on *axones*, wooden "axles." His appointment reflected pressures from both elite and *demos*. His homicide laws probably addressed ongoing elite violence after Cylon's failed coup (Plut. *Sol.* 12). The severity of his laws, confirmed by Solon who repudiated them (*Ath. Pol.* 7.1), may have reflected an elite reaction against mounting social chaos and any challenge to the traditional order. However, the *demos* also benefited, as the fixed procedures and penalties inherent in written laws necessarily limited arbitrary sentencing. Hesiod had complained of "crooked justice" by "gift-devouring" aristocrats. A generation after Draco, Solon proclaimed that he wrote down laws "alike for elite and *kakoi*, providing straight justice" for all, and legislating that verdicts by officials could be appealed to the *demos* (*Ath. Pol.* 9.1). Although Draco's laws were a step toward equal justice, Solon's *demos* remained concerned about unfair sentencing. Popular discontent forever blackened Draco's reputation. He fell from the group of charismatic lawgivers.

In 594/3, amid a massive uprising against the *eupatridai*, Solon was appointed "reconciler," lawgiver, and chief official, *archon* (Wallace 2007b). He published some hundreds of new laws on at least 21 *axones* (the thirteenth *axôn* contained at least 8 laws), arranged according to the officials charged with enforcing them, and with penalties much less severe than Draco's. For example, the penalty for theft was not death but double the value of a stolen item if recovered, ten times its value if not (frs. 23a–d Ruschenbusch). Detailed measures promoted social order and reflected systematic thought. One law specified the minimum distance from a neighbor's property of a house, wall, ditch, well, beehive, or certain kinds of trees (frs. 60–2 R). Another forbade speaking ill of the dead (fr. 32a R), arguably to curtail violence at elite funerals. Protecting all Athenians, Solon permitted "anyone who wanted" to prosecute crimes affecting the community, in case the immediate victim was weak or helpless (*Ath. Pol.* 9.1). Solon's concern for even the humblest Athenians is ever apparent, also reflecting traditional aristocratic ideologies. Although his source is unknown, Plutarch rightly remarked, "the lawgiver correctly accustomed citizens to understand and sympathize with one another as parts of one body" (*Sol.* 18.6). Solon also radically changed Athens' constitution, institutionalizing the *demos*'s voice and correlating power with wealth (Wallace 2007b).

Finally, as *aisumnêtês* (literally, "umpire") at Mytilene from 597/6 (see below), Pittacus also wrote laws. Aristotle calls him "a craftsman of laws" and quotes one of them; he notes that like Draco Pittacus did not change the constitution (*Pol.* 1274b). Diogenes Laertius says that Pittacus wrote a prose book "on laws for the citizens" (1.79). "When Croesus asked him what was the greatest rule (*archê*), he said the rule of the *poikilon xulon*, the shifting wood, by which he meant the law" (1.77, tr. Hicks). Much is legendary – but no classical laws were painted on wooden *axones*.

Sages

Despite great social progress, by the end of the seventh century tyrannies were mostly proving dysfunctional. Tyrants' autocratic powers sometimes corrupted, reverting to aristocratic abuse and degrading the *demos' timê*. Also, as Aristotle notes (*Pol.* 1312b21–3), most tyrants' sons lacked their fathers' talents. In consequence, many tyrannies were now eliminated and complaints about tyranny become common. At Mytilene no tyrant succeeded Myrsilos. After 597/6 Alcaeus (fr. 348) calls Pittacus "tyrant" to insult him. "Let Pittacus devour the city, as he did with Myrsilos" (fr. 70.7). Theognis repeated that image, calling Megara's tyrant *demophagos*, "people-eating" (1181), both poets turning against tyrants the complaints once heard against Homer's *demoboros* ("*demos*-eating") Agamemnon and Hesiod's "gift-eating" *basilees*. Alcaeus (fr. 296, cf. Sol. fr. 33) mentioned that Antileon tyrant of Chalcis had been skinned alive. In 594/3, despite some people's appeals, Solon refused a tyranny (Plut. *Sol.* 13–14) and granted amnesty to all disenfranchised persons (*atimoi*) except killers or would-be tyrants (19.4). "If I spared my fatherland and did not grasp the implacable violence of tyranny, bringing stain and disgrace upon my good name, then I am not at all ashamed. That way I think all people will win" (fr. 32 West). As we saw, he warned the *demos* against Peisistratus, of "slavery under a *monarchos*. Once a man is raised too high, it is not easy to restrain him" (fr. 9 W). At Corinth Periander came to employ a bodyguard as his father had not (Arist. *Pol.* 1315b.). In a famous story (e.g., Hdt. 5.92) Thrasyboulos tyrant of Miletus recommended that he lop off the heads of prominent citizens, whether to eliminate hostile aristocrats or to promote equality (so Arist. *Pol.* 1284a). No tyrant succeeded Periander's nephew Psammetichos, who ruled only three years, until 582 (Arist. *Pol.* 1315b26):

> He was tyrant over the Corinthians until some of them joined together and killed him after he had held the tyranny for a short while, and freed the city. The *demos* tore down the house of the tyrants and made public their property; they threw [Psammetichos'] body out of the country without burial, dug up the graves of his ancestors, and cast out their bones.
>
> (Nicolaus *FGrH* 90 F 60.1)

They also removed Cypselus' name from their treasury at Delphi (Plut. *Mor.* 400de).

These reversals account for our sources' schizoid assessment of the early tyrants. Herodotus' account of Cypselus and Periander is mostly negative: "anything Cypselus had left undone in the way of killing or banishing, Periander completed for him" (5.92). Yet, as we have noted, his narrative of baby Cypselus' survival and rise to power is positive, as are early sources for Periander. As Salmon says (1997: 62), "it is most unlikely that favorable traditions about tyrants were invented" after tyrants were discredited. Stories of Cypselus' and Periander's cruelties reflect revisionist, anti-tyranny sentiment starting in the early sixth century.

As for laws, they were not discredited but proved inadequate to resolve social problems. Solon's contemporary Anacharsis allegedly observed that they were like spiderwebs, snaring the weak but torn to pieces by the rich and powerful (Plut. *Sol.* 5.2–3).

At this time of crisis and stalemate, a new charismatic figure appeared: the sage or *sophos*.[12] Although twenty-seven men came to be called *sophoi* (D.L. 1.42), the core group included Thales of Miletus, Pittacus of Mytilene, Bias of Priene (near Miletus), Kleoboulos tyrant of Lindos on Rhodes, Solon of Athens, and Periander tyrant of Corinth. Their traditional number seven, first attested in Plato (*Prt.* 343c), was unknown to Herodotus (1.29).

Although many legends accrued to the *sophoi*, the original and most famous *sophoi* were a historical early-sixth-century phenomenon. Of the core six, four came from Ionia, and all were active between 597 and 582. No later fabricator would have limited the group to so narrow a period or region. Solon governed in 594/3. Pittakos was *aisumnêtês* for ten years from 597/6. Periander lived until 585. Bias lived at the time of Alyattes, who ruled ca. 610–580. Thales was linked with the eclipse of 585 (Hdt. 1.74). Diogenes Laertius 1.22 states that he was first to be called *sophos*, and in Damasias' archonship (582/1) "the epithet was applied to all the seven, as Demetrius of Phaleron says." According to Clement of Alexandria (*Strom.* 1.129) citing the fourth-century dramatist Andron, "those enrolled with Thales as *sophoi* were synchronous with him." In addition, the semi-legendary *sophos* Anacharsis is said to have visited Athens in 592–588 (D.L. 1.101); as we shall see, he was associated with the group by the mid-sixth century. Although Chilon may have been ephor in 556 (D.L. 1.68), in Herodotus (1.59) he is prominent at the time of Peisistratus' birth in the early sixth century. The obscure *sophos* Myson of Chên – a place even the ancients could not locate – was known to the sixth-century Ionian poet Hipponax as "he whom Apollo named the wisest of men" (D.L. 1.107). The panhellenic prestige of the core six soon attracted outside figures like Chilon, included because of traditions of Spartan wisdom. Lycurgus was patently too early.

The core *sophoi* are also represented as a group, most famously in the story of the tripod (see below). Plato (*Prt.* 343a) says they met at Delphi to dedicate the first fruits of their wisdom.

Periander supplies one final argument for the historicity of the early *sophoi*. His mediation – as we shall see, a classic function of *sophoi* – between Athens and Mytilene in 607/6 indicates that so far from being judged abusive, he succeeded in (re)presenting himself as *sophos* when that type emerged. Kleoboulos tyrant of Lindos presumably did the same. However, already for Solon "tyrant" and *sophos* clashed. Periander's self-transformation was quickly forgotten, and he was soon blackened by sixth-century hostility to tyrants. From this time on, he could never have been listed as *sophos*.

The one quality the *sophoi* shared was wisdom, although none was an ivory-tower philosopher, a type invented by Plato (Dicaearchus of Messene in D.L. 1.40; Nightingale 2000: 138–9). To be sure, Thales worked on philosophical and cosmological problems (D.L. 1.23–4), probably influenced by eastern wisdom traditions. Herodotus actually calls him "Phoenician by remote descent" (1.170, cf. D.L. 1.22). As Nightingale notes, however, he becomes an impractical contemplative first in Plato (*Theaet.* 174a–b). The *sophoi* cultivated useful wisdom. Plutarch writes, "in philosophy, like most of the wise men of that age, Thales was concerned above all with applying morals to politics . . . he seems to have been the only sage of that period who pursued his speculations beyond the limits of strictly practical problems; all the rest gained their reputation for wisdom from their prowess as statesmen" (*Sol.* 3). Thales reportedly advised the Milesians not to ally with Croesus (D.L. 1.25), and the Ionians to create a federation with a common government at Teos (Hdt. 1.170). Bias responded to Persian conquest by suggesting that the Ionians emigrate en masse to Sardinia (Hdt. 1.170).

So far from absent-minded, *sophoi* are also associated with "cunning intelligence," *mêtis*.[13] Pittacus used a concealed net to defeat an opponent; Kleoboulos' daughter was nicknamed *Eumêtis*; Solon feigned madness to convince the Athenians to attack Salamis (an illegal proposal); Thales anticipated a good year for olives and rented all the oil mills, scoring a fortune; Bias saved Priene from Alyattes' siege by sending out two fattened mules, implying that even Priene's animals were well fed. Although a dark streak can be detected in some of these episodes, most involved good causes. "It is also said that Bias was a very effective pleader; but he was accustomed to use his powers of speech to a good end" (D.L. 1.84).

Amid corrupted tyrannies and ineffective legislation at the end of the seventh century, *sophoi* opened a third path, above all to reconciliation. The *sophos* Solon promised Athens' aristocracy he would not become tyrant; he promised the *demos* redress for their economic, judicial, and political grievances. In consequence, *demos* and elite together appointed him *diallaktês*, "reconciler." His poetry repeatedly proclaims his mediating role. If anyone else had gained his post,

> he'd not have held the people back, nor stopped
> until he'd stirred the milk and lost the cream.
> But I took up my post in No-Man's Land
> just like a boundary stone.
>   (fr. 37.6–10)

> Both sides I strove to surround with a strong shield.
> I did not permit an unjust victory to either's demands.
>   (fr. 5)

> Yet had another held the goad as I,
> a man of bad intent and filled with greed,
> would he, like me, have held the people back?
> Had I supported what then pleased their foes
> or even what their own extremists planned,

> Athens had been bereaved of many men.
> Therefore I warded off from every side,
> a wolf at bay among the packs of hounds.
>
> (fr. 36.20–6)

According to *Ath. Pol.* 5.2, one poem "argues the case of each side in turn against the other and goes on to exhort them to join in putting an end to the quarrel that had arisen."

Similarly, in 597/6 at Mytilene the *demos* appointed the *sophos* Pittacus *aisumnêtês*, "umpire" for ten years. Alcaeus begged them not to do so (fr. 74), and when they persisted he lamented: "they established Pittacus the base-born as tyrant of the gutless and ill-starred city, praising him greatly all together (*aolles*)" (fr. 348). Along with Solon's poems on Peisistratus, these lines clearly document the early *demos*'s power.[14] Pittacus had collaborated with the tyrant Myrsilos. He had engaged in aristocratic strife and helped kill the tyrant Melanchros. After 597, however, we hear only that he foreswore violence, freeing the killer of his son Tyrraios ("better to pardon now than repent later": D.L. 1.76), and arresting but releasing his enemy Alcaeus ("pardon is better than punishment": D.L. 1.76, Diod. 9.12.3). Alcaeus fr. 70 confirms that, although of Thracian blood, he married a Penthilid, from the former ruling *genos*. Diodorus writes, "Pittacus was admired for his *sophia* . . . In his dealings with individual citizens he was affable and kindly, and he freed his native land from the three greatest evils, tyranny, civil strife, and war" (9.11.1). Valerius Maximus (4.1 ext. 6) preserved the tradition that "Pittacus had a heart full of moderation."

It is further intriguing that the two cities known to have appointed *sophoi* as reconcilers had earlier appointed Periander *sophos* to mediate their dispute over Sigeion. According to Himerios (*Or.* 28.2, p. 128 Colonna = Alc. fr. 448), "Alcaeus sang the glory of Thales, in the panegyric of Lesbos." If so, even a murderous aristocrat now commended a *sophos*.

A third, although fictional, example of the type is Cretan Thales.[15] Plutarch writes:

> One of those regarded as *sophos* and *politikos* was Thales, whom Lycurgus persuaded, out of favor and friendship, to come to Sparta. Now Thales appeared to be a poet of lyric songs and screened himself behind this art, but in reality he did the work of one of the mightiest lawgivers. For his odes were speeches exhorting to good obedience and civic harmony, through songs and rhythms having much of the orderly and tranquility, so that those who listened to them were insensibly softened in their characters, and renouncing the mutual bad feelings so rife at the time, lived together in the common pursuit of what was fair. In some way, therefore, Thales was a forerunner of Lycurgus and his education.
>
> (*Lyc.* 4)

Probably from the start *sophoi* were linked with "apophthegms," pithy phrases advocating restraint, moderation, and wisdom. Clement (*Strom.* 5.8.44) cites from Pherecydes of Syros – Pherecydes flourished ca. 544 or earlier, and was himself sometimes counted a *sophos* (D.L. 1.116–22) – that "Anacharsis the Scythian, when going to sleep, held his private parts with his left hand and his mouth with his right, riddling that one must control both, but it was better to control the tongue than pleasure." If Clement cites correctly, Anacharsis was known as *sophos* already by the mid-sixth century.[16] Plato's Socrates remarks that in the past some people realized

> that to frame such utterances is a mark of the highest culture . . . Among these were Thales, Pittacus, Bias, our own Solon, Kleoboulos, and Myson, and a Spartan, Chilon . . . Their wisdom consisted of pithy and memorable dicta . . . They met together and dedicated the first-fruits of their wisdom to Apollo . . . inscribing these words which are on everyone's lips: "Know thyself" and "nothing too much" . . . In particular this saying of Pittacus, "hard is it to be noble," got into circulation privately and earned the approval of the wise.
>
> (*Prt.* 343a)

In the hellenistic era, some 147 *apophthegmata* of the *sophoi* were inscribed around the Greek world, as far as Aï Khanoum in northern Afghanistan (Oikonomides 1980; see Stobaeus 3.1.172). Many reflect traditional wisdom: "most men are bad" (Bias, cf. *Od.* 2.277); "nothing too much" (cf. *Theog.* 335); Chilon's "call only the dead happy," echoing Herodotus' Solon (1.32). Moral proverbs advocating good behavior supplemented written laws, which did not begin to regulate private conduct until the second half of the fourth century.

Finally, contrasting with the tyrant's now debased image, the *sophoi* are represented as neither vain nor greedy. In a famous story (e.g., D.L. 1.27–8), Milesian fishermen recovered a golden tripod from the sea. The Milesians sent to Delphi to discover its owner, and were told it belonged to the wisest man. They gave it to Thales, who passed it to another *sophos*, and so on. Finally, Thales (or another) deposited it at Delphi. Resistance to greed is probably an original component of the *sophos* type. Solon wrote: "wealth I desire to have, but wrongfully to get it I do not wish. Justice, even if slow, is sure" (fr. 13.7–8). "For often evil men are rich and good men poor; but we will not exchange with them our virtue for their wealth, since one abides always, while riches change their owners every day" (fr. 15). Solon surrendered power after his year of office; so did Pittacus after his ten. Diogenes Laertius (1.75, cf. Plut. *De mal. Hdt.* 858b) writes that afterwards

> Pittacus received from the people of Mytilene a grant of land, which he dedicated as sacred domain . . . Sosicrates relates that he cut off a small portion for himself and pronounced the half to be more than the whole. Furthermore, he declined an offer of money made him by Croesus, saying that he had twice as much as he wanted; for his brother had died without issue and he had inherited his estate.

Other qualities were attributed to some *sophoi*, including lawgiving (D.L. 1.40), for example by Pittacus and Solon. Stobaeus (3.1.172) attributes to Periander the proverb "Keep to old law but fresh fish." In addition, ever since Odysseus – "many were they whose cities he saw, whose minds he learned of" (*Od.* 1.3) – and Gilgamesh, wandering to learn or teach was linked with wisdom. Solon, Thales, and Anacharsis all reportedly wandered.[17] Anacharsis represents a related type, the foreign wisdom expert, some of them listed as *sophoi*. Epimenides of Crete (Maeandrius counted him *sophos*: D.L. 1.41) reportedly helped the Athenians before Solon.

The *sophos*-type proved influential, not least for sixth-century tyrants. Although we cannot document "some people's" claim (D.L. 1.122) that Peisistratus was *sophos*, that claim remains significant, suggesting that like Periander and Kleoboulos, some people repackaged Athens' tyrant as sage. More impressively, in [Plato] *Hipparchos*, a quality dialogue of the later fourth century, Peisistratus' son Hipparchus set up herms on the roads around Attica, inscribed with pithy sayings: "Walk thou with honest thoughts," "Do not deceive a friend" (229a–b). He and his brother reconciled with their political enemies in what Wade-Gery called "a union of hearts" (see ML 6). Thus Hipparchus also reconfigured himself as sage. Lasos of Hermione, a music theorist at the Peisistratid court, was also the author of pithy witticisms ("Lasismata") and was sometimes counted a *sophos* (D.L. 1.42). Although the later impact of the *sophos*-type cannot be considered here, the fifth-century "sophists" (Plato's term) in fact called themselves *sophoi* and were wandering thinkers, offering among other things practical counsel in governing. When Socrates doubted Delphi's claim that he was the wisest man, he was appropriating the tripod-tradition of the early *sophoi*.

Conclusion

This chapter has examined the emergence of three powerful seventh-century types: tyrant, lawgiver, and sage. The appeal of charismatic individuals is evident down through Greek history. A hero was a mortal deemed so great that his bones forever possessed magic powers. At Mytilene, Myrsilos was thus honored, as was Pittacus (D.L. 1.175). A sacred precinct, the "Teutameion," was dedicated to Bias son of Teautames (D.L. 1.88). Settlements abroad were led not by communities but by a "founder," *oikistês*, many also receiving heroic honors (Malkin 1987: 210). The oikist "occupies the position of the consensual social arbitrator, similarly occupied by formal 'arbitrators' and lawgivers such as Pittacus or Solon and emulated by tyrants" (Malkin 2002b: 216). Archaic *demoi* empowered charismatic individuals especially during social crises. Lawgivers promised straight justice or fair government. Tyrants promised to end elite violence and rule in the *demos*'s interest, toward peace and prosperity. In Herodotus, we have seen, the Medes appointed Deioces so they could "get on with [their] work under orderly government, and not lose [their] homes altogether in the recent chaos." But laws proved weak and some tyrants turned abusive. *Sophoi* met with better success. After Pittacus, Mytilene's aristocracy did not resume internecine violence. After Solon, Athens' aristocracy did revert to violence, and the *demos* responded by installing a tyrant. However, Peisistratus promised to work for them, to obey Solon's laws, and to retain Solon's governmental institutions. His rule was later judged a Golden Age (*Ath. Pol.* 16.7; [Pl.] *Hipparch.* 229b). The aristocrats eliminated his sons, elite in-fighting resumed, and the *demos* finally seized power.

If tyranny was an ambiguous legacy of archaic Greece, written laws were a permanent contribution. The *sophoi* caught everyone's imagination. Their intellectual and political descendants were active down through the fifth century. As literary figures, as Plutarch's *Banquet of the Seven Sages* makes clear, they flourished into the Roman period.

NOTES

1 For the (often left-leaning) scholars supporting this interpretation of tyranny, see Andrewes 1956: e.g. 36–8 ("mainly hoplite revolutions"); Finley 1970 [1981]: 102–5; Ste. Croix 1981: 278–83; Murray 1993: 143–58; Salmon 1997; J.-P. Wilson, *CR* 50 (2000) 641 ("strong evidence . . . of a reciprocal relationship between tyrant and *demos*"); and cf. Meier 1990a: 48 ("those who espoused the people's cause were usually intent upon tyranny"). Unattributed translations are my own, often adapted from standard versions.

2 For this view of tyranny see Berve 1967; Pleket 1969; Libero 1996: 400–2 (and e.g. 226–7 on Theagenes of Megara); Anderson 2005: 193–8; and references in Stein-Hölkeskamp 1996: 655 n. 15; cf. Drews 1972. For lawgivers, see esp. Hölkeskamp 1992b ("the image of the great lawgiver" was "a philosophical and historiographical construct," "a pseudo-historical invention": 88); 1999; and e.g. Anderson 2005: 179.

3 On Solon's fictional biography, see Raaflaub 1996b: 1035–8; for lawgivers, see Szegedy-Maszak 1978 and below.

4 For more detailed discussion, see Raaflaub and Wallace 2007: ch. 2; Stein-Hölkeskamp 1989 esp. part III "Die Aristokraten in der archaischen Gesellschaft."

5 Also Sarpedon at *Il.* 12.310–21. Compare Pindar *Pyth.* 10.110–11: "among the *agathoi* [the nobility] lies the careful ancestral governing of cities."

6 For details, see Wallace 2007a.

7 Not foreign mercenaries: Lavelle 1992.

8 Nic. Dam. fr. 61.4; cf. Paus. 6.19.1–4 (including an inscription) with Griffin 1982: 40–2.

9 Van Wees (1999a: 34–5) discusses this breakdown of relations between rich and poor.

10 *Pol.* 1302b30, 1304b34–40, cf. 1300a16–9; for details, see above all Robinson 1997; Raaflaub and Wallace 2007.

11 Oost 1972: 13; Salmon 1984: 63–5; Hölkeskamp 1999: 151.

12 Compare Meier 1990a: 41–43, mentioning the contribution of the sages and others in the emergence of political thought and as political conciliators. The dense and wide-ranging section including these remarks ("The Social History of Political Thought as the Engine of Change": 40–52) repays careful study.

13 Detienne and Vernant 1974: 42–3, 291–2; Nightingale 2000: 141–2.

14 Quite possibly because of Pittacus' success, *aisumnêtai* later became regular officials, in sixth-century Miletus, Cumae, Olympia, and elsewhere. An early fifth-century inscription from Teos forbids the appointment of an *aisumnêtês* even if the majority (*polloi*) wish it (for references, see Faraguna 2005).

15 Apparently Tynnondas of Euboea was also this type (Plut. *Sol.* 14), but little is known of him.

16 "The factual basis of [Anacharsis's story] may be impossible to recover, but there is no reason to doubt that it had one": J. G. F. Powell (*CR* 32 [1982] 203), reviewing J. F. Kindstrand, *Anacharsis: The Legend and the Apophthegmata* (Uppsala 1981). Kindstrand supposed that Anacharsis was a shaman. See Hartog 2001: 108–16 for Anacharsis in Greek culture.

17 E.g., D.L. 1.43–4; Hdt. 1.29–30; 2.177.2; 4.76; see Lloyd 1975: 49–60; Montiglio 2000.

CHAPTER TWENTY-TWO

Sanctuaries and Festivals

François de Polignac

The Age of Sanctuaries

The archaic period might be called the "age of sanctuaries" in the Greek world. No other phase of Greek history saw so many new sacred spaces appear in most areas, and many of these remained in use for most of antiquity. This trend can partly be ascribed to the creation of new settlements, as a result of the greater density of occupation in most parts of continental Greece and the Aegean and of course the so-called colonization movement on various shores of the Mediterranean. But demography and the history of settlement provide only a partial explanation. New sanctuaries appear in places that had long been inhabited, and new types of sanctuaries are created, such as the Thesmophoria, frequented only by women honoring Demeter Thesmophoros. The change is therefore also of a different kind.

The absence or scarcity of identifiable sanctuaries does not necessarily reflect the absence or rarity of religious practices; it may mean that these practices cannot be easily distinguished from other types of activity at this particular stage of a society's history. However, the formal appearance of spaces clearly and exclusively devoted to cult does imply that religious activities in general, and more specifically the cults associated with these places, receive a new visibility and autonomy, and consequently a new social significance. It is to these spaces only that the terms "sanctuary" or "cult place" can be applied. Archaeologists usually identify them by the very specific nature of the finds: concentrations of ashes, burnt material, bones, and artifacts such as fine ceramics, figurines and bronzes found in assemblages quite distinct from those found in domestic or other mundane contexts. The identification is sometimes made easier by specific forms of architecture or furbishing: built altars, enclosure walls, temples, small shrines or other kinds of buildings. But it must be stressed that temples or buildings are not necessary to define a sanctuary and are not always attested: many small sanctuaries retained a very simple open-air form throughout their existence, and some important sanctuaries, such as Olympia, remained without temple for quite a long time.

It is true that the number of cult places dating back to the Bronze Age or Early Iron Age known through archaeological discoveries has greatly increased recently. Only a handful were known some twenty or thirty years ago; continuity or discontinuity between Bronze Age cults and archaic sanctuaries was a highly controversial issue, with much debate revolving around a very few cases. These discussions, insofar as they aimed to identify a general trend, are outdated. There is now enough evidence to illustrate every conceivable situation from, at one end of the spectrum, clear and long-lasting continuity on the same spot between a Bronze Age, Iron Age and historical cult – the sanctuary at Kato Syme in Crete, known as a cult place of Hermes and Aphrodite in historical times, and the cults of Apollo Maleatas on Mount Kynortion near Epidaurus and of Aphaea on the island of Aigina are representative cases, despite periods when cult activity seems to decline – to, at the other extreme, the creation in the archaic period of a new sanctuary on a site never before occupied.[1]

In between, various intermediate situations have been identified, though the state of the archaeological documentation does not always allow us to make clear-cut distinctions between them. Some sanctuaries were founded in new locations shortly after the collapse of the Mycenean palatial system, as part of the changes in political situation and settlement patterns in the last century of the Late Bronze Age: one might mention the sanctuaries at Kalapodi near Hyampolis (commonly identified as the sanctuary of Artemis Elaphebolos, on the northern limit of later Phocis), of Athena Itonia at Philia in Thessaly, or Kommos and quite a few other sanctuaries in Crete.[2] From the eleventh century onwards, cults were also established at former Bronze Age sites which had been abandoned (or frequented only in a very discrete way) sometimes for a short while (perhaps one or two generations in the case of the sanctuaries of Poseidon at Isthmia or Apollo at Amyclae near Sparta), sometimes for a much longer period (several centuries in the case of Olympia and its Middle Helladic village). In some of these cases, the new cult marks the return of religious activities, or at least its return to a more visible form if one supposes some kind of undetectable frequentation, on the site of a Bronze Age sanctuary whose memory had been kept: this relative continuity seems attested at Amyclae, for instance. But most cases are ambiguous, since no clear trace of religious activity has been identified in the Bronze Age levels preceding the sanctuary; Isthmia for example is established in the eleventh century on top of a small settlement, far from any palatial centre, where no evidence of cult has been found (Morgan 1999b). For the sanctuaries similarly appearing later in the ninth and eighth centuries at the site of Mycenean settlements, like Delphi, Eleusis, Delos, the Heraion at Prosymna in Argolis, the distance in time raises questions about the forms of transmission of religious tradition and cultic continuity *stricto sensu* when no material trace can be identified.

In fact, one must not focus on the question of apparent continuity or discontinuity, since the real issue is to understand why cults become more visible and formalized at a given place and time, whether this process results from the revival or reshaping of a pre-existing but discrete or decayed religious activity or from the creation of a brand new cult place. Various attempts have been made to understand which factors would make a cult more or less visible in the Early Iron Age. It has been often noted, for instance, that most cult places known at that time are situated outside settlements, and usually in regions where no large and dominant settlement played the role of a central place: the sanctuary in these cases functions as a central gathering place for the inhabitants of the settlements in its neighborhood and sometimes in distant areas as well – Olympia, Isthmia, the sanctuaries of Apollo on Mount Kynortion and of Artemis at Kalapodi, Kato Syme in Crete clearly illustrate this role in the social organization of more or less wide areas, and they had no strict equivalent in Argolis or Attica where important settlements were already exercising some influence on the regional organization. Conversely, formal sanctuaries within settlements seem rare, except in Crete. The idea that cults were one of the activities performed in or around buildings associated with the local "chiefs" or *basileis*, whether they were the "rulers' dwellings," as Alexander Mazarakis-Ainian put it (Mazarakis Ainian 1997), or rather large "halls" for the gathering and banqueting of the local élite, as in the case of the long apsidal buildings found at Lefkandi in Euboea or at Thermos in Aetolia, may help to explain the absence of distinct sanctuaries in some proto-urban or small settlement contexts. Similarly, cults practiced by women, like those in honor of Demeter Thesmophoros mentioned above, may have been celebrated in domestic contexts before their formalization in specific sanctuaries: the famous terracotta models of granaries found in the tombs of wealthy Athenian women of the ninth century might illustrate the connection of women with the growth of grain and the goddess who cared for it, before it was transferred to a more public expression in proper cult places.

The religious life in Iron Age Greece might thus correspond to the double ritual context depicted in the *Odyssey* (3.1–67, 404–72; Sourvinou-Inwood 1993: 2–4). When Telemachus arrives at Pylos during his visits to former companions of his father, he finds king Nestor performing a large sacrifice to Poseidon on behalf of all the cities of the kingdom and in front of all the Pylians; this cult takes place outdoors, on the seashore – an external location typical of the large collective gathering and where altars and sacrificial remains would allow its identification as a cult place. Later, back in Pylos, Nestor has a cow sacrificed in honor of Athena, and this sacrifice takes place in front of his palace; the king, his sons and Telemachus attend to the ceremony, then the sacrificial meat is shared by the participants in the banquet inside the palace. The banquet, which plays an essential part in establishing and entertaining relations within the elite, is also a sacrificial meal, but there is no separate cult place.

This hypothesis however cannot account for all the diverse situations. A few urban sanctuaries are known as well, and all cults were not necessarily under the control of a local chief; different forms of social organization of cult may also have existed even if they are hard to identify. This is why the debate on continuity, whatever the currently dominant view (there are distinct pendulum swings in the historiography), does not really affect the analysis of sanctuaries in the archaic period, when formal visibility becomes the rule for cults at most levels. If this change does not necessarily correspond to the creation of new cults, it certainly reflects a more general change in the nature of the relation to the sacred in society, and the expression of new needs and new functions, which the historian must try to identify.

Hierarchies and Functions:
Apollo Ptoios as a Case Study

In the study of classical Greek religion, a common approach to defining functional distinctions and hierarchies between sanctuaries is to evaluate the relation between the cults and the polis. On the one hand, the civic cults which defined the religious identity of each polis were controlled by the city itself; all cities, large or small, had sanctuaries which were the symbols of their civic identity and unity, whether on their acropolis, in their urban space or in their territory. On the other hand, there were also cults whose functions, audience and sometimes administration were situated either on higher levels, including cities in larger units, or lower levels, including smaller groups within the city. Among the former were, naturally, the great panhellenic sanctuaries such as Olympia, with its famous games, or Delphi, with its renowned oracle. There were also sanctuaries which gave a religious identity and unity to whole regions and groups of cities, like Delos for the Ionians in the Aegean, or Thermos for the Aetolians. In most of these cases – except Delos when the Athenians took control of the sanctuary – the activity and influence of the sanctuary were not completely subordinated to the politics and the culture of a single city, even when its administration belonged to one polis (for example Elis for Olympia). Other sanctuaries, on the contrary, owned by powerful cities, were used by them to reinforce their international prestige and influence in the Greek world, such as Isthmia where the Corinthians held the panhellenic Isthmian games, the Heraion at Prosymna where the Argives displayed their control over the Argive plain and organized their own games, or, in a different way, the sanctuary of Demeter at Eleusis whose famous Mysteries greatly enhanced the religious prestige of Athens. At the other end of the scale, one would find the purely local cults of restricted range, such as the cults of the Attic demes, and the cults of the various associations which played an important part at the junction between public and private.[3]

The value of this approach is debatable, since it appears a bit too schematic to give a satisfactory account of the diversity of cult organization in classical Greece. But more fundamentally, it is inadequate for an understanding of cults and sanctuaries in archaic Greece. It presupposes a fully developed conception of "civic" affairs, and a clear-cut distinction between various levels and types of communities and collective organizations – two requisites that do not correspond to the realities of archaic societies. The example of the sanctuary of Apollo Ptoios (or Ptoieus) in Boeotia, which too seldom receives as much attention as its importance and interest deserve, will show the diversity of functions a sanctuary could fulfill simultaneously or at different times, and its entanglement in various and evolving relations within and between different communities (see figure 22.1).[4]

This sanctuary sheltered a renowned oracle whose activity is well attested in classical and hellenistic literature and incriptions. It is located in the mountains which form the northern border of the Theban plain, beside a road which linked the plain to the districts further north, along the Euboean strait, which belonged to Locris in the classical period. More precisely, the sanctuary is at the southern end of the

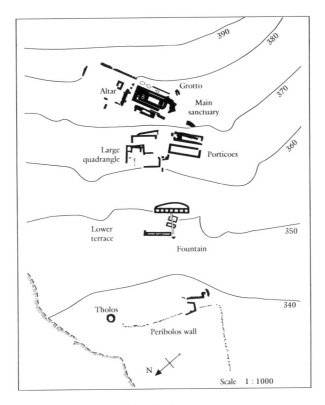

Figure 22.1 Plan of the sanctuary of Apollo Ptoios
Source: After Ducat (1971).

narrow gully at the foot of Mount Ptoion which allows the road to pass through the mountain. Though not very far from the settlement of Acraephia, some 2 miles west as the crow flies, the sanctuary stands isolated, on the eastern bank of the ravine. The appearance of the cult, at the end of the eighth century, is clearly related to the existence of the road and to relations with the northern regions. The cult indeed does not start as a modest local practice which might later have gained more importance and a wider audience. A few but remarkable prestige offerings are to be found among the very first votives, especially bronzes (figurines, fragments of tripods, large pins). Some of these have parallels in Thessaly or further north while others illustrate the long-distance exchanges with the Near East in which the Euboeans played an active part at that time and which brought highly praised oriental artifacts to Greece. Especially interesting are a few figurines (sirens, griffins) and handles which adorned oriental bronze cauldrons, testifying to the presence of a prestigious type of offering which can be found only at a very limited number of early archaic sanctuaries, mainly at Olympia, and in lesser quantities at the Heraion on Samos and in the Argolid, at Delphi and on the Athenian Acropolis. The quality of these votives shows that the sanctuary, situated half-way between the Boeotian plains and the Thessalian/Euboean area, was created in an "interregional" context (perhaps under a strong

Thessalian influence) where it stands in a central position: an important break with the classical view which, considering its position in relation with the spatial organization of historical Boeotia and the central role of Thebes, would place it at the periphery, on the border of a territory.

It is tempting to imagine that the interregional audience was attracted by early activity of the oracle at the Ptoion, but judging from the available evidence the cult seems to vanish after one generation and does not resume before ca. 640, thus reopening the question of what makes a cult visible or invisible to archaeologists. Its reappearance is once more signalled by innovative and prestigious offerings: immediately after the sanctuary on Delos, the Ptoion is the second cult place in Greece where the dedication of monumental stone sculptures starts, around 640/630. Both sanctuaries receive the earliest statues of young girls, *korai*, and later the first statues of young men, *kouroi*, whose accumulation in the Ptoion throughout the sixth and early fifth centuries forms an impressive collection (rivalling with that of the Delian sanctuary of Apollo) – about a hundred and twenty statues according to Jean Ducat. Another category of prestigious dedications reappears almost simultaneously in the late seventh century: large bronze tripods, whose metallic parts have usually disappeared but whose existence is known from their stone bases and central supporting columns, which reinforced their monumentality and stability.

But the context of these offerings has changed when compared with the first phase of the sanctuary. Many recent studies have demonstrated that style, especially for sculptures, is an important component in the definition of cultural identities and in the field of competition between élites.[5] The statues found at the Ptoion, though mostly produced locally, show a great stylistic diversity, some with markedly local features, others clearly inspired by Cycladic or Attic models, still others combining all these traditions and influences in various ways. It is therefore most plausible that the Ptoion was regarded as a central place for competitive aristocratic display and public assertion of a special relationship with the god and its oracle through prestigious offerings, and there are several reasons to think that it played this role at least for a large part of Boeotia. No other sanctuary in the region is known to have received monumental sculpture, let alone in such quantity, and the nearby city of Acraephia, though rather important and prosperous during the archaic period, cannot be considered the only source of a monumental display which puts the Ptoion on a par with panhellenic or regional sanctuaries like Delphi or Delos. Nor did Thebes exert any predominant influence in the area before the late sixth century and the Theban presence alone therefore cannot account for the richness of the offerings.

Moreover, the sanctuary was on the border between the two districts which later together formed classical Boeotia, but which during the archaic period were not yet politically unified and retained very distinct historical and cultural traditions, and therefore strongly differentiated identities: the Theban plain in the south-east, centered on Thebes and its "Cadmean" traditions, and the Copais plain with "Minyan" Orchomenos in the west, which remained under Thessalian influence until around 570. The legends of the origins of the sanctuary and its founder, the hero Ptoios, seem originally more oriented towards the area of Orchomenos (Schachter 1981: 58–9), but the cult was also in direct connection with the Theban plain and obviously frequented by Thebans and inhabitants of the neighboring cities. Its "in-between" position again reveals one of the major issues at stake at the sanctuary. As a common sanctuary, it created a cultural community that could acquire some kind of shared identity through its use, and its function as a central place for competitive display also played a unifying role for the élites of the various cities. The Ptoion seems therefore to be one of the places where a Boeotian cultural identity – not yet implying political unification – was progressively elaborated during the archaic period. The final stage in this evolution is the appearance, around 500, of the first dedications by the Boeotians as a group, bearing testimony to the beginnings of the Boeotian confederation (*koinon*) as the result of the process that led from the elaboration of a common cultural identity to political unification under the guidance of Thebes. These offerings however were not dedicated to Apollo himself, but to Athena Pronaia ("in front of the temple"): the Boeotians as a group were at first admitted only, one might say, as far as the threshold. The history of the Ptoion as an official sanctuary of the Boeotian confederacy belongs to later times.

Far from excluding other relations and functions, either on a broader international level or on a more local basis, the role of the Ptoion in the making of a regional identity makes it especially interesting to examine how all these levels were combined within the same sanctuary. On one side, the "central" and independent position of the sanctuary and its oracle (admitting as a hypothesis that this functioned from the time of the visible renewal of the cult in the second half of the seventh century), half-way between the major political centres of the region, attracted members of leading families from other areas who wanted to insert themselves into the Boeotian network of aristocratic relations and competitions to extend their influence: the Alcmeonidae and the Peisistratidae of Athens are thus represented in the second half of the sixth century by the offerings of Alcmeonides, son of Alcmeon and brother of Megacles, and of Hipparchus, son of Peisistratus.

On the other hand, the reinforcement of the local connections of the sanctuary with the city of Acraephia can be traced through the archaic period. The part the Acraephians may have played in the creation and early history of the sanctuary remains obscure, since the cult, as said above, did not appear originally as a purely local concern. The Acraephians are known to have administered the sanctuary and its oracle in the late classical and hellenistic periods; their implication in the archaic period seems plausible, but its nature, extent and evolution are not precisely documented. Some elements however might indicate a stronger presence in the sixth century. Inscriptions of that period show that dedications of statues and tripods were made by Acraephians acting as individuals. But the most interesting change is the creation, at the very beginning of the sixth century, of a sanctuary of the hero Ptoios, the legendary founder of the cult, half-way between the city and the sanctuary of Apollo. A remarkable feature of the new sanctuary, in the second half of the century, is the dedication of tripods that eventually formed a long double row along the entrance; the inscriptions on their supporting columns show that they were all offered by the Acraephians as a collective body. The foundation of the hero cult was therefore an initiative of the polis of Acraephia. Sophisticated stories have been elaborated by some modern scholars to explain the meaning of this foundation, conceiving of the relation between Ptoios and Apollo as one of rivalry and imagining that the local Acraephian hero, first "owner" of the oracle, had been expelled by the god and had taken refuge in the new sanctuary closer to the city.[6] In fact, as all the other examples of roads linking cities to the main sanctuaries in the territory show, it is much simpler and more convincing to explain the official foundation of the hero sanctuary as a landmark symbolizing the strong interest that the city was taking in Apollo's cult. Whether this interest was programmatic, as a claim for a stronger presence of Acraephia in the administration of the sanctuary, or reflected the reality of a closer relationship already established, as in most similar cases, cannot be precisely determined and is of secondary importance here; in any case, however important the involvement of Acraephia, the sanctuary of Apollo was obviously not a purely "civic" sanctuary of the Acraephians. But a clear result of the creation of the new sanctuary was to enhance, through the figure of Ptoios, the local dimension and identity of a cult until then more characterized by its regional and interregional implications and wide-ranging contacts.

Several levels of meaning, audience, and function were therefore imbricated around Apollo and the growing "sacred landscape" which his presence induced. The case of the Ptoion sanctuary points towards several topics to which we shall now turn in order to identify the specificities of archaic sanctuaries and festivals and to analyze their evolution: debate about the validity of notions of central or peripheral situation: questions of communication, competition and identity; and reflections on offerings and their visibility.

Centrality, Territoriality: Changing Paradigms

The focus on the polis has deeply determined our way of analyzing space and using territorial terminology, ancient or modern. Concepts of centre and periphery, territory, limits, borders, seem to coincide perfectly with ancient terms such as *chora* for the cultivated areas surrounding an urban centre or *eschatia* for the faraway areas assimilated to territorial boundaries, often associated with representations of wilderness – perfect grounds for encounters with unsettling and potentially dangerous deities such as Artemis the Huntress, Dionysos or Pan. It is therefore tempting to think that the territorial organization of the polis corresponded with cultural values wich remained unchanged throughout the history of ancient Greece, and that sanctuaries located within a territory or close to its historical borders should always be studied through their relations with the centre on which they depended. Thence the use of terms such as sub-urban or peri-urban, extra-urban, rural or territorial, to classify these sanctuaries.[7] Many of these were viewed as purely local in the first stage of their existence, and their history was one of progressive integration into the larger cultic organization of the city through the archaic period. The well known sanctuary of Artemis at Brauron on the eastern coast of Attica and its full integration into the civic religion of Athens in the sixth century, formalized by the creation of an urban Brauronion and a procession between the city and the coastal sanctuary, is often quoted as an example of this process.

Without denying the coherence of the cultural representations attached to mountainous areas, seashores or other kinds of geographical features which *we* consider as "natural" boundaries when looking out from an urban centre, the case of the Ptoion has shown that one must question the peripheral character "naturally" conferred on sanctuaries located in such areas. As said above, even in mountainous areas or on a seashore, sanctuaries usually correspond to easily accessible places that allowed the gathering of people from surrounding areas and communities, sometimes on a large scale. Recent studies have therefore questioned our spatial paradigms. P. Horden and N. Purcell (2000) have emphasized the importance of maritime "connectivity" in the Mediterranean, and this is obviously true of the ancient Aegean and other parts of ancient Greece. Catherine Morgan has made a plea for a reversal of our viewing of spatial organization in areas not entirely determined by the system of the polis, thus giving to sanctuaries the role of central places for various kinds of exchange, services and shared practices, including cults, a role elsewhere played by urban centers (C. Morgan 2003). But this reversal can also be extended to areas and periods where the organizing power of the cities did play an increasing part from the eighth century onwards, to give a broader view of the processes and issues at stake in the functioning of sanctuaries and celebrations of festivals.

Various types of "sacred centrality" thus appear to function in different contexts and periods. Naturally, some regional cults did occupy a central position amidst the various communities which built a shared cultural identity (and sometimes later a political unity) around them: the sanctuary at Thermos in Aetolia certainly belongs to this category. One of the best examples remains the Heraion in the Argolid, located on a hill from which the goddess overlooked the Argive plain (in the same way as she overlooked the sea in some of her sanctuaries on promontories such as at Perachora or on Cape Lacinion); however, the original extent of the Heraion's centrality in the Late Geometric and archaic period – did it cover the entire plain, including Argos, to whose growing influence the sanctuary would come to testify, or only its eastern communities, strengthening their common identity against Argos? – remains a debated issue.[8] But some of the sanctuaries which Morgan studied to support her analysis present many similarities with the Ptoion example. Such is the case of the sanctuary of Apollo and Artemis at Kalapodi (Hyampolis), on the edge of the valley which links the areas known in historical times as Phocis and Locris. Though the history of the cult starts quite early, at the end of the Bronze Age, or maybe still earlier, the offerings of the late eighth century show striking similarities with those of the Ptoion and denote a similar convergence from both the northern areas, Thessaly and Euboea with their maritime connections, and the more continental areas in the south (C. Morgan 2003: 114–19). Later however, this central position gave way to another perception of the cult. If one accepts the identification with the sanctuary of Artemis Elaphebolos, closely associated with the war which allowed the Phocians to free themselves of Thessalian domination around 570, the sanctuary would have appeared from that time onwards as a sacred protection on the northern edge of Phocis as well as an important gathering place for all Phocians, and thus as a decisive component of their *ethnos* identity as it emerged in the sixth century (Ellinger 1993). On the southern edge of Phocis, Delphi too may owe its initial development to its position at the junction of a dynamic maritime area on one side – in this case the Corinthian gulf which witnessed the rapid expansion of Corinthian activity and influence in the eighth century – and central Greece on the other (Morgan 1990: 113–18, 161–6).

Another type of central sanctuary can be found in the Aegean: Delos, in its "Ionian circle" including the Cyclades and the tips of Attica and Euboea, played an important part in the early history of the surrounding islands, and was more especially at the very heart of the competition between Paros and Naxos. But many other sanctuaries which seem to have been, at least for a while, equally accessible by sea and by land, or even more accessible by sea, well illustrate the necessity to look at ancient Greece from various points of view. The early spatial orientation of the sanctuary of Hera on Samos clearly points towards the seashore, a few hundred meters away south of the cult place: the sea provided the main access to the sanctuary until the late seventh century, and many offerings (full-scale and model ships) and rituals (like the procession which brought a statue of Hera to the sea to be bathed) underline the early maritime connections of the sanctuary (Kyrieleis 1993). The exceptional wealth of the sanctuary in oriental offerings (or Greek imitations) from the late eighth to the late seventh centuries may illustrate the part played by Samian Hera in protecting relations between the Eastern Aegean, Cyprus and the Near East, without the need to postulate frequent visits by Eastern traders.[9] Similarly, the well known sanctuary of the so-called "Polis cave" (which apparently was not a cave, but an open place by the seashore) in Polis Bay on Ithaca, located on an important maritime route and apparently in use during most of the Early Iron Age (Malkin 1998: 94–119), or the large and rich sanctuary recently excavated close to a well protected bay on the small island of Despotiko, not far from Paros, all bear witness to the importance of maritime connections in the history of sanctuaries.

The consequences of the growing influence of cities, starting with the most powerful ones like Corinth, Athens, Argos, and Sparta, from the eighth century onwards, as central places structuring the spatial and cultic organization around them, cannot therefore be reduced to a single process of gradual integration of local cults which eventually produces polis religion as a global and neatly hierarchical system. It played on several levels, in different contexts, and gave birth to a variety of situations, as can be illustrated by a few examples, especially now that recent discoveries have thrown light on the early history of some sanctuaries (Kyrieleis 2002a).

One interesting situation is characterized by the absence of any important city in the immediate vicinity of a sanctuary: Olympia is of course the best known case. As in other areas, the rise of the cult in its historical location, apparently in the eleventh century, can be associated with the regional reorganization of settlement and population patterns in the Western Peloponnese after the destruction of the Mycenaean palace in Pylos and the departure of some of the Pylian populations (the "Neleid migration"). The cult, which seems to have been attracted and stabilized by the presence of a still visible Early Bronze Age tumulus (mid-third millenium BC), was probably frequented by the inhabitants of small settlements dispersed over the area (Kyrieleis 2002b). But it quickly gained a larger audience: from the tenth and still more the ninth centuries onwards, the offerings of bronzes (animal figurines, and later the famous tripod cauldrons which accumulated in the sanctuary throughout the Geometric period) show increasing connections with areas such as Messenia, Arcadia and the Argolid (Morgan 1990: 57–99). For reasons that cannot be determined with precision, Olympia quite early on became a meeting place and site of competition for elites of various parts of the Peloponnese, without any centre of power in its vicinity. This situation brings to mind various questions about the functioning of the sanctuary in early times. Who was responsible for practical matters such as the safety of the sanctuary and its offerings? Who kept the memory of the donors? (The function of sanctuaries as places of memory, especially for the donors of the most prestigious offerings, is an important issue to which we will turn later.) What form did competition between these elites take? The "official" date for the beginning of the Olympic Games, fixed at 776 BC by deduction from the classical Greek calendar based on Olympiads, does not correspond to anything visible in the life of the sanctuary; rather, important new buildings and extensions show that the sanctuary was adapted for public competition, especially through the creation of a stadium, around 700. Several scholars have therefore suggested that the historical games were founded at that time, and were held annually for some twenty years before their transformation into a penteteric festival, thus making the number of Olympiads fit with this new chronology (Mallwitz 1988: 98–101). But the question of the existence of some earlier kind of competition, restricted to elite practices (chariot races?), remains open; anyway, competition is also visible throughout the eighth century in the evolution of tripod offerings towards increasingly monumental, elaborate and decorated artifacts, reaching heights of up to 2.50 m.

In Olympia, as in our Ptoion-case, the presence and activity of local populations cannot be denied but do not take a clearly identifiable shape until a later phase of the sanctuary's history. The traditions about the conflict between the two cities of Pisa and Elis over control of Olympia in the early archaic period are rather vague and cannot be given a precise chronology; but they reveal the claims of locally emerging cities for a greater role and visibility in the sanctuary, its administration and its cults. Quite interestingly, as at the Ptoion, it is the creation (or formal appearance) of a distinct cult at the beginning of the sixth century which officially signals the role played by the Eleans in the administration of the sanctuary. A temple of Hera was built in the northern part of the Altis and this cult was apparently purely or mainly Elean. The building of this temple antedates the building of the temple of Zeus, thus confirming that architectural monumentality and cultic hierarchy should not be systematically equated. Once again, the claim for, or recognition of, an official role in the administration of an interregional (or international) cult plays an important part in the transformation of local communities into more self-conscious cities, but it is the formalization of a secondary cult which defines and symbolizes their civic identity. One might say that, in these cases, it is not the city which contributes to the rise of the sanctuary, but the sanctuary which contributes to the rise of local cities.

Conversely, it is also in the period around 600 BC that important changes show how powerful cities were taking control of external sanctuaries and transforming them into manifestations of their influence, wealth and prestige. These changes modified both the internal organization of the sanctuaries and their territorial orientations, through the creation of sacred ways and processions between city and sanctuary. A classic example has been the sacred way between Athens and Eleusis, whose creation should ideally coincide with the foundation of the urban Eleusinion in Athens and the building of a new Telesterion in Eleusis at the time of Solon; but the chronology of the Eleusinian sanctuary and of the Athenian interventions is not as obvious as once thought. Most illuminating now are the cases of Samos and Miletos. As said before, the earliest orientation of the Samian Heraion was towards the sea, with one minor access route inland, towards the north, added during the seventh century, but a complete reorientation took place at the turn of the seventh and sixth centuries. The road to the sea kept its ritual function, but a sacred way was traced between the city and the sanctuary (some 4 miles away) and led to a new entrance on the eastern side of the sanctuary. Offerings of monumental sculpture by rich Samians (including gigantic *kouroi*) immediately gathered along the avenue between this entrance and the temple (Kienast 1992: 193–8; Duplouy 2006: 190–203). The new sacred way did not modify the "sacred landscape" only in the sanctuary or its immediate vicinity: at the other end, it may have played a role in the creation of a sanctuary of Artemis at the gate of the city (Zapheiropoulou 1997). The case is even clearer for Miletus, thanks to the discoveries made along the sacred way which, by the mid-sixth century at the latest, linked the city to the important sanctuary of Apollo at Didyma, some 10 miles south. The previous access to the sanctuary was apparently through a harbor situated 2 miles to the north-west. The new sacred way was at the origin of the foundation of sanctuaries and meeting places, frequented by religious associations in charge of public cults such as the Molpoi, which were built at regular distances between the city and the sanctuary during the second half of the century. The presence of groups of seated statues of a similar kind in several of these places as well as the ritual songs and dances performed there by the cultic associations reinforced the feeling of cultural continuity all along the road travelled every year by the great civic procession.[10]

Not all situations, however, are as clear-cut as these, and an appropriate analysis of the many different contexts and deities is necessary to understand the role of sanctuaries. In some cases, for instance sanctuaries of Artemis as in Ephesos, Mounichia and Brauron in Attica, or Amarynthos in Euboea, one may wonder about the relation between the symbolic meaning and functional aspect of the proximity of the sea: Artemis, as the goddess of all kinds of transitions, passages and boundaries, can easily stand on a seashore or by a harbor, but does this mean that these sanctuaries effectively served as meeting places between local inhabitants and regular or occasional visitors landing nearby, at least at one stage of their history? If this function ever existed, it left no clear evidence and all these sanctuaries are narrowly associated with the nearest polis from the late archaic period onwards. Quite interesting too is the case of the mountain and hill-top sanctuaries frequently attested in central Greece in the archaic period. Some may have existed in the Early Iron Age, if not earlier (e.g. the Hymettos in Attica); but their most flourishing period covers the late eighth and seventh centuries (Polignac 2002). At that time, they form an almost continous chain in central Greece, from Boeotia to the north-eastern Peloponnese, with frequent visual links between the highest mountain peaks, such as Parnes between

Boeotia and Attica, and perhaps also Cithaeron and Helicon, Hymettos in Attica, Ochi and probably Dirphys in Euboea, Oros in Aegina, Naxos in the Cyclades and so on. In central and eastern Attica, similar cults appear at the same time on many lower summits. Most of these cults were dedicated to Zeus (or Zeus and Hera) and, in view of their position, probably took the form of festivals which periodically gathered the surrounding populations; the visual connections make it tempting to think that these festivals were held at the same moment, especially since they might correspond to seasonal activities in higher zones, such as transhumance. The practicing of cult on Mt. Parnes, for instance, can be related to the seasonal use of the Skourta plateau, on its western slopes, by people coming from Boeotia as well as Attica, when the area was not yet a strategic place disputed by Athens and Thebes for the control of the border between the two regions. These cults would therefore create yet another kind of cultic community independently from city or *ethnos* or regional identity. A notable feature is the diversity in the later evolution of these cults: some retained their importance through their integration in the civic religion of a polis (Zeus Panhellenios at Aegina); some disappeared (Parnes); some survived at a low level or knew some phases of revival as local and rural cults dedicated to Zeus as rain-giver ; and some eventually gained a new importance thanks to a complete reinterpretation of their meaning – a good example would be, if we accept its existence in the archaic period, the Cithairon cult which became, in Late Hellenistic and Roman times, the great pan-Boeotian festival of the Daidala.[11]

To conclude, the spatial paradigm confirms the diversity of cultic communities and identities which could take shape around sanctuaries in the archaic period. The polis was one of them, but others could transcend the polis; though an evolution is often visible towards a greater integration of cults in the civic system, many sanctuaries may have retained for a while a "multi-dimensional" function, serving different kinds of communities simultaneously. The historian must therefore try to identify the various contexts or "horizons" of a cult practice. Besides the spatial paradigm, other elements may help to apprehend this diversity.

Competition, Offerings, and Memory

The spirit of the *agón* is a well known characteristic of Greek culture and the importance of competition has already been mentioned. When dealing with sanctuaries, the idea of competition brings to mind first of all the famous games which were created during the archaic period: the Olympic games, the other panhellenic games – Delphic, Isthmian and Nemean – all founded, according to the traditions, at the beginning of the sixth century, and the games created by an ever increasing number of cities wishing to enhance their prestige and attractiveness, such as the panathenaic games in Athens, to mention only one of the best known. Recent excavations have thrown light on the early history of some of these, often reassessing their chronology: in Olympia, as we saw, but also at Isthmia and Nemea where the evidence for the organization of competitions does not seem to appear before the second quarter or the middle of the sixth century. In Nemea, the excavations underneath the classical "*heróon* of Opheltes" revealed that an artificial mound had been created at that time, in the shape of a funerary tumulus (Miller 2002).[12] Both the stadium and the track for the horse- and chariot-races seem to have been placed originally on either side of this "tumulus," thus consciously imitating the early situation in Olympia. The lowering of the chronology is of some historical significance for the Isthmian games, since the traditional dating would mean that they were a creation of the Cypselid tyrants, while the new date implies that they were founded after the fall of the dynasty (Gebhard 2002). In Delphi too, the traditional view, which associates the creation of the games with the so-called First Sacred War against Krisa and the foundation of the Delphic Amphictyony to rule and protect the sanctuary at the beginning of the sixth century, is far from solidly based, since the "history" of the Sacred War has been heavily reinvented by later propaganda. But the second half of the century undoubtedly witnessed rapidly increasing agonistic activity, which gave to athletes and to the poets who sang their victories a new social importance: the late archaic and early classical period sees the flourishing of the *epinikia*, victory odes, through which the glory and praise of the victor was shared by his fellow-citizens, thus striking a balance between individual glory and the collective pride of the city (Kurke 1991).

Naturally, competitions of all kinds existed in earlier periods, but they were associated instead with funerals of dominant personalities, as in the *Iliad*. Hesiod's testimony about his victory at Amphidamas' funeral in Chalcis and his offering of the tripod he had won to the Muses of the Helicon is corroborated by a few seventh-century bronze cauldrons found in Boeotia and on the Athenian acropolis, which bear a double inscription, one relating to the funeral games where the cauldron had been won and the other to its dedication in the sanctuary (Polignac 2005a: 20–1). The tumuli, whether real or fake, in Olympia and Nemea, may therefore have served to mark a symbolic transition of the *agón* from the funeral to the cultic sphere.

Moreover, games are but one manifestation of the competitive mind. Others played on the generosity and emulation in display of rich and powerful individuals or groups who wished to obtain, reinforce or maintain a high position in society. Recent studies show Greek elites as occupying a constantly renegotiated position won (or lost) through the acquisition (or loss) of prestige by a variety of means, not strictly hierarchized: it was not the hereditary belonging to an established aristocracy which gave power, wealth and prestige; nor did power and wealth guarantee membership in the elite. Only a specific social and public use of wealth, prestige or authority, by whatever process they were gained and maintained, could create the collective recognition of one's belonging to the leading group in the community – in other words, confer the quality of being *aristos*, "best" (Duplouy 2006). Organizing large sacrifices which could feed a fair number of people during the main city festivals, or offering important contributions of any kind for the building of a temple, were obviously good opportunities to prove one's generosity. In this regard, there is no great difference between the Alcmeonidae taking in hand the rebuilding of the temple at Delphi and the Lydian king Croesus contributing lavishly to the building of the celebrated Artemision at Ephesos.

Competition was also embodied by prestige offerings. Whether or not games existed in Olympia before the end of the eighth century (see above), the idea of competition is visible in the cauldron tripods which accumulated there and became especially impressive during the Late Geometric period. At that time, besides Olympia, several other sanctuaries (Isthmia, the Heraion in the Argolid, the Athenian Acropolis, Delphi, Dodona) were receiving the same kind of offerings and can therefore be identified as places where the elites of the major cities were displaying their authority and were competing for prestige, both amongst themselves (between leading families) and on an "international" level. But it was also at this moment that forms of competition widened, revealing possible identifications with new models of society. Thus, the last quarter of the eighth century witnessed the arrival of the first oriental offerings, especially the cauldrons with protomes which were rapidly imitated by Greek bronzesmiths with such skill that it is often difficult to distinguish between genuinely oriental and Greek productions. Since few traditional tripod cauldrons clearly belonging to the early archaic period have been found, it has sometimes been thought that these had been replaced by oriental or orientalizing cauldrons, most fashionable in the "orientalizing period." There are however good reasons to think that both kinds of cauldrons coexisted, embodying different values and images of social prestige. From then onwards, a succession of new kinds of offerings renewed the expression of competition in sanctuaries, especially the monumental sculptures whose importance in the "sacred landscape" from the second half of the seventh century onwards has been noted above, and still later numerous monuments and buildings, including the large temples which allowed whole cities to mark their presence and stake their claims in the sanctuaries they controlled or in international contexts like Delphi and Olympia.

All these facts are well known but raise a few questions. Offerings to the gods are at the heart of a triangular relation: between dedicator and deity, whether the former is asking for or reciprocating a favor; between dedicator and community, since the offering said something about his identity, status and role in this community; and also between god and community, when the latter could recognize in the wealth and the fame of its sanctuary a sign of its close relation with the deity. Prestige offerings represent only a small part of the huge quantities of offerings found in sanctuaries, but they were the most conspicuous, made to be exhibited as testimonies of the exceptional favor bestowed by the divinity on an individual, a family or other group, and shared by the community to which they belonged. They can therefore hardly be conceived without some kind of commemoration of the people who had brought them. Dedicatory inscriptions and inventories could fulfill this function. But, if one excepts the graffiti on pots and sherds which reflect another use of writing, formal dedicatory inscriptions on offerings are extremely rare until the end of the seventh century and none has yet been found for earlier periods (Polignac 2005a). Inventories are not known to have existed at that time either, though they may have been set down on perishable materials (leather, clay). Conversely, the function of memorization and catalogues are at the roots of early poetry (*katalegein* describes the poetic performance of the bard), and since most of the early dedicatory inscriptions are hexametric, it seems quite probable that the memory of the most prestigious offerings was kept through poetic compositions, maybe performed on ritual occasions, in a form retained for the inscriptions (Papalexandrou 2005: 108–14, 194–9). The oral tradition, obviously predominant until the late seventh/early sixth century, does not completely preclude the use of writing: the earliest dedicatory inscription dates back to the early seventh century, according to the traditional dating of the so-called "Manticlos Apollo," a bronze figurine found in Boeotia and bearing on its legs two hexametric verses recording Manticlos' gift to the god. Orality and writing rather seem to have played complementary roles, even when the use of inscriptions tended to become more general: in many cases, as for the Manticlos figurine, the dedicatory inscription fails to provide important information such as the donor's father's name, which defines the social identity of the donor, the circumstances of the offering and so on. These inscriptions could be fully understood only by those who shared a more general knowledge which was transmitted by other channels and other devices; and sanctuaries may have been the places where this common knowledge was preserved and passed on.[13] The study of the interactions between songs, memory, disposition of monuments and inscriptions and ritual behavior in space also opens new horizons in the understanding of sanctuaries (Giannisi 2006).

This debate on orality and writing confirms one phenomenon which has been noted several times in this chapter and opens up broader considerations. This phenomenon is the importance of the period which covers the end of the seventh and the beginning of the sixth centuries, and which witnessed complete change in many respects. Full comprehension of the meaning of these correlated changes needs further study, since they often extend to many other social practices. The wider considerations concern sanctuaries and festivals as places of communication. In a way, everything in a sanctuary can convey a message: the offerings, the iconography, the architecture, the ritual itself (Stavrianopoulou 2006). Once more, a full understanding of the message requires identification of its addressees, its *contexte de réception*: the specifics of ritual might be elaborated by contrast or comparison with other practices (cultic or funerary) within or outside the community; offerings could be chosen in order to display cultural references shared with other groups or communities within or outside the city. Songs and dances performed at festivals frequently reshaped and renewed the *mythoi* and representations which gave meaning to the cult, in a constant renegotiation between the communities and their historical environment, a movement of permanent re-creation of the tradition on which various social groups, cities, *ethnè*, built their identity. The role of sanctuaries and festivals in archaic Greece cannot be analyzed either by isolating one element, or by general categorizations determined by rigid and constant parameters (the so-called "nature" of a deity, for instance). It should rather be seen as a system in which the meaning of each element is determined by complex interactions with other components, combining long-lasting religious conceptions and rapid shifts in cult practices and organization. Sanctuaries are certainly among the places where the extraordinary vitality and inventiveness of archaic Greece are most visible.

NOTES

1 For a thorough review of the different situations, see Schnapp-Gourbeillon 2002: 183–253, with a marked emphasis on continuities.

2 At Kalapodi, however, earlier levels have recently been excavated by Wolf-Dietrich Niemeier, who suggests placing the sanctuary in the category of cult places created in the Mycenaean period – but the cultic caracter of the finds has yet to be confirmed.

3 The great diversity of these "local sanctuaries" is clearly shown by Baumer 2004.

4 The last monograph on the sanctuary is Ducat 1971.

5 Viviers 1992; Müller and Prost 2002; Duplouy 2006: 217–49.

6 This view results from a frequent confusion between the realities of cult history and Greek ideas on Apollo and his way of establishing sanctuaries and creating a symbolic order by overpowering the previous owner of the place (e.g. at Delphi, Telphoussa). Though criticized by Ducat 1971: 441–2, the theory that the hero Ptoios had preceded Apollo in the oracular function finds some support in Schachter 1981: 54–7.

7 It is worth remembering that these terms were coined first in the 1960s and 1970s for the study of the Greek foundations in Southern Italy and Sicily, where these distinctions appeared neatly established thanks to the archaeology of early urbanism and territorial organizations which developed at that time. They can still provide useful categories but for purely descriptive purposes (Pedley 2005: 39–52).

8 My own analysis, following a well-established scholarly trend, illustrated the first view (Polignac 1998) while the idea of a discontinuity or an opposition between Argos and the Heraion was sustained, on different grounds, by I. Strøm (1995; 1998) and J. Hall (1995; Hall 1997: 99–106).

9 The role of Eastern visitors in the diffusion of oriental offerings in archaic Greek sanctuaries is another debated issue. S. Morris 1992 gives them a predominant role while I tend to minimize their presence, considering that most oriental offerings rather illustrate Greek practices.

10 Tuchelt, Schneider, Schattner 1996; Duplouy 2006: 203–14; Giannisi 2006: 28–33.

11 On this transformation, see Chaniotis 2002. Another case is the Mt Lykaion cult which became the central pan-Arcadian cult in classical times, but no clear evidence of archaic activity has been found.

12 According to the most widespread legend, the death of the child Opheltes, son of the local king, was supposed to be at the origin of the foundation of the games by the Argive heroes marching against Thebes.

13 The well-known episode of the reading by Herodotus (5.59–61) of the "Cadmean inscriptions" on tripods dedicated to Apollo Ismenios in Thebes illustrates this process.

CHAPTER TWENTY-THREE

The Economy

Hans van Wees

Archaic Greece is often imagined as a world of subsistence farmers struggling to survive, ruled by a small landed elite whose "aristocratic" values abhor sordid profit-making. Hesiod's peasants and Homer's heroes are the respective models. This simple and static picture of archaic Greece has featured heavily in the long debate about the differences between ancient and modern economies. For "primitivists," the fundamental characteristic of ancient economic life is that the vast majority of people were farmers who aimed for no more than subsistence and self-sufficiency, whose families themselves consumed what they produced, and engaged in as little exchange as possible. For "modernists," by contrast, ancient farmers produced a large proportion of their crops for the market, and accordingly relied heavily on trade. For a primitivizing school of thought called "substantivism," most kinds of exchange in the ancient world were not profit-oriented but took the form of reciprocity or redistribution, in which the guiding principle was generosity. For modernizing "formalists," however, most kinds of exchange were as much motivated by profit in antiquity as they are in the modern world, and equally subject to the laws of supply and demand. Scholarship is similarly divided on the economic roles of the ancient city and the ancient state.[1]

It will be argued here that from the very beginning the archaic economy was far more complex than the usual picture suggests, and that its further development into something still more complex, and in some but certainly not all ways more "modern," was a central phenomenon of the period. In particular, we shall see that intense and escalating competition for wealth characterized economic life throughout and was a driving force behind many of major historical developments and crises of the age.

Economic Ethics in Hesiod's *Works and Days*

Almost all surviving early epic Greek poetry is filled with tales of gods and heroes, but there is one great exception: Hesiod's *Works and Days*, an 828-verse exhortation to "toil with toil after toil" (382). The premise of this poem is that the poet has a brother, Perses, who has greedily taken more than his fair share of the inheritance (34–40), yet manages his estate so poorly that he is forever begging his neighbors and brother for help (394–403), and is clearly in need of advice. Whether the figure of Perses was real or fictional, he was the perfect foil for Hesiod's emphatically repeated message: there are no shortcuts to riches; lasting wealth can come only from an honest, pious life and constant hard work on the farm. Why a poem on such a mundane subject was composed, ca. 700 BC, and why it uniquely survived amongst countless songs of legend and myth are questions crucial to the study of archaic economic attitudes.[2]

Perses' first priority, according to Hesiod, is to accumulate a year's supplies (30–4). He must work to avoid hunger and debt;[3] his goal is to escape "poverty" (*penia*, 497; cf. 638), and to gain a "sufficient livelihood" (*bios arkios*, 501, 577). In short, Perses sounds like a small farmer who aims at self-sufficiency but struggles merely to feed his wife and children (399).[4]

Yet Hesiod's advice on how to run a farm assumes throughout that Perses will be employing slaves (*dmôes*) and hired laborers (*thêtes*). The first thing a farm needs is a "bought woman," he says (405–6). Ploughing is a job for "your slaves and you yourself" (459–60): one slave ploughs (441–5), one sows (445–7), and one covers over the seeds (469–71). Perses must "sharpen the sickles and wake up the slaves" at harvest time (573), "order the slaves to thresh the grain" (597–9, 607–8) and "instruct the slaves" to build sheds (502–3). He must also hire a couple of free laborers on an annual contract (602–3).[5] Clearly a man with six or more full-time staff must own quite a large farm, and what Hesiod had in mind when he spoke of a "sufficient" livelihood was much more than bare subsistence. His concerns about "poverty" and "hunger" must be understood in the light of the quite high standard of living which he expected.

Poverty is a relative concept, of course. In classical Greece everyone who could not afford to live off the labor of others was deemed to live in "poverty," and Hesiod may have used the term in the same sense.[6] Even hunger is a relative term. Among modern Cretan shepherds a perceived struggle against "hunger" (*pina*) is integral to their self-image, although in objective terms they are quite prosperous. Their "hunger" is not physiological but expresses a perception of themselves as fighting to survive, in contrast to the ruling classes who "eat" at their expense (Herzfeld 1985: 21–3). Hesiod's "hungry" farmer, too, stands in contrast to the rulers of his community who are repeatedly called "gift-eaters" (*dôrophagoi*; 39, 221, 264). When Hesiod warns against hunger, he is thinking not so much of literal starvation, but of a more metaphorical "hunger": the relative deprivation of those outside the ruling class.

Works and Days thus addresses a farmer who owns a sizeable estate and employs at least half a dozen laborers, free and slave; the poem tells him to devote himself to work in order to maintain his property and independence. The question is why a hymn to the virtues of toil was meaningful and important to a landowner at this economic level. The answer is that he faced a competing ideology of leisure, as well as intense rivalry for wealth.[7]

The work ethic and the leisure class

Once upon a time there had been no need to work, according to Hesiod: "the tribes of men used to live on earth far removed from . . . hard toil and painful illnesses" (90–2; cf. 109–13). But now the gods "keep hidden from men the means of living" (42, 47) and people "will never stop being worn down by toil and misery" (176–8). For Hesiod, work is thus not merely an economic necessity for the poor, but a religious obligation owed by all mankind.

> Gods and men are filled with indignation at one who would live without working, his disposition like that of stingless drones who devour what the bees have toiled for, eating without working . . . When you work, you will be much better loved by the gods . . . There is no reproach in work; there is reproach in idleness (*aergia*) . . . Whatever your lot in life (*daimôn*), it is better to work.
>
> (299–314)

"Whatever your lot in life": these precepts apply to rich and poor alike.[8] The elevation of toil to a form of piety makes work obligatory even for those who could afford to abstain.

Hesiod's insistence that "there is *no* reproach in work" shows that he was not concerned with men who were simply lazy, but with men who regarded work as socially unacceptable. Better-off landowners might well feel, as many did in classical Greece, that a life of leisure was more appropriate to their status than a life of work, and indeed that physical labor was shameful. It was people like these whom Hesiod tried to convince that their fellow-men and the gods would not admire them for their lives of "leisure," but hold them in contempt for their "idleness." Those who struggled to make a good living, he added, could in any case not afford to feel "shame" (*aidôs*) at engaging in physical labor, because greater shame lay in not being rich:

> Shame is no good at providing for a needy man – shame which both harms and benefits men greatly – shame comes with poverty, but confidence with wealth.
>
> (317–19)

Hesiod's exhortations to work hard were thus aimed at landowners who aspired to a leisured life style – whether or not they could afford it – which involved spending time away from the farm and taking an active part in public life. Hence he disapproved of Perses "closely watching disputes, listening in an assembly" (29–34) and repeatedly warned against idling in the "warm communal meeting hall" (*leschê*, 495, 501) or in semi-public places such as "the bench in the smithy" (493) and "benches in the shade" (574). Humble as these settings may sound, they were visited by both rich and poor. Even a king and his guests might go out after dinner to "the bench and the talk of the people" (Homer, *Odyssey* 15.468), and even an official Spartan envoy to neighboring Tegea might visit the local smithy (Herodotus 1.67.5–68.1).

How actively did Hesiod expect a farmer who employed slaves and free laborers to be involved in agricultural labor? In the preface to his farming calendar, he seems to want the landowner to engage in unremitting toil personally and energetically.

> If your heart is set on wealth, do as I say, and toil at toil after toil.
>
> (381–2)

> Strip off to sow, strip off to plough, strip off to reap the harvest, if you wish to take care of all the labours of Demeter in due season.
>
> (388–93)

> Toil, foolish Perses.
>
> (397–8)

He imagines the farmer himself driving the oxen (467–9), making clothes (538) and storing grain and fodder (600–7). Yet the ploughing was in fact done by a team of slaves, as we saw (441–7, 469–71); clothes were woven by the women of the household (779), as they were throughout Greek history; and slaves took care of threshing and storage (597–9, 607–8) while the farmer relaxed in the shade, enjoying good food and wine (582–96).[9] Hesiod's rhetoric of "toil," then, cannot be taken at face value any more than his rhetoric of "hunger."

The landowner may occasionally have shared his slaves' labor, and his sons might help out on the farm (379–80) or take the livestock to graze on the mountainside, as according to the *Theogony* Hesiod himself did in his younger days (22–6). Otherwise, his commitment to work evidently takes the form of energetic *supervision* of the laborers: he rises before the slaves do (*W&D* 573), reminds them of work to be done (502–3), and issues instructions (597). His job is "to *arrange (kosmein)* tasks in due measure" (306), i.e. to organize the work to be done by others. The introduction to the poem's final section, on auspicious and inauspicious days, goes so far as to assume that the landowner might visit his estate only on the last day of each month, to hand out supplies and leave instructions for work to be done in the month ahead: "You must explain to your slaves the days given by Zeus, observing them duly; the thirtieth of the month is the best to supervise work (*erga epopteuein*) and to distribute rations" (765–7).

In short, the strict work ethic advocated by *Works and Days* required, not manual labor, but hands-on farm management. It was essentially the same ethos commended, centuries later, by Xenophon, for whom "toil" (*ponos*) was the way to wealth and physical fitness (*The Estate Manager* 11.12–13): his idea of "toil" was a walk to the farm early in the morning to see whether the slaves were working satisfactorily, followed by a recreational horse-ride around the estate and a walk or run back to the town-house for a mid-morning meal (11.14–18). Xenophon's landowner, like Hesiod's, wasted no time idling in public places but was seen in the *agora* only "when doing some business or at any rate not being entirely at leisure" (7.1).

Both authors were clearly addressing primarily "those who practice agriculture through supervision," as Xenophon called them, rather than those who work their own land (*autourgoi*, 5.4). Poorer men could no doubt relate to Hesiod's message, and indeed Hesiod's theology of "work" may well have drawn on ideas widely held by working farmers, who often see their struggle to survive as god's will.[10] But the main aim of *Works and Days* was not to remind poor peasants that they would starve if they did not work; it was to persuade landowners who enjoyed – or at least aspired to – a life of leisure to devote their time instead to close supervision of agricultural labor, with an eye to maximum productivity.

Beyond self-sufficiency: wealth as an economic goal

To avoid "hunger" and "poverty," i.e. to rise to an economic level at which work is a matter of choice rather than necessity, is the landowner's first goal, but he wants more than this: he competitively pursues "wealth" (*ploutos, aphenos*) with the aim of becoming richer than others in his community. This goal is emphasized at the start of *Works and Days*, where the poet distinguishes two kinds of "competition" (*eris*), one leading to war and conflict, the other a force for good, set "in the roots of the earth" (11–19):

> It drives even a lazy man to work, for one wants to work when one sees another who is rich and makes every effort to plough and plant and look after his estate. Neighbor envies neighbor as he strives for wealth. This competition is good for mortals.
>
> (20–4)

The reference to "envy" shows that this kind of rivalry is not merely for a large livelihood, but for greater prestige and social superiority, a theme which is picked up later:

> If you work, the idle man will soon envy you as you become rich – wealth is accompanied by excellence (*aretê*) and prestige (*kudos*).
>
> (312–13; cf. 287–92)

Conversely, if your harvest is small, "few will admire you" (482), and poverty brings not only shortages but "shame" (*aidôs*, 319). Increasing wealth is also the main consideration in family planning. The farmer should have only one son, so that his estate will not be divided, "for thus wealth will increase in your halls" (376–7), but alternatively he may take a risk and have several sons, for "Zeus might easily give prosperity beyond words to greater numbers: more people, more attention to work, larger surplus (*epithêkê*)" (379–80).

Crucially, this surplus is not simply stored or given away, but invested in expansion of the farm: it may be exchanged for livestock – hence "work makes people rich in sheep and wealthy" (308; cf. 120) – or for land, because with the help of the gods "you may buy the estate of other men, not another man yours" (341).[11]

Most modern scholars play down such references to wealth as very much secondary to the supposed main message of *Works and Days*, which is to prevent the household from falling below subsistence level, or to aim for a marginal increase of wealth at best.[12] Yet Hesiod mentions striving for wealth at least as often as avoiding hunger and poverty, and his emphasis is clearly not just on preserving an adequate livelihood but on competitively increasing one's property. He seeks "prosperity beyond words" (*aspetos olbos*, 379). His remark to Perses that "when you have enough" grain stored at home you can start trying to appropriate other people's property (33–4) is doubly ironic: it is never acceptable to seize the property of others, and it is not possible to have "enough" wealth (Fisher 1992: 187).

Rivalry for wealth is also pursued by means other than productive work, and this is why Hesiod introduces the second, "blameworthy," kind of competition which turns to deceit and violence (13–15). Perses is accused of resorting to such behavior (27–38, 274–8) and so are the judges who ruled in his favor (202–12; cf. 189, 192). All are urged to avoid perjury (219, 282–5; cf. 190–4), injustice, arrogant aggression (*hybris*, 213–85), and shameless greed.[13] In the light of these concerns Hesiod's famous comment that "half is much more than whole, and there is great goodness in mallow and asphodel" (40–1) is clearly not a glorification of poverty nor an exhortation to resign oneself to a life in humble circumstances, but yet another warning that half a farm legitimately inherited is better than an entire estate unjustly appropriated, and that even a pauper's meal, honestly earned, is better than a dishonest life of affluence. Getting rich at any cost is wrong, but getting rich remains the goal (West 1978: 152–3).

Productive and destructive rivalry clearly spring from the same competitive impulse and inspire the same emotions.[14] Farmers not merely compete to preserve their holdings but engage in a rivalry to expand and excel so fierce that it often spills over into litigation and violence. It is this problem to which *Works and Days* responds by advocating self-enrichment through productive "toil," at the cost of forgoing the display of wealth through leisure.

Other archaic poets also frequently comment on the intense general striving for "wealth" and warn against acquiring property illegitimately. In the early seventh century, Semonides mocks the vanity of human aspirations (fr. 1.6–10):

> Hope and faith rouse everyone to strive for the impossible: . . . there is no one who does not believe that, this time next year, he will associate with wealth and the upper classes.

Solon similarly notes that "if someone is poor and the labors of poverty coerce him, he fully expects to acquire much property" (fr. 13.33–4, 41–2). The rich are no less ambitious: "no clear limit to wealth is set for men; those of us who now have the greatest livelihood double their efforts. Who could satisfy all?" (13.71–3). Nor does Solon exclude himself from the general pursuit of riches: "I *yearn* for property," he says, provided that it is not acquired unjustly (13.7–32). Theognis echoes Solon's lines about unlimited desire for wealth, warns against unjust gains, and sums up: "One can have enough of everything – except wealth."[15]

By the late seventh century, poets were lamenting that the love of wealth had got out of hand to the extent that property had become the *only* thing that mattered, and whole communities were in danger of being destroyed by unbridled greed. "Aristodemos, they say, once put it very effectively in Sparta: 'A man is what he owns, and not a single poor man is noble or respected,'" Alcaeus reports (fr. 360), while a contemporary poem included the line "Greed will destroy Sparta; nothing else."[16] Solon and Theognis also expressed the fear that their cities would be destroyed "by the townsmen themselves . . . for the sake of wealth" and they insisted that personal "excellence" ought to count for more than property alone. Nevertheless, Solon himself institutionalized a system in which political rights were assigned strictly on the basis of property qualifications, not birth or other criteria of status.[17]

Archaic poetry leaves no doubt that a powerful acquisitive drive, rather than a struggle for mere self-sufficiency, shaped the archaic economy. We shall see that it encouraged maximum productivity and profit-seeking, extreme exploitation of labor, and conspicuous consumption.

Land and Labor: The Agricultural Regime

By the standards of modern commercial agriculture, archaic Greek cultivation was far from intensive, but in comparison with the practices of cultivation prevailing in the Mediterranean before the twentieth century it was quite demanding. Biennial fallow was the norm, i.e. agricultural land was left bare every other year, but archaic farmers adopted the most intensive form of these low-intensity regimes.[18] Repeated ploughing in spring and summer, a long ploughing and sowing season in autumn, and careful manuring improved moisture-levels, fertility and friability, and allowed a farmer with a single span of oxen to cultivate some 10–15 ha (25–40 acres), when his modern counterpart could only manage 4–6 ha (10–15 acres).[19] Viticulture, the other main activity mentioned by Hesiod, is inherently labor-intensive, especially when it relies on artificial irrigation, as according to Homer it did. The construction of terraces and enclosure walls placed considerable additional demands on the workforce.[20]

On the other hand, animal husbandry, a low-intensity element of the agricultural regime, was practiced on a notably large scale in early Greece, at least by the elite. Hesiod frequently alludes to the rearing of sheep and goats, and occasionally cows and pigs.[21] Homer's Odysseus owns thousands of animals, and it is these rather than his farms which are cited as proof of exceptional wealth. Livestock were a major prestige symbol, and were therefore reared in the greatest possible numbers: when they exceeded the limits of what local resources could sustain, arrangements were made for the animals to be pastured abroad.[22]

Some scholars argue that the economy of Greece in the "Dark Age" was mainly pastoral, and that a fundamental shift to a predominantly agricultural regime occurred in the eighth century. The much greater emphasis on livestock in Homer than in Hesiod is cited as evidence for this, but the contrast is a matter of poetic emphasis rather than historical reality: Homer conjures up a picture of wealth on a "heroic" scale by describing vast herds and constant feasts of meat, but leaves no doubt that the staple foods are grain and wine rather than meat; Hesiod preaches his gospel of work by concentrating on cereals and vines as the most labor-intensive

crops, but reveals that livestock are reared and eaten as well. There is some archaeological evidence that cattle grew in importance in the early Dark Age and had declined
again by 800 BC, but this is hardly enough to support the idea of a fundamental
economic change.[23] The tradition that "the livestock of the rich" were resented by
the population of Megara and slaughtered by the popular leader Theagenes, ca. 630
BC (Aristotle, *Politics* 1305a8–28), suggests that large-scale animal husbandry was
a prestige enterprise which continued well into the archaic period.

The bulk of the labor force employed by the rich consisted of slaves. Homer and
Hesiod poetically call the workers *dmôes* rather than *douloi*, the usual term for slaves,
and Homer credits them with considerable independence in managing farms and
herds, which has led some scholars to argue that they were dependants rather than
outright slaves. Yet *dmôes* were bought and sold, and generally treated as chattels
(Fisher 1993: 10–14). In the classical period Sparta, Thessaly, and Crete drew their
main labor force from "enslaved" local populations, rather than from imported
chattel slaves, and there are hints that in the archaic period this type of forced labor
– whether imposed on the vulnerable poor or on defeated enemy populations – was
more widespread, an important alternative to chattel slavery (van Wees 2003).

Hired laborers on annual contracts formed a smaller but common part of the
work force. They received food and clothes, and at the end of their term of employment a wage (*misthos*) in kind, later perhaps in cash. For Homer, the lot of the hired
laborer was particularly miserable, at the mercy of unscrupulous employers who might
resort to threats and violence and send him away without payment.[24] Tenancy and
sharecropping were probably additional ways to raise a labor force. The *hektemoroi*,
"sixth-parters," attested in Attica are best explained as free men who cultivated other
men's land in exchange for a mere one-sixth of the harvest, as opposed to a half
share as is common in other share-cropping regimes (van Wees 1999a: 18–24): another
example of extreme exploitation of labor, slave or free.

The practice of forcing debtors to "work off" their obligations, so common throughout history, may also have existed in archaic Greece, although it is barely attested.
For all its warnings about avoiding debt, there is no sign in *Works and Days* that
the repayment of loans, let alone the payment of interest, could be enforced by
any sanction other than the refusal of further credit (349–51, 448–57). By about
600 BC, however, the situation had changed dramatically. In Megara, people protested
against paying interest, while in Athens and elsewhere, non-repayment of loans was
punished by selling the debtor or his family as slaves.[25] One would expect many debtors
to avoid this ultimate sanction by agreeing to work for their creditors as "debt-
bondsmen," but the sources make no explicit mention of this type of labor.[26]

The idea that loans could carry interest and that (re)payment could be legally enforced
evidently only emerged in the course of the seventh century and is tangible evidence
that competition for wealth was rapidly escalating at the time. Rather than remain
content with the gratitude of their borrowing neighbors, the rich increasingly
sought to make a profit from the extension of credit. The same process would account
for more severe exploitation of labor through the creation of serf-like statuses in
some parts of Greece and the creation of new kinds of dependent and free labor in
others, including Athens' sixth-parters and perhaps debt-bondsmen. The influential

thesis that a spectrum of dependent statuses, including debt-bondage, was a legacy of the Dark Age, which declined in the course of the archaic period to be replaced by a sharp division between free men and slaves – as argued by Moses Finley in the 1960s – is thus probably wrong, and certainly has little basis in the ancient evidence.[27]

Craftsmen and Other Specialists

Competition for wealth was not confined to landowners: "potter resents potter and joiner joiner; beggar envies beggar and bard bard" (Hesiod, *W&D* 25–6). The rewards of rivalry among craftsmen and other specialists could be great, because wealthy individuals and entire communities competed for their services. "A diviner, or a healer of ills, or a joiner of wood, or indeed an inspired bard" might be asked to come and work abroad, for "such people are invited by mortals across the boundless earth" (*Od.* 17.382–7). These are not "itinerant" artisans forced to travel in search of work, but specialists in such demand that the best of them are "invited" all over the world. The same passage calls them "public workers" (*demioergoi*), men whose services benefit the whole community, a title shared with public officials. By the end of the archaic age, diviners, healers, poets, sculptors and painters traveled across the Greek world, commanding high wages and achieving fame far beyond their own communities. This competitive climate inspired striking technical and cultural developments, including a degree of professionalization and specialization, even in the less highly regarded and less profitable crafts.

In the world of Homer and Hesiod, the range of craftsmen seems narrow and levels of specialization low, and archaeological evidence confirms that around 700 BC metalwork and pottery were indeed usually produced in small, unspecialized work-shops. Despite scholars' occasional reference to "industrial quarters," the largest excavated smiths' workshops of the time, at Pithecusae and Skala Oropou, each consisted of a domestic dwelling with two forges in close proximity; in both, bronze and iron, and possibly gold and silver, were worked at the same time (figure 23.1).[28] Evidence for potters' workshops is limited to scattered kilns and dumps of waste products in otherwise residential areas.[29] No other kind of workshop is attested. The simple nature of houses and temples around 700, small and made largely of wood and mudbrick with limited use of mostly unworked stone, is another indication of low levels of specialization.[30]

Subsequently, competition between craftsmen to meet the demand for new ways of displaying wealth produced spectacular developments, especially in sculpture and architecture. Corinth was the first to display its exceptional riches by building temples with all-stone walls and tiled roofs in the city and at the Isthmus around 680 and 650 BC. Rooftiles were a new invention. Not until ca. 580 did any other city match this, but then an all-stone temple of Artemis on Corcyra was quickly followed by a series of very large sanctuaries at Samos, Ephesus and Miletus, which raised the stakes by being surrounded with vastly expensive double colonnades of a hundred or more stone columns. The marble used often needed to be brought to the site from overseas at great expense. Such lavishing of resources on temple-

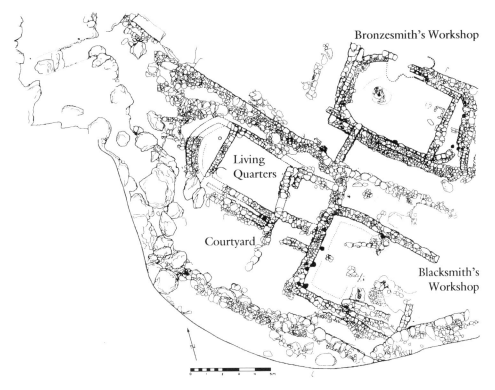

Figure 23.1 The Mazzola "industrial quarter" at Pithecusae, ca. 750–700 BC
Source: Drawing by F. Gehrke in Ridgway (1992: fig. 25).

building, accompanied by increasing use of stone also for other public buildings and private houses, led to an important innovation in construction technology: from around 515 BC, blocks were no longer put in place via ramps, but lifted up by mechanical hoists and pulleys.[31]

Monumental stone statues from ca. 650 onwards joined the small wooden, terracotta and bronze statuettes which had previously served as cult images and votives. Lifesize or larger stone images of standing youths (*kouroi*) and seated or standing young women (*korai*) were widely set up as dedications in temples, and in Attica also as grave markers (figure 23.2). Competition at first concentrated on size, and quickly escalated to the point where a colossal 10 m tall *kouros* was dedicated to Apollo on Delos by the Naxians, ca. 580. After this, scale came to matter less than quality in sculpture, as is evident from a new concern to render in detail the musculature of the *kouroi* and the elaborate dress of the *korai*, much helped by the invention of the claw chisel and perhaps the rasp, ca. 575–550. Finally, around 500, the limited range of static poses represented so far was abandoned in favor of more complex postures and freer movement. The role of competition between craftsmen in driving these changes is nicely ilustrated by the boast of a sculptor who used extreme foreshortening to

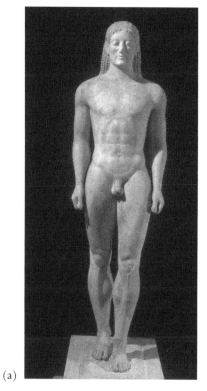 

(a)   (b)

Figure 23.2   (a) Life-size *kouros* from Anavyssos in Attica, ca. 530 BC (Athens, National Museum 3851). The base of this statue carries the following inscription: "Stand and mourn at the grave monument of Kroisos, who is dead. Brutal Ares once destroyed him among the front-line fighters." (b) Small *kore*, dedicated by a woman, Iphidike, on the Acropolis at Athens, ca. 520–510 BC (Acropolis Museum 675). This statue was originally placed alongside a winged victory figure on a column. The piece was signed by the sculptor, Archermos of Chios
Source: Acropolis Museum. © akg-images/Nimatallah.

render a particularly tricky pose in relief and inscribed his work: "Alxenor of Naxos made this. Just look at it!"[32]

Developments in metalwork are harder to trace because little of it escaped being melted down and reused by later generations. Literary evidence suggests that bronze tripod-cauldrons and mixing-bowls were being cast on a monumental scale by the late seventh century. The most notable innovation was the casting of lifesize bronze statues, when previously large "metal" statues had consisted of hammered sheets of bronze or gold attached to a wooden core. The new process was probably made possible by the invention of piece-moulding around 550. By the end of the century bronze had overtaken marble as the favorite medium for votive and commemorative statues.[33]

Potters continually devised new shapes and styles of decoration – above all, for tableware (figure 23.3). The competitive spirit noted by Hesiod had occasionally led

(a)

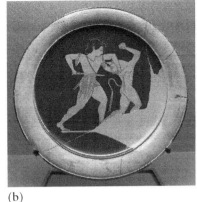

(b)

Figure 23.3 (a) An Athenian black-figure amphora of the so-called Tyrrhenian type, ca. 560 BC, showing three men with round hoplite shields fighting three men with "Boeotian" shields. (b) An Athenian red-figure plate by Paseas, ca. 520–510 BC, showing Theseus killing the Minotaur, an important national Athenian myth

Source: Staatliche Antikensammlungen, Munich, inv. 1429 (= J127); photo by Bibi Saint-Pol. Louvre G67; photo by Bibi Saint-Pol.

potters to sign their work at least since 720 BC, but not until the 570s did an Athenian potter sign as the decorator rather than maker of a vase ("Sophilos drew this"), and it was another few years before separate signatures by painter and potter show that these are two different persons. A degree of specialization was the result of rivalry to produce higher-quality decoration. The sophistication and complexity of black-figure decoration on Attic pottery developed so fast over the next few decades that Athenian tableware, especially drinking-cups, came to be in much greater demand across the Greek world than previously sought-after Corinthian and Laconian wares, which went out of production. Between 535 and 520, Athenian potters developed a whole range of new decorative techniques, surely not least in order to gain an edge over their rivals: coral red gloss, polychrome decoration, relief effects, moulded ornaments, vases in the shape of human and animal heads, and white-ground and red-figure painting all made their first apperance in these years. Red-figure decoration became dominant from ca. 500 onwards, and painters continued to compete in producing more complex imagery in the new style: "Euphronios could never do this!", Euthymides proudly wrote on one of his showpieces.[34]

Domestic spinning and weaving was increasingly supplemented by professional cloth production and associated industries. From the end of the seventh century onwards, poets refer to items of dress imported from far away, or made with exotic materials: cloaks of Scythian wool; clothes colored with Scythian dye; Scythian shoes; Lydian sandals; and most notably costly headscarves imported from Lydia, mentioned by Sappho as having recently taken the place of locally produced headgear. We also hear of cloaks made in Miletus which were in high demand as luxury garments in distant cities such as Sybaris and Syracuse.[35] Cloth and clothing bought at great expense thus became an important means of displaying wealth. By the end of the sixth century, fashions in dress were highly elaborate and afforded a good living to pro-fessional weavers, cobblers, fullers, tanners, and even washerwomen. In Athens, some of these – and other craftsmen, too – were rich enough to dedicate marble basins and statues on the Acropolis, right alongside those dedicated by men of the very highest rank.[36]

Given a growing demand for a greater variety of ever more sophisticated skills, increasing specialization in craft-production was inevitable. A recently discovered "rural" pottery workshop of 525–475 BC at Kavala on Thasos produced tableware, storage vessels, rooftiles, terracotta ornaments and models, but neither cooking vessels nor transport amphoras, probably because special techniques were required to make such vessels respectively heat-resistant and impermeable (Perreault 1999). Even in this humble industry and in this rustic environment, ornamental and utilit-arian items were produced by separate workshops. In more urban settings craft production by the end of the sixth century must have moved some way towards the situation found in Athens in the late fifth century, where workshops with dozens of slaves were devoted to producing one single product each, be it shields, knives, couches, or lamps.

As for other specialists, by the late sixth century competition for their services was frantic. Poets like Simonides earned large sums of money by composing victory odes for rich men, tyrants and cities; poets explicitly competed with sculptors for commissions, boasting that their songs were superior to statues as a medium of com-memoration.[37] The demand for physicians is illustrated by the career of Democedes of Croton, who settled in Aegina around 530:

> In the first year he surpassed the other healers, although he was untrained and owned none of the tools of this craft. In the second year, the Aeginetans hired him publicly for a wage of 6,000 drachmas; in the third year, the Athenians did so for 10,000 drach-mas; in the fourth year Polycrates [of Samos] for 12,000 drachmas.
>
> (Herodotus 3.125, 131)

His further adventures took him to Persia, before he finally returned a wealthy man to his native Croton where he married into the local elite (3.129–30, 136–7). No less striking is the competition between cities to hire the best diviners for their armies: in 479, the Corinthians managed to hire the popular Deiphonus of Apollonia, who "got work all over Greece"; the Persians paid "no small amount" to Hegesistratus of Elis; and the Spartans were so desperate to hire Teisamenus of Elis that they uniquely granted him and his brother Spartan citizenship.[38]

Neither craftsmen nor other specialists can have been very numerous in any Greek community. Even the production of decorated Athenian tableware, much in demand across the Mediterranean, seems to have involved at most 200 people at any time, less than 1 percent of the inhabitants of Athens.[39] But even if the total number of specialists did not exceed a few percent of the population, they consti-tuted a significant element of a city's economy insofar as they provided services and commodities which were vital to the competitively escalating displays of wealth in which cities and individuals engaged throughout the period.

Traveling Farmers, Adventurers, and Merchants: Forms of Exchange

A farmer in the seventh century presumably paid in kind for the services and commodities provided by specialists, and engaged in occasional barter with his neighbors or in a local market, but we have no explicit evidence for such types of exchange. We do hear, however, of many landowners taking to the seas and trading their surpluses abroad at a more profitable rate. They were joined by "adventurers," who combined trading with raiding, and in the course of the archaic period increasingly also by professional merchants.

Hesiod claims that his father used to trade overseas "because he lacked a fine livelihood" and suffered "bad poverty" (*W&D* 633–40); others might do the same (647; cf. 686). He himself takes pride in having sailed only once, not for the sake of trade (648–62), and imagines an ideal world in which farms produce such abundance that no one need ever "travel in ships" (43–6, 236–7). Trade here seems a last resort for struggling farmers, and some scholars infer that Hesiod advocates keeping trade to the minimum required for subsistence.[40] Yet the poet acknowledges that a farmer may be motivated by "a desire (*himeros*) for sea-travel," rather than by necessity (618), and will not limit himself to acquiring specific commodities for his own consumption but aim to make as much gain as possible. "Drag your swift ship to the sea and prepare a cargo to fit in it, so that you may win profit (*kerdos*) to bring home" (631–2); "put your cargo in a big ship, for the bigger the cargo, the bigger will be your profit upon profit" (643–5). Hesiod imagines that some might even consider trading their *entire* harvest abroad, but advises against this because the danger of losing everything at sea is too great: one should "leave behind most and make a cargo of the lesser part" (689–90). Unlike certain classical Greek writers, Hesiod clearly approves of profit-making in exchange as such, and his dislike of overseas trade is due purely to the fact that it is a risky enterprise.[41] His advice on sailing is thus not confined to "poor" farmers forced to engage in trade to make ends meet, but includes rich farmers who could afford to abstain but nevertheless also engage in it because it offers potentially great profits. Even at the highest social levels landowners sell their surpluses abroad, although they may employ agents rather than make the trip in person.[42]

The agricultural calendar has a regular slot for seaborne trade, the slack period between the threshing in late June and the vintage in early September, which coincides with a season of mild and steady winds (414–22, 571–81, 609–14, 663–77). Another opportunity comes in late April, when the weather begins to improve, in a quiet spell before the grain harvest in mid-May (678–86). The farmer's almanac features auspicious days for cutting ship timbers, making a start on ship-building, and setting sail (805–9, 814–18), among activities which are otherwise confined to the household and the farm. Here and elsewhere, Hesiod imagines a farmer who has his own ship (43–6, 622–32, 671–2). When he advises to "praise a small vessel, but put your cargo in a big one" (643), however, he must be thinking of a less well-off farmer facing this choice when taking passage on another man's ship.

The Greek word for "trade," *emporia*, which literally means "passenger travel," shows that this was common practice.

Since much of the agricultural surplus was evidently traded by farmers themselves, there was in early Greece relatively little scope for making a living as a professional merchant. Metals, too, may have been traded directly by those who exploited the mines, judging by Homer's story of a king sailing in person with a cargo of iron "to Temesa in search of copper" (*Od.* 1.180–4). Full-time traders did exist, but the only merchants featured in Homer – Phoenicians rather than Greeks – sell "trinkets" such as jewelry: exotic craft products were among the few commodities traded not by producers but by middlemen.[43]

Alongside the farmers and merchants who traveled "on business" (*kata préxin*), we encounter overseas travelers who sail the seas "at random" (*mapsidiôs*) in search of opportunities to raid for booty, compete in games, obtain gifts, and incidentally engage in a little trade as well.[44] Adventurers of this kind remained recognizable figures throughout the archaic age – from Homer's Odysseus to Philippos of Croton, an Olympic victor who traveled the Mediterranean in his private warship, joined at least one war and two colonizing ventures, and was worshiped as a hero after falling in battle in Sicily in 510 BC (Herodotus 5.47). Private raiding for booty was regarded as a legitimate practice, explicitly recognized as such in for example the laws of Solon.[45] The Greeks make their first appearance in Assyrian records in the late eighth century as sea-raiders, and two centuries later relentless raiding provoked major military action by Etruscans and Carthaginians against the Phocaeans on Corsica in 535 and by Sparta against the Samians in 525 BC (Herodotus 1.70, 166; 3.47). Private plundering expeditions brought wealth and fame to the rich men who provided the ships and much-needed supplementary income for the poor men who formed the crews. The main forms of booty were livestock and slaves, and since raiders regularly sold off their plunder, rather than bringing it home, slave trade was an important economic activity in archaic Greece. Homer imagined Achilles making a fortune selling Trojan captives in nearby islands, and for the prophet Ezekiel the "Ionians" were major suppliers of slaves to the cities of Phoenicia.[46]

Not all "random" travel involved violence. Sightseeing trips to Egypt and elsewhere were a regular part of the archaic Greek upper-class lifestyle. Later sources tell us that such voyages might be funded by incidental trade along the way, which seems likely enough.[47] Reciprocal hospitality between guest-friends (*xeinoi*) was equally important, however, and the gifts which visitors could expect to receive from their hosts could be a great source of wealth and prestige. Although gifts would have to be reciprocated if the former host came to visit in turn, adventurous travelers could collect more and greater gifts than they would ever need to repay. Their kind of profit-seeking was a notable feature of the archaic economy (van Wees 2002a).

In certain societies, trade and gift-giving are constrained by the existence of distinct categories of commodity which circulate only within separate "spheres of exchange." It has been argued by some that early Greece, too, recognized one sphere for prestige wealth, another for subsistence goods, without scope for exchange ("conversion") between the two. The Homeric epics, however, clearly show that there was no such separation of spheres, and that the rules of exchange placed no limit on the accumulation of wealth.[48]

The ubiquity of trading farmers, raiders and adventurers left only a marginal role for the professional merchant at the start of the archaic period, but his significance soon increased. Growing demand for high-status commodities made by specialists was one factor encouraging the intervention of middleman traders. Another was the expansion of exchange networks, from ca. 650 onwards, into the Black Sea and the far Western Mediterranean, where not only Greek craft products but also Greek wine and olive oil could be traded at highly profitable rates: the first Greeks to sail beyond the Straits of Gibraltar, in the late seventh century, reputedly made a staggering profit of 360,000 drachmas in a single voyage (Herodotus 4.152). These markets could only be reached by professional merchants for the distances and risks involved were too great to be covered by landowners traveling in the slack farming season. Conversely, by the end of the archaic period many parts of Greece no longer produced enough wheat for local consumption and relied on merchants to import it from the Black Sea.[49]

The rise of the professional trader led to the development of specialized merchant ships in the mid-sixth century. The "large vessels" in which Hesiod advised the farmer to take passage were apparently twenty- or fifty-oared galleys of the kind also used for raiding, but around 550 we find the first evidence in art and archaeology for Greek sailing ships with large hulls and without rowers, designed purely to transport goods (figure 23.4).[50] At roughly the same time, the professionalization of Greek trade led to the handing over to Greek control of Naucratis, the main trading-station (*emporion*) on the Nile. Greeks had been visiting and living here since the late seventh century, but now apparently became the dominant presence.[51]

Figure 23.4 One of the earliest surviving Greek representations of a specialized merchant ship, sail-powered and with a large hull. The merchant is about to be attacked by an oared galley of the kind traditional in archaic Greece; this one has rowers at two levels, and a ram shaped like a boar's head. Late sixth-century Attic black-figure cup
Source: British Museum, B436.

Late archaic Greek shipwrecks mostly contain amphoras, which must have contained wine or oil, and some ceramic tableware. An Egyptian customs register from 475 BC confirms and amplifies this pattern. From mid-February to mid-December three or four Greek ships a month passed through this customs station, with a peak of five at the end of summer, compared to a total of only six Phoenician ships for the entire year. All Greek ships brought wine, olive oil (possibly scented) and "empty" pottery; their return cargoes are not recorded in full but always included some natron, a food preservative and ingredient in the manufacture of glass and glaze. The bulk of the return freight will have been wheat, which Egypt produced in great quantity. The duty levied was steep: the

larger ships paid an amount of silver equivalent to 1,000 Attic drachmas plus a similar sum in gold, and also handed over a proportion of the wine, oil and pottery.
Profit margins must have been high to make this level of taxation viable.[52]

Much discussion has been devoted to the significance of pottery as an item of
trade. The view that it was mere "saleable ballast," traded in small quantities on the
back of more valuable commodities, was disproved by the discovery of a shipwreck
dating to ca. 515 BC at Pointe Lequin near Marseilles. This ship, one of the largest
wrecks known from this period, carried about 100 amphorae and other storage jars,
and a few terracotta figurines and lamps, but was otherwise crammed full with 2,500
Attic and Ionian drinking cups.[53] Ceramic tableware was evidently well worth trading
in its own right. The exponential rise in production of Athenian painted pottery in
the second half of the sixth century must have been driven by the demands of traders,
who may well have commissioned batches of pots for specific overseas markets,
judging by the creation in Athens of so-called Tyrrhenian and Nikosthenic amphoras
which imitate Etruscan vessels and are found almost exclusively in Etruria (Scheffer
1988; Osborne 1996b). If the letters SO scratched on many late sixth-century vases
are the trademark of Sostratus of Aegina, the only trader to make even greater profits
than the explorers who first went beyond Gibraltar, this man may have made much
of his fortune selling Greek tableware.[54]

The role of trade in archaic Greece therefore cannot be judged by the apparently
small number and marginal status of professional merchants in early poetry. Trade
was a vital element of the Greek economy from the very beginning of the period,
but it was largely in the hands of non-professionals, especially farmers traveling seasonally. Professional merchants increasingly supplemented and perhaps replaced
producers selling their own wares, as a result of the search for greater profits and
for new ways to display wealth through conspicuous consumption of imported goods.
The latter were not confined to a few precious "luxuries" for a narrow elite, but
extended to much more widely affordable "semi-luxuries" such as the imported wine
which Hesiod's farmer drinks, the imported cup from which he might drink it, or
the oil with which his daughter anoints herself.[55] The volume of trade and number
of merchants are unquantifiable, but by the late sixth century professional traders
were an integral part of the economy, and their commodities indispensable to the
lifestyle of many.

Markets, Coins, Laws, and Wars:
The Economy and the State

The "state" in archaic Greece is not the highly developed set of governmental
institutions and procedures which we associate with the modern word. What did exist
from the very beginning of the archaic age, however, was a clear distinction between
matters "private" (*idia*) and "public" (*dêmia*) and a sense that those in power made
their decisions on behalf of the people (*dêmos, laos*) and ought to manage public
affairs in the people's interest.[56] And the economic well-being of the community was
certainly amongst the rulers' concerns. For Homer and Hesiod, agricultural prosperity

depended on how the "lords" exercised their power: if they ruled justly, land and animals would flourish; if they ruled unjustly, barrenness, plague and famine would ensue. By the mid-sixth century, if not earlier, some states were able to make more pragmatic contributions to the prosperity of their people: on Siphnos, the government raised so much revenue from local silver and gold mines that it could fund an impressive programme of public building and distribute the surplus among its citizens. Until 483 BC, the Athenians dealt similarly with the revenue from their silvermines.[57]

How far governments would intervene in economic matters in order to maximize public revenue is hard to tell, but large-scale public spending on infrastructure is attested as early as 600 BC, when the Corinthians built their famous slipway (*diolkos*) across the Isthmus, making travel between the eastern to the western Mediterranean much quicker and safer. So successful was the investment that according to a credible later tradition Periander of Corinth "exacted no other tax and was satisfied with those from the *agora* and the harbours," the latter no doubt including tolls imposed for crossing the Isthmus.[58]

If states were perhaps not often major economic agents in their own right, they did take an active role in regulating the private economic behavior of their citizens. Exchange in local markets and harbors needed to be closely monitored in order to limit the scope for conflict. An early example of state intervention here is Solon's creation of a new system of weights and measures, and regulation of the relative values of grain, livestock and silver.[59] Such measures imply the existence of boards of officials like the later *agoranomoi* or *metronomoi* who amongst other things enforced the use of officially sanctioned measures.

The best-known and most-studied form of state intervention in economic life is the introduction of coinage, beginning around 600 BC with gold and electrum coins struck by Greek cities in Asia Minor, and followed from ca. 550 onwards by numerous silver coinages struck in mainland Greece (figure 23.5). Great claims have sometimes been made for coinage as transforming not only economic life but Greek culture in general.[60] Yet long before they used coins the Greeks already used money, in the sense of a conventional measure of value and medium of exchange. In Homer, values are expressed as so many "oxen-worth"; in Solon's laws, they are measured in both a "barley-standard"; *drachma*-weights of silver and other fixed weights of

(a)   (b)

Figure 23.5   (a) Two sides of a silver stater from Teos, dated to ca. 510–475 BC.
(b) Two sides of a late archaic coin from Clazomenae
Source: CNG Coins: www.cngcoins.com.

metal are also attested.[61] Coinage did not introduce fundamentally new attitudes towards trade, value, or wealth; it merely introduced a more convenient medium of exchange. Its only advantage over uncoined metal was that one did not need to weigh it.

The smaller the difference between coined and uncoined metal as a means of exchange, the more remarkable it is that archaic states went to the trouble of minting coins at all – no simple matter for the vast majority of cities which did not have their own mines and therefore needed to acquire gold or silver from abroad.[62] The reason must have been that transactions involving silver or gold were too numerous, too contentious, or both, to rely on weighing. The finds confirm that the number of transactions was large: although it used to be thought that relatively few coins were minted, and only in large denominations, it is now clear that from the beginning tiny fractions – down to 0.15 grammes of silver – were produced and that some early issues already consisted of 100,000s, if not millions, of coins.[63] Public transactions by state officials cannot account for much of this, or have provided the original impetus for minting, since not even the wealthiest tyrants did much more than pay monthly wages to a few hundred construction workers or mercenaries. Nor can coins have been designed primarily for trade with other communities, since their value was by definition guaranteed only within the state which coined them, and they were treated as bullion, and weighed, when used abroad.

This leaves as the only likely explanation for the introduction of coinage that from the beginning it was designed for the same purpose which it served in classical Greece, namely to facilitate private transactions within the community. The use of pieces of metal with a guaranteed value would greatly reduce marketplace dispute about inaccurate weights and impure metal. So long as trade was small-scale and often confined to direct barter, market officials could deal with such disputes easily enough, but as it grew in volume and complexity, maintaining order would have required a vast number of enforcers – or a guaranteed medium of exchange. Coinage, rather than "the root of all evil" which stimulated greed, was one of the means by which Greek states tried to contain the effects of escalating competition for wealth, an invention which helped prevent the market-place from turning into a battlefield.[64]

Another, much more radical but generally less successful, strategy to reduce competition for wealth was to curb private expenditure: one has less incentive to accumulate wealth when one is not allowed to display it. From the late seventh century onwards, we hear of sumptuary laws limiting various uses of cloth and gold. Costly funerary practices were restricted, while maximum prices for the hire of female entertainers inhibited the display of wealth at symposia, as did the imposition of double fines for offenses committed while drunk. Radical sumptuary legislation is attributed to Periander of Corinth who, as part of a general drive against "luxury" around 600 BC, "forbade the citizens to acquire slaves and live in leisure" (Nicolaus of Damascus *FGrH* 90 F58), and set up a board of magistrates to monitor excessive private spending – a role also associated with the Areopagus Council in Athens. A different but equally radical approach was adopted in Sparta where a sixth-century reform prescribed a life of leisure for all male citizens but imposed a uniform lifestyle which allowed no conspicuous consumption which could reveal differences of wealth among them.[65] The evidence for many of these laws is of late date and sometimes far from reliable, yet by about 500 BC, archaeo-logy does reveal a much more egalitarian material culture in Greece, and alongside general social pressure and preaching against luxury by the likes of Pythagoras of Samos, intervention by public authorities must have contributed much to bringing this about.[66]

Direct intervention in production and exchange is also attested. The most notable example is a law, reliably attributed to Solon, forbidding the export of all produce except olive oil, on pain of being formally put under a curse by the chief magistrate.[67] Athens may have been concerned to secure a grain supply already around 600 BC, as it certainly was in the classical period. Yet the extension of Solon's export ban to all "produce" (*ta ginomena*), perhaps including the products of mining and quarrying as well as of agriculture, rather than just grain, suggests a different motivation. By confining the owners of land and other resources to trading their surpluses in the relatively small domestic market, the law in effect lim-ited the profits they could hope to make, so that acquisition of ever larger estates would produce diminishing returns and become less attractive. An exception was made for olive oil, surely not in order to encourage its production but because trade in oil, the country's most exportable commodity, was already so important to the rich, and perhaps to many poorer farmers as well, that its prohibition was not feasible or indeed desirable.[68] Although there are few known parallels for such direct intervention in trade, there is no reason to think that only Athens was capable of, or in need of, this kind of legislation: its near-absence from the archaic record may be due to its lack of interest to later sources, rather than its rarity in the archaic world.

Perhaps the most important way of relieving the internal tensions created by eco-nomic competition was to acquire new land and other resources by force at the expense of outsiders. Alongside widespread private raiding by sea and land, we also find public campaigns of plunder, conquest and overseas settlement.[69] Sparta's conquest of Messenia is the most dramatic example. Even if this was a much more piecemeal process than tradition suggests, it was by the late seventh century at least regarded as a public enterprise and served in part to silence popular agitation for an internal redistribution of land.[70] Whether Athens' conquests and settlements abroad from ca. 600 BC onwards were public ventures from the start is open to debate, but by the end of the sixth century these territories were under public control. Similarly, although many of the countless new towns settled by Greeks across the Mediterranean throughout the archaic age were probably the creation of private groups of settlers, the preserved oath of the original settlers of Cyrene shows that by the late seventh century publicly enforced emigration was also conceivable as a solution to desperate economic problems – in this case prolonged drought.[71]

It would be wrong to see overseas settlement and war exclusively as means to solve internal economic problems. They were also in themselves forms of collective competition for wealth, and for prestige and power. Moreover, states justified their campaigns in terms of honor and revenge, justice and punishment, rather than in terms of economic policy. Yet escalating economic pressures were a significant force behind the predatory and expansionist activity of archaic Greek states and individuals, and the economic impact of such activity is undeniable: Athens' conquests must have done much to solve its social and economic problems, and the subjugation of Messenia completely transformed the material basis of Spartan society.

Conclusion: The Nature and Development of the Archaic Economy

The conventional "primitivist" image of masses of peasants seeking only self-sufficient subsistence, presided over by elites without interest in anything as vulgar as making money, seriously misrepresents the economic world of archaic Greece. It is based largely on readings of Hesiod and Homer unduly influenced by models – not to say stereotypes – of typical "peasant" and "aristocratic" culture and society which on closer examination prove not to account adequately for archaic economic behavior and attitudes.

Archaic farmers aspired to produce as large as possible a surplus and to sell this at the most favorable rate. In doing so, they were part of an intense competition for wealth which permeated all levels and sections of society. The elite liked to stress its ability to forgo profit for the sake of honor occasionally, and looked down on those who could not afford to be so high-minded. Archaic poets lamented that profit-seeking was the root of all society's evils. But all this only confirms that competition for wealth was pervasive: it does not imply a pre-modern rejection of the profit-motive any more than modern moralizing about greed implies that our own economy is not overtly driven by the search for the largest possible gain.

The competitive display of wealth was another dynamic force in the archaic economy. It was not confined to the use of rare luxury items but extended to the consumption of imported commodities which lent prestige through their relatively high cost and "exotic" origins but were nevertheless quite widely affordable. From the start of the archaic age, the various regions of mainland Greece not only produced their own range of local specialities but were part of the economically even more varied eastern Mediterranean world. By the end of the period, they were part of Mediterranean-wide networks. This could not fail to encourage agricultural specialization, attested especially by the proliferating export of local wines, and it caused both craft production and trade to develop rapidly to exploit new opportunities for profit.

The state, which on conventional views had no role to play in either the subsistence economy of the masses or the exchange of prestige goods among the elite, intervened extensively, if not always successfully, in order to manage the consequences of these developments. The introduction of coinage to facilitate increasingly complex and competitive exchange; sumptuary legislation to alter patterns of consumption; legislation designed to limit production for export; the measures of Solon and others to reduce inequality and rein in the worst excesses of labor exploitation – all were attempts to mitigate the impact of escalating economic competition.

Of course the archaic economy was not the same as the economy of the contemporary western world. Its smaller scale, more limited technology and slower flow of information, its different political institutions and cultural values, and not least its extensive reliance on slave labor are among a range of vital differences. But there are fundamental similarities as well, and it is these, above all, which made the archaic period such a dynamic age. A closed world of subsistence peasantry and of aristocrats content to preserve the status quo would have seen no change, unless it had been forced to change by an external force, as has often happened in traditional societies in the modern world. In Greece, however, change came from within, and this could only happen because competitive economic values and behavior, potentially productive and destructive in equal measure, drove the transformation.

NOTES

1 Primitivism goes back to Karl Bücher (1893); substantivism to Karl Polanyi (esp. 1944); Max Weber (1921) and Johannes Hasebroek (1928) developed related views on the city and the state, respectively. All these lines of argument were combined by Moses Finley (1973a) into an interpretation of the ancient economy which dominated the field until recently. Modernism is associated with Eduard Meyer (1895) and Michael Rostovtzeff (1941); a moderate form of it is prominent in recent scholarship (e.g. Morley 2007).

2 Countless ancient quotations from the poem (gathered in West 1978) disprove the notion that it was a work of parody (Nisbet 2004) and count heavily against the view that it expressed the values of a marginal group (Tandy 1997: 207–8) or Dark Age values which were about to be superseded (Edwards 2004: 77–9); cf. n. 7 below. Date: West 1966: 40–8; Janko 1982.

3 Hunger: 298–302, 363–5, 404, 647; debt: 366–7, 394–404, 477–8, 647.

4 This aspect of Hesiod's poem is stressed by most scholars: e.g. Edwards 2004: 50–62, 88, 114, 166; Tandy 1997: 6, 211–17; Millett 1991: 31–4; 1984: esp. 93–103; Walcot 1970: 6, 8. See n. 12 below for different views.

5 See West 1978: 602. The ploughmen are explicitly "slaves" (459, 470). An estate which employs so many slaves and full-time hired laborers cannot be called a "family farm," contra e.g. Walcot 1970: 42; Hanson 1995: 96, 107–8; Edwards 2004: 105–6, 133.

6 See esp. Finley 1973a: 40–1; van Wees 2004: 34–6.

7 Rather than because agriculture was new and unfamiliar in his day (e.g. Snodgrass 2006: 207; Tandy 1997: 209, 226; Howe 1958), or because a newly intensive regime was being introduced (Starr 1977: 156–61; Hanson 1995: 32–41, 108), or because he addressed impoverished aristocrats who knew nothing about farming (Bravo 1977: 10–13; Mele 1979: 18–27): Hesiod does not offer a useful practical guide to agriculture, but *moral* advice.

8 See West 1978: 311, 314; Nussbaum 1960: 217.

9 The farmer's period of relaxation begins ca. 21 June; the slaves' threshing and storing begins ca. 20 June (West 1978: 582, 598), so the farmer does not take an active part in their work (contra West 1978: 54).

10 See e.g. Walcot 1970; Millett 1984.

11 Contra Millett 1984: 95; Edwards 2004: 34, the prospect of acquiring more land, not the danger of losing what one has, is emphasized here.

12 Millett 1984: 94–5, and other scholars cited in n. 4; the importance of wealth, however, is stressed by Starr 1977: 48–9, 126–8; Hanson 1995: 101 (cf. Bravo 1977; Mele 1979). Individual expansion is not to be confused with overall economic "growth."

13   352, 356, 359–60; cf. 320–6. These passages clearly refer to illegitimate seizure of prop-
     erty, not the receipt of gifts which one is unable to return (contra Millett 1984: 101–3;
     1991: 33–4).
14   E.g. Walcot 1978: 8–21; Konstan and Rutter 2003.
15   Theognis 227–32; 596. Warnings: 27–30, 145–6, 197–203, 466, 753.
16   Aristotle fr. 544 Rose; Diodorus 7.12.6; Plutarch, *Mor.* 239f; see van Wees 1999b: 3–4.
17   Solon, fr. 4.1–6; cf. 4.11; 4b; Theognis 41–50, 833–6, 1141–9. Excellence v. wealth:
     Solon fr. 15; Theognis 53–8, 185–92, 1109–12. Property-classes: van Wees 2006; Raaflaub
     2006.
18   *W&D* 462–4; with Edwards 2004: 127–58; West 1978: 462–3, 464. Cf. ch. 4, above.
19   See van Wees 2006: 382–5. Manuring: Plut. *Solon* 23.6; Homer, *Od.* 17.297–9.
     Modern ploughing regimes: Forbes 2000: 63, 212; Foxhall 2003: 80–3.
20   Irrigation: Homer, *Od.* 7.129–30; *Il.* 21.257–62. Walls: *Od.* 7.112–13; 18.357–9;
     24.222–5; *Il.* 5.88–92; 18.561–6; 21.441–57; cf. Donlan 1999: 311–14; Richter 1968:
     104–7.
21   Sheep: *Theogony* 22–3; *W&D* 775, 786–7, 795–7. Goats: *W&D* 516, 543–5, 585, 590,
     592, 786; cows: 406, 591; pigs: 790–1.
22   *Od.* 4.634–7; 14.100–2; 20.185–8.
23   The archaeological evidence is set out by Snodgrass 1987, 193–209; it seems to me equally
     compatible with the extension of livestock-rearing as a prestige enterprise (below).
24   Homer, *Il.* 21.441–55; cf. *Od.* 11.489–91.
25   Megara: Plut. *Mor.* 295d; Athens: Solon frs. 4.23–5; 36.8–12; elsewhere: Diod. 1.79.4.
26   Solon F 36.13–15 may or may not allude to debtors serving as debt-bondsmen. See Harris
     2002 for the distinction between legal sale into slavery for debt and informal debt-bondage.
27   van Wees 1999a; 2003; contra Finley 1973a: 70; 1982: 114–15, 132, 149, 166; 1998:
     271–3.
28   Ridgway 1992: 91–100; Mazarakis Ainian 2002b: 154–65. Literary evidence: Eckstein
     1974. On crafts generally: Burford 1972.
29   See surveys by Crielaard 1999b: 54–8; Morgan 1999c: 220–34; Johnston 1991.
30   See esp. Mazarakis Ainian 1997; Fagerström 1988.
31   Construction technology: Snodgrass 1980a: 149–50; Coulton 1974. Marble transport:
     Snodgrass 1983a. Development of architecture: Hurwit 1985: 179–202, 210–13.
32   Surveys of developments: Boardman 1991 (for Alxenor, ca. 490, see fig. 244); Stewart
     1990. Tools: Adam 1966: 18–22 (claw chisel, ca. 560), 75 (rasp, ca. 550).
33   Colossal bowls: Hdt. 1.70; 4.152. Piece-moulding (rather than indirect lost-wax cast-
     ing) as the decisive development: Haynes 1992: 48–9; bronzework: also Mattusch 1988;
     metalwork generally, e.g. Stibbe 2006; Rolley 1986.
34   Earliest signatures: Ridgeway 1992: 94, 96; Boardman 1974: 11–12. Decorative styles:
     Cohen et al. 2006. Euthymides: Boardman 1979: 33–4; fig. 33.2.
35   See Hipponax fr. 2 West; Sappho fr. 39, 98, 125, 210 L-P; Alcaeus fr. 318 L-P; Alcman
     fr. 1.67–9 Page; Timaeus *FGrH* 566 F50 (ap. Athenaeus 519b); Diodorus 12.21.1.
36   For the development of archaic dress, see Van Wees 1998b; 2005a; 2005b. Dedications
     by fuller, tanner, washerwomen, potters in late sixth century: Raubitschek 1949: 465;
     Keesling 2003: 69–77; Johnston 2006: 28–33.
37   Poets' status and fees: Thomas 1995; rivalry with sculptors: Morgan 2007; Thomas 2007.
38   Hdt. 9.33, 35, 37–8, 92, 95; cf. 3.132.
39   See Hannestad 1988: 223 for possible levels of workshop production.
40   E.g. Tandy 1997: 224–5; Edwards 2004: 52, 61–2.
41   *W&D* 247, 618–22, 667–77, 682–8, 691–4.

42 For "agent" trade, see Bravo 1977; Mele 1979.

43 Full-time traders: *Od.* 8.161–4; Solon fr. 13.49–52; Phoenicians: *Od.* 15.415–84.

44 "At random": *Od.* 3.71–4; 9.252–5; cf. *Hymn to Apollo* 452–5; cf. *Od.* 8.159–60. For the interpretation of this formula, see Nowag 1983: 168; Mele 1979: 71; contra Bravo 1980: 976.

45 Ulpian in *Digest* 47.22.4; cf. van Wees 1992: 207–17; contra de Souza 1999: 17–20.

46 Ezekiel 27.12–24. For Achilles, see Hom. *Il.* 21.40–1, 58, 78–9, 102; 22.45; 23.741–7; 24.751–3. Benefits of raiding to rich and poor: Thuc. 1.5.1; *Od.* 17.286–9.

47 Sightseeing: e.g. Hdt. 1.30 (funded by trade: Plut. *Sol.* 25); 2.135; 3.139. Friends abroad: Solon fr. 23.

48 van Wees 1992: 223–7; contra Morris 1986: 8–9; Kurke 1999: 10–23.

49 See e.g. Garnsey 1988: 89–164; Whitby 1998a.

50 Shipwrecks: A. J. Parker 1992: nos. 441, 835, 846, 870, 915, 1042, 1243; also Long, Miro and Volpe 1992: 229. The earlier Giglio Campese A wreck, ca. 600 (A. J. Parker 1992: no. 451) carried Greek pots as part of a mostly Etruscan cargo. Iconographic and literary evidence for merchant ships: Humphreys 1978: 166–9; Gray 1974; challenged by Reed 1984.

51 Hdt. 2.178–9; see Möller 2000: 182–215; Bresson 2000: 13–84.

52 See Yardeni 1994; Briant and Descat 1998; Bresson 2000: 67–9.

53 Pointe Lequin shipwreck: Long, Miro and Volpe 1992. "Saleable ballast," esp. Gill 1991.

54 Herodotus 4.152, with Harvey 1976. Trademarks: Johnston 1977; 2006.

55 *W&D* 522 (oil, not explicitly imported), 589 (wine). "Semi-luxuries": Foxhall 1998.

56 On perception of power in Homer, see esp. Hammer 2002; van Wees, forthcoming: ch. 3.

57 Homer, *Od.* 19.109–14; Hesiod *W&D* 225–47. Distribution of surplus: Hdt. 3.47; 7.144.

58 Periander: Aristotle fr. 611.20 Rose = Heracleides *FHG* ii F 5; *diolkos*: Salmon 1984: 136–9.

59 *Ath Pol* 10; Plut. *Sol.* 15.4.

60 E.g. Kurke 1999; Seaford 2004; cf. von Reden 1995: 171–3.

61 Oxen-worth: Homer, *Il.* 6.235–6; 23.702–5, 885; *Od.* 1.428–31. Barley-standard: de Ste Croix 2004: 33–41. Silver weights: Kim 2001: 13–19; Seaford 2004: 88–101.

62 A point developed in detail by Errietta Bissa in her UCL doctoral dissertation (2007).

63 Kim 2001: 12–13; 2002; Howgego 1995: 6–7.

64 "Invention" or rather a borrowing from the Lydians: Hdt. 1.94. Other views on origins of coinage: e.g. Martin 1996b; Schaps 2004.

65 For all these laws, see the critical discussion in Bernhardt 2003: 23–51, 71–91, 109–21; for Sparta, see Hodkinson 2000: 209–368.

66 Contra skepticism of Bernhardt 2003; cf. Blok 2006 for religious aspects. Pythagoreans: Bernhardt 2003: 51–67; material culture: Morris 1998a: 31–6; 2000: 109–54.

67 Solon F 65 Ruschenbusch (Plut *Sol.* 24.1); cf. Tean curses of ca. 475: ML 30 = Fornara 1983a: 63.

68 See Stanley 1999: 155–7, 229–34; Garnsey 1988: 8–16, 109–11; differently Descat 1993.

69 Private enterprise: Frost 1984; de Souza 1998 – but these studies underestimate the significance of public warfare: van Wees 2004: 95–7, 203–6.

70 This is implied by Tyrtaeus frgs. 1 (redistribution), 5 (original conquest attributed to king Theopompus, i.e. a public venture); see van Wees 1999b; 2003.

71 Oath: Faraone 1993, contra Osborne 1996a. Private settlement versus public colonization: Osborne 1998b contra Malkin, ch. 19 in this volume.

CHAPTER TWENTY-FOUR

Class[1]

Peter W. Rose

For Walter Donlan In Memoriam

Class as a Concept

Reading through almost any of the numerous treatments of the archaic period of Greece, I am struck by a paradox: class emerges as a virtually indispensable concept, yet the content, the implications of the concept, are rarely if ever discussed. It is not given separate treatment and virtually never appears as such in the indices of even substantial accounts of the period. To be sure, there are fulsome listings under "aristocrats," and usually some notice taken of "peasants" and "slaves," but rarely any account of the conceptual framework within which the relations of these classes are to be understood.

The most obvious reason for this glaring lacuna is the cold war and its heritage. The late Moses Finley, whose influence on the field of ancient history would be difficult to exaggerate, was hounded out of the United States for a brief flirtation with Marxism despite the fact of his conversion to the far safer work of Weber and to some extent Polanyi (Finley 1982: ix–xix). The lesson was not wasted. The equation of Marxism with totalitarianism and of capitalism with freedom is alive and well in the consciousness of millions of adults throughout the world – both those whom the equation ill serves and those who flourish because of it. With the striking exception of the work of G. E. M. de Ste Croix (1981), Marxist treatments of ancient Greece (e.g., Thomson 1946; and Wason 1973) have done little to encourage the use of Marx, and this is compounded by the nearly total ignorance of Marx's own work – let alone of the best work of those in the Marxian tradition – on the part of classics scholars in England and the United States. In Europe, for historical reasons we cannot explore here, even the most conservative intellectuals are likely to know more of Marx's texts than some of the most progressive scholars in the United States. Thus, for example, Marx's concept of class struggle is arbitrarily reduced to violent clashes between self-consciously organized groups and accordingly dismissed as irrelevant for archaic Greece.[2] The complex concept of ideology has gained a certain currency in the last 1980s, but usually as the "world view" of the elite who account for most of our texts or in an abstracted and homogenized form as the "ideology of the *polis*" or "civic ideology."

Following Marx and what I take to be the best of the twentieth-century Marxist tradition,[3] I will try to set forth very briefly what I take to be the essential features of a properly[4] Marxist view of class. Central to a Marxist view of class is that classes arise from a relationship of exploitation in the way in which a society produces both its necessities for survival and a surplus. If the society remains at a pure subsistence level or the surplus produced is shared equally by the entire community, there are no classes in the Marxist sense.[5] The centrality of the notion of exploitation – the extraction of surplus value – means that classes are inherently plural and relational. Moreover, the exploiters and the exploited, in relation to the means of production (e.g., land, farm animals, tools) and the relations of production (e.g., subservience, intimidation, paternalism, castes) are in an inherently antagonistic relationship. Specific individuals are of course in a whole array of other relationships that in any particular social formation may mitigate, mystify, or exacerbate this antagonistic relationship. Indeed one obvious function of ruling class ideology is precisely to act as "glue" holding together the potentially antagonist elements in a society under the strain of fundamental changes – and, as we shall see, the archaic age was a period of profound changes.[6] Shared symbols, religious practices and beliefs, kinship, nationality, or a shared external threat may loom larger in any given historical moment than the relationship to production. Marx speaks of this antagonist relationship – i.e., the class struggle – as "now hidden, now open" (Marx/Engels 1975: 6. 482). By "hidden" I take him to refer to the process by which, for example, a slave tends to do as little work as possible or commit individual acts of sabotage of the work process.[7] This is the thrust of Eumaeus' oft-cited declaration in the *Odyssey* that "the day of slavery takes away half a man's excellence (*aretê*)." This sort of resistance is more or less unconscious and individual. By "open" I take Marx to refer to concerted, relatively self-conscious resistance implying some level of organization. Though we do not know the specific political mechanisms at work, we must infer from the sources about the Solonian crisis in the early sixth century that Athenian peasants exerted sufficient political pressure as a *class* to force those in control of Athenian society to have recourse to the expedient of appointing Solon as mediator with very broad powers. Thus the distinction between "hidden" and "open" class warfare corresponds roughly to the distinction often drawn between a "class-in-itself" and a "class-for-itself."

Closely related to this distinction is the issue of consciousness. During much of history people are not conscious of the mode of production into which they are born: it appears natural and inevitable, a matter of destiny, or God's will. So too, many of the changes that take place at the level of production – changes that shape the fundamental conditions of existence of a society – remain unconscious. The shift from bronze tools to iron, the shift from leaving fields fallow for a season to the extensive use of animal manure to enable using the same land every year, the gradual move from primary dependence on a meat diet to a primary reliance on grains – these are changes that took place over several generations and at different speeds in different parts of Greece, but cumulatively they had very substantial consequences for the conditions of possibility in the various Greek societies. Yet those involved in these changes are unlikely to have been fully conscious of the process in which they were engaged until it was largely complete. It is precisely the blindness of conscious actors to such factors that suggests the inadequacy of the emphasis on status and struggles over status that is so much more congenial to classical scholars. There is no doubt that our surviving sources offer far more data for self-conscious struggles over status; the problem is that these struggles offer little explanatory power for significant long-term changes. On the contrary, again and again in moments of genuine threat to class interests, squabbles over status are temporarily suspended by elites who becomes conscious of their collective interests.

The issue of unconscious changes in the mode of production raises the vexed question of the degree to which a Marxist approach to classes is "deterministic." Marx's best formulation of this is the following: "Human beings (*die Menschen*) make their own history, but they do not make it just as they please; they do not make it under circumstances chosen by themselves, but under circumstances directly encountered, given and transmitted from the past" (Marx/Engels 1975: 11. 103). This implies that human beings are neither pawns of vast unconscious forces nor totally free agents, but make real choices within a severely circumscribed set of specific historical circumstances. The choices they make then alter the historical circumstances. This dialectic of human action and specific conditions of possibility is central to Marx's conception of the historical movement arising from class struggle. It is by no means an inevitably "progressive" process; the consequences of the history of class struggles in specific historical eras are "a fight that each time ended *either* in a revolutionary re-constitution of society at large, *or in the common ruin of the contending classes*" (Marx/Engels 1975 [1847]: 6. 482; emphasis added). Particularly after the disillusionments accompanying the defeated revolutions of 1848, Marx emphasized the gap between changes at the level of the mode of production which could entail a "revolutionary re-constitution of society at large" and the *ideological* level on which people normally carry on class struggle: "in studying such transformations it is always necessary to distinguish between the material transformation of the economic conditions of production, which can be determined with the precision of natural science, and the legal, political, religious, artistic, or philosophic – in short *ideological* forms in which men *become conscious of this conflict and fight it out* (Marx/Engels 1975 [1859]: 29. 263; emphasis added). A common misconception of Marx's notion of class struggle is that it *only* refers to violent – usually armed – conflict with a clear winner. Yet the vast majority of Marx's writings, both those published in his lifetime and those unpublished (especially *The German Ideology* and the *Grundrisse*) are best understood as critiques of ideology. The subtitle of the first volume of *Capital* is "A Critique of Political Economy," by which Marx meant the full range of discourses committed to the defense of capitalism. For complex historical reasons I cannot discuss here (see Anderson 1984), by far the richest intellectual work done by Marxists in the twentieth century has been in the area of ideological critique, particularly of cultural critique. From this vast discussion I would emphasize two insights. One is from the octogenarian Claude Lévi-Strauss: when asked what he retained from his study of Marx, he replied, "only a few lessons from Marx's teaching have stayed with me – above all that consciousness lies to itself" (Lévi-Strauss and Eribon 1991: 108). The key implication of this is that ideology is not the same as propaganda, the conscious distortion of truth for explicit political ends. It entails self-deception along with the will to convince others. Thus for example, to suggest that a certain version of religion enormously facilitated the consolidation of the *polis* in the interest of the aristocracy is not to imply a cynical and conscious conspiracy to manipulate the *dêmos*, but it does argue that this process was not entirely innocent of self-serving political motives.

A second insight comes from Theodor Adorno: in advocating what he called "immanent critique" he argued, "It takes seriously the principle that it is not ideology in itself which is untrue but rather its pretension to correspond to reality" (Adorno 1981: 32). Neither literary texts nor the apparently more objective data of archaeology (Morris 1998a) give us direct access to the real: both are imbedded in social processes designed to present a partial vision as the whole truth of society.

In the following text I will attempt to apply this model of class conflict to those developments of the archaic period in which it seems to me to offer a valuable explanatory perspective, though I am well aware that in other chapters of this volume there are fuller and inevitably more nuanced treatments of virtually all the areas I will discuss. Given the paucity and ambiguity of the available evidence, I am painfully aware as well that any efforts at explanation are necessary tentative and entail a substantial speculative component, but I believe that the quest for understanding is worth the risk of error.

The "Dark Age"

A central debate about the Dark Age is over the degree of social stratification that survived the cataclysmic destruction of the Mycenaean palace societies – a revolutionary transformation that may have extended over a hundred-year period – roughly 1200–1100. Some scholars believe that the Mycenaean ruling elite and along with it subordinated peasants and slaves survived this major trauma intact and maintained relations of domination throughout the Dark Age down into the eighth century "renaissance" or "revolution" as it is now frequently called (Latacz 1977). Some, while acknowledging the massive disruption associated with destruction of palace civilization, argue that "a considerable degree of social hierarchy survived the twelfth-century catastrophes" (Morris 1987: 2). Others, focusing on the poverty of the remains of the so-called "Dark Age," believe the society of at least the early Dark Age was essentially egalitarian and meritocratic.[8] Relying on comparative anthropology, they offer a model of social organization in which "big-men" or "chiefs," who have to demonstrate regularly their abilities in battle and in effecting relative economic security and social harmony for their followers, arrogate to themselves some of the meager social surplus but function primarily as a means of redistribution of social wealth in bad years or in good times through generous public feasts, presumably with a religious component (Donlan 1985; 1989; 1997b). Where a Marxist approach to classes may be relevant to this debate is in its focus on the necessity of substantial social surplus to sustain the gross inequalities associated with a fully developed class system. The archaeological evidence for the early Dark Age (for example, the excavation of Nichoria) suggests for the period 1075–975 such small numbers (some sixty people: Thomas and Conant 1999: 36) and such meager architectural differentiation between the ordinary homes and the home of the leader of the community (with storage pits that fit well with a redistributive role) that little room is left for the high degree of social differentiation posited by some. On the other hand, the sheer size of the structure and the relative wealth of the burials (including gold ornaments and two slaughtered horses) at the so-called "heroön" of Lefkandi (dated roughly to about 950: Thomas and Conant 1999: 97) suggest that in this community at least – and it was probably not unique – the process of consolidation, presumably through heredity, had led to a very sharp differentiation of the local chief and the concentration of far more of the social surplus in his hands and probably in the hands of a small elite of his closest allies who had the most stake in perpetuating his memory as more than human. Horses in a poor mountainous land like Greece were always a mark of wealth and prestige, ideological markers of status. The appearance of bronze horse figurines at the end of the ninth century and throughout the eighth centuries suggests a new self-consciousness of a class wealthy enough to own horses (Osborne 1998a: 24–7).

The Rise of the *Polis*

At some time between the destruction of the Mycenaean world of centralized fortifications surrounded by peasant settlements and the appearance of substantial stone temples, communal stone altars, and walls encompassing a whole community, a majority of Greek communities organized themselves into something generally called *poleis*. Associated with this process was the widespread replacement of monarchic forms of political organization by the collective control of political life by the largest landowners who styled themselves as the *aristoi* or by the plural use of the word *basileus*, which seems to have been the most common designation for big men, chiefs, or monarchic rulers in the post-Mycenaean period. Instead of one-man rule, authority was dispersed among a number of annually rotated offices. Aside from the highly ambiguous and endlessly debated evidence of Homer, we have only archaeological evidence of the consequences of this major shift. Beyond temples, walls and shrines, major changes in burial practices about 700 suggest significant shifts in the social symbols by which the elite celebrated its exalted status: horse figurines disappear (Osborne 1998a: 27); wealthy graves in general seem to disappear at the same time that there is a dramatic increase in the overall number of graves. This has been interpreted either as a change in the condition of admission to burial to permit previously excluded lower-status persons (Morris 1987: 184–9) or a sign of a dramatic increase in population, a phenomenon inferred already from the massive "colonization" process occurring in this same period (Snodgrass 1980a: 19–25). As in the debate about the class character of life in the Dark Age, one side sees the creation of the *polis* as the work of a well established aristocracy with roots going back to the Mycenaean period (esp. Morris 1998a; 1987), while the other sees in the process itself the signs of the emergence of an essentially new and presumably highly self-conscious class (Snodgrass 1993b; 1980a). While one must always allow for differential developments and different timeframes in so highly fragmented a world as archaic Greece, the latter alternative makes more sense to me as a general account of the rise of the *polis*. One has to imagine a gradual process in which the inheritance of wealth and status by warrior big men or chiefs eventually consolidates more and more power in fewer hands, which in turn depend more and more on the support of allied lesser chiefs to maintain domination over a peasant majority. The *relative* security achieved over time would seem to have encouraged a gradual but decisive shift in the mix of animal husbandry and agriculture in favor of agriculture, which lead to an overall increase in the level of surplus produced by the society. As Qviller (1981) has pointed out, the Homeric poems speak of many raids to steal cattle but no wars over the possession of land, and it is precisely in the latter half of the eighth century that we first hear of such wars. Since the primary source of value in an increasingly agricultural society is land, the donation of land (Qviller 1981) by the chiefs to their most crucial supporters eventually puts them on a more and more equal footing with those supporters, who then demand an equal share in power. The result is the system of alternating annual magistracies shared out among an elite. But at the same time the institution of *citizenship* is somehow tied to a notion of some sort of ownership of what at that time constituted at least the minimum amount of land (a *klêros* – literally an "allotment") to sustain a family (Snodgrass 1983: 38–9).

How fragile and potentially contentious this process was is suggested first of all by the massive movement of population associated with radically expanded trade of this new surplus and "colonization" – a mostly informal process[9] which led ultimately in about a century and a half to the establishment of some fifteen hundred new Greek *poleis* scattered all around the Mediterranean and Black seas like "frogs around a pond" as Plato was to describe it (*Phaedo* 109b2). The process of consolidating poleis in Greece itself seems dialectically linked with the exclusion of many thousands of persons from these new communities of "citizens." In some cases this exclusion was presumably managed directly by the new aristocracy as in the case of the settlement of Cyrene from Thera about 630. The fourth-century inscription speaks of a decision by the "assembly," but it would be unrealistic at this period to envision an open democratic decision by the entire adult male community.[10] The death penalty for refusal to comply suggests the coercive character of the process. In other cases individuals or groups of individuals opted to seek their fortunes elsewhere than in the new poleis (Osborne 1998b).

Within these new mainland and eastern Greek communities legitimation of control of all the best land by so few required a major ideological offensive that set the terms of ideological struggle throughout the entire archaic period. We see this most clearly perhaps in the archaeological evidence. I have already alluded to the evidence of burials, but more dramatic evidence of the new social formations is a new heavy emphasis on the religion of *polis*-protecting divinities (de Polignac 1995a) manifested in temples of sufficient size and impressiveness of materials to imply a radical redivision of the social surplus in the direction of communal values.

At the same time we find significant material evidence of the worship of actual or imagined Mycenaean shrines of heroes (Antonaccio 1995a) claimed as legitimating ancestors of the self-styled *aristoi*. This would entail an ideological juggling act that in various forms will characterize the rest of the archaic period: on the one hand, asserting through religion the ties that bind the poorest peasant to the richest landowner; on the other, insisting on the genealogically based superiority and therefore "legitimacy" of the ruling elite. Forgoing displays of wealth in burials in the interest of communal solidarity would then be balanced by cult rituals that affirm the special links with divinity of the "best" families.

   That this juggling act produced a radically new way of conceiving of the relation of human beings to their world is suggested in the striking shifts in the creative response manifested in the only art surviving from this period. As one scholar has put it, the Geometric art of the eighth century entailed "a rather cozy domestication of the world . . . and imagery of control." But, "we find people in the seventh century surrounding themselves with images which, both by their exuberant style and by the creatures they chose to depict, go beyond the bounds of human control" (Osborne 1998a: 65). More broadly, the ideological struggle over the next two centuries has been characterized as one between an "elite" ideology and a "middling" ideology.[11] In place of "anti-aristocratic" thought (Donlan 1973 [1999]) this view emphasizes a conflict *within* the ruling class between those who see their best interest in fostering a (mystified) sense of solidarity and common interest within the *polis* and those determined to celebrate their superiority and "otherness." The first group gives up many of the external signs of their real privilege, while the second flaunts it in lifestyle – celebrated most obviously in sympotic vase-painting and poetry – , in dedications, in Panhellenic games, and in funeral monuments (Osborne 1998a: 77–85, 133–55). Much compelling evidence has been brought forth in support of this "middling/ elite" opposition. Particularly suggestive is the argument that the fostering of the "middling" ideology had the *unintended* consequence of preparing those outside the elite for the emergence of democracy (Morris 1996b: 36–42). What is troubling about this analysis is its implicit or potential Hegelianism: ideologies contend with each other and at certain point cast up a new formation that is "realized" in the institutional form of democracy. Only, it seems, as an afterthought does Morris rightly acknowledge the continuing reality of oligarchic domination: "Many *poleis* entrusted themselves to the guardianship of oligarchies throughout the classical period. On the whole, it seems that democracy was only tried out when a military crisis raised the stakes and made it impossible for the guardians to claim to represent the middle" (Morris 1996b: 41). The reality of oligarchy throughout the whole period – in particular the unique prestige of Sparta (see below) – casts serious doubt on the alleged collapse of elitist ideology. To be sure, Persian domination of Ionia required an adjustment of the class-based celebration of "orientalizing" values, but the mystification of continuing aristocratic domination of landownership in response to pressure from below – hardly acknowledged or explored by Kurke or Morris – took many forms that with hindsight seem contradictory but attest perhaps better to the flexibility and adaptability of rulers vis-à-vis ruled than to clear-cut conflicts within the ruling class.

Homer has often been claimed as a major element in this self-conscious ideological offensive (e.g., Morris 1986). My own view, which space does not permit me to elaborate, is that both the probable conditions of performance (large panhellenic festivals which are first attested in the eighth century)[12] and the texts themselves reflect at best a highly ambivalent and more deeply a hostile response to the shift from monarchy to oligarchy, the religious celebration of protective deities, and the legitimation of the *aristoi* by claims of inherited superiority. The *Iliad*, which I am still inclined to see as a poem of the second half of the eighth century,[13] looks back to an idealized Dark Age meritocracy where the best warrior is acknowledged as worthy of the best prizes and highest status in a process conceived as ultimately controlled by the community of fellow warriors ("the sons of the Achaians"). Agamemnon, with his inherited scepter and numerous followers despite his relative incompetence as a warrior and leader, suggests the process that was leading inexorably toward the consolidation of an aristocracy, while numerous details point toward a movement away from a fortress dependent on a warrior-chief to the emergence of true poleis, in which citizens share some sense of collective responsibility for their community.[14]

By contrast the *Odyssey* seems to me a poem fully immersed in the next major historical development that appears to have followed hard upon the formation of the *polis* if not contemporaneous with it, namely, the simultaneous and interconnected massive expansion of Mediterranean trade and so-called colonization. Odysseus, who unambiguously displays the consciousness of a potential colonist (9.116–41), is insultingly taken for a trader (8.159–64) and plausibly presumed the bosom friend of traders (1.180–7), embodies the same Dark Age ideal of the meritocratic monarchic *basileus* as the *Iliad*.[15] But the process of aristocratic consolidation is assumed to have progressed so far that the modest-sized island of Ithaca is said to contain many *basilêes*, any of whom might occupy the preeminent position seemingly abandoned by Odysseus (1.394–6), though the plans of the suitors to divide up his wealth once they have disposed of Telemachus (2.335–6) suggests that they also envision doing away with the very idea of the paramount *basileus*. Odysseus' long build-up of rage in the guise of a beggar against these leisured playboys with their fancy servants and lives filled with sports and feasting, who are grimly and systematically slaughtered to the last man, seems to me to reflect the deep resentments of the substantial portion of the Greek population who had lost their livelihoods in the consolidation of aristocratic power and had to seek survival as colonists or traders.

Hesiod, Tyranny, and the Solonian Crisis

If this reading is at all to the point, the celebration in the *Odyssey* of what looks like nostalgia for the Dark Age may in fact anticipate what is usually seen as one of the next major political development, the rise of tyranny. Tyranny, whatever its other causes, was especially associated with the suppression of aristocratic power and the support of discontented peasants.[16] What is frustrating from the perspective of anyone seeking to understand the nature of these developments from a class perspective is the absence of any clear evidence of the *means* by which aristocrats oppressed the peas-antry. Here the evidence of Hesiod is both tantalizing and ultimately a great source of frustration. A recent study by Anthony Edwards (2004) has rightly stressed that the text of Hesiod confines its specific critique of the *basilées* to bribe-taking and the manipulation of the judicial process. At the same time the sense of totalitarian power evoked in the parable of the hawk and the nightingale (*WD* 202–12), the sweeping sense of the centrality of justice to the prosperity or failure of the whole community (*polis* 227, 240) suggest to me that the power exercised by the collective *basilées* is perceived in terms essentially compatible with the vision of the *Odyssey* – just as the idealization of the single *basileus* of the cosmos in the *Theogony* suggests a consciousness ready to return to the rule of one man. An approach to Hesiod that emphasizes the specificity of his individual conflict with his brother fails to explain his enormous and enduring popularity, his citation, for example, by such aristocrats as Alcaeus and Plato. The breadth of Hesiod's vision of the struggle of justice and injustice seems to have struck a cord that resonated far beyond the squabbles of Ascra.

A relatively recent study of the self-presentation of the tyrants (McGlew 1993) has stressed the centrality of claims to bring "justice" to societies where its abuse is rampant. Again we may feel frustrated by the abstraction with which this sweeping concept masks any account of the specific forms of aristocratic abuse. Even the data of Solon's poems, supplemented by the reflections of the later authors who quote them, though far more specific in suggesting the economic sphere of aristocratic abuses, have provoked widely disparate interpretations. The words *hektêmoroi* and *hektêmorioi* appear first in the Aristotelian *Athenaiôn Politeia* and in Plutarch's *Solon* respectively, not in Solon's own words. But scholars are not agreed on so basic an issue as whether the aristocratic landowners *took* one-sixth from the peasants so designated or *left* them only one-sixth of the harvest (van Wees 1999a: 22; Osborne 1996a: 223). Given that the Spartans seem to have taken a half the harvest of the helots and that this form of agricultural exploitation is widely attested in other parts of the world in other eras, I find it hard to believe that taking only a sixth would have provoked so deep a crisis that the aristocrats had recourse to the extreme measures implied in the sweeping powers entrusted to Solon. Whatever the correct meaning of this term, no one doubts the direct evidence of Solon that native Athenians were being reduced to slavery within Attica (Solon fr. 36.13–15 West) and as well were being sold abroad – and for a long enough period prior to the mediation of Solon that these Athenians had even lost their Attic dialect (Solon fr. 36.8–12 West).

Thus for the whole period I am persuaded by van Wees' application of the mafia analogy (1999a): aristocrats with a very high opinion of their own worth and moral rectitude were engaged in relentless competition with each other to extract wealth from the peasants by any means possible. Tyrants – whether opportunists or not – gained dominant positions by the claim, and sometimes perhaps by the reality, of restraining these greed-driven depredations. We are best informed about the Athenian picture, but Alcaeus and Theognis give an equally rich sense of the ferocity of the struggles. Given the monopoly of discourse by the aristocracy, it is not surprising that their struggles with each other and especially against the "traitors" who achieve or aspire to tyranny are the central focus of their poetry. One does not need to assume, for example, that "Pittacus [of Mytilene] was at any time the leader of a popular party, the champion of the oppressed, the spokesman of the spirit of democracy" (Page 1955: 176), or misconstrue Alcaeus' rare references to the *damos* (1955: 177) to recognize that "the story of the noble families fighting against each for supreme power in the State" (1955: 176) is not the whole story. Indeed, only scholars who never ask themselves where the *wealth* of aristocrats came from and what were the *means* by which they might gain "supreme power in the State" could be so confident that class conflict is irrelevant to these struggles. The winners take all in these struggles, exiling or killing the losers. Either they seize the land of the losers (cf. Theognis 1199–1201) and take over their slaves and dependent peasants or – as is likely, if the peasant supporters are swept up in armed struggles – they too are killed or exiled. Some specific sense of the dimensions of the costs to the poorer dependents of aristocrats embroiled in struggles for supremacy is Herodotus' statement that the Spartan king Cleomenes, at the instigation of Isagoras, rival of Cleisthenes, drove out 700 families from Athens (5.72.13–14). Scholars have of course disputed the figure as too high (e.g., Stanton 1990: 141), but that such a figure seemed credible to Herodotus and presumably to his audience suggests that it was recognized as "normal" that all those connected with the losing aristocrats would suffer the consequences.[17]

The impact of the tyrants on the terms on which class struggle was pursued in the wake of their fall is an important consideration. While generalizations are always open to exceptions, I think McGlew (1993) makes a persuasive case that the experience of tyranny, in particular such measures as reorganizing and renaming the tribes that made up the population, building projects such as temples, aqueducts, sewers, public fountains as well as the organization of community-wide religious festivals inevitably fostered a greater sense of identification with the power and prestige of the *polis*. The only problem with this just observation is that, like the "middling/elite" opposition, it may lead to the impression that this effort at creating a homogenized consciousness in the *polis* somehow ended class struggle. As long as the aristocracy continued to hold the best land, and through the leisure won from the labor of slaves (Ste Croix 1981) exercised control of cultural and political life, the struggle continued.

Sparta and the Consolidation of the Aristocratic Ideal

In the case of Sparta we have in the poems of Tyrtaeus evidence for the means by which internal class conflict in the *polis* was "solved" by directing hostility outward into conquest and the systematic exploitation of those outside the community to extract the wealth necessary to "homogenize" a seriously divided *polis*. Aristotle, in a section of the *Politics* where he is discussing how "in aristocracies revolutions are stirred up when a few only share in the honors of the state," elaborates his point with specific examples. It is striking that *all* the examples he gives are from Spartan history, ranging from the "so-called Partheniai" who were expelled and founded the colony of Tarentum late in the eighth century, to the rebellion of Cinadon in 398. Apart from inequitable sharing of honors, to which he had given pride of place as a cause of revolutions in aristocracies, he also cites economic causes: "when some are very poor and others very rich, a state of society which is most often the result of war, as at Lacedaemon in the days of the Messenian War; this is proved from the poem of Tyrtaeus, entitled 'Good Order'; for he speaks of certain citizens who were ruined by the war and wanted to have a redistribution of the land."[18] It is very frustrating that Aristotle does not quote directly from Tyrtaeus: he does not spell out how citizens were ruined by the war or why he believes war is the most common cause of such economic disparities, but the demand for redistribution of the land suggests that long-standing disparities in the division of land were exacerbated by the war. Despite the emphasis in Tyrtaeus on the apparent motive of land hunger in attacking Messenia, a land "of broad dancing places . . . good for plowing, good for sowing," fr. 5.2–3 West) it is hard to believe there was any absolute shortage of land in Laconia. Rather, as has been effectively argued a propos of Attica during the Solonian crisis,[19] it was the dramatic inequality of the division of existing land that triggered the decision to seek new land and use external war as a vehicle for imposing internal unity. Though the relationship of the two Messenian Wars remains murky, it appears that the eighth–century conquest was sufficiently arduous and lengthy to produce a whole generation of sons of dubious legitimacy, who were a sufficient threat to the status quo to be shipped off to found Tarentum, traditionally in 706. The second war, probably in the mid-seventh century, which Tyrtaeus describes as requiring twenty years (fr. 5.4–8 West), seems to have been intimately connected with the internal crisis that led to the measures collectively described as the "Spartan system" or the "*eunomia*" ("good-order"), a term Hesiod uses to characterize the utopian world order after the triumphant succession of Zeus to the kingship of heaven (*Th.* 902). Since the chronology of the implementation of specific components of this system is irretrievable, the best way of formulating the process is to stress the consistent underlying logic of the system (Hodkinson 1997: 86). Given Tyrtaeus' explicit – gloating? – description of the burdens imposed on the Messenians, "bringing to their masters, under the pressure of grim necessity, half of all the crop the field yields" (fr. 6 W), it seems a reasonable inference that the economic foundations of the system were laid first. A leisured class of "peers" was created by allotting enough helot-worked land to ensure – at least by seventh-century criteria – sufficient income to free all members of this class from the necessity of agricultural labor. The consequences of enslaving a substantial population to work the land of their ancestors for the benefit of foreigners presumably were clear by the time of the second Messenian War if not sooner. Thus more or less simultaneous with the economic arrangements must have been various measures aimed at the full militarization of this new class of peers. The thoroughness of the efforts to implement a "middling" ideology – to erase all signs of class differences within this group – is breath-taking: homogenized clothing, diet, living quarters, education, sexual rules. Central to the socialization process was the celebration of communal over individual interests. This is clear from Tyrtaeus' relentless efforts to "sell" death as a brave hoplite as the greatest imaginable male achievement (fr. 10; 11; 12 W) and his sweeping dismissal of athletic prowess so dear to the elite (fr. 12 W). Yet a central lever of that socialization process was the valorization of that quintessential aristocratic value, competition with one's peers. Over the long run the continued substantial inequalities in landholdings, allowing some the enormous luxury of competing in horse-racing, the most extravagant of ancient sports, and a marriage system[20] that encouraged the consolidation of family wealth led to fewer and fewer "peers" being able to sustain their required contribution to the Spartan fraternity system, so that in the relatively short period between 480 to 371 the true Spartiates declined from 8,000 to some 1,500.[21]

The ascendancy of Sparta during the archaic period was intimately connected with the "Spartan mirage" (Ollier 1933; 1943), an illusion of Spartan inherent uniqueness and – usually – superiority that consolidated various elements in the aristocratic ideal on the ideological level despite the absence of any apparent discursive contributions by Spartans themselves, who seemed to have remained at the minimal level of literacy. Supremacy in warfare, total independence from all other sorts of physical labor, the complete antisepsis from the corruption of trade or money, systematic homosexuality (Cartledge 1981) combined with a celebration and public display of female beauty (Pomeroy 2002: 132–3) – all seemed to fulfill the aspirations of aristocrats from the rest of Greece to represent a true meritocracy while enjoying what they considered the most important of pleasures. Moreover, Sparta's ingenuity in forming the first inter-*polis* extensive alliance devoted to fostering oligarchy and combating first tyranny then democracy had the effect of transforming class struggle within individual Greek poleis into a panhellenic struggle.

Athenian Developments

We have already touched upon the Solonian crisis and the phenomenon of tyranny in Athens. The element of class struggle is perhaps nowhere more self-evident than in the circumstances that induced the ruling aristocracy of Athens, self-styled the Eupatridai (sons of noble fathers), to risk empowering a single individual, who, as Solon himself emphasizes, was in a perfect position to make himself tyrant, in the hopes of a peaceful solution to the perceived threat of those they were exploiting and oppressing. To be sure, the details of those circumstances, as described by Solon himself and by our ancient sources, are by no means as clear as one would like. But Solon's fragments are clear enough evidence that the threat of massive bloodshed was imminent (fr. 36.22–5 W).

The alternative of tyranny had already been attempted by Cylon, an aristocratic Olympian victor, in 632, and the wording of Thucydides' account (1.126) suggests that at that point the peasantry "all came in from the countryside and joined in besieging" Cylon and his partisans, all of whom, with the possible exception of Cylon himself, were killed. Again one wonders how many of those killed were themselves aristocrats and how many were peasant pawns in the games of their leaders. The subsequent written law code of Dracon, judging from what little has survived, seems far less about giving ordinary citizens access to unambiguous laws than dealing with the crisis within the ruling elite provoked by these killings.[22]

Solon's solutions to the crisis entailed a trade-off of increased political power and access to justice for the peasants in return for preserving as much as possible of the unequal division of property: the ending of debt-slavery, probably a limited redivision of the land,[23] establishment of an executive committee (*boulê*) for the assembly, an apparently very explicit law code, establishment of an appeals court (*êliaia*) are some of the advantages for the *dêmos* which Solon claimed they could never have "seen in dreams" (37 W). The reorganization of citizenry in terms of income rather than ancestry, while it seems to have benefited primarily those with wealth lacking pedigrees (Foxhall 1997), could have meant little to the peasant majority. At the same time Solon claimed that "it did not please him to [act] with the violence of tyranny, or for the base (*kakoisin*) to have an equal share of their country's fertile soil with the noble (*esthlous*)" (fr. 34.7–9 W), from which we can assume that the best the peasants achieved was free title to the little they had earlier had. It appears from his defensive tone that these measures satisfied neither side. Though most scholars attribute to Solon the creation of an "independent" peasantry,[24] the bitter struggles of the sixth century which saw three separate attempts to establish the tyranny of Peisistratus are unlikely to have entailed only the deaths of aristocrats: again it seems most likely that the feuding aristocrats played off their respective peasant followers against each other. Even if the threat of debt-slavery was removed, peasants without adequate land to feed themselves in years of bad harvest – which seem to have been a regular phenomenon (Garnsey 1988: 9 and passim) – remained subordinated to the bigger landowners.[25] The fact that Peisistratus saw fit to establish travelling judgeships attests to the continued oppression of the peasantry through manipulation of "justice."

The class character of the Cleisthenic revolution is still hotly debated, but I believe the focus on Cleisthenes' motives[26] is somewhat misplaced. It seems plausible enough that faced with the prospect of a Spartan-backed return to the narrowest sort of oligarchic rule under Isagoras and his faction, Cleisthenes resorted to strategies that had worked for some tyrants in their struggles with aristocratic rivals – appeals to the masses, reorganization of tribes (Corinth and Sicyon), massive building programs, religious festivals. He was, however, constrained by the fact that Athens had already had a very negative experience of tyranny: hence the guarantee implicit in the law of ostracism that neither he nor his family would assume such a role. He may well have been confident that his success in verbal manipulation of the assembled citizenry would be a sufficient source of future power – as indeed in the long run it was for his family, if not for himself. Like Solon he gambled on a trade-off of expanded political power for the *dêmos* in exchange for preserving the property relations of his own class, but this time the consequences undoubtedly far exceeded his expectations. The exploration of the consequences would take us beyond our period. I would say only that the implication built into so many accounts of the emergence of democracy (e.g., Manville 1990) that its arrival heralded the end of class warfare in Athens vastly overstates the case (Rose 1992: chs. 4–6).

The all-too-present threat of Spartan-backed reaction and the unanticipated rise of the threat of Persia had the effect of dramatically accelerating the democratic consciousness of the peasantry in Athens. For the aristocracy of Greece it created an identity crisis: for the Aleuadai of Thessaly and the ruling elite in Thebes support from the authoritarian Persian regime seemed the better option than risking annihilation for the sake of what was after all primarily an assault provoked by democratic Athens. On the other hand, for Sparta and other aristocratic poleis the threat of the loss of their precious autonomy ultimately made risks assumed in solidarity with Athens worth the price. But the very necessity of taking sides accelerated the process already begun with Sparta's intervention in Athens – and perhaps already with her expedition against Polycrates – in which a Panhellenic class war was in the making.

NOTES

1 Special thanks to David Roselli and the editors of this volume for helpful feedback on an earlier, much longer version of this text.
2 E.g., Starr 1977: 19, 200–1 n. 31; Donlan 1999 [1980]: 189–90 n. 7; Hopkins 1983: xiii.
3 For useful overviews and debates see McLellan 1979; 1983; Anderson 1976; 1980; 1983; Jameson 1971; Jones 1977.
4 There is almost literally not a word of my account that would not be passionately disputed by some other self-styled Marxist. While it is tempting and often comforting to mock Marxist "in-fighting," it is one of the characteristics of Marx's heritage that it is self-reflexive and constantly attempts to historicize and critique its own categories of analysis.
5 See Turnbull 1962 for an account of a classless society.
6 Clifford Geertz's much admired essay (1973: 193–233) on ideology especially stresses the role of ideology as a response to *strain* through the generation of symbolic maps of confusing new realities, but he is at pains to minimize any relation of these responses to specifically economic structures of specific societies.
7 For Cuban slaves during the sugar cane harvest when they were often literally worked to death, doing as little as possible was an absolute condition of survival (Foner 1962: 189).
8 Desborough 1972: 329–55; Snodgrass 1971: 380–8; 1993b: 35; see also chs. 3–4, above.
9 Osborne 1998b; Wilson 1997a.
10 *Pace* Murray 1980 (1993): 116; text of oath: 114–15.
11 Morris 1996b; Kurke 1999: 19–21; cf. 1992.
12 Wade-Gery 1958; Taplin 1992.
13 *Pace* Burkert 1976; M.L. West 1995; et al.
14 Rose 1992: 43–91; 1997; Scully 1990; Haubold 2000; see also ch. 5, above.
15 See Dougherty 2001 for a rich exploration of connections between trade, colonization and the *Odyssey*. Rose 1992: 92–140. Thalmann's interesting exploration of class relations in the *Odyssey* (1998) glances only in passing at the phenomenon of colonization and ignores Odysseus' association with trade. See Rose 1999.
16 Aristotle, *Politics* 1305a22–3; Salmon 1997; see also ch. 6, above.
17 See also van Wees 2000b.
18 Aristotle, *Politics* 1306b 23–1307a2; Tyrtaeus fr. 1 West; cf. van Wees 1999b.
19 Foxhall 1997; Osborne 1996a: 222–3.
20 Hodkinson 1989; cf. Ste. Croix 1981: 102.

21   Cartledge 1979: 307–18; Hodkinson 2000; see also ch. 7, above.
22   Gagarin 1986; Andrewes 1982a: 1982b; Osborne 1996a: 185–96; 1997.
23   van Wees 1999a; Osborne 1996a: 225.
24   Osborne 1996a: 225; Wood 1988: 95 and passim; see also ch. 8.
25   I am convinced by Rhill 1996: 94–5; Harris 2002 that Solon did not end debt-bondage
     as opposed to debt-slavery.
26   E.g., Stanton 1990 vs. Osborne 1996a: 299–304.

CHAPTER TWENTY-FIVE

Gender[1]

Lin Foxhall

Self-evident as it appears, how we understand the specific roles of women and men in the archaic Greek world depends entirely on how we reconstruct Greek societies of the period. In practice this is a difficult exercise. Different scholarly approaches to archaic Greece have resulted in radically different visions of gender, age, and social organization. Arguments have been put forward to support opposing positions that women held a worse or, frequently, a better position in pre-classical Greek societies than in later periods. Our diverse but fragmentary source material presents a bee's-eye view: each kind of source projects a different picture and these are not always easily integrated into a coherent narrative.

This chapter will investigate the representation of gender and social organization in a range of sources from the archaic period. Each is explored in some depth as a case study and analyzed to suggest how gender might have functioned in relation to age, rank, status and other social variables in archaic Greek culture. The aim is to understand the impact which the ideology of gender division and the principles of gender roles might have had on people's lives. The result is a partial picture which only skims the surface of this fascinating and profoundly complex aspect of social life.

Women and Men in Homer

Gender is a key element in epic poetry. The masculinity of heroes is highlighted by setting them amidst a spectrum of male and female characters, human and divine, of varying ages, ranks and statuses. Recent scholarship on gender in epic has often focused on the *Odyssey*, perhaps because the characters and their situations seem more approachable than those of the *Iliad* and female characters play more prominent roles in the story line.[2] However the representation of men, women, and gender on the battlefields of the *Iliad* are as useful for analyzing ideologies of gender as the cosy domesticity of the *Odyssey*. Most importantly, Homeric epic established a base line for ideologies of gender which not only permeated the world of archaic Greece, but also lasted for the whole of classical antiquity.[3]

Iliad *1: causality and gender relations*

From the outset the *Iliad* involves relationships between men and women. The Trojan War was itself initiated by the abduction of a woman (Helen of Sparta, wife of Menelaus). So too, the action of the *Iliad* begins with an abducted woman, her return to her father and the subsequent quarrel between Achilles and Agamemnon. The roles of male and female characters, both human and divine, in this chain of events are worth exploring in some detail. At the beginning of the *Iliad*, the poet explains the background to the anger of Achilles, the outcome of his quarrel with Agamemnon over a woman (1.8–13). The Achaeans had taken Chryseis, the daughter of Chryses, priest of Apollo, as part of the booty from earlier raids on cities. The girl had been handed over to Agamemnon, leader of the Achaean Greeks, as part of his share (1.125–6, 366–9). Agamemnon had rejected her father's attempt to ransom her (1.12–33). But the old priest Chryses prayed to Apollo for revenge on the Achaeans, and the god answered his prayer by striking them and their animals with plague (1.35–52). To propitiate the god, the Achaeans had to send the girl back home to her father with a hecatomb (one hundred sacrificial animals; 1.54–100). Agamemnon is furious at this.

Despite Achilles' protests that no other prize is available (1.121–9), Agamemnon insists that if Chryseis returns home he must have a replacement even if that means taking someone else's prize (1.130–9). Achilles complains that Agamemnon is greedy and has always taken the best booty, threatening to return home with his men (1.149–71). Agamemnon retaliates:

> But here is my threat to you.
> Even as Phoebus Apollo is taking away my Chryseis,
> I shall convey her back in my own ship, with my own
> followers; but I shall take the fair-cheeked Briseis,
> your prize, I myself going to your shelter, that you may learn well
> how much greater I am than you, and another man may shrink back
> from likening himself to me and contending against me.
>
> (1.181–7)[4]

While the outraged Achilles ponders whether or not to run his sword through Agamemnon, the goddess Athena grabs his hair instructing him to stick to verbal abuse, and not to kill Agamemnon (1.188–214). Achilles obeys. Despite the old king Nestor's attempts to reconcile the two warriors, neither will give way (1.247–305). Achilles retires, proclaiming that he will not use force to stop Agamemnon taking his girl Briseis, but neither will he obey Agamemnon's commands nor fight for the Greeks in the future (1.233–41, 292–303). Agamemnon prepares to return Chryseis to her father, and instructs his heralds to take Briseis from Achilles, who duly lead her away, much to Achilles' shame and distress (1.308–48):

> But Achilles
> weeping went and sat in sorrow apart from his companions
> beside the beach of the grey sea looking out on the infinite water.
> Many times stretching forth his hands he called on his mother.
>
> (1.348–51)

Achilles' mother, the minor sea goddess Thetis, rises out of the waves in response to his entreaties (1.357–63). Achilles asks for her help (1.364–412). As soon as she can, Thetis goes to Olympus to call in the favor Zeus owes her, asking him to strengthen the Trojans, thus forcing the Achaeans to ask for Achilles' help and to restore his damaged honor:

> She came and sat beside him with her left hand embracing
> his knees, but took him underneath the chin with her right hand
> and spoke in supplication to lord Zeus son of Cronus:
> "Father Zeus, if ever before in word or action
> I did you favour among the immortals, now grant what I ask for . . .
>
> Deeply disturbed Zeus who gathers the clouds answered her:
> "This is a disastrous matter when you set me in conflict
> with Hera, and she troubles me with recriminations.
> Since even as things are, forever among the immortals
> she is at me and speaks of how I help the Trojans in battle.
> Even so, go back again now, go away, for fear she
> see us. I will look to these things that they be accomplished.
>
> (1.500–4, 517–24)

Zeus then returns home to face his suspicious wife Hera in the company of the family of gods.

> Thus he took his place on the throne; yet Hera was not
> ignorant, having seen how he had been plotting counsels
> with Thetis the silver-footed, the daughter of the sea's ancient,
> and at once she spoke revilingly to Zeus son of Cronus:
> "Treacherous one, what god has been plotting counsels with you?
> Always it is dear to your heart in my absence to think of
> secret things and decide upon them. Never have you patience
> frankly to speak forth to me the thing that you purpose."
>
> (1.536–43)

In response to Hera's repeated nagging, Zeus finally threatens her with physical violence. Hera is frightened, but is comforted by her son Hephaistos:

> Then in return, Zeus who gathers the clouds made answer:
> "Dear lady I never escape you, you are always full of suspicion.
> Yet thus you can accomplish nothing surely, but be more
> distant from my heart than ever, and it will be the worse for you.

If what you say is true, then that is the way I wish it.
But go then, sit down in silence and do as I tell you,
for fear all the gods, as many as are on Olympus, can do nothing
if I come close and lay my unconquerable hands upon you."
He spoke, and the goddess the ox-eyed lady Hera was frightened
and went and sat down in silence wrenching her heart to obedience,
and all the heavenly gods in the house of Zeus were troubled.
Hephaistus the renowned smith rose up to speak among them,
to bring comfort to his beloved mother, Hera of the white arms.

                                                    (1.560–72)

Women, men and the ideologies of gender

Scholars agree that we cannot read Homeric epic literally, but differ significantly
in their views of the degree to which it might or might not represent a coherent
and/or historical society. My personal view is that epic bears approximately the same
relationship to "real life" as contemporary TV soap operas: both genres are larger-
than-life fantasies peopled by characters who are not individuals so much as "types."
In epic, these characters are always set in the past, at an earlier stage of human social
development. Their behavior is contrasted to that of "real people, today" by the
poet (Graziosi and Haubold 2005: 97, 115). The poems thus do not portray a "real"
or "historical" society in the modern sense. However, both soap opera and epic draw
for their impact on themes and perspectives which are prevalent in and relevant
to the societies which generate them in the first place. Even if the plots stretch
credibility and most of the situations in which the characters find themselves do not
accurately portray the banal realities of everyday life, they reflect, challenge and to
some extent shape the ideologies and concerns of mainstream society. Therefore,
what we can learn from this episode of the *Iliad* is *not* "how men really treated women"
in any particular period or place in early Greece. Rather, Homeric epic informs us
about deeply embedded social and moral values, including the principles of social
hierarchies and gender relations, which more generally underpinned the societies of
the archaic Greek world.

   As noted above, in the *Iliad* women are essential to the way in which events unfold
for the warriors who are the central characters. The poet sets us up to perceive women
as crucial elements in a chain of causality, but not the movers and shakers of events.
Women are portrayed as the cause of problems among men: because of their very
existence men behave badly and do rash things. The young women of noble birth
(in true epic style) abducted by the Achaeans, Chryseis and Briseis, are portrayed
as objects, toys of the heroes. Agamemnon wants to keep Chryseis because she is
ornamental: "I like her better than Clytemnestra my own wife, for in truth she
is no way inferior, neither in build nor stature nor wit, nor in accomplishment"
(1.113–15). Heroes are autonomous, but there are no epic heroines (Graziosi and
Haubold 2005: 99). The poet shows these young female captives as subject to men,
and only just acknowledges that they might have feelings (e.g., Briseis' distress when
led away from Achilles to Agamemnon, 1.346–8).

The representation of the older women in this episode is less clear-cut. Hera is portrayed as a nagging, suspicious wife, and Zeus seems to be rather afraid of her when he tells Thetis to go away lest Hera see them. Hera is no shrinking violet, and confronts him face-to-face. Zeus acknowledges her status as his wife and the privileges which that position commands, but he quickly runs out of reasonable arguments and then addresses her complaints and questions not with sensible discussion, but with threats of violence.

Among both deities and mortals, wives in Homer appear to participate in semi-public gatherings in male company, in contrast to the way the women of later classical Athens were often represented as secluded from men and public life. However, the context is generally firmly within the household, in the company of other family members. Thus, Hera speaks out among the family of the gods, as did Thetis in the house of Peleus (*Il.*1.396–400). In the *Odyssey* Penelope holds a prominent position in the house of Odysseus (*Od.* 2.129–37), although Telemachus, her grown-up son, claims authority in the absence of his father (1.325–361). Odysseus is told that the way to gain favor in Phaeacia is to approach the queen, Arete, as she sits by the hearth in the public rooms of the palace which is her home (*Od.* 6.297–315; 7.48–77), although Arete herself does not speak out until the assembled Phaeacians have departed (7.233–9). As this last example shows, hierarchies of rank and status may temper gender relations: Athena can grab Achilles' hair because she is a goddess, while among the gods, Hera is more senior than Thetis. However, all of these women hold their positions in relation to the men in their lives (Naerebout 1987: 124). Nor can they get their way with men by direct action; instead they persuade, cajole, manipulate, or deceive. Frequently they engage men's attention by direct bodily contact, as when Thetis meets Zeus, Athena stops Achilles, or Chryseis and her father Chryses embrace on her return. Sons are represented as very close to their mothers (Hephaestus comforts and advises Hera), and they in turn support their sons (Thetis and Achilles). Although Penelope is portrayed as the paradigm of the faithful and virtuous wife, Telemachus, her son, is as important to her as her husband (*Od.* 4.727–8, 762–6).

In contrast, masculinity, power and authority go together in epic. Men achieve positions of power and authority by fighting and violence (Naerebout 1987: 125), but at the same time they are not ashamed to show strong emotion (van Wees 1998a). Agamemnon, outwitted by Chryses and overpowered by Apollo, is shamed by losing his prize. He receives Achilles' challenges as a threat and an insult. To regain his position of power, he seizes Achilles' prize, taking advantage of the fact that Achilles is younger, with less authority (as Nestor's attempts at reconciliation make clear). Achilles, when shamed, turns first to thoughts of violence, then to fighting with words, then to his divine mother, whose immortal status outranks even Agamemnon. For these heroes, their masculinity propels them into a constant competitive struggle to maintain their position in relation to other men, regularly played out through physical force. This can easily lead to the kind of destructive "excessive masculinity" displayed by Achilles and Agamemnon in their quarrel, in contrast to responsible masculinity which considers the needs of others (Graziosi and Haubold 2003; 2005: 106–9).

Homeric epic, therefore, sharply differentiates male and female roles. These roles are complex and the expectations associated with them are mitigated by age and status. However, the perspective of epic is masculine (Naerebout 1987: 111) and women are usually defined by their relationships to men of equal or superior status.

Hesiod and the Institutionalization of Misogyny

In his cosmological hexameter poems the *Theogony* (535–616) and the *Works and Days* (42–105), Hesiod presents an origin-myth of women as a curse (disguised as a gift) given to mankind by the gods. These passages have been the subject of considerable scholarly analysis.[5] The story is the culmination of a series of reciprocal deceptions, beginning with Zeus' anger when Prometheus attempts to deceive him by dividing the sacrificial ox so that the gods choose the unappetizing bones wrapped in the attractive fat while men keep the meat. In response Zeus takes fire away from men, but Prometheus steals it back again. Zeus then orders the gods to make Pandora from clay, in the shape of a beautifully adorned bride on the surface but with nothing but badness inside. This beautiful image is handed over to Epimetheus, Prometheus' foolish brother, who accepts her without remembering Prometheus' instructions not to take any gift from Zeus. Pandora, in one sense herself a pottery vessel made to trap men, brings with her a *pithos*, a ceramic storage jar, which she opens despite instructions not to do so. The result is that all the evils which plague humans are let loose into the world, although she replaces the lid in time to keep Hope in the jar.

For Hesiod, women are a different species from men, with a different origin. They are a necessary evil. Without them a man cannot have children to support him in his old age, but women consume a man's substance and sap his strength.

> For from her is descended the female sex, a great affliction to mortals as they dwell with their husbands – no fit partners for accursed Poverty, but only for Plenty . . .

> And he gave a second bane to set against a blessing for the man who, to avoid marriage and the trouble women cause, chooses not to wed, and arrives at grim old age lacking anyone to look after him. He is not short of livelihood while he lives, but when he dies, distant relatives share out his living. Then again, the man who does partake of marriage, and gets a good wife who is sound and sensible, spends his life with bad competing constantly against good; while the man who gets the awful kind lives with unrelenting pain in his heart and spirit, and it is an ill without a cure.
>
> (Hes. *Theog.* 590–3, 602–12; tr. West 1988a)

Gender in Early Greek Poetry: Iambic and Lyric Verse

The appropriate and inappropriate behavior of men and women *as* men and women, is a recurring theme in Greek poetry of the seventh and sixth centuries. However, different genres and works present diverse and sometimes contradictory aspects of gender ideology. Most of these poems were composed by men, although a substantial body of verse is attributed to one of the few named Greek women poets, Sappho. Not surprisingly it is impossible to compress these into a unified, coherent narrative, and it is not easy to understand the connections between the ideals and ideas expressed in poetry and "real life." The following sections explore these issues in two case studies.

Semonides and the tradition of misogyny

The seventh-century iambic poem attributed to Semonides, preserved in Stobaeus (4.22.193), stands near the start of a line of misogynistic expression that runs from Hesiod straight through classical antiquity and beyond.[6] It begins by presenting women as virtually a different species (cf. Hesiod): "From the first god made the temperament (*nóon*) of woman separately (*chôris*)" (fr. 7.1–2, my translation). The meaning of the word "separately" in this passage is ambivalent – it could mean "separately from men" or it could mean different types of women were made separately from each other – perhaps both meanings are intended. The poem then compares different types of women to (mostly) unpleasant animals and natural forces, perhaps implying that at one level *all* women are sub-human. We hear of the slovenly woman made from a pig, the clever but nasty woman made from a fox and the woman made from a dog:

> and the one made from a bitch, whining (?), just like her mother,
> she who wants to hear everything and know everything
> and everywhere peeking and prowling she barks, even if she sees no one.
> A man could not stop her either with threats
> nor if, angered, he knocked out her teeth with a stone,
> not by speaking to her sweetly, not even if she chances to be sitting among guests,
> but constantly she keeps up her unstoppable yapping.
>
> (fr. 7.12–19)[7]

These are followed by the useless woman made of earth, the unpredictable woman made from the sea, the stubborn and greedy woman made from a donkey, the sex-mad weasel woman, and the dainty woman, fit only for kings or tyrants, made from a mare:

> She sends work and trouble somewhere else
> and she wouldn't touch a handmill, take up a sieve,
> and sitting by the oven she avoids getting covered in soot.
> She makes a man her lover by compulsion;
> she washes off the dirt two or three times a day
> anoints herself with perfume
> and always wears her hair combed out long,
> shaded with flowers.
>
> (fr. 7.58–66)

Next comes the devious woman made from a monkey, followed by the only decent type of woman, the one made from the bee:

> The one taking her is fortunate,
> since on such a one blame does not settle.
> Under her life flourishes and increases
> and she grows old loving a loving man
> having borne a good (*kalon*) family (*genos*), famed in name.
> She becomes very distinguished among all women
> and divine grace surrounds her.
> She takes no pleasure sitting among the women where they are talking sex.
> Such women, the best and most sensible, Zeus grants as a favour to men.
>   (fr. 7.83–93)

But, after this optimistic note, the poem ends with a scathing condemnation of the whole species of womankind as "the greatest evil Zeus made" (fr. 7.96–7, 115) to plague men. Even if you think a woman is sensible, says the poet, she will let you down, consume your resources, make your life a misery and behave outrageously when her husband is not looking (fr. 7.96–109; cf. Hes. *Theog.* 590–3, 602–12, quoted above). When Zeus created women

> he placed an unbreakable fetter round our feet
> from the time when Hades received those
> who fought with each other on account of a woman.
>   (fr. 7.116–18)

These "types" of women echo some of the female portraits in Homer and Hesiod. The bitch woman is reminiscent of Hera, the nagging wife (including the "justifiable" male reaction of threatening her with violence). The delicate and beautiful mare woman has her counterpart in Helen of Troy, also referred to indirectly at the end of Semonides' poem[8] – the woman on whose account the Trojan War was fought – driving men mad with desire. Both of these "types" recall different aspects of Pandora, her beautiful exterior (like the mare) with the heart of a bitch (Hes. *WD* 62–8). And Penelope, the faithful and industrious wife who is not led astray even when her husband is not there to guide her is reflected in the bee-woman, locating women's virtue within the setting of family relationships.

The performative context of this poetry is not easy to ascertain. In ancient Greece iambic verse was associated with raunchy satirical humor, and some may have been performed in ritual settings.[9] Frequently it is associated with cults of Demeter and festivals restricted to women, especially the widespread Greek rites of the Thesmophoria, and later Greek writers regularly depict women's songs and activities associated with these cults as overtly hostile to men (Burkert 1985: 244). Such festivals seem a most unlikely setting for the misogynistic iambic verses attributed to Semonides; and the all-male company of the *symposion*, which provided a refuge from women, seems the most obvious context for their performance.[10] One possibility is that this misogynistic iambic poetry was itself a satire of satire – a masculine parody of the songs women were believed (by men) to sing in the Thesmophoria and similar festivals, but this interpretation is speculative. More certainly, early Greek iambic poetry was divided both in use and in its subsequent history along gendered lines: the iambic verses of women in ritual settings have not been preserved, while the probably symposiastic iambic poetry attributed to Semonides has been handed down to us through literary and manuscript traditions. This schism suggests that a strong gender divide affected other aspects of social life in Greek communities of the archaic age.

Alcaeus and Sappho

Elite society of late seventh- and early sixth-century Lesbos has left us a collection of poetic fragments written in the Aeolic dialect attributed to two poets, male and female respectively, Alcaeus and Sappho. Later Greek writers, as well as the famous inscription known as the Parian Marble, describe them both as individuals and set them in a specific historical context. However, it is not clear how reliable this information is: much of it may have been derived by later authors from the poems themselves, most of which have not survived to modern times. Most scholars now believe that we cannot read these poems literally or autobiographically (duBois 1995: 3–4) and it is not certain that the fragments attributed to, e.g., "Sappho" were all written by a single individual (Lardinois 1994: 62) – the same may well be true for other lyric poets of the archaic age. In any case, ancient Greek poetry was generally commissioned for public performance with musical accompaniment; thus the poets (like poets of later times) take on many different voices. However intimate this poetry might appear, we should not assume that any particular poetic voice represents the personal feelings of the poet her- or himself (Lardinois 2001: 78, 92). Nonetheless, despite the difficulties of interpreting this material, early Lesbian poetry offers important insights into contemporary social and political life of wealthy social groups, and the operation of gender within that society.

Alcaeus' poetry covers a range of topics and occasions but several substantial fragments appear to be overtly political, representing political rhetoric in poetic form redolent of Solonic verse, or the complaints of a man in exile railing about his political opponents:

> This wave in turn comes (like?) the previous one, and it will give us much trouble to bale out when it enters the ship's . . . Let us strengthen (the ship's sides) as quickly as possible, and let us race into a secure harbour; and let soft fear not seize any of us; for a great (ordeal) stands clear before us. Remember the previous (hardship): now let every man show himself steadfast. and let us not disgrace (by cowardice) our noble fathers lying beneath the earth.
>
> (fr. 6)[11]

> the Lesbians established this great conspicuous precinct to be held in common, and put in it altars of the blessed immortals . . .
>
> Come, with gracious spirit hear our prayer, and rescue us from these hardships and from grievous exile; and let their Avenger pursue the son of Hyrrhas, since once we swore, cutting . . . never (to abandon?) any of our comrades, but either to die at the

hands of men who at that time came against us and to lie clothed in earth, or else to
kill them and rescue the people from their woes. But Pot-belly did not talk to their
hearts; he recklessly trampled the oaths underfoot and devours our city.

(fr. 129)

I, poor wretch, live with the lot of a rustic, longing to hear the assembly being sum-
moned, Agesilaidas, and the council: the property in possession of which my father and
my father's father have grown old among these mutually destructive citizens, from it I
have been driven, an exile at the back of beyond, and like Onomacles I settled here
alone in the wolf-thickets(?) . . . to the precinct of the blessed gods . . . keeping my feet
out of trouble, where Lesbian women with trailing robes go to and fro being judged
for beauty, and around rings the marvelous sound of the sacred yearly shout of the
women; . . . from many (troubles) when will the Olympian gods (free me?)?

(fr. 130)

This poetry portrays a world in which wealthy men from prominent families were
the primary actors in a factionalized, competitive polis. The stability of the state
(metaphorically depicted as a ship at sea), its governance, the world of citizen landowners, the assembly and the council, the threats of and attacks on political enemies
– all were entirely the concern of a masculine elite (cf. Stehle 1997: 230–3). Women,
performing the rituals of the polis in an extra-mural sanctuary, were clearly a key part
of the social and cosmological order. They were crucial for maintaining relationships
between men, as well as between gods and humans, but they were excluded from
the cut and thrust of politics.

Like other lyric poets, Alcaeus elaborates on Homeric themes, and it is revealing
to compare his treatment of Helen of Troy with that of Sappho. In two similar poems
he writes of Helen in derogatory terms as the destroyer of Greek and Trojan men,
who, led astray by a man because of her feminine weakness, selfish passion and evil
actions, caused the Trojan War.

As the story goes, because of evil deeds bitter grief came once to Priam and his sons
from you, Helen, and Zeus destroyed holy Ilium with fire. Not such was the delicate
maiden whom the noble son of Aeacus, inviting all the blessed gods to the wedding,
married, taking her from the halls of Nereus to the home of Chiron; he loosened the
pure maiden's girdle, and the love of Peleus and the best of Nereus' daughters flourished; and within the year she bore a son, the finest of demigods, blessed driver of
chestnut horses. But they perished for Helen's sake – the Phrygians and their city.

(fr. 42)

. . . and excited the heart of Argive Helen in her breast; and crazed by the Trojan man,
the deceiver of his host, she accompanied him over the sea in his ship, leaving in her
home her child (desolate?) and her husband's bed with its rich coverlet, (since) her heart
persuaded her (to yield?) to love (through the daughter of Dione?) and Zeus . . . many
of his brothers (the dark earth?) holds, laid low on the Trojans' plain for that woman's
sake, and many chariots (crashed?) in the dust, and many dark-eyed (warriors) were
trampled, and (noble Achilles rejoiced in?) the slaughter.

(fr. 283)

The fragments attributed to Sappho represent almost the only surviving poetry from the Greek world likely to be written by a woman. Her account of Helen is very similar in outline to that of Alcaeus, but the perspective is completely different (duBois 1995: 121–3):

> Some say a host of cavalry, others of infantry, and others of ships, is the most beautiful thing on the black earth, but I say it is whatsoever a person loves. It is perfectly easy to make this understood by everyone: for she who far surpassed mankind in beauty, Helen, left her most noble husband and went sailing off to Troy with no thought at all for her child or dear parents, but (love?, Aphrodite?) led her astray . . . lightly . . . (and she?) has reminded me now of Anactoria who is not here; I would rather see her lovely walk and the bright sparkle of her face than the Lydians' chariots and armed infantry . . . impossible to happen . . . mankind . . . but to pray to share . . . unexpectedly.
>
> (fr. 16)

In this poem Sappho presents a distinctively feminine set of values, focused not on the conventions of masculine ideals of warfare and public life, but on love and desire.[12] It is hard not to think of Alcaeus' fragment 283 (above), to which this poem provides an alternative viewpoint. Helen is not presented as a wicked woman, the bane of men, but as a woman with a mind of her own (duBois 1995: 124), and the poet makes no moral judgment on her actions. Although she is an active agent, she is not entirely autonomous, nor by implication, was Anactoria, the absent woman whom Sappho recalls with longing. This is a recurring theme in Sappho's work – women who are active agents, but lack full autonomy. It may be one of the elements which is distinctively feminine:

> ". . . and honestly I wish I were dead." She was leaving me with many tears and said this: "Oh what bad luck has been ours, Sappho; truly I leave you against my will." I replied to her thus: "Go and fare well and remember me, for you know how we cared for you. If not, why then I want to remind you . . . and the good times we had. You put on many wreaths of violets and roses and (crocuses?) together by my side, and round your tender neck you put many woven garlands made from flowers and . . . with much flowery perfume, fit for a queen, you anointed yourself . . . and on soft beds . . . you would satisfy your longing (for?) tender . . . There was neither . . . nor shrine from which we were absent, no grove . . . nor dance . . . sound."
>
> (fr. 94)

As in the case of Helen above, the poet here presents women who have minds and strong feelings of their own but who are caught in a net of powerful social obligations and are thus not entirely in control of their life circumstances. As with Helen, to take complete control would be to transgress the social and political order of the polis, but that does not mean that women were always happy to accept that order passively.

There are hints that Sappho is aware of Lesbian public life and political discourse, but she does not present herself as an active participant. The following poem about her brother, who was perhaps in trouble, has political implications. However, it is formulated as a prayer, thus conforming with the public, religious roles of women visible in Alcaeus' poetry. It is probably also significant that the poem focuses on a close family member, in contrast to the wide-ranging political invective of Alcaeus.

> (Cypris and) Nereids, grant that my brother arrive here unharmed, and that everything he wishes in his heart be fulfilled, and grant too that he atone for all his past mistakes and be a joy to his friends and a bane to his enemies, and may no one ever again be a grief to us; grant that he may be willing to bring honour to his sister . . . grievous sufferings . . . formerly sorrowing . . . hearing . . . millet-seed . . . (accusation?) of the citizens . . . and do you, (august?) Cyprian, putting aside (your former enmity?) (free him?) from evil (sufferings?).
>
> (fr. 5)

Alcaeus' poetry fits the settings of elite male public life, but it is more difficult to locate Sappho and her work (Stehle 1997: 262–3). For many years scholars ancient and modern imagined Sappho as a kind of "school mistress" in charge of teaching young women of the Lesbian elite, though this interpretation is no longer widely accepted (H. N. Parker 1993). Lardinois (2001) has convincingly argued that many of Sappho's poems are formulated as accepted female genres of public discourse: prayers, laments and the praise of brides/wedding songs. This might also give a clue as to where we place her, her friends/lovers and her work: in the private and public religious festivals and roles allocated to the women of the polis, especially to prominent women (cf. Stehle 1997: 265–88). In fragment 94 (above), these are the settings where the two women about to be separated had met and developed their relationship. If this is correct, what is extraordinary about Sappho is not that she wrote songs nor that she expresses explicitly feminine perspectives including homoerotic affection and attachments, but that her work was written down. We know that many women throughout Greek history composed songs, prayers and laments which vanished without a trace. What was distinctive about Lesbian society in the late seventh and early sixth century which preserved the poems of Sappho the woman? As yet, we do not know, though it might be that the outstanding quality of the poetry in combination with her position in a wealthy, high-status family superseded her femininity.

Alcman

Alcman, writing in Sparta in the late seventh century, about contemporary with Alcaios and Sappho, offers another perspective on men's and women's roles in archaic Greek societies. It is clear from both later literary accounts (Calame 2001: 141) and contemporary visual representations (Pipili 1987) that music and dance were tremendously important for many occasions in the communal life of archaic Sparta, for men and women of all ages. Such activities were often performed in groups of the same age, gender and status, thus reifying important social groups and divisions within Spartan society. Alcman F1 (Campbell) is a long poem written for a chorus of young women to perform at a religious festival. In this poem, the poet takes on the voices of the girls in the form of a feminine prayer, depicting their conversations, affection and relationships.

[36] There is such a thing as the vengeance of the gods: that man is blessed who devoutly weaves to the end the web of his day unweeping.

And so I sing of the [40]brightness of Agido: I see her like the sun, which Agido summons to shine on us as our witness; but our illustrious choir-leader by no means allows me either to praise or to fault her; [45]for she herself seems pre-eminent, just as if one were to put a horse among grazing herds, a sturdy, thunderous-hoofed prize-winner, one of those seen in rock-sheltered dreams. [50]Why, don't you see? The race-horse is Venetic; but the hair of my cousin Hagesichora has the bloom of undefiled gold, [55]and her silver face – why do I tell you openly? This is Hagesichora here; and the second in beauty after Agido will run like a Colaxaean horse against an Ibenian; [60]for the Pleiades, as we carry a robe (or plough?) at daybreak (or: to Orthria?), rise through the ambrosial night and fight against us just like the star Sirius.

For abundance of purple [65]is not sufficient for protection, nor intricate snake of solid gold, no, nor Lydian headband, pride of dark-eyed girls, [70]nor the hair of Nanno, nor again godlike Areta nor Thylacis and Cleesithera; nor will you go to Anesimbrota's and say, "If only Astaphis were mine, [75]if only Philylla were to look my way and Damareta and lovely Ianthemis"; no, Hagesichora guards me. For is not fair-ankled Hagesichora present here? [80]Does she not remain (near) Agido and commend our festival? Come, you gods, accept their (prayers): to the gods belong fulfilment and accomplishment. Choir leader – [85]if I may speak – I am myself only a girl screeching pointlessly, an owl from the rafter, but even so I long to please Aōtis most of all for she proved the healer of our sufferings; [90]but it was thanks to Hagesichora that girls trod the path of lovely peace.

For like the trace-horse . . . and in a ship too [95]one must obey the helmsman most of all; and she is of course (not) more melodious than the Sirens, for they are goddesses; but this our choir of ten sings as well as eleven girls: [100]why, its song is like that of a swan on the waters of the Xanthus; and she . . . her lovely yellow hair.

(Alcman 1.36–101, Campbell)

It is difficult to be certain about the context in which this poem was performed, and the interpretation of the internal clues has been much disputed. The poem seems to represent a chorus of ten or eleven teenage girls (70–7, 98–9) performing at a religious festival to a goddess. They are led by Hegesichora – a name, or perhaps a title, which means "chorus leader." The role of Agido (another female name) is not clear: she does not seem to be a member of the chorus, so perhaps she is a priestess or holds some other position in the cult.

Which goddess is the object of their ritual is not certain – the poem mentions "*Aōtis*," which is probably the Lakonian form of Eos, "dawn" (87), and "*orthriai*" (61). The latter term is puzzling, since the word is an adjective meaning "at daybreak," and could thus be translated as either "for Orthria" (an otherwise unknown dawn goddess), or more convincingly as "at dawn" (Hamilton 1989: 469). The situation is complicated because one anonymous ancient commentator emended *orthriai* to *orthiai* – thus identifying the dedicatee with the famous and well-documented Spartan deity Artemis Orthia. This is a tempting solution, but must probably be eliminated because the word *orthiai* does not fit the metre of the poem (Calame 2001: 5; Hamilton 1989: 469).

The association with dawn may be underpinned by lines 60–3 where it is made clear that the song was performed at night, perhaps just before dawn, when both the Pleiades and the dog-star Sirius were visible in the eastern sky. This probably also fixes the time of year at late July or early August. An alternative interpretation of the "Pleiades" as the name of a rival chorus (Calame 2001: 6) need not rule out the astronomical association: it is plausible that a rival chorus would choose a name associated with the season of the festival. The element of competition, common in musical festivals but perhaps also implying athletic competition as part of the festival, may also be suggested by the comparison of the girls to race horses (Hamilton 1989 467–8), but the metaphor might also highlight the "semi-wild" nature of teenage girls.

The summer-time performance of the festival may clarify another puzzling element: the term *pharos* (61). Normally the word means "robe," and this makes most sense in the cultic context. Clothing was regularly dedicated to goddesses, while in many cults statues were ritually "dressed," and these practices are well documented for archaic Sparta (Cole 2004: 213–25). Indeed from the temple of Artemis Orthia we have many dedications of lead votives representing model textiles as well as dedications of loom weights and other equipment for making textiles from both Artemis Orthia (fig. 12.2a) and Athena Chalkioikos (Foxhall and Stears 2000). It is probably also relevant in this context that the start of this section of the poem (36–9) compares the course of a person's life to a piece of weaving, an activity specifically associated with women and the realm of the feminine. The lavish descriptions of the girls' clothing (64–8), a common concern of teenage girls in all periods of history, may also be significant for the cultic context. Similarly, the representations of female clothing in the tiny lead votives are carefully crafted to emphasize that they are rich and ornate (fig. 12.2b). However, one late antique commentator has suggested that the word "*pharos*" means "plough" here, and this has been accepted by some modern scholars (Calame 2001: 5). But, since this is the time of year at which ploughs and ploughing are least significant in Greek farming for the earth is baked hard, this seems less relevant than the cultic association with clothing.

One of the most interesting features of this poem (cf. Alcman 3) is the way in which the relationships of the girls with each other are portrayed. The chorus addresses Hegisichora as "cousin" in line 52, and though we should not necessarily read this literally to assume that the girls are all related, it does imply that they are very close and accustomed to doing a number of activities as a group. The whooper swan (*Cygnus cygnus*) to which the chorus compares itself (100–1, in contrast to the lone girl screeching like an owl, 86–7) is a significant image here, for these swans sing only when they are in large groups; in the breeding season they are solitary and silent (Peterson et al. 1965: 43). The mimicry of teenage girls' conversation in lines 64–91 also highlights the intense, erotic bonds of affection between the girls, expressed in terms reminiscent of Sappho's poetry. It is probable that this reflects the Spartan social system in which both boys and girls were educated in age-groups, spending a considerable amount of time with their age-mates and away from their own families, and thus developing strong affective relationships with each other (Calame 2001: 214–19). It may well be the case that the rite for which this poem was written served to mark a transition in age and life stage – the performance of the poem happening as night turned into day must have served to emphasize its transitory nature.

The poems for young girls by Alcman are complemented by some of his more fragmentary lyrics apparently written for choruses of young men. F2 seems to be dedicated to the Dioskouroi and F46, F47, F48 feature Apollo; these are all deities whose cults were significant for young men and their developing masculinity in Sparta.

> Most worthy of reverence from all gods and men, they dwell in a god-built home (beneath the earth, always alive), Castor – tamers of swift steeds, skilled horsemen – and glorious Polydeuces.
>
> (Alcman F2, Campbell)

The survival of all this poetry probably indicates the very great importance attached to gender- and age-related social groupings in archaic Spartan society, and the marking through cultic performance of the transition from one life stage to the next. For the smooth operation of Spartan society, each different age/gender group had its own specific functions: girls developed into women who married, wove, and bore children while boys grew into men who were warriors. The orderliness of gendered hierarchies and categories is reflected in the dedications found in Spartan sanctuaries. For Artemis Orthia, the rites most often described by later authors (Pausanias 3.16.10) focus on boys and men and these have often been associated with the numerous dedications of lead votives in the shape of warriors starting in the late seventh century (fig. 12.2c). However, as noted above, there are also numerous dedications of model textiles and textile-making equipments such as loom weights (fig. 12.2a). Loomweights, many inscribed, also appear in the sanctuary of Athena Chalkioikos, but here there are also distinctively male votives, notably Athenian Panathenaic amphorae won by Spartan men in the famous Panathenaic games (Dickins 1906–7; 1907–8). In contrast the series of disturbing, grotesque masks from Artemis Orthia are regularly indeterminate in gender, and this may have enhanced their scariness (fig. 12.1). None of this implies gender equality in archaic Sparta; rather it highlights the primacy of order, each group in its place fulfilling its allotted role ostensibly for the benefit of the community as a whole.

Gender and Material Culture

Exploring gender through material objects is a difficult exercise in the best of circumstances, but for the world of archaic Greece the problems are compounded by the particularly skewed and fragmentary nature of the archaeological record. Many successful settlements of archaic times have been obliterated by the classical, Roman and later cities which succeeded them; so it is difficult to see the "urban" and rural landscapes of the period. Moreover, classical archaeologists have traditionally focused on monumental buildings, sanctuaries, cemeteries and the art associated with them, which offer only a partial view of the operation of gender and social organization.

Gender and housing in archaic Greece

In an important article and a book Ian Morris (1999a; 2000: 280–6) presents what he sees as a new mode of gender relations emerging in eighth century Greece. In contrast with the "more flexible" (Morris 1999a: 265) structures of gender he perceives in Iron Age Greece, Morris argues that the new sense of community focused on the male citizen made life more restrictive for women. This, he claims, can be discerned in the social construction of space, in particular with what he identifies as the emergence of the "courtyard house." Following Nevett (1999), he associates this development with structures of gender characteristic of the classical world (especially Athens) in which women become associated with private domestic space (to which access was controlled by men) while simultaneously they were excluded from public spaces. Morris tracks the evolution of domestic architecture from the one-room apsidal houses characteristic of iron age Greece, to rectilinear houses, followed by the "appearance" of courtyard houses at Zagora on Andros in the later eighth century.

One obvious problem with this hypothesis, which Morris himself acknowledges (1999a: 265), is that few Iron Age and eighth-century houses are known or published, and there are even fewer from the seventh and sixth centuries. This makes it hard to locate those we have securely within larger social and political contexts or to test Morris' assumption that these houses were designed for nuclear families. Concomitantly, it is difficult to understand the development of houses and households over the period. Moreover, there is considerable regional variation, so that rectilinear houses emerge at different times in different parts of the Greek world. At Old Smyrna the eighth-century town contained a mix of apsidal, oval, and rectilinear houses (Coldstream 1977: 304). At Zagora virtually all units were rectilinear from the earliest occupation of the site before 800 (Cambitoglou et al. 1971: 27), perhaps in part because the local schist and marble fractures easily into squared blocks. Examples from Magna Graecia, where the use of space was complex and sometimes rather different from "old Greece," may also muddy the waters. For example, the best known sixth-century houses in the *chora* of Metapontion consist of three rows of three rooms, a type which persisted into classical times alongside the "courtyard house" (figure 25.1).

A closer look at the intriguing site of Zagora (figure 25.2) does, however, raise some interesting questions about gender and social organization in early archaic times, and allows a re-examination of Morris' ideas. The cluster of rooms and courtyards at Zagora was not built all at once but grew organically over the course of just over a century (from shortly before 800 to the abandonment of the site early in the seventh century), and was constantly under modification. This is clear from the many walls which butt up against other walls but are not keyed into them, as well as the many units which are subsequently subdivided. The excavators of the site were consequently able to work out an elaborate relative chronology of the various walls and units.[13] Indeed the excavators of the site talk about "units" rather than houses, rooms, or courtyards since it is not always clear where one "house" stops and another starts (Cambitoglou et al. 1971: 13; 1988: 154). None of this should be very surprising

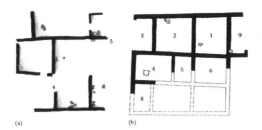

Figure 25.1 Farmhouses in the chora of Metaponto: (a) Cugno del Pero, sixth century BC; (b) Fattoria Fabrizio, fourth century BC, perhaps built on the plan of a sixth-century house on the site
Source: After Adamesteanu (1974) and Carter (2006: 139, fig. 4.3).

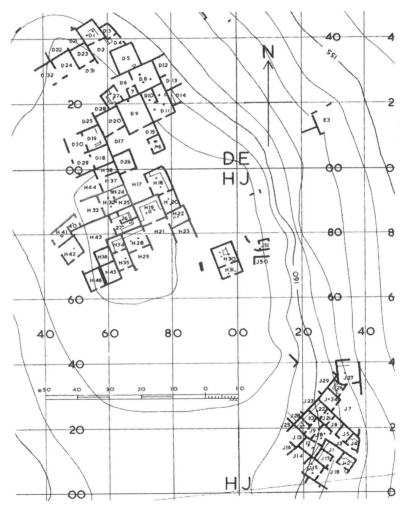

Figure 25.2 Zagora, Andros
Source: After Coldstream (1977: 307, fig. 97).

since families' perceived needs for space change rapidly over the course of their lifecycles. The example that Morris cites[14] to demonstrate the supposed change from a "*megaron*-type" house to a "courtyard type" house is the division of units H32 to create in addition units H24 and H25, with modifications to H43/H26/H27, and the addition of H40/H41/H42 (figure 25.2).[15] However, these changes could as easily be interpreted as the subdivision and extension of a "house" to accommodate changing family needs over time (see below). The result of the modification bears little resemblance to the courtyard houses of classical times.

It is perhaps more useful to ask what kinds of families might have lived at Zagora. Unroofed courtyards were a feature of the site from the beginning. Moreover, some rooms are very large: a good example is H19 built with a substantial bench and a central hearth but also containing a number of spindle whorls as well as a (masculine?) drinking assemblage (fine ware amphora, *skyphoi*, kraters) and cooking pots. In front of H19 is a large court (H21). By the final phase of the site, three two-room units (H34–H35; H28–H29; H22–H23) are arranged on either side of H19–H21.[16] The location of and finds in H19–H21, as well as the large size of the area strongly suggest that a range of different activities was performed in this space by different people at different times. It is possible that groups of people closely related to each other lived in the three adjoining units (H34–H35; H28–H29; H22–H23) but shared H19–H21 as common space for particular kinds of activities such as men's drinking parties or women's textile working groups (figure 25.2). In light of this interpretation, the modification and extension surrounding the large courts H43 (figure 25.2) and H33 (figure 25.2) might represent similar extended family groups living in the adjacent smaller units, but sharing courtyard and other room space (H41?) for joint activities.

We know that family relationships were important for archaic social and political organization, and we should therefore expect close family relationships to be significant for housing. It would not be unreasonable to suppose that parents, adult children with families of their own, siblings and even cousins might live close to each other and engage in some activities in kin-groups larger than the nuclear family. Hence, one could envisage the courts and rooms of Zagora as a series of kin-based compounds rather than as a group of nuclear-family houses, though any such interpretation is speculative at the present state of our knowledge.

The Athenian agora: inventing public space

It is clear from the example of Zagora that conceptualizations of domestic living space and how it was entwined with ideologies of family, gender, and political and social order may have been somewhat different in archaic times than in the classical period. The long-term excavations of the Athenian agora offer another example of how notions of space and gender changed in early Greece, and in particular how the developing distinction between public and private space might relate to notions of gender.[17]

Down to the end of the eighth century the Athenian agora, located at the heart of the ancient city of Athens, was full of graves and remains of private houses, and there is no indication that the public, civic space of political activities was physically separated from the private space of households (figure 25.3).[18] The area of the later Tholos in the south-west corner of the agora housed a cemetery in late Geometric times (Young 1939) (figures 25.3, 25.4). Just south-west of the later agora precinct, on a main road leading into it at the foot of the Areopagus, a cemetery was also established in the eighth century (Young 1951) (figure 25.5, table 25.1).

Table 25.1 Archaic cemetery south-west of the Athenian agora

Graves of the sixth century BC							Total
Men	9 [I, ad]	10 [I, ad]	11 [I]	16 [I]	17 [I]		5
Women	4 [I, ad]	5 [I]	12 [I]	14 [I]	21 [I]		5
Child	3 [urn]	15 [I]					2
Unknown	6 [C]	7 [C]	8 [?]	13 [I]	18 [I]	19 [C] 20 [C]	7
Total							19

Numbers are grave numbers assigned by Young.
I = inhumation; C = cremation; ad = adolescent; urn = urn burial.
Source: From Young (1951).

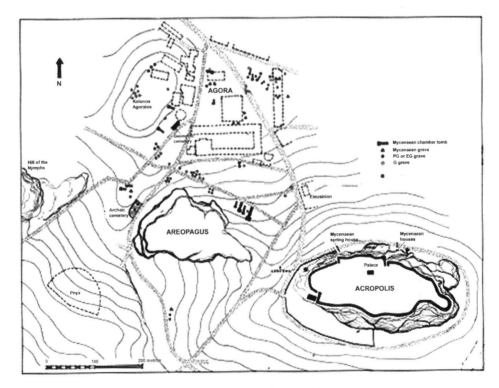

Figure 25.3 Early burials in and around the Athenian Agora
Source: After Camp (1986).

Archaeologically the seventh century is an enigmatic period in Athens. However, (1) the remains of a seventh century house near the Geometric cemetery in the south-west corner of the agora, (2) the presence of seventh-century wells and graves, along with traces of residential debris scattered around the precinct,[19] and (3) evidence for graves in the cemetery south-west of the agora and on the lower, eastern slope of Kolonaios agoraios dating to the seventh and even the sixth centuries, all suggest that at this time the separation of civic, public space from private space had not yet developed in Athens.[20]

Building C, D, and F are the earliest "public" buildings in the agora, located in its south-west corner. Building C (located under the "Old Bouleuterion") dates to the early sixth century, and its function is unclear. The earliest phases of Buildings D and F date to the middle of the sixth century.[21] By the later sixth century the south side of this complex (Building F) consisted of a large hall with a double colonnade oriented roughly E–W, with a line of smaller rooms on the S side and a cluster of rooms and out-buildings on the W side (figure 25.4). On its N side were two large barbecue pits, suggesting some kind of communal or civic dining on a large scale. Its function is uncertain, but since it is situated on the site of the later Tholos, adjacent to the site of the Old Bouleuterion, both associated in classical times with the Council and the Prytany, it is often assumed that Buildings C, D, and F housed some of the same functions for an early Athenian council (Thompson and Wycherley 1972: 27). Another possibility, not necessarily mutually exclusive with the first, is that it housed the Peisistratid family, who ruled Athens as tyrants between 546 and

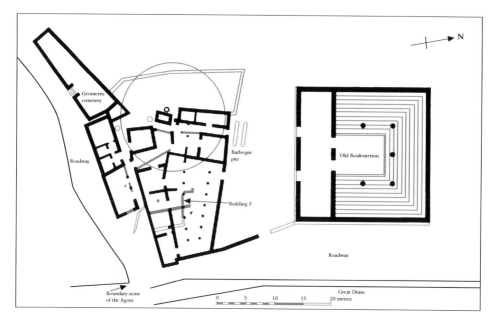

Figure 25.4 Athenian Agora, area of the Tholos (south-west corner), end of the sixth century BC
Source: After Camp (1986).

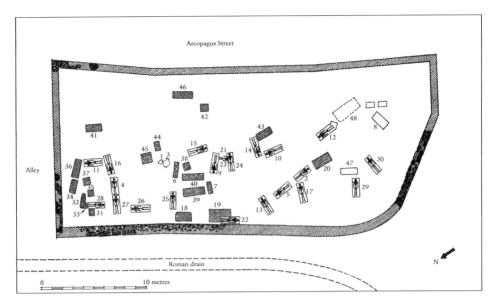

Figure 25.5 Schematic plan of the archaic cemetery south-west of the Athenian Agora
Source: After Young (1951: 71).

510 (Camp 2001: 35). Significantly, these structures respected the boundaries of the late Geometric cemetery and did not impinge on it.

Two interesting things happened in and around the agora about this time. The first is that the cemetery south-west of the agora was enclosed by a wall and became more heavily used (Young 1951: 74, 78) (figure 25.5). Some of the sixth century graves disturbed earlier burials of the eighth and seventh centuries. The latest burials in the cemetery date to about 500. It does not appear that this cemetery was reserved for "great heroes" (Morris 1987: 68) or important men. Of the 19 burials belonging to the sixth century, skeletal remains could not be sexed for seven, five were men of various ages, five were women of various ages and two were children (table 25.1). The idea that graves belonged well away from public, civic space, indeed outside the city walls because they were a potential source of ritual pollution, thus seems to be an idea of the fifth century and later which had not yet developed (Young 1951: 68). On the other hand, it is interesting that once buildings with a public function were constructed in the south-west corner of the agora, apparently it did not seem appropriate to re-use the adjacent Geometric cemetery, even though its boundaries were acknowledged by the builders. This might suggest the need to put at least some physical distance between the dead and the living as part of a developing ideology of civic space, and the separation of "public" and "private" realms.

It is possible that the Peisistratid family appropriated the cemetery just south-west of the agora as a family grave plot (Morris 1987: 68). If they resided in the buildings in the south-west corner of the agora, this cemetery would have been conveniently close, and highly visible, given its location on a main road leading to the agora. Against this interpretation, it is clear that in the fifth century Athenians recognized and respected the integrity of this cemetery: after the destruction of the city by the Persians in 479 part of the west wall enclosing the cemetery was rebuilt and the cemetery survived intact until the late fifth century (Young 1951: 73–4, 77). Given the fifth century Athenian rejection of tyranny and the Peisistratid family associated with it, this careful treatment of the cemetery would be surprising for grave plots closely associated with the Peisistratids. An alternative possibility is that Building F constituted the residence of the Archon *and his family* for the year in which he held office. Any members of the family who died during that time might have been buried in this cemetery. If this suggestion is correct, it implies that elite status was more important than gender for access to "public space," insofar as that notion was developed in sixth century Athens. This is not to suggest that women took part in political life, but rather that civic space was not yet defined as exclusively male. Instead, it could have been the territory of high-status families, although men alone were active in politics.

The second development, dating to the third quarter of the sixth century, was the erection of the south-east Fountain House, just on the southern edge of the agora. Water was conveyed a considerable distance into the building from the east in terracotta pipes running under the street (Camp 2001: 35). At about this time there is a spate of black-figured Athenian vases featuring women collecting water from fountain houses (figure 25.6; Boardman 1974: 112), and the Roman author

Figure 25.6 Women collecting water from a fountain house; black-figure painting on a hydria (water jar) attributed to the Priam Painter, 520–510 BC
Source: Toledo Museum of Art, 1961.23.

Pausanias (1.14.1) credited Peisistratus with improving the Athenian water supply by the construction of fountain houses at this time (Tölle-Kastenbein 1994: 73–4). Whether or not this particular fountain can actually be attributed to Peisistratus, it is interesting that by the end of the sixth century, the public buildings of the agora cluster for the most part on the western side, while the south-east Fountain House, though still within the precinct of the agora, is at the margins of the space on which civic activity apparently focused. The boundary stones which by now separated off the agora as designated public space situated at its south-west entrance date to the very end of the sixth century.

Collecting water, and making sure that families have adequate supplies of water was a stereotypically feminine job in archaic and classical Greece, as the numerous images on vases indicate (Lewis 2002: 71–4). Fountain houses were therefore places associated with feminine activities, where it was legitimate for women to go and to socialize. The insertion of a fountain house into an area where male-oriented public and civic activities were already located at the time of its construction is thus remarkable. The south-east Fountain House could have been built outside the agora, to the east closer to the spring which was its source of water. That it was deliberately set within the agora constitutes an important statement about the significance and place of women in civic and communal life: certainly included but literally at the edges. It also suggests that improvements undertaken communally need not be solely for the benefit of men, since fountain houses would have had their most immediate and positive impact on the lives of women in the city.

Conclusions: Gender in Context

The demarcation of gender, alongside age and status, was extremely important as an organizing principle in archaic Greek societies. Clearly delineated categories of gender signified social order. An ideology of gender dichotomy comes through strongly in our written sources: the realm of feminine activities, behaviors and concerns was different and often separate from those of the male world. These discrete realms at times engaged with each other and at other times came into conflict. Although men generally seem to maintain overall control, women are not simply passive. Public roles for women appear to have centered in religion and ritual – where a feminine public voice was acceptable. Women were never rulers or openly part of political life as far as we know – Sappho's possible "political" comments are veiled and focused on her brother, a close relative (fr. 5), just as women who appear in male company do so at home within the family. However the extent to which these ideologies were actually played out in "real life" is impossible to ascertain. The strong dichotomies which come through in written sources are perhaps not so strong in the material cultural record.

Although, not surprisingly, there are strong similarities with the ideologies of gender we know from classical times, we should not think that gender operated in exactly the same ways in the archaic period. On the other hand, I do not believe that gender roles were "more flexible" in archaic times. For example, acceptance of the idea that women could be considered legitimate objects of physical violence seems to be more obvious in archaic sources than in classical times, whatever the reality.

In archaic Greece, gendered behavior was set within different social and political contexts, where the network of social relations in which a person was embedded gave a different significance to the individual or the household than we know from classical times. In communities like Zagora, related families may have lived in close proximity to each other. It is likely that family networks placed limits on the autonomy of both men and women, though it is likely that these limits imposed more on women if we are to believe Sappho's voice. Moreover, we have seen a different relationship of family/kin group to community than we see in classical times, though we cannot presume that these relationships were the same in all archaic communities. Many poleis seem to have been little more than a consensus between rival groups of elite families, competing with each other, as depicted in the poetry of Alcaeus, Solon and others. Women were caught up in these rivalries and sometimes must have been important players.

Were there dramatic changes in ideologies of gender in the eighth century? I think not. Certain themes appear to span the period: Homer's Hera locates herself and operates within the Olympian family as much as Sappho does; the girls of Alcman's choruses are not depicted as individuals, they are a group, albeit a significant one within the community, crucial for its continuity and reproduction (Calame 2001). But the operation of gender was not static either: what changed gradually over time was the shape of political settings themselves. This in turn had a profound impact on how deeply embedded gender ideologies were fitted to the changing notions of community which eventually became the classical polis.

NOTES

1   I am grateful to Lorna Hardwick, André Lardinois, and Kurt Raaflaub for their helpful and supportive comments on this chapter.
2   On women and gender in Homer, see Graziosi and Haubold 2005: 95–119; Graziosi and Haubold 2003; Schein 1996; Cohen 1995; Doherty 1995; Austin 1994; Felson-Rubin 1994; Katz 1991; Easterling 1991; Winkler 1990: 129–61; Naerebout 1987; Murnaghan 1986; Foley 1978; Beye 1974.
3   Naerebout 1987: 126–7; Graziosi and Haubold 2005: 115–18.
4   Quotations from the *Iliad* are in the translation of Lattimore 1951.
5   On Pandora and the origin and nature of women in Hesiod see Clay 2003: 101–3, 116–25; Ogden 1998; Brown 1997; Zeitlin 1995; Vernant 1980: 168–85; Loraux 1981: 75–117; Arthur 1973.
6   Remarkably little has been written specifically about Semonides' misogynistic iambic; see Hubbard 1994 (mostly focused on the date of the poem); Easterling 1989; Lloyd-Jones 1975.
7   Quotations from Semonides are in the translation of Gerber 1999b.
8   Fr. 7.116–18, quoted above, and in the poetry of Alcaeus and Sappho, see below.
9   Bartol 1992: 66; West 1974: 22–39.
10 Stehle 1997: 237–40; Bartol 1992: 66–7, 70.

11 Quotations from Alcaeus and Sappho are in the translation of Campbell 1982.

12 Winkler 1990: 176–8; duBois 1995: 101, 104–5; Greene 2002: 98–9.

13 Cambitoglou *et al.* 1971: 13–20, 29–31, 33–6; 1988: 71, 151–4.

14 Morris 1999a: 268–9 and figs. 14.3a and 14.3b; 2000: 282 and figs. 7.7a and 7.7b.

15 Developed by Morris from the discussion of the excavators, but not following their interpretation (Cambitoglou et al. 1988: 107–16).

16 H34–H35 are in fact the earliest rooms of this complex in its present configuration (Cambitoglou et al. 1988: 151, 153), but H19 and H22 had Middle Geometric floors, and the present Late Geometric walls may have replaced Middle Geometric walls (Cambitoglou et al. 1988: 154).

17 On notions of "public" and "private" space in ancient Greece see Vernant 1983; Jameson 1990a and 1990b; Nevett 1994; Morris 1998c; Goldberg 1999; Ault 2000; Antonaccio 2000; Foxhall 2000; Cahill 2002.

18 On the Athenian agora see Camp 1986; 1990; 2001; Thompson and Wycherley 1972; Wycherley 1957. There is no reliable evidence for the existence of an "old agora" pre-dating the site of the classical agora. The idea is based on a fragment of the second century BCE writer Apollodoros (*FGrH* 244 F 113; see also Wycherley 1957: 224–5, no. 731), who located the shrine of Aphrodite Pandemos in an "old agora," probably in a misguided attempt to explain the cult title. See Thompson and Wycherley 1972: 19; Wycherley 1957: 1.

19 Brann 1961; Young 1939.

20 Young 1951; Thompson and Wycherley 1972: 15–20.

21 Camp 2001: 34–5; Thompson and Wycherley 1972: 24–9.

CHAPTER TWENTY-SIX

The Culture of the *Symposion*

Oswyn Murray

The Study of the *Symposion*

The *symposion* was, together with the gymnasium and the circuit of international festival games, the focus of aristocratic culture in the archaic age. The modern recognition of the importance of this phenomenon began with the first attempts to define a specific period of archaic Greek history which could be seen as differing from the classical age, in the lectures of Jacob Burckhardt, which were first given at Basel University in 1872, but not published until thirty years later (1898–1902), after his death.[1] Thereafter little attention was paid to the *symposion* until the late 1960s, when various trends in archaic cultural history began to come together (Murray 1990: 1–13). Under the influence of studies on oral poetry, the importance of understanding the place and purpose of performance of early Greek poetry led to an increasing interest in the relation between Greek drinking customs and the forms and genres of Greek lyric and elegiac poetry.[2] In art history the study of the relation between shape, function, and iconography in Greek vases began to focus on the fact that most archaic Greek pottery was intended for use in the drinking party (Fehr 1971; Lissarrague 1990a). Finally the identification by archaeologists of a type of room specifically designed for male drinking parties (the *andron*), and of later groups of such rooms intended for use at sanctuaries such as Brauron, Perachora and Corinth, provided a physical location for the rituals of the drinking party.[3] These various trends towards an interest in the *function* of cultural artifacts were brought together for the first time in a conference held in 1984, when scholars working on all the various disciplines involved in the study of early Greek history became aware of the interlocking nature of their separate discoveries. Since 1990 the study of the *symposion* has become a preoccupation of researchers working in all areas of archaic cultural history, and has come to be seen as the centre of aristocratic artistic patronage, and the focus of a specific aristocratic lifestyle.

The Evidence

It is indeed strange that this interest is so recent. The Greeks themselves were fascinated by the variety of rituals of conviviality that they observed both within their own culture and in other cultures; they often had a tendency to define periods within their own history and the characteristics of other civilizations in terms of their eating and drinking habits. In the second century AD this literature on conviviality was distilled into the encyclopaedic work of Athenaeus of Naucratis: his book, the *Deipnosophistae* or "Professors at the Feast," one of the longest surviving books from antiquity, was organized as a banquet of words, according to the order of the various dishes or topics that might be found in a contemporary banquet, and presented in the form of imagined conversations during it. That is, like many ancient encyclopedias and collections, its organization is based, not on the arbitrary order of the alphabet, but on a principle derived from its own subject matter; this enabled the reader to find quickly the topic that interested him, while allowing the possibility of more or less continuous reading as a literary work.[4] The sheer length and comprehensiveness of this compilation has meant that, like the interest of the Greeks themselves, our interest in many areas of research is inevitably focused on the literary fragments of lost works and descriptions of rituals or customs which concern food and drink. We know more about Greek conviviality than about any other aspect of ancient Greek life, and we have more fragments of archaic poetry (and of comic poetry) concerned with this subject than any other.

The functions of early Greek poetry involved both entertainment and instruction, together with the presentation of cultural values; in an oral society attempts to disseminate or preserve statements of value are often expressed in rhythmic or poetic form, in order to facilitate their memorizing and transmission. Although writing existed in archaic Greece for a variety of purposes (not least the preservation of poetic texts), poetry remained a dominant means of disseminating information; and many of the characteristic forms of poetic discourse are related to the *symposion* and developed within it. Elegiac poetry, designed to be performed to the accompaniment of the flute, was the main focus for descriptive, normative, and hortatory discourse. Military exhortation, whose characteristic is its second person plural address to the listeners, is now believed to be intended for performance at the military *symposion* in Asia Minor, Sparta and elsewhere.[5] The collection of sympotic poetry which has come down under the name of Theognis of Megara is concerned with the social and moral values of an aristocratic elite which felt increasingly threatened by the power of new money and low birth; the poetry of Solon and others expresses wider political concerns using the traditional sympotic framework; the poetry of Alcaeus reflects the concerns of the political *hetaireia* (Rösler 1980). While choral lyric is related to the dances performed at religious festivals, the various monodic lyric metres reflect the songs sung in *symposia*. This lyric poetry, designed to be sung by solo performers to the lyre, offers many more personal themes: reflections on death and the transitory nature of human pleasures, and on the power of love (always from the point of view of the lover whether the object of his love is male or female) produced a poetry of refinement and elegance. Many of the poetic forms reflect the context of the *symposion*, for instance the catena in which each couplet or stanza sets a theme to be taken up by the next singer in the group, or the Attic form known as the *skolion* or drinking song, commemorating exploits of the Athenian aristocracy.

Since the eighteenth century the collecting, description, and cataloguing of Greek vases has been a major preoccupation of the art world: the majority of these vases were found in funerary contexts, initially in Etruscan tombs, but later also in a number of major Greek sites in Italy such as Spina and Agrigento.[6] The representations on these vases were originally studied for their contribution to the history of Greek religion, and *symposion* scenes were neglected, classified among "scenes of reality" or "everyday life." More recently it has become obvious that these *symposion* scenes are the commonest single set of representations on Attic Black and Red Figure vases, as well as being strongly represented on Corinthian and Laconian vases (figures 26.1 and 26.2); scenes of a sympotic nature are also frequent in representations of the gods and heroes, notably of course Dionysus. Moreover the designation "scenes of reality" is fundamentally misleading; for these representations are highly stylized and formulaic, manipulating a set of stock attributes of the sympotic world, at the same

Figure 26.1 Symposium, featuring a cuirass and two helmets behind the diners, Middle Corinthian krater, Athana Painter, ca. 600–570 BC
Source: Louvre E629; photo *La Licorne*, courtesy Musée du Louvre.

Figure 26.2 Boeotian symposium: a man talking to a new arrival while reclining on a couch, being served wine by an adult male attendant, Boeotian kantharos of ca. 560 BC
Source: Louvre MNE 1172; photo by Bibi Saint-Pol.

time as being intensely original and competitive: each painter seeks to create a new mode of representation, and so to demonstrate his superiority over his rivals. François Lissarrague has shown in a fundamental study that these images themselves participate in the rituals of the *symposion*: they play games and make jokes for the amusement of the drinkers; they are themselves part of the entertainment (1990a; see below). For the first time humor, visual jokes, and puns have been shown to be an essential component of Greek art; and the artist is revealed as being at least as sophisticated a participant in the entertainment of the *symposion* as his contemporaries, the poets. In order to understand the thought-world of the *symposion* we therefore need to study vase-painting and lyric poetry together, and neither of these two art forms makes sense outside their context.

The painted vase was of course decorated in respect of its practical use within the *symposion*. Particular shapes were created for particular functions: the krater or mixing bowl served to mix wine and water; the hydra and the amphora contained the liquid; various forms of jug were used for serving it, and Athenaeus devotes the whole of book 11 of his *Deipnosophistae* to an alphabetical catalogue of cup-shapes used for drinking. Many of the surviving representations themselves show cups and jugs lined up along the base of the vase, or hanging on the walls of the room portrayed. Etruscan tombs in many centres (such as Tarquinia and Caere) were decorated as *symposion* rooms, and furnished with the necessary vessels together with large quantities of wine in storage amphorae for drinking in the Etruscan version of the afterlife.[7] From such evidence it is possible to reconstruct the activities of symposiasts and the uses of their utensils. Other cups are far too large for use, and must have hung on the walls of the *andron* as decoration.

The *andron* itself or specialized drinking room is marked out by a number of characteristics, which are not of course all present in each example. These include the existence of a water supply, drainage and a washable floor, and stone benches or fixings for the legs of wooden couches around the walls of the room. Above all the size of the room is conditioned by the needs of the drinking party: it is normally square in shape; each wall holds an equal number of couches together with the end of the couch on the next wall, while the entrance wall has its door placed off centre to accommodate the door in relation to the number of couches on that wall. It has long been noticed that standard sizes of these rooms can be expressed in terms of the number of couches they could accommodate, from 7 to 11 to 15 (McCartney 1934); Birgitta Bergquist has pointed out another consequence of the principle of mutual communication required by the *symposion*, that the diagonal across the room must be compatible with the participation of all the group in the conversations, singing rituals and games: later and larger banqueting halls can often be shown by their plans and floor decoration to have been intended to be divided in use for more than one sympotic group.[8] Another common characteristic of these rooms is that they are often positioned close to the street entrance and away from the women's quarters: in many cases they have grander decoration and even vestibules with architectural features.[9] From the late fifth century public dining rooms of this type are found in city centres or religious sanctuaries, arranged in rows within *hestiatoria*, presumably for dining by an elite of magistrates or priests.[10] It has indeed been suggested that such rooms were also used for other purposes, and that is no doubt true (Jameson 1990b: 188–91). But the particular features mentioned above mean that the rooms were architecturally designed with a specific function in mind, much as the dining-room in modern bourgeois architecture may be defined by its size, its lack of provision for soft furnishings, its closeness to the kitchen and the presence of a hatchway, or the front parlor in working-class nineteenth-century terrace houses by its superior decoration and closeness to the front door: the fact that both may be used for many functions (bicycle storage, television, multigym) does not affect their original architectural functions or their designation in estate agent's jargon as a place for special ritual occasions like the dinner party, or for the reception of important visitors like the vicar or laying out the dead.

Basic Rules

"Drinking Greek style" (*Graeco more bibere*) meant adopting a specific set of customs which were regarded as quintessentially Greek. Whereas (as the Greeks themselves insisted) the Greek gods and the Homeric heroes had feasted seated on chairs or benches, later Greeks at the *symposion* reclined on the left elbow, lying on couches containing never more than two to a couch, facing from left to right along the walls of the room. There was an insistence on equality among the participants, with no more than the selection of one member as *basileus* or *symposiarchos* to guide the group activities, mainly by deciding the mixture of wine and water, and the forms of entertainment for the evening: the number in the group was restricted by the need to participate in the various activities to no more than 30 (3, 7, 11, or 15 couches with 2 to a couch). Other essential features of this ritualized drinking include the absolute prohibition on respectable citizen women being present, and the separation of the time of eating (the *deipnon*) from the time of drinking; many of these aspects distinguish the Greek *symposion* from the rituals of conviviality among the Etruscans and the Romans, despite the fact that these are derived from Greek practices and are in many respects deeply influenced by them. The ritual was centred around the krater or mixing bowl in which wine and water were mixed according to traditional criteria. The food served at this point seems to have been limited to nuts, barley cakes, chickpeas, and other thirst-creating snacks, although the scenes on vases display a wider range of breads and large slabs of meat, perhaps in a composite representation of different stages in the *deipnon* and *symposion*, or in an evocation of heroic or divine feasting.

Origins

Ritual forms of feasting or commensality are common to most societies, ancient and modern: from a cultural point of view they are basically forms of display and/or enjoyment, and in relation to other aspects of the culture they can be classified in terms of their functions of emphasizing either shared values in relation to the community or the group, or the superiority of the individual ruler or elite group over those excluded from the feast. It is clear that Greek culture possessed from its origins two forms of feasting. The first is related to practices of sacrifice, in which the worshipers either ate on site the sacrificial meat, or sometimes took it away for consumption elsewhere: priests might receive special privileges or cuts, but others seem to have shared equally as members of the community; other feasts of a similar religious nature also existed, with the characteristic of being inclusive of all community members, at least of the male sex. These rituals may be said to perform the function of creating communal values.[11]

The Homeric feast on the other hand appears to be exclusive, in that it relates to the self-definition of an elite group within the society: this group is naturally that of the leaders (*basileis*) and their warrior retainers.[12] The feast takes place in the *megaron* or great hall: it appears to be an intrinsic part of the lifestyle of the Homeric aristocracy:

> Eumaeus, this must surely be the fine house of Odysseus: it would be easy to recognize and pick out even among many. There are buildings on buildings, and the court is well fenced with a wall and cornice, and the double gates are well protected: no man could force it. And I see that many men are feasting within, for the smell of fat is there, and the lyre sounds, which the gods have made as companion of the feast.
>
> (*Odyssey* 17.264–71)

As the Greeks themselves noted, the participants in these feasts are seated, the portions of meat reflect the honor or merit of the warriors, and there is no separation between eating and drinking. Women are not entirely excluded, but seem already to play a minor role: only married women are usually present, they take no part in the action and appear to be excluded from the eating of meat and drinking of wine.[13] Nevertheless the picture given in the *Odyssey* already seems to reflect the importance of pleasure and of poetic performance within the feasting rituals.

Within this context the archaic aristocratic *symposion* seems best regarded as a continuation of the Homeric warrior feast involving the adoption and elaboration of specifically new types of luxurious behavior from the near east; it was initially practiced more in elite circles than in the community as a whole; and, although the rituals came to be more widely adopted and certainly influenced forms of sacrificial feasting, they seem to have continued to be seen as an aristocratic activity even into the classical period. The origin and date of introduction of these new social rituals can be traced most clearly through iconography (Dentzer 1982). It seems that the practice of reclining at the feast is derived from the near east, where the earliest datable representation is the seventh-century scene of the victorious king Assurbanipal in glory, reclining alone with attendants and musicians beside a tree decorated with the heads of his enemies in the palace of Nimrud; but the eighth-century Hebrew prophet Amos (6.3–7) already denounces the Jews of Samaria as feasting in luxury with music and wine on couches inlaid with ivory; the semitic word *marzeah* is used in a number of texts to describe such luxurious feasts. Greek representations of the reclining banquet are not however directly derived from the Assyrian and near eastern motif of the king in solitary glory, and only later use this motif as a way of representing heroic status on funerary monuments; the Greek portrayals start with the depiction of the group banquet, in which all appear equal. The earliest Greek representations of such scenes of the reclining banquet are found on early middle Corinthian kraters in the late seventh century, and the first poet specifically to describe it is the contemporary Alcman:

> seven couches and as many tables crowned with poppy cakes and linseed and sesame and among the cups . . . honey cakes.
>
> (fr. 19 L–P)

This provides a lower fixed point for the adaptation of the eastern motif of the solitary reclining figure to a depiction of that communal celebration which seems to be a characteristic contribution of the Greeks.

However, the main period of oriental influences on Greek culture belongs to the late eighth and early seventh centuries; and I have argued that one of the earliest Greek inscriptions, that on "Nestor's cup" of about 725 BC shows a fully developed sympotic self-referentiality, and suggests by its emphasis on Aphrodite that the practice of reclining was now established in Greece; and also that, from early in the seventh century, the poetry of Archilochus and Callinus already refers to reclining. The tomb evidence from Etruria and Latium suggests that the developed feasting rituals of the reclining banquet began to be widely practiced in Italy among the elite in the late eighth and early seventh centuries, and it has normally been assumed that these rituals derive from Greek rather than Phoenician practices. The distribution of pendent semi-circle Euboic pottery seems to demonstrate a widespread trade in wine and drinking vessels as well as slaves from this period. It is therefore easier to see the Greek adoption of a new and specifically eastern form of reclining feasting ritual as occurring from the late eighth century onwards, and to view the entire production of archaic Greek vase painting and of archaic Greek poetry as being influenced from the start by the rituals of the reclining *symposion* (Murray 1994). Indeed the relation of these new practices to the fundamental banquet structure of the *Odyssey* and its contrast in this respect with the *Iliad* may suggest sympotic influence on the *Odyssey* itself, and a combination of innovation and continuity within the Greek poetic tradition which requires further exploration.[14]

Rituals of Consumption

The occasion as it is presented in the literary evidence is always a special one, a festival or the celebration of a sporting or poetic victory, the regular meeting of a *thiasos* or other groupings of a religious nature: but Aristotle (*NE* 8.1160a) makes it clear that many religious groups met specifically for the dual purpose of sacrifice and pleasure, and not all religious rituals connected with the *symposion* were taken seriously – in the fifth century the profanation of the Mysteries was carried out in a sympotic context, and there were even drinking groups which met specifically on days of ill omen (Murray 1990: 149–61).

In its fully developed form the *symposion* began with the clearing away of the remains of the *deipnon*, and the arrival of the second tables (*deuterai trapezai*). The leader poured libations in unmixed wine to the gods, and decided the strength of the mixture of wine and water to be used. The wine was mixed with water in the krater in proportions discussed by Athenaeus, from two or three of water to one of wine, to stronger mixes, half-in-half, or two to three or even four or five (Athen. 10.430–1). Since Greek wine was naturally fermented and sweet, it must normally have reached the maximum alcohol content at which the yeast is killed off at around 16–17 percent of alcohol (distillation was unknown before the alchemists of the Middle Ages). Dilution by three to one would have put its alcohol content in the range of modern beers, and it was drunk in similar quantities.[15] The quality was not high: we hear of no vintages, only local characteristics such as wines from particular islands (the vintage is a Roman sophistication); the wine was usually drunk young, and must often have tasted of the various containers in which it was stored – resin-painted porous amphorae or goatskins. Sieves were commonly used to remove floating debris.

Unmixed wine was reserved for the gods and heroes; among mortals it was regarded as a sign of barbarian uncouthness (drinking in the Scythian fashion) and likely to lead to madness, as with king Cleomenes of Sparta; the tendency of Macedonians such as Philip and Alexander to drink their wine neat proved their lack of Greek culture, and inevitably led to excesses such as murder or death by drinking. However, it is clear that unmixed wine was permitted as part of one practice, the *proposis* or toast, often to the beloved in a ritual connected with homosexual pairing between *erastes* and *eromenos*; it seems that this is represented on the many vases which contain "*kalos* inscriptions," such as *Miltiades kalos* or similar statements, both serious and playful. Later poets deplored the Athenian habit of multiple *proposeis*, which led to drunken behavior, and praised the decorum of the Spartan habit of forbidding the *proposis* (Critias in Athenaeus 10.432–3).

There has been no systematic study of the capacity of ancient wine containers, but personal experiment suggests that there are two main sizes of krater, corresponding perhaps to the number of men in the 7 and 15 couch models for *symposia*: the smaller could contain approximately 7 litres, the larger 14. Each emptying of the krater therefore represented a round of between a half and 1 litre for each participant, and it is clear that the successive kraters were considered as a form of sympotic time, marking successive stages in the *symposion*:

Three kraters only do I mix for the temperate – one to health, which they empty first,
the second to love and pleasure, the third to sleep. When this is drunk up wise guests
go home. The fourth krater is ours no longer, but belongs to hybris, the fifth to uproar,
the sixth to drunken revel, the seventh to black eyes. The eighth is the policeman's,
the ninth belongs to biliousness, and the tenth to madness and hurling the furniture.

(Eubulus in Athenaeus 2.36)

Dionysus was recognized as a wild and untamed god and the dangers of wine in
provoking quarrels, strife and an uncomfortable display of the truth both in word
and character were well known; the true aim of the *symposion* was rather a measured
release from inhibitions in a communal setting, leading to a form of heightened
consciousness that could on occasion become possession by the god, or even a
mystical ecstasy such as is evoked towards the end of Plato's *Symposium*. But despite
this goal of self-control there are plenty of scenes on Attic vases of wild behavior
and of vomiting or of *kraipale*, the hangover.[16]

The furniture of the *symposion* was the ultimate expression of aristocratic luxury:
cushions and baskets for transporting provisions together with the walking stick often
appear in the background on vases as shorthand symbols for a sympotic scene where
the attention is directed to other aspects such as sex. Luxury and sophistication marked
the *symposion*: in Aristophanes' *Wasps* the old man Philokleon is taught how to behave
at aristocratic *symposia*:

Come and lie down, and learn how to be a symposiast and a socialite.
How do I lie then? Come on, tell me.
Elegantly.
You want me to lie like this?
Oh *no*.
How then?
Straighten your knees and pour yourself over the cushions, limply and athletically.
Then praise one of the bronzes, inspect the ceiling, admire the hangings in the hall.

(*Wasps* 1208–15)

There were gradations of comfort: characteristically it was alleged that the Spartans
reclined "on the wood" without cushions, in order to demonstrate their toughness
and simplicity. The couch or *kline* was the most important item of furniture, often
decorated with inlay: in Plato's *Republic* the word usually unsuspectingly translated
as "bedmaker" in fact refers to the skilled trade of making couches for the aristocratic *symposion*. The wealthy father of Demosthenes owned two factories, one for
making swords, the other a couch factory employing 22 slaves; the stock in hand
on his death included ivory (for inlay), iron and wood, gall (for staining) and copper (Demosthenes 27.9–10). In Plato the archetypal skilled craftsman is the "couch
maker" (*Republic* 597a), who makes not the perfect idea of a couch but simply the
physical couch itself, which is merely an imitation of the form of the couch: the true
sympotic couch is ultimately a single and unique reality, an idea in the mind of God.
Similarly the tables of which Plato talks are the low tables seen beside the couches
in sympotic representations on vases.

The wealth of potters was proverbial: "potter competes with potter" says Hesiod (*W&D* 25); they signed their works with pride both as potters and as painters, and dedicated monuments on the Athenian acropolis carved by the best and most expensive sculptors. The concept of pleasure expressed in the archaic word *euphrosyne* combines wine, women and song as experienced in the rituals of the *symposion*: Plato may disapprove of pleasure but he finds it difficult to conceive of any form of pleasure which is not connected with the *symposion*.[17] The art of conversation itself, especially on themes literary and philosophical, found its natural home and highest expression in the *symposion* (Ford 2002: 25–45). Ultimately art and custom, imagery, and word, combine in the Greek *imaginaire* to create a conception of the quintessentially Greek form of pleasure.

Entertainments

Other forms of luxury became part of the sympotic culture: there was a whole science of wreaths and the different meanings of various flowers, of which Athenaeus gives a glossary in book 15. Perfumed oils and unguents already belonged to the near eastern tradition. The various types of entertainment at the *symposion* seem to have evolved over time. The earliest sympotic poetry was composed by participants who are full and equal members of the group; the poets exhort their fellow drinkers and describe their own unmediated emotions. This at least is the impression given by the surviving fragments of poets down to the mid-sixth century. But thereafter the tone of the poetry changes and elements of professionalism emerge: Ibycus and Anacreon portray generic emotions adapted for performance by others as well as themselves; Simonides, Bacchylides, and Pindar are clearly poets who composed and performed as entertainers, and who used their skills to gain entry to the sympotic group (Svenbro 1984). Anecdotal and other evidence shows that by the late sixth-century poets could command high fees for their compositions on special occasions, and were retained as court poets in the retinues of tyrants. Thus Ibycus was associated with the father of Polycrates; Anacreon and Simonides were among the poets patronized by Hipparchus of the Pisistratid dynasty; Anacreon moved to the court of Polycrates where the two are found reclining in the *andron* when the fateful message arrived which lured Polycrates to his death (Herod. 3.121). Simonides' travels were famous; he spent some time with the Aleuadai of Thessaly before returning to Athens as poet laureate of the victorious Greeks, and then joining Aeschylus at the court of Hieron in Syracuse: he was notorious for his willingness to travel and his meanness with the money he earned. The careers of Pindar and Bacchylides in the early fifth century belong to the same pattern of aristocratic patronage centred on victories at the games and the arts of the *symposion*. This combination of sport and alcohol is found in the most famous description of a tyrannical *symposion*, the year-long athletic contests and feasting held for the hand of the daughter of Cleisthenes of Sicyon, at the end of which the drunken Hippokleides of Athens danced such obscene dances that he threw away his chances with the famous remark "Hippokleides doesn't care" (Herod. 6.127–9). Perhaps the ultimate symbol of the late archaic aristocratic age of refinement is the *psykter* or wine cooler, a pottery container designed to float in the wine and cool it: this was fashionable only for a brief period from the 520s to about 460; its running decoration on the outside was meant to give an illusion of movement to the hazy vision of the drinkers as the figures floated round on the surface of the wine in the krater – a succession of hoplites on dolphins, a mirror image of the drinkers themselves or grotesque satyrs balancing wine cups on improbable erections – all painted by the greatest artists of the age, the Kleophrades Painter, Oltos, Douris, and others.

The best known game of skill played at *symposia* was *kottabos*, the art of flicking drops of wine at a target such as a metal pan, so as to make it fall off its stand; the skill has so far defeated modern devotees. Athenaeus spends almost half a book (15.665–8) on this Sicilian invention. There were prizes of eggs, cakes, nuts, or kisses, and the name of a loved one was often uttered at the same time as throwing; there were complex varieties of the game and even specially designed rooms: *kottabos* cups with rings to help direct the droplet are known.

The cups themselves play games with their shapes. There are joke or trick cups designed to prevent drink from reaching the mouth, or deposit it on the user's lap; turning the cup into a mask was a favorite fantasy, by painting eyes on the outside of cups so that the drinker appears to wear a cup mask as he tilts it back, with the base (sometimes in the shape of a set of genitals) suggesting a misshapen nose.

There were other forms of professional entertainment. Grotesque padded dancers appear on Corinthian, Attic, Boeotian, and Laconian pottery from the late seventh century; they are perhaps the precursors of those acrobats and mime artists found for instance in Xenophon's *Symposium*, and may indeed have influenced the development of the choral and dramatic festivals. The *akletos*, or uninvited guest, appears as almost a standard feature from Odysseus the beggar onwards (and is still retained in the only surviving modern example of the classical reclining banquet, the Jewish Seder or Passover); he was expected to entertain the drinkers as a form of licensed fool, and can be found portrayed in the painted Tomb of the Diver (Paestum), as in the figure of Alcibiades entering Plato's *Symposium* late and already drunk.[18]

The practice of reclining restricted the size of the group; the long rituals, intimate space and competitive elements of the *symposion* created a powerful psychological unifying effect on the participants which is discussed by Plato in the *Laws*, and resulted in a form of bonding outside the norms of the polis and the social constraints of the family. The *symposion* was a place apart with its own rules and code of behavior: Andocides (*On the Mysteries* 48–69) claims that breaking the relation of trust (*pistis*) uniting the group was morally so dreadful that it could be weighed against being responsible for the death of one's own father and other innocent family members.

Citizen women were prohibited from participating in the *symposion*;[19] but the pleasures of Aphrodite were one of its defining characteristics: slave women are present from the earliest artistic representations. Sometimes they practice a musical skill, as the flute players whose hiring price was regulated by Athenian law; sometimes they dance. But for the most part they are simply present as *hetairai*, a word coined to reflect the male *hetairoi* (companions) who are the members of the drinking group: they climb on the couches, are often shown naked (the symposiasts until very drunk are normally represented as at least half clothed) and are expected to engage in sex. This explains the absence of the missionary position in Greek art, for the woman is the active and dominant member of the partnership. Often they are shown indulging in group activities: it has been said that the only team sport known to the Greeks is sex, and they play a full part in the *komos* or drunken procession. *Hetairai* were courtesans rather than prostitutes: they were often highly trained in the various skills of the *symposion*, and commanded great prestige and high prices: Corinth, the home of sacred prostitution in the temple of Aphrodite, was a famous training ground. They were often owned by individuals, or (since they were expensive to purchase, and were unlikely to be needed every evening) they could be shared between a couple of men; it was however thought proper to get rid of one's *hetaira* on marriage. Their lives were in many respects more free than those of citizen women, and their opportunities greater: but the distance between their status and that of the free citizen woman, together with the problems of crossing this boundary are portrayed in deliberately shocking form by Apollodorus in the famous case against Neaera, a politically motivated exposure of a rival for illegally taking a *hetaira* as his wife (Demosthenes 59).[20] The aged Pindar wrote a choral ode for performance in 464 by the sacred prostitutes whom Xenophon of Corinth dedicated to Aphrodite when he won his double victory at Olympia in the stadion and the pentathlon:

> Young girls with many lovers, servants of persuasion in wealthy Corinth who burn the golden tears of fresh incense, often flying in your thoughts to the heavenly mother of desires, Aphrodite, you my children she has permitted without blame in delightful acts of love to pick the fruit of soft youth. When compulsion calls, all is fair . . . But I wonder what the lords of the Isthmus will say of my finding such a beginning as this for my honey-sweet drinking song, as accompaniment to women shared in common. We test gold on a pure touchstone . . . O mistress of Cyprus, here to your grove Xenophon has brought a hundred-limbed herd of girls, rejoicing at the fulfilment of his prayers.
> (*Encomia* F 122)

For the men (as for the slave women involved) the skills and attitudes displayed in the *symposion* required training: Aristophanes describes the education of his generation of Marathon-warriors spent healthily in music and poetry and preparations for the gymnasium, leading to "a shining chest, clear skin, broad shoulders, a weak tongue, a broad arse and a small cock" (*Clouds* 1010–14). In his admittedly comic description of the two competing types of education it is clear that the aim of the ancient *paideia* is preparation for the sympotic and sporting life.

It was a young man's world, opposed to old age and even more to death (Murray 1988a), a world of life well adapted to the age class systems that were widespread in the archaic world, and whose most extreme example is found in Sparta (Bernardi 1985). Within such groups homosexuality is considered normal: the lover (*erastes*) initiates the loved one (*eromenos*) into the adult male world. Sexual activity may often be involved, but the essential relationship is one of education. Jealousy and sublimation, the idealization of the pursuit, belong to the competitive world of fellow drinkers where all are equal. Youths are initiated into the group by sitting among the participants, and are admired for their beauty; they become the object of desire,

but are named as equals rather than remaining anonymous. For more casual relationships the slave boy who serves the wine is available to be chatted up, for instance
by the poet Sophocles, caught at a *symposion* on Chios in the memoirs of his rival
Ion (Athenaeus 13.603–4); to judge from the universal convention on Greek
vase-painting these slave boys (like the female slaves of eighteenth century Danish
colonial society) performed their duties naked. It is for such reasons that literary
descriptions of *symposia*, from Plato's *Symposium* and that of Xenophon to the various comic portrayals in Aristophanes and in Euripides' *Cyclops*, emphasize sex and
sexual desire: it is the natural subject for sympotic discourse, just as it is the natural
subject for artistic representation or for celebration in song and music.

The end of the *symposion* is officially marked by libations to Hygieia (health) and
the departure of the guests home to bed – in the case of Xenophon's *Symposium*
hastening home to their wives after being aroused by a mime of the love of Dionysus
and Ariadne, a favorite scene on Attic vases – lit by torchbearers along the darkened
streets. Other parties ended less decorously, with everyone except Socrates asleep
among the debris (Plato's *Symposium*), or engaging in orgiastic sex with the male
and female slaves in the *symposion* given by Chabrias to celebrate his chariot victory
at the Pythian Games of 373 (Demosthenes 59.33).

One disadvantage of the *symposion* from the point of view of a politically active
class was its private nature: this could be overcome by a display of drunken aristocratic behavior in the sleeping streets in a ritual known as the *komos*. The most
famous representation in art is the return of Hephaistos, which appears in some 130
scenes on Attic vases. Hera had hurled Hephaestus from Mt. Olympus because of
his lameness; in revenge he made a golden throne which trapped her when she sat
on it: in order to secure her release, Dionysus had to make Hephaestus drunk and
escort him back to Olympus on a donkey surrounded by satyrs. Many sympotic vases
portray the procession of revelers carrying the paraphernalia of the *symposion* and
accompanied by girls, flute players and other hangers on, and displaying all manner
of riotous behavior. The *komos* was a display of aristocratic power and privilege over
ordinary citizens; it involved ritualized violence against innocent passers by. In the
Wasps Philokleon comes home drunk from his first experience of the *symposion* with
a flute girl on his arm, pursued by outraged citizens threatening writs (1326ff). The
behavior of the *hetaireiai* of Lesbos led to a law prescribing double penalties for
offences committed when drunk. This form of display of aristocratic power and
disregard for the conventions and laws of the city caused a crisis in democratic
Athens in 415 with the famous scandals of the mutilation of the *Hermai* and the
desecration of the Mysteries (Murray 1990: 149–61).

Social Functions

The earliest description of the Spartan army in Herodotus (1.65) shows that it was
based on sympotic drinking groups (Murray in Slater 1991: 83–103). Elsewhere the
bonding achieved by communal drinking remained important in the organization of
aristocratic groups of *hetairoi*, whose aim was to control the political life of the city:

the poetry of Alcaeus of Lesbos was composed for performance in the *symposion* and reflects the struggles of such aristocratic groups to maintain control of the city against the rise of popular leaders (Rösler 1980). The importance of organizations such as the aristocratic phratries of Athens, apparently controlling local government and the citizenship lists until the age of Cleisthenes, seems similarly to have been based on a social system which reflected the power of aristocrats to organize their retainers through rituals of conviviality; many of these groupings continued later in the democratic polis to have their basis in such forms of communality.

The public rituals of the aristocratic state were based on the *prytaneion*, where public dining was an honor or a privilege granted to magistrates and priests, ambassadors, victors at the Olympic and other games, and to the kin of public heroes such as the descendants of the tyrannicides at Athens. These privileged aristocrats were known as *parasitoi* because they dined "alongside" at state expense: the word was originally a status designation before it became a term of abuse.[21] Similarly the aristocratic priests of the various religious cults appropriated the sympotic style to their religious feasting; and many religious *thiasoi* and *eranoi* dedicated to heroes and lesser deities followed suit, finding their main purpose in a form of sacrificial conviviality.

Although the sympotic culture seems to have originated in the practices of a warrior elite, under the influence of luxury and the pleasure principle it became essentially a spectacle apart, a separate world opposed to that of the public sphere. Within the aristocratic polis the *symposion* therefore developed a dual function: on the one hand it was a place of *euphrosyne* devoted to pleasure, a lifestyle designating the privilege of the leisure class (Veblen 1899), basically outside the structures of family and kinship, and an alternative to the polis. On the other hand, because the archaic polis was essentially controlled by the aristocracy, the *symposion* was interwoven with all the structures of the polis, and provided a focal space for common action both on behalf of and against the polis. Greek society thus displays the fundamental opposition recognized by anthropologists between kinship and the *Männerbund* or brotherhood.[22] This dual function is well recognized in the first two books of Plato's *Laws*, which set out to create a social system based on the good use and benefits of alcohol.

In economic terms the *symposion* was the foundation of the Mediterranean-wide trade in luxury goods that developed from the eighth century onwards; the expansion of early Greek trade was based on metals for armaments, slaves, and luxuries serving the needs of developing aristocratic elites everywhere, as the cultures in contact with the Mediterranean basin progressively adopted Greek cultural norms, from northern Spain and the interior of Gaul to the Scythian nomads of south Russia (Wells 1980). From the eighth century the chief export of Greece (in return for metals and slaves) was wine and the style of drinking that went with it: it is no chance that the presence of Greek merchants is signaled everywhere in the archaeological record by the spread of drinking cups, from the pendent semi-circle skyphoi of Euboea to Corinthian and Attic ware. The native chieftains of Gaul and south Russia increasingly marked their aristocratic status through a process of acculturation to Greek customs brought about by trade. From the eighth century onwards the Etruscan aristocracy imported huge numbers of Greek wine amphorae, as they established their emerging status through the wholesale adoption of Greek sympotic practices. Sostratus of Aegina was the richest man in Greece, specializing in supplying the Etruscan market (Harvey 1976). The Etruscans imported large quantities of the finest Attic black-figure and red-figure pottery, some of which was specially made for them; this led to the creation of a native pottery modeled on that of the Greeks. Unlike the Greeks (before the development of mystery cults) they also adapted the sympotic style to their conception of the afterlife, with the consequence that most of our evidence for sympotic furnishings and pottery comes from the tombs of the Etruscan-dominated area of Italy, from the Po valley to Campania.

Decline

The *symposion* remained a characteristic social practice among the Greeks throughout the classical period, and hence there is no problem about using fifth- and fourth-century evidence to explain its workings. But with the gradual decline of aristocratic dominance it began to lose much of its cultural importance (Murray 1995). In Athens it remained the chief focus of the aristocratic lifestyle until the mid-fifth century, with the democratic reforms of Ephialtes (462) and the establishment of a new aggressive Athenian imperialism; its demise may be symbolized in the death of the last great sympotic poet, Pindar, around 446 (Van Groningen 1960). The artistic and cultural patronage of the new democratic Athens focused instead on public festivals, especially tragedy (Herington 1985), and on public wall-painting, instead of lyric poetry and vase-painting; politicians like Pericles and Cleon shunned the *symposia* for the assembly and the law courts. There was a brief revival in the late fifth century with the rise of "laconism" (the cult of Sparta) as a cultural fashion among the elite and the development of *hetaireiai* as oligarchic terrorist groups, associated with men such as Alcibiades and Andocides: the poetry of Critias, extreme oligarch and Plato's relative, attempts to re-establish a purer normative *symposion* based on idealization of Sparta.[23] But with the end of the aristocratic age the *symposion* passed from dominant cultural form to a simple private articulation of the bourgeois pleasure principle and a theme in the literary world of aristocratic nostalgia (Martin 1931). By the mid-Hellenistic period even the rituals of the *symposion* were largely forgotten or subsumed into those of royal feasting and the Roman *convivium*.[24] Occasional literary revivals and a few rituals in Byzantine court life and in traditional Judaism remained to recall the traditional manners of high Greek culture, until the High Renaissance revival of an antiquarian interest in dining "in the Greek style" (Jeanneret 1991).

NOTES

1   Burckhardt 1902; a definitive publication of the manuscripts of the lectures is in progress.
2   Gentili 1988 (originally published 1969); Rösler 1980.
3   Robinson and Graham 1938; Miller 1978.

4　A. Lukinovich in Murray (ed.) 1990: 263–71; Braund and Wilkins 2000; Romeri 2002.

5　E. L. Bowie in Murray (ed.) 1990: 221–9; Murray in Slater (ed.) 1991: 83–103.

6　*Spina* 1958; *Agrigento* 1988; Vierneisel and Kaeser 1990.

7　A. Rathje and A. Pontrandolfo in Murray and Tecusan 1995: 167–75; 176–95.

8　Bergquist in Murray 1990: 37–65.

9　Walker 1983; Robinson and Graham 1938.

10　Prominent examples can be found at Perachora, Brauron, Corinth and Athens (Prytaneion, Pompeion).

11　For this aspect see especially Schmitt Pantel 1992 and *ThesCRA*.

12　Murray in Slater 1991: 83–103; Van Wees 1995. I do not think there is actually much difference between our views, since we both seem agreed that the elite is a warrior elite.

13　Detailed reconstructions in Seymour 1907: 208–34; van Wees 1995.

14　See now Murray 2008.

15　There is a special class of undecorated black pottery known as the *amis* or pisspot, which was brought in by slaves when needed.

16　There is, however, no clear reference in antiquity to alcoholism as a condition (as opposed to binge drinking), which may be explained by the social rituals surrounding the drinking of alcohol and by the absence of spirits or fortified wine. In contrast those who drank outside the *symposion*, such as women or slaves, were commonly portrayed in art and literature as antisocial addicts, because they drank unmixed wine alone and in secret.

17　*Republic* 372–3 with Burnyeat 1997: 217–49; Tecuşan in Murray 1990: 238–60.

18　Fehr in Murray (ed.) 1990: 185–95; Napoli 1970.

19　Schmitt Pantel 2001; there is here a clear contrast with Etruscan and Roman practices based on the family and the *convivium*: Murray 2000.

20　For the different statuses of *pallakai* (long-term partners), *hetairai*, and *pornai* see Demosth. 59.122; Davidson 1997: 73–136.

21　Athenaeus 6.234–48 on *parasitoi*; Schmitt Pantel 1992: 147–77; Miller 1972.

22　Schurtz 1902; Völger and von Welck 1990.

23　Calhoun 1913; Murray 1990: 149–61.

24　Zaccaria Ruggiu 2003; Dunbabin 2003.

CHAPTER TWENTY-SEVEN

The Culture of Competition

Nick Fisher

Peleus the old man would ever be telling his son Achilles
always to be the best (*aristeuein*) and to be superior to all others
                    (Nestor to Patroklos, in Homer, *Iliad* 11.783–4)

There was not then one kind of Strife (*Eris*), but over the earth
there are two. One a man would praise when he understood her,
but the other is blameworthy: and they have wholly different spirits.
One stirs up evil warfare and battle conflict,
a cruel being: her no mortal loves; but of necessity
through the will of the Immortals, men pay honour to harsh Strife.
But the other, the elder, was given birth by dark Night,
and Zeus son of Kronos who sits high and lives in the aether
placed her in the roots of the earth, a being far better for men.
She arouses even the helpless man to labour.
For any one, looking at another, though he lacks work,
Looking at a a rich man who hurries to plough and plant
and put his house in good order, emulates the other, neighbour to neighbour
hurrying after wealth. This is the good Strife for men.
Potter gets angry with potter, and craftsman with craftsman,
and beggar envies beggar, and bard with bard.
                    (Hesiod, *Works and Days*, 11–26)

Introduction: The Origins of Greek Athletics

The casual visitor to any Greek city from the sixth century onwards (such as the Scythian wise man Anacharsis pictured as a visitor to Solon of Athens in Lucian's second-century AD essay of that name) would have been struck forcibly by some peculiar activities. First, in open spaces, often attached to a sanctuary, naked boys and men would be training or competing in athletic contests, or watching, conversing and pursuing friendships and homosexual affairs (typically between young men and younger youths); second, in similar settings, groups of males and females, divided by gender and by age, would be practicing or competing in elaborate contests of choral singing and dancing; third, later in the day, inside private houses or public or sacred buildings, mostly all-male groups would be engaged in ritualized dining and drinking (see ch. 26). The archaic period has with good reason been characterized as the age of "agonal man," when the Greeks began to devote massive energies and resources to an astonishingly wide range of contests inside and beyond their many communities: so named by the Swiss historian Jacob Burckhardt in his nineteenth-century classic *Griechische Kulturgeschichte*.[1] As the passages quoted above indicate, from the start of the archaic period intense personal rivalry operated both where the elite competed for honor in the public spheres of warfare and debate, and where those of less standing competed for wealth and status in villages and towns. The values associated with the competitive spirit, manly success and courage (*aretê*, *andreia*), honor (*timê*), competitiveness for honor (*philotimia*), love of victory (*philonikia*), strife (*eris*) should not be seen – as they are sometimes – as exclusively aristocratic or elitist values. These contests contributed greatly to the tensions and political conflicts of the archaic period, but equally, and no less importantly, to the distinctive social practices of the Greeks and to the political and social cohesion which many states enjoyed at least some of the time.

The social value of such intense yet controlled contests is already clear in the Homeric poems. Book 23 of the *Iliad* is devoted to Achilles' intense performance of the funeral of his dead comrade Patroklos (including the sacrifice of twelve noble Trojan youths and Patroclus' two favorite dogs), and his management of extensive funeral games. There are contests in chariot-racing, boxing, wrestling, running, armed combat, throwing of iron weights, archery, and spear-throwing. This long scene, the presentation of some games in the Phaeacian episode of the *Odyssey*, and briefer references to games in the *Iliad*,[2] all testify to the centrality of trials of manly strength, speed, weapon skills, and courage in "Homeric society." Many contests, like those for Patroclus, are funeral games, but some, like bardic recitations and performances by singing and dancing choruses, form part of the general entertainment for guests (as with the Phaeacians in *Odyssey* 8).

There are archaeological indications of combat sports (bull-leaping and boxing) in the Bronze Age in Crete and mainland Greece, but the events in Homer correspond rather to those which developed in the archaic age. The Homeric poems may well have been composed at a time when regular organized contests, featuring many of these events, were getting under way, at least at Olympia (ca. 700?, see below); if so, these poets felt that regular festival events were too "modern" to be brought into their "epic" world, and displayed only funerary and other forms of social competitions featuring their heroes. Nestor's allusion, however, to his father's sending a four-horse chariot team to Elis to compete for a tripod in a race (*Iliad* 11.698–702) should be seen both as carefully differentiated from the "later" Olympic games (Elis is close to, but not the same as, Olympia, the prize is a tripod, not a crown: this was pointed out in antiquity, by Strabo 8.3.30), but also as "a validating mythological forerunner" of them.[3] The games for Patroclus effect the transformation of Achilles away from his isolated hatred of Agamemnon's divisive leadership and his obsessive grief for Patroclus; the rift is made up and the Greeks reunited, as Achilles operates as a noble master of ceremonies and resolves potentially dangerous conflicts with tact and generosity. Similarly in the Phaeacian games, tact is needed from Odysseus and Alkinous to defuse insults and prevent violence. The contests themselves imitate forms of combat, but the absence of death and serious injury forms a striking contrast with the rest of the *Iliad*. This all prepares the way for the agreement of Achilles to the release of Hector's body to Priam in book 24.[4]

Hence these fictional games provide intimations of the later value to Greek communities of their great games, whose memory, interpreted and misinterpreted from the first celebration of "Modern Olympics" in 1896 in Athens to the recent Games again in Athens in 2004 and in Beijing in 2008, has contributed so much to sport and politics across the modern world. The supposed ideals of amateurism, and "it's not the winning but the taking part," associated above all with Baron de Coubertin and the founding of the modern Olympics (Young 1984), in fact played as small a part in the ideology and practice of the ancient games as it has in practice in the modern. In the ancient games the rewards for the victors could be enormous, and the shame of defeat felt intense;[5] one must remember however that such language suits Pindar's rhetorical aim to praise the victor, there were prizes for second places at local games such as the Panathenaia, and some Greeks could claim that competitors took pleasure at having trained and taken part.[6] More generally, inter-state games and collective musical contests and shows were of great value in creating cohesion of spirit and co-operation inside Greek communities, and building ideals of Panhellenic unity across the Greek world, however often these tendencies towards consensus were threatened or destroyed by wars and civil conflicts.

The Development of Crown and Money Games

The first date in Greek history has long been conventionally fixed at 776. This was apparently established by the fifth-century sophist Hippias of Elis as the date of the foundation of the Olympic Games, celebrated thereafter every four years, and hence the "first year" of the chronographic system adopted by Greek writers from the third century BC, dating known events by four-year periods called "Olympiads." Mythological tradition associated the games with Zeus, in whose honor they were held, and with two earlier "heroic" founders, Heracles and Pelops (after which the games had in theory lapsed); Pelops' hero-shrine had a central place at Olympia between the temples of Zeus and Hera.[7] The founding date of 776, however, is far from certain. First there are doubts about the accuracy and consistency of the lists of "victors" on the basis of which Hippias and later writers drew up their systems and calibrated Olympiads and other dates (such as the sack of Troy), and there is a good case for supposing that the conventional calibration of Olympiad dates with our Julian system is deeply uncertain, because Greek writers used conflicting systems without necessarily being aware of it (see Shaw 1999; 2003; Christesen 2007). Second, archaeologically, the dating of a spread of wells at the area of competition ca. 700 strongly suggests that events only began around that time, and that Elis was previously a small place. Probably the games were originally annual rather than quadrennial and smaller in scope.[8] Whatever the date, the facts that records were kept, and that the games came eventually to provide the most authoritative Greek dating system well into the Christian era, attest the centrality of these contests in Greek life and in the formation of Greek identity, and the primacy of Olympia among the Pan-Hellenic festivals.

Olympia, a shady grove at the junction of the rivers Alpheios and Kladeos in the north-west of the Peloponnese, seems to have been an important sanctuary of Zeus from the late eleventh century, and its first location was related to an earlier Mycenaean tumulus, which became later identified as Pelops' tomb (Kyrieleis 2002a). Originally, it probably provided a neutral place for sacrifices, dedications, meetings, and exchanges for the elites of the western Peloponnese; in the later part of the eighth century it came under the control of Elis (Strabo 8.3.30), and became the major sanctuary in southern Greece. The contests remained for some time local Peloponnesian affairs, but gradually increased their significance (Morgan 1990: chs. 2–3). According to tradition, initially there was only the short foot race (one length), and from the seventh to the fifth centuries they added two longer races, the *pentathlon* and the wrestling (figure 27.1), the boxing, the chariot race, the *pankration* (all-in fighting) and the horse race; similar events for boys; and, finally, the race in hoplite armor, mule-cart race and mares race (Paus. 5.8.6–11). Originally the prizes were valuable objects, but Olympia was the first to offer symbolic prizes, the wreath or crown (*stephanos*) of wild olive,[9] from which derived the name "crown games." A sign that Olympia's fame and importance had grown across Greece is the beginning of monumental building ca. 600 with a large temple for Hera, and soon afterwards a series of individual "treasuries" were built and maintained by individual states to

Figure 27.1 Wrestlers and spectators on the shoulder of a black-figure Athenian vase, Munich 1468
Source: Blow Up GmbH, courtesy of Staatliche Antikensammlungen, Munich.

house their dedications. The treasury of the Sicyonians was followed over the next century and a half by those of Megara in central Greece, Epidamnos in north west Greece, Cyrene in North Africa, Byzantium in the north-east, and states in the far west including Syracuse, Metapontion, and Selinus. Control of the sanctuary and the games remained mostly with Elis, who provided a range of officials and Judges (*Hellenodikai*) to manage the sacred truce, the training period, and the festival events, though there were repeated periods of disruption and conflict during the archaic period. The various disputants were neighboring Pisa, Argos (under its ruler Pheidon) and Sparta, but the chronology of these events is uncertain (see most recently Crowther 2003; Christesen 2007).

The second most important setting was Apollo's shrine at Delphi, in a remote spot some way up the slopes of Mt. Parnassos to the north of the Korinthian gulf, which became during the archaic period the most famous oracle in the Greek world, and the one most consulted by Greek and non-Greek states. Mythological traditions focused on how Apollo gained control there by destroying a serpent, the Python (hence his cult-title Pythios, and the Pythian Games – see the sixth-century *Homeric Hymn to Apollo* 300–87), and then by a wrestling competition with Herakles over the "Delphic tripod." Further confused traditions, contaminated by political pro-paganda in the fifth and fourth centuries, described a ten-year war (the "First Sacred War") involving local communities around Delphi and some more powerful states in central Greece (including Athens, Sicyon, and Thessaly); the historical substra-tum of this largely invented tradition seems to be a relatively local struggle in the early sixth century (hinted at in the *Homeric Hymn to Apollo* 531–44) for control over the oracle and its sanctuary. The result was that control was shared between Delphians and the supposedly safe and neutral hands of a collective organization, the "Amphiktionic Council" (Herodotus 7.200, 213, 228). This body had already existed as the "Pylaean amphiktiony," operating at the sanctuary of Demeter at Anthela near Thermopylae, and constituted by representatives from peoples in Thessaly and central Greece.[10]

Probably at this time (the traditional date is 582), athletic contests were added to pre-existing musical events to create the large-scale "Pythian" games, modeled on those at Olympia, also open to all Greeks and not dominated by any single power-ful state. Every four years, dovetailed to fit in between the Olympics, these "crown" games offered a prize of Apollo's laurel. Delphi also embarked on a major building programme. The temple of Apollo was built (and rebuilt after a fire) during the sixth century, and as at Olympia individual states built "treasuries" as a public store for their offerings and booty from wars; an especially impressive one with elaborate sculptures was built ca. 525 by the small island state of Siphnos which possessed gold and silver mines.[11]

Soon afterwards, local games at a sanctuary of Zeus at Nemea, in the northern Peloponnese east of Argos, and a sanctuary of Poseidon at Isthmia, close to Korinth and the commercial hub of Greece, achieved upgrading to "crown" status. The archae-ological evidence for Nemea is compatible with the traditional date of 573 (Miller 1990; 2004: 105–12); that at Isthmia suggests perhaps expansion to large-scale games after the middle of the sixth-century (Gebhard 2002). Each offered their distinctive honorific crowns, of fresh celery at Nemea and of pine or dry celery (at different

Table 27.1 The cycle of Panhellenic games

Olympiad 75.1	480	July/August	Olympia
Olympiad 75.2	479	July/August	Nemea
Olympiad 75.2	478	April/May	Isthmia
Olympiad 75.3	478	July/August	Pythia
Olympiad 75.4	477	July/August	Nemea
Olympiad 75.4	476	April/May	Isthmia

times) at Isthmia (Plutarch *Moralia* 675d–676d). Both operated every two years, and developed founding mythologies comparable to those at the other sites, linking the games to the deaths respectively of a heroic boy (Melikertes/Palaimon at Isthmia) or a baby (Opheltes at Nemea), and also to activities of major heroes like Herakles (subjugation of the Nemean lion) and Theseus (defeat of the brigand Sinis at Isthmia). These four formed the grand athletic cycle (*periodos*) of Panhellenic games; a four-year period of the *periodos* is presented in table 27.1 (the Greek new year began in the summer).

There were also many local games. Poetic competitions for valuable prizes are attested as early as Hesiod, who claims to have won at the funeral games conducted for "warlike Amphidamas" by his sons, at Chalkis on Euboea (*Works and Days* 654–5). By the sixth century many states and supra-state religious organizations based on sanctuaries organized competitions in athletic events, choral singing and dancing, instrumental performances, epic recitations, or beauty contests. As they offered prizes in cash or kind, they were known collectively as "money games" (*chrematikoi agones*). Prizes might be very substantial. At the Panathenaia at Athens they were gold crowns or painted *amphorae* filled with olive oil. The winner of the footrace received 100 *amphorae*, each containing around 39 litres of olive oil: such a prize was perhaps worth 1,200–2,000 drachmai, or 1/5–1/3 of a talent. This festival was significantly expanded in the mid-sixth century (trad. date 566–565), becoming both an annual, lesser event and a Greater Panathenaia every four years, which invited competitors from far afield. Pindar often mentions victories won at local games as preliminaries to a Panhellenic triumph; a good example is in *Nemean* 10, where the praise of a major Argive wrestling victor, Theaios and his family, in addition to Panhellenic victories at Nemea, Isthmia, and a hoped-for one at Olympia, mentions a bronze shield won at the Argive Heraia, the oil-filled amphorae of Athens, silver wine-bowls of Sicyon, woollen clothes from Pellene in Achaia, and in Arkadia bronze prizes from Kleitor, Tegea, and the sanctuary of Zeus on Mt. Lykaios, high above the city of Lykosoura. In short, there were hundreds of festivals offering various contests and prizes all over the Greek world. Thus the leading athletes and musicians had many opportunities for continuous training and competition, and a great many more had chances for irregular competition at a lower level. Good awareness of the importance of such contests at major sanctuaries is revealed by Thucydides' account of the history of festivals and contests at Apollo's sanctuary on Delos.[12]

The processes of announcing such festivals and the traveling and entertaining of state representatives were marked by formality, rituals, and further contests. Sacred heralds (*kerukes*), "treaty-bearers" (*spondophoroi*) or delegates (*theoroi*) traveled around the states to announce the "sacred truces" and invite participation (in the early fourth century this produced a specific contest for heralds); everywhere they were received by officially appointed "delegate-receivers," *theorodokoi*. Cities then sent their representatives (*theoroi*) to many festivals, often in the form of a performing chorus, to be entertained there.[13] In a divided, insecure and often violent world, full of wars and internal political divisions, these inter-state festivals and processions provided periods of general peace, added considerably to the growing sense of a common Greek identity based on their distinctive shared rituals and social life (most famously enunciated at Herodotus 7.144), and offered multiple opportunities for individual Greeks of different states to develop social, political and economic ties with each other.

The Rewards to the Victors

The high value attributed by all Greek communities to all these contests is attested above all by the remarkable honors and material rewards on offer, matching or out-stripping the adulation and wealth lavished on Olympic medallists in the modern professional era. As we have seen, valuable prizes were on offer in the "money games"; and though the "crown games" marked their distinctiveness by offering merely honorific garlands, victors were usually richly rewarded by their cities. Already at the end of the sixth century Xenophanes complained:

> But if some one were to win a victory through speed of foot
>   Or in the pentathlon, where there is the sanctuary of Zeus
> By the streams of Pisa at Olympia, or by wrestling
>   Or by engaging in pain-bringing boxing,
> Or in the terrible contest which they call the *pankration*,
>   He would become more brightly famous in the gaze of fellow-citizens,
> And would win front seats at the public games,
>   And there would be food for him from the public stores,
> From the city, and a present which will be a treasure for him,
>   And again if he won with the horses, he would get all these things,
> Though he is not as worthy as I.
>
>   (fr. 2.1–11 W)

A fifth-century inscription confirms that the Athenians had long given Panhellenic victors free meals for life in the Civic Hall (*Prytaneion*),[14] and Plutarch (*Solon* 23) asserts that Solon (ca. 594–580) imposed cash limits on bonuses of 500 drachmai for Olympia and 100 for Isthmia (and presumably something comparable for the other two). Any reward fixed in coined money must in fact be later than Solon, as Athenians did not mint coins before the mid-sixth century, but the idea of the Athenian state setting a substantial reward may well go back to Solon; on a sixth-century bronze plaque from Sybaris in South Italy an Olympic victor called Kleombrotos recorded his dedication to Athena of 10 percent of his prize.[15]

In addition, victors were frequently memorialized with one or both of two types of permanent artistic records. A bronze or marble statue might be dedicated at the sanctuary (Pausanias in book 6 describes over 200 statues he saw in his tour of Olympia), or set up in the agora or a sanctuary in the athlete's home community, at his family's or the community's expense. Rare surviving examples of such fine sculptures include the famous charioteer at Delphi and the charioteer found more recently at Motya in Sicily (Bell 1995). Secondly, at least in the period between the mid-sixth century and towards the end of the fifth, the victory celebration often included a performance by a chorus of an elaborately composed victory ode (*epinician*), at the site or, perhaps more usually, on the triumphant return home. The most famous composers of such songs were Simonides and his nephew Bacchylides of Keos, and Pindar of Thebes, active between ca. 520 and 440; four books of Pindar's epinicians, fourteen songs by Bacchylides, and some fragments of Simonides have been preserved. These (above all Pindar's) are complex works, weaving together praise of the victor, his family, trainer and city, praise of the craft of the poet, along with accounts of the event and the games, and appropriate mythical narratives. The myths frequently suggest a form of heroicization of the victor, indicating that his virtues and achievements, won with the active support of the gods, came close to matching those of past heroes (especially those related somehow to the family or to the city); or in contrast they praise the victor by emphasizing his avoidance of the outrageous behavior indulged in by those heroes who committed exemplary crimes against men or gods. A few spectacularly strong or fearsome athletes, who went on to perform great or frightful deeds, ended up receiving heroic honors after their deaths, and their statues were believed to have strange powers (Miller 2004: 160–5). Exemplary here is the boxer Kleomedes of Astypalaia, who was disqualified in 492 because he killed his opponent, and then went mad, pulled down a school, killed sixty children, and disappeared inside a chest. On Delphi's advice, he was honored as "the last of the heroes" (Pausanias 6.9.7). As Pindar regularly observes, there was a similarity of function and a metaphoric equivalence between the epinician song and the victory statue in the conveyance of lasting honor (Steiner 1993; 1998; 2001); naturally the poet often asserts the superiority of his songs because they are not static, but travel across the Greek world, and last for ever, suggesting the songs might be given subsequent performances elsewhere and be read as texts.[16]

Purposes, Training, and Professionalism

To hope for athletic success, culminating in an Olympic victory, was naturally then a strong ambition for most Greeks.[17] A major justification offered for these honors became the belief that athletics and collective dancing were useful because they provided transferable skills for disciplined soldiers.[18] Many events at the crown games featured forms of fighting (boxing [figure 27.2], wrestling [figure 27.1], *pankration*) or rewarded what were apparently useful skills (running, especially the race in armor, jumping with weights, equestrian events, and javelin-throwing); all these events would create strong, fit bodies. The case should not be overstated. Most of these events did not really impart the detailed skills supposedly needed in a hoplite battle, the disciplined, cohesive fighting with shield and sword in an infantry battle. Some local games provide more useful arguments. At Sparta, the state which apparently took military training of its citizens most seriously, there were brutal team fighting games at the Platanistas (Pausanias 3.14.8–10), and tests of endurance for their young men at festivals such as the cheese-stealing contests for Artemis Orthia or the lengthy choral dancing in the summer heat at the Gymnopaedia.[19] At the Athenian Panathenaia the boat-race, equestrian contests, and the war-dance with spear and shield known as the *pyrrhiche*, which was practiced all over Greece and involved leaps and feints (see Ceccarelli 2004), approximated rather more closely to non-hoplite military needs.[20] Choral singing and dancing inculcated practices of cohesive, synchronized and disciplined action, as Xenophon was to point out repeatedly.[21] Two recent and plausible arguments should also be noted, first that the standard close-order hoplite battles of two tightly packed phalanxes may not have been fully developed until the Persian wars, and second that all Greek soldiers, including hoplites, regularly engaged in many flexible forms of manoeuvre as well as combat in tight formation. Hence training in speed of movement, leaps and feints, and covert movements was not unhelpful.[22]

Even so, the argument that athletic and other contests played a major part in training Greek soldiers derived much of its plausibility from the reluctance of the Greek states (other than Sparta) to organize specific military training, as was observed by Plato.[23] Its appeal may also have been heightened by stories of famous athletes, such as the six-times Olympic victor Milo of Kroton who did great deeds as a leader in a battle against Sybaris, ca. 510, allegedly wearing his Olympic crowns and dressed as Herakles (Diodoros 12.9.5). Strong voices were raised from early times against the excessive rewards for athletes. Tyrtaios the Spartan poet of patriotism (second half of the seventh century) argued that athletic skills were useless unless accompanied by courage to face the enemy (fr. 12 W), and the philosopher Xenophanes (in the poem cited earlier) urged that despite their pretensions and rewards athletes in fact contributed nothing to their communities, unlike poets and intellectuals (fr. 2 W). These arguments were repeated and extended in Euripides' satyr play *Autolykos* (fr. 441 N); it cannot be assumed these were Euripides' own views. These arguments were strengthened as more specialized training and diets for athletes were felt by many to make their skills and bodies even less readily "transferable" to the battlefield.[24] They seem, however, to have made little impact on popular enjoyment of sport. Non-contestants enjoyed the spectacles, and everyone in a community derived vicarious satisfaction from their champions' victories, in the beliefs that Panhellenic successes pleased the gods and brought lasting honor and benefit to the city.

Greek athletics were often violent and ended in fatalities or serious injuries, and thus clearly offered a useful outlet for aggressive drives. But it was not a free-for-all. The Olympic judges drew up written rules, probably in the early sixth century (an inscription containing the rules on wrestling has recently been discovered), and these were adopted by organizers of other games. The rules defined and banned excessively violent acts, bribery and other forms of foul play, and sanctions could be imposed by the referees and organizing committee, including the establishing of statues of

Figure 27.2 Boxers and umpires, red-figure kylix, Triptolemos painter, ca. 490 BC
Source: Toledo 61.26; photo courtesy of Toledo Museum of Art.

Zeus ("Zanes") out of the fines, to stand between the sanctuary and the stadium as a warning to other athletes.[25] The games may thus be viewed as an alternative to warfare which emphasizes that here competitiveness and violence must be balanced by respect for laws and rules, which are all sanctioned by Zeus (Poliakoff 1987: 112–15).

Training facilities had to be provided for the many men and boys who wished to prepare for these contests. Our knowledge of the development of Greek *gymnasia* (general training grounds, changing areas, baths) and *palaistrai* (outside training areas for wrestling and other combat sports, often with rooms for school classes as well) is sadly limited in the archaic period. Archaeologically, at Olympia there are remains of a bath house from the classical period, and the surviving *palaistra* and *gymnasion* are Hellenistic, but there must have been training areas already in the sixth century; similarly at Delphi, where the surviving terraced *gymnasion* and *palaistra* were started in the later fourth century. There is some textual evidence for the development in the sixth century of three *gymnasia* in Athens, the Kynosarges, the Academy, and the Lykeion, the latter two of which would later have the philosophical schools of Plato and Aristotle attached to them.[26] But open air training, changing and washing facilities must have existed in many or most cities at least from the sixth century onwards, the beginnings of what was to remain a central, defining Greek institution until the end of the Roman Empire. Legislation concerning access to the *gymnasia* also probably goes back to the early sixth century. Fourth-century and later sources attributed to the Athenian lawgiver Solon laws which sought to preserve status-distinctions by preventing slaves from training at *palaistrai* and from pursuing free boys as lovers;[27] such attributions are often retrojections, but these laws may well be sixth century, since Aeschines' citation includes a rare archaic verb (*xeraloiphein*) meaning "to rub dry with oil."

Gymnasion, and the verb for athletic training *gymnazesthai*, both derive from the word *gymnos* meaning "naked," and competing nude was a innovation of the archaic period which came to be widely seen as a distinctive feature of Greek culture, as is claimed by both Thucydides (1.6) and Plato (*Rep.* 452c). They both claim it was introduced "not long ago" (Plato taking the idea from Thucydides), rather inaccurately, as the evidence of vase-painting clearly indicates that it was well established by the middle of the sixth century.[28]

Thucydides claims the practice started among the Spartans, Plato among the Cretans and Spartans. Plato and other fourth-century sources also held that Cretan cities and Sparta were places where homosexual love-relationships between older and younger youths had long been part of institutionalized upbringing of future male citizens and warriors, where the older partner offered affection and training in military skills and discipline.[29] Many scholars argue that homosexual relations between males of unequal ages originally developed across Greece as part of secretive, ritualized, "rites of passage" for young men; then, perhaps from the sixth century onwards, in many cities they developed into more optional and open relationships centred on the public activities of nude athletes at the *gymnasia*, especially among the more leisured classes.[30] In Cretan cities and in Sparta, on the other hand, homosexual relations remained located in mandatory socialization procedures for all young citizens, but adapted to fit new military and social needs. Young Cretans and Spartans spent much of their boyhood and youth living together in male houses, called *phitidia* or *syssitia* at Sparta, and *andreia* in Crete.[31]

One of the first surviving uses of the verb *gymnazesthai*, "to exercise naked," plays with the erotic connotations of gymnastic activities: "Happy is the man who, in love, exercises naked (*gymnazetai*), going home and sleeping all day with a beautiful boy" (Theognis 1335–6). Sixth- and fifth-century poetry, later anecdotes about sixth-century aristocrats and tyrants, and contemporary illustrations on black-figure and early red-figure vases all suggest the prevalence of homosexual contacts and rivalry at these settings. Whatever may be the case with the "initiatory" hypothesis, the decision taken across the Greek world to adopt athletic nudity was surely central to the public legitimation of idealized homosexual love from the sixth century onwards.[32] The muscular, bronzed and oiled bodies of the athletes, gleaming like statues, must have had a powerful erotic appeal for many, if not all, of the thousands of spectators, and decorous allusion to such erotic attractiveness can be found in Pindar's victory poems.[33]

At the Athenian *gymnasion* of the Academy the association was allegedly blazoned forth by the erection there of an altar to Eros by a polemarch called Charmos (an aristocrat who in one story had been the lover of the tyrant Peisistratos' son and heir, Hippias): this carried the inscription: "Eros of many devices, for you Charmos has established this altar at the shady boundaries of the *gymnasion*."[34] Charmos' supposed connections, political and erotic, with the family of Athenian sixth-century tyrants indicate that the pederastic connotations of nude athletics could have political implications. But such associations were contradictory. There is no doubt that the most powerful men in the states were prominent among those who participated in the games, especially those events such as chariot-racing which involved the greatest expense and carried most prestige; equally no doubt such men engaged vigorously in love affairs. The leading poets, Ibycus, Simonides, Anacreon, Pindar, and Bacchylides, competed to celebrate the athletic victories, the physical attractiveness and the loves of tyrants such as Polycrates in Samos, Peisistratus and his sons in Athens, Hieron, Gelon and Thrasydaios in Sicily, as well as of many other aristocrats across the cities and larger regions such as Thessaly. Ambitious men found that the *éclat* of a spectacular athletic victory gave them great honor (*time*), indeed an especially grand form of spectacular distinctiveness often called *kudos*, a term which also hints at divine approval; such renown might provide sufficient "symbolic capital" to form the basis for a profitable marriage alliance, a military command, or an attempt at political power.[35] An early instance is Kylon at Athens, the son-in-law of Theagenes the tyrant at neighboring Megara. He followed a victory in the four-horse chariot at Olympia (some time between 640 and 620) with an unsuccessful attempt to win power: Herodotus' wording "Kylon was an Olympic victor from Athens, who grew his hair long for a tyranny" implies an intimate connection between an Olympic triumph, an aristocratic hairstyle and a bid for supreme political power.[36] Kleisthenes the tyrant of Sikyon, at much the same time as the proliferation of Panhellenic and other games ca. 580–560, chose the occasion of his own chariot victory at Olympia to invite all the "best men in Greece" to become suitors for his daughter Agariste, and tested the thirteen candidates extensively. The younger ones were tested on his specially built running-track, *palaistra* and *gymnasia*, though performance at the *symposion* carried most weight in the selection procedure (Herodotus 6.126–7).

On occasions, however, some tyrants feared, or had cause to fear, intense homosexual relations between young men and youths. According to Athenaeus (602), such passions were behind many plots against tyrants, the most famous of which was the assassination of Hippias the tyrant's younger brother Hipparchos at Athens by the insulted lovers Harmodios and Aristogeiton (see also Thucydides 6.54–9); other tyrants such as Polycrates of Samos allegedly tried to forestall the danger by shutting down the *palaistrai*.

But the elites may not have monopolized every competition. The most prestigious events, above all the chariot racing, involved very considerable expense in purchase and upkeep of horses and equipment, and must have been pretty much monopolized by the wealthy elites (it was the owner who claimed the prize, while often employing a relation, friend, or paid expert as charioteer: see Nicholson 2003). But the non-equestrian events at the crown and the local games may have attracted a considerably wider range of participants, though evidence is thin and scholarly opinion deeply divided.

The traditional view that in the archaic period the elites totally dominated all events in top-flight athletics was challenged by Young's provocative book (1984). This pointed out, first, that this view was developed in the early twentieth century by scholars who shared sympathies with the founders of the new amateur Olympic movement in their admiration for the "amateur ideal" and hostility to the spread of "professionalism" and the extension of sport to poorer competitors; they idealized and misrepresented

Greek sport accordingly.[37] Second, Young suggested that the traditional view rested largely on the praise in Pindar's epinician poems of the family traditions and political connections of very many of his victors; but the clientele of the most successful poet may not be a fair sample. Third, he argued positively that even in the archaic period talented non-aristocratic youths could have won victories and become wealthy, given the high value of the prizes at many local games such as the Panathenaia. Some successful athletes are said by later sources to have come from humbler backgrounds, for example Glaukos of Karystos, whose remarkable strength was witnessed when he mended a plough, and who became first a champion boxer and later held political office in Kamarina;[38] the goat-herd and hare-catcher Polymestor of Miletos who ran an Olympic short race;[39] and the Olympic long-distance runner for whom, allegedly, Simonides wrote an epigram, celebrating how he had previously carried fresh fish from Argos to Tegea in a rough basket on his shoulders.[40] Young suggested that the remarkable number of victories won by some small cities, especially the South Italian cities Kroton and Sybaris (which we saw earlier offering large rewards to its victors), may be explained by the hypothesis that they spent money on sponsorship deals to persuade talented athletes to transfer allegiance (see also Miller 2004: 216–18). One may add (Fisher 1998) that the strongly homosexual atmosphere of the *gymnasia* combined with the civic pressures to produce victors may have helped to counteract aristocratic prejudice and encouraged older and richer athletes, trainers, or other sponsors to advance the careers of attractive and talented youths of more humble origins. Arguably too some of the distinguishing markers of wealth and breeding, such as expensive clothes, may have seemed less evident and divisive when all were naked together for long periods of time, and such equality may even have helped to foster political egalitarianism and the growth of more democratic regimes (Miller 2000; 2004: 232–4).

These views have been challenged, however.[41] Some of these cases of alleged humble successes may well reflect later mythologizing; Aristotle explicitly adduces the fish porter's achievement as an exceptional case. Many scholars remain unconvinced that a significant number of youths from unleisured backgrounds could have found the time to attend *gymnasia* at all, to be spotted and supported to compete at the highest levels. The issues remain open, in large part because of the lack of detailed information; a sure assessment remains beyond our grasp.

Competition and Politics in the Late Archaic Period: Pindar's Epinicians

It is hard to overstate the political significance of these games and contests, or their importance to Greek life and to the identities and fame of individual cities and larger groupings such as the amphiktionies. It is striking, for example, how many of the critical disturbances we hear of in Athenian politics interact with celebrations of the Athenian Panathenaia or other major festivals (e.g. Kylon's attempted coup – at the "wrong" festival – or Peisistratos' coup[42]), or took place in panathenaic years (the assassination of Hipparchos). The sudden increase in popularity an aristocrat gained from an Olympic victory seems to have been a major threat to an existing regime (e.g. Kylon's attempted coup; the elder Miltiades' departure to the Chersonese; his nephew Kimon's triple victory in exile, his diplomatic ceding of the third to the tyrant Peisistratos, his return, shortly followed, after the tyrant's death, by his own assassination allegedly authorized by the new tyrants)[43]. Other tyrants, from Kleisthenes of Sikyon to the very powerful early fifth-century tyrants in Sicily, spared no efforts to have Olympic and other victories proclaimed in their names, above all in the chariot-races; and there are a good many instances where victors go on to major military or political careers or become involved in political *stasis*.

In such contexts, and especially in cities where political tensions were running high, it is readily understandable that poets celebrating the triumphant return of an adult Panhellenic victor to his city had to avoid excessive praise which might arouse hostility, envy or fear. These are central themes of Pindar's epinicians.[44] The assertion of the victor's *arete* (virtue, achievements), his natural talents (*physis, phya*), training, effort (*ponos*) and expense (*dapana*), leading to his deserved honor (*time*), and rewards from his city, must be balanced by mention of the decency of his general life and his refusal to abuse his social position. Victors are repeatedly said to show appropriate values of social respect (*aidos*) and control of excessive desires (*sophrosyne*), and avoidance of *hybris*, deliberately aggressive behavior which gives the perpetrator pleasure by inflicting shame or harm on those taken to be socially inferior.[45] Envious suspicions of the wealth or luxury of the victor and his family are allayed by emphasis on the collective reciprocal pleasures of the songs and banquets, uniting the victor and poet with the wider community. Finally, on the divine level, the praise of the victor had to balance the achievement of as much glory as a mortal could attain with the awareness of the limits of mortality and the necessity to respect the superior power and honor of the gods, if one were to avoid their justified anger or envy at a man's excessive *hybris* or excessively high thoughts; these ideas were typically conveyed through the pointed retelling of myth. A particularly prominent moral concept encapsulates the ideal of social harmony (in practice no doubt often mitigating or masking serious conflicts or tensions), that of *charis*. The concept embraces at once brightness, reciprocity and pleasure, as do its personifications – the single goddess *Charis*, or the three *Charites*, who also appear regularly in their individual forms of *Aglaia* (joy, brightness, beauty), *Euphrosyne* (good spirits, pleasures of the *symposion*), and *Thalia* (feasting, festivity). *Charis* can denote the effect which beauty and charm (such as that of athletes) have on the viewers, any shared delight in song, dance, poetry, feasting, and sex, and any element in positive, mutually reinforcing, chains of benefactions, gratitude and rewards. A primary example of such a reciprocity was the understanding that athletic, military, or political success, or major financial contributions from the rich, rightly produced honorific and monetary rewards in return from their communities.[46]

Many Pindaric praise poems display an elegant interplay of all these meanings. For example, *Olympians* 14, composed for a boy runner from Boeotian Orchomenos, is a short ode which largely takes the form of a hymn to the *Charites*, who received special cult at that site, and emphasizes the point that the community of the gods, as well as those of all men, depend on these goddesses for all their social pleasures such as choruses and feasts: A more ambitious poem, *Olympians* 7, in honor of the celebrated boxer Diagoras of Rhodes, starts with an elaborate analogy in the first two stanzas which compares the gift of a foaming wine-cup at a wedding *symposion* to the bridegroom and his friends, with the gift from the poet of the nectar of the Muses, the song, to the victor: over both celebrations fruitful *Charis* presides with her music and song. At the end of the ode, after a long account of the mythical founding of Rhodes, the poet asks Zeus to grant to Diagoras a "respectful recipro-city" (a *charis* full of *aidos*), linking him together with both citizens and foreign friends (*astoi* and *xenoi*), because he "travels straight on a road which hates *hybris*"; he and his ancestry deserve their fame because "along with the *charites* of the Eratidai the city too has its feasts (*thaliai*)" (*Olympians* 7.88–94). The beginning and the end of this ode thus emphasize that *charis* casts its reciprocal and harmonious pleasures over marriages and epinician celebrations alike, where it brings together the victor's noble family, his friends and foreign guests, and members of the wider community. Kurke (1991: 210) sees a tension in the poem between more "aristocratic" cele-brations, such as the initial wedding or the more private feasts of the family (or pseudo-kinship group) of the Eratidai, and the distinct, perhaps inferior, festivities of the "city," but there is no reason to see the wedding as an exclusive occasion, and the last lines suggest that as the restraint and generosity of the victor and his family has averted envy and hostility, it enables the community to share equally in the delight and the glory of the victory in public feasts (on which see Schmitt-Pantel 1990; 1992). How far such hopes were in fact fulfilled may naturally be doubted, and there must always have been a fluctuating balance between tension and harmony in relations between elite victors and the wider citizen population. Pindar's strategy is to ally himself with the victor and family as all alike figures of talent and success, blessed by the gods, who should not arouse envy because of their justice, respect for the honor of others and avoidance of *hybris*; he does this especially in cases where there are reasons to suppose major opposition existed, for example towards tyrants like Hieron of Syracuse, responsible for much killing and mass deportation of popula-tions, his general Chromios, or Theron of Akragas; leading figures in exile, such as Megacles of Athens; and cities where there was much political tension, such as Aegina.[47]

Competitive Participation and the Advance to Democracy: Cleisthenes' Athens

The contribution made to civic harmony and the absence of civil strife (*stasis*) by shared musical performance in competitive choral song-dance received more atten-tion in Greek political theory from the late fifth century onwards than it has in modern scholarship at least until recently. Plato's *Laws* explores in detail how sacrifice and choral song-dance are fundamental to a community's relations to its many gods, to homogeneity between its members and to the proper education of its young. Book 8 of Aristotle's *Politics* contains recommendations for the educational role of music's harmonies and rhythms in providing communal pleasures and developing the ethi-cal characters and responses of the educated citizenry.[48] According to a remarkable passage in the second-century historian Polybios (4.20–1; Kowalzig 2004: 41–2), most of the Arkadian cities exemplified these social benefits, as they had always had a great devotion to "choruses of boys and young men singing and dancing every year with great enthusiasm for honor (*philotimia*) to the pipes-players of the Dionysiac guilds in the theatres"; they celebrated men's and women's choruses at regular festivals and all sang at their private entertainments. These practices had created a softer and more civilized character. But one Arkadian city, the small city of Kynaitha, was the exception which proved the rule; it did not practice *choreia* and was destroyed in an outburst of lawlessness, *stasis* and savage violence ca. 220 BC.

Late archaic Athens is a particularly interesting case, where an increase in the number of civic competitions for male citizens went hand in hand with a startling increase in equality and political participation. The second half of the sixth century, and especially the reforms of Kleisthenes (ca. 508–500), saw a considerable expansion of contestants and prizes, and correspondingly a wider spread of participation across the class levels of citizens, in choral singing and dancing (especially in dithyrambs and in the new form of tragic drama, which began in the 530s or (less probably) ca. 508–500,[49] as well as in athletics, torch races, and gymnastics. This was accompanied by a diminution, in comparison with many other states, in the numbers of choruses of girls and women, which earned Plato's disapproval.[50]

Kleisthenes' radical reorganization of Athens made its citizens all members of their local "demes" and linked them through these with 30 larger regional units ("trittyes"), 3 of which combined to form 10 "tribes" (*phylai*), created in ways which deliberately brought together a mix of Athenians from three different sectors of Athenian territory: city, coast, and uplands (e.g. Anderson 2003). These new tribal units became the basis not only of the more democratic political institutions of the deme, the tribe, and the council of 500, but also of many new contests, of lavish dithyrambic choruses, each of 50 men or boys, of dramatic choruses, of dancers in the *pyrrhiche*, torch races, and an exhibition of group manliness (the *euandria*, found in places beyond Athens: Crowther 1985). These programmes in the state-run festivals must have demanded the participation of a considerably expanded number of citizens and their sons, many involving intense team-work (Osborne 1993b). It seems that every year 2,000 or more chorus-members were needed in dithyramb, tragedy, and comedy in city-run festivals (especially the Dionysia, Panathenaia and Thargelia); others were needed for sacred processions to outside sanctuaries (*theoriai*) to places like Delphi and Delos.[51] The implications of this for the social levels of participants are debated.[52] The funding of all the activities of these festivals, like the funding of the greatly expanded war fleet in the period 493–480, was shared between state expenditure and the peculiar Athenian institution developed in this period known as the "liturgy." The richest 1,000 or so citizens were required to expend substantial amounts of money, time, and effort, paying for and organizing choruses' costumes and training, the *theoriai* to sanctuaries, feasts for all participants in a tribal contest, or the maintenance of a warship; but they were also strongly encouraged to contribute much more than what was legally required, and a good many seem to have done so.[53] The Athenians made effective use of the social mechanism of the reciprocal exchange of *charis*. According to the ideology of the city, contributions of the rich were driven by a complex motivation which came to be labeled (good) *philotimia* (reminiscent of Hesiod's "good Strife"), which can be unpacked in this context to mean "enthusiasm to do good for the community from the desire for honor"; the rich expected significant rewards in the material form of statues and other memorials and more uncertain but arguably more significant forms of increased political support or social recognition. This is a striking example of how the Greek passion for competition and honor was harnessed to achieve social cohesion, and to persuade many of the elite to cooperate with egalitarian and democratic practices. One piece of evidence about a hundred years later strongly suggests that this increased focus on community-sponsored competition in the late archaic period had considerable success in uniting elites and more middling citizens.[54] According to Xenophon, just before the battle in the Piraeus during the civil war in 404 between the supporters of the "Thirty Tyrants" and the democratic insurgents, a respected herald of the Eleusinian mysteries appealed to the oligarchs as follows:

> Citizens, why are you driving us out? Why do you want to kill us? We have never done you any harm, but have shared with you in the most solemn rituals and sacrifices and the finest festivals, and have been chorusmen together, as boys we have trained together and we have served as soldiers together and shared many dangers with you by land and sea for the sake of our common security and freedom.

> (*Hellenica* 2.4.20–1)

NOTES

1 See the reissue of selections in English, 1998: ch. 2; also Poliakoff 1987: 105–15; Golden 1998: 28–33; Spivey 2004: 1–16.
2 *Od.* 8.97–249 (also 24.84–92); *Il.* 4.385–90, 23.629–45, 678–80, 22.162–4.
3 Taplin 1992: 39; also Hornblower 2004: 9–10.
4 Macleod 1982: 28–32; also Golden 1998: 88–95.
5 E.g. Pindar, *Pythians* 8.83–7; *Olympians* 8.68–9, with Young 1984: 163–70.
6 E.g. Plato, *Theages* 128e; see Kyle 1992; Crowther 1992; Golden 1998: 70–1.
7 E.g. Pindar, *Olympians* 1; 2; 10.29–92; Pausanias 5.7.7, 5.8.1–2, 5.13.1.
8 Morgan 1990: 46–9, 89–90; Mallwitz 1988: 98–101; Golden 1998: 63–5.
9 Pausanias 1.7.7, 1.8.6; Pindar, *Olympians* 3.1–230.
10 C. Morgan 1990: 135–6; 2003: 129–30; Tausend 1992: 34–47; Davies 1994; McInerney 1999: 154–72; Sanchez 2001: 32–80.
11 Herodotus 3.57–8; Neer 2003.
12 Thuc. 3.104, with Hornblower 1991: 516–31.
13 Dillon 1997; Perlman 2000; Rutherford 2004.
14 *IG* I³ 131; Miller 1978; Kyle 1987: 145–7.
15 Jeffery 1990: Supplement p. 456 no. 1a and Plate 79.1; Moretti 2002: 123.
16 O'Sullivan 2003; Currie 2005; Hubbard 2004.
17 Pindar, *Olympians* 1.1–9, 10.22–30; *Nemeans* 10.31–3; Plato, *Apology* 36d–e; *Republic* 465c–e.
18 Lucian, *Anacharsis* 14–15, 30; Xenophon, *Memorabilia* 3.12.1–8. See also ch. 30.
19 Parker 1989; Kowalzig 2004: 58–9.

20 E.g. Golden 1998: 23–8; Poliakoff 1987: 94–103; van Wees 2004: 87–95.

21 *Memorabilia* 3.3.11–12, 3.4, 3.5.6; *Oikonomikos* 8.3–5.

22 Rawlings 2000; van Wees 2000a; 2004: 89–93, 166–77; Krentz 2002.

23 Plato, *Laws* 813–6, 829–31, and Aristotle, *Politics* 1338b25–39.

24 Plato, *Republic* 404c–e; Aristotle, *Politics*, 1335b1–5, 1338b9–a10; Kyle 1987: 137–41.

25 *SEG* 48: 541; Pausanias 5.21; Siewert 1992.

26 Delorme 1960: 36–42; Kyle 1987: 21–2, 64–92; Glass 1988.

27 Aeschines 1.138–9; Plutarch, *Solon* 1.3–4; *Moralia* 152d, 751b.

28 Bonfante 1989; McDonnell 1991; Golden 1998: 65–6.

29 Plato, *Laws* 636a–b, 836b; Aristotle *Pol.* 1273a23–6; Ephoros *FGH* 70 F 149, quoted by Strabo 10.4.21; Timaeus *FGH* 566 F 144, quoted by Athenaeus 602f.

30 Bremmer 1980; 1990; Stewart 1997: 27–9; Calame 1999: 96–9, 101–9; Scanlon 2002: 66–87.

31 Cartledge 2001: 91–105 (Sparta); Leitao 1995 and Carter 1997 (Crete).

32 Stewart 1997: 27–34; Scanlon 2002: 205–19.

33 E.g. Pindar, *Olympians* 8.19–21; *Pythians* 10.56–60; *Isthmians* 7.21–4: see Instone 1990; Steiner 1998; 2001: 222–34.

34 Athenaeus 609d; see also Plutarch, *Solon* 1, 6–7; Pausanias 1.30.1.

35 Kurke 1991; 1993; Osborne 1996a: 244.

36 Herodotus 5.71; different versions of the story in Thucydides 1.126 and Plutarch, *Solon* 12.

37 Prime representatives of such views are Gardiner 1930; Harris 1964.

38 Pausanias 6.10; Aeschines 3.189–90 and *Scholia*: Moretti 1959: no. 134.

39 Philostratos, *Gymnastics* 13; Moretti 1959: no. 79.

40 Aristotle, *Rhetoric* 1365a20–6; Simonides, *Epigrams* 41 Page.

41 For example by Kurke 1991; 1993; Pritchard 2003; balanced treatments in Kyle 1987: 124–54; Golden 1990: 71–2; 1998: 141–5; Pleket 1992; 1998.

42 Thucydides 1.126; Herodotus 1.59–61.

43 Herodotus 6.36 (Miltiades); 6.103 (Kimon); see Connor 1987; Phillips 2003.

44 E.g. Crotty 1982; Mullen 1982; Most 1985; Kurke 1991.

45 On these concepts see North 1966; Dover 1974; Fisher 1992; Cairns 1993.

46 Kurke 1991; MacLachlan 1993.

47 Pindar, *Olympians* 1; *Pythians* 1; 2; 3 (Hiero); *Nemeans* 1; 9 (Chromios); *Olympians* 2 (Theron); *Pythians* 7 (Megacles); *Pythians* 8 (Aegina); see Fisher 1992; Most 2003.

48 Wallace 1998b; Brulé and Vendries 2001; Wilson 2003; and Murray and Wilson 2004, esp. essays by Kowalzig, Ford, Wallace and Wohl.

49 Connor 1990; Sourvinou-Inwood 1994.

50 Kowalzig 2004; for women's choruses in general see above all Calame 1997.

51 Xenophon, *Mem.* 3.3.12; cf. 3.5 for praise of the discipline of Athenian choruses.

52 E.g. Fisher 1998 argues for wider levels, Pritchard 2003 for more restricted.

53 Kallet 1998; Wilson 2000a.

54 Cartledge 1985a: 115–19; Fisher 2003: 202–3; Wilson 2003: 182–4.

CHAPTER TWENTY-EIGHT

Literacy

John-Paul Wilson

The Greek alphabet was conceived at some point prior to the mid-eighth century BC. It was not a completely new "invention," derived as it undoubtedly was from a script used by the Semitic peoples of the Levantine coast. Most Greek letter names and letter forms are similar, if not identical, to those used in this so-called north-west Semitic script, as is the letter order (see table 28.1). The north-west Semitic script is normally separated into three main branches, Phoenician, Aramaic and Hebrew (Naveh 1982), and there is some debate about from which specific branch the Greek alphabet was derived. Herodotus (5.60) states that the Greeks called their alphabet "Phoenician letters" (*phoinikeia grammata*), an expression that also crops up in a fifth century BC inscription from Teos.[1] The term "Phoenician," however, need not exclusively describe those who dwelt in the region, roughly equivalent to modern Lebanon, which modern scholars most readily associate with this term (Markoe 2000: 11). Aramaic inscriptions have been found in the Greek world from ninth- and eighth-century contexts (Amadasi Guzzo 1987), and linguistic arguments have been offered in support of a specifically Aramaic origin of the Greek alphabet (Driver 1976: 267). On the other hand, a number of letter endings "show an evolution characteristic of Phoenician and not of the Aramaic dialect" (Amadasi Guzzo 1991: 296); so it seems probable that the Greek alphabet was derived from the Phoenician script.

The Greek alphabet worked differently from the Phoenician script (table 28.1). It had specific signs for vowels, whereas the Phoenician did not, vowels being implied by the context. The Greek consonantal inventory was slightly smaller and indeed different from the Phoenician; hence a number of Semitic signs had no equivalent sound value in Greek. Five such redundant signs were consequently used to represent the vowel sounds.[2]

The arrival of the alphabet in the Greek world, it has often been argued, was the impetus for a cultural and intellectual revolution (Goody and Watt 1968). Indeed, it has been characterized as a, if not *the*, seminal moment in the development not only of Greek society, but also of western civilization (Havelock 1982). "Without

Table 28.1 Comparison of Phoenician and Greek letter names and letter forms

Phoenician letter names	Phoenician letter forms	Greek letter forms	Greek letter names
aleph	Ӿ	α	*Alpha*
beth	⊲	β	*Beta*
gimel	∧	γ	*Gamma*
daleth	◢	δ	*Delta*
he	⊒	ε	*Epsilon*
waw	Y	Ϝ	*Digamma*
zayin	I	ζ	*Zeta*
heth	⊟	η	*(h)eta*
teth	⊗	θ	*Theta*
yodh	⋌	ι	*Iota*
kaph	⋋	κ	*Kappa*
lamedh	(	λ	*Lambda*
mem	⋌	μ	*Mu*
nun	⋀	ν	*Nu*
samekh	⧧	ξ	*Xi*
'ayin	○	ο	*Omicron*
pe	⋌	π	*Pi*
tsade	⋏	ϻ	*San*
qoph	φ	ϙ	*Qoppa*
resh	◁	ρ	*Rho*
sin	W	σ	*Sigma*
taw	×	τ	*Tau*
		υ	*Upsilon*
		φ	*Phi*
		χ	*Chi*
		ψ	*Psi*
		ω	*Omega*

There is great variation in the letter forms of the Phoenician and Greek alphabets. The forms presented here are common but do not reflect any one epichoric script.

writing," Ong (1982: 78) observes, "the literate mind would not and could not think as it does, not only when engaged in writing but normally even when it is composing its thoughts in oral form. More than any other single invention, writing has transformed human consciousness." Whereas earlier pictographic and ideographic writing systems, such as Mesopotamian cuneiform, Egyptian hieroglyphics and Linear B remained the preserve of a scribal class because of their complexity, the Greek alphabet was remarkably easy to learn, and therefore, it is argued, led to a much wider transformation of "human consciousness."[3] Some suggest that the Greek alphabet was fundamentally better suited to the expression of abstract thoughts and ideas than any earlier writing system, because it was fully (if not always perfectly) phonetic.[4]

It is no longer fashionable to think of the arrival of the alphabet in Greece in quite such dramatic terms. The Greek alphabet is now widely regarded as *not* intrinsically superior to the earlier middle eastern scripts; complex thought can be and indeed was expressed using these scripts.[5] It is also generally accepted that only a very small percentage of Greeks in any period could in fact read or write (Harris 1989: 43–146). Greek society remained what modern scholars would call an "oral" culture. Long after the alphabet came to Greece, the written word supported the spoken word rather than supplanting it (Thomas 1992: 88–93).

More generally, writing itself is no longer thought to be necessarily a catalyst for intellectual revolution and increased freedom.[6] Literacy can and has had such an impact in different cultures, at different times, but only in combination with a variety of other factors (Lloyd 1979).

This chapter will look in more detail at the uses to which writing was put and at levels of literacy in archaic Greece, while also addressing the broader questions of how one defines the terms "literacy" and "literate," and whether one can usefully describe archaic Greek culture as "literate" or "oral." We will begin by asking how, when, where, and why the alphabet came to Greece.

The Origins of the Greek Alphabet

How?

The alphabet was probably developed in a single place, at a single time. Some have advocated a single "innovator,"[7] while others have viewed it as the product of a group or community.[8] The latter seems to me more acceptable since it allows for an immediate audience for this new "technology." That the alphabet was the product of a single "invention" may seem counter-intuitive since the early Greek alphabet is notable for its distinct regional variations, the so-called epichoric scripts.[9] For example, the alphabet used in archaic Corinth is subtly, and sometimes not so subtly, different from that used in Attica (Osborne 1996a: 110–11). These differences, however, have been deemed by many less striking and significant than the similarities: all epichoric scripts use the same Phoenician signs for the vowels; all misapply the names and the sound values of the Semitic sibilants, *zayin*, *samek*, *sade* and *shin*; all split the Semitic *waw* into two forms, *upsilon* and *vau* (later *digamma*); and all use the Semitic cursive forms for certain letters, such as *iota* and *vau*.[10] All this would imply that there was a single "mother-script" from which all local Greek scripts evolved, the differences being a secondary development.[11]

The process of transmission and adaptation could hardly have occurred if the "innovator," or more likely "innovators," did not have at least a broad appreciation of how the Phoenician script worked. As already noted, the adaptor seems to have had some misapprehensions about the north-west Semitic script which surely rule out the possibility that he himself was Semitic (contra Powell 2002: 114). It seems likely, however, that the process occurred in a context where Greeks and Phoenicians were living in close proximity, if not in a bilingual community.

When?

If one accepts the "monogenesis" theory of the Greek alphabet then it should theoretically be possible to locate a point in time and in space for the transmission and adaptation of the alphabet. In the last hundred years dates as divergent as 1800 and 700 have been suggested, and most points in between.[12] The earliest inscription now known seems to date to no later than 775,[13] which rules out later datings, but the argument remains far from resolved.

Despite the diversity of opinion, there have been just two basic approaches to this question. The first, an approach adopted by most classical scholars and initially suggested by Carpenter in 1933, is essentially an argument from silence: one cannot place the transmission much earlier than the earliest inscriptions that have been discovered. As noted, the earliest known example of Greek alphabetic writing, from Gabii in central Italy, is dated securely to the first quarter of the eighth century. After this rather isolated find, there are something like one hundred inscriptions (excluding single letter inscriptions) from 750 to 650 from all over the Greek world. The argument from silence then currently suggests that the alphabet cannot have arrived in the Greek world much before 775, and a date around the beginning of the eighth century can be posited. Clearly, such an argument is always likely to be shattered by new discoveries, but extensive excavations have taken place at many major Early Iron Age sites and as yet none have produced an inscription from before the eighth century, and while the possibility of a site such as Gabii producing an earlier inscription remains, the probability of an inscription from the ninth century or earlier being discovered is diminishing (contra Bernal 1990).

The second approach involves a comparison between letter forms in the earliest Greek inscriptions and in the fairly firmly dated corpus of Semitic inscriptions. Such an approach leads McCarter (1975) to suggest an early eighth-century date, which fits perfectly with the argument from silence, but has led Naveh (1982: 175–86) to a very different conclusion. He argues, on the basis of the form and stance of Greek letters and the direction of writing, that the Greek alphabet was not based on the linear Phoenician alphabet at all but on its precursor, the pictographic Proto-Canaanite alphabet, and therefore the transmission of the alphabet to Greece has to be dated to before 1050 when this pictographic script gave way to the linear script. Naveh's arguments have been widely supported by Semitic epigraphists, but have received little attention from classical scholars who have maintained a belief in a late ninth/early eighth century transmission.[14] There are indeed problems with Naveh's arguments. The features of letter stance and direction of writing which he notes can be explained as independent Greek developments, and in any case we cannot be sure that the Phoenician script developed in a perfectly linear manner. For example, in the Aramaic inscription on a statue from Tell Fakhariyah (ancient Sikan) the presence of a dotted *ayin* and of a trident-shaped *kaph* would suggest an early eleventh-century date, but iconographic criteria suggest a ninth-century date.[15] If one accepts this later dating then it throws into question the whole of the Naveh's argument, since this inscription would demonstrate the continued existence of "archaic" letter forms into the ninth century.[16]

In epigraphic terms alone Naveh's argument is far from water-tight, but in historical terms – and Naveh (1982: 184) himself says "the antiquity of the Greek alphabet is not a question of epigraphy alone; it is also, and primarily, a historical issue" – it appears barely tenable. Naveh must explain why, if the alphabet was transmitted to Greece in the eleventh century, no inscription earlier than 775 has yet emerged. One possible explanation for such a *lacuna* might be to suggest that only in the eighth century did the Greek alphabet enter the public domain, while prior to this it had had a restricted usage, and was written only on perishable writing materials. Konishi (1993) has argued that the alphabet was adopted in the tenth century by forgetful oral poets who used the alphabet as some kind of *aide mémoire*, keeping it a closely guarded secret until someone let things slip in the eighth century, but this does not seem a very plausible scenario. Naveh's suggested date of ca. 1050 places the transmission in a period of rapid cultural, economic, and demographic decline; a period when contacts with the outside world appear minimal and inter-regional exchange was negligible. It is difficult to see how the alphabet could have come to Greece at this time or who used it and with what purpose.

In historical terms, a date in the early eighth century seems far more probable. Contacts between the Aegean and the outside world were growing: indeed there is evidence for Phoenician settlers in the Aegean, and Greek settlers in northern Syria.[17] It is also much easier to posit a motivation for the transmission and to identify an audience for this new technology. The balance of the evidence therefore favors a date of ca. 800.

Where?

The case for the place of transmission must be judged on three criteria. First, on the evidence of Graeco-Phoenician interaction at the site, since the transmission and adaptation must have taken place in a community where Greeks and Phoenicians were in close contact. Second, on the potential for the rapid and extensive dissemination of the alphabet from that site, since it is evident, if one accepts a date of ca. 800, that the alphabet spread very quickly across the Greek world. Third, it must be judged on epigraphic grounds – how closely does the local script resemble the Phoenician alphabet?

The literary sources suggest extensive Phoenician settlement throughout the Aegean (Jeffery 1990: 8–10). At Rhodes this is strongly corroborated by archaeological evidence (Coldstream 1969) and it is unquestionable that Rhodes was an important point on the east–west trade route, with Rhodian pottery present from Al Mina to Pithekoussai. On the other hand, the Rhodian epichoric script is notable from an early stage for its straight *iota*, when it is the crooked form that is recognized as closest to the Phoenician letter *yod* from which *iota* is derived (Jeffery 1990: 356). The straight form probably only emerged later to prevent confusion with the letter *sigma*, so that the Rhodian form of *iota* is a mark of a derivative alphabet, not the original Greek model.

There is purely archaeological evidence for Greeks and Phoenicians co-existing in the eighth century in Crete, north Syria, Cyprus, and also in the western

Mediterranean at Pithekoussai, although the Greek settlement there seems to be too late to be considered as the place of transmission. A ninth-century Phoenician temple has been identified at Kommos in south-east Crete, along with a diverse array of pottery types, including Phoenician red slip ware, which might mark it out as some kind of trading-post (Shaw 1989). There is also a Phoenician inscription from the Tekke cemetery, near Knossos, perhaps as early as 900 (Snycer 1979), which Coldstream (1982) sees as evidence of a Phoenician family of metalworkers settled here. There is no doubting Crete's connections with the rest of the Aegean, and it was clearly an important stop-off on trade routes west. The Cretan script itself is "the closest of all to the Semitic alphabet," with its crooked *iota* and its lack of the so-called "new" or supplementary letters (Jeffery 1990: 9).

Al Mina, at the mouth of the Orontes in northern Syria, offers another possibility. The archaeological evidence suggests that the settlement was some kind of port-of-trade, dating back perhaps to the ninth century. Debate among scholars has focused on the nature of the Greek presence at the site. Boardman (1990) argues for an enclave of Greek merchants, while Kearsley (1999) suggests that the Greeks at Al Mina were mercenaries. Others, however, deny any direct Greek contact with the site, arguing that the Greek pottery at Al Mina was carried there by Levantine traders (e.g. Graham 1986). There is little doubt that Al Mina was not a Greek settlement: the architecture of the site is Levantine. To deny any Greek presence there at all, however, is to go too far. The quantities of Greek pottery at Al Mina, and the ratio of Greek to non-Greek pottery at the site, are considerably higher than for any other settlement in the Levant, so there ought to have been at least a temporary or seasonal Greek presence. As the place of transmission, it has in its favor a probably mixed population, and also the fact that Greek traders would have been more likely to learn the rudiments of the spoken and even written Phoenician language in this context than on their home soil in Rhodes or Crete, for example. It can also be placed at the eastern end of important Mediterranean and Aegean trade routes.

A good case can also be made for Cyprus. There is a strong Phoenician presence there from the ninth century, and contacts with the Aegean and the western Mediterranean are strong. Johnstone (1978) has argued that the presence of an indigenous writing system on the island, the so-called Cypriot syllabary, may have acted as a catalyst for the adaptation of the Phoenician alphabet, a view recently expanded upon by Woodard (1997). One possible objection to the role of Cyprus in the transmission is the paucity of Greek alphabetic inscriptions from the island, in stark contrast to the number of Phoenician inscriptions, and to a lesser extent the number of inscriptions in the syllabary. Woodard explains this in terms of Cypriot conservatism, and the endurance of the syllabary might point towards this, but it remains a troubling factor.

My own feeling is that the transmission must have taken place in a context where Greeks and Phoenicians lived side by side, and where Greeks had at least a working knowledge of Phoenician or Aramaic. It strikes me as intrinsically less likely that this would have occurred in the Aegean, and I favor a non-Greek context, either northern Syria, and specifically Al Mina, or in the east of Cyprus where the Phoenician presence was strong both culturally and perhaps politically.

Why?

The question of why the Greeks adopted and adapted the north-west Semitic script has received relatively little scholarly attention. General accounts of archaic Greece often express the likelihood of commercial reasons for the transmission, without fully exploring the question.[18] Studies that directly address the question for the most part argue against a mercantile origin in favor of the more romantic notion of a "poetic" origin.[19]

The theory of a mercantile origin starts from the belief that the Greek alphabet was derived from the Phoenician script. The Phoenicians were the great traders of both the Old Testament and the Homeric epics, and it was therefore in a commercial context, so the argument runs, that the Greeks must have first encountered Phoenician writing. Seeking to emulate their principal competitors, they adapted it to their own language in order to keep accounts, send business letters and so forth. The rapid diffusion of the alphabet might also add weight to the mercantile origin theory, since it is plausible to imagine the alphabet spreading along Aegean and Mediterranean trade routes, disseminated by the very men who adapted it in the first place.

The problem with this theory, in the form laid out above, is that it rests on a single piece of circumstantial evidence – the adaptation from the Phoenician script. Both Powell (1991) and Robb (1994) reject the mercantile theory out of hand because there is no material evidence to support it. Powell (1991: 182) says of the earliest Greek (eighth and seventh century) alphabetic inscriptions, "there is nothing in these . . . to suggest mercantile interests, public or private: no financial accounts, not even any numbers or evidence that a numeral system existed."[20] They argue instead for a poetic origin, suggesting that the alphabet was invented to write down oral poetry. Powell (1991) asserts that a single individual created the Greek alphabet in order to record Homer. Robb (1994) regards the writing down of hexameter verse in general, initially in a dedicatory context, as the impetus for the "invention." The theory of poetic origin again relies initially on circumstantial evidence. As noted, the Greek alphabet differs from the Phoenician script insofar as it has signs to notate vowel sounds, and the absolute necessity of vowels for the recording of hexameter verse might explain the impetus for their "invention": it would have been impossible to write Greek poetry using the Phoenician consonantal script. Some of the earliest Greek inscriptions do indeed record hexameter verse: the verses on the Dipylon oinochoe[21] and "Nestor's cup,"[22] and the inscriptions of Mantiklos[23] and Nikandre.[24] Powell (1991: 183) believes that numerous shorter inscriptions can also be identified as hexametrical.

There are, however, a number of objections to this theory. First, it might be argued that vowels are grammatically essential for recording any sort of Greek, not just verse (Thomas 1992: 55). Second, early Greek scripts do not seem to distinguish vowel length (Osborne 1996a: 112). Third, as already noted, Greek vowel signs may have been a product of a misunderstanding of the Phoenician glottal stops and not some incredible invention after all. Finally, there is a danger of over-emphasizing the importance of the surviving verse inscriptions to the argument because it privileges "texts" written on non-perishable materials, i.e. pottery, metal, and stone. If all the "texts" written on papyrus, leather and wooden writing tablets had also survived they might well have provided a very different perspective on early use of the alphabet.

Neither of these theories appears compelling and other possible explanations have been offered. For example, Woodard (1997) views the alphabet as the product of experimentation by Cypriot scribes, while Johnston (1983) suggests that the alphabet was initially created for the simple purpose of denoting ownership. This suggestion deserves further attention, given the frequency of inscriptions that claim ownership of an object, by stating "I belong to *x*." Personal names or alphabetic marks, even more numerous, may function in the same way. Such a practice is evident in contemporary Phoenician inscriptions.[25] One way of explaining this practice of marking ownership is to identify the inscribers as traders distinguishing their cargo from that of other traders, while traveling on a large ship. Evidence would seem to suggest that the *emporos*, the Greek for trader, was in origin a man who bought passage on another man's ship: with the cargo of numerous *emporoi* stored in the hold, some means of distinguishing who owned what may have been required. At some point, the captain of the ship may have functioned as a "memorizer" of the cargoes.[26] Greeks traveling alongside Phoenicians may have adopted their practice of marking or inscribing their name upon their cargo, a process which required learning the Phoenician writing system. On this model, the initial catalyst is once more "mercantile," but this does not deny the possibility that these traders saw the further possibilities of this new technology; they had after all to look no further than the Phoenicians who utilized this "art" for a range of purposes, including the religious and the magical.[27]

Literacy in Archaic Greece

The uses of writing

When exploring the uses to which alphabetic writing was put in archaic Greece one must look primarily to the body of surviving inscriptions. Such inscriptions, however, survive only on stone – whether on dressed slabs (*stelai*), on the side of buildings, on statue bases, or very occasionally on the living rock – on pots or on potsherds (*ostraka*), very rarely on clay plaques, and infrequently on metal, sometimes fashioned into bowls, tripods, statuettes and so forth, or occasionally into purpose-made "sheets" or plaques. This corpus must constitute a tiny proportion of the written texts produced in archaic Greece; anything written on papyrus, leather or wood has not survived, and this must also be true of the vast majority of texts inscribed on potsherds, metal etc. It is not, however, merely a question of volume. Certain categories of evidence are vastly underrepresented or potentially altogether invisible. The Homeric epics were written down, perhaps as early as 730, as was much other poetry, yet only the few fragments of hexameter verse already mentioned have survived. One can only speculate as to whether a small number of letters written on lead, dating to the sixth and early fifth century, are extraordinary or reflect the wider but otherwise unattested use of writing as a means of communication in the archaic period (Wilson 1997a). Similarly, a small collection of *ostraka*, dating from the mid-sixth through to the fifth century, found in the Athenian agora, inscribed with short messages may be a serendipitous glimpse at what was a widespread use of writing for the everyday and mundane.[28]

With these words of caution in mind, we will now look at the surviving archaic inscriptions. I have divided these into 24 categories, which are not necessarily discrete – as we will see, there is clear overlap between some of them – but distinct enough to be useful.

1   *Single letters recorded in isolation.* A large number of inscriptions consist of a single letter, which may be no more than experimentation: the "author" practicing his writing. In other instances the letter may represent a numeral, since the letters of the Greek alphabet doubled as numbers in the so-called "Ionian" or "Milesian" numeral system,[29] or some kind of trademark (category 23). Beyond such practical explanations for these shortest of inscriptions, it has been suggested that these single letters held some kind of symbolic power; that the very act of inscribing a letter on an object gave it greater magical or ritual importance.[30] Sometimes a letter may have stood for the name of a deity: "A" for "Athena" (Lehmann 1960: 29). That so many of these inscriptions come from dedicatory contexts would seem to support such views.

2   *Nonsense inscriptions.* The earliest known Greek inscription, from Gabii in central Italy, might be read as either "*euoin*" or "*eulin*," which readings have respectively been interpreted as a "Bacchic cry" (Peruzzi 1992) and as an abbreviated form of the name Eulinos, "deft-spinner" (Ridgway 1996). Yet it is just as likely that, like several other inscriptions, this is a string of letters with no meaning. Such inscriptions, like single letters, may be examples of "doodling" or they may be attempts to imbue an object with a magical importance. This earliest inscription was after all found in a grave on a locally manufactured and otherwise unremarkable pot.

3   *Abecedaria.* There are numerous examples of inscriptions listing the letters of the alphabet, occasionally in full but more often incomplete and sometimes even inaccurate.[31] One must suspect that these abecedaria are examples of "students" learning this new skill of writing by much the same method as schoolchildren have ever since, by writing out the alphabet in order. An ivory writing tablet found in an Etruscan grave at Marsiliana in central Italy has a full 26-letter alphabet inscribed along its upper border (Jeffery 1990: 236–7). The deposition of such a "school-tablet" (Jeffery 1990: 240, no. 18) in an adult's grave may suggest that the deceased's ability to read and write was worth emphasizing. On the other hand, the grave was rich in other ivory items and the inclusion of an ivory writing tablet may have been incidental to what was primarily an expression of the deceased's wealth.

4   *Proper names.* The vast majority of inscriptions are simply personal names, most often found individually but sometimes in a list. Many of these are found in dedicatory contexts. At the sanctuary on Mount Hymettos in Attika a significant number of inscriptions have a name followed by "*egraphse*" meaning "x wrote this" (Langdon 1976). Since this was the shrine of Zeus Semios, "Zeus of the [weather]

signs," the "signs" of writing may have been thought especially appropriate here (Thomas 1992: 60). A list of names of ca. 550–500, cut by different hands into the tufa blocks of a building in the sanctuary of Apollo at Delphi, might be the names of those who paid for the erection of the building or those who built it (Jeffery 1990: 101). Writing out one's name is an essential part of becoming literate, so some inscribed names may be further examples of writing practice. In other instances, the name is a statement that "so-and-so was here," as in the case of the "signatures" of Greek mercenaries at Abu Simbel in Egypt, dating to the early seventh century, some of which add an ethnic to the personal name: "Elesibios the Teian," "Tambis the Kolophonian" (Bernand and Masson 1957). It is also possible that names functioned as tags denoting ownership of an object (category 5).

5 *Declarations of ownership.* Some inscriptions denote ownership more explicitly. One of the earliest inscriptions, not much later than 750, found on Pithekoussai etched in a fragment of a crude, probably locally manufactured amphora, reads "I am of Mima[l]lon."[32] Buchner (1978: 135) has suggested that this inscription is a writing-exercise, since he sees a second line of text as repeating the first. This, however, seems to go beyond what can be observed on the amphora, and it is likely that Mimallon was simply laying claim to the amphora and its contents, probably wine. One may imagine Mimallon carrying his goods on a ship not his own, alongside those of other individuals, a common practice in archaic Greece (Bravo 1977). Elsewhere statements of ownership are backed up by a curse: an inscription on a Corinthian *aryballos* (perfume flask) from Kyme, ca. 675, reads "I am the *lekythos* of Tataie; whoever should steal me will be blind."[33]

6 *Dedications.* A number of inscriptions from categories already discussed formed part of a dedication to a god or goddess. Around 700 more explicit dedications appear. Some simply state the name of the god or goddess; others take the form "Person X dedicated this to God/Goddess Y" or a variation on this: an inscribed gold bowl found in the sanctuary at Olympia reads, "the Kypselids dedicated it to Herakles" (Jeffery 1990: 131, no. 13). Others are more complex, such as the two-line dedication by Mantiklos to Apollo in hexameter verse.[34]

7 *Curses.* Lead curse-tablets, *defixiones*, although essentially a later phenomenon, are attested as early as the sixth century (Jordan 1985). Even earlier inscriptions on *ostraka*, however, might be viewed as curses, such as the seventh century example from Mount Hymettos in Attika, which declares someone a *katapugôn*, a "bugger" (Thomas 1992: 59).

8 *Epitaphs.* Inscribed tombstones, like explicit dedications, emerge ca. 700, but only appear in significant numbers in the latter part of the seventh century. The earliest examples are rough stone markers bearing only a name, such as those from a necropolis at Thera (Jeffery 1990: 317, nos. 3–4). Others, however, are inscribed with sometimes quite complex texts. One of the earliest examples of these more detailed epitaphs is that of Dweinias, a Corinthian, dating to ca. 650, which announces that "the shameless sea destroyed him" (Jeffery 1990: 131 no. 6).

9 *Craftsmen's signatures.* Potters, stonemasons, sculptors, and other craftsmen often left their mark on their creations. This might simply be their name but in some instances their role as creator was made more explicit. A *krater* dating to ca. 725–700 features

an inscription, painted on before firing, in the later common form "[. . .]inos made me" (Arena 1994: 19–20).

10   *Labels (dipinti).* A feature of some sixth century Attic Black Figure vases is the name-label, attached to the mythical characters represented on the vase. The extreme case is the François vase which has 129 such inscriptions (Cristofani 1981: 177–8). Some such name labels are not names at all but simply a collection of letters with no meaning (Boardman 1974: 200–1).

11   *Sympotic inscriptions.* A small number of inscriptions may be products of the symposion. Etched on a Rhodian *kotyle*, found in a Pithekoussan grave, is the so-called Nestor's cup inscription.[35] Written in hexameter verse, it reads: "I am the drink-worthy cup of Nestor; whosoever should drink from this cup, desire for fair-crowned Aphrodite shall seize." This inscription might be a symposiast's pun on the cup of Nestor in the *Iliad* (11.634–40).[36] A symposiast, given a first line of hexameter verse, is challenged to add a second, ideally amusing, line of his own. So impressed is he with his effort that he immortalizes it by inscribing it on his favorite drinking cup. This heightens the "joke" since his drinking cup is nondescript, in contrast to the magnificent four-handled, gold-embossed version of the *Iliad*. The inscription on the "Dipylon oenochoe" also begins in metre: "Who of all the dancers dances most delicately."[37] A second line trails off into apparent nonsense; one might venture to suggest that the second writer was not less skilled so much as drunk! Whether or not one accepts such specific interpretations, these inscriptions do seem to be connected with the world of the symposium.

12   *Graffiti.* This term is used by epigraphists for informal writing not inscribed on stone: as such, many inscriptions in the categories above are also *graffiti*. It is used here, however, in its more modern sense. Declarations of love (or hate) daubed on bus shelters and nicknames of graffiti artists covering railway bridges have parallels in the ancient world. On a rock plateau at Thera, near what would later become the *gymnasion*, a series of inscriptions, perhaps as early as the late eighth century, expresses the "admiration" of young men for each other in increasingly explicit terms (Powell 1991: 173–80). One set begins "Laqudidas is fine (*agathos*)," which is trumped by "Eumelos is best in the dance," which in turn is outdone by the claim "Krimon, best at the *konialos* [a bawdy dance with strong sexual overtones], warms the loins of Simias." The names of the mercenaries cut into the leg of a monumental statue outside a temple at Abu Simbel (category 4) might also slot into this category.

13   *Laws.* The earliest example of an inscribed law dates to the second half of the seventh century and was engraved on a temple wall in Dreros on Crete. A growing body of secular and sacred law is attested for the first half of the sixth century. The epigraphic evidence fits in well with the literary tradition for codification of law, which places legendary lawgivers in this same period. It seems likely then that it was only from the mid seventh century that writing came to serve the *polis*, although it is worth noting that there is some tradition of the Greeks recording their laws on wood (e.g. Plut. *Solon* 25). Two broad observations can be made with regard to these early laws. First, they are for the most part poorly inscribed and not the work of professional stonecutters. Second, these laws are mostly concerned with procedure and with the penalties for breaking laws, and not with what we would regard as criminal law.

14 *Honorific decrees.* Decrees which celebrate citizens and outsiders who have benefited the *polis*, and bestow various honors on them, are among the most common type of inscription in the Classical and Hellenistic periods. They are less common in the archaic period, but a number are attested for the sixth century. For example, a late sixth-century inscription from Crete records the extensive honors granted to one Spensithios (Jeffery and Morpurgo Davies 1970).

15 *Records of public works.* A number of sixth-century inscriptions record the work done by an individual or group (sometimes public officials), often the erection or repair of a civic building or temple. An inscription from the sanctuary of Athena Aphaia, dating to ca. 550, for example, states that building was carried out "when Kleiotas was priest" (Jeffery 1990: 112, no. 4). Other inscriptions report the fulfilment of particular public duties, such as the organization of the first Great Panathaneia by a group of Athenian magistrates, the *hieropoioi* (Jeffery 1990: 77, no. 18).

16 *Lists of public figures.* Inscriptions recording lists of *polis* officials, such as magistrates and priests, are strikingly few in the archaic period, given that lists composed in the fifth century and later cite the names of these officials from as early as the seventh century.[38] Perhaps records of officials were kept but have simply not survived in any great number; alternatively, such lists were the product of the imaginations of later officials or historians. The use of eponymous officials in some archaic inscriptions, such as the dedicatory inscription of Damonon in which victories are listed by eponymous ephor, may presuppose the existence of such lists (Jeffery 1990: 60), or else it was a short-term mnemonic aid rather than a system used for dating (Thomas 1992: 67; 1989). The few lists of names that have survived may be lists of victors in games rather than lists of officials (Jeffery 1990: 60), and date to the very end of the archaic period.

17 *Treaties.* Inter-state treaties are rare in the archaic period and the few there are date to no earlier than the late sixth century. These earliest treaties, such as that between Elis and Heraia, were found at Olympia (Jeffery 1990: 220, no. 6).

18 *Temple inventories.* A common phenomenon in the classical period, the temple inventory – a record of valuables dedicated at a sanctuary – is relatively rare in the archaic period. There are, however, a few examples, most notably an inscription on a silver plaque from Ephesos of ca. 550, which lists the silver and gold collected for the temple, perhaps to pay for its construction.[39]

19 *Boundary markers.* Inscribed boundary stones, *horoi*, might be characterized as public inscriptions, marking out as they do the physical and legal limits of a public space, whether sacred – the *temenos* of a temple – or civic – for example, an agora. In origin, uninscribed stones may have fulfilled this function, but there are relatively early examples of inscribed *horoi*, such as that from the precinct of Herakles at Aigina, marked simply "*Herakleos*," dating to the seventh century (Jeffery 1990: 112, no. 3). Such examples of inscribed boundary stones as there are from the archaic period seem for the most part to demarcate sacred rather than civic space.

20 *Coin legends.* Some of the earliest Greek coins, found in Lydia, and dating to ca. 600, are inscribed with a name, perhaps denoting the issuer, whether king, *polis* official, or military leader. The presence of a "legend" – the technical term for

such inscriptions – only becomes the norm towards the end of the sixth century, when abbreviations denoting the *polis* which issued the coin start to appear: for example, ATH, on the coins of Athens (Kraay 1976).

21 *Correspondence.* A small number of archaic inscriptions, incised on lead sheets, and a similarly modest number of *ostraka*, might be reasonably classified as letters. The former date from the very end of the sixth century and are notable for coming from the fringes of the Greek world: two from Olbia and its environs, on the northern shores of the Black Sea, one from Emporion, in north-east Spain, and one from Himera, in Sicily.[40] The letters from Olbia and Emporion seem to have been exchanged between men involved in some sort of transaction: one might call them "business" rather than personal letters. The rarity of letters is not unexpected: most letters would have been written on papyrus or perhaps on waxed writing tablets. It is also worth emphasizing that a letter which reached its destination, particularly one written on lead, was likely to be erased and the material reused. It is probable that this small corpus only survives because these letters never reached their intended recipient. Those found on *ostraka* are of a different nature and seem to be letters or rather notes left for one neighbor by another – "Thamneus, put the saw under the threshold of the garden gate" – or by a master for a slave – "Boy, bring other new couches for Phalanthos."[41]

22 *"Contracts."* An even smaller body of inscriptions might be categorized as "contracts," or perhaps less contentiously as records of transactions. Again inscriptions of this type are attested only from the late sixth century. A series of lead tablets from Corcyra, dating to ca. 500, record the amounts of loans made and the names of debtors. The paucity of such evidence may suggest that few businessmen were literate, but again it may merely be an issue of survival. An account of the purchase of a boat, on a lead tablet from Pech-Maho in southern France, replete with information as to where stages of the transaction took place, and with a list of witnesses, implies a developed set of institutions for the administration of exchange in this area. This in turn suggests that this inscription is the tip of an iceberg rather than an anomaly (Wilson 1997a).

23 *Trademarks.* Numerous alphabetic marks found on amphorae and on painted pottery have been identified as trademarks. These presumably acted to identify the vendor of either the contents of the container or, in the case of fine-ware, the vase itself (Johnston 1979). Single letters found on amphorae or vases may have functioned as trademarks, and the phenomenon may date back to the second half of the eighth century. More complex marks are attested in the latter part of the seventh century and in the sixth, ranging from straightforward abbreviations of the trader's name – so "SO," perhaps the mark of the famed merchant Sostratos – to ligatures of two or more letters, presumably abbreviations, to combinations of letters and non-alphabetic marks.[42]

24 *Oracular questions and responses.* The literary tradition states that questions to and replies of the Delphic oracle were written on leather. Consequently the voice of this oracle (and of its visitors) is known only from the literary sources. Those of the oracle at Dodona, however, were written on bronze or lead plaques and survive in small number from the late sixth century and early fifth (Jeffery 1990: 230, nos.

13, 15–17). Isolated examples of such inscriptions from more obscure oracles are also known: a bronze disk, dating to the early sixth century, probably from Kyme, states simply, "Hera does not allow further prophecy" (Jeffery 1990: 238, 240, no. 5).

Harris has said of the archaic period that "written texts were employed for a very limited range of purposes and by a very limited number of people" (1989: 46). The brief inventory above suggests otherwise: writing was utilized for religious, magical, symbolic, artistic, economic, political, practical and frivolous purposes.

Its religious function is most evident in the relative frequency of inscribed dedications after ca. 700. Quickly, if not immediately, writing became a tool of the worshiper: votive objects could be personalized by the addition of a few words, immortalizing the very act of dedication and the dedicator himself. Emphasis might also be placed on the apparent ritual or even magical power of writing. As noted, curses are attested from the seventh century – perhaps earlier if we accept Thomas' view that the Nestor's cup inscription parodies the curse form (1992: 59). Ownership inscriptions might be interpreted as another "magical" use of writing. Even when not accompanied by an explicit written curse, such inscriptions may have functioned alongside a spoken curse: the inscription would warn any potential thief that the object belonged to someone else, while the accompanying spoken curse would lay out the consequences of theft. Writing then might have been seen as reinforcing the power of a curse that would also have been uttered out loud (Thomas 1992: 79–81). The potentially destructive force of writing is emphasized in a passage of the *Iliad* (6.170–5) where a writing tablet instructs the recipient to kill the bearer: here the letters are described strikingly as "lethal marks (*semata*)" (Bellamy 1988). At a more basic level, the very presence of alphabetic signs on an object – single letters, a word, phrase or sentence, or even a nonsense inscription – might have added to, or shaped, its ritual power.

A further symbolic function of writing is that letters may have functioned "as an additional artistic element" in some archaic inscriptions.[43] The orientation of the writing, size of the letters, and visibility of the inscription in some instances suggest that ease-of-reading was not the first consideration, and that their primary function was decorative.

Any desire to characterize the uses of archaic writing as principally non-rational, however, seems mistaken. One observes numerous practical, rational uses of writing throughout the archaic period. It has already been suggested that Greek traders first adapted the alphabet in order to denote ownership of a cargo. The craftsman's signature also appears an eminently pragmatic form of writing: an advertisement of the maker's skills. Sixth-century business letters and records of transaction may also reasonably be characterized as commercial.

Writing was also used in the political sphere from perhaps as early as ca. 700. Public inscriptions are only attested from ca. 650 onwards, but some earlier inscriptions also had a conspicuous "political" function in the wider ancient Greek sense. Dedicatory inscriptions, explicitly naming the dedicator(s), were produced for the audience of those who frequented the sanctuary at which the object had been dedicated. The sanctuary became a kind of "political" arena in the latter part of the eighth century: a place where one could communicate one's piety but also one's wealth to others through the act of dedication. The addition of an inscription to a dedication might be viewed as the most explicit example of such an ethos, as it presented very clearly, to those who could read, the identity of the dedicator, and with it his/her piety and wealth.

Writing was also used for light-hearted purposes from an early date, as the eighth-century sympotic inscriptions and Theran graffiti show. From the introduction of the alphabet, writing seems to have been utilized for varied, perhaps even conflicting purposes: can one, for example, reconcile the symbolic or magical power of writing with its purely practical applications?

Whatever the conflicts, early uses of writing have this in common: they feature within existing customs (Thomas 1992: 72). Memorials to the dead and dedications to the gods, for example, existed before writing. The addition of writing to the physical object, whether tombstone or vase, enhanced the effect of that object but did not fundamentally change its function. Written curses existed alongside spoken curses and essentially allowed the creation of a physical object, the curse tablet, which represented the spoken curse. It is striking that in a number of inscriptions the object is made to speak: "I am the drink-worthy cup of Nestor," or "[. . .]inos made me." A number of tombstones speak directly to the passer-by, even "engaging" in conversation.[44] In these instances, writing directly represents the spoken word.

Written law also added to rather than replaced unwritten law, which remained of great importance: in late sixth-century Crete, the duties of the community's scribe (*poinikastas*), Spensithios, were "to write down *and* to memorize the affairs of the city."[45] Written law did not attain any greater authority than unwritten. Thomas (1992: 71) observes that much early written law is found within sanctuaries, even inscribed on the walls of temples, emphasizing the need of divine sanction to consolidate its force. One wonders also whether the "memorizer of cargoes," described in the *Odyssey* (8.160), continued to exist even when names and/or claims of ownership had been inscribed on the goods. It is only in the longer term that we see uses of writing that might be considered independent of visual or oral forms, uses which emerge because of the very existence of writing. Correspondence, inventories and accounts, for example, might fall into such a category. It is only later still, perhaps in the fourth century, that writing finally usurps the dominance of the spoken word.

Levels of literacy

Some estimates of levels of literacy have been offered. Harris (1989: 61) suggests that "it would be astonishing if as much as 10 percent of the population as a whole was literate"; and that there was "a rather low level of craftsmen's literacy," defined as "the condition in which the majority, or near-majority, of skilled craftsmen are literate, while women and unskilled laborers and peasants are mainly not" (Harris 1989: 8). Murray, on the other hand, states that "archaic Greece was a literate society in the modern sense" (1993: 98), which means greater than 20 percent literacy (Goody and Watt 1968). Without attempting to define "literacy," or indeed "literate," in quantifiable terms, however, such estimates do not mean a great deal.

Is a literate person someone who can both read *and* write? How much does some-one have to be able to read and/or write to make them literate?[46] Some scholars have suggested that basic literacy is implied by the ability to write one's own name,[47] but there is little value in classifying someone who can just about decipher his or her own name alongside someone who can read the entire text of the *Iliad*. The application of a broad, absolute definition of "literate" is ultimately less helpful than the identification of different levels of literacy. Harris (1989: 5) develops three main categories: literate, illiterate, and semi-literate; the last includes "persons who can write slowly or not at all, and who can read without being able to read complex or lengthy texts." I will offer a slightly more nuanced set of definitions, in addition to the term "general literacy" which covers the first four categories below:

1   *Developed literacy*: the ability to read long texts – whether public inscriptions or poetry – and to write texts of a non-standard type, for example a letter or a note.
2   *"Political" literacy*: the ability to read and understand long and detailed texts, in particular those produced by the *polis*, such as laws, decrees, treaties. The ability to write is incidental.
3   *Practical literacy*: the ability to read and to write short texts of a standard type, such as a statement of ownership, a dedication or even a curse.[48]
4   *Kindergarten literacy*: the ability, at a minimum, to make out alphabetic signs, and at a maximum to write one's own name.
5   *Non-literacy*: the inability to read or write.

It should be emphasized that the order of these definitions does not necessarily reflect descending levels of literacy but rather different *types* of literacy. This set of definitions could be refined much further: "developed literacy" encompasses a potentially wide range of abilities, within which a Euripides would be placed along-side someone who never wrote more than a scribbled note to a friend. Also, a greater distinction may need to be drawn between the ability to read and the ability to write (Thomas 1992: 10–11). In the discussion which follows, however, these definitions may help to illuminate the varied impact writing had on archaic Greek society.

Two broad points can be made about levels of "general literacy" in archaic Greece. First, the number of Greek inscriptions from the period 800–500 relative to the number from later periods strongly suggests that "general literacy" was at a lower level in this era than in any subsequent period of classical antiquity. Second, "general literacy" increased across the archaic period, and levels made a particular jump at the beginning of the sixth century. The first point, I think, needs no further inves-tigation. The second point requires some further consideration.

The magical and symbolic use of writing in early inscriptions suggests that only a small number of Greeks had any understanding of the alphabet at the time, and that the majority were "non-literate." Comparative evidence shows that writing only retains such magical/symbolic power when it is little or not at all understood (Holbek 1989). As more people become able to read and write, writing loses some if not all of its magical and symbolic force (Goody 1968b). Nonsense inscriptions and single-letter inscriptions, which may have imbued an object with magical or symbolic power, become less frequent from the middle of the seventh century onwards, which may suggest that a greater proportion of the population reached at least "kindergarten literacy."

The emergence of public inscriptions in the second half of the seventh century, and particularly in the sixth century, might be one of the primary indices of increasing "general literacy" if laws were written down to protect the masses from the whims of the ruling elite. This would only have the desired effect if the masses were able to understand these laws, that is if there was widespread "'political' literacy" (e.g. Gagarin 1986). This view has been challenged, however, because of the nature of early law, and because of the nature of public inscriptions themselves. Eder (1986) has argued that law was written down not to protect the masses but as a means to prevent change, a product of aristocratic conservatism. A variation on this position suggests that the elite used written law to protect themselves against the threat of one of their own number growing too powerful. The earliest attested law, for example, defines the terms of office of the chief magistrate, the *kosmos*, and the consequences of breaching those terms, and as such would presumably have been of limited significance to those without access to power, that is, to the vast majority (Osborne 1996a: 186–7). If we assume either of these positions then there is no need to believe that the masses were expected or were able to read these laws (cf. Whitley 1998a).

Such a conclusion is amplified if we also accept Thomas's view that inscriptions had as much a symbolic as a practical function; that they acted as "memorials of a decision rather than simply documents intended to record important details" (1992: 84). Many written laws do not seem to have been inscribed with the reader in mind: the lettering is often small and barely legible, and there is no punctuation. Fifth-century inscriptions from Teos which curse officials who do not read out the public inscriptions (Herrmann 1981) may indicate a wider practice of reciting public inscriptions. On this view, the inscribed stele acted as a communal reminder of the enactment of law and need not suggest anything about the level of literacy. Even if the emergence of written law is not necessarily indicative of high levels of "'political' literacy," however, it may have encouraged the development of such skills among those with a political interest.[49]

Thus far, we have argued that writing became more widely known and used within the Greek world as the archaic period progressed, particularly in the sixth century. A closer look at the surviving inscriptions, however, gives a clearer sense of the nature of archaic literacy, and of the different levels of literacy suggested by the evidence. Many archaic scribes are notable for their ineptitude. Many appear ill at ease with the technology they are using, producing letters of uneven size, continually shifting the orientation of these letters and the direction of writing, being unable to write in a straight line, and unable to judge how much space they will need for their words such that the endings of some inscriptions have to be squeezed into too small a space. Some of this may be a product of the media on which surviving inscriptions are scrawled – an *ostrakon* is a far from perfect writing surface. Another factor may be the "aesthetic handling of writing" (Thomas 1992: 78): letters may be re-orientated and their direction changed to suit overall artistic aims. Even with these factors in mind, however, these inscriptions do not suggest high levels of literacy, but individuals who have learnt a little writing to suit their specific purposes: a potter enough to put his signature on his work; a vase-painter to label his characters; a trader to lay claim to his cargo; a citizen to display his name on a dedication and to proclaim his piety. In other words, these inscriptions are evidence of a level of "practical literacy."

The brevity of the vast majority of archaic inscriptions drives home this conclusion. The Nestor's cup inscription and the Mantiklos dedication at approximately thirteen words each are notably longer than most other inscriptions of the early archaic period and it is only in the latter part of the seventh century that we start to get examples of more than a few lines. Most of these longer inscriptions are public, in the form of laws or honorific decrees, and one must suspect that they were produced by public scribes, such as the Cretan *poinikastas* (see above). Of course, it is possible that long, complex texts of a non-public nature were being produced on papyrus and other perishable surfaces throughout the archaic period – someone, after all, was writing down the text of the *Iliad* and the *Odyssey* in the late eighth or early seventh century. The inscriptional evidence, however, implies that levels of "developed literacy" were low.

Only in the sixth century do we see the first clear inscriptional evidence for "developed literacy" in the form of letters, whether written on lead, presumably to be sent over some distance, or scratched on *ostraka*, perhaps used to pass on short notes to a friend, neighbor, or slave. Not all these inscriptions appear to be the work of frequent letter-writers. The text of a letter of ca. 500 on lead found at Berezan on the northern shores of the Black Sea is a good example of this.[50] Written in the third person, it has poor syntax and grammar, and inconsistent spelling. The author, one Achillodoros, can be forgiven since his plight is serious – he claims that he is wrongly "being enslaved" and the letter asks another man to save him from this fate – and it is easy to envisage the letter being written in a hurry, with little regard for niceties. The key point is that this man, if not a slave then of low enough status to be taken for one, is able to write a fairly long, detailed letter. Other letters on lead are also written by or sent to traders, or at least those involved in exchange, and low level exchange at that. Similarly, the author of a "contract" from Pech-Maho in southern France is not a big businessman by anyone's standard (Wilson 1997a). These documents are few in number and come from the margins of the archaic Greek world but they insinuate a more widespread practice of letter-writing among traders, perhaps on papyrus. The wider implication is that there was "developed literacy" among a group of relatively low social (and perhaps economic) status.

The "letters" on *ostraka* from the Athenian agora are also few in number – just two date to the sixth century – but they also hint at the wider use of writing for this everyday purpose (see n. 42). Their authors demonstrate a comfort with writing – the short texts follow no fixed formula – and a familiarity that is surely evidence of "developed literacy." One of these "letters" is probably addressed to a slave ("boy"): here is at least one domestic slave who is able to read a short note.

The general observation may be made that levels of "developed literacy" and of "'political' literacy" appear to be low relative to levels of "practical" and "kindergarten literacy." Absolute figures, however, are difficult to come by. Only at the regional or *polis* level might we be able to advance hard numbers, and even then no more

Table 28.2 Literacy: Athens and Attica

| Date | Athens And Attica | | | | |
	Dedications	Epitaphs	Laws	Graffiti	Dipinti
700–650	2	0	0	49	2
650–600	8	2	0	64	6
600–550	35	12	0	63	45
550–500	101	66	4	32	531
500–480	249	2	4	32	174

Data from Whitley 1998a: 314 (revised from Stoddart and Whitley 1988).

than tentatively. The statistical analyses of Simon Stoddart and James Whitley have gone some way in this direction.[51]

From the data for Athens and Attica (table 28.2) Whitley (1998a: 316–17) draws some broad conclusions. First, basic literacy was widespread in Attika. Second, this literacy "was . . . concerned with naming and commemorating the actions and achievements of named individuals," as reflected by the number of dedications and epitaphs. Third, this literacy "was bound up with the oral, narrative and visual culture of the time"; a fact reflected in particular by the widespread practice of Attic painters labeling the characters on their vases, notably in the period 550–500 when some 531 such *dipinti* are attested. Fourth, writing was little used in the public sphere, at least not to "monumentalize" Attic law. Using broadly the same data, Stoddart and Whitley (1988) suggested that a few thousand Athenians were literate.

The figures for Crete (see table 28.3) provide very different conclusions. There is little or no evidence of literacy among the general populace: there are tiny numbers of epitaphs, dedications, and graffiti and no dipinti. In contrast, significant numbers of written laws are attested. At first glance, these two observations might seem in conflict: if there is limited literacy for whom are these laws being put up? Whitley

Table 28.3 Literacy: Crete

| Date | Crete | | | | | |
	Dedications (a)	(b)	Epitaphs	Laws	Graffiti	Dipinti
700–650	0	0	0	0	5	0
650–600	2	13	1	3	2	0
600–550	0	0	0	7	0	0
550–500	2	0	1	16	4	0
500–480	2	0	3	12	2	0

(a) standard dedicatory inscriptions; (b) inscribed armor.
Data from Whitley 1998a: 317 (revised from Stoddart and Whitley 1988).

(1998a: 322) suggests that these laws should be seen as monuments and not texts: "there to represent the majesty of the law to a population that was largely illiterate." Such literacy as is evident on Crete he views as scribal literacy: "where literacy is virtually confined to a small, specialist group, for whom the practice of writing is a specialist (and sometimes hereditary) skill" (Whitley 1998a: 322). In the communities of Crete then the vast majority would seem to fall into the category of "non-literate."

These two contrasting models of literacy drive home the point that writing was utilized for different purposes in different regions; that levels and types of literacy could vary dramatically from place to place; and that although literacy could be socially confined in some *poleis*, in others it was "democratized" and widespread.

Literacy and Orality

If the arrival of the alphabet in the early eighth century affected the way in which Greeks thought, this is not reflected in the surviving inscriptional evidence. On the contrary, the new technology, perhaps adopted in the first instance for the pragmatic reasons set out above but quickly utilized for a variety of other functions, was incorporated into existing cultural practices. The epitaph and the written dedication did not replace their un-inscribed counterparts, just as written law did not supersede unwritten. Archaic Greece did not become a literate culture insofar as writing did not become the dominant form of communication. It is reasonable to suggest that more people listened to poetry than read it, made oral rather than written agreements, and passed on messages, if at all possible, by word of mouth rather than by a note scratched on a potsherd. To suggest, however, that archaic Greece was and remained fundamentally an oral culture is to oversimplify the situation. This is not merely because, in certain spheres of Greek life, writing grew more important than oral communication – in the commercial sphere, writing, whether of letters or contracts, was of some importance by the end of sixth century – or because in certain regions levels of basic literacy were perhaps high – such as Attica in the second half of the sixth century. Rather, it is because literate and oral, literacy and orality, are not antithetical.[52] No one should doubt that, in the archaic period, "the written word was subordinate to the spoken" (Thomas 1992: 91). But nor should anyone doubt that writing had considerable impact on existing cultural practices: that it amplified the power of the curse, gave greater political meaning to a dedication, and added to the communal significance of a law. This places writing at the heart of Greek culture in the archaic period. Ultimately, writing may not have transformed Greek society in the spectacular fashion sometimes claimed for it, but it did have a pervasive and lasting influence.

NOTES

1 Dittenberger *SIG* 38.37. It has been suggested, however, that these are not "Phoenician letters" but rather "Red letters": see Edwards and Edwards 1974; Edwards 1979.

2 The process may have been accidental rather than deliberate: Jeffery 1990: 2; Sampson 1985: 101.
3 See Daniels and Bright 1996: 19–134.
4 Goody and Watt 1968; Havelock 1982; cf. Kerckhove 1981 who suggests that a completely phonetic alphabet lends itself to left-hemisphere brain activity, the side of the brain which promotes abstract, analytic thought.
5 See Goody 1977 for a partial retraction of his earlier views. Harris 1986 suggests that a kind of alphabetic snobbery has governed the way in which western scholars approach the problem.
6 Street 1984; Thomas 1992: 18–22.
7 Powell 1991: Euboean "rhapsode" as inventor; Powell 2002: 114: single Semitic adaptor.
8 E.g. Woodard 1997: Cypriot scribes.
9 Kirchhoff 1970 for the categorization of these epichoric alphabets into Green, Red, Dark Blue and Light Blue families; cf. Woodard 1997: 140–1 for a concise discussion.
10 Jeffery 1990: 6–7, for a fuller discussion; Woodard 1997: 133–204 (esp. 171–4) challenges some of Jeffery's observations.
11 Some challenge the monogenesis thesis: e.g. Isserlin 1991.
12 700 BC: Carpenter 1933; 1800 BC: Bernal 1990. Overview in Heubeck 1979: 75–6.
13 Ridgway 1996, but cf. Peruzzi 1992; Bietti Sestieri 1992: T.482.
14 E.g. Powell 1991. Bernal 1990 attributes adherence to a late transmission of the alphabet to an anti-Semitic desire to undermine the role of the Phoenicians in the process.
15 Kaufman 1982; Naveh 1987; another example in Gibson 1982: 12–17; cf. Burkert 1992: 28.
16 Kaufman 1986 suggests that Greeks may have borrowed the alphabet from a community like Tell Fakhariyah, where an archaic form of the Phoenician alphabet was enshrined.
17 Phoenician settlers: Coldstream 1969; Greek settlers: Boardman 1990.
18 E.g. Glotz 1926: 116–17; Finley 1970 (1981): 87; Murray 1980 (1993): 95.
19 Robb 1978; 1994; Heubeck 1979; Havelock 1982; Schnapp-Gourbeillon 1982; Powell 1991; 2002.
20 See Lombardo (1988) for detailed criticism of the mercantile origin theory.
21 Ca. 740–730: Jeffery 1990: 15–16, 68, 76; Powell 1991: 158–62. See also Powell 1988.
22 Ca. 735–720: Jeffery 1990: 235–6; Powell 1991: 163–6. See Buchner and Ridgway 1993: 751–9, for a full bibliography by O. Vox.
23 Ca. 700–675: Jeffery 1990: 90–1, 94; Powell 1991: 167–9.
24 Ca. 650: Jeffery 1990: 291, 303; Powell 1991: 169–71.
25 See for example Amadasi Guzzo and Karageorghis (1977: 134–5) for an eighth century inscription on a red slip jar that reads: "belonging to *NTŠ*," one of a number from Cyprus.
26 This is one of the roles assigned to the "captain of merchants" in the *Odyssey* (8.159–64).
27 See Amadasi Guzzo (1967: 150–1) for an example of an early eighth century dedication, and Coote (1975) for a magical text of ca. 800 BC.
28 Lang 1976: 8–9 (esp. B1, B2, B7, B9).
29 On the Milesian system, see Tod 1911; 1913 and Johnston 1977: 27–31; cf. 1973.
30 Thomas 1992: 60. Goody 1968b: 201–2, notes the use of scraps of writing as amulets.
31 For an example of a 27-letter abecedarium, see Jeffery 1990: 471.
32 See Buchner 1978: 135; Jeffery 1990: 436, A; Arena 1994: 17.
33 See Jeffery 1990: 236, 240, no. 3; Arena 1994: 29.
34 Jeffery 1990: 90–1, 94; Powell 1991: 167–9.
35 A second "Nestor's Cup," from Eretria in Euboia, has recently been found.

36 See Hansen 1976; Murray 1996.

37 Jeffery 1990: 15–16, 68, 76; Powell 1991: 158–62; cf. Powell 1988.

38 See for example the Athenian archon list: Merritt 1939.

39 Hogarth 1908: 45; cf. Jeffery 1990: 339.

40 Olbia and Emporion: see Wilson (1997a); Himera: see Jeffery 1990: 421.

41 Lang 1976: 8–9; the first inscription (B1) dates to the mid-sixth century; the second
     (B2) dates to the later sixth century.

42 On Sostratos, see Johnston 1972; Harvey 1976.

43 Thomas (1992: 78); see further Svenbro 1988.

44 See Friedländer 1948 for examples of such tombstones.

45 See Jeffery and Morpurgo Davies 1970; Thomas 1992: 69–70.

46 See Harris 1989: 3–7 for a good discussion of definitions. UNESCO (1990: 2) have
     defined an "illiterate" as someone "who cannot with understanding both read and write
     a short simple statement on everyday life."

47 See esp. Cressy 1980. The ability to write someone else's name as part of the procedure
     of ostracism has been viewed as a potential mark of high levels of literacy in fifth cen-
     tury Athens, since a quorum of 6,000 was required. The discovery of a mass of *ostraka*
     inscribed with the name Themistokles in just a few different hands, however, suggests
     that political factions might simply hand out ready-inscribed *ostraka*: see Broneer 1938.

48 The distinction between standard and non-standard is important here since it distinguishes
     between the ability to compose a text freely and the ability simply to mimic a recognized
     formula, such as "X dedicated me to Y" or "I am the vase of Z."

49 Thomas 1977 suggests that written law can be a catalyst for increased demands for
     equality rather than a product of such demands.

50 See Wilson 1997a for text, translation and bibliography of earlier work on this text.

51 See Stoddart and Whitley 1988; Whitley 1997; 1998a.

52 As argued in general terms by Finnegan 1988, and, for Greece, by Thomas 1992: 88–93.

CHAPTER TWENTY-NINE

Intellectual Achievements

Kurt A. Raaflaub

> The development of thought and ideas during the period in which the city state came into being . . . must have been heavily affected by three factors: the continuing influence of the epic tradition, the spread of literacy, and the social, political and economic changes associated with the polis itself. Individuals, too, obviously played their part – poets like Hesiod and Archilochus as well as self-declared sages like the earlier Presocratics. The period was one of major changes in the whole literary and intellectual sphere, beginning as it did with Homer and ending with the rise of philosophy and drama. Accompanying developments in religion and ritual . . . have to be taken into account in attempting to reconstruct the whole intellectual background – a precarious and demanding operation in any event, but valuable if absurdity and one-sidedness can be avoided.
>
> (Kirk 1988: 389)

Kirk's statement, rightly emphasizing the hazards involved in such an undertaking, omits one major influence on intellectual developments in archaic Greece (although mentioning it frequently in the chapter's argument): interaction with Egypt and west Asia (Anatolia, the Levant, and Mesopotamia). Drama, although institutionalized in Athens in the course of the sixth century (Osborne 1993b; Wilson 2000b; cf. Csapo and Slater 1995: 89–101), is only preserved from the post-Persian War period. I shall focus on a few highlights: Homer, Hesiod, Solon, and the beginnings of political and constitutional thought, philosophy, science, geography, and history.[1]

Homer

Two works of monumental accomplishment and enduring importance stand at the very beginning of the Greek literary tradition: the *Iliad* and *Odyssey*.[2] Both are attributed to "Homer," about whom, if he was a real person, we know very little (Vogt 1991; Latacz 1996: ch. 2). For my present purposes it does not matter whether the epics were created by one or two poets and when exactly they should be dated between the mid-eighth and the first third of the seventh century (Janko 1982; Raaflaub 1998: 187–8). I shall here use "Homer" simply as a practical label.

Homer followed upon a long tradition of oral epic whose practitioners composed their songs in performance, recreating traditional tales and at the same time adapting, expanding, and elaborating them in reaction to the mood, expectations, and needs of their audiences (Lord 2000). Whether, and how exactly, he also made use of the new technique of writing (ch. 28, above) to build the massive and complex edifice of his masterpieces remains debated.[3] It lies in the nature of oral poetry (as in that of all oral traditions: Vansina 1985; Ungern-Sternberg and Reinau 1988) that it both preserves ancient elements and adapts to changing conditions. In my view, the element of constant adaptation and transformation is much stronger on all levels than that of preservation. Hence it is impossible to draw from the epics themselves firm conclusions concerning a "historical core" (the or a Trojan War). Most probably the society they depict is historical and (near-)contemporary with the poet and his audiences.[4] Being deliberately panhellenic, they shed local or regional peculiarities and thus were attractive and accessible to all Greeks (Nagy 1990b: esp. chs. 2–3).

Finally, epic song was performed both in the great halls of elite leaders and at public events such as festivals. The prevailing view attributes to Homer an elite perspective if not the propagation of elite values and power (Morris 2001b; van Wees 1992). Although both are quite prominent at times, both epics are also quite critical of the elite. I suggest that, apart from their artistic quality (below), they were successful and remained popular because they served the needs not only of the elite but of all on whom the well-being of the community depended. It was important not only to the community but also to the elite to propagate positive patterns of behavior and to illustrate the disastrous consequences of negative ones. In this sense Homer represents a communal perspective (Raaflaub 1991: 250).

For all these reasons, Homer, although embedded in an age-old tradition of oral song, lets us hear the voice of early Greek society. This society was in transition, experiencing a veritable "structural revolution" (Snodgrass 1980a; Morris 1998a). Our question here is in what ways Homer offers us insight into Greek intellectual achievements at the dawn of history. I mention but three aspects.

First of all, both epics are exceptional pieces of art, produced by a true genius with remarkable skills, inspiration, and imagination. It suffices to examine the songs mentioned and performed in the epics (Edwards 1987: 17–19) and what we know of the songs comprising the "epic cycle" (Latacz 1997; Burgess 2001) to understand the massive difference. The *Iliad* is neither an epic on the Trojan War nor a song about great deeds of great heroes – although, of course, both aspects are central. It is a poem on the anger of Achilles, on a single episode in the ten year-long war, that takes place over a span of a few weeks. It offers some 16,000 lines of dramatic and highly complex narrative, adorned with flashbacks and flashforwards, speeches, changes of place and perspective, and comprising, besides extensive battles and numerous meetings of councils and assemblies, stories set in the past, a parallel series of diverse interactions among gods, and some of the most memorable scenes in world literature: Hector's farewell to his wife Andromache and son Astyanax (Book 6), and the meeting between

Achilles and Priam (Book 24). The composition of this intricate structure is in itself a major intellectual achievement (Latacz 1996: ch. 3; Morris and Powell 1997: ch. 15). The same is true for the *Odyssey*. These two epics offered a model that deeply influenced subsequent Greek literature and with which all subsequent epic poets – and not only they – had to contend (Morris and Powell 1997: ch.2; Fowler 2004: chs. 15–19).

The *Iliad* is also in more than one sense a predecessor of later Greek historiography.[5] The ancients always thought that it described a historical war, and, although often aware that the epics should be read as poetry, not history, they learned from them the basic techniques of writing history. Herodotus, the first historian, was also considered the "most Homeric" of historians (Ps.-Dion. *On the Sublime* 13.3). Homer's influence is visible, among much else, in Herodotus' use of language, direct speech, motifs, and a similar construction of episodes. "The most fundamental similarity linking the two works, however, concerns the *means* of description employed, for Herodotus accommodated Homer's instruments of poetic representation to his prose work" by creating "the illusion that he was the observer of the deeds under description."[6] Thucydides took Homer seriously enough historically to use his evidence to support his own argument (1.9–12). And, indeed, one might well recognize in Homer a conscious effort to come to terms with problems familiar to the historian, such as the reliability of sources, the securing of knowledge, and the arranging of a multitude of details into a coherent dramatic narrative (Lendle 1992: 3–5). In a recent monograph, Jonas Grethlein (2006) illuminates impressively many historical dimensions and perspectives in and of the *Iliad*. Even if some of Homer's devices belonged among the stock tools of epic song their elaboration, combination, and sophisticated use again betray an intellectual achievement of the highest order.

Finally, in a very substantial way Homer is also the "father" of Greek political reflection and thus the ancestor of the more advanced political thought, theory, and philosophy we know from later centuries. I focus on two strands of thought.[7] One begins with Odysseus' description of Cyclops society (*Od.* 9). Blessed by the gods, they live in golden age-like abundance (107–11) but they are lawless and outrageous (106), despise the gods (273–8), disrespect foreigners (273–370), and do not communicate with their own neighbors (115) or with other peoples (125–9). Most of all, they lack laws, councils, and assemblies; each lives by himself with his family and according to his own norms (112–15). The Cyclopes thus live in a completely atomized society, in a non-community that consists of autonomous, unconnected households. This is, in every respect, the extreme opposite of normal human society. Description – and thus conceptualization – of non-society presupposes an ability to conceptualize what society is or should, ideally, be. This Homer does in his description of the Phaeacians. They were originally neighbors of the Cyclopes but, harassed by the monsters, moved away. The two societies that structurally represent extreme contrasts were thus initially juxtaposed, just as we find cities at war and peace juxtaposed on the shield of Achilles (*Il.* 18.490–540) or a just and unjust city forming one vignette in Hesiod (below). The Phaeacians founded a new polis (as Greeks would do in the age of "colonization"): perfect both as settlement (*Od.* 6.262–8) and community. They honor the gods, are generous and hospitable to strangers, meet in assembly, are governed by a council of elders and a recognized leader, communicate with and respect each other, and are masters of sailing (Books 6–13).

Since none of his tales required the singer to expand on these aspects, his effort to conceptualize ideal polis and non-polis is significant. It is part of his world view: the epic world is organized in poleis just as his own world was (Raaflaub 1993b; Hölkeskamp 2002). A person is identified by his polis, and the polis is a marker of civilization: it represents culture, community, communication, and justice; not to be part of a polis is identical with lawlessness, isolation, lack of community, and primitiveness (Scully 1990). Not accidentally, therefore, the poet also pays close attention to council and assembly meetings[8] as well as to the "middle," the center of the community (*meson, koinon*, Detienne 1965).

The second strand of political thought I wish to single out here begins with the proem of the *Iliad* (1.1–7). It focuses not on heroic deeds but on the disastrous consequences for the community of two leaders' inability to subordinate their pride to the common good. Before entering battle, the Lycian leaders Sarpedon and Glaucus "review" the conditions of their eminent status among their people: they are honored because they work hardest defending the community (12.310–21; cf. Redfield 1994). Agamemnon too knows his duty: "I myself desire that my people be safe, not perish" (1.117; tr. Lattimore 1951), and even lowly Thersites reminds him of this: "It is not right for you, their leader, to lead in sorrow the sons of the Achaians" (2.233–4). But, having made a serious mistake and caused harm to his community (1.8–100), Agamemnon fears his rival and a loss of honor. He insists on protecting his status and humiliating his opponent (1.185–7; cf. 287–9). Achilles in turn lambasts Agamemnon as "devourer of his people" (1.231), refuses to "be called of no account and a coward" by obeying Agamemnon's despotic orders (1.293–6), almost kills him, and in anger withdraws from the fighting – although he is fully aware that this will cause death and grief to many Achaeans (1.240–4).

Both leaders place their own honor above the common interest and refuse to heed good advice (1.252–84). Yet Agamemnon, having initiated the quarrel and dishonored his most important follower, bears greater responsibility. As a result, his leadership is severely damaged, and the Achaeans suffer campaign-threatening defeat. Soon Agamemnon realizes his mistakes and begins to repair the damage, closely collaborating with the other leaders. He offers reconciliation and generous compensation to Achilles. Although the latter is at first unable to overcome his anger, eventually, after Patroclus' death, the rift in the community will be healed. At that point, Agamemnon, who after his initial mistakes does everything right, is praised as "more just" (*dikaioteros*, 19.181–83) – that is, he has reached a higher level of justice and communal recognition: everybody makes mistakes but the community depends on its leaders' ability to correct such mistakes and overcome the consequences. In this sense, Agamemnon in the end offers a positive model.

An important parallel on the Trojan side involves Hector. Presented for the longest time as a perfect leader, he bears the quality of protector in his name (Nagy 1979: 146) and is recognized for it by the community (6.401–3). He too, however, gets carried away by ambition and considerations of honor, fails to listen to justified warnings, makes a bad decision, and causes his army to be routed by Achilles' fury.

In the end, unable to face the blame for having destroyed half his army through his "recklessness," he chooses to fight and die honorably (22.99–110). Unlike Agamemnon, Hector thereby compounds his first mistake by a second one. He saves his honor but deprives his community of its strongest defender and seals its ultimate defeat. From the perspective of the community, like Agamemnon he should have swallowed his pride, admitted his mistake, and carried on, learning from the experience. Again it is the communal perspective that determines the singer's elaboration of the story.

The epics thus pay close attention to communal problems and relationships. Using traditional narrative to dramatize ethical and political problems that are important to the audience, the poet depicts positive and negative models; he helps his listeners think through such problems and guides them to solutions; he illuminates the causes and consequences of certain attitudes and actions and connects these with the well-being of the community. In doing so, he raises his listeners' critical awareness and educates them. Communal interests clash with individual aspirations, as they will throughout Greek history, and this tension, dramatic, dangerous, but productive, combined with the poet's role as a voice of communal concern and responsibility, goes a long way in explaining the emergence of Greek political thought (Raaflaub 2000: 27, 34, 57–9).

Homer and West Asia

Scholars have demonstrated impressively in how many ways Homer is connected not only with a distant Indoeuropean past (Nagy 1990a) but also with west Asian texts and ideas.[9] The importance of such connections can and will not be doubted. But doubts may be expressed about the consequences some scholars are willing to draw from them. Forty years ago, Martin West declared (1966: 31): "Greek literature is *near eastern literature*." More recently, Johannes Haubold (2002) made a similar argument. Both authors adduce strong evidence. Yet their conclusions seem too global. Rather, one might say with Walter Burkert (1991: 174; 1992: 128–9) that we can no longer study Greek literature in isolation from its wider context. All this raises important questions which I can only mention briefly here. Is the evidence adduced able to support such general and far-reaching conclusions? How does it affect the question of the creativity of Greek poets? And how do we imagine the transmission of motifs and ideas to Greece? After all, most of the evidence we have for Mesopotamian, Hurrite, and Hittite myths and epics that suggest close correspondences with Greek epic, dates centuries earlier than Homer (and Hesiod, below). In Mesopotamia, such texts were transmitted in scribal schools far into the first millennium but Greeks (or, more likely, their eastern informers) would not have had access to such specialized texts. Scholars disagree about whether versions of these texts were transmitted orally as well, and how such oral and written strands of transmission might have interacted with each other.[10] Moreover, we mostly read these eastern texts in much earlier versions. They may have been preserved in the scribal schools quite faithfully over centuries, although there too, as the Babylonian creation epic demonstrates (Cohen 1993:

406–53), adaptations to changing conditions were inevitable. In orally transmitted songs or tales, such adjustments would have been more frequent, rapid, and fundamental (above). But this oral tradition is, with few exceptions (e.g., Sanchuniathon and Philo of Byblos: M. West 1997: 283–6; Baumgarten 1981), not accessible to us. Whether we are thinking of a "cultural bridge" in the Bronze Age or in the "Orientalizing Period," or both, we are thus forced to "compare apples and oranges."

At any rate, the mere fact that Greek epic reflects much eastern influence seems to prove widespread oral tradition – but of texts unknown to us and perhaps rather different from those preserved on Hittite or Mesopotamian tablets. While the transmission of motifs and ideas is easily demonstrable, this is more difficult for more complex issues, such as the structure of epic composition (but see Burkert 1992: ch. 3). And finally, as Hesiod shows (below), when being integrated into Greek contexts, such cultural borrowings were, whenever necessary, thoroughly adapted to Greek conditions and needs. I would suggest tentatively that all three areas of Homer's "intellectual achievement" sketched above would largely have risen above the sphere of eastern influence. To my knowledge, west Asian epic did not reach the complexity and sophistication of Homer's epic composition. Nor do present, past, and future there interact in the conscious and elaborate ways characteristic of Homer. In political thought, one would *a priori* expect the poet to focus on issues that were of concern to his audiences and thus to adjust to such specific uses whatever foreign motifs he integrated.

Hesiod

Epic poets, often reproducing traditional songs, downplayed their own creative contribution. They were "singers" par excellence; their names and identities were unimportant for their songs. By contrast, Hesiod wants to convey insights, wisdom, and advice. For this, the poet's persona matters. Thus he informs us of his name (*Theog.* 22), his personal background, especially his meeting with the Muses on Mount Helicon (22–34), and his quarrel with his brother Perses (*Works and Days* [*WD*] 37–41). Whether these biographical details (also 633–40, 650–9) are authentic or intended to create a fictitious persona appropriate to this specific type of panhellenic poetry is much debated.[11] Hesiod's world is certainly not that of Homer's elite warrior heroes and adventurers. Rather, it is a world of small farmers who work hard to survive, are suspicious of town and elite (*WD* 27–32, 39), and seek their support primarily among their neighbors (342–51).

From a social perspective, Hesiod's works thus complement the Homeric epics; they offer invaluable insight into the mentality, world view, and concerns of a class that is almost completely ignored in Homer (Millett 1984; ch. 5, above; but contrast ch. 23, above). Moreover, trying to understand the world in which he lives, Hesiod asks penetrating questions: what are the factors and values that sustain human well-being and a good community? Why is the world full of evils, and who is responsible for human suffering? What qualities must a good leader have, and how can bad leaders be convinced to change their ways? Such questions prompted Hesiod to write his epics, *Theogony* and *Works and Days*.[12]

Cosmogonies and theogonies had a long prehistory in ancient west Asia and far beyond (West 1966: 1–16). So did literature conveying wisdom, exhortation, and advice (West 1978: 3–25). Even more than Homer, Hesiod abounds in motifs and stories that clearly originated in the east and south of the Mediterranean.[13] We need think only of the "myth of the Ages," featuring four metals (*WD* 110–201, though enlarged by an age of heroes: 160–73), or the "succession myth" (below). In most cases, though, such foreign elements are thoroughly adapted to their Greek context, serving the poet's specific purposes.

Thus, for example, the "succession myth" in the *Theogony* is based on west Asian myths that are preserved in Hittite texts, with antecedents among the Hurrites and in Mesopotamia:[14] the succession of Uranos (sky), Kronos (fertility), and Zeus (weather) corresponds to that of Anu (sky, here preceded by Alalu), Kumarbi (fertility), and Tessop (weather); Typhoeus, the earth-born monster that challenges Zeus' reign, corresponds to Ulikummi, the rock-born monster; a sickel that was used to separate earth and sky plays an important role, to name just a few of the analogies.[15] Correspondences with the Babylonian creation myth (*Enuma elish*, Foster 2005: 436–86; M. West 1997: 282–3) are obvious in the election of the gods' king by their assembly and in his victory over an earlier generation of gods that seals his supremacy. While the Hittite texts tell the story without moral or political elaboration (which may have been added in oral recitation) and the *Enuma elish* praises the divine king's qualities and justice in a long series of epithets at the end, in Hesiod's version a political interpretation pervades the entire story (Scully, forthcoming; Raaflaub 2008).

Contrasting Zeus' positive characteristics and leadership skills with the wickedness of his predecessors, Hesiod paints a carefully constructed image of a good leader who is able to gain power and popularity and whose wisdom and justice guarantee the permanence of his rule. Undoubtedly, this image is intended as a model for elite leaders in human society: it presents a stark contrast to the injustice and corruption that characterizes the leaders in *Works and Days*. Hesiod thus integrates the basic components of the west Asian succession myth into his poem because they are useful for his purposes, but he interprets the story in a new way and fits it into an ethical and political framework that is crucial in his own context.

As West's catalog of correspondences shows (1997: ch. 6), external influence accounts for only a fraction of the *Theogony*. Most importantly, no outside model exists for Hesiod's comprehensive effort to categorize and systematize the forces and factors that affect nature and human society. He does this by adapting the traditional format of genealogy, using family relation as symbol for dependence, close connection, causality, or chronological sequence. For example, the list of "children of *eris*" (strife, 226–32) serves to describe the many forms of appearance and effect of strife; in modern terms, this constitutes a "conceptual field." By marrying Themis to Zeus and giving them three daughters, Eunomia, Dike, and Eirene (901–3), Hesiod connects an earlier, traditional order, characterized by divine or customary law, with Zeus' new order, in which good order, justice, and peace appear as primary communal values. Although it remains rooted in myth and traditional forms of thought, Hesiod's system betrays a developed ability for abstraction, philosophical speculation, and, with its focus on the evolution of a just world order and central social values, for political thought.

In *Works and Days* Hesiod, critical of the elite whose corruption and "crooked verdicts" (220–1) threaten the well-being of their community (27–39, 219–64), reflects on the connection between justice and prosperity of both individuals and community. Zeus, the protector of justice, and his daughter, Dike, bless the just and punish the unjust (259–62). "Many times one man's wickedness ruins a whole city" (240, probably referring to mythical or epic examples, such as Paris or Oedipus), when Zeus hits it with plague, barenness, famine, and defeat in war (238–47). Conversely, the polis of "those who give straight verdicts and follow justice" enjoys peace, fertility, and happy feasts (225–37; cf. *Il.* 16.384–92; *Od.* 19.109–14). The myth of Prometheus, the champion of humankind, makes clear that humans themselves are responsible for their misery and the origin of evil in the world (*Theog.* 521–616; *WD* 47–106; Clay 2003: ch. 5). While in the Sumerian myth about the origin of evils responsibility lies entirely with the gods (Jacobsen 1946: 161–5), Hesiod (like Homer, *Od.* 1.22–43) does not doubt that the gods are benevolent; it is the humans themselves whose evil deeds continually attract divine punishment and who have to correct their ways themselves. The poet's task is to expose the causes, to warn, and to admonish. Lacking power himself, he has to rely on his firm belief in the justice of Zeus (1–9), who not only sees all and knows all (267) but will not allow the unjust to prevail (273).

Works and Days is thus an "instruction to princes" that advocates the principles of justice and communal reponsibility (Martin 1984; but see Heath 1985). But Hesiod also admonishes his peers: farmers like himself and Perses, whose responsibility it is to realize the "good order" in their own small worlds (213–18, 274–335, 394–413), focusing on work, family, farm, and neighborhood (243–51).

Hesiod's significance in Greek intellectual history thus lies in his effort at systematization, his progress toward abstract thinking, and his emphasis on human responsibility and the connection between justice and communal well-being. Like the singers in Homer's epics (*dēmiourgoi*, "workers among the people"; Gschnitzer 1981: 33–4), and thus perhaps Homer himself, Hesiod too is (or presents himself as) a man of the people, respected but low on the social ladder. Men of wisdom favored by the Muses, singers and educators of the people, thus initially are not elite leaders; the earliest intellectual achievements in Greece must be credited to commoners, and the first insights of Greek political thought are fostered by a perspective that is communal and often critical of the elite.

Solon

Solon, one of the "Seven Sages" (Martin 1993) was appointed archon and mediator in 594 BCE and charged with resolving a difficult social, economic, and political crisis that had brought Athens to the brink of civil war. His function as a "reconciler" and his legislation are discussed in this volume, chs. 21 and 8, respectively. I shall focus here briefly on the political ideas that are formulated in his poetry (West [W] 1992; tr. West 1994). Here, for the first time in history, we find expressions of explicit political thought, not woven into epic narrative or genealogical schemes but directly addressed to the citizens of Athens.

In an important poem containing programmatic statements (4 W²; Vlastos 1946; Jaeger 1966: 75–99; Stahl 1992), Solon says: "My mind orders me to teach this to the Athenians" (30). The statesman and legislator is also a poet and educator of his people, and he is one of them. "Our city will never fall" by divine will! On the contrary: Athena stands ready to protect her city (1–4). The first lesson, emphasized already in the *Odyssey* (1.22–43) and by Hesiod, thus is: the woes that trouble the community are caused not by the gods but by the citizens themselves, most of all by the greedy and abusive leaders, the elite (5–13), who ignore Dike's ordinances. But, silent and knowing, she "comes in time with certainty (*pantōs*) to exact punishment." The result is "an inescapable wound for the entire polis" (enslavement by a tyrant, *stasis*, civil war, death of young men, enslavement of debtors; 14–25). The second lesson thus contradicts Hesiod (*WD* 259–60): Dike does not need to appeal to her father Zeus to uphold justice and punish evildoers. She stands on her own, is almost an abstract principle, she knows and she will act, with certainty.

Violations of justice thus have inevitable consequences, comparable to natural phenomena: as snow or hail come from a dark cloudbank and thunder follows upon lightning, so a polis whose citizens have elevated one man too high will be enslaved by a tyrant (9 W²; cf. 11; 13.8, 17–32). Whether in the realm of justice, social relations, or politics, the consequences of specific actions can be expected – and thus predicted – with a degree of certainty that resembles the cause and effect relationships in the realm of nature: political laws are like natural laws.

Where Hesiod had to trust in Zeus' wisdom and power (*WD* 273), Solon knows. Where Hesiod had to refer to mythical examples (*WD* 240–1), Solon observes what is happening in many poleis around him and bases his political conclusion on "empirical data." Where Hesiod emphasized physical suffering and prospering of polis, people, and nature (*WD* 225–47), Solon thinks politically. Moreover, "the public ill comes home to every man" and finds him "for sure" (*pantōs*) wherever he hides (Sol. 4.26–9). With certainty, therefore, the entire community (17) and every citizen will suffer. Lesson three: Hesiod was wrong. It will not do to avoid the *agora* (*WD* 27–31), hide in one's farm, and rely on neighbors (342–51). On the contrary: it is crucial to be alert and involved and to assume communal responsibility.

Solon thus established a pattern of political causes and consequences that enabled him to understand political processes, predict the outcome of certain actions or patterns of behavior, and take appropriate action. He too, had to appeal to the nobles to change their ways. But, based on logical arguments, not just belief in divine retribution, this appeal was much more compelling: the elite too was threatened by its own transgression; elite abuse of power, followed by civil strife and tyranny, was bound to hurt the elite as much as the others. Unlike Hesiod, as an appointed lawgiver Solon was in a position to draw the consequences and realize necessary reform. Whether or not these reforms were entirely successful, they were, for the first time as far as we know, based on more than religious and moral concerns: they were founded on political experience and calculation and something approaching a political theory.[16]

Constitutional Thought

Written laws, inscribed on stone or bronze, appear in Greece from around the mid-seventh century.[17] The idea to inscribe laws on durable material probably came from west Asia, where it had been practiced for millennia (Westbrook 1988; 1989). The purpose probably was not least to demonstrate the communal importance of such laws and to place them under the protection of the gods (Thomas 1996). In addition, they were published and accessible, and citizens who made the effort could learn what the law was. The law thus was literally placed "in the middle" (*es meson*) of the community, and it was the community, through its elected officials, that controlled the law and could change it if it wished. Unlike in West Asia and Egypt, where all-powerful kings initiated and controlled the law, in the Greek polis the law was enacted by the assembly or, upon the mandate of the assembly, by a lawgiver (ch. 21, above). Although publication increased the security and equality of law and thus benefited the less powerful in the polis, the elite probably was as much interested in legislation that helped prevent abuses and thus maintained communal peace (Eder 2005).

Probably in the third quarter of the seventh century, we find the first attestation of a rudimentary constitution: the "Great Rhetra" in Sparta.[18] Sparta was suffering from a long and difficult war against the Messenians and from domestic unrest that expressed itself not least in the demand for redistribution of land. Reliance on the citizen army to control the subjected populations became ever more important. Changes were necessary, and they were encoded in the Rhetra. Buttressed by the installation of new cults and a territorial restructuring of the community, the demos, meeting in assembly at fixed dates and a fixed place, now was formally empowered to make the final decisions that concerned the community, although with certain limitations. As citizens, land-owners, soldiers, and assemblymen, they were equal ("peers," *homoioi*; Cartledge 2001: 68–75), despite social and economic differences. Most importantly, the communal decision making process was here regulated, the powers of leaders, council, and assembly in this process determined for the first time. However the Rhetra was presented to the community (as an oracle from Delphic Apollo, as the restoration of the initial "polis charter"), most likely it was also hailed as a return to *eunomia*, the traditional good order.[19]

One or two generations later, Solon, also aiming to overcome a severe crisis (above), introduced constitutional changes in Athens as well (ch. 8, above). Tradition attributes to him a new popular council with 400 members that balanced the aristocratic Areopagus Council, a system of four classes that linked military to political capacity, and various other measures that increased popular involvement in politics and communal responsibility (Wallace 2007b).[20] Yet, overall, despite ancient and modern claims to the contrary, Solon's constitution, like the Spartan Rhetra, was far from a democracy in any strict sense of the word.[21] Like Sparta's Rhetra, it was hailed by its creator as the restoration of *eunomia*. What Solon achieved was consonant with his position as a mediator: a system that curtailed elite abuses, introduced appropriate protections, and balanced aristocratic leadership with popular power while emphasizing the citizens' responsibility for the common good.

Political and constitutional legislation proliferated in the sixth century. Many poleis adopted constitutions that were characterized by a considerable amount of equality for substantial parts of the citizen body (Robinson 1997).[22] Most of these constitutions are attested only partially, by inscriptions regulating a particular aspect or by references in later sources (especially Aristotle's *Politics*). In the case of Athens, though, we have enough information to reconstruct the entire scheme, even if details remain agonizingly unclear (ch. 8, above). Again reform was prompted by emergency: disruptive aristocratic rivalry, outside intervention, and popular revolt. Empowered by broad support, Cleisthenes realized a reform plan he had proposed earlier, apparently to great acclaim.[23] This plan was complex and sophisticated.

Attica had been divided by regions and pockets of aristocratic influence. The margins were still not fully integrated (Anderson 2000). In order to unify country and citizen body, Cleisthenes organized the territory into some 140 local districts (demes) and combined them (supposedly by lot) into new artificial units: regional "thirds" and national "tribes." Each of the latter comprised districts from the three major regions of the country (Traill 1975). The demes had important functions in exercising "grassroots democracy." Most importantly, through their tribes, the citizens of the demes were represented proportionally, in a remarkably high density of representation (roughly 1: 60), in the new Council of 500 that played an enhanced political role. They also formed tribal regiments in the newly constituted citizen army and tribal contingents competing in national festivals. The council members, serving for a year (and no more than twice so that over time more than a third of all citizens over eighteen served at least once; Hansen 1999: 249), gained valuable political experience and, commuting between their demes in the large Attic territory and Athens, carried information out and citizen reactions in, thus connecting country and center and creating a "civic presence" in Athens (Meier 1990a: 73–8). All this was enhanced by religious innovations and building activity that turned Athens into the civic center of a large but thoroughly integrated polis (Anderson 2003). As a result, Athens emerged united, triumphed in 506 against attacks by Sparta and hostile neighbors and in 490 mustered the courage to ward off a Persian invasion at Marathon.

Civic subdivisions were typical of Greek poleis (Jones N. F. 1987; Davies 1996), but the scheme designed by Cleisthenes was so complex and sophisticated that it must have been quite exceptional. It was based on a rational assessment of the problems that plagued the Athenian community after the expulsion of the tyrants and of the difficulties posed to communal unity by the large size and topographical diversity of Attica and the economical and social differences among various parts of the citizen body. Hence Cleisthenes created institutions that forced citizens from various areas and backgrounds to collaborate in civic, military, and cultic events. Such collaboration fostered mutual familiarity and trust; it helped integrate the community. Ostracism, a kind of "negative election" to remove temporarily inidividuals that were perceived as dangerous and/or to avoid political paralysis (Eder 1998: 118–21; Dreher 2000; Forsdyke 2005) reveals the same spirit of rational innovation and ingenuity. That Cleisthenes was able to make his bold proposals palatable to his fellow citizens attests to his political skills and ability to sense the needs and will of both people and elite – and to their readiness to demand and accept change for the common good. Overall, his reforms represent an extraordinary intellectual and political achievement, indispensable for the fully developed democracy of the fifth century.

Philosophy

The sixth century witnessed the beginning of philosophical and scientific thinking. Most of its representatives lived in Greek Asia Minor, the most advanced area in the Greek world until Miletus was destroyed after defeat in the Ionian Revolt against Persia (499–494 BCE; Murray 1988b; Gorman 2001). Miletus founded many colonies in the Black Sea area (ch. 17, above) and traded with the eastern and southern Mediterranean, including the Greek trade post in Naucratis (Möller 2000; ch. 23, above). Hence this part of the Greek world was particularly rich in knowledge and international connections. Eastern influences on religion and art accumulated there, Milesians first draw maps of the known world and wrote geographical works, and the conditions for scientific (below) and philosophical thought, both highly developed in west Asia and partly in Egypt, were especially favorable.[24] For example, Thales of Miletus (first half of the sixth century) was a mathematician and astronomer (he is credited with various geometrical discoveries and with predicting the solar eclipse of 585: Hdt. 1.74; Stephenson and Fatooki 1997); he was counted among the Seven Sages, was practical in resolving difficult problems (Hdt. 1.75), and gave good political advice (1.170). All this, however, does not explain why he sought the first principle of all things, determined it to be water, and insisted on physical rather than religious explanations for natural phenomena (Arist. *Met.* 13.983b6ff; for an explanation, see Kirk 1988: 410).

Next to nothing is known about individual early philosophers. What was transmitted in antiquity was mostly anecdotal and drawn out of their writings of which only pitiful fragments are preserved; they offer glimpses into their thought but rarely permit reconstruction of coherent arguments or entire works. Nor do we know the circumstances of their philosophizing. Still, they were pathbreakers and innovators, and later authors such as Plato and Aristotle built on their ideas, often in critical discussion. Many of them were primarily interested in *physis*, the natural world and its origin and functioning; man and human society were part of *physis*, subject to its laws, and not considered separately.[25] I shall highlight here three areas in which their discoveries were particularly influential.

To begin with, first principles, the emergence of the world, and the structure of the cosmos (Wright 1995; Algra 1999). Thales suggested water, perhaps inspired by near eastern thought. He imagined the earth, kept in perfect balance, as floating on water as well. Aristotle considered him the founder of natural philosophy because he postulated a material principle for all existing things and broke with the tradition of explaining natural phenomena by divine action (*Met.* 983b17ff). His insistence on physical causes proved most influential,[26] but it may well be that his speculation was less systematic and that it was really his contemporary Anaximander who set the tone by appealing systematically to rational principles and natural processes. He wrote a prose treatise "On the Nature of Things" (*peri physeos*), drew a world map (below) and perhaps constructed a visual representation of the sky (*sphaira*). His speculation extended to meteorological phenomena and zoogony but he is best known for his one extant sentence (perhaps the earliest in European prose):

> ... some other *apeiron* nature, from which come into being all the heavens and the worlds in them. And the source of coming-to-be for existing things is that into which destruction, too, happens, "according to necessity; for they pay penalty (*dikē*) and retribution (*tisis*) to each other for their injustice (*adikia*) according to the assessment of Time."
>
> (DK 12 B1; tr. Kirk et al. 1983: no. 110)

The origin of all things thus is the *apeiron* which, ungenerated, eternal, and infinite, surrounds the generated world and governs all its processes. In a biological and mechanical process of separating out opposites, the world is created, while huge wheels of fire produce the celestial phenomena (Kahn 1960; Hölscher 1968: 9–89). Anaximenes (second half of the sixth century) in turn postulated elemental air (*aēr*) as the first principle that started the process of world formation, causes change through condensation and rarefaction, turning into fire, wind, water, earth, and rock, and supports the earth from below (Wöhrle 1993). Reacting against him, Heraclitus of Ephesus (around 500), "arguably the most important of all Presocratics" (Kirk 1988: 410–11), in dense and often cryptic aphorisms insisted on fire as the primary element. More importantly, he believed that a universal, all-penetrating *logos* structures and rules this world. His views on *physis* were closely tied to his theory of constant change ("In the same river we both step and do not step, we are and we are not," DK 22 B49a; hence the saying attributed to him: *panta rhei*, "all is in flux") and to his epistemology (Hölscher 1968: 130–72; Kahn 1979). Finally, Xenophanes of Colophon (ca. 570–467), who brought Ionian natural philosophy to the Greek west, saw earth and water as the origin of things and explained meteorological and celestial phenomena by the formation of clouds from the sea.

Second, religious speculation. Heraclitus, we saw, postulated that the world is structured and ruled by a universal *logos* (DK 22 B1–2). Xenophanes (Lesher 1992; Schäfer 1996) is famous for his polemics against Homer's and Hesiod's representation of gods as similar to humans in their habits and vices (DK 21 B 11–12, cf. 14), and for his critique of a culture-specific anthropomorphic conception of gods (B 15–16). Instead, in a first step toward philosophical theology and monotheism, Xenophanes postulated a radically different kind of divinity:

> There is one god, among gods and men the greatest, not at all like mortals in body or in mind.
> He sees as a whole, thinks as a whole, and hears as a whole.
> But without toil he sets everything in motion, by the thought of his mind.
> And he always remains in the same place, not moving at all, nor is it fitting for him to change his position at different times.
>
> (B 23–6)

Pythagoras, born on Samos in the mid-sixth century, emigrated to southern Italy ca. 530, where he presented himself as sage, seer, teacher, and charismatic miracle-worker with supernatural abilities, and became, through the society he founded, an important force in the social, political, religious, and intellectual life of Magna Graecia. Since neither he nor his successors before the late fifth century left any writings, it is impossible to know how much of the Pythagorean tradition in various areas of thought goes back to him. It seems likely that he had the "extraordinary intuition of the mathematical structure of the universe" (Kirk 1988: 412), and certain that he introduced into Greek religion the doctrine of the transmigration of souls. His society with its highly regulated cult organization was greatly influential.[27]

Finally, political ideas. Heraclitus, like other archaic aristocrats, such as Alcaeus (Page 1955) or Theognis (Figueira and Nagy 1985), was highly critical of the demos – but also of everyone else (DK 22 B 29, 104; cf. 121). Xenophanes, in turn, found little to praise in the values and attitudes of the elite (1–3 W²). He polemicized against the public honors heaped upon victorious athletes because, unlike his own expertise (*sophiē*), the athlete's skills help to maintain neither the polis' good order (*eunomiē*) nor the public treasury (2 W²). Traditional elite values are here criticized not from an individual perspective, as in the case of Archilochus (Burnett 1983), but from a communal standpoint. More importantly, since disciplines like physics, ethics, religion, and politics were not yet separated, laws of nature were thought to operate in human society as well and natural processes could be explained by relations and rules valid in society. Thus in Anaximander's fragment (above) the cosmos is conceptualized as a system regulated by principles of justice. Things emerge from the *apeiron* in a perfect balance of opposites. Such balance represents justice, the prevalence of one opposite over the other injustice which will require punishment or compensation over time. This cosmic concept was rooted in an analogous perception of social and political order that was based on justice and equality (*isonomia*; Vlastos 1947; Vernant 1965: 185–206); this is one of the earliest testimonia for a political concept of equality (Raaflaub 1996a: 143–5). Similarly, Heraclitus postulated a correspondence between the structures and relationships in nature or cosmos and human societies: justice, balance, and retaliation were the operating principles in both spheres. Like several archaic poets, he expressed a strong preference for the middle (*meson*) and moderation (*metrion*), urged respect for law and the common good, and used trade and war as metaphors for natural processes (Raaflaub 2000: 50). It is a great pity that so little is known reliably about Pythagoras' society; that it was based on unusual social and political ideas seems clear but what these were exactly remains doubtful (Riedweg 2002: ch. 3).

In the sphere of early Greek philosophy too, therefore, Greek thinkers quickly went beyond the undeniable and important stimuli they received from the east (West 1971). Based on their insights and speculation, their successors in the fifth century laid the foundations of a long and extremely fertile and influential philosophical tradition.

Science and Technology

Science (*Wissenschaft*) is a modern term. The Greeks talked about knowledge (*epistēmē*) and skills (*technē*). In a somewhat specific sense, science did not begin in Greece before the evolution of medicine in the second half of the fifth century. By contrast, the ancients thought that Thales, Pythagoras, and their contemporaries had laid the foundations of science and that its roots went back to the old civilizations of west Asia and Egypt (e.g., Hdt. 2.109; Arist. *Met.* 981b23–5). Both views are correct: mathematics and astronomy were highly developed in Mesopotamia long before they reached the Greeks.[28] Egyptian medicine was famous in the ancient world.[29] There is no question that the Greeks learned from them in every respect (e.g., Lloyd 1979: ch. 4; Marganne 1993). Yet Thales' and Pythagoras' reputations rested not least on their mathematical and geometrical theorems. According to Herodotus (3.129–37), at the Persian King Darius' court the Greek physician Democedes, after a remarkable career, succeeded where Egyptian doctors had failed (Griffiths 1987). Greek medicine had thus reached a significant level already in the late sixth century (Kudlien 1967; Conrad et al. 1995). During Darius' expedition against the Scythians, the Samian engineer Mandrokles gained fame for building a bridge over the Bosporus (4.87–9). Harpalos of Tenedos constructed the bridge over the Hellespont for Xerxes when that built by Phoenician and Egyptian engineers had been destroyed (7.34–6; Hofstetter 1978: no. 130; Hammond and Roseman 1996). Even if Herodotus' reports may be tainted by Greek patriotism, there can be no doubt that Greek engineers, architects, artists, masons, and shipwrights were active in the Persian empire under Darius at the latest (Hofstetter 1978; Walser 1984: ch. 5) and apparently much earlier in Mesopotamia (Raaflaub 2004a: 204–6). Greek skills and ingenuity were thus sought after even in the east with its long-standing tradition of accomplishments in these areas.

Herodotus (3.60; Tölle-Kastenbein 1976) praises Samos (Shipley 1987) for "three of the greatest building and engineering feats in the Greek world," perhaps all dating to the time of the tyrant Polycrates (ca. 537–22): the great breakwater that created an artificial harbor, the long tunnel that secured the town's water supply, constructed by Eupalinus of Megara (Kienast 1995), and the temple of Hera, one of the largest in Greece, built by the Samian Rhoecus (Kyrieleis 1981; 1993; Furtwängler 1984). Samos was also home to one of the largest *kouroi* ever erected (Kyrieleis 1996). Water supply systems are known from elsewhere too (e.g., Athens: Tölle-Kastenbein 1994). Monumental temples were built competitively by several poleis in the sixth century. Greek temples were developed out of earlier wooden structures; in their monumental form they emerged in the contact zone of east and west in Asia Minor and incorporated significant Egyptian influences (Coldstream 1985; Höcker 1998). In Jeffrey Hurwit's view, however, the Doric order was invented not in imitation but in emulation of Egyptian architecture. "That is, its formulation was a means of rivaling and responding to what the Greeks saw along the Nile, a means of asserting Greek differences in Greek terms, even as the Greeks borrowed from the Egyptians some of the very techniques that allowed them to respond better and on a monumental scale" (1985: 179–86, quote 185–6).

Moreover, monumental temples are rightly seen as an expression of communal vigor, collaboration, and identity (Snodgrass 1980a: 33, 58–62; ch. 22, above). Greek *kouroi*, nude male statues, and *korai*, clothed female statues, erected on tombs and in sanctuaries as dedications honoring the dead and the gods, were inspired by Levantine and Egyptian sculpture, but what the Greek artists did with the *kouros* "was to absorb the monumental conception and the thousand-year-old tradition of rendering the male body and transform it into something entirely new, purely Greek, in an act of creative synthesis" (Kyrieleis 1993: 150–1; Hurwit 1985: 186–202); moreover, the Greek *kouros* had in Greek society a function that differed greatly from that of the Egyptian "model" in its own society (Fehr 1996; Osborne 1998a: 75–85).

Geography, Ethnography, and Historiography

Already Homer, considered the "founder of geography" by no less an expert than Strabo (*Geography* 1–2; Biraschi 2005), reflects a lively interest in geographical exploration (e.g., *Od.* 5.400–23, 438–53; 9.116–41) and the characterization of various peoples. Odysseus' tales of his adventures on the way home from Troy (*Od.* 9–12) recall far-flung travels in the western Mediterranean as well as sailors' yarn (Heubeck and Hoekstra 1989: 3–11; Dougherty 2001; Hartog 2001), while the famous shield of Achilles suggests a schematic conceptualization of earth and sky, if not elements of a map (a circular earth surrounded by the ocean: *Il.* 18.483–607; Edwards 1991: 200–9; Harley and Woodward 1987: 131–2), and the "catalog of ships," listing the Achaean contingents at Troy, follows a geographic route through the Greek world.[30] In the seventh and sixth centuries, colonizing and trading expeditions (Raaflaub 2004a: 202–4, 210–11) added enormously to the knowledge of the Mediterranean. In the second half of the sixth century, Persian conquests and an active interest of Egyptian and Persian kings in exploration expanded such knowledge far beyond the sphere hitherto familiar to the Greeks (Cary and Warmington 1963). Phoenicians sailed around Africa (Hdt. 4.42), while in 519–516 Scylax of Caryanda in Caria explored the coast between India and Egypt (4.44; *FGrH* 709). Probably in the early fifth century (Ameling 1993: 256 n. 92), the Carthaginian Hanno led a celebrated expedition along the African coast, perhaps as far as Cameroon,[31] the Achaemenid Sataspes another (Hdt. 4.43), while Hanno's contemporary Himilco traveled from Gibraltar to Britain (Cary and Warmington 1963, 45–9; Ameling 1993, 267 with n. 151). Greek descriptions of coastlines with comments on distances, sailing and harbor conditions, settlements, and peoples (called *periplous*) may thus have been preceded by Carthaginian and perhaps Phoenician or Persian versions. Scylax wrote the earliest attested Greek *periplous*; that of Pseudo-Scylax in the fourth century (covering the entire Mediterranean and Black Sea; Pereti 1979; Marcotte 1986), and another, of an anonymous first century CE author, on the coast from Suez to India (Casson 1989) offer an impression of the sparse and handbook-like nature of these works.

Nevertheless, reports such as these, and oral information pouring into sixth-century Miletus as the center of a "worldwide" net of colonial and trade connections, must have enabled Anaximander to draw the first world map. Simple and schematic though it was, nothing comparable in scope and ambition is known from other areas of the Mediterranean orbit.[32] This map was improved by Hecataeus (below), used for political purposes by Aristagoras of Miletus, the instigator of the Ionian Revolt (Hdt. 5.49–50), and heavily criticized by Herodotus (4.36). In opposition to the concept of a flat, circular earth surrounded by ocean, perhaps already Pythagoras postulated a spherical earth; certainly Parmenides (born ca. 515) did so, dividing it into five zones (two cold, two temperate, and one hot; Dilke 1985: 25).

The *periegesis* or *periodos ges* ("Circuit of the Earth") authored by Hecataeus of Miletus (ca. 560–480) is likely to have gone far beyond the pattern set by the early *periplous* literature.[33] As Fornara writes (1983b: 13),

> Hecataeus's work was by any standard a stupendous achievement. Consisting of two books, one dealing with Europe, the other with Asia, Egypt, and Libya . . . [it] was a narrative geography with map attached. Unlike the writers of utilitarian voyage-accounts . . . , Hecataeus attempted a comprehensive description of the entire known (and unknown) world. Naturally, it incorporated the results of the author's travels and the reports of others, published and oral; it also contained the heavy admixture of theory proper to an essentially scientific work.

Descriptions of country, flora, fauna, rulers, and inhabitants with their customs formed the core elements of each entry. Although Hecataeus did not write an ethnography but "a geography containing subordinate ethnographies," perhaps based on an already established genre (Fornara 1983b: 14), he is often seen as founder of the genre of ethnography (Trüdinger 1918: 10ff; Müller 1972: 94–101).

Hecataeus also wrote a *Genealogia*, a systematization of the family relationships among mythical heroes (as Hesiod and various authors after him had done for the gods, combining cosmogony, theogony, and divine genealogy). This work too marked a break and new beginning. The opening sentence of the preface, "I write what follows as it seems to me to be true; for the stories of the Greeks are varied, and, as is manifest to me, absurd" (*FGrH* 1 F1), perhaps aims less at radical rationalization than at the establishment of clear chronology in a period that was remote and distorted by myth but, in general Greek understanding, still reflected real persons and events. Logically, therefore, Hecataeus separated, for the first time, "heroic" or "mythical" from more strictly "historical time" that was accessible by historical memory – a distinction Herodotus would later use (e.g., 1.5; 3.122) and complicate (Marincola 1997: 117–27; Cobet 2002). Although the *Genealogia* has little to do with genuine history, its author reveals the kind of critical historical thinking that would later prompt the generation of historical works. Together with Homer's epics, elegies and other poetry dealing with historical events (Bowie 2001; Marincola 2006), and other works of rudimentary history (such as accounts of the foundation of colonies: Giangiulio 2001), Hecataeus' work claims an indispensable position in the ancestry of Greek historiography and its influence on Herodotus was significant – despite the latter's often biting criticism (West 1991; Fowler 2006).

Conclusion

Kirk finds well established already in Homer the roots of the "intensely personal confrontation between individual and outside world . . . the Greek habit of self-analysis" that breaks through so powerfully in the earliest extant representatives of lyric poetry (1988: 393). In other ways, too, we saw, Homer signals new beginnings; his influence on later poetry and thought cannot be overestimated. According to Jean-Pierre Vernant, we see in Hesiod's work "what may be described as a learned mythology richly and subtly elaborated that possesses all the finesse and rigor of a philosophical system while at the same time remaining totally committed to the language and mode of thought peculiar to myth" (1990: 217). Even if Kirk rightly warns against turning Hesiod into a real predecessor of the early philosophers, they still followed along Hesiod's path of seeking a single origin of the world and using some form of a genetic paradigm to explain its formation. It was not until the very end of the sixth century that Xenophanes and Heraclitus broke decisively away from patterns set by the two epic poets (1988: 397–400, 410–11).

Yet Homer's and Hesiod's influence is far from sufficient to explain the steady, if far from consistent, progress in the use of reason that Kirk sees as the hallmark of the intellectual achievement of the archaic period (412–13), or the independence and individualism in thought and behavior that I would emphasize. Moreover, this achievement extends to virtually all areas of artistic and literary activity. Various scholars have compared Homer with geometric art, seeing, for example, similar mastery of a difficult intellectual task in the complex and monumental structures of the epics and the great geometric vases that served as grave markers in the Kerameikos cemetery (Whitman 1958: ch. 5; Andreae and Flashar 1977). The composition of monumental epics or sophisticated lyric songs, the design of an elaborate reorganization of polis structures or a new polis constitution, the observation of political cause and effect relations amounting to laws of politics, the conceptualization of the cosmos and its evolution, the drawing of a world map, monumental architecture and refined sculpture, feats of engineering, the adaptation of writing (ch. 28, above), the invention of techniques that made monumental bronze sculpture possible or enabled potters to develop black and red figured vases (Schneider 2002: 70) – all these are significant intellectual achievements with far-reaching consequences (Hall 1975; H. Schneider 1991).

When looking for the social conditions that encouraged these developments, surely the rise of the polis (chs. 18 and 20, above) must be considered decisive – in several ways. Poleis developed in clusters and in constant competition with each other; each differed from the others in subtle but crucial ways, and comparison stimulated critical thinking. Moreover, in the "age of colonization" new poleis were founded in large numbers, each built from scratch by citizens who often came from different backgrounds and had joined for different reasons; each foundation, though sponsored by one polis and led by one leader, was thus the result of complex negotiations and careful thought (ch. 19, above). Geographical mobility as well as opportunities offered by trade, emigration, and service abroad translated into social mobility and the weakening of traditional values and social structures. The tension between individual and collective aspirations, often erupting in violent social conflicts, accelerated social change and proved productive in stimulating the search for new solutions. The elite, despite ambition and power, never rose far above the large class of "middling" farmers, on whom they depended for the defense of the polis and who therefore played an important role in the assembly as well (Raaflaub 1999: 132–41). All this made it possible not only for members of the elite (such as Alcaeus or Solon) but also for outsiders and "underdogs" (a *dēmiourgos* bard such as the Homeric singers, a farmer like Hesiod's character, or a mercenary like that of Archilochus) to raise their voices and express their thoughts in public, whether affirmatively or critically. In some poleis, even in a male-dominated society women were able to reach fame for their outstanding skills (we need only think of Sappho). A society in ferment, undergoing rapid change and a vast expansion of its horizon, offered fertile ground for individualism and independent thinking. The will to high achievement was further stimulated by a pervasive spirit of competitiveness, emphasized already by Hesiod's distinction between a bad and a good form of strife (*eris; WD* 11–26).

All these tendencies were encouraged (and not discouraged or suppressed, as they were in the great civilizations of Egypt and west Asia, or even in Israel's theocracy) by two factors. One was that far into the sixth century the Greek poleis developed on their own, in a "power vacuum," that is, outside the control of great empires with absolute, divinely sanctioned monarchies. This was crucial for the formation of societies that were in important ways egalitarian and became even more so by the end of the archaic period, and for the creation of concepts such as equality and freedom. Justice, we saw, was communally based, and obedience was not a prime value (not even in Sparta where it became one only towards the end of the period if not even later).[34] The other factor was that religion, though important in various ways, did not play a central role in legitimizing power and hierarchy. Hence Greek thinkers were free to emphasize, for example, human responsibility for their own and their community's well-being. Such freedom became a powerful force in prompting the evolution of independent thought, political reflection, and philosophical speculation (Raaflaub 2000: 57–9).

As we saw, Greek thinkers and artists of all types eagerly learned from the older and more highly developed civilizations east and south of the Mediterranean. In fact, such external influences were a *sine qua non* for the development of Greek culture. But, largely for the reasons outlined above, Greek culture never became a near eastern culture. The Greeks transformed and adapted what they learned. In the process they created a new culture that was rooted in both foreign and ancient Greek traditions, was elevated by impressive intellectual achievements in many areas, quickly assumed distinctive characteristics, and, within a few decades of the great confrontation between east and west in the Persian wars, developed into something that bore little similarity with its eastern forebears – even if the Greeks continued to be inspired by the east in religion, crafts, and much else.[35]

NOTES

1   For surveys of archaic Greek literature, Fränkel 1973; Lesky 1966 are still useful. W^2 = West 1992. – My main purpose is to give a survey of important aspects and to guide the reader to relevant bibliography. I thank Deborah Boedeker and Hans van Wees for valuable suggestions.

2   Generally on Homer, see Latacz 1996; Morris and Powell 1997; Taplin 2000b; Fowler 2004; ch. 5, above.

3   See Latacz 2002: 58–9. Powell 1991; 1997 (early and comprehensively) and Nagy 1996a (much later) advocate extreme positions. For brief summaries of the debate, see Edwards 1987: 23–8; Saïd 1998: 31–5.

4   On "homeric society," see Finley 1978; more recently, Ulf 1990b; van Wees 1992; Raaflaub 1991; 1997b; 1998; Donlan 1999; Hölkeskamp 2002; Osborne 2004; ch. 5, above. Despite the likely origin of epic and hexametric song as early as the sixteenth century BCE (West 1988b; Janko 1992: 8–19), Latacz's thesis (2004) that the hexameter served as a "straightjacket" that enabled such poetry to carry detailed memories over exceptionally long periods of time, like some of his other views, has met serious objections: Cobet and Gehrke 2002; Ulf 2003. Nor is it convincing that much of the material culture reflected in the epics stems from the Bronze Age (so recently Shear 2000). For comparison with other epic traditions, see Raaflaub 2005a. Despite exciting and important new discoveries, which Latacz rightly highlights, we are still far from resolving the puzzle of the "historical" Trojan War.

5   Homer's influence on later Greek literature, however, goes far beyond poetry and historiography; for geography and ethnography, see the end of this chapter.

6   Fornara 1983b: 31; cf. Strasburger 1972; Hartog 2000; Boedeker 2002; Pelling 2006.

7   See Raaflaub 1988; 2000: 27–34; 2001: 73–89. See now also Hammer 2002; Balot 2006: ch. 2, and, among important earlier work, Vernant 1982. Christian Meier's seminal work on the emergence of Greek political thought (1989; 1990a; 2001) does not include Homer.

8   Ruzé 1997; Raaflaub 1997c; 2001: 80–5; Hölkeskamp 2002.

9   Burkert 1991; 1992; 2002; West 1997; also Penglase 1994; Bachvarova 2005.

10   See now relevant chs. in Foley 2005 (esp. Noegel 2005) and, on this debate, Alster 1992; 1995; Michalowski 1992; 1995, as well as other chs. in Vogelzang and Vanstiphout 1992.

11   E.g., Gagarin 1974; West 1978: 30–40; Erler 1987; Nagy 1990a: ch. 3.

12   On Hesiod, see, apart from the introductions to West's commentaries (1966; 1978), Brown 1953; Lamberton 1988; Solmsen 1995; Tandy and Neale 1996; Clay 2003, Stoddard 2004; chs. 5 and 23, above. Tr. Athanassakis 1983; West 1988a.

13   Walcot 1966; West 1997: chs. 3, 6; Schmitz 2004a.

14   Heubeck 1955; Lesky 1955; Walcot 1966; West 1997: ch. 6.

15   Hoffner 1990: 38–61; Haas 1994: 82–90, 96–8, 113–15.

16   Constraints of space force me to omit a section on the broad range of Greek "lyric poetry" that is also characterized by innovation, experimentation, and brilliance in style and content, and impressively displays the spirit of independence and individualism that must have been typical of the archaic age as an "age of experiment" (Snodgrass 1980a). See, e.g., Fränkel 1973: chs. 4, 6; Lesky 1966: 107–54, 168–208; Burnett 1983; Podlecki 1984; Knox 1985: chs. 5–8; Fowler 1987; Gerber 1997; Kurke 2000.

17   Collected by Koerner 1993; van Effenterre and Ruzé 1994–95. For interpretation and significance, see Hölkeskamp 1999 and ch. 21, above. On the necessary conditions, Gehrke 1993; Hölkeskamp 1994.

18   E.g., M. Meier 1998; Cartledge 2001: 29–34; ch. 7, above, with a different interpretation.

19   *Eunomia*, emphasized as a communal value by Hesiod (above), is prominent in two Spartan poets: Alcman (64 Campbell 1988) and Tyrtaeus (1–4 W). In the latter *eunomia* seems to be connected with a summary of the Rhetra. This connection is questioned by van Wees 1999b and defended by Raaflaub 2006.

20 Whether Solon's timocracy already included fixed agrarian income assessments, as Arist. *Ath. Pol.* 7.4 claims, is debated: de Ste. Croix 2004: ch. 1; Raaflaub 2006: 404–23; *contra:* van Wees 2006.

21 See ch. 8, above, and Wallace 2007b for Solonian democracy; for discussion, Raaflaub, Ober, and Wallace 2007.

22 The founding of hundreds of new settlements abroad in the "colonizing" movement of the late eighth to sixth century offered many opportunities for constitutional innovation and experimentation that in turn affected political developments in Greece proper (ch. 19, above). These colonies were usually built largely on the principle of equality.

23 Hdt. 5.66–73; Arist. *Ath. Pol.* 20–2; Ober 1996; 2007. See also Meier 1990a: ch. 4; Loraux 1996; Welwei 1999: 1–21; Anderson 2003.

24 West 1971; Hussey 1972: esp. 1–11; 1995; Emlyn-Jones 1980.

25 Fragments: Diels and Kranz 1951–2 (DK), tr. Freeman 1948; tr. and interpretation: Kirk et al. 1983; see further Guthrie 1962; Fränkel 1973; Barnes 1979; Long 1999; informative entries in *DNP*. All these should be consulted on individual thinkers mentioned below.

26 Snell 1944; Hölscher 1968: chs. 8–10; Mansfeld 1985.

27 Burkert 1972; Zhmud 1997; Riedweg 2002.

28 Neugebauer 1957; van der Waerden 1966; 1967; 1988; Pichot 1991.

29 Nunn 1996; Westendorf 1999; see also Köcher 1963–80.

30 Giovannini 1969; cf. Kirk 1985: 168–87; Visser 1997.

31 Parts of his description survive in a Greek translation: Ameling 1993: 255–6; tr. Cary and Warmington 1963: 63–8; Blomquist 1979; Bayer and Huss 1993.

32 Dilke 1985: 22–5; Harley and Woodward 1987: 132–5; for Mesopotamia and Egypt, ibid. 107–29; Horowitz 1998: ch. 2.

33 Hecataus' fragments: *FGrH* 1; Nenci 1954; interpretation: Jacoby 1956: 186–237 (reprint of *RE* 7: 2666ff); Pearson 1939: ch. 2; von Fritz 1967: ch. 3; Fornara 1983b: 4–12; Bertelli 2001.

34 Obedience as the prime virtue in Mesopotamia: Jacobsen 1946: 202–4; diverse concepts of justice: Irani and Silver 1995. For the late evolution of Sparta's rigid *kosmos* based on obedience (Xen. *Lak. Pol.* 8.1–2; Plut. *Lyc.* 30.3–4), see, e.g., Thommen 1996; ch. 7, above. Power vacuum etc.: e.g., Vernant 1982; Meier 1990a: 29–52; 2001.

35 Miller 1997; Munn 2006; ch. 9, above, and 31, below.

CHAPTER THIRTY

War and International Relations

Henk Singor

Introduction

The world of archaic Greece is often seen through the prism of the age that succeeded it. This is perhaps unavoidable, since most of our literary sources on the seventh and sixth centuries come from the fifth century or later and many elements of classical Greek civilization first took shape in the archaic age. But teleological perspectives and backward projections from a later age are liable to misrepresent the seventh and sixth centuries. There were indeed some constants in land warfare from the early seventh to the late fourth centuries, not the least the role of heavy-armed infantry in pitched battles, but that does not mean "hoplite warfare" was more or less static for nearly four centuries. Features peculiar to archaic warfare were an overlap between the private and the public spheres in war and international relations, and a predominance of relatively limited warfare, both in the frequency of wars and in their scope. The end of this period saw the rise of larger and more homogeneous hoplite armies, of interstate leagues and power politics on a grander scale, phenomena that were to characterize the classical age as well.

A World of Small Communities

The strong sense of community which the epic conveys in its images of local ruler, elders and people indicates the presence already in Homer of the type of political life which we associate with the polis, and the archaeological record confirms that the city-state was beginning to emerge in the second half of the eighth century.[1] The number of *poleis* known to us from the archaic and classical ages runs into the hundreds and most must have been very small indeed.[2] All these countless petty states actively engaged, or so we may assume, in war and diplomacy.

It has often been said that war in ancient Greece was a natural condition and peace in fact an artificial interruption. Such a view is primarily based on the undoubted frequency of wars fought by imperial Athens in the fifth century and on such customs as truce- or peace-treaties for fixed periods, often thirty years, after which a new generation was supposed to have a chance at waging war.[3] The situation in the archaic age was probably less clear-cut. There were at least three different types of war or collective violence. First, booty-raids were usually undertaken not by a community as a whole but by one or a few of its leading men with their personal followers (Rihll 1993; Tandy 1997). Secondly, public wars with limited goals, often border conflicts, were waged on behalf of the community but nevertheless involved only a portion of the community's warriors. Finally, wars in which the very existence of the community was at stake naturally involved all those who could be of any help with whatever weapons they had.

All-out war with the aim of wiping out the opponent seems to have been rare. Although in the epic tradition total destruction of the city, the slaughter of its men and the enslavement of women and children, is the fate of Troy (and is mentioned in a casual remark as the normal fate of a city taken by its assailants: *Il.* 9.591–5), historical tradition tells us of only a handful of Greek cities destroyed by other Greeks in the whole archaic period. Melia, on the peninsula of Mycale, was destroyed by a coalition of Miletus, Samos, and Priene (Vitruvius, *De architectura* 4.1.3–5). Asine and Nauplia were destroyed by neighboring Argos and their inhabitants settled by Sparta on the coasts of Messenia, shortly before 700.[4] Arisbe on Lesbos was destroyed by Methymna and its inhabitants enslaved at an unknown date in the achaic age (Hdt 1.151.2). Crisa was destroyed by the Delphic Amphictions around 590 and its territory turned into pastureland.[5] Pellene suffered destruction through the hands of neighboring Sicyon once in the early sixth century but was later rebuilt. Among the western Greek colonies wars of annihilation seem to have been more common: we know of the fate of Camarina in 553, destroyed by its mother-city Syracuse, of Siris, destroyed around 550 by a coalition of Sybaris, Croton and Metapontum, and of the famous destruction of Sybaris by Croton, in probably 510.[6]

Undoubtedly there were other cases, including wars that did not end in the physical destruction of the defeated community but in its absorption by a neighboring state, as happened probably to Eleusis, incorporated by Athens in the seventh century, or Eleutherae and Oropus, annexed in the sixth. Nevertheless, such a fate was probably exceptional. The very existence of that multitude of mostly small *poleis* during the archaic age, among which only a few were in the end able to evolve to a status of "regional powers," suggests the rarity of warfare and aggression on a grand scale, leading to the subjugation, absorption or annihilation of neighbors.[7] Instead, we have traditions of the unification of neighboring settlements by peaceful merger or *synoikismos*.[8] A notorious exception is Sparta. Having subjugated Laconia probably in the course of the eighth century, it turned to Messenia and started a series of campaigns that was to end only in the late seventh century with the incorporation of most of Messenia's fertile lands and the enslavement of the population as helots. In seventh-century Greece this was like an echo of what probably had been more common in the Dark Age with its unsettled conditions and migrations, just as the epic images of the destruction of Troy conjured up the harsh practices of an earlier age probably more than the every day realities of Greece ca. 700.

This is not to say that warfare at large was rare in the archaic age. Raids by private bands, especially raids overseas, must have been common. In the epic tradition both cattle raids and piratical enterprises figure prominently and the latter endured in the archaic age as a normal and even respected way of life and of production. Among its "products" were Greeks and non-Greeks kidnapped and enslaved on foreign shores. The differences between such raids, more commercial enterprises, or outright warfare must have been slight indeed, and one could shade into the other depending on what opportunities presented themselves. For the victims there was no difference at all. There were also public wars with limited goals, especially to settle border disputes between the emerging *poleis*, to which we shall return.

In all this warfare there was a considerable overlap of private and public spheres. The heroes who assembled for the expedition against Troy took part on the basis of kinship obligations or other personal bonds with the leader. Agamemnon himself had gone to Ithaca to persuade Odysseus to join (*Od.* 24.102–19), whilst Achilles was persuaded to participate by an embassy of Odysseus and Nestor (*Il.* 11.765–82). The princes brought along the warriors of their respective communities, and these communities may have had some say in the matter, even if only by shouting their approval, but the great coalition still looks like an enterprise of private adventurers in the style of a raid for booty. Thus, war could come suddenly in the shape of a landing of raiders, or leading men could force a war on their communities from sheer personal motives. This brings us back to the question whether war was a "natural" condition of interstate relations in archaic Greece.

In order to conclude an alliance, first a formal "friendship" (*philotês*) had to be established. Without it, there could be no question of a treaty whatsoever (Baltrusch 1994: 7–8). The inhabitants of Ithaca, for instance, recognized the Thesprotians as bound to them in friendship and hence would not allow raiding of Thesprotian territory (*Od.* 16.427; Raaflaub 1997c: 21–2). By implication, all those not recognized as "friends" were fair game for plundering (Rihll 1993). Such bonds of friendship are to be expected primarily between neighbors rather than between more distant communities, but this does not necessarily mean that in the absence of *philotês* there was a "natural" state of war. In the epic war against Troy, Menelaus and Odysseus were first sent on a formal mission to ask for the return of Helen and her treasures; only when their mission met with no success did war become inevitable (*Il.* 3.205–24). Moreover, it seems likely that wars between Greek communities had to be formally declared in the archaic age, as was the norm in the classical period. And an official institution for helping and protecting members of other communities, the *proxenia*, which implies state-level bonds of friendship, existed already in the seventh century.[9] All this suggests not a natural state of war but rather settled interstate relations.

A formal bond of friendship between states was probably established by means of *spondai*, an invocation of the gods with libations. Such occasions called for the presence of "heralds" (*kêrykes*) from both sides. In the person of the herald, the private sphere again mingled with the public domain. In Homer, Agamemnon had his personal *kêrykes*, Thalthybius and Eurybates, but the community as such also had its herald: the Trojans, for example, had Idaeus. At one point in the Trojan War a truce was declared and *spondai* performed with the assistance of the heralds; the *philotês* thus established would have permanently ended the conflict, if the truce had not subsequently been broken (*Il.* 3.67–323). The episode throws light on the primary function of the herald in war: establishing contact with the opposing party and arranging truces or treaties under invocation of the gods. With his sacred staff, the *kêrykeion*, he was inviolable and thus able to undertake such dangerous missions and to provide inviolability to any envoys he might accompany.[10] The herald's presence was a reminder that contact with the enemy was still possible and that the conflict could in principle be suspended or even put to an end. Whenever a party was so outraged that it was determined to destroy its opponent utterly, it could decide to do without heralds, resorting to a "war without heralds and without treaties" (*polemos akêryktos kai aspondos*), i.e. a war without limits or *à outrance*. We shall meet a few instances of this in the later archaic age.

The opposite of war-to-the-finish was the practice of arbitration between states. Its origins are not clear, but in the archaic age it was not uncommon for two parties in a conflict to invoke the mediation of a third, often sponsored, so to speak, by the oracle at Delphi (Piccirilli 1973). The role of Delphi in this can hardly surprise, given its function as an interstate oracular centre that was in the seventh and sixth centuries increasingly consulted for a variety of topics, from colonization enterprises to constitutional reforms. Arbitration sanctioned by the god also presupposed a certain awareness of community between the various *poleis*. A broadly shared common background of language and material culture, religion and literary tradition – personified by Homer – greatly enhanced that awareness. Interstate sanctuaries and festivals reinforced it further, especially where permanent forms of cooperation developed between communities that maintained a common sanctuary. Known as Amphictyonies such cooperations are attested for a number of sanctuaries in the archaic age, the most important of which were those of Delphi, Delos, and the Panionion at Mycale.[11] It is tempting to assume that such forms of cooperation in religious matters paved the way for more political forms of interstate relations, but this is hard to prove. Where amphictyonies were more or less coextensive with well-defined regions and clusters of communities they may indeed have facilitated the creation of regional federations, as in the case of Boeotia in the late sixth century. But in other respects their political impact was probably more indirect. Notions of restraint in warfare among neighbors were easily connected with the common bonds created by an amphictyony, and again Apollo at Delphi played an important role in this; in any case, the Delphic amphictyony was later believed to have formally introduced a set of limiting conventions for warfare among its member states (to which we shall come back below). When in 481 most of the states of mainland Greece concluded a grand alliance against the Persian invaders, the ensuing Hellenic League took over this feature of the Delphic amphictyony in its decision to suspend warfare amongst the anti-Persian Greeks for the moment and for the future, when wars were expected to be resumed again (!), to abide by the rules of Delphi.[12]

Cooperation between communities in the form of an alliance must have been common from a very early date. Already the epic tradition pictured the great coalition of Greeks against Troy, and from ca. 700 onwards various coalitions between two or more *poleis* are known (Tausend 1992: 64–187). They were always incidental forms of cooperation, meant to expire when their purpose was achieved. More permanent organizations arose only slowly and towards the end of the archaic age. We have a few treaties between Greek communities that are preserved in inscriptions set up in Olympia, of which an alliance "for hundred years" between Elis and Heraea in the western Peloponnese is the oldest (ca. 550?). Olympia more than other sacred places served as a religious authority sanctioning such treaties.[13] Clearly, it could claim that role because of the prestige of its cults and related games. The well-known Olympic truce or *ekecheiria*, suspending warfare for all those traveling to and from Olympia for the games surely underlined this, although there were parallels in truces applied to the visitors of other holy games at the Isthmus and in Delphi and indeed to all those on religious missions (*theôroi*) to a sanctuary (Brodersen 1991: 10–14). Perhaps in the case of Olympia as a repository of interstate treaties there was some influence of an older amphictyonic organization, but if so, we do not know anything more precise about it.

Sparta's interference in Olympic affairs in the late seventh and sixth centuries surely had a propagandistic purpose as it ran parallel to Sparta's expansionist policies in the Peloponnese. These policies created in the second half of the sixth century a network of alliances between Sparta and most of the other *poleis* of the peninsula. Traditionally, the wars between Sparta and Tegea are seen as the beginnings of that system, but in fact the origins of the so-called Peloponnesian League are obscure.[14] Although the constitution of this league would develop further during the fifth century, we may assume that from the start the relation between Sparta and her allies was an unequal one. Clearly, Sparta acted as the *hêgemôn* or "leader" of her "allies" (*symmachoi*), a normal situation for any Greek alliance or *symmachia*, in which always a leading power had bound to itself other communities that by the very act of their "alliance" had handed over most of their external freedom of action. Typically, the alliance would be officially known as "The Spartans and their allies." Such hegemonial aspirations required more propaganda, and apart from a close connection between Sparta and Olympia, references to the heroic past could serve as such: in the sixth century we find Sparta claiming the inheritance of Agamemnon (the bones of his son Orestes were "discovered" in neighboring Tegea and transferred to Sparta) and king Cleomenes could call himself an "Achaean." But the existence of the Peloponnesian League clearly enhanced Spartan power and prestige in such a way that in 481 the coalition of anti-Persian Greeks naturally accepted Sparta as its *prostates*, "leader" or "champion," thus adding a new element of propaganda in Greek interstate relations.

Phenomena such as the rise of the Peloponnesian League in the later sixth century, or the subordination of the Boeotian cities to Thebes in a federal league in the same period thus restricted the freedom of a number of communities. But in many other parts of Greece and certainly in the period before ca. 550, political fragmentation, sudden wars and incidental coalitions still were the norm. On the whole, archaic Greece was a world in which war could come swiftly and unexpectedly over a community in the shape of a raid or, more rarely, in the form of a campaign of utter destruction by enemy states, or again, in the form of a challenge to battle by a neighbor over a disputed border or some matter of honor or revenge. But we have no indication that such wars happened frequently, and perhaps the custom of concluding peace-treaties or "truces" for periods of 30 years even speaks against it.[15] At the same time, a growing network of *xenia-* and *philia-*relations bonded more and more *poleis* together in an "interstate community" that was partly designed to prevent wars and partly to regulate them to some extent: it was the world of the heralds who kept communications open and arranged truces. This network of relations was established and maintained mostly by local elites, and these also put their stamp on the nature of warfare.

Hoplites, Horsemen, and the Rise of the Phalanx

The Homeric picture of the battlefield has been the subject of numerous studies in recent years.[16] It is now generally recognized that the mass of common soldiers plays a much more important, if not more decisive, role in the epic battles than the *Iliad*'s emphasis on the individual prowess of its heroes would suggest. But the images are not always consistent, ranging from the individual exploits of princes in their chariots chasing across the battlefield to filmic panoramas of huge armies rolling in waves across the plain of the Scamander. Setting aside both of these extremes, one is left with the impression that most fighting is done by bands of warriors, each representing the fighting men of a single community. They are drawn up in two groups: the "front-rank fighters" (*promachoi*), who are armed with spears and swords and usually equipped with metal armor, and behind them the "mass" (*laos* or *plêthys*) of light-armed, who throw or shoot their javelins, stones and arrows over the heads of the warriors in front. The named heroes of the epic are invariably *promachoi*, whether fighting in front of the army as a whole or fighting at the head of their local levy.

The heavy-armed fighters in front seem to fight in close order, in essence not unlike the hoplite phalanx of classical times. They are described as *phalanges* ("lines," "ranks," or more vaguely "troops") and *stiches* ("lines," "ranks," or sometimes "files") which conveys the impression of dense formations. These formations are, however, on a far smaller scale than the classical phalanx, sometimes reduced to a single "rank" with less well-equipped fellow-fighters pressing behind. Sometimes, too, the *promachoi* act on their own, more or less as duelists apart from the mass of the warriors. This, and the apparent mobility of the great heroes, roaming the battlefield in search of worthy opponents, differentiates the image of epic battle from the more homogeneous masses of hoplites in the classical period. Instead of the single decisive clash which characterized classical battles, we have a near-endless series of charges, flights and rallies, a mobility that allows for the use of chariots, archers, javelin-throwers, and so on, as well as the hand-to-hand fighting of the heavy-armed.

A fragment of the Ephesian poet Callinus (mid-seventh century) confirms that the epic picture reflects the historical reality of the late eighth and seventh centuries. Here, we find an exhortation to fight to the death in front of the *laos*: the victorious warrior will be considered "a demi-god in worth"; if he meets his death on the battlefield he will be lamented and missed by "the people" (Callinus F 1 West). The Homeric parallel is obvious. In the Spartan poems of Tyrtaeus, Callinus' younger contemporary, we again hear of *promachoi* and "people behind" (Tyrtaeus F 11.13 West); the latter are the light-armed: *gymnêtes* or *gymnomachoi*, F 11.35; 23a.14). This combination of heavy- and light-armed troops is not what one would expect of the classical Spartan army but is consistent with the epic picture, although Tyrtaeus stresses much more the role of the dense formation of the *promachoi*. They have to stick together (F 10.15; 11.11) and stand fast, for fleeing means a loss of "excellence" (*aretê*, F 11.14; 19), whereas it is good to be killed while facing the enemy (F 10.1–2; 30). For deeds of individual bravery there is little space. We can see the hoplite phalanx emerging, but it is not yet complete, given the role of the light-armed (who at one point even "run in front," F 23a. 14).[17]

Archaeological evidence seems to confirm this picture. Bronze cuirasses appear from around 720; a certain shift away from swords to spears with iron points suggests the growing importance of the ranks of "spearmen" (*doryphoroi*), in the archaic age the normal term for the heavy-armed warriors fighting in close combat; the round bronze-clad shield with double grip (*aspis* or *hoplon*, from which the classical term *hoplitês* may have been derived) were likewise introduced towards the end of the eighth century, almost certainly answering the needs of close-formation fighting. Bronze armor was expensive, and for the later years of the eighth century we may confidently assume that possession of hoplite armor was the privilege of a small minority of leading men and their most trusted friends or retainers. The small groups of soldiers in close order shown in vase paintings of the early seventh century must correspond to the select bands of *promachoi* of our poetic sources.[18]

In the course of the seventh century, hoplite armor and tactics spread. It has been suggested that from an early stage a broad segment of the population must have been enrolled as hoplites. It is supposed to have been a military necessity for any *polis* to maximize their hoplite levies, since these were the new decisive force on the battlefield, and this is thought to have become economically possible by a spread of landed property that provided a larger percentage of the population with the means to equip themselves than was possible later.[19] But we know too little about the economic conditions in early archaic Greece to warrant such assumptions about the distribution of land-ownership. In classical Athens, only the three highest property classes served as hoplites, and if the minimum income for even the lowest of these classes (the *zeugitai*, with harvests of at least 200 bushels of barley) is anything to go by, they were very wealthy and represented only a small minority of the population (Foxhall 1997: 130–1; van Wees 2001; 2006). In any case, these property classes may not originally have had a military dimension at all.[20]

Likewise, vase paintings and figurines of heavy-armed warriors can only tell us that hoplites existed, not how numerous they were. In the case of Sparta, the large number of small lead figurines found at the sanctuary of Orthia suggests, but does not prove, an increase of hoplite equipment in the seventh century. Sparta is exceptional, however, since the conquest of Messenia uniquely provided all the citizens with the means to equip themselves as hoplites. We may therefore tentatively date the origin of the all-hoplite Spartan army to the end of the seventh or first half of the sixth century, and imagine that it gave an incentive to others to try to catch up. But we cannot say how the "hoplite classes" of the fifth century *poleis* had arisen during the archaic age, except that a steady growth in number of those owning hoplite armor, with probably occasional leaps forwards, seems most plausible. Perhaps anyone who acquired the necessary equipment could freely join the ranks of his fellow-citizens, or else, bearing in mind the disdain of the classical hoplite for his social inferiors, admission may have been somehow regulated and ordered from above.

The shield blazons depicted on archaic vases, which show a great variety of individual emblems in contrast to the city-emblems which were the norm in classical hoplite armies (Anderson 1970: 16–20), are suggestive of rather small, elite forces. Glimpses of archaic warfare in our sources, especially Herodotus, also convey an impression of smaller hoplite forces than could be raised in the classical period. In the early fifth century, Athens had 8–9,000 hoplites (Hdt 9.28.6), almost half of whom had evidently become hoplites in 506, when Athens settled 4,000 colonists in Chalcis (Hdt 5.77.2; 6.100.1). This leaves us with only 4–5,000 Athenian hoplites before 506. The number must have been even lower before 508, when Cleisthenes enrolled many new citizens (Arist. *Pol.* 1275b36–7; *Ath. Pol.* 21.2, 4). As hoplites, these new citizens must in all probability have become landholders as well. Conceivably, part of the land came from confiscations of the property of Isagoras' party, driven from power by Cleisthenes, whereas the tyrant Peisistratus might have distributed land already among his Argive *doryphoroi*, who had established the sanctuary of their Apollo Lykeios just outside Athens – which was to remain the rallying-point and parade ground of the Athenian hoplite army – and perhaps the tyrant's grants of land were only now, by Cleisthenes, ratified or legalized by the extension of citizenship. In any case, the Athenian hoplite class was considerably extended by political measures shortly after the fall of the tyrants. How many hoplites there had been before the tyranny, we can only guess, but 1,000 to 2,000 or so might not be far off the mark.[21]

These small numbers of full hoplites continued to be supported when necessary by poorly equipped spearmen, javelin-throwers, archers, and slingers at the back or on the flanks. The few indications we have of archaic army-organization point to the involvement of all able-bodied men. For it was the "tribes" (*phylai*), those basic subdivisions of the citizenry at large, which provided the archaic *polis* with its army units: the Spartan army at the time of Tyrtaeus was organized in the three Dorian *phylai* (F 19.8), and the Athenian army must have had four tribal regiments before Cleisthenes' reforms, just as it had ten afterwards.[22] On occasions of all-out war, when the very existence of the community was at stake, motley formations including all kind of troops would thus have taken the field.

But all-out warfare was rare, and much more common were wars in which only part of the potential forces were involved. In such conflicts one turned naturally to full hoplites. It was these elite "professionals" who put their mark on the nature of fighting in general, conveying many of the norms and ideals of heroic *promachoi* to a wider citizen levy, imbuing it to some extent with an aristocratic ethos, while at the same time hardening the boundaries between those considered fit to join in such an honorable force and those excluded. This would explain why in the archaic age the class of citizens liable to serve as hoplites only gradually expanded and never

Figure 30.1 Fifth-century clay model from Boeotia, showing a hoplite with double-grip shield mounted beside a charioteer with a Boeotian shield slung behind his back
Source: Athens National Museum, inv. 200; photo Deutsches Archäologisches Institut.

incorporated all free men – Sparta again constituting the great exception, thanks to the labors of its helots, which made it possible for all citizens to become hoplites.

In the *Iliad* most of the heroes own chariots, from which, as a rule, they dismount to fight (figure 30.1). The presence of chariots on the Homeric battlefield is rather awkward and often at odds with the images of fighting in massed formations. In the real world of the late eighth and seventh centuries, chariots had no military use, so far as one can tell, and served only as highly prestigious attributes of the elite in ceremonial processions and chariot racing.[23] But the possession of horses always remained a mark of the aristocracy, and the role of horsemen in war underwent a remarkable development in archaic Greece.

Hippeis, "horsemen" or "horse-owners," a general term for an aristocratic elite in Archaic Greece, could use their mounts in the same way as heroes had used their chariots: as impressive means of transport to the scene of battle. On seventh-century vases one sees these "knights" riding out to battle with their "squires" to dismount and duel with similarly equipped opponents while the squires take care of the horses. The epic connotations are all too clear when, sometimes, names of epic heroes are inscribed next to the figures in such scenes (Greenhalgh 1973: 84–99). It is often supposed that they reflect historical reality as well. In the seventh century, it is said, riders were "mounted hoplites," whereas true cavalry appeared only

in the sixth century. This seems unlikely. Cavalry already existed in the seventh
century in the Near East and it is hard to see why Greek horse-owners would have
waited so long to put their mounts to more practical use in war. Presumably, the
vase paintings were chosen because of their heroic flavor and we should not press
this evidence too hard. On the other hand, some elite hoplites in the sixth century
and later, such as Sparta's "Knights" or Thebes' "Charioteers and Chariot-fighters,"
were called after their precious horses and chariots although they fought on foot.[24]
Two contradictory developments seem to have affected the use of horses in Greek
warfare in this age. One trend was to use horses in the manner of chariots only for
transport and display, which ended in giving up the horses altogether, making their
owners pure hoplites. The other was to use horses "for real" – mostly by harassing
fleeing or dispersed opponents with javelins or sometimes thrusting spears – and
this trend gained in importance in the archaic age (Greenhalgh 1973: 99–145; Worley
1994: 21–58). As was often the case in the classical period, it would have been the
younger members of the elite who provided such a cavalry, whilst their fathers served
as hoplites.

At the end of the archaic age, this latter trend was reversed and the cavalry
provided by the elite of the communities all but disappeared, at least in southern
mainland Greece. Athens had no cavalry to speak of in the first half of the fifth
century, Sparta none at all. This can hardly have been for military reasons, because
later in the fifth century these states would again organize regular cavalry units. The
explanation must be that the spread of hoplite equipment and tactics had created a
hoplite mentality and with it an egalitarian ethos that tended to exclude both the
mounted "knight" and the socially inferior "rabble" of the light-armed. This ethos
easily translated itself into the political ideals of a state of *Homoioi* ("Equals") as in
Sparta or a "hoplite democracy" as in Cleisthenes' Athens.

It was perhaps not a coincidence, therefore, that cavalry did play an important
role under the tyranny of the Peisistratids at Athens. These tyrants also employed
specialized light-armed troops, Scythian archers, and Thracian peltasts, and experi-
mented with tactical combinations of hoplites and archers and hoplites and cavalry.[25]
Clearly, they were less hindered by socio-political inhibitions and had an open mind
for the practical applications of military developments and innovations. Similarly, the
Greek cities in Sicily and Italy, always more threatened in their existence than those
in the Greek motherland, and also frequently governed by tyrants, maintained from
the sixth century onwards important cavalry forces and employed from an early age
numbers of mercenaries from their hinterlands.[26]

Hoplite tactics thus asserted themselves in Central and Southern Greece in the
late sixth and early fifth centuries against light-armed troops and cavalry, to the extent
of practically excluding these other troops. This raises the question why such tactics
had developed in the first place. A common view is that hoplite warfare was the expression of the solidarity of the citizen-farmers who in the early archaic age, against the
background of a steadily rising population, had to defend their agricultural base against
competitors. It is not obvious, however, why this should have led to the employment of heavy-armed infantry in close-order formation. Line-formations in general
were common enough for infantry in many parts of the world, but the densely-packed

hoplite phalanxes of Greece, increasingly excluding other troops, were a different matter and understandably left non-Greeks in awe and astonishment.[27] The rise of hoplite tactics is better explained by the cultural influence of heroic notions of *promachoi* fighting for their own glory as well as acting as champions on behalf of their communities. This ideal from epic and elegiac poetry was sustained during the archaic age and adhered to by a growing segment of these communities. The relative lack of intensive warfare, certainly of wars of annihilation in the seventh and sixth centuries, meant that hoplite tactics could develop in a protected environment, as it were, growing from small elite bands until finally almost the entire levies of most *poleis* of mainland Greece were involved.

Archaic Greek Wars

Warfare in the archaic age does not exhibit many of the grim and often ghastly features that shimmer through in quite a few passages of the epic: heads of fallen enemies cut off to be displayed on stakes, bodies left unburied as food for dogs and birds of prey.[28] Often, such treatment of the slain in Homer is presented as a threat which is not carried out. Indeed, the armies once even conclude a solemn truce in order to bury their dead (*Il.* 7.372–441). This latter practice was the rule in historical times. In the Dark Age, such threats may well have been more often realized; a memory of these horrors may have haunted archaic imagination in the shape of the dog-like, winged demons of the battlefield, the Harpies, Sphinxes, and Keres. Perhaps Homer's rejection of the more horrific deeds of his heroes, such as Achilles' treatment of Hector's body, contributed to their final disappearance. In any case, the Spartan victor at Plataea, Pausanias, in 479 expressly refused to decapitate the body of the fallen Mardonius as a deed unworthy of a Greek (Hdt 9.78–79.1).

Various "irrational" or magical elements of warfare of the kind that figure so prominently in war-epics and sagas from Ireland to India – ecstatic dances, incantations, magical instruments, and so on – have left only few traces in the Homeric epic.[29] A certain humanizing trend is unmistakable already in the *Iliad*. It may not be out of place to signal the absence in Greek history of any idea of a "holy war," of warfare bent on the utter destruction of the opposing side at the command of, or in devotion to, a god. Such notions were known to peoples in the Near East and to Germanic tribes. Conceivably, their absence in Greece facilitated the emergence of norms and practices that served to mitigate to some extent the realities of war.

What we know of wars in archaic Greece after Homer seems to confirm this trend. Wars of annihilation, as we saw, were very probably rare. An alternative to complete destruction of a city is hinted at in the *Iliad* and might well have been practiced in archaic times, i.e. the equal division of all its movable goods between attackers and defenders (cf. *Il.* 18.509–12; 22.114–21). The custom of a truce after battle to enable both sides, but especially the defeated, to bury their dead, must have become standard in the archaic age. So too the custom, absent in Homer, of marking with a "trophy" (*tropaion*) the "turning-point" (*tropê*), the spot at which the enemy first turned and fled and battle was decided, by the victor after battle. The *tropaion* is testimony to the emergence of pitched hoplite battles, in which the break-up of a formation signaled its irreversible defeat. In general, archaic warfare as practiced by the hoplites became a more "open" affair until, in the early fifth century, it could be said that the Greeks first agreed upon a suitable place and time for battle and then fought it out (Hdt 7.9B) – as a bloody tournament, one might say. This is certainly an exaggeration, but not without an important element of truth. Ruses and tricks became a standard feature of military strategy in the classical period and they were probably not lacking in the archaic age, but their rarity and simplicity at this early stage of hoplite warfare suggest that they were not yet common, and probably frowned upon by many.[30]

Archaic battle was an affair of man-to-man fighting between the heavy-armed (figure 30.2). A fragment of Archilochus (mid-seventh century) says that the "spear-renowned" lords of Euboea will exclude bows and slings from combat and will leave Ares' work to the swords (F 3 West). A restriction of warfare to the heavy-armed seems implied. Later tradition told of an agreement between the Euboean cities Chalcis and Eretria not to use missiles (*télebola*) in their war over the Lelantine plain. This agreement is almost certainly a fourth-century invention,[31] and the famous statement by Polybius that "the Ancients" did not use missiles or tricks but fought "openly"

Figure 30.2 Sixth-century Corinthian battle scene, showing 12 hoplites fighting hand-to-hand in a dense melee, Corinthian krater by Tydeus painter, ca. 575–550 BC
Source: Louvre E622; photo Musée du Louvre.

(13.3.2–4), is usually thought to have been based on this dubious tradition, but such claims may still reflect a mode of fighting practiced in the seventh century, given Archilochus' description of the Euboean lords' disdain for the use of missiles. Exclusion of the light-armed is also suggested by a story about early fighting in the Megarid, where the warriors did battle "in a mild and friendly way," "invariably releasing their prisoners against ransom and not at all causing harm to those working the fields" (Plut. *Mor.* 295b–c).

Sparing the non-combatants is suggestive of some code of honor. In the classical period we find references to "the laws (or customs) of the Greeks" which should be, but surely often were not, respected by the parties in war. A set of conventions did indeed develop in the archaic age, which, although not often violated, nevertheless influenced Greek warfare to a considerable extent. The most important of these conventions were: to allow the defeated party to bury its dead under truce; to release prisoners of war against a ransom; to refrain from sacking a town completely; and, finally, not to attack by surprise.[32] Later tradition called these rules specifically *Amphiktyonikoi nomoi*, "laws (or customs) of the Amphictyons," i.e. the twelve states which supervised the sanctuary of Apollo at Delphi (Dion. Hal. 4.25.3–6). This might well be the fruit of Delphic propaganda. In the fourth century Aeschines mentioned "the oath of the Amphictyons" by which they swore not to destroy each other's cities, nor to try to reduce them by starvation or deprive them of their water supply (Aesch. 2.115, cf. 3.109–10), but its date is unknown and even its historicity uncertain. Still, such an agreement would be in line with the practices observed in archaic Greek warfare and reflects a deference to Delphi in these matters that almost certainly goes back to the sixth century (Tausend 1992: 34–43).

That these rules were observed, by and large, in most wars between the *poleis* of southern and mainland Greece is suggested by the unsophisticated way in which many of those wars were conducted. The near-absence of ruses and stratagems has already been mentioned. The absence of city-walls is probably another indication. City-walls were well known among the Greeks in Ionia in the eighth century, as well as in Sicily in the seventh and sixth, but in the Greek motherland they were practically nonexistent.[33] According to Thucydides, city-walls were a recent phenomenon in his day (1.2.1–2; 1.7.1). Presumably, many archaic communities had not considered it imperative to protect themselves with walls, either because wars were rare or limited in their objectives or both. Release of prisoners against ransom, too, is well attested in the archaic age – though admittedly it was also frequently practiced in later centuries.[34]

The decisive role of hoplites in battles fought by general levies which mustered all sorts of fighters stimulated a tendency to restrict combat to hoplites alone, or even to select troops of hoplites. To leave the outcome of a battle to a duel (*monomachia*) is a feature of "heroic" warfare known in many cultures and attested already in the *Iliad* (*Il.* 3.1–222) and in Greek legends (e.g. Echemus and Hyllus; Melanthus and Xanthius). It survived here and there in Archaic Greece: the duel between Pittacus of Mytilene and the Athenian Phrynon for the possession of Sigeum was a famous example. But more peculiar to the archaic age, it seems, were set combats between troops of hoplites of equal number, selected to decide the outcome of a conflict.

Such battles between picked troops (*logades*) were an attempt to avoid all-out war and at the same time conjured up scenes of heroic combat.

Around the middle of the sixth century Sparta and Argos agreed on a battle between twice three hundred champions for the possession of Thyreatis. According to Herodotus, two Argives and one Spartan survived. The two Argives then went to their city to proclaim victory, the Spartan remained alone on the battlefield and claimed victory on that ground; thus, the outcome was still undecided and a massive battle between the full armies ensued in which the Spartans defeated their opponents (Hdt 1.82). There are obvious legendary elements involved, but in essence the "battle of the champions" must have been a historical event long remembered – as late as 421 BC Argos proposed to the Spartans another such battle "just like once in the past," a proposal that this time was rejected (Thuc. 5.41.2). We may assume that more such battles by *logades* occurred, especially in the Peloponnese, where traditions of formal duels[35] and legendary fights to the last man by picked troops[36] were particularly strong. Where in the archaic age opponents of unequal military strength waged prolonged wars against each other, it may have been the involvement of *logades* which allowed the weaker party to sustain the conflict. The wars between Sparta and Tegea in the sixth century may have been instances of this (Hdt 1.66; 67.1–2; 68.6; cf. 9.26.2).

The existence in many Greek states of the classical period of standing forces of elite troops, usually three hundred strong, again called *logades* or *epilektoi*, can hardly be dissociated from the tradition of elite or champion-combat in the archaic age. Some states maintained a standing elite force, like the "Knights" in Sparta or the "Charioteers and Chariot Fighters" in Thebes (see above), but still also selected *logades* ad hoc, for instance the 300 Spartans at Thermopylae in 480 (Hdt 7.205.1–2) or the 300 champions for the battle for Thyreatis.[37]

The tournament-like manner of waging hoplite battle speaks for a conception of war as closely related to a sporting contest. There is indeed a considerable overlap in terminology and spirit between sports and hoplite warfare in late archaic and early classical times. *Agôn*, "contest," can mean battle as well as sporting competition; *aethlon*, "prize," denotes the prizes to be won in both. Victors in war were hailed in the same manner as winners at the games. Prizes for "the bravest" or even "the most beautiful" warriors were awarded after the great battles of the Persian Wars: in all, Herodotus mentions 21 of such *aristeia* or distinctions for valor, both for individuals and for city-contingents.[38] Conversely, an Olympic victor could be put at the head of his city's army, his valor in sport apparently not distinguished from that in war; thus, for example, the Olympic wrestling champion Milon of Croton was made commander of the Crotoniate levy in its war on Sybaris in 510 (Diod. 2.9.5). The connection between warfare and sport is further suggested by the introduction at the Olympic games in 520 of the *hoplitodromos* or race in armor. Finally, victors in both wars and games dedicated offerings from their prizes to the gods.

Sport at the level of interstate festivals like Olympia was in the archaic age still mainly an aristocratic affair (see ch. 27), and this may give us a clue to the origins of the regulation and limitation of warfare in archaic Greece. There are many instances of such limitations in other cultures and they normally occur between parties that share the same language, religion, modes of fighting and a whole set of cultural values.

In Greece, these conditions obviously prevailed as well. Yet, it would be rash to explain the agonistic or ritualistic features of archaic Greek warfare solely by reference to a common cultural background. The existence of a multitude of mostly small agrarian communities bordering each other and apparently seldom able or willing to achieve large-scale territorial gains may well have contributed to the rise of limited warfare, but again this is not a sufficient explanation. Some other factor must have been involved as well and this can only have been the influence of aristocratic traditions, norms, and ideals as conveyed above all by Homer and the elegiac poets.[39]

Aristocratic culture dominated political life and interstate relations in the archaic age. Aristocrats maintained in large measure the relations between states. Their intermarriages – one thinks of the famous wedding contest for Agariste, daughter of the tyrant Cleisthenes of Sicyon – guest-friendships, missions to supra-local sanctuaries, and their attendance or participation in the great games all served to strengthen a network of personal relationships that could have impact in the political sphere as well. By the same token, personal obligations and personal conflicts between aristocratic members of different communities could trigger war or military intervention by their *poleis*.[40] Aristocratic honor played a large role here, but notions of honor and revenge were shared by the community at large. Even egalitarian Sparta went to war against Samos for having been wronged by Samian pirates who hijacked a bronze bowl sent by Sparta to the Lydian king and a corselet sent by Amasis of Egypt to Sparta (Hdt 3.47). The endless conflicts about borderlands, too, were surely "a matter of honor rather than of economic or strategic interests" (Connor 1988: 9), because the bones of contention in these conflicts not seldom were pieces of land with relatively little value in themselves, like the Orgas contested between Athens and Megara and probably also the Thyreatis contested between Argos and Sparta. For most of the archaic period, then, it was aristocratic values which dictated international relations and the rules of war.

Changes in Warfare at the End of the Archaic Age

In the end, many long-contested borderlands were incorporated by the stronger states. Megara lost the Orgas and the island of Salamis to Athens, and some western borderland to Corinth; the Thyreatis became Spartan. Thus, an element of pragmatism or *Realpolitik* emerged towards the end of the archaic period especially among the stronger *poleis*, initially alongside ritualized and limited warfare, but eventually making the latter more and more obsolete.

A "war without heralds" was started shortly after 500 by Aegina against Athens on the grounds of the Aeginetans' "long-standing hatred" towards the Athenians, according to Herodotus (5.81.2). The war opened with the capture of Athenian religious envoys (*theôroi*) by the Aeginetans (in itself an act of sacrilege, certainly in Athenian eyes) and developed into a series of raids and counter-raids (5.85–93). The threat of the Persian invasion forced a suspension of warfare, but after the Persian wars tensions remained until Athens, greatly enhanced in maritime power, drove the Aeginetans off their island to Cynouria at the beginning of the Peloponnesian War and finally massacred many of them there in 424 (Thuc. 1.108.4; 2.27.1; 4.57). Clearly, we have another type of war here, not bound by traditional inhibitions.

A further instance, also from the early fifth century, is the war between the Phocians and the Thessalians (Hdt 8.27–8; Paus. 10.1.3–4), during which the Phocians, fearing total defeat, at one point made preparations for collective suicide (Plut. *Mor.* 244b–e), before ultimately achieving victory with the help of some simple but brutal stratagems. The story of their despair (*aponoia*) inspired Plutarch to speak of a *polemos aspondos* or war without treaties. In these wars the very existence of the communities was at stake and therefore the normal "laws (or customs) of the Greeks" did not apply.

What could be called a counter-movement, away from the restrictions of ritualized land warfare in the archaic age, can already be detected in the sixth century. The role of tyrants, employing a variety of troops, including mercenary soldiers from abroad, sometimes in combined forces and in destructive warfare, has already been pointed out. In Greece proper, the subordination of the aristocracy to the *polis*-community made room for regimes based on wider participation by hoplite citizens and ushered in a new stage in warfare. Sparta probably was ahead of others in this. Its hoplite army, as we meet it in our fifth-century sources, must go back to a major reorganization at some time in the sixth (Singor 2002). Even here, the ambitions of powerful personalities could still be a major factor in politics, as can be seen by the actions of king Cleomenes and his campaigns against Athens and Argos. But after Cleomenes' ignominious end by suicide, shortly after 494 BC, decisions of war and peace, including the supervision of the allies in the Peloponnesian League, seem to have been firmly in the hands of the ephors and the assembly (Thommen 1996: 87–98). In Athens, towards the end of the sixth century, Cleisthenes' reforms created a citizen-hoplite army that first defeated Chalcis and Thebes in 506 and then the Persians at Marathon in 490. Among the many *poleis* of Greece clearly some now rose to a status of regional powers. Alliances on a more permanent basis, like the Peloponnesian League, became feasible, and with them power politics entered a new phase.

A new development that contributed in no small measure to this change was the appearance of navies and maritime power. Before the sixth century, as far as we know, there had been no specialized warships and no navies in any Greek state. Predatory warfare and piracy there had certainly been, but the ships used were multi-purpose vessels owned by private individuals.[41] Ships solely meant for war and maintained by the state appear in the second half of the sixth century, first among the Ionians in Phocaea, and in Samos under the tyrant Polycrates. The costs of building and maintaining warships, especially triremes (invented sometime in the sixth century, possibly by the Carthaginians: Wallinga 1993: 111–14) must have been such that only wealthy communities or "pirate-states" under the ruthless control of tyrants, could afford substantial navies. Probably it was the threat of Persia and Carthage that triggered Greek navy-building in the sixth century and, after the opportune discovery of silver-ores at Laurium, the creation of the Athenian navy in the years after 490. Naval power then enabled Athens to spring the bonds of traditional land-based warfare and to shape, after 480, a new and increasingly unscrupulous policy aimed at domination (*archê*) of a multitude of sea-bordering communities.

Early fifth-century Greece, then, differed greatly from that world of small communities in which wars had been mostly limited affairs which in general did not substantially change the political map. Now, new aspirations came to the fore: hegemony and domination. The larger *poleis* had absorbed smaller neighbors or subordinated these in a league. Boundaries had become hardened and communities defined themselves more than before as citizens against non-citizens. This again made further absorptions of other communities less palatable and stimulated new forms of domination: hegemonies in formal alliances under the leadership of a dominant state (Raaflaub 1990: 525). Herein too, Sparta had taken the lead in the later sixth century with the creation of the Peloponnesian League under its leadership, that eventually comprised the whole of the Peloponnese with the exception of Argos. In 481–480, most of mainland Greece united in a Hellenic League under Spartan leadership against a common foe. An element of ideology entered politics with slogans about "panhellenic" identity as defined in opposition to the Persians and their threat to Greek "freedoms." The allies formally promised to suspend their mutual wars and in future to abide by "the customs of the Greeks." The *nomoi tôn Hellênôn* thus became a standard recognized by all – but only to be discarded more and more in the contests for hegemony and domination that ensued.

NOTES

1 For the political community in Homer, see van Wees 1992: 32–4; Raaflaub 1997c: 2–8, 20–7; and ch. 5 above. For the archaeology of the *polis*, see esp. chs. 3–4, 18 and 22, above.

2 Ruschenbusch 1978; cf. van Wees 1992: 270–2, for Homeric population sizes.

3 E.g. de Romilly 1968: 207–20; contra Ilari 1980: 38–41 and Bravo 1980: 977–83, who also explains another piece of evidence, a much misunderstood passage in Plato's *Laws* (625e).

4 Theop. *FGrH* 115 F 383; Paus. 4.24.4; 27.8; 35.2.

5 For the war on Crisa, see Brodersen 1991: 4–6; Tausend 1992: 34–47. Howe 2003 convincingly argues that it sprang from the need to create space for the numerous herds serving the growing demands of the oracle at Delphi.

6 Camarina: Thuc. 6.5.3; Philistus *FGrH* 3 B 556 F 5; Siris: Justin 20.2.4; Schol. Lycophron 984; Sybaris: Hdt 5.44; 6.21; Diod. 13.9.1–10.1; Strabo 263. For destructions and the fate of prisoners, see also Ducrey 1968.

7 As pointed out by Meier 1990b: 569–71.

8 Moggi 1976 lists 51 cases of *synoikismos* before 338; 16 of these date from before 500, including 5 or 6 which are legendary.

9 See ML 4 for the earliest known *proxenos*, Menecrates of Corcyra, who died ca. 625–600. For the institution, see further Marek 1984; Herman 1987.

10 For *kérykes* and envoys in Homer, see van Wees 1992: 32–4; 277–89; Wéry 1979. For their role in the classical period, see Mosley 1973; for classical declarations of war, see Troncoso 1995.

11 See Tausend 1992: 8–63 for a survey of all the material.

12 Boeotia: Tausend 1992: 26–34; the Hellenic League against Persia: Baltrusch 1994: 30–51.

13 See Bengtson 1962: nos. 110 (Elis-Heraia), 111 (friendship "for fifty years" between the Anaitoi and the Messapioi in the south of Italy) and 120 (friendship "forever" between Sybaris and the Serdaioi).

14 For the Peloponnesian League, see Baltrusch 1994: 19–30; Thommen 1996: 55–64.

15 For the relative infrequency of wars in the archaic period, see Frost 1984; Connor 1988: 6–8; Meier 1990b: 563–79.

16 Detienne 1968; Latacz 1977; Pritchett 1985a: 7–44; Snodgrass 1993a; Bowden 1993; van Wees 1994; 2000a. The following summarizes my own views, for which see Singor 1995.

17 Contra Pritchett (1985b: 1–68), one cannot take Pausanias' account of the Second Messenian War as evidence for the nature of early Greek battle, despite his use of Tyrtaeus.

18 Rather than the fully developed hoplite phalanx, as is usually assumed (e.g. Lorimer 1947; Hanson 1989; 1995; Snodgrass 1993a). For the iconographic evidence, see van Wees 2000a.

19 See Raaflaub 1997c: 54; 1999: 136; Donlan 1997b: 45–6; Hanson 1995; Bowden 1993: 48; Detienne 1968: 120.

20 Whitehead 1981 derives the term *zeugitai* from *zygon* or "rank" of the hoplite phalanx, but the term surely denotes the *zeugos* or yoke of oxen as a property criterion.

21 For the possible military implications of Cleisthenes' reforms see Siewert 1982; further on Athens before Cleisthenes: Frost 1984; Singor 2000.

22 Compare also Nestor's advice to Agamemnon, *Il.* 2.362. For Athens, n. 21 above.

23 On chariots and early cavalries there is a growing body of literature: Gaebel 2002: 44–60.

24 Sparta: Hdt 1.67.5; 8.124.3; Thuc. 5.72.3; Xen. *Lac. Pol.* 4.1–3.Thebes: Diod. 12.70.1.

25 Cf. Vos 1963; Best 1969; for the light-armed generally: Lissarrague 1990b.

26 For Athens, see Singor 2000; and above, ch. 8; for Sicily, see above, ch. 16.

27 For the common view, see e.g. de Polignac 1995a: 45–60; Raaflaub 1997c: 53. Sensible remarks in Dawson 1996: 47–64. For the perception of hoplite combat as unique, see Hdt. 7.9B.

28 Lopping off of heads: *Il.* 11.145–6, 261; 13.202–5; 14.498–500; 18.176–7, 335. Fights over dead bodies threatened with non-burial or mutilation: e.g. *Il.* 16.492 ff; 18.5ff.

29 Cf. the references to heroes as "dancers" (*Il.* 7.241; 16.617) and as men "outstanding in the war-cry," or to Apollo "casting a spell" on the Greeks (15.306, 322).

30 Pritchett 1974: 177–89 (ambuscades); 156–76 (surprise attacks), mostly post-archaic. For simple archaic ruses, see e.g. Hdt 1.63.9 (Pallene, 546 BC), 6.77–8 (Sepeia, 494 BC?). For the norms of late archaic and classical hoplite warfare, see Connor 1988; Hanson 1989; Hanson (ed.) 1991; Meissner 2002; *contra* Krentz 2002; van Wees 2004.

31 Wheeler 1987; for the Lelantine War, see now in detail Parker 1997: 59–152.

32 See Ilari 1980: 358–72; Connor 1988: 11–16; *contra* Krentz 2000.

33 Winter 1971: 61–4, 289–99; Lawrence 1979: 30–8; see further ch. 18, above.

34 See Ducrey 1968; after the release of prisoners their fetters could be displayed as votive offerings in a sanctuary (Hdt 1.67 and 5.77.4, with the epigram ML 15).

35 Ephorus *FGrH* 70 F 54; Athen. 154d; cf. Ps.Plut. *Mor.* 309cd; Stobaeus 39.32 (three brothers from Tegea dueling with three brothers from Pheneos, in a double of the famous Roman legend of the Horatii and Curiatii); Plut. *Mor.* 675c (*monomachiai* to the death in Pisa).

36 100 *logades* from Oresthasium fought to the death against the Spartans (we are not told when) and received hero-status in Phigalia (Paus. 8.39.3–4; 41.1); 360 *logades* from Cleonae had assisted Heracles in his fight with the Moliones and were killed to the last man (Ael. *VH* 4.5); *logades* from Argos were all killed in combat with the Phlegyads (Paus. 9.36.2).

37   For an overview see Alonso and Freitag 2001.

38   Pritchett 1974: 276–90; after Herodotus only individual distinctions are mentioned.

39   See Morris 1996b for the two strands of lyric poetry: one elitist, the other community-oriented.

40   Personal obligations: e.g. Thuc. 1.126.2; Paus. 1.28.1 (Cylon and Theagenes); cf. Singor 2000 (Peisistratus' friends and in-laws abroad). Personal wrongs: e.g. Plut. *Mor.* 254b–e (adultery of Neaira of Miletus with Promedon of Naxos causes war between the two states).

41   See Wallinga 1993, and briefly De Souza 1998.

CHAPTER THIRTY-ONE

Ethnicity and Cultural Exchange

Jonathan M. Hall

Ethnic and Cultural Identities

The question of what constitutes Greek ethnicity is probably more of a preoccupation for modern scholars than it was for the ancients themselves. In day-to-day interactions, the average Greek citizen identified himself primarily with his family and with his *polis* or local community (and the possible tensions that could arise between these two levels of self-identification represent a popular theme in Attic tragedy of the fifth century). Beyond that, he might sometimes take cognizance of his affiliation to a broader collectivity known as the *ethnos*, be it regionally based (e.g. the Boeotians or Thessalians) or more dispersed and "diasporic" (e.g. the Dorians or Ionians). Yet there were also some occasions on which the ancient Greeks reflected more generally on a consubstantiality that ran deeper than the internecine conflicts that so often characterized relations between and among *poleis* and *ethné*.

Writing around the outbreak of the Peloponnesian War in 431, Herodotus seems to have had a particular reason for wanting to define and promote a common Greek identity that he feared was soon to dissolve in the bloody conflict that pitched the Athenians and their allies against the Spartan-dominated Peloponnesian League. Indeed, one of the most explicit definitions of Greek identity in our extant literary sources is placed in the mouth of an Athenian delegation, shortly before the battle of Plataea in 479: "Then again, there is the matter of Greekness (*to Hellénikon*) – that is, our common blood, common tongue, common cult places and sacrifices and similar customs; it would not be right for the Athenians to betray all this" (8.144.2). The passage is justly famous, but so much attention has been paid to its fourfold definition of Greek identity in terms of kinship, language, religion, and culture that two features have often gone unnoticed. The first is that the Athenians' appeal to Greekness is actually an afterthought: their primary concern is with avenging the Persian sack of their temples. The second is that, when set against the broader background of the *History* and especially the ethnographic digressions, the four "ingredients" of Greekness are not normally accorded equal weight in defining populations. Instead, cultural considerations consistently outrank linguistic or religious ones, while kinship is given scant regard (Hall 2002: 189–94). That this had not always been the case is illustrated by another episode from the *History*. When, earlier in the fifth century, the Macedonian king Alexander I wanted to compete in the Olympic games, he demonstrated his *bona fide* Greek credentials – a prerequisite for admission to the games – in terms of his ancestry and of his family's original derivation from Peloponnesian Argos (5.22.1–2). It is no coincidence that in 380 the Athenian orator Isocrates was to claim that "those who are called Greeks are those who share our culture rather than a common biological inheritance" (*Paneg.* 50). The proclamation would have had little rhetorical effect had not notions of shared blood and kinship once constituted a crucial criterion of Greekness.

In modern scholarship, there is sometimes a tendency to conflate ethnic and cultural identities, defining the former in terms of the latter. This is, in part, a reaction to the iniquitous racial philosophies of the early twentieth century in which a people's destiny was thought to be determined by biological descent. But a moment's thought will reveal that there are cultural groups or "movements" (e.g. bohemians, hippies, punks, goths, etc.) that can hardly be described as ethnic. If we define a cultural group as one which grounds its identity in a set of shared symbols (ideas, beliefs, values, attitudes, and practices), selected from the totality of social existence and endowed with a particular signification for the purposes of communicating distinctiveness (Hall 2004a: 46), then it would be fair to say that the ethnic group represents a specific type of cultural group. What defines it as ethnic – as opposed to linguistic, religious, or occupational – is the fact that the symbols by which it communicates its distinctiveness revolve around notions of kinship (however fictive), a primordial territory and a common history, rather than language, theological dogma, or profession. This is not to deny that language, religion, customs and even physiognomy may be important to ethnic classification, but such elements are secondary markers or "indicia" because they are highly variable in different contexts and lack the universality of such core-elements or definitional "criteria" as putative kinship (Horowitz 1975: 119–21). We could do a lot worse than follow the German sociologist Max Weber's definition of ethnic groups as "human groups that entertain a *subjective belief* in their common descent . . . whether or not an *objective* blood relationship exists" (1978: 389 [emphasis added]). Consequently, it is important to realize that ethnicity and cultural identity, though related, are not homologous and should not therefore be analyzed as if they were.

The Birth of the Hellenes

There are two moments in the history of Archaic Greece that tend to be regarded as particularly critical for fostering a sense of Greek identity. The first is the last third of the eighth century, when waves of overseas settlement, predominantly in Sicily and south Italy, led to a situation in which Greek settlers were confronted by indigenous populations. This, it is often argued, forced the newcomers to reflect on what it was that might account for the differences between themselves and their neighbors. The second is the Persian War of 480–479, when a relatively small coalition of Greek city-states, headed by Sparta, managed to repel the onslaught of Xerxes' army, prompting the creation of a "barbarian" antitype against which Greeks might define themselves. The attention given to both events is due in no small part to the legacy of French structuralism, which became popular in classical scholarship from the 1970s and privileged difference over similarity, as well as to a now entrenched anthropological orthodoxy that ethnic groups are defined by their boundaries and hence through opposition with other ethnic groups (Barth 1969). Nevertheless, the significance of both events may have been overestimated.

The *Odyssey* is often regarded as a product of the "age of colonization." The dichotomy drawn between the "cultured" civic world of Odysseus and his companions and populations such as the Cyclopes, who "have no deliberative assemblies or laws, but inhabit the peaks of the tall mountains in hollow caves, each one of them legislating over his own children and wife without taking account of others" (9.112–15), could conceivably articulate the differences that Greek settlers perceived between themselves and the indigenous residents of the west. Yet this would be to ignore the fact that the Greeks were hardly unaware of the Italian peninsula prior to its intensive exploitation in the later eighth century. Mycenaean Greeks had frequented the region and imported Greek pottery in Puglia testifies to a resumption of traffic across the Adriatic by at least the end of the ninth century (D'Andria 1995). Furthermore, while the act of establishing a settlement overseas often involved a great deal of violence towards the native community, it seems that a relatively stabilized equilibrium between Greek settlers and indigenous residents was normally established within a generation or two at most sites.

Literary sources talk about intermarriage and this is the interpretation that some archaeologists have given for the presence of indigenous styles of female jewelery in graves at early colonial sites (Coldstream 1993). Some linguistic evidence points in a similar direction. The existence of mixed names, such as the Rutile Hipukrates known from a graffito on a seventh-century oinochoe at Tarquinii (Morel 1984: 147), or of Greek names written according to non-Greek phonology – e.g. the name Eurumakes, attested in a "Sicel" inscription from eastern Sicily (Agostiniani 1988–9: 195–6) – is most reasonably interpreted as the product of "mixed" marriages. Three graffiti from the acropolis of the Greek city of Gela on Sicily appear to employ the dative case to indicate possession, a construction that is uncommon in Greek but is well documented in the so-called "Elymian" languages of western Sicily (Piraino Manni 1980), and this is highly suggestive of the sort of bilingual environment that intermarriage favors. None of these cases would lead us to suppose a climate of apartheid or ethnic chauvinism on the part of Greek settlers. In fact, the Greek cities in south Italy and Sicily were more frequently engaged in hostilities with one another than with indigenous populations and, despite claims to the contrary,[1] the supposed evidence for "panhellenic" sanctuaries outside the cities of Naxos and Croton is far from compelling (Hall 2002: 122–4). Even the gaudy and ostentatious western treasuries at Olympia project more of a sense of smug satisfaction on the part of self-made communities than a yearning to participate in an exclusively Greek confraternity.

Turning to the other end of the archaic period, there can be no doubt that the conflict with Persia had a profound effect on Greek self-consciousness. The word *barbaros*, attested only rarely in earlier literature, becomes far more frequent in literature written after 479 (see further below). Yet the current vogue for viewing identities as constructed "oppositionally" through perceived differences has tended to occlude the fact that they can also – albeit less efficiently – be generated "aggregatively" through perceived similarities.

Nomenclature is important here, because it would appear that there have seldom, if ever, existed ethnic groups whose "essence" was not expressed through a specific name (Smith 1986: 23). "Hellenes," the name that the Greeks applied to themselves, does not appear in our literary sources until the sixth century. There is a single exception in the *Iliad* (2.681–5) though, as Thucydides (1.3.3) had already pointed out, it there denotes the population of a small region by the estuary of the Sperchius river, south of Thessaly. In literature of the seventh century, instead, the word that we find is "Panhellenes"[2] – a term whose prefix emphasizes not the unity but the diversity of the various populations inhabiting the southern Balkans. The earliest extant attestation of "Hellenes" in its more inclusive sense is in a fragment of Hecataeus (1 *FGrH* 119), writing in the late sixth or early fifth centuries but, provided that Pausanias (10.7.5–6) has correctly cited (and dated) a victory dedication set up at Delphi by the Arcadian musician Echembrotus, the term should already have entered into currency by 586. It can hardly be a coincidence that this is precisely the period in which a consortium of Greek cities in the eastern Aegean collaborated in founding a sanctuary to "the gods of the Hellenes" in the Egyptian trading-post of Naucratis.[3] Nor can it be accidental that a literary notice which provides the first explicit testimony regarding the *nature* of Greek identity can almost certainly be dated to the sixth century.[4]

The *Catalogue of Women*, erroneously attributed in antiquity to Hesiod, was a poem that sought to reconcile local genealogical traditions within a broader and overarching Hellenic framework. In it, we read that "the sons of the war-loving king Hellen were Dorus, Xuthus and Aeolus who fights from the chariot" (fr. 9 M–W) and that "by the will of the gods, Xuthus took as his wife Creusa of beautiful form, the fair-cheeked daughter of godlike Erechtheus, and she lay with him in love and bore him Achaeus, Ion of the noble steeds and the beautiful Diomede" (fr. 10(a) 20–4). Although genealogies could serve a number of purposes for the ancient Greeks – from expressing hereditary claims on the part of elite families to explaining relationships between features of local landscapes – they are a particularly efficacious way of articulating notions of consubstantiality based upon putative kinship. Indeed, the fact that figures such as Dorus and Achaeus are purely eponymous constructions, lacking any mythological "depth," provides a strong indication that this was the primary function of the genealogy. By linking their eponymous founding-fathers to one another in a single genealogy, then, the four principal *ethné* of the Greeks –

the Aeolians, Dorians, Ionians and Achaeans – could both take cognizance of their ethnic relatedness and express their affiliation to a larger Hellenic family, embodied in the personage of the eponymous Hellen.

There are, however, three indications to suggest that this awareness of a common Greek identity, based on kinship, was a relatively recent phenomenon at the time the *Catalogue* was composed. Firstly, while the name "Hellenes" is, as we have seen, unattested prior to the sixth century, the groups that would later be regarded as ethnic constituents of the Greeks appear earlier. It is well known that the term "Achaeans" is freely employed in the Homeric epics to denote the Greeks generally but there are also single references to the Ionians (*Il.* 13.685) and to the Dorians (*Od.* 19.177), while Hesiod (*W&D* 636) describes Kyme, his father's birthplace, as Aeolian. Secondly, the relegation of the eponymous Ion and Achaeus to the third generation and the intrusion of the non-eponymous Xuthus almost certainly betray a process of fusion between two originally independent stemmata – one which linked the Dorians with the Aeolians, and one which stressed an affinity between the Ionians and Achaeans. Thirdly, by subscribing to a gradual and aggregative development of Greek consciousness, we can better explain why there were certain groups, such as the Arcadians or the Aetolians, whose eponymous founders were never incorporated within the lineage of Hellen. We are always, of course, held hostage by the differential survival rates of our sources, but the apparently simultaneous appearance of both this genealogical tradition and the earliest attestations of the ethnonym "Hellenes," together with the foundation of the Hellenion at Naucratis, all argue strongly for the sixth century as the critical watershed in the emergence of Greek ethnic consciousness.

Explaining how and why this genealogical tradition was coined is far from easy but all the signs point towards Thessaly. It is through the figure of Aeolus that the *Catalogue* traces the ancestry of the most illustrious mythical lineages of Greece and Herodotus (7.176.4) argues that Aeolis was the original name for Thessaly. Furthermore, Strabo (9.5.6) and the Scholiast to Apollonius Rhodius (4.265; citing Hesiod and Hecataeus) both describe Thessaly as having once been ruled by Deucalion, the father of Hellen, and by his descendants. There is some reason to believe that Deucalion was also associated with a separate genealogical tradition that told how another of his sons, Amphictyon, was the father of Malus, Itonus and Physcus and that Itonus' son was Boeotus while Locrus and Ion were the sons of Physcus. Since Itonus was a town in Achaea Phthiotis and Physcus the site of a sanctuary in West Locris, this genealogy would appear to explain the original membership of the "amphictyony" or federation of *ethné* (Malians, Phthiotid Achaeans, Locrians, Boeotians, and the Ionians of Euboea) that was charged with administering the sanctuary of Demeter at Anthela and, eventually, the sanctuary of Pythian Apollo at Delphi. Although this genealogical tradition can only be reconstructed from fragments preserved in authors of widely varying dates,[5] it can hardly have served any functional utility *after* the later seventh century, when Thessaly began to dominate the Delphic Amphictyony and to exercise hegemony over the previously independent states of Malis and Achaea Phthiotis (Hall 2002: 134–54). In other words, the Thessalians seem to have appropriated the figure of Deucalion (probably originally a Locrian hero) and provided him with a new lineage, derived from Hellen and Aeolus, that served to bypass an earlier genealogical tradition and thereby promote their own claims over their fellow members within the Delphic Amphictyony.

If so, the most likely venue for the promotion of the new Hellenic genealogy was probably Olympia, where Thessalian elites began to win a string of victories from the early decades of the sixth century (Moretti 1957). The Olympic Games were, as we have seen, explicitly restricted to those who could adduce Hellenic descent and, in fact, the vast majority (91.3 percent) of the Olympic victors recorded for the period 776–475 could claim a direct affiliation to one of the four *ethné* represented in the pseudo-Hesiodic genealogy. The corollary of this is that there were *ethné* resident in Greece that could not formally declare a Hellenic affiliation and it is interesting that several of the groups that fall into this category were immediate neighbors of the Thessalians. Such is the case with the Magnesians, whose eponymous founding-father, Magnes, according to the *Catalogue* (fr. 7 M–W), was the son of Zeus and Deukalion's sister Thuia. Although related to Hellen (his maternal uncle), Magnes cannot adduce strict lineal descent from him and this effectively denies Hellenic ancestry to the Magnesians who, by the later Archaic period, had been brought into a position of dependency upon the Thessalians. It should be no surprise that no Magnesian is credited with an Olympic victory in the Archaic period; the same is true of other Thessalian satellite populations (*perioikoi*) such as the Perrhaebi or the Dolopes.

The inference would be, then, that it was the Thessalians who sought to promote a common Greek ethnicity, first with the Dorians of the Peloponnese and then with the Ionians and Achaeans, in order to exclude from full recognition those neighboring populations over whom they exercised hegemony. Although serving an exclusionary function, such an appeal was predicated on perceptions of similarity between various Greek-speaking groups rather than differences, since any differences that the Thessalians might have imagined between themselves and populations such as the Magnesians or the Malians would hardly have been significant to the geographically distant Dorians or Ionians. No doubt appeals were made to apparently common *indicia* such as language, cult, and customs, but the deciding criterion was ultimately genealogical. The important point is that, while the promotion of Greek ethnicity must have been sponsored by the elites (who, initially at any rate, were the only class that possessed the leisure and revenues to compete at Olympia), there was no mechanism by which this genealogical conception of Greekness could be restricted to them alone.

Whose Culture?

"Culture" is one of those words that is seemingly instantly comprehensible while at the same time extraordinarily difficult to define. I doubt that many students of classical antiquity lose much sleep over how to define Greek culture even if the specific aspects highlighted would probably be different for the specialist in literature, who might focus on epic, lyric, and epinician poetry, than for the classical archaeologist or art historian, who would likely point to canonical forms of architecture, "naturalizing" sculptural representations and painted figured pottery. "Greek culture" is normally treated simply as an ensemble of diagnostic traits, some inherited from the Late Bronze Age, others borrowed from the near east and yet others donated to more "primitive" populations in the colonial orbit.

Yet it ought to be a sobering thought that this "shopping list" characterization of culture conforms to anthropological conceptions that were current in the early decades of the twentieth century and that cultural anthropologists have been insisting for some time now that culture is inherently "contradictory, loosely integrated, contested, mutable, and highly permeable" (Sewell 1999: 53). The issue is compounded by the fact that the sort of theoretical sophistication that has been displayed with such good effect in discussions of ancient ethnicity has rarely been extended to the realm of culture. It is now commonplace to privilege the "emic" (internally perceived) over the "etic" (externally observed) view of ethnicity: Sir John Myres' attempts (1930) to chart the "becoming" of the Greeks by reference to objectively observable indices such as cranial type, dialects, cults, and material culture strike the modern reader as unsatisfactory precisely because they pay so little attention to what and how the Greeks thought about themselves. When it comes to culture, on the other hand, it is invariably the externally observable traits that are considered. Take, for example, what an eminent archaeologist has to say about the indigenous populations of eastern Sicily: "The impact of Greek ideas and culture was immediate. On many Sicel sites near the early colonies we find Greek vases, and often too vases which are native in shape but quite Greek in decoration . . . In the mid fifth century there was a nationalist Sicel movement, but by then the natives had been almost completely hellenized" (Boardman 1980 (1999): 190).

There are essentially two factors that have hindered investigations of Greek culture. The first has been the tendency to regard those elements that have survived from the past – be they works of literature, inscriptions, sanctuaries, sculpture, or ceramics – as the passive trace-elements of behavioral patterns. Yet this is to ignore the potential for individual agency and the fact that people *do* things with culture. Put another way, certain symbols can be actively and deliberately selected and employed to communicate distinctiveness and the categories that are delineated in this process do not always take the same shape as those which the modern archaeologist, applying descriptive and typological classifications, identifies. The second is a lingering legacy of the "settlement archaeology" method pioneered by Gustav Kossinna, Professor of Archaeology at the University of Berlin in the early decades of the twentieth century, and imported into Anglo-American scholarship by the Australian archaeologist Gordon Childe. According to this method, "a plurality of well-defined diagnostic types that are repeatedly and exclusively associated with one another" should constitute the "material expression of what today would be called a people" (Childe 1956: 123; 1929: v–vi).

Quite apart from the fact that there seldom exists archaeological consensus as to what should count as a "well-defined diagnostic type" (Jones 1997: 108–9), a series of case studies has made it blatantly clear that ethnic and cultural boundaries do not always coincide.[6] On Sicily, it is not difficult for the modern archaeologist to discern the formal and stylistic influences that Greek ceramic traditions exercised on local pottery. During the Early Iron Age (i.e. the eleventh to eighth centuries), the "Pantalica II" or "Cassibile" culture of eastern Sicily appears to betray its derivation from the "Ausonian" culture of the Italian mainland but intensive contacts with Greek settlers, from the last third of the eighth century, prompted the adoption of a new ceramic style – known as "Finocchito," after an indigenous site near Syracuse – which owed many of its features to the pottery of the newcomers (Bernabò Brea 1957: 147–85).

Yet to focus on ceramics alone would be misleading. In the sixth-century settlement at the "Sicel" site of Morgantina, nine miles north-east of Piazza Armerina, the indigenous practice of multiple inhumation in chamber tombs was retained alongside the adoption of Greek burial practices such as cremation and inhumation in fossae, sarcophagi, and vases (Antonaccio 2001; 2003). Conversely, Greek settlers at Syracuse and Leontini felt no compunction about adopting indigenous mortuary practices (Shepherd 1995). Further west, at Sabucina, imports and local imitations of Protocorinthian, Rhodian, and Cretan wares indicate the existence of contacts with the Greek city of Gela to the south, but the seventh- and sixth-century architecture at the site expresses a hybrid mélange of both Aegean and indigenous traditions (De Miro 1983). Again, however, this would be to adopt too "passive" a view. The fact that the "Sicel" leader Ducetius could, in the mid-fifth century, spearhead a "nationalist" movement of secession makes it most unlikely that the Sicels conceived of themselves as "almost completely hellenized."

Interestingly enough, there is one area where a more active or "knowledgeable" agency is credited to the Greeks within the process of cultural exchange. From the tenth century, near eastern – and particularly north Syrian – grave goods are found in burials at Lefkandi on the island of Euboea and at sites in Crete, Attica, and the Dodecanese. In some cases, it is clear that such eastern objects were accompanied by their manufacturers: a tenth-century burial in the Tekke cemetery at Cnossus was associated with items of jewelry and unworked gold and silver which have been attributed to a Levantine craftsman on Crete; in Athens, a pair of granulated and filigreed gold earrings found in a ninth-century female burial may also point to a resident Levantine craftsman in the city (Coldstream 1982: 267; 2003: 56). There are also indications that easterners frequented Greek sanctuaries: at the sanctuary of Hera at Perachora near Corinth, near eastern objects of predominantly Levantine origin account for around 75 percent of the metal finds, while no less than 85 percent of the metal dedications at the Samian Heraion are of non-Greek manufacture (Kilian-Dirlmeier 1985). Some may have been dedicated by Greek elites who had acquired them through trade or exchange, but the sheer quantities, together with the presence in both sanctuaries of Egyptian mirrors with hieroglyphic dedications to the goddess Mut, make it probable that the dedicators were not Greeks (Strøm 1992: 57).

Towards the end of the eighth century, exposure to the artistic and cultural traditions of the near east in the form of imported objects resulted in their adoption into, and accommodation within, Greek styles. The impressive north Syrian bronze cauldrons with siren attachments that had begun to appear in sanctuaries such as

Olympia were swiftly imitated by Greek craftsmen who modified them by adding attachments in the shape of griffins – a mythical beast of near eastern origin (Muscarella 1992). Other eastern motifs such as chimeras, Tritons, lions, animal friezes, and lotus and palmette friezes begin to adorn Greek – and especially Corinthian – pottery, while north Syrian models are generally adduced in the development of the "Daedalic" style of sculpture that arises on Crete in the seventh century. New Semitic loan-words were borrowed along with their corresponding objects and techniques – for example, *chiton* (a linen tunic), *kanon* (a measuring rod), *deltos* (writing-tablet) and *chrysos* (gold) – and some scholars have even identified western Asiatic elements in the poetry of Homer and Hesiod.[7] Had the same operating assumptions been applied to this phenomenon as are employed in discussing Greek settlement of the west, we might have described Greece as being thoroughly "orientalized." Instead, the term that is generally used is "orientaliz*ing*" – emphasizing the conscious, active and creative nature of Greek initiative (and, incidentally, the Hellenocentric bias of many modern scholars).

It is not that it is wrong to emphasize the "creative transformation" (Burkert 1992: 7) by which near eastern elements were incorporated within Greek cultural traditions. It is simply that it seems unwarranted to credit unduly the Greeks with such an initiative unless we are also prepared to recognize a similar creativity among the indigenous populations of south Italy and Sicily (modern aesthetic judgements are inappropriate to analyses of cultural exchange). But perhaps one of the most damaging aspects to the whole discussion of culture contact has been the tendency to elide the distinction between geographical provenance and ethnicity. Put differently, it is one thing to say that a certain artifact appears first in the near east and is then imported and eventually imitated by craftsmen resident in the Aegean basin. It is quite another to claim that *the* Greeks defined themselves according to an eclectic culture that selected, usurped and transformed elements of near eastern cultural traditions.

This begs the question: did the Greeks – or the Sicels, Oenotrians, or Etruscans, for that matter – recognize, let alone emphasize, any "ethnic" essence in the items that they imported or imitated? Time is an important dimension here because it should be fairly obvious that extraneous elements, once accommodated within local traditions and practices, become increasingly familiar. Willow pattern wares are probably more redolent now of the faddish tastes of the British bourgeoisie than of their Chinese origins. Similarly, it is unlikely that the originally oriental connotations of the palmette were uppermost in the minds of ancient Greeks when, in the sixth century, palmette anthemia begin to crown funerary stelai in Attic cemeteries. But what about originally, at the time of adoption or imitation?

Already by the time of the earliest lyric poets, the east was a byword for *habrosuné*, or "luxury," and the poetess Sappho was one of its most eloquent champions. "I am in love with *habrosuné*," she gushes (fr. 58 L–P), as she extols the virtues of Lydian sandals (fr. 39), saffron robes and purple cloaks (fr. 92) and a decorated headband from the Lydian capital of Sardis (fr. 98). Sappho is clearly aware that good things are to be had from Lydia, and Sardis in particular, but that does not necessarily mean that these luxury items carried an ethnic connotation for her. Indeed, when Sappho refers to Lydia in the same breath as Lesbos and the Greek cities of

Ionia (frs. 98, 132), it is difficult to discern any significant differentiation between what are, for us, the Greek and non-Greek worlds. This is not terribly surprising. Sappho, like her compatriot Alcaeus or the Spartan poet Alcman, belonged to an aristocratic milieu in which intermarriage, guest-friendship and gift exchange delineated class distinctions rather than ethnic boundaries, and for which a constellation of abstract values such as *areté* ("excellence"), *philotimia* ("ambition"), and *kudos* ("glory") were valorized as a model of, and for, elite behavior. According to one view, the Homeric epics themselves represent an elite tool of exclusion, identifying in both behavioral and genealogical terms the leading families of contemporary Greece with the great heroes of the mythical past (Tandy 1997: 166–93), while it has been suggested that one of the functions of Pindar's epinician odes was to resolve the potential tension between a victor's claims to participate in a transregional elite and the necessity of reintegrating him within his local community (Kurke 1991).

It is not so much the precise provenance of Sappho's luxuries that is at issue as the fact that they are difficult to obtain without the benefit of interpersonal relationships that extend well beyond the borders of the local community. Parallel phenomena can be documented in the west. In south Italy, for example, "Greek"-style hoplite armor begins to appear from the seventh century, but it was employed not by infantrymen of middling means but by mounted elite warriors. Similarly, the Greek practice of communal wine consumption, almost certainly in association with the institution of the symposium, would appear to be a thoroughly aristocratic pursuit to judge from the wealthy burials in which spits, firedogs, cups, wine-jugs, and later mixing-bowls appear (Greco 1993: 105–8). At Pontecagnano in Campania, a specifically "Homeric" style of burial, involving inurned cremation in bronze and silver vessels, was reserved for a few "princely" tombs of the early seventh century in a cemetery where inhumation had prevailed since the middle of the eighth century (D'Agostino 1996: 536–7). In all these cases, the items that are adopted function as prestige symbols within indigenous cultural traditions rather than indicating any contrived assimilation with donor cultures. The Etruscans were not trying to "pass" as Greeks, nor was Sappho seriously attempting to persuade her readers that she was a Lydian, but both were conversant in a symbolic vocabulary that transected ethnic and linguistic boundaries. To describe both cultural universes as "Greek" would be seriously misleading.

The distinctive symbols by which this supraregional and transethnic elite communicated its distinctiveness were not lost on those who did not – or claimed not to – participate in such distinguished company. Phocylides' protestation that "a small *polis*, settled orderly on a rock, is mightier than foolish Nineveh" (fr. 4 West) may be a response to Alcman's contrast between "lofty Sardis" and "boorish Thessaly" (fr. 16 L–P). Anacreon (fr. 481 Page) sneers at the *lydopatheis* – i.e. those with a pathological addiction to the Lydian way of life – while Xenophanes (fr. 3 West) levels a similar criticism at his fellow citizens of Colophon: "having learned useless luxury from the Lydians, so long as they were without hateful tyranny, they used to go to the meeting-place wearing all-purple robes, no fewer than a thousand for the most part, proud and rejoicing in their luxuriant hair, drenched with the scent of sumptuous unguents." A similar gibe may underlie a scene on an Attic black-figure oinochoe, signed by Xenocles the potter and Cleisiphus the painter and dated ca. 520, on which symposiasts are represented wearing oriental items of apparel such as a Lydian turban, loose boots and a loincloth.[8]

One might be tempted to think that it is here, among supposedly "middling" poets (Morris 2000: 155–91), that the "authentic Greek culture" of the Archaic period is to be found, but the issue is not so simple. Some of the elegiac poets may seem to adopt an anti-aristocratic stance, but most scholars are agreed that their poetry was disseminated by means of that thoroughly aristocratic institution, the symposium. Perhaps we come closest to the perspective of the average Greek Joe in the representation of daily life that the Hesiodic persona (if not the poet himself) proffers in the *Works and Days*, but what is striking in this poem is how narrow, parochial and introspective the regular farmer's horizons are. Evidence for a conscious reflection on the symbols that constituted a uniquely and universally "Greek" culture in the Archaic period continues to remain elusive.

Enter the Barbarian

The creation of a barbarian antitype that facilitated the process of Greek self-definition is largely a phenomenon of the period after the Persian War and therefore lies, strictly speaking, outside the limits of this volume. Nevertheless, it is worth briefly "looking ahead" since in doing so, the contours of Greek ethnic and cultural identity during the Archaic period will emerge in sharper relief.

It is generally argued that the word *barbaros* is onomatopoeic, deriving from the seemingly incomprehensible babblings of non-Greek speakers, and that this indicates that the primary criterion in Greek self-definition was therefore linguistic (e.g. Hall 1989: 4). Indeed, Strabo (14.2.28) says as much. Yet, the linguistic tests for determining onomatopoea are as scientifically imprecise as they are for the false etymologies that ancient authors – Strabo included – were so fond of providing. The first (and only) time that the term appears in the Homeric epics, it is as part of a compound adjective used to describe the Carians – *barbarophonoi*, meaning "barbarian with regard to speech" – and the fact that the poet has to specify the precise aspect in which the Carians are barbarians should cause us to hesitate before assuming a primarily linguistic connotation. The word does not appear again in extant literature until the later sixth century, when Anacreon's invocation to Zeus to "silence the solecian speech lest you utter barbarisms" (fr. 423 Page) does appear to indicate a linguistic usage, but this is not necessarily true of Heraclitus' maxim that "men's eyes and ears are poor witnesses if they have barbarian souls" (fr. 107 D–K) or of Hecataeus' belief that Greece was originally inhabited by barbarians (*FGrH* 1 F 119). It has been suggested that *barbaros* may, in fact, be a loan-word from a Sumerian term that simply meant "strange" or "foreign" (Weidner 1913). It is worth remembering that what we term the Greek language was, in reality, a collection of myriad local dialects – not all of which were mutually intelligible[9] – and that there is no strong evidence for an awareness of a common, albeit abstract, Greek language until the fifth century (e.g. Hdt 2.154.2).

In contrast to its scarcity during the Archaic period, the word *barbaros* is attested with increasing frequency in the decades immediately after the expulsion of the Persian forces from Greece. In Aeschylus' *Persians*, performed in 472, the term appears no fewer than 10 times while there are as many as 103 occurrences of *barbaros* or its cognates in the extant plays of Euripides. In both tragedy and comedy, the figure of the barbarian is represented as foolish, cowardly and cruel, lacking justice and intelligence – in short, as embodying the precise opposite of all the virtues that the Greeks claimed for themselves.[10] On red-figure vases, depictions of Persians, Phrygians, and Thracians become ever more common, identified by specific items of dress, such as caps, cloaks, and boots (DeVries 2000). This is also the period in which the Trojans, who had previously been represented with little in the way of ethnic stereotyping, became thoroughly easternized and were assimilated – in Athenian thought, at least – with the Phrygians (Erskine 2001).

The invention of a barbarian "other," against which the Greeks could define themselves, represented an effective response to some of the limitations that were inherent in the formerly "aggregative" construction of Greek identity through genealogical kinship. As we have seen, such genealogical conceptions could never be truly inclusive since they were incapable of accommodating the ethnic eponyms of all the groups that resided in Greece. The Greeks cannot have been unaware of the irony that the Arcadians of Tegea, who played a crucial role in defeating the Persians at the Battle of Plataea (Hdt 9.71), were unable to trace their ancestry back to Hellen. On the other hand, genealogical definitions of Greekness were not exclusive either. According to Herodotus (7.150.2), there was a rumor that the Argives had remained neutral during the war because of an embassy sent by Xerxes shortly before its outbreak: the Persian heralds had argued that bonds of kinship existed between themselves and the Argives because their ethnic eponym, Perses, had been the son of the Argolic hero Perseus. While there is no question here of the Persians attempting to be incorporated within the lineage of Hellen himself, the episode demonstrates how flexible, and ultimately incapable of being policed, genealogical traditions could be. By focusing on opposition and difference, rather than confraternity and similarity, a new, more inclusive definition of the Hellenic community arose. At the same time, however, "blood-lines" were hardly a very visible criterion of differentiation: language, cultic observances and, above all, cultural practices provided far more concrete mechanisms for constructing a boundary between Hellenism and barbarism.

The vast majority of our evidence comes, of course, from Athens but there are some reasons for believing that Athens played a major role both in the invention of the barbarian and in the substitution of cultural for ethnic criteria in Greek self-definition. Xerxes' invasion had been particularly traumatic for the Athenians: unlike their Peloponnesian allies to the south, the Athenians had voluntarily abandoned their city and watched it being sacked by the Persian occupiers and there are some grounds for believing that a greater percentage of the Athenian citizen-body was involved in direct confrontation with the Persian invaders than was the case with most other cities. The creation and perpetuation of a barbarian antitype also served two other purposes that were very much to Athens' advantage. The first was the *kudos* that the

Athenians derived from their virtually sole stand against the Persians at Marathon in 490 and their critical contribution at the Battle of Salamis, ten years later, which signaled a major shift in the fortunes of the Persians.[11] More than two generations later, the Spartans could appeal to the heroic service shown by the Athenians during the Persian invasion and employ it as a pretext for not meting out the savage treatment to the city that the Corinthians and Thebans were demanding (Xen. *Hell.* 2.2.19–20). The second was the need to portray the barbarian as a constant and eternal menace in order to justify the continued existence of the hegemonic league that the Athenians led and from which they derived much of their prosperity during the fifth century (Hall 1989: 62). But part of the explanation also lies in political developments at Athens itself.

I have argued that while it was probably the elites who frequented Olympia that were responsible for fostering a Greek ethnic consciousness, exclusion from this aggregatively-constructed and genealogically-imagined Greek family was not based on considerations of class. Instead, the elites expressed their distinctiveness through the employment of cultural symbols linked to a prestige goods economy: to be a member of the ruling classes was to participate in a symbolic universe that did not terminate at ethnic or cultural boundaries. Over the span of five decades, from the popular uprising against Spartan occupation in 508, which triggered the institutional reforms of Cleisthenes, to the attacks of Ephialtes on the last bastion of aristocratic rule, the Areopagus, in 462/1, the Athenian masses seized the government of their state. A growing realization among the poorer, rowing classes that the defense of the city would henceforth rest on their shoulders almost certainly contributed to this process (Ceccarelli 1993). The shift in the balance of power was not sudden but it was revolutionary, as shown by the slogan that was adopted – *démokratia*, or "power of the *démos*." In the literature of the Archaic period, *démos* is the word that often describes the non-aristocratic population of a city (Donlan 1970): the victory of the *démos* could only be achieved at the expense of the Athenian elite and it was in the cultural sphere that their behavior might now be viewed as transgressive and inconsistent not only with Athenian, but also with Greek, standards and norms.

One of the first symptoms of this assault on aristocratic behavior is witnessed in the ostracisms dating to the decade after Marathon, which imposed a ten-year exile without loss of property rights on one individual, subject to a quorum, each year (Siewert 2001). Particularly interesting are some of the "votes" cast for one Callias, son of Cratias, from the deme of Alopece, who was probably ostracized in 485. Four of these actually describe him as a "Mede" – the ethnonym the Greeks normally used of the Persians – and one even graphically depicts him in Persian costume. At a specific level, these ostraka accuse Callias of treason and collaboration with the enemy, but at a more general level they are an attack on the entire aristocratic way of life, characterized by intermarriage, guest-friendship and the adoption of easternizing customs and practices. With Pericles' citizenship law of 451, by which Athenian citizenship was restricted to those whose parents were both Athenian, the attempt to curb the aristocratic practice of intermarriage was complete. Those practices that had hitherto been emblematic of a transregional elite, conversant in symbolic codes that transcended local communities, had now successfully been marginalized (see Miller

1997). The fact that it was in the cultural sphere that such elite, orientalizing transgressions could most easily be scrutinized ensured that from now on culture would serve as the most distinctive boundary marker between Hellenism and barbarism.

It is probably the case that there is a natural limit to the growth of the ethnic community (Connor 1994: 202). That is to say, there is a stage beyond which even an imagined kinship community becomes unimaginable. It was precisely at the moment when a new, "oppositional" construction of Greek identity became a feasible option for those who had formerly been excluded on genealogical grounds that the very ethnic basis of Greek identity collapsed and gave way to newly universalized cultural criteria that had previously constituted a monopoly of the elites. But the promotion of cultural criteria in Greek self-definition was to have a momentous historical impact, spreading Greek ideas and practices throughout the territories conquered by Alexander the Great and eventually permitting far-flung populations – regardless of genealogical origins – to participate in a Hellenism that would long survive, in Christianized form, the collapse of the Roman empire.

NOTES

1 Malkin 1986; Lomas 1993: 11, 32.
2 E.g. Hes. *W&D* 526–8; fr. 130 M–W; Archil. fr. 102 West.
3 Hdt 2.178.2–3; cf. Möller 2000: 105–8.
4 West 1985: 168–71; Fowler 1998: 1.
5 Hecataeus *FGrH* 1 F 16; Paus. 5.1.4; 9.1.1; Steph. Byz. s.v. *Malos.*
6 E.g. Arnold 1978; DeCorse 1989.
7 Burkert 1992: 88–117; West 1997.
8 DeVries 2000 with Cohen 2001.
9 Thuc. 3.94.5; Pl. *Prt.* 341c.
10 Hall 1989; Georges 1994.
11 Podlecki 1966: 8–26; Picard 1980: 117–22; Miller 1997: 6, 31–2.

Bibliography

ABBREVIATIONS

For technical reasons, all modern Greek titles have had to be transliterated; the transliteration is phonetic, with the exception of diphthongs which for the sake of clarity have been represented as such, rather than converted into single vowels.

A&A	*Antike und Abendland*
AA	*Archäologischer Anzeiger*
AAA	*Arkhaioloyika Analekta ex Athenon*
AArch	*Acta Archaeologica*
ABSA	*Annual of the British School in Athens*
AD	*Arkhaiologikon Deltion*
AEMTH	*Arkhaioloyiko ergo stin Makedonia kai Thraki*
AEph	*Arkhaioloyiki Efimeris*
AETHSE	*Acts of the Archaeological Meeting of Thessaly and Central Greece*
AFO	*Archiv für Orientforschung*
AION (archeol.)	*Annali dell'Istituto Universitario Orientale di Napoli, Dipartimento di Studi del mondo classico e del Mediterraneo antico, Sezione di archeologia e storia antica*
AJA	*American Journal of Archaeology*
AK	*Antike Kunst*
AM	*Archäologische Mitteilungen (= MDAI)*
Annales(ESC)	*Annales (Économies, Sociétés, Civilisations)*
AR	*Archaeological Reports*
ASAA	*Annuario della Scuola Archeologica di Atene e delle Missioni Italiane in Oriente*
ASNP	*Annali della Scuola Normale Superiore di Pisa, Classe di Lettere e Filosofia*
AWE	*Ancient West and East*

BASOR	*Bulletin of the American Schools of Oriental Research*
BCH	*Bulletin de correspondance hellénique*
BICS	*Bulletin of the Institute of Classical Studies of the University of London*
C&M	*Classica et Medaevalia*
CAH	*Cambridge Ancient History*, 2nd edn. Cambridge 1970–
CAJ	*Cambridge Archaeological Journal*
ChrEg	*Chronique d'Egypte*
ClAnt	*Classical Antiquity*
CPh	*Classical Philology*
CQ	*Classical Quarterly*
CRAI	*Comptes rendus de l'Académie des Inscriptions et Belles-Lettres*
CW	*Classical World*
DdA	*Dialoghi di archeologia*
DHA	*Dialogues d'histoire ancienne*
DNP	*Der Neue Pauly*
FGrH	*Die Fragmente der griechischen Historiker* (ed. F. Jacoby)
GeogrAnt	*Geographia Antiqua*
GFA	*Göttinger Forum für Altertumswissenschaft*
G&R	*Greece and Rome*
GRBS	*Greek, Roman and Byzantine Studies*
IA	*Iranica Antiqua*
IG	*Inscriptiones Graecae*
JDAI	*Jahrbuch des Deutschen Archäologischen Instituts*
JHS	*Journal of Hellenic Studies*
JMA	*Journal of Mediterranean Archaeology*
JÖAI	*Jahreshefte des Österreichischen Archäologischen Instituts*
JRA	*Journal of Roman Archaeology*
JRS	*Journal of Roman Studies*
MDAI(A) (R) (Ist.)	*Mitteilungen des Deutschen Archäologischen Instituts, Athenische Römische Abteilung, Abteilung Istambul*
MedArch	*Mediterranean Archaeology*
OCD	*Oxford Classical Dictionary*, 3rd edn. Oxford 1996
OJA	*Oxford Journal of Archaeology*
PAAH	*Praktika tis en Athinais Arkhaioloyikis Etaireias*
PCPhS	*Proceedings of the Cambridge Philological Society*
PP	*La Parola del Passato*
REA	*Revue des études anciennes*
REG	*Revue des études greques*
RFIC	*Rivista di filologia e di istruzione classica*
SO	*Symbolae Osloenses*
TAPhA	*Transactions of the American Philological Association*
ThesCRA	*Thesaurus Cultus et Rituum Antiquorum*
VDI	*Vestnik Drevnei Istorii*
WS	*Wiener Studien*
ZA	*Zeitschrift für Assyriologie*
ZPE	*Zeitschrift für Papyrologie und Epigraphik*
ZRG	*Zeitschrift der Savigny-Stiftung für Rechtsgeschichte, Romanistische Abteilung*

Abrams, P. 1978. "Towns and Economic Growth: Some Theories and Problems." In Abrams and E. A. Wrigley (eds.), *Towns in Societies: Essays in Economic History and Historical Sociology*, 9–33. Cambridge.

Abulafia, D. (ed.). 2003. *The Mediterranean in History*. London.

Abulafia, D. 2005. "Mediterraneans." In Harris 2005: 61–93.

Adam, S. 1966. *The Technique of Greek Sculpture in the Archaic and Classical Periods*. London.

Adamesteanu, D. 1974. *La Basilicata antica: storia e monumenti*. Cava dei Tirreni.

Adams, L. 1978. *Orientalizing Sculpture in Soft Limestone from Crete and Mainland Greece*. Oxford.

Adkins, A. W. H. 1960. *Merit and Responsibility: A Study in Greek Values*. Oxford.

Adorno, T. 1981. *Prisms*. Tr. S. and S. Weber. Cambridge, MA.

Adrymi-Sismani, V. 2006. "The Palace of Iolkos and Its End." In Deger-Jalkotzy and Lemos 2006: 465–81.

Agelarakis, A. P. 1999. "Reflections of the Human Condition in Prehistoric Thasos: Aspects of the Anthropological and Palaeopathological Record from the Settlement of Kastri." In *THASOS: Matières premières et technologie de la préhistoire à nos jours*, 447–57. Paris.

Agostiniani, L. 1988–89. "I modi del contatto linguistico tra Greci e indigeni nella Sicilia antica." *Kokalos* 34–5: 167–206.

Agrigento 1988. *Veder Greco – Le necropoli di Agrigento*. Rome.

Akurgal, E. 1983. *Alt-Smyrna*, I: *Wohnschichten und Athenatempel*. Ankara.

Akurgal, E. 1987. *Griechische und römische Kunst in der Türkei*. Munich.

Akurgal, M. 1998. "Bayrakli kazısı 1997." *Kazı Sonuçları Toplantısı* 20–2: 33–47.

Albanese Procelli, A. M. 2003. *Sicani, Siculi, Elimi*. Milan.

Alcock, S. E. 1999. "The Pseudo-history of Messenia Unplugged." *TAPhA* 129: 333–41.

Alcock, S. E. 2002a. *Archaeologies of the Greek Past: Landscape, Monuments, and Memory*. Cambridge.

Alcock, S. E. 2002b. "A Simple Case of Exploitation?" In P. Cartledge, L. Foxhall, and E. Cohen (eds.), *Money, Labour and Land: Approaches to the Economies of Ancient Greece*, 185–99. London.

Alcock, S. E. and R. Osborne. (eds.). 1994. *Placing the Gods: Sanctuaries and Sacred Space in Ancient Greece*. Oxford.

Alcock, S. E. and J. Cherry. (eds.). 2004. *Side-by-side Survey: Comparative Regional Studies in the Mediterranean World*. Oxford.

Alekseev, A. Y. 2003. *Khronografiya Evropeiskoi Skifii VII–IV vekov do n.e.* St. Petersburg.

Alexiou, S. 1958. "I minoiki thea meths' ipsomenon kheiron." *Kritika Khronika* 12: 179–299.

Alexiou, S. 1972. "Anaskafi eis Ayian Pelayian Irakliou." *Arkheologika Analekta Ex Athinon* 5: 230–44.

Alexiou, S. 1984. "Une nouvelle inscription de Panormos-Apollonia en Crète." In Nicolet et al. 1984: 323–7.

Alfieri, N., P. E. Arias, and M. Hirmer. 1958. *Spina*. Florence and Munich.

Algra, K. 1999. "The Beginnings of Cosmology." In Long 1999: 45–65.

Almagra-Gorbea, M. 2001. "Cyprus, Phoenicia, and Iberia: From 'Precolonization' to 'Colonization' in the 'Far West'." In Bonfante and Karageorghis 2001: 239–70.

Almeida, J. A. 2003. *Justice as an Aspect of the Polis Idea in Solon's Political Poems: A Reading of the Sources in Light of the Researches of New Classical Archaeology*. Leiden.

Aloni, A. 2001. "The Proem of Simonides' Plataea Elegy and the Circumstances of Its Performance." In D. Boedeker and D. Sider (eds.), *The New Simonides: Contexts of Praise and Desire*, 86–105. Oxford.

Alonso, V. and K. Freitag. 2001. "Prolegomena zur Erforschung der Bedeutung der Eliteeinheiten im archaischen und klassischen Griechenland." *Gerión* 19: 199–219.

Alster, B. 1992. "Interaction of Oral and Written Poetry in Early Mesopotamian Literature." In Vogelzang and Vanstiphout 1992: 23–69.

Alster, B. 1995. "Epic Tales from Ancient Sumer: Enmerkar, Lugalbanda, and Other Cunning Heroes." In Sasson 1995: 2315–26.

Amadasi Guzzo, M. G. 1967. *Le iscrizioni fenicie e puniche delle colonie in occidente*. Rome.

Amadasi Guzzo, N. G. 1987. "Iscrizioni semitiche di nord-ovest in contesti greci e italici (X–VII sec. a.c.)." *DdA* 3rd ser. 5.2: 13–28.

Amadasi Guzzo, N. G. 1991. " 'The Shadow Line': Réflexions sur l'introduction de l'alphabet en Grèce." In C. Baurain, C. Bonnet, and C. Krings (eds.), *Phoinikeia Grammata: Lire et écrire en Méditerannée*, 293–311. Namur.

Amadasi Guzzo, N. G. and V. Karageorghis. 1977. *Kition*, III. Nicosia.

Amandry, P. 1987. "Trépieds de Delphes et du Péloponnèse." *BCH* 111: 79–131.

Ameling, W. 1993. *Karthago. Studien zu Militär, Staat und Gesellschaft*. Munich.

Ampolo, C. 1996. "Per una storia delle storie greche." In Settis 1996: 1015–88.

Ampolo, C. 1997. *Storie greche: La formazione della moderna storiografia sugli antichi Greci*. Turin.

Ancient Macedonia, V. 1993. Thessaloniki.

Anderson, G. 2000. "Alkmeonid 'Homelands,' Political Exile, and the Unification of Attica." *Historia* 49: 387–412.

Anderson, G. 2003. *The Athenian Experiment: Building an Imagined Political Community in Ancient Attica, 508–490 BC*. Ann Arbor.

Anderson, G. 2005. "Before *Turannoi* Were Tyrants: Rethinking a Chapter of Early Greek History." *ClAnt* 24: 173–222.

Anderson, G. 2006. "Why the Athenians Forgot Cleisthenes: Literacy and the Politics of Remembrance in Ancient Athens." In Craig Cooper (ed.), *The Politics of Orality*, 103–28. Leiden.

Anderson, J. K. 1970. *Military Theory and Practice in the Age of Xenophon*. Berkeley.

Andersen, Ø. and M. Dickie. (eds.). 1995. *Homer's World: Fiction, Tradition, Reality*. Bergen.

Anderson, P. 1976. *Conversations on Western Marxism*. London.

Anderson, P. 1980. *Arguments within English Marxism*. London.

Anderson, P. 1983. *In the Tracks of Historical Materialism*. London.

Anderson, P. 1984. *In the Tracks of Historical Materialism*. Chicago.

Andrea, Z. 1993. "Aspects des relations entre l'Albanie et la Macédoine avant l'Âge du Fer." In *Ancient Macedonia* V: 109–23.

Andreae, B. 1982. *Odysseus. Archäologie des europäischen Menschenbildes*. Frankfurt.

Andreae, B. and H. Flashar. 1977. "Strukturäquivalenzen zwischen den homerischen Epen und der frühgriechischen Vasenkunst." *Poetica* 9: 217–65.

Andrewes, A. 1954. *Probouleusis: Sparta's Contribution to the Technique of Government*. Oxford.

Andrewes, A. 1956. *The Greek Tyrants*. London.

Andrewes, A. 1982a. "The Growth of the Athenian State." *CAH*[2] III.3: 360–91.

Andrewes, A. 1982b. "The Tyranny of Pisistratus." *CAH*[2] 3.3: 392–416.

Andronikos, M. 1969. *Veryina: To nekrotafeion ton timvon*. Athens.

Andronikos, M. 1984. *Veryina: The Royal Tombs and the Ancient City*. Athens.

Anghel, S. 1999–2000. "*Euergetai* in the Greek Cities in the Black Sea." In *Il Mar Nero* IV: 89–115.

Antonaccio, C. M. 1995a. *An Archaeology of Ancestors: Tomb Cult and Hero Cult in Early Greece*. Lanham.

Antonaccio, C. M. 1995b. "Lefkandi and Homer." In Andersen and Dickie 1995: 5–27.

Antonaccio, C. M. 2000. "Architecture and Behaviour: Building Gender into Greek Houses." *CW* 93: 517–34.

Antonaccio, C. M. 2001. "Ethnicity and Colonization." In Malkin 2001: 113–57.

Antonaccio, C. M. 2003. "Hybridity and the Cultures within Greek Culture." In Dougherty and Kurke 2003: 57–74.

Antonaccio, C. M. 2007. "Elite Mobility in the West." In Hornblower and Morgan 2007: 265–85.

Antonetti, C. 1997. "Megara e le sue colonie: un'unità storico-culturale?" In Antonetti (ed.), *Il dinamismo della colonizzazione greca*, 83–94. Naples.

Arapogianni, X. 1999. "A Dedicatory Inscription from Prasidaki." *Horos* 13: 167–72 (in Greek).

Aravantinos, V. L., L. Godart, and A. Sacconi. 2001. *Thèbes: Fouilles de la Cadmée*, I: *Les tablettes en linéaire B de la Odos Pelopidou*. Pisa.

Archibald, Z. H. 1998. *The Odrysian Kingdom of Thrace: Orpheus Unmasked*. Oxford.

Archibald, Z. H. 2000. "Space, Hierarchy and Community in Archaic and Classical Macedonia, Thessaly and Thrace." In Brock and Hodkinson 2000: 212–33.

Arena, R. 1994. *Iscrizioni greche arcaiche di Sicilia e Magna Grecia*, III: *Iscrizioni delle colonie euboiche*. Pisa.

Arnason, J. and P. Murphy. (eds.). 2001. *Agon, Logos, Polis: The Greek Achievement and Its Aftermath*. Stuttgart.

Arnheim, M. T. W. 1977. *Aristocracy in Greek Society*. London.

Arnold, D. 1978. "Ceramic Variability, Environment and Culture History among the Pokom in the Valley of Guatemala." In I. Hodder (ed.), *The Spatial Organization of Culture*, 39–59. London.

Aro-Valjus, S. 1999. "Gūgu or Guggu." In Radner 1999: 427–28.

Arthur, M. B. 1973. "Early Greece: Origins of the Western Attitude towards Women." *Arethusa* 6: 7–58.

Artzy, M. 2000. "Routes, Trade, Boats and 'Nomads of the Sea'." In S. Gitin, A. Mazar, and E. Stern (eds.), *Mediterranean Peoples in Transition, Thirteenth to Early Tenth Centuries* BCE, 439–48. Jerusalem.

Asheri, D. 1966. *Distribuzioni di terre nell'antica Grecia*. Turin.

Asheri, D. 1988. *Erodoto: Le Storie, Libro I (Introduzione e Commento)*. Milan.

Asheri, D. 1996. "Colonizzazione e decolonizzazione." In S. Settis (ed.), *I Greci: Storia Cultura Arte Società*, I: *Noi e i Greci*, 73–115. Turin.

Athanassakis, A. N. 1983. *Hesiod*, Theogeny, Works and Days, Shield. *Translation, Introduction, Notes*. Baltimore.

Auberson, P. and K. Schefold. 1972. *Führer durch Eretria*. Bern.

Aubet, M. E. 1987. *Tiro y las colonias fenicias de Occidente*. Barcelona.

Aubet, M. E. 1993 (2001). *The Phoenicians and the West: Politics, Colonies and Trade*. Tr. Mary Turton of Aubet 1987. Cambridge.

Aubet Semmler, M. E. 2002. "The Phoenician Impact on Tartessos: Spheres of Interaction." In Bierling 2002: 225–40.

Auda, Y., L. Darmezin, J.-C. Decourt, B. Helly, and G. Lucas. 1990. "Espace géographique et géographie historique." In J.-L. Fiches and S.E. van der Leeuw (eds.), *Archéologie et espaces*, 87–126. Juan les Pins.

Ault, B. A. 2000. "Living in the Classical Polis: The Greek House as Microcosm." *CW* 93: 483–96.

Austin, N. 1994. *Helen of Troy and Her Shameless Phantom*. Ithaca, NY.

Avram, A., J. Hind, and G. Tsetskhladze. 2004. "The Black Sea Area." In Hansen and Nielsen 2004: 924–73.

Bäbler, B. 1998. *Fleißige Thrakerinnen und wehrhafte Skythen: Nichtgriechen im klassischen Athen und ihre archäologische Hinterlassenschaft*. Stuttgart.

Bachvarova, M. 2005. "The Eastern Mediterranean Epic Tradition from *Gilgamesh* and *Akka* to the *Song of Release* to Homer's *Iliad*." *GRBS* 45: 131–53.

Badian, E. 2000. "Back to Kleisthenic Chronology." In Flensted-Jensen et al. 2000: 447–64.

Bailo Modesti, G. and P. Gastaldi. 1999. *Prima di Pithecusa: I più antichi materiali greci del golfo di Salerno*. Naples.

Bakhuizen, S. C. 1985. *Studies in the Topography of Chalkis on Euboea*. Leiden.

Bakker, E. J., I. J. F. De Jong, and H. van Wees. (eds.). 2002. *Brill's Companion to Herodotus*. Leiden.

Balcer, J. M. 1984. *Sparda by the Bitter Sea*. Chico.

Balcer, J. M. 1985. "Fifth Century Ionia: A Frontier Redefined." *REA* 87: 31–42.

Balkas, A. (ed.). 1998. *Andros kai Khalkidiki*. Andros.

Balot, R. 2001. *Greed and Injustice in Classical Athens*. Princeton.

Balot, R. 2006. *Greek Political Thought*. Malden and Oxford.

Baltrusch, E. 1994. *Symmachie und Spondai: Untersuchungen zum griechischen Völkerrecht der archaischen und klassischen Zeit (8.-5. Jahrhundert v. Chr.)*. Berlin.

Bammer, A. 1998. "Sanctuaries in the Artemision of Ephesos." In Hägg 1998: 27–47.

Bammer, A. 2001. "Kosmologische Aspekte der Artemisionfunde." In U. Muss (ed.), *Der Kosmos der Artemis von Ephesos*, 11–26. Vienna.

Bammer, A. and U. Muss. 1996. *Das Artemision von Ephesos*. Mainz.

Bareş, L. 1999. *Abusir*, IV: *The Shaft Tomb of Udjahorresnet at Abusir*. Prague.

Barkworth, P. R. 1993. "The Organization of Xerxes' Army." *IA* 27: 149–67.

Barletta, B. 1990. "An 'Ionic Sea' Style in Archaic Doric Architecture." *AJA* 94: 45–72.

Barnes, J. 1979. *The Presocratic Philosophers*, I. London.

Barth, F. (ed.). 1969. *Ethnic Groups and Boundaries: The Social Organization of Culture Difference*. London.

Bartol, K. 1992. "Where was Iambic Poetry Performed? Some Evidence from the Fourth Century BC" *CQ* 42: 65–71.

Bartoloni, G. (ed.). 1982. *Enea nel Lazio: Archeologia e mito*. Rome.

Baslez, M.-F. 1986. "Présence et traditions iraniennes dans les cités de l'Egée." *REA* 87: 137–55.

Bats, M. and B. D'Agostino. (eds.). 1998. *Euboica: L'Eubea e la presenza Euboica in Calcidica e in Occidente*. Naples.

Baumer, L. 2004. *Kult im Kleinen. Ländliche Heiligtümer spätarchaischer bis hellenistischer Zeit*. Rahden.

Baumgarten, A. J. 1981. *The Phoenician History of Philo of Byblos: A Commentary*. Leiden.

Baumgarten, F., F. Poland, and R. Wagner. 1908 (1913). *Die hellenische Kultur*². Leipzig. 3rd edn. 1913.

Baurain, C. 1997. *Les Grecs et la Méditerranée orientale: Des siècles obscurs à la fin de l'époque archaïque*. Paris.

Bayer, K. and W. Huss. 1993. "Der Fahrtenbericht des Hanno"; "Das afrikanische Unternehmen des Hanno." In G. Winkler and R. König (eds., tr.), *C. Plinius Secundus d.Ä., Naturkunde, Buch V*. Munich and Darmstadt.

Beazley, J. D. 1956. *Attic Black-figure Vase-painters*. Oxford.

Beazley, J. D. 1963. *Attic Red-figure Vase-painters*. 2 vols. Oxford.

Beck, H. 1997. *Polis und Koinon. Untersuchungen zur Geschichte und Struktur der griechischen Bundesstaaten im 4. Jahrhundert v. Chr.* Stuttgart.

Beister, H. and J. Buckler. (eds.). 1989. *Boiotika.* Munich.

Bell, M. 1995. "The Motya Charioteer and Pindar's *Isthmian 2*." *Papers and Monographs of the American Academy in Rome* 40: 1–42.

Bellamy, R. 1988. "Bellerophon's Tablet." *Classical Journal* 84: 289–307.

Beloch, K. J. 1912. *Griechische Geschichte*, I.1: *Die Zeit vor den Perserkriegen*, 2nd revd. edn. Strassburg, Repr. with Nachtrag, Berlin and Leipzig, 1924.

Beloch, K. J. 1913. *Griechische Geschichte*, I.2: *Die Zeit vor den Perserkriegen*, 2nd revd. edn. Strassburg, Repr. with Nachtrag, Berlin and Leipzig, 1926.

Bengtson, H. 1950 (1960; 1965; 1969; 1977). *Griechische Geschichte von den Anfängen bis in die römische Kaiserzeit.* Munich; 2nd edn. 1960; 3rd edn. 1965; 4th edn. 1969; 5th edn. 1977.

Bengston, H. 1962. *Die Verträge der griechisch-römischen Welt von 700 bis 338 v. Chr.*, II. Munich.

Benzi, M. 2001. "LH IIIC Late Mycenaean Refugees at Punta Meliso, Apulia." In Karageorghis and Morris 2001: 233–40.

Bérard, C. 1970. *Eretria*, III: *L'Héröon à la Porte de l'Ouest.* Bern and Lausanne.

Bérard, C. et al. 1989. *A City of Images: Iconography and Society in Ancient Greece.* Tr. D. Lyons. Princeton.

Berent, M. 2000. "Anthropology and the Classics: War, Violence and the Stateless Society." *CQ* 50: 257–89.

Bergquist, B. 1992. "The Archaic Greek Temenos in Western Greece. A Survey and Two Inquiries." In A. Schachter (ed.), *Le Sanctuaire grec*, 109–52. Geneva.

Bernabé, A. 2004. "Hittites and Greeks: Mythical Influences and Methodological Considerations." In Rollinger and Ulf 2004b: 291–310.

Bernabò Brea, L. 1957. *Sicily before the Greeks.* Tr. C. M Preston and L. Guido. New York.

Bernal, M. 1987. *Black Athena: The Afroasiatic Roots of Classical Civilization.* London.

Bernal, M. 1990. *Cadmean Letters: The Westward Diffusion of the Semitic Alphabet before 1400 BC.* London.

Bernand, A. and O. Masson. 1957. "Les inscriptions grecques d'Abou-Simbel." *REG* 70: 1–46.

Bernardi, B. 1985. *Age Class Systems.* Cambridge.

Bernhardt, R. 2003. *Luxuskritik und Aufwandsbeschränkungen in der griechischen Welt.* Historia Einzelschriften 165. Stuttgart.

Berranger, D. 1992. *Recherches sur l'histoire et la prosopographie de Paros à l époque archaïque.* Clermont-Ferrand.

Bertelli, L. 2001. "Hecataeus: From Genealogy to Historiography." In Luraghi 2001c: 67–94.

Bertelli, L. 2004. "La Sparta di Aristotele: un ambiguo paradigma o la crisi di un modello?" *Rivista Storica dell'Antichita* 34: 9–71.

Berve, H. 1937. *Miltiades. Studien zur Geschichte des Mannes und seiner Zeit.* Berlin.

Berve, H. 1967. *Die Tyrannis bei den Griechen.* 2 vols. Munich.

Berve, H. and G. Gruben, with M. Hirmer. 1961. *Griechische Tempel und Heiligtümer.* Munich.

Beschi, L. 1998. "Arte e cultura di Lemno arcaica." *La parola del passato* 53: 48–76.

Beschi, L. 2004. "Ceramiche arcaiche di Lemno: Alcuni problemi." *ASAA* LXXXI ser. III, 3.1: 309–49.

Best, J. G. P. 1969. *Thracian Peltasts and Their Influence on Greek Warfare.* Amsterdam.

Beye, C. R. 1974. "Male and Female in the Homeric Poems." *Ramus* 3: 87–101.

Beyer, I. 1976. *Die Tempel von Dreros und Prinias A und die Chronologie der kretischen Kunst des 8. und 7. Jhs. v. Chr.* Freiburg.

Bianchi Bandinelli, R. 1978a. *Storia e civiltà dei Greci: Origini e sviluppo della città*. Il Medievo Greco. Milan.

Bianchi Bandinelli, R. 1978b. *Storia e civiltà dei Greci: Origini e sviluppo della città. L'arcaismo*. Milan.

Bichler, R. 1985. "Der Synchronismus von Himera und Salamis. Eine quellenkritische Studie zu Herodot." In E. Weber and G. Dobesch (eds.), *Römische Geschichte, Altertumskunde und Epigraphik*, 59–74. Vienna.

Bichler, R. 1996. "Wahrnehmung und Vorstellung fremder Kultur: Griechen und Orient in archaischer und frühklassischer Zeit." In M. Schuster (ed.), *Die Begegnung mit dem Fremden*, 51–74. Stuttgart and Leipzig.

Bichler, R. 2000. *Herodots Welt: Der Aufbau der Historie am Bild der fremden Länder und Völker, ihrer Zivilisation und ihrer Geschichte*. Berlin.

Bichler, R. 2004a. "Das chronologische Bild der 'Archaik' in der Historiographie der griechischen Klassik." In Rollinger and Ulf 2004b: 207–48.

Bichler, R. 2004b. "Ktesias 'korrigiert' Herodot. Zur literarischen Einschätzung der *Persika*." In Heftner and Tomaschitz 2004: 105–16.

Bichler, R. 2004c. "Some Observations on the Image of the Assyrian and Babylonian Kingdoms within the Greek Tradition." In Rollinger and Ulf 2004a: 499–518.

Bicknell, P. J. 1972. *Studies in Athenian Politics and Genealogy*. Stuttgart.

Bierling, M. (ed.). 2002. *The Phoenicians in Spain: An Archaeological Review of the Eighth to Sixth Centuries BCE*. Winona Lake.

Bietti Sestieri, A. M. (ed.). 1992. *La necropoli laziale di Osteria dell'Osa*. 3 vols. Rome.

Bietti Sestieri, A. M. 1997. "Italy in Europe in the Early Iron Age." *Proceedings of the Prehistoric Society* 63: 371–402.

Bilabel, F. 1920. *Die ionische Kolonisation*. Leipzig.

Binder, J. 1998. "The Early History of the Demeter and Kore Sanctuary at Eleusis." In Hägg 1998: 131–39.

Bintliff, J. 1999. "Pattern and Process in the City Landscapes of Boeotia from Geometric to Late Roman Times." In M. Brunet (ed.), *Territoires des cités grecques*, 15–33. Paris.

Bintliff, J. 2002. "Settlement Pattern Analysis and Demographic Modeling." In P. Attema, G.-J. Burgers, E. van Joolen, M. van Leusen, and B. Mater (eds.), *New Developments in Italian Landscape Archaeology*, 28–35. Oxford.

Bintliff, J. and A. M. Snodgrass. 1988. "Mediterranean Survey and the City." *Antiquity* 62: 57–71.

Bintliff, J. and A. M. Snodgrass. 1989. "From Polis to Chorion in South-west Boeotia." In Beister and Buckler 1989: 285–99.

Bintliff, J., P. Howard, and A. M. Snodgrass. 1999. "The Hidden Landscape of Prehistoric Greece." *JMA* 12: 139–68.

Bintliff, J., P. Howard, and A. M. Snodgrass (eds.). 2007. *Testing the Hinterland: The Work of the Boeotia Survey (1989–1991) in the Southern Approaches to the City of Thespiai*. Cambridge.

Biraschi, A. M. 2005. "Strabo and Homer: A Chapter in Cultural History." In Daniela Dueck, Hugh Lindsay, and Sarah Pothecary (eds.), *Strabo's Cultural Geography: The Making of a Kollossourgia*, 73–85. Cambridge.

Blackman, D. 2001. "Archaeology in Greece, 2000–2001." *AR* 47: 1–144.

Blaise, F. 1996. "Individualité d'un sens ou individu historique?" In F. Blaise et al. 1996: 255–62.

Blaise, F., P. Judet de la Combe, and P. Rousseau (eds.). 1996. *Le Métier du mythe: Lectures d'Hésiode.* Lille.

Blandin, B. 2005. "Espace des vivants, demeures des morts: Les pratiques funéraires d'Erétrie à l'époque géométrique." Diss. University of Lausanne.

Blanton, M., G. Feinman, S. Kowalewski, and P. Peregrine. 1996. "A Dual-processual Theory for the Evolution of Mesoamerican Civilization." *Current Anthropology* 37: 1–14.

Blavatskii, V. D. 1964. *Pantikapei.* Moscow.

Bleicken, J. 1985 (1988, 1991, 1994). *Die athenische Demokratie.* Paderborn. 2nd edn. 1988; 3rd edn. 1991; rev. and enlarged edn. 1994.

Bleicken, J. 1989. "Die Herausbildung der Alten Geschichte in Göttingen: von Heyne bis Busolt." In Classen 1989: 98–127.

Bleicken, J. (ed.). 1993. *Colloquium aus Anlass des 80. Geburtstages von Alfred Heuß.* Kallmünz.

Bleicken, J. 1995 (1998). "Wann began die athenische Demokratie?" *Historische Zeitschrift* 260: 337–64. Repr. in Bleicken, *Gesammelte Schriften*, I: 13–40 Stuttgart, 1998.

Blok, J. H. 2006. "Solon's Funerary Laws: Questions of Authenticity and Function." In Blok and Lardinois 2006: 197–247.

Blok, J. and A. Lardinois (eds.). 2006. *Solon of Athens: New Historical and Philological Approaches.* Leiden.

Blok, J. and P. Mason (eds.). 1987. *Sexual Asymmetry: Studies in Ancient Society.* Amsterdam.

Blome, P. 1982. *Die figürliche Bildwelt Kretas in der geometrischen und früharchaischen Periode.* Mainz.

Blomquist, J. 1979. *The Date and Origin of the Greek Version of Hanno's Periplus.* Lund.

Blumenthal, E. 1963. *Die altgriechische Siedlungskolonisation im Mittelmeerraum unter besonderer Berücksichtigung der Südküste Kleinasiens.* Tübingen.

Blümer, W. 2001. *Interpretationen archaischer Dichtung: Die mythologischen Partien der Erga Hesiods.* 2 vols. Münster.

Boardman, J. 1952. "Pottery from Eretria." *ABSA* 47: 1–48.

Boardman, J. 1957. "Early Euboean Pottery and History." *ABSA* 52: 1–29.

Boardman. J. 1959. "Chian and Early Ionic Architecture." *Antiquaries Journal* 39: 170–218.

Boardman, J. 1961. *The Cretan Collection in Oxford: The Dictaean Cave and Iron Age Crete.* Oxford.

Boardman, J. 1963. "Artemis Orthia and Chronology." *ABSA* 58: 1–7.

Boardman, J. 1964 (1980/1999). *The Greeks Overseas: Their Early Colonies and Trade.* London. 3rd edn. 1980; 4th edn. 1999.

Boardman, J. 1967a. *Excavations in Chios, 1952–1955: Greek Emporio. ABSA* suppl. 6. London.

Boardman, J. 1967b. "The Khaniale Tekke Tombs II." *ABSA* 62: 57–75.

Boardman, J. 1968. *Archaic Greek Gems: Schools and Artists in the Sixth and Early Fifth Centuries* BC. Evanston.

Boardman, J. 1970 (2001). *Greek Gems and Finger Rings: Early Bronze Age to Late Classical.* London. 2nd edn. 2001.

Boardman, J. 1974. *Athenian Black Figure Vases: A Handbook.* London.

Boardman, J. 1979. *Athenian Red Figure Vases: The Archaic Period.* London.

Boardman, J. 1983. "Symbol and Story in Greek Geometric Art." In W. Moon (ed.), *Ancient Greek Art and Iconography,* 15–36. Madison.

Boardman, J. 1990. "Al Mina and History." *OJA* 9: 169–90.

Boardman, J. 1991. *Greek Sculpture: The Archaic Period.* London.

Boardman, J. 1994. *The Diffusion of Classical Art in Antiquity.* London.

Boardman, J. 2000. *Persia and the West: An Archaeological Investigation of the Genesis of Achaemenid Persian Art.* London.

Boardman, J. and J. Hayes. 1966. *Excavations at Tocra 1963–65: The Archaic Deposits,* I. London.

Boardman, J. and J. Hayes. 1973. *Excavations at Tocra 1963–65: The Archaic Deposits,* II. London.

Boardman, J. and F. Schweizer. 1977. "Clay Analyses of Archaic Greek Pottery." *ABSA* 68: 267–83.

Boardman, J. and C. E. Vaphopoulou-Richardson (eds.). 1986. *Chios: A Conference at the Homereion in Chios 1984.* Oxford.

Boedeker, D. 2002. "Epic Heritage and Mythical Patterns in Herodotus." In Bakker et al. 2002: 97–116.

Boedeker, D. and K. Raaflaub (eds.). 1998. *Democracy, Empire, and the Arts in Fifth-Century Athens.* Cambridge, Mass.

Boedeker, D. and D. Sider. 2001. *The New Simonides: Contexts of Praise and Desire.* Oxford.

Boegehold, A. 1962. "The Nessos Amphora: A Note on the Inscription." *AJA* 66: 405–6.

Boehringer, D. 2001. *Heroenkulte in Griechenland von der geometrischen bis zur klassischen Zeit: Attika, Argolis, Messenien.* Berlin.

Bol, C. 1974. "Die Giebelskulpturen des Schatzhauses von Megara." *AM* 89: 64–75.

Bolmarcich, S. 2005. "Thucydides 1.19.1 and the Peloponnesian League." *GRBS* 45: 5–34.

Bommeljé, S., P. Doorn, M. Deylius, J. Vroom, Y. Bommeljé, R. Fagel, and H. van Wijngaarden. 1987. *Aetolia and the Aetolians: Towards the Interdisciplinary Study of a Greek Region.* Utrecht.

Bonetto, J., and I. Oggiano. 2004. "Reise nach Westen. Die Koloniestadt Nora auf Sardinien ist eindrucksvolle Zeugin des phönizischen Kulturtransfers." *Antike Welt* 35: 29–35.

Bonfante, L. 1989. "Nudity as a Costume in Classical Art." *AJA* 93: 543–70.

Bonfante, L. and V. Karageorghis (eds.). 2001. *Italy and Cyprus in Antiquity: 1500–450 BC.* Nicosia.

Bonias, Z. 1998. *Ena ayrotiko iero stis Aiyies Lakonias.* Athens.

Bonnet, C. 1988. *Melqart: Cultes et mythes de l'Héraclès tyrien en Méditerranée.* Namur.

Bookidis, N. 1990. "Ritual Dining in the Sanctuary of Demeter and Kore at Corinth: Some Questions." In Murray 1990b: 86–94.

Bookidis, N. 1993. "Ritual Dining at Corinth." In Marinatos and Hägg 1993: 45–61.

Bookidis, N. 2003. "The Sanctuaries of Corinth." In C. K. Williams and N. Bookidis (eds.), *Corinth,* XX: *Corinth, the Centenary, 1896–1996,* 247–59. Princeton.

Borgeaud, P. 1988. *The Cult of Pan in Ancient Greece.* Chicago and London.

Borza, E. 1990. *In the Shadow of Olympus: The Emergence of Macedon.* Princeton.

Bosanquet, R. C. 1905. "Excavations at Palaikastro IV: The Temple of Dictaean Zeus." *ABSA* 11: 298–308.

Bosanquet, R. C. 1939–40. "Dicte and the Temples of Dictaean Zeus." *ABSA* 40: 60–77.

Bosch Gimpera, P. 1976. "Cronologia e historia de Emporion." *Revista de la Universidad Complutense de Madrid* 35: 37–57.

Boss, *see* Boß

Boß, M. 2000. *Lakonische Votivgaben aus Blei.* Würzburg.

Bourriot, F. 1976. *Recherches sur la nature du génos: Étude d'histoire sociale athénienne, périodes archaïque et classique.* 2 vols. Lille.

Bouzek, J. 1997. *Greece, Anatolia and Europe: Cultural Interactions during the Early Iron Age.* Jonsered.

Bouzek, J. 2000–1. "The First Thracian Urban and Rural Dwellings and Stonecutting Techniques." In Tsetskhladze and de Boer 2000–1: 243–52.

Bouzek, J., M. Domaradzki, and Z. H. Archibald (eds.). 1996. *Pistiros*, I: *Excavations and Studies.* Prague.

Bowden, H. 1993. "Hoplites and Homer: Warfare, Hero Cult, and the Ideology of the Polis." In Rich and Shipley 1993: 45–63.

Bowden, H. 1996. "The Greek Settlement and Sanctuaries at Naukratis: Herodotus and Archaeology." In Hansen and Raaflaub 1996: 17–37.

Bowersock, G. 2005. "The East–West Orientation of Mediterranean Studies and the Meaning of North and South in Antiquity." In W. Harris (ed.), *Rethinking the Mediterranean*, 167–78. Oxford.

Bowie, E. L. 2001. "Ancestors of Historiography in Early Greek Elegiac and Iambic Poetry?" In Luraghi 2001c: 45–66.

Bowra, C. M. 1961. *Greek Lyric Poetry: From Alcman to Simonides.*[2] Oxford.

Boyd, T. D. and M. H. Jameson. 1981. "Urban and Rural Land Division in Ancient Greece." *Hesperia* 50: 327–42.

Bradley, R. 1999. *Paleoclimatology.*[2] New York.

Brann, E. 1961. "Protoattic Well Groups from the Athenian Agora." *Hesperia* 30: 305–79.

Braudel, F. 1972. *The Mediterranean and the Mediterranean World in the Age of Philip II.* Tr. S. Reynolds. 2 vols. Glasgow.

Braudel, F. 2001. *Memory and the Mediterranean.* New York.

Braund, D. (ed.). 2005. *Scythians and Greeks: Cultural Interactions in Scythia, Athens, and the Early Roman Empire (Sixth Century BC–First Century AD).* Exeter.

Braund, D. and J. Wilkins (eds.). 2000. *Athenaeus and His World.* Exeter.

Bravo, B. 1977. "Remarques sur les assises socials, les formes d'organisation et la terminologie du commerce maritime grec – l'époque archaïque." *DHA* 3: 1–59.

Bravo, B. 1980. "Sylān: Représailles et justice privée contre les étrangers dans les cités grecques." *ASNP* 10: 673–987.

Bravo, B. 1983. "Le Commerce des céréales chez les Grecs de l'époque archaïque." In Garnsey and Whittaker 1983: 17–29.

Bravo, B. and A. S. Chankowski. 1999. "Cités et emporia dans le commerce avec les barbares à la lumière du document dit à tort 'inscription de Pistiros'." *BCH* 123: 275–317.

Brea, B. 1957. *Sicily before the Greeks.* New York.

Bredow, I. von. 1997. "Das Emporion Pistiros in Thrakien." *Orbis Terrarum* 3: 109–20.

Bremmer, J. 1980. "An Enigmatic Indo-European Rite: Pederasty." *Arethusa* 13: 279–98.

Bremmer, J. 1990. "Adolescents, *Symposion* and Pederasty." In Murray 1990b: 135–48.

Bresson, A. 2000. *La cité marchande.* Bordeaux.

Briant, P. 1997. "Bulletin d'histoire achéménide I." In *Recherches récentes sur l'Empire achéménide. Topoi* suppl. 1: 5–127.

Briant, P. 2002a. *From Cyrus to Alexander: A History of the Persian Empire.* Tr. P. T. Daniels. Winona Lake. Orig. French edn. Paris, 1996.

Briant, P. 2002b. "History and Ideology: The Greeks and 'Persian Decadence'." In T. Harrison (ed.), *Greeks and Barbarians*, 189–210. Edinburgh.

Briant, P. 2003. "Histoire et archéologie d'un texte: La Lettre de Darius à Gadatas entre Perses, Grecs et Romains." In Giorgieri et al. 2003: 107–44.

Briant, P. and R. Descat. 1998. "Un registre douanier de la satrapie d'Égypte à l'époque achéménide (*TAD* C3, 7)." In N. Grimal and B. Menu (eds.), *Le commerce en Égypte ancienne*, 59–104. Cairo.

Bringmann, K. 1975 (1986a). "Die grosse Rhetra und die Entstehung des spartanischen Kosmos." *Historia* 34: 513–38. Repr. in Christ 1986: 351–86.

Bringmann, K. 1980 (1986b). "Die soziale und politische Verfassung Spartas – ein Sonderfall der griechischen Verfassungsgeschichte?" *Gymnasium* 87: 465–84. Repr. in Christ 1986: 448–67, with "Nachtrag," 468–69.

Brize, P. 1980. *Geryoneis des Stesichoros und die frühe griechische Kunst*. Würzburg.

Brize, P. 1997. "Offrandes de l'époque géométrique et archaïque à l'Héraion de Samos." In J. de la Genière (ed.), *Héra, images, espaces, cultes*, 123–39. Naples.

Brock, J. K. 1957. *Fortetsa: Early Greek Tombs Near Knossos*. Cambridge.

Brock, J. K. and G. Mackworth Young. 1949. "Excavations in Siphnos." *ABSA* 44: 1–92.

Brock, R. and S. Hodkinson (eds.). 2000. *Alternatives to Athens: Varieties of Political Organization and Community in Ancient Greece*. Oxford.

Brodersen, K. 1991. "Heiliger Krieg und Heiliger Friede in der frühen griechischen Geschichte." *Gymnasium* 98: 1–14.

Broneer, O. 1938. "Excavations on the North Slope of the Acropolis, 1937." *Hesperia* 7: 161–263.

Brown, A. S. 1997. "Aphrodite and the Pandora Complex." *CQ* 47: 26–47.

Brown, N. O. 1953. *Hesiod:* Theogony. Indianapolis.

Brulé, P. and C. Vendries (eds.). 2001. *Chanter les dieux: Musique et religion dans l'Antiquité grecque et romaine*. Rennes.

Brunet, M. (ed.). 1999. *Territoires des cités grecques*. BCH suppl. 34. Paris.

Bryce, T. 1998. *The Kingdom of the Hittites*. Oxford.

Bücher, K. 1893. *Die Entstehung der Volkswirtschaft*. Tübingen.

Buchner, G. 1978. "Testimonianze epigrafiche semitiche dell'VIII sec a. C. a Pithekoussai." *PP* 33: 130–42.

Buchner, G. and D. Ridgway. 1993. *Pithekoussai*, I. Rome.

Buck, R. J. 1979. *A History of Boeotia*. Edmonton.

Budd, P., A. M. Pollard et al. 1995. "Lead Isotope Analysis and Oxhide Ingots: A Final Comment." *JMA* 8: 70–5.

Bunbury, E. H. 1883. *A History of Ancient Geography among the Greeks and Romans from the Earliest Ages till the Fall of the Roman Empire*. London.

Burckhardt, J. 1898–1902 (1956). *Griechische Kulturgeschichte*. Ed. J. Oeri. 4 vols. Berlin and Stuttgart. Repr. Basel, 1956.

Burckhardt, J. 1958. *Griechische Kultur*. Berlin.

Burckhardt, J. 1963 (2002). *History of Greek Culture*. Tr. P. Hilty. New York. Repr. Mineola, 2002.

Burckhardt, J. 1998. *The Greeks and Greek Civilization*. Ed. O. Murray. Tr. S. Stern. London.

Burford, A. 1972. *Craftsmen in Greek and Roman Society*. London.

Burford, A. 1993. *Land and Labor in the Greek World*. Baltimore.

Burgers, G.-J. 1998. *Constructing Messapian Landscapes*. Amsterdam.

Burgess, J. S. 2001. *The Tradition of the Trojan War in Homer and the Epic Cycle*. Baltimore.

Burkert, W. 1972. *Lore and Science in Ancient Pythagoreanism*. Tr. E. L. Minar. Cambridge.

Burkert, W. 1976. "Das hunderttorige Theben und die Datierung der Ilias." *WS* N.F. 10: 5–21.

Burkert, W. 1985a. "Das Ende des Kroisos: Vorstufen einer herodoteischen Geschichtserzählung." In C. Schäublin (ed.), *Catalepton*, 4–15. Basel.

Burkert, W. 1985b. *Greek Religion*. Tr. J. Raffan. Oxford.

Burkert, W. 1988. "The Meaning and Function of the Temple in Classical Greece." In M. V. Fox (ed.), *Temple in Society*, 27–47. Winona Lake.

Burkert, W. 1991. "Homerstudien und Orient." In Latacz 1991: 155–81.

Burkert, W. 1992. *The Orientalising Revolution: Near Eastern Influence on Greek Culture in the Early Archaic Age*. Tr. M. E. Pinder and W. Burkert. Cambridge, Mass.

Burkert, W. 1995. "Greek *Poleis* and Civic Cults: Some Further Thoughts." In Hansen and Raaflaub 1995: 201–9.

Burkert, W. 1996. "Greek Temple-builders: Who, Where and Why?" In Hägg 1996: 21–9.

Burkert, W. 1997. "From Epiphany to Cult Statue." In A. B. Lloyd (ed.), *What Is a God? Studies in the Nature of Greek Divinity*, 15–34. London and Swansea.

Burkert, W. 2001 (1985). "The Making of Homer in the Sixth Century BC: Rhapsodes versus Stesichorus." In D. von Bothmer (ed.), *Papers on the Amasis Painter and his World*, 43–62. Maliby 1985. Repr. in Cairns 2001c: 92–116. Revd. and corrected repr. 1978.

Burkert, W. 2002. *Babylon–Memphis–Persepolis: Eastern Contexts of Greek Culture*. Cambridge, Mass.

Burkert, W. 2003. *Die Griechen und der Orient*. Munich.

Burn, A. R. 1960. *The Lyric Age of Greece*. London.

Burn, A. R. 1965. *A Traveller's History of Greece*. London.

Burnett, A. P. 1983. *Three Archaic Poets: Archilochus, Alcaeus, Sappho*. Cambridge, Mass.

Burnyeat, M. 1997. "Culture and Society in Plato's Republic." *The Tanner Lectures on Human Values* 20: 216–324.

Burr, D. 1933. "A Geometric House and a Proto-Attic Votive Deposit." *Hesperia* 2: 542–640.

Burstein, S. M. 1999. "*IG* I³ 61 and the Black Sea Grain Trade." In Mellor and Tritle 1999: 93–104.

Bury, J. B. 1900 (1913, 1957, 1975, 1978). *A History of Greece to the Death of Alexander the Great*. London; 2nd edn. 1913; 3rd edn., ed. R. Meiggs, 1951; 4th edn. 1975; revd. and corrected repr. 1978.

Buschor, E. 1913. *Griechische Vasenmalerei*. Munich.

Busolt, G. 1885–1904 (1967). *Griechische Geschichte bis zur Schlacht von Chaironeia*. 4 vols. Gotha. Repr. Hildesheim, 1967.

Busolt, G. and H. Swoboda. 1926. *Griechische Staatskunde*, II. Munich.

Cabrera Bonet, P. 1996. "Emporion y el comercio griego arcaico en el nordeste de la Península Ibérica." In R. Olmos and P. Rouillard (eds.), *Formes archaïques et arts ibériques*, 43–54. Madrid.

Cahill, N. D. 2002. *Household and City Organization at Olynthus*. New Haven. Website: www.stoa.org/olynthus/.

Cahill, N. H. and J. H. Kroll. 2005. "New Archaic Coin Finds at Sardis." *AJA* 109: 589–617.

Cairns, D. 1993. *AIDOS: The Psychology and Ethics of Honour and Shame in Ancient Greek Literature*. Oxford.

Cairns, D. 2001a. "Affronts and Quarrels in the *Iliad*." In Cairns 2001c: 203–19.

Cairns, D. 2001b. "Introduction." In Cairns 2001c: 1–56.

Cairns, D. (ed.). 2001c. *Oxford Readings in Homer's* Iliad. Oxford.

Calame, C. 1977. *Les chœurs de jeunes filles en Grèce archaïque: Morphologie, fonction religieuse et sociale*. Lanham.

Calame, C. (ed.). 1983. *Alcman*. Rome.

Calame, C. 1999. *The Poetics of Eros in Ancient Greece*. Princeton.

Calame, C. 2001. *Choruses of Young Women in Ancient Greece: Their Morphology, Religious Role and Social Functions*. Tr. D. Collins and J. Orion. Lanham.

Calder, W. M. and A. Demandt (eds.). 1990. *Eduard Meyer: Leben und Leistung eines Universalhistorikers*. Leiden.

Calhoun, G. M. 1913. *Athenian Clubs in Politics and Litigation*. Austin.

Callaghan, P. J. 1978. "KRS 1976: Excavations at a Shrine of Glaukos, Knossos." *ABSA* 73: 1–30.

Callaghan, P. J. 1992. "Archaic to Hellenistic Pottery." In Sackett 1992: 89–136.

Callaghan, P. J. and A. W. Johnston. 2000. "The Iron Age Pottery from Kommos, I: The Pottery from the Greek Temples at Kommos." In Shaw and Shaw 2000: 210–335.

Calligas, P. 1984–5. "Anaskafes sto Lefkadi Evoias, 1981–1984." *Arkheion Evoikon Meleton* 26: 253–69.

Calligas, P. 1988. "Hero Cult in Early Iron Age Greece." In Hägg et al. 1988: 229–34.

Calligas, P. 1988–9. "I proimi arkhaia Khalkida," *Anthropoligika Kai Arkhaiologika Khronika* 3: 88–105.

Camassa, G. 1988. "Aux origines de la codification écrite des lois en Grèce." In M. Detiénne (ed.), *Les savoirs de l'ecriture en Grèce ancienne*, 130–55. Lille.

Cambitoglou, A. 1981. *Archaeological Museum of Andros*. Athens.

Cambitoglou, A., J. J. Coulton, J. Birmingham, and J. R. Green. 1971 (1992). *Zagora*, I: *Excavation of an Island Settlement on the Island of Andros, Greece*. Sydney; 2nd edn. Athens, 1992.

Cambitoglou, A. and J. K. Papadopoulos. 1988. "Excavation at Torone 1986: A Preliminary Report." *MedArch* 1: 180–217.

Cambitoglou, A., J. J. Coulton, J. Birmingham, and J. R. Green. 1988. *Zagora*, II: *Excavation of a Geometric Town on the Island of Andros; Excavation Season 1969; Study Season 1969–1970*. Athens.

Cambitoglou, A. et al. 1971 (1992). *Zagora*. Sidney; 2nd edn. Athens.

Cambitoglou, A. et al. 1991. *Archaeological Museum of Andros: Guide to the Finds from the Excavations of the Geometric Town at Zagora*. Athens.

Camp, J. M. 1979. "A Drought in the Late Eighth Century BC." *Hesperia* 48: 397–411.

Camp, J. M. 1986 (1998). *The Athenian Agora: Excavations in the Heart of Classical Athens*. London; rev. edn. 1998.

Camp, J. M. 1990. *The Athenian Agora: A Guide to the Excavations and Museum*.[4] Athens.

Camp, J. M. 2000. "Walls and the *Polis*." In Flensted-Jensen et al. 2000: 41–57.

Camp, J. M. 2001. *The Archaeology of Athens*. New Haven.

Campbell, D. A. 1982. *Greek Lyric*, I: *Sappho, Alcaeus*. Cambridge, Mass.

Campbell, D. A. 1988. *Greek Lyric*, II: *Anacreon, Anacreonta, Choral Lyric from Olympus to Alcman*. Cambridge, Mass.

Carawan, E. 1998. *Rhetoric and the Law of Draco*. Oxford.

Carlier, P. 1984. *La Royauté en Grèce avant Alexandre*. Strasbourg.

Carlier, P. 2006. "*Anax* and *basileus* in the Homeric Poems." In Deger-Jalkotzy and Lemos 2006: 101–9.

Carpenter, R. 1933. "The Antiquity of the Greek Alphabet." *AJA* 37: 8–29.

Carradice, I. and M. Price. 1988. *Coinage in the Greek World*. London.

Carrington, R. 1971. *The Mediterranean*. New York.

Carter, J. B. 1997. "*Thiasos* and *Marzeah*: Ancestor Cult in the Age of Homer." In Langdon 1997b: 72–112.

Carter, J. C. 2000. "The Chora and the Polis of Metaponto." In Krinzinger 2000: 81–94.

Carter, J. C. 2006. *Discovering the Greek Countryside at Metaponto*. Ann Arbor.

Cartledge, P. 1977. "Hoplites and Heroes: Sparta's Contribution to the Technique of Ancient Warfare." *JHS* 97: 11–27.

Cartledge, P. 1978. "Literacy in the Spartan Oligarchy." *JHS* 98: 25–37.

Cartledge, P. 1979 (2002). *Sparta and Lakonia: A Regional History*. London; 2nd edn. 2002.

Cartledge, P. 1980. "The Peculiar Position of Sparta in the Development of the Greek City-state." *Proceedings of the Royal Irish Academy* 80: 91–108. Repr. in Cartledge 2001: 21–38.

Cartledge, P. 1981. "The Politics of Spartan Pederasty." *PCPhS* 30: 17–36.

Cartledge, P. 1982. "Sparta and Samos: A Special Relationship." *CQ* 77: 243–65.

Cartledge, P. 1985a. "The Greek Religious Festivals." In Easterling and Muir 1985: 98–127.

Cartledge, P. 1985b. "Rebels and *Sambos* in Classical Greece: A Comparative View." In P. Cartledge and F. D. Harvey (eds.), *CRUX: Essays in Greek History Presented to G.E.M. de Ste. Croix on his 75th Birthday*, 16–46. Exeter. Repr. in Cartledge 2001: 127–52.

Cartledge, P. 1987. *Agesilaos and the Crisis of Sparta*. London.

Cartledge, P. 1991. "Richard Talbert's Revision of the Sparta–Helot Struggle: A Reply." *Historia* 40: 379–81.

Cartledge, P. 1992. "Early Lakedaimon: The Making of a Conquest State." In Sanders 1992: 49–52.

Cartledge, P. 2001. *Spartan Reflections*. London.

Cartledge, P. 2002. *The Spartans: An Epic History*. London.

Cartledge, P. 2003. "Raising Hell? The Helot Mirage: A Personal Re-View." In Luraghi and Alcock 2003: 12–30.

Cartledge, P. and A. Spawforth. 1989. *Hellenistic and Roman Sparta: A Tale of Two Cities*. London.

Cary, M. and E. H. Warmington. 1963. *The Ancient Explorers*. Baltimore.

Caskey, M. 1986. *The Temple at Ayia Irini*. Part I: *The Statues – Keos* II. Princeton.

Caskey, M. 1998. "Ayia Irini: Temple Studies." In Mendoni and Mazarakis Ainian 1998: 123–38.

Cassimatis, H. 1982. "Figurines dédaliques de Gortyne: Essai de typologie." *BCH* 106: 446–64.

Casson, L. 1971. *Ships and Seamanship in the Ancient World*. Princeton.

Casson, L. 1989. *The* Periplus Maris Erythraei: *Text with Introduction, Translation, and Commentary*. Princeton.

Castro, María Cruz Fernández. 1995. *Iberia in Prehistory*. Oxford.

Catling, H. W. 1996. "Bronze." In Coldstream and Catling 1996: 543–74.

Catling, H. W. 2002. "Zeus Messapeus at Tsakona, Laconia, Reconsidered." *Lakonikai Spoudai* 16: 67–99. In Cavanagh et al. 2002: 151–256.

Catling, R. 1998. "The Typology of the Protogeometric and Subprotogeometric Pottery from Troia and Its Aegean Context." *Studia Troica* 8: 151–87.

Catling, R. 2002. "The Survey Area from the Early Iron Age to the Classical Period (c. 1050–c. 300 BC)." In W. Cavanagh, J. Crouwel, R. W. V. Catling, and G. Shipley (eds.), *Continuity and Change in a Greek Rural Landscape: The Laconia Survey*, I: 151–256. London.

Catling, R. 2005. "Emborio and Kambos: Two Archaic Sites on Melos." In Yeroulanou and Stamatopoulou 2005: 69–77.

Catling, R. and I. S. Lemos. 1990. *Lefkandi*, II.1: *The Protogeometric Building at Toumba – The Pottery*. Ed. M. R. Popham, P. G. Calligas and L. H. Sackett. London.

Cavanagh, W. G. 1996. "The Burial Customs." In Coldstream and Catling 1996: 651–75.

Cavanagh, W. G., J. Crouwel, R. Catling, and G. Shipley. 1996. *Continuity and Change in a Greek Rural Landscape: The Laconia Survey*, II: *Archaeological Data*. London.

Cavanagh, W. G., J. Crouwel, R. Catling, and G. Shipley. (eds.). 2002. *Continuity and Change in a Greek Rural Landscape: The Laconia Survey*, I: *Methodology and Interpretation*. London.

Cawkwell, G. 1993. "Sparta and Her Allies in the Sixth Century." *CQ* 43: 364–76.

Ceccarelli, P. 1993. "Sans thalassocratie, pas de démocratie? Le rapport entre thalassocratie et démocratie à Athènes dans la discussion du Ve et du IVe siècles av. J.-C." *Historia* 42: 444–70.

Ceccarelli, P. 2004. "Dancing the *Pyrrhiche* in Athens." In Murray and Wilson 2004: 91–118.

Chambers, M. 1990a. *Aristoteles. Staat der Athener: Übersetzt und erläutert.* Berlin.

Chambers, M. 1990b. *Georg Busolt: His Career in His Letters.* Leiden.

Chamoux, F. 1953. *Cyrène sous la monarchie des Battiades.* Paris.

Chandezon, C. 2003. *L'élevage en Grèce (fin V^e–fin Ier s. a.C.): L'apport des sources épigraphiques.* Bordeaux.

Chaniotis, A. 2002. "Ritual Dynamics: The Boiotian Festival of the Daidala." In H. W. Singor, F. T. Van Straten, and J. H. M. Strubbe (eds.), *Kykeon. Studies in honour of H. S. Versnel,* 23–48. Leiden.

Chankowski, V. and E. Fouache. 2000. "Pistiros (Bulgarie)." *BCH* 124: 643–54.

Chapman, R. 2003. *Archaeologies of Complexity.* London.

Charalampidou, X. 2003. Simvoli stin topoyrafia tis Eretrias ton arkhaikon khronon, in *AETHSE* 1: 993–1018.

Charbonneaux, J., R. Martin, and F. Villard. 1968. *Grèce archaïque (620–480 avant J.-C.).* Paris.

Chatzidimitriou, A. 1997. "Zarakes." *AD* 52B: 407–409.

Chatzidimitriou, A. 2003. "Khalkino enepiyrafo stathmio apo tous Zarakes Karistias." *AETHSE* 1: 1077–92.

Chatzidimitriou, A. 2003–4. "Anaskafika dedomena kai porismata apo tin arkhaiologiki erevna stous Zarakes Karistias." *Arkheion Evoikon Meleton* 35: 53–68.

Cherry, J. F. 1988. "Pastoralism and the Role of Animals in the Pre- and Protohistoric Economies of the Aegean." In C. R. Whittaker (ed.), *Pastoral Economies in Classical Antiquity,* 6–34. Cambridge.

Cherry, J. F. 1990. "The First Colonization of the Mediterranean Islands." *Journal of Mediterranean Archaeology* 3: 145–221.

Cherry, J. F., J. L. Davis, and E. Mantzourani. 1991. *Landscape Archaeology as Long-term History: Northern Keos in the Cycladic Islands.* Los Angeles.

Cherry, J. F. and J. L. Davis. 1998. "Northern Keos in Context." In Mendoni and Mazarakis Ainian 1998: 217–21.

Childe, V. G. 1929. *The Danube in Prehistory.* Oxford.

Childe, V. G. 1942. *What Happened in History.* Harmondsworth.

Childe, V. G. 1950. "The Urban Revolution." *Town Planning Review* 21: 3–17.

Childe, V. G. 1956. *Piecing Together the Past.* London.

Christ, K. 1972. *Von Gibbon zu Rostovtzeff.* Darmstadt.

Christ, K. (ed.). 1986. *Sparta.* Darmstadt.

Christesen, P. 2007. *Olympic Victor Lists and Ancient Greek History.* Cambridge.

Christien, J. 2002. "Iron Money in Sparta: Myth and History." In Powell and Hodkinson 2002: 171–90.

Chrysostomou, A. 2000. "Konstandia 1998–2000: The Mound Cemetery and the Wider Area." *AEMTH* 14: 505–18.

Chrysostomou, A. and P. Chrysostomou. 2002. "Excavations in the West Cemetery of Arhondiko Near Pella in 2002." *AEMTH* 16: 465–78.

Clarke, M. L. 1962. *George Grote: A Biography.* London.

Classen, C. J. (ed.). 1989. *Die klassische Altertumswissenschaft an der Georg-August-Universität Göttingen.* Göttingen.

Clay, J. S. 2003. *Hesiod's Cosmos.* Cambridge.

Cobet, J. 1997. "Milet 1994–1995: Die Mauern sind die Stadt: Zur Stadtbefestigung des antiken Milet." *AA* 1997: 249–84.

Cobet, J. 2002. "The Organization of Time in the *Histories*." In Bakker et al. 2002: 387–412.

Cobet, J. and H.-J. Gehrke. 2002. "Warum um Troia immer wieder streiten?" *Geschichte in Wissenschaft und Unterricht* 53: 290–325.

Cohen, B. (ed.). 1995. *The Distaff Side: Representing the Female in Homer's* Odyssey. New York.

Cohen, B. 2001. "Ethnic Identity in Democratic Athens and the Visual Vocabulary of Male Costume." In Malkin 2001: 235–74.

Cohen, B. et al. 2006. *The Colors of Clay. Special Techniques in Athenian Vases*. Los Angeles.

Cohen, M. E. 1993. *The Cultic Calendars of the Ancient Near East*. Bethesda.

Coja, M. "Greek Colonists and Native Populations in Dobruja (*Moesia Inferior*): The Archaeological Evidence." In Descoeudres 1990: 157–68.

Coldstream, J. N. 1968. *Greek Geometric Pottery. A Survey of Ten Local Styles and Their Chronology*. London; updated 2nd edn., Exetb 2008.

Coldstream, J. N. 1969. "The Phoenicians in Ialysos." *BICS* 16: 1–8.

Coldstream, J. N. 1972. "Knossos 1951–61: Protogeometric and Geometric Pottery from the Town." *ABSA* 67: 63–98.

Coldstream, J. N. 1973a. *Knossos: The Sanctuary of Demeter*. London.

Coldstream, J. N. 1973b. "Knossos 1951–61: Orientalizing and Archaic Pottery from the Town." *ABSA* 68: 33–63.

Coldstream, J. N. 1977 (2003). *Geometric Greece*. London; 2nd edn. 2003.

Coldstream, J. N. 1982. "Greeks and Phoenicians in the Aegean." In H. G. Niemeyer (ed.), *Phönizier im Westen*, 261–72. Mainz.

Coldstream, J. N. 1983. "The Meaning of the Regional Styles in the Eighth Century BC." In Hägg 1983b: 17–25.

Coldstream, J. N. 1984a. "Dorian Knossos and Aristotle's Villages." In Nicolet et al. 1984: 311–22.

Coldstream, J. N. 1984b. "A Protogeometric Nature Goddess from Knossos." *BICS* 31: 93–104.

Coldstream, J. N. 1985. "Greek Temples: Why and Where?" In Easterling and Muir 1985: 67–97.

Coldstream, J. N. 1990. "The Beginnings of Greek Literacy: An Archaeologist's View." *Ancient History: Resources for Teachers* 20: 144–59.

Coldstream, J. N. 1992. "Early Hellenic Pottery." In Sackett 1992: 67–87.

Coldstream, J. N. 1993. "Mixed Marriages at the Frontiers of the Early Greek World." *OJA* 12: 89–107.

Coldstream, J. N. 1995. "The Rich Lady of the Areiopagos and Her Contemporaries: A Tribute in Memory of Evelyn Lord Smithson." *Hesperia* 64: 391–403.

Coldstream, J. N. 1996. "The Protogeometric and Geometric Pottery." In Coldstream and Catling 1996: 2. 311–420. London.

Coldstream, J. N. 1998. "Eating and Drinking in Euboean Pithekoussai." In Bats and D'Agostino 1998: 303–10.

Coldstream, J. N. 1999. "Knossos 1951–61: Classical and Hellenistic Pottery from the Town." *ABSA* 94: 321–51.

Coldstream, J. N., P. J. Callaghan, and J. N. Musgrave. 1981. "Knossos: An Early Greek Tomb on the Lower Gypsades Hill." *ABSA* 76: 141–65.

Coldstream, J. N. and P. Bikai. 1988. "Early Greek Pottery in Tyre and Cyprus: Some Preliminary Comparisons." *Report of the Department of Antiquities, Cyprus* 1988: 35–44.

Coldstream, J. N. and H. W. Catling (eds.). 1996. *Knossos North Cemetery: Early Greek Tombs*. London.

Coldstream, J. N. and C. F. MacDonald. 1997. "Knossos: Area of South-West Houses: Early Hellenic Occupation." *ABSA* 92: 191–245.

Coldstream, J. N. and G. Huxley. 1999. "Knossos: the Archaic Gap." *ABSA* 94: 289–307.

Coleman, Carter, J. 1994. "Sanctuaries in the *Chora* of Metaponto." In Alcock and Osborne 1994: 161–98.

Collignon, M. 1881. *Manuel d'archéologie grecque*. Paris.

Conerman, S. (ed.). 1999. *Mythen, Geschichte(n), Identitäten: Der Kampf um die Vergangenheit*. Asien und Afrika 2. Hamburg.

Connor, W. R. 1987. "Tribes, Festivals and Processions: Civic Ceremonial and Political Manipulation in Ancient Greece." *JHS* 107: 40–50.

Connor, W. R. 1988. "Early Greek Land Warfare as Symbolic Expression." *Past and Present* 119: 3–29.

Connor, W. R. 1990. "City Dionysia and Athenian Democracy." In Connor et al., *Aspects of Athenian Democracy*, 7–32. Copenhagen.

Connor, W. R. 1994. *Ethno-nationalism: The Quest for Understanding*. Princeton.

Conrad, L. I., R. Porter, V. Nutton, and A. Wear. 1995. *The Western Medical Tradition: 800 BC–18 AD*. Cambridge.

Conophagos, C. 1980. *Le Laurium antique*. Athens.

Cook, J. M. 1958-9. "Old Smyrna, 1948–1951." *ABSA* 53–4: 1–34.

Cook, J. M. and R. V. Nicholls. 1998. *Old Smyrna Excavations: The Temples of Athena*. London.

Cook, R. M. 1960 (1966, 1997). *Greek Painted Pottery*. London; 2nd edn. 1966; 3rd edn. 1997.

Cook, R. M. and P. Dupont. 1998. *East Greek Pottery*. London.

Coote, R. B. 1975. "The Kition Bowl." *BASOR* 220: 47–58.

Corinto e l'Occidente. 1995. Taranto.

Cornell, T. J. 1995. *The Beginnings of Rome: Italy and Rome from the Bronze Age to the Punic Wars, c. 1000–264 BC*. London.

Corsten, T. 1999. *Vom Stamm zum Bund: Gründung und territoriale Organisation griechischer Bundesstaaten*. Munich.

Cosmopoulos, M. B. 2003. *Greek Mysteries: The Archaeology and Ritual of Ancient Greek Secret Cults*. London.

Costa, V. 1997. *Nasso dalle origini al V sec. a. C.* Naples.

Coucouzeli, A. 2004. "From Tribe to State in the Greek Early Iron Age: The Archaeological Evidence from Lefkandi and Zagora." In Stampolidis and Yannikouri 2004: 461–80.

Coulson, W. 1985. "The Dark Age Pottery of Sparta." *ABSA* 80: 29–84.

Coulson, W. 1988. "Geometric Pottery from Volimidia." *AJA* 92: 53–74.

Coulson, W. 1996. *Ancient Naukratis*, vol. II, part 1: *The Survey at Naukratis*. Exeter.

Coulson, W. and H. Kyrieleis (eds.). 1992. *Proceedings of an International Symposium on the Olympic Games*. Athens.

Coulson, W., D. Haggis, M. S. Mook, and J. Tobin. 1997. "Excavations on the Kastro at Kavousi: An Architectural Overview." *Hesperia* 66: 315–90.

Coulton, J. J. 1974. "Lifting in Early Greek Architecture." *JHS* 94: 1–19.

Coulton, J. J. 1976. *The Architectural Development of the Greek Stoa*. Oxford.

Coulton, J. J. 1977. *Greek Architects at Work: Problems of Structure and Design*. London.

Coulton, J. J. 1993. "The Toumba Building: Description and Analysis of the Architecture." In M. R. Popham, P. G. Calligas, and L. H. Sackett (eds.), *Lefkendi II: The Protogeometric Building at Toumba. Part 2: The Excavation, Architecture and Finds*, with J. Coulton and H. W. Catling, 33–70. British School of Athens.

Courbin, P. 1963. "Stratigraphie et stratigraphie: méthodes et perspectives." In Courbin (ed.), *Etudes archéologiques: Recueil de travaux*, 59–102. Paris.

Courbin, P. 1993. "Fragments d'amphores protogéométriques grecques à Bassit (Syrie)." *Hesperia* 62: 95–113.

Courtils, J. des and J.-C. Moretti (eds.). 1993. *Les grands ateliers d'architecture dans le monde égéen du VIe siècle av. J.C.* Paris.

Cressy, D. 1980. *Literacy and the Social Order: Reading and Writing in Tudor and Stuart England*. Cambridge.

Crielaard, J. P. 1995a. "Homer, History and Archaeology: Some Remarks on the Date of the Homeric World." In Crielaard 1995b: 201–88.

Crielaard, J. P. (ed.). 1995b. *Homeric Questions: Essays in Philology, Ancient History and Archaeology*. Amsterdam.

Crielaard, J. P. 1998. "Surfing on the Mediterranean Web: Cypriot Long-distance Communications during the Eleventh and Tenth Centuries BC." In Karageorghis and Stampolidis 1998: 187–204.

Crielaard, J. P. 1999a. "Early Iron Age Pottery in Cyprus and North Syria: A Consumption-oriented Approach." In Crielaard, van Wijngaarden and Stissi 1999: 261–90.

Crielaard, J. P. 1999b. "Production, Circulation and Consumption of Early Iron Age Greek Pottery (Eleventh to Seventh Centuries BC)." In Crielaard, van Wijngaarden and Stissi 1999: 49–81.

Crielaard, J. P. 2000. "Honour and Valour as Discourse for Early Greek Colonialism (8th–7th Centuries BC)." In Krinzinger 2000: 499–506.

Crielaard, J. P. 2002. "Past or Present? Epic Poetry, Aristocratic Self-representation and the Concept of Time in the Eighth and Seventh Centuries BC." In Montanari 2002: 239–96.

Crielaard, J. P. 2006. "Basileis at Sea: Elites and External Contacts in the Euboian Gulf Region from the End of the Bronze Age to the Beginning of the Iron Age." In Deger-Jalkotzy and Lemos 2006: 271–97.

Crielaard, J. P. and J. Driessen. 1994. "The Hero's Home: Some Reflections at Toumba, Lefkandi." *Topoi* 4: 251–70.

Crielaard, J. P., G.-J. van Wijngaarden, and V. Stissi (eds.). 1999. *The Complex Past of Pottery: Production, Circulation and Consumption of Mycenaean and Greek Pottery (Sixteenth to Early Fifth Centuries BC)*. Amsterdam.

Cristofani, M. 1981. "Appendice. Le iscrizioni." In *Materiali per servire alla storia del Vaso François*, 175–78. Rome.

Crotty, K. 1982. *Song and Action: The Victory Odes of Pindar*. Baltimore.

Crouwel, J., M. Prent, et al. 1995–2002. "Geraki, an Acropolis Site in Lakonia: Preliminary Report." Various reports in *Pharos*, vols. 3–10.

Crowther, N. B. 1985. "Male 'Beauty' Contests in Greece: The *Euandria* and *Euexia*." *L'Antiquité classique* 54: 285–91.

Crowther, N. B. 1992. "Second-place Finishes and Lower in Greek Athletics (Including the Pentathlon)." *ZPE* 90: 97–102.

Crowther, N. B. 2003. "Elis and Olympia: City, Sanctuary and Politics." In Phillips and Pritchard 2003: 61–74.

Csapo, E. 1991. "An International Community of Traders in Late 8th–7th c. BC Kommos in Southern Crete." *ZPE* 88: 211–16.

Csapo, E. 1993. "A Postscript to 'An International Community of Traders in Late 8th–7th c. BC Kommos.'" *ZPE* 96: 235–36.

Csapo, E. and W. J. Slater (eds.). 1995. *The Context of Ancient Drama*. Ann Arbor.

Csapo, E., A. W. Johnston, and D. Geagan. 2000. "The Iron Age Inscriptions." In Shaw and Shaw 2000: 101–34.

Cultraro, M. 2004. "The Northern Aegean in the Early Iron Age: An Assessment of the Present Picture." In Stampolidis and Giannikouri 2004: 215–26.

Cunliffe, B. 1979. *The Celtic World*. London.

Cunliffe, B. 1994a. "Iron Age Societies in Western Europe and Beyond, 800–140 BC." In Cunliffe 1994b: 336–72.

Cunliffe, B. (ed.). 1994b. *The Oxford Illustrated Prehistory of Europe*. Oxford.

Cunliffe, B. 2001. *Facing the Ocean: The Atlantic and Its Peoples*. Oxford.

Cuozzo, M. 2003. *Reinventando la tradizione: Immaginario sociale, ideologie e rappresentazione nelle necropoli orientalizzanti di Pontecagnano*. Paestum.

Currie, B. 2005. *Pindar and the Cult of Heroes*. Oxford.

Curtins, E. and J. A. Kampert. 1881–1903. *Karten von Attika*. Berlin.

Cuyler Young, T. 1980. "A Persian Perspective." *IA* 15: 213–39.

D'Agata, A. L. 1998. "Changing Patterns in a Minoan and Post-Minoan Sanctuary: The Case of Ayia Triada." In Cavanagh et al. 1998: 19–26.

D'Agostino, B. 1996. "L'incontro dei coloni greci con le genti anelleniche della Campania." In G. Pugliese Carratelli (ed.), *I Greci in occidente*, 533–40. Milan.

D'Agostino, B. 1999a. "I principi dell'Italia centro-tirrenica in epoca Orientalizzante." In Ruby 1999: 81–8.

D'Agostino, B. 1999b. "Euboean Colonisation in the Gulf of Naples." In G. R. Tsetskhladze (ed.), *Ancient Greeks West and East*, 207–27. Leiden.

D'Agostino, B. and D. Ridgway (eds.). 1994. *Apoikia: I più antichi insediamenti Greci in Occidente. Funzione e modi dell'organizzazione politica e sociale. Scritti in onore di G. Buchner. AION (archeol.)* 1. Naples.

D'Andria, F. 1990. "Greek Influence in the Adriatic: Fifty Years after Beaumont." In Descoeudres 1990: 281–90.

D'Andria, F. 1995. "Corinto e l'occidente: la costa Adriatica." In *Corinto e l'Occidente* 457–508.

D'Andria, F. and K. Mannino (eds.). 1996. *Ricerche sulla casa in Magna Grecia e in Sicilia*. Galatina.

D'Ercole, M. C. 2005. "Identités, mobilités et frontières dans la Méditerranée antique: L'Italie adriatique, VIIIᵉ–Vᵉ s. av. J.-C." *Annales d'histoire économique et sociale* 60: 165–81.

D'Onofrio, A. M. 1982. "Korai e kouroi funerari attici." *AION(archaeol)* 4: 135–70.

D'Onofrio, A. M. 1988. "Aspetti e problemi del monumento funerario attico arcaico." *AION(archaeol)* 10: 83–96.

D'Onofrio, A. M. 1993. "Le trasformazioni del costume funerario ateniese nella necropoli pre-soloniana del Kerameikos." *AION(archaeol)* 15: 143–71.

D'Onofrio, A. M. 1995. "Santuari 'rurali' e dinamiche insediative in Attica tra il Protogeometrico e l'Orientalizzante (1050–600 a.C.)." *AION(archaeol)* 2: 57–88.

D'Onofrio, A. M. 1997. "The 7th Century BC in Attica: The Basis of Political Organization." In Damgard Andersen et al. 1997: 63–88.

Dakoronia, F. 1993a. "Elateia." *Fokika Khronika* 5: 25–39.

Dakoronia, F. 1993b. "Homeric Towns in East Lokris: Problems of Identification." *Hesperia* 62: 115–27.

Dalby, A. 1995. "The *Iliad*, the *Odyssey* and Their Audiences." *CQ* 45: 269–79.

Dalby, A. 1998. "Homer's Enemies: Lyric and Epic in the Seventh Century." In Fisher and van Wees 1998: 195–211.

Dalongeville, R. and G. Rougemont. 1993. *Recherches dans les Cyclades*. Lyon.

Damgard Andersen, H., H. Horsnæs, S. Houby-Nielsen, and A. Rathje (eds.). 1997. *Urbanization in the Mediterranean in the 9th to 6th Centuries BC.* Copenhagen.

Dandamaev, M. A. 1989. *A Political History of the Achaemenid Empire.* Tr. W. J. Vogelsang. Leiden.

Daniels, P. T. and W. Bright (eds.). 1996. *The World's Writing Systems.* Oxford.

Danner, P. 1997. "Megara, Megara Hyblaea and Selinus: The Relationship between the Town Planning of a Mother City, a Colony and a Sub-colony in the Archaic Period." In Damgard Andersen et al. 1997: 143–65.

Darcque, P. and R. Treuil (eds.). 1990. *L'habitat égéen préhistorique.* Paris.

Davaras, C. 1972. *Die Statue aus Astritsi.* Bern.

David, E. 1979. "The Pamphlet of Pausanias." *PP* 34: 94–116.

Davidson, J. N. 1997. *Courtesans and Fishcakes.* London.

Davies, J. K. 1994. "The Tradition about the First Sacred War." In S. Hornblower (ed.), *Greek Historiography*, 193–212. Oxford.

Davies, J. K. 1996. "Strutture e suddivisioni delle 'poleis' arcaiche. Le ripartizioni minori." In Settis 1996: 599–652.

Davies, J. K. 1997. "The 'Origins of the Greek *Polis*': Where Should We Be Looking?" In Mitchell and Rhodes 1997: 24–38.

Davies, J. K. 1998. "Ancient Economies: Models and Muddles." In Parkins and Smith 1998: 225–56.

Davies, J. K. 2000a. "Geschichtswissenschaft/Geschichtsschreibung, II: Griechische Geschichte." *DNP* 14: 188–98.

Davies, J. K. 2000b. "A Wholly Non-Aristotelian Universe: The Molossians as Ethnos, State, and Monarchy." In Brock and Hodkinson 2000: 234–58.

Davies, J. K. 2001a. "Rebuilding a Temple. The Economic Effects of Piety." In D. J. Mattingly and J. Salmon (eds.), *Economies beyond Agriculture in the Classical World*, 209–29. London.

Davies, J. K. 2001b. "Temples, Credit, and the Circulation of Money." In Meadows and Shipton 2001: 117–28.

Davies, J. K. 2002. "Greek History: A Discipline in Transformation." In Wiseman 2002: 225–46.

Davies, J. K. 2003. "Democracy without Theory." In Derow and Parker 2003: 319–35.

Davies, J. K. 2004. "The Concept of 'Citizen.'" In S. Cataldi (ed.), *Poleis e politeiaia. Esperienze politiche, tradizioni litterarie, progetti costituzionali. Atti convegno internazionale di Storia Greca.* Turin, May 29–31, 2002. Alessandria.

Davies, J. K. 2005. "The Gortyn Laws." In M. Gagarin and D. Cohen (eds.), *The Cambridge Companion to Ancient Greek Law*, 305–27. Cambridge.

Davies, J. K. 2007. "The Origins of the Festivals, especially Delphi and the Pythia." In C. Morgan and S. Hornblower (eds.), *Pindar's Poetry, Patrons and Festivals: From Archaic Greece to the Roman Empire*, 47–69. Oxford.

Davies, M. 1991. *Poetarum Melicorum Graecorum Fragmenta*, I. Oxford.

Davies, W. V. and L. Schofield (eds.). 1995. *Egypt from the Aegean and the Levant: Interconnections in the Second Millennium BC.* London.

Davis, J. (ed.). 1998. *Sandy Pylos: An Archaeological History from Nestor to Navarino.* Austin.

Davis, J. and J. Bennet. 1999. "Making Mycenaeans: Warfare, Territorial Expansion and Representations of the Other in the Pylian Kingdom." In R. Laffineur (ed.), *Polemos: Le contexte guerrier en Egée à l'Age du bronze*, 107–20. Liège.

Dawkins, R. (ed.). 1929. *The Sanctuary of Artemis Orthia at Sparta.* London.

Dawson, D. 1996. *The Origins of Western Warfare: Militarism and Morality in the Ancient World.* Boulder.

De Angelis, F. 2000. "Estimating the Agricultural Base of Greek Sicily." *Papers of the British School at Rome* 68: 111–48.

De Angelis, F. 2002. "Trade and Agriculture at Megara Hyblaia." *OJA* 21: 299–310.

De Angelis, F. 2003. *Megara Hyblaia and Selinous: The Development of Two Greek City-states in Archaic Sicily.* Oxford.

De Caro, S. and C. Gialanella. 1998. "Novità pitecusane: L'insediamento di Punta Chiarito a Forio d'Ischia." In Bats and D'Agostino 1998: 337–53.

De Jong, I. 1995. "Homer as Literature: Some Current Areas of Research." In Crielaard 1995b: 127–46.

De Jong, I. 2001. *A Narratological Commentary on the* Odyssey. Cambridge.

De Libero, L. 1996. *Die archaische Tyrannis.* Stuttgart.

De Miro, E. 1983. "Forme di contatto e processi di trasformazione nelle società antiche: l'esempio di Sabucina." In *Modes de contacts et processus de transformation dans les sociétés antiques,* 335–44. Pisa and Rome.

De Sanctis, G. 1912. *Atthis: Storia della repubblica ateniese dalle origini alla età di Pericle.*[2] Turin.

De Souza, P. 1998. "Towards Thalassocracy? Archaic Greek Naval Developments." In Fisher and van Wees 1998: 271–93.

De Souza, P. 1999. *Piracy in the Graeco-Roman World.* Cambridge

Debord, P. 1999. *L'Asie Mineure au IVe siècle (412–323 a.C.).* Bordeaux.

DeCorse, C. 1989. "Material Aspects of Limba, Yalunka and Kuranko Ethnicity." In S. Shennan (ed.), *Archaeological Approaches to Cultural Identity,* 125–40. London.

Deger-Jalkotzy, S. 1995. "Mykenische Herrschaftsformen ohne Paläste und die griechische Polis." In R. Laffineur and W.-D. Niemeier (eds.), *Politeia: Society and State in the Aegean Bronze Age,* 367–77. Liège and Austin.

Deger-Jalkotzy, S. 2006. "Late Mycenaean Warrior Tombs." In Deger-Jalktozy and Lemos 2006: 151–79.

Deger-Jalkotzy, S. and I. Lemos (eds.). 2006. *Ancient Greece from the Mycenaean Palaces to the Age of Homer.* Edinburgh.

Delcourt, M. 1938. *Sterilités mysterieuses et naissances maléfiques dans l'antiquité classique.* Liège.

Delorme, J. 1960. *Gymnasium: Etude sur les monuments consacrés à l'éducation en Grèce.* Paris.

Demakopoulou, K. 1982. *To Mikinaiko iero sto Amikleo kai i YE IIIG periodos sti Lakonia* Diss. University of Athens.

Demargne, P. and H. van Effenterre. 1937. "Recherches à Dreros II." *BCH* 61: 333–48.

Demetriou, D. 2005. "Negotiating Identity: Greek Emporia in the Archaic and Classical World." Diss. Johns Hopkins University.

Den Boer, W. 1954. *Laconian Studies.* Amsterdam.

Dengate, C. F. 1988. "The Sanctuaries of Apollo in the Peloponnesos." Diss. University of Chicago.

Dentzer, J.-M. 1982. *Le Motif du banquet couché dans le Proche-Orient et le monde grec du VIIe au IVème siècle avant J.-C.* Paris.

Derow, P. and R. Parker (eds.). 2003. *Herodotus and His World.* Oxford.

Desborough, V. R. d'A. 1952. *Protogeometric Pottery.* Oxford.

Desborough, V. R. d'A. 1972. *The Greek Dark Ages.* London.

Descat, R. 1993. "La loi de Solon sur l'interdiction d'exporter les produits attiques." In A. Bresson and P. Rouillard (eds.), *L'emporion,* 145–61. Paris.

Descoeudres, J.-P. (ed.). 1990. *Greek Colonists and Native Populations.* Canberra and Oxford.

Detienne, M. 1965. "En Grèce archaïque: Géométrie, politique et société." *Annales(ESC)* 20: 425–41.

Detienne, M. 1968. "La phalange: Problèmes et controverses." In Vernant 1968: 119–42.

Detienne, M. 1998. *Apollon, le couteau à la main: Une approche expérimentale du polythéisme grec*. Paris.

Detienne, M. (ed.). 1990. *Tracés de fondation*. Louvain.

Detienne, M. and J.-P. Vernant. 1974. *Les ruses de l'intelligence: La mètis des Grecs*. Paris.

Develin, B. and M. Kilmer. 1997. "What Kleisthenes Did." *Historia* 46: 3–18.

Dever, W. 1992. "The Late Bronze Age–Early Iron I Horizon in Syria/Palestine: Egyptians, Canaanites, Sea Peoples and Proto-Israelites." In W. A. Ward and M. S. Joukowsky (eds.), *The Crisis Years: The 12th Century BC*, 99–110. Dubuque.

DeVries, K. 2000. "The Nearly Other: The Attic Vision of Phrygians and Lydians." In B. Cohen (ed.), *Not the Classical Ideal: Athens and the Construction of the Other in Greek Art*, 338–63. Leiden.

Dewald, C. 2003. "Form and Content: The Question of Tyranny in Herodotus." In K. Morgan 2003: 25–58.

Dewald, C. and J. Marincola (eds.). 2006. *The Cambridge Companion to Herodotus*. Cambridge.

Dickie, M. 1995. "The Geography of Homer's World." In Andersen and Dickie 1995: 29–56.

Dickinson, O. T. P. K. 1994. *The Aegean Bronze Age*. Cambridge.

Dickinson, O. T. P. K. 2007. *The Aegean from Bronze Age to Iron Age*. London.

Diels, H. and W. Kranz (eds.). 1951–2 (1961). *Die Fragmente der Vorsokratiker*, 3 vols. Berlin. Vol. I 10th edn. 1961.

Dietler, M. 1997. "The Iron Age in Mediterranean France." *Journal of World Prehistory* 11: 269–357.

Dietz, S. and I. Papachristodoulou. 1988. *Archaeology in the Dodecanese*. Copenhagen.

Dilke, O. A. W. 1985 (1998). *Greek and Roman Maps*. London. Repr. Baltimore: 1998.

Dillon, M. 1997. *Pilgrims and Pilgrimage in Ancient Greece*. London.

Dillon, M. and L. Garland (eds.). 2000. *Ancient Greece. Social and Historical Documents from Archaic Times to the Death of Socrates*.[2] London.

Dinsmoor, W. B. 1927 (1950, 1975). *The Architecture of Ancient Greece: An Account of Its Historic Development*[2]. New York; 3rd edn. 1950, London and New York. Repr. 1975.

Di Vita, A. 1996. "Urban Planning in Ancient Sicily." In G. Pugliese Carratelli (ed.), *The Western Greeks*, 263–308. London.

Docter, F. and H. Niemeyer. 1994. "Pithekoussai: The Carthaginian Connection." In D'Agostino and Ridgway 1994: 101–16.

Dodds, E. R. 1951. *The Greeks and the Irrational*. Berkeley.

Dohan, E. H. 1931. "Archaic Cretan Terracottas in America." *Metropolitan Museum Studies* 3: 209–28.

Doherty, L. E. 1995. *Siren Songs: Gender, Audiences, and Narratives in the* Odyssey. Ann Arbor.

Domínguez, A. J. 1986. "La ciudad griega de Emporion y su organizacion politica." *Archivo español de arqueología* 59: 3–12.

Domínguez, A. J. and C. Sánchez. 2001. *Greek Pottery from the Iberian Peninsula: Archaic and Classical Periods*. Ed. G. R. Tsetskhladze. Leiden.

Dommelen, P. van. 1998. *On Colonial Grounds: A Comparative Study of Colonialism and Rural Settlement in First Millennium BC West Central Sardinia*. Leiden.

Donlan, W. 1970. "Changes and Shifts in the Meaning of *Demos* in the Literature of the Archaic Period." *PP* 25: 381–95.

Donlan, W. 1973. "The Tradition of Anti-aristocratic Thought in Early Greek Poetry." *Historia* 22: 145–54. Repr. in Donlan 1999: 237–48.

Donlan, W. 1981. "Reciprocities in Homer." *CW* 75: 137–75.

Donlan, W. 1985. "The Social Groups of Dark Age Greece." *CPh* 80: 293–308.

Donlan, W. 1989. "The Pre-state Community in Greece." *SO* 64: 5–29. Repr. in Donlan 1999: 283–302.

Donlan, W. 1997a. "The Homeric Economy." In Morris and Powell 1997: 649–67.

Donlan, W. 1997b. "The Relations of Power in Pre-state and Early State Polities." In Mitchell and Rhodes 1997: 39–48.

Donlan, W. 1998. "Political Reciprocity in Dark Age Greece." In Gill et al. 1998: 51–71.

Donlan, W. 1999. *The Aristocratic Ideal and Selected Papers.* Wauconda.

Donlan, W. 2002. "Achilles the Ally." *Arethusa* 35: 155–72.

Doonan, R. C. P. and A. Mazarakis Ainian. 2007. "Forging Identity in Early Iron Age Greece: Implications of the Metalworking Evidence from Oropos." In Mazarakis Ainian 2007: 361–78.

Dothan, T. and M. Dothan. 1992. *People of the Sea: The Search for the Philistines.* New York.

Dougherty, C. 1993. *The Poetics of Colonization: From City to Text in Archaic Greece.* Oxford.

Dougherty, C. 2001. *The Raft of Odysseus: The Ethnographic Imagination of Homer's* Odyssey. Oxford.

Dougherty, C. and L. Kurke (eds.). 1993. *Cultural Poetics in Archaic Greece: Cult, Performance, Politics.* Cambridge.

Dougherty, C. and L. Kurke (eds.). 2003. *The Cultures within Ancient Greek Culture: Contact, Conflict, Collaboration.* Cambridge.

Doukellis, P. N. and L. G. Mendoni (eds.). 1994. *Structures rurales et sociétés antiques.* Paris.

Dover, K. J. 1974. *Greek Popular Morality in the Time of Plato and Aristotle.* Oxford.

Dover, K. J. 1978. *Greek Homosexuality.* London.

Dreher, M. 2000. "Verbannung ohne Vergehen. Der Ostrakismos (das Scherbengericht)." In L. Burckhardt and J. von Ungern-Sternberg (eds.), *Grosse Prozesse im antiken Athen,* 66–77. Munich.

Drews, R. 1972. "The First Tyrants in Greece." *Historia* 21: 129–44.

Drews, R. 1983. *Basileus: The Evidence for Kingship in Geometric Greece.* New Haven.

Drews, R. 1993. *The End of the Bronze Age: Changes in Warfare and the Catastrophe ca. 1200 BC.* Princeton.

Driver, G. 1976. *Semitic Writing.*² London.

Dubois, L. 1996. *Inscriptions grecques dialectales d'Olbia du Pont.* Geneva.

Dubois, P. 1995. *Sappho is Burning.* Chicago.

Ducat, J. 1971. *Les Kouroi du Ptoion.* Paris.

Ducat, J. 1974. "Le Mépris des hilotes." *Annales ESC* 29: 1451–64.

Ducat, J. 1990a. "Esclaves au Ténare." In M.-M. Mactoux and E. Geny (eds.), *Mélanges P. Lévêque,* IV: 175–93. Paris.

Ducat, J. 1990b. *Les Hilotes.* Athens.

Ducat, J. 1994. *Les Pénestes de Thessalie.* Paris.

Ducat, J. 1999. "Perspectives on Spartan Education in the Classical Period." In Hodkinson and Powell 1999: 43–66.

Ducat, J. 2006. *Spartan Education: Youth and Society in the Classical Period.* Swansea.

Ducrey, P. 1968. *Le Traitement des prisonniers de guerre dans la Grèce antique des origines à la conquête romaine.* Paris.

Dunbabin, K. M. T. 2003. *The Roman Banquet: Images of Conviviality.* Cambridge.

Dunbabin, T. J. 1948. *The Western Greeks.* Oxford.

Dunbabin, T. J. 1950. "An Attic Bowl." *ABSA* 45: 193–202.

Dunbabin, T. J. 1957. *The Greeks and Their Eastern Neighbours: Studies in the Relations between Greece and the Countries of the Near East in the Eighth and Seventh Centuries BC.* London.

Dunn, J. (ed.). 1992. *Democracy: The Unfinished Journey, 508 BC to AD 1993.* Oxford.

Duplouy, A. 2006. *Le Prestige des élites: Recherches sur les modes de reconnaissance sociale en Grèce entre les Xe et Ve siècles avant J.-C.* Paris.

Durrell, L. 1977. *Sicilian Carousel.* New York.

Dušanić, S. 1970. *The Arcadian League of the Fourth Century.* Belgrade. In Serbian with English Summary.

Dušanić, S. 1997. "Platon, la question messénienne et les guerres contre les Barbares." In P. Brulé and J. Oulhen (eds.), *Esclavage, guerre, économie en Grèce ancienne*, 75–86. Rennes.

Dusinberre, E. R. M. 2003. *Aspects of Empire in Achaemenid Sardis.* Cambridge.

Easterling, P. E. 1989. "Semonides." In Easterling and B. M. W. Knox (eds.), *The Cambridge History of Greek Literature*, I.1: 112. Cambridge.

Easterling, P. E. 1991. "Men's κλέος and women's γόος: Female Voices in the *Iliad.*" *Journal of Modern Greek Studies* 9: 145–51.

Easterling, P. E. and J. V. Muir (eds.). 1985. *Greek Religion and Society.* Cambridge.

Ebert, J. 1972. *Griechische Epigramme auf Sieger an gymnischen und hippischen Agonen.* Berlin.

Ebert, J. and P. Siewert. 1997 (1999). "Eine archaische Bronzeurkunde aus Olympia mit Vorschriften für Ringkämpfer und Kampfrichter." In Ebert, *Agonismata: Kleine philologische Schriften zur Literatur, Geschichte und Kultur der Antike*, 200–36. Stuttgart. Repr. in A. Mallwitz and K. Herrmann (eds.), *XI. Bericht über die Ausgrabungen in Olympia*, 391–412. Berlin, 1999.

Eckstein, F. 1974. *Handwerk*, Teil I: *Die Aussagen des frühgriechischen Epos.* Archaeologia Homerica L. Göttingen.

Eder, B. 1998. *Argolis, Lakonien, Messenien vom Ende der mykenischen Palastzeit bis zur Einwanderung der Dorier.* Vienna.

Eder, B. 2006. "The World of Telemachos: Western Greece 1200–700 BC." In Deger-Jalkotzy and Lemos 2006: 549–80.

Eder, B. and V. Mitsopoulos-Leon. 1999. "Zur Geschichte der Stadt Elis vor dem Synoikismos von 471 v. Chr." *JÖAI* 68: 1–39.

Eder, W. 1998. "Aristocrats and the Coming of Athenian Democracy." In Morris and Raaflaub 1998: 105–40.

Eder, W. 2005. "The Political Significance of the Codification of Law in Archaic Societies: An Unconventional Hypothesis." In K. A. Raaflaub (ed.), *Social Struggles in Archaic Rome: New Perspectives on the Conflict of the Orders*, 239–67; expanded and updated edn. Malden and Oxford.

Eder, W. and K.-J. Hölkeskamp (eds.). 1997. *Volk und Verfassung im vorhellenistischen Griechenland.* Stuttgart.

Edwards, A. T. 1993. "Homer's Ethical Geography: Country and City in the *Odyssey.*" *TAPhA* 123: 27–78.

Edwards, A. T. 2004. *Hesiod's Ascra.* Berkeley.

Edwards, G. D. and R. D. Edwards. 1974–5. "Red Letters and Phoenician Writing." *Kadmos* 13: 48–57.

Edwards, M. W. 1987. *Homer: Poet of the* Iliad. Baltimore.

Edwards, M. W. 1991. *The* Iliad: *A Commentary*, V: *Books 17–20.* Cambridge.

Edwards, R. B. 1979. *Kadmos the Phoenician: A Study in Greek Legends and the Mycenaean Age.* Amsterdam.

Effenterre, H. van and F. Ruzé (eds.). 1994–5. *Nomima: Recueil d'inscriptions politiques et juridiques de l'archaïsme grec.* 2 vols. Rome.

Ehrenberg, V. 1925. *Neugründer des Staates: Ein Beitrag zur Geschichte Spartas und Athens im VI. Jahrhundert.* Munich.

Ehrenberg, V. 1933. "Der Damos im archaischen Sparta." *Hermes* 68: 288–305. Repr. in Ehrenberg 1965a: 202–20.

Ehrenberg, V. 1937. "When Did the Polis Rise?" *JHS* 57: 147–59. Repr. in Ehrenberg 1965a: 83–97.

Ehrenberg, V. 1946. *Aspects of Antiquity: Essays and Reviews*. Oxford.

Ehrenberg, V. 1960 (1969). *The Greek State*. Oxford. 2nd edn. 1969.

Ehrenberg, V. 1965a. *Polis und Imperium*. K. F. Stroheker and A. J. Graham (eds.). Zurich and Stuttgart.

Ehrenberg, V. 1965b. "Wann entstand die Polis?" In Ehrenberg 1965a: 83–97. Repr. in Gschnitzer 1969: 3–25.

Ehrhardt, N. 1988. *Milet und seine Kolonien*. Frankfurt.

Ehrhardt, N. 2003. "Milet nach den Perserkriegen: ein Neubeginn?" In E. Schwertheim and E. Winter (eds.), *Stadt und Stadtentwicklung in Kleinasien*, 1–19. Bonn.

Ehrhardt, N. 2005. "Die Ionier und ihr Verhältnis zu den Phrygern und Lydern." In E. Schwertheim and E. Winter (eds.), *Neue Forschungen zu Ionien*, 93–111. Bonn.

Ekschmitt, W. 1986. *Kunst und Kultur der Kykladen*, II: *Geometrische und archaische Zeit*. Mainz.

Eliopoulos, T. 1998. "A Preliminary Report on the Discovery of a Temple Complex of the Dark Ages at Kephala Vasilikis." In Karageorghis and Stampolidis 1998: 301–13.

Eliot, C. W. J. 1962. *Coastal Demes of Attika: A Study of the Policy of Kleisthenes*. Toronto.

Ellinger, P. 1993. *La légende nationale phocidienne. Artémis, les situations extrêmes et les récits de guerre d'anéantissement*. Paris.

Emlyn-Jones, C. J. 1980. "Myth and Reason: The Ionian Origin of Greek Philosophy." In Emlyn-Jones, *The Ionians and Hellenism: A Study of the Cultural Achievement of the Early Greek Inhabitants of Asia Minor*, 97–132. London.

Eremin, A. 2002. "Settlements of Spartan *perioikoi*: *poleis* or *komai*?" In Powell and Hodkinson 2002: 267–83.

Erickson, B. L. 2000. "Late Archaic and Classical Crete: Island Pottery Styles in an Age of Historical Transition, ca. 600–400 BC." Diss. University of Texas.

Erickson, B. L. 2002. "Aphrati and Kato Syme: Pottery, Continuity, and Cult in Late Archaic and Classical Crete." *Hesperia* 71: 41–90.

Erickson, B. L. Forthcoming. *Late Archaic and Classical Crete*. Princeton.

Erler, M. 1987. "Das Recht (*Dike*) als Segensbringerin für die Polis." *Studi Italiani di filologia classica* 3rd ser. 5: 5–36.

Errington, M. 1990. *A History of Macedonia*. Berkeley.

Erskine, A. 2001. "Trojans in Athenian Society: Public Rhetoric and Private Life." In Papenfuss and Strocka 2001: 113–22.

Euben, J. P., J. R. Wallach, and J. Ober (eds.). 1994. *Athenian Political Thought and the Reconstruction of American Democracy*. Ithaca, NY.

Fagerström, K. 1988. *Greek Iron Age Architecture: Developments through Changing Times*. Göteborg.

Faraguna, M. 2005. "La figura dell'aisymnetes tra realtà storica e teoria politica." In R. Wallace and M. Gagarin (eds.), *Symposion 2001: Vorträge zur griechischen und hellenistischen Rechtsgeschichte*, 321–38. Vienna.

Faraone, C. 1993. "Molten Wax, Spilt Wine and Mutilated Animals: Sympathetic Magic in Near Eastern and Early Greek Oath Ceremonies." *JHS* 113, 60–80.

Faure, P. 1960. "La Crète aux cent villes." *Bulletin de l'Association Guillaume Budé* 4th ser. 2: 228–49.

Faustoferri, A. 1996. *Il trono di Amyklai e Sparta: Bathykles al servizio del potere*. Naples.

Fehling, D. 1985. *Die Sieben Weisen und die frühgriechische Chronologie*. Bern.

Fehr, B. 1971. *Orientalische und griechische Gelage*. Bonn.

Fehr, B. 1996. "Kouroi e korai. Formule e tipi dell'arte arcaica come espressione di valori." In Settis 1996: 785–843.

Felsch, R. C. S. 1983. "Zur Chronologie und zum Stil geometrischer Bronzen aus Kalapodi." In Hägg 1983b: 123–29.

Felsch, R. C. S. 1991. "Tempel und Altäre im Heiligtum der Artemis Elaphebolos von Hyampolis bei Kalapodi." In R. Etienne and M. T. Le Dinahet (eds.), *L'Espace sacrificiel dans les civilisations Méditerranéens de l'antiquité*, 85–91. Paris and Lyon.

Felsch, R. C. S. 1999. "To Mikinaikon leron sto Kalapodi. Latreia kai Teletouryikon." In *I perifereia tou mikinaikou kosmou: A' diethnes diepistimoniko sibosio Lamia, 25–29 Septemvriou 1994*, 163–70. Lamia.

Felsch, R. C. S. 2001. "Opferhandlungen des Alltagslebens im Heiligtum der Artemis Elaphebolos von Hyampolis in den Phasen SHIIIC – Spätgeometrisch." In Laffineur and Hägg 2001: 193–200.

Felsch, R. C. S., H. J. Kienast, and H. Schuler. 1980. "Apollon und Artemis oder Artemis und Apollon? Bericht von den Grabungen im neu entdeckten Heiligtum bei Kalapodi, 1973–1977." *AA* 1980: 38–123.

Felsch, R. C. S. et al. 1987. "Bericht über die Grabungen im Heiligtum der Artemis Elaphebolos und des Apollon von Hyampolis." *AA* 1987: 1–99.

Felson-Rubin, N. 1994. *Regarding Penelope: From Character to Poetics*. Princeton.

Figueira, T. J. 1981. *Aegina: Society and Politics*. Salem.

Figueira, T. J. 1985. "The Theognidea and Megarian Society." In Figueira and Nagy 1985: 112–58.

Figueira, T. J. 1991. *Athens and Aigina in the Age of Imperial Colonization*. Baltimore.

Figueira, T. J. 1999. "The Evolution of the Messenian Identity." In Hodkinson and Powell 1999: 211–44.

Figueira, T. J. 2002. "Iron Money and the Ideology of Consumption in Laconia." In Powell and Hodkinson 2002: 137–70.

Figueira, T. J. 2003. "The Demography of the Spartan Helots." In Luraghi and Alcock 2003: 193–239.

Figueira, T. J. 2004a. "The Nature of the Spartan *kleros*." In Figueira 2004b: 47–76.

Figueira, T. J. (ed.). 2004b. *Spartan Society*. London and Swansea.

Figueira, T. J. and G. Nagy (eds.). 1985. *Theognis and Megara: Poetry and the Polis*. Baltimore.

Finley, M. I. 1954 (1962, 1978, 2002). *The World of Odysseus*. New York; 2nd edn. 1962; 3rd edn. 1978; 4th edn., with intro. by Simon Hornblower, London 2002.

Finley, M. I. 1968. "Sparta." In Vernant 1968: 143–60. Repr. in Finley, *The Use and Abuse of* History,[2] 161–78. London, 1986. Also repr. as "Sparta and Spartan Society" in Finley 1982: 24–40, 253–55.

Finley, M. I. 1970 (1981). *Early Greece: The Bronze and Archaic Ages*. New York; 2nd edn. London, 1981.

Finley, M. I. 1973a (1985). *The Ancient Economy*. London; 2nd rev. edn. London, 1985.

Finley, M. I. 1973b (1985). *Democracy Ancient and Modern*. London; 2nd edn. 1985.

Finley, M. I. 1977. "The Ancient City: From Fustel de Coulanges to Max Weber and Beyond." *Comparative Studies in Society and History* 19: 305–27.

Finley, M. I. 1982. *Economy and Society in Ancient Greece*. B. D. Shaw and R. P. Saller, eds. New York.

Finley, M. I. 1998. *Ancient Slavery and Modern Ideology*. Expanded edn., ed. B. D. Shaw. Princeton.

Finnegan, R. 1988. *Literacy and Orality*. Oxford.

Finster-Hotz, U. 1984. *Der Bauschmuck des Athenatempels von Assos. Studien zur Ikonographie.* Rome.

Fischer-Hansen, T. 1996. "The Earliest Town-planning of the Western Greek Colonies, with Special Regard to Sicily." In Hansen 1996: 317–73.

Fisher, E. 1988. "A Comparison of Mycenaean Pottery from Apulia with Mycenaean Pottery from Western Greece." Diss. University of Minnesota.

Fisher, N. R. E. 1989. "Drink, Hybris and the Promotion of Harmony in Sparta." In Powell 1989: 26–50.

Fisher, N. R. E. 1992. *Hybris: A Study in the Values of Honour and Shame in Ancient Greece.* Warminster.

Fisher, N. R. E. 1993. *Slavery in Classical Greece.* London.

Fisher, N. R. E. 1994. "Sparta Re(de)valued: Some Athenians' Public Attitudes to Sparta between Leuctra and the Lamian War." In Powell and Hodkinson 1994: 347–400.

Fisher, N. R. E. 1998. "Gymnasia and Social Mobility in Athens." In P. Cartledge, P. Millett, and S. von Reden (eds.), *KOSMOS: Essays in Order, Conflict and Community in Classical Athens,* 84–104. Cambridge.

Fisher, N. R. E. 2003. "'Let Envy Be Absent': Envy, Liturgies and Reciprocity in Athens." In D. Konstan and K. Rutter (eds.), *Envy, Spite and Jealousy: The Rivalrous Emotions in Ancient Greece,* 181–215. Edinburgh.

Fisher, N. R. E. and H. van Wees (eds.). 1998. *Archaic Greece: New Approaches and New Evidence.* London.

Flaig, E. 1993. "Die spartanische Abstimmung nach der Lautstärke (Überlegungen zu Thukydides 1,87)." *Historia* 42: 139–60.

Flaig, E. 2001. "Unsere fremd gewordene Antike: Warum wir ihr mehr verdanken, als wir noch wahrhaben wollen." *Neue Zürcher Zeitung,* Oct. 6.

Flensted-Jensen, P. (ed.). 2000. *Further Studies in the Ancient Greek* Polis. Stuttgart.

Flensted-Jensen, P., T. H. Nielsen, and L. Rubinstein (eds.). 2000. *Polis and Politics: Studies in Ancient Greek History.* Copenhagen.

Fletcher, R. 2006. "The Cultural Biography of a Phoenician Mushroom-lipped Jug." *OJA* 25: 173–94.

Flower, M. A. 2002. "The Invention of Tradition in Classical and Hellenistic Sparta." In Powell and Hodkinson 2002: 191–217.

Foley, A. 1988. *The Argolid 800–600 BC: An Archaeological Survey.* Gothenburg.

Foley, H. P. 1978 (1984). "'Reverse Similes' and Sex Roles in the *Odyssey.*" *Arethusa* 11: 7–26. Repr. in J. Peradotto and J. P. Sullivan (eds.), *Women in the Ancient World: The Arethusa Papers,* 59–78. Albany, 1984.

Foley, J. M. (ed.). 2005. *A Companion to Ancient Epic.* Malden and Oxford.

Foner, P. S. 1962. *A History of Cuba and Its Relations with the United States,* I: *1492–1845.* New York.

Fontenrose, J. 1978. *The Delphic Oracle: Its Responses and Operations, with a Catalogue of Responses.* Berkeley.

Forbes, H. 2000. "The Agrarian Economy of the Ermionidha around 1700: An Ethnohistorical Reconstruction." In S. Sutton (ed.), *Contingent Countryside. Settlement, Economy and Land Use in the Southern Argolid since 1700,* 41–70. Stanford.

Ford, A. 2002. *The Origins of Criticism.* Princeton.

Ford, A. 2004. "Catharsis: The Power of Music in Aristotle's *Politics.*" In Murray and Wilson 2004: 309–36.

Fornara, C. W. 1983a. *Archaic Times to the End of the Peloponnesian War*[2]. Translated Documents of Greece and Rome 1. Cambridge.

Fornara, C. W. 1983b. *The Nature of History in Ancient Greece and Rome*. Berkeley.

Fornasier, J. and B. Böttger (eds.). 2002. *Das Bosporanische Reich: Der Nordosten des Schwarzen Meeres in der Antike*. Mainz.

Forrest, W. G. 1957. "Colonisation and the Rise of Delphi." *Historia* 6: 160–75.

Forrest, W. G. 1960. "The Tribal Colonisation of Chios." *ABSA* 55: 172–89, with pl. 48–50.

Forrest, W. G. 1963. "The Date of the Lykourgan Reforms in Sparta." *Phoenix* 17: 157–79.

Forrest, W. G. 1966. *The Emergence of Greek Democracy*. London.

Forrest, W. G. 1968 (1980, 1995). *A History of Sparta 950–192 BC*. London; 2nd edn. 1980; 3rd edn. 1995.

Forsdyke, S. 2005. *Exile, Ostracism, and Democracy: The Politics of Expulsion in Ancient Greece*. Princeton.

Forsén, B. 2003. "The Road Network of the Valley." In J. Forsén and B. Forsén, *The Asea Valley Survey*, 63–75. Stockholm.

Forsén, J., B. Forsén, and E. Østby. 1999. "The Sanctuary of Agios Elias: Its Significance and Its Relations to Surrounding Sanctuaries and Settlements." In Nielsen and Roy 1999: 169–91.

Forster, E. S. 1902. "Praesos: The Terracottas." *ABSA* 8: 271–81.

Forster, E. S. 1905. "Terracotta Plaques from Praesos." *ABSA* 11: 243–57.

Förtsch, R. 1998. "Spartan Art: Its Many Different Deaths." In W. G. Cavanagh and S. E. C. Walker (eds.), *Sparta in Laconia: The Archaeology of a City and Its Countryside*, 48–55. London.

Förtsch, R. 2001. *Kunstverwendung und Kunstlegitimation im archaischen und frühklassischen Sparta*. Mainz.

Fossey, J. M. 1990. *The Ancient Topography of Opountian Lokris*. Amsterdam.

Foster, B. R. 2005. *Before the Muses: An Anthology of Akkadian Literature.*[3] Bethesda.

Fouchard, A. 2003. "Homère et le bon ordre politique." *Gaia* 7: 75–86.

Fowler, R. L. 1987. *The Nature of Early Greek Lyric: Three Preliminary Studies*. Toronto.

Fowler, R. L. 1998. "Genealogical Thinking, Hesiod's *Catalogue*, and the Creation of the Hellenes." *PCPhS* 44: 1–19.

Fowler, R. L. 2006. "Herodotus and His Prose Predecessors." In Dewald and Marincola 2006: 29–45.

Fowler, R. L. (ed.). 2004. *The Cambridge Companion to Homer*. Cambridge.

Foxhall, L. 1995. "Bronze to Iron: Agricultural Systems and Political Structures in Late Bronze Age and Early Iron Age Greece." *ABSA* 90: 239–50.

Foxhall, L. 1997. "A View from the Top. Evaluating the Solonian Property Classes." In Mitchell and Rhodes 1997: 113–36.

Foxhall, L. 1998. "Cargoes of the Heart's Desire: The Character of Trade in the Archaic Mediterranean World." In Fisher and van Wees 1998: 295–309.

Foxhall, L. 2000. "The Running Sands of Time." *World Archaeology* 31: 484–98.

Foxhall, L. 2003. "Cultures, Landscapes, and Identities in the Mediterranean World." *Mediterranean Historical Review* 18: 75–92.

Foxhall, L. and K. Stears. 2000. "Redressing the Balance: Dedications of Clothing to Artemis and the Order of Life Stages." In M. Donald and L. Hurcombe (eds.), *Gender and Material Culture*, 3–16. London.

Fränkel, H. 1973. *Early Greek Poetry and Philosophy*. Tr. M. Hadas and J. Willis. New York.

Frau, B. 1982. "Graviscae: Porto Greco di Tarquinia." In B. Frau (ed.), *Gli antichi porti di Tarquinia*, 1–81. Rome.

Frederiksen, R. 2003. "Walled *Poleis* of the Archaic Period: Architecture, Distribution and Significance." Diss. University of Copenhagen.

Freeman, K. 1948. *Ancilla to the Pre-Socratic Philosophers*. Cambridge.

Freitag, K., P. Funke, and N. Moustakis. 2004. "Aitolia." In Hansen and Nielsen 2004: 379–90.

French, E. 1981. "Mycenaean Figures and Figurines: Their Typology and Function." In R. Hägg and N. Marinatos (eds.), *Sanctuaries and Cults in the Aegean Bronze Age*, 41–8. Stockholm.

Freyer-Schauenburg, B. 1974. *Bildwerke der archaischen Zeit und des Strengen Stils*. Samos XI. Bonn.

Friedländer, P. 1948. *Epigrammata: Greek Inscriptions in Verse from the Beginnings to the Persian Wars*. Berkeley.

Friis Johansen, K. 1923. *Les vases sicyoniens*. Paris and Copenhagen.

Friis Johansen, K. 1957. "Exochi. Ein frühgriechisches Gräberfeld." *Acta Archaeologica* 28: 1–192.

Fritz, K. von. 1967. *Die griechische Geschichtsschreibung*, I. Berlin.

Frödin, O. and A. Persson. 1938. *Asine: Results of the Swedish Excavations 1922–1930*. Stockholm.

Frost, F. 1984. "The Athenian Military before Cleisthenes." *Historia* 33: 283–94. Repr. in F. Frost, *Politics and the Athenians. Essays on Athenian History and Historiography*, 175–90. Toronto 2005.

Funke, P. 1993. "Stamm und Polis. Überlegungen zur Entstehung der griechischen Staatenwelt in den 'Dunklen Jahrhunderten.'" In Bleicken 1993: 29–48.

Funke, P. 1997. "Polisgenese und Urbanisierung in Aitolien im 5. und 4. Jh. v. Chr." In Hansen 1997: 145–88.

Funke, P. 2001a. "Acheloos' Homeland. New Historical-Archaeological Research on the Ancient Polis Stratos." In Isager 2001: 189–204.

Funke, P. 2001b. "Wendezeit und Zeitenwende: Athens Aufbruch zur Demokratie." In Papenfuß and Strocka 2001: 1–16.

Funke, P. 2002. "Europäische *lieux de mémoire* oder *lieux de mémoire* für Europa im antiken Griechenland?" In *Jahrbuch für Europäische Geschichte* 3: 3–16.

Furtwängler, A. 1984. "Wer entwarf den grössten Tempel Griechenlands?" *MDAI(A)* 99: 97–103.

Fusaro, D. 1982. "Note di architettura domestica greca nel periodo tardo-geometrico e arcaico." *DdA* n.s. 1: 5–30.

Fustel de Coulanges, N. D. 1873 (1864). *La cité antique: étude sur le culte, le droit, les institutions de la Grèce et de Rome*. Paris.

Gaebel, R. E. 2002. *Cavalry Operations in the Ancient Greek World*. Oklahoma.

Gagarin, M. 1974. "Hesiod's Dispute with Perses." *TAPhA* 104: 103–11.

Gagarin, M. 1981. *Drakon and Early Athenian Homicide Law*. New Haven.

Gagarin, M. 1986. *Early Greek Law*. Berkeley.

Gallet de Santerre, H. 1958. *Délos primitive et archaïque*. Paris.

Galloway, P. 1986. "Long-term Fluctuations in Climate and Population in the Preindustrial Era." *Population and Development Review* 12: 1–24.

Galloway, P. 1988. "Basic Patterns in Annual Variation in Fertility, Nuptiality, Mortality, and Prices in Preindustrial Europe." *Population Studies* 42: 275–303.

Gardiner E. N. 1930. *Athletics in the Ancient World*. Oxford.

Garnsey, P. 1988. *Famine and Food Supply in the Graeco-Roman World: Responses to Risk and Crisis*. Cambridge.

Garnsey, P., K. Hopkins, and C. R. Whittaker (eds.). 1983. *Trade in the Ancient Economy*. Cambridge.

Garnsey, P. and C. R. Whittaker (eds.). 1983. *Trade and Famine in Classical Antiquity.* Cambridge.

Gates, C. 1983. *From Cremation to Inhumation: Burial Practices at Ialysos and Kameiros During the Mid-Archaic Period, ca. 625–525 BC.* Los Angeles.

Gauger, J.-D. 2000. *Authentizität und Methode. Untersuchungen zum historischen Wert des persisch-griechischen Herrscherbriefs in literarischer Tradition.* Hamburg.

Gauss, W. and F. Ruppenstein. 1998. "Die Athener Akropolis in der frühen Eisenzeit." *MDAI(A)* 113: 1–60.

Gavrilyuk, N. A. 1999. *Istoriya ekonomiki Stepnoi Skifii VI-III vv. do n.e.* Kiev.

Gawantka, W. 1985. *Die sogenannte Polis: Entstehung, Geschichte und Kritik der modernen althistorischen Grundbegriffe der griechische Staat, die griechische Staatsidee, die Polis.* Stuttgart.

Gebhard, E. 2002. "The Beginnings of Panhellenic Games at the Isthmus." In Kyrieleis 2002b: 221–37.

Geertz, C. 1973. *The Interpretation of Cultures.* New York.

Gehrke, H.-J. 1985. *Stasis: Untersuchungen zu den inneren Kriegen in den griechischen Staaten des 5. und 4. Jahrhunderts v. Chr.* Munich.

Gehrke, H.-J. 1986. *Jenseits von Athen und Sparta.* Munich.

Gehrke, H.-J. 1993. "Gesetz und Konflikt: Überlegungen zur frühen Polis." In Bleicken 1993: 49–67.

Gehrke, H.-J. (ed.). 1994. *Rechtskodifizierung und soziale Normen im interkulturellen Vergleich.* Tübingen.

Gehrke, H.-J. 1994–5. "Die kulturelle und politische Entwicklung Akarnaniens vom 6. bis zum 4. Jahrhundert v. Chr." *GeogrAnt* 3–4: 41–7.

Gehrke, H.-J. 1995a. "Der Nomosbegriff der Polis." In O. Behrends and W. Sellert (eds.), *Nomos und Gesetz: Ursprünge und Wirkungen des griechischen Gesetzesdenkens,* 13–35. Göttingen.

Gehrke, H.-J. 1995b. "Zwischen Altertumswissenschaft und Geschichte: Zur Standortbestimmung der Alten Geschichte am Ende des 20. Jahrhunderts." In E.-R. Schwinge (ed.), *Die Wissenschaften vom Altertum am Ende des 2. Jahrtausends n. Chr.,* 160–96. Stuttgart and Leipzig.

Gehrke, H.-J. 1997. "Gewalt und Gesetz. Die soziale und politische Ordnung Kretas in der Archaischen und Klassischen Zeit." *Klio* 79: 23–68.

Gehrke, H.-J. 2000a. "*Ethnos, phyle, polis.* Gemäßigt unorthodoxe Vermutungen." In Flensted-Jensen et al. 2000: 159–76.

Gehrke, H.-J. 2000b. "Verschriftung und Verschriftlichung sozialer Normen im Archaischen und Klassischen Griechenland." In E. Lévy (ed.), *La Codification des lois dans l'Antiquité,* 141–59. Paris.

Gehrke, H.-J. 2001. "Myth, History, and Collective Identity: Uses of the Past in Ancient Greece and Beyond." In Luraghi 2001c: 286–313.

Gehrke, H.-J. 2003a. "Marathon (490 v.Chr.) als Mythos: Von Helden und Barbaren." In G. Krumeich and S. Brandt (eds.), *Schlachtenmythen: Ereignis – Erzählung – Erinnerung,* 19–32. Cologne.

Gehrke, H.-J. 2003b. "Sull'etnicità elea." *GeogrAnt* 12: 5–22.

Gehrke, H.-J. 2005. "*Zur elischen Ethnizität.*" In T. Schmitt, W. Schmitz, and A. Winterling (eds.), *Gegenwärtige Antike – antike Gegenwarten,* 17–47. Munich.

Gehrke, H.-J. and E. Wirbelauer. 2004. "Akarnania and Adjacent Areas." In Hansen and Nielsen 2004: 351–78.

Gentili, B. 1988. *Poetry and Its Public in Ancient Greece: From Homer to the Fifth Century.* Baltimore.

Gentili, B. and C. Prato (eds.). 1988. *Poetae Elegiaci: Testimonia et Fragmenta*, I.² Leipzig.

Georganas, I. 2002. "Constructing Identities in Early Iron Age Thessaly: The Case of the Halos Tumuli." *OJA* 21: 289–98.

Georges, P. 1994. *Barbarian Asia and the Greek Experience from the Archaic Period to the Age of Xenophon.* Baltimore.

Gerber, D. E. 1997. *A Companion to Greek Lyric Poets.* Leiden.

Gerber, D. E. 1999a. *Greek Elegiac Poetry: From the Seventh to the Fifth Centuries* BC. Cambridge.

Gerber, D. E. 1999b. *Greek Iambic Poetry.* Cambridge.

Gerkan, A. von. 1915. *Der Poseidonaltar bei Kap Monodendri.* Berlin.

Gernet, L. 1968 (1952, 1981). "Sur le symbolisme politique: Le foyer commun." In Gernet, *Anthropologie de la Grèce antique*, 382–402. Paris. Originally in *Cahiers internationaux de sociologie* 11 (1952): 22–43. English as "Political Symbolism: The Public Hearth." In Gernet, *The Anthropology of Ancient Greece*, 322–39. Tr. J. Hamilton and B. Nagy. Baltimore, 1981.

Gialanella, C. 2003. "Pittekoussai." In N. Stampolidis (ed.), *Sea Routes from Sidon to Huelva: Interconnections in the Mediterranean 16th–6th c. BC*, 178–83. Athens.

Giangiulio, M. 1996. "Avventurieri, mercanti, coloni, mercenari: Mobilità umana e circolazione di risorse nel Mediterraneo antico." In Settis 1996: 497–525.

Giannisi, Ph. 2006. *Récits des voies. Chant et cheminement en Grèce archaïque.* Grenoble.

Gibson, J. C. L. 1982. *Textbook of Syrian-Semitic Inscriptions*, III. Oxford.

Gierth, L. 1971. "Griechische Gründungsgeschichten als Zeugnisse historischen Denkens vor dem Einsetzen der Geschichtsschreibung." Diss. Fribourg.

Gigon, O. (ed.). 1987. *Aristoteles: Librorum deperditorum fragmenta.* Berlin and New York.

Gill, C., N. Postlethwaite, and R. Seaford (eds.). 1998. *Reciprocity in Ancient Greece.* Oxford.

Gill, D. W. J. 1991. "Pots and Trade: Spacefillers or Objets d'art?" *JHS* 111: 29–47.

Gill, D. W. J. 1994. "Positivism, Pots and Long-Distance Trade." In Morris 1994: 99–107.

Gill, D. W. J. and M. Vickers. 2001. "Laconian Lead Figurines: Mineral Extraction and Exchange in the Archaic Mediterranean." *ABSA* 96: 229–36.

Gillett, A. 2002. *On Barbarian Identity in the Early Middle Ages.* Turnhout.

Ginouvès, R. (ed.). 1994. *Macedon from Philip II to the Roman Conquest.* Princeton.

Giorgieri, M., M. Salvini, M.-C. Trémouille, and P. Vannicelli (eds.). 2003. *Licia e Lidia prima dell'ellenizzazione.* Rome.

Giovannini, A. 1969. *Etude historique sur les origines du catalogue des vaisseaux.* Bern.

Glaser, F. 1983. *Antike Brunnenbauten in Griechenland.* Vienna.

Glass, S. L. 1988. "The Greek Gymnasium: Some Problems." In Raschke 1988: 155–73.

Glotz, G. 1926. *Ancient Greece at Work: An Economic History of Greece from the Homeric Period to the Roman Conquest.* New York.

Glotz, G. and R. Cohen. 1925. *Histoire Ancienne*, II: *Histoire grecque*, I: *Des origines aux guerres médiques.* Paris.

Goette, H. G. 1993. *Athen–Attika–Megaris: Reiseführer zu den Kunstschätzen und Kulturdenkmälern im Zentrum Griechenlands.* Cologne.

Goette, H. G. 2000a. *Athens, Attica and the Megarid: An Archaeological Guide.* London.

Goette, H. G. 2000b. *Ho axiologos demos Sounion: Landeskundliche Studien in Südost-Attika.* Rahden.

Goldberg, M. Y. 1999. "Spatial and Behavioural Negotiation in Classical Athenian Houses." In P. M. Allison (ed.), *The Archaeology of Household Activities*, 142–61. New York.

Golden, M. 1990. *Children and Childhood in Classical Athens.* Baltimore.

Golden, M. 1998. *Sport and Society in Ancient Greece.* Cambridge.

Goldstone, J. 2002. "Efflorescences and Economic Growth in World History: Rethinking the 'Rise of the West' and the Industrial Revolution." *Journal of World History* 13: 323–89.

Goldstone, J. and J. F. Haldon. 2008. "Ancient States, Empires and Exploitation: Problems and Perspectives." In I. Morris and W. Scheidel (eds.), *The Dynamics of Ancient Empires*, 3–29. New York.

Goody, J. (ed.). 1968a. *Literacy in Traditional Societies*. Cambridge.

Goody, J. 1968b. "Restricted Literacy in Northern Ghana." In Goody 1968a: 198–264.

Goody, J. 1977. *The Domestication of the Savage Mind*. Cambridge.

Goody, J. and I. Watt. 1968. "The Consequences of Literacy." In Goody 1968a: 69–84.

Gorman, V. B. 2001. *Miletos, the Ornament of Ionia: A History of the City to 400 BCE*. Ann Arbor.

Gorman, V. B. and E. W. Robinson (eds.). 2002. *Oikistes: Studies in Constitutions, Colonies, and Military Power in the Ancient World*. Leiden.

Gosden, C. 2005. *The Archaeology of Colonialism*. Cambridge.

Gounaris, A. P. 1999. "Erevnes oikistikis ton Protoyeometrikon – Yeometrikon Kikladon kai ta zitoumena tis Kikladikis protoistorias." In Stampolidis 1999: 96–113.

Gounaris, A. P. 2002. *Stoikheia oikistikis – poleodomias – arkhitektonikis kata tin protogeometriki – geometriki periodo kai i simvoli tous stin ermineia yenesis tis poleos*. Diss. University of Crete.

Gounaris, A. P. 2005a. "I apousia ton Kikladon apo ton Nion Kataloyon. Ermineftiki prosegisi basei tou mithou." *Epetiris Etaireias Kikladikon Meleton* 18: 94–142.

Gounaris, A. P. 2005b. "Cult Places in the Cyclades during the Protogeometric and Geometric Periods: Their Contribution in Interpreting the Rise of the Cycladic *Poleis*." In Yeroulanou and Stamatopoulou 2005: 13–68.

Graham, A. J. 1960. "The Authenticity of the *horkion ton oikisteron* of Cyrene." *JHS* 80: 94–111. Repr. in Graham 2001: 83–112.

Graham, A. J. 1964a (1983). *Colony and Mother City in Ancient Greece*. Manchester; 2nd enlarged edn. Chicago 1983.

Graham, A. J. 1964b. "ΟΙΚΗΙΟΙ ΠΕΡΙΝΘΙΟΙ." *JHS* 84: 73–75. Repr. in Graham 2001: 257–62.

Graham, A. J. 1978. "The Foundation of Thasos." *ABSA* 73: 61–98. Repr. in Graham 2001: 165–229.

Graham, A. J. 1982a. "The Colonial Expansion of Greece." *CAH*² III.3: 83–162.

Graham, A. J. 1982b. "On the Great List of Theori at Thasos." *The Ancient World* 5: 103–21. Repr. in Graham 2001: 231–56.

Graham, A. J. 1982c. "The Western Greeks." *CAH*² III.3: 163–95.

Graham, A. J. 1984. "Religion, Women, and Greek Colonization." In *Religione e città nel mondo antico. Atti, Centro ricerche e documentazione sull'antichità classica* 11. Rome 1981–2 (1984) 293–314. Repr. in Graham 2001: 327–48.

Graham, A. J. 1990. "Pre-Colonial Contacts: Questions and Problems." In Descoeudres 1990: 45–60.

Graham, A. J. 2001. *Collected Papers on Greek Colonization*. Leiden.

Graham, A. J. 2002. "The Colonization of Samothrace." *Hesperia* 71: 231–60.

Gras, M. 1995. *La Méditerranée archaïque*. Paris.

Gras, M. 1997. *Il Mediterraneo nell'età arcaica*. Paestum.

Gras, M. 2002. "Périples culturels entre Carthage, la Grèce et la Sicile au VIIIᵉ siècle av. J.-C." In C. Müller and F. Prost (eds.), *Identités et cultures dans le monde Méditerranéen antique*, 183–98. Paris.

Gras, M., H. Tréziny, and H. Broise. 2004. *Mégara Hyblaea, V: La ville archaïque*. Paris.

Gray, D. 1974. *Seewesen*. Archaeologia Homerica, G. Göttingen.

Gray, V. 1996. "Herodotus and Images of Tyranny: The Tyrants of Corinth." *American Journal of Philology* 117: 361–89.

Grayson, A. K. 1975. *Assyrian and Babylonian Chronicles.* Locust Valley.

Graziosi, B. and J. Haubold. 2003. "Homeric Masculinity ἠνορέη and ἀγηνορίη." *JHS* 123: 60–76.

Graziosi, B. and J. Haubold. 2005. *Homer: The Resonance of Epic.* London.

Greaves, A. M. 2002. *Miletos: A History.* London.

Greco, E. 1993. *Archeologia della Magna Grecia.*[2] Rome and Bari.

Greco, E. (ed.). 1999. *La città greca antica: Istituzioni, società e forme urbane.* Rome.

Greco, E. 2001. "Abitare in campagna." In *Problemi della chora coloniale dall'Occidente al Mar Nero*, 171–201. Taranto.

Greco, E. (ed.). 2002. *Gli Achei e l'identità etnica degli Achei d'Occidente.* Paestum.

Greco, E., T. Kalpaxis, N. Papadakis, A. Schnapp, and D. Viviers. 2000. "Itanos (Crète Orientale)." *BCH* 124: 551–5.

Greenblatt, S. 1991. *Marvelous Possessions: The Wonder of the New World.* Chicago.

Greene, E. 2002. "Subjects, Objects, and Erotic Symmetry in Sappho's Fragments." In N. S. Rabinowitz and L. Avanger (eds.), *Among Women: From the Homosocial to the Homoerotic in the Ancient World*, 82–105. Austin.

Greenewalt, C. H. 1992. "When a Mighty Empire Was Destroyed: The Common Man at the Fall of Sardis, ca. 546 BC." *Proceedings of the American Philosophical Society* 136: 247–71.

Greenewalt, C. H. 1995a. "Croesus of Sardis and the Lydian Kingdom." In Sasson 1995: 1173–83.

Greenewalt, C. H. 1995b. "Sardis in the Age of Xenophon." In P. Briant (ed.), *Dans les pas des Dix-Mille*, 125–45. Toulouse.

Greenewalt, C. H. and M. L. Rautman. 2000. "The Sardis Campaigns of 1996, 1997, and 1998." *AJA* 104: 643–81.

Greenhalgh, P. A. L. 1973. *Early Greek Warfare: Horsemen and Chariots in the Homeric and Archaic Ages.* Cambridge.

Greifenhagen, A. 1965. "Schmuck und Gerät eines lydischen Mädchens." *AK* 8: 13–19.

Grethlein, J. 2006. *Das Geschichtsbild der Ilias: Eine Untersuchung aus phänomenologischer und narratologischer Perspektive.* Göttingen.

Griebel, C. G. and M. C. Nelson. 1998. "The Ano Englianos Hilltop after the Palace." In J. L. Davis (ed.), *Sandy Pylos: An Archaeological History from Nestor to Navarino*, 97–100. Austin.

Griffin, A. 1982. *Sikyon.* Oxford.

Griffiths, A. 1987. "Democedes of Croton: A Greek Doctor at Darius' Court." In Sancisi-Weerdenburg and Kuhrt 1987: 37–51.

Griffiths, A. 1995. "Nonaristocratic Elements in Archaic Poetry." In Powell 1995: 85–103.

Groningen, B. A. van. 1960. *Pindare au Banquet.* Leiden.

Grote, G. 1846–56 (1872). *A History of Greece.* 12 vols. London; 4th edn. 1872.

Grove, A. T. and O. Rackham. 2001. *The Nature of Mediterranean Europe: An Ecological History.* New Haven.

Gruben, G. 2001. *Griechische Tempel und Heiligtümer.*[5] Munich.

Gschnitzer, F. 1955. "Stammes- und Ortsgemeinden im alten Griechenland." *WS* 68: 120–44. Repr. in Gschnitzer 1969: 271–97 and in Gschnitzer 2001–3: 1. 24–50.

Gschnitzer, F. 1960. *Gemeinde und Herrschaft. Von den Grundformen griechischer Staatsordnung.* Sitzungsberichte Österreichische Akad. Wiss. Wien, phil.-hist. Kl. 235.3. Graz. Repr. in Gschnitzer 2001–3: 2. 203–53.

Gschnitzer, F. (ed.). 1969. *Zur griechischen Staatskunde.* Darmstadt.

Gschnitzer, F. 1981. *Griechische Sozialgeschichte von der mykenischen bis zum Ausgang der klassischen Zeit.* Stuttgart.

Gschnitzer, F. 2001–3. *Kleine Schriften zum griechischen und römischen Altertum.* Ed. by C. Trümpy and T. Schmitt. 2 vols. Stuttgart.

Guarducci, M. (ed.). 1935–50. *Inscriptiones Creticae.* 4 vols. Rome.

Guarducci, M. (ed.). 1967–78. *Epigrafia greca.* 4 vols. Rome.

Guarducci, M. 1987. *L'epigrafia greca dalle origini al tardo impero.* Rome.

Guenon, H. 1976. *La Libye.* Paris.

Guglielmino, R. 1996. "Materiali egei e di tipo egeo da Roca Vecchia (Melendugno, Lecce). Nota preliminare." *Studi di antichità, Università di Lecce* 9: 259–86.

Guillon, P. 1943. *Les trépieds du Ptoion.* Paris.

Guthrie, W. K. C. 1962. *A History of Greek Philosophy,* I: *The Earlier Presocratics and the Pythagoreans.* Cambridge.

Guzzo, P. G. "Myths and Archaeology in South Italy." In Descoeudres 1990: 131–41.

Haarer, P. 2000. "Obeloi and Iron in Archaic Greece." Diss. Oxford.

Haas, V. 1994. *Geschichte der hethitischen Religion.* Leiden.

Haber, S., I. Morris, and W. Scheidel. Forthcoming. *Ancient Empires.* Stanford.

Hadzis, C. 1995. "Fêtes et cultes à Corcyre et à Corinthe: Calendrier d'Epire, calendriers des cités coloniales de l'Ouest et calendrier de Corinthe." In *Corinto e l'Occidente,* 445–52.

Hägg, R. 1983a. "Burial Customs and Social Differentiation in 8th-century Argos." In Hägg 1983b: 27–31.

Hägg, R. (ed.). 1983b. *The Greek Renaissance of the Eighth Century* BC: *Tradition and Innovation.* Stockholm.

Hägg, R. (ed.). 1996. *The Role of Religion in the Early Greek Polis.* Stockholm.

Hägg, R. (ed.). 1998. *Ancient Greek Cult Practice from the Archaeological Evidence.* Stockholm.

Hägg, R. (ed.). 2002. *Peloponnesian Cults and Sanctuaries.* Stockholm.

Hägg, R., N. Marinatos, and G. Nordquist (eds.). 1988. *Early Greek Cult Practice.* Stockholm.

Haggis, D. 1996. "Archaeological Survey at Kavousi, Crete: Preliminary Report." *Hesperia* 65: 373–432.

Haggis, D. 2001. "A Dark Age Settlement System in East Crete and a Reassessment of the Definition of Refuge Settlements." In Karageorghis and Morris 2001: 41–59.

Haggis, D., M. S. Mook, C. M. Scarry, L. M. Snyder, and W. C. West. 2004. "Excavations at Azoria, 2002." *Hesperia* 73: 339–400.

Hahn, I. 1983. "Foreign Trade and Foreign Policy in Archaic Greece." In Garnsey and Whittaker 1983: 30–6.

Haider, P. W. 1996. "Griechen im Vorderen Orient und in Ägypten bis ca. 590 v. Chr." In Ulf 1996b: 59–115.

Halbherr, F. 1888. "Scavi e trovamenti nell' antro di Zeus sul Monte Ida in Creta." *Museo Italiano di Antichità Classica* 2: 689–768. Florence.

Halbherr, F. 1901. "Cretan Expedition XVI: Report on the Researches at Praesos." *AJA* 5: 371–92.

Hall, A. R. 1975. *A History of Technology from Early Times to the Fall of Ancient Empires.* Oxford.

Hall, E. 1989. *Inventing the Barbarian: Greek Self-definition through Tragedy.* Oxford.

Hall, J. 1995. "How Argive was the 'Argive' Heraion? The Political and Cultic Geography of the Argive Plain, 900–400 BC" *AJA* 99: 577–613.

Hall, J. 1997. *Ethnic Identity in Greek Antiquity.* Cambridge.

Hall, J. 2000. "Sparta, Lakedaimon and the Nature of Perioikic Dependency." In Flensted-Jensen 2000: 73–89.

Hall, J. 2001. "Contested Ethnicities: Perceptions of Macedonia within Evolving Definitions of Greek Identity." In Malkin 2001: 159–86.

Hall, J. 2002. *Hellenicity: Between Ethnicity and Culture.* Chicago.

Hall, J. 2003a. " 'Culture' or 'Cultures'? Hellenism in the Late Sixth Century." In Dougherty and Kurke 2003: 23–34.

Hall, J. 2003b. "The Dorianization of the Messenians." In Luraghi and Alcock 2003: 142–68.

Hall, J. 2004a. "Culture, Cultures, and Acculturation." In Rollinger and Ulf 2004b: 35–50.

Hall, J. 2004b. "How 'Greek' were the Early Western Greeks?" In Lomas 2004: 35–54.

Hall, J. et al. (1998). Review feature on Hall 1997. *CAJ* 8: 265–83.

Halliday, W. R. 1923. *The Growth of the City State.* Liverpool.

Halperin, D. 1990. *One Hundred Years of Homosexuality.* London.

Halstead, P. 2001. "Mycenaean Wheat, Flax and Sheep: Palatial Intervention in Farming and Its Implications for Rural Society." In Voutsaki and Killen 2001: 38–50.

Hamilakis, Y. and E. Konsolaki. 2004. "Pigs for the Gods: Burnt Animal Sacrifices as Embodied Rituals at a Mycenaean Sanctuary." *OJA* 23: 135–51.

Hammer, D. 2002. *The* Iliad *as Politics: The Performance of Political Thought.* Norman, OK.

Hammond, N. G. L. 1950 (1973). "The Lycurgan Reform at Sparta." *JHS* 70: 42–64. Repr. as "The Creation of Classical Sparta." In Hammond, *Studies in Greek History*, 47–103. Oxford 1973.

Hammond, N. G. L. 1967. *Epirus: The Geography, the Ancient Remains, the History and Topography of Epirus and Adjacent Areas.* Oxford.

Hammond, N. G. L. 1988. "The Expedition of Xerxes." *CAH*² IV: 518–91.

Hammond, N. G. L. 1994. "Illyrians and North-West Greeks." *CAH*² VI: 422–43.

Hammond, N. G. L. and G. T. Griffith. 1979. *A History of Macedonia*, II: *550–336 BC.* Oxford.

Hammond, N. G. L. and L. J. Roseman. 1996. "The Construction of Xerxes' Bridge over the Hellespont." *JHS* 116: 88–107.

Hanell, K. 1934. *Megarische Studien.* Lund.

Hanfmann, G. 1983. *Sardis from Prehistoric to Roman Times.* Cambridge.

Hannestad, L. 1988. "The Athenian Potter and the Home Market." In J. Christiansen and T. Melander (eds.), *Ancient Greek and Related Pottery*, 222–30. Copenhagen.

Hannestad, L. 1996. "Absolute Chronology: Greece and the Near East c.1000–500 BC." *AArch* 67: 39–49.

Hansen, M. H. 1981–2. "The Athenian *heliaia* from Solon to Aristotle." *C&M* 33: 9–47.

Hansen, M. H. 1989. "Solonian Democracy in Fourth-century Athens." *C&M* 40: 71–99.

Hansen, M. H. 1991 (1999). *The Athenian Democracy in the Age of Demosthenes.* Oxford. New exp. edn. Norman 1999.

Hansen, M. H. (ed.). 1993a. *The Ancient Greek City-state.* Copenhagen.

Hansen, M. H. 1993b. "The Polis as a Citizen-state." In Hansen 1993a: 7–29.

Hansen, M. H. 1994. "The 2500th Anniversary of Cleisthenes' Reforms and the Tradition of Athenian Democracy." In Osborne and Hornblower 1994: 25–37.

Hansen, M. H. 1995. "Boeotian *Poleis*: A Test Case." In M. H. Hansen (ed.), *Sources for the Ancient Greek City State*, 13–63. Copenhagen.

Hansen, M. H. (ed.). 1996. *Introduction to an Inventory of Poleis.* Copenhagen.

Hansen, M. H. 1997. "The *Polis* as an Urban Centre: The Literary and Epigraphical Evidence." In Hansen (ed.), *The* Polis *as an Urban Centre and as a Political Community*, 9–86. Copenhagen.

Hansen, M. H. (ed.). 1997. *The Polis as an Urban Centre and as a Political Community.* Copenhagen.

Hansen, M. H. 2002. "Was the *Polis* a State or a Stateless Society?" In Nielsen 2002b: 9–47.

Hansen, M. H. 2004. "The Perioikic *Poleis* of Lakedaimon." In T. H. Nielsen (ed.), *Once Again: Studies in the Ancient Greek Polis*, 149–64. Stuttgart.

Hansen, M. H. and K. Raaflaub (eds.). 1995. *Studies in the Ancient Greek Polis.* Stuttgart.

Hansen, M. H. and K. Raaflaub (eds.). 1996. *More Studies in the Ancient Greek Polis.* Stuttgart.

Hansen, M. H. and T. H. Nielsen (eds.). 2004. *An Inventory of Archaic and Classical Poleis.* Oxford.

Hansen, P. A. 1976. "Pithecusan Humour: The Interpretation of 'Nestor's Cup' Reconsidered." *Glotta* 54: 25–44.

Hanson, V. D. 1989. *The Western Way of War: Infantry Battle in Classical Greece.* New York.

Hanson, V. D. (ed.). 1991. *Hoplites: The Classical Greek Battle Experience.* London.

Hanson, V. D. 1995 (1999b). *The Other Greeks: The Family Farm and the Agrarian Roots of Western Civilization.* New York; 2nd edn. Berkeley 1999.

Hanson, V. D. 1999a. "No Glory That Was Greece: The Persians Win at Salamis, 480 BC." In R. Cowley (ed.), *What if? Military Historians Imagine What Might Have Been*, 15–35. London.

Harding, A. 1994. "Reformation in Barbarian Europe, 1300–600 BC." In Cunliffe 1994b: 304–35.

Harley, J. B. and D. Woodward (eds.). 1987. *The History of Cartography*, I: *Cartography in Prehistoric, Ancient, and Medieval Europe and the Mediterranean.* Chicago.

Harris, E. M. 1997. "A New Solution to the Riddle of the Seisachtheia." In Mitchell and Rhodes 1997: 103–12.

Harris, E. M. 2002. "Did Solon Abolish Debt-Bondage?" *CQ* 52: 415–30.

Harris, H. A. 1964. *Greek Athletes and Athletics.* London.

Harris, R. 1986. *The Origin of Writing.* London.

Harris, W. V. 1989. *Ancient Literacy.* Cambridge.

Harris, W. V. (ed.). 2005. *Rethinking the Mediterranean.* Oxford.

Harrison, T. 2000. *Divinity and History: The Religion of Herodotus.* Oxford.

Harrison, T. 2002. "The Persian Invasions." In Bakker et al. 2002: 551–78.

Hartog, F. 2000. "The Invention of History: The Pre-history of a Concept from Homer to Herodotus." *History and Theory* 39: 384–95.

Hartog, F. 2001. *Memories of Odysseus: Frontier Tales from Ancient Greece.* Tr. Janet Lloyd. Chicago.

Harvey, F. D. 1976. "Sostratos of Aegina." *PP* 31: 206–14.

Hasaki, E. 2002. *Ceramic Kilns in Ancient Greece.* Diss. University of Cincinnati.

Hasebroek, J. 1928. *Staat und Handel im alten Griechenland.* Tübingen.

Hasebroek, J. 1933 (1965). *Trade and Politics in Ancient Greece.* Tr. L. M. Fraser and D. C. MacGregor. London. Repr. New York 1965.

Hatzopoulos, M. B. 1996. *Macedonian Institutions under the Kings.* 2 vols. Athens and Paris.

Hatzopoulos, M. B. 1997. "L'Etat macédonien antique: Un nouveau visage." *CRAI* 1997: 7–25.

Hatzopoulos, M. B. 1999. "Le macédonien: Nouvelles données et nouvelles théories." *Ancient Macedonia* 6: 225–39.

Hatzopoulos, M. B. and P. Paschidis. 2004. "Makedonia." In Hansen and Nielsen 2004: 794–809.

Haubold, J. 2000. *Homer's People: Epic Poetry and Social Formation.* Cambridge.

Haubold, J. 2002. "Greek Epic: A Near Eastern Genre?" *PCPhS* 48: 1–19.

Hauser, S. R. 1999. "Der hellenisierte Orient. Bemerkungen zum Verhältnis von Alter Geschichte, Klassischer und Vorderasiatischer Archäologie." In H. Kühne, R. Bernbeck, and K. Bartl (eds.), *Fluchtpunkt Uruk: Archäologische Einheit aus methodischer Vielfalt. Schriften für Hans-Jörg Nissen*, 316–41. Rahden.

Hauser, S. R. 2001a. "'Greek in Subject and Style, but a Little Distorted': Zum Verhältnis von Orient und Okzident in der Altertumswissenschaft." In S. Altekamp, M. R. Hofter, and M. Krumme (eds.), *Posthumanistische Klassische Archäologie: Historizität und Wissenschaftlichkeit von Interessen und Methoden*, 83–104. Munich.

Hauser, S. R. 2001b. "Orientalismus." In *DNP* 15.1: 1233–43.

Havelock, E. A. 1963. *Preface to Plato*. Oxford.

Havelock, E. A. 1982. *The Literate Revolution in Greece and Its Cultural Consequences*. Princeton.

Haynes, D. 1992. *The Technique of Greek Bronze Statuary*. Mainz.

Head, B. V. 1911. *Historia Numorum*^{2}. Oxford. Various reprints.

Healy, J. F. 1978. *Mining and Metallurgy in the Greek and Roman World*. London.

Heath, M. 1985. "Hesiod's Didactic Poetry." *CQ* 35: 245–63.

Hedreen, G. 2001. *Capturing Troy: The Narrative Functions of Landscape in Archaic and Early Classical Greek Art*. Ann Arbor.

Heftner, H. and K. Tomaschitz (eds.). 2004. *Ad Fontes: Festschrift für G. Dobesch*. Vienna.

Heitsch, E. (ed.). 1966. *Hesiod*. Darmstadt.

Helly, B. 1994. "Quinze années de géographie historique en Thessalie." In *La Thessalie: Quinze années de recherches archéologiques, 1975–1990: Bilans et perspectives*, 13–20. Athens.

Helly, B. 1995. *Aleuas le Roux: Les tétrades et les Tagoi*. Lyon.

Henderson, J. 2003. "*Demos*, Demagogue, Tyrant in Attic Old Comedy." In K. Morgan 2003: 155–79.

Henige, D. P. 1974. *The Chronology of Oral Tradition: The Quest for a Chimera*. Oxford.

Henkelman, W. 2003. "Persians, Medes and Elamites: Acculturation in the Neo-Elamite Period." In Lanfranchi et al. 2003b: 181–231.

Herington, J. 1985. *Poetry into Drama: Early Tragedy and the Greek Poetic Tradition*. Berkeley.

Herman, G. 1987. *Ritualised Friendship and the Greek City*. Cambridge.

Herman, G. 1996. "Reciprocity." *OCD*^{3}: 1295.

Hermary, A. 2000. "Les naïskoi votifs de Marseille." In Hermary and Tréziny 2000: 119–33.

Hermary, A. and H. Tréziny (eds.). 2000. *Les cultes des cités phocéennes*. Aix-en-Provence.

Herrmann, P. 1981. "Teos und Abdera im 5. Jahrhundert v. Chr." *Chiron* 11: 1–30.

Herzog, R. 1971. *Allgemeine Staatslehre*. Frankfurt.

Herzfeld, M. 1985. *The Poetics of Manhood: Contest and Identity in a Cretan Mountain Village*. Princeton.

Heubeck, A. 1955. "Mythologische Vorstellungen des Alten Orients im archaischen Griechentum." *Gymnasium* 62: 508–25.

Heubeck, A. 1979. *Schrift*. Archaeologia Homerica 3.X. Göttingen.

Heubeck, A. and A. Hoekstra. 1989. *A Commentary on Homer's* Odyssey, II: *Books ix–xvi*. Oxford.

Heuss, A. 1946 (1969). "Die archaische Zeit Griechenlands als geschichtliche Epoche." *A&A* 2: 26–62. Repr. in Gschnitzer 1969: 36–96.

Heuss, A. 1981. "Vom Anfang und Ende 'archaischer' Politik bei den Griechen." In G. Kurz, D. Müller, and W. Nikolai (eds.), *Gnomosyne: Menschliches Denken und Handeln in der frühgriechischen Literatur*, 1–29. Munich.

Hignett, C. 1952. *A History of the Athenian Constitution to the End of the Fifth Century* BC. Oxford.

Hind, J. 1994. "The Bosporan Kingdom." *CAH*² VI: 476–511.

Hind, J. 1999. "The Dates and Mother Cities of the Black Sea Colonies (Pseudo-Scymnus and the Pontic Contact Zone)." In O. Lordkipanidzé and P. Lévêque (eds.), *La Mer Noire: Zone de Contacts*, 25–34. Besançon.

Hinz, W. and H. Koch. 1987. *Elamisches Wörterbuch*. 2 vols. Berlin.

Höcker, C. 1998. "Sekos, Dipteros, Hypaethros. Überlegungen zur Monumentalisierung der archaischen Sakralarchitektur Ioniens." In R. Rolle and K. Schmidt (eds.), *Archäologische Studien in Kontaktzonen der antiken Welt*, 147–63. Göttingen.

Höckmann, U. and D. Kreikenbom (eds.). 2001. *Naukratis: Die Beziehungen zu Ostgriechenland, Ägypten und Zypern in archaischer Zeit*. Möhnesee.

Hodder, I. 1986. *Reading the Past*. Cambridge.

Hoddinott, R. F. 1981. *The Thracians*. London.

Hodge, A. T. 1998. *Ancient Greek France*. London.

Hodkinson, S. 1983. "Social Order and the Conflict of Values in Classical Sparta." *Chiron* 13: 239–81.

Hodkinson, S. 1989. "Inheritance, Marriage, and Demography: Perspectives upon the Success and Decline of Classical Sparta." In Powell 1989: 79–121.

Hodkinson, S. 1992. "Sharecropping and Sparta's Economic Exploitation of the Helots." In Sanders 1992: 123–34.

Hodkinson, S. 1997. "The Development of Spartan Society and Institutions in the Archaic Period." In Mitchell and Rhodes 1997: 83–102.

Hodkinson, S. 1998. "Lakonian Artistic Production and the Problem of Spartan Austerity." In Fisher and van Wees 1998: 93–117.

Hodkinson, S. 1999. "An Agonistic Culture? Athletic Competition in Archaic and Classical Spartan Society." In Hodkinson and Powell 1999: 147–87.

Hodkinson, S. 2000. *Property and Wealth in Classical Sparta*. London and Swansea.

Hodkinson, S. 2003. "Spartiates, Helots and the Direction of the Agrarian Economy: Towards an Understanding of Helotage in Comparative Perspective." In Luraghi and Alcock 2003: 248–85.

Hodkinson, S. and A. Powell (eds.). 1999. *Sparta: New Perspectives*. London and Swansea.

Hodos, T. 2006. *Local Responses to Colonization in the Iron Age Mediterranean*. London.

Hoffman, G. L. 1997. *Imports and Immigrants: Near Eastern Contacts with Iron Age Crete*. Ann Arbor.

Hoffmann, H. 1972. *Early Cretan Armorers*. Mainz.

Hoffner, H. A. 1990. *Hittite Myths*.² Ed. G. M. Beckman. Atlanta.

Hofstetter, J. 1978. *Die Griechen in Persien: Prosopographie der Griechen im persischen Reich vor Alexander*. Berlin.

Hogarth, D. 1900. "The Dictaean Cave." *ABSA* 6: 94–116.

Hogarth, D. 1908. *Excavations at Ephesus*. London.

Högemann, P. 1992. *Das alte Vorderasien und die Achämeniden: Ein Beitrag zur Herodot-Analyse*. Wiesbaden.

Holbek, B. 1989. "What the Illiterate Think of Writing." In K. Schousboe and M. T. Larsen (eds.), *Literacy and Society*, 183–96. Copenhagen.

Hölkeskamp, K.-J. 1992a. "Arbitrators, Lawgivers and the 'Codification of Law' in Archaic Greece. Problems and Perspectives." *Metis* 7: 49–81.

Hölkeskamp, K.-J. 1992b. "Written Law in Archaic Greece." *PCPhS* 38: 87–117.

Hölkeskamp, K.-J. 1994. "Tempel, Agora und Alphabet. Die Entstehungsbedingungen der Gesetzgebung in der archaischen Polis." In Gehrke 1994: 135–64.

Hölkeskamp, K.-J. 1997. "*Agorai* bei Homer." In Eder and Hölkeskamp 1997: 1–19.

Hölkeskamp, K.-J. 1999. *Schiedsrichter, Gesetzgeber und Gesetzgebung im archaischen Griechenland.* Stuttgart.

Hölkeskamp, K.-J. 2002. "*Ptolis* and *agore*: Homer and the Archaeology of the City-state." In Montanari 2002: 297–342.

Hölkeskamp, K.-J. 2005. "What's in a Code? Solon's Laws between Complexity, Compilation and Contingency." *Hermes* 132: 280–93.

Holloway, R. R. 1981. "Motives for Colonization." In Holloway, *Italy and the Aegean 3000–700 BC*, 133–54. Louvain-la-Neuve and Providence.

Hölscher, T. 1989. *Die unheimliche Klassik der Griechen.* Bamberg.

Hölscher, T. 1991. "The City of Athens: Space, Symbol, Structure." In A. Molho, K. Raaflaub, and J. Emlen (eds.), *City States in Classical Antiquity and Medieval Italy*, 355–80. Stuttgart.

Hölscher, T. 2000. "Feindwelten – Glückswelten: Perser, Kentauren und Amazonen." In Hölscher (ed.), *Gegenwelten zu den Kulturen Griechenlands und Roms*, 287–320. Munich and Leipzig.

Hölscher, U. 1968. *Anfängliches Fragen. Studien zur frühen griechischen Philosophie.* Göttingen.

Homann-Wedeking, E. 1968. *Archaic Greece.* Tr. J. R. Foster. London.

Hopkins, K. 1983. *Death and Renewal.* Cambridge and New York.

Horden, P. and N. Purcell. 2000. *The Corrupting Sea: A Study of Mediterranean History.* Oxford.

Hornblower, S. 1991. *A Commentary on Thucydides*, I: *Books I–III.* Oxford.

Hornblower, S. 2004. *Thucydides and Pindar.* Oxford.

Hornblower, S. and C. Morgan (eds.). 2007. *Pindar's Poetry, Patrons, and Festivals: From Archaic Greece to the Roman Empire.* Oxford.

Horowitz, D. 1975. "Ethnic Identity." In N. Glazer and D. Moynihan (eds.), *Ethnicity: Theory and Experience*, 111–40. Cambridge.

Horowitz, W. 1998. *Mesopotamian Cosmic Geography.* Winona Lake.

Houby-Nielsen, S. 1992. "Interaction between Chieftains and Citizens?" *Acta Hyperborea* 4: 343–74.

Houby-Nielsen, S. 1995. "'Burial Language' in the Archaic and Classical Kerameikos." *Proceedings of the Danish Institute at Athens* 1: 129–91.

Houby-Nielsen, S. 1996. "The Archaeology of Ideology in the Kerameikos: New Interpretations of the Opferrinnen." In Hägg 1996: 41–54.

Houby-Nielsen, S. 1998. "Revival of Archaic Funerary Practices in the Hellenistic and Roman Kerameikos." *Proceedings of the Danish Institute at Athens* 2: 127–45.

Houby-Nielsen, S. 2000. "Child Burials in Athens." In J. Sofaer Derevenski (ed.), *Children and Material Culture*, 151–66. London.

Houby-Nielsen, S. 2001. "Sacred Landscapes of Aetolia and Achaia: Synoecism Processes and Non-Urban Sanctuaries." In Isager 2001: 257–76.

Houby-Nielsen, S. Forthcoming. *The Significance of the Topography of the Sanctuary of Ay. Irini in Cyprus.* Focus on the Mediterranean 6. Stockholm.

Howe, T. P. 1958. "Linear B and Hesiod's Breadwinners." *TAPhA* 89: 44–65.

Howe, T. 2003. "Pastoralism, the Delphic Amphiktyony and the First Sacred War: The Creation of Apollo's Sacred Pastures." *Historia* 52: 129–46.

Howgego, C. J. 1995. *Ancient History from Coins.* London.

Hubbard T. K. 1994. "Elemental Psychology and the Date of Semonides of Amorgos." *American Journal of Philology* 115: 175–97.

Hubbard, T. K. 2004. "The Dissemination of Epinician Lyric: Pan-Hellenism, Reperformance, Written Texts." In C. J. Mackie (ed.), *Oral Performance and Its Context*, 71–93. Leiden.

Hüber, F. 1997. *Ephesos. Gebaute Geschichte*. Mainz.

Huber, S. 2003. *L'Aire sacrificielle au Nord du sanctuaire d'Apollon Daphnéphoros*. Eretria XIV. Basel.

Hughes, J. D. 1975. *Ecology in Ancient Civilizations*. Albuquerque.

Humphreys, S. C. 1978. *Anthropology and the Greeks*. London.

Humphreys, S. C. 1991. "A Historical Approach to Drakon's Law on Homicide." In M. Gagarin (ed.), *Symposion 1990: Papers on Greek and Hellenistic Legal History*, 17–45. Cologne.

Hurst, H. and S. Owen (eds.). 2005. *Ancient Colonizations: Analogy, Similarity, and Difference*. London.

Hurwit, J. M. 1985. *The Art and Culture of Early Greece, 1100–480 BC*. Ithaca, NY.

Hurwit, J. M. 1999. *The Athenian Acropolis: History, Mythology, and Archaeology from the Neolithic Era to the Present*. Cambridge.

Hussey, Edward. 1972. *The Presocratics*. London.

Hussey, Edward. 1995. "Ionian Inquiries: On Understanding the Presocratic Beginnings of Science." In Powell 1995: 530–49.

Huttner, U. 1997. *Die politische Rolle der Heraklesgestalt im griechischen Herrschertum*. Stuttgart.

Hutzfeldt, B. 1999. *Das Bild der Perser in der griechischen Dichtung des 5. vorchristlichen Jahrhunderts*. Wiesbaden.

Huxley, G. L. 1962. *Early Sparta*. London.

Iakovidis, S. 1981. *Excavations of the Necropolis at Perati*. Los Angeles.

Iakovidis, S. and E. French. 2003. *Archaeological Atlas of Mycenae*. Athens.

Ilari, V. 1980. *Guerra e diritto nel mondo antico*, I: *Guerra e diritto nel mondo greco-ellenistico fino al III secolo*. Milan.

Immerwahr, S. 1990. *Aegean Painting in the Bronze Age*. Philadelphia.

Instone, S. 1990. "Love and Sex in Pindar: Some Practical Thrusts." *BICS* 37: 34–42.

Intzesiloglou, B. 2002. "The Archaic Temple of Apollo at Ancient Metropolis." In Stamatopoulou and Yerolanou 2002: 109–15.

Irani, K. D. and M. Silver (eds.). 1995. *Social Justice in the Ancient World*. Westport.

Isaakidou, V., P. Halstead, J. Davis, and S. Stocker. 2002. "Burnt Animal Sacrifice at the Mycenaean 'Palace of Nestor,' Pylos." *Antiquity* 76: 86–92.

Isager, J. (ed.). 2001. *Foundation and Destruction: Nikopolis and Northwestern Greece*, III. Aarhus.

Isager, S. 1998. "The Pride of Halikarnassos: Editio Princeps of an Inscription from Salmakis." *ZPE* 123: 1–23.

Isserlin, B. S. J. 1991. "The Transfer of the Alphabet to the Greeks: The State of Documentation." In *Phoinikeia Grammata: Lire et Écrire en Méditerranée*, 281–91. Liège.

Jackman, T. 2005. "Burial and Social Diversity in Western Greece, 700–300 BC." Diss. Stanford University.

Jackson, D. A. 1976. *East Greek Influence on Attic Vases*. London.

Jacobs, B. 1994. *Die Satrapienverwaltung im Perserreich zur Zeit Darius' III*. Wiesbaden.

Jacobs, B. 2003. "Die altpersischen Länder-Listen und Herodots sogenannte Satrapienliste (Historien III 89–94)." In R. Dittmann, C. Eder, and B. Jacobs (eds.), *Altertumswissenschaften im Dialog: Festschrift für W. Nagel*, 301–43. Münster.

Jacobsen, T. 1946. "Mesopotamia." In H. Frankfort, H. A. Frankfort, J. A. Wilson, T. Jacobsen, and W. A. Irwin, *The Intellectual Adventure of Ancient Man: An Essay on Speculative Thought in the Ancient Near East*, 125–219. Chicago.

Jacobson, E. 1995. *The Art of the Scythians: The Interpretation of Cultures at the Edge of the Hellenic World*. Leiden.

Jacobsthal, P. 1956. *Greek Pins and Their Connexions with Europe and Asia*. Oxford.

Jacobsthal, P. and A. Langsdorff. 1929. *Die Bronzeschnabelkannen. Ein Beitrag zur Geschichte des vorrömischen Imports nördlich der Alpen*. Berlin.

Jacoby, F. 1902. *Apollodors Chronik. Eine Sammlung der Fragmente*. Berlin.

Jacoby, F. 1923–54. *Die Fragmente der griechischen Historiker*. 3 vols. Berlin, then Leiden.

Jacoby, F. 1956. *Griechische Historiker*. Stuttgart.

Jacquemin, A. 1993. "Repercussions de l'entrée de Delphes dans l'amphictionie sur la construction à Delphes à l'époque archaïque." In Courtils and Moretti 1993: 217–25.

Jacquemin, A. 1999. *Offrandes monumentales à Delphes*. Paris.

Jaeger, W. 1966. *Five Essays*. Tr. A. M. Fiske. Montreal.

James, P. 2003. "Naukratis Revisited." *Hyperboreus* 9: 235–64.

Jameson, F. 1971. *Marxism and Form: Twentieth-century Dialectical Theories of Literature*. Princeton.

Jameson, M. H. 1974. "The Excavation of a Drowned Greek Temple." *Scientific American* 231: 110–19.

Jameson, M. H. 1990a. "Domestic Space in the Greek City-State." In S. Kent (ed.), *Domestic Architecture and the Use of Space*, 92–113. Cambridge.

Jameson, M. H. 1990b. "Private Space and the Greek City." In Murray and Price 1990: 171–95.

Jameson, M. H., C. N. Runnels, and T. H. van Andel. 1994. *A Greek Countryside: The Southern Argolid from Prehistory to the Present Day*. Stanford.

Janko, R. 1982. *Homer, Hesiod and the Hymns: Diachronic Development in Epic Diction*. Cambridge.

Janko, R. 1992. *The* Iliad: *A Commentary*, IV: *Books 13–16*. Cambridge.

Janko, R. 1998. "The Homeric Poems as Oral Dictated Texts." *CQ* 48: 1–13.

Jantzen, U. 1955. *Griechische Greifenkessel*. Berlin.

Jeanneret, M. 1991. *A Feast of Words*. Oxford.

Jeffery, L. H. 1956. "The Courts of Justice in Archaic Chios." *ABSA* 51: 157–67, pl. 43.

Jeffery, L. H. 1961a (1990). *The Local Scripts of Archaic Greece*. Oxford; 2nd edn., with additional material by A. W. Johnston. Oxford 1990.

Jeffery, L. H. 1961b. "The Pact of the First Settlers at Cyrene." *Historia* 10: 139–47.

Jeffery, L. H. 1976. *Archaic Greece: The City-states c. 700–500 BC*. London.

Jeffery, L. H. and A. Morpurgo-Davies. 1970. "POINIKASTAS and POINIKAZEN: A New Archaic Inscription from Crete." *Kadmos* 9: 118–54.

Jellinek, G. 1914. *Allgemeine Staatslehre*.[3] Berlin.

Johannowsky, W. 1955–56. "Frammenti di un dinos di Sophilos da Gortina." *ASAA* 33–34: 45–51.

Johannowsky, W. 2002. *Il Santuario sull'acropoli di Gortina*, II. Athens.

Johnson, A. W. and T. Earle (eds.). 1987. *The Evolution of Human Societies: From Foraging Group to Agrarian State*. Stanford.

Johnston, A. W. 1972. "The Rehabilitation of Sostratos." *PP* 27: 416–23.

Johnston, A. W. 1973. "Two and a Half Corinthian Dipinti." *ABSA* 68: 186–88.

Johnston, A. W. 1979. *Trademarks on Greek Vases*. Warminster.

Johnston, A. W. 1983. "The Extent and Use of Literacy: The Archaeological Evidence." In Hägg 1983b: 63–8.

Johnston, A. W. 1991. "Greek Vases in the Marketplace." In T. Rasmussen and N. Spivey (eds.), *Looking at Greek Vases*, 203–31. Cambridge.

Johnston, A. W. 1999. "Epichoric Alphabets: The Rise of the Polis or a Slip of the Pen?" In N. Dimoudis (ed.), *The History of the Hellenic Language and Writing*, 419–33. Altenburg.

Johnston, A. W. 2006. *Trademarks on Greek Vases: Addenda*. Oxford.

Johnston, A. W. and R. E. Jones. 1978. "The 'SOS' Amphora." *ABSA* 73: 103–41.

Johnstone, W. 1978. "Cursive Phoenician and the Archaic Greek Alphabet." *Kadmos* 17: 151–66.

Jones, A. H. M. 1967. *Sparta*. Oxford.

Jones, D. 2000. *External Relations of Early Iron Age Crete, 1100–600 BC*. Dubuque.

Jones, G. 1982. "Cereal and Pulse Remains from Protogeometric and Geometric Iolkos, Thessaly." *Anthropologika* 3: 75–8.

Jones, G. 1987. "Agricultural Practice in Greek Prehistory." *ABSA* 82: 115–23.

Jones, N. F. 1987. *Public Organization in Ancient Greece: A Documentary Study*. Philadelphia.

Jones, S. 1997. *The Archaeology of Ethnicity: Constructing Identities in the Past and Present*. London.

Jongman, W. and M. Kleijwegt (eds.). 2002. *After the Past: Essays in Ancient History in Honour of H. W. Pleket*. Leiden.

Jordan, D. R. 1985. "A Survey of Greek *defixiones* not Included in the Special Corpora." *GRBS* 26: 151–97.

Jurado, J. 2002. "The Tartessian Economy: Mining and Metallurgy." In Bierling 2002: 241–62.

Kahn, C. H. 1960 (1985). *Anaximander and the Origins of Greek Cosmology*. New York. Repr. 1985.

Kahn, C. H. 1979. *The Art and Thought of Heraclitus: An Edition of the Fragments with Translation and Commentary*. Cambridge.

Kahrstedt, U. 1922. *Griechisches Staatsrecht*, I: *Sparta und seine Symmachie*. Göttingen.

Kallet, L. 1998. "Accounting for Culture in Fifth-century Athens." In Boedeker and Raaflaub 1998: 43–58.

Kamp, J. S. van der. 1996. "Anonymous Tomb Cults in Western Messenia: The Search for a Historical Explanation." *Pharos* 4: 53–88.

Karageorghis, V. (ed.). 1994. *Cyprus in the 11th Century BC*. Nicosia.

Karageorghis, V. 2003. "Heroic Burials in Cyprus and Other Mediterranean Regions." In Stampolidis and Karageorghis 2003: 339–51.

Karageorghis, V. and N. Stampolidis (eds.). 1998. *Eastern Mediterranean: Cyprus–Dodecanese–Crete 16th–6th cent. BC*. Athens.

Karageorghis, V. and C. E. Morris (eds.). 2001. *Defensive Settlements of the Aegean and the Eastern Mediterranean after c. 1200 BC*. Nicosia

Karagiorga, T. G. 1972. "Anaskafi periokhis arkhaiou Doriou." *AEph* 1972: *Chronika* 12–20.

Karamitrou-Mentesidi, G. 1993. *Kozani, City of Elimiotis: Archaeological Guide*. Thessaloniki.

Karamitrou-Mentesidi, G. 1996. "The Macedonian City of Aeane: Historical Identity and Significance." *AEMTH* 10A: 23–33.

Karamitrou-Mentesidi, G. 1999. *Voion – Notia Orestis. Arkhaioloyiki Erevna kai Istoriki Topoyrafia*. Thessaloniki.

Karakasi, K. 2001. *Archaische Koren*. Munich.

Karakasi, K. 2003. *Archaic Korai*. Los Angeles.

Karouzos, C. 1939. "Anaskafai en Naxo." *PAAH* 1939: 119–24.

Kasper-Butz, I. 1990. *Die Göttin Athena im klassischen Athen*. Frankfurt.

Katz, M. 1991. *Penelope's Renown*. Princeton.

Kaufman, S. A. 1982. "Reflections on the Assyrian-Aramaic Bilingual from Tell Fakhariyah." *Maarav* 3: 137–75.

Kaufman, S. A. 1986. "The Pitfalls of Typology: On the Early History of the Alphabet." *Hebrew Union College Annual* 57: 1–14.

Kearns, E. 1989. *The Heroes of Attica*. London.

Kearsley, R. 1999. "Greeks Overseas in the 8th Century BC: Euboeans, Al Mina and Assyrian Imperialism." In G. Tsetskhladze (ed.), *Ancient Greeks West and East*, 109–34. Leiden.

Keen, A. G. 2000. "'Grain for Athens': The Importance of the Hellespontine Route in Athenian Foreign Policy before the Peloponnesian War." In G. J. Oliver, R. Brock, T. J. Cornell, and S. Hodkinson (eds.), *The Sea in Antiquity*, 63–74. Oxford.

Keesling, C. M. 2003. *The Votive Statues of the Athenian Acropolis*. Cambridge.

Keller, D. 1985. "Archaeological Survey in Southern Euboea, Greece: A Reconstruction of Human Activity from Neolithic Times through the Byzantine Period." Diss. Indiana University.

Kennell, N. 1995. *The Gymnasium of Virtue*. Chapel Hill.

Kennell, N. 1999. "From Perioikoi to Poleis. The Laconian Cities in the Late Hellenistic Period." In Hodkinson and Powell 1999: 189–210.

Kenzelmann Pfyffer, A., T. Theurillat, and S. Verdan. 2005. "Graffiti d'époque géométrique provenant du sanctuaire d'Apollon Daphnéphoros à Érétrie." *ZPE* 151: 51–86.

Kenzler, U. 2000. "Vom dörflichen Versammlungsplatz zum urbanen Zentrum. Die Agora im Mutterland und in den Kolonien." In Krinzinger 2000: 23–8.

Kerckhove, D. de. 1981. "A Theory of Greek Tragedy." *Sub-Stance* 29: 23–36.

Kiechle, F. 1959. *Messenische Studien: Untersuchungen zur Geschichte der Messenischen Kriege und der Auswanderung der Messenier*. Kallmünz.

Kiechle, F. 1963. *Lakonien und Sparta: Untersuchungen zur ethnischen Struktur und zur politischen Entwicklung Lakoniens und Spartas bis zum Ende der archaischen Zeit*. Munich.

Kienast, H. J. 1992. "Topographische Studien im Heraion von Samos." *AA*: 171–213.

Kienast, H. J. 1995. *Die Wasserleitung des Eupalinos auf Samos*. Samos XIX. Bonn.

Kilian, K. 1975. *Fibeln in Thessalien von der Mykenischen bis zur Archaischen Zeit: Praehistorische Bronzefunde* XIV. ii. Munich.

Kilian, K. 1977. "Zwei italische Kammhelme aus Griechenland." In *Etudes Delphiques*, 429–42. BCH Supp. 4. Paris.

Kilian, K. 1983. "Weihungen aus Eisen und Eisenverarbeitung im Heiligtum zu Philia (Thessalien)." In Hägg 1983b: 131–46.

Kilian, K. 1985. "Magna Grecia, Epiro e Macedonia durante l'età del ferro." In *Magna Grecia, Epiro e Macedonia*, 237–88. Taranto.

Kilian, K. 1988. "Mycenaeans up-to-date: Trends and Changes in Recent Research." In E. French and K. Wardle (eds.), *Problems in Greek Prehistory*, 115–52. Bristol.

Kilian-Dirlmeier, I. 1985. "Fremde Weihungen in griechischen Heiligtümern vom 8. bis zum Beginn des 7. Jahrhunderts v.Chr." *Jahrbuch des Römisch-Germanischen Zentralmuseums Mainz* 32: 215–54.

Killen, J. 1994. "Thebes Sealings, Knossos Tablets and Mycenaean State Banquets." *BICS* 39: 69–86.

Kim, H. S. 2001. "Archaic Coinage as Evidence for the Use of Money." In Meadows and Shipton 2001: 7–21.

Kim, H. S. 2002. "Small Change and the Moneyed Economy." In P. Cartledge, E. Cohen, and L. Foxhall (eds.), *Money, Labour and Land: Approaches to the Economies of Ancient Greece*, 44–51. London.

Kimmerle, R. 2005. *Völkerrechtliche Beziehungen Spartas in spätarchaischer und frühklassischer Zeit.* Münster.

Kinch, K. F. 1914. *Vroulia.* Berlin.

King, C. 2004. *The Black Sea: A History.* Oxford.

Kinzl, K. H. 1979. "Betrachtungen zur älteren griechischen Tyrannis." In Kinzl (ed.), *Die ältere Tyrannis bis zu den Perserkriegen: Beiträge zur griechischen Tyrannis,* 298–325. Darmstadt.

Kinzl, K. H. (ed.). 1995. *Demokratia: Der Weg zur Demokratie bei den Griechen.* Darmstadt.

Kirchhoff, A. 1970. *Studien zur Geschichte des griechischen Alphabets.* Amsterdam.

Kirk, G. S. 1985. *The* Iliad*: A Commentary,* I: *Books 1–4.* Cambridge.

Kirk, G. S. 1988. "The Development of Ideas, 750–500 BC." *CAH*[2] IV: 389–413.

Kirk, G. S., J. E. Raven, and M. Schofield. 1983. *The Presocratic Philosophers.*[2] Cambridge.

Kisov, K. 2004. *Trakiiskata kultura v regiona na Plovdiv i techenieto na r. Stryama prez vtorata polovina na I khil.pr.khr.* Sofia. Summary in English.

Kistler, E. 1998. *Die Opferrinnen-"Zeremonie." Bankettideologie am Grab, Orientalisierung und Formierung einer Adelsgesellschaft in Athen.* Stuttgart.

Kistler, E. 2004. " 'Kampf der Mentalitäten': Ian Morris' 'elitist' versus 'middling ideology.' " In Rollinger and Ulf 2004b: 145–76.

Klinkott, H. Forthcoming. "Der König, das Reich und die Länder. Überlegungen zum Selbstverständnis des achaimenidischen Grosskönigtums." In R. Krautkrämer and S. Stark (eds.), *Zwischen Bithynien und Baktrien: Studien zur Geschichte und Kultur des antiken Orients.* Stuttgart.

Klippel, W. and L. Snyder. 1991. "Dark Age Fauna from Kavousi, Crete." *Hesperia* 60: 179–86.

Knappett, C. 2005. *Thinking through Material Culture: An Interdisciplinary Perspective.* Philadelphia.

Knoepfler, D. 1988. "Communication sur les traces de l'Artémision d'Amarynthos près d'Erétrie." *CRAI* 1988: 382–421.

Knoepfler, D. 1989. "Le calendrier des Chalcidiens et de Thrace. Essai de mise au point sur la liste et l'ordre des mois eubéens." *Journal des Savants* 1989: 23–59.

Knoepfler, D. 1990. "The Calendar of Olynthus and the Origin of the Chalcidians in Thrace." In Descoeudres 1990: 99–115.

Knox, B. M. W. (ed.). 1985. *The Cambridge History of Classical Literature,* vol. 1. Cambridge.

Köcher, F. 1963–80. *Die babylonisch-assyrische Medizin in Texten und Untersuchungen.* 6 vols. Berlin.

Koerner, R. 1993. *Inschriftliche Gesetzestexte der frühen griechischen Polis.* Ed. K. Halloff. Cologne.

Kõiv, M. 2003. *Ancient Tradition and Early Greek History: The Origins of States in Early-Archaic Sparta, Argos and Corinth.* Tallinn.

Kokkorou-Aleura, G. 1993. "Fragment of a *Kouros* from Tourkoleka at Megalopolis." In O. Palagia and W. Coulson (eds.), *Sculpture from Arcadia and Laconia.* 13–24. Oxford. In Greek.

Kolb, F. 1984. *Die Stadt im Altertum.* Munich.

Kolb, F. 1999. "Bemerkungen zur archaischen Geschichte Athens: Peisistratos und Dionysos, das Heiligtum des Dionysos Lenaios und das Problem der Alten *Agora* in Athen." In Mellor and Tritle 1999: 203–18.

Kolodny, E. Y. 1966. "La population des îles en Méditerranée." *Méditerranée* 1: 3–31.

Kolodny, E. Y. 1974. *La population des îles de la Grèce: Essai de géographie insulaire en Méditerranée orientale,* 3 vols. Aix-en-Provence.

Bibliography				663

Konishi, H. 1993. "The Origins of the Greek Alphabet: A Fresh Approach." *Liverpool Classical Monthly* 18.7: 102–5.

Konstan, D. and K. Rutter (eds.). 2003. *Envy, Spite and Jealousy: The Rivalrous Emotions in Ancient Greece*. Edinburgh.

Kontoleon, N. 1939. "Anaskafai en Naxo." *Praktika*: 119–24.

Kontoleon, N. and C. Karouzos. 1937. "Anaskafai en Naxo." *PAAH* 1937: 115–22.

Koparal, E. and E. Iplikçi. 2004. "Archaic Olive Oil Extraction Plant in Klazomenai." In A. Moustaka et al. (eds.), *Klazomenai, Teos and Abdera: Metropoleis and Colony*, 221–34. Thessaloniki.

Kophiniotis, I. K. 1892. *Istoria tou Argous*. Athens.

Kopcke, G. and I. Tokumaru (eds.). 1992. *Greece Between East and West: 10th–8th Centuries*. Mainz.

Korres, M. 1997. "An Early Attic Ionic Capital and the Kekropion on the Athenian Acropolis." In O. Palagia (ed.), *Greek Offerings: Essays on Greek Art in Honour of John Boardman*, 95–107. Oxford.

Kottaridi, A. 2002. "Discovering Aegae, the Old Macedonian Capital." In Stamatopoulou and Yeroulanou 2002: 75–81.

Kourayos, Y. 2004a. "Despotiko. I anakalipsi enos neou ierou." In Stampolidis and Yannikouri 2004: 437–52.

Kourayos, Y. 2004b. "Despotiko. Ena neo iero se mia akatoikiti nisida ton Kikladon." *Evlimeni* 5: 27–89.

Kourayos, Y. 2005. "Despotiko Mandra: A Sanctuary Dedicated to Apollo." In Yeroulanou and Stamatopoulou 2005: 105–33.

Kourinou, E. 2000. *Sparte: symvole ste mnemeiake topographia tes didaktorike diatrive*. Athens.

Kourou, N. 1990–1. "Evoia kai Anatoliki Mesoyios stis arkhes tis protis khilietias." *Arkheion Evoikon Meleton* 29: 237–79.

Kourou, N. 1994. "Sceptres and Maces in Cyprus." In Karageorghis 1994: 203–15.

Kourou, N. 2001a. "To palaiotero tikhos tou Xobouryou sta plaisia ton Kikladikon okhiroseon." In *Tinos. Kato Meri. Etaireia Tiniakon Meleton* 3: 25–41. Athens.

Kourou, N. 2001b. "Tenos–Xobourgo: A New Defensive Site in the Cyclades." In Karageorghis and Morris 2001: 171–89.

Kourou, N. 2002. "Tenos–Xobourgo: From a Refuge Place to an Extensive Fortified Settlement." In Stamatopoulou and Yeroulanou 2002: 255–68.

Kourou, N. and A. Karetsou. 1998. "An Enigmatic Stone from Knossos: A Reused Cippus?" In Karageorghis and Stampolidis 1998: 243–53.

Kowalzig, B. 2004. "Changing Choral Worlds: Song-dance and Society in Athens and Beyond." In Murray and Wilson 2004: 39–66.

Kraay, C. M. 1964. "Hoards, Small Change and the Origin of Coinage." *JHS* 84: 76–91.

Kraay, C. M. 1976. *Archaic and Classical Greek Coins*. London.

Krause, C. 1982. "Zur städtebaulichen Entwicklung Eretrias" *AK* 25: 137–44.

Krentz, P. 2000. "Deception in Archaic and Classical Greek Warfare." In van Wees 2000c: 167–200.

Krentz, P. 2002. "Fighting by the Rules: The Invention of the Hoplite Agon." *Hesperia* 71: 23–39.

Krinzinger, F. (ed.). 2000. *Akten des Symposions "Die Ägäis und das westliche Mittelmeer: Beziehungen und Wechselwirkungen, 8. bis 5. Jh. v. Chr."* Vienna.

Kristiansen, K. 1998. *Europe Before History*. Cambridge.

Kroll, H. 1993. "Kulturpflanzen von Kalapodi." *AA* 1993: 161–82.

Kroll, W. (ed.). 1905. *Die Altertumswissenschaft im letzten Vierteljahrhundert*. Leipzig.

Kron, U. 1988. "Kultmahle im Heraion von Samos archaischer Zeit: Versuch einer Rekonstruktion." In Hägg, Marinatos and Nordquist 1988: 135–47.

Kryzhitskij, S. D. 2001. "Khram Afrodity na Berezani. Rekonstruktsiya." *VDI* 1: 165–75.

Kucan, D. 2000. "Rapport synthétique sur les recherches archéobotaniques dans le sanctuaire d'Héra de l'Ile de Samos." *Pallas* 52: 99–108.

Kudlien, F. 1967. *Die Anfänge des medizinischen Denkens bei den Griechen*. Zurich and Stuttgart.

Kuhrt, A. 1988. "Earth and Water." In Kuhrt and Sancisi-Weerdenburg 1988: 87–99.

Kuhrt, A. 1995. *The Ancient Near East c. 3000–330 BC*, II. London.

Kuhrt, A. 2002. *"Greeks" and "Greece" in Mesopotamian and Persian Perspectives*. Oxford.

Kuhrt, A. and H. Sancisi-Weerdenburg (eds.). 1988. *Achaemenid History*, III: *Method and Theory*. Leiden.

Kullmann, W. 1984. "Oral Poetry Theory and Neoanalysis in Homeric Research." *GRBS* 25: 307–23.

Kunze, E. 1931. *Kretische Bronzereliefs*. 2 vols. Stuttgart.

Kurke, L. 1991. *The Traffic in Praise: Pindar and the Poetics of Social Economy*. Ithaca, NY.

Kurke, L. 1992. "The Politics of *habrosunē* in Archaic Greece." *ClAnt* 11: 90–121.

Kurke, L. 1993. "The Economy of *Kudos*." In Dougherty and Kurke 1993: 131–63.

Kurke, L. 1999. *Coins, Bodies, Games, and Gold: The Politics of Meaning in Archaic Greece*. Princeton.

Kurke, L. 2000. "The Strangeness of 'Song Culture': Archaic Greek Poetry." In Taplin 2000a: 58–87.

Kurz, I. 2000. *Vom Umgang mit den Anderen: Die Orientalismus-Debatte zwischen Alteritätsdiskurs und interkultureller Kommunikation*. Würzburg.

Kuznetsov, V. D. 2002. "Phanagoreia." In Fornasier and Böttger 2002: 59–68.

Kyle, D. G. 1987. *Athletics in Ancient Athens*. Leiden.

Kyle, D. G. 1992. "The Athletic Events." In J. Neils (ed.), *Goddess and Polis: The Panathenaic Festival in Ancient Athens*, 80–101. Princeton.

Kyrieleis, H. 1981. *Führer durch das Heraion von Samos*. Athens.

Kyrieleis, H. 1988. "Offerings of the 'Common Man' in the Heraion at Samos." In Hägg et al. 1988: 215–21.

Kyrieleis, H. 1993. "The Heraion at Samos." In Marinatos and Hägg 1993: 125–53.

Kyrieleis, H. 1996. *Der grosse Kuros von Samos*. Bonn.

Kyrieleis, H. 2002a. "Zu den Anfängen des Heiligtums von Olympia." In Kyrieleis 2002b: 213–20.

Kyrieleis, H. (ed.). 2002b. *Olympia 1875–2000: 125 Jahre Deutsche Ausgrabungen*. Berlin.

Kyrou, A. and D. Artemis. 1998. "The Silver Coinage of Kythnos in the Early 5th Century BC." In R. Ashton and S. Hunter (eds.), *Studies in Greek Numismatics in Memory of Martin Jessop Price*, 233–6. London.

Labarbe, J. 1974. "Un putsch dans la Grèce antique: Polycrate et ses frères à la conquête du pouvoir." *Ancient Society* 5: 21–41.

LaBianca, S. and S. Scham. 2006. *Connectivity in Antiquity: Globalization as Long-term Historical Process*. London and Oakville.

Lacroix, L. 1965. *Monnaies et colonization dans l'occident grec*. Brussels.

Laffineur, R. and R. Hägg (eds.). 2001. *Potnia: Deities and Religion in the Aegean Bronze Age*. Liège.

Lambert, S. D. 1993 (1998). *The Phratries of Attica*. Ann Arbor; 2nd edn. 1998.

Lamberton, R. 1988. *Hesiod.* New Haven.

Lambrinoudakis, V. 1988. "Veneration of Ancestors in Geometric Naxos." In Hägg et al. 1988: 235–46.

Lambrinoudakis, V. 1991. "The Sanctuary of Iria on Naxos and the Birth of Monumental Greek Architecture." In D. Buitron-Oliver (ed.), *New Perspectives in Early Greek Art*, 173–88. Hanover and London.

Lambrinoudakis, V. 1992. "Exi khronia anaskafikis erevnas sta Iria tis Naxou." *AEph* 1992: 201–16.

Lambrinoudakis, V. 2001 (2004). "The Emergence of the City-state of Naxos in the Aegean." In Lentini 2001: 13–22; 2004: 61–74.

Lambrinoudakis, V. 2005. "A New Early Archaic Building on Naxos. Some Thoughts on the Oikos of the Naxians on Delos." In Yeroulanou and Stamatopoulou 2005: 79–86.

Lambrinoudakis, V. and G. Gruben. 1985–7. "Anaskafi arkhaikou ierou sta Iria Naxou." *Arkhaiognosia* 5: 133–91.

Lambrinoudakis, V. and G. Gruben. 1987. "Das neuentdeckte Heiligtum von Iria auf Naxos." *AA* 1987: 569–621.

Lane Fox, R. 2000. "Theognis: An Alternative to Democracy." In Brock and Hodkinson 2000: 35–51.

Lanfranchi, G. B. 2000. "The Ideological and Political Impact of the Assyrian Imperial Expansion on the Greek World in the 8th and 7th Centuries BC." In S. Aro and R. Whiting (eds.), *The Heirs of Assyria*, 7–34. Helsinki.

Lanfranchi, G. B., M. Roaf, and R. Rollinger. 2003a. "Afterword." In Lanfranchi et al. 2003b: 397–406.

Lanfranchi, G. B., M. Roaf, and R. Rollinger (eds.). 2003b. *Continuity of Empire: Assyria, Media, Persia.* Padua.

Lang, F. 1996. *Archaische Siedlungen in Griechenland: Struktur und Entwicklung.* Berlin.

Lang, F. 2001. "The Dimensions of the Material Topography." In Isager 2001: 205–17.

Lang, F. 2005. "Structural Change in Archaic Greek Housing." In B. A. Ault and L. C. Nevett (eds.), *Ancient Greek Houses and Households: Chronological, Regional, and Social Diversity*, 12–35. Philadelphia.

Lang, M. 1967. "Kylonian Conspiracy." *CPh* 62: 243–49.

Lang, M. 1976. *Graffiti and Dipinti.* The Athenian Agora 21. Princeton.

Langdon, M. K. 1976. *A Sanctuary of Zeus on Mount Hymettos.* Athens.

Langdon, S. (ed.). 1993. *From Pasture to Polis: Art in the Age of Homer.* Columbia.

Langdon, S. 1997a. "Introduction." In Langdon 1997b: 1–8.

Langdon, S. (ed.). 1997b. *New Light on a Dark Age: Exploring the Culture of Geometric Greece.* Columbia MO.

Lapatin, K. 2001. *Chryselephantine Statuary in the Ancient Mediterranean World.* Oxford.

Lardinois, A. 1994. "Subject and Circumstances in Sappho's Poetry." *TAPhA* 124: 57–84.

Lardinois, A. 2001. "Keening Sappho: Female Speech Genres in Sappho's Poetry." In Lardinois and L. McClure (eds.), *Making Silence Speak: Women's Voices in Greek Literature and Society*, 75–92. Princeton.

Larenok, P. A. and O. Dally. 2002. "Taganrog." In Fornasier and Böttger 2002: 86–91.

Laroche, D. and M.-D. Nenna. 1993. "Études sur les trésors en Poros à Delphes." In Courtils and Moretti 1993: 227–45.

Larsen, J. A. O. 1949. "The Origin and Significance of the Counting of Votes." *CPh* 44: 164–81.

Latacz, J. 1977. *Kampfparänese, Kampfdarstellung und Kampfwirklichkeit in der Ilias, bei Kallinos und Tyrtaios.* Munich.

Latacz, J. (ed.). 1991. *Zweihundert Jahre Homer-Forschung: Rückblick und Ausblick*. Stuttgart.

Latacz, J. 1996. *Homer: His Art and His World*. Tr. J. P. Holoka. Ann Arbor.

Latacz, J. 1997. "Epischer Zyklus." *DNP* 3: 1154–56.

Latacz, J. (ed.). 2002. *Homers Ilias. Gesamtkommentar: Prolegomena*². Munich.

Latacz, J. 2004. *Troy and Homer: Towards a Solution of an Old Mystery*. Tr. K. Windle and R. Ireland. New York and Oxford.

Lattimore, R. (tr.). 1951. *Homer: The* Iliad. Chicago.

Lauffer, S. 1979. *Die Bergwerkssklaven von Laureion*.² Wiesbaden.

Lauter, H. 1985. *Lathuresa: Beiträge zur Architektur und Siedlungsgeschichte in spätgeometrischer Zeit*. Mainz.

Lavas, G. P. 1974. *Altgriechisches Temenos: Baukörper und Raumbildung*. Basel and Stuttgart.

Lavelle, B. M. 1992. "Herodotos, Skythian Archers, and the Doryphoroi of the Peisistratids." *Klio* 74: 78–97.

Lavelle, B. M. 2005. *Fame, Money, and Power: The Rise of Peisistratos and "Democratic" Tyranny at Athens*. Ann Arbor.

Lawrence, A. W. 1979. *Greek Aims in Fortification*. Oxford.

Lawrence, A. W. 1996. *Greek Architecture*.⁵ Revised by R. A. Tomlinson. New Haven.

Lazenby, J. F. 1996. "Miltiades." *OCD*.³ 981–2.

Le Rider, G. and S. Verdan. 2002. "La trouvaille d'Erétrie: Réserve d'un orfèvre ou dépôt monétaire?" *AK* 45: 133–52.

Leahy, A. (ed.). 1990. *Libya and Egypt c. 1300–750 BC*. London.

Lebessi, A. 1969. "Afrati." *AD* 24B: 415–18.

Lebessi, A. 1970. "Afrati." *AD* 25B: 455–61.

Lebessi, A. 1973. "Ieron Ermou kai Afroditis eis Simin Viannou." *PAAH* 1973: 188–99.

Lebessi, A. 1981. "I Sinekheia tis Kritomikinaikis Latreias: Epibioseis kai Anabioseis." *AEph* 1981: 1–24.

Lebessi, A. 1985. *To Iero tou Ermi kai tis Afroditis sti Simi Viannou*, I.1: *Khalkina kritika torevmata*. Athens.

Lebessi, A. 2002. *To Iero tou Ermi kai tis Afroditis sti Simi Viannou*, III: *Ta khalkina anthropomorpha eidolia*. Athens.

Lee, H. M. 1988. "The 'First' Olympic Games of 776 BC." In Raschke 1988: 110–18.

Lefèvre, F. 1998. *L'Amphictionie pyléo-delphique: Histoire et institutions*. Paris.

Legon, R. P. 1981. *Megara: The Political History of a Greek City-State to 336 BC*. Ithaca NY.

Legouilloux, M. 2000. "L'alimentation carnée au Iᵉʳ millénaire avant J.-C. en Grèce continentale et dans les Cyclades: Premiers résultats archéozoologiques." *Pallas* 52: 69–95.

Lehmann, L. 1960. *Samothrace*, II.2. New York.

Lehmann, Ph. W. and D. Spittle. 1982. Samothrace 5: *The Temenos*. Princeton.

Leitao, D. D. 1995. "The Perils of Leukippos: Initiatory Transvestism and Male Gender Ideology in the *Ekdusia* at Phaistos." *ClAnt* 14: 130–63.

Lemos, A. A. 1986. "Archaic Chian Pottery on Chios." In Boardman and Vaphopoulou-Richardson 1986: 233–49.

Lemos, A. A. 1991. *Archaic Pottery of Chios: The Decorated Styles*. 2 vols. Oxford.

Lemos, A. A. 1997. "Rizari. A Cemetery in Chios Town." In *Greek Offerings. Essays on Greek Art in Honour of John Boardman*, 73–85. Oxford.

Lemos, I. 1998. "Euboea and Its Aegean Koine." In Bats and D'Agostino 1998: 45–58.

Lemos, I. 2001. "The Lefkandi Connection: Networking in the Aegean and the Eastern Mediterranean." In Bonfante and Karageorghis 2001: 215–26.

Lemos, I. 2002. *The Protogeometric Aegean: The Archaeology of the Late Eleventh and Tenth Centuries BC*. Oxford.

Lemos, I. 2004–5. "Lefkandi." In J. Whitley (ed.), "Archaeology in Greece," *AR* 2004–2005: 50–2.

Lemos, I. 2006. "Athens and Lefkandi: A Tale of Two Sites." In Lemos and Deger-Jalkotzy 2006: 505–30.

Lemos, I. 2007. "Recent Archaeological Work on Xeropolis, Lefkandi: A Preliminary Report." In Mazarakis Ainian 2007: 123–33.

Lendle, O. 1992. *Einführung in die griechische Geschichtsschreibung.* Darmstadt.

Lendon, J. E. 1994. "Thucydides and the 'Constitution' of the Peloponnesian League." *GRBS* 35: 159–77.

Lendon, J. E. 2000. "Homeric Vengeance and the Outbreak of Greek Wars." In van Wees 2000c: 1–30.

Lenschau, T. 1905. "Griechische Geschichte." In Kroll 1905: 154–92.

Lenschau, T. 1913. "Zur Geschichte Ioniens." *Klio* 13: 175–83.

Lentini, M. C. (ed.). 2001. *The Two Naxos Cities: A Fine Link Between the Aegean Sea and Sicily.* Palermo.

Lentini, M. C. (ed.). 2004. *Le due città di Naxos.* Giardini Naxos.

Lepore, E. 2000. *La Grande Grèce: Aspects et problèmes d'une "colonisation" ancienne.* Naples.

Lesher, J. H. 1992. *Xenophanes of Colophon, Fragments: A Text and Translation with a Commentary.* Toronto.

Lesky, A. 1955. "Griechischer Mythos und Vorderer Orient." *Saeculum* 6: 35–52.

Lesky, A. 1966. *A History of Greek Literature.* Tr. J. Willis and C. de Heer. New York.

Lévêque, P. 1999. *La colonisation grecque en Méditerrané occidentale.* Rome.

Lévêque, P. and P. Vidal-Naquet. 1964. *Clisthène l'athénien.* Paris.

Lévêque, P. and P. Vidal-Naquet. 1996. *Cleisthenes the Athenian: An Essay on the Representation of Space and Time in Greek Political Thought from the End of the Sixth Century to the Death of Plato.* Tr. D. A. Curtis. Atlantic Highlands.

Levi, D. 1969. "Un pithos iscritto da Festos." *Kretika Chronika* 21: 153–6.

Lévi-Strauss, C. and D. Eribon. 1991. *Conversations with Claude Lévi-Strauss.* Chicago.

Lévy, E. 1977. "La Grande *Rhétra*." *Ktèma* 2: 85–103.

Lévy, E. 2003. *Sparte: Histoire politique et sociale jusqu'à la conquête romaine.* Paris.

Lewis, D. 1985. "Persians in Herodotus." In M. Jameson (ed.), *The Greek Historians: Literature and History,* 101–17. Saratoga.

Lewis, D. 1988. "The Tyranny of the Pisistratidae." *CAH*[2] IV: 287–302.

Lewis, S. 1996. *News and Society in the Greek Polis.* London.

Lewis, S. 2002. *The Athenian Woman: An Iconographic Handbook.* London.

Liampi, K. 1988. "Oi nomismatikes ekdoseis ton Kikladon kai i Kikloforia tous." In Mendoni and Margaris 1988: 208–93.

Liberman, G. 1997. "Plutarque et la 'Grande Rhétra'." *Athenaeum* 65: 204–7.

Link, S. 1991. *Landverteilung und sozialer Frieden im archaischen Griechenland.* Stuttgart.

Link, S. 1992. "Die Gesetzgebung des Zaleukos im epizephyrischen Lokroi." *Klio* 74: 11–24.

Link, S. 1994. "Zur archaischen Gesetzgebung in Katane und im epizephyrischen Lokroi." In Gehrke 1994: 165–77.

Link, S. 2000. *Das frühe Sparta. Untersuchungen zur spartanischen Staatsbildung im 7. und 6. Jahrhundert v.Chr.* St. Katharinen.

Link, S. 2003. "Eunomie im Schoss der Rhetra? Zum Verhältnis von Tyrt. frgm. 14 W und Plut. Lyk. 6,2 und 8." *GFA* 6: 141–50.

Link, S. 2004. "Snatching and Keeping: The Motif of Taking in Spartan Culture." In Figueira 2004b: 1–24.

Lintott, A. 1982. *Violence, Civil Strife and Revolution in the Classical City.* Baltimore.

Lipka, M. 2002a. "Notes on the Influence of the Spartan Great Rhetra on Tyrtaeus, Herodotus and Xenophon." In Powell and Hodkinson 2002: 219–25.

Lipka, M. 2002b. *Xenophon's Spartan Constitution: Introduction, Text, Commentary.* Berlin.

Lissarrague, F. 1990a. *The Aesthetics of the Greek Banquet.* Princeton.

Lissarrague, F. 1990b. *L'Autre guerrier: Archers, peltastes, cavaliers dans l'imagerie antique.* Paris.

Livadiotti, M. and G. Rocco (eds.). 1996. La *presenza italiana nel dodecaneso tra il 1912 e il 1948.* Catania.

Livadiotti, M. and G. Rocco. 1999. "Il tempio di Athena Polias a Ialiso. Un contributo alla conoscenza dell'architettura rodia." In *Rhodos 2.400 chronia: e pole tes Rhodou apo ten idryse tes mechri ten katalepse apo tous Tourkous (1523). Diethnes Epistemoniko Synedrio, Rhodos, 24–29 Oktovriou 1993,* 110–11. Athens.

Liverani, M. 2003. "The Rise and Fall of Media." In Lanfranchi et al. 2003b: 1–12.

Lloyd, A. B. 1975. *Herodotus: Book ii. Introduction.* Leiden.

Loyd, A. B. 1980. "M. Basch on Triremes: Some Observations." *JHS* 100: 195–8.

Lloyd, C. 1983. "Greek Urbanity and the *Polis.*" In R. T. Marchese (ed.), *Aspects of Graeco-Roman Urbanism: Essays on the Classical City,* 11–41. Oxford.

Lloyd, G. E. R. 1979. *Magic, Reason and Experience: Studies in the Origin and Development of Greek Science.* Cambridge.

Lloyd-Jones, H. 1975. *Females of the Species: Semonides on Women.* Park Ridge.

Lobel, E. and D. Page. 1955. *Poetarum Lesbiorum Fragmenta.* Oxford.

Lohmann, H. 1993. *Atene: Forschungen zur Siedlungs- und Wirtschaftsstruktur des klassischen Attika.* Cologne.

Lohmann, H. 1997. "Survey in der Chora von Milet: Vorbericht über die Kampagnen der Jahre 1994 und 1995." *AA* 1997: 285–311.

Lohmann, H. 1999. "Survey in der Chora von Milet: Vorbericht über die Kampagnen der Jahre 1996 und 1997." *AA* 1999: 439–73.

Lohmann, H. 2004. "Melia, das Panionion und der Kult des Poseidon Helikonios." In: E. Schwertheim and E. Winter (eds.), *Neue Forschungen zu Ionien. Kolloquium (01.03.–03.03.2004). Landhaus Rothenberge/Münster* (Asia Minor Studien 54): 57–91. Bonn.

Lolos, Y. G. 2001. "Dark Age Citadels in Southern Salamis." In Karageorghis and Morris 2001: 115–36.

Lomas, K. 1993. *Rome and the Western Greeks, 350 BC–AD 200: Conquest and Acculturation in Southern Italy.* London.

Lomas, K. (ed.). 2004. *Greek Identity in the Western Mediterranean.* Leiden.

Lombard, M. 1974. *Les Métaux dans l'ancien monde du Ve au XIe siècle.* Paris and The Hague.

Lombardo, M. 1988. "Marchands, transactions économiques, écritures." In M. Detienne (ed.), *Les Savoirs de l'écriture en Grèce ancienne,* 159–87. Lille.

Lombardo, M. 2002. "*Emporoi, emporion, emporitai:* forme e dinamiche del commercio greco nella penisola iberica." In G. Urso (ed.), *Hispania terris omnibus felicior: Premesse ed esiti di un processo di integrazione,* 73–86. Pisa.

Long, A. A. (ed.). 1999. *The Cambridge Companion to Early Greek Philosophy.* Cambridge.

Long, L., J. Miro, and G. Volpe. 1992. "Les épaves archaïques de la pointe Lequin (Porquerolles, Hyères, Var)." In M. Bats et al. (eds.), *Marseille grecque et la Gaule. Études Massaliotes* 3: 199–234.

Loraux, N. 1981. *Les Enfants d'Athéna: Idées athéniennes sur la citoyenneté et la division des sexes.* Paris.

Loraux, N. 1993. *The Children of Athena: Athenian Ideas about Citizenship and the Division between the Sexes.* Tr. C. Levine. Princeton.

Loraux, N. 1996. "Clistene e i nuovi caratteri della lotta politica." In Settis 1996: 1083–1110.

Lord, A. B. 2000. *The Singer of Tales.*[2] Ed. S. Mitchell and G. Nagy. Cambridge.

Lorimer, H. L. 1947. "The Hoplite Phalanx with Special Reference to the Poems of Archilochus and Tyrtaeus." *ABSA* 42: 76–138.

Lotze, D. 1959. Metaxu eleutheron kai doulon: *Studien zur Rechtsstellung unfreier Landbevölkerungen in Griechenland bis zum 4. Jahrhundert v.Chr.* Berlin.

Lotz, D. 2000. *Bürger und Unfreie im vorhellenistischen Griechenland: ausgewählte Aufsätze.* ed. W. Ameling and K. Zimmermann. Stuttgart.

Loukopoulou, L. D. 1989. *Contribution à l'histoire de la Thrace propontique durant la période archaïque.* Athens.

Loukopoulou, L. D. 1999. "Sur le statut et l'importance de l'emporion de Pistiros." *BCH* 123: 359–71.

Loukopoulou, L. D. 2004. "Thrace from Strymon to Nestos." In Hansen and Nielsen 2004: 853–69.

Louyot, D. 2005. "Archéologie des fortifications et défense du territoire des Cyclades durant l'antiquité grecque." Diss. University of Bordeaux.

Louyot, D. and A. Mazarakis Ainian. 2005. "Les structures défensives antiques dans les Cyclades: L'exemple de Kythnos." *REA* 107: 691–715.

Luce, J.-M. 2002. "A partir de l'exemple de Delphes: La question de la fonction des pièces." *Pallas* 58: 49–97.

Luke, J. 2003. *Ports of Trade: Al Mina and Geometric Pottery in the Levant.* Oxford.

Lupi, M. 2003. "L'*archaia moira*: Osservazioni sul regime fondiario spartano a partire da un libro recente." *Incidenza dell'Antico* 1: 151–72.

Luraghi, N. 2001a. "Die Dreiteilung der Peloponnes: Wandlungen eines Gründungsmythos." In H.-J. Gehrke (ed.), *Geschichtsbilder und Gründungsmythen*, 37–63. Würzburg.

Luraghi, N. 2001b. "Der Erdbebenaufstand und die Entstehung der messenischen Identität." In Papenfuss and Strocka 2001: 279–301.

Luraghi, N. (ed.). 2001c. *The Historian's Craft in the Age of Herodotus.* Oxford.

Luraghi, N. 2002a. "Becoming Messenian." *JHS* 122: 45–69.

Luraghi, N. 2002b. "Helotic Slavery Reconsidered." In Powell and Hodkinson 2002: 229–50.

Luraghi, N. 2003. "The Imaginary Conquest of the Helots." In Luraghi and Alcock 2003: 109–41.

Luraghi, N. 2008. *The Ancient Messenians: Constructions of Ethnicity and Memory.* Cambridge.

Luraghi, N. and S. E. Alcock (eds.). 2003. *Helots and Their Masters in Laconia and Messenia: Histories, Ideologies, Structures.* Washington, DC.

Luther, A. 2002. "Chilon von Sparta." In A. Goltz, A. Luther, and H. Schlange-Schöningen (eds.), *Gelehrte in der Antike*, 1–16. Cologne.

Luther, A. 2004. *Könige und Ephoren: Untersuchungen zur spartanischen Verfassungsgeschichte.* Frankfurt a. M.

Maass, M. 1977. "Kretische Votivdreifüsse." *AM* 92: 33–59.

MacLachlan, B. 1993. *The Age of Grace: Charis in Early Greek Poetry.* Princeton.

Macleod, C. 1982. *Homer:* Iliad *XXIV.* Cambridge.

Maddoli, G. 1992. "L'epigramma dei Clitori a Olimpia (Paus. V 23,7)." *PP* 47: 256–62.

Maffi, A. 1992. "Leggi scritti e pensiero giuridico." In G. Cambiano, L. Canfora, and D. Lanza (eds.), *Lo spazio letterario della Grecia antica*, I.1: 419–32. Rome.

Malakasioti, Z. and A. Mousioni. 2004. "Nea evrimata tis Epochis tou Khalkou kai tis Epokhis tou Sidirou stin Alo." In Stampolidis and Yannikouri 2004: 353–68.

Malkin, I. 1985. "What's in a Name? The Eponymous Founders of Greek Colonies." *Athenaeum* 63: 115–30.

Malkin, I. 1986. "Apollo Archegetes and Sicily." *ASNP* 16: 959–72.

Malkin, I. 1987. *Religion and Colonization in Ancient Greece*. Leiden.

Malkin, I. 1989. "Delphoi and the Founding of Social Order in Archaic Greece." *Métis* 4: 129–53.

Malkin, I. 1994a. "Inside and Outside: Colonisation and the Formation of the Mother City." In D'Agostino and Ridgway 1994: 1–9.

Malkin, I. 1994b. *Myth and Territory in the Spartan Mediterranean*. Cambridge.

Malkin, I. 1996. "Territorial Domination and the Greek Sanctuary." In P. Hellström and B. Alroth (eds.), *Religion and Power in the Ancient Greek World*, 75–82. Uppsala.

Malkin, I. 1998. *The Returns of Odysseus: Colonization and Ethnicity*. Berkeley.

Malkin, I. (ed.). 2001. *Ancient Perceptions of Greek Ethnicity*. Washington, DC.

Malkin, I. 2002a. "A Colonial Middle Ground: Greek, Etruscan, and Local Elites in the Bay of Naples." In C. L. Lyons and J. K. Papadopoulos (eds.), *The Archaeology of Colonialism*, 151–81. Los Angeles.

Malkin, I. 2002b. "Exploring the Validity of the Concept of 'Foundation.' A Visit to Megara Hyblaia." In Gorman and Robinson 2002: 195–225.

Malkin, I. 2003a. "Herodotus and 'Tradition'." In Derow and Parker 2003: 153–70.

Malkin, I. 2003b. "Pan-Hellenism and the Greeks of Naukratis." In M. Reddé, L. Dubois, D. Briquel, et al. (eds.), *La naissance de la ville dans l'antiquité*, 91–6. Paris.

Malkin, I. 2004. "Postcolonial Concepts and Ancient Greek Colonization." *Modern Language Quarterly* 65: 341–64.

Malkin, I. 2005a. "Herakles and Melqart: Greeks and Phoenicians in the Middle Ground." In E. S. Gruen (ed.), *Cultural Borrowings and Ethnic Appropriations in Antiquity*, 238–58. Stuttgart.

Malkin, I. (ed.). 2005b. *Mediterranean Paradigms and Classical Antiquity*. London.

Malkin, I. 2005c. "Networks and the Emergence of Greek Identity." In Malkin 2005b: 56–74.

Mallwitz, A. 1988. "Cult and Competition Locations at Olympia." In Raschke 1988: 79–111.

Mann, C. 2001. *Athlet und Polis im archaischen und frühklassischen Griechenland*. Göttingen.

Mansfeld, J. 1985. "Aristotle and Others on Thales." *Mnemosyne* 38: 109–29.

Manville, P. B. 1990. *The Origins of Citizenship in Ancient Athens*. Princeton.

Maran, J. 2000. "Das Megaron im Megaron: Zur Datierung und Funktion des Antenbaus im mykenischen Palast von Tiryns." *AA* 2000: 1–17.

Maran, J. 2001. "Political and Religious Aspects of Architectural Change in the Upper Citadel of Tiryns: The Case of Building T." In Laffineur and Hägg 2001: 113–22.

Marangou, L. 2002. *Amoryos*, I. Athens.

Marcotte, D. 1986. "Le périple de Scylax." *Bolletino dei Classici* 7: 166–82.

Marek, C. 1984. *Die Proxenie*. Frankfurt.

Marganne, M. H. 1993. "Links between Egyptian and Greek Medicine." *Forum* 3.4: 35–43.

Margomenou, D. et al. 2005. "Reflections on the 'Aegean' and Its Prehistory: Present Routes and Future Destinations." In J. Cherry et al. (eds.), *Prehistorians Round the Pond: Reflections on Aegean Prehistory as a Discipline*, 1–21. Ann Arbor.

Mari, M. 2002. *Al di là dell'Olimpo: Macedoni e grandi santuari della Grecia dall'età arcaica al primo ellenismo*. Athens.

Marinatos, N. and R. Hägg (eds.). 1993. *Greek Sanctuaries: New Approaches.* London.

Marinatos, S. 1936. "Le temple géométrique de Dréros." *BCH* 60: 214–85.

Marincola, J. 1997. *Authority and Tradition in Ancient Historiography.* Cambridge.

Marincola, J. 2006. "Herodotus and the Poetry of the Past." In Dewald and Marincola 2006: 13–28.

Markoe, G. 2000. *Phoenicians.* London.

Marsilio, M. S. 2000. *Farming and Poetry in Hesiod's* Works and Days. Lanham.

Martelli, M. 1988. "La stipe votiva dell' Athenaion di Ialiso: Un primo bilancio." In Dietz and Papachristodoulou 1988: 104–20.

Martelli, M. 1996. "La stipe votiva dell' Athenaion di Ialiso." In Livadiotti and Rocco 1996: 46–69.

Martin, Jochen. 1974. "Von Kleisthenes zu Ephialtes. Zur Entstehung der athenischen Demokratie." *Chiron* 4: 5–42.

Martin, Josef. 1931. *Symposion: Die Geschichte einer literarischen Form.* Paderborn.

Martin, Richard. 1984. "Hesiod, Odysseus, and the Instruction of Princes." *TAPhA* 114: 29–48.

Martin, Richard. 1993. "The Seven Sages as Performers of Wisdom." In Dougherty and Kurke 1993: 108–28.

Martin, Roland. 1951. *Recherches sur l'agora grecque.* Paris.

Martin, Roland. 1974. *L'Urbanisme dans la Grèce antique.*[2] Paris.

Martin, Roland. 1983. "Espace civique, religieux et profane dans les cités grecques de l'archaïsme à l'époque hellénistique." In P. Gros (ed.), *Architecture et société de l'archaïsme grec à la fin de la république romaine*, 9–41. Paris.

Martin, Roland. 1987. *Architecture et urbanisme.* Rome.

Martin, T. 1996a. *Ancient Greece: From Prehistoric to Hellenistic Times.* New Haven.

Martin, T. 1996b. "Why Did the Greek Polis Originally Need Coins?" *Historia* 45: 257–83.

Marx, K. and F. Engels. 1975. *Collected Works*, III: *Marx and Engels: 1843–44*; V: *Marx and Engels: 1845–47*; XI: *Marx and Engels 1851–1853.* New York.

Masaracchia, A. 1958. *Solone.* Florence.

Mason, P. 1987. "Third Person/Second Sex: Patterns of Sexual Asymmetry in the *Theogony* of Hesiodos." In Blok and Mason 1987: 147–89.

Masson, O. 1976. "Nouveaux graffites grecs d'Abydos et de Bouhen." *ChrEg* 51: 305–9.

Matsas, D. 2004. "E Samothrake sten proime epoche tou siderou." In Stampolidis and Gianikouri 2004: 227–57.

Mattusch, C. 1988. *Greek Bronze Statuary.* Ithaca, NY.

Mayrhofer, M. 1979. *Iranisches Personennamenbuch*, I: *Die altiranischen Namen.* Vienna.

Mazarakis Ainian, A. 1987. "Geometric Eretria." *AK* 30: 3–24.

Mazarakis Ainian, A. 1993. "Epifaneiakes erevnes sti niso Kithno: To tikhos tis arkhaias Kithnou." *AEph* 1993: 217–53.

Mazarakis Ainian, A. 1995. "Epifaneiakes arkhaioloyikes erevnes stin Kithno." *PAAH* 1995: 137–209.

Mazarakis Ainian, A. 1997. *From Rulers' Dwellings to Temples: Architecture, Religion and Society in Early Iron Age Greece (1100–700 BC).* Jonsered.

Mazarakis Ainian, A. 1998a. "Anaskafi Skala Oropou." *PAAH* 1998: 51–81.

Mazarakis Ainian, A. 1998b. "The Kythnos Survey Project: Poleodomia kai teikhi tis arkhaias poleos Kithnou." In Mendoni and Mazarakis Ainian 1998: 363–78.

Mazarakis Ainian, A. 1998c. "Oropos in the Early Iron Age." In Bats and D'Agostino 1998: 179–215.

Mazarakis Ainian, A. 2000. *Omiros kai arkhaiologia.* Athens.

Mazarakis Ainian, A. 2001. "From Huts to Houses in Early Iron Age Greece." In J. R. Brandt and L. Karlsson (eds.), *From Huts to Houses: Transformations of Ancient Societies*, 139–61. Stockholm.

Mazarakis Ainian, A. 2002a. "La fonction des périboles dans les agglomérations du début de l'Age du Fer." In *Habitat et urbanisme dans le monde grec de la fin des palais mycéniens à la prise de Milet*, 183–227. Toulouse.

Mazarakis Ainian, A. 2002b. "Recent Excavations at Oropos, Northern Attica." In Stamatopoulou and Yeroulanou 2002: 149–78.

Mazarakis Ainian, A. 2003. "Yeometriki Eretria. Arkhitektoniki, poleodomia kai koinoniki oryanosi." *AETHSE* 1: 955–77.

Mazarakis Ainian, A. 2004a. "From the Beginnings to the Archaic Age: Hero Cults of Homeric Society." In *Thesaurus Cultus et Rituum Antiquorum*, II.3d: *Heroisierung und Apotheose*, 131–40. Basel and Los Angeles.

Mazarakis Ainian, A. 2004b. "I simvoli tou Oropou sti meleti ton oikismon tou Aigaiou tis Proimis Epokhis tou Sidirou." In Stampolidis and Yannikouri 2004: 369–87.

Mazarakis Ainian, A. 2005. "Inside the Adyton of a Greek Temple: Excavations on Kythnos (Cyclades)." In Yeroulanou and Stamatopoulou 2005: 87–103.

Mazarakis Ainian, A. 2006. "The Archaeology of Basileis." In Deger-Jalkotzy and Lemos 2006: 181–211.

Mazarakis Ainian, A. (ed.). 2007. *Oropos and Euboea in The Early Iron Age: Acts of an International Round Table*, University of Thessaly, June 18–20, 2004. Volos.

Mazarakis Ainian, A. and A. Matthaiou. 1999. "Enepiyrafo alieftiko varos ton yeometrikon khronon." *AEph* 1999: 143–53.

Mazzarino, S. 1947. *Fra Oriente e Occidente: ricerche di storia greca arcaica*. Florence.

McCartney, E. S. 1934. "The Couch as Unit of Measurement." *CPh* 29: 30–5.

McCarter, P. K. 1975. *The Antiquity of the Greek Alphabet and the Early Phoenician Scripts*. Missoula.

McDonald, W. A. and W. D. E. Coulson. 1983. "The Dark Age at Nichoria: A Perspective." In McDonald, Coulson, and J. Rosser (eds.), *Excavations at Nichoria in Southwest Greece*, III: *Dark Age and Byzantine Occupation*, 316–29. Minneapolis.

McDonald, W. A., O. T. P. K. Dickinson, and R. J. Howell. 1992. "Summary." In McDonald and N. C. Wilkie (eds.), *Excavations at Nichoria in Southwest Greece*, II: *The Bronze Age Occupation*, 757–69. Minneapolis.

McDonnell, M. 1991. "The Introduction of Athletic Nudity: Thucydides, Plato and the Vases." *JHS* 111: 182–92.

McGlew, J. F. 1993. *Tyranny and Political Culture in Ancient Greece*. Ithaca, NY.

McHardy, F. 2008. *Revenge in Athenian Culture*. London.

McInerney, J. 1999. *The Folds of Parnassos: Land and Ethnicity in Ancient Phokis*. Austin.

McLellan, D. 1979. *Marxism after Marx*. Boston.

McLellan, D. 1983. *Karl Marx: The Legacy*. London.

Meadows, A. and K. Shipton (eds.). 2001. *Money and Its Uses in the Ancient Greek World*. Oxford.

Mee, C. 1998. "Anatolia and the Aegean in the Late Bronze Age." In E. Cline and D. Harris-Cline (eds.), *The Aegean and the Orient in the Second Millennium BC*. London.

Meier, C. 1980. *Die Entstehung des Politischen bei den Griechen*. Frankfurt a. M.

Meier, C. 1989. "Die Entstehung einer autonomen Intelligenz bei den Griechen." In Meier, *Die Welt der Geschichte und die Provinz des Historikers*, 70–100. Berlin.

Meier, C. 1990a. *The Greek Discovery of Politics*. Tr. D. McLintock. Cambridge, MA.

Meier, C. 1990b. "Die Rolle des Krieges im klassischen Athen." *Historische Zeitschrift* 251: 555–605.

Meier, C. 1998. *Athens: A Portrait of the City in Its Golden Age.* Tr. R. and R. Kimber. New York.

Meier, C. 2001. "The Greeks: The Political Revolution in World History." In Arnason and Murphy 2001: 56–71.

Meier, M. 1998. *Aristokraten und Damoden: Untersuchungen zur inneren Entwicklung Spartas im 7. Jahrhundert v.Chr. und zur politischen Funktion der Dichtung des Tyrtaios.* Stuttgart.

Meier, M. 2000. "Zwischen Königen und Damos. Überlegungen zur Funktion und Entwicklung des Ephorats in Sparta (7. – 4. Jh. v. Chr.)." *ZRG* 117: 43–102.

Meier, M. 2002. "Tyrtaios fr. 1B G/P bzw. fr. °14 G/P (= fr. 4 W) und die grosse Rhetra – kein Zusammenhang?" *GFA* 5: 65–87.

Meiggs, R. 1982. *Trees and Timber in the Ancient Mediterranean World.* New York.

Meiggs, R. and D. M. Lewis (eds.). 1969 (1988). *A Selection of Greek Historical Inscriptions to the End of the Fifth Century B. C.* Oxford. Rev. edn. 1988.

Meissner, B. 2002. "Krieg und Strategie bei den Griechen." *Seminari Romani di cultura Greca* 5: 107–35.

Melander, T. 1988. "Vroulia: Town Plan and Gate." In Dietz and Papachristodoulou 1988: 83–7.

Mele, A. 1979. *Il commercio greco arcaico: prexis ed emporie.* Naples.

Mellor, R. and L. Tritle (eds.). 1999. *Text and Tradition: Studies in Greek History and Historiography in Honor of Mortimer Chambers.* Claremont.

Mendoni, L. and N. Margaris (eds.). 1998. *Kiklades: Istoria tou topiou kai topikes istories.* Athens.

Mendoni, L. and A. Mazarakis Ainian (eds.). 1998. *Kea–Kythnos: History and Archaeology. Kea–Kithnos: Istoria kai Arkhaiologia.* Athens.

Meriç, R. and P. A. Mountjoy. 2002. "Mycenaean Pottery from Bademgediği Tepe (Puranda) in Ionia: A Preliminary Report." *MDAI (Istambul)* 52: 79–98.

Merritt, B. D. 1939. "Greek Inscriptions (14–27)." *Hesperia* 8: 48–82.

Mersch, A. 1997. "Urbanization of the Attic Countryside from the Late 8th Century to the 6th Century BC." In Damgard Andersen et al. 1997: 45–62.

Mertens, N. 2002. "*Ouk homoioi agathoi?* The Perioikoi in the Classical Lakedaimonian *Polis.*" In Powell and Hodkinson 2002: 285–303.

Meyer, E. 1892. "Lykurgos von Sparta." In Meyer, *Forschungen zur alten Geschichte,* I: 211–86. Halle.

Meyer, E. 1895. *Die wirtschaftliche Entwicklung des Altertums: ein Vortrag.* Jena.

Michalowski, P. 1992. "Orality, Literacy and Early Mesopotamian Literature." In Vogelzang and Vanstiphout 1992: 227–45.

Michalowski, P. 1995. "Sumerian Literature: An Overview." In Sasson 1995: 2279–91.

Mieroop, M. van de. 2004. *A History of the Ancient Near East.* Oxford.

Mierse, W. E. 1983. "The Persian Period." In G. M. A. Hanfmann (ed.), *Sardis from Prehistoric to Roman Times: Results of the Archaeological Exploration of Sardis 1958–1975,* 100–8. Cambridge.

Millender, E. G. 2001. "Spartan Literacy Revisited." *ClAnt* 20: 121–64.

Miller, M. C. 1997. *Athens and Persia in the Fifth Century: A Study in Cultural Receptivity.* Cambridge.

Miller, S. G. 1978. *The Prytaneion: Its Function and Architectural Form.* Berkeley.

Miller, S. G. 1990. *Nemea: A Guide to the Site and the Museum.* Berkeley.

Miller, S. G. 1991. *Arete: Greek Sports from Ancient Sources.* Berkeley.

Miller, S. G. 2000. "Naked Democracy." In Flensted-Jensen et al. 2000: 277–96.

Miller, S. G. 2002. "The Shrine of Opheltes and the Earliest Stadium of Nemea." In Kyrieleis 2002b: 239–50.

Miller, S. G. 2004. *Ancient Greek Athletics.* New Haven.

Millett, P. 1984. "Hesiod and His World." *PCPhS* 30: 84–115.

Millet, P. 1991. *Lending and Borrowing in Ancient Athens.* Cambridge.

Mitchell, L. G. and P. J. Rhodes (eds.). 1997. *The Development of the* Polis *in Archaic Greece.* London.

Mitchell, S. 1985. "Archaeology in Asia Minor 1979–1984." *AR*: 70–105.

Mitten, D. G. and S. F. Doeringer. 1967. *Master Bronzes from the Classical World.* Mainz.

Moggi, M. 1976. *I sinecismi interstatali greci.* Pisa.

Moignard, E. 1996. "The Orientalizing Pottery." In Coldstream and Catling 1996: 421–62.

Moignard, E. 1998. "Native Wit: Some Orientalising Pottery from the Knossos North Cemetery." In Cavanagh et al. 1998: 80–6.

Möller, A. 2000. *Naukratis: Trade in Archaic Greece.* Oxford.

Möller, A. 2001. "Naukratis, or How to Identify a Port of Trade." In D. W. Tandy (ed.), *Prehistory and History: Ethnicity, Class and Political Economy,* 145–58. Montréal.

Momigliano, A. 1952. *George Grote and the Study of Greek History.* London. Repr. in Momigliano 1955: 213–31 and in Momigliano 1966: 56–74.

Momigliano, A. 1955. *Contributo alla storia degli studi classici.* Rome.

Momigliano, A. 1966. *Studies in Historiography.* London.

Montanari, F. (ed.). 2002. *Omero tremila anni dopo.* Rome.

Montiglio, S. 2000. "Wandering Philosophers in Classical Greece." *JHS* 120: 86–105.

Moortel, A. van de. 2005 (2006). "Mitrou." In J. Whitley (ed.), "Archaeology in Greece," *AR* 51 (2004–5): 52–5; (2005–6): 64–6.

Moortel, A. van de and E. Zahou. 2003–4. "2004 Excavations at Mitrou, East Locris." *Aegean Archaeology* 7: 39–48.

Morel, J.-P. 1984. "Greek Colonization in Italy and in the West (Problems of Evidence and Interpretation)." In T. Hackens, N. D. Holloway, and R. R. Holloway (eds.), *Crossroads of the Mediterranean,* 123–61. Louvain and Providence.

Moretti, L. 1959. *Olympionikai: I vincitori negli antichi agoni olimpici.* Rome.

Moretti, L. 2002. "Nuovo supplemento al catalogo degli olympionikai." In Kyrieleis 2002b: 119–28.

Morgan, C. 1988. "Corinth, the Corinthian Gulf and Western Greece during the Eighth Century B.C." *BSA* 83: 313–38.

Morgan, C. 1990. *Athletes and Oracles: The Transformation of Olympia and Delphi in the Eighth Century BC.* Cambridge.

Morgan, C. 1991. "Ethnicity and Early Greek States: Historical and Material Perspectives." *PCPhS* 37: 131–63.

Morgan, C. 1993. "The Origins of Panhellenism." In Marinatos and Hägg 1993: 18–44.

Morgan, C. 1997. "The Archaeology of Sanctuaries in Early Iron Age and Archaic *ethne*: A Preliminary View." In Mitchell and Rhodes 1997: 168–98.

Morgan, C. 1998. "Euboians and Corinthians in the Area of the Corinthian Gulf." In Bats and D'Agostino 1998: 281–302.

Morgan, C. 1999a. "Cultural Subzones in Early Iron Age and Archaic Arkadia?" In Nielsen and Roy 1999: 382–456.

Morgan, C. 1999b. *Isthmia,* VIII: *The Late Bronze Age Settlement and Early Iron Age Sanctuary.* Princeton.

Morgan, C. 1999c. "Some Thoughts on the Production and Consumption of Early Iron Age Pottery in the Aegean." In Crielaard, van Wijngaarden and Stissi 1999: 213–59.

Morgan, C. 2000. "Politics without the Polis: Cities and the Achaean Ethnos, c. 800–500 BC." In Brock and Hodkinson 2000: 189–211.

Morgan, C. 2001a. "Ethne and Early Greek States, ca. 1200–480 BC: An Archaeological Perspective." In Malkin 2001: 75–112.

Morgan, C. 2001b. "Symbolic and Pragmatic Aspects of Warfare in the Greek World of the 8th–6th Centuries BC." In L. Hannestad and T. Bekker Nielsen (eds.), *War as a Cultural and Social Force: Essays on Warfare in Antiquity*, 20–44. Copenhagen.

Morgan, C. 2002a. "Ethnicity: The Example of Achaia." In Greco 2002: 95–116.

Morgan, C. 2002b. "The Origins of the Isthmian Festival." In Kyrieleis 2002b: 251–71.

Morgan, C. 2003. *Early Greek States beyond the Polis*. London.

Morgan, C. 2007. "Debating Patronage: the Cases of Argos and Corinth." In Hornblower and Morgan (eds.) 2007, 213–63.

Morgan, C. and J. M. Hall. 1996. "Achaian Poleis and Achaian Colonisation." In Hansen 1996: 164–232.

Morgan, C. and J. J. Coulton. 1997. "The *Polis* as a Physical Entity." In Hansen 1997: 87–144.

Morgan, K. A. (ed.). 2003. *Popular Tyranny: Sovereignty and Its Discontents in Ancient Greece*. Austin.

Morley, N. 2007. *Trade in Classical Antiquity*. Cambridge.

Morris, I. 1986. "Gift and Commodity in Archaic Greece." *Man* 21. 1–17.

Morris, I. 1987. *Burial and Ancient Society: The Rise of the Greek City-State*. Cambridge.

Morris, I. 1991. "The Early Polis as City and State." In Rich and Wallace-Hadrill 1991: 24–57.

Morris, I. 1992. *Death Ritual and Social Structure*. Cambridge.

Morris, I. (ed.). 1994. *Classical Greece: Ancient Histories and Modern Archaeologies*. Cambridge.

Morris, I. 1996a. "The Absolute Chronology of the Greek Colonies in Sicily." *AArch* 67: 51–9.

Morris, I. 1996b. "The Strong Principle of Equality and the Archaic Origins of Greek Democracy." In Ober and Hedrick 1996: 19–48.

Morris, I. 1997a. "An Archaeology of Equalities? The Greek City-states." In D. Nichols and T. Charlton (eds.), *The Archaeology of City-States*, 91–105. Washington, DC.

Morris, I. 1997b. "The Art of Citizenship." In Langdon 1997b: 9–43.

Morris, I. 1997c. "Periodization and the Heroes: Inventing a Dark Age." In M. Golden and P. Toohey (eds.), *Inventing Ancient Culture: Historicism, Periodization, and the Ancient World*, 96–131. London and New York.

Morris, I. 1998a. "Archaeology and Archaic Greek History." In Fisher and van Wees 1998: 1–92.

Morris, I. 1998b. "*Burial and Ancient Society* after Ten Years." In S. Marchegay, M.-T. Le Dinahet, and J.-F. Salles (eds.), *Nécropoles et pouvoir*, 21–36. Paris.

Morris, I. 1998c. "Remaining Invisible: The Archaeology of the Excluded in Classical Athens." In S. R. Joshel and S. Murnaghan (eds.), *Women and Slaves in Greco-Roman Culture*, 193–220. London.

Morris, I. 1999a (2003a). "Archaeology and Gender Ideologies in Early Archaic Greece." *TAPhA* 129: 305–17. Repr. in M. Golden and P. Toohey (eds.), *Sex and Difference in Ancient Greece and Rome*, 264–75. Edinburgh 2003.

Morris, I. 1999b. "Iron Age Greece and the Meanings of "Princely Tombs'." In Ruby 1999: 57–80.

Morris, I. 2000. *Archaeology as Cultural History: Words and Things in Iron Age Greece*. Malden and Oxford.

Morris, I. 2001a. "The Athenian Empire (478–404 BC)." www.stanford.edu/group/sshi/empires2.html.

Morris, I. 2001b. "The Use and Abuse of Homer." Rev. version. In Cairns 2001a: 57–91.

Morris, I. 2003. "Mediterraneanization." *Mediterranean History Review* 18: 30–55.

Morris, I. 2004a. "Archaeology, Standards of Living, and Greek Economic History." In J. Manning and I. Morris (eds.), *The Ancient Economy: Evidence and Models*, 91–126. Stanford.

Morris, I. 2004b. "Economic Growth in Ancient Greece." *Journal of Institutional and Theoretical Economics* 160: 709–42.

Morris, I. 2005. "Mediterraneanization." In Malkin 2005b: 30–55.

Morris, I. 2006a. "The Collapse and Regeneration of Complex Society in Greece, 1500–500 BC." In Schwartz and Nichols 2006: 72–84.

Morris, I. 2006b. "The Growth of Greek Cities in the First Millennium BC." In G. Storey (ed.), *Urbanism in the Preindustrial World: Cross-cultural Approaches*, 27–51. Tuscaloosa.

Morris, I. 2007. "Early Iron Age Greece." In Morris et al. 2007: 211–41.

Morris, I. In preparation. "Population Growth in the Iron Age Mediterranean."

Morris, I. and B. Powell (eds.). 1997. *A New Companion to Homer*. Leiden.

Morris, I. and K. A. Raaflaub (eds.). 1998. *Democracy 2500? Questions and Challenges*. Dubuque.

Morris, I., R. Saller, and W. Scheidel (eds.). 2007. *The Cambridge Economic History of the Greco-Roman World*. Cambridge.

Morris, S. P. 1984. *The Black and White Style: Athens and Aigina in the Orientalizing Period*. New Haven.

Morris, S. P. 1992. *Daidalos and the Origins of Greek Art*. Princeton.

Morris, S. P. 1997. "Greek and Near Eastern Art in the Age of Homer." In Langdon 1997b: 56–71.

Morris, S. P. 2001. "The Prehistoric Background of Artemis Ephesia: A Solution to the Enigma of Her 'Breasts.'" In Muss 2001: 135–51.

Morrison, J. S. and R. T. Williams. 1968. *Greek Oared Ships 900–322 BC*. Cambridge.

Morrow, G. 1960. *Plato's Cretan City*. Princeton.

Morton, J. 2001. *The Role of the Physical Environment in Ancient Greek Seafaring*. Leiden.

Moschonissioti, S. 1998. "Excavations at Ancient Mende." In Bats and D'Agostino 1998: 255–71.

Mosley, D. J. 1973. *Envoys and Diplomacy in Ancient Greece*. Wiesbaden.

Mosshammer, A. A. 1979. *The Chronicle of Eusebius and Greek Chronographic Tradition*. Lewisburg.

Most, G. 1985. *The Measures of Praise: Structure and Function in Pindar's Second Pythian and Seventh Nemean Odes*. Göttingen.

Most, G. 1989. "Zur Archäologie der Archaik." *A&A* 35: 1–23.

Most, G. 2003. "Epinician Envies." In D. Konstan and K. Rutter (eds.), *Envy, Spite and Jealousy: The Rivalrous Emotions in Ancient Greece*, 123–42. Edinburgh.

Mülke, C. 2002. *Solons Politische Elegien und Iamben (fr. 1–13; 32–37 West)*. Munich.

Mullen, W. 1982. *Choreia: Pindar and Dance*. Princeton.

Müller, C. and F. Prost (ed.). 2002. *Identités et cultures dans le monde méditerranéen antique*. Paris

Müller, K. E. 1972. *Geschichte der antiken Ethnographie und ethnologischen Theoriebildung*, I. Wiesbaden.

Müller, R. (ed.). 1976. *Kulturgeschichte der Antike*, I: *Griechenland*. Berlin.

Munn, M. 2006. *The Mother of the Gods, Athens, and the Tyranny of Asia: A Study of Sovereignty in Ancient Religion*. Berkeley.

Murnaghan, S. 1986. "Penelope's *agnoia*: Knowledge, Power and Gender in the *Odyssey*." *Helios* 13: 103–15.

Murray, O. 1980 (1993). *Early Greece*. London; 2nd edn. 1993.

Murray, O. 1988a. "Death and the Symposion." *AION (archeol)* 10: 239–57.

Murray, O. 1988b. "The Ionian Revolt." *CAH²* IV: 461–90.

Murray, O. 1990a. "Cities of Reason." In Murray and Price 1990: 1–25.

Murray, O. (ed.). 1990b. *Sympotica: A Symposium on the* Symposion. Oxford.

Murray, O. 1994. "Nestor's Cup and the Origins of the Greek Symposion." In D'Agostino and Ridgway 1994: 47–54.

Murray, O. 1995. "Forms of Sociality." In J.-P. Vernant (ed.), *The Greeks*, 218–53. Chicago.

Murray, O. 1997. "The Rationality of the Greek City: The Evidence from Camarina." In Hansen 1997: 493–504.

Murray, O. 2000. "La Convivialité dans les cultures de l'antiquité: La Méditerranée et la Chine." In P. Sauzeau (ed.), *Bacchanales*, 7–21. Cahiers du GITA 13. Montpellier.

Murray, O. 2001. "Herodotus and Oral History Reconsidered." In Luraghi 2001: 314–25.

Murray, O. 2008. "The *Odyssey* as Performance Poetry." In M. Revemann and P. Wilson (eds.), *Performance, Iconography, Reception: Studies in Honor of Oliver Taplin*, 161–76. Oxford.

Murray, O. and S. Price (eds.). 1990. *The Greek City from Homer to Alexander*. Oxford.

Murray, O. and M. Tecuşan (eds.). 1995. *In Vino Veritas*. London.

Murray, P. and P. Wilson (eds.). 2004. *Music and the Muses*. Oxford.

Muscarella, O. 1992. "Greek and Oriental Cauldron Attachments: A Review." In Kopcke and Tokumaru 1992: 16–45.

Muscarella, O. 2003. "The Date of the Destruction of the Early Phyrgian Period at Gordion." *AWE* 2.2: 225–52.

Musgrave, J. H. 1996. "The Human Bones." In Coldstream and Catling 1996: 677–702.

Muss, U. 1999. "Zur Dialektik von Kultstatue und Statuetten im Artemision von Ephesos." In H. Friesinger and F. Krinzinger (eds.), *100 Jahre österreichische Forschungen in Ephesos*, 597–603. Vienna.

Muss, U. 2007. "Kleinplastik aus dem Artemision von Samos." In J. Cobet, V. von Graeve, W.-D. Niemeier, and K. Zimmermann (eds.), *Frühes Ionien: Eine Bestandsaufnahme*. Mainz, 211–20.

Muss, U. (ed.). 2001. *Der Kosmos der Artemis von Ephesos*. Vienna.

Musti, D. 1996. "Regole politiche a Sparta: Tirteo e la *Grande Rhetra*." *RFIC* 124: 257–81.

Musti, D. and M. Torelli (eds.). 1991. *Pausania, Guida della Grecia, libro IV: La Messenia*. Milan.

Musti, D., A. Sacconi, L. Rocchetti, M. Rocchi, E. Scafa, L. Sportiello, and M. E. Giannotta (eds.). 1991. *La transizione dal miceneo all'alto arcaismo: Dal palazzo alla città*. Rome.

Mustilli, D. 1932–3. "La necropoli tirrenica di Efestia," *ASAA* 15–16: 1–278.

Mylonas, G. E. 1959. *Aghios Kosmas: An Early Bronze Age Settlement and Cemetery of Attica*. Princeton.

Mylonas, G. E. 1974. *Eleusis and the Eleusinian Mysteries*. Princeton.

Myres, J. L. 1930. *Who Were the Greeks?* New York.

Naerebout, F. G. 1987. "Male–Female Relationships in the Homeric Epics." In Blok and Mason 1987: 109–46.

Nafissi, M. 1991. *La nascita del* kosmos: *Studi sulla storia e la società di Sparta*. Perugia.

Nafissi, M. Forthcoming. "The Great Rhetra (Plut. *Lyc.* 6): A Retrospective and Intentional Construct? In L. Foxhall, H. J. Gehrke and N. Luraghi (eds.), *Intentionale Geschichte: Spinning Time*. Stuttgart.

Nagy, G. 1979 (1999). *The Best of the Achaeans: Concepts of the Hero in Archaic Greek Poetry*. Baltimore. Rev. edn. 1999.

Nagy, G. 1990a. *Greek Mythology and Poetics*. Ithaca, NY.

Nagy, G. 1990b. *Pindar's Homer: The Lyric Possession of an Epic Past*. Baltimore.

Nagy, G. 1996a. *Homeric Questions*. Austin.

Nagy, G. 1996b. *Poetry as Performance: Homer and Beyond*. Cambridge.

Napoli, M. 1970. *La tomba del tuffatore*. Bari.

Naso, A. (ed.). 2006. *Stranieri e non-cittadini nei santuari greci*. Florence.

Naveh J. 1982. *Early History of the Alphabet: An Introduction to West Semitic Epigraphy and Palaeography*. Jerusalem.

Naveh, J. 1987. "Proto-Canaanite, Archaic Greek, and the Script of the Aramaic Text of the Tell Fakhariyah Statue." In P. D. Miller, P. D. Hanson, and S. D. McBride (eds.), *Ancient Israelite Religion: Essays in Honor of F. M. Cross*, 101–13. Philadelphia.

Nazarov, V. V. 2001. "Svyatilishche Afrodity v Borisfene" *VDI* 1: 154–65.

Neer, R. T. 2003. "Framing the Gift: The Siphnian Treasury at Delphi and the Politics of Public Art." In Dougherty and Kurke 2003: 129–49.

Nenci, G. 1954. *Hecataei Milesii fragmenta: Testo, introduzione, appendice e indici*. Florence.

Neugebauer, O. 1957. *The Exact Sciences in Antiquity²*. Providence.

Nevett, L. C. 1994. "Separation or Seclusion? Towards an Archaeological Approach to Investigating Women in the Greek Household in the Fifth to Third Centuries BC." In M. Parker-Pearson and C. Richards (eds.), *Architecture and Order: Approaches to Social Space*, 98–112. London.

Nevett, L. C. 1999. *House and Society in the Ancient Greek World*. Cambridge.

Nicholls, R. V. 1970. "Greek Votive Statuettes and Religious Continuity." In B. Harris (ed.), *Auckland Classical Essays Presented to E. M. Blaiklock*, 9–14. Auckland and Oxford.

Nicholson, N. 2003. "Aristocratic Victory Memorials and the Absent Charioteer." In Dougherty and Kurke 2003: 101–28.

Nicolet, C. et al. 1984. *Aux origines de l'Hellénisme: La Crète et la Grèce. Hommage à H. van Effenterre*. Paris.

Niels, J. (ed.). 1992. *Goddess and Polis: The Panathenaic Festival in Ancient Athens*. Hanover, NH.

Nielsen, T. H. 1996. "A Survey of Dependent *Poleis* in Classical Arkadia." In Hansen and Raaflaub 1996: 63–105.

Nielsen, T. H. (ed.). 1997. *Yet More Studies in the Ancient Greek Polis*. Stuttgart.

Nielsen, T. H. 2002a. *Arkadia and Its* Poleis *in the Archaic and Classical Periods*. Göttingen.

Nielsen, T. H. (ed.). 2002b. *Even More Studies in the Ancient Greek Polis*. Stuttgart.

Nielsen, T. H. and J. Roy. 1998. "The Azanians of Northern Arkadia." *C&M* 49: 5–44.

Nielsen, T. H. and J. Roy (eds.). 1999. *Defining Ancient Arkadia*. Copenhagen.

Niemeier, W.-D. 1999. "'Die Zierde Ioniens': Ein archaischer Brunnen der jüngere Athenatempel und Milet vor der Perserzerstörung." *AA*: 373–413.

Niemeier, W.-D. 2003. *Der Kuros vom Heiligen Tor*. Mainz.

Niemeyer, H. G. 1990a. "The Greeks and the Far West: Towards a Revaluation of the Archaeological Record from Spain." In G. Pugliese Carratelli (ed.), *La Magna Grecia e il lontano Occidente*, 29–54. Taranto.

Niemeyer, H. G. 1990b. "The Phoenicians in the Mediterranean: A Non-Greek Model For Expansion and Settlement in Antiquity." In Descoeudres 1990: 469–90.

Niemeyer, H. G. 1995. "Phoenician Toscanos as a Settlement Model? Its Urbanistic Character in the Context of Phoenician Expansion and Iberian Acculturation." In B. Cunliffe and S. Keay (eds.), *Social Complexity and the Development of Towns in Iberia: From the Copper Age to the Second Century AD*, 67–88. Oxford.

Niemeyer, H. G. 2002. "The Phoenician Settlement at Toscanos: Urbanization and Function." In Bierling 2002: 31–48.

Nietzsche, F. 1969. "Götzen-Dämmerung: Was ich von den Alten lernte." In G. Colli and M. Montanari (eds.), *Werke*, 6.3: 49–156. Berlin.

Nietzsche, F. 1997. *Twilight of the Idols, Or, How to Philosophize with the Hammer*. Tr. R. Polt. Intro. by T. Strong. Indianapolis.

Nightingale, A. W. 2000. "Sages, Sophists, and Philosophers: Greek Wisdom Literature." In Taplin 2000a: 138–73.

Nilsson, M. P. 1941 (1955, 1967). *Geschichte der griechischen Religion*, I: *Bis zur griechischen Weltherrschaft*. Munich; 2nd edn. 1955; 3rd edn. 1967.

Nippel, W. 1980. *Mischverfassungstheorie und Verfassungsrealität in Antike und früher Neuzeit*. Stuttgart.

Nisbet, G. 2004. "Hesiod, *Works and Days*: A Didaxis of Deconstruction." *G&R* 51: 147–63.

Nixon, L. and S. Price. 2001. "The Diachronic Analysis of Pastoralism through Comparative Variables." *ABSA* 96: 395–424.

Noegel, S. 2005. "Mesopotamian Epic." In Foley 2005: 233–45.

North, D. 1981. *Structure and Change in Economic History*. New York.

North, H. 1966. *Sophrosyne: Self-knowledge and Self-restraint in Greek Literature*. Ithaca, NY.

Nowag, W. 1983. *Raub und Beute in der archaischen Zeit der Griechen*. Frankfurt am Main.

Nowicki, K. 1999. "Economy of Refugees: Life in the Cretan Mountains at the Turn of the Bronze and Iron Ages." In A. Chaniotis (ed.), *From Minoan Farmers to Roman Traders: Sidelights on the Economy of Ancient Crete*, 145–71. Stuttgart.

Nowicki, K. 2000. *Defensible Sites in Crete c.1200–800 BC. (LMIIIB through Early Geometric)*. Liège and Austin.

Nunn, J. F. 1996. *Ancient Egyptian Medicine*. Norman.

Nussbaum, G. 1960. "Labour and Status in the *Works and Days*." *CQ* 10: 213–20.

Nutton, V. 1995. "Medicine in the Greek World, 800–50 BC." In L. Conrad et al., *The Western Medical Tradition, 800 BC–AD 1800*, 11–38. Cambridge.

Nylander, C. 1970. *Ionians in Pasargadae: Studies in Old Persian Architecture*. Uppsala.

Nylander, C. 1974. "Anatolians in Susa – and Persepolis (?)." *Acta Iranica* 6: 317–23.

Ober, J. 1996. "The Athenian Revolution of 508/7 BC: Violence, Authority, and the Origins of Democracy." In Ober, *The Athenian Revolution: Essays on Ancient Greek Democracy and Political Theory*, 32–52. Princeton.

Ober, J. 1998. "Revolution Matters: Democracy as Demotic Action." In Morris and Raaflaub 1998: 67–85.

Ober, J. 2007. "'I besieged that Man': Democracy's Revolutionary Start." In Raaflaub et al. 2007: 83–104.

Ober, J. and C. Hedrick (eds.). 1996. *Dēmokratia: A Conversation on Democracies, Ancient and Modern*. Princeton.

Oelsner, J. 1999–2000. "Review of Rollinger 1993." *AfO* 46–7: 373–80.

Ogden, D. 1994. "Crooked Speech: The Genesis of the Spartan *Rhetra*." *JHS* 114: 85–102.

Ogden, D. 1997. *The Crooked Kings of Ancient Greece*. London.

Ogden, D. 1998. "What Was in Pandora's Box?" In Fisher and van Wees 1998: 213–30.

Ohnesorg, A. 2005. "Naxian and Parian Architecture: General Features and New Discoveries." In Yeroulanou and Stamatopoulou 2005: 135–52.

Oikonomides, A. N. 1980. "The Lost Delphic Inscription with the Commandments of the Seven and P. Univ. Athen. 2782." *ZPE* 37: 179–83.

Oliva, P. 1971. *Sparta and Her Social Problems*. Amsterdam and Prague.

Ollier, F. 1933 (1943). *Le Mirage spartiate: Etude sur l'idéalisation de Sparte dans l'antiquité grecque de l'origine jusqu'aux cyniques*. Paris.

Onasoglou, A. 1981. "Oi Yeometrikoi Tafoi tis Trayanas stin Anatoliki Lokrida." *AD* 36A: 1–57.

Ong, W. 1982. *Orality and Literacy: The Technologizing of the Word*. London.

Onyshkevych, L. 2002. "Interpreting the Berezan Bone Graffito." In Gorman and Robinson 2002: 161–79.

Oost, S. 1972. "Cypselus the Bacchiad." *CPh* 67: 10–30.

Oost, S. 1973. "The Megara of Theagenes and Theognis." *CPh* 78: 186–96.

Orrieux, C. and P. Schmitt Pantel. 1999. *A History of Ancient Greece*. Tr. J. Lloyd. Oxford.

Osanna, M. 2001. "Fattorie e villaggi in Magna Grecia." In *Problemi della chora coloniale dall'Occidente al Mar Nero*, 203–20. Taranto.

Osborne, R. 1985. *Demos: The Discovery of Classical Attica*. Cambridge.

Osborne, R. 1987. *Classical Landscape with Figures: The Ancient Greek City and Its Countryside*. London.

Osborne, R. 1989. "A Crisis in Archaeological History? The Seventh Century BC in Attica." *ABSA* 84: 297–322.

Osborne, R. 1993a. "Archaeology, the Salaminioi, and the Politics of Sacred Space in Archaic Attica." In Alcock and Osborne 1994: 143–60.

Osborne, R. 1993b. "Competitive Festivals and the Polis: A Context for Dramatic Festivals at Athens." In A. Sommerstein, S. Halliwell, J. Henderson, and B. Zimmermann (eds.), *Tragedy, Comedy and the Polis*, 21–37. Bari.

Osborne, R. 1995. "The Economics and Politics of Slavery at Athens." In Powell 1995: 27–43.

Osborne, R. 1996a. *Greece in the Making, 1200–479 BC*. London.

Osborne, R. 1996b. "Pots, Trade, and the Archaic Greek Economy." *Antiquity* 70: 31–44.

Osborne, R. 1997. "Law and Laws. How Do We Join up the Dots?" In Mitchell and Rhodes 1997: 74–82.

Osborne, R. 1998a. *Archaic and Classical Greek Art*. Oxford.

Osborne, R. 1998b. "Early Greek Colonization? The Nature of Greek Settlement in the West." In Fisher and van Wees 1998: 251–70.

Osborne, R. 2004. "Homer's Society." In R. Fowler (ed.), *The Cambridge Companion to Homer*, 206–19. Cambridge.

Osborne, R. and S. Hornblower (eds.). 1994. *Ritual, Finance, Politics: Athenian Democratic Accounts Presented to David Lewis*. Oxford.

Osborne, R. and B. Cunliffe (eds.). 2005. *Mediterranean Urbanization 800–600 BC*. Oxford.

Østby, Erik. 1980. "The Athenaion of Karthaia." *Opuscula Atheniensia* 13.4: 189–223.

Østby, Erik. 1990–1. "I templi di Pallantion." *ASAA* n.s. 51–52: 53–94.

Østby, Erik. 1997. "Early Iron Age in the Sanctuary of Athena Alea at Tegea: Recent Excavations." *Acta ad archaeologiam et artium historiam pertinentia* 9: 79–107.

Østergård, U. 1991. *Akropolis – Persepolis Tur/Retur: Hellenismeforskningen mellem orientalisme, hellenisme, imperialisme og afkolonisering*. Aarhus.

Ostwald, M. 1969. *Nomos and the Beginnings of the Athenian Democracy*. Oxford.

Ostwald, M. 1986. *From Popular Sovereignty to the Sovereignty of Law*. Berkeley.

Ostwald, M. 1988. "The Reform of the Athenian State by Cleisthenes." *CAH*² IV: 303–46.

O'Sullivan, P. 2003. "Victory Statue, Victory Song: Pindar's Agonistic Poetics and Its Legacy." In Phillips and Pritchard 2003: 75–100.

Owen, S. 2005. "Analogy, Archaeology and Archaic Greek Colonization." In Hurst and Owen 2005: 5–22.

Owens, E. J. 1991. *The City in the Greek and Roman World*. London.

Özgen, J. and J. Öztürk. 1996. *Heritage Recovered: The Lydian Treasure*. Ankara.

Özyigit, Ö. and A. Erdogan. 2000. "Les Sanctuaires de Phocée à la lumière des dernières fouilles." In Hermary and Tréziny 2000: 11–23.

Page, D. L. 1955. *Sappho and Alcaeus*. Oxford.

Page, D. L. (ed.). 1962. *Poetae Melici Graeci*. Oxford.

Palagia, O. and W. Coulson (eds.). 1993. *Sculpture from Arcadia and Laconia*. Oxford.

Paliokrassa, L. 1991. *To iero tis Artemidos Mounikhias*. Athens.

Panaino, A. 2001. "Greci e Iranici: Confronto e conflitti." In S. Settis (ed.), *I Greci*, III: *I Greci oltre la Grecia*, 79–136. Turin.

Panaino, A. 2003. "Herodotus I, 96–101: Deioces' Conquest of Power and the Foundation of Sacred Royalty." In Lanfranchi et al. 2003b: 327–38.

Papachatzis, N. D. 1980. *Pausanias' Periegesis of Greece, Books 7 and 8: Achaia and Arkadia*. Athens. In Greek.

Papadakis, N. 1989. "Roussa Ekklisia." *AD* 37: 389.

Papadimitriou, A. 1998. "I oikistiki exelixi tis Tirinthas meta ti Mikinaiki epokhi. Ta arkhaioloyika evrimata kai i ermineia tous." In A. Pariente and G. Touchais (eds.), *Argos et l'Argolide: Topographie et urbanisme*, 117–30. Paris.

Papadimitriou, A. 2006. "The Early Iron Age in the Argolid: Some New Aspects." In Deger-Jalkotzy and Lemos 2006: 531–47.

Papadopoulos, J. K. 1989. "An Early Iron Age Potter's Kiln at Torone." *Mediterranean Archaeology* 2: 9–44.

Papadopoulos, J. K. 1996a. "Euboians in Macedonia? A Closer Look." *OJA* 15: 151–81.

Papadopoulos, J. K. 1996b. "The Original Kerameikos of Athens and the Siting of the Classical Agora." *GRBS* 37: 107–28.

Papadopoulos, J. K. 1997a. "Innovations, Imitations and Ceramic Style: Modes of Production and Modes of Dissemination." In R. Laffineur and P. B. Bétancourt (eds.), *Technē: Craftsmen, Craftswomen and Craftsmanship in the Aegean Bronze Age*, 449–62. Liège and Austin.

Papadopoulos, J. K. 1997b. "Phantom Euboians." *JMA* 10: 191–219.

Papadopoulos, J. K. 1998. "A Bucket, by Any Other Name, and an Athenian Stranger in Early Iron Age Crete." *Hesperia* 67: 109–23.

Papadopoulos, J. K. 2003. *Ceramicus Redivivus: The Early Iron Age Potter's Field in the Area of the Classical Athenian Agora*. Princeton.

Papadopoulos, T. J. and L. Kontorli-Papadopoulou. 2001. "Death, Power and Troubles in the Late Mycenaean Peloponnese. The Evidence of Warrior-Graves." In P. Fischer (ed.), *Contributions to the Archaeology and History of the Bronze and Iron Ages in the Eastern Mediterranean*, 127–38. Vienna.

Papadopoulou, Z. 2002. *Sifnion asti: Filologikes, arkhaiologikes kai topoyrafikes martiries yia tin arkhaia poli tis Sifnou*. Athens.

Papaephthimiou, V. 2001–2. "Sibleyma trion kathiston eidolion apo to iero tis Dimitros kai ton Dioskouron tis arkhaias Messinis'." In *Praktika tou 6. diethnous sinedriou Peloponnisiakon spoudon: Tripolis, 24–29 Septemvriou 2000*, II, 129–46. Athens.

Papaephthimiou-Papanthimou, A. and A. Pilali-Papasteriou. 2002. "Arhondiko 2002: Present and Future." *AEMTH* 16: 457–64.

Papakonstantinou, H. 1982. "A Late Archaic Sima from Triphylia." *AAA* 15: 238–43. In Greek.

Papalexandrou, N. 2005. *The Visual Poetics of Power: Warriors, Youths and Tripods in Early Greece*. Lanham.

Papenfuss, D. and V. M. Strocka (eds.). 2001. *Gab es das griechische Wunder? Griechenland zwischen dem Ende des 6. und der Mitte des 5. Jahrhunderts v. Chr*. Mainz.

Parke, H. W. 1933. *Greek Mercenary Soldiers: From the Earliest Times to the Battle of Ipsus*. Oxford.

Parke, H. W. 1967. *The Oracles of Zeus*. Oxford.

Parke, H. W. and D. E. W. Wormell. 1956. *The Delphic Oracle*. Oxford.

Parker, A. J. 1992. *Ancient Shipwrecks of the Mediterranean & the Roman Provinces*. Oxford.

Parker, H. N. 1993. "Sappho Schoolmistress." *TAPhA* 123: 309–51.

Parker, R. 1989. "Spartan Religion." In Powell 1989: 142–72.

Parker, R. 2000. "Greek States and Greek Oracles." In R. Buxton (ed.), *Oxford Readings in Greek Religion*, 76–108. Oxford.

Parker, V. 1991. "The Dates of the Messenian Wars." *Chiron* 21: 27–47.

Parker, V. 1992. "The Dates of the Orthagorids of Sicyon." *Tyche* 7: 165–75.

Parker, V. 1993. "Some Dates in Early Spartan History." *Klio* 75: 45–60.

Parker, V. 1994. "Some Aspects of the Foreign and Domestic Policy of Cleisthenes of Sicyon." *Hermes* 122: 404–24.

Parker, V. 1997. *Untersuchungen zum Lelantischen Krieg und verwandten Problemen der frühgriechischen Geschichte*. Stuttgart.

Parkins, H. and C. Smith (eds.). 1998. *Trade, Traders and the Ancient City*. London.

Parlama, L. 1973–4. "Arkhaiotites kai mnimeia Messinias." *AD* 29B: 315–16.

Parlama, L. and N. Stampolidis. 2000. *The City beneath the City*. Athens.

Patterson, O. 2003. "Reflections on Helotic Slavery and Freedom." In Luraghi and Alcock 2003: 289–309.

Patzek, B. 1992. *Homer und Mykene: Mündliche Dichtung und Geschichtsschreibung*. Munich.

Patzek, B. 2004. "Griechischer Logos und das intellektuelle Handwerk des Vorderen Orients." In Rollinger and Ulf 2004b: 427–45.

Payne, H. 1927–8. "Early Greek Vases from Knossos." *ABSA* 29: 224–98.

Payne, H. 1931. *Necrocorinthia*. Oxford.

Pearson, L. 1939. *Early Ionian Historians*. Oxford.

Pearson, L. 1962. "The Pseudo-history of Messenia and Its Authors." *Historia* 11: 397–426.

Pedley, J. G. 1993 (1998). *Greek Art and Archaeology*. New York; 2nd edn. 1998.

Pedley, J. 2005. *Sanctuaries and the Sacred in the Ancient Greek World*. Cambridge.

Pedrizet, P. and G. Lefebvre. 1919. *Les Graffites grecs du Memnonion d'Abydos*. Paris.

Pelling, C. 2006. "Homer and Herodotus." In M. J. Clarke, B. G. F. Currie, and R. O. A. M. Lyne (eds.), *Epic Interactions: Perspectives on Homer, Virgil, and the Epic Tradition Presented to Jasper Griffin by Former Pupils*, 75–104. Oxford.

Peña, M. J. 1992. "Ampurias: De la polis à la civitas." *Index* 20: 135–45.

Penglase, C. 1994. *Greek Myths and Mesopotamia: Parallels and Influence in the Homeric Hymns and Hesiod*. London.

Peretti, A. 1979. *Il periplo di Scilace. Studio sul primo portolano del Mediterraneo*. Pisa.

Perlman, P. 1992. "One Hundred-citied Crete and the Cretan πολιτεία." *CPh* 87: 193–205.

Perlman, P. 2000. *City and Sanctuary in Ancient Greece: The Theorodokia in the Peloponnese*. Göttingen.

Perlman, P. 2002. "Gortyn: The First Seven Hundred Years, II: The Laws from the Temple of Apollo Pythios." In Nielsen 2002b: 187–227.

Perlman, P. 2004. "Crete." In Hansen and Nielsen 2004: 1144–95.

Pernier, L. 1914. "Templi arcaici sulla Patela di Prinias: Contributo allo studio dell'arte deda-lica." *ASAA* 1: 18–111.

Perreault, J. Y. 1999. "Production et distribution à l'époque archaïque: le cas d'un atelier de potier de Thasos." In Crielaard, van Wijngaarden and Stissi (eds.) 1999: 291–301.

Peruzzi, Emilio. 1992. "Cultura greca a Gabii nel secolo VIII." *PP* 47: 459–68.

Petropoulos, M. 2001. "Yeometrikos naos Rakitas – latrevomeni theotita." In V. Mitsopoulos-Leon (ed.), *Forschungen in der Peloponnes*, 39–45. Athens and Vienna.

Petropoulos, M. 2002. "The Geometric Temple of Ano Mazaraki (Rakita) in Achaia during the Period of Colonization." In Greco 2002: 143–64.

Petzold, K. E. 1990. "Zur Entstehungsphase der athenischen Demokratie." *RFIC* 18: 145–78.

Phillips, D. 2003. "Athenian Political History: A Panathenaic Perspective." In Phillips and Pritchard 2003: 197–232.

Phillips, D. and D. Pritchard (eds.). 2003. *Sport and Festival in the Ancient Greek World*. Swansea.

Picard, O. 1980. *Les Grecs devant la menace perse*. Paris.

Piccirilli, L. 1973. *Gli arbitrati interstatali greci*, I: *Dalle origini al 338 a.C.* Pisa.

Pichot, André. 1991 (1995). *La Naissance de la science*. Paris. German edn. tr. S. Summerer and G. Kurz. Darmstadt, 1995.

Piepenbrink, K. 2001. *Politische Ordnungskonzeptionen in der attischen Demokratie des vierten Jahrhunderts v. Chr.* Stuttgart.

Piérart, M. 2003. "Genèse et développement d'une ville à l'ancienne Argos." In M. Reddé (ed.), *La Naissance de la ville dans l'antiquité*, 49–70. Paris.

Pikoulas, G. (Y.) A. 1981–2. "Arkadian Azania." In *Praktika B' Diethnous Sinedriou Peloponnisiakon Spoudon*, 269–81. Athens. In Greek.

Pikoulas, G. (Y.) A. 1991. "I Dentheliati kai to odiko tis diktio." In *Praktika tou 3. Topikou Sinedriou Messeniakon Spoudon*, 279–88. Athens.

Pikoulas, G. (Y.) A. 1995. *Road Network and Defence: From Corinth to Argos and Arkadia*. Athens. In Greek.

Pikoulas, G. (Y.) A. 1999. "The Road-network of Arkadia." In Nielsen and Roy 1999: 248–319.

Piraino Manni, M. T. 1980. "Nuove iscrizioni dall'Acropoli di Gela." In *Philias Charin: Miscellanea di studi classici in onore di Eugenio Manni*, 1767–1832. Rome.

Platon, N. 1954 (1955, 1956). "Anaskafi Onithi Youledianon Rethimnis," *PAAH* 1954: 377–82; 1955: 298–305; 1956: 226–8.

Pleket, H. W. 1969. "The Archaic Tyrannis." *Talanta* 1: 19–61.

Pleket, H. W. 1975. "Games, Prizes, Athletes and Ideology." *Stadion* 1: 49–89.

Pleket, H. W. 1992. "The Participants in the Ancient Olympic Games: Social Background and Mentality." In Coulson and Kyrieleis 1992: 147–52.

Pleket, H. W. 1998. "Sport and Ideology in the Greco-Roman World." *Klio* 80: 315–24.

Podlecki, A. J. 1966. *The Political Background of Aeschylean Tragedy*. Ann Arbor.

Podlecki, A. J. 1975. *The Life of Themistocles: A Critical Survey of the Literary and Archaeological Evidence*. Montreal and London.

Podlecki, A. J. 1984. *The Early Greek Poets and Their Times*. Vancouver.

Pohl, W. and H. Reimitz (eds.). 1998. *Strategies of Distinction: The Construction of Ethnic Communities 300–800*. Leiden.

Pöhlmann, R. 1889 (1896, 1914). "Grundzüge der politischen Geschichte Griechenlands." In F. Hommel et al. (eds.), *Geographie und politische Geschichte des klassischen Altertums*, 353–464. Nördlingen; 2nd edn. as *Grundriss der griechischen Geschichte nebst Quellenkunde*. Munich, 1896; 5th edn. 1914.

Pöhlmann, R. von. 1902. *Griechische Geschichte im neunzehnten Jahrhundert*. Munich.

Polanyi, K. 1944. *Origins of Our Time: The Great Transformation.* New York.

Poliakoff, M. 1987. *Combat Sports in the Ancient World: Competition, Violence and Culture.* New Haven.

Polignac, F. de. 1984. *La Naissance de la cité grecque: Cultes, espace et société, VIIIᵉ–VIIᵉ s. av. J.-C.* Paris.

Polignac, F. de. 1995a. *Cults, Territory, and the Origins of the Greek City-State.* Tr. J. Lloyd. Chicago.

Polignac, F. de. 1995b. "Repenser 'la cité'?" In Hansen and Raaflaub 1995: 7–19.

Polignac, F. de. 1998. "Cité et territoire à l'époque géométrique. Un modèle argien?" In A. Pariente and G. Touchais (eds.), *Argos et l'Argolide. Topographie et urbanisme,* 145–62. Paris.

Polignac, F. de. 1999. "L'Installation des dieux et la genèse des cités en Grèce d'Occident: Une question résolue? Retour à Mégara Hyblaea." In G. Vallet (ed.), *La Colonisation grecque en Méditerranée occidentale,* 209–30. Rome.

Polignac, F. de. 2002. "Cultes de sommet en Corinthie et Argolide." In Hägg 2002: 119–22.

Polignac, F. de. 2005a. "Usages de l'écriture dans les sanctuaires du haut archaïsme." In V. Dasen and M. Piérart (eds.), *Idia kai demosia. Les cadres "privés" et "publics" de la religion grecque antique. Kernos* suppl. 15. Liège.

Polignac, F. de. 2005b. "Forms and Processes: Some Thoughts on the Meaning of Urbanization in Early Archaic Greece." In Osborne and Cunliffe 2005: 45–69.

Pomeroy, S. B. 2002. *Spartan Women.* Oxford.

Popham, M. 1994. "Precolonization: Early Greek Contact with the East." In Tsetskhladze and De Angelis 1994: 11–34.

Popham, M., L. H. Sackett, and P. G. Themelis (eds.). 1980. *Lefkandi,* I: *The Iron Age Settlement. The Cemeteries.* London.

Postgate, J. N. 2001. "System and Style in Three Near Eastern Bureaucracies." In Voutsaki and Killen 2001: 181–94.

Pottier, M. E. 1915. "Fouilles archéologiques sur l'emplacement de la nécropole d'Éléotonte de Thrace. *BCH* 39: 135–240.

Poulsen, F. 1906. "Eine kretische Mitra." *AM* 31: 373–91.

Powell, A. (ed.). 1989. *Classical Sparta: Techniques behind Her Success.* London.

Powell, A. (ed.). 1995. *The Greek World.* London.

Powell, A. 1998. "Sixth-century Lakonian Vase-painting: Continuities and Discontinuities with the 'Lykourgan' Ethos." In Fisher and van Wees 1998: 119–46.

Powell, A. and S. Hodkinson (eds.). 1994. *The Shadow of Sparta.* London.

Powell, A. and S. Hodkinson (eds.). 2002. *Sparta beyond the Mirage.* London and Swansea.

Powell, B. 1988. "The Dipylon Oinochoe Inscription and the Spread of Literacy in Eighth Century Athens." *Kadmos* 27: 65–86.

Powell, B. 1991. *Homer and the Origin of the Greek Alphabet.* Cambridge.

Powell, B. 1997. "Homer and Writing." In Morris and Powell 1997: 3–33.

Powell, B. 2002. *Writing and the Origins of Greek Literature.* Cambridge.

Prent, M. 2003. "Glories of the Past in the Past: Ritual Activities at Palatial Ruins in Early Iron Age Crete." In R. M. Dyke and S. E. Alcock (eds.), *Archaeologies of Memory,* 81–103. Malden and Oxford.

Prent, M. 2005. *Cretan Sanctuaries and Cults: Continuity and Change from Late Minoan IIIC to the Archaic Period.* Leiden.

Prinz, F. 1979. *Gründungsmythen und Sagenchronologie.* Munich.

Pritchard, D. 2003. "Athletics, Education and Participation in Classical Athens." In Phillips and Pritchard 2003: 293–350.

Pritchett, W. K. 1974. *The Greek State at War*, II. Berkeley.

Pritchett, W. K. 1979. *The Greek State at War*, III. Berkeley.

Pritchett, W. K. 1985a. *The Greek State at War*, IV. Berkeley.

Pritchett, W. K. 1985b. *Studies in Ancient Topography*, V. Berkeley.

Pugliese Carratelli, G. 1976. "Cadmo: prima e dopo." *PP* 31: 5–16.

Pugliese Carratelli, G. 1996. *The Greek World: Art and Civilization in Magna Graecia and Sicily*. New York.

Pugliese Carratelli, G. (ed.). 1990. *La Magna Grecia e il lontano Occidente*. Taranto.

Pugliese Carratelli, G. 1996. *The Western Greeks*. London.

Pugliese Carratelli, G. and M. Bats (eds.). 1998. *Confini e frontiera nella Grecità d'occidente* (Convegni di Studi sulla Magna Grecia, Atti 37). Taranto.

Purcell, N. 1990. "Mobility and the Polis." In Murray and Price 1990: 29–58.

Purcell, N. 1997. "Review of *The Archaeology of Greek Colonisation: Essays Dedicated to Sir John Boardman*." *Antiquity* 71: 500.

Purcell, N. 1998. "Mobilità e Magna Grecia." In G. Pugliese Carratelli and Bats 1998: 573–9.

Py, M. 1993. *Les Gaulois du Midi*. Paris.

Quass, F. 1971. *Nomos und Psephisma: Untersuchungen zum griechischen Staatsrecht*. Munich.

Qviller, Bjørn. 1981. "The Dynamics of Homeric Society." *SO* 56: 109–55.

Raaflaub, K. A. 1987. "Herodotus, Political Thought, and the Meaning of History." In D. Boedeker (ed.), *Herodotus and the Invention of History. Arethusa* 20: 221–48.

Raaflaub, K. A. 1988. "Homer and the Beginning of Political Thought in Greece." *Boston Area Colloquium of Ancient Philosophy* 4: 1–25.

Raaflaub, K. A. 1990. "Expansion und Machtbildung in frühen Polis-Systemen." In W. Eder (ed.), *Staat und Staatlichkeit in der frühen römischen Republik*, 511–45. Stuttgart.

Raaflaub, K. A. 1991. "Homer und die Geschichte des 8. Jh.s v. Chr." In Latacz 1991: 205–56.

Raaflaub, K. A. (ed.). 1993a. *Anfänge politischen Denkens in der Antike: Die nahöstlichen Kulturen und die Griechen*. Munich.

Raaflaub, K. A. 1993b. "Homer to Solon: The Rise of the Polis. The Written Sources." In Hansen 1993a: 41–105.

Raaflaub, K. A. 1995. "Einleitung und Bilanz: Kleisthenes, Ephialtes und die Begründung der Demokratie." In Kinzl 1995: 1–54.

Raaflaub, K. A. 1996a. "Equalities and Inequalities in Athenian Democracy." In Ober and Hedrick 1996: 139–74.

Raaflaub, K. A. 1996b. "Solone, la nuova Atene e l'emergere della politica." In Settis 1996: 1035–81.

Raaflaub, K. A. 1997a. "Greece." In C. G. Thomas (ed.), *Ancient History: Recent Work and New Directions*, 1–35. Claremont.

Raaflaub, K. A. 1997b. "Homeric Society." In Morris and Powell 1997: 624–48.

Raaflaub, K. A. 1997c. "Politics and Interstate Relations among Early Greek Poleis: Homer and Beyond." *Antichthon* 31: 1–27.

Raaflaub, K. A. 1997d. "Soldiers, Citizens, and the Evolution of the Early Greek Polis." In Mitchell and Rhodes 1997: 49–59.

Raaflaub, K. A. 1998. "A Historian's Headache: How to Read 'Homeric Society'"? In Fisher and van Wees 1998: 169–93.

Raaflaub, K. A. 1999. "Archaic and Classical Greece." In K. Raaflaub and N. Rosenstein (eds.), *War and Society in the Ancient and Medieval Worlds*, 129–61. Washington, DC.

Raaflaub, K. A. 2000. "Poets, Lawgivers, and the Beginning of Political Reflection in Archaic Greece." In C. Rowe and M. Schofield (eds.), *The Cambridge History of Greek and Roman Political Thought*, 23–59. Cambridge.

Raaflaub, K. A. 2001. "Political Thought, Civic Responsibility, and the Greek Polis." In Arnason and Murphy 2001: 72–117.

Raaflaub, K. A. 2002a. "Herodot und Thukydides: Persischer Imperialismus im Lichte der athenischen Sizilienpolitik." In N. Ehrhardt and L.-M. Günther (eds.), *Widerstand–Anpassung–Integration: Die griechische Staatenwelt und Rom*, 11–40. Stuttgart.

Raaflaub, K. A. 2002b. "Philosophy, Science, Politics: Herodotus and the Intellectual Trends of His Time." In Bakker et al. 2002: 149–86.

Raaflaub, K. A. 2003a. "Freedom for the Messenians? A Note on the Impact of Slavery and Helotage on the Greek Concept of Freedom." In Luraghi and Alcock 2003: 169–90.

Raaflaub, K. A. 2003b. "Stick and Glue: The Function of Tyranny in Fifth-century Athenian Democracy." In K. Morgan 2003: 59–93.

Raaflaub, K. A. 2004a. "Archaic Greek Aristocrats as Carriers of Cultural Interaction." In Rollinger and Ulf 2004a: 197–217.

Raaflaub, K. A. 2004b (1985). *The Discovery of Freedom in Ancient Greece*. First English edn., revd. and updated. Chicago; German edn. Munich, 1985.

Raaflaub, K. A. 2004c. "Zwischen Ost und West: Phönizische Einflüsse auf die griechische Polisbildung?" In Rollinger and Ulf 2004b: 271–90.

Raaflaub, K. A. 2005a. "Epic and History." In Foley 2005: 55–70.

Raaflaub, K. A. 2005b. "Homerische Krieger, Protohopliten und die Polis: Schritte zur Lösung alter Probleme." In B. Meissner, O. Schmitt, and M. Sommer (eds.), *Krieg–Gesellschaft–Institutionen: Beiträge zu einer vergleichenden Kriegsgeschichte*, 229–66. Berlin.

Raaflaub, K. A. 2006. "Athenian and Spartan *Eunomia*, Or: What to Do with Solon's Timocracy?" In Blok and Lardinois 2006: 390–428.

Raaflaub, K. A. 2008. "Zeus und Prometheus: Zur griechischen Interpretation vorderasiatischer Mythen." In M. Bernett, W. Nippel, and A. Winterling (eds.), *Christian Meier zur Diskussion: Autorenkolloquium am Zentrum für Interdisziplinäre Forschung der Universität Bielefeld*, 33–60, Stuttgart.

Raaflaub, K. A. and R. W. Wallace. 2007. " 'People's Power' and Egalitarian Trends in Archaic Greece." In Raaflaub et al. 2007: 22–48.

Raaflaub, K. A., J. Ober, and R. W. Wallace. 2007. *Origins of Democracy in Ancient Greece*. Berkeley.

Rackham, O. 2003. "The Physical Setting." In Abulafia 2003: 11–32.

Radner, K. (ed.). 1999. *The Prosopography of the Neo-Assyrian Empire*, I.2 (B–G). Helsinki.

Raepsaet, G. 1993. "Le Diolkos de l'Isthme à Corinthe: Son tracé, son fonctionnement." *BCH* 117: 233–56.

Rahe, P. A. 1992. *Republics, Ancient and Modern: Classical Republicanism and the American Revolution*. Chapel Hill.

Rainbird, C. P. 1999. "Islands out of Time: Towards a Critique of Island Archaeology." *Journal of Mediterranean Archaeology* 12.2: 216–34.

Ramage, A. and P. Craddock. 2000. *King Croesus' Gold: Excavations at Sardis and the History of Gold Refining*. London.

Raphtopoulou, S. 1996–7. "Tafes tis epokhis tou sidirou sti Sparti." In *Praktika tou 5. Diethnous Sinedriou Peloponnisiakon Spoudon* II, 272–82. Athens.

Raschke, W. (ed.). 1988. *The Archaeology of the Olympics*. Madison.

Rasmussen, S. W. 2003. *Public Portents in Republican Rome*. Rome.

Raubitschek, A. 1949. *Dedications from the Athenian Akropolis: A Catalogue of the Inscriptions of the Sixth and Fifth Centuries* BC. Ed. with the collaboration of L. H. Jeffery. Cambridge, MA.

Rawlings, L. 2000. "Alternative Agonies: Hoplite Martial and Combat Experiences beyond the Phalanx." In van Wees 2000c: 233–60.

Reden, S. von. 1995. *Exchange in Ancient Greece*. London.

Reden, S. von. 2002. "Money in the Ancient Economy: A Survey of Recent Research." *Klio* 84: 141–74.

Redfield, J. M. 1994. *Nature and Culture in the* Iliad: *The Tragedy of Hector*. Expanded edn. Durham.

Reed, C. M. 1984. "Maritime Traders in the Archaic Greek World." *Ancient World* 10: 31–44.

Reed, C. M. 2003. *Maritime Traders in the Ancient Greek World*. Cambridge.

Reeder, E. D. (ed.). 1995. *Pandora: Women in Classical Greece*. Baltimore.

Reese, D. S. 2000. "The Iron Age Fauna." In Shaw and Shaw 2000: 415–646.

Reger, G. 1997. "Islands with One Polis versus Islands with Several Poleis." In Hansen 1997: 450–92.

Reher, D. and J. Ortega Osona. 2000. "Malthus Revisited: Exploring Medium-range Interaction between Economic and Demographic Forces in Historic Europe." In T. Bengtsson and O. Saito (eds.), *Population and Economy: From Hunger to Modern Economic Growth*. 183–212. Oxford.

Reichert-Südbeck, Petra. 2002. *Kulte von Korinth und Syrakus: Vergleich zwischen einer Metropolis und ihrer Apoikia*. Dettelbach.

Renfrew, C. 1972. *The Emergence of Civilisation: The Cyclades and the Aegean in the Third Millennium BC*. London.

Renfrew, C. and M. Wagstaff (eds.). 1982. *An Island Polity: The Archaeology of Exploitation in Melos*. Cambridge.

Reyes, A. B. 1994. *Archaic Cyprus: A Study of the Textual and Archaeological Evidence*. Oxford.

Rhodes, P. J. 1972. *The Athenian Boule*. Oxford.

Rhodes, P. J. 1981 (1993). *A Commentary on the Aristotelian* Athenaion Politeia. Oxford; 2nd edn. 1993.

Rhodes, P. J. 1984. *Aristotle, The Athenian Constitution. Trans. with Introduction and Notes*. Harmondsworth.

Rhodes, P. J. 2003. *Ancient Democracy and Modern Ideology*. London.

Rhomiopoulou, K. 1999. "Oi apoikies tis Androu sto boreio Aigaio." In Stampolidis 1999: 126–31.

Riccardi, M. 1986–7. "Il tempio di Apollo Pizio a Gortina." *ASAA* 64–5: 7–130.

Rich, J. and A. Wallace-Hadrill (eds.). 1991. *City and Country in the Ancient World*. London.

Rich, J. and G. Shipley (eds.). 1993. *War and Society in the Greek World*. London.

Richer, N. 1998. *Les éphores: Etudes sur l'histoire et sur l'image de Sparte (VIIIᵉ–IIIᵉ siècles av. J.-Chr.)*. Paris.

Richter, G. M. A. 1931. "Greek Bronzes Recently Acquired by the Metropolitan Museum of Art." *AJA* 35: 189–201.

Richter, G. M. A. 1961. *Archaic Gravestones of Attica*. London.

Richter, G. M. A. 1968. *Korai: Archaic Greek Maidens*. London.

Richter, G. M. A. 1970. *Kouroi: Archaic Greek Youths.*[3] London.

Richter, G. M. A., with I. A. Richter, and G. M. Young. 1942 (1960). *Kouroi: A Study of the Development of the Greek Kouros from the Late Seventh to the Early Fifth Century BC*. New York. Repr. 1960.

Richter, W. 1968. *Die Landwirtschaft im homerischen Zeitalter*. Archaeologia Homerica, H. Göttingen.

Ridgway, B. S. 1977. *The Archaic Style in Greek Sculpture*. Princeton.

Ridgway, D. 1990. "The First Western Greeks and Their Neighbours, 1935–1985." In Descoeudres 1990: 60–72.

Ridgway, D. 1992. *The First Western Greeks*. Cambridge.

Ridgway, D. 1994. "Phoenicians and Greeks in the West: A View from Pithekoussai." In Tsetskhladze and De Angelis 1994: 35–46.

Ridgway, D. 1996. "Greek Letters at Osteria dell'Osa." *Opuscula Romana* 20: 87–97.

Ridgway, D. 2000a. "The First Western Greeks Revisited." In D. Ridgway et al. (eds.), *Ancient Italy in Its Mediterranean Setting*, 179–91. London.

Ridgway, D. 2000b. "Riflessioni sull'orizzonte 'precoloniale' (IX–VIII sec. a.C.)." In *Magna Grecia e Oriente mediterraneo prima dell'età ellenistica*, 91–109. Taranto.

Ridgway, D. 2004. "Euboeans and Others along the Tyrrhenian Seabord." In Lomas 2004: 15–33.

Ridgway, D. and Ridgway, F. (eds.). 1979. *Italy before the Romans: The Iron Age, Orientalizing and Etruscan Periods*. London and New York.

Riedweg, C. 2002. *Pythagoras: His Life, Teaching, and Influence*. Tr. S. Rendall. Ithaca, NY.

Rihll, T. 1993. "War, Slavery, and Settlement in Early Greece." In Rich and Shipley 1993: 77–107.

Rihll, T. 1996. "The Origin and Establishment of Ancient Greek Slavery." In M. I. Bush (ed.), *Serfdom and Slavery: Studies in Legal Bondage*, 89–111. London.

Rihll, T. and J. V. Tucker. 1995. "Greek Engineering: The Case of Eupalinos' Tunnel." In Powell 1995: 403–31.

Risberg, C. 1992. "Metal-working in Greek Sanctuaries." In T. Linders and B. Alroth (eds.), *Economics of Cult in the Greek World*, 33–40. Uppsala.

Risberg, C. 1997. "Evidence of Metal Working in Early Greek Sanctuaries." In C. Gillis, C. Risberg, and B. Sjöberg (eds.), *Trade and Production in Premonetary Greece*, 185–96. Jonsered.

Rizakis, A. D. (ed.). 1991. *Achaia und Elis in der Antike*. Athens.

Rizza, G. and S. Scrinari. 1968. *Il Santuario sull' Acropoli di Gortina*, I. Rome.

Roaf, M. D. 1983. *Sculptures and Sculptors at Persepolis*. London.

Robb, K. 1978. "Poetic Sources of the Greek Alphabet." In E. Havelock and J. Herschell (eds.), *Communication Arts in the Ancient World*, 223–36. New York.

Robb, K. 1994. *Literacy and Paideia in Ancient Greece*. New York and Oxford.

Robertson, M. 1975. *A History of Greek Art*. 2 vols. Cambridge.

Robertson, N. 1978. "The Myth of the First Sacred War." *CQ* 28: 38–73.

Robertson, N. 1998. "The City Center of Archaic Athens." *Hesperia* 67: 283–302.

Robinson, D. M. and J. W. Graham. 1938. *The Hellenic House: A Study of the Houses Found at Olynthos*. Baltimore.

Robinson, E. W. 1997. *The First Democracies: Early Popular Government outside Athens*. Stuttgart.

Rocco, G. 1996. "Il tempio di Athana Polias e Zeus Polieus." In Livadiotti and Rocco 1996: 43–46.

Roebuck, C. 1959. *Ionian Trade and Colonization*. New York.

Rolley, C. 1969. *Fouilles de Delphes*, V.2: *Les statuettes de bronze*. Paris.

Rolley, C. 1977. *Fouilles de Delphes*, V.3: *Les trépieds à cuve clouée*. Paris.

Rolley, C. 1986. *Greek Bronzes*. London.

Rollinger, R. 1993. *Herodots babylonischer Logos*. Innsbruck.

Rollinger, R. 1999. "Zur Lokalisierung von Paršuma in der Fārs und einigen Fragen der frühen persischen Geschichte." *ZA* 89: 115–39.

Rollinger, R. 2001. "The Ancient Greeks and the Impact of the Ancient Near East: Textual Evidence and Historical Perspective (ca. 750–650 BC)." In R. M. Whiting, (ed.), *Mythology and Mythologies: Methodological Approaches to Intercultural Influences*, 233–64. Helsinki.

Rollinger, R. 2003a. "Herodotus." In *Encyclopaedia Iranica*, XII: 254–88. Costa Mesa.

Rollinger, R. 2003b. "The Western Expansion of the 'Median Empire': A Re-Examination." In Lanfranchi et al. 2003b: 289–319.

Rollinger, R. 2004. "Herodot (II 75f, III 107–9), Asarhaddon, Jesaja und die fliegenden Schlangen Arabiens." In Heftner and Tomaschitz 2004: 927–44.

Rollinger, R. 2008. "The Median 'Empire', the End of Urartu and Cyrus the Great's Campaign in 547 BC. (*Nabonidus Chronicle* II 16)." *AWE* 7: 49–63.

Rollinger, R. and C. Ulf (eds.). 2004a. *Commerce and Monetary Systems in the Ancient World: Means of Transmission and Cultural Interaction*. Stuttgart.

Rollinger, R. and C. Ulf (eds.). 2004b. *Griechische Archaik: Interne Entwicklungen – Externe Impulse*. Berlin.

Romano, I. B. 2000. "The Dreros *sphyrelata*: A Re-examination of Their Date and Function." In C. C. Mattusch, A. Brauer, and S. E. Knudsen (eds.), *From the Parts to the Whole: Acta of the 13th Intern. Bronze Congress*, I, 40–50. Portsmouth.

Romeri, L. 2002. *Philosophes entre mots et mets*. Grenoble.

Romilly, J. de. 1968. "Guerre et paix entre cités." In Vernant 1968: 207–20.

Roobaert, A. 1977. "Le danger hilote?" *Ktèma* 2: 141–55.

Rose, P. W. 1992. *Sons of the Gods, Children of Earth: Ideology and Literary Form in Ancient Greece*. Ithaca, NY.

Rose, P. W. 1997. "Ideology in the *Iliad*: Polis, *Basileus, Theoi*." *Arethusa* 30: 151–99.

Rose, P. W. 1999. Review of W. G. Thalmann, *The Swineherd and the Bow: Representations of Class in the* Odyssey. *Phoenix* 53: 3–4.

Rose, V. (ed.). 1886. *Aristotelis qui ferebantur librorum fragmenta*.³ Leipzig.

Rosen, R. M. 1997. "Homer and Hesiod." In Morris and Powell 1997: 463–88.

Rösler, W. 1980. *Dichter und Gruppe: Eine Untersuchung zu den Bedingungen und zur historischen Funktion früher griechischer Lyrik am Beispiel des Alkaios*. Munich.

Rostovtzeff, M. 1941. *Social and Economic History of the Hellenistic World*. Oxford.

Rouet, P. 2001. *Approaches to the Study of Attic Vases: Beazley and Pottier*. Oxford.

Rouillard, P. 2001. "Greci, Iberi e Celti." In Settis 2001: 499–534.

Roussel, D. 1976. *Tribu et cité: Etudes sur les groupes sociaux dans les cités grecques aux époques archaïque et classique*. Paris.

Rousset, D. 2002. *Le Territoire de Delphes et la Terre d'Apollon*. Paris.

Roy, J. 1972. "An Arkadian League in the Earlier Fifth Century?" *Phoenix* 26: 129–36.

Roy, J. 1997. "The *Perioikoi* of Elis." In Hansen 1997: 282–320.

Roy, J. 1999. "Les cités d'Elide." In J. Renard (ed.), *Le Péloponnèse: Archéologie et histoire*, 151–76. Rennes.

Roy, J. 2000a. "The Frontier between Arkadia and Elis in Classical Antiquity." In Flensted-Jensen et al. 2000: 133–56.

Roy, J. 2000b. "Problems of Democracy in the Arcadian Confederacy 370–362 BC." In Brock and Hodkinson 2000: 308–26.

Roy, J. 2002a. "The Pattern of Settlement in Pisatis: The 'Eight *Poleis*'." In Nielsen 2002a: 229–47.

Roy, J. 2002b. "The Synoikism of Elis." In Nielsen 2002a: 249–64.

Roy, J. and D. Schofield. 1999. "IvO 9: A New Approach." *Horos* 13: 155–65.

Rubensohn, O. 1962. *Das Delion von Paros*. Wiesbaden.

Ruby, P. (ed.). 1999. *Les Princes de la protohistoire et l'émergence de l'état.* Naples and Rome.

Rudolph, H. 1971. "Die ältere Tyrannis in Sikyon." *Chiron* 1: 75–83.

Ruggeri, C. 2004. *Gli stati intorno a Olimpia: Storia e costituzione dell'Elide e degli stati formati dai perieci elei* (400–362 a.C.). Stuttgart.

Ruiz, A. and M. Molinos. 1998. *The Archaeology of the Iberians.* Cambridge.

Ruiz Mata, D. 2002a. "The Ancient Phoenicians of the 8th and 7th Centuries BC in the Bay of Cádiz: State of the Research." In Bierling 2002: 155–98.

Ruiz Mata, D. 2002b. "The Beginnings of the Phoenician Presence in Southwestern Andalusia." In Bierling 2002: 263–98.

Runciman, W. G. 1990. "Doomed to Extinction: The Polis as an Evolutionary Dead End." In Murray and Price 1990: 347–67.

Ruschenbusch, E. 1958. "*Patrios politeia.* Theseus, Drakon, Solon und Kleisthenes in Publizistik und Geschichtsschreibung des 5. und 4. Jh. v. Chr." *Historia* 7: 398–424.

Ruschenbusch, E. 1966. ΣΟΛΩΝΟΣ ΝΟΜΟΙ: *Die Fragmente des solonischen Gesetzeswerkes mit einer Text- und Überlieferungsgeschichte.* Wiesbaden.

Ruschenbusch, E. 1978. *Untersuchungen zu Staat und Politik in Griechenland vom 7.-4. Jh. v. Chr.* Bamberg.

Rusyaeva, A. S. 1999. "Proniknovenie Ellinov na territoriyu Ukrainskoi lesostepi v arkhaicheskoe vremya (k postanovke problemy)" *VDI* 4: 84–97.

Rutherford, I. 2004. "Song-dance and Pilgrimage at Athens." In Murray and Wilson 2004: 67–90.

Ruzé, F. 1984. "Plethos. Aux origines de la majorité politique." In Nicolet 1984: 247–63.

Ruzé, F. 1997. *Délibération et pouvoir dans la cité grecque de Nestor à Socrate.* Paris.

Ryan, F. 1994. "The Original Date of the *demos plethyon* Provisions of *IG* I³ 105." *JHS* 114: 120–34.

Sackett, L. H. (ed.). 1992. *Knossos: From Greek City to Roman Colony. Excavations at the Unexplored Mansion II.* London.

Sackett, L. H., V. Hankey, and R. J. Howell. 1966. "Prehistoric Euboea: Contribution towards a Survey." *ABSA* 61: 33–112.

Sahlins, M. 1972. "On the Sociology of Primitive Exchange." In Sahlins (ed.), *Stone Age Economics*, 185–275. London.

Saïd, S. 1998. *Homère et l'Odyssée.* Paris.

Ste. Croix, G. E. M. de. 1972. *The Origins of the Peloponnesian War.* London.

Ste. Croix, G. E. M. de. 1981. *The Class Struggle in the Ancient Greek World: From the Archaic Age to the Arab Conquests.* Ithaca, NY.

Ste. Croix, G. E. M. de. 2004. *Athenian Democratic Origins and Other Essays.* Ed. D. Harvey and R. Parker. Oxford.

Sakellarakis, J. A. 1988. "Some Geometric and Archaic Votives from the Idaean Cave." In Hägg et al. 1988: 173–93.

Sakellariou, M. B. 1989. *The Polis-state: Definition and Origin.* Athens.

Salapata, G. 1992. "Lakonian Votive Plaques with Particular Reference to the Sanctuary of Alexandra at Amyklai." Diss. University of Pennsylvania.

Salapata, G. 2002. "Myth into Culture: Alexandra/Kassandra in Lakonia." In Gorman and Robinson 2002: 131–59.

Sallares, R. 1991. *The Ecology of the Ancient Greek World.* London.

Saller, R. 2002. "Framing the Debate over Growth in the Ancient Economy." In W. Scheidel and S. von Reden (eds.), *The Ancient Economy*, 251–69. Edinburgh.

Salmon, J. B. 1977. "Political Hoplites?" *JHS* 97: 84–101.

Salmon, J. B. 1984. *Wealthy Corinth: A History of the City to 338 BC.* Oxford.

Salmon, J. B. 1997. "Lopping off the Heads? Tyrants, Politics and the *Polis*." In Mitchell and Rhodes 1997: 60–73.

Salmon, J. B. 2000. "Pots and Profits." In G. R. Tsetskhladze, A. J. N. W. Prag, and A. M. Snodgrass (eds.), *Periplous: Papers on Classical Art and Archaeology Presented to Sir John Boardman*, 245–52. London.

Salt, A. and E. Boutsikas. 2005. "Knowing When to Consult the Oracle at Delphi." *Antiquity* 79: 564–72.

Salviat, F. 1948. "Une nouvelle lois thasienne: institutions judiciaires et fêtes religieuses à la fin du IVᵉ s. av. J.-C." *BCH* 72: 193–267.

Salviat, F. 1992. "Sur la religion de Marseille grecque." In M. Bats, G. Bertucchi, G. Conges et al. (eds.), *Marseille grecque et la Gaule*, 141–50. Lattes and Aix-en-Provence.

Salviat, F. 2000. "La source ionienne: Apatouria, Apollon Delphinios et l'oracle, l'Aristarcheion." In Hermary and Tréziny 2000: 25–31.

Sampson, A. 1980. *I Neolithiki kai i Protoelladiki I stin Evoia*. Athens.

Sampson, A. 1981. *Evoiki Kimi* I. Chalcis.

Sampson, G. 1985. *Writing Systems: A Linguistic Introduction*. London.

Samuel, A. E. 1972. *Greek and Roman Chronology: Calendars and Years in Classical Antiquity*. Munich.

Sánchez, P. 2001. *L'Amphictionie des Pyles et de Delphes: Recherches sur son rôle historique, des origines au IIᵉ siècle de notre ère*. Stuttgart.

Sancisi-Weerdenburg, H. 1988. "Was There Ever a Median Empire?" In Kuhrt and Sancisi-Weerdenburg 1988: 197–212.

Sancisi-Weerdenburg, H. 1989. "The Personality of Xerxes, King of Kings." In L. de Meyer and E. Haerinck (eds.), *Archaeologia Iranica et Orientalis*, 549–61. Gent.

Sancisi-Weerdenburg, H. 1994. "The Orality of Herodotos' Medikos Logos or: The Median Empire Revisited." In Sancisi-Weerdenburg, A. Kuhrt, and M. C. Root (eds.), *Achaemenid History*, VIII: *Continuity and Change*, 39–55. Leiden.

Sancisi-Weerdenburg, H. 1995. "Medes and Persians in Early States?" In M. A. van Bakel and J. G. Oosten (eds.), *The Dynamics of the Early State Paradigm*, 87–104. Utrecht.

Sancisi-Weerdenburg, H. (ed.). 2000. *Peisistratos and the Tyranny: A Reappraisal of the Evidence*. Amsterdam.

Sancisi-Weerdenburg, H. 2001. "Yaunâ by the Sea and across the Sea." In Malkin 2001: 322–46.

Sancisi-Weerdenburg, H. and A. Kuhrt (eds.). 1987. *Achaemenid History*, II: *The Greek Sources*. Leiden.

Sanders, J. M. (ed.). 1992. *Philolakon: Lakonian Studies in Honour of Hector Catling*. London.

Sanders, N. K. 1985. *The Sea Peoples: Warriors of the Ancient Mediterranean*. London.

Sanmartí, E. 1990. "Emporion, port grec à vocation ibérique." In *La Magna Grecia e il lontano occidente*, 389–410. Taranto.

Sapouna-Sakellaraki, E. 1997. *Khalkis: istoria, topoyrafia kai mouseio*. Athens.

Sapouna-Sakellaraki, E. 1998. "Geometric Kyme: The Excavation at Viglatouri, Kyme, on Euboea." In Bats and D'Agostino 1998: 59–104.

Sapouna-Sakellaraki, E. et al. 2002. "Skyros in the Early Iron Age." In Stamatopoulou and Yeroulanou 2002: 117–48.

Sapouna-Sakellaraki, E., J. J. Coulton, and I. A. Metzger. 2002. *The Fort at Phylla, Vrachos: Excavations and Researches at a Late Archaic Fort in Central Euboea*. London.

Sasson, J. (ed.). 1995. *Civilizations of the Ancient Near East*. 4 vols. New York.

Scanlon, T. F. 2002. *Eros and Greek Athletics*. Oxford.

Schachter, A. 1981. *Cults of Boiotia*, I. London.

Schachter, A. 1986. *Cults of Boiotia*, II. London.

Schachter, A. 1989. "Boeotia in the Sixth Century BC." In H. Beister and J. Buckler (eds.), *Boiotika: Vorträge vom 5. Intern. Böotien-Kolloquium zu Ehren von S. Lauffer*, 73–86. Munich.

Schachter, A. (ed). 1990. *Le sanctuaire grec*. Entretiens sur l'Antiquité classique 37. Vandoeuvres.

Schäfer, C. 1996. *Xenophanes von Kolophon: Ein Vorsokratiker zwischen Mythos und Philosophie*. Stuttgart.

Schäfer, J. 1992. "Areal D: Das 'Heiligtum des Zeus Thenatas'." In Schäfer (ed.), *Amnisos: Nach den archäologischen, historischen und epigraphischen Zeugnissen des Altertums und der Neuzeit*, I: 159–78. Berlin.

Schallin, A.-L. 1993. *Islands under Influence: The Cyclades in the Late Bronze Age and the Nature of Mycenaean Presence*. Göteborg.

Schama, S. 1996. *Landscape and Memory*. Toronto.

Schaps, D. 2004. *The Invention of Coinage and the Monetization of Ancient Greece*. Ann Arbor.

Schaudig, H. 2001. *Die Inschriften Nabonids von Babylon und Kyros' des Grossen samt den in ihrem Umfeld entstandenen Tendenzschriften: Textausgabe und Grammatik*. Münster.

Schaus, G. 1985. "Evidence for Laconians in Cyrenaica in the Archaic Period." In G. Barker, J. Lloyd, and J. Reynolds (eds.), *Cyrenaica in Antiquity*, 395–403. Oxford.

Scheffer, C. 1988. "Workshop and Trade Patterns in Athenian Black Figure." In J. Christiansen and T. Melander (eds.), *Ancient Greek and Related Pottery*, 536–46. Copenhagen.

Scheidel, W. 2001. *Death on the Nile: Disease and the Demography of Roman Egypt*. Leiden.

Scheidel, W. 2002. "A Model of Demographic and Economic Change in Roman Egypt after the Antonine Plague." *JRA* 15: 97–114.

Scheidel, W. 2003. "The Greek Demographic Expansion: Models and Comparisons." *JHS* 123: 120–40.

Scheidel, W. 2004a. "Demographic and Economic Development in the Ancient Mediterranean World." *Journal of Institutional and Theoretical Economics* 160: 743–57.

Scheidel, W. 2004b. "Gräberstatistik und Bevölkerungsgeschichte: Attika im achten Jahrhundert." In Rollinger and Ulf 2004b: 177–86.

Scheidel, W. 2007. "Demography." In I. Morris, R. Saller, and W. Scheidel (eds.), *The Cambridge Economic History of the Greco-Roman World*, 38–86. Cambridge.

Scheid-Tissinier, E. 1994. *Les Usages du don chez Homère: Vocabulaire et pratiques*. Nancy.

Schein, S. (ed.). 1996. *Reading the* Odyssey: *Selected Interpretive Essays*. Princeton.

Schilardi, D. U. 1975. "Paros, Report II: The 1973 Campaign." *Journal of Field Archaeology* 2: 83–96.

Schilardi, D. U. 1983. "The Decline of the Geometric Settlement of Koukounaries at Paros." In Hägg 1983b: 173–83.

Schilardi, D. U. 1984. "The LH IIIC Period at the Koukounaries Acropolis, Paros." In J. A. MacGillivray and R. L. N. Barber (eds.), *The Prehistoric Cyclades*, 184–206. Edinburgh.

Schilardi, D. U. 1988. "The Temple of Athena at Koukounaries." In Hägg et al. 1988: 41–8.

Schilardi, D. U. 1995. "Il culto di Atena a Koukounaries e considerazioni sulla topografia di Paros nel VII sec. a.C." In Schilardi and Lanzillotta 1995: 33–64.

Schilardi, D. U. and E. Lanzillotta (eds.). 1995. *Le Cicladi ed il mondo Egeo*. Rome.

Schmid, B. 1947. *Studien zu griechischen Ktisissagen*. Diss. Freiburg.

Schmidt, J. U. 1986. *Adressat und Paraineseform: Zur Intention von Hesiods "Werken und Tagen."* Göttingen.

Schmidt-Dounas, B. 2004. "Frühe Peripteraltempel in Nordgriechenland." *AM* 119: 107–37.

Schmitt, R. 1973. "Deiokes." *Anzeiger der Österreichischen Akademie der Wissenschaften* 110: 137–47.

Schmitt, R. 1996a. "Bemerkungen zu dem sog. Gadatas-Brief." *ZPE* 112: 95–101.

Schmitt, R. 1996b. "Deioces." In *Encyclopaedia Iranica*, VII: 226–27.

Schmitt, R. 2002. *Die iranischen und Iranier-Namen in den Schriften Xenophons*. Vienna.

Schmitt, R. 2003a. "Lyder und Lykier in achaimenidischen Quellen." In Giorgieri et al. 2003: 291–300.

Schmitt, R. 2003b. "Die Sprache der Meder – eine grosse Unbekannte." In Lanfranchi et al. 2003b: 23–36.

Schmitt-Pantel, P. 1990. "Sacrificial Meal and *Symposion*: Two Models of Civic Institutions in the Archaic City?" In Murray 1990b: 14–36.

Schmitt-Pantel, P. 1992. *La cité au banquet: Histoire des repas publiques dans les cités grecques*. Rome.

Schmitt-Pantel, P. 2001. "Les femmes grecques et l'*andron*." *Clio* 14: 155–81.

Schmitt-Pantel, P., F. Lissarrague, L. Bruit, and A. Zografou. 2005. "Le banquet en Grèce." *Thesaurus Cultus et Rituum Antiquorum* II: 218–50. Los Angeles.

Schmitz, W. 2001. "'Drakonische Strafen': Die Revision der Gesetze Drakons durch Solon und die Blutrache in Athen." *Klio* 83: 7–38.

Schmitz, W. 2004a. "Griechische und nahöstliche Spruchweisheit. Die,*erga kai hemerai*' Hesiods und nahöstliche Weisheitsliteratur." In Rollinger and Ulf 2004b: 311–33.

Schmitz, W. 2004b. *Nachbarschaft und Dorfgemeinschaft im archaischen und klassischen Griechenland*. Berlin.

Schnapp, A. 1996. "Città e campagna: L'immagine della *polis* da Omero all'età classica." In Settis 1996: 117–63.

Schnapp-Gourbeillon, A. 1982. "Naissance de l'écriture et fonction poétique en Grèce archaïque: Quelques points de repère." *Annales ESC* 37: 714–23.

Schnapp-Gourbeillon, A. 2002. *Aux origines de la Grèce (XIIIe–VIIIe siècles avant n. e). La genèse du politique*. Paris

Schneider, H. 1991. "Die Gaben des Prometheus: Technik im antiken Mittelmeerraum zwischen 750 v. Chr. und 500 n. Chr." In D. Hägemann and H. Schneider, *Landbau und Handwerk 750 v. Chr. bis 1000 n. Chr.*, 19–313. Berlin.

Schneider, H. 2002. "Technik, Technologie." *DNP* 12.1: 68–74.

Schneider, J. 1985. "La Chronologie d'Alcman." *REG* 98: 1–64.

Schneider, T. 1991. "Félix Bourriots 'Recherches sur la nature du génos' und Denis Roussels 'Tribu et cité' in der althistorischen Forschung der Jahre 1979–1989." *Boreas* 14: 15–31.

Schoinas, C. 1999. "Eikonistiki Parastasi se Ostraka Kratira apo tin Ayia Triada Ileia." In *I Perifereia tou Mikinaikou Kosmou*, 257–62. Lamia.

Schuller, M. 1985. "Die dorische Architektur der Kykladen in spätarchaischer Zeit." *JDAI* 100: 319–98.

Schuller, M. 1991. *Der Tempel der Artemis im Delion auf Paros*. Berlin.

Schuller, W. 1980 (1990). *Griechische Geschichte*. Munich; 3rd edn. 1990.

Schuller, W. 1985. *Frauen in der griechischen Antike*. Konstanz.

Schürmann, W. 1996. *Das Heiligtum des Hermes und der Aphrodite in Syme Viannou*, II: *Die Tierstatuetten aus Metall*. Athens.

Schurtz, C. H. 1902. *Altersklassen und Männerbünde*. Berlin.

Schwartz, E. 1899. "Tyrtaios." *Hermes* 34: 428–68.

Schwartz, G. M. and J. J. Nichols (eds.). 2006. *After Collapse: The Regeneration of Complex Societies*. Tucson.

Schweitzer, B. 1969. *Die geometrische Kunst Griechenlands*. Cologne.

Scott, L. 2000. "Were There Polis Navies in Archaic Greece?" In. G. J. Oliver et al. (eds.), *The Sea in Antiquity*, 93–116. BAR International Series (suppl.) 899. Oxford.

Scully, G. 1979. *The Earth, the Temple and the Gods: Greek Sacred Architecture*[3]. New Haven.

Scully, S. 1990. *Homer and the Sacred City*. Ithaca, NY.

Scully, S. Forthcoming. "Hesiod's *Theogony* and the Enuma Elish: City Creation Myths." In Scully, *Hesiod's* Theogony. Oxford.

Seaford, R. 1994. *Reciprocity and Ritual: Homer and Tragedy in the Developing City-state*. Oxford.

Seaford, R. 2003. "Tragic Tyranny." In K. Morgan 2003: 95–115.

Seaford, R. 2004. *Money and the Early Greek Mind: Homer, Philosophy and Tragedy*. Cambridge.

Sealey, R. 1976. *A History of the Greek City States, 700–338 BC*. Berkeley.

Sealey, R. 1979. "Zum Datum der solonischen Gesetzgebung." *Historia* 28: 238–41.

Sekunda, N. V. 2000. "Land Use, Ethnicity and Federalism in West Crete." In Brock and Hodkinson 2000: 326–47.

Semple, E. C. 1932. *The Geography of the Mediterranean Region: Its Relation to Ancient History*. London.

Senff, R. 2000. "Die archaische Wohnbebauung am Kalabaktepe in Milet." In Krinzinger 2000: 29–37.

Service, E. R. 1975. *Origins of the State and Civilization: The Process of Cultural Evolution*. New York.

Settis, S. (ed.). 1996. *I Greci: Storia cultura arte società*, II: *Una storia greca*. 1: *Formazione*. Turin.

Settis, S. 2001. *I Greci: Storia cultura arte società*, III: *I Greci oltre la Grecia*. Turin.

Severin, T. 1985. *The Jason Voyage: The Quest for the Golden Fleece*. London.

Sewell, W. H. 1999. "The Concept(s) of Culture." In V. E. Bonnell and L. Hunt (eds.), *Beyond the Cultural Turn: New Directions in the Study of Society and Culture*, 35–61. Berkeley.

Seymour, T. D. 1907. *Life in the Homeric Age*. London.

Sgourou, M. 2002. "Excavating Houses and Graves: Exploring Aspects of Everyday Life and Afterlife in Ancient Thasos." In M. Stamatopoulou and M. Yerolanou (eds.), *Excavating Classical Culture: Recent Archaeological Discoveries in Greece*, BAR IS 1031: 1–11. Oxford.

Shanks, M. 1996. *Classical Archaeology of Greece: Experiences of the Discipline*. London.

Shanks, M. 1999. *Art and the Greek City State: An Interpretive Archaeology*. Cambridge.

Shanks, M. and C. Tilley. 1987. *Archaeology and Social Theory*. Albuquerque.

Shapiro, H. A. 1989. *Art and Cult under the Tyrants in Athens*. Mainz.

Shaw, B. 1996. "Seasons of Death: Aspects of Mortality in Imperial Rome." *JRS* 86: 100–38.

Shaw, J. 1989. "Phoenicians in Southern Crete." *AJA* 93: 165–83.

Shaw, J. 1998. "Kommos in Southern Crete: An Aegean Barometer for East–West Inter-connections." In Karageorghis and Stampolidis 1998: 13–24.

Shaw, J. and M. C. Shaw. 2000. *Kommos*, IV: *The Greek Sanctuary*, part I. Princeton.

Shaw, P.-J. 1999. "Olympiad Chronography and 'Early' Spartan History." In Hodkinson and Powell 1999: 273–309.

Shaw, P.-J. 2003. *Discrepancies in Olympiad Dating and Chronological Problems of Archaic Peloponnesian History*. Stuttgart.

Shear, I. M. 2000. *Tales of Heroes: The Origins of the Homeric Texts*. New York and Athens.

Shear, T. L. et al. 1978. *Athens Comes of Age: From Solon to Salamis*. Princeton.

Shelmerdine, C. 2006. "Mycenaean Palatial Administration." In Deger-Jalkotzy and Lemos 2006: 73–86.

Shepherd, G. 1995. "The Pride of Most Colonials: Burial and Religion in the Sicilian Colonies." In T. Fischer-Hansen (ed.), *Ancient Sicily*, 51–82. Copenhagen.

Shepherd, G. 2000. "Greeks Bearing Gifts: Religious Relationships between Sicily and Greece in the Archaic Period." In C. J. Smith and J. Serrati (eds.), *Sicily from Aeneas to Augustus: New Approaches in Archaeology and History*, 55–70. Edinburgh.

Shepherd, G. 2005. "Hellenicity: More Views from the Margins." *AWE* 4: 437–45.

Sherratt, S. 1994. "Commerce, Iron and Ideology: Metallurgical Innovation in 12th–11th century Cyprus." In Karageorghis 1994: 59–107.

Sherratt, S. and A. Sherratt. 1993. "The Growth of the Mediterranean Economy in the Early First Millennium BC." *World Archaeology* 24: 361–78.

Shimron, B. 1979. "Ein Wortspiel mit homoioi bei Herodot." *Rheinisches Museum* 122: 131–3.

Shipley, G. 1987. *A History of Samos 800–188 BC*. Oxford.

Shipley, G. 1992. "*Perioikos*: The Discovery of Classical Laconia." In Sanders 1992: 211–26.

Shipley, G. 1997. "Other Lakedaimonians: The Dependent Perioikic *Poleis* of Laconia and Messenia." In Hansen 1997: 189–281.

Shipley, G. 2000. "The Extent of Spartan Territory in the Late Classical and Hellenistic Periods." *ABSA* 95: 367–90.

Shipley, G. 2004a. "Lakedaimon." In Hansen and Nielsen 2004: 569–98.

Shipley, G. 2004b. "Messenia." In Hansen and Nielsen 2004: 547–68.

Shramko, B. A. 1987. *Bel'skoe gorodishche skifskoi epokhi (gorod Gelon)*. Kiev.

Siapkas, J. 2003. *Heterological Ethnicity: Conceptualizing Identities in Ancient Greece*. Uppsala.

Siewert, P. 1982. *Die Trittyen Attikas und die Heeresreform des Kleisthenes*. Munich.

Siewert, P. 1992. "The Olympic Rules." In Coulson and Kyrieleis 1992: 111–17.

Siewert, P. 1994. "Eine archaische Rechtsaufzeichnung aus der antiken Stadt Elis." In G. Thür (ed.), *Symposion 1993: Vorträge zur griechischen und hellenistischen Rechtsgeschichte*, 17–32. Cologne.

Siewert, P. 2001. *Ostrakismos-Testimonien: die Zeugnisse antiker Autoren, der Inschriften und Ostraka über das athenische Scherbengericht*. Stuttgart.

Sigalas, C. 2000. "Un sanctuaire d'Aphrodite à Thera." *Kernos* 13: 241–5.

Simantoni-Bournia, E. 1998. "Oi Kiklades apo tous Proimous Istorikous Khronous mekhri to telos tis arkhaikis epokhis." In Mendoni and Margaris 1998: 173–207.

Simantoni-Bournia, E. 2001–2. "Kosmimata apo to iero ton Irion Naxou." *Arkhaiognosia* 11: 141–53.

Simantoni-Bournia, E. 2004. *La céramique grecque à reliefs: Ateliers insulaires du VIIIᵉ au VIᵉ siècle avant J.-C.* Geneva.

Simpson, P. L. P. 1997. *The Politics of Aristotle: Translated with Introduction, Analysis, and Notes*. Chapel Hill.

Singor, H. W. 1995. "*Eni Prôtoisi Machesthai*: Some Remarks on the Iliadic Image of the Battlefield." In Crielaard 1995: 183–200.

Singor, H. W. 2000. "The Military Side of the Peisistratean Tyranny." In H. Sancisi-Weerdenburg (ed.), *Peisistratos and the Tyranny: A Reappraisal of the Evidence*, 107–29. Amsterdam.

Singor, H. W. 2002. "The Spartan Army at Mantinea and Its Organisation in the Fifth Century BC." In Jongman and Kleijwegt 2002: 235–84.

Sinn, U. 1978. "Das Heiligtum der Artemis Limnatis bei Kombothekra." *AM* 93: 45–83.

Sinn, U. 1981. "Das Heiligtum der Artemis Limnatis bei Kombothekra." *AM* 96: 25–71.

Sjögren, L. 2003. *Cretan Locations: Discerning Site Variations in Iron Age and Archaic Crete*. Oxford.

Skinner, M. 2004. *Sexuality in Greek and Roman Culture*. Oxford.

Sklalet, C. H. 1928. *Ancient Sicyon*. Baltimore.

Skorda, D. 1992. "Recherches dans la vallée du Pléistos." In J.-F. Bommelaer (ed.), *Delphes: Centenaire de la "Grande Fouille,"* 39–66. Leiden.

Slater, W. J. (ed.). 1991. *Dining in a Classical Context*. Ann Arbor.

Sloan, R. and M. Duncan. 1978. "Zooarchaeology of Nichoria." In G. Rapp and S. Aschenbrenner (eds.), *Excavations at Nichoria in Southwest Greece*, I: 60–77. Minneapolis.

Smith, A. D. 1986. *The Ethnic Origins of Nations*. Oxford.

Smith, J. A. 1989. *Athens under the Tyrants*. Bristol.

Smith, M. 2004. "The Archaeology of Ancient State Economies." *Annual Review of Anthropology* 33: 73–102.

Smith, R. C. 1985. "The Clans of Athens and the Historiography of the Archaic Period." *Echos du monde classique* 29: 51–61.

Snell, B. 1944. "Die Nachrichten über die Lehren des Thales und die Anfänge der griechischen Philosophie- und Literaturgeschichte." *Philologus* 96: 170–82.

Snell, B. and H. Maehler (eds.). 1975. *Pindarus*, II: *Fragmenta, Indices*. Leipzig.

Snodgrass, A. M. 1964. *Early Greek Armour and Weapons*. Edinburgh.

Snodgrass, A. M. 1965. "The Hoplite Reform and History." *JHS* 85: 110–22.

Snodgrass, A. M. 1971 (2000). *The Dark Age in Greece: An Archaeological Survey of the Eleventh to the Eighth Centuries BC*. Edinburgh; 2nd edn. 2000.

Snodgrass, A. M. 1974. "An Historical Homeric Society?" *JHS* 94: 115–25.

Snodgrass, A. M. 1977a. *Archaeology and the Rise of the Greek State*. Cambridge.

Snodgrass, A. M. 1977b. "Cretans in Arcadia." In *Antichità Cretesi: Studi in onore di Doro Levi*, II: 196–201. Catania.

Snodgrass, A. M. 1980a. *Archaic Greece: The Age of Experiment*. Berkeley.

Snodgrass, A. M. 1980b. "Iron and Early Metallurgy in the Mediterranean." In T. Wertime and J. Muhly (eds.), *The Coming of the Age of Iron*, 335–74. New Haven.

Snodgrass, A. M. 1983a. "Heavy Freight in Archaic Greece." In Garnsey et al. 1983: 16–26.

Snodgrass, A. M. 1983b. "Two Demographic Notes." In Hägg 1983b: 167–71.

Snodgrass, A. M. 1986a. "The Historical Significance of Fortifications in Archaic Greece." In P. Leriche and H. Tréziny (eds.), *La fortification dans l'histoire du monde grec*, 125–31. Paris.

Snodgrass, A. M. 1986b. "Interaction by Design: The Greek City State." In C. Renfrew and J. F. Cherry (eds.), *Peer Polity Interaction and Socio-Political Change*, 47–58. Cambridge.

Snodgrass, A. M. 1987. *An Archaeology of Greece: The Present State and Future Scope of a Discipline*. Berkeley.

Snodgrass, A. M. 1989. "The Coming of the Iron Age in Greece: Europe's Earliest Bronze/Iron Transition." In M. Sørensen and R. Thomas (eds.), *The Bronze Age–Iron Age Transition in Europe*, 22–35. Oxford.

Snodgrass, A. M. 1991. "Archaeology and the Study of the Greek City." In Rich and Wallace-Hadrill 1991: 1–23.

Snodgrass, A. M. 1993a. "The 'Hoplite Reform' Revisited." *DHA* 19: 47–61.

Snodgrass, A. M. 1993b. "The Rise of the *Polis*: The Archaeological Evidence." In Hansen 1993: 30–40.

Snodgrass, A. M. 1994a. "The Nature and Standing of the Early Western Colonies." In G. R. Tsetskhladze (ed.), *Greek and Roman Settlements on the Black Sea Coast*, 1–10. Bradford.

Snodgrass, A. M. 1994b. "A New Precedent for Westward Expansion: The Euboeans in Macedonia." In D'Agostino and Ridgway 1994: 87–93.

Snodgrass, A. M. 1996. "Iron." In Coldstream and Catling 1996: 575–97.

Snodgrass, A. M. 1998. *Homer and the Artists*. Cambridge.

Snodgrass, A. M. 1999. *Arms and Armour of the Greeks*.[2] Baltimore.

Snodgrass, A. M. 2005. "'Lesser Breeds': The History of a False Analogy." In Hurst and Owen 2005: 45–58.

Snodgrass, A. M. 2006. *Archaeology and the Emergence of Greece*. Edinburgh.

Snycer, S. 1979. "L'inscription phénicienne de Tekke, près de Cnossos." *Kadmos* 18: 89–93.

Snyder, L. and W. Klippel. 2000. "Dark Age Subsistence at the Kastro Site, East Crete." In S. Vaughn and W. Coulson (eds.), *Palaeodiet in the Aegean*, 65–83. Oxford.

Solin, H. 1981. "Sulle dediche greche di Gravisca." *PP* 36: 185–87.

Solmsen, F. 1949 (1995). *Hesiod and Aeschylus*. Ithaca, NY; 2nd edn. 1995, with a new foreword by G. M. Kirkwood.

Solovyov, S. L. 1998. "Archaic Berezan: Historical-archaeological Essay." In Tsetskhladze 1998a: 205–26.

Sommer, S. 2001. *Das Ephorat: Garant des spartanischen Kosmos*. St. Katharinen.

Sordi, M. 2004. "Pausania II e le leggi di Licurgo." In Heftner and Tomaschitz 2004: 145–50.

Sørensen, L. W. 2002. "The Archaic Settlement at Vroulia on Rhodes and Ian Morris." *Acta Hyperborea* 9: 243–53.

Soueref, K. 2000. "Toumba, Thessaloniki, 2000: Excavations in the Ancient Cemetery." *AEMTH* 14: 215–25.

Soueref, K. and K. Havela. 2002. "Souroti 2002." *AEMTH* 16: 267–76.

Sourvinou-Inwood, C. 1990. "What is *Polis* Religion?" In Murray and Price 1990: 295–322.

Sourvinou-Inwood, C. 1993. "Early Sanctuaries, the Eighth Century and Ritual Space. Fragments of a Discourse." In Marinatos and Hägg 1993: 1–17.

Sourvinou-Inwood, C. 1994. "Something to Do with Athens: Tragedy and Ritual." In Osborne and Hornblower 1994: 269–90.

Souza, P. de. 1998. "Towards Thalassocracy? Archaic Greek Naval Developments." In Fisher and van Wees 1998: 271–94.

Spencer, N. 1995. *A Gazetteer of Archaeological Sites in Lesbos*. *BAR* International Series 623. Oxford.

Spencer, N. 2000. "Exchange and Stasis in Archaic Mytilene." In Brock and Hodkinson 2000: 68–81.

Spivey, N. 2004. *The Ancient Olympics: War Minus the Shooting*. Oxford.

Stahl, M. 1987. *Aristokraten und Tyrannen im archaischen Athen: Untersuchungen zur Überlieferung, zur Sozialstruktur und zur Entstehung des Staates*. Stuttgart.

Stahl, M. 1992. "Solon F 3 D – die Geburtsstunde des demokratischen Gedankens." *Gymnasium* 99: 385–408.

Stahl, M. 2003a. *Gesellschaft und Staat bei den Griechen: Archaische Zeit*. Paderborn.

Stahl, M. 2003b. *Gesellschaft und Staat bei den Griechen: Klassische Zeit*. Paderborn.

Stählin, F. 1924. *Das hellenische Thessalien. Landeskundliche und geschichtliche Beschreibung Thessaliens in der hellenischen und römischen Zeit*. Stuttgart.

Stählin, F. 2002. *I arkhaia Thessalia*. Tr. G. Papasoteriou and A. Thanopoulou. Thessaloniki.

Stamatopoulou, M. 2007. "Thessalian Aristocracy and Society in the Age of Epinikian." In Hornblower and Morgan 2007: 309–41.

Stamatopoulou, M. and M. Yeroulanou (eds.). 2002. *Excavating Classical Culture: Recent Archaeological Discoveries in Greece*. Oxford.

Stampolidis, N. 1996. *Antipoina "Reprisals": Contribution to the Study of Customs of the Geometric-Archaic Period*. Rethymnon.

Stampolidis, N. (ed.). 1999. *Fos Kikladikon: Timitikos tomos sti mnimi tou Nikou Zafiropoulou*. Athens.

Stampolidis, N. (ed.). 2001. *Praktika tou simposiou Kafseis stin epokhi tou Khalkou kai tin proimi epokhi tou Sidirou: Rodos, 29 Apriliou–2 Maiou 1999*. Athens.

Stampolidis, N. 2002. "The Greeks in the Aegean prior to the Colonization Movement." In Vassos Karageorghis (ed.), *The Greeks beyond the Aegean: From Marseilles to Bactria*, 1–5. New York.

Stampolidis, N. 2003a. "On the Phoenician Presence in the Aegean." In Stampolidis and Karageorghis 2003: 217–30.

Stampolidis, N. 2003b. "A Summary Glance at the Mediterranean in the Early Iron Age." In Stampolidis and Karageorghis 2003: 41–79.

Stampolidis, N. and V. Karageorghis (eds.). 2003. *Ploes . . . Apo ti Sidona sti Khouelva: Skheseis laon tis Mesoyiou 16os–6os e. p.Kh./ Sea Routes from Sidon to Huelva: Interconnections in the Mediterranean, 16th–6th c. BC*. Athens.

Stampolidis, N. and A. Yannikouri (eds.). 2004. *To Aigaio stin Proimi Epokhi tou Sidirou*. Athens.

Stanley, P. V. 1999. *The Economic Reforms of Solon*. St. Katharinen.

Stanton, G. R. 1984. "The Tribal Reform of Kleisthenes the Alkmeonid." *Chiron* 14: 1–41.

Stanton, G. R. 1990. *Athenian Politics c. 800–500 BC: A Sourcebook*. London.

Starr, C. G. 1961. *The Origins of Greek Civilization*. New York.

Starr, C. G. 1965. "The Credibility of Early Spartan History." *Historia* 14: 257–72.

Starr, C. G. 1977. *The Economic and Social Growth of Early Greece: 800–500 BC*. Oxford.

Starr, C. G. 1986. *Individual and Community: The Rise of the Polis*. New York.

Starr, C. G. 1987. *Past and Future in Ancient History*. Lanham.

Staveley, E. S. 1972. *Greek and Roman Voting and Elections*. London.

Stavrianopoulou, E. (ed.). 2006. *Ritual and Communication in the Graeco-Roman World*. *Kernos* suppl. 16. Liège.

Stehle, E. 1997. *Performance and Gender in Ancient Greece: Nondramatic Poetry in Its Setting*. Princeton.

Steiner, D. 1993. "Pindar's 'Oggetti Parlanti'." *Harvard Studies in Classical Philology* 95: 159–80.

Steiner, D. 1998. "Moving Images: Fifth-century Victory Monuments and the Athlete's Allure." *ClAnt* 17: 123–53.

Steiner, D. 2001. *Images in Mind: Statues in Archaic and Classical Greek Literature and Thought*. Princeton.

Stein-Hölkeskamp, E. 1989. *Adelskultur und Polisgesellschaft. Studien zum griechischen Adel in archaischer und klassischer Zeit*. Stuttgart.

Stein-Hölkeskamp, E. 1996. "Tirannidi e ricerca dell' *eunomia*." In Settis 1996: 653–79.

Stein-Hölkeskamp, E. 1997. "Adel und Volk bei Theognis." In Eder and Hölkeskamp 1997: 21–35.

Stein-Hölkeskamp, E. 1999. "Polykrates." In K. Brodersen (ed.), *Grosse Gestalten der griechischen Antike: 58 historische Portraits von Homer bis Kleopatra*, 105–12. Munich.

Steinwenter, A. 1925. *Streitbeendigung durch Urteil, Schiedsspruch und Vergleich nach griechischem Rechte*. Munich.

Stephenson, F. R. and L. J. Fatooki. 1997. "Thales' Prediction of a Solar Eclipse." *Journal of the History of Astronomy* 28: 279–82.

Stewart, A. 1990. *Greek Sculpture: An Exploration*. New Haven.

Stewart, A. 1997. *Art, Desire and the Body in Ancient Greece*. Cambridge.

Stibbe, C. M. 1985. "Chilon of Sparta." *Mededelingen van het Nederlands Historisch Instituut te Rome* 46: 7–24.

Stibbe, C. M. 1996. *Das andere Sparta*. Mainz.

Stibbe, C. M. 2002. "The 'Achilleion' near Sparta: Some Unknown Finds." In R. Hägg (ed.), *Peloponnesian Sanctuaries and Cults*, 207–19. Stockholm.

Stibbe, C. M. 2006. *Agalmata: Studien zur griechisch-archaischen Bronzekunst*. Leiden.

Stika, H.-P. 1997. "Pflanzenreste aus dem archaischen Milet." *AA* 1997: 157–63.

Stoddard, K. 2004. *The Narrative Voice in the* Theogony *of Hesiod*. Leiden.

Stoddart S. and J. Whitley. 1988. "The Social Context of Literacy in Archaic Greece and Etruria." *Antiquity* 62: 761–72.

Strasburger, H. 1972 (1982). *Homer und die Geschichtsschreibung*. Wiesbaden. Repr. in Strasburger, *Studien zur Alten Geschichte*, II: 1057–97. Hildesheim, 1982.

Street B. 1984. *Literacy in Theory and Practice*. Cambridge.

Strøm, I. 1992. "Evidence from the Sanctuaries." In Kopcke and Tokumaru 1992: 46–60.

Strøm, I. 1995. "The Early Sanctuary of the Argive Heraion and Its External Relations." *Proceedings of the Danish Institute at Athens* I: 37–127.

Strøm, I. 1998. "The Early Sanctuary of the Argive Heraion and Its External Relations." *Proceedings of the Danish Institute at Athens* II: 37–125.

Stroud, R. S. 1968. *Drakon's Law on Homicide*. Berkeley.

Stroud, R. S. 1998. *The Athenian Grain-Tax Law of 374/3 BC*. Princeton.

Sulimirski, T. and T. Taylor. 1991. "The Scythians." *CAH²* III.2: 547–90.

Sullivan, R. D. 1996. "Psammetichos I and the Foundation of Naukratis." In W. D. E. Coulson (ed.), *Ancient Naukratis*, II.1: *The Survey at Naukratis*, 177–95. Exeter.

Svenbro, J. 1982. "A Mégara Hyblaea, le corps géometrique." *Annales ESC* 37: 953–64.

Svenbro, J. 1984. *La Parola e il marmo*. Turin.

Svenbro, J. 1988. *Phrasikleia: Anthropologie de la lecture en Grèce ancienne*. Paris.

Svenbro, J. 1993. *Phrasikleia: An Anthropology of Reading in Ancient Greece*. Tr. J. Lloyd. Ithaca, NY.

Swoboda, H. 1905. "Griechische Staatsaltertümer." In Kroll 1905: 234–87.

Symeonoglou, N. 2002. "Early Iron Age Pottery and the Development of the Sanctuary at Aetos, Ithaka (Greece)." Diss. Washington University.

Szegedy-Maszak, A. 1978. "Legends of the Greek Lawgivers." *GRBS* 19: 199–209.

Szemerényi, O. 1974. "The Origins of the Greek Lexicon: *ex oriente lux*." *JHS* 94: 144–57.

Tainter, J. 1988. *The Collapse of Complex Societies*. Cambridge.

Talbert, R. J. A. 1989. "The Role of the Helots in the Class Struggle at Sparta." *Historia* 38: 22–40.

Tandy, D. W. 1997. *Warriors into Traders: The Power of the Market in Early Greece*. Berkeley.

Tandy, D. W. and W. C. Neale. 1996. *Hesiod's* Works and Days: *A Translation and Commentary for the Social Sciences*. Berkeley.

Taplin, O. 1992. *Homeric Soundings: The Shaping of the* Iliad. Oxford.

Taplin, O. (ed.). 2000a. *Literature in the Greek and Roman Worlds: A New Perspective*. Oxford.

Taplin, O. 2000b. "The Spring of the Muses: Homer and Related Poetry." In Taplin 2000a: 22–57.

Tasia, A., Z. Lola, and O. Peltekis. 2000. "Thessaloniki: The Late Archaic Temple." *AEMTH* 14: 227–46.

Tausend, K. 1992. *Amphiktyonie und Symmachie: Formen zwischenstaatlicher Beziehungen im archaischen Griechenland*. Stuttgart.

Tausend, K. 1993. "Zur Bedeutung von Lousoi in archaischer Zeit." *JÖAI* 62: 13–26.

Taylor, M. C. 1997. *Salamis and the Salaminioi: The History of an Unofficial Athenian Demos.*
   Amsterdam.

Taylor, T. 1994. "Thracians, Scythians, and Dacians, 800 BC–AD 300." In Cunliffe 1994b:
   373–410.

Televantou, C. 1993. "Andros: O yeometrikos oikismos tis Ipsilis." *Andriaka Khronika* 21:
   187–208.

Televantou, C. 1996. "Andros: L'antico insediamento di Ipsili." In Schilardi and Lanzillotta
   1995: 79–100.

Televantou, C. 1998. "Andros kai Khalkidiki," Ανδριακά Χρονικά 29: 31–55.

Televantou, C. 1999. "Andros. To iero tis Ipsilis." In Stampolides 1999: 132–9.

Televantou, C. 2001. "Ayios Andreas on Sifnos: A Late Cycladic III Fortified Acropolis." In
   Karageorghis and Morris 2001: 191–213.

Televantou, C. 2004. "I Andros kata tin proimi epokhi tou sidirou." In Stampolidis and
   Yannikouri 2004: 421–6.

Televantou, C. 2005. "I akropolis tou Ayiou Andrea Sifnou: oikistikes faseis." In *Praktika B'
   Diethnous Sifnaikou Sibosiou, Sifnos 27–30 Iouniou 2002*, I: 61–70. Athens.

Thalmann, W. G. 1998. *The Swineherd and the Bow: Representations of Class in the* Odyssey.
   Ithaca, NY.

Themelis, P. 1965. "Arkhaiotites kai mnimeia tis Messinias." *AD* 20B: 207–8.

Themelis, P. 1981. "Ergastirio khrisokhoias tou 8ou aiona p.Kh. stin Eretria." *AAA* 14:
   185–208.

Themelis, P. 1983. "An 8th Century Goldsmith's Workshop at Eretria." In Hägg 1983b:
   157–65.

Themelis, P. 1994. "Hellenistic Architectural Terracottas from Messene." In N. A. Winter
   (ed.), *Proceedings of the International Conference on Greek Architectural Terracottas of the
   Classical and Hellenistic Periods*, 141–69. Princeton.

Themos, A., H. Zavvou, et al. 1992–7. Annual Reports of the Fifth *Eforeia* Proistorikon kai
   Klasikon *Arkhaiotiton*. *AD* 47B [1997]–52B [2002].

Theurillat, T. 2007. "Early Iron Age Graffiti from the Sanctuary of Apollo at Eretria." In
   Mazarakis Ainian 2007: 331–44.

Thomas, C. 2007. *Alexander the Great in His World*. Oxford.

Thomas, C. and C. Conant. 1999. *Citadel to City-state: The Transformation of Greece,
   1200–700 BCE*. Bloomington.

Thomas, R. 1992. *Literacy and Orality in Ancient Greece*. Cambridge.

Thomas, R. 1995. "The Place of the Poet in Archaic Society." In Powell 1995: 104–29.

Thomas, R. 1996. "Written in Stone? Liberty, Equality, Orality, and the Codification of Law."
   In L. Foxhall and A. D. E. Lewis (eds.), *Greek Law and Its Political Setting*, 9–31. Oxford.

Thomas, R. 2000. *Herodotus in Context: Ethnography, Science and the Art of Persuasion.*
   Cambridge.

Thomas, R. 2007. "Fame, Memorial and Choral Poetry: The Origins of Epinikian Poetry –
   an Historical Study." In Hornblower and Morgan 2007: 141–66.

Thommen, L. 1996. *Lakedaimonion Politeia: Die Entstehung der spartanischen Verfassung.*
   Stuttgart.

Thommen, L. 2003. *Sparta: Verfassungs- und Sozialgeschichte einer griechischen Polis*. Stuttgart.

Thompson, H. A. and R. E. Wycherley. 1972. *The Agora of Athens: The History, Shape and
   Uses of an Ancient City Center*. The Athenian Agora XIV. Princeton.

Thomson, G. 1946. *Aeschylus and Athens: A Study in the Social Origins of Drama*. London.

Thomson, G. 1955. *Studies in Ancient Greek Society*, II: *The First Philosophers*. London.

Thomson, G. 1961. *Studies in Ancient Greek Society*, I: *The Prehistoric Aegean*.[3] New York.

Tigerstedt, E. N. 1965–78. *The Legend of Sparta in Classical Antiquity*, 2 vols. and index. Stockholm.

Tilly, C. 1992. *Coercion, Capital, and European States*, AD *990–1990*. Oxford.

Tiverios, M. and S. Gimatzidis. 2002. "Excavations on the Double Table of Anchialos in 2002." *AEMTH* 16: 203–32.

Tiverios, M., E. Manakidou, and D. Tziafaki. 2002. "Archaeological Investigations at Karabournaki in 2000: The Ancient Settlement." *AEMTH* 16: 257–66.

Tod, M. N. 1911. "The Greek Numerical Notation." *ABSA* 18: 98–132.

Tod, M. N. 1913. "Three Greek Numeral Systems." *JHS* 33: 27–34.

Todd, J. A. et al. (eds.). 2002. *Greek Archaeology without Frontiers*. Athens.

Toepffer, J. 1889 (1973). *Attische Genealogie*. Berlin. Repr. New York 1973.

Tölle-Kastenbein, R. 1969. *Die antike Stadt Samos. Ein Führer*. Mainz.

Tölle-Kastenbein, R. 1976. *Herodot und Samos*. Bochum.

Tölle-Kastenbein, R. 1994. *Das archaische Wasserleitungsnetz für Athen und seine späteren Bauphasen*. Mainz.

Tolstikov, V. P. 2002. "Pantikapaion." In Fornasier and Böttger 2002: 39–58.

Tomkinson, J. L. 2002. *Attica*. Athens.

Tomlinson, R. A. 1972. *Argos and the Argolid: From the End of the Bronze Age to the Roman Occupation*. London.

Tomlinson, R. A. 1976. *Greek Sanctuaries*. London.

Tonkova, M. 2005. "Problem't za choveshkoto zhertvoprinoshenie v Trakiya." In G. Kitov and D. Dimitrova (eds.), *Zemite na B'lgariya: Lyulka na trakiiskata kultura*, II: 67–73. Sofia.

Torelli, M. 1971. "Il santuario di Hera a Gravisca." *PP* 26: 44–67.

Torelli, M. 1977. "Il Santuario greco di Gravisca." *PP* 32: 398–458.

Torelli, M. 1982. "Per la definizione del commercio greco-orientale: il caso di Gravisca." *PP* 37: 304–25.

Torelli, M. 1988. "Riflessioni a margine dell'emporion di Gravisca." *Revue du Groupe européen d'études pour les techniques physiques, chimiques et mathématiques appliquées à l'archéologie* 20: 181–90.

Torelli, M. (ed.). 2000. *The Etruscans*. London.

Touloupa, E. 2002. *Ta enaetia ylipta tou naou tou Apollonos Dafniforou stin Eretria*. Athens.

Traill, J. S. 1975. *The Political Organization of Attica: A Study of the Demes, Trittyes, and Phylai, and Their Representation in the Athenian Council*. Princeton.

Traill, J. S. 1986. *Demos and Trittys: Epigraphical and Topographical Studies in the Organization of Attica*. Toronto.

Travlos, J. 1950. "Anaskafi stin Elevsini." *PAAH* 1950: 122–7.

Travlos, J. 1971. *Pictorial Dictionary of Ancient Athens*. London.

Travlos, J. 1988. *Bildlexikon zur Topographie des antiken Attika*. Tübingen.

Treister, M. Y. 1998. "Ionia and the North Pontic Area. Archaic Metalworking: Tradition and Innovation." In Tsetskhladze 1998a: 179–99.

Treister, M. Y. 2001. *Hammering Techniques in Greek and Roman Jewellery and Toreutics*. Leiden.

Treister, M. Y. 2002. "Excavations at Pantikapaion, Capital of the Kingdom of the Bosporus: Old Finds, Recent Results and Some New Observations." In Todd et al. 2002: 151–74.

Treister, M. Y. and F. Shelov-Kovedyaev. 1989. "An Inscribed Conical Clay Object from Hermonassa." *Hesperia* 58: 289–96.

Trigger, B. 2003. *Understanding Early Civilizations*. Cambridge.

Tronchetti, C. 2003. "Sardinia from the 8th c. BC." In Stampolidis (ed.), *Sea Routes from Sidon to Huelva: Interconnections in the Mediterranean 16th–6th c. BC*. In Stampolidis and Karageorghis 2003: 162–3.

Troncoso, V. A. 1995. "Ultimatum et déclaration de guerre dans la Grèce classique." In E. Frézouls and A. Jacquemin (eds.), *Les Relations internationales. Actes du Colloque de Strasbourg, 1993*, 211–95. Paris.

Trüdinger, K. 1918. *Studien zur griechisch-römischen Ethnographie*. Diss. University of Basel.

Trundle, M. 2004. *Greek Mercenaries: From the Late Archaic Period to Alexander*. London.

Tsakos, K. 2001. "Die archaischen Gräber der Westnekropole von Samos und die Datierung der samischen Athemienstelen." *AA*: 451–66.

Tsetskhladze, G. R. 1994. "Greek Penetration of the Black Sea." In Tsetskhladze and De Angelis 1994: 111–36.

Tsetskhladze, G. R. (ed.). 1998a. *The Greek Colonisation of the Black Sea Area: Historical Interpretation of Archaeology*. Stuttgart.

Tsetskhladze, G. R. 1998b. "Greek Colonisation of the Black Sea Area: Stages, Models, and Native Population." In Tsetskhladze 1998a: 9–68.

Tsetskhladze, G. R. 1998c. *Die Griechen in der Kolchis (historisch-archäologischer Abriss)*. Amsterdam.

Tsetskhladze, G. R. 1998d. "Trade on the Black Sea in the Archaic and Classical Periods: Some Observations." In Parkins and Smith 1998: 52–74.

Tsetskhladze, G. R. 2000–1. "Black Sea Piracy." In Tsetskhladze and de Boer 2000–1: 11–15.

Tsetskhladze, G. R. 2002a. "Ionians Abroad." In G. R. Tsetskhladze and A. M. Snodgrass (eds.), *Greek Settlements in the Eastern Mediterranean and the Black Sea*, 81–96. Oxford.

Tsetskhladze, G. R. 2002b. "Phanagoria: Metropolis of the Asiatic Bosporus." In Todd et al. 2002: 129–50.

Tsetskhladze, G. R. 2003. "Greeks beyond the Bosporus." In V. Karageorghis (ed.), *The Greeks beyond the Aegean: From Marseilles to Bactria*, 129–66. New York.

Tsetskhladze, G. R. 2004. "On the Earliest Greek Colonial Architecture in the Pontus." In C. J. Tuplin (ed.), *Pontus and the Outside World: Studies in Black Sea History, Historiography and Archaeology*, 225–78. Leiden.

Tsetskhladze, G. R. and F. De Angelis (eds.). 1994. *The Archaeology of Greek Colonisation*. Oxford.

Tsetskhladze, G. R. and J. G. de Boer (eds.). 2000–1. *The Black Sea Region in the Greek, Roman and Byzantine Periods*. Amsterdam.

Tsetskhladze, G. R. and M. Y. Treister. 1995. "The Metallurgy and Production of Precious Metals in Colchis before and after the Arrival of the Ionians (Towards the Problem of the Reasons for Greek Colonisation)." *Bulletin of the Metals Museum* 24: 1–32.

Tsipopoulou, M. 1984. "Tafoi tis proimis epokhis tou Sidirou stin Anatoliki Kriti: Sibliroma." *AD* 39: 232–45.

Tsipopoulou, M. 1987. "Tafoi tis proimis epokhis tou Sidirou stin Anatoliki Kriti." In *EILAPINI: Tomos Timitikos yia ton Kathiyiti Nikolao Platona*, 253–69. Heraklion.

Tuchelt, K. 1992. *Branchidai-Didyma*. Mainz.

Tuchelt, K., P. Schneider, and T. G. Schattner. 1996. *Didyma*, III.1. *Ein Kultbezirk an der Heiligen Strasse von Milet nach Didyma*. Mainz.

Tuna-Nörling, Y. 1995. *Die Ausgrabungen von Alt-Smyrna und Pitane: Die attisch-schwarzfigurige Keramik und der attische Keramikexport nach Kleinasien*. Tübingen.

Turnbull, C. M. 1962. *The Forest People: A Study of the Pygmies of the Congo*. New York.

Turner, F. M. 1981. *The Greek Heritage in Victorian Britain*. New Haven.

Tziaphalias, A. 1994. "Ayios Yeoryios Larisa." In *THESSALIA Dekapente khronia arkhaiologikis erevnas 1975–1990*, 179–88. Athens.

Tzouvara-Souli, C. 2001. "The Cults of Apollo in Northwestern Greece." In Isager 2001: 233–45.

Ulf, C. 1990a. "Die Abwehr von internem Streit als Teil des 'politischen' Programms der homerischen Epen." *Grazer Beiträge* 17: 1–25.

Ulf, C. 1990b. *Die homerische Gesellschaft: Materialien zur analytischen Beschreibung und historischen Lokalisierung.* Munich.

Ulf, C. 1996a. "Griechische Ethnogenese versus Wanderungen von Stämmen und Stammstaaten." In Ulf 1996b: 240–80.

Ulf, C. (ed.). 1996b. *Wege zur Genese der griechischen Identität. Die Bedeutung der früharchaischen Zeit.* Berlin.

Ulf, C. 1997. "Überlegungen zur Funktion überregionaler Feste im archaischen Griechenland." In Eder and Hölkeskamp 1997: 37–61.

Ulf, C. 2001. "Gemeinschaftsbezug, soziale Stratifizierung, Polis – drei Bedingungen für das Entstehen aristokratischer und demokratischer Mentalität im archaischen Griechenland." In Papenfuss and Strocka 2001: 163–86.

Ulf, C. (ed.). 2003. *Der neue Streit um Troia. Eine Bilanz.* Munich.

Ulf, C. 2004. "Ilias 23: Die Bestattung des Patroklos und das Sportfest der 'Patroklos-Spiele'." In Heftner and Tomaschitz 2004: 73–86.

UNESCO. 1990. *Compendium of Statistics on Illiteracy.* Paris.

Ungern-Sternberg, J. von and H.-J. Reinau (eds.). 1988. *Vergangenheit in mündlicher Überlieferung.* Stuttgart.

Ure, P. N. 1921. *The Greek Renaissance.* London.

Ure, P. N. 1922. *The Origin of Tyranny.* Cambridge.

Vagnetti, L. 1989. "A Sardinian askos from Crete." *ABSA* 84: 355–60.

Vallat, F. 1996. "Nouvelle analyse des inscriptions néo-élamites." In H. Gasche and B. Hrouda (eds.), *Collectanea Orientalia: Histoire, arts de l'espace et industrie de la terre*, 385–95. Neuchâtel.

Vallet, G. (ed.). 1978. *Les céramiques de la Grèce de l'est et leur diffusion en Occident.* Paris.

Vallet, G., F. Villard, and P. Auberson. 1976. *Mégara Hyblaea, I: Le quartier de l'agora archaïque, avec la collaboration de M. Gras et H. Tréziny.* Paris.

Valmin, M. N. 1938. *The Swedish Messenia Expedition.* Lund.

Vansina, J. 1985. *Oral Tradition as History.* London.

Varela, J. L. M. 2003. *Consideraciones acerca del origen y la naturaleza de la ciudad planificada en las colonias griegas de occidente.* Oxford.

Vasić, R. 1993. "Macedonia and the Central Balkans: Contacts in the Archaic and Classical Period." In *Ancient Macedonia*, V: 1683–91.

Vatin, C. 1969. *Médéon de Phocide.* Paris.

Veblen, T. 1899. *The Theory of the Leisure Class.* New York.

Verbanck-Piérard, A. and D. Viviers (eds.). 1992. *Culture et cité. L'avènement d'Athènes à l'époque archaïque.* Bruxelles.

Verbruggen, H. 1981. *Le Zeus Crétois.* Paris.

Verdan, S. 2007. "Eretria: Metalworking in the Sanctuary of Apollo Daphnephoros during the Geometric Period." In Mazarakis Ainian 2007: 345–59.

Verdenius, W. J. 1985. *A Commentary on Hesiod*, Works and Days, *vv. 1–382.* Leiden.

Vernant, J.-P. 1965. *Mythe et pensée chez les Grecs*, I. Paris.

Vernant, J.-P. (ed.). 1968. *Problèmes de la guerre en Grèce ancienne.* The Hague and Paris.

Vernant, J.-P. 1980. *Myth and Society in Ancient Greece.* Tr. J. Lloyd. Sussex and Atlantic Highlands.

Vernant, J.-P. 1982. *The Origins of Greek Thought.* Ithaca, NY.

Vernant, J.-P. 1983. "Hestia-Hermes: The Religious Expression of Space and Movement in Ancient Greece." In Vernant, *Myth and Thought among the Greeks,* 127–75. London.

Vernant, J.-P. 1990. *Myth and Society in Ancient Greece.* Tr. J. Lloyd. New York.

Versakis, F. 1916. "To ieron tou Korinthou Apollonos." *AD* 2: 65–118.

Vestergaard, T. 2000. "Milesian Immigrants in Late Hellenistic and Roman Athens." In G. J. Oliver (ed.), *The Epigraphy of Death,* 81–109. Liverpool.

Vidal-Naquet, P. 1986. "Land and Sacrifice in the *Odyssey*: A Study of Religious and Mythical Meanings." In Vidal-Naquet, *The Black Hunter,* 15–38. Tr. A. Szegedy-Maszak. Baltimore.

Vierneisel, K. and B. Kaeser (eds.). 1990. *Kunst der Schale, Kultur des Trinkens.* Munich.

Vinogradov, Y. G. 1998. "The Greek Colonisation of the Black Sea Region in the Light of Private Lead Letters." In Tsetskhladze 1998a: 153–78.

Vinogradov, J. G. and S. D. Kryzickij. 1995. *Olbia.* Leiden.

Visser, E. 1997. *Homers Katalog der Schiffe.* Stuttgart and Leipzig.

Viviers, D. 1992. *Recherches sur les ateliers de sculpteurs et la cité d'Athènes à l'époque archaïque.* Bruxelles.

Viviers, D. 1994. "La cité de Dattalla et l'expansion territoriale de Lyktos en Crète centrale." *BCH* 118: 229–59.

Vlachopoulos, A. (ed.). 2005. *Nisia tou Aigaiou: Arkhaiologia.* Athens.

Vlachou, V. 2007. "Oropos: The Infant and Child Inhumations from the Settlement (Late 8th–Early 7th Centureis BC)." In Mazarakis Ainian 2007: 213–40.

Vlassopoulos, K. 2005. *Unthinking the Greek Polis: Ancient Greek History beyond Eurocentrism.* Diss. Cambridge.

Vlastos, G. 1946. "Solonian Justice." *CPh* 41: 65–83. Repr. in Vlastos 1995: 32–56.

Vlastos, G. 1947. "Equality and Justice in Early Greek Cosmologies." *CPh* 42: 156–78. Repr. in Vlastos 1995: 57–88.

Vlastos, G. 1995. *Studies in Greek Philosophy,* I. D. W. Graham ed. Princeton.

Vogelzang, M. E. and H. L. J. Vanstiphout (eds.). 1992. *Mesopotamian Epic Literature: Oral or Aural?* Lewiston.

Vogt, E. 1991. "Homer – ein grosser Schatten? Die Forschungen zur Person Homers." In Latacz 1991: 365–77.

Voigt, E. (ed.). 1971. Sappho et Alcaeus. Amsterdam.

Voigt, M. M. and R. C. Henrickson. 2000. "The Formation of the Phrygian State: The Early Iron Age at Gordion." *Anatolian Studies* 50: 1–18.

Voigtländer, W. 2004. *Teichiussa: Näherung und Wirklichkeit.* Rahden.

Vokotopoulou, J. 1985. "La Macédoine de la protohistoire à l'époque archaïque." In *Magna Grecia, Epiro e Macedonia,* 133–66. Taranto.

Vokotopoulou, J. 1986. Vitsa: Ta Nekrotafeia tis Molossikis Komis. Athens.

Völger, G. and K. von Welck. 1990. *Männerbande Männerbünde.* Cologne.

Vos, M. F. 1963. *Scythian Archers in Archaic Attic Vase-Painting.* Groningen.

Voutsaki, S. and J. Killen (eds.). 2001. *Economy and Politics in the Mycenaean Palace States.* Cambridge.

Vox, O. 1984. *Solone autoritratto.* Padua.

Voyatzis, M. 1999. "The Role of Temple Building in Consolidating Arkadian Communities." In Nielsen and Roy 1999: 130–68.

Voza, G. 1999a. *Nel segno dell'antico: Archeologia nel territorio di Siracusa.* Palermo.

Voza, G. (ed.). 1999b. *Siracusa 1999: Lo scavo archeologico di Piazza Duomo*. Palermo and Syracuse.

Wace, A. 1937. "A Spartan Hero Relief." *AEph* 1937: 217–20.

Wachter, R. 2001. *Non-Attic Greek Vase Inscriptions*. Oxford.

Wade-Gery, H. T. 1943–4. "The Spartan Rhetra in Plutarch *Lycurgus* VI." I: *CQ* 37: 62–72; II: *CQ* 38: 1–9; III: *CQ* 38: 115–26. Repr. in Wade-Gery 1958: 37–85.

Wade-Gery, H. T. 1958. *Essays in Greek History*. Oxford.

Waerden, B. L. van der. 1966. *Erwachende Wissenschaft*, I: *Ägyptische, babylonische und griechische Mathematik*.[2] Basel and Stuttgart.

Waerden, B. L. van der. 1967. *Erwachende Wissenschaft*, II: *Die Anfänge der Astronomie*. Groningen.

Waerden, B. L. van der. 1988. *Die Astronomie der Griechen: Eine Einführung*. Darmstadt.

Wagner-Hasel, B. 1997. "Die Macht der Penelope: Zur Politik des Gewebes im homerischen Epos." In R. Faber and S. Lanwerd (eds.), *Kybele–Prophetin–Hexe: Religiöse Frauenbilder und Weiblichkeitskonzeptionen*, 127–46. Würzburg.

Wagner-Hasel, B. 2000. *Der Stoff der Gaben: Kultur und Politik des Schenkens und Tauschens im archaischen Griechenland*. Frankfurt.

Walbank, F. W. 2000. "Hellenes and Achaians: Greek Nationality Revisited." In Flensted-Jensen 2000: 19–33.

Walberg, G. 1995. "The Midea Megaron and Changes in Mycenaean Ideology." *Aegean Archaeology* 2: 87–91.

Walcot, P. 1966. *Hesiod and the Near East*. Cardiff.

Walcot, P. 1970. *Greek Peasants, Ancient and Modern: A Comparison of Social and Moral Values*. Manchester.

Walcot, P. 1978. *Envy and the Greeks: A Study of Human Behaviour*. Warminster.

Walker, H. J. 1995. *Theseus and Athens*. Oxford.

Walker, K. G. 2004. *Archaic Eretria: A Political and Social History from the Earliest Times to 490 BC*. London.

Walker, S. 1983. "Women and Housing in Classical Greece: The Archaeological Evidence." In A. Cameron and A. Kuhrt (eds.), *Images of Women in Antiquity*, 81–91. London.

Wallace, M. B. 1970. "Early Greek *Proxenoi*." *Phoenix* 24: 189–208.

Wallace, R. W. 1983. "The Date of Solon's Reforms." *AJAH* 8: 81–95.

Wallace, R. W. 1989. *The Areopagus Council to 307 BC*. Baltimore.

Wallace, R. W. 1998a. "Solonian Democracy." In Morris and Raaflaub 1998: 11–29.

Wallace, R. W. 1998b. "The Sophists in Athens." In Boedeker and Raaflaub 1998: 203–22.

Wallace, R. W. 2004. "Damon of Oa: A Music Theorist Ostracised?" In Murray and Wilson 2004: 249–68.

Wallace, R. W. 2006. "The 'Sophists', Fifth-century Intellectual Developments, and Sokrates." In L. J. Samons (ed.), *The Cambridge Companion to Periclean Athens*. Cambridge.

Wallace, R. W. 2007a (still forthcoming in 2009). "Politics at Mytilene ca. 650–587/6: Pittakos *sophos*." In A. Pierris (ed.), *Archaic Lesbos: Sappho, Alcaeus and Pittacus*. London.

Wallace, R. W. 2007b. "Revolutions and a New Order in Solonian Athens and Archaic Greece." In Raaflaub et al. 2007: 49–82.

Wallace, S. 2003. "The Perpetuated Past: Re-use or Continuity in Material Culture and the Structuring of Identity in Early Iron Age Crete." *ABSA* 98: 251–77.

Wallace, W. P. 1954. "Kleomenes, Marathon, the Helots, and Arkadia." *JHS* 74: 32–5.

Wallinga, H. 1984. "The Ionian Revolt." *Mnemosyne* 37: 401–37.

Wallinga, H. 1987. "The Ancient Persian Navy and Its Predecessors." In H. Sancisi-Weerdenburg and A. Kuhrt (eds.), *Achaemenid History*, I: 47–78. Leiden.

Wallinga, H. 1989. "Persian Tribute and Delian Tribute." In P. Briant and C. Herrenschmidt (eds.), *Le tribut dans l'Empire perse*, 173–81. Paris.

Wallinga, H. 1993. *Ships and Sea-power before the Great Persian War*. Leiden.

Walser, G. 1984. *Hellas und Iran: Studien zu den griechisch-persischen Beziehungen vor Alexander*. Darmstadt.

Walser, G. 1987. "Persischer Imperialismus und griechische Freiheit." In Sancisi-Weerdenburg and Kuhrt 1987: 155–65.

Walter, U. 1993a. *An der Polis teilhaben: Bürgerstaat und Zugehörigkeit im archaischen Griechenland*. Stuttgart.

Walter, U. 1993b. "Herodot und die Ursachen des Ionischen Aufstandes." *Historia* 42: 257–78.

Walter, U. 1998. "Der Begriff des Staates in der griechischen und römischen Geschichte." In T. Hantos and G. A. Lehmann (eds.), *Althistorisches Kolloquium aus Anlass des 70. Geburtstages von Jochen Bleicken*, 9–27. Stuttgart.

Walter-Karydi, E. 1985. "Geneleos." *AM* 100: 98–104.

Wason, M. O. 1947. *Class Struggles in Ancient Greece*. London.

Watrous, L. V. 1996. *The Cave Sanctuary of Zeus at Psychro: A Study of Extra-urban Sanctuaries in Minoan and Early Iron Age Crete*. Liège and Austin.

Watrous, L. V. 1998. "Crete and Egypt in the Seventh Century BC: Temple A at Prinias." In Cavanagh et al. 1998: 75–9.

Waywell, G. B. 1993. "The Ada, Zeus and Idrieus Relief from Tegea in the British Museum." In O. Palagia and W. Coulson (eds.), *Sculpture from Arcadia and Laconia. Proceedings of an International Conference Held at the American School of Classical Studies at Athens, April 10–14, 1992*, 83–85. Oxford.

Webb, V. 1978. *Archaic Greek Faience: Miniature Scent Bottles and Related Objects from East Greece, 650–500 BC*. Warminster.

Weber, M. 1921. "Die Stadt." *Archiv für Sozialwissenschaft* 47, 621–772. Repr. in Weber 1972.

Weber, M. 1972. *Wirtschaft und Gesellschaft*[5]. Tübingen.

Weber, M. 1978. *Economy and Society*. G. Roth and C. Wittich, eds. Tr. E. Fischoff et al. Berkeley.

Webster, G. 1996. *A Prehistory of Sardinia, 2300–500 BC*. Sheffield.

Webster, T. B. L. 1972. *Potter and Patron in Classical Athens*. London.

Wedde, M. 2000. *Towards a Hermeneutics of Aegean Bronze Age Ship Imagery*. Mannheim.

Wees, H. van. 1992. *Status Warriors: War, Violence and Society in Homer and History*. Amsterdam.

Wees, H. van. 1994. "The Homeric Way of War: The *Iliad* and the Hoplite Phalanx." *G&R* 41: 1–18, 131–55.

Wees, H. van. 1995. "Princes at Dinner: Social Event and Social Structure in Homer." In Crielaard 1995: 147–82.

Wees, H. van. 1997. "Homeric Warfare." In Morris and Powell 1997: 668–93.

Wees, H. van. 1998a. "A Brief History of Tears: Gender Differentiation in Archaic Greece." In L. Foxhall and J. Salmon (eds.), *When Men were Men: Masculinity, Power and Identity in Classical Antiquity*, 10–53. London.

Wees, H. van. 1998b. "Greeks Bearing Arms: The State, the Leisure Class, and the Display of Weapons in Archaic Greece." In Fisher and van Wees 1998: 333–78.

Wees, H. van. 1998c. "The Law of Gratitude: Reciprocity in Anthropological Theory." In Gill et al. 1998: 13–49.

Wees, H. van. 1999a. "The Mafia of Early Greece: Violent Exploitation in the Seventh and Sixth Centuries BC." In K. Hopwood (ed.), *Organized Crime in Antiquity*, 1–51. London.

Wees, H. van. 1999b. "Tyrtaeus' Eunomia: Nothing to Do with the Great Rhetra." In Hodkinson and Powell 1999: 1–42.

Wees, H. van. 2000a. "The Development of the Hoplite Phalanx: Iconography and Reality in the 7th Century." In van Wees 2000c: 125–66.

Wees, H. van. 2000b. "Megara's Mafiosi: Timocracy and Violence in Theognis." In Brock and Hodkinson 2000: 52–67.

Wees, H. van (ed.). 2000c. *War and Violence in Ancient Greece*. London.

Wees, H. van. 2001. "The Myth of the Middle-class Army: Military and Social Status in Ancient Athens." In T. Bekker-Nielsen and L. Hannestad (eds.), *War as a Cultural and Social Force*, 45–71. Copenhagen.

Wees, H. van. 2002a. "Greed, Generosity and Gift-exchange in Early Greece and the Western Pacific." In Jongman and Kleijwegt 2002: 341–78.

Wees, H. van. 2002b. "Gute Ordnung ohne Grosse Rhetra – Noch einmal zu Tyrtaios' *Eunomia.*" *GFA* 5: 89–103.

Wees, H. van. 2002c. "Homer and Early Greece." *Colby Quarterly* 38: 94–117.

Wees, H. van. 2003. "Conquerors and Serfs: Wars of Conquest and Forced Labor in Archaic Greece." In Luraghi and Alcock 2003: 33–80.

Wees, H. van. 2004. *Greek Warfare: Myths and Realities*. London.

Wees, H. van. 2005a. "Clothes, Class and Gender in Homer." In D. Cairns (ed.), *Body Language in the Greek and Roman Worlds*, 1–36. Swansea.

Wees, H. van. 2005b. "Trailing Tunics and Sheepskin Coats: Dress and Status in Early Greece." In L. Cleland, M. Harlow, and L. Llewellyn-Jones (eds.), *The Clothed Body in the Ancient World*, 44–51. Oxford.

Wees, H. van. 2006. "Mass and Elite in Solonian Athens: The Property Classes Revisited." In Blok and Lardinois 2006: 351–89.

Wees, H. van. forthcoming. *The World of Achilles*. Cambridge.

Wehrli, F. 1944–59 (1967–78). *Die Schule des Aristoteles: Texte und Kommentare*. 10 vols. Stuttgart; 2nd edn. 1967–78.

Weidner, E. 1913. "*Barbaros.*" *Glotta* 4: 303–4.

Weinberg, J. 1999. "The International Elite of the Achaemenid Empire: Reality and Fiction." *Zeitschrift für die Alttestamentische Wissenschaft* 111: 583–608.

Wells, B. 1983. *The Protogeometric Period*, part 2: *An Analysis of the Settlement. Asine 11: Results of the Excavations East of the Acropolis 1970–1974*. Fasc. 4. Stockholm.

Wells, P. S. 1980. *Culture Contact and Culture Change*. Cambridge.

Welsch, W. 1999. "Transculturality: The Puzzling Form of Cultures Today." In M. Featherstone and S. Lash (eds.), *Spaces of Culture: City, Nation, World*, 194–213. London.

Welter, G. and U. Jantzen. 1951. "Das Diktynnaion." In F. Matz, *Forschungen auf Kreta 1942*, 106–17. Berlin.

Welwei, K.-W. 1979 (1986). "Die spartanische Phylenordnung im Spiegel der Großen Rhetra und des Tyrtaios." *Gymnasium* 86: 178–96. Repr. with addendum in Christ 1986: 426–47.

Welwei, K.-W. 1983 (1998). *Die griechische Polis: Verfassung und Gesellschaft in archaischer und klassischer Zeit*. Stuttgart; 2nd edn. 1998.

Welwei, K.-W. 1988. "Ursprünge genossenschaftlicher Organisationsformen in der archaischen Polis." *Saeculum* 39: 12–23.

Welwei, K.-W. 1990 (2000). "Die Staatswerdung Athens – Mythos und Geschichte." In G. Binder and B. Effe (eds.), *Mythos. Erzählende Weltdeutung im Spannungsfeld von Ritual, Geschichte und Rationalität*, 162–87. Trier. Repr. in Welwei, *Polis und Arché: Kleine Schriften zu Gesellschafts- und Herrschaftsstrukturen in der griechischen Welt*, 108–33. Stuttgart, 2000.

Welwei, K.-W. 1992. *Athen: Vom neolithischen Siedlungsplatz zur archaischen Grosspolis.* Darmstadt.

Welwei, K.-W. 1999. *Das klassische Athen: Demokratie und Machtpolitik im 5. und 4. Jahrhundert.* Darmstadt.

Welwei, K.-W. 2004. *Sparta: Aufstieg und Niedergang einer antiken Grossmacht.* Stuttgart.

Wenskus, S. R. 1961. *Stammesbildung und Verfassung: Das Werden der frühmittelalterlichen gentes.* Cologne.

Wéry, L.-M. 1979. "Die Arbeitsweise der Diplomatie in homerischer Zeit." In E. Olshausen and H. Biller (eds.), *Antike Diplomatie*, 13–55. Darmstadt.

West, M. L. 1966. *Hesiod*, Theogony: *Edited with Prolegomena and Commentary.* Oxford.

West, M. L. 1970. "Review" of C. Prato (ed.), *Tyrtaeus* (1968). *Classical Review* n.s. 20: 149–51.

West, M. L. 1971. *Early Greek Philosophy and the Orient.* Oxford.

West, M. L. 1974. *Studies in Greek Elegy and Iambus.* Oxford.

West, M. L. 1978. *Hesiod*, Works and Days: *Edited with Prolegomena and Commentary.* Oxford.

West, M. L. 1983. *The Orphic Poems.* Oxford.

West, M. L. 1985. *The Hesiodic Catalogue of Women: Its Nature, Structure and Origins.* Oxford.

West, M. L. 1988a. *Hesiod*: Theogony *and* Works and Days. Tr. with intro. and notes. Oxford and New York.

West, M. L. 1988b. "The Rise of the Greek Epic." *JHS* 108: 151–72.

West, M. L. 1992. *Iambi et Elegi Graeci Ante Alexandrum Cantati*, II.² Oxford.

West, M. L. 1995. "The Date of the *Iliad*." *Museum Helveticum* 52: 203–19.

West, M. L. 1997. *The East Face of Helicon: West Asiatic Elements in Greek Poetry and Myth.* Oxford.

West, M. L. (tr.). 1994. *Greek Lyric Poetry.* Oxford.

West, S. 1991. "Herodotus' Portrait of Hecataeus." *JHS* 111: 144–60.

West, S. 2002. *Demythologisation in Herodotus.* Xenia Toruniensia 6. Torun.

West, S. 2003. "Croesus' Second Reprieve and Other Tales of the Persian Court." *CQ* 53: 418–28.

Westbrook, R. 1988. "The Nature and Origins of the XII Tables." *ZRG* 105: 74–121.

Westbrook, R. 1989. "Cuneiform Law Codes and the Origins of Legislation." *ZA* 79: 201–22.

Westendorf, W. 1999. *Handbuch der altägyptischen Medizin.* Leiden.

Wheeler, E. L. 1987. "Ephorus and the Prohibition of Missiles." *TAPhA* 117: 157–82.

Wheeler, E. L. 1991. "The General as Hoplite." In V. D. Hanson (ed.), *Hoplites: The Classical Greek Battle Experience*, 121–70. London.

Whitbread, I. K. 1995. *Greek Transport Amphorae: A Petrological and Archaeological Study.* London.

Whitby, M. 1994. "Two Shadows: Images of Spartans and Helots." In Powell and Hodkinson 1994: 87–126.

Whitby, M. 1998a. "The Grain Trade of Athens in the Fourth Century BC." In Parkins and Smith 1998: 102–28.

Whitby, M. 1998b. "An International Symposium? Ion of Chios fr. 27 and the Margins of the Delian League." In E. Dabrowa (ed.), *Ancient Iran and the Mediterranean World*, 207–24. Kraków.

Whitby, M. (ed.). 2002. *Sparta.* Edinburgh.

White, E. 2001. *The Flâneur: A Stroll through the Paradoxes of Paris.* London.

Whitehead, D. 1981. "The Archaic Athenian *zeugitai*." *CQ* 31: 282–6.

Whitehead, D. 1986. *The Demes of Attica 508/7–ca. 250 BC: A Political and Social Study.* Princeton.

Whitehead, D. 1996. "Demes, Demoi." *OCD³*: 446–7.

Whitley, J. 1991a. "Social Diversity in Dark Age Greece." *ABSA* 86: 341–65.

Whitley, J. 1991b. *Style and Society in Dark Age Greece: The Changing Face of a Pre-literate Society 1100–700 BC.* Cambridge.

Whitley, J. 1994. "Protoattic Pottery: A Contextual Approach." In Morris 1994: 51–70.

Whitley, J. 1996. "Gender and Hierarchy in Early Athens." *Métis* 11: 209–31.

Whitley, J. 1997. "Cretan Laws and Cretan Literacy." *AJA* 101: 635–61.

Whitley, J. 1998a. "Literacy and Lawmaking: The Case of Archaic Crete." In Fisher and van Wees 1998: 311–32.

Whitley, J. 1998b. "From Minoans to Eteocretans: The Praisos Region 1200–500 BC." In W. G. Cavanagh, M. Curtis, J. N. Coldstream, and A. W. Johnston (eds.), *Post-Minoan Crete*, 27–39. London.

Whitley, J. 2001. *The Archaeology of Ancient Greece.* Cambridge.

Whitley, J. 2002. "Objects with Attitude: Biographical Facts and Fallacies in the Study of Late Bronze Age and Early Iron Age Warrior Graves." *CAJ* 12: 217–32.

Whitley, J. 2004. "Style Wars: Towards an Explanation of Cretan Exceptionalism." In G. Cadogan, E. Hatzaki, and A. Vassilakis (eds.), *Knossos: Palace, City, State*, 433–42. London.

Whitley, J. 2006a. "Before the Great Code: Public Inscriptions and Material Practice in Archaic Crete." In E. Greco and M. Lombardo (eds.), *La Grande Iscrizione di Gortyna: Centoventi anni dopo la scoperta*, 41–56. Athens.

Whitley, J. 2006b. "Praisos: Political Evolution and Ethnic Identity in Eastern Crete, c.1400–300 BC." In Deger-Jalkotzy and Lemos 2006: 597–617. Edinburgh.

Whitman, C. H. 1958. *Homer and the Heroic Tradition.* Cambridge.

Wickens, J. M. 1986. "The Archaeology of Cave Use in Attica, Greece, from Prehistoric through Late Roman Times." Diss. University of Michigan.

Wickert, K. 1961. "Der Peloponnesische Bund von seiner Entstehung bus zum Ende des archidamischen Krieges." Diss. University of Erlangen-Nürnberg.

Wickert-Micknat, G. 1982. "Die Frau." In H.-G. Buchholz (ed.), *Archaeologia Homerica: Die Denkmäler und das frühgriechische Epos*, vol. 3 R: 1–147. Göttingen.

Wickham, C. 2005. *Framing the Early Middle Ages: Europe and the Mediterranean 400–800.* Oxford.

Wiesehöfer, J. 1988. "Das Bild der Achaimeniden in der Zeit des Nationalsozialismus." In Kuhrt and Sancisi-Weerdenburg 1988: 1–14.

Wiesehöfer, J. 1990. "Zur Geschichte der Begriffe 'Arier' und 'arisch' in der deutschen Sprachwissenschaft und Althistorie des 19. und der ersten Hälfte des 20. Jahrhunderts." In H. Sancisi-Weerdenburg and J. W. Drijvers (eds.), *Achaemenid History, V: The Roots of the European Tradition*, 149–65. Leiden.

Wiesehöfer, J. 1999. "Kyros, der Schah und 2500 Jahre Menschenrechte: Historische Mythenbildung zur Zeit der Pahlavi-Dynastie." In S. Conermann (ed.), *Mythen, Geschichte(n), Identitäten: Der Kampf um die Vergangenheit*, 55–68. Hamburg.

Wiesehöfer, J. 2002. "Griechenland wäre unter persische Herrschaft geraten . . . : Die Perserkriege als Zeitenwende?" In H. Brinkhaus and S. Sellmer (eds.), *Zeitenwenden*, 209–32. Hamburg.

Wiesehöfer, J. 2003a. "The Medes and the Idea of the Succession of Empires in Antiquity." In Lanfranchi et al. 2003b: 391–6.

Wiesehöfer, J. 2003b. "Vom 'Oberen Asien' zur 'gesamten bewohnten Welt': Die hellenistisch-römische Weltreich-Theorie." In M. Delgado, K. Koch, and E. Marsch (eds.), *Europa, Tausendjähriges Reich und Neue Welt: Zwei Jahrtausende Geschichte und Utopie in der Rezeption des Danielbuches*, 66–83. Fribourg and Stuttgart.

Wiesehöfer, J. 2004a. *Ancient Persia.*[3] London.

Wiesehöfer, J. 2004b. "Daiukku, Deiokes und die medische Reichsbildung." In M. Meier and U. Walter (eds.), *Deiokes, König der Meder*, 15–26. Stuttgart.

Wiesehöfer, J. 2004c. "O Master, Remember the Athenians: Herodotus and Persian Foreign Policy." In V. Karageorghis and I. Taifacos (eds.), *The World of Herodotus*, 209–22. Nicosia.

Wiesehöfer, J. 2004d. "Persien, der faszinierende Feind der Griechen: Güteraustausch und Kulturtransfer in achaimenidischer Zeit." In Rollinger and Ulf 2004a: 295–310.

Wiesehöfer, J. 2005. "Daniel, Herodot und Dareios der Meder: Auch ein Beitrag zur Abfolge von Weltreichen." In R. Rollinger (ed.), *Von Sumer bis Homer*, 647–53. Altenberge.

Wiesehöfer, J. 2006. *Das frühe Persien.*[3] Munich.

Wikander, Ö. (ed.). 2000. *Handbook of Ancient Water Technology*. Leiden.

Wilcken, U. 1924 (1939, 1951, 1958, 1962). *Griechische Geschichte im Rahmen der Altertumsgeschichte*. Munich; 4th edn. 1939; 7th edn. 1951; 8th edn. 1958; 9th edn. 1962.

Wilkes, J. 1992. *The Illyrians*. Cambridge, MA.

Will, E. 1955. *Korinthiaka: Recherches sur l'histoire et la colonization de Corinthe des origines aux guerres médiques*. Paris.

Willetts, R. F. 1955. *Aristocratic Society in Ancient Crete*. London.

Willetts, R. F. 1962. *Cretan Cults and Festivals*. London.

Willetts, R. F. 1967. *The Law Code of Gortyn: Edited with Introduction, Translation and a Commentary*. Berlin.

Williams, C. K. 1995. "Archaic and Classical Corinth." In *Corinto e l'Occidente*, 31–45. Taranto.

Williams, R. T. 1965. *The Confederate Coinage of the Arcadians in the Fifth Century*. New York.

Wilson, J.-P. 1997a. "The 'Illiterate Trader'?" *BICS* 44: 29–56.

Wilson, J.-P. 1997b. "The Nature of Greek Overseas Settlements in the Archaic Period: *emporion* or *apoikia*?" In Mitchell and Rhodes 1997: 199–209.

Wilson, P. J. 2000a. *The Athenian Institution of the* Khoregia: *The Chorus, the City and the Stage*. Cambridge.

Wilson, P. J. 2000b. "Powers of Horror and Laughter: The Great Age of Drama." In Taplin 2000a: 88–132.

Wilson, P. J. 2003. "The Politics of Dance: Dithyrambic Contest and Social Order in Ancient Greece." In Phillips and Pritchard 2003: 163–96.

Wilson, R. J. A. 1981–2. "Archaeology in Sicily, 1977–1981." *AR* 28: 84–105.

Winkler, J. 1990. *The Constraints of Desire*. New York.

Winter, E. 1999. "Ta ikhni ton poleon tis A. Khalkidikis," *Archaeological Research in Macedonia and Thrace* 13: 282–94.

Winter, F. E. 1971. *Greek Fortifications*. London.

Winter, N. A. 1993. *Greek Architectural Terracottas from the Prehistoric to the End of the Archaic Period*. Oxford.

Wiseman, T. P. (ed.). 2002. *Classics in Progress: Interpreting the Ancient World*. Oxford.

Wöhrle, G. (ed., tr.). 1993. *Anaximenes aus Milet: Die Fragmente zu seiner Lehre*. Stuttgart.

Wolf, A. 1995. *Heldensage und Epos: Zur Konstituierung einer mittelalterlichen volkssprachlichen Gattung im Spannungsfeld von Mündlichkeit und Schriftlichkeit*. Tübingen.

Wood, E. M. 1988. *Peasant-citizen and Slave: The Foundations of Athenian Democracy*. London.

Woodard, R. 1997. *Greek Writing from Knossos to Homer: A Linguistic Interpretation of the Origin of the Alphabet and the Continuity of Ancient Greek Literacy.* Oxford.

Worley, L. J. 1994. *Hippeis: The Cavalry of Ancient Greece.* Boulder.

Wright, G. R. H. 2003. "The Formation of the Classical Greek Temple: Beginning Another Century of Discussion." *Thetis* 10: 39–44.

Wright, J. (ed.). 2004. *The Mycenaean Feast.* Princeton.

Wright, M. R. 1995. *Cosmology in Antiquity.* London.

Wycherley, R. E. 1957. *Literary and Epigraphical Testimonia.* The Athenian Agora III. Princeton.

Xanthoudides, S. A. 1918. "Dreros." *AD* 4: 18–25.

Yalouris, N. 1956. "Excavation at Bambes Makrysia." *PAAH* 1956: 187–92. In Greek.

Yalouris, N. 1958. "Excavation at Bambes Makrysia." *PAAH* 1958: 194–8. In Greek.

Yalouris, N. 1971. "A Classical Temple in the Area of Lepreon." *AAA* 4: 245–51. In Greek.

Yalouris, N. 1973. "A Guide to the Antiquities of Ancient Triphylia (Modern Olympia)." *Olympiaka Chronika* 4: 149–82. In Greek.

Yardeni, A. 1994. "Maritime Trade and Royal Accountancy in an Erased Customs Account from 475 BC on the Ahiqar Scroll from Elephantine." *BASOR* 293: 67–87.

Yates, D. C. 2005. "The Archaic Treaties between the Spartans and their Allies." *CQ* 55.1: 65–76.

Yeroulanou, M. and M. Stamatopoulou (eds.). 2005. *Architecture and Archaeology in the Cyclades.* Oxford.

Yntema, D. 2000. "Mental Landscapes of Colonisation: The Ancient Written Sources and the Archaeology of Early Colonial-Greek Southeastern Italy." *Bulletin Antieke Beschaving* 75: 1–49.

Yoffee, N. and G. Cowgill (eds.). 1988. *The Collapse of Ancient States and Civilizations.* Tucson.

Young, D. C. 1984. *The Olympic Myth of Greek Amateur Athletics.* Chicago.

Young, D. C. 2004. *A Brief History of the Olympic Games.* Malden and Oxford.

Young, R. S. 1939. *Late Geometric Graves and a Seventh-century Well.* Princeton.

Young, R. S. 1951. "Sepulturae intra urbem." *Hesperia* 20: 67–134.

Yunis, H. (ed.). 2003. *Written Texts and the Rise of Literate Culture in Ancient Greece.* Cambridge.

Zaccaria Ruggiu, A. 2003. *More regio vivere: Il banchetto aristocratico e la casa romana di età arcaica.* Rome.

Zahrnt, M. 1992. "Der Mardonioszug des Jahres 492 v. Chr. und seine historische Einordnung." *Chiron* 22: 237–79.

Zangger, E., M. Timpson, S. Yazvenko, E. Kuhnke, and J. Knauss. 1997. "The Pylos Regional Archaeological Project, II: Landscape Evolution and Site Preservation." *Hesperia* 66: 549–641.

Zapheiropoulou, N. 1997. "La relation entre l'Heraion et la ville de Samos." In J. de La Genière (ed.), *Héra. Images, espaces, cultes,* 151–62. Naples.

Zapheiropoulou, P. 1985. *Provlimata tis Miliakis Ageioyrafias.* Athens.

Zapheiropoulou, P. 1999. "I due 'Polyandria' dell'antica necropolis di Paros." *AION (archeol)* NS 6: 13–24.

Zapheiropoulou, P. 2000a. "To arkhaio nekrotafeio tis Parou stin geometriki kai arkhaiki epokhi." *AEph* 2000: 283–93.

Zapheiropoulou, P. 2000b. "Paros archaïque et son rôle dans la colonisation du nord de la mer Égée." In A. Avram and M. Babis (eds.), *Civilisation grecque et cultures antiques périphériques,* 130–3. Bucharest.

Zapheiropoulou, P. 2002. "Recent Finds from Paros." In Stamatopoulou and Yeroulanou 2002: 281–4.

Zapheiropoulou, P. 2003. *La céramique "mélienne." Exploration Archéologique de Délos*, Fasc. XLI. Paris.

Zapheiropoulou, P. and A. P. Matthaiou. 2000. "Parische Skulpturen." In A. H. Borbein (ed.), *Antike Plastik*, 27: 7–35. Munich.

Zeitlin, F. 1995. "The Economics of Hesiod's Pandora." In E. D. Reeder (ed.), *Pandora: Women in Classical Greece*. Princeton.

Zhmud, Leonid. 1997. *Wissenschaft, Philosophie und Religion im frühen Pythagoreismus*. Berlin.

Zimmermann, J.-L. 1989. *Les Chevaux de bronze dans l'art géométrique grec*. Mainz.

Zuntz, G. 1971. *Persephone: Three Essays on Religion and Thought in Magna Graecia*. Oxford.

Indices

Source Index

General Index

Abdera, 234, 308, 337
Abulafia, D., 327
Acanthus, 235
Acarnania, 203, 205, 265, 294, 303,
    307–8, 310, 359, 407–8
Achaea, 56, 61, 119, 194, 202–3, 228,
    255–7, 260, 263–70, 323–4, 377, 391,
    407
Achaean League, 119
Acharnae, 158
Achilles, 39, 72, 75, 84–5, 87–9, 91, 93,
    96, 303, 330, 352, 355, 412, 458,
    484–7, 524–6, 565–7, 569, 587, 595
Acrae, 324
Acraephia, 297–8, 431–3
Acragas, 13, 209, 324–5, 387, 538
Actium, 197
Adorno, T., 471
Adrastus, 105
Adriatic Sea, 23, 26, 33–4, 57, 265–6,
    323, 606
Aegina, 183, 191–3, 198–9, 209, 263,
    266, 267, 274, 289, 319, 341, 343, 361,
    376, 428, 439, 456, 460, 522, 538,
    553–4, 599
Aegium, 61
Aegyptus, 90
Aelius Aristides, 356
Aeolis, Aeolians, 169, 225–6, 233–5, 608;
    see also dialect, Aeolic
Aeolus, 86, 318
Aeschines, 534, 597
Aeschines the Orthagorid, 107
Aeschylus, 167, 178, 330, 517, 615
Aetolia, 15, 194, 202, 205, 228, 294–5,
    299, 303, 307–8, 407, 429–30, 435
Afrati, 55, 275–7, 282–5, 289
Africa, 22–5, 31–2, 36, 197, 288, 314–18,
    322, 326–7, 390–1, 528, 579
Agamemnon, 72, 84, 87–9, 118–19, 134,
    412, 416, 420, 475, 484, 486–7, 526,
    567–8, 587, 589
Agamemnon of Cyme, 28
Agariste, 106, 264, 535, 599
age groups, 45, 47, 53, 88, 90, 208, 216,
    355, 404, 447, 483, 486–8, 494, 496–7,
    505–6, 519, 525

Agesilaus, 9
Agiadae, 124
agōgē, 240
agōn, 14, 439, 525, 598
agoranomoi, 461
agriculture, *see* economy, agriculture and
aidōs, 14, 446, 448, 537–8
Ainis, 302
aisymnētēs, 401, 419, 421, 423, 426n.14
Akurgal, E., 226
Al Mina, 32, 58, 59, 214–15, 317, 546–7
Alalia, 325–6; battle of, 326
Alcaeus, 55, 112, 355–9, 411–12, 415–16,
    420, 423, 450, 476–7, 491–4, 506, 509,
    521, 577, 582, 613
Alcamenes, 119
Alcibiades, 9, 518, 522
Alcman, 128, 357–9, 494–6, 506, 514,
    613
Alcmeonidae, 140, 152, 153, 264, 302,
    312, 413, 416, 433, 440
Aleuadae, 304, 481, 517
Alexander I of Macedon, 177, 312, 605
Alexander the Great, 18, 30, 196, 515,
    617
Alexandria, 196, 421
alliance, 55, 60, 92, 101, 153, 171,
    175, 263, 269, 407, 585, 587–90,
    601
alphabet, xxii, 43, 57–8, 290, 509,
    542–61; origins of, 15, 77–8, 214–15,
    288–9, 542, 544–9; see also literacy
Alyattes, 365, 421–2
Amarynthus, 193–4, 203, 205, 438
Amasis, 181, 599
Amazons, 330
Ambracia, 33, 103, 265, 310, 323
Ambracian Gulf, 198, 296
Amisus, 335–6
Amphiaraus, 190, 298
Amphipolis, 377
Amorgos, 213–14, 363–4, 388
Amyclae, 52, 105, 119, 134, 134n.12,
    243–4, 247–8, 251–2, 428
Anacharsis, 421, 423–4, 524
Anacreon, 110, 358, 517, 535, 613–14
Anactorium, 103, 265

Made in the USA
Las Vegas, NV
09 April 2021